Gothic Grandeur

A Rare Tradition in American Catholicism

An Historical Narrative of the Administrative Life
of
The Mother Church
of
The Diocese of Buffalo, New York

**A Commemorative Work for the 175th Anniversary
of St. Louis Roman Catholic Church
Main and Edward Streets / Buffalo, New York**

Authored and Co-Edited by
C. EUGENE MILLER Ph.D.
Professor Emeritus
University of Louisville / Louisville, Kentucky

and

Co-Edited by
MICHAEL A. RIESTER M.A., M.S.W.
Archivist
St. Louis Roman Catholic Church / Buffalo, New York

Dedication

To all parishioners of St. Louis Church past and present,
to all clergy who celebrated Mass and administered the Sacraments within its walls,
to all trustees who attended to its temporal affairs,
to all lay and religious who taught in its school,
and to all Roman Catholics in the Diocese of Buffalo,
this narrative is dedicated.

Copyright © 2003 by The Canisius College Press

For more information, contact:
Canisius College Press
2001 Main Street
Buffalo, New York 14208

Publisher: Joseph F. Bieron
Book Design and Layout: Mary Lu Littlefield

Printed in the United States of America
Library of Congress Catalog Number Pending
ISBN 0-9740936-1-0

St. Louis Church as it appears today

Gothic Grandeur

St. Louis Church Altar in the 20th Century

iv

Acknowledgments

The author and editors wish to acknowledge and thank all the authors, publishers, librarians, curators, secretaries, parishioners, historians, and critics who have helped to bring this work to fruition.

We have singled out the following institutions for special mention: Buffalo and Erie County Public Library; Buffalo and Erie County Historical Society; Archives of the Catholic Diocese of Buffalo; Archives of St. Louis Church, Buffalo, New York; Ekstrom Library, University of Louisville, Louisville, Kentucky; Cardinal Hayes Library, Manhattan College, Bronx, New York; Archives of Manhattan College, Bronx, New York; Archives of St. Joseph's Collegiate Institute, Buffalo, New York; Archives of the Sisters of St. Joseph, Clarence, New York.

Although all individuals who have provided us with research material have been credited for their contributions in the *References and Notes* sections that follow each chapter, we would like to list here the names of those whose contributions were extensive: Chris Andrle, Robert McCarthy, Bill Kurzdorfer, Jack and Arline Hoyt, John Pax, Mike Mikos, Molly B. Hauck, Patrick Kavanaugh, Sister Martin Joseph, Sister Ann Louise, Sister Regina Murphy S.S.M.N., Robert Ruzala, Donald Killian, Michael Zobel Thomas McKeon Jr., Brother Luke Salm F.S.C., Brother Edward Martin F.S.C., and Sister Mary Anne Butler S.S.J.

Because of his most prestigious position and his invaluable contribution concerning the final days of *A Rare Tradition in American Catholicism at St. Louis Church*, we wish to give special recognition to The Most Reverend Donald W. Trautman, Catholic Bishop of Erie, Pennsylvania.

The editorial journey from a first rough draft of a manuscript to a product which can be confidently given to a prospective publisher is neither a jaunt nor a stroll; it is more like a trek in a jungle. Spelling, grammar, clarity, and precise expression of one's thesis needs to be checked, reconsidered, and revised. The author's nephews and niece, Timothy Miller, John Miller, and Lora Buchheit Winkler graciously supplied the needed computer hardware and software to achieve success. The use of the computer as an aide to satisfactory editing is not a panacea. Human readers are still needed. We therefore thank Sylvina Godfrey Miller, Marie Buchheit Miller, and Michael and Carol Zobel for their devoted attention that they gave to the text by reading it and offering invaluable suggestions. Likewise we wish to express gratitude to Edward Zimmermann, *Professor Emeritus* of Canisius College for his literary criticism.

We must add, however, that this is a final product from the hands of humans. No matter what errors may be found in the text, those persons acknowledged above deserve no condemnation. Only we, the author and editors, are accountable for any malapropism or anachronism which may have crept into the final treatise. For each we offer our *"mea culpa."*

Trustees of St. Louis Church 1906

Preface

*I*t is only fitting that, on the occasion of its one hundred and seventy-fifth celebration, this compendium of the parish history of St. Louis Church, Buffalo, New York, should be presented. In this the fourth year of the new millennium, when parochial unity and cooperation are so vitally necessary, the knowledge of what our forebears struggled for and accomplished in the cause of religion must be regarded not only as interesting information but as an inspiration and encouragement to those who now carry the burdens associated with not only survival of the parish but its development and influence in the lives of Americans. It is their story. It begins in an age when Catholicism in America was just a seed, and the United States of America was still a missionary land whose number of clergy were a trickle and whose copious number of laity flocked to America's shore escaping the trials and tribulations abounding in Europe.

*T*here was no Catholic Church in Buffalo, New York, the terminus of the Erie Canal that in 1825 had opened trade and industry from the Atlantic to the Midwest. For ten years following the deeding of land to Bishop John Dubois, third bishop of New York, by Louis Stephen Le Couteulx de Chaumont in 1829, Catholic laymen, accompanied by Father John Nicholas Mertz, all immigrant Alsatians, Lorrainers, French, Swiss, and Irish, built and cared for the temporalities and spiritualities of a small church known as the *Lamb of God*. Later, after a more prestigious structure was completed and dedicated, its name was changed to *Saint Louis* in honor of Louis IX, King of France and patron saint of Le Couteulx. About this time, the trustees incorporated the parish according to a law enacted by the New York State Legislature in 1813. In doing so they combined American republican politics and government with their desire to uphold European traditions of their culture represented by communal customs of lay governance.

*F*rom the time of the death of Le Couteulx on November 16, 1840 until 1855, the action of the lay trustees to govern the church according to the provisions of the incorporation law of 1813 caused grave controversy and conflict between the laity, clergy, and the hierarchy of the American ecclesia. With the exception of some lulls in argumentation, the battle of clashing cultures and wills went on continuously. Although the trustees appealed both to democratic innovations and native traditions in their argumentation, they were unwilling to view the conflict as a struggle over abstract principles. They made the parish's traditions, developed during Mertz's pastorship, ends in themselves. It was these precedents and customs rather than political ideals that were at stake. They used, however, politics and public opinion as tools to achieve their goal. The struggle rose to a crescendo when the New York State Legislature enacted the Putnam Law in 1855 assuring the legitimacy of the trustees' right to govern the church as they had proposed. Before this, however, the black flag of interdict had hung over the face of St. Louis Church. The priest had been withdrawn by the bishop, the parishioners had been denied the reception of the sacraments, and the trustees had been excommunicated. Freemasons, Nativists, and Protestants reveled in the opportunity to acclaim the church's lay trustees as pioneer Protestants in a reactionary church.

Louis LeCouteulx

All through this period of stress one gnawing concern, deeply embedded in the hearts and minds of the parishioners and their trustees, continued to erode their pride in holding tenaciously to their will which was in conflict with the hierarchy. They did not want to be Protestants! Although they had become tainted with materialism and nationalism in their adopted land, they did not wish to fall into the heresy which, in glorifying God, would find life possible without the saving efficacy of Christ's grace in the sacraments. In the end, although ideological differences were not reconciled, a compromise was effected between the trustees and Bishop John Timon, who had become bishop of Buffalo following its creation as a diocese separate from New York in 1847. It was brought about by arbitration between bishop and trustees initiated by Father Francis Xavier Wenninger S.J., a missionary from Kentucky. Timon had the trustees sign documents that gave the bishop a greater role in the parish's government, but the trustees remained entrenched as a system. It was one which lasted until 1979 when the parish's property and assets were transferred to the diocese under the direction of Bishop Edward D. Head. Monsignor William A. Schwinger became pastor and guided the church through its new phase for sixteen years after which it was assigned in 1995 to Monsignor Robert A. Mack.

The basic plan of this book envisions the narration of the externals which took place at the parcel of land donated by Louis Le Couteulx through one hundred and seventy-five years, so as to reflect the internals of faith which daily integrated the lives of those in the congregation. The stones of the church, the bricks of the school, the framing of the rectory, and the landscaping of the property were seen as visible proofs of conviction, loyalty, and sacrifice of both clergy and laity. Within the walls of the four churches built on this site during its long history, infants were baptized and children instructed for confirmation; human souls were absolved of their sins and nourished with the Bread of Life; young men and women pronounced their vows in marriage pledging their lives till death made them part; many young men, newly ordained, said their first Mass; the dying received their last earth-given flow of heavenly grace, and the dead underwent funeral rites that religiously honored their mortal remains as their souls leaped into eternal life. All through its history, the Sacrifice of the Mass served as the solidifying ritual of the parish's spiritual activity and its way of celebrating the most honored feasts of Easter, Pentecost, Christmas, Corpus Christi, and St. Louis, King of France.

The final church building which now exists at Main and Edward Streets is a gothic structure modeled upon the great German Cathedral in Cologne; a type of architecture which began in France and spread throughout Europe. In its structure, St. Louis Church has a sense of being rude, barbarian, rugged, misshapen, and grotesque. It has the characteristics of the Middle Ages; it is medieval and romantic rather than classical, as was the previous church that burned to the ground in 1885. It is characterized by the converging weights and strains at isolated points under slender vertical piers and counterbalancing buttresses and by pointed arches and vaulting. In this intriguing sense of slenderness and weakness so combined to form strength and stability, we vision the whole history of St. Louis Church. In the grotesque we see the rough and tumble of its beginnings. The counterbalances give us a sense of the paradox in the conflict between the laity and the clergy for which there was, in compromise, a solution. The parish had a French beginning, its Germanic ethnic period, and its assimilation into the modern diocesan system. Its history is mundane and sublime; it is the story of body and soul. Today, after all the vicissitudes of one hundred and seventy-five years, it stands physically, spiritually, and inspirationally as a Spire in the City, a Steeple in the City, and a Tower in the City. It, with the devotion of its parishioners, has ascension, aspiration, and surge; and, as such, it has grandeur.

That is why we have chosen to title its historical development as *Gothic Grandeur: A Rare Tradition in American Catholicism.*

We, the author and editors of this literary work, wish to conclude this preamble by paraphrasing the authors of the *St. Louis Bazar Chronicle* written in 1888, upon whose shoulders we stood while traveling back in time. How very few people there are who, glancing at the completed pages of history, can fathom the long, hard, continuous labor there represented. The days and nights of search and research, the consulting of high authorities on disputed points, the minute gathering of particles which when united by the master hand form so beautiful and instructive a picture of the past. Imaginative writing leaves the mind free to follow its own behest's while the historian has but one course to pursue; facts are his food and truth his constant companion. Thoughts like these suggested themselves while contemplating the progress of our work termed *Gothic Grandeur: A Rare Tradition in American Catholicism.* The readers of this carefully compiled history should experience only pleasure and comfort; the facts have all been gathered, and sifted, and weighed; the work is done. Now to enjoy the results! But, what of the historians? How can their hours of patient toil and of vexatious disappointment be suitably repaid? The sleepless nights and thought-burdened days are spent and cannot be reclaimed or altered. Nature may be restored, but each infraction of its laws leaves a mark on the surface. And so the delvers in the history of days gone by, the students of ages past and of men nigh forgotten, bring forth from their studies a creation which all must admire, but which none can hope to reward. We historians seek no equitable reward other than that self-consciousness which arises from the knowledge of a difficult and overpowering task completed. With the struggle past, however, our faces brighten up again like the earth after a storm. We historians once more wear our proverbial smile that the work has gone forth; we sigh with relief at the thought of a great weight lifted from our shoulders. [1]

REFERENCES AND NOTES ⚜ PREFACE

1. *The St. Louis Bazar Chronicle*, October 25, 1888, vol. 1. no.4. p. 2; This chronicle had thirteen issues, each of which was distributed daily over the two week period of the Bazaar held inside the partially completed gothic structure which now stands at the corner of Main and Edward Streets in Buffalo, New York. The members of the publication committee for the chronicle were: D. Edward Metzger, M.F.Boechat, Peter B. Seereiter, Charles J. Fix, and Peter Paul. The historical period is 1888; the language at St. Louis Church is still predominately German. In German the word Bazaar is *Der Bazar*; it means Verkaufshalle or Warenmarkt, or Wohltaetigkeitsbazar, a beneficent, charitable or charity market.

C. Eugene Miller Ph.D.
Michael A. Riester M.A., M.S.W.
Buffalo, New York
October 17, 2003

Table of Contents

Bishop John Dubois

PROLOGUE

Ancestry of Tradition

The Catholic Church is the oldest institution in the Western World. It began almost two thousand years ago when a small nucleus of men and women clung with shared faith and emotion to the teachings of a man named Jesus Christ following his crucifixion in Jerusalem by the authority of Pontius Pilate, the Roman procurator of Judea. The center of their faith was their belief that the Christ had risen on the third day after his death and had been seen in his risen state by many. Starting as a sect of Judaism, it spread rapidly to countless regions of the Roman Empire.

Although for two centuries it suffered much at the hands of the emperors of Rome, it won a decisive victory over paganism in 312 when Constantine, the reigning emperor, granted it complete religious liberty. With the invasions of the barbarians, the Empire declined, fell apart, and the Church, which found its fortunes linked to the state, fell into a period of confusion. It was, however, undaunted, survived, and for one thousand years held Western Civilization together as a conglomerate kingdom called Christendom. The Catholic Church animated its laws, institutions, customs, literature, art, and architecture with faith in Jesus Christ as God and Man, and regulated the moral and social behavior of medieval kings, princes, peasants, and townspeople.

In the fourteenth and fifteenth centuries, social, religious, economic, and cultural forces in Christendom, along with a decline in spirituality and morality in the Church, ripened Western Civilization for a great religious upheaval led by Martin Luther and John Calvin. Although Christendom was torn asunder, the Catholic Church saved itself by a thoroughgoing reform inaugurated at the Council of Trent, which began in 1545 and ended in 1563. It continued for two centuries following the end of the Council to weather crisis after crises right up to the French Revolution in 1789. The Church's attitude toward the outside modern world was negative and condemnatory, but it effected a vast missionary activity in the world which among other achievements brought Catholicism to the shores of the Americas that had been discovered by Columbus in 1492, and was progressively colonized by Spain, Portugal, Holland, France, and England. The missionary activity of the Catholic Church in the region of North America between the Atlantic Ocean and the Mississippi River, bordered by the Gulf of Mexico in the South and Canada in the North, is the origin of the traditions in American Catholicism.

One such tradition is the relationship and interaction of clergy and laity in the development of American Catholicism from the years following the American Revolution to the present day. In order to understand the beginnings of this tradition one must have a flash-back into European history where for many centuries, the rise and fall of empires, the political, philosophical, and social upheavals, the wars and counter-wars in the name of religion, and the interplay between Church and State developed different cultural attitudes which clung to the colonizers and immigrants like heavy baggage as they began their lives in the New World.

Reverend Stephen Theodore Badin as he would have appeared when he visited Buffalo, New York, in the late fall of 1828, stayed at the home of Louis LeCouteulx, and encouraged LeCouteulx to donate property to Bishop Dubois so as to provide a church for the Catholic community.

In regards to defining its authority, the Catholic Church was in flux for its first two hundred years of existence. By the beginning of the third century leadership for its many spiritual and temporal activities had taken on a structure whereby bishops, priests, and deacons correlated the works of apostles, prophets, teachers, healers, miracle workers, comforters, and linguists. Through the missionary work of Peter and Paul, the Church had spread across most of the landmass surrounding the Mediterranean Sea. As years turned into decades following the first century, however, Christians realized that the world had not come to an end and the experience of the Second Coming of Jesus was to be the subject of faith for the future. Further, they had seen the demise of the Apostles and other eyewitnesses to the resurrection of the Christ. The charismatic leadership developed by Paul and the notion of a royal priesthood of all Christians, which did not make distinction between clergy and laity, and had evolved as a presbyterial system, needed reorganization so that the veracity of the oral tradition promoted by these eyewitnesses would be preserved.

Communities of Christians led by their presbyters defined the existence of a church. Certain churches assumed authority over other churches with some obtaining metropolitan status. Gradually, specific cities of large population and economic growth became the centers for more Christian activity, and they took on suprametropolitan status. Such were the congregations of Rome, Alexandria, and Antioch; and, at each one, a monarchial episcopate became the guarantor of the veracity of the oral traditions. Soon, however, these episcopates gathered in synods to recognize and approve the distribution of a certain limited body of writings, containing that oral tradition which they called Scripture. Subsequently the episcopates collectively agreed to uphold their authority and safeguard their orthodoxy by formulating a creed of faith. It asserted faith in God, a Father and Creator, faith in an incarnate God, Christ Jesus, and faith in a manifestation of God, Holy Spirit,

who had inspired prophets to foretell salvation history and be a source of grace to all Christian communities whose members formed the earthly arm of a communion of saints. After the Council of Nicaea in 325, the episcopate at Rome gained the most elite status among all the other suprametropolitan episcopates because it had been the See of Peter and Paul, it was the capital of the Roman Empire, and it enjoyed material wealth by which it was able to assist all the other churches in the Empire.

Emperor Constantine donated his Lateran palace in Rome as a residence for the bishop of Rome. He recognized the Christian clergy as a distinct social class and exempted them from military service. He clothed the decisions of the bishop with civil authority and modified Roman law so as to conform to Christian values. Under his rule the Church was firmly set on the road to cooperative union with the state. At this time Sylvester I was the bishop of Rome and the thirty-second successor there to Peter, the Apostle. Although by the third century the bishop of Rome had maintained leadership over other churches toward understanding the will of Christ in controversial questions, he did not reach the high profile of supreme patriarch until the fifth century. In 496, Pope Gelasius I opened the way to the theology of "the two powers" according to which political or temporal power was subordinated to the spiritual power. This doctrine permeated the Church between the years when Rome fell victim to barbarian invasions and Frankish kings established order in Europe.

Pope Leo III as Emperor of Rome crowned Charlemagne, the greatest of the Frankish kings, on Christmas Day in the year 800. The age of Christendom was first established with the union of the temporal and the spiritual in one commonwealth with two heads. Charlemagne and his successors exercised authority over the Church in spiritual matters in opposition to the doctrine of Gelasius I, but several of the reigning Popes procrastinated in exerting their supremacy because they enjoyed on a limited basis the ability to intervene in the affairs of state. After ninety years of existence, this first attempt at Christendom fell into decay and the papacy became a victim of political intrigue, losing all moral and spiritual authority. The rulers of the Saxons, Bavarians, Swabians, and Franconians, however, after a long bout with feudalism, revived the Empire in the tenth century. This new kingdom became the first of the three German Reichs. At first the emperors found the Church to be a most effective force in the struggle against disorder and they found the bishops to be the most suitable collaborators by reason of their education and their state of celibacy.

Although order was achieved, it was done so at the expense of Church authority. Lay power was dominant. The old canon law, which required the bishops to be elected by the clergy and the people, was forgotten. Lay investiture was on the rise; newly anointed bishops knelt in homage before kings and vassals. The bishops were not only responsible for the spiritual welfare of their subjects but they were also given feudal obligations, which took precedence over ecclesiastical ones. The rule of proprietary ownership was established whereby even parish priests were considered as subjects to the lords who hired them and owned the Church property. Cardinal Humbert condemned both lay investiture and proprietary ownership in the first half of the ninth century as manifestations of the perversion of proper order. He demanded that laymen be obedient to the clergy; and, whenever the spiritual and the temporal came into conflict, the spiritual authority must have the final word.

In order to put Humbert's theory into practice, however, the Church had to wait until 1073 when Hildebrand was elected and named Pope Gregory VII. He came into direct conflict with Henry IV, the reigning emperor. The clergy were waging war against the papacy; they resisted the papal decrees against simony and clerical marriages. Henry showed little sympathy for reform; sided with the clergy and continued to keep royal control over episcopal nominations. Bickering between Henry and Gregory rose to a crescendo and Gregory excommunicated Henry and all the bishops who had sided with him. Henry knew that with this dictum came the Pope's declaration to the subjects of Henry's kingdom that he was being deposed as emperor. Others, such as Rudolf, the Duke of Swabia, were waiting in the wings to snatch the crown. Kneeling in the snows at Canossa on a January evening before the castle of Countess Mathilda, where Gregory was vacationing, Henry begged the Pope's forgiveness. Although he received it, he quickly defied the Pope again. Consequently, the Pope approved Rudolf as emperor. Henry was again excommunicated, fought against Rudolf and won, deposed the Pope, and installed an anti-Pope, Clement III, in his place. Robert Guiscard, a Norman ruler of southern Italy, came to Gregory's aid and drove Henry out of Rome but left the city in ashes. The populace blamed Gregory for the destruction and drove him out and replaced him with an anti-Pope. Gregory died in 1085 in exile. Henry was deserted by his wife and son and floundered around Italy pursued by his enemies. He finally abdicated in 1105, one year before he died. Finally, Urban II, a moderate and a pragmatic man, who was elected Pope in 1088, partially emancipated the Church from lay control. The question of lay investiture was reconciled by compromise. Although the clergy became the principal electors of the bishops with participation by the laity, the emperor still exercised great influence over the choice of the bishop. The German version of this settlement was embodied in the Concordat of Worms in 1122.

Hildebrand was also successful in asserting absolute papal power over the Church. His *Dictatus Papae* states that the pope can be judged by no one; the Roman Church has never erred and never will err until the end of time; the Roman Church was founded by Christ alone; the pope alone can depose and restore bishops; he alone can make new laws, set up new bishoprics, and divide old ones; he alone can transfer bishops; he alone can call general councils and authorize canon law; he alone can revise his judgments; his legates, even though in inferior orders, have precedence over all bishops; an appeal to papal courts inhibits judgment by all inferior courts; a duly ordained pope is undoubtedly made a saint by the merits of St. Peter. By the fourteenth century these concepts were well entrenched in the discipline of the Church in Western Civilization. The ancient concept of collegiality of bishops was lost and the Pope was indeed a world ruler who dominated both the spiritual and temporal life of Europe.

The papal monarchy, however, went into decline; storm clouds gathered over Christendom; they were an omen of the demise of this proud and romantic idea of temporal and spiritual power working together to effect a Camelot on earth. Although the papacy survived the great schism generated by the concepts of conciliarism in the fifteenth century, it failed to establish its moral and spiritual leadership over Christendom. The development of nationalism and the modern state was being conceived. People began to look upon popes and emperors as figureheads with empty titles. It appeared that every city-state had its king and there were as many princes as there were households. The Roman Church did not reform itself in time and the Reformation split Europe into the two camps of Catholicism and Protestantism. The decrees of the Council of Trent put the Church onto a course of reform, but it was a course based upon a medieval structure; the ideas of humanists and liberals were not heeded. [1]

The bishop was given absolute control over his diocese; no room was left for participation of the laity in the top echelon of the administration of the Church. Because the Council wanted the Church to become more parish-centered, however, it reinforced on the local administrative level the medieval tradition of lay management. It was found that this form of management strengthened the parishioner's faith by increasing individual involvement. The post Council of Trent Church, in opposition to Protestantism, became a rigoristic and authoritarian institution that brought it into the seventeenth century as a strong, self-confident, spiritually revitalized organization. It did not come into existence, however, without violence generated by religious, political, and emotional upheavals in the camps of both Protestants and Catholics. For thirty years, combatant armies took to the field and raped the countryside. By the settlement of the Thirty Years War in 1648 at the Treaty of Westphalia all people living in each local community were allowed only the freedom of religious faith and practice which was that of the reigning prince, duke, or other established civil authority. A strong rivalry existed between Protestants and Catholics. Many contested areas required the strong religious involvement of the laity provided for by the Council of Trent's encouragement of lay management. [2]

Another example of the interrelationship between clergy and laity in the Catholic Church in Europe existed in England and Ireland. A brief look at the history of Catholicism in these two countries further sheds light on the management of church congregations at the local level. The Church of England had a continuous history with the Roman Catholic Church from the sixth century with Augustine of Canterbury's mission from Rome until the Crown and parliament rejected papal authority in the sixteenth century. In 1534, King Henry VIII denounced papal authority and schismatically tore the Church of England away from its roots in Rome. Roman Catholicism in England was driven underground but never died. It survived through the establishment of a remarkable network of seminaries, monasteries, and convents on the Continent which were filled with English and Irish youth. By the eighteenth century, however, Roman Catholics were considered by the civil authorities to be such a minority that four Catholic districts emerged and were ruled by a vicar apostolic appointed by the papacy. Although a Roman Catholic emancipation act was proclaimed in 1829, it was not until 1850 that dioceses and a hierarchy were re-established. Likewise, the history of Catholicism in Ireland is strongly linked to the history of the civil authority in England.

St. Patrick, a missionary of the Roman Catholic Church, converted the Irish people about the year 432. He organized the Church of Ireland around an episcopal structure; but, monasteries, which had come into existence during his lifetime, became dominant in authority after his death. These monasteries were the homes to abbots, bishops, priests, monks, and friars. Living together within their walls was a mixture of clergy and laity whose daily succor was provided by and controlled by laymen, many of whom were descendants of the house's founder. In 1128, the white and black robed Cistercians arrived on Ireland's shores. These monks, withdrawn from the world, were educated and respected. They maintained an ascetic discipline of wandering and had outposts in Scotland and England. So also, members of other religious orders, known as friars, who arrived in Ireland professed renunciation, poverty, and self-sacrifice and went about begging and preaching. All had a strong interest in evangelization. The faith did not spread throughout Ireland from cities because it was not urbanized. From the monastic centers, however, preaching radiated outward to the surrounding agrarian population. The peasants became very familiar with Franciscans, Dominicans, Carmelites, and Augustinians. A form of democratic rule existed within the monasteries, and the monks brought these principles into the countryside where they preached. Each year, as an example, the monks held chapters or assemblies in a democratic fashion; and, in collegiality, they could depose an autocratic abbot if reasons for doing so were found sufficient.

In 1111, a synod divided the island into provinces and dioceses. In 1155, Pope Adrian IV, an Englishman, wanted Ireland under English rule. After the Norman invasion of 1171 dioceses and tithing continued in the South but monasteries continued to hold sway in the North and West. After a period of moral decay during the fourteenth and fifteenth centuries, bishops, priests, and laity reformed. Following the schism of Henry VIII, the Dublin parliament recognized him as head of the schismatic Church of Ireland. For the next three hundred years Ireland's religious practice was in the hands of those who held the crown in England. Cardinal Reginald Pole attempted reconciliation with Rome during the reign of Mary Tudor. Queen Elizabeth I, in establishing a monarchial episcopal polity which included both Lutheran and Reformed doctrines, tried to be as inoffensive as possible to Roman Catholics. In taking the throne, James II attempted an unsuccessful restoration and unification with Rome. Others, however, such as Oliver Cromwell and William of Orange brought only military force and persecution to the Catholics.

At the Battle of the Boyne in 1690, William of Orange was victorious over all Irish resistance and the Church of Ireland was no longer an identity. Bishops and clerics were officially banished from the realm. Catholic laymen were not allowed to vote, hold political office, purchase land, or serve as lawyers or military officers. The Mass was proscribed. As in England, the Catholic Church in Ireland went underground and continued to offer sophisticated pressure on the British Crown. While waiting for relief to come, laymen assumed leadership roles and worked closely with priests who administered in secret. Together they kept the flame of faith alive on the Emerald Isle. In 1793, all bans on Roman Catholic laymen were lifted except for the one proscribing political office. In 1829 this last barrier was also removed due to the pressure of Daniel O'Connell's Catholic Association. The flood of clergy and laity emigrating from Ireland during the seventeenth and eighteenth centuries was enormous. Great numbers fled to France when King James II went into exile. Several of these were military officers. Presbyterians and Congregationalists moved into Northern Ireland and confiscated property, which no longer could be owned by Catholics. Impoverished, these Catholics took to the high seas; many came to America. Religious congregations left Ireland and went to Rome where they established seminaries for young laymen who followed them. Their plan was to raise up an army of clergy that could follow the Irish emigrants to America and other parts of the world. [3]

*T*he Ancestry of Tradition ends here. During the two thousand years of its existence, the Roman Catholic Church established and consistently defended a monarchial form of leadership with a vertical chain of command. It began at an apex with the Pope, the Vicar of Christ, descended through the bishops, titulars in their dioceses, and ended with the priests, pastors of their parishes. These were the clergy, and the laity had to follow exactly all clerical decisions concerning faith, morals, and liturgical affairs. Latitude in terms of lay management of temporal affairs in the parishes was permitted and in many cases encouraged. In mission countries where the priest arrived and evangelized the pagan natives, he became their shepherd. The pagans once Christianized worked with the priest catechizing, providing managerial skills, and developing a charismatic leadership along the lines of the ancient Paulian church. In other missions, where the immigrants arrived before the priest, a different model of management emerged. The immigrants had already been baptized and had received the grace of some of the sacraments. Within their ranks leaders arose to gather congregations and construct churches. When priests were assigned to them, they did not look upon them as shepherds but as partners. The laity, void of a priest, had already initiated its educational programs, its health needs, its economic development, and its community organization. The heterogeneous polyglot immigrants

did not need conversion; they were already Catholic. Now they wished to share their talents with their pastors in the spiritual and temporal development of their parishes. Their pastor would bring the Body and Blood of Christ onto the altars in their homes and eventually into the churches that they would build. He would bring the Church with all its grace to them in the seven sacraments. He would lead them in devotions, remind them of the significance of feast days in the Church, and motivate their spiritual enthusiasm through his sermons. He did not need to develop a self-reliant people, break the cycle of poverty, illness, educational deprivation, and substitute a willingness to progress. He needed only to give them good example through his asceticism and devotion.

*B*ased upon this backdrop of European history, immigration, and evangelization, American Catholicism formulated its own traditions in the colonies following their successful revolution against England. As a Christian tradition, community, and a way of life spawned in Europe, it emphasized the universality of the Church, but its faith recognized the Pope as the visible head of that Church and the foundation of unity of the bishops and faithful. Many American Anglican, Protestant, Orthodox, and Oriental Christians claimed catholicity, but they did not recognize the Pope of Rome as their head; and, in many cases actually despised him. As such they professed sectarian catholicism, and they distinguished themselves by demanding that Petrine Catholics be called Roman Catholics. By whatever name, Petrine or Roman Catholic, immigrants faithful to the Pope of Rome continued to develop in a missionary setting from the American Revolution to the beginning of the twentieth century. Any traditions, which were initiated in their individual parishes during the missionary period that outlasted it, and lived many decades beyond it, can be considered as rare traditions in American Catholicism.

REFERENCES AND NOTES ❦ PROLOGUE

1. The above paragraphs reflect a summary of a text on Church History. Thomas Bokenkotter, *A Concise History of the Catholic Church*, Revised and Expanded Edition, Image Books, Doubleday, New York, 1990. Chapters 1-3.

2. L. Pfleger, "Untersuchungen zur Geschicte des Pfarrei-Institute in Elsass," 3 parts, "Die Einkommensquellen, i. Das Kirchenvermoegen," part 3, *Archiv fuer Elsassiche Kirchengeschicte* VIII (1932): 14; Andre Schaer, "Le Chapitre Rural Ultra Colles Ottinis en Haute-Alsac, Apres La Guerre de Trente Ans Jusque a La Revolution. La Vie Paroissale dans Un Doyen Alsacien D'Ancien Regime (1648-1789)," *Archv. de L'Eglise D'Alsace,* XVI (new series) (1967-68): 200; Rev. H.J. Schroeder, *Canons and Decrees of the Council of Trent* (St. Louis, 1941), pp.157, 429; John Bossy, "the Counter-Reformation and The Catholic People of Europe," *Past and Present* (1970): 51-70; Michael P. Fogarty, *Christian Democracy in Western Europe, 1820-1953* (London, 1957), p.7.

3. The above paragraphs reflect a summary of encyclopedic articles. Richard P. McBrien, *Encyclopedia of Catholicism*, HarperCollins, New York, NY, 1995, "England, Catholicism;" "Ireland, Catholicism;" "Celtic Spirituality;" "St. Patrick."

CHAPTER ONE

Catholicism Comes to Buffalo

On October 12, 1492, three small vessels, *Nina*, *Pinta*, and *Santa Maria* that had sailed from Spain in August anchored in shallow waters surrounding the Bahama Islands in the West Indies. The small fleet was under the command of Christopher Columbus, an Italian from Genoa, who had been commissioned by Queen Isabella of Castile to sail west, discover new lands, and possibly find a watery passage to Asia. Three months later, Columbus returned to Spain. Quickly word spread throughout all Europe that a Western World, hitherto unknown, had now been found. At the dawn of the sixteenth century many entrepreneurs and emissaries of Spain, France, Portugal, Belgium, Sweden, Italy, England, and the Netherlands began to explore and exploit the North and South American Continents that today are known as the Western Hemisphere. John Cabot, an Italian navigator, under the employ of the English Crown, was the first to reach the East Coast of Canada in 1497. Ten years later Jacques Cartier, sailing from France, discovered the St. Lawrence River. In 1608 a Frenchman, Samuel de Champlain, who in 1603 had surveyed the length of the St. Lawrence River, established the settlement at Quebec. He later developed a trading center at Montreal, discovered the Lake which bears his name, and became lieutenant governor of New France.

Louis de Buade Comte de Frontenac became governor of French Canada in 1672. He commissioned Louis Joliet to go west and explore the areas surrounding the Mississippi, Fox, Illinois, and Wisconsin Rivers. Rene Robert Cavelier De La Salle

and Father Louis Hennepin joined Joliet. They not only discovered the Mississippi but they traveled throughout the Great Lakes Region erecting forts and settlements along Lake Michigan, in Arkansas, and in the valley of the Illinois River. In 1682 they reached the Gulf of Mexico and claimed all the territory they had traveled through for France and gave it the name Louisiana. Traveling southwest from Quebec, they stayed for a time at Fort Niagara, a formidable stone trading post established by the French in 1669 at the mouth of the Niagara River as it entered Lake Ontario. Having received new provisions they moved up river until they saw for the first time the great cascade of Niagara. The river after flowing twenty miles downstream from Lake Erie split into two channels before cascading with awesome power. One channel, one thousand one hundred and eighty feet wide, fell one hundred and sixty-seven feet, while the other, three thousand one hundred feet wide, plummeted one hundred and fifty eight feet. Father Hennepin filled with emotion and reverence offered thanksgiving to God for such a wondrous spectacle; never had he seen such a vast volume of water moving with such power.

In 1609, Henry Hudson, a British explorer financed by the Dutch, while attempting to find a North East passage to the Pacific Ocean, discovered the Hudson River which runs from the Adirondack Mountains in New York State three hundred and fifty miles to the Atlantic Ocean. The West Indian Company was chartered in Holland and settlements were made in the New World all along the full length of the Hudson River.

In 1626 Peter Minuit bought Manhattan Island from the Indians for twenty-five dollars and co-established, with Cornelius Jacobsen Mey, the colony of New Amsterdam at the mouth of the Hudson River. The Netherlands declared it a province in 1643. In 1664, however, the English fleet appeared in the harbor and Peter Stuyvesant, the governor, surrendered it to the British who returned Dutch Guiana in South America to the Netherlands as a token gesture. New Amsterdam was renamed New York in honor of the Duke of York who received it as a gift from Charles II, King of England. Although the Dutch reclaimed it in 1673, they returned it again to English rule one year later.

$\mathcal{P}$ortugal established colonies in Brazil beginning in 1500. In 1513 Vasco Nunez Balboa crossed the Darien Isthmus, today known as the Isthmus of Panama, from the Atlantic Ocean to find another ocean which later was named by Ferdinand Magellan, a Portuguese navigator in Spanish employ, as the Pacific Ocean. While Hernando Cortez landed at Vera Cruz in Mexico in 1519, Magellan brought the Spaniards to Argentina. In 1520 he brought them to Chiloe, now known as Chile. Spaniards also explored the lands of Central America; they established Guatemala City in 1524. Cuba became a Spanish stronghold from which conquerors set sail to subdue the Incas Empire in Peru, Colombia, Venezuela, Ecuador, and Bolivia. Sebastian Cabot, son of John Cabot, opened Paraguay and Uruguay for exploitation, in 1527. In 1536 a fort was built at the present site of Asuncion in Paraguay. Ponce de Leon sailed to North America and discovered Florida in 1513. It was later settled by Spaniards, Englishmen, and French Huguenots. It remained a possession of Spain until it was ceded to the United States in 1819.

$\mathcal{S}$ir Walter Raleigh, an English explorer, led five expeditions to Virginia under the encouragement of Queen Elizabeth I. Although he planted the English flag in North America, he was a failure at his several attempts of colonization. In 1595, he did, however, make a successful expedition and settlement in Guiana in South America. The French Huguenots made a settlement on Paris Island, at Port Royal Harbor and established Fort Carolina in honor of King Charles IX. This is considered as the first colony of South Carolina. The first permanent English colony in North America was settled at Jamestown, Virginia in 1607. Captain John Smith acting as emissary of the London Company brought the first settlers to the colony. In 1614, he sailed along the full coast of New England; and, subsequently, James I, King of England, gave the Plymouth Company the rights to settle in the area that today is occupied by six states. On December 21, 1620, the *Mayflower* landed at Plymouth, Massachusetts, with a band of Puritans seeking religious freedom in North America. It became the second permanent English settlement in the New World. The Dutch and Swedes first settled Pennsylvania in 1614. After 1681 the territory was acquired by the British and Charles II, King of England, granted the territory to William Penn. In 1682 he brought a group of Quakers to form settlements. In 1608, Captain John Smith explored the area known today as Maryland. It was so named by him in honor of Henrietta Maria, queen consort to Charles I, King of England. The king deeded the land to Sir George Calvert, the first Lord Baltimore, who was born in Yorkshire, England. He died before the first settlement could be made there. In 1634, his youngest son, Leonard Calvert, accompanied by Andrew White, a Jesuit, brought the first colonists to that settlement that was Saint Mary's on the Potomac River. By 1770 the colony was attended to by twenty-three Jesuit priests. [1]

$\mathcal{T}$he explorers from France, Spain, and Portugal were predominantly Roman Catholics. They were staunch believers in the grace which came from the sacraments, particularly the Sacrament of Penance. Through this sacrament they had, by faith, the assurance that their sins would be forgiven when it was administered by a priest who rendered to them absolution. Their fear of being cast into hell upon death for serious unforgiven sins, should their demise result from some unforeseen disaster while at sea, prodded them into taking with them a priest as a confessor on their voyage to the New World. Many other priests, filled with an ardent missionary zeal, joined the excursions to find adventure and evangelical success among the natives of the lands chosen for discovery. Priests from the Religious Orders of Franciscans, Dominicans, and Jesuits came to the New World aboard Spanish and Portuguese vessels. When these vessels returned to Europe filled with booty taken from the explored and exploited lands, many priests, not engaged as confessors to the ships crew, remained with those who made settlements, living side by side with the natives. Franciscans focused their attention on Mexico, Ecuador, and Bolivia. Peru and Colombia were evangelized by the Dominicans. The expeditions of Sabastian Cabot brought the Jesuits to Paraguay and Brazil. In 1530, however, Charles I, King of Spain, forbade foreign priests from going to America unless they had received his royal permission. He also required that liturgical and sacramental practices in the communities in Spanish America follow those in vogue in Spain, particularly those exercised at Toledo and Seville. The first dioceses in both Spanish and Portuguese America were founded about 1550.

The Society of Jesus, commonly known as Jesuits, sent missionaries to New France. Between 1636 and 1649 several priests came, lived, and evangelized the native American Indians such as the Hurons, Algonquins, Mohawks, and Iroquois. Enthusiastic and idealistic Catholic laymen accompanied several of them. The names of those devout missionaries who worked among the Indians will forever be remembered as part of North American history. Isaac Jogues, Rene Goupil, John de la Land, Anthony Daniel, John de Brebeuf, Gabriel Lalemant, Charles Garnier, and Noel Chabanel suffered torture and death as they left their mark in the sands of that history. Other French priests traveled in close consort with the bands of explorers that discovered and surveyed the Great Lakes region and the Louisiana territory. Jacques Marquette, who was ordained a priest in France in 1666, traveled with Louis

Jolliet and founded missions at Sault Ste. Marie and Saint Ignace in Michigan, at Kaskaskia, Illinois, and in many villages down the Mississippi River as far south as the Arkansas River.

As the world welcomed the dawn of the eighteenth century, it saw that South and Central America, along with the islands of the West Indies, were well entrenched with the culture of Spain, while Brazil remained under the mantle of Portuguese education, training and language. Florida in North America was in Spanish hands, but Britain claimed the entire east coastal region above Florida to New England. In this region religious affiliation was shared by Puritans, Quakers, Huguenots, Low Church Anglicans, Scotch-Irish Presbyterians, Baptists, Methodists, Congregationalists, and Unitarians. Canada and the Louisiana Territory were in the hands of the French, and Catholicism was the religion of most settlers who liturgically practiced it provided that a priest was available. Catholics were never a majority in Maryland, neither were they a majority of passengers on the *Dove* and the *Ark* that brought the first settlers to Saint Mary's. Religious freedom in Maryland ended in 1692 when the Church of England became the established religion of the colony.

Until the American Revolution, Catholics in Maryland, although not persecuted, were penalized. The Quakers of Pennsylvania, however, were tolerant toward Catholics. A similar toleration existed in the colony of New York during the governorship of Thomas Dongan. In 1689, however, Catholicism was proscribed; a situation which lasted until after the American Revolution. Catholics were also scattered in areas of New Jersey and Virginia; and, in all of English America, only a few priests were available. Some English Jesuits supported themselves on slave operated farms and exercised an itinerant ministry. Six German Jesuits and a few Franciscans administered to a well-dispersed flock of Dutch farmers in Pennsylvania. Prior to the Revolution the only area in New England where some Catholics could be found was in Abnaki, Maine. These natives had been converted by French Jesuits from Canada. Between 1754 and 1760, Britain and France brought their disputes of the Seven Years War being carried on in Europe to North America. Historians referred to the engagement between these two powers in America as the French and Indian War. When it ended England was the victor, and French Canada became a British province. The French, however, continued to rule over the Louisiana Territory west of the Mississippi River. The United States of America purchased this territory, comprising one million square miles, from France in 1803.

At the signing of the Declaration of Independence by the colonists in 1776, all the territory from the Atlantic Ocean to the Mississippi River, which had been claimed by England prior to the American Revolution, contained only twenty-five thousand Roman Catholics. They represented only one-percent of the total population, and they were administered to by twenty-six priests, all former members of the Society of Jesus, which had originated in the sixteenth century following the Reformation in Europe, but had been suppressed before the American Revolution. By the eighteenth century the Society's membership had risen to thirty thousand. In 1715 Pope Clement XI showed his displeasure with the controversial missionary strategies of the Jesuits in China. They had attempted to adapt Catholicism to Chinese culture that for centuries had been wrapped in Confucianism. Franciscan and Dominican missionaries who had also evangelized in China jealously criticized this Jesuit practice, and brought their complaints to the papacy. In 1742 Pope Benedict XIV condemned the Jesuits' methods. In 1750 they were driven out of Paraguay because both the Spanish and Portuguese governments had complained to Rome that the Jesuits accused them of being inhuman to the native Indians. It was a fact that was true, but Rome sided with the governments. The final blow to the Society came, however,

following its complete financial collapse in France in 1764. Under pressure from France, Spain, and Portugal, Pope Clement XIV finally suppressed the Jesuits in 1773. Pius VII however, again restored them in 1814. At this time the most important newly restored Jesuit in the United States was John Carroll.

John Carroll was born in Upper Marlboro, Maryland in 1736. He was educated at Jesuit academies in Maryland and France. While attending school in France in 1753 he entered their Society and was ordained in 1761. When it was suppressed he returned, with twenty-two ex-Jesuit companions, to Maryland; and, as secular priests they took up missionary pastoral duties. Catholicism in America had not yet had a distinct identity. In 1776, Carroll accompanied his cousin Charles Carroll of Carrollton, the only Catholic to sign the Declaration of Independence, to Canada. Charles Carroll's mission, assigned by the Continental Congress, was to encourage the Canadians to join with the English Colonists in their war for independence. John Carroll acted as the confessor and spiritual advisor to the mission. It was further assumed that he would have an influence with the French Catholics in Canada. Charles Carroll, who was born at Annapolis in 1737, was a senator from Maryland to the first United States Congress, and was considered to be the richest man in the colonies. John Carroll's older brother, Daniel Carroll, educated in France, was a wealthy planter and merchant. He and Thomas Fitzsimmons were the only Roman Catholics to help frame and sign the Constitution of the United States in 1789.

In 1783 John Carroll was asked by the Papacy to organize the Catholic clergy in the colonies. The following year Pope Pius VII chose him to be the ecclesiastical head of the Catholic Mission Church in America. In 1789, he was raised by papal edict, *Ex Hoc Apostolicae,* to be the bishop of the first Catholic See in United States. His missionary diocese ran from the Atlantic Ocean to the Mississippi River. Carroll was ordained to his episcopal position at Lulworth Castle, England, on August 15, 1790 and acclaimed Bishop of Baltimore. In 1808, when he created four new dioceses besides his own, he was given the title of archbishop. The five dioceses were Baltimore, Bardstown, Boston, New York, and Philadelphia. Baltimore was considered an archdiocese and exercised its authority over all the other four, but it was, in itself, most attentive to the territories in the South. Philadelphia was to oversee all of Pennsylvania and the western countryside of New Jersey. When appointed, a bishop residing in New York City would govern throughout the State of New York and the eastern half of New Jersey. The Boston diocese would be responsible for the entire New England area. Bardstown, Kentucky serviced all the territory from the Allegheny Mountains to the Mississippi River. Between 1820 and 1829 six more dioceses were formed by Baltimore's archbishops who were Carroll's successors. They were: Charleston, South Carolina; Richmond, Virginia; Cincinnati, Ohio; St. Louis, Missouri; New Orleans, Louisiana; and Mobile, Alabama.

During his tenure as archbishop, John Carroll advocated universal religious toleration, and promoted the theory of the separation of Church and State. He attempted to introduce a republican style in Church government, but he was not successful. He would have liked to see the vernacular used in Church liturgy; but, from this, he had to retreat because it did not meet with papal approval. When he was aware that Rome would not approve of his allowing the laity to have a hand in choosing pastors for parishes, he left the choice in the hands of the individual bishops. In this way he allowed all of his parishes to assume a "mission status." He did, however, encourage lay trustees to build churches and care for their physical needs. Despite difficulties that were generated by some trustees who sought to use this encouragement to usurp their bishops' authority over temporal affairs, he never repudiated the system. When his tenure as archbishop came to an end with his death in 1815, it could be said that he, with serenity and skill, had been successful in accomplishing a most

remarkable and awesome task of adjusting an ancient faith to a new political order.

Some priests from Ireland who had studied in seminaries on the continent came directly to America. Others first returned to England, settled quietly into country villages where, as being a very small minority in the eighteenth century, they were no threat to the Protestants. Once in America, however, they felt threatened by the several French priests who had fled to the United States after choosing not to take the oath required by the *Constitution of the Clergy* decreed by the French Revolutionary government. These were mostly Sulpicians or educated by them, and had proven themselves heroic missionaries. The Irish, however, who had escaped the tyranny of Britain had no desire to live under any kind of continental domination. To them the French clergy represented that domination because they had become predominant favorites of Carroll and his successors, who whenever there was a need to appoint bishops to newly formed dioceses sought them from the ranks of Continental priests rather than from those of the Irish. Examples of the notable French bishops were Jean Louis Cheverus, Boston; Benedict Flaget, Bardstown; Louis William Du Bourg, New Orleans; Simon Brute, Vincennes; Michael Portier, Mobile; and Ambrose Marechal. Two other Continentals who were not Frenchmen were Joseph Rosati, an Italian bishop at St. Louis and Frederick Rese, a German bishop at Detroit. [2]

Although the continental clergy retained a majority of the ruling episcopal powers in the mission church in America, the Irish clergy of lesser rank outnumbered them and filled the episcopal positions when the aging French influence waned. The Irish clergy who reached episcopal prominence were either ordained in Ireland before emigration; or, following their immigration into America, received Holy Orders after being trained in Sulpician seminaries. Noteworthy among them were: Patrick Kenrick, John England,

Martin Spalding, John Purcell, William Quarter, Henry Conwell, and Benedict Fenwick. One outstanding Englishman was James Whitefield who became bishop of Boston after Cheverus returned to France. It was from the ranks of the Irish clergy of the Dominican Order located in Rome that the first and second bishops for the diocese of New York were directly chosen by papal authority. Luke Concanen, an Irish Dominican, first received the nod in 1808. He, however, died before crossing the Atlantic Ocean, and Pope Pius VII, who was in exile, had to wait until 1814 to appoint another Dominican Friar, John Connolly. He arrived in New York one year later. During the intervening seven years the vicar generals, Anthony Kohlmann and Benedict Fenwick governed the diocese. Connolly served as bishop for seven years and died suddenly at his residence at Saint Patrick's Cathedral located on Mott Street. Father John Power, an Irishman, assumed authority over the diocese for two years, until 1826, when John Dubois, a French Sulpician and expatriate of the French Revolution was ordained the third Bishop of New York by Ambrose Marechal in Baltimore on October 26, 1826.

John Dubois was born in Paris, France on the eve of the feast of Louis IX, king and saint, on August 24, 1764. He was the son of a bourgeois widow; his father had died while he was very young. At the age of seven he entered Louis Le Grand, a primary and secondary educational establishment in Paris. The Seine River was only a short distance down the hill from his school; and, from his dormitory window, he could gaze upon the towers of Notre Dame Cathedral. As a scholar, he was a precocious lad; he had a quick mind and had achieved a scholarship. Although he was of small size, his innocent brown eyes, soft face, and a sense of humor allowed him to fit in well with his fellow students. In 1783 following his graduation, he entered the seminary of Saint Magloire, Paris. He was ordained at the age of twenty-three in 1787. Following his ordination he became a priest in residence at Saint Sulpice, the largest and most elite parish in France with approximately ninety thousand parishioners. He remained there until he left France in 1791 at the height of the French Revolution.

Dubois belonged to the lowest estate in France. Although he was a member of the clergy he was not of the nobility; he was a commoner. Noble clergy could look forward to being appointed bishops while commoner clergy remained for a lifetime as parish curates. He made friends with his classmates among who were Camille Desmoulins, Maximilien Robespierre, and John Cheverus. On July 12, 1789, Desmoulins gave his vivacious speech, *A Call to Arms;* two days later a fired up mob stormed the Bastille and liberated the political prisoners. Robespierre was a leader of the revolutionaries in the beginning of the revolution but with shifts in the power struggle, he too ended his career as a victim of the guillotine. Before he died, however, he forged papers for Dubois, allowing him to leave France, unharmed, for America. At the height of the blood bath in Paris in 1792, Dubois was safe in exile in Virginia. He brought with him a letter of introduction to James Monroe from the Marquis de Lafayette. Adrienne Lafayette, wife of the Marquis, had been a member of the parish of Saint Sulpice and had become quite friendly with Dubois; sometimes he was her confessor. She interceded for him to her husband to receive this letter. Lafayette and Monroe had been comrades at the battle of Brandywine during the American Revolution.

Upon his arrival in Virginia, Dubois learned that Monroe was a United States Senator residing in Richmond, Virginia. Upon making his acquaintance, Dubois resided in that city. He said Mass in rented rooms and in the homes of the few Catholics whom he met. Upon the suggestion of Monroe, the State Legislature allowed Dubois to offer Mass in the courtroom of the new Capitol; it was the first time that Mass had been said in Richmond. He also became friendly with some Protestant ministers such as John Buchanan and John

Blair. While learning English he spent time with Patrick Henry. Later he rode circuit to Catholics in Norfolk, Alexandria, and Harpers Ferry. He supported himself by teaching French, Latin, Greek, writing, arithmetic, and bookkeeping in a rented building which he called his school. The only other priest who rode on the circuit was Jacob Frambach, a German. Technically Catholicism was proscribed in Virginia, but because of their friendship with Protestant ministers, and because the number of Catholics they administered to was insignificantly small, the authorities overlooked their evangelical activity.

In 1794, Bishop Carroll requested Dubois to center his missionary activity at Frederick, Maryland. It was there that Dubois made the acquaintance of Roger Brooke Taney who married Anne Key, sister of Francis Scott Key. Dubois presided at their wedding. Taney became a financial and legal advisor for Dubois and assisted him in building St. John's Church in Frederick. In 1836, Taney was appointed Chief Justice of the United States Supreme Court. Dubois spent the next ten years giving service to the growing Catholic population in northwest Maryland. In 1805, after purchasing land in what was called St. Mary's Valley, Dubois built a chapel on a small mountainside outside of Emmitsburg. From that year until 1821 he worked hard in establishing Mount Saint Mary's College, helped Elizabeth Ann Seton to establish her Order of the Daughters of Charity adjacent to his college, became the Sisters' superior, wrote their first set of regulations, built up his faculty especially after the arrival of Simon Brute, and finally gave last rites and witnessed the death of Mother Seton. Although his heart was broken in 1824 when the main building of his college was destroyed by fire, he started a new one immediately. The money to support the project poured in. With the help of Simon Brute, Dubois' seminary and college at St. Mary's was highly competitive with the Sulpician seminary in Baltimore. Jealousy within the Baltimore faculty reared its ugly head. Dubois and Brute were drummed out of the Sulpician Order. Two years later Dubois was

installed as bishop of the New York Diocese. Brute eventually was chosen Bishop of Vincennes.

In 1808, while Carroll waited for Rome to choose a bishop for the New York Diocese, he was dissatisfied with his Irish clergy. Protestants, who disliked Catholic laymen, were even more appalled with the priests. Several of the clergy that showed up in New York were an unproven lot. They had had problems with their ecclesiastical authority in Ireland and England and proved themselves to be scoundrels in America. They acted individually and often in opposition to episcopal authority. Two such priests, Matthew O'Brien and William O'Brien, would not communicate with Carroll. Matthew O'Brien was an acclaimed drunkard and a public scandal. Another priest, Patrick Kelly, who was pastor of St. Peter's Church in New York City, would lambaste his personal enemies from the pulpit. Although Carroll was most relieved when Bishop Connolly finally arrived from Rome, he did not know that these kinds of problems would become worse.

After the American Revolution most Catholic laymen had administered the temporal affairs of their churches in absence of local hierarchy. In New York the Irish population grew and so did resentment against the French clergy, especially the episcopate. The Irish did not wish to live under any foreign domination. As more dioceses were created, they did not want to hand over their authority to the new bishops or to the pastors who were assigned to their parishes. Shortly after becoming a resident bishop of New York, Connolly wrote a letter to the *Propaganda Fide,* the Roman curia charged with the administration of missionary activities, stating that if the bishops in America continued to prefer priests from the continent to those of Ireland it would harm the Church. He was emphatic in letting the papacy know that in New York the population consisted chiefly of Irishmen; they had built the churches, and they expected to have pastors who understood Irishmen. When Connolly died on

February 5, 1825, Father John Power, the Vicar General and an influential Irish priest, governed the diocese for two years, and moved to gain the episcopate. He was handsome, fair, with blue eyes, and dark curly hair. He had come to New York in 1818; he was intelligent, popular, ambitious, and courted public favor. John England, bishop of South Carolina, promoted Power's cause with Rome. On St. Patrick's Day, 1825, the combined Irish clergy of New York sent off a petition to Rome requesting that Power become their bishop. There was, however, a great deal of fraud in the claim of signatures on the petition.

*W*hen Cheverus left Boston in 1823 and returned to France to be appointed Cardinal at Bordeaux, Dubois' name was placed on the list for the bishopric of Boston. Conwell, an Irish bishop of Philadelphia, highly approved of this decision and Rome had a chance to look into the virtues of this man from Emmitsburg. Power kept up the pressure for the job in New York but Dubois' name continued to be considered. Archbishop Marechal, however, insisted that it was essential that he, as archbishop, be the one to decide whose names were to be presented to the Roman Curia as candidates to the American Sees. He insisted that there should be no lobbying with Rome, particularly an Irish lobby. He believed that Benedict Fenwick, president of Georgetown University, would make a good candidate, however, because of an insufficient number of Catholics in the New York Diocese, DuBourg backed by Flaget and David wanted to combine it and Boston into one diocese.

*T*he papacy asked Anthony Kohlmann, a Jesuit and former vicar general of New York, then living in Rome, to consider the criteria required for a bishop to be assigned to New York. After much consideration he spelled out three things required of a new bishop. He concluded that any new bishop should have the desire and ability to found a seminary in New York for young men with a vocation to the priesthood. The candidate should also have ability and a desire to establish a nunnery for the education of young ladies who would devote their lives to teaching and charitable activities. Finally, the candidate should be a person who would see that the orphanage being conducted by the nuns would be expanded. Kohlmann had only one person in mind that had shown abilities in these areas; that person was Dubois. Kohlmann sent his opinions and recommendation to *Propaganda Fide* on December 25, 1825 and again on March 31, 1826. On April 24, 1826, Pope Leo XII named the sixty-two year old Dubois as the third bishop of New York. At Dubois' consecration ceremony at Baltimore, William Taylor, a New York priest, an Irish activist and confidant of John Power, delivered the sermon. He was chosen by Dubois to do so as a way of placating the Irish hatred toward his appointment. Dubois realized that he had been placed as captain to an immigrant church swirling in a sea of fierce Irish nationalism. The choice backfired. Taylor, a convert from Protestantism who had been ordained a priest, expounded with words of meanness toward Dubois rather than uplifting ones. He wanted his words to be heard all the way to the Vatican. His theme was clear; no Frenchman should have been placed in charge as bishop of Irishmen. The entire text of his sermon appeared the following week in the *Truth Teller,* a New York Catholic paper edited by John Power.

*A*fter his consecration by Archbishop Ambrose Marechal, Dubois was installed in his cathedral in November 1826; Power, as vicar general, surrendered the reins to him. Dubois quickly pleaded with the Irish. He said, "Let there be one heart and one soul between bishop, priests, and laity. If so, the Catholics in New York might almost work miracles." He was now the leader of a Catholic population of twenty-five thousand souls. He had, however, only seven priests to share his labors in a diocese, which covered more than thirty million acres with nine churches, spread two hundred to three hundred miles apart. He did not quit the confessional from Saturday morning until Sunday night except for meals and divine services. To show the Irish that they should accept him even though he was a Frenchman he said, "St. Patrick, patron of Ireland, was born in Gaul!"

He also wrote many very good pastoral letters of kindness to the Irish people as a means of appeasing them; he spoke of the good qualities they brought to New York as immigrants. He appealed to their sense of fairness as a means of achieving cooperation. His letters never reached the laity's ears; Fathers Thomas Levin and John Power controlled the only Catholic paper, and they refused to print his letters. Dubois tried to especially reach out to those living at Five Points, which was an area of New York City at the intersection of five streets: Anthony, Little Water, Orange, Cross, and Mulberry. It contained a sprawling mass of filthy tenements with dark and dank cellars where tunnels led to the sewers; rats and disease were rampant. Nearby were an endless number of pawnbrokers, children who were ragged and barefoot, beggars, thieves, drunkards, and sex offenders. It was the Irish ghetto. Relating to it, Dubois observed a continued neglect of public instruction that led the Irish Catholics to almost total neglect of frequenting the sacraments and ignorance of the truths of religion. As the poor class they had to work on Sundays and therefore missed Mass. Marriages were attended with levity. Baptisms were performed in private homes, with refreshments, rather than in a church. Irish wakes were loaded with booze and lack of prayers. From his pulpit at St. Patrick's Cathedral, Dubois tried consistently to reach out to their spiritual needs. He said, "You have come to America in search of civil and religious freedom and liberty, but you have fallen into double slavery; the slavery of poverty and slavery of your own passions which have deprived you of both freedom and liberty."

The Erie Canal had been opened in 1825. It was a water system from the Hudson River to Buffalo on Lake Erie. Many Irish had been hired to bring this tremendous New York State project to completion. After it was finished these Irish workers spread far and wide throughout the State; many remained at the terminus of their work schedule. Dubois did not only administer to the Irish in New York City where he had three churches: St. Patrick's Cathedral, St. Peter's Church, and Christ Church, but visited them throughout the State following this canal system. When he found goodness among them he praised it; when he found evil he condemned it. In Albany, he removed Father John Savage from his pastorship. Because Dubois had no other priest to give to the church, he assigned laymen to conduct the administration of the congregation and promised occasional visits by a circuit priest. In Rochester, the trustees announced to him that the pastor, Father John McCormick, had eloped with a young woman in violation of morality and the obligations of his sacred office. Again Dubois dismissed the pastor, and assigned laymen to provide prayer services until a priest could be sent there.

In 1827, Dubois, while following the Erie Canal, found ten times the number of Catholics than he had expected in many scattered areas. In Buffalo, he found eight hundred of them who were Irish, French, Swiss, Alsatians, Lorrainers, and Germans. The three languages predominate among them were English, French, and German. Dubois was fluent in English and French, but for those speaking German, he heard their confessions using an interpreter in a manner that did not violate the seal of confession. He did the same when he heard the confessions of converted Indians. He also found that the French who had moved over the border from Canada to New York State refused to build churches because they were accustomed to receiving everything gratis in Canada where the Church and clergy were supported by government taxation. A year later, Dubois traveled to Baltimore for the consecration of Archbishop James Whitefield. Upon his return to New York City, he immediately set out to visit Canada; it was a begging and borrowing mission. It was while returning from this mission that he again visited Buffalo where Louis Le Couteulx, a fellow émigré from

France during the French Revolution, became his benefactor at the encouragement of Stephen Theodore Badin, a Kentucky missionary priest who had also fled Europe during that revolution. Badin had stayed six weeks, and conducted prayer services and said Mass at the courthouse and in the home of Louis Le Couteulx. He suggested that Le Couteulx donate and deed property to Bishop Dubois for the purpose of constructing on it a church for the conglomerate of Catholics whom had immigrated into Western New York. Because of the efforts of these three men, Dubois, Le Couteulx, and Badin, the seed of Roman Catholicism, which had been sown in the village of Buffalo prior to Dubois' visitations now blossomed forth. [3]

Buffalo had been founded by Joseph Ellicott, an agent for the Holland Land Company, in 1801. He named it New Amsterdam in courtesy to the Dutch land speculators who controlled the company. In 1810 its name was changed to Buffalo; reasons for choosing this name have several interpretations. When Dubois arrived for his visit the village had a population of three thousand. Although the Catholics had no church in which to congregate, they represented nearly twenty-seven percent of the total population which was mainly made up of Protestants who worshiped in five churches.

For several years after the American Revolution the western third of New York State remained in isolation. Activities of commerce and trading centered more around Fort Niagara than along the shore of Lake Erie. Western New York was essentially the home and hunting grounds to the Seneca Indians. The Commonwealth of Massachusetts laid claim to the ownership of the four million acres of land between the Genesee and Niagara Rivers but in practice financial claim could not be achieved unless the land was surrendered by purchase from the Indians. This seemed like a technicality to civilized financiers who negotiated the ownership of lands that their forefathers had claimed the right to simply because they had walked across them. In 1791, Robert Morris, born in Liverpool, England, émigré to the colonies in 1747, finance commissioner for the newly formed government of the United States, and senator from the Commonwealth of Pennsylvania, bought the four million acres from Massachusetts, and immediately sold it to the Holland Land Company, a multimillion dollar Dutch syndicate headquartered in Amsterdam, Europe. Wilhelm Willink, Pieter Stadnitski, Hendrick Vollenhover, Rutger Jan Schimmelpenninckm, Nicholas Van Straphorst, Pieter Eeghen, Gabriel Van Straphorst, Jan Willink, and Hendrick Seye were members of the board for the company. They represented six banks in Holland, and they sent Theophilus Cazenove to America as their agent. He set up an office in Philadelphia and appointed Joseph Ellicott as the chief surveyor, overseer, and developer of these millions of acres.

Before Ellicott could proceed with his work, the dummy holding company formed by the Dutch had to be legitimatized, the land had to be purchased from the Indians canceling their claim to it, and Morris had to remain financially solvent. In 1797, Thomas Morris, son of Robert Morris, made the purchase from the Senecas. He offered them $100,000. It was a bargain at two and one-half cents per acre. In 1798 the New York State legislature accommodated the Dutch speculators. It changed State law so that a foreign company could purchase land in the State. In that year Robert Morris was sent to debtor's prison in Philadelphia. Borrowing money on credit destroyed him when his creditors foreclosed, before his bank, which he had founded in North America in 1782, could find the cash to bail him out. His reputation of having been a signer of the Declaration of Independence, a mercantile businessman who had provided money to the Continental Army during the Revolution, and Superintendent of the Continental Congress in 1781 could not save him from this disgrace.

Following these financial settlements, Ellicott went

to work with a passion. He cleared trees, built roads along the Indian trails, and constructed bridges to span the rivers, streams, and creeks. Because of his achievements the price of the land tripled in value. He alone determined the location of counties, towns, and villages. He alone set the criteria for sales of property; he chose to sell in small parcels to families rather than give large holdings to manorial landlords. When he laid out the streets and packages of land in New Amsterdam, he modeled his work after the design of Washington D.C. whose architect had been Pierre L'Enfant. Ellicott was his assistant on that project originated in 1793. Although founded in 1801, the village of Buffalo was not laid out until 1803. Tragically it was burned to the ground in 1813 by a combined force of British and Indian troops who had captured Fort Niagara and proceeded down the Niagara peninsula laying waste to all the settlements in its path. The five hundred residents of Buffalo had fled before the British arrived. The newspaper office, the several taverns, the hotel, the jail, the homes of two physicians, the stores of two apothecaries, and the mercantile trade center became a pile of charred beams and smoldering ashes. The abandoned homes of the settlers who had come to Buffalo from the New England States, beginning around 1805, were looted by the Indians and destroyed by fire. By 1820, however, not only most of the original settlers returned, but also many others joined them. In a census that year, two thousand names were recorded. The village began once again to prosper, but it remained isolated.

In 1817, the New York State Legislature proposed the construction of the Erie Canal. It was to follow a route from the Hudson River at a point above Albany, travel west to the Mohawk River, follow the river to Oneida Lake, cutting into and following the Oswego River, passing through Syracuse known then as Salina, traveling to Rochester, and continuing on to Buffalo. Dewitt Clinton was the governor of New York and his opponents to its construction called the canal "Clinton's Big Ditch." When completed in 1825, it was three

hundred and sixty-three miles long and forty feet wide. A barrel of flour could be shipped by barge on the canal from Buffalo to New York City for thirty cents. Using overland travel the same barrel of flour would have cost ten dollars. This ninety-seven percent cost reduction in shipping made the canal an overnight success. Barge travel was nearly bow-to-stern moving in two directions. From New York City to Buffalo such a low cost travel fare made possible the transportation of thousands of immigrants who fled Europe and sought residence in the Midwestern States. Many of these seekers of farmland and fortunes found that the terminus of their western quest was Buffalo; they needed to seek no farther. In 1825 Buffalo's population had increased twenty percent in one year. By 1828, over three thousand people had become residents in the city; many others took up residence in the countryside.

Among the many real estate entrepreneurs of the post Revolutionary period in Western New York who dealt with Ellicott and the Holland Land Company was Louis Le Couteulx. When he arrived in New Amsterdam, as Buffalo was known in 1803, the residents were mainly land investors of English origin, immigrant Protestants from the New England States. Although Le Couteulx was French and a Catholic, he was a wealthy nobleman who figured prominently among the citizenry. Tall, erect, habited in black outer garment with cambric shirt front showing, ruffled wristbands, knee-breeches, hair tied in a queue, and in one hand a jeweled gold snuff box, the gift of his *bon ami,* Louis XVI, he was labeled by his peers as a "gentleman," a term used to express his elegance and propriety befitting his position. Born on the eve of the feast of Saint Louis, King of France, August 24, 1756 in Rouen, France, he belonged to a prestigious and wealthy family. Previous to the rise of the Rothchilds and other banking families, Le Couteulx family members had been financiers to the kings of France, in gratitude for which they were granted the title of nobility. During the American Revolution, they financially supported, through a complex series of loans, the colonists in their struggle for independence.

*B*eing fluent in English, Louis Le Couteulx was sent to America to secure payments of these loans after the war ended. Attracted by the many opportunities which he found in America and knowing of the dangers to his life on the eve of the French Revolution he became a United States citizen in 1789. After a brief return visit to France, he settled in America in 1790. Before coming to Buffalo, however, he lived in Albany, New York, where he commanded the esteem of many people as a druggist and sergeant-at-arms of the State Senate. His name on the cornerstone of St. Mary's Church bears witness to his beneficence to the Catholics in that area. When he moved to Western New York, he became the first county clerk of the newly created Niagara County. Immediately following the War of 1812, he suffered great financial loss, yet he quickly regained his prestige. His farsightedness and sense of enterprise, coupled with his great generosity, won for him the admiration of his fellow Buffalonians. As early as 1803, he was a central figure in a group of financiers who envisioned Buffalo's eventual destiny as a great commercial center, using the city's lake port as a prime attraction, once the sand bar to the entrance was removed.

*U*pon arriving in Buffalo, he entered into the service of Joseph Ellicott as an agent for the Holland Land Company. On many occasions he wrote letters to the directors and managers of the company such as Theophilus Cazenove, and L. Van Staphorst in order to encourage them to give him a free hand in building a church, school, and cemetery in the village to service the members of a small Catholic population. They had preceded the arrival of any priest to the village and had gathered with Le Couteulx in the privacy of their own homes to worship. Whenever a missionary arrived, however, such as Badin, they had the privilege of attending Mass. With the completion of the Erie Canal and the increased number of Catholics to the area, the need for a specific house of worship became apparent. During the late fall and early winter of 1828, Badin discussed the situation with Le Couteulx. He pointed out that only after a church was established would the congregation have an opportunity to have a resident priest appointed to serve as its pastor. Quickly Le Couteulx made his decision to make a generous donation of land for this purpose. On January 1, 1829 he had the deed to a specific piece of property owned by himself and his wife, Jane Eliza, transferred to John Dubois, the Roman Catholic Bishop of New York. In making the transfer he specified that the plot of land in Buffalo distinguished as Outer Lot twenty-five with two hundred and sixteen feet fronting Main and Delaware Streets with a four hundred foot depth would be used only for the purpose of establishing a Roman Catholic church, school, and cemetery. A portion of the cemetery was to be reserved for a vault which would, as years passed, act as the resting place for the bodily remains of the members of the Le Couteulx family. Another portion of Outer Lot twenty-five was to be set aside for rental, the proceeds of which would pay a salary to a resident priest. On January 5, 1829 the deed was filed at Erie County Court House in the presence of George R. Babcock. Louis and Jane Eliza then informed John Dubois of the completion of the deed's transaction, and offered it to him as a New Year's Day gift.

*O*n July 21, 1829, Dubois again came to Buffalo to ceremoniously accept and bless the land that had been deeded to him. He preached and said Mass at the courthouse and administered the sacraments of Baptism, Penance, and the Eucharist. A procession was formed which moved from the courthouse to the lot specified in Le Couteulx's donation, upon which a church was destined. Dubois consecrated the ground. Irish, Swiss, French, Alsatian, Lorraine, and German Catholics as well as many friendly and inquisitive Protestants attended the ceremonies. While in Buffalo, he was the ecclesiastical witness at the marriage of Anthony Crique and Elizabeth Beidz, both of who had been born in Alsace and had immigrated to America. The other witnesses were Jean Gaspar Pfeffer and Joseph Wandling. It was the first recorded wedding that took place while Dubois visited the village.

Dubois was so elated that upon returning to New York City he wrote to the Pope. He described his elation, telling him how he found in Buffalo, a village near the Falls of the Niagara, a good and pious Frenchman who had donated to him a superb tract of land for building a church for over eight hundred Catholics in the area. He described the joy that came to his heart when he administered the sacraments to so many, and his surprise at the number of baptisms he was requested to make. He praised the great emotion he saw among the people present when he celebrated the Holy Sacrifice of the Mass; their voices were firm; their singing was true, pious, and melodious; and their faces were filled with modesty, recollection, and devotion. He knew that he had found a gold mine of spirituality in Western New York, the far-off outpost of his vast diocese. In return, the Catholic colony of Western New York knew that it had found a sympathetic ecclesiastical friend in him.

As bishop he acted quickly in finding a priest to be resident in Buffalo; one who would be both fluent in French and German languages. He chose Reverend John Nicholas Mertz who quickly arrived to take pastorship of the immigrant flock. He was one of the only four European German-speaking priests who were in the United States at that time. He had been born in Bondorf near Trier in 1764, ordained in 1790, and immigrated into America in 1811. For three years he served among the German Catholics in Conewago, Pennsylvania followed by fifteen years of service in Baltimore before coming to Buffalo. Although he was advanced in years, he was a dedicated clergyman full of all the sacrificial spirit needed by a frontier priest. He was respected and loved by the majority of people with whom he came in contact; not only did Catholics love

him, but so also did members of other denominations recognize his virtues. By many, he was considered a saint because in all things he found consolation in Jesus Christ. Through humility he acquired patience; in suffering patiently his tribulations were no longer suffering. He bore the afflictions of life with indescribable equanimity in order to please his Christ and spiritually feed his flock to which Christ had entrusted him. He sought only the flock's salvation while continuing to understand the vicissitudes of the lives of the men, women, and children under his care. Being content with the possessions of the necessities of life, he sought only the fulfillment of the will of God.

At first, finding no rectory reserved for his lodging, Mertz took up shelter in a log house on the west side of Pearl Street between Court and Eagle Streets; it was Charles Miller's livery stable. His evening meal usually consisted of a few potatoes, roasted in the ashes of his fireplace, accompanied with a cup of tea. When Le Couteulx heard of the scantiness of his menu, he lost no time in perfecting arrangements whereby the larder of the pastor was properly supplied. In a former Methodist meeting house, Mertz set up his first place of worship with a school for the children. Although furnishings were few, Vespers were often sung with the accompaniment of a small reed organ. Soon his church was too small for the rapidly increasing Catholic population including those from the farm areas that would drive their teams to the village on Sundays. By the beginning of 1830 it was obvious that a larger church had to be built. A canonical circular was posted in the village spreading the good news of the Catholic populous' intentions concerning its plans of religious expansion. It contained the plan to build a church on the property, valued at $1,000, donated by Le Couteulx and deeded to Bishop Dubois. It's design called for a structure fifty feet by fifty feet in length and width and twenty-six feet high containing three galleries, several pews, and finished in the most smooth and economical manner, suitable without pomp or extravagance. The document ended with a profound statement that had prophetic overtones. It read, "This immortal monument of Christian philanthropy will show our brethren, friend, foe, sojourner, and traveling stranger that our hearts are devoted to our Christian religion."

*I*n the fall of 1831, Mertz undertook the task of building a permanent church at a cost of $180. The expense was partly covered by money he had brought with him from Europe and partly from donations provided by families in the congregation, many of who were relatively poor. Like most of the construction activities on the frontier, labor and materials were supplied by the parishioners as were meals and lodging for the workers, several of who came in from the neighboring farm country. By the spring of 1832, a small wooden church was completed. Its exterior appearance resembled a primitive log house with timbers exposed on the outer surface. The walls were covered with a rough coating of plaster between the beams; an air of solidity, comeliness, and comfort pervaded the entire edifice. When the congregation first viewed the building, nicknamed the *Wigwam,* it resembled an Iroquois tribe's Long House. Upon completion, however, the church was named the Lamb of God suggested by the figure of a lamb on a bronze tabernacle brought by Mertz from Europe. It was under this title that it was consecrated by Bishop Dubois on his visit to Buffalo, following his return to New York after his European tour where he had spent his time begging for funds and priestly personnel so vitally needed in his large diocese. In 1835, Mertz was seventy-one years old; he could not continue alone because his duties were too arduous. Dubois sent Father Alexander Pax to Buffalo to be his assistant. A year later Mertz made a short visit to his homeland in Europe after which he returned to Western New York and took up residency in Eden. He spiritually labored there until his death in 1844. It was with the act of consecration of the Lamb of God by Dubois that Catholicism found a permanent home in Western New York; and, from this first site of residency, it spread far and wide across the Niagara Frontier, and into the southern counties of New York State to the border of Pennsylvania, and it lasted uninterruptedly for one hundred and seventy-five years. *Ad Multos Annos!* [4]

Above: **The Most Reverend John Hughes** who succeeded John DuBois as Bishop of the vast New York Diocese in August of 1839.

REFERENCES AND NOTES ✣ CHAPTER ONE

1. Names, dates, and events in preceding paragraphs taken from entries in the encyclopedic sources: A. H. McDannald, Editor-in-Chief, *The Modern Encyclopedia*, W.H. Wise and Co., New York, NY, 1935; Francis J. Reynolds, Editor-in-Chief, *World's Popular Encyclopedia*, The World Syndicate Publishing Co., New York, NY, 1937, 10 vols.; Harold J. Blum, Exec. Editor, *Illustrated World Encyclopedia*, The National Lexicographic Board, Woodbury, NY, 1970, 21 vols.

2. Names, dates, events, and biographical sketches in preceding paragraphs were taken from the following indexed sources: Thomas Bokenkotter, *A Concise History of the Catholic Church*, revised and expanded edition, Image Books, Doubleday, New York, NY, 1990, Ch. 31, "The American Church;" Richard P. McBrien, Gen. Editor, *Encyclopedia of Catholicism*, HarperCollins, New York, NY, 1995, "Catholicism in the United States," and other topics as listed; R.R. Palmer and Joel Colton, *A History of the Modern World Since 1815*, Alfred Knopf, New York, NY, 1978; Prologue, xii, and topics found in index through 19th C., as located in the text.

3. For extended biographical information concerning Bishop Dubois see: Richard Shaw, *John Dubois, Founding Father*, United States Catholic Historical Society, Yonkers, NY, and Mount St. Mary's College, Emmitsburg, MD, 1983; Richard Shaw, *Dagger John, The Unquiet Life and Times of Archbishop John Hughes of New York*, Paulist Press, New York, NY, 1977. The author/editor was first introduced to these preceding texts by Frank Mason, a lay minister at St. Pius X Church, Loudenville, New York; personal friend to Richard Shaw; and former teacher of Bishop Howard Hubbard, Albany, New York. For Stephen T. Badin's biographical material see: op. cit. *Encyclopedia of Catholicism*. For the living conditions of the Irish in New York City see: C. Eugene Miller and Forrest Steinlage, *Der Turner Soldat; A Turner Soldier in the Civil War; Germany to Antietam*, Calmar Publications, Louisville, KY, 1988, p. 36. For Dubois at school in France see: Robert R. Palmer, *The School of the French Revolution*, Princeton, 1975, pps. 75ff. For Dubois' escape from France see: James R. Bayley, *A Brief Sketch of the Early History of the Catholic Church on the Island of Manhattan*, New York, 1870, pps. 104ff. For Dubois' relation with John Carroll see: Peter Guilday, *The Life and Times of John Carroll*, New York, 1922, vol. 2, pps. 167, 405. For the Daughters of Charity at Emmitsburg see: Sarah Trainer Smith, "Philadelphia's First Nun," *Records of the American Catholic Historical Society of Philadelphia*, 1894, vol. 5, pps. 417ff; Sister Mary Agnes McCann, *The History of Mother Seton's Daughters*, New York, 1917, vol. 1, p.23ff. For Irish resentment of the French clergy and hierarchy see: Ronen John Murtha, *The Life of the Most Reverend Ambrose Marechal*, Ann Arbor, MI, 1975, p.221ff. For Dubois traveling through the wilderness of his vast Diocese of New York, see: "Association for the Propagation of the Faith," *Historical*

Records and Studies, New York, 1909, vol. 5, p. 220. For the problems of Bishop Connolly, first resident bishop of the New York Diocese, with the laity and clergy see: Rev. William Taylor, *An Address to the Roman Catholics of New York*, New York, 182, p.3. According to Kohlmann, Dubois was the man who as bishop could fulfill the three requirements as the third bishop of the Diocese of New York. See: "Anthony Kohlmann to Propaganda Fide," New York Archdiocesan Archives, 1815.

4. For the City of Buffalo, the Holland Land Company and Le Couteulx land grant see: C. Eugene Miller, Gen. Editor, *Good Shepherd, The Church on the Canal, 1847-1997*, Good Shepherd Roman Catholic Church Society, Pendleton, NY, 1997, pps. 1-10; Richard C. Brown and Bob Watson, *Buffalo: Lake City in Niagara Land*, Windsor Publication, Buffalo, 1981, p.72; Mark Goldman, *High Hopes, The Rise and Decline of Buffalo, New York*, State University of New York Press, Albany, NY, 1983, pps. 1-47; "The Holland Land Company," *Buffalo Evening News*, October 3, 1953; Anita Louise Beaudette, *A Man And a Church Named Louis*, Unpublished Paper, D'Youville College, Buffalo, NY, 1954; "St. Louis Deed Valid," *Buffalo Express*, Aug., 12, 1914; Letter of John Dubois Bishop of New York, *Annals of the Association for the Propagation of the Faith*, Lyon, Rusand, 1830, vol. 4, p. 449ff. For biographical Material on Louis Le Couteulx see: Molly B. Hauck, Historian, *Louis Le Couteulx, Buffalo Pioneer and Philanthropist*, Mount Calvary Archives, Buffalo, NY, 1999; excerpts of her text are included in Chapter Three of this text. Information concerning John Nicholas Mertz, the erection of the Lamb of God Church, and the work of Father John Neumann see: *Andenken Hockw. Herrn Joh. Nik. Mertz einem der ersten deutschen Priester der Ver. Staaten und ersten Mission-Priester von Buffalo, N.Y.*, Kath. Volks-Ztg, Baltimore, MD, 1868, pps. 1-72; Translation of the preceding pages was done for the author/editor by Karla Braun-Kolbe, a student of linguistics and law at the State University of New York at Buffalo. "Letter from Rev. Alig, " St. Louis Church Archives, Buffalo, NY, dated 1844; St. Louis Dramatic Circle, *Anniversary Souvenir and Programme of St. Louis Dramatic Circle*, St. Louis Church Archives, 1896, p.16; *The St. Louis Bazar Chronicle*, Buffalo, NY, Oct., 30, 1888, vol.1, no.8; *The St. Louis Bazar Chronicle*, Buffalo, NY, 1888, vol.1, no.2; *St Louis Bazar Chronicle*, Buffalo, NY, Nov. 2, 1888, vol. 1, no.11; Glen Atwell and Ronald Elmer Batt, *The Chapel: A Comprehensive History of the Chapel and Pilgrimage of Our Lady Help of Christians, Cheektowaga, New York and the Alsatian Immigrant Community at Williamsville, New York*, The Holling Press Inc., Buffalo, NY, 1981, p.14; J. Berger, *Leben und Wirken des hochseligen Johannes Nep. Neumann, C.SS.R., Bischofs von Philadelphia*, New York, NY, 1883, p. 121. The canonical circular distributed in the City of Buffalo announcing the construction of the Lamb of God Church as presented in *The St. Louis Bazar Chronicle*, Buffalo, NY, Oct., 27, 1888, vol.1, no., 6 is given here: " To all Benevolent and Charitable Christians of every denomination whom this may concern. We of the Roman Catholick profession, Citizens of the village of Buffalo, Erie County, and State of New York, Greeting.

Seeing our depraved situation, degenerating from our duty as Christians, destitute of that care which a pastor of our church could render, and also destitute of a House of Worship belonging to our profession, in this section of that County and only Country on the Globe, which the great Creator of mankind has doomed to be blessed with Liberty of Conscience. DO firmly and unanimously intend, with the assistance of God and our Christian Brethren, of all denominations, to build a CHURCH, 50 feet by 50 feet, and 26 feet high, and three galleries, several pews, and finished in the most smooth and economical manner, suitable without pomp or extravagance, on a certain commodious lot of ground in the aforesaid village of Buffalo, the lot in extent of two acres, beautifully situated, and valued at $1,000. Rendered and granted to the Roman Catholick Church by a member of said Church a native of France, Doctor Louis Le Couteulx. The foregoing being a true statement of our Religious intentions, hoping under God that we may prosper in this good design, we do solicit the assistance of all Charitable Christians to erect an immortal monument of Christian Philanthropy, and show our Brethren, the friend, the foe, the sojourner and travelling stranger, that our hearts were devoted to the Christian Religion."

Most Reverend John Timon who was appointed the first Bishop of the newly formed Diocese of Buffalo created by Pope Pius IX on April 23, 1847. Timon consecrated St. Louis Church on December 21, 1847.

CHAPTER TWO

Mother Church of Western New York

$\mathcal{T}$oday as in centuries gone by, when Catholics reach the end of their proclamation of faith at each Sunday Mass, they pronounce their belief in the Communion of Saints. They believe that there is one body made up of many members; those who are members of the Catholic Church on earth, those members of the Church who have died and reached a nebulous place called Purgatory, awaiting their release to enjoy the Divine Vision, and those who have died and are now participating in all the satisfaction of that Vision. Categorically they are called the Church Militant, the Church Suffering, and the Church Triumphant. One hundred and seventy-five years ago a band of Irish, Alsatian, Lorraine, French, Swiss, and German Catholics, residents of Buffalo, New York, and the environs thereof formed a Church Militant which founded the Catholic parish which today is known as St. Louis Church. When the doors of its predecessor, the Lamb of God Church, opened in 1832, there was no other edifice in Western New York that could be called a Roman Catholic Church. From that year, throughout the decades, touching three centuries and the construction of three more replacement churches, an expanding Church Militant consisting of a flood of European immigrants and their descendants came to worship at the corner of Main and Edward Streets. The present day structure stands proudly in all its Gothic Grandeur as the Historic Mother Church of the Buffalo Diocese, waiting to welcome to liturgical service members, friends, foes, sojourners, and traveling strangers.

$\mathcal{T}$he early history of this church is a treatise in perplexity, a labyrinth in which minds, wills, hearts, and emotions clashed, but the goal of all involved was the same —the preservation of Catholicism where grace through the sacraments flowed into the core of everyone's soul. As a Mother Church in a missionary land, St. Louis was like a woman who is about to give birth. She has anxiety because her hour is come. As a Mother Church she had to lay down the policies, principles, and attitudes by which her militant must live, worship, and die. These became the beginnings of a Rare Tradition in American Catholicism; they were established with pain. When her child is born into the world, the mother no longer remembers her anguish because of the joy that she feels holding it close to her bosom. So also the Mother Church had joy because the Catholicism she spawned permeated through the entire Communion of Saints of Western New York.

$\mathcal{P}$ost Revolutionary War Catholics in an evolving country, which was based on the principle of everyone having the inalienable right to life, liberty and the pursuit of happiness, needed to be aggressively active, almost combative. They were truly the Church Militant. In Western New York in 1829 they were the minority of the frontier's population, and they were of foreign extraction. Many French Catholics had come from French Canada, others were émigrés of the French Revolution, and a few were descendants of early French fur traders. Irish Catholics had made Buffalo the terminus of both their labors in building the Erie Canal and their quest to move west. Although most lived in poverty, they carved out an existence in the byways along the Buffalo harbor. Several Swiss families had fled Europe, came first to Canada, and finally sought refuge in Buffalo. They, however, were also prone to travel west. The German-speaking people, however, made up the largest faction of the Catholic population in Buffalo. These were Alsatians, Lorrainers, and Rheinlanders, and they outnumbered the other ethnic groups three to one. Also the Alsatians and Lorrainers were somewhat wealthy, mobile, and ambitious, and they were particularly liked by Le Couteulx because, being French by citizenry in Europe, he considered them as fellow countrymen.

With the arrival of Nicholas Mertz as pastor the Alsatians and Lorrainers began to dominate the parish by promoting and showing leadership in spiritual, intellectual, and cultural activities. Among those families which grew to prominence in leadership during a ten year period following the completion of the Erie Canal were the Haberstros, Handels, Sandracks, Webers, Ottenots, Allenbrandts, and Mesmers. Although the Alsatians and Lorrainers had been French subjects in Europe, they, in America, maintained their German traditions, especially their language. They were well educated and developed high economic standards. With the decline of trade on the Upper Rhein after the defeat of Napoleon, thousands of them immigrated to America. In Buffalo, they were almost indistinguishable from their German counterparts, mainly the Rheinlanders who had emigrated from the lands drained by the Rhein, Moselle, and Saar Rivers. There were, however, other Germans who came to America from Bavaria's Palatinate, a province on the west side of the Rhein River north of Alsace. In both groups one found those who had been farmers of sugar, hops, flax, and fruits or had worked as laborers in coal mines, iron shops, or textile factories. The Alsatians and Lorrainers, however, concentrated in the skilled trades to a degree greater than other Germans, Anglo Saxon Americans, or the

Irish. By the late 1840's several had established their houses of business such as dry goods stores, cobbler shops, and clockwork factories on Main Street. They also remained longer in Buffalo than did those from the other groups who in subsequent years found greener pastures in the West. Although many of them, such as Joseph Haberstro, had immigrated directly to Buffalo and assiduously accumulated capital, they were somewhat reluctant to maintain all their European customs especially in their homes that were void of high *Fachwerk* designs, and sloping roofs.

Joseph Haberstro was born in Altkirch, Alsace, and attended a home school for his early education. When he came to America in 1828 he was a distinguished mastercraftsman in the art of designing and manufacturing rifles. Upon arriving in Buffalo he took up residence on Washington Street near Carroll. In 1830 he made a fifteen-year contract with Louis Le Couteulx to lease and operate a shop at 193 Main Street. Later, he established a second business at 523 Main between Mohawk and Genesee Streets. In 1830, he married Catherine Mesmer. They exchanged their vows in the Sacrament of Matrimony witnessed by Mertz. Between 1830 and 1845, Haberstro held a lucrative contract to produce rifles for the army of the German Confederation. During these years he was a leader of the trustees of the congregation which worshiped in the Lamb of God and St. Louis churches. The members of the congregation claimed that they rested upon his shoulders. He died on March 29, 1862.

These pioneer Alsatians and Lorrainers, like Haberstro, regarded economic power as the catalyst of their existence in Western New York. Although they did not seem to be unduly devout, they knew that a church would not appear unless they developed it. They wanted to enjoy the religion of their forebears in the Old World; they wanted to live life with the Catholic Sacraments. Otherwise, how would their children be baptized, confirmed, absolved of sins, receive the

Eucharist, marry, and die anointed deaths? For those fostering their children to consider life among the clergy, how were they to seek ordination without a place of worship? They knew that the answer lay in their hands and theirs alone. Stephen Badin, a circuit priest, knew this when he encouraged Le Couteulx to donate the land on Main and Edward Streets for a church, school, and cemetery. The donation of this land to Bishop Dubois for the sole purpose of doing this was given to him "in trust." When the people would come forth and build their church upon this land, they, by civil law, would be the responsible owners of it.

When the congregation of mixed nationalities received from Dubois their first priest, Nicholas Mertz, controversy quickly erupted. Although the German-speaking element considered themselves as the leaders, each of the other nationalities saw themselves as having a profound claim on any church that was to be built. The Irish were the most disturbed; Mertz was a priest who not only had trouble hearing confessions in English, but he was reluctant to give sermons in English. When he preached for the benefit of the English-speaking portion of the congregation, he would give very short sermons in that tongue. In his humble way to do his best, he would often tax and confuse himself as well as the listeners. The result of his mixing up words brought forth from his lips crude phrases that caused much merriment, particularly among the Irish. The German-speaking element in the congregation were also not pleased with his efforts of sermonizing in English, stating that the Irish being a minority in the church should learn German, and then they could understand and enjoy the sermons. Further the Germans pointed out that the rest of the Mass was said in Latin and all were at an equal disadvantage there if they had not read the translations of that language. Mertz disapproved of this logic, and admonished their vocal outcries. He said, "This is not a church for the Germans, or the French, or the Irish, or any nationality, or party. This is simply a Catholic Church, for all Catholics in Buffalo and the environs thereof."

Although Mertz seemed comfortable with his French, the Frenchmen in the parish believed that the appointment of a German priest was inappropriate since it was the French influence which contributed the land. In the faces of the more jolly Palatinate Bavarians redness appeared. They saw in Mertz only a stern Jansenistic Rheinlander. He, however, tried to be impartial, but turned his back on innovation and continued to don the three cornered hat, the breeches, and the knee buckles of the Rheinland clergy. Although the German attendance at Mass tripled during his tenure as pastor, his asceticism was lionized. He refused to allow the congregation to put a furnace in the church and would not accept an offer to have a new organ built. He contended that the reed organ would suffice. For many years after he had left Buffalo, the story was told and retold as to how the congregation had to huddle together on one Christmas Eve at Midnight Mass because they were freezing in his unheated church. It was well established in the story that the congregation on that night worshiped with great intensity; the warmth of divine grace was needed in their bodies as well as in their hearts. In spite of his asceticism, trivial upheaval, and childish cynicism, the parish never ceased to enjoy a functional calm and prosperity. Mertz assumed the role of spiritual leader and left the administration of the temporalities of the church completely into the hands of the leaders who called themselves the trustees. Although he refused to have certain things done such as the installation of a furnace and a new organ, he made his refusal to the trustees in such a way as to appeal to their reason and not unravel their anger. He profoundly believed that "one in the hand was worth two in the bush!" Besides, in 1833, he gave tacit approval of the request of an organized group of laymen at the Lamb of God to handle the finances of the parish. Louis Le Couteulx also approved of lay management of the new church, even though he was aware that very little money had been provided for its construction. He knew that the congregation's labor and donation of materials was of equal value. This unruffled beginning of trusteeism at the Mother Church, however, was immediately brought under scrutiny by Father Johann Raffeiner.

*U*pon Dubois' visit to Buffalo in 1833, Raffeiner ridiculed the trustees at the Lamb of God Church. He asked them how much each had donated toward the construction of the church. The trustees only replied with confusion; they said they had given nothing. Unlike Le Couteulx, they did not consider their labor and materials as a financial contribution, but Dubois, who heard their answer to Raffeiner, was well appreciative of their efforts. Because of his own French background and the difficulties of administering such a large diocese as New York from a distance of four hundred and twenty miles away, Dubois approved of the trustee system as it was developing in Buffalo, even though he disapproved of it in New York City. Raffeiner, however, was wary of the evils of it. He was an Austrian by birth and a physician during the Napoleonic Wars. Although he had a lucrative post-war practice in Europe, he decided to enter the seminary and study philosophy and theology. He was ordained in 1825 and came to New York City in 1833. Immediately Dubois put him in charge of visiting all the German congregations scattered in the far-flung Diocese of New York. In this position Raffeiner formulated his opinions in opposition to the evils of trusteeism and felt that the system should be abolished. It was this type of thinking which later made him very much liked by Archbishop John Hughes who subsequently replaced Dubois and made Raffeiner a vicar general and liaison among the German flock. He worked in the diocese for thirty years. With his own money, he financed the construction of St. Nicholas Church in New York City and assumed its pastorship by appointment from Hughes.

*T*rusteeism in Post Revolutionary War America, from the Atlantic Ocean to the Mississippi River, was an inevitable and logical outcome of Catholic laymen preceding clergy to a location where eventually a Catholic parish would be formed and a church constructed. The will on the part of the laymen to administer a church easily followed after they had financed or built with their own hands a place of worship. Furthermore, Catholics were a minority, and they looked to the methods whereby Protestant churches were being administered. In New York State, Catholic laymen found that laws protecting churches, mainly Protestant, which had been incorporated, dated as far back as 1784. It was well established in English Law that a church itself could not be incorporated, only specific groups of churchmen could enjoy this privilege. They were the trustees. Although Catholic bishops understood the value of incorporation, they also felt their authority threatened by a conflict of civil law with ecclesiastical law when the trusteeism of stubborn laymen would clash with self-determined clergy. The Catholic bishops' fears were not unwarranted because these clashes did occur causing much embarrassment.

*T*rusteeism was not necessarily the culprit; it was the abuse of the system that was wrong. In many cases laymen regarded it as ideal. In other cases the clergy was excluded from all control except for spiritual concerns. In all abusive cases there was a tendency to regard as justifiable the appeal to the civil power in order to protect the trustees' course of action. Ecclesiastical authority looked upon trusteeism as an evil that had to be squelched. In its eyes it was a disease, but it lasted in American Catholicism from 1785 until it was finally subdued in 1863. The hierarchy began its cure with the First Provincial Council of Baltimore held in 1829. The provisions made that year were reiterated and expanded in subsequent councils and finally applied to the entire American Church in the First Plenary Council held in 1852. Whatever legal basis may have existed, lay power was not in the minds of the nation's Catholic hierarchy, and this conclusion was supported by Catholic Tradition. In the minds of the laity, however, it seemed very reasonable to formulate a type of lay trusteeism as a compromise between total and partial clerical control of both spiritual and temporal activity. It would consist of partial temporal control by the laity with clerical conciliation so stipulated in the form of a contract. Such a contract, so established in the early nineteenth century and maintained uninterruptedly through more than three-quarters of the twentieth century would be considered as a Rare Tradition in American Catholicism.

Until his departure from Buffalo in 1836, Mertz, besides attending to the duties of a pastor at the Lamb of God in cooperation with the trustees, he also was required to administer to rural Catholics in the environs of the city. There were clusters of Catholics in the environs of Buffalo in Erie and Niagara Counties. At these places he periodically attended to the sick, said Mass, and consoled them with the sacraments. Under his leadership a parish church named for St. John the Baptist was started at Lockport in 1834, and a log-church which carried the same name was built at North Bush in 1836. In the same year a chapel was constructed in Williamsville. It was called the parish of Sts. Peter and Paul. Also in that year Dubois sent a secular priest, John Neopomecene Neumann, to Western New York. Neumann was born in Bohemia March 28, 1811. After studying the basic humanities and philosophies under the Paulist Fathers at Budweis, he began his studies in theology. On July 21, 1832, he was tonsured and received the four minor orders leading to the priesthood in the Catholic Church. Subsequently he took courses at the University of Prague but returned to Budweis in 1835. At this time he expressed his desire to go to America to do missionary work among the many German-language Catholics who had immigrated there and had set up permanent residences.

On April 20, 1836, Neumann sailed from Le Havre, France, on the ship *Europe*. When it landed in New York in May, Dubois immediately ordained him and sent him via the Erie Canal to Buffalo with a brief stopover in Albany and Schenectady. On July 13, 1836, he said his first Mass in the Lamb of God Church, and proceeded directly to Williamsville to minister to the spiritual needs of its German settlers. For four years, accompanied only by his horse that carried his backpacks, he trudged along

the roadways with his walking stick giving service to the clusters of Catholics organized by Mertz at North Bush, Lancaster, Sheldon, Pendleton, Swormville, Batavia, Java, Medina, and Tonawanda. In 1837, when Dubois visited Buffalo for the last time, he made a special effort to visit with Neumann. He saw that Neumann needed assistance and called upon Father Lutgen to come and work with him. Neumann, however, found Lutgen, a native of Luxemburg, unworthy both in preaching and moral conduct. Quickly he had him removed and sent back to New York. Also in 1837, St. Patrick's Church was erected in Buffalo for the sole purpose of establishing a spiritual refuge for the Irish population that had felt that they were disenfranchised at the Lamb of God. In the following year, Neumann was overjoyed when he saw the erection of a chapel at Java. It was also named St. Patrick.

In 1840, on Easter Sunday, Neumann was diagnosed with a severe case of fever that lasted for three months. Besides his sickness he was unhappy with his inability to create the spiritual fervor which he wanted his parishioners to have. Further he was plagued with a tremendous, almost overpowering depression, produced by a feeling of loneliness. He decided to find comfort and strength by joining the Order of the Most Holy Redeemer known as Redemptorists. On October 9, 1840, he moved to Pittsburgh, Pennsylvania, and then on to Baltimore. Before he left Western New York, however, he witnessed the construction of St. Mary's Church at Medina.

In 1836, Reverend Alexander Pax succeeded Mertz as pastor of the Lamb of God. The life of Pax, like that of his predecessor Mertz, was reflective of the struggles and pastoral challenges of the immigrant church in the United States. He was born in Sarreingsming in Sarregemund, Lothringen, on February 10, 1799, grew and waxed strong, studied philosophy and theology, and was ordained February 22, 1823. After his ordination

Pax was assigned as pastor in the small village of Bliesbrucken, where he received letters from friendly priests who had gone on mission to America encouraging him to come to the United States and join them in their activities. After many days in prayer, he decided to write to his bishop, Besson of Metz, requesting permission to leave Europe and sail for the New World. Pax received no reply. Although disappointed, he presented his request before the bishop in person, who was quick to reply that he hesitated to release Pax for missionary activity in the United States because new priests had a difficult task of adjusting to the trials and tribulations associated with American Presbyterianism and Trusteeism. It was with this reasoning that Besson refused to sponsor him. Pax withdrew from the bishop's quarters, returned to his parish church, knelt before a statue of the Most Blessed Virgin, and wept bitterly. He asked, "How can I obtain sponsorship? Is it the will of your Son most gracious lady?" In the days that followed, fellow priests who knew of his intentions appealed to Bishop Raess of Strassbourg to intercede with Besson on Pax's behalf. Besson finally relented and granted Pax's request, but he stipulated that in the event that Pax found himself unhappy in his missionary work, he would be welcomed back to Metz with open arms.

Upon arriving in America, Pax met with Dubois who invited him to proceed to Western New York and give assistance to Mertz who was finding his apostolic work to be exhausting. He arrived in the summer of 1835. Immediately Mertz saw that Pax's energy and devotion were untiring, and that he had a keen eye for temporal affairs with tact and aptitude for business. Pax took upon his shoulders the strenuous responsibilities of serving those Catholics scattered throughout the rural areas surrounding Buffalo. After Mertz went to Europe in 1836, Pax assumed all pastoral duties at the Lamb of God Church, plus continuing to administer in the rural countryside, where he was obliged to traverse through swamps and wilderness. Loaded down with wearisome toil from early morn, throughout the day,

and oft far into the night, he never complained; but, when Neumann arrived at Williamsville, he was most happy that he had a staunch supporter and counselor who was ever ready to stand by him and aid in furthering the missionary work. When Neumann left Western New York, Pax was assisted by Father Theodore Noethen. [1]

Having obtained some relief in serving the rural community, Pax turned his attention to the planning of the construction of a new church at the site of the Lamb of God Church. In his mind it was a necessity; the congregation was growing rapidly and the small church was unable to accommodate it. When he presented his ideas to the trustees, who had been elected in 1832 and were still in office, they, Michael Wehrle, Peter Kramer, Peter Esslinger, George Zahm, George Bemgesser, John Dingens, and Peter Zinns, at first thought that his plan was too stupendous, but later whole heartily agreed that even though it was a tremendous undertaking, it would result in the largest Catholic church building in America. Pax went door-to-door collecting money, materials, and recruiting workmen. He encouraged the trustees to form a building committee that they did. The contractor chosen for the masonry work was Peter Kramer, a conscientious mastercraftsman who assigned specific duties to Andrew Mayer, Peter Miller, and John Ambrose.

When Pax and the trustees had decided to build this grandiose church, the Germans, French, and Irish were still one congregation, even though a very tense one. Louis Le Couteulx's health had failed and his two sons, by his first wife, who had at first stayed in France, had come to live with their father in Buffalo. They were William Benedict Le Couteulx, the elder, and Pierre Alphonse Le Couteulx, the younger. As early as 1836, both began to play primary roles in the administration of affairs at the Lamb of God Church. In that year, William came to Buffalo after having served as an officer in the French navy. In France, he had also been elected as a Knight of the Legion of Honor and a Knight of the Order of St. Louis. When he arrived in Buffalo, he was asked by the trustees to preside over their body as an honorary president and spokesman for the trustees. These were posts that he continued to hold for many years. Upon assuming these honors, he was quick to point out that the church was suffering from financial instability and could not continue with Pax's and the trustees' plan to build a new church until a remedy was found.

At Mass, on August 21, 1836, William lectured the congregation on their failure to provide financial support for the construction of the new church, school, and maintain a salary for the pastor. He even prodded the trustees saying that only after he saw the largess of their offerings would he himself pay his share. He then turned his attention to the congregation and said, "Every member of this congregation, married or single, must feel the want of such an establishment, because of the influence it will have upon the morals and welfare of the Catholic children." He then turned his wrath on to those who had failed to pay their pew rent, an appropriation, part of which paid the salary of the pastor. He pointed out that since Pax had replaced Mertz, he received only forty dollars in salary, forcing him to draw upon financial support from France. William pounded his fist upon the pulpit and said, "Shame to those who unjustly retain part of the pastor's lawful income! If those who are indebted for their pews do not come and settle their accounts within this and next Sunday, their names shall be struck up, together with the amount of their debt at the door of this church, so that every member in the congregation may know them. Further it shall be the duty of the Board of Trustees to prosecute them as common debtors."

The corner stone of the new church was laid on August 31, 1838; it was blessed by Pax and in agreement with the trustees the church was designated as St. Louis Church in deference to Louis Le Couteulx

who, although retired and ill, was present for the occasion. As work progressed on the new brick church, it was constructed around the little roughcast structure that had served as the Lamb of God Church. Until the exterior of the new church was completed, Mass was said, worship continued, and Vespers sung in the little church. Only when demolition was absolutely necessary were the walls torn down and the debris thrown, shoveled, or wheeled out the doors and windows of the new structure. On August 26, 1840, Monsignor Forbin Sanson, Bishop of Nancy, France, came to Buffalo to administer the Sacrament of Confirmation to two hundred adults in the newly opened edifice. It was on this occasion that he dedicated it to St. Louis, King of France. It, however, was not completed until 1843, at which time an epigraph designating it as *St. Louis German Catholic Church* was carved in the stone façade above the main entrance. The expression German Catholic reflected the congregation's strong ethnic identity with German-speaking parishioners in distinction to French-speaking ones; whose numbers had fallen into minority status. Louis Le Couteulx did not live to witness the event; he died on November 16, 1840.

While the congregation at the Lamb of God Church began its drive to finance and construct Pax's dream church, the trustees began to feel uneasy about information which had filtered into Western New York concerning events which were taking place in New York City. At St. Patrick's Cathedral on January 7, 1838, Dubois consecrated as coadjutor bishop, John Hughes, the Irish youth that twenty years earlier he had hired as an overseer of his slaves at Emmitsburg. In the last week of January, while Dubois and Hughes visited Philadelphia, Dubois suffered a minor stroke. Although he was warned that he was seriously ill, he refused to lighten the load of his activities; and, two weeks later in February, he was felled by a more serious one which left him with his right side partially paralyzed. In May he suffered still another which left him almost completely immobilized. Because of these crippling attacks, John Hughes, for all practical purposes, became the functioning bishop of the vast New York Diocese. The Pope, however, did not remove Dubois from authority of the diocese until August 1839, at which time John Hughes became bishop.

The trustees in Buffalo were in fear that an Irish bishop, especially John Hughes, whom they disliked because of his antagonistic attitude toward their beloved Bishop Dubois, would begin to curtail the building plans and administration of the new church. Further, they were distressed by the dictums which had been formulated at the First Provincial Council of Baltimore in 1829, and which by 1838, were concertedly being applied in various dioceses. Bishops were urged not to sponsor churches whose deed was not in their hands, to inform the faithful that donations by the faithful were not to be considered as a right to title of the land or structures which these donations purchased, and to advocate canonical penalties to bring errant trustees to terms. Finally, however, they also realized with much satisfaction that although English Law did not provide for the protection of churches as institutions, it stated that certain groups of churchmen of an institution could enjoy such protection and privilege from incorporation laws. [2]

Until 1689, only the Anglican Church in New York State was recognized as an acceptable religious body. In that year, however, all other dissenting Protestant sects were granted religious freedom by the *Toleration Act*. These groups, however, could not secure incorporation of their church property; but beginning in 1696 several sects were given charters. From the War of Independence until the *Religious Incorporation Act* was passed by the State legislature on April 6, 1784, religious corporations could be organized in New York State only by special legislation. It was under this act, however, that the trustees of the first Catholic Church in New York City, St. Peter's Church, were incorporated; the property of

which rested in their hands. In 1813, the New York State legislature went further and passed into law, *An Act for the Incorporation of Religious Societies*. It regulated all religious bodies including the Catholic Church. Control of the temporal affairs of the religious societies was placed in the hands of the lay corporators, independent of priest, bishop, presbytery, synod, or other ecclesiastical judicatory. Under a trustee corporation system, the law considered a church under three aspects: the spiritual organization, the society, and the trustee corporation. The law regulated nothing concerning the spiritual, took cognizance of the society, and made the trustee corporation the legal representative of the society.

On December 2, 1838, three months after the corner stone was laid for the new St. Louis Church, a group of seven men, all German-speaking, applied and were granted a charter of incorporation according to the Law of 1813. Under the provisions of that law, the trustees formulated an extensive application for the charter. It read, "We whose names and seals are herewith affixed do certify that in pursuance of notice duly given according to law for that purpose, immediately after the time of divine service, on two Sunday mornings last past, in the church commonly called the Roman Catholic Church of St. Louis situated on Main Street in the city of Buffalo in the County of Erie and the State of New York, and in pursuance of the said notice the male persons of full age belonging to said church, in which Divine service is usually celebrated according to the rights of the Roman Catholic Church met for the purpose of associating themselves together and forming a religious incorporation under the act entitled *An Act to Provide for the Incorporation of Religious Societies*, passed April 5, 1813, and an act to amend same, at which meeting by a majority of voices George Zahm, and Peter Lux were nominated and did preside at the said meeting and election, and counted the votes which were cast. And we hereby certify that the following named persons by a plurality of voices were regularly chosen as trustees of said society for one year ensuing the first year and commencing on the first Sunday in October last to wit John Dingens, Nicholas Goetz, Michael Wehrle, Joseph Berst, George Bemgesser, Francis Handel, and Peter Kramer. And we hereby further certify that the said meeting fixed upon and determined that seven persons would constitute the board of trustees, and they and their successors should forever thereafter be called and known as *The Trustees of the Roman Catholic Church of St. Louis in the City of Buffalo.*" The application was received and the State of New York duly recognized the trustees' corporation. It appears that there was no formal opposition to this act from Bishop Hughes who was administering the New York Diocese for the ailing Bishop Dubois.

Two years after the incorporation, Louis Le Couteulx died at the venerable age of eighty-four. His passing marked the end of an era, not only for the church that was forever indebted to his generosity and charity, but also for the City of Buffalo, which richly benefited from his philanthropy. In addition to the large tract of land given "in trust" to Dubois and his successors for the construction of St. Louis Church, his legacy and largess included the establishment of a public school, the Buffalo Orphan Asylum, the Immaculate Conception Church and School, the Le Couteulx Institute for Deaf Mutes, and St. Mary's Maternity Hospital and Kindergarten. Following his death an obituary appeared in the local press on November 17, 1840. It read, "With the most unaffected sorrow we announce the death of our venerable and beloved fellow-citizen Louis Etienne Le Couteulx de Chaumont. The model of a perfect gentleman of irreproachable life, unostentatious yet diffusive in his charities, with purity and simplicity in his manners bordering on the patriarchal relieved by the most finished courtesy, and a firm faith and devout believer in God, full of years he sank to rest last night, honored and loved by all who knew him." [3]

For several years before his death his sons William and Alphonse had interested themselves in their father's affairs and assisted him in the discharge of many financial obligations, social commitments, and leadership concerns. As such, although their philosophies were different, they were highly regarded by the trustees at St. Louis Church. One such difference between the two sons was consideration of the French-speaking and German-speaking elements in the church, especially the use of language during the exercise of the liturgy and devotional services. Alphonse favored the French while William proposed German. The congregation was also divided, with the majority opinion resting with the Germans. On Sundays, by way of compromise, Pax instituted the custom of alternating the language of the sermons. When a sermon was read in German, however, conduct befitting a political rally, that is, booing, clapping, and whistling, ensued from the French group. The same held true when the situation was reversed. Alphonse often claimed that tensions between the two groups resulted from the trustees, all Germans, who failed to represent the French minority of the church. It was his belief that in their hearts they wished that the French element would be driven out of the congregation. William on the other hand sided with the trustees who had made him an honorary president. He was committed to be an advocate for them with Hughes who had replaced Dubois as bishop of the Diocese of New York.

The diocese, which was entrusted to Hughes' care, was in great need of his administrative abilities. With incoming ships loaded with Catholic immigrants, it was growing by leaps and bounds. Under his predecessor, Dubois, Catholicism had grown from the religion of the relatively few to the religion of the masses. Under Dubois, parishes scattered throughout the diocese received little supervision because of the lack of available priests. Hughes saw the need for bringing this loosely bound collection of churches, operating independently across the state, under diocesan regulations and statutes. In accomplishing this monumental task, he was faced with two major obstacles: resistance on the part of the non-English speaking immigrants to assimilate into American society; and, perhaps more difficult, combating the growing anti-Catholic sentiment of the Nativists, a group of Americans who possessed a form of xenophobia directed especially at Catholic immigrants in the United States. Prior to Hughes' becoming bishop they had burned a large convent in Charlestown, Massachusetts, in 1834. He, however, pursued these two problems with relentless zeal and oratorical skill that commanded the respect of Catholics and Protestants alike.

A naturalized citizen himself, he strongly advocated immigrants to learn the language and customs of their adopted country and forsake former loyalties that proved divisive. He encouraged them to follow through with their choice to become full Americans without reservation. His insistence on assimilation into American society by speaking English was no problem for the Irish, but met with strong resistance from the Germans who insisted that the preservation of their language meant safeguarding their faith. In addition to his assimilation policy, he also expressed both to the Irish and the Germans his dislike of the evils of trusteeism. Immediately upon assuming his ecclesiastical duties he applied his talents to break the trustees' hold on the parishes in New York City and eventually eradicated the system in them. Determined to carry out his convictions, he convoked a three-day synod of his priests. It was the first of its kind in the diocese. A total of sixty-four priests gathered at St. John's College in Fordham, north of New York City, in August 1842.

Each one arrived at the convocation with copies of the decrees of the Council of Trent and the decrees of the 1829 Provincial Synod at Baltimore. The agenda included clarifying church discipline and diocesan regulations concerning the clergy, restricting Irishmen from frequenting secret societies, and making a strong statement against lay-trusteeism. A list of statutes regulating and guiding the administration of churches followed. Among the specific norms, there were those that restricted the authority exercised by trustees. They could no longer hire or fire church employees or use certain sums of money without permission of the pastor. Their financial books were to be subject to inspection by the bishop and meetings could not be held without the approval of the pastor. These regulations signified a centralization and transfer of power into the bishop's hands. Following the conclusion of the proceedings, a pastoral letter was sent to every priest in the diocese on September 8, 1842 with an instruction that it would be read from every pulpit.

The letter did not arrive in Buffalo until early December. After reading it from the pulpit, Pax attempted to summarize its contents. Doing so, he concluded by saying that the bishop desired to obtain a *Verwaltung* of the St. Louis Church, which Pax had understood to mean that the discharge of the temporal affairs of the church and the discipline that should govern it would be under the surveillance and cooperation of the pastor and the congregation through the trustees. In Pax's mind the bishop's *Verwaltung* would change nothing in the administration at the church that had existed since 1832 and had been formalized by incorporation in 1838. The trustees, however, when they heard of a bishop's *Verwaltung,* saw red! Their translation was the bishop's usurpation of their administration, management, and stewardship; it was an attack on their trusteeship. They visioned that the land donated by Le Couteulx to Dubois and his successors "in trust," which reverted to the trustees by the incorporation laws of New York State, was now to be stolen by ecclesiastical edict by John Hughes, bishop of New York. In their Alsace-Lorraine dialect, *Verwaltung* was a legal term associated with an equitable right in property distinct from legal ownership thereof. Pax, however, did not think that this interpretation was in the mind of the bishop. Hughes' pastoral letter had not addressed the issue of church property even though, in the Synod of Baltimore, bishops were advised not to sponsor churches whose deed was not in their hands, nor to acknowledge that trustees had title to land and structures on the land simply because they had made donations to acquire them. It was, however, forefront in the minds of the trustees of St. Louis Church, and they thought of it as abominable. They could not rest until the situation was clarified. Pax, however, could not understand their voracious desire for having the word *Verwaltung* stricken from the document because he had no intention of making any changes in the parish administration since receiving the bishop's letter.

On December 11, 1842, a meeting of the trustees was held, with the entire congregation present, to discuss the pastoral letter. It was decided that a reply to the bishop had to be made in writing. In a document, composed by six members of a committee formed by the trustees, eight resolutions were listed which supposedly expressed the opinion of the entire congregation. John Dingens, T.L. Schreck, and William Le Couteulx signed it. On December 29, Pax forwarded it to Hughes adding his own note expressing his dismay over the anger of his parishioners which was caused in the reading of the pastoral letter and the disturbing interpretations given to it by William Le Couteulx. Hughes responded to Pax on January 28, 1843. He told Pax that the trustees' letter reflected a spirit of resistance to the statutes of the diocese, which were agreed upon at the synod. Hughes expressed his dismay because he previously held the congregation at St. Louis in high esteem for their piety and faith. He doubted that the majority of the congregation had supported the resolutions and presumed that they were formulated based upon a serious misunderstanding of his pastoral letter. He, however, stated that the statutes contained in it were meant for all churches in the diocese and wondered if, because of some special circumstance, a separate law for the congregation of St. Louis was necessary.

He then made it very clear that, while he would not dispute the words which the authors chose to employ in their letter, he would not hesitate to withdraw the Catholic Ministry from the walls of St. Louis if the congregation pursued a system of governance separate from that of the rest of the diocese. Any move to govern itself apart from the statutes given to it, or any proposed hindrances, would result in immediate transfer of its pastor to another congregation more deserving of his services. He made it most clear that the path which Pax's church had chosen was outside the Catholic Church, and it must determine for itself whether it is in fact Catholic or not. In conclusion, he ordered Pax to read his letter on three different occasions to the congregation without comment, in order that the parishioners may understand for themselves what was being requested of them and decide accordingly. The last line of his letter, directed to Pax, read, "But I forbid you absolutely to remain for one hour in the church if they make any physical opposition to complying with the statutes of the diocese." Pax carried out the bishop's wishes and read the letter on three consecutive Sundays at the Eucharistic liturgy.

Following Vespers on the evening of February 12, 1843, a second general meeting of the congregation was held in order to determine its opinion of the bishop's reply that was read by Pax without commentary. After the congregation was dismissed, William Le Couteulx and the committee that had drawn up the set of resolutions in the letter of December 11, 1842 met in private. Besides Le Couteulx, present were Francis Handel, Joseph Haberstro, Peter Zinns, George Zimmermann, John Dingens, and T.L. Schreck. A second letter to be sent to Hughes in the name of the entire congregation was composed. They requested and insisted that the transfer to the pastor the right, which they now enjoyed to administer the property of their church, was not acceptable. They stressed that they wanted to maintain the peace and union that now existed between the congregation and Pax, however, they were unwaveringly committed to their resolutions provided in their letter of December 11. They went on to rebut Hughes' insinuation that he doubted the Catholicity of the congregation at St. Louis simply because of the manner in which the trustees wished to interpret the method by which they would carry out the statutes of the diocese. They said, "As true Roman Catholics, we sincerely deplore to be at variance with our clergy, as regards the administration of our temporal affairs, but consider it as a painful duty devolved upon us, persuaded as we are that we are bound to maintain for our children and great-grandchildren a privilege which we consider as held by us only in trust." They concluded with the hope that the bishop would reconsider his position, and his threats to withdraw their pastor and deprive the congregation of religious assistance.

After reading their letter, Hughes sent the trustees a definitive statement. He said, "I read your letter with surprise because my pastoral letter was an intimation of an ecclesiastical law which is to be adhered to in general throughout the diocese. It is not yet in force, but when it will be, I trust it will be of greatest advantage to the peace of the congregation. Should it prove otherwise, however, in your judgment, you will have it in your power to resist its execution; and when you do, it will be time enough for me to ascertain what shall be my duty in the case. Should you determine that your church shall not be governed by the general law of the diocese, then we shall claim the privilege of retiring from its walls in peace." This letter intensified the trustees' rage. They were unable at this point to let the matter drop and continue with church affairs as if they had never heard the word *Verwaltung*; no argument however potent, no assurance however sincere, could dislodge their tenacity to make the bishop understand their point of view. It was also unfortunate

that their anger and frustration was directed in large part towards Pax. They were very verbal expressing their views, not only to the congregation, but also to members of the general public. Soon followed a violent response against Pax; the windows of his residence were smashed and he received life threatening letters.

Under this mounting tension, Pax fled his residence and took refuge with Theodore Noethen who was pastor in Williamsville. Pax took final leave of St. Louis Church on March 21, 1843. His health had deteriorated; he returned to his native land, where, on February 18, 1874, he died. With his departure from Buffalo, Hughes took swift action, placing the church under interdict on April 4. By his action, which was an ecclesiastical penalty, the congregation at St. Louis Church was prohibited from ministerial participation in public worship and reception of the sacraments, and sacramentals. Mass was no longer conducted within the church's walls and the Eucharist no longer resided in the tabernacle. No priest was given jurisdiction to function in any ecclesiastical way in regards to parishioners of St. Louis. George Deuther, a member of a group of parishioners who did not sign any former petitions, wrote to the bishop, asking him to reconsider his action. The bishop replied, "Much as I feel for the good, pious people, I cannot allow any priest to officiate at St. Louis until I am assured that the congregation, in its trustees as well as in its members, are Catholics in their souls as well as by their outward profession. There are many other good German congregations without a pastor, and I must provide for those congregations who make it their pride to be governed by their pastors rather than attempting to govern them."

News of the interdiction quickly spread throughout the city. The *Buffalo Daily Gazette* interviewed William Le Couteulx. He informed the editor of what happened to the parish and explained his opinion as to why the bishop had taken such drastic ecclesiastical action. The *New York Commercial Advertiser,* quoting Bishop Hughes, took variance with the opinions of Le Couteulx. The article denied that Hughes had demanded the property at St. Louis to be turned over to him and that he had withdrew Pax as pastor of the church. Hughes made it clear that the dispute was the issue of church governance in conformity with ecclesiastical law. The articles stirred public opinion but did not change either the will of the trustees or the determination of the bishop. The trustees, however, proceeded to elect two new members to the board in order to determine the feelings of the congregation. Two sets of nominees were proposed. Candidates George Zimmermann and George Bemgesser supported the bishop. Joseph Haberstro and John Dingens advocated the position held by the trustees. The latter won the election receiving nearly three hundred votes each. On October 19, 1843, the results were published in the *Buffalo Daily Gazette* with an editorial comment which admonished the Catholic clergy for its action of interdiction and showed elation that a line dividing temporal from spiritual power had been drawn and that the congregation at St. Louis Church was defending the firm position which it had taken. By doing so the newspaper claimed that the church was acting according to the principles of American liberty.

*P*ublic opinion generated by the news articles must have stirred up some diplomacy behind the scenes. On October 20, 1843, the trustees received a letter from Rev. Adalbert Inamu, pastor of the congregation in Utica, New York. It contained a proposal from Hughes through which he hoped a peaceful settlement could be made. It contained only two articles concerning the administration of church affairs. If the trustees at Buffalo signed these, peace would be immediately restored to their church. The trustees, however, still contended that although the conditions stated were satisfactory to them, the proposal, in general, was in conflict with the constitutions of their incorporation.

They did not sign Hughes' proposal; but sent instead, a letter to him through Inamu. They assured the bishop that they were satisfied with his articles, however, they were not sure that this was all that he wanted. They told him that they would not raise objections to their assigned pastor supervising the church money; they would go so far as to have their secretary send him copies of their financial negotiations. Finally, they agreed to allow the pastor to have influence in the election of sexton, schoolteachers, organists, singers, and members of the managerial and maintenance staff. Their letter went unanswered and was followed by six months of silence. The trustees also went silent and had no meetings with the congregation again until Sunday, June 30, 1844, when William Le Couteulx chaired one that began shortly after morning prayer at ten o'clock.

*T*he meeting was held in the church; a very large crowd was in attendance. It was unanimously decided by all present that a petition be formulated and sent to Pope Gregory XVI through a cardinal, the papal nuncio at Paris. The petition was to contain a factual survey of the parish situation, the congregation's complaints against Bishop Hughes, and a request for appointment of a worthy Catholic priest to their church. Once a resolution had been made to write the petition, the meeting was adjourned until the following Sunday when it was agreed that the petition written in French, English, and German would be read, approved, and signed by its composers. On that following Sunday the trustees recognized: William Le Couteulx, Philip Born, Charles Esslinger, Lawrence Weber, Andreas Meyer, Caspar Pfeffer, Christian Blancan, T.L. Schreck, and Joseph Hartmann. Their petition was read and all present were told that it would be exhibited in Charles Esslinger's house for eight days. It contained an account of the beginnings of the parish and the basis for the congregation's right to control the church property, a description of the deplorable spiritual state of the parish for which Hughes was to be held responsible, the facts of the scandal the interdict had caused in the city, and an inference that the Roman

Catholic religion in the area was in grave danger of extinction. The congregation was then informed that only those who signed the petition to the Holy Father would be considered real and legal members of St. Louis Church. Once signed, the petition was immediately sent to Paris.

This letter sent to Pope Gregory XVI was concluded with the inclusion of a prophetic insight from the leaders of the congregation at St. Louis, which eventually through much agony would establish for their parish a Rare Tradition in American Catholicism. It read, "In this essay we do not want to speak about the good or the bad which was caused by our resistance against the will of our bishop, for a right we enjoyed under his Most Reverend predecessor, John Dubois. Yet we cannot refrain from making this natural observation that in France where most of us were born, as well as in other countries in Europe, the temporal affairs of the churches are administered by church councils consisting of lay persons; and yet everything is in very good order, without any difficulties which we are made to feel here. While we would not approve of it, we might still be able to understand that a parish church which is to be founded in the future, because it is required that way, could not be consecrated if the members were not willing to cede the administration of their temporal affairs to the clergy. However we will never be able to understand that the same could be required of us, namely the condition without which we cannot obtain any religious help, since we already were, according to the laws of the country, an incorporated parish long before the notification of this rigid requirement; this would mean that we defy the existing laws and cause disharmony everywhere. If only a single member objected to the bishop's will, that would be sufficient to uphold the Act of Incorporation. Although our bishop has never been able to understand it, why should we be condemned to suffer so much?"

While St. Louis remained under interdict, the Redemptorist Fathers were invited by Bishop Hughes to come to Buffalo with the intention of forming a church that would attract the German element wary of the conditions that existed at St. Louis Church. No one, however, except Rev. Benedict Bayer, C.SS.R., knew what was in the mind of the bishop. At first Bayer said Mass and preached in German in the basement of the Irish Church, St. Patrick. He invited any Germans of the city, who felt that they had no other affiliation, to attend. The Sacrament of Penance was also offered. On February 22, 1844, Bayer with the assistance of George Deuther purchased land at Broadway and Pine for the erection of a new church. Within three months a rough establishment was completed and named St. Mary's. From its first day it attracted a sizeable number of German families who were dissatisfied with the affairs at St. Louis. When the Redemptorist priests saw this response, they began preaching long sermons in French also. This attracted a second element to the new church. This was exactly what Bishop Hughes had hoped for; he wished to divide and conquer. His plan worked well. There were shifting loyalties in families, even among some in the same family. The shift from St. Louis to St. Mary's actually caused families to break up and be set at odds with each other. By the middle of July the trustees at St. Louis Church saw that even those who had chosen to stay were isolating them. Pew rents began to drop, and the trustees saw the handwriting on the wall. If they did not obtain a priest quickly, they would be standing alone at their altar having a prayer service for an empty church and their funds so dwindled would curtail them from even keeping up the maintenance.

Fearing for their extinction and that of their congregation, they decided on applying for an unconditional surrender to the bishop. Using the vehicle of the *Buffalo Commercial Advertiser* they wrote, on August 10, 1844, an apology to Bishop Hughes and asked him for his pardon. They expressed their belief that they had misunderstood what he had requested and they expressed their willingness that the church and congregation be regulated according to the provisions of his former pastoral letter, and that the administration of the temporal affairs be conducted conformable to it. They further added their regrets that they, by mistaken impressions, had caused any scandal or offense to their Catholic brethren. They confessed that they would be the last ones to oppose the authority of religion, either intentionally or deliberately. With this apology, the interdict that began on April 4, 1843 came to an end. Their apology, written in English, was translated into German and placed on the door of St. Mary's Church as well as on the door of St. Louis Church. On the Sunday following the reply, Hughes arrived in Buffalo to greet the reunited congregation. He preached, and then released the church officially from interdict. Before he left, he blessed all those who had gathered to welcome him. Within a short time he assigned Father Francis Guth to be the pastor at St. Louis Church.

Western New York now had nine churches. There were three in the City of Buffalo; St. Louis, the Mother Church, encouraging German and French patronage, St. Mary's, administering to German exiles from the Mother Church, and St. Patrick's, serving Irish and other English-speaking members. In the rural areas six churches had sprung up by 1844; St. John the Baptist, Lockport, Sts. Peter and Paul, Williamsville, St. John the Baptist, North Bush, St. Patrick, Java, St. Mary's Medina, and St. Joseph's, Day Brook Pond near Scio. Besides these churches there were circuit priests at Sheldon, Transit, Pendleton, and Lancaster spiritually caring for several groups of rural Catholics. The Mother Church was still in labor, but she had had the joy of seeing the steady birth of her children on the Western Frontier. [4]

The Lamb of God Church

REFERENCES AND NOTES ✣ CHAPTER TWO

1. Catechetical topic of the Communion of Saints as believed by the Catholic Church see: Joseph Ratzinger, *Cathechism of the Catholic Church*, Libreria Editrice Vaticana, Liguori Publications, Liguori, MO, 1992, p.247. For the early Church Militant in Buffalo see: Andrew P. Yox, "The Parochial Context of Trusteeism: Buffalo's St. Louis Church, 1828-1855," *Catholic Historical Review*, 76(4), pps. 712-733; op. cit. *World's Popular Encyclopedia*. For names of early parishioners at St. Louis Church and biography of Joseph Haberstro see: Philip Becker, *History of Germans of Buffalo and Erie County*, Verlag and Druck von Reinecke and Zesch, Buffalo, NY, 1898, reading section pps. 36-40, biography section, p.15. For John Nicholas Mertz at Lamb of God Church see: Michael A. Riester, *Lay Trusteeism at St. Louis Roman Catholic Church, Buffalo, New York*, M.A. Dissertation, Washington Theological Union, Silver Spring, Maryland, 1987, pps. 7-11. On Raffeiner see: op. cit. *Dagger John*, p. 179; op. cit. *John Dubois, Founding Father*, p. 158; Thomas Donohue, *History of the Catholic Church in Western New York*, Buffalo: Catholic Historical Publishing Inc., 1904, p. 115. For Trusteeism in Post-Revolutionary War Period in America see: Robert F. McNamara, "Trusteeism in the Atlantic States 1785-1863," *The Catholic Historical Review*, Vol. XXX, July 1944, no. 2, pps. 135-54. For John Neumann's and Theodore Noethen's missionary activities see: op. cit. *Good Shepherd*, pps. 2-4; J. Berger C.SS.R., *Theodore Noethen Report*, Berger Papers, Redemptorist Archives of Baltimore Province—Neumann section, Brooklyn, New York, 1833. Neumann had made North Bush his permanent residence while he visited his missions in Western New York. North Bush was a district, not a settlement. It was a region of swamps. Later, the North Bush Church became a mission of St. Joseph's Church in Ellysville, in an area known as Buffalo Plains, an area around the present day St. Joseph's Church on Main Street near the University of Buffalo, South Campus. The North Bush Church was abandoned in 1892. In 1927-8 the North Bush region was included in the section called Kenmore. Today the area is the home of St. John the Baptist Church of Kenmore; George Zimpfer, *History of the Roman Catholic Parish of Sts. Peter and Paul, From the Origins to 1928*, Archives of the Sts. Peter and Paul Church, Williamsville, NY, 1928. A painting hangs in the Kenmore-Tonawanda Historical Museum on Knoche Road, Tonawanda, which depicts Neumann standing beside his horse. Neumann disliked riding a horse; it carried his supplies; he walked beside it. In 1840, when Neumann left Western New York, Father Michael Guth, brother of Francis Guth, pastor at St. Louis Church, took over Neumann's parishes of North Bush, Lancaster, Sheldon, Pendleton, Transit, Swormville, Batavia, and Rochester. After two years, poor health required him to resign. Hughes replaced him with Father Theodore Noethen. He was born in Cologne, Germany and baptized in St. Mary's Church near the massive gothic cathedral. While a seminarian he defended, with firearms, the archbishop against civil authority; and, in doing so, he had his left arm so injured that it remained hanging limp for the rest of his life. He fled Cologne and went to Metz, France, where he studied at the seminary conducted by the Jesuits. From there he went to Rome and studied under Father Vincent Pallotti who was the spiritual director of the Propaganda Fide and founder of the Pallottine Fathers in 1835. Bishop Hughes of New York had asked Pallotti to send him candidates to the priesthood so as to do missionary work in his diocese in the United States. Pallotti sent Noethen. He arrived in New York in March 1841; by December he had finished his theology studies at St. Joseph's College (today the Fordham University Campus) under the direction of Father John McCloskey, who later became bishop of Albany and the first cardinal from the United States. Noethen was ordained by Hughes in St. Patrick's Cathedral on Mott Street, sent immediately to Western New York, and said his first Mass in St. Louis Church. After a short stay in Buffalo he took up residence in the rural countryside administering to all the parishes from which Michael Guth had resigned. In August 1845, he was transferred to Assumption parish in Salina, which today is called Syracuse, solved a very serious trustee problem in Utica, and went on to take up spiritual activities in Albany. He had a wonderful baritone voice and each year he was called upon to sing at the Holy Week services of Tenebrae at the Albany Cathedral. On Wednesday of Holy Week in 1879, he chanted the very moving and inspiring Lamentations of Jeremiah; however, he caught a cold and died the next day. It was Holy Thursday, April 10, 1879. These excerpts were taken from the notes of Rev. Barry Bossa, S.A.C., Our Lady of Mount Carmel Church, Yonkers, New York. He is writing a book on the life of Father Noethen. At St. Louis Church, in 1997, Bossa addressed the *Blue Army* on the 80th anniversary of the Fatima Apparition, into which he wove together the story of Mertz, Pax, Neumann, and Noethen. On Pax see: op. cit. *Lay Trusteeism at St. Louis*, p.14; *Andenken an den hochwuerdigen herrn Alexander Pax*, Buffalo Deutschen Press, Translation by Victor Pax; *Un Centenaire: Un pretre lorrain en Amerique: Alexander Pax, 1799-1874*; *St. Louis Bazar Chronicle*, Buffalo, NY, Nov. 2, 1888, vol. 1, no. 11.

2. For Pax and the construction of the brick church, the second St. Louis Church see: op. cit. *Anniversary Souvenir and Programme of the St. Louis Dramatic Circle*, St. Louis Church Archives, Buffalo, NY, 1896, pps. 17, 22; Robert T. Bapst, *One Hundred and Twenty Fifth Anniversary, St. Louis Church, 1829-1954*, St. Louis Church Archives, 1954, p.15; *St. Louis Bazar Chronicle*, Buffalo, NY, 1888, vol. 1, no. 11; For the names of trustees elected in 1832 see: op. cit. *History of Germans of Buffalo and Erie County*, p. 38. For Speech of William Le Couteulx delivered to the parishioners at St. Louis Church on August 21, 1836 see: Buffalo and Erie County Historical Society's Library, St. Louis Church File.

3. For Incorporation at St. Louis Church see: op. cit. *A Man and a Church Named Louis*; Charles G. Deuther, *The Life and Times of Rt. Rev. John Timon, D.D.*, Deuther Press, Buffalo, NY, 1870, p.103; op. cit. Glenn Atwell and Ronald Elmer Batt, *The Chapel: A Comprehensive History of the Chapel and Pilgrimage of Our Lady*

Help of Christians, p. 14; Joseph P. Murphy, *The Laws of the State of New York Affecting Church Property*, Dissertation Ph.D., Catholic University of America Press, Washington D.C., 1957, pps. 43-52. In the formation of the corporation at St. Louis Church, a committee was formed to set up an election procedure and write a set of by-laws. For the committee, George Zahm was the president and Peter Lux was the secretary. The by-laws were written as a set of resolutions: 1. The trusteeship, "Verwaltungsrath," was composed of seven members. 2. The pastor was considered a member of the board, but he would only be consulted; he had no vote. He would, however, preside at the meetings when he would be present. 3. There were three classes of selection; the congregation would elect one group of candidates for one year, a second for two years and a third for three years. This guaranteed an overlapping and continuity of the board. 4. If one member should die or be relieved for some other reason, his place would be taken by election of the members of the sitting board. 4. The board would meet on the first Sunday of each month after Vespers in the

schoolhouse. 5. The board would hold elections once each year on the first Sunday in October. The original members of the "Verwaltungsrath" of 1838 were: John Dingens, Nicholas Goetz, Michael Wehrle, Joseph Berst, George Bemgesser, Francis Handel, Peter Kramer. Alexander Pax was the pastor; one year later Francis Handel was replaced by Joseph Zimmermann, *Documents of St. Louis, Buffalo, New York*, St. Louis Church Archives, Buffalo, NY. Michael Riester, St. Louis Church's historian had a different list of trustees. They are: Joseph Haberstro, Francis Handel, John Dingens, Peter Kramer, Nicholas Goetz, George Bemgesser, and Fischer whose first name was either Frank, Jacob, or Martin. Throughout the history of the trustees, there were always seven members until late in the 20th century when a trustee, Paul Hardick, became ill and could not carry on. On the death of Louis Le Couteulx see: Martha J. F. Murray, *Memoire of Stephen Louis Le Couteulx de Chaumont*, Publication of the Buffalo Historical Society, 1906, p. 452.

Exterior of St. Louis Church 1843-1885, successor to the Lamb of God Church

33

4. On the Le Couteulx brothers, William and Alphonse see: op. cit. *Lay Trusteeism at St. Louis*, pps. 22-7 On Hughes, New York Diocese, and Nativitism see: op. cit. *Dagger John*, pps. 179, 180, 181. The account of the trustees at St. Louis opposing Hughes' pastoral letter, controversy with Hughes, interdiction, and reconciliation see: op. cit. *Lay Trusteeism at St. Louis*, pps. 28-49; *Records of the Trustees at St. Louis Church*, Archives of the St. Louis Church, Buffalo, NY, Feb., 12, 1843, pps. 16, 22-4, 154; Letter of the Congregation of St. Louis Church to Rt. Rev. John Hughes dated Feb., 12, 1843, St. Louis Church Archives, Buffalo, NY. It is important to note that the synod called by Hughes was in 1842 and not in 1841 as reported by Deuther and Donohue, see: op. cit. *History of the Catholic Church in Western New York*, pps. 152-55; and op. cit. *The Life and Times of Rt. Rev. John Timon*, pps.16, 105; The text of the letter sent by the Congregation of St. Louis Church to Pope Gregory XVI can be found in op. cit. *Records of the Trustees at St. Louis Church*, p. 24; *Buffalo Daily Gazette*, October 19, 1843; *Buffalo Commercial Advertiser*, August 10, 1844; For a listing of the origins of churches in the Diocese of Buffalo see: J. David Valaik et. al., *Celebrating God's Life in Us, The Catholic Diocese of Buffalo, 1847-1997*, The Heritage Press, Western New York Heritage Institute, Buffalo, NY, 1997, pps. 151-55. For Jesuits coming to Buffalo to preach a mission and influence the trustees see: George Krim S.J., "Diary of Fathers Fritsch, Frizzini, Kettner, and Ebner, 1848-51," *Canisius Monthly*, Canisius College Publication, Buffalo, NY, 1915-16.

Interior of St. Louis Church 1843-1885

CHAPTER THREE

Badin and Le Couteulx

Although the chance meeting of Stephen Theodore Badin with Louis Le Couteulx de Chaumont in Buffalo, New York, in the late fall of 1828 was simply a footnote in the biography of Badin, it was a milestone in the history of St. Louis Church and a monumental plateau in the philanthropic decisions of Le Couteulx. Badin had been the first ordained priest in the United States, who, in his old age, signed his letters *Proto-Sacerdos Baltimorensis,* first priest of the diocese of Baltimore. In 1904, his remains were transferred from the cathedral at Cincinnati, Ohio, and reverently interred in a replica log chapel on the site of its original structure on the campus of Notre Dame University, South Bend, Indiana. In Badin Hall, a building on the campus that was dedicated to him hangs his portrait as he appeared in his declining years. Gazing upon the painting, one sees a face characterized by a longish nose and a firm prominent jaw. His eyes are large and covered by heavy drooping lids. His countenance expresses grim determination rather than easy-going geniality. It is a true representation of a man who had been admired for his accomplishments rather than one who had been loved for a warm and friendly personality. In his youth he was a very small man, but his slight frame was possessed with boundless energy which allowed him to travel restlessly and endlessly from one part of the United States to another. As a Catholic missionary priest of the late eighteenth and early nineteenth centuries in America, he had a basic concern for spiritual things, but he felt the fascination of material progress by making new settlements and speculating in land for the benefit of the infant Catholic Church. The success of his restlessness, intellectual interests, a love for travel, and a zest for life were seen in his endless development of mission stations, churches, and schools. He truly caught the spirit of an adolescent nation that eventually conquered a continent.

It might be said that Badin met Le Couteulx on the rebound, in discouragement, and in-between jobs. Badin was returning from a long nine years stay in Europe, where after being a mendicant missionary, he found himself as an outcast, averted by Bishop Benedict Flaget of Bardstown, Kentucky, who should have welcomed him home with open arms to the land where he had faithfully served as a priest for twenty-six years before going abroad. After meeting with Le Couteulx, he had determined to go on to Monroe, Michigan, with the consent and incardination of his only episcopal friend, Bishop Edward Dominic Fenwick, a Dominican, who had been appointed head of the Diocese of Cincinnati which, after being formed in 1821, controlled the ecclesiastical activities in the Old Northwest Region of the United States. No other bishop wanted to see Badin even as a guest much less as a candidate for incardination. During the six weeks in which he resided at the home of Le Couteulx, he and his host had many conversations about the political situation in France. Badin told Le Couteulx that there was much talk that Charles X, the reigning Bourbon King, might be deposed. Le Couteulx agreed and predicted that within less than two years Charles would abdicate and be replaced by Louis Philippe who had fought with the Revolutionary Army, but left France in 1793 only to return in 1814 as a member of the Liberal Party. Badin agreed and added that while he had been in Europe he arranged for some paintings and other gifts given by Louis Philippe to be sent to Bardstown to adorn the interior of its St. Joseph's Cathedral. In 1797 Louis Philippe had made a visit to Kentucky, lived for a considerable amount of time at Bardstown, supported himself as a dancing instructor, and taught French to the local children.

One evening, Le Couteulx and Badin, while seated before the flames emanating from the fireplace, and sipping a glass of slowly aged wine as a digestive stimulant, turned to discussing missionary activity in America. Badin related the results of his survey of Catholicism in Kentucky. Before leaving for Europe in 1819, he had counted in his charge more than nine hundred and seventy-two Catholic families and more than three thousand souls. He told Le Couteulx that since coming to Kentucky in 1793, he had ridden more than one hundred thousand miles on horseback bringing the Gospel and the Sacraments to all parts of the State. At this point Le Couteulx told Badin that in the environs of Buffalo, more than eight hundred Catholic families were in residence. Badin suggested that Le Couteulx donate a sizeable amount of land to John Dubois, Bishop of New York, for the purpose of establishing a Catholic church, school, and cemetery. Badin praised Dubois' great efforts to develop Catholicism over the vast territory given to his charge, and he assured Le Couteulx that once the land would be secured, a priest, sent by Dubois, would immediately follow.

Badin explained in detail to Le Couteulx that, if he made the offer to Dubois, it would not be the first offering of its kind that had been proposed to him. In 1796, the settlers at Cartwright Creek in Kentucky had offered him two hundred acres of land for establishing a church, school, cemetery, and rectory along with an annual stipend if he would come and administer to them. Dubois, however, was unable to accept it at that time,

but praised the potential donors for their offer. Le Couteulx was touched, and promised Badin that his suggestion would become fact before the sun rose on New Year's Day of 1829. Realizing that no priest had been in the area of Western New York for some time, Badin spent the remaining days of his visit, saying Mass, hearing confessions, baptizing, and performing marriage ceremonies. He had no problem hearing confessions in English and French, but he was very shaky understanding German. In these latter cases he gave absolution conditionally saying, "An honest loving God knows the heart as well as the language of an honest man." On several occasions he sang Mass in the village courthouse to which a vast number of people attended, both Catholic and Protestant.

Badin was born at Orleans, France, July 17, 1768. He was the first boy and the third child in a family of fifteen children. The names of his mother and father have not been discovered; but, because of the type of schooling he received, they must have belonged to the well-to-do bourgeois caste. Following the traditional period of primary schooling at Orleans, he went to Paris and for three years studied the Classics at College Montaign. In 1789 he entered the Sulpician Seminary, however, the upheaval of the French Revolution caused its closure in 1791, two weeks before the second anniversary of Bastille Day. Returning to the home of his parents he feared that his bishop, who had taken the Oath of Allegiance to the Civil Constitution of the Clergy, would demand that his seminarians do the same. Badin had already received Minor Orders, but refused ordination at the hands of his bishop. Seeking advice from Jacques Andre Emery, Superior General of the Sulpicians, he and two ordained priests, John David and Benedict Flaget, set sail to America from Bordeaux, France, in January 1792. After landing at Philadelphia the trio proceeded immediately to Baltimore to meet with Bishop John Carroll; they arrived on March 28, 1792. Badin entered the Sulpician Seminary of St. Mary's and was ordained one year later on May 24, 1793. Badin was Carroll's first ordination following his own consecration as bishop.

Before September was three days old, Carroll had Fathers Stephen Badin and Michael Bernard Barriere on the road to missionary lands in Kentucky. After a two-month walk to Pittsburgh and a flatboat ride down the Ohio River, they entered Lexington, Kentucky, on November 27, 1793. They would have been there sooner; but, while sailing down river, they made a stop at Gallipolis at the junction of the Ohio and the Kanawha Rivers. Their purpose was to render spiritual service to a hapless group of French settlers who had been victims of a miserable land speculation. They sang Mass in the garrison, heard confessions, and baptized forty children. After arriving in Kentucky, Barriere remained in Scott County in northeastern Kentucky while Badin proceeded farther west to an area that became known as the Holy Land. It comprised a circle of land of twenty miles radius with Bardstown as the center. It boasted of villages and communities which carried the names: Lebanon, Holy Cross, St. Francis, Loretto, St. Mary's, New Hope, Gethsemane, Nazareth, and New Haven. Badin had three hundred families to care for when he arrived. When Barriere left Kentucky in April 1794, Badin's closest sacerdotal companion was Father John Rivet who resided in Vincennes, Indiana, nearly one hundred miles away.

At Holy Cross, Badin established his first church, St. Stephen's. By 1805, he had been made vicar general; and, at different times, had the assistance of four priests: Michael Fournier, Anthony Salmon, John Thayer, and Charles Nerinckx. He was not, however, fortunate to keep these men; Salmon died in an accident being thrown from his horse, Fournier bled to death after bursting a blood vessel during a construction accident, and Thayer, who seemed more interested in land speculation and profit than in preaching, left without permission. Only Charles Nerinckx remained as a faithful and efficient cleric. Before 1819, the Trappists had sought a home in

Kentucky but did not succeed in making a permanent settlement until 1848 at Gethsemane. In 1806, the Dominicans, led by Edward Dominic Fenwick, arrived in Kentucky coming from Bornheim, Belgium. They settled at Springfield on the eastern end of the Holy Land.

On May 1, 1811, Badin signed a contract to build a brick church at the corner of Main and Tenth Streets in Louisville, Kentucky. The church when completed was called St. Louis in honor of Louis IX, King of France. Badin took over the pastorship and remained there until he departed for Europe in 1819. The church remained on its present site, carrying its name of St. Louis until 1830. At that time, a new St. Louis Church was built on Fifth Street in Louisville, on the site of the present Cathedral of the Assumption, the seat of the diocese of Louisville. In 1811, Benedict Flaget arrived in Kentucky as the first bishop of the newly formed diocese of Bardstown. He had been consecrated by Carroll on November 4, 1810 but was unable to obtain sufficient funds to make his journey west until a year had passed. As he arrived Badin welcomed him to his "Episcopal palace," a log cabin sixteen feet square containing a bed, six chairs, two tables, and a few planks for book shelves. He greeted his traveling companion to America, his bishop, and his friend with these words, "You are now the poorest bishop in the Christian World!" Although the poorest, he had a very large diocese which covered all the territory of Kentucky, Tennessee, and the Old Northwest Territory. His diocese was advertised as the only one west of the Applachian Mountains.

As Flaget's authority became prominent in the new diocese, Badin's influence became more obscure. He was forced to take a back seat in the management of sacerdotal and temporal affairs; new men, the bishop's men, were in charge. Badin, however, still held the deeds to several properties in Lexington, Danville, Louisville, and in small villages in the Holy Land. Flaget wanted these deeds, but they were not forthcoming. Badin lost his post as vicar general and the property question carved a large incision in a nineteen-year friendship between himself and Flaget. In 1819 Badin sailed for Europe; it was supposed to be a moment of rest and rehabilitation, but it extended into a pattern of wanderlust for a mendicant missionary. Once in Europe, Flaget pronounced that Badin had been again raised to the rank of vicar general in charge of fund raising for the Diocese of Bardstown. Badin went to France, Italy, Flanders, Holland, and England. He received two thousand francs from Charles X, King of France, collected many more thousands in the parishes he visited. In one year alone, 1827, he appropriated one hundred and three thousand francs for the missions in his Western United States. He used his book, *Origine et Progres de la Mission du Kentucky*, which he published at Paris in 1821, as the springboard of his campaign of apostolic beggary. Among the many churches in his itinerary were those in his hometown of Orleans, in the Loire Valley, at Paris, and at Bornheim, Belgium.

When he returned to America, no bishop except Edward Dominic Fenwick offered him incardination. When Badin arrived in New York, Dubois asked him to stop in Buffalo on his way to Cincinnati and gave him temporary jurisdiction to administer the sacraments while traveling. He may have stayed in Buffalo, but his lack of fluency of the German language prodded his decision to move on. By February 6, 1829 he was well established at Monroe, Michigan. It was a small village located on the Raisin River, south of Detroit, near Lake Erie. On one occasion Badin sang Mass in honor and for the intentions of the American prisoners who had been massacred there during the War of 1812. While at Monroe in 1830, he wrote his address to the populace titled *An Affectionate Address to Every Inquirer After Truth*. After leaving Monroe, he purchased land at South Bend, Indiana, and had built a school and an orphanage there. Collectively they were named Ste. Marie des Lacs, but it was a short-lived

endeavor. In 1834, he gave the property to Bishop Simon Brute of Vincennes with the condition that the land be used for some philanthropic purpose. Later Bishop Celestine Hailandiere, Brute's successor, deeded the property to the Congregation of the Holy Cross. Upon it the congregation built the University of Notre Dame. In 1837 Flaget asked him to return to Kentucky and assume his post as vicar general. Although it was more an honorary position than an active one, he accepted. In 1841, he donated his property in Portland, a village west of Louisville, so that a church called Our Lady of Portland could be built. He did not, however, hand over the deed until 1848.

The University of Notre Dame was founded in 1842 and Badin was invited there as a guest of Father Edward Sorin, the director. Following his stay, Badin returned to his wandering ways visiting and giving sermons throughout Ohio, Michigan, and Illinois. He returned to Kentucky in the winter of 1848-49. He was enfeebled and expected to remain there until he died. He had, however, one more disappointment. Benedict Flaget had so declined in health that John Martin Spalding his coadjutor bishop became the real power within the diocese. Spalding leased the first church Badin had built on Tenth and Main Streets for secular use, and sent in the wrecking crews to raze the second St. Louis Church built on Fifth Street. Although Badin opposed both actions, Spalding would not pay him any heed because he had planned to build his cathedral on the latter site. Louisville had become the center of the diocese; and, although Bardstown with its St. Joseph's Cathedral had been reduced to parish status, it remained an historical landmark. When the cornerstone for the cathedral in Louisville was laid, Badin, thoroughly disgruntled, refused to be present at the ceremony. Later in the day, when everyone had left, he came out bareheaded, dressed in his surplice, and carrying his breviary. As he walked around the foundation he mumbled to himself the *Miserere*. He paraphrased the Gospel by St. Luke: "If they do not receive your word, go into the streets and say, 'Even the very dust of the city that cleaveth to me, I wipe off against you!'" Three days later he did just that. His departure was quite colorful. His baggage was piled high on a dray cart with himself perched on top of all his belongings. A large, forlorn, and aged horse pulled the cart unceremoniously with a slow methodical pace through the city to the steamboat landing; at which point, he got down, shook the dust of Kentucky from his feet, and walked up the plank of the packet scheduled to sail for Cincinnati. He never returned, except to attend the funeral of his old friend and sometime opponent, Benedict Flaget.

*B*adin spent the last fourteen years of his life traveling, giving sermons, and writing on Catholic missionary work, discipline, and apologetics. He also wrote an almost endless number of personal letters. Since he never believed that they would be published, he wrote without guile. They display a strange combination of astuteness and naivete and clearly reveal his pettiness and at the same time his really important contributions to the development of the Catholic Church in the Mid-West. He shows himself to be a man of strong hates and even stronger loves. For him evil was evil and good was good; there were no shades of gray between the blacks and whites. He displays a combination of his intense and unchangeable conviction about things with a shifting, changeable attitude towards persons. In some letters he gushes warm effusions of affection toward Flaget, Fenwick, and Chabrat; in others, he strongly expresses how piqued he is with them. In many ways his pen reveals his childishness. He has sudden swings in attitudes, showing that he is very sensitive to the most insignificant cut. He is like a boy sitting in a corner, always pouting over some imagined slight. He tells his ecclesiastical superiors just what he thinks they should know, and he was completely convinced that he knew best in all matters. He tells them what they should do even though it does not concern him; and, he does so without epistolary deference to their rank. Neither does he display the meek humility that was so characteristic of clerical correspondence of his time. Badin was

convinced that this kind of humility approached hypocrisy. While he was living in the house of Bishop Purcell, the successor of Fenwick, at Cincinnati in 1853, his end finally came. He was eighty-five years old, but he had not lost his sense of sarcastic humor. After he had received the last rites he lay in a semi-conscious state. Looking up he saw his slow-working attendant attempting an action of concern for his health. He said in a clear voice, "Is it possible that you haven't got through yet!" With that he fell into a coma and never regained consciousness. Several days later, as a violent thunderstorm raged outside, he died in the afternoon of April 21, 1853.

*T*he second important personage at the meeting of 1828 with Stephen Theodore Badin was Louis Etienne Le Couteulx de Chaumont. The first Roman Catholic Church, The Mother Church, of Buffalo, New York, cannot be mentioned without referring to this man because he is its benefactor. Initially called the Lamb of God Church and evolving through four buildings on the same site, it grew into the impressive structure of Gothic Grandeur which stands there today at Main and Edward Streets. Le Couteulx was born in Rouen, France, August 24, 1756, on his family's estate near Etrepagny. Ironically, this was the eve of the feast of St. Louis, King of France, for whom the structure of Gothic Grandeur was named and dedicated. His birthplace was at the center of Normandy, the province of northern France between Brittany and French Flanders, whose coast is washed by the English Channel. Besides the varied coast scenery, one enjoyed the pastureland and orchards. Here near Rouen, William the Conqueror was laid to his final rest and Joan of Arc was burned at the stake. It was the birthplace of many great Frenchmen: La Salle, Corneille, Frontenelle, Boieldieu, Carrel, Lemonnier, and Gustave Flaubert. At the time of Louis Le Couteulx's birth, the streets of Rouen were narrow, picturesque, with timber-fronted buildings, and ennobled by magnificent churches such as St. Maclou, St. Ouen, and St. Gervais. It was an active city devoted to the spinning and weaving of cottons, velvets, woolens, linens, and mixed silk. It lay on the Seine River, half way between Paris and the port of Le Havre on the English Channel.

The father of Louis Le Couteulx was Francois Leon Le Couteulx de Chaumont, General Attorney at the Parliament of Normandy. He was enormously wealthy; for years his family had made its fortune in banking. It had made many loans and other financial favors to King Louis XII who was known as *Le Pere du Peuple*. He came to the throne in 1498 and was soon involved in the Italian Wars. France had been meddling in the internal affairs of Italy, and the Two Sicilies were fought over by the Houses of Aragon, Spain, and Anjou, France. In 1505, after he ennobled the Le Couteulx family that was so generous to him, Louis XII married Mary Tudor, the sister of Henry VIII. Affluence bred affluence in the Le Couteulx family; its sons mounted success upon success in banking, shipping, trading, and law. As a young man, age twenty, Louis Le Couteulx went to Cadiz, Spain, bordering the Atlantic Ocean and the Strait of Gibraltar. There his family ran a counting house, in which he kept records of loans for industries involving sherry wine, fishing, and fruits. When his tenure was finished there, he sailed to England and took a position with his cousin, Le Couteulx de La Norrayes, in London. While Louis was in residence, the English colonies in America revolted against the taxation policy of King George III. They demanded their independence and went to war to achieve it. Louis returned to France, where, after meeting with the Marquis de Lafayette who had much compassion towards the American Revolution, encouraged his family to grant loans to the colonists so as to finance their war. Later it also financed the endeavors of King Louis VII to assist the American cause. When the war ended with the colonists victorious, Louis Le Couteulx was chosen by his family to cross the Atlantic, meet with Robert Morris, Superintendent of Finance, who had been elected by the members of the Continental Congress, and collect the debts incurred by the Americans during their Revolution.

Le Couteulx arrived in New York City in the summer of 1786 with his bride, Marie Antoinette Clouet, daughter of a magistrate of the royal administration in Paris, and niece of General Chevalier of Tousard, who fought at the side of the colonists in the American Revolution on June 17, 1775. After this battle at Breed's Hill near Boston, Massachusetts, British forces occupied Rhode Island. During one of the battles there Tousard lost his right arm. After a few weeks in New York City, Le Couteulx and his wife traveled to Philadelphia to meet with Robert Morris who, besides handling finances for the Congress, was serving his fourth term in the Pennsylvania Assembly and was director of his Bank of North America. Needless to say, actual cash exchanges between Morris and Le Couteulx were skimpy; money backed by solid credit was a rare commodity in the new Republic. Land, however, was plentiful and could be used as barter and payment of debt. Morris, who was a speculator in real estate, had been successful in paying war debts in this way both to foreigners and veteran soldiers of the Revolutionary Army. Le Couteulx and his family were satisfied with Morris' offerings. Concluding his business with Morris, Le Couteulx stayed in America, became a citizen, first lived in New Jersey, and later purchased an estate outside Philadelphia, near Morris' home called *The Hills*. Le Couteulx named his estate *La Petite France*. He was witness to the framing and signing of the American Constitution in 1789, and saw his friend Morris elected one of the first Senators of the Federal Government from the State of Pennsylvania.

Louis' correspondence with his family in France kept him informed of the dangers of the tumultuous political changes and the uncertainty the country was undergoing in the early years of the French Revolution. Their position as wealthy nobles and financiers, loyal to the throne, made them quite vulnerable with regards to the edicts issued forth from the National Assembly. The Bastille had been stormed on July 14, 1789, many political factions vied for power, and the peasants revolted. On October 6, 1789, the revolutionary mob marched to Versailles and dragged King Louis XVI and his Queen, Marie Antoinette, from their home and imprisoned them in the Tuileries at Paris. It was at this time that Louis Le Couteulx, concerned for his parents and with the insistence of his wife, left the United States and returned to France. By this time, Marie Antoinette Clouet, his wife, had born him two sons, Pierre Alphonse and William Benedict. They traveled with their parents on this perilous journey. They found Paris in turmoil; Louis' father and other family members had been imprisoned because, having a financial establishment at Cadiz, they were accused of spying for Spain. Friends warned him that it was impossible to have them released, and that the mob, which ruled the National Assembly, would not respect his American citizenship if he stayed in Paris. Secretly, the Le Couteulx family of four sailed down the Seine to Le Havre. With the help of two fishermen they fled to England where they remained in exile for a year. When Victor Riqueti Mirabeau, author and statesman, had apparently brought some order and calm to the French situation in 1790, Louis and his family again returned to France. Upon arriving he found that he was in the midst of the lull before the storm, and decided to leave and return to America. His wife, however, struck with illness, refused to go. Louis went alone, leaving his two sons with her at the French town of Dieppe, a harbor town on the English Channel at the mouth of the Arques River. Never would he return to France again!

After leaving, Le Couteulx sailed to America via England, Spain, and the West Indies. He arrived in New York City on February 17, 1791. Returning to Philadelphia, he sold *La Petite France* to the dismay of Morris, his friend. While Le Couteulx had been exiled in England, he sent Morris an expensive pair of Merino sheep to be used at Morris' summer residence. They were a breed of short wool sheep, which were introduced into Spain from Africa; although the male had horns, the ewe did not. With the money gained from the sale of his estate Le Couteulx, accompanied by his servant and with the encouragement of Morris, set out

to see the new frontier adjacent to the Niagara River in Western New York. When Morris had resigned from the office of finance commissioner of the Federal Government, he, as director of the American Land Company, purchased four million acres of land between the Genesee and Niagara Rivers in New York State which had been claimed by the Commonwealth of Massachusetts. The company had also purchased six million acres in Georgia, Pennsylvania, Virginia, Maryland, and the two Carolinas. Included in the Western New York purchase was the one and a quarter million acres that had been owned by two other land speculators, Phelps and Gorham. Because of financial difficulty, however, Morris found himself required to sell off these large holdings.

Local investors were not affluent enough to buy, and alien speculators were banned from doing so by the New York State Legislature. Morris, however, found a way. A group of Americans had bound themselves together and set up a trust for a group of Dutch businessmen who later called themselves the Holland Land Company. It was part of a multimillion dollar Dutch syndicate headquartered in Amsterdam, Holland, of which Wilhelm Willink, Pieter Stadnitski, Hendrick Vollenhover, Rutger Jan Schimmelpenninckm, Nicholas Van Straphorst, Pieter Eeghen, Gabriel Van Straphorst, Jan Willink, and Hendrick Seye were members of the board of directors. In America it was never an authentic company bound by incorporation laws. Instead, it consisted of three sets of proprietors holding their property as joint tenants, meaning that the survivor took the whole; the shares could not be subjects of a will nor sale until the last survivor met his demise. All deeds were issued in the name of the individual proprietor. Jointly, the board of directors appointed agents to conduct their business. Expenses and profits were charged to and paid from the individual proprietor in accordance with his land holdings. In 1792 the board of directors chose Theophilus Cazenove as their agent in America, and he set up his office in Philadelphia. It was with him that Robert Morris conducted the sale of his Western New York property in 1798.

A year before the sale, Cazenove hired Joseph Ellicott to survey and negotiate with the Seneca Indians for title to their lands for which they received two and one-half cents per acre. In 1798 when the New York State Legislature rescinded its ban on alien ownership, the Holland Land Company took absolute control. Ellicott, besides being the chief surveyor, took complete charge of being overseer and developer of the millions of acres under the company's ownership. He cleared away trees, built roads along Indian trails, and constructed bridges to span rivers, creeks, and streams. Through his efforts the value of the land tripled. On November 1, 1800, the Holland Land Company chose Ellicott as their Western New York agent. The State assumed sovereignty over the entire region of Western New York naming it Ontario County with Canandaigua as the county seat. In 1802, the area west of the Genesee River was separated to form Genesee County with Batavia as its headquarters. Further division took place in 1808 producing Niagara County as a separate entity of two parts; one north of Tonawanda Creek and the other south of it. Later with more division, the southern section was subdivided into Erie, Chautauqua, Cattaraugus, and Allegany Counties. Unfortunately after Morris sold his interests in Western New York to the Holland Land Company, he was faced with financial ruin. He was incarcerated for three years in a debtor's prison in Philadelphia. Upon release he was a broken man and died in 1806. What a tragic end for a member of the Continental Congress, a signer of the Declaration of Independence, a member of the Finance Committee of Congress, and financier of the American Revolution! Likewise tragedy awaited Joseph Ellicott. After having been asked to resign from the Holland Land Company, he resided in New York City where, following admittance into Bloomingdale mental asylum, he committed suicide in 1826.

While the initial land speculations were being concocted in Western New York, Louis Le Couteulx moved to Albany, New York, where he set up his first pharmacy compounding and dispensing medicines. Besides Le Couteulx, other Frenchmen of importance, fleeing the onslaught of the French Revolution, found haven in and about Albany. They were Duke de La Roche-Foucauld-Liancourt, Marquis de Lafayette, and Perigord de Tallyrand. While residing in Albany, Le Couteulx joined some other philanthropists in founding St. Mary's Parish; his name distinctively appears on the certificate of incorporation. He would have personally visited Canada to collect funds for the construction of a church building that was proposed, but he was not allowed to do so. At the time, no Frenchmen were allowed to enter Canada. He arranged for a non-French friend to make the visit in his place. In 1800, near the end of summer, he decided to expand his business pursuits, an endeavor that required him to travel to Detroit, Michigan. Traveling overland from Albany through Utica, he reached the port town of Oswego on Lake Ontario. There he boarded the *Saint-Laurent* bound for Fort George, Upper Canada, at the mouth of the Niagara River opposite Fort Niagara.

When he disembarked on October 8, 1800, he was immediately searched and arrested by the British as a spy. Among the papers which he carried was a correspondence from Le Couteulx & Company, Bankers in Paris, introducing the French philosopher and traveler, Constantin Francois Chasseboeuf, Compte de Volney, to Louis Le Couteulx. Because of the anarchistic ideas expressed in Volney's book, *Les Ruines, ou Meditations sur les Revolutions des Empires*, the British were convinced that Volney had proposed a conquest and humiliation of Great Britain by the French that included an invasion of Canada. They interpreted other lines in the personal correspondence that Le Couteulx carried, which described activities between the bankers in Paris and Volney, as the guilt of Le Couteulx by association with Volney. Under heavy guard Le Couteulx was transported to Quebec where he spent two years in a dark and dank dungeon. Although the American government tried to have him released, it was unsuccessful. It was not until 1802, following the Peace of Amiens between France and England, that he gained his freedom. Walking forth from his prison cell, one could see how traumatized his ordeal was; his dark hair which he had had at Fort George had turned completely gray.

*W*hile he was in prison his securities, gold bullion, and credit certificates were well taken care of by friends and co-advisors in Albany. Once again Le Couteulx turned west to the Niagara Frontier. He found lodging at Crows Tavern in New Amsterdam, the former name of Buffalo. During his stay he penned a letter to Joseph Ellicott of the Holland Land Company declaring his wish to purchase outer lot number two on the East Side of Main Street at the corner of Crow. He expressed to Ellicott his desire to build on it in the spring of 1803. The price was $250.00, a sum, which although it also included an outer lot of four acres up stream on Buffalo Creek, seemed excessive to Le Couteulx. Nevertheless he made a deposit of $50.00 with an agreement to pay the balance in equal installments plus interest. Being on his way to Detroit, Le Couteulx requested Ellicott to send the contract to him there. He further requested Ellicott to procure for him a farm of about eighty acres.

*T*his was the beginning of a relationship with the Holland Land Company that eventually blossomed into a sub-agency position for himself with the company. Soon a voluminous amount of correspondence was exchanged between Ellicott and Le Couteulx. Ellicott had his office in Batavia, and Le Couteulx quickly befriended Theophilus Cazenove, and the Van Straphorst brothers, Nicholas and Gabriel, members the board of directors of the Holland Land Company. Land was cheap and could be bought on credit. In the next few years, Le Couteulx bought many lots and farms,

and became a prominent voice in the economic affairs of New Amsterdam. He reiterated the need of the village to have a Roman Catholic Church. He advocated the removal of the sandbar blocking the mouth of Buffalo Creek that prevented the successful use of the inner harbor. Once he prophesied, "If the Hollanders can't do it, the Yanks will!" He suggested that a canal be cut from the mouth of the Buffalo Creek to Black Rock. Although he donated one half acre of his outer lot number one for the enterprise, he complained bitterly, when the project was underway, that it ruined his chicken yard.

*B*y 1804 Le Couteulx had taken a second wife, Jane Eliza. They lived in his house at the northeast corner of Crow and Willink Streets. His large building consisted of living quarters and a pharmacy, which faced Crow Street. Besides making sales in the store, he made house calls, performed surgery, dispensed prescriptions, and acted as a veterinarian. In addition he sold flour, whiskey, pork, hams, bacon, shingles, and butter. By 1806, his house and store were one of sixteen in the village. In that year he received permission from Ellicott to cut timber away from the "point" at the foot of Main Street so that he would be able to see the Lake from his home. After a few more years he replaced his wooden structure with a brick house, the bricks for which he purchased from William Hodge, who owned a large farm, brick-works, and a tavern on the main east-west road into New Amsterdam, about three miles east of the heart of the village. It was hard, burnt brick, for which Hodge charged an extra fifty cents per thousand. His wife wanted a garden around the house; he gave her one that became renowned for its beauty. As the town grew and moved its boundaries north on Main Street, the road grades surrounding his house were lowered so much that his mansion eventually sat on a hill surrounded by the garden protected by a large retaining wall. Today the HSBC bank building occupies the site. Besides William Hodge's family, other neighbors to Le Couteulx were the families of Samuel Fletcher Pratt, Ebenezer Johnson and Juba Storrs.

Prior to 1813, the village boasted of a hotel, a jail, two physicians, two pharmacists, newspapers, taverns, and a thriving mercantile trade. In 1810, *Buffalo Town* was created by an act of the Legislature, and it was incorporated as a village in 1813. Buffalo had become the seat of Niagara County and Le Couteulx who had been chosen the first clerk of the county served two consecutive terms. His office was located at the corner of Main and Swan Streets, which was only a few blocks from his home. In 1812, war broke out again between the New United States and Great Britain. In September of that year, with fear of an imminent attack on Buffalo being launched by the British from Canada, he sent the county records to Ellicott whose office was in Batavia. The attack did not come immediately as expected. In 1813, therefore, the village was incorporated. Soon after, however, the British regulars and Indians, who had crossed over from Canada, swept up the Niagara River from Lewiston burning and pillaging everything in their path. On December 30, 1813, they reached Buffalo. When they were finished with their fury, only a few of the ninety-three structures in the city were left unburned. The citizens and the remnants of any American army had fled into the winter night.

Le Couteulx and his wife returned to Albany where he still had the refuge of his property and his pharmacy. For the remainder of the war he assumed, by appointment of the Federal Government, the position of Forage Master. It was his responsibility to procure, purchase, make storage, and provide transportation of food, clothing, and equipment to the militia in areas ravaged by the war. His name became well known; and, in 1817, he was appointed Sergeant-of-Arms of the Senate. In 1824, he returned to Buffalo, and set about rebuilding his business. The opening of the Erie Canal in 1825, brought almost instant prosperity to Buffalo, and Le Couteulx with his shrewd sense of business capitalized on commerce with the flood of immigrants from the Northeast and European emigrants. He never forgot, however, one of his primary requests for Buffalo, the establishment of a Roman Catholic Church.

The topic was ripe in his mind when Badin came to Buffalo in the late fall of 1828, and stayed at his home. Le Couteulx thought that he could persuade Badin to remain in Buffalo and be the priest that the growing Catholic community so desperately needed. Badin said that he had a former commitment with his friend Bishop Edward Dominic Fenwick of Cincinnati to take upon himself the mission at Monroe, Michigan. He assured Le Couteulx, however, that if land was available for a church and the people were willing to build a structure upon it, Dubois would find and send a priest who could speak French and German.

On January 5, 1829, Bishop Dubois received the deed of the property, owned by Le Couteulx, which ran from Main Street to Delaware Avenue as a New Year's Day gift. Dubois sent Father Nicholas Mertz to Buffalo, and a crude but useful structure named the Lamb of God Church became a reality in 1832. A second church, built over the first, was completed by 1843. Le Couteulx, however, did not live to see the first service conducted in it; he died on November 16, 1840, following his wife, Jane Eliza, who had preceded him to the grave by a few years. Two days after his death, Mayor Sheldon Thompson called a special meeting of the Common Council to pay tribute to him. In his memory a painting of his portrait was commissioned and placed in the Council Chambers. Today this portrait hangs in the hall of St. Mary's School for the Deaf on Main Street at Dewey. It displays him as a man who was refined, dignified, and genial. One who was tall, erect, and dressed elegantly. His silver hair tied in a queue. He wore a long French surcoat, unbuttoned, showing the finest linen cambric shirt with ruffles. His dress displayed a wristband with jeweled links, black cloth knee breeches, silk stockings, and high heeled shoes with wide silver buckles. He carried a chapeau in his right hand; and, in the other, he held exquisitely a fine linen cambric handkerchief. Between thumb and forefinger of the left hand he held his snuffbox, a gift from his friend, King Louis XVI.

In donating his property between Main Street and Delaware Avenue, in trust, to Bishop Dubois, he stipulated that a Catholic burial ground be placed at the site as well as a church. In the area reserved for graves, a plot especially reserved for himself and his family was set aside. When Le Couteulx and his wife died, it was impossible to fulfill this request. In 1832 the village of Buffalo was newly incorporated as the City of Buffalo. One of the provisions of incorporation was that all public cemeteries would be banned within the city's limits. This was a direct result of the first great cholera epidemic that attacked the city in that year. The two public cemeteries which had existed before that date were the Franklin Square burial grounds, at the present site of City Hall, and the Catholic cemetery adjacent to the Lamb of God Church. Property, however, was purchased outside the city's limits on farm lot number thirty. A portion of this plot, also known as Potters Field, was given to the Catholics so that they could bury according to their custom; it was given in retribution for the condemnation of their cemetery next to the Lamb of God Church. The Catholic portion encompassed about an acre. Because the Lamb of God Church was the only church in 1832 which had Catholic membership, the cemetery eventually became known as the New St. Louis Church Cemetery. The trustees of St. Louis Church claimed ownership of it because since its founding they had provided the necessary care of all gravesites. In one of these the Le Couteulx family was first buried. Cholera again visited the City of Buffalo with epidemic proportions in 1849 and 1854. Because of these events and the expansion of the city, the Common Council decided to condemn Potters Field and the New St. Louis Cemetery in 1859.

During the winter of that year, six Catholic parishes in the city, including St. Louis' parish made plans to provide their members with a new burial ground. By springtime the United German and French Roman Catholic Cemetery was formed on farm property which had been purchased on Pine Ridge Road at the city's edge in the township of Cheektowaga. It

took nearly twenty years to make the complete transfer of all the remains at the New St. Louis Cemetery to the United German and French Roman Catholic Cemetery. Finally on August 3, 1879, the remains of Louis Le Couteulx, his wife Jane Eliza, and their son William Benedict Le Couteulx were re-interred in this cemetery. On November 2, 1894, hundreds of spectators gathered at the New York Central Railroad Station to watch Frank Snyder unload what was considered the largest stone crucifix in the world. Weighing thirty tons and having a height of twenty-six feet, it was installed at the Le Couteulx family plot. In transport it rested in the bed of a wooden wagon called "a truck" which was pulled by twenty-four workhorses. It had been sculptured by James Gilbert Hamilton at the Empire Granite Company of Barre, Vermont, and had been two years in the making. Hamilton was born in Scotland in 1851, immigrated to the United States, and took up residences at various times in Philadelphia, Cleveland, and New York City.

Le Couteulx had willed his entire estate to his two sons, Pierre Alphonse and William Benedict with the exception of a trust fund that was set up for William's wife, Charlotte, to last for her lifetime. After her death the trust was to be transferred to Jenny, her daughter, who was living in France. Charlotte, who had moved to France after William died, met her demise in 1861. Four children including one minor, Barthelemy and her brother survived her. Her will was probated under the direction of her daughter, Marie Louise Damainville. Pierre Alphonse married Antoinette Adelaide Dupont on October 2, 1827. They had three children. The date of his death and place of interment are unknown. Louis Etienne Le Couteulx, considered as the Founding Father of St. Louis Church, had promoted several philanthropic endeavors besides his initiation of the Catholic Mother Church of Buffalo with her school, rectory, cemetery, and rental properties, which provided the trustees and pastor with financial aid. He also owned more lots circumscribing that which he donated in trust to Bishop Dubois. On Pearl Place, near Virginia, today known as St. Louis Place, he owned a plot of land, on which was built a structure which was first used as a school and later purchased by Bishop Timon to be used as a hospital under the direction of the Sisters of Charity.

*W*hen Timon brought the Sisters of Charity to Buffalo, the trustees of St. Louis Church allowed them to set-up their first hospital in a tent on the church grounds. In 1848, the hospital moved to a brick structure on Pearl Place that was incorporated with Pierre Alphonse Le Couteulx as one of the trustees. In that same year, The Sisters of Charity opened St. Mary's Asylum for widows, foundlings, and infants at 126 Edward Street. Louis Le Couteulx had also donated this property to Bishop Timon for that purpose. One year later, the present Immaculate Conception Church at 150 Edward Street was founded under the name of St. Mary's of the Lake for the purpose of catering to the spiritual needs of Irish families which were expanding

their residences into areas west of Main Street. In 1839, however, the property upon which the church, school, and rectory are built was donated provisionally by Louis Le Couteulx to Reverend John Hughes, who was Bishop of the Diocese of New York. The land was intended for the erection of a church for the use of the Irish who were dissatisfied with the lack of English being spoken at St. Louis Church. The Irish, however, felt that the lot was too far away from their residences along the lakefront, and they opted to build elsewhere. The land therefore reverted back to Louis Le Couteulx who willed it to his son, Alphonse, who in turn deeded it to Timon in 1849. Next to St. Mary's Asylum on Edward Street was another large lot that also had been donated by the Le Couteulx family. On this site, St. Mary's Institute for Deaf Mutes was established in 1857. It evolved into a four-story building to which many additions were added by 1880. One of the wings became a boarding school for young ladies. When the Sisters of St. Joseph arrived in 1854, at the request of Bishop Timon, they used the building as a novitiate and a convent. [3]

Badin and Le Couteulx

REFERENCES AND NOTES ✣ CHAPTER THREE

1. Badin's suggestion to Le Couteulx concerning other land donations to Dubois is taken from a letter from Badin written to Carroll on April 11, 1796; see: *Records of the American Catholic Historical Society of Philadelphia*, vol.19, 1908. Any other references to this text will be cited in the future as op. cit. or ibid. followed by the identification *Records*, vol. number and date.

2. Biographical material for Stephen Theodore Badin was mainly taken from David Read Driscoll Jr., *Stephen Theodore Badin*, Thesis, Master of Arts Degree, Department of History, Graduate School of the University of Louisville, Louisville, Kentucky, 1953. A second source of the biographical material was taken from Badin's own work. see: Badin, S. T., *Origine et Progres de la Mission du Kentucky*, Paris, 1821. A third source of material was gleaned from Sister Mary Ramona Mattingly, *The Catholic Church on the Kentucky Frontier 1785-1812*, Catholic University of America, Studies in American Church History, vol. 25, Washington, D.C., 1936. Archival sources concerning Badin's life and his activities in Kentucky and the Old Northwest are a) Loretto Motherhouse, Nerinckx, Kentucky; an original of *Origine et Progre etc.* are kept there. b) Nazareth Motherhouse, Nazareth, Kentucky. The Sisters at this establishment have a large collection of Badin's letters, newspaper clippings, and Catholic Church history of the early days of Kentucky. c) The University of Notre Dame, South Bend, Indiana, a complete set of the *Badin Papers*. For a reference for the condition which Badin found in Gallipolis, Ohio, see: Rev. Laurence Kenny, "The Gallipolis Colony," *Catholic Historical Review*, vol. 4, 1918-19, pps. 415-50.

3. These paragraphs describing the life and activities of Louis Le Couteulx and his family have resulted from editing a scholarly paper titled *Louis Etienne Le Couteulx de Chaumont: 1756-1840*, written by Molly B. Hauck and submitted to Professor C. Eugene Miller, author/editor, on 12/21/2001. At the time she completed her work she was an Independent Researcher/ Mount Calvary Cemetery Inc./ Historian/ Archivist. She graciously gave the editors permission to place her work into this St. Louis Church History: *Gothic Grandeur: A Rare Tradition in American Catholicism*. Her source material was obtained from the following: Severance, Frank, ed., *Publications of the Buffalo and Erie County Historical Society*. Murray, Martha J.J., *Memoir of Stephen Louis Le Couteulx de Chaumont*, Buffalo and Erie County Public Library, Special Collections Department. Donohue, Thomas D.D., *History of the Catholic Church in Western New York, Diocese of Buffalo*, Buffalo Historical Publishing Company, Buffalo, New York, 1904. Buffalo and Erie County Public Library, *Newspaper clippings*, scrapbook prepared by WPA during the depression years. *The Buffalo News*, Thursday, August 15, 1996. Riester, Michael, *The 167th Anniversary History of St. Louis Church*, St. Louis Church Archives. From the Buffalo and Erie County Historical Society, *News Clippings, Maps, and Vertical Files*. Direct conversations with: Patrick Wiessend, Director of the

Holland Land Company Museum, Batavia, New York; Michael Riester, Archivist and Historian, St. Louis Church; Copies of Molly Hauck's works can be found in the Mount Calvary Cemetery Archives. During Louis Le Couteulx's time, Le Couteulx Street ran from Rock Street to Water Street in the harbor area. Carolina Street ran from Tupper Street to the Erie Canal, and Exchange Street was formerly Crow Street. There were two Morgan Streets; one at Virginia, running south a short distance where it crossed Louis Street, now known as Edward Street, dead ended shortly thereafter at the intersection of Morgan Street, now known as Elmwood Avenue, and Edward Street. It was eventually extended to join the other Morgan Street to the south, becoming Elmwood Avenue. Louis Street ran from Virginia to Delaware; from Delaware to Main it was called Walden Alley. In 1836-7, these narrower streets were straightened and widened from Main to Virginia; in 1855 they became Edward Street. Louis Le Couteulx's home was located on a block that was purchased by developers in the early 1800's and became known as Le Couteulx Block. It was demolished in 1889. Time has erased the Le Couteulx home, his history, his name, and even the streets named for him, but he continues to live on at St. Louis Church. The records, which Le Couteulx sent to Batavia when he was clerk for Niagara County, did not remain there. The legal community of Buffalo demanded that they be returned and so they were. The trustees of the United German and French Roman Catholic Cemetery were elected to the board of directors from representatives of those parishes existing in Buffalo at the time of its incorporation. Today, although the original cemetery retains its original name, the non-profit organization that began as the United German and French Roman Catholic Cemetery changed its name to Mount Calvary Cemetery, Inc., in 1982. The cemetery has been consecrated five times, each time a new section was added. Louis Le Couteulx's sons may have come to live with him and his second wife, Jane Eliza, after the death of their mother, Marie Antoinette Clouet. Both were born in the United States, Pierre Alphonse on Dec. 29, 1788 in Pennsylvania, and William Benedict on June 20, 1787, in Trenton, New Jersey. William, the elder appears to have lived his adult life in Buffalo. Both men were in Buffalo when their father died. The 1850-55 *City Directory* lists Alphonse Le Couteulx as living on Eleventh and Hudson Streets. Louis Le Couteulx died at his home on Crow Street. William was a French Naval Officer of the Legion of Honor; trustee of St. Louis Church; had many rental properties in the city, which he inherited from his father; he married Charlotte Laure Gaudry on February 8. 1818; they had four children: Barthelemy-William, Jenny-Blanche, Marie-Louise, and Mathilde-Alphonsine. Barthelemy-William was their only son and the youngest. He was born in Buffalo on Dec. 6, 1840. He was fourteen years younger than Jenny-Blanche, the youngest daughter. Two of the daughters married and lived in France; Mathilde married a baron. Barthelemy lived in France with his mother. Marie-Louise married Augustin Damainville, and lived in Buffalo. Her husband was one of the appraisers of William Benedict Le Couteulx's will. She and Augustin had four children. William B. Le Couteulx died in 1859 and was buried next to his father and Jane Eliza in the New St. Louis Cemetery, Lot 1, Sec.

MM. St. Mary's Asylum was south of Edward Street just east of Morgan then Elmwood. It evolved into St. Mary's Infant Asylum and Maternity Hospital after the consolidation of the Buffalo Widows and Orphan Asylum with St. Mary's Lying Hospital. It was reincorporated in 1897. At St. Mary's Maternity Hospital one of the attending physicians was Doctor Julian A. Riester, who charged $40 for delivery and follow-up, including house calls. He was an ancestor of Michael Riester, present historian at St. Louis Church and co-editor of this text. The house which was used as a novitiate and convent of the Sisters of St. Joseph is today called St. Mary's Square; it is an apartment complex. In her paper, op. cit. *Louis Etienne Le Couteulx de Chaumont: 1756-1840*, Molly Hauck refers to the ownership of the property and building on St. Louis Place previously Pearl Place, which in 1848 was incorporated by the Sisters of Charity as a hospital, as that of Louis Le Couteulx. In the paper, Steffan, Jacob P., *Michael Steffan History*, unpublished, Buffalo, 1939, the author refers to the Steffan family purchasing this property and building in 1875. A copy of the paper is in the St. Louis Church Archives. Jacob Steffan claims that his mother,

Frances Mary Kloepfer, had been employed there as a cook or maidservant prior to its being transformed into a hospital. Putting the two facts together, the writer/editor of this book would contend that the building on the property was there before 1848. Frances Kloepfer must have worked for either Le Couteulx or for whoever was renting or who had purchased it from Le Couteulx. It is also known that a school was there before the Sisters used it as a hospital. If Le Couteulx did not own it at the time, he probably had sold it to the school's corporation. For conditions and personages in Buffalo prior to the War of 1812, the burning of Buffalo and the aftermath see: op. cit. *High Hopes*, pp. 21-5. For additional information concerning the Holland Company see: *Abstract of Title to Property in Pendale, Pendleton, New York, No. 93-04643*, Ticor Guarantee Company, Buffalo, New York, 1993; Goldman, Mark, *The Rise and Decline of Buffalo, New York*, State University of New York Press, Albany, New York, 1933, p.27; "The Holland Land Company," *Buffalo Evening News*, October 3, 1953; Powell, Roland, "Were the Indians Given Fair Price for WNY? U.S. Reopens the Case," *Buffalo Evening News*, July 18, 1970.

CHAPTER FOUR

The Missionary Clergy

The missionary clergy who immigrated into post-revolutionary United States from the continent of Europe, in distinction from the Irish clergy, were mainly alumni of seminaries founded on the French interpretation of the principles put forth at the Council of Trent in 1563 concerning the priesthood and the Sacrament of Holy Orders. The Council had concluded that the priesthood in the Catholic Church should be one that is visible and external. An ordained priest definitely had the power of consecrating the body and blood of Jesus Christ, and the power of forgiving sins in Christ's name. It did not, however, stress the priest's responsibility of preaching or community leadership. It proclaimed further that Holy Orders is indisputably one of the seven sacraments instituted by Christ; and those who received it were impregnated with the grace it conferred. Additionally, the Council defined the hierarchical structure in the Catholic Church in which all clergy were at some stage of minor and major orders with bishops being superior to the priests. It also made a clear distinction between the priesthood of the lay baptized and the ordained in the Church. For four hundred years following the Council of Trent, the priesthood so defined was propagated in seminaries that were established in every diocese. After a young recruit had passed through several years of formation in one of these seminaries, he was ready to receive minor and major orders, culminating in final reception of the Sacrament of Holy Orders, which was his introduction into the priesthood.

During the eighteenth century, the Sulpician seminaries which had been founded in France took the lead in developing the educational system under which the candidate for Holy Orders studied. In one phase of it known as the minor seminary, he digested the classics, humanities, and sciences; Latin and Greek were his textbook languages. While studying he lived a life detached from the world; it was one regulated, in a quiet reverent atmosphere from early morning rising to late evening bedtime. He lived by a preordained schedule that included morning prayer, meditation, recitation of the rosary, daily Mass, classroom lectures, sermons, spiritual reading, and committing passages of scripture to memory. He learned a special seminary language; he ate in a refectory, did dishes in a scullery, studied in a common room, and slept in a cell. At meals, he did not speak to his tablemates; he listened to a lector reading aloud.

Similarly, but more intensely this routine was continued in the major seminary where the curriculum included philosophy, theology, related science, and discipline. Each day, in private, the seminarian begged pardon from the superior of the house for the faults that he had committed that day. This act was not a confession of those sins that would be exposed in the Sacrament of Penance, but they were the many foibles, indiscretions, and peccadilloes related to the house disciplinary code. Once a week, the seminarian knelt in front of his colleagues and announced aloud his disciplinary failures of the week; and, prayerfully, he begged them to ask God to forgive him. Unique to the French seminary was the insistence upon structured mental prayer in which the seminarian identified himself with Jesus Christ who was considered as a real man, a real historical figure. He being present in the Eucharist, was to be followed, listened to, and imitated. Although He died, He rose from the dead. He is God the Son, the second person of the Blessed Trinity, the only path by which the seminarian could reach God the Father in unity with the Holy Spirit.

At the climax of this intense period of study the seminarian was admitted to minor orders. The Council of Trent had prescribed four minor orders: porter, lector, exorcist, and acolyte. Porters had maintenance and security responsibilities; lectors read during liturgical worship; exorcists assisted at rites of initiation and repentance; acolytes served as secretaries and messengers for the bishop. The subdiaconate, which prior to the Council was a minor order, had been raised to the status of a major one; the subdeacon being the assistant to the deacon. At his ordination ceremony by the bishop, he was clothed in the vestments that the subdeacon wore at Mass which were the amice, alb, and dalmatic, a form of tunic. The bishop handed the young cleric a book of epistles, chalice, paten, and a pair of filled cruets. These items symbolized the activities which he performed at a Solemn High Mass. Upon receiving the order of subdeacon, the candidate was sealed to celibacy by solemn promise and was required to daily recite from his breviary the liturgy of the hours. Conferring of the diaconate followed almost immediately upon the reception of the subdiaconate. At its ceremony of ordination, the bishop laid hands on the candidate, prayed, and presented him with the stole, dalmatic, and a book of gospels. As deacon, the candidate was given the mission to exercise a limited leadership role in designated pastoral responsibilities in the absence of the priest. He was, however, limited to performing only the liturgies associated with preaching, baptism, and administration of communion. Historically, the original duty of the deacon was to distribute alms to the poor. Liturgically, awarding the diaconate was

considered just a second step in the completion of the reception of Holy Orders.

After a period of time, the head of the seminary determined which deacons were ready to be ordained to the priesthood by the bishop. The ceremony was regularly performed on one of the Ember Days that were three days of a week occurring four times during the year. The bishop, however, had the discretion to ordain at any time, other than Ember Days if he found it necessary to do so. At the ordination ceremony the deacon was presented to the bishop by the head of the seminary, who vouched that the candidate was worthy and ready to seek this holy office. The bishop requested all those present, clergy and laity, to give any reason why this man should not be given the sacrament. Upon hearing no opposition, the bishop proceeded to the liturgy of the imposition of hands upon the candidate. First he imposed his hands. Then he requested all priests present to come forward and impose their hands upon the candidate. Prayers whereby God was asked to rain down His graces upon the candidate and give him the fullness of heavenly gifts and divine grace followed this action.

Then the bishop crossed the deacon's stole to symbolize that he took upon himself the yoke of the Lord whose burden was sweet and light. Next the bishop presented him with the chasuble, representing charity. At this point the *Veni Creator* was intoned and while the choir sang the verses, the bishop took oil and began anointing the deacon's hands. First he anointed the thumb, then the index finger of each hand, and then the palms of both hands. Into these anointed hands, he placed the chalice filled with wine and water. Setting it down on the altar, the deacon received from the bishop the paten with the bread, and pronounced the words that directed him to receive the powers to consecrate. After these symbolic actions had been performed, the bishop said Mass accompanied by the newly ordained priest who received communion at the hands of the bishop. At the end of Mass, there was a second imposition of hands, which at its conclusion the bishop addressed the new priest saying, "Beloved son! Diligently consider the office to which you have been promoted, and the burden which has been placed upon your shoulders; let it be your first care to lead a holy and religious life, and to please the Almighty, that you may be made worthy of his grace, which, through his mercy, he may grant you."

Following the reception of the Sacrament of Holy Orders, the newly ordained priest was assigned by the bishop to a parish as an assistant to a registered pastor. The priest had no choice but to obey because he had been incardinated at the time of his reception of the diaconate. Incardination was the canonical bond that existed between cleric and a given diocese. No cleric was allowed to minister without this bond and under the supervision of its bishop. After a few years of ministry as an assistant, the priest was assigned by his bishop to a pastorship. As pastor, he was responsible for the care of his parish community. Besides entering into a sacramental and catechetical ministry, he was also responsible for finances, building maintenance, parish programs, coordinating the parish mission, and fostering lay ministries. If a priest, either assistant or pastor decided to leave his parish for a ministry in a missionary country, he would first have to obtain a letter of excardination from his bishop and receive a new incardination from the bishop of the diocese to which he desired to go.

Once these official papers were established the priest was on his own to seek funds for travel, prepare for land transportation to a port city on the continent, and arrange passage on a ship headed to his missionary country. He either had to personally subsidize his travel, or he could receive money from the Sacred Congregation for the Propagation of the Faith at the Vatican, which was first established by Pope Gregory XV in 1622. In 1829, there were only four German

priests functioning in the Missionary Catholic Church in the United States. They were Reverend Fathers Ludwig de Barth, Baltimore; Rese, Cincinnati; Mertz, Buffalo; and Demetrius Gallitzin, Pennsylvania. In addition there were only two German seminarians, who were soon to be ordained at Bardstown, Kentucky. They were J.M. Henin and M. Kundig. Also, although the number of priests speaking English or French was greater than the Germans, they too were very scarce. [1]

There was much rejoicing among Catholics of Buffalo when Bishop Dubois sent John Nicholas Mertz there to be the first pastor of their growing congregation. Although at the time of his arrival, he was sixty-five years of age, he still was hearty, rugged, and always well. During his eighteen years of experience in his former ministries at Conewago, Pennsylvania, and Baltimore, Maryland, he had accustomed himself to many situations in America, and was prepared for the emergency of advancing holy religion in Western New York. In his outward appearance, however, he had not modernized. Being at the age of forty-seven on his first arrival in America, and of such stern character that he cared little for the world's verdict, he retained his priestly clothing as had been the custom in a previous century in his European home. He was tall, of a tendency to be lean. Coming to Buffalo, he was rather slightly stooped and round shouldered, wearing his three-cornered hat, black neck cloth without turned down collar, black vest buttoned in full, a long brown overcoat, short black pants, buckles at his knees, and heavy buckled shoes. His appearance left an involuntary deep impression upon one's mind. His habits of life were of the plainest and most severe. His look was always of an earnest, grave, and solemn nature.

Mertz was born at Bondorf near Trier on the Moselle River in 1764. Bondorf was in Rheinpfalz, which had been a province of Bavaria until 1801 when France annexed it under the authority of Napoleon

Bonaparte. In 1790, he was ordained at Metz. It was a fortified city in Lorraine, France, which had come under French rule in 1648 as a result of the treaty of Westphalia, ending the thirty years war. Its bishopric boasted of its gothic cathedral. After his ordination Mertz spent twenty-one years in religious service in France being able to speak both French and German. He witnessed the bloody French Revolution and the downfall of the Bourbon monarchy. He saw his ministry fall into ill repute because the influence of the hierarchy of the Catholic Church had been intricately interlaced with the fortunes of the aristocracy and monarchy.

*I*n 1805, he was forty-one years old; an age when one looks over the past and questions if and how changes should be made in one's life. While he struggled with his thoughts, Napoleon defeated the Russians and Austrians at Austerlitz, followed by the Peace at Pressburg. Under Napoleon's protection the Confederation of the Rhein was formed and Napoleon made his own brother, Joseph, King of Spain. Both these changes effected the business, social, and religious community in which Mertz served. Many disenchanted laborers and craftsmen gathered up their belongings and financial savings and immigrated to America. When news came to him in 1809 that Napoleon had occupied Vienna, destroying aristocratic rule there, he knew that he too must make preparations to go to the United States, and minister to his French and German expatriates. He was then forty-five years old and he requested his bishop to consider his excardination. Two years later he was accepted by Archbishop Carroll of Baltimore to come to Pennsylvania and serve the German element settled there; he remained in the area of Conewago for three years after which he spent fifteen years in Baltimore. By 1829, James Whitefield had become archbishop. He asked Mertz to report to Bishop Dubois in New York City.

*W*hile Mertz was in Pennsylvania, he experienced many of the trials and tribulations that other Continental European missionaries experienced in America. The settlers of Conewago had come across the Atlantic to seek out cheap fertile land for farming. No matter how rustic, it was better than they had in Europe, and they knew that in their old age they could be looked after by their children who were bound to settle about them. Although there were only twenty-five priests available in 1787, these settlers set aside tracts of land to be used for the establishment of chapels or station-churches so that when itinerant priests would wander into their locale a place was available for conducting services. Some priests, who came from France, Alsace, and Lorraine, had aristocratic or bourgeois backgrounds. They came with family patrimonies, and could purchase acres of land for churches, schools, and cemeteries. They also had sufficient acuteness and business-mindedness for handling these ecclesiastical properties. Other priests, however, wanted to bind their congregations and settlements by contract to pay them a salary for conducting their ministry. Many times the fee they required was too high, but the poor farmers agreed to it because they were eager to participate fully in the sacraments. Soon, however, they found that they could not meet the payments. Because of their default, these priests took them to court, which caused much scandal and was usually disapproved by Carroll, the archbishop of Baltimore, and his successors. News of parochial problems traveled slowly to the archbishop from the frontier and many harms were done before a cure could be rendered. Some disgruntled priests simply left the place to which the bishop had sent them without informing him; they went to find greener pastures; they refused to share in the poverty of their laity.

*W*hen errant priests found richer patrons in areas to which the bishop had not sent them, they performed their priestly functions without jurisdiction. One major concern was in regards to the Sacrament of Matrimony. It was debatable whether marriages performed by them were legal according to Church standards. Later, when a properly incardinated priest came into these areas, many marriages were redone on a conditional basis. Some married couples, however, when they heard that their marriage by a vagabond priest had been most likely null and void, decided then to separate and remarry other partners. Many a conscience was most disturbed because the laity also considered their absolutions in confessions by errant priests to be null and void. The administration of sacramental absolution was even difficult for those priests who had proper jurisdiction. Many had to tend to their flocks who were dispersed over several hundred miles; each priest usually saw each group only once every two months. In making the circuit they suffered much. They rode on horseback or walked. Crossing rivers, their horses lost their footing. Traveling through the forests the horses sometimes bolted and threw their riders to the ground. Many a priest fell from his saddle with his foot caught in the stirrups, and dragged to great lengths before his horse came to rest. The missionary priest battled falling rocks, got lost in the woods, tramped through heavy rain, and slept on wet leaves or on the limbs of trees. Priests were prey for hostile Indians and antagonistic non-Catholics. After being attacked they, in a wounded state, were left to die, and did so unless tended to by some good samaritan.

One pressing concern for the missionary priest was the burden of deciding who were the ones most in need of Extreme Unction, commonly known as the last rites. He was required to practice a kind of sacerdotal triage whereby the most needy would receive it first. In many cases his decision, no matter how well reasoned, would clash with relatives of the sick who saw only their need, and refused to understand his dilemma. To bring some pacification into a community, the missionary outlined simple rules to be followed by the laity. When they were in need of him during a sickness, they were required to send someone to fetch him, make payment of a nominal fee, have a doctor's certificate proving that the call was genuinely critical, and provide a horse for his transportation. In some cases exceptions were made;

understanding and charity guided the devoted missionary. Other disciplinary rules, which the missionary had to devise, were associated with the attendance at Mass under the penalty of grave sin. These involved the mode of transportation available to the laity and the distance one had to travel. If a family had a horse and wagon, and lived within ten miles of the church or station where Mass was conducted, it had the obligation to be present whenever the priest was available. Likewise, members of families who lived within five miles but had no horses were still required to be present; a five-mile walk was not considered excessive. Since the priest could not conduct Mass every Sunday in the same place, he had to outline other religious exercises for the laity when he was not present. He recommended family prayer, catechism, nightly examination of conscience, and spiritual reading. Pious persons added to these the recitation of the rosary and other devotions in honor of the Blessed Virgin Mary. Often when the priest would instruct the children, he would say "My children, mind this; no morning prayer, no breakfast; no evening prayer, no supper; my children be good, and you will never be sorry for it."

One of the most troublesome problems for the missionary priest oozed forth from within himself; it was his own emotion of loneliness. Ideally in this regard, those most safeguarded in missionary work were members of religious orders who entered a missionary field with a band of clerics rather than as single individuals, as was the case with many early missionary priests in the United States. In most cases, they were assigned to their task by a bishop whose residence was extremely far away, they found themselves alone in a vast territory with few pleasures, and confined by all the hardships and moral codes imposed on them by their state in life. History has shown that some missionary priests turned to alcohol as a way of handling loneliness. Others indulged in suspicious and intriguing activities of entrepeneurships while several just disappeared or lost their senses. A few sought the company of local women and sullied their holy vow of celibacy. Psychologists and psychiatrists have claimed that one of the leading causes for an individual to seek illicit sexual pleasure privately is loneliness and an inability to have available, stable, and well-meaning companionships. Well-intentioned missionary priests intensely feared these moral disorders, and used a combination of prayer and fasting as a deterrent and a deliverance from temptation. If they did fall, their condition was compounded by the fact that the only confessor available to them was in most cases some two hundred miles away. Often missionary priests, who could not go to confession for as long as twenty-one months at a time, would reflect on the words in Ecclesiastes (4:10), "If one should fall, another will help him up; but woe to the man who has no one to help him when he falls down." For this reason several missionary priests, such as John Nepomucene Neumann, joined religious orders whose missionaries labored together in small groups.

After his arrival in Buffalo, Mertz lived for a short time in a log house upon the west side of Pearl Street, between Court and Eagle Streets, near the livery stable of Charles W. Miller. Divine services were held in a frame house near his residence for which the rent was paid by the Catholic congregation that gathered there. Among those who attended Sunday Mass were Germans, French, and Irish. In 1831, Mertz decided that he wished to have a church built on the lot provided by Louis Le Couteulx at the junction of Main and Edward Streets. It was at a location considered quite far north from the residential area, and it had to be reached by wagon or buggy. The church was built of oak wood, obtained from the Jammertal forest and quarry section of Buffalo. The forest covered the area of the present site of Forest Lawn Cemetery and Delaware Park. The quarries were northeast of the forest in an area that is located on the east side of Main Street north of Humboldt Parkway. Large logs were drawn from there to the area of construction by ox teams, furnished by different members of the congregation. They were then

hewn into shape with broad axe. When finished, the church had the appearance of a log house because some of the installed timbers, which were reported to be eight and twelve inches square, were exposed on the surface. The walls were covered with a rough coating of plaster between these beams giving it a very substantial and attractive appearance. The height on the outside was twenty feet from the foundation to the eaves, which projected somewhat over the sides of the building. The roof was shingled. It was placed far enough back from Main Street so that a larger church could eventually be built around and above it. It was begun in the fall of 1831 and completed in the spring of 1832.

When it was completed some wondered why it had no chimney. It was Father Mertz who believed that a fireplace and chimney were out of place in a church. He had a small sized pulpit built on the left in the forward part of the church, and the seats in front, the width of one bench length, were at right angles, facing the middle aisle from north and south. He did not allow instrumental music; the organ was of a reed construction and the violin was banished from the church. Only voices were encouraged to intone a psalm or a hymn. In 1832, the number of people who attended Mass each Sunday was about seventy or eighty. One Protestant who used to come by the church about the time services were concluded, and watched the members file out, remarked in amazement, "Where do all the Catholics come from?" A few years later, he would have been more shocked because from seven hundred to eight hundred people congregated on Sundays, and the little building was filled to over-flowing. A large number of people were obliged to stand outside about the windows and doors. Several knelt around the church to get as near as possible to hear the divine service and the teaching of the gospel as presented by Mertz.

Since quite a number of Irish came to church each Sunday, Mertz, who had but a limited command of the

English language, would discourse for their benefit in that language. It was a short sermon that often taxed and confused him to find the proper words to express himself. The result of his endeavor, filled with improper mixing of words, brought about considerable merriment among the Irish. Likewise, the sermons were not pleasing to the Germans; they said that the Irish should either learn German or be satisfied with the rest of the Mass that was said in Latin. They claimed that the church was German. Mertz was displeased with this remark because he said that it was there for all the Catholics of Buffalo whether they were Irish, French, or German.

John George Schneider and Brumpter Zimmermann had supervised the work of building the church. Not only did the Catholics work with great earnestness and zeal to put up the building, but also their Protestant friends and neighbors assisted them in every way possible. Mertz had allocated quite a sum of money that he had collected while he was in Europe visiting churches explaining the needs of the Missionary Church in America. Although Buffalo was not his first choice of a missionary field of endeavor, nonetheless, he was generous in establishing his church that he named The Lamb of God Church. It was appropriate because he had brought with him from Europe a tabernacle whose bronze door depicted Jesus Christ as a lamb. On the part of the parishioners, their time was generously given, but money was not plentiful. Those that had brought some money with them from Europe had it only in a limited degree. When on Sunday the collection was taken, as much as fifteen sous were realized. Being the equivalent of seventy-five cents, it was considered by the congregation as a large amount. The girls on first communion day, which was held after their thirteenth birthday, wore ordinary calico dresses and white lace caps; extravagance was not indulged in, the wherewith being out of the question. Entertainment was on a no cost basis. After Mass on Sundays there was activity among the members by way of greeting, hand shaking, and general visiting. In this they found considerable satisfaction; many of the people coming from miles around had fascinating stories to tell.

In 1888, the writers of *The St. Louis Bazar Chronicle* interviewed several elderly parishioners who remembered some vignettes concerning Mertz and the parishioners of The Lamb of God Church in the years between 1831 and 1838. One person told how Mertz had lived the simplest life, eating but a few potatoes roasted in the hot ashes of his open fireplace. These he would roll about in his hands when sufficiently roasted, and blow between them to cool them enough so he could partake of them with his cup of tea. Another old lady told her version of one of his baptisms. While in the act of baptizing a child held in the arms of its mother, the baby became very troublesome and unruly. Because nothing would quiet it, the venerable Mertz resorted to a pucker of his mouth for a whistle to silence it; but, because of his old age and his loss of teeth, it was not a success. Many old-timers related facts about early immigration of Catholics into Buffalo who were Alsatians. They said, "Many were encouraged to come to America because they were venturesome and believed that financial success would be at the end of the rainbow of their travels." One successful resident told how he had written to his brother still in Alsace. He told his brother that in Buffalo he could sell *holz schuhe*, wooden shoes, for thirty or forty sous and that he paid nothing for the wood which he used to make them. Upon receiving the letter, the brother had much encouragement to emigrate. In Alsace, he had to pay for his wood to make shoes and only received ten or twelve sous. In part, it was by a series of such letters relating financial successes in the New World that the floodgates of immigration were opened.

After immigrants were settled into their new environment they soon realized that they were being addressed by a name which recalled their former European residence or occupation. In the grocery stores or at the street markets one often heard the names such as Schumacher George, Schreiner Peter, Schuetze Franz, Uhrmacher Franz, Canal Schneider, Brumpter Sep, or Posauna Jake, which were occupationally descriptive. On other occasions one would see persons who graciously responded to Ingweiler Schumacher, Werther Schumacher, Hagenau Andres, or Wasseler Weber, which indicated their place of emigration. Once given in this manner, the names did not die out until a decade had passed away, and the new generation became heads of households.

When Mertz arrived in Buffalo, many Catholics had great relief; now they could again receive the sacraments and live lives according to the moral code to which they had been accustomed to in Europe. Before he arrived there was, most of the time, no priest at all; only occasionally would one wander into the territory. He stayed so briefly that the Catholics could not rectify their lives, particularly their marital status. Many people had lived together as man and wife, having been married by their acquaintances, who performed the marriage rites as best they could, but not properly witnessed according to the Doctrines of the Catholic Church. Those who were not married and had fallen into sexual abuses had no way of reconciliation except to assume that God would not punish them if they were sorry for their sins. They had, however, much more confidence in salvation after receiving the Sacrament of Penance. To them, in this regard, Mertz was their salvation.

Before Mertz left The Lamb of God Church to travel to Europe and subsequently return to Western New York to take the pastorship of St. Mary's Church in Eden, Father Alexander Pax was sent by Bishop Dubois to act as his assistant. Pax was born at Sarreinsming, a small village about two miles southeast of Saareguemines, Alsace, on January 2, 1799. He was the son of Nicholas Pax and Anne Madeleine Bock. The leadership of the French Revolution, which changed the administrative structure of France, and

eventually all Europe, had fallen apart; the democratic dream had evaporated. Gone also was the monarchy; King Louis the XVI and his wife Marie Antoinette had previously perished at the guillotine. This reign of terror caused a scarcity of priests in France; it drove the parish vicar, J.P. Lauer, from his church in Sarreinsming. Consequently Pax was baptized at Auersmachen, Prussia, on February 10, 1799. As a young man, he first studied at Aachen under the tutelage of Abbe Bayer, from whence he attended the Latin school at Bitche. When his studies were finished he entered the seminary at Metz and was ordained by Monsignor Andre Jauffret at the Cathedral of Metz on February 27, 1823. Eight days later he found himself as an assistant at the parish in Forbach. By 1825 he had become pastor at Soucht, a small village near Bitche. Here with arduous labor, he built a handsome new church that was consecrated by Monsignor Jean-Francois Besson and named the Assumption of the Blessed Virgin. Not long after this he was appointed pastor at Bliesbrucken.

After completing his church at Soucht, he mentally wrestled with the consideration of becoming a missionary to the United States, which at the time of his ordination had startled the world with its proclamation of the Monroe Doctrine, which stated that attempts by European powers to return parts of America to colonial status would be viewed as a very unfriendly act. Pax had heard the sounds of *liberte-egalite* sounded from the rooftops in France, but it was in America where a less bloody revolution seemed to have had the true sense of liberty and freedom. Following the reign of terror, a new regime, the Directory, tried to hold the First Republic of France on a middle ground between equalitarian revolution and aristocratic-clerical-royalist reaction. It failed and gave way to the Consulate of which Napoleon Bonaparte, rising in influence, took the rein of leadership. By 1823 the empire of Napoleon had risen and fallen. He had been exiled; and, although the monarchy of the Bourbons was once again in shaky control of France, the Catholic Church was very wary of the future. Pax did not wish to be a victim in another political upheaval. [2]

Pax had heard of many young priests asking their bishops for permission to leave France and go to the United States where the hierarchy was mainly in the hands of émigré Frenchmen. Fellow countrymen already ministering in America had sent letters to priests and seminarians in Europe asking them to come over the Atlantic Ocean and reinforce their efforts of evangelization. These letters were published, by Father Weis, future bishop of Speyer, and Father Raess, bishop of Strasbourg, in *Journal von Mainz*. They also edited *Der Katholik*, a journal well known to the clergy of Lorraine, which encouraged missionary activity. Articles written by Pauline Jaricot, concerning the French and German missions in East and North Africa, appeared in *Bulletin des Missions*. Writing a letter, Pax requested Bishop Besson of Metz for permission to be released from his duties so as to join the missionaries in America; he was refused, but, in turn, the bishop offered him a better post in the diocese. He then traveled to Metz, and begged his bishop's permission in person. Still he was denied. Disheartened, he visited one of the local churches, knelt before the altar of the Blessed Virgin, prayed, and wept bitterly. Suddenly, he felt a hand touch his shoulder; he turned and saw a priest, whom, some years before, he had befriended, looking down upon him and speaking words of cheer and encouragement.

The priest advised Pax to write to Raess, bishop of Strasbourg and a man who never lost interest in gathering priests who wished to volunteer for service in America. Raess was in constant communication with the archbishop of Baltimore in the United States. After nine months and several frustrating negotiations between Metz and Strasbourg, Pax was granted a letter of excardination, by which he was released by the bishop of Metz, and allowed to be accepted by any diocese which would have him. It was Pax's permission to go

to America. Giving it, his bishop said, "Father, if it should not be as you anticipate in America, entirely to your liking and satisfaction, a good parish will ever be ready for you in your homeland." After a long and perilous voyage of fifty days, Pax arrived in New York City and prepared to proceed directly to Cincinnati, Ohio. Bishop Dubois, however, derailed his intentions and urged him not to go to Cincinnati, but to stay in Buffalo and give assistance to Nicholas Mertz whom, because of his age and health, needed him. Pax arrived at The Lamb of God Church in 1835. His first experience of ministry was being the clerical witness at a reception of the Sacrament of Matrimony on August 6, 1835.

The following summer, Mertz sailed for Europe and Pax made preparations to build a large brick church around The Lamb of God, while it remained intact and usable during construction. He contended that in doing so this new church, which would be named St. Louis Church in honor of Louis IX, King of France and patron saint of Louis Le Couteulx, would still contain The Lamb of God even though its walls would be torn down and flushed out the windows and doors of the new church. The parishioners, although they wanted a new church, were very skeptical that the project could be done since money was very scarce. Pax's spirit, however, was undaunted; he went to work with such earnestness that he brought confidence to the laity that saw the need for a larger church. On many Sundays, because of the large gatherings, they deplored having left their own country where they could attend services so nicely and have their comfort in a roomy church. At The Lamb of God, it was just the contrary. The parishioners took up the challenge and once again were ready to gather supplies, tools, and equipment. Pax often assisted in the work with his own hands, but mainly in going house to house in the city collecting money. Several times he went out into the countryside, going on foot for miles, encouraging workmen to come to his assistance and lend their services without remuneration. He seemed to know no such thing as rest and, whether night or day, he was continually more than busy with planning, working, and encouraging the workmen. When the church was finished, one parishioner remarked, "There is not a brick in that great structure which has not felt the sweat of *Pfarrer Pax*; and, while he gave his all, he did not decrease his personal assistance to the spiritual affairs of the congregations in the city and to those scattered far and wide over a vast countryside filled with swamps and forests." Until 1840, Pax was assisted by Father John Neumann, who had assumed missionary work in the countryside around Buffalo in 1836.

Pax, in the earnestness and zealousness of his work, oftentimes neglected his own comforts, developed serious disorders of the stomach, and suffered intensely from swollen feet, which no doubt was brought on by his many long and wearisome tramps in swamp and forest. Because he had ruined and exhausted his constitution, he was obliged to confine himself to his bed and remain indoors, very much against his own will, for some considerable time. This was a cause of great anxiety to him, as he thereby was prevented from giving his work the superintendence he so desired. During his illness, however, he had the comfort of having his trusted friend, Neumann, with him to administer to the affairs of his charge; they cherished each other's companionship, and a warmer friendship than ever was the result of their being thrown together. To their delight, Bishop De Forbin, of Nancy, France, came to Western New York and confirmed two hundred persons at St. Louis Church on August 26, 1840. Sometime during the month of September 1841, Bishop Hughes, of New York, called on Pax and conferred with him, regarding the advisability of forming an association or society of German priests, for the purpose of attracting to the New York Diocese priests speaking the German language. Although Pax favored the idea and encouraged it very much, it seems that nothing ever came of it, and the assistance that was expected as a result of such an association never developed.

During Pax's administration of about eight years in Buffalo, the parish records show that he baptized one thousand six hundred and six persons, administered four hundred and eight marriages, and conducted last rites and funeral services for three hundred and eighty-eight. During these years, he was a most zealous worker in looking after the spiritual welfare of his people, but his health was undermined and almost beyond repair. He had a growing anxiety come over him; he determined to return to the Fatherland and end his missionary work in America. After arranging carefully his affairs, he sailed for Europe near the end of March 1843. Upon his departure one lady, who knew him well, wanted to visit him and bid him farewell. The weather, however, was so bad that it was next to impossible to get around, and she could not go out to see him. Her sister who lived closer, however, did go to bid him farewell. His last words to her were, " It seems that my years of labor here have not been hard enough; even the elements conspire to greet me with a farewell storm."

Upon his arrival in Europe Pax first visited family and friends in his native village. After a short time, he undertook a trip to Rome, however, he only went as far as Strasbourg. His ankles had swollen as far as his thighs and his face gave every appearance that he had a severe case of dropsy. With rest Pax recovered and took a ministry at Schorbach and later at Diebling. Here he built a schoolhouse and also renovated and improved considerably the condition of the church. These have remained monuments to his zeal and energy. During the fall of 1858, he, plagued by tuberculosis, became so exhausted that only with the greatest difficulty could he preach. He retired to private quarters on Rue Sainte-Croix at Sarreguemines. Finally his illness attacked his digestive system; an attack from which he never rallied. On February 14, 1874, at seven o'clock in the evening of Ash Wednesday, he died. Pax was attended by two priests who administered the last sacraments. He was always zealous for the good of his fellowman, polite, and talented. He had a keen memory, retaining acute recollection of every detail; and, above all, he was a pious man to the end. His last wishes were that his remains rest at Sarreinsming with those of his mother. His wish was granted and next to her his body lies. (3)

At St. Louis Church, his memory remains of his labors, works, and good deeds, among which, as was the case with all missionary priests, the exercise of administering the sacrament of baptism. For him, it was this one act which gave him the most joy. Prior to the day of the ceremony, Pax had asked the parents to supply the child with a Christian name because it would be under it that he would perform the rite. He told the parents that under that name the child would be changed into a new person who would have a patron saint whose virtues in life could be imitated. He also requested that the parents have two sponsors present at the service. These were the child's godparents, who, if in the future the parents should die, they would be responsible for the Christian upbringing of the baptized. On the day of the ceremony, however, they would be necessary witnesses to the administration of the Sacrament of Baptism, which had been instituted by Christ, and conferred inward grace through the application of an outward sign. When all the preparations had been made, the child, parents, sponsors, and priest met at the door of the church. Pax explained to them that meeting at the door had been a custom since the early days of Christianity; it represented that the child, like the catechumens, was passing through the door into the communion of the faithful so as to be entitled to receive the other six sacraments as it grew to maturity. Pax quoted St. John's gospel, "Except a man be born again of water and the Holy Ghost, he cannot enter into the kingdom of God." Breathing three times on to the child, Pax said that it represented the Creator breathing life into Adam, Christ breathing the Holy Ghost into the disciples, and his breathing of the Holy Ghost directly into the soul of the child being held by its parents.

Entering a little farther into the church, Pax then made the sign of the cross onto the breast and forehead of the baby saying, "Receive the sign of the cross upon thy forehead, and in thy heart; receive the faith of the heavenly commandments, and let thy manners be such that thou mayest now be the temple of God." He told the sponsors that, through the baptism that he was performing, the child belonged to Christ; it would carry His cross, His battleflag! Under this sign the baby would belong to Christ, as a member of His kingdom which was the sum total of all souls who had been saved by the shedding of His blood on the cross. Quoting St. Matthew's gospel, Pax said, "Whosoever shall deny Me before men, I shall also deny him before My Father who is in heaven." He then placed salt into the mouth of the baby saying, "Let your speech be always in grace, seasoned with salt." The child being too young to understand, Pax turned to the godparents and explained that salt represented the preservation of the child's soul from the corruption of sin. He said, "Salt is the emblem of wisdom which gives relish to all things; Christ therefore fills the soul with true wisdom and prudence." Following this, Pax performed what was known as the exorcisms; a set of prayers which begged for the release of the child's soul from the bond of Satan and original sin, and a transfer of that soul to the kingdom of God and the communion of saints.

Following these rites, Pax escorted the entourage to the baptismal font in the front of the church near the altar. He placed the extremities of his stole upon the child, representing its introduction into the church. He said, "Come into the temple of God, that thou mayest have part with Christ, unto everlasting life." All present answered, "Amen!" After which together, Pax, godfather, and godmother recited the Apostles' Creed and the Lord's Prayer. Then Pax put his hands to his mouth, made saliva on his fingers, and touched the baby's ears and nose saying, "Ephpheta, be thou opened," while touching the ears, and, "Unto the odor of sweetness," while touching the nose. He then turned to the parents and godparents and instructed them saying; "We are unto God the good odor of Christ; to them who are saved the odor of life." He then asked them in the name of the child to denounce Satan and all his works and pomps. This he followed by anointing the baby on the breast and between the shoulders saying, "I anoint thee with the oil of salvation in Christ Jesus our Lord, that thou mayest have eternal life." Turning once again to the entourage, he explained that anointing with oil symbolized the preparing of the gladiators and wrestlers of early Christianity in Rome so as to make them supple, fortify their hearts, and to bear resolutely their yoke in combat. For the baby being baptized the anointing was to make it resilient and responsible for its actions in its fight against Satan, to give it heart to resist his attacks, and to receive divine grace to bear the yoke of God's law.

After these preliminaries, the child was finally administered the actual baptism, that is the pouring of water upon its forehead. Three times Pax did so, announcing the baby's Christian name, and saying, "I baptize thee in the name of the Father and of the Son, and of the Holy Ghost." He anointed the top of its head with holy chrism, a mixture of oil and balm. He covered the child's head with a white cloth that symbolized the early catechumens who, having been accepted into the church for the first time, were dressed in a white robe. Pax explained to the parents that the child's soul was now a chosen vessel into which one day it would receive in Holy Communion the body and blood of Jesus Christ. To the baby he said, "Receive this white garment, which thou mayest carry unspotted before the judgment-seat of our Lord Jesus Christ, that thou mayest have eternal life." Lighting candles, Pax placed them into the hands of the godparents saying to them as representatives of the soul baptized, "Receive this burning light, and keep the baptism without reproof; keep the commandments of God, that when our Lord shall come to His nuptials, thou mayest meet Him, together with all the saints, in the heavenly court, and

mayest have eternal life, forever and ever, Amen." With this concluding prayer, Pax ended the ceremony and congratulated all present, inviting them to a short repast at the rectory. [4]

By the time Pax left for Europe in 1843, Roman Catholicism in the city of Buffalo was solidly established and ready for expansion and growth. Together, Mertz and Pax had brought the Mass and the sacraments to the many scattered families in the environs of the city. Mertz was the first missionary, operating with St. Louis Church as a base, to bring the Good News to the Alsatians, Lorrainers, and Germans dwelling on the farms in the area of East Eden, twenty miles south of Buffalo. On one of his first visits to the area in 1830, he was prepared to offer the Sacrifice of the Mass in the local schoolhouse. One of the Protestant officials sent his son to the building with the order to remove the table from the room where Mertz was to conduct his service. The boy did as his father ordered; and, a few hours later, he came down with a serious malady. Mertz made a reference to his condition at the congregation's next gathering. He said, "In regards to our table which vacated the premises on my last visit, I can only say that the judgment of God is on the people of Eden." Mertz loved the area so much that when he returned from Europe he purchased fifteen acres there and spent the rest of his life tending to his flock in the vast territory around him: Eden, Hamburg, Collins, Boston, and Langford.

In 1830, Hamburg was known as White's Corners. Mertz was the first priest to visit the early settlers who were the families of B. Friedmann, J. Friedmann, S.G. Burnhardt, F. Huber, E. Sauer, M. Conrad, M. Schmidt, and T. Cassiday. After Mertz died, Father Rudolph Follenius visited the village and found twenty-two families most desirous of his services. From his home in Hamburg, Mertz often went to North Evans where he said Mass in the homes of Joseph Guiney, Andrew Schappacher, John Kinny, and James Ryan. It was also

Mertz who first came to Lancaster and Sheldon, and administered the sacraments to small isolated groups of Catholics eager to worship. He found ten families in Sheldon, and said his first Mass in Lancaster at the home of Henry Riding. After 1834 it was Pax who helped Mertz in these endeavors, and Pax continued to carry on the work which Mertz had begun at Williamsville and North Bush where he had built small log chapels. In 1836 Father John Neumann arrived in Western New York and relieved Pax of much of the duties of tending to the flocks in these rural areas.

*N*eumann first settled at Williamsville. After only seven months, however, he found a better reception for his work at North Bush. Here he was given a small residence and he could conduct services in Mertz's chapel. From here he made regular visits to Lancaster and said Mass in a barn-like structure that had been put up by the people on July 18, 1836. In 1838 he was the first cleric to officially visit Catholic settlers at Niagara Falls. During the same year he went to Sheldon, met with the congregation organized by Mertz and named it St. Cecilia's parish. On his first visit he said Mass at the home of Mr. Peter George and promised that he would continue to do so every second month in the summer season. He instructed the villagers to construct a log chapel for him to conduct the worship. During his stay in Western New York from 1836 until 1840, Neumann was also credited for making visits to the Good Shepherd Congregation in Pendleton, the farmers in Swormville, which was also known as Transit, and to villagers as far east as Batavia. On one occasion, sick and weary, Neumann lay beneath a tree, when a party of passing Indians wrapped him in a blanket, and carried him to a neighboring farmhouse where he was nursed back to health. In his lectures at Batavia, he often referred to this event when he sermonized the gospel story of the Good Samaritan. When Neumann left Western New York in 1840 to join the Redemptorist Order, his duties were taken up first by Father Michael Guth, brother of Francis Guth, the third pastor of St. Louis Church, and later by Father

Theodore Noethen who stayed in the region until 1845.

*A*nother tireless missionary of Western New York was Father T. McEvoy. He was an Irishman who, for five years, seemed to be everywhere in all the counties of the Southern Tier, which included the southern half of Erie County and Chautauqua, Cattaraugus, and Allegany Counties. At the time Neumann was leaving Western New York, McEvoy was invading the southern territory bringing Roman Catholicism to the many scattered Irish families. He was the first priest at Belmont, Angelica, Greenwood, East Aurora, Springbrook, Ellicottville, Perry, Dunkirk, Friendship, Scio, Limestone, and Java. He made Java his base of operations. He didn't have any churches or chapels; he was satisfied to conduct worship in the homes of the settlers. He was at Timothy Culbert's home in Scio where William Clancy and Mr. McCasson brought nearly one hundred souls to attend Mass. Some had to travel over twenty miles so as to be present. In 1849 it was the likes of Thomas Flanigan and John Devins who rallied the men, women, and children to receive the sacraments at McEvoy's hand at East Auora and Springbrook. At Ellicottville it was Fitzsimmons and McIvers who announced the coming of McEvoy. He shared, along with the Franciscans, the benevolence of Nicholas Deveraux, a Frenchman from Utica, New York, who owned large tracts of land in Allegany and Cattaraugus Counties into which he desired to relocate colonies of Catholics. In order to encourage them to settle in the district, Deveraux went to Rome in 1845, and applied at the Irish Franciscan College of St. Isidore for a group of monks to found a monastery on his property. He offered them $5,000 and presented them with a deed to two hundred acres of land. Without hesitation his offer was accepted; and, on May 9, 1850, Fathers Pamphilo de Magliano, Sisto de Gagliano, Samuel de Prezza, Salvatore de Manarola, and a lay Brother, left Rome; their destination was a beautiful spot near the northern bank of the Allegany River. Here they laid the cornerstone for a college and a seminary that in years to come would be called St. Bonaventure's

College. From this vantage point the Order spread its sacred influence over towns and villages where McEvoy had first evangelized: Allegany, Ellicottville, Olean, Cuba, Scio, Andover, Greenwood, Randolph, Jamestown, Chapelsburg, Limestone, and Chipmunk.

As it has been stated before, clerical religious orders provided the ideal missionary force for evangelization. Western New York was fortunate to have had several of them come within its borders and preach, teach, conduct Mass, and administer the sacraments. By 1855 Jesuits, Franciscans, Oblate Missionaries of Mary Immaculate, Redemptorists, Dominicans, and Vincentians had come to the Niagara Frontier and the Southern Tier. They had numbers of well-educated workers, financial backing, and prestige so as to build and operate churches, catechetical schools, and seminaries. Through them vocations would be generated and the secular clergy perpetuated. Fathers Lucas Caveng, Bernard Fritsch, Joseph Fruzzini, William Kettner, and Rupert Ebner were the first Jesuits to come into Western New York from Stevensville and Chippewa in Ontario, Canada. They were members of the Canadian Mission of the French Jesuit Province whose headquarters was among the German immigrants at Petersburg, Ontario. From this base they carried their evangelization into all areas of the Canadian Niagara Peninsula. After arriving in Buffalo at the request of Bishop Timon they spread their influence over the rural areas including North Bush, Williamsville, Ellysville, Transit, and Pendleton. Their labor influenced the development and stabilization of several churches: St. Francis Xavier, Black Rock; St. Joseph's, Ellysville; St. Michael's, Buffalo; St. Louis Church, Buffalo, St. Ann's, Buffalo; Sts. Peter and Paul, Williamsville; Good Shepherd, Pendleton; and St. Mary's, Swormville.

Prior to 1850, the settlers at Ellysville and the surrounding area called Buffalo Plains usually attended Sunday Mass after 1836 at North Bush or at St. Louis

Church. In that year, property was secured on Main Street and construction started on a building under the direction of the Jesuits. The Jesuits, however, were not the only Order to have an influence at St. Joseph's Church. In 1855, the Redemptorists took over the church, and they were followed by the Franciscans and once again by the Jesuits. As early as 1851, Bishop John Timon had asked the Oblate Missionaries of Mary Immaculate to come to Buffalo and begin a seminary. This Order had been founded by Father Charles Eugene de Mazenod, who later became bishop of Marseille, France. A group from the Order led by Father Edward Chevalier came to Buffalo from Montreal and purchased land at a place where the County Poor House once stood. They turned it into a seminary for the diocese and later developed Holy Angels parish around it. Other Redemptorists had come to Buffalo from Rochester, New York. They were invited by Bishop Hughes to build a church at Batavia and Pine Streets so as to drain dissatisfied German parishioners from St. Louis Church. Father Benedict Bayer led this effort. Later they were also influential in the development of the parish and church of Sts. Peter and Paul at Hamburg, New York. Before 1850 an Irish Dominican, Father Urquhart who had made his residence at Java was known to be visiting and administering the sacraments to settlements of Catholics in Allegany, Steuben, and Wyoming Counties. Likewise in 1855, the Vincentians, under the direction of Father John Joseph Lynch who later became bishop of Toronto, Canada, purchased land high above the gorge of the Niagara River downstream from the mighty falls. On it they built the initial building as a seminary for the diocese of Western New York known as Our Lady of the Angels. Later it became Niagara University.

The historic discussion above has centered on the most westerly parts of the diocese of Buffalo that was formed by Pope Pius IX at Rome in 1847. It was at this time that the vast diocese of New York was divided into three parts: New York, Albany, and Buffalo. Hughes remained as archbishop of New York, John McCloskey became bishop of Albany, and John Timon, a Vincentian, governed the See at Buffalo that included all the territory around the two rival cities of Rochester and Buffalo. The area about Rochester had been evangelized much earlier than that around Buffalo. When Timon was consecrated bishop on October 17, 1847, Buffalo boasted of a population of forty thousand while Rochester claimed thirty thousand residents. Rochester, however, insisted that its Catholic population was greater than Buffalo, more centrally located, and should have been chosen as the episcopal residence of the See of Western New York. After all it had four churches: St. Patrick's, St. Joseph's, St. Mary's, and Sts. Peter and Paul. Buffalo only had three churches: St. Louis', St. Patrick's, and St. Mary's. Later when Timon began collecting funds for the construction of his cathedral in Buffalo, Catholics in Rochester reminded him of their distaste for the selection of the center of the diocese. They were very reluctant to contribute. He had to forcefully remind them that he was appointed Bishop of Buffalo, not Bishop of Rochester, and that the naming of the See was not of his choice, but that it was the selection of Rome. [5]

Of all the efforts of the missionary clergy, the one which they were most faithful to, other than Mass, and which consumed much of their time was the administration of the Sacrament of Extreme Unction. It was the third and last great unction, the consecration of Catholics prior to their death, following the unction of baptism and confirmation. All priests and laity looked upon it as a most desirable sacrament, but it put the priest on the road at some uncomfortable hours, during bad weather, and took him over long distances. It seems fitting, therefore, not to end this discussion concerning missionary priests with a note of competition between two rival cities. Rather it is more fitting to describe the last moments of a dying friend among a group of faithful Catholics, who are gathered together to bid farewell. It is uplifting to read of their great

consolation when the missionary priest performed in their presence the last rites, the supreme unction or consecration by which supernatural grace flowed lavishly into the soul of a sick and departing person.

It was early on a cold day in November, 1833, when Andrew Schappacher arrived at the Lamb of God Church in Buffalo to fetch Father Nicholas Mertz to come with him to North Evans. Andrew's mother, Cecilia, was very ill and the doctor had predicted that she had not more than a day to live. Mertz obtained his sacred oils from the church, and immediately set out in Andrew's wagon, drawn by two burly horses, on the journey south. By the time they reached the Schappacher house darkness had already fallen upon the countryside. Entering, Mertz immediately heard Cecilia's confession and rendered her absolution. After saying the "Confiteor, Miseratur, and Indulgentiam" for her, he extended his hands over her and made the sign of the cross three times saying, "In the Name of the Father and of the Son and of the Holy Ghost, may all power of the devil be extinguished in thee, by the laying on of our hands, and by the invocation of all the holy angels, archangels, patriarchs, prophets, apostles, martyrs, confessors, virgins, and all the saints." To this prayer the gathered group responded, "Amen." Then dipping his thumb into the vial of holy oil, he anointed her in the form of the cross upon, each in turn, her eyes, ears, nose, mouth, hands, and feet. At each unction he prayed for the pardon of the sins which that sense may have committed. Upon completion of this prayer the gathered friends said, "Amen," and recited the Litany of the Saints followed by the Our Father in silence.

After a moment of reflection, Mertz continued with prayer saying, "Save thy servant, trusting in thee, O my God! Send her, O Lord! help from thy sanctuary, and do thou defend her from Zion. Be to her, O Lord! a tower of strength from the face of the enemy; let not the enemy have power over her, nor the son of iniquity be able to hurt her. Lord, hear my prayer, and let my cry come unto Thee." Mertz then turned away from Cecilia, looked upon her friends, and said, "The Lord be with you." They responded, "And with your spirit." Following this salutation Mertz continued, "Let us pray. O Lord God! who hast said by thy apostle James, 'Is any one sick among you, let him bring in the priests of the church, and let them pray over him, anointing him with oil in the name of the Lord, and the prayer of faith will save the sick one, and the Lord shall raise him; and if he be in sins, they shall be forgiven him,' heal we beseech thee, O Lord our Redeemer! by the grace of the Holy Ghost, the maladies of this sick woman; cure her wounds, and forgive her sins; drive away from her all pains of mind and body, and mercifully restore unto her perfect health both as to the interior and the exterior; that being recovered by Thy mercy, she may return to her former duties; who, with the Father and the Holy Ghost, livest and reignest one God, for ever and ever." All present announced, "Amen!" Without pause Mertz went on, "Look down, we beseech thee, O Lord! on thy servant, Cecilia, fainting under the infirmity of her body, and refresh her soul which thou hast created; that she, being improved by thy chastisements, may be saved by thy medicine; through Christ Our Lord." Again the ones gathered said, "Amen!" Finally Mertz concluded, "O holy Lord, almighty Father, everlasting God! who, by imparting

the grace of thy benediction to sick bodies, preservest, according to the multitude of thy mercies, the work of thy hands, favorably attend to the invocation of thy name; and, delivering thy servant from her illness, and restoring her to health, raise her up by thy right hand, strengthen her by thy virtue, defend her by thy power, and restore her with all desired prosperity to thy Holy Church; through Christ our Lord." With this came the final "Amen!"

Although these prayers of the Church contained encouraging words of restoration to health, a condition which many times occurred after the invocations were made; in this case, however, they only brought comfort to Cecilia who was truly dying. She reached her hand out to Mertz who grasped it with his large, rough, fingers. In a muffled voice she said, "Father, thank you! I now see the coming of the Lord!" Andrew came to her and with tears in his eyes, kissed her on the cheek. Although her health was not restored that night, the extreme or last unction did not terrify her; she knew that all those around her would witness her passing into eternal life and entering into the lot of the triumphant souls. Mertz turned to the relatives and friends. He said, "Tonight she sees the Beatific Vision!" [6]

The Rev. John Mertz
Pastor of St. Louis Church 1829-1836

The Rev. Alexander Pax
Pastor of St. Louis Church 1836-1843

REFERENCES AND NOTES ✤ CHAPTER FOUR

1. For a discussion of the missionary period in the United States, Diocese of New York, and Western New York see: op. cit. *History of the Catholic Church in Western New York*, pps. 114-33; For a discussion of the Sacrament of Holy Orders, European Seminaries, minor order, major orders, and priesthood especially from the Council of Trent see: Shadler, F.J., *The Beauties of the Catholic Church*, Frederick Pustet & Co., Cincinnati, Ohio, 1881, 415-56; for a catechetical study of Holy Orders during the 19th C. see: Deharbe, Joseph S.J., *L'Arge Catechism*, Benziger Brothers, Cincinnati, Ohio, 1921, pps. 115-16; for a complete historical study of the Sacrament of Holy Orders see: Martos, Joseph, *Doors to the Sacred*, Triumph Books, Liguori, Missouri, 1991, 392-439.

2. Source material for the discussion of the life of Father John Nichols Mertz was taken from the op. cit. *Bazar Chronicles*; these appeared daily except Sunday from October 23, 1888 until November 3, 1888. These were vol. 1., nos. 1-8, however, vol. 1, no. 13, appeared on December 29, 1888; copies of these chronicles are in the St. Louis Church Archives. For a discussion of conditions in Europe in locations where emigrants left their homeland for the United States see: op. cit. *A History of the Modern World*, Prologue, xii-xxvi, "Reaction Versus Progress," pps. 419-47, "Revolution and the Reimposition of Order," pps. 462-93. For further information about the life and times of John Nicholas Mertz see: op. cit. *Andenken an Hochw. Herrn Joh. Nik. Mertz*, pps.1-10. In this text, a review is made of early German priests in America. In 1799 Father Peter Heilbron was located in Westmoreland County, PA. He arrived in Goshenhoppen, Berks Co., PA (Pennsylvania), in 1787. From 1791-1799 he was pastor at Holy Trinity Church in Philadelphia. He took the place of Johannes Carolus Heilbron who went to Spain on Nov. 13, 1791. Other priests were Fathers Peblenz, Frambach, Graessel, Van Huftel, John Nepomucene Goetz, and William Elling. In 1897 Goetz and Elling were in Philadelphia and had trouble with church trustees. Goetz went West, Elling remained until 1806. Peblenz was vicar general at Baltimore. Graessel was the youngest of the German priests. He became Bishop Carroll's co-adjutor but he died before his confirmation came from Rome. Also helpful were German Capuchins. Other German priests involved in activities of the early church are: Fathers Caesar Reuter, Baltimore, Franz Fromm, Youngstown, PA, and Theodore Brouwers, who brought Fromm to PA against Bishop Carroll's will. Capuchins were a breakaway group of the original Franciscan Order. They began in 1525 at Marche, Italy. Approved by Pope Paul III in 1536. For Febronianism see: op. cit. *Encyclopedia of Catholicism*. The City Trier in modern times is known as Treves. The year before Mertz's birth near Trier, Johann Nickolaus von Hontheim, auxiliary bishop of Trier, who under the penname of Justinius Febronius published his book, *Justini Febronii de statu praesenti ecclesiae et legitima potestate romani pontificas liber singularis*, began the movement in France and Germany whereby the Catholic Church should become a conciliar church. Papal authority was restricted to supervising church unity and promulgating decrees of the general councils to be called by the bishops or emperors. Papal announcements had no binding effect unless approved by the local bishops. In effect the concept called for the establishment of National Churches. Although the works of Hontheim were condemned by Pius VI, and he recanted in 1778 when Mertz was 14 years old, the inroads which it had made remained until after the French Revolution. This is one reason why Mertz was ecclesiastically schooled and ordained in 1790 at Metz rather than at Trier. The section devoted to an understanding of the problems of the missionary priest in post-revolutionary times in America was mainly derived from op. cit. *Stephen Theodore Badin*, a thesis by David Driscoll, pp. 24-46. Other references to this topic can be found in op. cit. *Records*, vol. 19, 1908; Martin Spalding, *Catholic Missions*, pps. 47, 71-2, 115. Also see: Letters of Stephen Theodore Badin to Carroll, Rolling Fork, KY, Aug. 24, 1796; Badin to Neale, Sept. 2, 1808; these letters are in the Baltimore Cathedral Archives; others like them are contained in op. cit. *Records*, vol. 19, 1908. For a relationship between loneliness and temptation as stated by Father John Neumann see: op. cit. *Good Shepherd: the Church on the Canal*, p.3. In op. cit. *Bazar Chronicles*, 1888, it is stated that wood was brought from the Jammerthal forest on Delavan Avenue to construct the Lamb of God Church. It is also stated there that the stone footings for the gothic church was called Yammerthal stone. These are "old" German words. In modern German they would be written Jammertal. Using it in terms of a kind of wood, forest, or stone is also incorrect unless the writers were referring to the location where these items came from. The translation of the German word Jammertal is "Valley of Sadness." This name was possibly given by a set of Germans who lived in the area of Buffalo that today would be land in the vicinity of Canisius College. The Jammertal forest, which also has the name Iroquois forest, was located at the present site of Forest Lawn Cemetery and Delaware Park. The Jammertal quarries would have been located north of Humboldt Parkway in the region east and south of Main and Fillmore.

3. Source material for the discussion of biographical information concerning Father Alexander Pax see: op. cit. *Bazar Chronicles*, vol. 1., nos. 10-12; Also see: Rev. Victor Pax, *Andenken an der hochwuerdigen Herrn Alexander Pax*, printed by the German Press, 515 Main Street, Buffalo, NY, and preserved in the archives of John H. Pax, Buffalo, NY. A copy is also attached to op. cit. *Lay Trusteeism at St. Louis Roman Catholic Church, Buffalo, New York*. Also see: Alexander Pax, *Un Centenaire: Un pretre lorrain en Amerique Alexander Pax (1799-1874)*, La Societe d'Histoire et d'Archeologie de Sarreguemines, France, 1967, researched by Jean Houpert. In 1836, Rev. Alexander Pax succeeded Fr. Mertz as pastor of St. Louis. The life of Rev. Pax, like that of his predecessor Fr. Mertz, was reflective of the struggles and pastoral challenges of the immigrant church in the United States. Fr. Pax was born in Sarreingsming in Sarregemund, Lorraine, on February 10, 1799. He was ordained a priest on February 22, 1823. As pastor in the small village of Bliesbrucken, most likely inspired by

reports from his fellow priests in America, he made the decision to become a missionary to the United States.

4. This description of the administration of the Sacrament of Baptism follows the rite approved by the Council of Trent as found in: op. cit. *The Beauties of the Catholic Church*, pps. 290-303. The passages of Scripture used in the ceremony are found in John III, 5; Matt. X, 33; Colossians IV, 6; 2 Cor. II, 15-16; 1 Pet. II, 9; and Matt V, 16. The lighted candles signified that the neophyte had been born from darkness to light, faith must not be cold and lifeless, but living and active, virtuous deeds are a shining light to others, and good works are the bright flame of the soul as it appears before the heavenly Judge. Those who became sponsors at a baptism developed a relationship between themselves and the baptized and the parents of the baptized. This relationship was an impediment if by chance marriage was proposed between sponsor and baptized or between sponsor and parent of the baptized. The impediment could only be removed by a dispensation given by the bishop of the diocese. Further non-Catholics were not allowed to be sponsors. In the time of the Missionary Catholic Church in the United States it was the teaching of the Catholic Church that children who died without having been baptized were deprived of the beatific vision of God, which forms the essential happiness of heaven. This doctrine of the Church was based upon the Scripture," Unless a man be born again of water and the Holy Ghost, he cannot enter into the kingdom of God." (John III, 5). But the Church did not teach that unbaptized infants were condemned to the torments of the damned. For being guilty of no personal sin, the justice of God cannot visit them with the punishments these sins alone merit. The modern catechism of the Catholic Church is more considerate in regard to unbaptized persons and their relationship to the details of eternal life. There appears no reference to Beatific Vision and stresses that God has bound salvation to the Sacrament of Baptism, but he himself is not bound by the sacrament. See: Ratzinger, Joseph, Imprimi Potest for Interdicasterial Commission, *Catechism of the Catholic Church*, Liguori Publications, Liguori, Missouri, 1992, p. 320 no. 1257 and p. 224 nos. 847-8. The term Holy Ghost that was used in the 19th C. has now been upgraded to Holy Spirit when referring to the Third Person of the Blessed Trinity. It should be noted that the ordinary ministers of the Sacrament of Baptism are the priest and deacon. In necessity, however, laymen may perform the Sacrament; even Protestant laymen are also allowed provided they have the proper intention and use the Tridentine form of "I baptize thee in the name of the Father and of the Son and of the Holy Spirit. The breakdown of Pax's baptisms is as follows: During 1835, 15; in 1836, 233; in 1837, 218; in 1838, 166; in 1839, 193; in 1840, 238; in 1841, 216; in 1842, 261; and in 1843, 66.

5. The material in these paragraphs was researched in op. cit. *History of the Catholic Church in Western New York*. The missionary activities of Mertz, Pax, Neumann, Noethen, Guth, McEvoy, and the Religious Orders were found in Part III, "History of Parishes and Institutions." Information concerning the Jesuits activity in Western New York was taken from op. cit. *Good Shepherd: the Church on the Canal*, pps. 5-6; and Krim, George, S.J., *Diary of Fathers Fritsch, Fruzzini, Kettner, and Ebner, (1848-1851), Canisius Monthly*, Canisius College Publication, Buffalo, New York, 1915-16; Zimpfer, George, *History of the Roman Catholic Parish of Sts. Peter and Paul from the Origins to 1928*, Williamsville, New York, pps. 73-95. St. Mary's Church in East Eden is the second church in the Buffalo Diocese after St. Louis Church. Swormville was also known as Transit. Shortly after the death of Bishop Timon in 1867, the Diocese of Rochester was formed, but not all the churches in the eastern half of the original Buffalo Diocese were incorporated into it. Those in Steuben, Schuyler, Chemung, and Tioga Counties were placed into the Rochester Diocese shortly after the death of Bishop Ryan in 1896. The churches later included were: Sts. Peter and Paul, St. Mary's, St. John the Baptist, and St. Casimir's in Elmira; St. Catherine's in Addison; Sacred Heart in Perkinsville; St. Mary's of the Lake in Watkins along with a satellite church in Horseheads; St. Mary's in Bath; St. Gabriel's in Hammondsport; St. Ann's in Hornellsville; St. Pious in Cohocton; St. Joseph's in Wayland; St. James' in Waverly; St. Mary's in Rexville; St. Patrick's in Owego; and St. Mary's and St. Patrick's in Corning. see: op. cit. *History of the Catholic Church in Western New York*, pp. 308-318. For Mass being said at Sheldon, New York, in 1838 at the home of Peter George, an emigrant from Belgium, see: the genealogical studies of the George family by George Wilcox, Father Severin George S.J., and Barbara La Vigne Braun, 292 Hedstrom Drive, Eggertsville, New York. Also consult "St. Cecilia's celebrates anniversary,"*Western New York Catholic*, July 1998.

6. The prayers contained in these paragraphs were taken from op. cit. *The Beauties of the Catholic Church*, pps. 410-14.

CHAPTER FIVE

Immigrant Catholics in Antebellum Buffalo

The first Catholic Church Militant in Buffalo was composed of those who had come to America's shores to breathe the fresh air of freedom. As immigrants, they carried the heavy baggage of European Catholicism. It was a mix of cultural devotions, communal prayers, family rituals, and asceticism that they had learned and lived by in the Old World. Arriving in Buffalo, however, they were without a permanent church in which to conduct the Catholic liturgy and without a priest who could celebrate it, particularly the Mass. In 1829, eight hundred Catholics lived in residential areas and worked in stores, shops, and canal depots in Buffalo or on farms in the environs thereof. They became parishioners of the Lamb of God Church, which in 1838 was renamed St. Louis Church. By 1860, seventeen years beyond the end of the controversy between Bishop Hughes and the trustees of St. Louis Church, that number grew exponentially there and at other churches whose doors were opened to all Catholics who had migrated outward from that Mother Church. The Diocese of Buffalo was formed in 1847 and John Timon was consecrated as its first bishop. He pronounced a monarchical administration for it and renewed Hughes' *Verwaltung* in monolithic opposition to the trustees' corporation at St. Louis Church. It resulted in a second wave of interdiction with excommunication of the trustees. He opened more churches in Buffalo so as to bleed parishioners away from St. Louis' parish. A compromise, however, between the bishop and the trustees was reached in 1855. Even if a dispersion had not taken place because of this clergy-laity controversy, the vast increase in the

number of Germans, cascading into Buffalo and bulging the city's borders north and east, would have required more German-speaking parishes to evolve. The most massive tidal wave of immigrants hit Western New York between 1855 and 1860. They exceeded thirty-one thousand, which was more than half of the total number of the city's inhabitants.

In 1847 there were only two German-language Catholic churches in Buffalo, St. Louis Church on Main and Edward Streets and St. Mary's Church at Batavia and Pine Streets. By May of 1849, forty poor German families built a modest structure in the woods and called it St. John's Church. In 1851 it was enlarged; and, two years later, Father Rudolph Follenius, who had hailed from Fulda in Europe, inspired the congregation to complete a new brick church which was named St. Boniface in honor of the patron saint of the Germanic tribes on the continent. In October 1849, Father Fritsch S.J. gathered a small band of German Catholics together at Black Rock, a settlement north of Buffalo, to begin the parish known as St. Francis Xavier. There in 1852, a brick church was completed under the guidance of Father Francis Guth who went there after he had left St. Pierre's Church. In 1851, Father Lucas Caveng S.J., with the assistance of Father Fritsch S.J., took nineteen families, who had deserted the influence of the trustees at St. Louis Church, to experience the joy of participating at Mass in the basement of St. Pierre's French Church on Washington and Clinton Streets.

By January 1, 1852, these Jesuits had built a new church on Washington Street and named it St. Michael's Church. On that day Bishop Timon said the first Mass there following its dedication. Lucas Caveng S.J. remained the pastor until his death in 1862. From 1863 until 1870 the pastorship was in the hands of Father Joseph Durthaler who has been considered as the Father of St. Michael's Church because it was under his leadership that the structure, much like the present day church, was conceived and created. The cornerstone was laid on the feast of St. Ignatius in 1864 and the church was consecrated July 16, 1867. Although Timon did not live to see that day, he knew, before his death, that Bishop Lynch of Toronto, Canada, would perform that ceremony for him. Until 1868 all Jesuit activities in Western New York were under the authority of the Canadian Provincial Order. On September 16, 1868, however, that authority ceased and the German Provincial Order succeeded it. Caveng, at the direction of Timon, had begun St. Ann's Church in 1858; and, during the American Civil War, the St. Vincent de Paul congregation, comprising forty in number centered around Main and Eastwood Streets, sprang into existence under the influence of Father Joseph M. Sorg who was secretary to Bishop Timon. He later became pastor of St. Louis Church. [1]

By 1860, the United States had welcomed to her shores approximately two million German-speaking immigrants. A large majority of these, after a few months voyage, landed in New York City. Steamer transportation on the Hudson River and barge on the Erie Canal provided inexpensive travel for them to the western regions of America. Buffalo, at the terminus of the canal became the jumping-off point for their adventure in finding settlements in the states surrounding the Great Lakes. Of those who came only twenty thousand were Alsatians and Lorrainers, but a very representative proportion of these remained either in Buffalo or were scattered in the woods and farmlands in the environs of it. Some were known to settle in Canandaigua and Batavia, the first and second

major settlements of Western New York. In Buffalo, by 1850, it had been estimated that seven hundred of them lived in the city and the majority of these were Catholics and members of St. Louis Church. Although their national origin was French, their language was German and their ethnic identity was the product of a unique history. Furthermore, they were indistinguishable and easily lost among other German-speaking immigrants who had been their companions in the long voyage to their adopted country. With groups of Bavarians, Swiss, and German Rheinlanders, some mingled and migrated up the Rhein River to Rotterdam, a Dutch port of exodus from Europe to America. Others moved overland across France and departed from Le Havre. After making Buffalo their home, the Alsatians and Lorrainers became leaders in the establishment and maintenance of St. Louis Church's parish, in which they, after the 1840's, maintained that predominance, even though their immigration numbers decreased and the number of other German-speaking elements increased.

By 1860, almost two centuries had passed since France annexed Alsace-Lorraine. For two thousand years prior to annexation it had been a hotbed of European strife. For four hundred years it was occupied by Roman legions. By the time it was claimed by the Holy Roman Empire, following the domestication of the barbarians, it had acquired the Franco-German duality of language. Following the Treaty of Westphalia, marking the end of the Thirty Years War, it was restored to France, yet there was no conclusive resolution to the province's cultural identity. Although in French, it was called Alsace-Lorraine, in German, the territory was known as Elsass-Lothringen, which honored the many kings and emperors of the Holy Roman Empire who carried the name Lothair. Although French and German were spoken in both, Lorraine was inclined toward the French language in government and economics, whereas Alsace favored German. Alsatians rejected the French language and culture in education, business, and social activities. French-Alsatian intermarriage was parentally frowned upon. Under royal restoration of France under the reign of Louis Philippe between 1830 and 1848, determined efforts were made to draw the Alsatians to French culture through the education and propagation of the French language. The effort failed; they clung tenaciously to their Franconian dialect that was much like Palatine German spoken across the Rhein River in the Rheinpfalz.

The Alsatians who became the first parishioners at the Lamb of God Church and St. Louis Church had, in Europe, become more self-conscious in their homeland. Ethnically rejected by the French, and Louis Philippe's endeavors to change them into Frenchmen, they refused assimilation and stood up for cultural nationalism, and in so doing, feared political and economic persecution. In their minds, emigration was a solution. In America they were convinced that they could heighten their sense of cultural identity with an ample basis for communal feeling and collective action with Rheinlanders, Swiss, and Swabians who had also left their homelands. Above all else, at St. Louis Church, Alsatians, Lorrainers, and Germans shared a particularly devout Catholicism. These groups had come from an area of Europe where the results of the Reformation were inconclusive; the number of Protestants and Catholics, in the towns and villages in an arc of land from Holland in the northwest to the northern border of Italy, were approximately equal, in comparison to the rest of Western Europe. Because of this equality, Catholic Alsatians, Lorrainers, and Germans developed an intense sense of religious competition with Protestants that drove them to great religious concern, especially in regards to the observance of a tradition of lay management of temporal affairs in their churches. [2]

The Alsatians, Lorrainers, and Germans, who had come to Buffalo before 1850, became owners of land and business, above all they excelled in the concept of craftsmanship. The Germans, who came after 1850,

even though many were still considered occupationally desirable in the crafts, were more inclined to be seen in lower status positions of unskilled labor, domestic service, and teamsters. By 1855, those who had originally arrived became rooted in the nineteenth-century American community around them, and stayed as residents while the newer German population experienced a massive turnover. The homes of the original immigrants were more highly valued than those of the newcomers, and their children intermarried with well-rooted families rather than seeking out spouses from families of later arrivals. After 1855 until the Civil War, however, their records showing other points of European origin different from those who had preceded them indicated the influx of new faces at St. Louis Church. Before 1840, records of immigrants at St. Louis Church showed that they came from towns and villages around Metz, Strasbourg, Nancy, Pirmasens, and Saarbrucken in Alsace-Lorraine and the Rheinpfalz; those of later years indicate additional emigration from Baden, Bavaria, Hesse-Darmstadt, Rhenish Prussia, Vienna, and Wuerttemburg. Before the American Civil War broke out, more than a thousand parishioners who spoke German, French, or both, representing more than three hundred families, had occupied the pews of either the Lamb of God Church or St. Louis Church. Prior to 1837, they comprised eighty-three percent of the congregation. The remainder were English speaking, mainly Irish. Eleven families have been chosen for close scrutiny because they illustrate the motivation, courage, hardship, entrepreneurship, and deep Catholic faith of the immigrants who settled in Buffalo following the opening of the Erie Canal.

The history of the immigration of the Gittere family to Buffalo reveals much information that explains why so many Alsatians and Lorrainers left Europe and came to America between 1828 and 1832. Joseph Gittere Sr., who immigrated to Buffalo in 1830, was born at Dagsburg, Lorraine, on October 24, 1774. In that village, he married Maria Anna Lehrer on May 10, 1805. She was six years younger than he was. They had eight children; all born in Europe. Although they lived in a province of France where peasant farming was a way of life, the Gittere family did not work the land. Joseph Sr. and his sons were *maneuvres de profession*, workers at the trade of masonry; they built walls, buildings, dressed stone, or worked in quarries. Because of its isolation, their village prior to the beginning of the French Revolution in 1789, was usually insulated from the results of political events which took place in cities such as Paris, Lyons, Marseilles, and Bordeaux. One year later, however, these events began to impact more visibly in the provincial site of their village. Ecclesiastical estates and those of the nobles were confiscated. Religious Orders were dissolved. Priests and bishops were chosen by election of the people. Lorraine was divided into the Departments of Moselle and Meurthe. Neighboring Alsace was split into Haut Rhin and Bas Rhin. The calendar was changed; months were renamed and years were dated from the time of the establishment of the Republic. Although the government in the communes was left unchanged, the villages were renamed. Dagsburg became known as Dabo.

On April 20, 1792, France declared war against Austria and Prussia. At first it went badly for France with defeats at Kaiserslautern and Wissemburg which were within twenty miles of Dabo. The results of the battles did succeed, however, in bringing about *levee en masse*, national compulsory conscription of all young men. Until he married, Joseph Sr. was subject to this draft and service in the army. By that year, Napoleon had had great military success in Italy; however the treaties of Luneville and Amiens brought only a temporary hiatus to the war. Soon, all Europe was thrown into distress again until 1815 when the Napoleonic wars ended at Waterloo. With the coming of peace, however, the lives of the peasants at Dabo did not improve. Their houses were still poor and filthy and their pleasures confined to very simple village dances or church processions. No one had come to improve the education in the village. Knowledge of a trade was

only learned when parentally handed down. Proficiency in reading and writing was a luxury and mainly confined to religious subjects. These peasants and craftsmen still believed in elves, wizards, and goblins, but they were very obedient to Monsieur Le Curé, the parish priest. They desired only to be left alone, but an avalanche of events kept them in constant turmoil. Along the nearby German border, an incipient and unsettling liberalism, based on the ideas generated in the French Revolution, was oozing into German culture. Metternich, the Austrian Chancellor, instituted measures of repression and a system of secret informants to ferret out the reactionaries. He was solidly committed to slamming the door on the ideas of liberalism and democracy. Bavaria stationed troops in the Rhein districts, quartering them among the people. Public meetings were forbidden. In France the draft was reinstated in 1818, and the period of military service was raised from six to eight years. By 1828 there was a growing economic recession; the price of bread had risen one hundred and twenty-five percent.

The winter of 1829-30 was one of the coldest on record and produced extensive suffering at Dabo. Joseph Gittere's boys were in their teens and subject to military draft. He decided it was time to leave Lorraine. Although he was fifty-six years old, and had never traveled more than fifty miles from his village, he took his family across France to Le Havre, following the cotton industry's transportation route through Metz, Verdun, Rheims, Soissons, Beauvais, and Rouen. His family was not the only one to emigrate from Dabo. Baptismal records as early as 1830, retained in the files of St. Louis Church, list the names of some of his neighbors: Regina Kremer, Peter Kremer, Jacob and Elizabeth Morhaefer, Catherine Freyemuth, Marianne Lehrer, Wilhelm Rohr, Elizabeth Rebmann, and Gertrude Klein. Upon arriving at Le Havre it was not difficult to obtain passage to New York on one of the ships which had delivered and had already unloaded its cotton at the port. The ocean voyage to New York City took fifty-five days. After being cleared by health inspectors and landing, Gittere, his family, and friends, boarded a barge for passage up the Hudson River to Albany nearly one hundred and fifty miles away.

The barge was huge, towed by a steam operated, side-wheeler-tug which averaged seven miles-per-hour. As they traveled, they saw forests spread everywhere; and, once past the imposing Palisades, they viewed the great Catskill Mountains until they came to the gentle plains south of Albany. For their passage, they were required to pay approximately three dollars per family. Arriving at the city, they saw hundreds of canal boats docked wherever there was wharf space, teams of mules and donkeys moving back and forth on towpaths, and swarms of dock hands loading and unloading shipments of goods going West and coming East. In order to avoid the twenty-seven locks on the Erie Canal between Albany and Schenectady, the Gitteres took an over land stagecoach. It was a distance of fifteen miles, but it saved them a day of travel. At Schenectady, Joseph contracted with a hawker, a large muscular fellow, who offered the family space on his *line boat* going to Buffalo at the rate of one and one-half cents per mile. Line boats were canal boats, which took longer to travel the full length of the canal, but were less expensive than the *packet boats*, which were more luxurious and faster because they changed mules and horses every ten miles. On the line boats the passengers were stowed away with the freight. It took the Gitteres five days to reach Buffalo at the canal basin near the foot of Main Street.

Upon disembarking the family moved up Main Street and boarded with other Gitteres who had preceded them from Dabo. Among them were Helena, Anthony, and Nicholas Gittere, whose families were members of St. Louis Church. Immediately upon arrival, Joseph Gittere Sr. took up the trade of a leather tanner and morocco dresser. He worked for John Bush whose factory was on Crow Street, later to be called Exchange Street. Following him into the tannery

business was his son Joseph Jr. and his cousin Jacob Morhoefer. His other two sons, Jacob and Nicholas, trained by their father in the art of masonry, began in the employ of contractors eagerly building up the great emporium called Buffalo. All saved their earnings and on February 25, 1836, Joseph Gittere Sr. purchased his first home on Sycamore Street near Elm Street for $960.00. By 1838, Jacob, Joseph Jr., and Florenz had purchased homes on the same street. Their neighbors and fellow parishioners at St. Louis Church, John, George, and Joseph Zimmermann also owned homes there. By 1848, with more Gitteres buying homes, Sycamore Street had become known as Gitterey Lane. On February 21, 1860, Joseph Gittere Sr. died and was buried from St. Louis Church.

Jacob, his oldest son and third child was the most persevering, most frugal, most successful, and most domineering of all the other children. Like his father, he went to work immediately upon arriving in Buffalo, hewing, carving, shaping, and setting stone and brick in all weathers. He continued without surcease for forty years. On August 9, 1836, Reverend Alexander Pax joined him and Elizabeth Rebmann in the Sacrament of Matrimony at St. Louis Church. They had thirteen children of which six grew to maturity. The first was Jacob Alexander born on June 19, 1837. At the time of the interdiction of St. Louis Church in 1851, Jacob Gittere had his family worship at St. Michael's Church. He joined the Millers, Nicholas·Jr., Peter, and John in laying the bricks for that church which the Jesuits erected on Washington Street. He stayed in the congregation there until he died on January 19, 1875. His wife Elizabeth followed him in death on February 6, 1892. Both are buried in the United German and French Roman Catholic Cemetery on Pine Ridge Road, Section L, Lot twenty-nine. Over their graves is a large monument adorned with the statue of St. Jacob and a large letter "G" carved on the granite plinth. Jacob Alexander, however, rejoined St. Louis Church when he reached maturity.

Like the Gitteres another Lorrainer, Stephen Bettinger Sr., was born on November 11, 1821 in Gross-Bedringen, Lothringen. In 1830, he arrived with his parents, who first settled at Eden, New York; but, in 1832, he came into Buffalo and learned the trade of a drapery maker in the dry goods business. He worked with much diligence and had great sincerity. He moved up in the business, became a manager, and finally opened his own shop that for a long time was on the east side of Main Street between Genesee and Mohawk Streets. He attended the Lamb of God Church at Main and Edward Streets, stayed in the congregation for a long time, and was either married there or in the brick church, called St. Louis Church, to Margaretha Yager. They had ten children. In 1897, three of them, Stephen P. Bettinger, Albert A. Bettinger, and Mrs. Charles H. Ribbel, were still living in Buffalo. They had been married in St. Michael's Church because in 1851 their father, along with nineteen other families, left St. Louis Church to worship there. In 1864, when the cornerstone of the new St. Michael's was laid, on the feast of St. Ignatius, and blessed by Bishop Timon, Stephen Bettinger Sr. was one of the laymen attending the ceremony. On that day Francis Xavier Wenninger S.J. gave the sermon and Joseph Durthaler S.J. celebrated the Mass. Durthaler is called the father of St. Michael's Church because he was its pastor from August 15, 1863 until July 25, 1870. Caveng and Fritsch, however, actually founded the church in 1851 at Washington and Clinton when they first said Mass in the basement of the old St. Pierre's Church.

Among the Alsatians who came to Buffalo was Francis J. Kraft. He was born in Wangen, Wuerttemberg, on November 18, 1820. As a young adult in Europe, he learned the trade of a cabinetmaker. It was a talent that he brought with him to America in 1840. In Buffalo, he opened his own shop on Main Street near Mohawk. In 1844, however, he decided on a new career, that of a funeral director; he opened his first establishment on East-Huron Street and remained there in business until his death in 1898. He married Anna Rebstock in 1848 at St. Louis Church, which he, as a zealous worker, had helped to construct. She had been born in Stuttgart, Wuerttemburg. In 1896, Frank and Anna took a trip to Stuttgart to celebrate their fiftieth wedding anniversary. In his later years he took his son Frank A. Kraft, who was born on December 18, 1853 and attended St. Louis Church grammar school, into business with him. Following graduation his son attended Canandaigua Academy. For fifteen years Frank A. Kraft served in the United States Coast Guard, after which he married Elizabeth Cornelius and took up residence on Lexington Avenue. She had come to America with her father who at the time of emigration was residing at Gensingen near Bingen on the Rhein River. [3]

Another Alsatian, Nicholas Miller Sr. and his family arrived at New York City in 1829. They proceeded by way of the Erie Canal to Buffalo. Before emigrating from the canton of Wolmuenster in the Department of Moselle, he had worked as a mason. Wolmuenster was located ten miles due south of Zweibruecken, which was situated immediately inside the Rheinpfalz border in Germany. At Wolmuenster he was born in February 1777, attended school, learned the trade of masonry, and married Anna Maria Gross in 1803. She had been a resident of Obergailbach that was approximately five miles southeast of Wolmuenster. One year later their first of five children was born and named Peter. The other children were John, Anna Marie, Nicholas Miller Jr., and Elizabeth Marie. All were born in Wolmuenster. Peter married Magdalene Lindemann in 1828. They had nine children. The first, Peter Jr., was born aboard ship while the family was sailing to America. The other eight were born in Buffalo. After arriving in America, John married Anna Marie Yax at the Lamb of God Church on September 26, 1833. Later, Anna Marie married Andrew Egither. Nicholas Miller Jr. and his sister Elizabeth Marie were married in a double ceremony at St. Louis Church on May 5, 1840. He married Barbara Daveron and she married John Hensgen. Since the brick church had not been officially opened until August of that year, they had the distinction of being married in both the Lamb of God Church and St. Louis Church simultaneously.

After the Miller family arrived in Buffalo, Peter Miller and Magdalene Lindemann took up residence on Batavia Street, which was later named Broadway. He worked with his father and brothers as a mason and was successful in accumulating sufficient capital to purchase several lots on Pine Street. Peter worked with his brother John on the building committee for the construction of both the Lamb of God Church and St. Louis Church. In 1844, however, he moved his affiliation to the newly developed parish, St. Mary's, at the corner of Batavia and Pine Streets. In 1849 the Sisters of Notre Dame were invited by its pastor, Father Joseph Helmprecht C.SS.R. to come to the parish and open a school. In 1851, Peter Miller did the masonry work to complete a three-story building in which they would hold classes in the upper two floors. The first floor contained a large hall that was used for church related entertainment and meetings. The Sisters occupied a house next to the school as a convent. In 1852, Buffalo was again plagued with the third outbreak of cholera in twenty years. The disease again ravaged homes and many children were left orphans. The Sisters prevailed upon Helmprecht to build another building so as to develop an orphanage in which they could care for these destitute waifs. He purchased the land adjoining the Sister's residence from Peter Miller for $5,000, and asked him to construct the orphanage. After it was completed it remained intact until 1874 when it was closed and replaced by the German Roman Catholic Orphan Asylum on Dodge Street.

While Nicholas Miller Jr. assisted his father in the masonry business, he and Barbara Daveron had their residence on West Tupper Street. They remained parishioners of St. Louis Church. Their first child, John, was born on March 17, 1841, and was baptized eleven days later. He married Anna Mary LeJeune in 1861, and they reared a family of ten children. All of them

grew to maturity and married, bringing the following names into the Miller family circle: Hauck, Neukirchen, Wick, Egloff, Sturchler, Bilz, Maidwell, Quinlan, Coombs, and Keller. The last child of Nicholas Miller Jr. and Barbara Daveron was Charles Augustus Miller. He was born on April 30, 1862 and married Catherine Grimm at St. Louis Church on April 30, 1884. Following his marriage, he took up the trade of cabinetmaker; and, he and Catherine Grimm had nine children. They, however, were not as fortunate as their parents had been; they lost the first three in childbirth, the fifth died one day after birth, and the seventh died ten months after birth. Fortunately, all were baptized. Three of the four who lived to maturity were married at St. Louis Church; but, the second last, Eugene William, married Viola Irene Kramer in the rectory of St. Joseph's Church on Sixth Avenue in New York City on October 24, 1922. Eugene did not have the permission of his parents to marry; and, Father Henry B. Laudenbach, pastor of St. Louis Church, refused to perform the ceremony because he had had sad experience with Eugene's parents just one year before by witnessing Cecilia Miller's marriage to Warren Nason. She was Eugene's younger sister. Upon returning to Buffalo, Eugene and Viola continued to attend St. Louis Church, but lived on Thompson Street, Black Rock, with Viola's parents, Lewis and Florence Kramer. Their first son, Eugene William Jr. was born there on October 16, 1923. Prior to her marriage, Viola was Lutheran, like her parents, but eventually was baptized a Catholic by Father Laudenbach.

After their arrival in Buffalo, the lives of Nicholas Miller Sr. and his family were closely connected to developments in the city and events that involved the controversy between the trustees at St. Louis Church with both Bishop Hughes and Bishop Timon. The family first took up residence on Washington Street. Even prior to being married in the presence of Father Nicholas Mertz at the age of twenty-four, John Miller, second son of Nicholas Miller Sr., had become an active member in the parish. He and his brother Peter were members of the building committee for both the Lamb of God and St. Louis Churches. The witnesses at John's wedding to Anna Maria Yax were Nicholas Miller Jr. and Nicholas Daelinger. Anna Maria Yax had been born in Alsace on November 11, 1811 of German-speaking parents. She came to America encouraged by relatives living in Buffalo who had sent letters to her. These, however, had to be read to her because she could neither read nor write. John and Anna Maria's first two children, Catherine, born in January 1835, and Mary, born one year later, were both baptized by John Nicholas Mertz. Catherine, however, died one month after birth. Alexander Pax, the second pastor at Lamb of God Church, baptized the next four, Elizabeth, Nicholas, Barbara, and Mary Magdalene, who was baptized one year before the new church had been opened. Because of the controversy between the laity and the clergy, most of the Millers, at the insistence of Nicholas Miller Sr., attended services and gave their affiliation at St. Mary's Church when it opened in 1844. John Miller's remaining children, Catherine, named for her sister who had died, John Jr., Theresa, and Paul were therefore baptized by Benedict Bayer C.SS.R. at St. Mary's Church. Only Nicholas Miller Jr. remained a parishioner at St. Louis Church.

John Miller and Anna Maria Yax lodged with Nicholas Miller Sr. for a few years after their marriage until they established their own home in a small frame house at eleven Cherry Street which had been purchased by Nicholas Miller Sr. Buffalo's population had increased at an astounding rate, and there was an extraordinary amount of masonry work to be done. The Miller's worked long hours and accrued much profit. On September 24, 1839, John Miller paid Jabez Goodell $225 for a lot fifty feet wide by one hundred and twenty-one feet deep on Cherry Street which was a little east of the house he was living in. Goodell had purchased a vast portion of land in that area directly from the Holland Land Company in 1834 and developed it. He had laid out streets, subdivided the property, and built some houses. After purchasing the land from Goodell,

John Miller and his family continued living for several more years at eleven Cherry Street because there was no house on the property that he had purchased. All of his children attended Catholic schools. The older ones attended at St. Louis' school; but, after 1852, when St. Michael's Church opened a school, the younger ones went there. In the late summer of 1852, cholera once again ran rampant through the German population as it struck Buffalo with all of its fury. It particularly brought grave sadness into the Miller family. On September 1, 1852, John Miller's wife, Anna Maria Yax, died of the disease. Two days later Nicholas Miller Sr. fell victim to its scourge. After funeral services were held at St. Michael's Church, both were buried at the New St. Louis Cemetery. Later their remains were transferred to the United German and French Roman Catholic Cemetery. John who never again married was left with the task of raising to maturity his nine children who ranged in age from two to sixteen.

In April 1853, Buffalo's City Charter was modified and the boundaries of the city were extended four miles to engulf the town of Black Rock that had penetrated as far South as Riley Street. John Miller bought a considerable amount of land in that area. He took the advice of his younger brother, Nicholas Miller Jr., and returned his affiliation to St. Louis Church. On November 24, 1859, his daughter, Elizabeth, had a winter wedding there. She married Peter Egloff whose family had come to America from Switzerland. From that day forward, Peter was more of a son to John than just his son-in-law. Peter also became John's business partner. The Egloff family grew by one member every two years until the final number had reached twelve. Besides working with John, Peter was a cabinet varnisher; and, with his large family, resided on Boston Alley also known as Demond Place. John Miller and Peter Egloff made considerable amounts of money on land deals; and, by 1867, they owned many houses on Cherry Street in Buffalo and on Riley Street in Black Rock. Any houses on Cherry Street that had brick siding were Miller-Egloff houses. On November 26,

1884, John Miller made out his last will and testament. He bequeathed one-eighth of his estate to each of his surviving children. Theresa, the youngest daughter, had died about 1878. She had never married. John died on May 28, 1885 and is buried beside his wife in the United German and French Roman Catholic Cemetery. The remains of Nicholas Miller Sr., Nicholas Miller Jr., Barbara Daveron Miller, Andrew Miller, Anna Maria Gross Miller, John Miller, Anna Maria Yax Miller, Elizabeth M. Grimm, nee Miller, Peter X. Egloff, Anna B. Ring, nee Miller, and Mary Miller are side-by-side in Section D, Lot seven of the United German and French Roman Catholic Cemetery, Pine Ridge Road. [4]

*R*esearch of the families involved in the early history of St. Louis Church uncovered a rather interesting oddity. It relates to the ancestors of Carl Anthony Miller and his wife, Marie Magdalene Buchheit; both are presently parishioners at St. Louis Church. They were married there on April 29, 1969. Nicholas Miller Sr., was the patriarch of the Miller family of which Carl Anthony Miller is a direct descendant, coming through a paternal line from Nicholas Miller Jr., third son of Nicholas Miller Sr. Francis Buchheit was the patriarch of the Buchheit family of which Marie Magdalene Buchheit is a direct descendant coming through a paternal line from Charles Francis Buchheit son of Francis Buchheit, who was born in 1808 at Reifenburg, Rheinpfalz, to John Buchheit and Maria Beilmann, emigrated to America, and settled in Buffalo in 1835. On June 23, 1840, Francis Buchheit married Magdalena Chretien at St. Louis Church. She was the daughter of Jacob Charles Chretien and Maria Catherina Ochs. Ironically, two months before this date, Nicholas Miller Jr. and Barbara Daveron were also married there.

*F*rancis Buchheit and his brothers, Henry and John, emigrated from Reifenburg which is eight miles northwest of Pirmasens in Rheinpfalz and fifteen miles from Wolmuenster in Alsace, which was the birthplace of Nicholas Miller Sr. This short distance between the two families, who in life never knew each other because Alsace was in France and Rheinpfalz was a province of Bavaria, in death, continued to remain small. The present burial location of the Miller family in the United German and French Roman Catholic Cemetery, is in a section from which, across a narrow lane and only a stone's throw away, one finds a section where two generations of Buchheits descending from Francis and Magdalena Chretien Buchheit are buried. Marie Buchheit Miller's grandfather, Charles Francis Buchheit, who, in life was a painter, rests there with his wife Barbara Steffan. They had been married at St. Louis Church on June 22, 1869. They had six children who grew to maturity: Francis Michael, Charles John Michael, Frances Magdalene, George William, Rosina Maria, and Louis Anthony John. Rosina Maria, who never married, rests next to her mother and father in the family plot. Very little is known about John Buchheit except that he was a pattern maker and lived on German Alley with his sister-in-law Magdalena, after she was widowed by the death of her husband, Francis, in 1861. Henry Buchheit was born at Reifenburg on April 17, 1812. Upon coming to America, he stayed in Buffalo for awhile and married Maria Francisca Moll. Their son, also named Henry, was born on February 21, 1837 and baptized at the Lamb of God Church. All three moved west after Henry's birth and first settled in Bellville, Illinois. Later they moved to Perryville, Missouri, where they began the Buchheit clan whose general store, animal feed store, and trucking business are presently very famous in the Midwest. [5]

*M*arie Buchheit Miller's grandfather, Charles Buchheit, by marrying Barbara Steffan, entered into association with one of the first families to come to Buffalo prior to Le Couteulx's generous gift of land upon which St. Louis Church has prospered through one hundred and seventy-five years. In the year 1828, Barbara's father, Michael Steffan, who had emigrated from Oensbach, Baden, at the age of twenty-two, disembarked from a canal boat at the foot of Main Street.

It was the end of an adventure, which had begun with several days' travel to Le Havre, France, where he found a packet ship that gave him passage to America. After almost sixty days aboard the vessel he landed in New York City. After a steamship ride up the Hudson River he boarded a canal boat, pulled by mules, and settled down for a six day view of the Erie Canal, from Albany to Buffalo. Upon landing he could find no work. Strapping on his backpack, he walked to Dundas, Canada, where he had heard that work was available. After a trek of eighty miles he came upon a farm cut out from the wilderness which surrounded it. A farmer, an Englishman who knew no German, hired him for eight dollars a month. Michael did not know any English, and he had to learn it the hard way. The farmer asked him to bring up a tub from the cellar. After carrying nine different items up from the cellar, showing each of them to the farmer who rejected all nine, he finally brought up the tenth. The farmer gave Michael the nod of approval; it was then that he learned what tub was in English.

After two years, Michael earned enough money so that he could return to Baden. His parents had died and some money was left to him as an inheritance. He wished to settle up his share, visit with old friends, and return to America. Before leaving, his brothers and sisters and many of the villagers wished to know, "How is it going to America?" He told them, "If you want to know you will just have to come and see!" As a result, nearly one-half of the village of Oensbach decided to emigrate. Buffalo soon became the richer with family names such as Kloepfer, Wilhelm, Weber, Armbruster, and Krumholz, all led to this land of liberty by Michael Steffan. In Baden he had learned the trade of shoemaker and handler of leather products. He married Mary Barbara End on December 10, 1835 in the Lamb of God Church. She died, however, in 1837, leaving Michael without a child. On December 16, 1836, with his earnings and his patrimony, he purchased his first lot in the block fronting on Main Street between Goodell Street and Burton Alley and extending back to Washington Street. Jabez Goodell and his wife Diadama sold Michael the property for $352.95. On it he built a frame building which became his residence and his boot and shoe shop. On October 7, 1839, he married Frances Mary Kloepfer with whom he eventually had ten children, five sons and five daughters. She had been a native of Moos, Baden, being born there in 1813. Two years later he bought an adjoining lot to his Main Street residence from Henry Hearsey for $800.00, upon which he built a two and one-half story brick building with a driveway to the barns and sheds which he constructed in the rear of the property. A few years later he rented his business of shoe repairing to his employee, Frank Spoeri. Michael went into the old styled tavern business usually known as a general store.

Michael Steffan, Frank Spoeri, and many that had come from Oensbach became faithful parishioners of St. Louis Church. Likewise the surrounding farmers from Williamsville and other surrounding towns and villages would come to Buffalo on Sundays to attend Mass and Vesper service at St. Louis Church. Michael would accommodate them by having them put up their wagons and horses in his barns and livery stables. Going to church on a Sunday was a real opportunity to associate with community. After Mass in the morning, breakfast and dinner were served; each family bringing different kinds of foods and desserts. After much conversation in which the week's wages were discussed, types of crops that were in season were described, and weather predictions were evaluated, the community attended Vespers. Following this service, the farmers reclaimed their wagons and horses, said goodbye to their city friends and relatives, and returned to their homes.

In 1846, Michael Steffan in conjunction with Ernest G. Grey, Jacob F. Schoellkopf, and Charles Sigel, bought a strip of land between the Erie Canal and the Niagara River. An undivided one-eighth of this strip was allotted to Steffan and sold to him by Ebenezer Johnson, the first mayor of Buffalo, for the tidy sum of $750.

The entire piece of land in the purchase amounted to $6,000 and was later called *Sandy Town* because of the texture of the soil in the area. When the Buffalo and Lockport Railroad, later to be called the New York Central Railroad, and the State of New York purchased a small portion of this land fronting the canal, Steffan received a sum equal to his original purchase and retained most of his property. He divided his remaining share, land between Hudson and Virginia Streets, into three lots abutting the canal's towpath. Upon the largest of these he built a brick house with a barroom in the basement and living quarters upstairs. He and his family moved from Main Street and lived in their canal house for two years selling food and drink to the hungry and thirsty travelers on their way to the port of Buffalo. Boat travel was slow enough that a traveler could vacate the scow, stop for a bit of whiskey sold at three cents a pint, and be back on the boat with only a little shake of a lamb's tail.

*I*n 1846, Michael Steffan purchased a tannery in Patchin, New York, near the village of Boston, twenty miles from Buffalo, from his nephew, Fidelis Steffan, for the sum of $200. Michael Steffan then discontinued the restaurant and general store business and went into the leather business. George Fink, an expert tanner ran the factory for a few years; later this job fell to the able hands of John Kloepfer. By 1879, four of Michael Steffan's five sons were working in the leather business: Michael F., Anthony C., George L., and Jacob P. Steffan. The fifth son, John Steffan, went to St. Jerome College, seminary of the Resurrectionist Fathers in Berlin, Canada, and was eventually ordained a priest of that Order. The five daughters were Mary, Barbara, Blondina, Frances, and Josephine. By marriage, three of the girls brought the families of Anthony Weber, Charles John Michael Buchheit, and Michael Fornes into the Steffan family circle. All of Michael Steffan's children attended St. Louis Church school and were married with the witness and blessing of the St. Louis Church clergy. They also were devoted parishioners throughout their lives. In 1875, Michael Steffan and

Frances Mary Kloepfer purchased the brick building which the Sisters of Charity, who had come to Buffalo in 1847, used as a hospital on the corner of Pearl Place and Virginia Street. Previous to the Sisters' taking control of the property the building was a residence in which Frances Mary worked as a cook and servant girl from 1835 to 1838 for three dollars a week. The Steffan's purchased the building for $9,000; it was this building which became home for all the Steffan children and their spouses. It was the starting point of their young lives. Frances Mary died April 7, 1880 and Michael Steffan died on March 17, 1883. [6]

*O*ne of the first prominent, Buffalo born, children of an Alsatian family was Joseph Lambert Haberstro. On July 27, 1831, he was born to Joseph and Catherine Haberstro. John Nicholas Mertz baptized him at the Lamb of God Church. When he grew older he attended private school and learned the trade of gunsmith so as to follow in his father's footsteps. This he did for a short while, but he had other ambitions. He first found enjoyment and success in the drapery and dry-goods business; later, he became an insurance agent. In 1859, however, he decided to learn the art of beer making and became a self-made expert; he opened the great German-American Brewery at the corner of High and Main Streets. On September 1, 1853, he married Barbara Scheu. Although he found financial success in his various enterprises, he also had his eye on service and politics in and for the City of Buffalo and Erie County. From 1864 to 1867 he was an alderman on the City Council, becoming its president in 1866. From 1868 to 1871 he was property evaluator and tax appraiser for the City. From 1877 to 1879 he was Sheriff of Erie County. He concentrated much of his service endeavors in the volunteer fireman's association first being a member of Buffalo Engine Company Number Four organized in 1828; he remained active with it between the years 1847-1880. He was also a member in the Liedertafel, Orpheus, Harugari Maennerchor, and the Saengerbund. He participated in many of the singing competitions that were held in

Buffalo and other renowned cities in the eastern part of the United States. From 1853, he was a member of the Freemason's Concordia Lodge and Turnverein. He and his wife had eleven children of which six grew to maturity. [7]

*M*any parishioners at St. Louis Church spoke both German and French; some considering themselves more German than French and others who thought of themselves more French than German. Among the latter group was the Riester family. Eustache Riester and his wife Katharina nee Bierer had lived in Granheim, a Duchy of Wuerttemberg, in the Kingdom of Baden when they were married. After their son William was born on April 26, 1830, they moved to France where Eustache became an engineer at the Saline de Gouhenand, an important salt mine in the foothills of the northern portion of the Jura Mountains, a range which ran along the border of France and Switzerland between the Rhone and Rhein Rivers. Salt is mined much like coal. Men working in underground mines cut out blocks of salt, which are carried to the surface. The mines at Gouhenand had salt deposits that were hundreds of feet thick and covered a vast number of miles underground. Eustache, however, as an engineer, helped to drill wells into the deposits of salt. Water was sent down through these wells whereupon the salt was dissolved in the water, making brine. Using lift pumps the brine was brought to the surface and placed in large evaporating pans. As the water evaporated the salt remained behind to be collected; it usually had very few impurities.

*A*t the age of nineteen William Riester told his mother and father that he had decided to sail to America. He left Gouhenand and went to the Port of Le Havre where he embarked aboard the ship *Diademe* on August 18, 1849. In a diary, he described his travels through France. He left home very early in the morning of July 29, traveling with a friend who was going by carriage to Vesoul approximately eight miles away. It

was a small town, the capital of Haute-Saone, France. It was noted for its manufacture of tools especially files. He remained there only an hour until he was able to gain a seat on a coach going to Besancon for the sum of four franks. Six hours later he arrived there, a town on the Doubs River, known for its industry of watchmaking, metallurgical works, boots, paper, leather, and hosiery. It was one of the ancient cities of the Roman Empire. By way of transport on the Doubs and Saone Rivers and the Canal de Bourgogne he was able to arrive at Dijon near midnight on the same day that he began his travels. He saw nothing of the city that was known for its gothic cathedral and wineries. Immediately he continued on his journey on the canal toward Troyes a city on the Seine River in the district of Aube, France. He arrived there the next day. Troyes was a center for the manufacture of cotton and woolen textiles, yarn, and hosiery. It was here that the succession of the French crown was conferred on Henry V, king of England, in 1420.

*E*ach year shiploads of cotton would come from the United States to the port city of Le Havre. It was then loaded on river-craft and shipped to Troyes through Paris up the Seine River. From there the raw cotton would be scattered throughout the villages of Southern France and Alsace-Lorraine where an entrepreneur, known in German as a *Verlager,* would distribute it to those who had accepted from him weaving contracts. When the products were completed, he would collect them and return them to Troyes from which they would go down the Siene through Paris and be shipped to England and America from the port city of Le Havre. There was always more room on the ships for the return trip to America than there was for the imported raw materials. The extra room was profit for the sailing companies when it was filled with passengers paying a tidy sum of approximately $120 for the trip across the Atlantic Ocean. From Troyes, Riester sailed down the river to Paris where he spent six days waiting for passage to Le Havre. While in Paris he visited, Monsieur Bonnet Charles, a professor at the College de Suresne who advised him as to what books to purchase before going to America. These covered a broad scope of subjects such as industrial design, engraving, medicine, geometry, mechanics, and physics. Bonnet Charles also gave him the names and addresses of Monsieurs Hiacinte and Moure who resided at Rue Bosse du Rampart number sixteen at Le Havre Harbor.

It was very wise for a young man arriving alone in Le Havre to have a trusted friend to contact. Riester arrived in the port city about 6:00 A.M. on August 9, and he had to wait nine days before his ship, *Diademe,* set sail. When he disembarked, from the riverboat upon which he had traveled from Paris, he saw the likes of a French and German village. Innkeepers, merchants, and ship agents were everywhere. It was not like the quiet well-disciplined village of his parents from which he had left. Some people were stealing; others were gambling constantly. Many had miscalculated the cost of ocean travel and turned to crime to find money to pay their fare. Some losing at the gambling tables had to disappointedly leave the village and return to the towns from whence they had come. Women without husbands were raped, and men without wives were victims of shootings and knifings. Police protection was scant. Safety was found in a respectable hotel or at the home of friends such as Hiacinte and Moure.

At high tide, at 1:30 A.M. on August 18, 1849, his ship set sail. Many family groups were well prepared for the voyage with their meat salted, bread baked, cheese prepared, and butter neatly packed in kegs. Personal gear was stored in large chests with great iron bands and heavy locks. The ship's company provided the passengers, for a reasonable fee, with biscuits, rice, and potatoes. As part of the passage fare, fuel for cooking was provided; and, in good weather, cooking was allowed on deck. Other items such as packed hams, herring, flour, coffee, eggs, vinegar, chocolate, tea, and wine were considered luxuries for

which purchase was made at port before boarding the ship. Monsieur Moure had warned Riester not to forget his own chamber pot and a lantern. Riester was at sea only one day when he realized the wisdom of bringing these two items with him. In his diary, Riester gave an account of the food and drink that he brought aboard ship. They were: A whole ham; five pounds of rice, flour, and butter; one bag of potatoes; two liters of vinegar; two pounds of sugar; one bottle of schnapps, cognac, and absinthe, which was an alcoholic liquor flavored with wormwood and herbs. It was considered as a narcotic, forbidden to be used by members of the French military and navy, and condemned by Belgian law, but it was a sedative that attempted to cure the symptoms of seasickness.

While the ship began to unfurl its sails, the steamer *Hercules* pulled it out to sea. Through nice weather in the daytime and very windy weather at night, the ship cleared the English coast by August 22, at 4:00 P.M. Riester had already devoured one-half of his bottle of absinthe and he was very thankful for his chamber pot which was used for double duty, the contents of which were carefully disposed of downwind. By August 29, the fast pace which the good winds had provided subsequently became quite calm and the pace slackened. Riester's ship passed two English vessels heading for Europe before it came in sight, on September 8, of the Nova Scotia coastline. Between that day and September 17, the winds whipping around the edges of the sails and water splashing against the hull of the ship was a cacophony much like a orchestra tuning its instruments before the concert. But alas! On September 17, 1849 at 5:00 P.M., Riester saw the lighthouse at Montauk Point on the tip of Long Island, New York. The harbor was not very far away, and the voyagers leaped with joy.

At midnight the ship entered New York harbor and the surgeon representing the government came aboard to determine if the ship was free of disease.

Disembarkment took place at the foot of Manhattan Island at noon on September 18. Before leaving Europe, Riester was well instructed as to what he should do and whom he should meet upon arriving in New York. Quickly he boarded a steamer that took him up the Hudson River to Albany where he stayed for two days. His fare was a tidy sum of fifty cents. From Albany he made passage on the Erie Canal system and arrived in Buffalo on October 1, 1849, where he met a friend of his family, Monsieur Chevian who had arranged for Riester to take a position with the Eagle Furnace Company. Monsieur Chapper to whom Riester faithfully paid weekly rent, provided his lodging. In Riester's diary, he made mention of his wardrobe in those first months living in Buffalo. It consisted of eight pairs of slacks, four washcloths, twelve shirts, and seven handkerchiefs. He also stocked some remedies for chapped hands and eye diseases. In the summer of 1850, his liaison with his parents in France was Monsieur Rondat Mattheson from whom Riester heard that they were planning to come to America to be with him.

When Eustache and Katharina immigrated to Buffalo with the remainder of their children in 1851, they opened a grocery store at the corner of Burton and Washington Streets adjacent to the Steffan's livery stables. Although originally members of St. Pierre's Church, Eustache, who died in 1853 had his funeral service conducted by Father Lucas Caveng at St. Michael's Church. His wife Katharina died in 1877. William Riester's brother, Ferdinand Johannes Baptiste, had been born in France in 1840. After growing to adulthood, he became, with his partner Godfrey Frohe, proprietor of the Buffalo Stained Glass Institute. They designed and created the windows in the nave of St. Louis Church as well as in countless other churches in the Diocese of Buffalo. Another brother, Gustave, had been born in 1844. In Buffalo, he became a noted confectioner; and, upon his death, was buried from St. Louis Church in 1930 at the age of 86.

When Father Guth withdrew from St. Louis Church in 1850, and took the French congregation with him, William Riester was at his side. At St. Pierre's Church, Guth married William and Elizabeth Finsterbach on April 20, 1852. She had emigrated with her parents, Francois and Margarete nee Fete, from Hofmang-Belfort, France, a city close to the Saline de Gouhenard where Eustache Riester had been an engineer. While they lived on Seneca Street, William and Elizabeth Riester had fifteen children, nine of whom survived to adulthood. William was listed among the founding members of the United German and French Roman Catholic Cemetery in 1859 at Pine Hill. He died in 1898 and Elizabeth died in 1900. Their surviving sons were: William Jr., Julien, Leon F., Alexander, Emile Louis, Charles Ferdinand, Eugene Joseph, and Albert Louis. William Jr. became an engineer like his grandfather; Julien became a medical doctor who married Clara Kaiser at St. Louis Church in 1905; Leon became a noted inventor and surveyor who died in Mexico, a victim of yellow fever in 1894; Emile was a commercial advertiser and an accomplished musician; Albert, the youngest, married Julia Bischof a descendant of the Bleiler and Schranck families. Kasper Bleiler was one of the original members of the Lamb of God Church, and married Magdalene Phillipina Mueller there on August 14, 1837. They had a residence and grocery story at Prime and Lloyd Streets at the terminus of the Erie Canal. His sister, Maria Anna was married to Michael Schranck by Father Guth at St. Louis Church on October 19, 1844. Michael Schranck, was also an original member of the church; he made his fortune on land speculation and lived in a fashionable mansion on Main Street at the head of Goodrich Street until his death in 1874. [8]

One of the early families, which had its origin in Buffalo between the first and second period of interdiction of St. Louis Church, was the Grupp family. Joseph Grupp Sr. was the patriarch of the family. As a young man at the age of eighteen, he arrived in America in 1837. He was born February 19, 1819 at Reichbach, a Duchy of Wuerttemberg in the Kingdom of Baden, to Dominic and Christina Grupp. Upon arriving in Buffalo, he attended St. Louis Church, then known as the Lamb of God Church. In 1843, during the first period of interdiction of St. Louis Church by Bishop Hughes, he changed his affiliation to St. Mary's Church established on Broadway and Pine Streets under the direction of the Redemptorists. He was one of the first parishioners to be married there after Timon became bishop of the newly formed diocese. His wife was Maria Anna Friedmann who had been born to Joseph Friedmann and his wife Sabana nee Hauns at Oberwasser, Baden in 1823. They had two children, Joseph Grupp Jr. and Francis Wilhelm. Francis died in childbirth and his mother, Maria Anna, died one year later on January 10, 1854.

Joseph Grupp Sr. did not tarry in his desire to remarry and have more children. His choice for a new wife was the sister of Maria Anna, Theresa Friedmann, who was six years younger than she. At that time the disciplinary rules of marriage in Catholicism forbade the Sacrament of Matrimony to be executed between two persons who were related by affinity unless a dispensation was obtained. The impediment of affinity stated, however, that if a husband died, the wife could not marry anyone related to him within the fourth degree. Although there may have been some confusion as to what the impediment meant if the wife died, Grupp did not apply for a dispensation and his first child by Theresa, named Mary, born on October 18, 1854, was at first considered to be illegitimate by the Church. A dispensation was awarded, however, shortly thereafter. Joseph and Theresa then had a very productive marriage over the following fifteen years as she gave birth to six more children: Pauline, Wilhelmina, Maria Emma, Edward, Emil, and Wendeling Benjamin. All reached adulthood except Emil who died in 1869, three and one-half years after his birth. Tragedy again struck the life of Joseph Grupp Sr. when Theresa died a short time after Emil's demise.

Grupp waited two years before marrying again. On January 4, 1872, he married his third wife, Mary Ann Seitz, the daughter of George and Magdalena Seitz, nee Schwarzmann. The ceremony took place at St. Louis Church. Joseph Sorg, who had become pastor in 1867, celebrated the matrimonial Mass. Within the next five years, three of Joseph's daughters by his wife Theresa married at St. Louis Church. They were Mary Grupp with Michael Seitz, August 19, 1873; Pauline Grupp with Anthony Blatz, July 6, 1875; and Wilhelmina Grupp with Florian Truncer, July 3, 1877. Edward Grupp did not marry at St. Louis Church because he wed his wife, Josephine Dill, at her church in Kane, Pennsylvania on December 17, 1885. Joseph Grupp Sr. and Mary Ann Seitz had four children, three of which grew to adulthood. One son Joseph Anton Grupp married Frances Schasre at St. Louis Church on June 7, 1892.

Another son, Emil J. Grupp, who married Henrietta Ochs at St. Mary's Church, Lockport, New York, was of great importance to St. Louis Church. They had one child, Arthur Louis Grupp, who eventually carried on the business of the Emil J. Grupp Company, a paper distributing firm in Orchard Park, New York. Besides being a former treasurer of the Buffalo Rotary Club, a member of the Knights of the Holy Sepulchre, Arthur Louis Grupp was a trustee of St. Louis Church and a member of its Holy Name Society. He married Marie Angeline Faber. He died July 27, 1984, and she died on February 24, 1996. In their wills they were most generous to Canisius College, St. Louis Church, and Nardin Academy. After Arthur's death, Marie was also a trustee of St. Louis Church and served on the Board of Regents at Canisius College. The Grupp Fireside Lounge in the Canisius College Student Center was so named for the family in appreciation of Arthur and Marie's fidelity to the school. [9]

It is interesting to note that among the

parishioners who came to St. Louis Church between the years 1834 and 1863, at least fifteen claimed Baden as their European place of origin naming small towns such as: Hechingen, Oensbach, Oberhausen, Forchheim, Empfingen, Bucha, Breisach, Alt Breisach, Entschbach, Adelshausen, Oberwasser, Pforzheim, and Geschweir. In the twelfth century the Zaehringen family dwelt in the Breisgau, a name, given to the area, which today, surrounds the large city of Freiburg in southwestern Germany. The head of the family, Herman I, was a margrave, an hereditary noble of Verona, a commune in northeastern Italy on the Adige River. He won this title because he and members of his family militarily defended the country's borders. He named the area Baden in 1112. It is the entire landmass between Wuerttemberg and the Rhein River, with Mannheim in the north and Switzerland in the south. Its eastern portion lies in the Schwarzwald, the Black Forest. The Danube River drains the extreme southeast, and the remainder lies in the Rhein River basin whose tributaries are the Main, Neckar, Murg, and Kinzig Rivers. In German, Baden means to bathe, and one of its principal cities is Baden-Baden, a city of Baden in the State of Baden, built on the banks of the Oos River. The thermal baths in the area were known even to the Romans who named the village Aurelia Aquensis. In the north, Baden boasts of Heidelberg whose notable university was founded in 1386. The area produces grain, tobacco, hemp, rape, chicory, hops, grapes, and forests of pine, oak, beech, birch, and ash. Its mines are abundant in minerals such as limestone, gypsum, salt, soda, and mineral springs. It manufactures cottons, ribbons, paper, jewelry, pottery, tobacco, beer, wine, hats, wooden clocks and musical instruments, and chemicals.

*B*aden was devastated during the religio-political wars that followed the Reformation. From 1527 to 1771 the country was divided. The Baden-Baden area in the north was Roman Catholic, Baden-Durlach in the south was Protestant. Both, however, were united under Karl Friedrich of Baden-Durlach in 1771. By 1803 the entire country came under the influence of Napoleon Bonapart, the conqueror of Europe. By 1806, he urged Karl Friedrich to join the Confederation of the Rhein and in turn Napoleon made Karl a Grand Duke, a sovereign prince. In 1815, following Napoleon's defeat at Waterloo, Baden entered into the German Confederation and received a liberal constitution in 1818. Karl's successor, Grand Duke Leopold, *the Volksfreund*, introduced, into the country in 1832, the Prussian *Zollverein*, a custom union which was created in central Europe in 1819 by the thirty-nine autonomous German states. It determined economic and trade policies for the individual states with their mutual cooperation and input. Under strict regulation, the *Zollverein* allowed labor migration, proposed a minimum but fluctuating wage scale, and permitted work to be performed in all towns and villages by the *Auslaender* as well as the resident. An *Auslaender* was a transient worker who prior to the establishment of the *Zollverein* was unable to procure work in villages other than his own.

*A*lthough the policies of the *Zollverein* seemed to abolish the old practices of the guild system, it was soon found that the allocation of work assignments was still directed by the local mastercraftsman of each town and village. He could still require an *Auslaender* to apply for work only within the confines of a strict definition of the applicant's craft or trade specified by his years of apprenticeship. The mastercraftsman was required to give the applicant work only if the position could not be filled first by one of the local artisans. His judgment in this matter was final and the applicant had no means of appeal. These practices presented the *Auslaender* with a most distressing dilemma; if he did not get the work required as a journeyman to prove his skill through job performance, he could not get his own mastercraftsman license; if he did not get the license he could forever look forward to being a traveling, starving, and sporadically hired employee. Even though the system tried to improve the journeyman's lot through a *Wanderschaft* program, a probationary work schedule called a *Wanderjahre*, the difficulty of fulfilling the schedule was a Herculean task. Only the most devoted obtained total success and the license. For those who did so, their *Wanderbuch*, the booklet into which each employer gave his opinion of the journeyman's value, became a diploma always to be kept and honored. So many young men found that emigration to America, where they were told that work was in abundance, was easier than struggling through the labyrinthine channels carved out by the *Zollverein* policies. Buffalo and St. Louis Church became the terminus of the decisions that many of these hard pressed novice mastercraftsmen made between 1832 and the American Civil War. [10]

During the history of St. Louis Church, beginning with construction of the first building called the Lamb of God Church, through the years of parish consolidation and incorporation, interdiction, excommunication, and ending with Joseph Sorg having replaced Sergius Schoulepnikoff as pastor, the influential laymen of the parish were: William Le Couteulx, John Dingens, Nicholas Goetz, Michael Wehrle, Joseph Berst, George Bemgesser, Francis Handel, Peter Kramer, George Zahm, Peter Lux, Joseph Zimmermann, Philip Born, Charles Esslinger, Lawrence Weber, Andreas Weber, Casper Pfeffer, Christian Blancan, T.L. Schreck, Joseph Hartmann, Peter Zinns, George Zimmermann, Jacob Wilhelm, John Koch, Mathais Hausle, Anthony Diebold, Michael Mesmer, Nicholas Ottenot, Peter Munschauer, Martin Roth, Alexander Allenbrandt, and George Fischer. These were the immigrants who spanned twenty-three years of early Buffalo history establishing their businesses, providing for their families, and expressing their faith as Catholics, and volcanically defending, in resistance to clerical rule, their right to lay control of the temporal affairs of their church. Their mental capabilities, willful determination, and physical prowess, were as different as were the many areas of Europe from which they had emigrated. Of this group, one person for whom a most detailed genealogical record has been

obtainable is Mathais Hausle.

Hausle was born on February 24, 1798 at Loeffingen near Neustadt in the Schwarzwald, the Black Forest; the countryside being a province of Baden where great winding rivers, placid lakes, fertile table lands, and rich mountainous regions afforded a most enchanting picturesque view especially in winter when the slopes were covered with snow. Beautiful cascades, hot springs, wondrous valleys, precious metals, and fir trees abounded. This was the home of a mixed origin of people known as Swabians who were descendants of the inhabitants of the ancient duchy that generally corresponded to Wuerttemberg, Baden, and Western Bavaria. Folklore relates stories of secret and macabre events as dark as the Black Forest itself. Even today, on Shrove Tuesday, the day preceding Ash Wednesday, the residents of Loeffingen participate in a passionate carnival that features the re-enactment of *Hexenverbrennung*, the burning of witches at the gates of the city. It was in this village that Hausle, at the age of thirty-three, learned through letters written to him about the wonderful prosperity that one could obtain in America.

At the age of twenty, he had entered military service; and, eight years later on April 1, 1826, he was honorably discharged at Karlsruhe, Baden. For the next six years, he worked on his father's farm, learned tailoring from him; and, with two friends, formed a partnership in the manufacture of grandfather clocks. On February 23, 1832, he left his village, traveled through Neustadt and Freiburg to Karlsruhe. From there he proceeded to Strasbourg in Alsace. Then he joined the cotton merchants' convoy for Paris passing through Nancy, Dizier, Charlons-sur-Marne, and Chateau-Thierry. From Paris he sailed down the Seine River to the port of Le Havre. The vessel on which he sailed took two months before it arrived in New York harbor. Upon arriving he used the same canal route that others had taken in reaching Buffalo since 1825. He arrived in that city during the summer of 1832. With him he brought the inner-works for constructing grandfather clocks, and settled down to making and selling them. His sales' travels took him far and wide, even into Canada. It has been reported, that as the twentieth century dawned, two of Hausle's original clocks were in the possession of the members of the Steffan and Hagmeyer families, who were still members of St. Louis Church.

On December 29, 1834, at the Lamb of God Church, he married Magdalena Hoffmann, a young lady of eighteen years noted for her personal charm and physical beauty. Nicholas Mertz was the pastor and principal witness at their wedding. They had two children, Paul and John. In 1839, however, Magdalena fell victim to a progressive wasting away of her body caused by pulmonary tuberculosis, and died at the age of twenty-three. From necessity of caring for his two boys, Hausle entered into a second marriage three months after Magdalena died. His new wife was Magdalena Daniel, and the ceremony was held at Sts. Peter and Paul Church in Williamsville, her family's parish church, on November 5, 1839. Before their marriage, Magdalena Daniel, had been a housekeeper at the home of Millard Fillmore on Franklin Street. After marriage, she bore Hausle eight children between the years 1840 and 1858. They were Mathias Jr., Katharina, Magdalena, Mary, Amelia, Nicholas, Louise, and Rose.

Hausle's business prospered and his desire to return to Europe dissolved. In 1833, he signified his desire to seek citizenship in his adopted country; and, on August 20, 1838, he received full citizenship of the United States. His success as a clockmaker was enhanced by his partnership with Francis Handel and Jacob Koons. They had come to Buffalo from Alsace in 1828 and had invested wisely in city property. Handel owned land on Pearl Street near Huron and also on the east side of Main Street below Genesee Street. Koons bought land on the west side of Main Street below

Mohawk. Hausle was a more conservative thinker, and he bought land on Genesee Street between Elm and Michigan because it was inexpensive; and, although sandwiched in between two highly populated German settlements, it never proved to be a moneymaking investment. In 1836, however, Hausle built a commodious frame structure on his Genesee Street lot. Hausle finally gave up the clock business and opened a saloon with a grocery store attachment.

His saloon became popular with the German element and proved a most desirable meeting place for new arrivals from the Fatherland. Many a new immigrant drank his first glass of beer at Hausle's hostelry, and many a match between *die Johanns und die Gretchens* were negotiated within its walls. At the age of forty-five Hausle considered himself to be too old for military service, applied for an exemption, and was awarded it on February 28, 1843. His art of tailoring which he had learned from his father was not forgotten. The clothing for his boys and for himself was fashioned by his own hands. Magdalena Daniel often remarked that it looked more serviceable than beautiful. His sons had few pleasures, but their duties were many. In the tavern, beer, cherry wine and kummel were homemade and kept fresh and cool in the cellar. The boys took many an unwilling trip to where these commodities were stored when a patron's thirst had to be quenched, until they realized that a refreshing nip could be slyly taken in self-awarded compensation. The measure served by the hostelry was usually so large that the patron never knew a sip or two had been removed from the container.

By 1846, Hausle had canceled his indebtedness at Genesee Street, saved a considerable amount of capital, had a good cash flow, and purchased property at the northeast corner of Sycamore and Walnut Streets. He erected a small brick house, doing most of the work by himself with the aid of his sons. Sometime later he invested in a piece of property on the west side of

Johnson Street between Sycamore and Batavia Streets. He used this land for a massive vegetable garden. By the sweat and brawn of the older children, the garden was planted, weeded, hoed, fertilized, and watered. All winter long the family had an over supply of potatoes and the root cellar, which they dug and walled, preserved many of the other vegetables. Many times one could observe that this work was irksome to the children, but they obeyed their stern parents without question. Several pieces of property in the area were undeveloped; and, upon them, grew uncultivated bushes of currents and berries. Thrifty Mathias Jr. had the habit of picking these and selling them at the Elk Street market. In this way he saved enough pennies to buy a ticket for the circus which came to town.

In the summer of 1849, a terrible scourge visited the city; the cholera had returned. Within a few weeks after the outbreak, terror was in the air and a common dread pervaded the entire population. The weather was so hot and humid that it aggravated the disease and increased the mortality. Streets were deserted except for those administering to sick and dying or attending burials that were legion. Funerals, four, six, ten in number could be seen on multiple streets at the same time. The city was ripe for the spread of this pestilence. There were no closed sewers; open gutters and unpaved streets were filled with filth that filtered through the ground and reached the wells supplying potable water. No sanitary orders were given by the mayor or city council to check the spread of the plague. Flight from the city appeared to be the only solution for Hausle and his family. Immediately, with the exception of Paul who was employed at Bernheimer's dry goods store, the family moved to Williamsville where the Daniels had a home. They returned to the city in the fall; the scourge had passed. Hausle found that in his absence, the City had cleaned the streets, spread lime, and improved other sanitary conditions. Because of these preventative measures, the cholera epidemic of 1852 was less severe.

In 1860 Hausle rented his Genesee Street store and dwelling, and went into the dry goods and hardware business, in partnership with John Ortner, an uncle of his wife, using a store building on the opposite side of Genesee Street near Michigan Street. Hausle's family lived in rooms above the store for two years, at which time ten members in the family required larger accommodations. They moved back to their original home on Genesee Street. By this time the older sons were regularly employed; and, as it was a custom in German families, their entire earnings were turned over to their father. They were given a very skimpy allowance, never exceeding fifty cents, when their request was reasonable. After four years in the dry goods and hardware business, Hausle reoccupied his former store that he had rented and occupied himself with tailoring and selling rags. He continued in this endeavor until he died on August 15, 1867. Before his death, his older children had attended a private school conducted by Mr. and Mrs. T.L. Schreck; but, when St. Louis Church established its school his other children attended there. In 1843, Schreck had composed the letter of rebuttal sent to Bishop Hughes that defended the trustees' thesis.

All through his life in Buffalo, Hausle was a man of faith filled with religious zeal, although it was not worn upon his sleeve. Some may have considered him as stern, harsh, and severe. He, however, was just and upright. His rough exterior concealed a tender heart, which won for him the respect of his community, his friends, and his family. It was as big as his heavily framed body that carried about three hundred pounds. His name Hausle meant *Little House*, and, like a little house his heart was full of humility. He was not a rich man, nor was he ever attracted to public office. During the age when the black flag of interdict hung over St. Louis Church, however, he was one of the trustees. In the heat of authoritative battle waged by them with Bishop Timon over the temporalities of the church, he, along with other lay leaders, was excommunicated by

Bishop Timon. Once the interdict was lifted and a compromise was reached between the bishop and the laymen, he was reinstated. It was his personal victory that he had retained together his conviction and his Catholicism. [11]

*I*n the first years of his episcopate, Bishop Timon furiously purchased land to build churches encircling St. Louis Church so as to bleed away its parishioners. The Irish and French had already exited its walls. During the first half of the decade beginning with 1850, other German parishioners at St. Louis Church, discouraged by the years of interdiction, sought out havens in St. Mary's Redemptorist Church, St. Boniface's Church, and St. Michael's Jesuit Church in the city. German farmers from the countryside no longer had to make the long trek into the city on Sundays for Mass and Vespers. They had expanded their facilities, started by Nicholas Mertz and John Neumann, into sizeable churches such as Sts. Peter and Paul Church in Williamsville, St. Joseph's Church at Buffalo Plains, and St. John the Baptist Church at North Bush. Unexpectedly, Timon's diocese became the recipient of another small chapel that sprang, as it seemed, out of nowhere! On May 5, 1851, Joseph Batt Sr. deeded three acres of land to Bishop Timon, which were located at the junction of Union Road and Genesee Street. Upon this land, Batt, being a mason by trade, built that small chapel. It was dedicated on October 7, 1853 and named *Maria Hilf*, Our Lady Help of Christians. Immediately after this event, many Germans, especially those from St. Louis Church, made informal pilgrimages to *Maria Hilf*. Within the period of agonized struggle with interdiction, it had become a sacramental refuge for them.

*T*he history behind the decision of Joseph Batt Sr. to donate the land and build the chapel is fascinating. In 1789, he was born at Mertzweiler, Alsace, the only child of Michael Batt and Maria Anna Diebold. In that year the world witnessed the outbreak of the French

Revolution which led to the destruction of the monarchy and the creation of the radical French Republic. In 1792, it produced a sweeping social upheaval, changing and destroying age-old institutions such as church, calendar, monetary system, and family structure. Conservative farmers of the French countryside despised the Republic; and, in an ensuing war between France and Austria, sided with the Austrian monarchy. Many Alsatians fled their homeland and found refuge in the German lands east of the Rhein River. Michael Batt joined them in 1797; but, in doing so, lost all rights to his holdings in Mertzweiler; the Republic confiscated his land. Although he never returned to Alsace, his widowed wife, Maria Anna, with her son Joseph Batt returned to Morschweiler, Alsace, in 1800. She established a home there; it being only a few miles from their original home in Mertzweiler. It was here that Joseph Batt grew to maturity and carved out a living as a mason and a farmer.

*O*n March 9, 1813, he married Barbara Weber in the Catholic Church in Morschweiler. She had been born in Daugendorf that was also the birthplace of his mother, Maria Anna Diebold. Barbara was the daughter of Anton Weber and Barbara Schalk. Anton gave his daughter a charming dowry that included six hundred and sixty francs, wine, corn, linen press, a bed, and an expected inheritance of one thousand francs. In turn, Joseph Batt built a beautiful house in which both his mother and wife lived in harmony with him. In the twenty years that followed, he became a very prosperous farmer, accumulated many pieces of property including meadows, vineyards, and forests, and raised a family of ten children. When his oldest son was born and named Joseph, Barbara decided that it was time to call them Joseph Sr. and Joseph Jr.

*P*rosperity did not, however, bring Joseph Batt Sr. security. Napoleon Bonaparte's creation of the First Empire had led to France's embroilment in long and costly wars. Financially Alsace suffered much. Relief was hoped for following Bonaparte's defeat at Waterloo in 1815. The monarchy again reigned supreme in France. Although fifteen years of relative political stability resulted, and brought some security, clouds of revolution again darkened the land in 1830. Mobs once more stampeded the streets of Paris trying to bring down this monarchy. Peace, however, was found by liberalizing it and putting the *Citizen-King*, Louis Philippe, at the helm. Batt was not, however, impressed with this political maneuver; and, after his mother died on March 30, 1829, his mind turned to seriously considering emigration. He was not the only Alsatian thinking this way. One year before, he had seen many leaving his wife's village of Daugendorf for America, including a most respected friend, Johann Diebold. It, however, took him several more years to formulate positive plans for his family's departure.

In 1835, Joseph Batt Sr. had finally decided that it was time to leave France. He, however, first sent his oldest son, Joseph Batt Jr., to the United States to determine the most suitable place for the entire family to settle. After traveling through Ohio, Indiana, and Illinois, Batt Jr. returned to Buffalo, the initial entry point of his midwestern excursion. In Williamsville he found an area which he believed would be suitable for the Batt family to reside after immigrating. In much detail, he reported all his findings to his father in Europe. Batt Sr. sold all his property and in October 1836 he, his remaining seven children, married daughter, son-in-law, Joseph Gangloff, and one grandchild, John Gangloff, left their homeland bound for Le Havre, France. On November 11, 1836, they set sail on the *Mary Ann*, an American vessel under the command of Captain Arthur Child. Eighteen days later the ship reached a point in the Atlantic Ocean approximately four hundred miles west of the southern shore of Ireland. It was suddenly hit by a violent tropical storm with westward winds blowing a furious gale of hurricane severity. It was a dreadful electrified tempest with thunder booming all around for two and one-half hours from late morning to early afternoon.

The *Mary Ann* was stripped of her sails, masts toppled into the sea with rigging still attached, and the hull began to leak badly. Joseph Batt Sr. turned in prayer to the Blessed Virgin Mary to safeguard the ship, its crew, and all the families on board. Invoking the name of *Maria Hilf*, Our Lady Help of Christians and Star of the Sea, he made a solemn vow that if he and his family arrived safely in America, he would build a chapel there in her honor. Soon after his prayer, the storm abated and the ship limped back to Cork, Ireland, where after the leaks were repaired and the mizzenmast replaced, she once again began the journey to America.

On February 2, 1837, eighty-four days out of Le Havre with one hundred and twenty-nine passengers, the *Mary Ann* landed in New York City's harbor. Nine days later, the Batt family joined up with Joseph Batt Jr. in Williamsville, and settled on one hundred and thirty-eight acres of land which Batt Sr. had purchased from the Holland Land Company for the sum of $859.84. When he left France, he had an account of $4,800. This was quite a sizeable sum considering that the generality of immigrants began life in America with an account of $270. Before coming to America, he had been told by his son that their church, Sts. Peter and Paul, was in need of a bell. In Strasbourg, while traveling to Le Havre, Batt Sr. purchased one. It had survived the long voyage and was placed in the belfry of their new church. It ceremoniously rang at the wedding of Joseph Batt Jr. to Magdalena Snugg on January 14, 1840. She had been born in Surbourg, Alsace, in 1821. Father John Neumann officiated at their wedding which took place nine months before he departed Western New York and gave his missionary congregations over to the care of Father Michael Guth. At the time of the wedding Neumann also baptized the Gangloff grandchildren whose number had proliferated since the family's departure from Europe.

After the chapel, *Maria Hilf*, was completed Batt Sr. encouraged his friends in the city to come to it in pilgrimage. The first official one was held on May 24, 1864, the feast of Our Lady Help of Christians. As in Alsace, many who came and received special favors left votive-offerings and tokens, often in the form of wax or plaster representations of the limbs and organs in which disease had been relieved. In 1866, Batt saw that the chapel needed enlargement and he purchased the old stone church of Sts. Peter and Paul in Williamsville when a new church was completed on its sight. Using the stones from the old church he substantially enlarged his chapel. Batt Sr. died on July 29, 1872 at the age of eighty-three. Barbara Batt, his wife, preceded him in death by five months; she was eighty-four. Both were buried in the chapel cemetery, immediately behind the church. [12]

English speaking Catholics, mainly Irish, should not be ignored in an historical overview of antebellum Roman Catholics in Buffalo. Between 1825 and 1827 the Irish population of Buffalo increased rapidly. Completion of the Erie Canal and job offerings as laborers on its docks at the foot of Main Street offered quite an incentive for those who dug the canal and came to its terminus to stay in residence. The Irish, however, did not mix well with the Germans or French Catholics because of a language barrier. They also did not mix well with the WASPS, White Anglo Saxon Protestants, because of a religion barrier. As such, they stayed mainly to themselves as did the Germans and others were not seriously aware of them until after Bishop Timon arrived in 1847. It was then that Timon's voice frightened the Germans and the WASPS because it rallied and inspired the Irish to be more vocal and expressive. He championed the cause of all Irish families living mainly in the First Ward which was located on the south side of the city, near the terminus of the Erie Canal and the city's growing railroad network.

In contrast to the clergy of Continental European extraction, the Irish clergy slowly but gradually moved into Western New York from the eastern counties of the State. Bishop Conwell of Philadelphia was the first Catholic clergyman, who was not an explorer, to visit Buffalo. He came in 1821 while on a journey to Quebec, Canada, and baptized a child from the O'Rourke family. The same year Father Patrick Kelly came and stayed for some days at the home of the Episcopal rector, Rev. Doctor Babcock. He held a special Mass service for all English-speaking Catholics at the original St. Paul's Episcopal Church built on land fronting Pearl Street. This was the first public Mass said in Western New York since Father Louis Hennepin offered the Holy Sacrifice of the Mass on the banks of the Niagara River on December 11, 1678. Kelly had been educated in Ireland and ordained by Bishop Connolly in New York City in 1821. After he left Buffalo, no visiting priest came to the city until Father Michael McNamara, who was the first resident priest of Rochester, wandered into the area between 1825 and 1832. Fathers O'Donoghue, McGerry, O'Reilly, and Foley joined him in missionary work. In 1834, Father O'Reilly came into Lockport, New York, and organized a congregation and started the construction of a church. Later it became known as St. John the Baptist Church.

One priest, who came to Buffalo for a prolonged visit was Father Stephen Badin. He remained for six weeks starting in the late Fall of 1828. He was the first priest to be ordained in the United States. In 1819 he had gone to Europe for the purpose of collecting funds for his missions in Kentucky. After nine years there, he returned to America. On his way west, he stopped in Buffalo as the guest of Louis Le Couteulx who knew several of Badin's former French parishioners in Kentucky. It was Badin who encouraged Le Couteulx to donate property to Bishop Dubois so as to build a church for all Catholics of Buffalo, including the Irish as well as Continental European immigrants. Although fulfilled at first, it came to an end in 1837, when the Irish left the Lamb of God Church and began a separate congregation in rooms rented in a building on Main

Street near Niagara Street. Later they moved into another establishment at the corner of Main Street and the Terrace.

On May 1, 1837, Father Charles Smith came and said Mass for the first time in their rented rooms. He continued to do so once every month until the congregation was able to establish a church. In 1839, Bishop Hughes, who had been made coadjutor to Bishop DuBois, arrived in Buffalo. On the morning of August 15, 1839, he confirmed one hundred and ninety persons at the Lamb of God Church, and in the evening he preached to the Irish in a large rented hall. Following his sermon, he met with three representatives of the Irish contingent: Patrick Cannon, Patrick Milton, and Maurice Vaughan. Although these men wanted to build an Irish church on property donated to them by Louis Le Couteulx on Edward Street near Elmwood Avenue, Hughes thought that it would be too far away from their homes. He suggested that they buy property on the corner of Ellicott and Batavia Streets. They did so and their church named St. Patrick's opened its doors for the first time on May 1, 1841. Each Sunday the pews were filled to capacity and a school had been opened in the basement; the number of English-speaking Catholics had increased rapidly especially since much work was provided by the construction of the Boston and Buffalo Railroad.

The number of Irish that had attended the Lamb of God Church under the pastorships of John Nicholas Mertz and Alexander Pax represented seventeen per-cent of the total congregation. Marriage records from September 15, 1829 until May 17, 1836 show that Mertz celebrated seventy-one marriages. From June 4, 1836 until December 6, 1839 Pax performed only twenty-two marriages. For seven years the Irish population at the church remained quite representative; but during the next three years, a rapid decline set in. The records, however, show a distinct German influence in their preparation and filing. With

humor one reads the German spellings representing Irish names. McGloclyn or McGlochele was given for McLaughlin; Konly meant Connolly; Swiny meant Sweeney; Mury stood for Murray; and O'Konner was the German interpretation of O'Connor. In 1849, several Irish families opened St. Mary's of the Lake Church, later named the Immaculate Conception Church, on the property originally donated by Louis Le Couteulx to Bishop Hughes for the Irish but returned to him. Following Louis Le Couteulx's death, his son and heir, Alphonse Le Couteulx, deeded it to Bishop Timon for use by the many Irish that had moved north into the west side of Buffalo away from St. Patrick's Church at Ellicott and Batavia Streets. In 1855, Timon also closed St. Patrick's Church and absorbed its congregation into his St. Joseph's Cathedral located on Franklin Street. [13]

REFERENCES AND NOTES ✤ CHAPTER FIVE

1. For source material for the above paragraphs see: Paul V. Hale Ph.D., *St Michael's Church Bulletin*, The Jesuit Downtown Church of Buffalo, June 3, 2001 and June 10, 2001; Also consult: "The German Catholics of Buffalo," op. cit., *History of Germans of Buffalo and Erie County*, p.129ff and in the same text biographical sketches for those in attendance of the laying of the cornerstone of St. Michael's Church: Stephen Bettinger, Joseph Boot, Henry Diehl, Henry Georger, Louis Goetz, Francis Haefner, George Irr, Peter Kaesman, George Kold, Christopher Lang, Francis Lang, George Logel, John Lux, Casper Meyer, John Missert, Gregory Ritt, Michael Salles, John Streicher, Michael Wackerman, Benedict Weber, John Wild, Jacob Yax, and Martin Zinns. All these persons were originally members of St. Louis Church who because of interdiction problems gave service at St. Michael's Church. Bishop Timon laid the cornerstone on the feast of St. Ignatius in 1864. Many of these family names appear on the register at St. Louis Church following the solution of the problems between Bishop Timon and the trustees of St. Louis Church in 1855. Father Wenninger who was most influential in bringing a solution to the trustee problem was at the dedication of St. Michael's Church on June 16, 1867, see: *Leaves From an Old Diary*, Canisius College, Vol. II, p. 514. Henry Diehl was born in a building opposite but facing the *Free Press* building on Ellicott Street on January 14, 1835. His father was Conrad Diehl who came to Buffalo from Wittenborn, Hessen-Kassel. Henry went to private school and then

went into the tobacco-cigar sales business in the old American Hotel block. Later with his brothers he opened a large pharmacy. Henry married Salome Kabel of Buffalo Plains. In 1897 he was living at No. 391 Oak Street at the age of 62. He had four sons by his marriage. His brothers were John P. Diehl born in 1837; Jacob W. Diehl, and Dr. Conrad Diehl. At the dedication of the corner stone he was 29 years of age.

2. History and description of Alsace-Lorraine in Europe see: op. cit. *World' s Popular Encyclopedia*, Vol. 1., A-Bal, and op. cit. *Illustrated World Encyclopedia*, Vol. 1., A-Amm. The men who took leadership in Lothringen took the name of King Lothair. Each of these kings were also emperors of the Holy Roman Empire until 1137. The antebellum parishioners who spoke German and/or French at St. Louis Church were: Adler, Anna Mary; Aedelman, Anthony; Ailinger, Carrie; Allenbrandt, Alexander; Allenbrandt, Alois; Ambrose, John; Ambrose, Joseph; Ambrose, Norman; Ambs, Hiram; Ambs, Joseph; Ames, Joseph; Armbruster, Joseph; Baker, Henry; Ball, Charles; Ball, Joseph; Bartel, Victor; Barth, John; Bartell, Joseph; Bardol, Jacob; Bartol, Jacob; Batt, Joseph Sr.; Batt, Joseph Jr.; Batt, Nicholaus; Bauer, Mary; Baumann, Creszentia; Baumann, Regina; Becher, Celestin; Becker, Joseph; Behm, Margaret; Beilmann, John; Beingaesser, George; Beisinger, Mathias; Beiz, Lorenz; Bemgesser, George; Berst, Joseph; Bettinger, Stephen; Beyer, Joseph; Bibus, Michael; Biesang, Anton; Biesanz, Anton; Biesinger, Mathais; Blancan, Christian; Bleiler, Kaspar; Bleiler, Magdalena nee Mueller; Bork, Joseph; Born, Philip; Borsche, Franz; Breis, David; Breis, Caroline; Bronner, Gabriel; Bronner, Joseph; Brunner, Louis; Bubel, Anton; Buchheit, Barbara; Buchheit, Charles; Buchheit Francis; Buchheit, Henry; Buchheit, Magdalene; Burkhard, Mr.; Busher, P; Chretien, Carl; Chretien, Jacob C.; Chretien, John; Collignon, Frank; Cramer, Adam; Cramer, Peter; Cretien, Carl; Criqui, Anthony; Daveron, Barbara; Davis, Jacob; Davis, John; Davis, Peter; Deck, Frank; Deck, Jacob N; Deck, Josephine; Deck, Louisa; Deck, Magdalena; Decker, Joseph; Degenfiter, Mary; Dehlinger, Victor; Deigler, Anton; Deigler, Joseph; Delger, Anthony; Delger, George; Dellinger, Victor; Densinger, William; Diebold, Anthony; Diebold, Catherine; Diebold, George; Diebold, John; Diebold, Josephine; Dietle, Anton; Dietsche, Xavier; Dingens, John; Dittle, Anton; Doepp, Michael; Dole, Charles F; Doll, Frederick; Doll, Michael; Domedion, Antoinette; Domedion, F. W; Domedion Mrs. Jacob; Dossert, G.B; Druar, John; Eckert, Anthony; Eger, Mrs. A; Egether, Andrew; Egloff, Peter; Einsel, Joseph; Eisenmann, Nicholas; End, Aloysious; Entrup, Henry; Erb, Henry; Erb, Mary; Erisman, Martin; Erisman, Magdalena; Erman, Joseph; Ernewein, Ignatz; Esslinger, Carl; Fashero, John; Feldman, Anthony; Feldman, John; Fell, Joseph; Fertig, Regina; Fertig, Carl; Fiegel, John; Fink, Henry; Fischer, Frank; Fischer, Jacob; Fisher, John; Fisher, George; Fisher, Martin; Fix, Caroline; Fohl, Anton; Fougeron, Augusta; Fougeron, John; Forster, Joseph; Frank, John; Franz, Michael; Freimuth, George; Frey, John; Friedman, Joseph; Friesz, Joseph; Fuller, Andrew; Garono, Henry; Garono, Lorenz; Garono, Mary; Garono, Mary A.; Gastel, Joseph; Gattie, Joseph; Gattie, Mary; Gebhard, Lorenz; Gebhardt, Joseph; Gerber, Emil; Gerber, Antonia; Gerhard, Anna; Ginther, Jacob; Gittere, Anthony; Gittere, Florenz; Gittere, Elizabeth Schnur; Gittere, Helena; Gittere, Jacob Alexander; Gittere, Elizabeth Rebmann; Gittere, Catherine Mohaefer; Gittere, Joseph; Gittere, Maria Anna Lehrer; Gittere, Nicholas; Gittere, Maria Roll; Glass, Jacob; Glass, John; Glass, Peter; Glaess, Peter; Goetz, Nicholaus; Gramm, Maria Kathraina; Gross, Anna Maria; Grupp, Joseph; Haberkorn, Michael; Haberstro, Joseph; Hack, George; Hack, Theresa; Handel, Franz; Hausle, Mathias; Hausle, Paul; Hausle, Louise; Hausle, Magdalena; Hausle, Mary Ann; Hausle, Rosa; Halm, Johann; Handell, Franz; Hansgen, John; Hartmann, Joseph; Hasenfratz, Frank; Heim, Michael; Heinrich, Jacob; Heintz, Joseph; Heisle, Julia; Heittler, George; Hemmerlein, Lizzie; Herman, Anton; Herman, Valentin; Hibsch, Jacob; Hibsch, Michael; Hirsch, Johann; Hitchler, Magdalena; Hittler, Jacob; Holrat, Andreas; Huck, Charles; Huntzinger, Jacob; Huntzinger, John; Huntzinger, Mary; Jacob, Joseph; Jacobs, Emma; Jacobs, Mary; Jehle, Henrietta; Jost, Joseph; Jung, Lorenz; Jungmann, Johann; Jungmann, Catherine Gittere; Kammerer, Albert; Karlein, Michael; Kehl, Andreas; Kehl, Peter; Kerker, Mary; Kieffer, George; Kieffer, Peter; Kieffer, Simon; Killinger, Anthony; Kinske, Baldsar; Kinske, George; Kirn, Louisa; Kirsch, John; Kleber, Cecilia; Kloepfer, Jacob; Klug, Alois; Knauber, John; Knauber, Martin; Koch, Catherine; Koch, John; Kolb, Jacob; Kolb, Mary; Koons, Jacob; Kost, Philip; Kramer, Adam; Kramer, Jacob; Kramer, Peter; Kraemer, Adam; Kraemer, Peter; Kraft, Francis J.; Kraft, Joseph; Kraft, Ludwig; Kraft, B. Caspar; Kraus, Andrew; Kraus, Caroline; Kraus, Katie; Kraus, John; Kraus, Mary; Kreiner, Kaspar; Kremer, Elizabeth Gittere; Kremer, John Peter; Kretien, Carl; Krigi, Anton, Krumholtz, Ferdinand; Kugler, Adam; Kugler, Michael; Kuhn, Franz Anton; Lambert, George; Lang, Frederick; Lautz, John; Lautz, J.Adam; Le Couteulx, Alphonse; Le Couteulx, Louis; Le Couteulx, William; Lederle, Josie; Lederle, Bertha; Leichtnam, Joseph; Lenhard, Joseph; Lenhard, Louis; Lettau, Michael; Lienert, J.B.; Lienert, Mary B; Lindermann, Magdalena; Loesch, Anna; Loesch, Frank; Lorenz, John; Lossan, George; Lubel, Anton; Lutz, Joseph; Lutz, John; Lutz, Mathias; Lux, John; Lux, Peter; Marke, Joseph; Martin, Alexander; Marx, Lorenz; Mayer, Andreas; Mergenhagen, Barbara; Mesmer, Anton; Mesmer, Caspar; Mesmer, Michael; Metzger, Frank; Meyer, Andreas; Meyer, Anton; Meyer, Barbara; Meyer, Catherine; Meyer, Mary Ann; Meyer, Michael; Miller, Anna Maria; Miller Barbara; Miller, Catherine; Miller, Elizabeth; Miller, John; Miller, John Henry; Miller, Maria Magdalena; Miller, Mary; Miller, Nicholas Sr.; Miller, Nicholas Jr.; Miller, Paul; Miller, Peter; Miller, Rosa Catherine; Miller, Theresa; Morhaefer, Jacob; Morhaefer, Mariann Gittere; Mosbach, Thaddeus; Motsch, Joseph; Motsch, Louis; Motsch, Margaretta; Motsch, Michael; Munschauer, George; Munschauer, Nicholas; Munschauer, Peter; Muth, Jacob; Nagel, George; Nat, Martin; Neu, Anna Maria; Ochs, Andreas; Ochs, Maria Catherina; Ottenot, Nicolas; Ottenot, Augusta; Paul, Caroline; Paul, Mathias; Paul, Joseph; Paul, Mary M; Paul, Mathias; Pfeffer, Caspar; Pfohl, Jacob; Pfohl, Louis; Phillips, Johann; Plan, Ludwig; Ramon, Ludwig; Ramsperger, Elizabeth; Ramsperger, Joseph; Rauch, Joseph; Reif,

Michael; Richert, Christina; Richert, Louisa; Riester, Eustache; Riester, Katherina nee Bierer; Riester, William; Ring, Bartholomew; Ring, Joseph; Rink, Maria; Ritt, Nicholas; Rohr, Paul; Rohrer, Paul; Roos, George; Roos, Jacob; Rose, Joseph; Rose, Martin; Roth, Martin; Ruble, Mary A; Rusch, Joseph; Rusch, Sebastian; Sand, Katherine; Sand, Paul; Sandrock, George; Schaaf, Joseph; Schaefer, George; Schall, Andrew; Schennon, Clara; Scherer, A; Scherf, Rosa; Scheu, Joseph; Schildknecht, Lydia; Schill, Jacob; Schillo, Katie; Schlink, M.; Schmidt, Jacob; Schmidt, John, Bartholomew; Schmit, Anthony; Schmidt, Joseph; Schne, Mathias; Schneidewind, Anton; Schnur, Peter; Schoenacker A; Schoenacker, Hubert; Schranck, Michael; Schranck, Maria Anna nee Bleiler; Schreck, Franz (Schoolmaster); Schreck, T.L., Schreiber, Michael; Schreiner, Phillip; Schue, Matthias; Schum, Frank; Schwanz, Fannie; Schwanz, Martha; Schwanz, Vincent; Schwartz, John; Schwarz, Ludwig; Seckler, Johann; Singer, Frederick; Singer, Joseph; Singer, Henry; Smith, Alexander; Smith, Bernard; Smith, Bernard Sr.; Smith, Matilda; Smith, Sophia; Sorg, George; Speiser, Anton; Speth, Anton; Speth, Cyprian; Spoeri, Francis; Spoeri, Anna; Stadel, Mary M; Staedel, Wendelin; Stang, Joseph; Steinbach, Franz; Stemler, Anna M; Stephan, Martin; Stabel, Bernard; Stabel, Frank; Staedel, Wendelin; Steffan, Frances Mary; Steffan, Frank; Steffan, Joseph; Steffan, Michael; Vingert, Anton; Vingert, Sebastian; Vogel, Balthasar; Vogt, Peter A; Wachter, Joseph; Wachter, Lorenz; Wackermann, Michael; Waechter, Jacob; Walter, Theobald; Weber, Carrie; Weber, Henry; Weber, Karl; Weber, Lawrence; Weber, Louise; Weber, Mary; Wechter, Joseph; Wechter, Lorenz; Wehrle, Anthony; Wehrle, Michael; Wehrle, Peter; Weibel, Joseph; Weigel, William J; Weiller, Joseph; Weiland, Katherine; Weisbeck, Mr.; Weiss, John; Weppner, Arnold; Weppner, Jacob; Werle, Michael, Werle, John, Werrich, Joseph; Werrich, Henry; Weter, Peter, Wex, Lorenz; Weyand, Christian, Weyand, Louise; Wieder, Peter; Wilhelm, Anthony; Wilhelm, Jacob; Willman, Anthony; Winder, John; Winter, John; Wolfer, Jacob; Yax, Anna Maria; Yax, John; Yost, Joseph; Young, Lorenz; Young, John; Young, Victoria; Zahm, George; Zahm, John; Zahm, Nicholas; Zechman, Philip; Zeller, Mary M; Zent, Philip; Zimmermann, Anton; Zimmermann, George; Zimmermann, John L.; Zimmermann, Joseph; Zink, Henry; Zinns, Frank; Zinns, Fred; Zinns, Martin; Zinns, Peter; Zoellner, Heinrich; Zoll, John; Zuck, Joseph. These names and some biographies were obtained from three sources and incorporated into the above block covering the period of 1829 to 1855. They are: op. cit. *History of the Germans of Buffalo and Erie County*, p. 38 and biography section pps. 1-121; a partial list of the original parishioners of St. Louis Parish compiled from a recollection of an old timer circa 1888, *St. Louis Bazar Chronicle*, October 26, 1888; A list of the membership in the year 1829 was translated from the old records and repeated in *St. Louis Commandery, No, 204*, Elmwood Music Hall, October 27, 1925. A list of the church membership, attending the 1879 anniversary banquet, with dates on which they joined the church and their place of origin, *St. Louis Bazaar Herald*, September 19, 1900. Because of conflicting spellings of the names of the same person in the documents cited above, the author/editor included these

different spellings in his listing in these notes as if they were possibly different persons.

3. For the details of the family genealogy of the Gitteres see: Edward Zimmermann, *The Gitteres of Lorraine*, an unpublished manuscript written in Buffalo, New York, 1997. This document came to the editors from Msgr. James M. Connelly, Tonawanda, New York, on September 18, 2001; material for Chapter Five of *Gothic Grandeur* was extracted from pps. 1-48 of that text. See also references extracted from *The Gitteres of Lorraine*: Blaul, F., *Trauemen und Schauemen vom Rhein*, Germany, 1938; Coleman, Barry, *The Catholic Church and German Americans*, Milwaukee, 1952, p.21; Salzbacher, J., *Meine Reise nach Nord-Amerika im Jahre 1842*, Wien, 1845, pps. 80, 261; Dolan J., *The Immigrant Church*, Baltimore, 1875, p.33; Albion R., *The Rise of New York Port*, New York, 1970, p.350; Shaw, R., *Erie Water West*, Lexington, Kentucky, 1966, pps. 154, 206; Harlow, A., *The Road of the Century*, New York, 1947, p.3; Hill, H.W., *Municipality of Buffalo, New York*, New York, 1923, pps.165-6, 276-7. Edward Zimmermann is Professor Emeritus of Canisius College, Buffalo, New York. He was an educator in the English Department from 1965 to 1998. Msgr. Connelly and he are cousins such that Jacob Alexander Gittere Jr. is their great grandfather. In the text the city of Rheims may be spelled Reims, which is an older spelling for this city in France. The medieval kingdom of Lorraine, known in German as Lothringen, was known as Lotharingia. Francis J. Kraft's first residence was at No. 31 East-Huron Street. His son, Frank A. Kraft had his residence at No. 53 Lexington Avenue. Rheinpfalz was also known as the Palatinate.

4. The information concerning the Miller family from Nicholas Miller Sr. to the present day of Carl Anthony Miller aka C. Eugene Miller, author/editor of this book, was taken from the following sources: Genealogical studies by Alice Grupp Miller, Joseph Kellas, and Urban Lehner. Joseph Kellas lives at 156 Rosewood Drive, West Seneca, NY, 14224; Urban Lehner lives in Grand Rapids, Michigan, and Alice Miller lives at 74 Twla Place, Tonawanda, NY; Urban Lehner, *John Miller and Anna Maria Yax*, unpublished family history, 1985; op. cit. *History of Germans in Buffalo and Erie County*, p.37; Marriage, baptismal, citizenship, and burial records of various Millers starting with Nicholas Miller Sr. After marriage, Nicholas Miller Sr. and Anna Maria Gross had fivechildren: Peter, John, Anna Marie, Nicholas Jr., and Elizabeth. John Miller, son of Nicholas Miller Sr., married Anna Maria Yax and had ten children; they were: Catherine who died one month after birth, Mary, Elizabeth, Nicholas, Barbara, Mary Magdalene, Catherine II, John, and Theresa. Mary Miller married Thaddeus Mosbach, a tinsmith and immigrant from Baden. He died in 1859. Mary had a second marriage to Albert Kaemmerle. Barbara married Joseph Ring, a carpenter and immigrant from Alsace. Elizabeth married Peter Egloff, an immigrant from Switzerland. Nicholas married Mary Ann Nye and Theresa married Henry Weber. Also, Nicholas Miller Jr. and Barbara Daveron had nine children: John, Nicholas, Margaretha, Henry, Andrew Frederick,

Mary Elizabeth, George, Caroline, and Charles Augustus; Further, John Miller, son of Nicholas Miller Jr., and Anna Mary LeJune had ten children: Johanna, Henry J., Caroline Barbara, Louise B., Charles John Joseph, William Leonard, Mary A., Joseph Francis, Laura B., and George John; Also, Charles A. Miller, son of Nicholas Miller Jr., and Catherine Grimm, daughter of George Grimm, married at St. Louis Church and had nine children: Cecilia Rosalia, Edward George, Stella Maria, Lawrence Henry, Antoinette, Cornelius Francis, Elizabeth Maria, Eugene William, and Cecilia M.; Only Lawrence Henry, who married Laura C. Jenks, Cornelius Francis, who married Genevieve Butterworth, Eugene William, who married Viola Irene Kramer, and Cecilia M., who married Warren P. Nason grew to adulthood. Cornelius and Genevieve had a son, Edward who married Alice Grupp, the genealogist. Their other children were Helen, Cornelius, Charles, and Loretta. Eugene and Viola had a son, Carl Anthony who married Marie M. Buchheit. Carl Anthony, as aka C. Eugene Miller, is the author/editor of this book. Their other children were Eugene W. Miller Jr. and John E. Miller. Eugene W. Miller Jr. married Sylvina Godfrey and they had four children: Mark, William, Susan, and Barbara. Mark, William, and Susan were baptized at St. Louis Church; Barbara was baptized at St. Bartholomew's Church on Grider Street. Returning back in history, John Miller, son of Nicholas Miller Sr. and Anna Maria Yax had Elizabeth Miller whom married Peter Egloff. They in turn had Elizabeth O. Egloff who married Andrew P. Lehner, and had seven children, one of which is Urban Edward Lehner, genealogist and biographer of John Miller, who with Anna Maria Yax had seven more children besides Elizabeth. One of those was Theresa Miller who married in 1846. Her husband was Joseph Kellas Sr. with whom she bore Joseph Kellas Jr. who is the genealogist who gave the author/editor his contributions to this book. Peter Miller and his wife Magdalene Lindermann resided at 119 Batavia Street. Nicholas Miller Jr. and his wife Barbara Daveron resided at 216 West Tupper Street. Nicholas Miller Sr. had his first residence at 487 Washington Street. John Miller and his wife Anna Maria Yax resided for thirty years at 11 Cherry Street. Both Nicholas Miller Sr. and Anna Maria Yax Miller were buried at the New St. Louis Cemetery because the trustees surreptitiously gave permission to do so to Nicholas Miller Jr. who was still a member of St. Louis Church. Nicholas Miller Jr. had related to the trustees the fact that his brothers Peter and John laid the bricks for the St. Louis Church when it was built in the 1840's. In gratitude, they overlooked the fact that during periods of interdiction Nicholas Miller Sr. and many of his family had become members first at St. Mary's Church and later at St. Michael's Church.

5. Maps of Germany, Alsace-Lorraine, Rheinpfalz, Bavaria, pointing out the location of Reifenberg, Wolmuenster, Zweibruecken, Sarreguemines, Obergailbach, Gros-Rederching, Hornbach, and Saarbruecken, were supplied by the Genealogical Society of the Church of Jesus Christ of Latter Day Saints, Salt Lake City, Utah, USA. Also see: Deutsche Arbeitsgemeinschaft Genealogischer Verbande, *Pirmasens; Sippen in Dorf und Kirchspiel*, Frankfort am Main, 1959, vol. 15. and Walter Siegl,

der Pfaelzichen Ortssippenbuecher: 1640-1740, Frankfurt am Main, Band 1. also see: Hans Bahlow, *Deutsches Naemenlexikon, Familien-und Vornamen nach Ursprung un sinn erklaert*, Frankfurt am Main, 1972. These maps and papers were the result of studies made in Germany and the United States by Walter Hauber Jr., member of the Louisville Genealogy Society, 3023 Dale Ann Drive, Louisville, Kentucky, 40220, June 1992. Edward and Margie Welker, Perrysville, Missouri made genealogical studies on the Henry Buchheit family. Henry was the brother to Francis Buchheit, who is the first ancestor of the Buchheits in St. Louis Church. Genealogical sources gathered by Louis and Carmene Buchheit, Naples, Florida, Nov. 1977. Genealogical sources gathered by Cathy Steffan and Rosemary Grupp O'Connor. The parents of Francis, Henry, and John Buchheit who came to Buffalo, NY, from Reiefenberg, Rheinpfalz, Bavaria, in 1835, were John Buchheit and Anna Maria Beilmann. Henry was born on April 17, 1812. Francis Buchheit, Henry's brother was also born at Reifenberg in 1808 of the same parents. No information was obtained concerning John, but it is known from the 1860 *Buffalo Directory* that Magdelena Buchheit, widow of Francis Buchheit, was living on German Alley, Buffalo, with a John Buchheit who was not her son by Francis. Documentation from St. Louis Church shows that Francis Buchheit married Magdelena Chretien on June 23, 1840. She was a member of the Chretien family who were early members of St. Louis Church. One of their children was Charles Francis Buchheit who married Barbara Maria Steffan at St. Louis Church on June 22, 1869. Together they had six children: Francis Michael, Charles John Michael, Frances Magdalene, George William, Rosina Maria, Louis Anthony John. About 1910, George William Buchheit married Anna M. Schifferle. Their children were Paul, Robert, and Georgiana. Robert Buchheit was ordained a priest and was known as the builder of St. Gregory the Great Church on Maple Road in the town of Amherst, NY. About 1891, Francis Michael Buchheit married Anna Winterhalt. Their children were Joseph, Rudolph, John, Francis John, Barbara, Leo Louis, Gerald, and Mary. In 1926, Frances Magdalene Buchheit married George H. Koch. They had no children. Rosina Buchheit never married. Charles John Michael Buchheit married Mary Frances Futterer on June 25, 1912 at St. Louis Church. Their children were Charles F., Edward G., Richard J., and Marie M. On June 28, 1921, Louis Anthony Buchheit married Janet Hatten at St. Louis Church. On June 11, 1949, Louis John Buchheit married Carmene Didio at St. Louis Church. Their children were Kim, Clare Suzanne, and Louis John Jr. The meaning of the name Buchheit is similar to Buchheide, does not refer to books or libraries. It is a name that is rooted in the German noun, *die Buche* symbolizing the beech tree. The suffix, *Heit* a shortened form of *Heiter*, has the connotation of serenity, clearness, brightness, happiness, cheerfulness, or gladness. Hence the serenity of the beech forest.

6. Material for this section was summarized from Jacob P. Steffan, *Michael Steffan History* unpublished but circulated throughout the Steffan family since Jacob P. Steffan's death. A copy of this document is in the St. Louis Church Archives. Pearl Place in

Buffalo today is known as St. Louis Place. John Steffan attended the seminary in Berlin, Ontario, Canada. The name of this city was changed during the conduct of World War I to Kitchner, Ontario, Canada.

7. Op. cit. *History of the Germans in Buffalo and Erie County*, biographies section p. 15. Joseph Lambert Haberstro opened his dry goods store at 153 Main Street. In 1897, Haberstro and his family lived at 858 Washington Street.

8. Information concerning the Riester family was obtained from the genealogical collection of Michael Riester, co-editor of this book. See: Michael Riester, *A Short History of the Riester Family*, unpublished document in circulation during lectures on the History of St. Louis Church, Buffalo, NY, 1995. Also see: T*he Voyage to America*, a diary kept by William Riester who sailed to America from Le Havre, France on the *Diademe* October 1, 1849, a copy is in the Archives at St. Louis Church. The Schranck mansion was located at 1008 Main Street. Michael Schranck had one son, Michael, who in turn had only one son, another Michael, who hanged himself in the attic of the mansion. Today, Michael Riester, parishioner, member of the parish council, and historian of St. Louis Church is a direct descendant of Eustache Riester through his son William Sr.

9. A product of the Genealogical studies of Rosemary Grupp O'Connor, 1981. Also see: *The Buffalo News*, September 27, 1982 for Arthur L. Grupp and Marie Grupp being honored by the Church along with others invested as Knights and Ladies of the Equestrian Order of the Holy Sepulchre. Arthur L. Grupp memorial see: *Canisius College Chronicle*, October 1984. For a description of the Paper Distributing Firm owned by Arthur Grupp in his obituary see: *The Buffalo News*, July 29, 1984. For Marie Grupp as a member of Canisius College's Board of Regents see: *The Buffalo News*, Nov. 8, 1985. For Marie Faber Grupp as Distinguished Alumna of 1995 see: *Nardin Today*, Winter 1995, p.7. Marie Faber Grupp obituary see: *The Buffalo News*, February 25, 1996. "Marie A. Grupp, Canisius College Benefactor," see: *The Buffalo News*, Feb. 25, 1996. For other information concerning the original Grupp or Krupp family in Buffalo see the St. Louis Church Records of Baptisms, First Communions, Marriages, and Deaths. Before coming to America the Grupp name in Europe was spelled Krupp. Today Rosemary O'Connor and Alice Miller, both nee Grupp, trace their ancestry back through Edward Grupp. Alice Grupp married Edward Miller who traced his ancestry back through his father, Cornelius Miller to Nicholas Miller Jr. Anna Maria Friedmann Grupp was buried from St. Boniface Church because the Grupp family had again changed their affiliation after it was founded by Timon in 1849. Like several other families who had moved into the district around the church, a district known as the Fruitbelt, the Grupp family took up residence there in 1852.

10. Gerd Doerr, *Baden-Wuerttemberg*, Baden-Wuerttembergische Bank, Hamburg, 1995, Maps and Articles on towns, cities, villages, and environment, p.200. Indexed for names of places and events. Also see: op. cit. *Der Turner Soldat*, pps. 22-30.

11. The entire story of the Hausle family is contained in Leo H. Hausle, *Family Record Book of the Hausle Family: Biographical Sketches*, unpublished, Buffalo, NY, 1905. the Section "Mathias Hausle and his Family." A copy of this document is in the St. Louis Church Archives. Millard Fillmore was born in the Finger Lakes region of New York State in 1800. In 1830 he moved his law practice to Buffalo and took up residence at 180 Franklin Street. As a member of the Whig Party he was elected Vice President when Zachary Taylor was elected President of the United States in 1848. Taylor served for one year from 1849 until his untimely death in July 1850. Millard Fillmore assumed the presidency. He was not re-elected. The Whig Party fell apart; Fillmore did not join the Republican Party. In 1856 as a member of the American Party, known as the Know-Nothing Party, he ran for the presidency but lost. James Buchanan was elected president.

12. Glenn R. Atwell, ed., *The Batt Genealogy: A Record of the Descendants of Franz Joseph Batt Sr. and Barbara Weber and of Anthony Batt and Beatrice Glath, of Alsace and America*, published by the Batt Family Association of Alsace and America Inc., Buffalo, NY, 1976, Maps, and pps. 2-6. At the site of the chapel dedicated to Our Lady Help of Christians, Batt also built a frame schoolhouse, which was completed by July 10, 1853, at which time Father R. Follenius laid the cornerstone.

13. For a short history of the Irish in Buffalo see: op. cit. *High Hopes*, pps. 78-87, 93, 96-7. For Irish Catholicism on the Western Frontier and names of priests giving service in Western New York see: op. cit. *History of the Catholic Church in Western New York*, pps.114-127 and op. cit. *Celebrating God's Life in Us*, p.18. For early marriage records at St. Louis Church; 1829-1839 see: *Marriages, Book I*. It is preserved in the archives of St. Louis Church. These records were researched, compiled, and given to the author/editor by Christopher Andrle. The following is a list of Irish marriages at St. Louis Church. During Mertz's pastorship: William Michel and Margareta Karell; David Lyons and Philomena Conner; Edward Larenz and Helena Denys; Joannes William Killian and Maria Walsch; James Cunningham and Maria O'Rork; Philip Roger McMahon and Anna Sweeney; William Morrison and Eleanora Daley; Stephen Edmond and Catherine Flynn; Thomas Brady and Helena Flynn; Magnus Humbert and Maria Agnes Griffin; Jacob Sullivan and Anna Walsh; Andreas Finity and Maria Faden; Michael Carroll and Roas McGuire; Philip Michael Swift and Maria Shanehy; Owen McMeagen and Jean McNulty; Patrick Loughlin and Julia Morren; Patrick Nagel and Marianna McManus; Patrick Kelly and Margreta McCanna; Joannes Shey and Helena McManon; Christopher O'Harrison and Maria Regen; Patrick Galgan and Elizabeth Lenard; Michael Green and Anna O'Rourke; Patrick O'Connell and Anna McDaniel; Thomas McKane and Anna Jacob; Joannes McDorrmer and Maria Jacob; Jacob Comisky and Catherine Carrol; Patrick Sommers and Brigita O'Konner;

William Michel and Rosa Canday; Patrick McGloclyn and Maria Meesi; Joannes McKandry and Barbara Mader; Bernard McDonnel and Anna Flagnelly; Wilhelm Bengg and Anna Owens; Michael Cassedy and Sara McCanly; Bernard McGelan and Margreta Bredsche; Alexander McKeys and Rosanna Meesi; Patrick Scherdon and Brigitta Nealy; Joannes Kelly and Mary McCord; Philip Reilly and Brigitta McGinnis; Joannes Finigan and Catherine Crasly; Thomas Forrester and Brigitta Schmith; Patrick Trinner and Anna Weith; Jeremiah Seoul and Margreta Reagan; Dyonis Marohny and Anna Scherrer; Cornelius McGerty and Helena McGaven; Edward Wueth and Maria McFaden; Joannes Danahy and Anna Barens; Patrick Bourne and Brigitta O'Neil; Patrick Courayn and Margreta Megan; Joannes Connorton and Joanna Brenner; Joannes Selon and Margreta Malony; Dionis Denny Dokery and Maria Hand; Henry Morey and Annabel Nancy Kelly; Joannes Claer and Brigitta Kelly; George McKany and Joanna Haven; Samuel Bartholomew Beeston and Maria Kerey; Patrick McFile and Maria McGlochele; Jacob Grin and Maria McLeon; Joannes Cunningham and Maria McManus; Michael McCaffrey and Marianna McCornege; Patrick Sweyne and Annavel Nazy Regen; William Walsch and Maria Kechery; Bartholemew O'Grady and Rosanna McGinnis; Arthur Delany and Maria O'Neil; Michael Gogu and Anna Conly; Bernard Sweyne and Isabella Jasnsen; Patrick McNulty and Mary Dubin; Cornelius Murphy and Jean Butler; Cornelius McHarty and Maria Maginnis; Michael McWhire and Brigitta Hartney; Joannes Kenny and Judith Commanse. During Pax's pastorship: Dionis McKefrey and Alciano Swiny; Patrick Meloiser and Maria Mury; Martin Gallagher and Gratia Baruk; Thomas Lemon and Alciano Scaly; Joannes Carter and Brigitta Kalliser; Carnelius McKardy and Joanna Renn; Laurent Schmith and Margaretha Flynn; Jacob Cunningham and Maria Feagon; Peter Dagerty and Rosin Carigan; Peter Matter and Margaret McKiny; Jacob Dams and Maria Bradley.

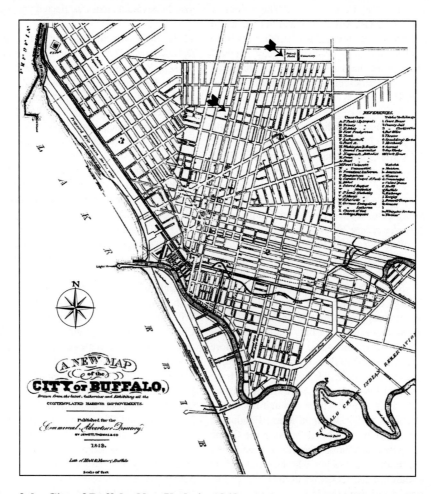

Map of the City of Buffalo, New York, in 1849, which was published by Jewett Thomas and Company for *Advertisers Directory*. Arrows point to St. Louis Church which was consecrated in 1847, located on Main Street opposite Goodell Street, and the new St. Louis Cemetery, located adjacent to North Street, north of the boundary line of the city.

CHAPTER SIX

A Rare Tradition in American Catholicism

In 1829, the year that Louis Le Couteulx deeded the property for the first Catholic Church in Buffalo to Bishop Dubois, the first Provincial Council in the United States, was convened. Ambrose Marechal, Archbishop of Baltimore, had died, and James Whitefield, who had replaced him as archbishop, held the Council at his home in Baltimore. Besides himself, six other bishops were present: William Du Bourg, New Orleans, Louisiana; Michael Portier, Mobile, Alabama; Joseph Rosati, St. Louis, Missouri; John England, Charleston, South Carolina; Benedict Flaget, Bardstown, Kentucky; and John Dubois, New York City, New York. Henry Conwell, Bishop of Philadelphia, Pennsylvania, had also been invited; but, in a letter to Whitefield, claimed that he was indisposed. Although not present at the opening of the meeting, his views were represented by Father William Matthews. Before the Council had adjourned, however, Conwell unexpectedly showed up to the surprise of all present. Besides the bishops, three lay lawyers were also present, one of which was Roger B. Taney who later became a Chief Justice of the Supreme Court of the United States. They were experts in the field of incorporation law. One important topic on the Council's agenda was corporate trusteeism.

The evils of trusteeism as defined by the hierarchy had spread rapidly in the United States following the War of Independence. When Dubois became bishop of the Diocese of New York in 1826, he found abuses of lay control in the parishes widespread. In New York, among the Irish, there were problems at St. Peter's, St. Patrick's Cathedral, and at Christ's Church. There was also a plague of disruption among the continental lay immigrants controlling activities at St. John's Church in Utica. Churches in New England were not immune, nor were they in Philadelphia, Pennsylvania, Charleston, South Carolina, Norfolk and Richmond, Virginia, and in many other parts of the country where the bishops were practicing ecclesiastical medicine in minor and major trouble spots. In order for the clerics to achieve the upper hand, a consultation on remedies and a concerted application of them was needed. The hierarchy refused to accept any lay leadership and the governance of the churches was to be by monarchy not democracy.

The First Council at Baltimore provided opportunity for that consultation and putting forth decrees. Bishops were urged to sponsor no church whose deed was not in their own hands, there would be no *jus nominandi* in the province, donations of the faithful should not establish title to such, and bishops were urged to use canonical penalties to bring errant trustees to terms. Four subsequent Provincial Councils, ending with the last in 1849, supplemented and modified these regulations. In that one, the possibility of lay ownership of land upon which churches were built was given extensive consideration and denounced. It was specifically decreed, "That all churches and all ecclesiastical property which had been acquired by donations or the offerings of the faithful, for religious or charitable use, belonged to the bishop of the diocese, unless it had belonged to some order of monks or religious congregation of priests. And henceforth it was the province of the bishops to acquire the title of all church property or in other ways secure control of the temporalities."

Eighteen years had passed since Le Couteulx had made his donation of land to Dubois. On December 21, 1847, being free of debt, St. Louis Church, Buffalo, the largest Roman Catholic Church in America, was consecrated by Bishop Timon, the first bishop of the newly formed diocese created by Pope Pius IX on April 23, 1847. It not only consisted of parishes in Buffalo but also extended over twenty counties of Western New York. The decision to subdivide the diocese of New York was first proposed to Rome by Hughes in May 1846. In the following year not only Western New York was the beneficiary of that proposal but so also was Albany for which John McCloskey was consecrated bishop. He was born in 1810, son of Irish immigrant parents. He attended Mount St. Mary's Seminary, Emmitsburg, Maryland, as a student of Dubois. He was ordained in 1834, studied in Rome, and assigned a ministry in New York City where he became coadjutor bishop to Hughes in 1844. After serving as bishop of Albany he replaced the deceased Hughes in 1864. He completed the construction of St. Patrick's Cathedral on Fifth Avenue and dedicated it in 1879. He became the first United States Cardinal in 1875.

When John Timon became bishop of Buffalo, he, an Irishman barely five feet tall, was a member of the Congregation of the Missions, known as Lazarists or Vincentians. He was born in Pennsylvania, one in a family of ten children. As he grew to maturity, his family moved to Baltimore, Maryland, then to Louisville, Kentucky, and finally settled in St. Louis, Missouri. At the age of twenty-six, he entered St. Mary's of Barrens Seminary and was ordained in 1825. He had a variety of ecclesiastical duties: seminary professor, circuit priest and missionary, and a superior performing canonical visitations of residencies of the Vincentian Order. He traveled to New Orleans, through

Texas, and circuited missions in Kentucky, Indiana, Illinois, Arkansas, and Mississippi. In 1832 he was nominated coadjutor bishop of St. Louis, but he declined the appointment. When the Republic of Texas was separated from the Mexican diocese of Monterey in 1840, he became its Prefect Apostolic.

He began his residency as Bishop of Buffalo in October 1847; the following year, he counted a Catholic population of forty-six thousand being attended to by sixteen priests assigned to an equal number of churches. Added to the nine previously described were: Sacred Heart, Angola; St. Mary, East Arcade; Our Lady Help of Christians, East Bennington; Sts. Peter and Paul, Hamburg; St. Mary of the Cataract, Niagara Falls; Good Shepherd, Pendleton; St. Cecilia, Sheldon; and St. Mary, Swormville. He invited the Sisters of Charity to come to Buffalo where they began an asylum for orphaned girls and in 1848 opened the first hospital in the city built on the corner of Virginia Street and Pearl Place. In 1849, he opened St. Joseph's Boys Asylum in Lancaster, brought the Brothers of the Christian Schools to teach at St. Joseph's College for boys, and had the Jesuits open Canisus High School and College while establishing St. Michael's Church on Washington Street. Finally the area was blessed with the labor and educational skills of the Sisters of St. Joseph, Daughters of the Heart of Mary, and the Grey Nuns. He built St. Joseph's Cathedral on Franklin Street. Patrick C. Keeley, an Irish architect, designed its gothic motif. Pope Pius IX made St. Joseph the patron saint of Timon's diocese. Timon died on April 16, 1867 and was buried within the cathedral that he built.

After his installation as bishop in New York City, Timon was eager to assume his ministerial duties in Buffalo. He arrived in the city accompanied by Bishops Hughes, Walsh, and McCloskey. They proceeded directly to the Mother Church, St. Louis. The *Buffalo Daily Courier* described their approach, "The carriage in which rode the bishop was drawn by four white chargers, and was the most conspicuous object in the procession. At a signal made for that purpose, the illuminated human mass moved on, and as it advanced up Main Street towards St. Louis Church beneath a canopy of blazing light, it produced an indescribably beautiful effect. It far surpassed our expectations, and reflected honor upon the distinguished individuals who were the occasion of it." Nearly twelve thousand greeted Timon on that day and took part in the procession. Next day he appointed the pastor of St. Louis Church, Francis Guth, as Vicar General of Germans in the diocese. On the following Sunday, Timon said a Pontifical High Mass at St. Louis Church, at which Hughes preached the sermon. At Vespers with the three bishops presiding and a massive number of people forming the congregation, Guth preached a sermon in both French and German. Finally, Timon consecrated the church and confirmed two hundred and twenty-seven persons.

After the ceremonies were completed, he took up residence with Guth and interrelated with the trustees who were courteous to him. That evening, however, while Guth and Timon were enjoying their repast, a message arrived from the trustees encouraging the bishop to find other lodgings. They did not like his presence at the rectory even though he had been willing to pay for the privilege of residing there. Timon told Guth, in a tone of firmness, that he should make it very clear to the trustees that the bishop had no intention of making St. Louis Church his permanent residence. They were to be assured that his greatest desire was to go and labor at St. Patrick's with his beloved flock, the Irish, who were in much greater need of his assistance than the Germans. Obviously he would be better at expressing himself to them in English than having his words interpreted in German at St. Louis Church. In speaking this way, he treated what he assumed as arrogance from the trustees with an apparent charity and goodwill. He wished to convey that he, unlike Hughes, was marked by a rare quality of diplomacy coupled with patience.

Hughes' presence at the installation of Timon had stirred the trustees' animosity toward him. Just the mention of his name sent these normally rational men into acrimonious rage. The sight and sounds of Hughes giving the sermon at the Pontifical High Mass, in English, recreated in them the vision of his claim to *Verwaltung* which had been hot branded into their brains. They may have had to apologize to him, but they had no intention of administering their church according to any dictums of his pastoral letter. Their only regret was that seventeen months of pain could have been avoided if they had taken Pax's advice and remained silent in December of 1842. Towering anger, however, had made these men bullheaded, obstinate, dogged, stubborn, and mulish. As pertinacious leaders they had a strong influence over the German psyche which honored to a fault the virtue of docility. Amongst Germans, leaders led and followers followed. Somehow, in temporal affairs, the trustees' authority rang more true in the minds of the members of the congregation than did Timon's ecclesiastical prowess. They accepted the trustees as their shepherds; they did not wish to be mere lambs of the bishop.

It was clear as early as January 1, 1848, that there would be a confrontation between the trustees and Timon over their concept of *Verwaltung*. Ecclesiastical ears were shut to their arguments in the past and so would they be again. They accepted canon law as superior to civil law on topics of morals and doctrine, but they believed that in certain matters, which were purely disciplinary, that civil law might prevail, and canon law be suspended. Such a case was embedded in the history of ownership of the property upon which St. Louis Church was built. Their argument was very clear to themselves. On January 1, 1829, Louis Le Couteulx and his wife executed a deed of the site of St. Louis Church to Bishop John Dubois and his successors forever. The deed was given "In Trust" for the purpose of a future church being erected on the premises; it was not an absolute conveyance.

On December 2, 1838, seven persons, constituting the Board of Trustees of St. Louis Church, incorporated according to the laws of the State of New York. Having done so, the trustees became the sole owners of the deed, and were empowered to take into their possession and custody all the temporalities belonging to the church, congregation, and society. Under their corporate name and title, they could sue in all courts of law, recover all debts, and have ownership of all buildings, burying places, and parsonages with their appurtenances. All of this they could claim just as if Le Couteulx, who, before giving the deed to Dubois had been a real estate operative in Buffalo for twenty-five years, had originally vested the right or title in them. He was well aware of the New York State Incorporation Law of 1813 for Religious Societies. Even though his son, Alphonse, claimed that this was not his father's will, the trustees considered it unreasonable to believe that a successful entrepreneur of real estate would have imagined otherwise. Timon's ears were as closed to the trustees' argument as were Hughes'. He felt bound by the ecclesiastical ordinance of Baltimore and insisted on control of the temporalities of St. Louis Church. According to him the trustees were to either dissolve their organization leaving the title in his hands or allow him, personally or through his appointees, to control the temporalities.

Determined to break the trustees' influence on the congregation, Timon arranged for a mission to be given at the church. Five Jesuits, Lucas Caveng, Bernard Fritsch, Joseph Fruzzini, William Kettner, and Rupert Ebner came to Buffalo from Canada to conduct a mission, an evangelical technique of conversion and renewal. It was similar to a Protestant revival whereby through a regular schedule of sermons, the preachers sought to brainwash their listeners, particularly the trustees. Unbeknown to the trustees, however, if it would succeed in its intended purpose, Timon was ready to entrust the parish to the Society of Jesus; and, as such, it would assume title and directorship of all the temporalities by his command based upon his understanding of canon law. The mission began in April 1848; it ended in failure. Caveng returned to Canada but the four other Jesuits moved to Williamsville where they opened a residence adjacent to Sts. Peter and Paul Church. Fritsch was assigned the pastorship at Good Shepherd Church in Pendleton and the others carried out mission work in the towns and villages of Niagara County.

The trustees, however, retained their temporal prowess at St. Louis Church with no further incident until the autumn of that year. Because the City of Buffalo was growing, the Common Council proposed to make an extension of its boundaries and lengthen certain streets. Since one such street was proposed to run through the property of St. Louis Church, the trustees planned to block it. They requested permission from the bishop to enlarge the church in such a way that it would be impossible for a street to cut through its property. They probably would not have bothered asking him except that they wanted to impress him with their graciousness to fulfill a rule of Hughes' pastoral letter which required that they incur no debt greater than $100 without the consent of the bishop. Timon refused their request saying that it would spoil the church that already was the largest in the United States. He did, however, suggest that they consider using the required funds to build a tower and construct a rectory on the property.

Having given the trustees his suggestion, Timon departed the city for a month-long visitation of rural parishes in his diocese. During his absence and without revealing the objections of the bishop, they obtained permission from Guth to begin the construction on the addition that the bishop did not approve. Timon returned to Buffalo on April 19, 1848. William Le Couteulx causally and unexpectedly met him on the street and informed him of the progress that had been made at St. Louis Church in his absence. "How large will the rectory be?" questioned the bishop. "There is no rectory," Le Couteulx, with an innocent smile, responded, "The church itself is taking on greater proportions with the pastor's permission." The bishop was infuriated and shouted, "Those trustees have beguiled their pastor; those plans were never approved by me." Timon told Le Couteulx to call a meeting of the pastor and the trustees; their bishop would be present. At the meeting he remonstrated with both the pastor and the trustees; he condemned the action of proceeding with the unauthorized construction, but sympathized with Guth who had mistakenly sanctioned the effort. The trustees acknowledged their irresponsibility and promised to end the work. How could it end however? It was impossible to dismantle walls, which had already reached a height of two to three feet above the ground. Timon had no choice but to ignore its completion. He told Guth to allow the trustees to carry on as they wished although in no way would he sanction the outcome or the method by which he and Guth were deceived.

In 1850, Timon traveled to Europe. While he was away the estranged relations between the French and German elements at St. Louis deteriorated. Alphonse Le Couteulx took up the banner on the side of the French. He told the congregation that the trustees had arrogated undo power to themselves; an action commenced with incorporation in 1838. He explained how gradually more Germans arrived and the French fell into a minority. Only if the invested interests of the congregation were in the hands of the authority of the bishop and the pastor would the French have proper representation. He tried hard to impress the German element of the congregation that it was the will of his father that the church remain French. "Look at your trustees," he said, "Since my father's death, they have determined to get possession of the property and chase away the French." One person listened intently to his plea given with profound elocution. He was Guth, the pastor, who decried the cleavage that had developed in the church because of language. He said, "Are we not Frenchmen, as Louis Le Couteulx perceived, even though we speak the German tongue?" The German element hissed and booed; Guth grew angry. In May, he left St. Louis Church, taking with him the French of the congregation. They retired to the corner of Washington and Clinton Streets where they established St. Pierre's French Church. Many years later the congregation increased in size, and it constructed a most beautiful church at the corner of Main and Best Streets; it was named Our Lady of Lourdes. With Guth's departure, Father Joseph Raffeiner assumed the pastorship at St. Louis Church.

With the French gone, the trustees became bolder. The next skirmish between the bishop and trustees developed over a situation that erupted at the school. Besides their duties at the hospital, Timon had asked the Sisters of Charity to teach classes at St. Louis Church. As with all religious Orders, one condition for assuming any responsibility of teaching or other charitable activity was the requirement that the religious would do so only if they had the freedom to operate according to their tradition. Although the bishop approved of this *laissez faire* policy, he failed to inform the trustees who were not aware of it or its meaning. Immediately they ran into conflict with the Sisters because their policies for the school did not agree with those of the Sisters. Therefore they asked them to retire from the school, and they replaced them with lay teachers. It was this incident, which prompted the trustees, on August 3, 1850, to propose to the bishop a set of rules, and regulations by which both he and the trustees could abide by.

According to these proposed rules, the trustees were to have no input in regard to spiritual matters without the permission and consent of the bishop; they were to truly and faithfully observe and fulfill his command in that regard. They proposed to administer the temporal affairs of the church, however, under the counsel and advice of their bishop, and to do so in a manner befitting themselves as the children of God.

They acknowledged that the bishop and the pastor are accountable to God as guardians of their flocks; and, as such, have the right to superintend the school attached to the church. They pledged their best to aid the clergy for the success of the school and the education of the youth. They, however, under the direction of the bishop, would select the teachers, and no teacher would be appointed without the sanction of the bishop or pastor. At all times the pastor would preside over the deliberations of the trustees and he would have his vote. They would also not expend anything over $100 on any improvements without the knowledge and consent of the bishop. They also pledged not to assist in the election of any person as a trustee who was known to be of immoral or unchristian character. Nicholas Ottenot, Joseph Haberstro, John Chretien, Jacob Wilhelm, and George Zimmermann drew up these proposals.

Although through these overtures it appeared that the trustees sought peace and accord with their bishop, information, which filtered out to the local press, painted a different picture. The German press reported a trustee victory over Timon concerning the completion of the church's addition and the dismissal of the Sisters of Charity. Timon took no action against the trustees because of the comments in the press, but he did not ignore them in his mind. He waited until February 1851. Once again he called upon the Jesuits to run a mission at St. Louis Church. The objective was the same as it had been in 1848. Although the Jesuits preached with greater fervor than they did before, they still failed in reaching the goal most desired by the bishop. The trustees seemed more hardened in their hearts, but Timon began to sense small cracks in the fidelity of many members of the congregation to their leadership. He was encouraged and composed a letter that was read from the pulpit, by Raffeiner, on Easter Sunday.

It stated, "Having long borne with patience from the trustees' acts of usurped authority which have plunged your church in debt, once the most flourishing congregation in my diocese, to gradually fall away, so that whilst St. Mary's Church has six or seven hundred children in the parish school, you have but a handful; and under incessant insinuations that your bishop wants to do now this, now that, the spirit of holy distrust and murmuring has entered the fold, and the piety of many has grown cold; it becomes our duty to remedy so sad a state of things. Many of you have had to assume the payment of a debt for a needless addition to this church; it was begun without my permission, and against the laws of the Roman Catholic Church and the diocese. I asked the Jesuits to take the administration of the church; they not only replied in the affirmative, but also said that they would assume the debt. They said that they would finance and build a school, yet they were rejected; their mission fell on deaf ears and hardened hearts. Your trustees should function no longer because we know not what presses those gentlemen to meddle with the affairs of God's house; the priest or bishop never thinks of meddling with the affairs of your houses, or with the affairs of houses consecrated to civic or political use. Bishop and priest leave the care of these houses to men of the world, but they are bound to care for God's house. We declare that the so-called trustees have no right in this church. The property is vested in us for our use. If they wish to be trustees, let them find a church in which to exercise their functions, but they will never have a priest who will minister in it." Then by ecclesiastical decree, Timon denounced the trustees, ousted them, and appointed Lucas Caveng of the Society of Jesus as pastor.

The bishop's Easter letter read by Raffeiner succeeded in causing the crack between the trustees and the members of the congregation to widen. It was becoming clear to the bishop that relatively few men were instigating the difficulties at the church. He saw William Le Couteulx as head of the opposition party. Again the bishop approached the congregation. He tried to make clear his true motivations in his condemnations of the trustees. He denied that he wanted to take the church away from the Germans and give it to the Irish; he did not want the revenues from the church; he did not wish to take away the freedom which they enjoyed as American citizens; he wanted the church to be debt free, and he sought only to discipline those who belonged to the opposition party.

The congregation listened, but seemed strangled by the ousted trustees who lost no time in drawing up a list of resolutions to unite the congregation behind them and slander their bishop. They praised their own indefatigable zeal in doing good, they accused Timon of lying when he said he would not give the parish to the Irish, and they contended that his actions were not only in opposition to the Laws of the State, but that they would produce very pernicious fodder to those opposed to the Holy Roman Catholic Religion in the Union. They then elaborated upon the bishop's sneakiness in deliberately putting a lay teacher out of his job for no good reason, replacing him by the Sisters of Charity who wanted to change school policy, and have the Jesuits usurp the control of their church for their own financial aggrandizement. They insisted that the congregation's troubles were not because of the trustees' leadership but because of the bishop's petty interference. Caveng was infuriated; and, on Sunday, May 4, 1851, he read a response of the bishop to these accusations. In it the bishop called for solidarity behind the clergy. Caveng added his own words, requesting a show of force by the majority. Only a few in the pews showed opposition; the few that did left the assembly. Not long after this confrontation Caveng received threats and was subjected to harassment. He responded by withdrawing from the church bearing the Blessed Sacrament. The tabernacle door was left open; God no longer dwelt within the walls of St. Louis Church. A deep sadness fell over the parish.

In the absence of Caveng, the trustees continued to function, holding quasi-religious services in the church. During this time no one in the congregation dared to contact the bishop against the will of the trustees. Faced with no other alternative, Timon sent a letter to the congregation on June 14, 1851, announcing that the church had been placed under interdict. He admonished, "No child of the church can without grievous sin, assist at any rites or prayers, whilst this sad state of things continues. May God save our beloved in Christ from awful punishment, such as He inflicted in times past on those who, in their worldly wisdom, rebelled against Moses and Aaron." From that day forward Protestants, Catholics, politicans, legislators, and editors within the entire city were aware of the bishop's action. The *Buffalo Morning Express* wrote," This church, the oldest of that persuasion in our city, and the only one perhaps incorporated according to the laws of this state, is involved in serious difficulties with Bishop Timon. We understand in consequence of a refusal to abandon to him their church property, and the administration of their temporal affairs, the hierarchy continues to deprive the congregation of their liberties; and, announces to all Catholic Churches in the diocese, an excommunication against the church and its congregation." On June 24, 1851, the same newspaper made a correction pointing out that the bishop had not excommunicated anyone, but rather warned Catholics not to participate in the unofficial services being held in the church during the absence of a priest.

At this point in the controversy, the two Le Couteulx brothers, William and Alphonse, took center stage, each one opposing the other. William submitted his views on the church to the *Buffalo Morning Express*; he traced the difficulties at St. Louis Church from the trustees' point of view, reiterated that any remarks made by Caveng were violently taxed with falsehoods, and described the severity endured by the congregation since the arrival of Timon to the city. He lambasted the bishop for sending Jesuits to the parish to correct trumped-up and petty evils of no consequence, for making one of them the pastor, for claiming his right of trust as if given by Louis Le Couteulx, for undermining the peace of our people, for sowing discord among them, and for dismissing the trustees and naming others without the election of the people. By the time his views were published a spontaneous meeting of the congregation had taken place, respectful but firm resolutions were adopted and transmitted to the bishop, maintenance of elected trustees was assured, and those appointed by the bishop were dislodged. At that moment open warfare succeeded debate. After reviewing the bishop's warning that worship was tantamount to excommunication, William replied, "I say to you that several attempts have been made with Bishop Timon to bring him to better feelings towards our congregation, but in vain. 'Submit to your bishop' was the only answer that could be obtained. Myself for one, took care to explain to him that our act of incorporation being a closed one, it required the unanimity of the congregation to alter it, and that my firm belief was that it could never take place."

By this time, the trustees were absolutely blinded to the intentions of the bishop; any action he could take would be, in their eyes, a threat to their authority in administrating the property and finances of the church. They only saw, as William did, that their incorporation in 1838 fulfilled the wishes of Louis Le Couteulx and gave them sole ownership over the property and the appurtenances thereon. Seeing the obstinacy of the trustees, Alphonse stepped forward. He said, "My father had often spoke to me of his desire to have marguilliers such as we had in France. Unlike these counselors, however, he never did wish that trustees by election should be invested with a power thus repugnant to the Holy Roman Catholic Church, an institution for which he had the greatest respect. If such an intention had been manifested to him, he would have opposed it with all his might. He knew that the congregation at St. Louis Church was composed of both French and Germans; a situation that necessitated administrative power in the hands of the bishop so as to maintain the just rights of all. It was evident that this was the reason my father made the donation of the property to Bishop Dubois and his successors. The

trustees knew, as well as I did, that this was the will of my father. Note that it was only after his death that they laid claim to the property and its administration." Boldly, Alphonse filed a second deed to the church property. In doing so he confirmed what he thought were the wishes of his father by making Timon the beneficiary of his deed. It was a *beau geste*; little did he realize that his deed was legally invalid. [1]

The report of interdiction spread not only through Buffalo but was heard in New York City, and found its way across the Atlantic Ocean even to the villages of France. On September 4, 1851, Alexander Pax, a curé at Diebling, a town in the Moselle area of France, wrote to Bishop Timon. Pax said, "Deign to permit a priest, who for eight years was a missionary in Buffalo, and under whom St. Louis Church was built, to express to you his sentiments of condolence for the grief which that church causes to your paternal heart. Permit me also to compliment you upon the wise firmness and apostolic zeal with which you defend the rights of the church from the usurpation of the trustees. I learned with extreme sorrow the excesses to which arrogant impiety impelled those trustees and their adherents. And also with joy, I read the letter by which you interdicted that profaned church. This measure was necessary in order to terminate usurpation and schismatic pride. I pray to God that He would deign to open the eyes of those senseless men, and call them from their wanderings to sincere repentance." Although Timon was overjoyed with Pax's letter and others expressing similar refrains, he saw no peaceful way to bring the dissidents to their knees. The trustees remained resolute in their opposition to him and continued to enjoy the backing of a large portion of the congregation. Having no priest, they and the congregation continued to meet for prayers on a regular basis. Under the direction of Mr. Leininger, the school remained in operation. The trustees continued to hold business meetings and administrate the finances; activities which by civil law they were not only allowed to do, but obligated to do by the charter of incorporation.

Timon, however, had decided on a more war-like approach to the situation that seemed stagnated. In an attempt to break the rebellious spirit of the trustees, he adopted the strong measures taken by Hughes, his predecessor, during the troubled times of 1843-44. He set out on a course of action that would destroy the trustees' base of support; he decided to found new Catholic parishes in the neighborhood of St. Louis Church, whose dissidents, wishing to remain Catholic, would be invited. He predicted that within the walls of St. Louis Church would only remain Protestants by choice. He felt sure that his plan would work because a significant number of pious families had left with Guth to organize St. Pierre's Parish. After Caveng left St. Louis Church nineteen families went with him and attended services that he conducted in the basement of St. Pierre's Church. Finally, Timon's deathblow to the trustees of St. Louis Church came when, under his insistence, the Jesuits built St. Michael's Church on Washington Street almost in the shadow of St. Louis Church for the sole purpose of attracting German patrons. On a piece of property known as the Squier estate they erected a small frame building in the latter half of 1851, and German families, mainly ex-parishioners of St. Louis Church, first attended Mass in it on January 1, 1852.

The interdict period at St. Louis Church is best described as one of impenetrable darkness and skepticism. The trustees attempted to dramatize the plight of the congregation in a resolution drawn up on November 7, 1852. Ten months had passed since the bloodletting of their congregation had made a transfusion into St. Michael's Church. They resolved to fly a black flag in front of the church to let all passersby know of their sorrow because they could not have the consolations of their sacred faith. They wanted all to consider them as the victims of an ecclesiastical plot. When the black infamous emblem deteriorated in the high winds of winter, they proposed a new flag to meet the new life of spring and the Easter season. It was white and carried the inscription *Where is our*

Shepherd? No sound, however, came forth from the pontiff of the cathedral on Franklin Street. Prior to the meeting that proposed the black flag, William Le Couteulx had sailed for Europe. He wanted to plead the trustees' case in the highest ecclesiastical court, Rome! On November 15, 1852, armed with a petition, he met with his holiness, Pope Pius IX. It was modeled after the one submitted to the papal nuncio in Paris in 1843.

His meeting failed to have the interdict on St. Louis Church lifted, but it did not go unnoticed. On December 14, 1852, Timon received a letter from the Sacred Congregation for the Propagation of the Faith informing him of the trustees' petition and provided sound advice as to how the bishop could proceed to rectify the situation. He was told that this controversy should not lie hidden; but for, the present, he should stand firm until it would be possible for some more positive directive to be handed down. Timon was assured that Rome would initiate diplomacy; and, while he was to wait, he was to know that he was being prayed for so that he could be kept longsuffering and unharmed. On June 30, 1853, the papal nuncio, Archbishop Gaetano Bedini, arrived in New York City and was greeted by Bishop Hughes. Would Timon's problems with St. Louis Church be on Bedini's schedule? [2]

Hughes had first met Bedini in Vienna in 1839, when Bedini was a fledgling monsignor and Hughes a newly consecrated bishop seeking funds in Europe for construction of colleges in America. Upon arriving, Bedini told Hughes that he had come as an unofficial representative of the Vatican who was assigned to handle temporal affairs with the government of the republic and to act as an ecclesiastical liaison between the Pope and the bishops. When this news was made public the question was asked, "If this were his reason for his visit, why was he first, before arriving in the United States, visiting Rio de Janeiro, where he was made nuncio to Brazil?" He replied that he had come to America to deliver special greetings from the Pope to President

Franklin Pierce and that he was to check on the internal affairs of the missionary Catholic Church. Not all of the country's hierarchy was convinced of the innocence of his claim. In Boston, Archbishop Peter Kenrick said, "His visit is one thing in appearance and another in effect." From the start it had never been made clear either to the ecclesiastical or the civil arm whether he was a visiting prelate or the emissary of a foreign nation. Italy at this time was a very divided nation. Sardinia was in the extreme north with Lombardy and Venetia. South of these states on the west coast of the peninsula was Tuscany and the duchies of Parma, Modena, and Lucca. In the far south covering one-half of Italy was Naples also known as the two Sicilies. Cutting through the center of the peninsula, separating the north and the south kingdoms were the Papal States, hereditary temporal possessions of the Roman See. Was Bedini, as a civil servant, representing the Pope, the ruler of these states or was he the ecclesiastic representing the Pope as the head of the missionary church in the United States?

Upon his arrival, Bedini was forty-seven years old, a timid, correct man, who had been engaged in papal administrative work throughout his entire priesthood. He was fluent in French, German, Italian, and Portuguese, but he had almost no knowledge of English. In 1848, during the many European revolutions, he had been governor of Bologna, capital of one of the Papal States, pontificating from the Cathedral of San Pietro. Bologna was the birthplace of Alessandro Gavazzi, who was a patriot during the revolutions and at the time of Bedini's visit was a dashing six-foot, ex-Franciscan priest. Following his unfrocking, he had moved to England and became a Protestant. He had come to the United States and Canada to spread with violence his anti-popery sentiments. In speeches he declared that the popish religion was the personification of monarchical government which was intended to overthrow the freedom of the immigrants who were coming in droves to the shores of the New World. He received much

backing and glorification from the Nativists who were making strong political inroads into the United States government.

Because of Gavazzi's rhetoric concerning executions in Bologna during the revolution, Nativists labeled Bedini the *Butcher of Bologna*. Against this cry he could not defend himself to the public wherever he visited. He first went to Baltimore to meet with Archbishop Francis Kenrick. In Philadelphia, he concerned himself with a trustee problem. His luxurious manner of living did not appeal to John Neumann, the bishop. During the summer months he was on a whirlwind tour of Chicago, Milwaukee, Green Bay, Detroit, Saratoga and Lake George, New York, and Quebec, Canada. By September, he was planning to bring his visit to a close. After a stop in Boston, he came to Buffalo; it was the last of his official assignments. After completing his work there he was encouraged by Hughes to stay longer in the country. Although he did so, he was never more than a few hours distant from the heckling and haggling of Gavazzi and the Nativists. The air was filled with defamation of Bedini and threats were made upon his life. On February 3, 1854, it was known that he was to leave for Europe on the *Atlantic* that would sail from Staten Island. An angry mob awaited his departure at the dock. Under the protection of United States Marshals, however, he outwitted them, by leaving earlier with his secretary in a row boat, which upon reaching deeper water was taken in tow by the steamship *Active*. It was in this humiliating manner that the papal nuncio departed after his seven months visit in America.

While staying in Buffalo, after having met with Timon on October 22, 1853, Bedini wanted to hear from the trustees of St. Louis Church. A committee formed of Michael Mesmer, Nicholas Ottenot, Peter Munschauer, and Martin Roth had an audience with Bedini at six o'clock. Respectful amenities were exchanged on both sides. The committee presented the archbishop with their *memorial*, a document that outlined the trustees' difficulties with Timon. They were encouraged when Bedini, in fluent German, assured them that he would carefully read their document and give it his full attention and consideration. He requested that they meet with him again in two days in the church between eleven and twelve o'clock; and, at that time, he would give them his response to their document. On October 24, 1853, they did so as requested accompanied with between fifty and sixty families. They waited and waited but Bedini did not come. After a reasonable time the trustees dismissed the congregation and sought an explanation from the archbishop; none was given. In the evening, however, he did inform them to meet with him the next day. He opened the meeting by reviewing the duties and responsibilities of Catholic laymen. Now the trustees felt a chill in the atmosphere surrounding the archbishop's chair. He told them that the rights they received by incorporation should aim at preserving the rights of the bishop according to the original deed. What the bishop may lawfully decide and require is what the congregation, either by consent or reaction, should conform. He then concluded, "Your submission to the laws of the Church will ever be a pledge of your submission to every other law which you are subject, as it is impossible to be a good Catholic, and not be at the same time a good citizen of your country." He then dismissed them, admonishing them to think about what he had said and send him a written reply.

The trustees were not impressed with his reasoning that their obligations toward Church and State were compatible. To agree with him would be a *Gueterabtretung*, a surrender of a bankrupt estate. They replied to the archbishop, "In Your Excellency's favored answer, we find only a repetition of all those summonses which have been made until now by the Reverend Timon, namely: complete surrender, and that our act of incorporation should be annulled, and that a committee should be instituted by the bishop, instead of a lawful board of trustees; all of which has been the reason for

our quarrelling from the very beginning until now. As far as the annulment of the act of incorporation is concerned, there can not be the slightest expectation for that, since we believe that the temporal administration of church matters has absolutely nothing to do with spiritual pastoral care. If Your Excellency should deem it necessary to permit us a further conversation in Bishop Timon's presence in order to effect reconciliation, it would be completely up to Your Excellency's decision. If that is to take place we would kindly request to be informed."

On October 26, 1853, a Redemptorist priest from St. Mary's Church, Reverend Nagel C.SS.R., informed the trustees that the archbishop would like to see them at eleven o'clock. Bedini never appeared. It was supposed that he was following the hierarchical rule that it is not the task of a bishop to debate in public with their laity. Nagel, however, spoke to the trustees and the parishioners who were in attendance. The trustees departed muttering words of disgust over being treated so shabbily by the archbishop. Later the same day Bedini sent his final reply to them. He said that what he had related to them earlier was his official word; it had not changed. Then he concluded, "Now then it becomes my duty to say that your answer is truly painful, especially to an envoy of the Holy Father, to whom you referred your case. The sad conviction forces itself on me that you disregard altogether Catholic principles, consequently that if you persist, it only remains for me to deplore the sad position in which you place yourselves in the face of the Church; but the responsibility of this rests entirely on yourselves." With these remarks ringing in the trustees' ears, Bedini left Buffalo on October 27, 1853. No peace had been restored between the disputing elements, but on his departure the trustees and their followers celebrated a picnic party which began with a march down Main Street. The marchers flew banners bearing inscriptions to the Papal Nuncio. The lead banner read, "Where is Archbishop Bedini?" Others carried these words: "Faith has nothing to do with temporalities;" "We will not abandon to our bishop;" "We maintained our civil rights and our bishop deprived us of all religious succor!"

*W*ith their appeal rejected by Bedini, the determined trustees of St. Louis Church attempted to overcome the spiritual power of the Catholic Church by petitioning the temporal power of the strongly nativistic legislature in New York State. For one to understand their decision to make this move, one must review events in American politics that took place at that time. In the 1840's Nativist's American politics was confined to the local and state levels; federal congressman were usually elected as representatives of either the Democratic or the Whig parties. Originally the Democratic Party was known as the party of Thomas Jefferson, third president of the United States. It went through many transformations until 1828 when it was officially declared totally Democratic. All candidates elected to the presidency of the United States from 1828 to 1860 were Democrats. With the demise of the Federalist Party in 1824, the Whig Party grew in strength and became a positive identity in 1828 and existed until 1860. In 1851, several secret societies promoted the attitude that the only families who should control American politics should be those who had been born in America or had been residents for more than fifty years; these were the Nativists.

*M*ysteriously in that year, these secret societies rose out of hiding, into the light of day, banding together as the Order of the Star Spangled Banner. Later when these groups decided to be a force in national politics they became the American Party. This was, however, only its conventional name; informally it was known as the Know-Nothing Party, given to it because when its members were asked about the secretiveness of its activities the reply was, "We know nothing." By the fall of 1854 the party had won a virtual monopoly of Massachusetts' government and secured a strong hold on legislative seats in New York State. Immediately gaining power, its representatives clashed with

Catholic clerics and bishops, especially Hughes and Timon. They were most upset with Hughes who claimed, "Catholics living in a democracy must be taught that democratic principles are not to be applied to the Roman Catholic Church." Because of statements like this, the Know-Nothing Party became extremely anti-Catholic, and it was willing to take up the cause of Catholic laymen who were ready to plead for their rights as members of Catholic Church incorporations and owners of Catholic Church properties. It was quite understandable that they would be anxious to take up the cause of the trustees at St. Louis Church. [3]

*I*n 1851, James O. Putnam, a State Senator from Buffalo, sponsored the *Roman Catholic Property Bill*, which would prevent any Catholic bishop or clergyman from holding property in his own name. It did not pass then, but was not forgotten. In 1852 at the urging of Bishop Hughes, the Tabor Bill was introduced in the New York Legislature. He knew of the Know-Nothing Party's inroads into politics, and he wished to fight it with civil law rather than theology. The bill, if passed, would guarantee the right of a bishop, by reason of his office, to hold church property in trust for religious and charitable purposes. It would have given the bishops corporate status and would have eliminated the need of lay trustees, as well as the danger for church property being transmitted to someone other than the bishop's successors. In 1853, the bill was defeated. On January 2, 1853, William Le Couteulx, representing the trustees of St. Louis Church approached Senators George Babcock and James Putnam requesting their permission to formulate a petition for a property bill as proposed in 1851. At a general meeting of the congregation on January 9, 1853, the petition, which was drawn up, was unanimously approved, and twenty men were appointed to gather signatures. It was then placed into the hands of Putnam and Babcock.

*T*he trustees were convinced that the success of the bill, if legislated, would absolutely place their church property legally into the hands of their corporation. An ensuing senatorial debate took place and gained immense notoriety around the country, particularly in Buffalo. Putnam, imbued with the Know-Nothing spirit of the times, argued in defense of the trustees' claim to rightful ownership on the grounds that they were maintaining their rights as American citizens in the face of papal encroachment. His speech before the Senate was deemed the most splendid of his career and exemplary of his skillful mastery of his profession. He concluded his arguments praising the trustees who as representatives of their congregation were victims of ecclesiastical authority. He said, "Here we see a band of men who have lived long enough in their adopted country to have the gristle of their liberal opinions hardened into bone; men devoted to the church of their fathers, but who love the State to which they have sworn allegiance and who respect its institutions. We see them resisting with heroism, which would honor the age of heroes, unitedly, unwaveringly, in defiance of bulls of excommunication from bishop, legate, and the Pope, every attempt to override their laws."

When Timon, who had been in Europe, returned and heard of Putnam's speech he wasted no time in drafting a rebuttal. He labeled Putnam's presentation as a harangue filled with inaccuracies, misrepresentations, and half-truths. He made it quite clear to the Senator that there was not a very definite separation between spiritual and temporal affairs in the Catholic Church. He said, "Many unthinking persons consider a church edifice and its revenues as entirely distinct from its spiritual character. If so, you may as well consider the body, its nourishment, its functions, and its actions, as entirely distinct from the soul. In fact, by God's eternal law, the soul acts on the body and the functions of the body have their powerful influence on the soul. If one legislates for the human body because it is flesh in the same manner, as one would legislate for an animal because it too is flesh, one would enslave the immortal soul. It is people like this who effect to consider the church, not as the house of God, but as the

house of Mr. Somebody, whom they represent, and the church revenues, not as something consecrated to God and belonging to Him, but as something belonging to them and theirs."

The bill, called the Putnam Bill, was passed into law on April 9, 1855, and in effect gave religious lay corporations the power to overrule the bishop if they felt so inclined. It also made it impossible for the bishop to hold property so as to transmit it to his successors in office. No church in New York State, however, in practice, applied all of the conditions of the law except St. Louis Church. One part of the law, however, was enacted; it was the provision that all Catholic Churches must incorporate in accordance to the trustee incorporation law of 1813 or suffer confiscation of their properties by forfeiture by the State of New York. Because of this provision, newly founded Catholic Churches in Western New York, during Timon's tenure of office, did so. Under a trustee corporation system, the law considered a church under three aspects: the *spiritual organization* of which the law said nothing; the *society*, of which the law took cognizance; and the *trustee corporation*, which was the legal representative of the society.

In 1863, the New York State Legislature, however, repealed the Putnam Law. In that same year because of the urging of Archbishop Hughes, Charles O'Connor, a New York lawyer, drafted a church incorporation bill which was passed into law on March 25, 1863, It was titled *An Act Supplementary to the Act entitled An Act to provide for the Incorporation of Religious Societies, passed April 5, 1813*. By the fourth section of that Act, a trustee system remained in place in all Catholic Churches and those trustees had the powers and authority granted to trustees of any other church, congregation, or society. The victory for the ecclesiastical hierarchy, however, lay in the component of the law which stated that the trustee body of each Catholic Church would consist of: archbishop or bishop of the diocese, the vicar general, the pastor of said church appointed by the bishop, and two laymen from the church congregation appointed by the pastor with the approval of the bishop. Only St. Louis Church enjoyed an exemption from this rule.

Although Hughes could call this a victory, he knew that it came about because he applied democratic principles to the Roman Catholic Church, a complete inversion of his former dictum. During the remainder of the nineteenth century going into the beginning of the twentieth century, several amendments were made to this law. In 1875, the trustees could apply the law according to the discipline, rules, and usage of the denomination to which the church members of the corporation belonged. In 1895, no act on the part of the board of trustees would be valid unless approved by the bishop. In 1902, the bishop could transfer, without consideration, property of a divided parish to a newly formed one. On July 29, 1911, the Sacred Congregation for the Propagation of the Faith, which had elevated the United States above missionary status in 1908, sent a message to the bishops of all dioceses in the country, requesting them to model parish corporations in their dioceses according to the laws of New York State. In 1917, the New York Law was extended to include not just *Roman Catholic Churches* but to include others which were *Catholic* but did not belong to the Latin rite.

It was, however, because of the Putnam Bill that the controversy at St. Louis Church was catapulted into the political arena and resulted in national newspaper exposure. In June 1854, while the debate of the bill was proceeding in the New York State Senate, Timon, in consultation with Father Francis Xavier Wenninger, a popular Jesuit from the Midwest and author of several books attacking Protestantism, excommunicated the seven resident trustees at St. Louis Church. This severe penalty, although it did not expel them from the Church, it did distance them from the Christian community because it excluded them from the life of the sacraments which is the life of the Church. By September, the congregation had dwindled to a discouraging number of families; it was time for Timon to deal directly with the members of the congregation barring the errant trustees from their influence. He asked Wenninger to take up residence in the rectory and negotiate directly with them. With the approval of Timon, Wenninger appointed a new set of trustees, who were moderate men, and then proceeded to reach the hearts of all through his preaching. Many in the congregation had already heard him preach at St. Michael's Church and were most captivated by him. His progress, however, was slow.

When one has felt that he is right for so long it is difficult for him to change. In the congregation were many Alsatian families who were the originators of it. They represented five-percent of the German community in Buffalo that represented forty-three percent of the total population. The Alsatians had persisted in the city longer than any other German-speaking group; they also had more land ownership than the Anglo-Americans. Although they prided themselves on their success as skilled tradesmen they also loved their Catholic religion. This is why they were so impressed with Wenninger's preaching which stressed that there was no salvation outside the Church. He told them that they were *Biedermeier Catholics*, would-be persons of quality, honor, and loyalty. He praised them for not being second-hand spokesmen for secular ideals, but he brought them back to the theme that they were being swallowed up by a vicious heresy; a concept by which, in glorifying God, finds life possible without the saving efficacy of Christ's grace in the sacraments.

All through the winter, Wenninger taught and preached. With the coming of spring he had made some progress and then the word came down from Albany on April 9, 1855; the Putnam Bill had become law.

Timon was displeased both with the announcement and Wenninger's slow pace of conversion. Wenninger assured the bishop that a settlement could be worked out; he asked him to be patient and leave the city for awhile. Timon went to Pittsburgh. On his return, Wenninger assured him that an agreeable compromise had been reached. Timon lifted the interdict on May 27, 1855. Wenninger gave a set of conditions outlining the regulation of parish life to Timon, who sent them to the congregation with his approval. Wenninger then brought other Jesuits into the parish for support; they remained there for several months until Timon appointed Father William Disters as the permanent pastor.

As Wenninger departed, he reviewed with the congregation the conditions of peace and reconciliation made with Bishop Timon. Referring to a signed document by both parties, he said, "St. Louis parish wants security for its church funds, it is assured; St. Louis parish wants peace, it will attain it; St. Louis parish wants its own pastor, it will get him; St. Louis parish wants to be and remain Catholic, it will remain so." Begging them that there would be no more dissention, he concluded, "Go forward on this road, St. Louis parish, as one man. In the name of God your hour has struck, now or never!" Although at times it was like walking on eggshells, the trustees continued to administrate the affairs of the church as a legal corporate entity in cooperation with their pastor and bishop according to the Incorporation Law of 1813. The excommunication of the dissident trustees was lifted. On July 18, 1859, William Le Couteulx was reconciled with the Church on his deathbed in the presence of Bishop Timon who heard his confession and gave him the last rites. Time proved a great healer. Old wounds began to heal and differences were set aside or forgotten as the church members increased rapidly with the tremendous infusion of German immigrants into the parish from 1855 to the outbreak of the War Between the States. As Timon prepared himself for his death that occurred on April 16, 1867, he recalled his conflict with

St. Louis Church. He prayerfully said, "I think I have done my duty. I beg pardon of God and man for any want of meekness or prudence that I may have possibly committed in this sad affair."

The conclusion of the sad affair, which the bishop referred to, was actually the initiation of a Rare Tradition in American Catholicism. A parish born of the French, open to all ethnic groups had become solidly German; more German than when it was incorporated in 1838. Like the problem developed in building the Tower of Babel, language caused, in part, ethnic groups to depart the walls of St. Louis Church and form other parishes. Ecclesiastical discipline against St. Louis Church brought about the construction of other churches in the city appealing to German-speaking Catholics. Going and almost lost Catholicism at St. Louis Church rose, like a phoenix, to great heights in the latter nineteenth century. With the lifting of the interdict and the repeal of excommunications, the trustee system remained in tact, and continued to administrate affairs as a legal corporate entity in cooperation with the pastor and bishop. Although the trustees mainly controlled "the how" of temporal affairs, they were not averse to listening to the pastor's suggestions. They also were most meticulous in providing for the temporal well being of the pastor; they had strong belief in the biblical phrase "the laborer is worthy of his hire." The corporation retained its deed to the property and was recognized by the episcopate as its legal owner. Haberstro and Mesmer, who had been excommunicated, returned for additional terms as trustees, but they proved, however, more circumspect. In turn, the congregation pledged to submit to the bishop rather than remain in apostasy. They abhorred the thought of Protestantism being their lot; their Catholicism was too well rooted in their souls.

It was this lay initiative at St. Louis Church that continued to be a force in the parish until late into the twentieth century. It was this documented compromise which formed the basis for a Rare Tradition in American Catholicism. The trustees, by persevering to the end and facing almost extinction, rallied to give a savory flavor of Americanism to Roman Catholicism in an era when laymen and clergy, episcopate and civil government, had to learn to respect and understand the needs of each other in an unstable democracy. In the documentation, further, the members of the congregation and their trustees agreed not to belong to any secret societies or be swayed by them. By September 21, 1855, both the Germans and the Irish in Buffalo united in opposition to the Know-Nothing Party. The political party had become not only abusively anti-Catholic, as before, but had no longer a need for Germans, such as those at St. Louis Church, who chose to remain Catholic rather than put on the cloak of Protestantism. They also became most violent against the massive number of German and Irish immigrants taking up residence in the city. As years passed the episcopates introduced and used civil legislation to solidify their ecclesiastical control over the increasing number of churches in their dioceses; evidence of which was their influence in passing new incorporation laws and amendments to old laws. Application of these, however, was not to St. Louis Church, but to all other churches, including those that had been incorporated during Timon's tenure of office. One such church, whose incorporation and trustee system has been well documented, is Good Shepherd Church, Pendleton in Niagara County. [4]

*T*hree important incidents in the history of the Diocese of Buffalo, involving the deed, ownership, and incorporation of St. Louis Church, have illustrated that well into the twentieth century this Rare Tradition in American Catholicism was alive and well. They are those which involved the Archbishop of New York, Michael Augustine Corrigan, who, in 1889, assigned a deed to Bishop Stephen Vincent Ryan, second bishop of Buffalo; the attempt to seize the deed to the church property in 1909, by Henry Le Couteulx de Chaumont,

Louis Le Couteulx de Chaumont, and Emanuel Baron de Bizi, descendants of Louis Etienne Le Couteulx, during the reign of Bishop Charles Henry Colton; and the execution of the dissolution of the trustee corporation of St. Louis Church and its surrender of ownership and administration to the diocese of Buffalo, in 1979, during the tenure of Bishop Edward D. Head.

*O*n August 13, 1889, twelve days before the first Mass was said at the newly constructed Gothic Church, replacing the one destroyed by fire on March 25, 1885, the Honorable James O. Putnam, author of the Putnam Law, explained the legality of Bishop Corrigan's granting a deed of St. Louis Church's property to Bishop Stephen Vincent Ryan, who had borrowed $60,000 from Jonathan Scoville, former mayor of Buffalo. Ryan gave the deed to Scoville as collateral, and advanced the money to the trustees of the church so they could pay the debt on the new church. Putnam explained, "As the Trust Estate was ended, as I have stated, on December 2, 1838, by the complete organization of the St. Louis Society, no interest whatsoever was vested in any successors after that date. Archbishop Corrigan had no interest, trust, or any other benefit to convey, and his deed to Bishop Ryan conveyed no interest, and the latter has no estate whatsoever in the church property. His deed is a nullity." Any mortgage assumed by Bishop Ryan on the church was therefore void; it was an attempt to mortgage the property of the Society in a method prohibited by law and the courts never permitted its foreclosure. Ryan, however, became the creditor of the society for the money advanced, but not as a mortgage. If the trustees, therefore, did not pay the loan of $60,000, by its due date, then Scoville had the right to sue the bishop but not the trustees. Ryan, however, had the right to sue the trustees in an ordinary manner, but he did not do so. By this incident the Rare Tradition in American Catholicism was recognized because no litigation arose out of any claim on Ryan's part.

Quite unexpectedly in 1909, Bishop Charles Henry Colton, was notified that members of the Le Couteulx family, living in France and direct descendants of Alphonse Le Couteulx sought to reclaim the property and assets of St. Louis Church. They claimed that because the church had sold parcels of land for purposes other than articulated in the original deed, the property reverted to the family. They also claimed that the gift of Louis Le Couteulx was a limited one, being invalidated upon the death of Bishop Dubois in 1842. An attorney, Edward Randall, in defense of Colton and the trustees, argued that the deed had been clearly made out to Dubois and his successors. He also stated that by incorporating in 1838, the trustees took legal possession of the church property. By this argument, the very act of incorporation, which Timon fought so desperately to break, became the central thrust of Randall's defense. Thus even if the title to the property was found to be invalid, which it was not, the construction of subsequent church buildings on the site entitled the trustees to control of the property on the grounds of adverse possessions. Such possessions included buildings, cemeteries, and appurtenances. The Supreme Court of New York State heard the case and decided in favor of the trustees. The Appellate division and the Court of Appeals later affirmed it in 1914. Again the Rare Tradition in American Catholicism was recognized.

In 1979, the Board of Trustees of St. Louis Church decided to explore the possibility of transferring the parish and its assets to the Diocese of Buffalo. Their reasons for dissolving the corporation were two-fold: to ensure the capable leadership of the church's assets and its tax-exemption status. The conditions of transfer contained two important conditions: the assets of the church, amounting to hundreds of thousands of dollars, were to be secured for the sole use of the parish and that a younger, more dynamic, pastor would be appointed to the church. Their ability to legally donate what was theirs to give proves their right to have had it. This Rare Tradition in American Catholicism had lasted uninterruptedly for one hundred and forty-one years, and served its purpose well, only to be replaced as the Catholic Church in America moved into the second decade following its revitalization according to the policy decisions reached in the Second Vatican Council.

On August 24, 1979, the eve of the feast of St. Louis, King of France, the trustees formulated a letter of transfer. On October 1, 1979, Bishop Edward D. Head, finalized the transfer of property and assets, and formed a new corporation, according to the revised laws of incorporation of 1863, under the title St. Louis Roman Catholic Church of Buffalo, New York. According to this law, the trustees of the corporation were the bishop, vicar general, pastor and two laymen. The by-laws of the new corporation were filed with the county clerk's office on October 4, 1979. Bishop Head addressed the congregation stating, "This action of transfer was taken to ensure the stability and longevity of your church. You can be assured that because of its historical background, good physical condition, and financial stability, St. Louis Church will remain open." On October 15, 1979, Head reported the climax of the transfer to the Roman Catholic Church's Apostolic Delegate, residing in Washington D.C., the Most Reverend Jean Jadot. In doing so Head remarked, "The tradition of St. Louis Church is a proud one, and a one hundred and fifty year chapter in the history of the diocese has come to an end." Four days later, Jadot, with Socratic irony, replied, "It certainly is a historic moment in the annals of the local community of faith. It would be of interest to me to learn whether or not there are any other parishes who are still legally under the control of trustees in New York State according to the laws of 1813." By his statement he recognized that the administration at St. Louis Church had been a Rare Tradition in American Catholicism. [5]

REFERENCES AND NOTES ✤ CHAPTER SIX

1. John Carroll was first succeeded by Leonard Neal and then by Ambrose Marechal. For the Councils at Baltimore and the evils of trusteeism see: op. cit. *Trusteeism in the Atlantic States, 1785-1863*, p. 146, and op. cit. *Dagger John*, p. 60. For biographical material on Bishop Timon see as indexed in op. cit. *The Life and Times of Rt. Rev. John Timon* and op. cit. *History of the Catholic Church in Western New York*; For the story line of this section see: op. cit. *Lay Trusteeism at St. Louis*, pps. 50-63 and for the specifics of the school problem with the Sisters of Charity see p. 87. For the Jesuits' intervention, Guth's pastorship, and the French leaving St. Louis Church to found St. Pierre's Church see: op. cit. *The Chapel* pps. 19, 21, and op. cit. *History of the Catholic Church in Western New York*, pps. 136, 157-60, 161-75, and op. cit. *The Life and Times of Rt. Rev. John Timon*, pps. 116, 117, 128, 134. When Caveng left the church with the Blessed Sacrament violence erupted among the parishioners; some took the side of the clergy and others favored the trustees. One person, in a letter written early in the twentieth century, recalled his siding with the trustees against Mr. McManus who approved of the clergy's actions in 1851 just prior to the pronouncement of interdiction. "It is not necessary for me to go into a long argument on this St. Louis Church matter. Able people have thrashed it out. Mr. McManus I think is biased, he gives the clerical side of the question. I do not think a man to be truthful, Catholic, and a good one must be a priest. The congregation at St. Louis asked nothing wrong in my opinion. Why were the descendants of Louis Le Couteulx on the side of the congregation? I knew William B., the son, ex-officer of the French navy, Knight of Lyon of Haver (sic); he resided here—Buffalo—during the time and was with the congregation all the time... Mr. McManus' presumption that a few people would take and appropriate the Church is farfetched and imaginary. It was said at the time that the new Bishop Timon wanted the church because it was the best and most suitable for a Cathedral. That then the congregation would be tricked and the French and Germans would eventually have to quit it... The Jesuits made an effort for the Church at another time; a meeting of the congregation was called to the church after Vespers on a certain Sunday. I was there. Rev. Caveng ascended the pulpit and harangued the congregation on fidelity, obedience and asked the question if they would submit to the bishop—upon that, the meeting was like one man and the cry a 'Hinaus mit ihm!' resounded in the church. Rev. Caveng with another priest made his exit through the rear of the church." This quote was taken from an unsigned letter of November 16, 1903, in the St. Louis file at the Buffalo and Erie County Historical Society, Buffalo, NY. At the time that Caveng left the church the trustees were: Jacob Wilhelm, George Zimmermann, Joseph Haberstro, John Koch, Mathias Hausle, A. Diebold, John Chretien, *Buffalo Democrat*, July 26, 1851. Caveng had been born in Switzerland on March 25, 1806. He entered the Society of Jesus, commonly known as Jesuits, on October 5, 1830. He was a professor at the college of Fribourg in Switzerland until he immigrated to Canada. In 1847, he was active with the

Canadian mission of the French Jesuit province, in a community of German immigrants at Petersburg, near Kitchener, Ontario. From that station, he and his associates, Fritsch, and Kettner, tended to many mission stations in the Niagara peninsula in Canada. Among them, Stevensville and Chippewa were not far from Buffalo. As early as 1848, Caveng and Fritsch had preached retreats and missions to the German-speaking Catholics of Williamsville. After a few weeks at St. Louis Church as pastor in 1851, Caveng abandoned his post because Timon asked him to take the leadership of St. Michael's Church, where he remained as superior of the Jesuit community and pastor until September 8, 1860. After a long illness, Caveng died at St. Michael's Church on January 27, 1862. He is buried in the priest's lot in the United German and French Roman Catholic Cemetery on Pine Ridge Road, Buffalo. For Alphonse Le Couteulx's filing a second deed to the St. Louis Church property see: *Catholic Union and Times*, January 23, 1913. Other references to the Le Couteulx brothers coming to front stage in the St. Louis Church controversy see: op. cit. *A Man and a Church Named Louis*, p.25. At the time of the interdict the trustees were Nicholas Ottenot, Joseph Haberstro, John Chretien, Jacob Whilhem, and George Zimmermann. For Pax's letter, September 4, 1851 sent from France see: op. cit. *The Life and Times of Rt. Rev. Bishop Timon*, p.154. The hospital founded by the Sisters of Charity in Buffalo was located on Pearl Place, a street several times in this text; later it was called St. Louis Place.

2. For the interdiction becoming public knowledge in the press see: *Buffalo Morning Express*, June 21, 1851; *Buffalo Morning Express*, June 24, 1851; *Buffalo Morning Express*, June 28, 1851. For the opening of St. Michael's Church in January 1852 and its effect upon the congregation at St. Louis Church see: op. cit. *The Chapel*, p. 23. Another part of the controversy over temporal affairs centered on the St. Louis Church cemetery. The following citation was not included in the text. "The trustees maintained that, through their incorporation, they were responsible for the administration of the cemetery. This claim stemmed from the original deed in which Louis Le Couteulx had stipulated land to be given for the use of a cemetery for Catholics. Because of the cholera epidemic of 1832, the cemetery became filled. On March 2, 1833, Mayor Ebenezer Johnson and the city clerk Dyre Tillinghast granted the Catholic Church an additional parcel of land outside the city limits for a cemetery. The trustees who assumed the responsibilities of the cemetery in 1838 held the deed, made out to Bishop Dubois and his successors. Being that St. Louis Church was the only Catholic Church in the city, the administration of the cemetery by the trustees posed no problem. The arrangement radically changed when the Diocese of Buffalo came into existence. In response to Bishop Timon's desire to manage the cemetery in the name of the diocese, the trustees resisted, claiming that they had sole right over the property. During the interdict period, resulting in the emergence of new parishes in the city, the trustees saw fit to enforce a restriction on burials only for St. Louis parishioners. The trustees petitioned the mayor and city council to restrict burials in the cemetery to their

parishioners only. In their petition they claimed that the omission of their name to the title of the cemetery, gave Bishop Timon the right to take the property away from them; and, by charging fees, to make a profit. Unlike the gifted deed of the St. Louis Church property to Bishop Dubois and his successors, 'In Trust,' there was no such statement in regards to the cemetery given by the City. Therefore the trustees did not have exclusive rights to the cemetery. Bishop Timon told the City Council that he had consecrated another new cemetery on August 15, 1849 and that any fees by individuals given as burial rights would go to liquidate the debt on the graveyard and subsequent to that time the revenue received would be used to keeping the cemetery in order and adorning it. The trustees, however, in defiance of the bishop continued to operate their cemetery. The issue, however, became a source of much misunderstanding and the cause of great grief for the families of seven Catholic Churches involved in burial needs. On April 5, 1852, a committee of forty-four former members of St. Louis Church sent a letter to the mayor and the City Council requesting that a definitive answer on their part be rendered in the matter. Having received no satisfactory answer, the committee organized to form the United German and French Roman Catholic Cemetery Association in 1853. It purchased land at Pine Hill for a new cemetery; the troubles at the old cemetery came to an end." op. cit. *Lay Trusteeism at St. Louis Church*, pps.68-71; "United German and French Roman Catholic Cemetery Association," *Verein der Deutsche und Franzoesische Romanische Katholische Friedhof*, Pamphlet and By-laws of 1853, St. Louis Church Archives, United German and French Roman Catholic Cemetery file. For description of the Black and White Flags of Interdict and the letter of William Le Couteulx to Pope Pius IX see: op. cit. *Records of the Trustees of St. Louis Church*, pps. 86-7 and for the reply of the Pope to Bishop Timon see: Letter to Rt. Rev. John Timon, December 14, 1852, from Cardinal Franzoni, Prefect of the Propaganda Fide, Archives of the Diocese of Buffalo.

3. For the visit of Archbishop Bedini to the United States and his meeting with the trustees in Buffalo, New York see: Thomas T. McAvoy, C.S.C., *A History of the Catholic Church in the United States*, University of Notre Dame Press, Notre Dame, Indiana, 1969, p. 172; James Hennessey, S.J., *American Catholics*, Oxford University Press, Toronto, Canada, 1981, p. 124; op. cit. *Dagger John*, pps. 278-88; op. cit. *History of the Catholic Church in Western New York*, pps. 177-180; op. cit. *Records of the Trustees of St. Louis Church*, pps. 89-92. Following the introduction of the Putnam Bill into the New York State Legislature, Timon, in 1854, excommunicated the seven trustees at St. Louis Church. They were: Martin Roth, Alexander Allenbrandt, Michael Mesmer, Jacob Wilhelm, George Fischer, Nicholas Ottenot, and Peter Munschauer. The Catholic Church had two types of excommunication, the lesser and the greater. The lesser deprived the recipients the right to receive the Eucharist; the greater, by absolute separation from the Church, deprived them of all rights and privileges of the Church. The seven trustees received the "greater excommunication," see: *The Sentinel*, June 2, 1854. The *Buffalo Sentinel* was the official

Catholic newspaper of Buffalo in 1854-55; The Rev. C. D. McMullen and Rev. Daniel Moore attended to the religious department; Rev. Peter Bede, secretary to Bishop Timon was the editor. Secular and Religious newspaper clippings in the St. Louis Church Archives concerning the controversy between Bishop Timon and the Trustees of St. Louis Church were compiled by William E. Swantz from the original collection of Peter Mergenhagen and given to Edward A. Rick. They were given to the archives in 1956. The trustees of the interdiction of Bishop Hughes in 1842-3, who had survived and were present for the compromise solution with Timon in 1855 were: Martin Fischer, Joseph Haberstro, Nicholas Haas, and Bartholomew Rinck, *Commercial Advertiser*, April 5, 1855. See also, *Taeglicher Buffalo Demokrat Und Weltbuerger*, June 7, 1854.

4. For the Putnam Bill and its effect on the St. Louis Church controversy see: op. cit. *American Catholicism*, p. 46; J.N. Larned, "James O. Putnam Memorial Evening," *Publications of the Buffalo Historical Society*, Buffalo, NY, 1903, p. 630; op. cit. *Lay Trusteeism at St. Louis Church*, pps. 77-80; op. cit. *The Laws of the State of New York Affecting Church Property*, pps. 47-51. For Wenninger's solution to the rift between Bishop Timon and the trustees at St. Louis Church see: Letter of F.X. Wenninger to the congregation of St. Louis Church dated June 1855, Archives of St. Louis Church; Leonard Riforgiato, "John Timon and the Problem of Trusteeism," a Paper presented at the meeting of the American Catholic Historical Association, Xavier University, Cincinnati, Ohio, April 20, 1985, p. 26; op. cit. *One Hundred and Twenty-fifth Anniversary*, p. 19. The Rare Tradition in American Catholicism initiated at St. Louis Church was a compromise between Bishop Timon and the trustees of the church. Four specific points were established in a written document outlining a balance of powers between the clergy and laity; trusteeism and trusteeship at the church remained intact, the pastor was given veto power, and the bishop assumed the role of arbitrator. The agreement included 1. The Trustees shall be elected from the members of the congregation, who are pew-holders of the church, but any member who belongs to any secret society, or neglects to observe his Easter confession and communion, shall not so be elected. 2. The Trustees shall render an account to the congregation, every six months, of the monies received and expended by them and to the Bishop at the end of every year. The Bishop reserves the right to examine the books and accounts at any time, at his own option. For every amount expended over $300, the Trustees shall procure the express consent of the Bishop. 3. The pastor shall attend all Trustees' meetings, *ex officio*, and if he deems fit to veto any action taken at the meetings, and does not afterwards withdraw his veto, the matter shall be submitted to the Bishop for his decision. 4. The pastor shall appoint the persons to serve the congregation, or instruct the youth of the congregation, as organist, sexton, and teachers, but with the consent of the Trustees. If the Trustees will not consent to the appointment of such persons by the priest, it shall be submitted to the decision of the Bishop. The congregation will remain incorporated under this administration; never can one

cent of the funds of the congregation be appropriated, without their consent, for any other purpose than the use of the congregation. For these four conditions see: *Buffalo Commercial Advertiser*, June 29, 1855, Archives of the St. Louis Church; also see: article pasted in the *Minutes of the Board of Trustees of St. Louis Church, 1838-1874*, book 1., "an attachment to the regular minutes, 1855." A provision included in the Putnam Law stated that Catholic Churches not incorporated according to the Act of 1813 would suffer escheatment of their church property to the State of New York. Escheatment was a confiscation of property by forfeiture. It was the seizure of private property to the public as being forfeited. Because of this provision, Timon had all Catholic Churches incorporated by the act of 1813. One such church was Good Shepherd, Pendleton. For incorporation and trusteeship at Good Shepherd Church, Pendleton, NY, see: op. cit. *Good Shepherd; The Church on the Canal, 1847-1997*, pps. 6-17, 41. A summary of the information contained therein follows: An example of churches in the Diocese of Buffalo, incorporated according to the New York State Law of 1813, and administrated by laymen in a manner similar to St. Louis Church is Good Shepherd Church, Pendleton, NY. The parish began in 1847 under the pastorship of Father Peter Kramer. In 1849, Joseph Leuthauser sold four acres of land to Bishop Timon. Although the purpose of the sale was to have a Catholic Church on the property, no stipulation was made of deeding the property "In Trust," as was the case at St. Louis Church. In that year Bernard Fritsch, one of the Jesuits who came from Canada and preached a mission to the trustees at St. Louis Church, became pastor of Good Shepherd parish and built a log church and said the first Mass in it on December 30, 1849. When the Jesuits left, Francis Stephen Uhrich became pastor; and, in 1854, he built a brick church that, with some improvements, remains the same today. Being free of debt the church was consecrated by Timon in 1859. In the previous year, however, the society of the church was incorporated according to the Law of 1813. The small congregation elected five laymen as trustees, and by-laws were written and approved retroactive to August 1, 1858. These men were responsible for the execution of the temporalities of the church in cooperation with the pastor appointed by the bishop. In 1863, Bishop Hughes had imposed upon the New York State Legislature to enact revisions to the 1813 law, which would provide a special arrangement for Catholic Churches in the State. Accordingly, the board of trustees in each church in the dioceses of New York would be composed of the bishop of the diocese, the vicar general, the pastor, and two appointed laymen from the respected parish. In the Buffalo diocese the bishop announced that all churches were compelled to be in conformity with this ruling within ten years. On November 2, 1873, Father Charles Geppert, pastor of Good Shepherd, told the congregation that they had to come into immediate conformity with the revised incorporation law. The parishioners were shocked; this was the first they had heard of the change. The cry went up, "The autocratic clergy now have the majority of the board in any decision that is to be made in the parish. Who can accept this tyranny?" Bishop Ryan, second bishop of the diocese of Buffalo, threatened the church with interdiction if the congregation did not reject all previous elections of trustees and consider past by-laws as null and void. Although the parish as well as all others, except St. Louis Church. did conform, a considerable amount of instability was experienced at Good Shepherd Church. The pastor, Charles Geppert, was transferred; Joseph Niebling became pastor but only stayed five months; Mathias Gessner who remained only one year replaced him. Herman Boemann, several Jesuits, and Francis Stephen Uhrich followed these pastors in rapid succession. True stability, however, did not come to the parish until the arrival of Conrad Kaelin in 1889.

5. For the survival into the late twentieth century of the "Rare Tradition in American Catholicism" generated by the trustees at St. Louis Church in 1838 see: *An Opinion Rendered By James O. Putnam*, presented to the trustees (Peter Paul, G. Frank Deck, Bud Jehle, Lawrence Wex, and Xavier Dietsche) of St. Louis Church, August 13, 1889, pps. 1-5; "The Title of the Church Property Absolute in the Trustees; The Question Thoroughly Explained by the Hon. James O. Putnam," *Buffalo Commercial Advertiser*, August 8, 1889 (Interpretation of the legal language contained in this document was made clear to the editors by G. Peter Higgins, Real Estate Lawyer, Pendleton, New York, 2001); *Buffalo Express*, "St. Louis Church Property in Suit," June 30, 1909; *Henry Le Couteulx de Chaumont, Louis Le Couteulx de Chaumont, and Emmanuel Baron de Bizi v. The Trustees of the Roman Catholic Church of St. Louis*, Sup. Ct. N.U., 1914, Archives of the Diocese of Buffalo, St. Louis file; *Buffalo Express*, "St. Louis Church Property Suit," June 30, 1909; *Buffalo Times*, "Two Claimants of St. Louis Church Property." January 7, 1913; *Buffalo Express*, "St. Louis Deed Valid," August 12, 1914; *Buffalo Times*, "Le Couteulx Heirs Now in French Army, Suit is Held Up," January 13, 1915; *Buffalo Express*, "St. Louis Church Wins," June 16, 1916. Memo to Bishop Head from Msgr. Donald Trautman, May 31, 1979, Archives of the Diocese of Buffalo, St. Louis file; A Letter of the Trustees of St. Louis Church, August 24, 1979, Archives of the Diocese of Buffalo, St. Louis file; *Buffalo Evening News*, "Historic St. Louis Church is Taken Over by the Diocese," October, 2, 1979; St. Louis Church, "Minutes of the Meeting of Board of Trustees," October 1, 1979 and October 9, 1979, Archives of the Diocese of Buffalo, St. Louis file; Letter of Bishop Edward D. Head to Rt. Rev. Jean Jadot, October 15, 1979, and a return letter from Jadot to Head, October 19, 1979, Archives of the Diocese of Buffalo, St. Louis file.

CHAPTER SEVEN

Gather Our Relics, We Rise Eternally

On April 9, 1865, General Robert E. Lee surrendered his Army of Northern Virginia to Ulysses Simpson Grant, commander-in-chief of the Union Forces, at Appomattox Courthouse, Virginia. Seventeen days later, Confederate General Joseph Eggleston Johnston surrendered to William Tecumseh Sherman and on May 4, 1865, the Confederate officer, Richard Taylor, had his troops stack their rifles in the presence of the Union General, Edward Richard Sprigg Canby. All Confederate resistance east of the Mississippi River had ceased; and, for all practical purposes, the great five year war called by some the American Civil War and by others the War Between the States, was over. Newspapers in Buffalo, New York, were extraordinarily busy and published extras between short intervals as they had done on April 15, 1861, when they gave an announcement and full account of the bombardment of Fort Sumter, guarding the harbor of Charleston, South Carolina. Headlines, larger in size and greater in excitement were continuously published. During the war, the city's population had watched for and read the reports of those volunteers who had joined regiments formed in Erie County and fell fatally or suffered serious wounds on the battlefields. Young Germans from Erie County were prominent in several New York infantry regiments such as the forty-ninth, thirty-third, and twenty-first. These units did their initial formation and training at Elmira, New York. Other artillery, cavalry, and sharpshooter units had called upon Buffalo and Erie County for recruits. The most famous of these was Wiedrich's Battery that was attached to General Louis Blenker's Division; Blenker was a former leader of a Bavarian Legion in the German Revolution of 1848 who came to America as a refugee.

The one single group of Germans in Western New York, which fostered active recruitment into regimental units, was the Turnverein, a gymnastic organization that was founded in Buffalo on March 3, 1853. It was first known as the *Social Turnverein.* Immediately upon organization it opened exercise classes, English classes, a singing group, drawing classes, and a debating society. In 1853, the Turnverein had one hundred and sixty members. Two years later it hosted the convention of the *North American Gymnastic Union* that had established the publication *Die Turnerzeitung* printed in Baltimore. Thirty delegates represented forty-seven societies in the United States. In their resolutions they condemned slavery as an institution, and gave strong opposition to Know-Nothings, and Prohibitionists, whom they called *Sunday Hypocrites.* In 1856, the gymnastic union threw its representation into action to promote the newly formed political party, the Republican Party, established in Pittsburgh, Pennsylvania. The anti-slavery faction within the Turners caused a split in Buffalo's group. *The Social Maenner Turnverein* had its headquarters at Gilig Hall at the corner of Genesee and Ash Streets. The breakaway element, *Turnverein Vorwaerts,* established itself at the bookbinding shop of Paul Wertsch at five hundred Main Street. The roster of war victims among the Turners almost completely depleted the ranks of the *Vorwaerts.* After hostilities ended, however, both groups were reunited; and, together, they were known as the *Buffalo Turnverein*. Before 1900, one found very few names of Catholics associated with the society because of its nineteenth century freethinking philosophy, which was anti-religious and anti-church as professed by its leaders.

In general, however, both freethinking and Catholic Germans had the spirit of republicanism that was one of progress and expansion. The products of invention, investment, and adventure carried the entrepreneur into the territories, sweeping along with him the immigrants, who were the laborers needed to bring his dreams to reality. The immigrants came by canal boat and railroad to Buffalo where they awaited passage into the Midwest so as to find their pot of gold. Many, however, stayed in Buffalo, swelling the ranks of the population. They were men who wanted the right of free labor and were resolved not to be bound in employer servitude. They needed power to gain that right and found it in the protection afforded by laws enacted by a strong Federal Government. Hence, at all costs, they wanted the Union to be preserved! They did not want the government to vacillate and compromise with slavery. They proposed that, only if every vestige of that institution was destroyed, could freedom of labor be guaranteed.

The parishioners at St. Louis Church were well pleased when they read in the *Catholic Union* that the bishop of Buffalo opposed slavery in theory and advocated freedom for black slaves. If in the South, the notion of slaves being owned, bought, and sold, using the laws of commerce, could persist without government control, could not the grasping monopolist of the North maintain a dominion over the immigrant worker? Every German felt that it would be more galling than black slavery. Under such a condition they would consider themselves as rented, victims of wage slavery. Those immigrants who came to Buffalo in the late 1850's knew what it meant to be a journeyman in Europe on a *Wanderjahr,* working to gain their

mastercraftsmenship papers. Job opportunities were limited, and they had to accept any wage offered by their employer. They had no rights to question his whim and fancy. They did not wish this to be their lot in America!

Much like all wars, where the battlefields are hundreds of miles away and the pinch on the pocketbook is not much felt, the daily results of the conflict held little pain to the readers of newspaper articles. It was only at the end of the war that the population of Buffalo felt pain. Approximately fifteen thousand young boys had donned blue uniforms and proudly marched off to war. Only ten thousand returned and most of those killed or seriously maimed in battle were members of poor families. In 1863, the streets of Buffalo had witnessed draft riots, and they had to be squelched by the action of the two-militia regiments, the 65th and 74th New York, which had just arrived from riot duty in New York City. Before they brought about calm, however, angry mobs of white dockworkers had stampeded away from the waterfront, crossed the Main Street business district, pushed into the small black section on the east side, and reeked havoc onto unsuspecting black residents who happened to be in the streets. For whites, it was one thing to hold the Union together, but to offer one's life for a black slave was a horse of a different color. In Buffalo's riot, however, only one fatality was reported by the newspapers, which indicated pleasure that its city's disturbance was a dwarf when compared to that of New York City.

By the time Lee had surrendered to Grant in 1865, Buffalo's lake-oriented economy, which had boomed during the war because the commercial outlet of the Mississippi River had been closed to raw materials coming from the Midwest, was considered the leading inland port-economy of the United States. The war was begun to save the Union, however, it ended with a devastated South which had to be reconstructed, a vast population of slaves who although free were vastly uneducated and poor, and an enormous number of dead and maimed soldiers. There were approximately seven hundred blacks living in Buffalo, some former slaves but mostly freed-men from the antebellum period, cramped together, as a community, on Michigan Street below Genesee Street on the East Side. They may have been small in number but they were well organized. Their homes were sandwiched in among the Germans, who had not moved, as several did, into the southern part of the *fruit belt*, a configuration of streets named Beech, Rose, Grape, Peach, Orange, Lemon, Locust, Mulberry, Maple, Michigan, Elm, Oak, Ellicott, and Cherry. All streets except Cherry ran parallel to Main Street in the west, and were bounded in the east by Jefferson Street. Cherry Street, in the south, intersected all the other streets and ran parallel to Genesee Street. North Street, the northern most extent of the city, intersected all parallel streets of the fruit belt. In 1865 the population of Buffalo was ninety-four thousand two hundred and ten of which approximately forty thousand were German. Most were Catholic and ranged in age between twenty and twenty-five years. Following the lifting of interdiction, St. Louis Church had become the recipient of a large number of these as parishioners. Many others who had gone to other German churches during interdiction returned to the Mother Church, bringing with them their children for baptisms, confirmations, and marriages. [1]

From 1864 to 1867, Father Sergius Schoulepnikoff served as pastor at St. Louis Church. He had replaced the early wartime pastors of J.E. Meshall and Francis Anthony Gerber. While acting as pastor, he had strong feelings for the black population of the city. Although only about fifteen of them were Catholic, and living in their isolated community among German families, he tried to help them. With his own money, he rented a house in their midst on the East Side, and turned it into a club-house named St. Augustine's Club. There he organized catechists who taught those who wished to learn doctrine and prayers. He developed a recreational program that kept the young off the streets while their parents worked. Most of those black parents with whom he worked had jobs as laborers or servants.

He became infuriated with articles such as the one that appeared in the *Buffalo Medical Journal* that comparatively described the cranial sizes of teutons, celts, and blacks. According to these articles, experiments had found that the smallest of the three belonged to members of the black race. The writers assumed that they were limited in mental capacity. The author's conclusion was, if they were not to be condemned to a life of slavery, at least, they should not receive the full approval of the other races. Both Schoulepnikoff and Timon forcefully denounced this medical attitude. In fact Timon was so appreciative of the work which was done at St. Augustine's, that he provided funds for the club's expenses using money designated for the Catholic Church's Black and Indian Apostolate. It was also suspected that prior to 1863, Schoulepnikoff, while pastor in the Southern Tier, was involved in processing blacks through the Underground Railroad, booking passage for them from safe house to safe house until they could reach Canada. After January of that year, this surreptitious maneuver was unnecessary because Abraham Lincoln's Emancipation Proclamation had already freed slaves in the Confederate States.

Schoulepnikoff had been born into a Russian noble family. He went to France and was ordained a priest in 1850; after which, he came to America, and proceeded directly to Buffalo to carry on his missionary desires. He was eloquent and eccentric, a renowned mathematician, and chess player. In his spare time he wrote two books describing the combination of moves in the game. While in Western New York, he served at St. Joseph's Cathedral, Buffalo, St. Mary of the Assumption, Lancaster, Good Shepherd Church, Pendleton, St. Patrick's, Java, Sacred Heart, Tonawanda, and Catholic communities in Dansville and Elmira. For a time he was the Vicar of French and Germans for the

Diocese of Buffalo. In Tonawanda, under the urging of Timon, he purchased property on Franklin Street and built a frame church that he called Sacred Heart. Later his building received a new pastor, Father Francis Stephen Uhrich, who literally cut the building in half, put one-half on a barge, and sailed it across to Grand Island to become a church that he named St. Stephen. While Schoulepnikoff was pastor at Good Shepherd Church, he initiated the concept that a collection should be taken for the pastor's salary. In the initial one, made by the church's trustees, he received the annual salary of $64.37.

Because his name was so difficult to pronounce and spell by the farmers in Pendleton, they affectionately knew him as Father Serge! At St. Louis Church, in conversation outside his presence, the congregation referred to him as *Der Russ*. This expression, however, was not said to him, face-to-face, until his last day at church. It was the occasion of the funeral of Mathias Hausle who, for a long time, was one of the trustees who had been excommunicated by Bishop Timon in the last days of controversy over ownership and maintenance of the church. Hausle, however, was reinstated after the compromise of 1855 that was negotiated by Wenninger. On August 15, 1867, Hausle died at the age of sixty-nine years following a long siege of kidney failure. He had been a member of the congregation since the church was founded. The lay leaders of the church wished to show him great honor because he had served well through troubled times. They appeared at his funeral, dressed in full regalia, accompanied by a band leading a congregational procession. After arriving at the church, *Der Russ* was not present. He refused to conduct the service until the trustees dispensed of their regalia and cast aside the band. He told them that wearing emblems and symbols of royalty, and carrying scepters in parade-like fashion did not meet the simplicity required of a Catholic burial, and savored and smacked of *Freimaurerei*, known to the English Protestants as Freemasonry. He was well aware that several of his congregations were members of the Mason's Concordia Lodge. They having been recruited by Joseph Lambert Haberstro, son of Joseph Haberstro, who had been one of the original trustees of St. Louis Church.

The trustees took the pastor aside privately, away from the casket and the mourners, and pleaded their case with him but to no avail. Suddenly a few of the less conservative of their membership no longer restrained themselves and shouted out, "*Herr Russ*, either do our bidding or *lossausen*," a slang expression meaning that he skip town hurriedly. Father Schoulepnikoff obliged them, but skipped very ungracefully with a few irate trustees at his heels endeavoring to belabor him with horsewhips. He never again returned to the parish or to any of the homes of the parishioners. Once again St. Louis Church was without a pastor. The mourners, waiting near the casket, wondered what had happened, and soon found that no priest would be available to conduct the service. Without introduction, Hausle's sister, Martha, arose, made a few remarks, offered prayers for the repose of his soul, and led the pallbearers and parishioners to the United German and French Roman Catholic Cemetery at Pine Hill for interment. It was this incident which closed the last chapter of the history of the mortal existence of Mathias Hausle, Catholic, Trustee, and Faithful Parishioner. One more vignette, however, needs to be added in the life of Father Schoulepnikoff. After his debacle at St. Louis Church, he entered the religious life as a Dominican and served in Cincinnati, Ohio. Two years later in 1869, however, he mysteriously disappeared; no trace of him was ever reported, however, the Dominicans made an identification of a pair of his shoes which he apparently abandoned near the railroad tracks at the city's depot. [2]

In the post Civil War days, the Catholic Church and, in fact, all Christian denominations thought highly of the dignity of the bodies of the departed faithful. To them the body was the medium or instrument of so many beautiful virtues, and so many good works performed during the life of the Christian. For that reason alone the body received the respect and reverence of family, friends, and mourners attending the funeral. Catholics, moreover, viewed each person's body as the vehicle by which the sacraments were received. The body was washed in baptism, in order to cleanse the soul. The body was anointed in oil, so that it became the temple of the Holy Ghost. The body was fed with the sacred flesh and nourished with the blood of Christ, to strengthen and fortify the soul. Through the Catholic's faith and hope, the body was venerated because of the assurance that on the last day it would rise again from the dust and mould of the grave, and would be clothed with splendor and glory so as to share with the soul the eternal joys it had merited. For these reasons, the manner of burial of the early Christians was distinguished from that of the pagans.

Pagans clothed the bodies of their departed in splendid and costly robes; Christians dressed their bodies plainly but neatly. One of the early Fathers of the Church, St. Jerome, speaking of pagan ritual, said, "How does this pride and vainglory suit affliction, tears, and sorrow? Cannot the bodies of the rich rot without being wrapped in costly silks?" In the conduct of funerals, the pagans employed certain men and women whose business it was to bewail and lament the deceased; these official mourners scratched their faces, tore at their hair, lacerated their arms with knives, and sang doleful and lugubrious songs; Christians sang psalms or prayerful hymns. Pagans did not believe in resurrection of the body nor in a future life; they deplored the death of their friends as an irrevocable misfortune; Christians looked upon death as a happy event, an entry into a better life. Another Father of the Church, St. Cyprian, comparing the attitudes of pagans and Christians toward death, said, "No, we should not bewail our deceased fellow-Christians, for they are not lost to us, for we have only sent them before us as our former associates in the pilgrimage of this life, and we

shall soon follow them; therefore we ought only to long after them, but not deplore them."

The early Christians placed the bodies of their deceased into the ground in such a manner that they faced the East. This signified that the dead placed their hope and trust in Christ, the light of their soul, who like the sun which rises in the east promised them bodily resurrection, and proved his power to do so by rising from the dead on the third day after His death on the cross. The Christians of early Rome, however, imitated the pagans in having cemeteries outside the city. Roman law forbade the interment of the dead inside the walls of the city. The pagans therefore set apart some field or garden near the high road. Christians, however, tunneled for miles around the walls of Rome, forming underneath the surface, a vast silent city of the dead known as the catacombs. These were a disconnected network of underground streets cut in the soft tufa rock, crossing each other at right angles, generally made on many levels which were reached by staircases. Into the walls, along these streets, were cut horizontal niches into which the bodies of the departed were laid. During the years of Christian persecution in Rome, the Church Militant assembled in the catacombs to participate at Mass and other prayer sessions. To accommodate for large numbers of gatherers, the subterranean highways were equipped with shafts communicating with the surface so that light and air could be supplied to the assemblage below.

Ever since the early days of Christianity, through schisms, reformations, political revolutions, and counter-reformations, the leaders of Catholicism, even as late as the nineteenth and early twentieth centuries, insisted upon burial of the bodies of deceased Catholics in cemeteries set aside and whose ground was blessed by the Church. To them, in life all Catholics held to the same faith, same hope, same charity, and all received the same divine grace through the same sacraments; so, in death, their earthly remains should be near each other. Therefore the Catholic Church insisted that the departed faithful be separated from pagans, protestants, schismatics, freethinkers, and anti-clerical antagonists. Catholics wanted a separate place for the remains of their departed so that they could, while standing at the tomb send up to God earnest and fervent prayers, honor their remains as instruments of virtuous lives, as venerable relics, and as sharers in eternal glory, and adorn the graves with symbols of redemption, particularly the cross, representing Christ, the first-born among the dead who casts His shadow over His sleeping brethren. Catholics were unwilling to share the last resting-place of their faithful with those who did not profess the same faith and were in life not in communion with them. It was for these reasons that Louis Le Couteulx, in granting his gift of land, in trust to Bishop Dubois, insisted that a parcel of that land be used for a Catholic cemetery to be filled with the bones of the parishioners of the church which would be built upon the remaining space provided by his grant; and, in which, he requested a special place there to be set aside for himself and his family. [3]

*P*rior to 1832 there were several small cemeteries in Buffalo. The first on the estate of Captain William Johnston, a British officer who owned a tract of land bounded on the north by Seneca Street, on the west by Washington Street, on the south by Little Buffalo Creek, and on the east by a line which ran parallel with Washington Street. At the corner of Exchange and Washington Streets, Johnston had established a small lot for use as a cemetery. One assumes that he and his infant son were buried there. Johnston had died in 1807. Interments continued in this lot until the village burial ground was established at Franklin Square, a section bordered by Church Street on the north, Eagle Street on the south, Delaware Avenue on the west, and Franklin Street on the east. On the Square today one finds the City and County Hall. The first Catholic Cemetery was the Old St. Louis Cemetery located on Edward Street near Main Street, occupying ground up to the present site of the rectory for St. Louis Church; it was part of

the land deeded in trust, as a gift, to Bishop Dubois by Le Couteulx. Burials were first made there in 1830.

*D*uring the cholera epidemic of 1832, the Buffalo City Council called for the closing of all cemeteries in the city. During this period, Ebenezer Johnson, the first mayor of Buffalo, had been a physician trained in New England, and settled in Buffalo in 1810. He abandoned his profession of medicine and went into the real estate business, becoming the senior partner in the banking firm of Johnson and Hodge. When called upon by his peers, he described the cause of the cholera epidemic in detailed fashion. He claimed that the dreaded disease originated in Quebec brought there by Irish immigrants who were flooding into the American continent from Europe. From there he assumed that it traveled down the St. Lawrence River, broke out among the workers digging the twenty-seven mile long Welland Canal starting at Port Dalhousie on Lake Ontario to Port Colborne on Lake Erie. From there it was transported into Buffalo by ships crossing the lake.

*H*is theory was well founded because the *comma bacillus* that initiates the cholera symptoms had been known to originate in India along the Ganges River. Intercontinental ship commerce brought the disease's organism to England in 1832, from which it spread rapidly to Ireland. In England two thousand five hundred deaths due to the disease were recorded. Johnson's theory, however, was held skeptical by some because in 1832 the first outbreak in the United States was observed in Kentucky, not in Buffalo. By whatever means it did arrive, by July of that year one hundred and twenty people had died and the community was frantic and paralyzed. Victims endured vomiting and diarrhea followed by severe cramps. Their pulses grew very weak, their skins became dry and cold, and their bodies took on a livid color. With their temperatures rising, their bowels suffered great constipation, and their excretions of urine became extremely meager; they found themselves at death's door. Several of those who were fortunate to receive salt solutions into their systems accompanied by drinking barley water seemed to respond favorably and fought off the final blow of the grim reaper. Undertakers worked around the clock, the city was quarantined, all traffic into and out of the city was stopped, and a makeshift hospital was opened and staffed by volunteers. Rich and poor alike fell victim to the plague that could kill within twenty-four hours of inception.

During the seven years prior to this disaster, Buffalo had grown in population from two thousand four hundred and twelve, to ten thousand. From Exchange Street, north and west, the roads were passable but unpaved. West of Franklin Street they were impassable, practically lying in the muck of swamp. Most of the population had homes on the west side of Main Street between Mohawk and Exchange Streets. When asked, people would say, "To get to Chippewa Street it is a long walk; when you get to Tupper Street you are out of town!" Below Exchange Street the heavy business and commerce was around the Erie Canal, lower Main and Commercial Streets, and on down to the Buffalo River. The newly incorporated City of Buffalo had six churches, eight institutions, two banks, one insurance company, ten elevators for grain at the harbor, one library with seven hundred volumes, sixteen public and private schools, sixty mail deliveries received in the winter months and eighty-eight deliveries during the season of navigation, ten store houses for lake and canal business, and forty manufacturing establishments. Among the craftsmen one could find seven blacksmiths, two cabinet makers, three wheelwrights and coach builders, two chair makers, one cooper, three hatters, two tanners, five boot and shoe makers, two painters, four tailors, one tobacco manufacturer, twenty-five carpenters and joiners, nineteen masons and stone cutters, one brush maker, and three butchers. Among the professionals there were doctors, pharmacists, and teachers.

In 1828, Leonard P. Cary was appointed constable; he was a one-man police force. By 1838 the force had grown to seven. It was not, however, until 1866 that a Niagara Frontier Police Department was created by an act of the State Legislature. The city's water supply system was also an evolving enterprise. In 1821, John Kuercherer was the first to supply it with potable water. In 1827 the Buffalo and Black Rock Jubilee Water Works supplied potable water from springs on Delaware Avenue; it was delivered to customers through wooden pipes. By January 2, 1852, The Buffalo Waterworks Company was established and delivered their potable water through a more extensive and modern system. Public transportation also evolved. Small railroad lines had sprung up in and around Buffalo starting in 1832. By 1834, four of them successfully expanded their operation: Buffalo and Erie, Buffalo and Aurora, Buffalo and Niagara Falls, and Buffalo and Black Rock. Only the Buffalo and Niagara Falls Railroad, however, was steam powered. Then the New York Central, hooked together short links, and established a complete run from Buffalo to Albany by 1853. By the time of the Civil War, with the help of both the canal and railroads, Buffalo's population increased to nearly eighty-two thousand. More immigrants arrived and stayed. Only the cruelty of the plagues tended to modulate the increase. Many who came died in the cholera epidemic of 1832, and more met their demise in the subsequent ones of 1849, 1852, and 1854.

When the city's cemeteries were closed in 1832, William Hodge, Johnson's partner, sold the city five acres of land known as farm lot number thirty, lying between North and Best Streets for Potter's field, a common burying ground. Set off from it, on its west side, was approximately one acre with an eighty-eight foot frontage on both North and Best Streets. The Common Council allocated it to the Catholics in recompense for closing their cemetery, the Old St. Louis Cemetery at Main and Edward Streets. Eventually it took on the name of the New St. Louis Cemetery. When the City gave this acre to the Catholics, the trustees of the Lamb of God Church, the only Catholic Church in Buffalo at that time had not yet been incorporated. The City, therefore, did not stipulate any condition of "in trust" as the original grant had carried for the Old St. Louis Cemetery. The trustees, however, believed, that it belonged to them because of their incorporation of 1838. They considered it simply as an extension of the Le Couteulx grant. Therefore they continued, as they had done since 1832, to care for the New St. Louis Cemetery as they did the old one, and regulate the conditions of burial of bodies in it until 1859.

Before the end of 1834, General Sylvester Matthews and Birdseye Wilcox purchased twelve acres of farm lot number thirty from Hodge for a private cemetery, adjoining the five acres of land which the City had purchased for Potter's Field. Many Buffalonians including the Hodge family purchased lots there. Being farmland it was, at the time of purchase, destitute of trees and shrubbery. Mathews, Wilcox, and Hodge planted locust trees because they grew quickly, needed little attention, and were inexpensive. By 1853 the cemetery had deteriorated; it had been sorely neglected in its maintenance. Several of the property owners and perspective owners joined together and formed the Buffalo Cemetery Association. In 1854 they bought the rights to all the lots in the cemetery for $5,000. The entire North Street Cemetery, including Potters field, the New St. Louis partition, and the Buffalo Association's section, however, was not used for interment after February 18, 1893. Other cemeteries outside the city had been created. The transfer of bodies was commenced in March of 1901 and completed by August of that year. Eventually on the site of these graves was constructed the armory of the sixty-fifth regiment. The law to carry out this action had been passed by the New York State Legislature and approved by the City of Buffalo on April 12, 1898.

After he had become bishop in 1847, Timon purchased land at Limestone Hill in Lackawanna for a cemetery; it was named the Bishop's Cemetery and reserved for the interment of deceased Irish. The unique use of this cemetery brought no argumentation from the trustees of St. Louis Church. It was, however, that one-acre abutting Potter's field which became a source of contention between them and Bishop Timon during his interdiction procedure. It became an additional vehicle through which they vented their resentment against the bishop and those Catholics, who, for various reasons, had left St. Louis Church and joined newly founded parishes. The trustees maintained that, through their incorporation of 1838 and the stipulations of the original deed of 1829, they were responsible for the administration of the New St. Louis Cemetery. Although they admitted that Mayor Ebenezer Johnson and the City Clerk Dyre Tillinghast had granted that parcel of land outside the city limits on March 2, 1833 for a Catholic cemetery, they assumed that they still held the same legal privileges over it which applied to their ownership of the old deeded cemetery. They argued further that between the years 1839 and 1847, Bishop Hughes did not specifically voice an opinion over their administration of it. They said that when Timon had accepted the position of bishop over the newly formed diocese, only then did they resist his command to allow interment of all deceased Catholics in the diocese. The trustees, therefore, restricted stubbornly the burials in their cemetery to only their parishioners; and, by doing so, refused the right of burial there to Catholics from other churches; a right which they claimed was created by Timon as a ploy to make them submit to his will. [4]

In 1852, however, when Timon claimed that there was an omission of the words "in trust" placed in the deed for the New St. Louis Cemetery, the trustees were infuriated, and they responded by appealing to the City Council. They said, "The consequence of that unfortunate omission is that Right Reverend Bishop

Timon, now Catholic Bishop of the new See of Buffalo, has lately claimed said cemetery as his own, turned out the grave-digger and appointed another, and otherwise having taken the whole control of said premises permitting to be buried there only those he pleases, and mostly from congregations not in existence in the city at the time of the grant, to the exclusion of that of the church of St. Louis, for which it was intended, and creating himself a revenue out of said cemetery, by charging a fee of $2.00 for each body buried there! That Bishop Timon should buy lands, as he has already done, to make cemeteries, and speculate upon the sale of them into small lots to those willing to buy them, we have nothing to say; but, when the spirit of speculation extends to that cemetery given by the City for the use of our congregation, surely we have a right to complain, and to seek redress at the hands of the donors."

Hearing of their approach to the City Council, Timon was quick to reply. He said, "In August, 1849, I was informed by the trustees that the New St. Louis Cemetery allotted by the City of Buffalo was full." He then proceeded to explain that he had consecrated another piece of ground which he had purchased elsewhere for burials, and on the occasion of its consecration he had publicly and before a large crowd of people stated the rules to be followed in the government of that cemetery. He further told the City Council that when the pastor of St. Louis Church had informed him that it was no longer decent to be buried in the New St. Louis Cemetery in sections reserved only for members of St. Louis Church, he ordered the pastor to close it, but if Catholics from any parish in the city wished to be buried in other parts of it, near their friends, that he should grant them that permission. The pastor then told the bishop that these had also been closed. Later the bishop found out that the trustees had deceived him and the pastor and that the New St. Louis Cemetery still had available spaces. They had used the ploy of unfitness as a weapon in their war of wills against the bishop!

The cemetery issue became the source of much misunderstanding; and, inevitably, the cause of much grief for the families involved. Since 1832 to the time of the solution of the interdiction problem at St. Louis Church, the former members of the church were scattered into seven churches within and surrounding Buffalo. These were: St. Patrick's, the Irish Church at Broadway and Ellicott Streets; St. Mary's, the Redemptorist Church at Broadway and Pine Streets; St. Peter's, the French Church at Washington and Clinton Streets; St. Michael's, the Jesuit Church at six hundred and fifty-one Washington Street; St. Boniface, one hundred and twenty-four Locust Street; St. John the Baptist, the North Bush Church, on Englewood Avenue; St Joseph's, the Buffalo Plains Church, at three thousand two hundred and sixty-nine Main Street; and St. Mary's of the Lake at one hundred and fifty Edward Street, which in 1854 became known as the Immaculate Conception Church. Although the bodies of those interred at the Old St. Louis Cemetery had been moved to the New St. Louis Cemetery, many wives, children, friends, and relatives who would later die, stipulated that they wished to be buried side-by-side or in the neighborhood of their loved ones, even though they themselves had left St. Louis Church and had given affiliation to one of the other Catholic churches.

On April 5, 1852, therefore, a committee of forty-four former members of St. Louis Church, then members of other churches, sent a letter to the mayor and the city council requesting that a definitive answer be rendered by them concerning this matter. They said, "Our kindred and friends lie buried in the said grounds; our wives and children there rest in peace, and this is were we wish that our bodies may be interred. Because in said ground our kindred and friends have found a common resting place, we feel that by your grant, which has been in effect for twenty years, we are entitled to rest there also. You, the representatives of the City of Buffalo are now, however, called upon by the trustees of St. Louis Church to act disgracefully in the sight of God and man and say that you have repudiated your act and deed, and have permitted a self-constituted body of priestless men, without any ecclesiastical power or authority, to assume the control of that which now belongs to, and is held in trust for, the members of all Catholic churches which have been properly organized. We do not know the reason why the grave-digger was dismissed, but we do know that this same man left the bodies of the dead so near the surface of the ground that you, representatives of the City of Buffalo, were compelled at great expense to cover those exposed bodies with earth during the summer of 1849."

The committee received no satisfactory answer from the City Council. The frustration among Catholics in Buffalo continued to exist for the next seven years until it was decided to organize an incorporation known as the United German and French Roman Catholic Cemetery Association. It was formed on February 21, 1859 in the schoolhouse of St. Mary's Church by six parishes: St. Louis, St. Mary's, St. Boniface, St. Ann's, St. Peter's, and St. Michael's. It had purchased fourteen acres on the west side of Pine Ridge Road for the interment of their loved ones and to rebury their relatives and friends from the New St. Louis Cemetery, which was closed to the purchase of new plots in that year. By 1879 all lots in the original section of the United German and French Roman Catholic Cemetery had been sold. Of those who had been buried in the New St. Louis Cemetery were Louis Le Couteulx and his family. It had been stipulated in deeding the property "in trust" to Bishop Dubois and his successors that a place be reserved in the Old St. Louis Cemetery for this purpose. Le Couteulx, however, died in 1840 and could not be buried there because all bodies buried in Buffalo's cemeteries were required to be moved after the cholera epidemic of 1832 to Potter's Field.

Thirty years later, the trustees of the United German and French Roman Catholic Cemetery, therefore, gave a plot of land in their cemetery to St. Louis Church on agreement that the church would build a suitable monument there within a certain number of years and have Le Couteulx's remains moved to it. Father Joseph Sorg, pastor at St. Louis Church, chose Sunday September 14, 1873 as the first day to begin the preparations for the movement of the earthly remains of the Le Couteulx family from the New St. Louis Cemetery to their new grave site in the United German and French Roman Catholic Cemetery. He made it clear to the parishioners that sufficient funds would have to be raised so as to transfer the bodies from the old cemetery to the new one, pay for the preparations of the grave site and monument, and have money for the annual Mass and Office of the Dead said for the repose of the souls of the family. He titled the entire thrust of their action as the *Founder's Commemoration*. From 1873 until 1879 the annual commemoration of the Mass and Office was held at St. Louis Church and the donations of the parishioners were gathered over and above their pew rent. All members of the congregation who donated $5.00 or more toward the program were awarded a special written memento of their names. When the great *Uebertragung*, the transfer was completed, the celebration before the new gravesite took place on Sunday afternoon August 3, 1879.

The total expenditures made prior to the celebration of the *Founders Commemoration Day* were $593.68. All but $72.47 was secured prior to the event. The details of the expenditures were recorded: $10.00 for the removal of the iron fence around the old burial site, $153.75 for the preparations of the new site including a new iron fence, $5.00 for a tree, and $424.93 for the transfer of the bodies. Some large contributions from a few totaled $283.00. The remainder of the congregation, however, each donating less than $5.00, contributed the total sum of $218.21. Adding $20.00 for the sale for the old *Eisengitters*, the iron fence around the burial ground that was vacated, the total gift toward the ceremony was $521.21. Such action on the part of the parishioners was a true expression of their faith which they expressed every Sunday while they heard the priest or the choir sing that part of the Nicene Creed which states, "And I believe in One, Holy, Catholic, and Apostolic Church. I confess one baptism for the remission of sins. I look for the resurrection of the dead, and the life of the world to come." Since, however, the parishioners of St. Louis Church could not raise a sufficient amount of money to pay for a monument, but had paid for all the other necessities, the trustees of the cemetery financed the "largest crucifix in the world," sculptured in Barre, Vermont, transported to Buffalo, and placed at Le Couteulx's gravesite. [5]

Although reason tells one that the grave contains only the decayed flesh and bones of the deceased, living Catholics cannot separate in their minds the bodies and the souls of their loved ones who have died. They cannot see death having any victory! They continue to believe that their loved ones, who had crossed the river to lie under the shade of the elm tree, have their souls experiencing a new active life either as saints or as saved personalities awaiting sanctification. The Roman Catholic Church each year sets aside two days to specifically honor all who have died in Christ and in communion with the Church. These are called *All Saints Day* and *All Souls Day,* celebrated respectively on the first and second day of November. *All Saints Day* venerates the names of all those who died, are saints, but are not officially canonized. They are those who have fought the good fight and have been admitted to the Beatific Vision of God. In honoring their departed ancestors and making mental visits to their mansions of bliss, living Catholics reflect on the fact that they too can be numbered among the saints. They resolve to persevere in the service of God and observe His holy law. The feast was instituted in Rome during the reign of Pope Boniface IV. At the beginning of the seventh century, the Pantheon, that had stood as a heathen temple to honor the Roman god Jupiter was opened as a church, dedicated to the Blessed Virgin Mary and the martyrs. Pagan temples such as the Pantheon had been destroyed in the eastern half of the Roman Empire by Theodosius at the beginning of the

fifth century; but, in the West, they remained as monuments of the magnificence of the former empire. It was in this temple that the pope had twenty-six wagonloads of bones deposited as relics of unknown martyrs who had been buried in the catacombs during the years of Christian persecutions. In 834, Pope Gregory IV extended the feast day to the whole Church.

All Souls Day was instituted to remember the souls of the departed who may not have been sufficiently pure and holy enough so as to be, immediately upon death, ushered into the sight of the Beatific Vision of God. Although the sufferings and death of Christ had saved them, they began their experience of Purgatory, a state of resignation, patience, and hope while they waited for their total purification. Although the Catholic believes that all are saved by the Incarnate God from eternal punishment for sins committed in life, they also contend that besides eternal punishment there is temporal punishment for these sins which must be accounted for. It has an analogy in criminal justice whereby the criminal can be forgiven, but he must serve time in prison. In the biblical book of Macabees one finds the passage which states, "It is a holy and wholesome thought to pray for the dead that they may be loosed from their sins." (2 Mach., XII: 46). Judas Macabee, a Jewish leader, fighting for independence against Antiochus Epiphanes in 164 B.C., wanted his people to pray for his departed soldiers who had died in battle. He realized that night had come to them, a time when no one can work. Although the souls in purgatory can suffer for their friends on earth, they cannot help themselves. They depend upon the Church Militant to intercede for them before the throne of God. The Catholic Church has always championed their cause and placed their Remembrance Day on the day after the festival of *All Saints.*

Prayer cards or memorials given to those who attended the wakes of the departed were to be distributed to friends so that they would pray for the departed whose souls may be in purgatory. They were also posted in the vestibules of the churches for the same purpose. In the early centuries of the Catholic Church, the Fathers and Doctors of the Church encouraged such devotions. St. John Chrysostom said, "Let us also pray for those who have died in Christ." Tertullian, who lived in the next age after the Chosen Twelve, told how the widow prays for the soul of her husband and begs refreshment for him. St. Augustine promoted the use of prayers for those lavishing in purgatory especially his mother, Monica. Later she was claimed a canonized saint by papal authority. Even the schismatic Greeks and the Jews were convinced that the concept of purgatory was grounded in the nature of rational man. It seemed a basic ingredient of the virtue of justice. The solemn celebration of prayers for the dead in the Catholic Church was the Mass of Requiem said on the third, seventh, and thirtieth day after death. On the third day it represented the resurrection of Jesus Christ. Being said on the seventh day it represented God's resting on the seventh day after his creation of the world. On the thirtieth day it reminded the faithful of the thirty days of mourning of the children of Israel who lamented the death of Moses and Aaron. Catholicism has always considered death as the birthday of the soul into eternal life. The absolute and final victory over death will come on the last day when the body rusted and decayed in the tomb will gloriously be reunited with the soul; and, once again as both matter and form, the person will live a life which here on earth is unimaginable.

Unfortunately, until that day comes, fallible humans who are prone to covetousness must handle our sacred cemeteries. So was the case in the transfer of bodies from the North Street Cemetery to newly approved land sites. Grand larceny was one of the crimes committed by contractors in their removal and reburying of bodies. Presentation of false claims to the city ran into many thousands of dollars. In the transfer, poorly prepared grounds were planned for the reception of the bodies and head stones were not set up, but just placed on the ground. It was also noted that several coffins were broken open and the bones separated into other boxes so that the contractor could claim the burial of more bodies than actually were moved. Many contractors were convicted; some received sentences up to ten years in Auburn Prison. It was pointed out that one contractor had stolen between forty and sixty thousand dollars of taxpayers' money. Because he was paid by poundage in the transfer of bodies, many caskets were filled with cow bones, sheep bones and other non-human materials so as to increase the laborers profit. Before transfer, several caskets were unlocked and looted of all valuables that were treasures of the deceased, and which loved ones had placed inside the casket at the time of burial. Many bodies were not properly buried; some being only between fourteen inches and four and one-half feet underground. In the removal from the old cemetery many caskets were poorly marked and located incorrectly in the new cemetery. Several of those that were properly placed were identified with an incorrect tombstone. Finally, if bones were not properly identified they were simply mingled with others and reburied.

Although crimes of this type have been recorded in history, they are not the pattern in the modern world. More care is presently taken and most cemeteries are well looked after. Historically, respect for the dead has won out over the criminal element. Since the time of Solomon, man has pondered his words, "One generation passeth away, and another generation cometh, but the earth abideth forever." Forever, yes, until the last day, for even then the earth shall pass away! Until then, however, Catholics reverently cherish the memory of those who died, emulating their virtues, while attempting to avoid their errors, and seek to be ready so that when the summons comes they can say, "Oh! Lord, we are ready to pass the torch to others, let them run the race as we have done. Let us join our many ancestors who have already come into Your heavenly kingdom." [6]

With respectful levity one might assume that Catholics can paraphrase an old slogan to read, "you can take it with you!" Like most other people, they know that when they die their wealth remains behind to be distributed to survivors and charitable organizations according to wills and codicils. Engrained, however, in their psyches is the faith that grace, like a mighty Niagara, continually flows through the Church reaching out to the souls in purgatory, cleansing those already saved but awaiting transport to the Beatific Vision. They believe that after death purification of their souls depends upon the spiritual benefits of the Church. Prior to death, therefore, they take out a spiritual insurance policy; they set up foundations so that the Sacrifice of the Mass will be offered on set occasions for their intentions after their death and the death of their loved ones. They may know that none buy their way into heaven, but they believe that earthly wealth will perpetuate the Church, the Church will perpetuate its sacred prayers and good works to God, and God will be pleased to perpetuate the cleansing of the souls in purgatory in the name of the Church.

It was in this faith that the pastor of St. Louis Church with the approval of the trustees and the consent of the bishop set up the policy known as *Stiftung*, the policy of bequests for Masses to be said and sung according to a set plan; these were the St. Louis Church's Foundations which began with the death of Elizabeth Flexing on June 17, 1868 when she donated in her will the sum of $139.56 for Masses to be said for her intentions, one each year, for ten years following her death. Her money was placed in the treasury of the church controlled by the trustees. The financial transaction was approved by Jacob Davis, president of the trustees, by J.L. Jacobs, secretary of the corporation, and by Father Joseph Sorg, the pastor. During these ten years the pastor received the stipend of $8.34 from the trustees each time he said one of the Masses, and recorded and signed his action in the Foundations Book in which all records were meticulously entered, guarded, audited, and preserved.

All Masses said or sung were, prior to the occasion, announced in the church's bulletins.

Each Foundation was an individual act on the part of the trustees, the pastor, and the bishop. Each amount of money received was accepted first by the approval of the trustees and then by the pastor and bishop. In general it was the reigning pastor who said or sang the Masses which were requested. Many foundations were made several years before the death of the beneficiaries. Many were approved and initiated after a person's will had been probated. Some were set up prior to death naming several family members as beneficiaries, with Masses to be offered subsequent to their deaths. In some cases the words "in perpetuity" were used to indicate that the Masses were to be offered forever on indicated occasions. Other bequests stipulated terms of years such as twenty-five, fifty, or one hundred. In other wills, terms such as, "until St. Louis Church exists," or "as long as St. Louis Church is incorporated," appeared indicating that the beneficiaries of the spiritual favors were also controlling the earthly aspects of the grant and not forgetting the controversy over authority in the early days of the church's existence. The manner in which the bequests were made further showed the dichotomy of the parishioners' attitudes toward the authority in the church since the great compromise of 1855. Some were made directly to the pastor while others were initially directed to the trustees.

One bequest reflected the religious attitudes of the nineteenth century when anti-Catholicism was ideologically based on xenophobic and ethnic prejudice. Protestants vented their hatred on the poisons of popery. They claimed the Roman Catholic Church to be apostate and not really Christian. The bishops of the Catholic Church denounced or strongly curtailed mixed marriages of Catholics and Protestants; and, by the tone of their pastoral letters, isolated Catholics from Protestant sponsored activities. These attitudes were mildly exposed in the conditions of Rosalia Kurtzman's Foundation. Prior to her death on February 3, 1893, she had given $1,200 to St. Louis Church with the stipulation that as long as she was living, Masses were to be said according to her intention from the interest earned on the investment of the money; and, that after her death, the capital was to be used for Foundation Masses: a Requiem High Mass was to be sung annually as long as St. Louis Church should exist for Roaslia Kurtzman and her husband, and another to be sung annually for the duration of fifty years for the repose of the souls of the deceased members of the Kurtzman family. In regards to this contract, the bishop gave his approval *viva-voce*, by word of mouth, with the stipulation that Mr. Kurtzman's name not appear in the announcements of the Masses because he was a Protestant, the victim of a mixed marriage. The contract was accepted and signed by Father Paul Hoelscher, pastor, Charles Lautz, president of the trustees, and J.H.Ullenbruch, secretary of the corporation.

Some Foundations offered bequests that provided large sums of money that went to the beautification of St. Louis Church after its reconstruction following the great fire of 1885. One such bequest was the Lang and Lautz Foundation. Gerhard Lang, founder of Lang's brewery, and Charles Lautz, president of the trustees, and his wife Susanna donated $5,000. With this money the side altars consecrated to the Sacred Heart of Jesus and the Immaculate Heart of Mary, built of oak-wood and marble, were installed in 1893. By this time, Gerhard Lang had already died; but, in compliance with the stipulations of Lautz, the trustees, pastor, and the bishop wholeheartedly approved the bequest that two Requiem High Masses would be sung annually, one for Lang on July 14, and the other for Lautz and his wife after their deaths. Until then the money would remain in the church's treasury, be invested, and draw interest. When the bishop gave his approval that year, he also suggested that as soon as the financial condition of the church stabilized a special amount of money should be

set aside so that from its interest all Foundation Masses at St. Louis Church could be paid. Further, on November 3, 1893, Paul Hoelscher, pastor, made a motion to the trustees that henceforth money should be taken from the treasury for a Requiem High Mass to be sung for all former pastors of St. Louis Church on one day each year during November. The stipend was to be paid by the trustees to the pastor who would celebrate the Mass.

On February 23, 1903 Emma Lang died. In her last will and testament $25,000 was donated to St. Louis Church with the stipulation that three-fifths of it would be used to design, construct, and install the marble high altar in the sanctuary. The remaining two-fifths of the money was to be used to pay the debts on the church. This was an important contribution because the loan to build the new gothic church structure had not yet been completely paid back to the banks and lenders. On March 3, 1903, Jacob G. Lang, Emma's brother and executor of her will paid the first $15,000 to the trustees of the church; the remaining amount was paid the following year. In return, the trustees set up a Foundation whereby for as long as St. Louis Church existed an anniversary High Mass was to be sung annually on February 23, for the repose of her soul. Also in 1903, Mrs. Emma Weppner gave the trustees the sum of $6,000 to be used to purchase a new Communion Rail separating the sanctuary from the nave of the church. It extended across the width of the two side altars and the main altar. For her donation she received an annual living expense of $300 for the remainder of her life which ended in death on November 24, 1913. Following her demise, an annual Requiem High Mass was said for the repose of her soul and that of her husband Jacob Weppner.

The two altars in the transepts of the Church resulted because of the contributions of Catherine Feist and Mrs. Frank T. Hartman, nee Elizabeth Esser. Catherine's Foundation was set up on April 1, 1908 when she donated the sum of $3,500. With this money the trustees were able to install Saint Joseph's Altar in the left transept as one views the main altar. In the remainder of her lifetime Catherine received an annual pension of $120 and following her death three Requiem High Masses were sung annually and in perpetuity for herself, her husband, John Feist, and her deceased son, Louis Henry Davis. The $4,000 which Elizabeth Esser donated to the trustees on January 31, 1909 went to pay for the beautiful altar, in the right transept, featuring the *La Pieta*, Our Lady of Sorrows, modeled after the masterpiece of Michaelangelo displayed in St. Peter's Basilica in Rome. On May 11, 1909 her Foundation was approved and finalized. Upon her death an annual Requiem High Mass was sung, in perpetuity, for the repose of her soul and those of her father, John Esser, and all the deceased members of her family.

Requiem High Masses were also requested and approved in several other important Foundations. Among these were Charles Lautz's contribution of $1,000 in 1901 and Catherine Neunder's donation of $1,000, both of which were applied to the Organ Fund in 1902, and Rosalia Bortzmeier's $1,000 which gave added assistance to the altar fund in 1895. On January 1, 1903, Catherine increased her Foundation by adding an extra $20,000. She died on December 19, 1918. In the summer of 1909, Edward M. Hager completed the construction of the beautifully carved wooden pulpit that adorns the nave of the church. He made it according to the design and drawings of William Schickel, the architect of the Church. On the pulpit one sees the figures of the four Evangelists, Matthew, Mark, Luke, and John, and some Fathers and Doctors of the Catholic Church. For material and labor the pulpit had upon completion an estimated worth of $4,000. Because Hager donated the cost of all his materials and labor, the trustees, pastor, and bishop wholeheartedly created a Foundation whereby both he and his wife Ottilia shared in the fruits of anniversary requiem Masses annually as long as St. Louis Church existed. Edward Hager died on June 14, 1919, and Ottilia died on

January 19, 1945.

The wording in some of the wills and codicils which gave the basis for setting up Foundations involved much concern to the trustees and the clergy, especially when the words of the donors vented near impossible control of the use of the funds. One such case was the John Kraus Foundation. John died on April 15, 1910 and was buried in the United German and French Roman Catholic Cemetery. In his will, he left $500 to the *St. Louis German and French Roman Catholic Church*. For this amount the trustees had little problem carrying out his wishes for requiem Masses being sung for the repose of his soul and the souls of his family whose names were so stipulated. They did have a problem, however, with the extra $2,000 which he willed to the church with the stipulation that it be placed in interest bearing securities so that the interest would go to the care and maintenance of his and his family's grave sites. For these he detailed how they should be kept with the application of flowers, urns, vases, watering, and grass cutting. He also requested like maintenance for the grave of his father. Further he wanted his pew in St. Louis Church, number one hundred and seventy-seven, to be continually rented in his family's name.

The pastor and the trustees carefully discussed the ramifications of his requests. They had no authority over the operational procedures at the United German and French Roman Catholic Cemetery, nor were they going to be responsible for paying the cemetery an arbitrary sum for the upkeep of individual graves. The trustees discussed the situation with the cemetery board. The members of the board said that they would take upon themselves the upkeep if the trustees of St. Louis Church would pay a lump sum of $1,200. The trustees agreed, and then set up Kraus' Foundation based on the remaining $800. For this, plus the original $500, they were willing to carry out his other wishes concerning the pew and the Masses. Therefore John and Caroline Kraus, John and Elizabeth Kraus, and Alexander Kraus,

John Kraus, and Delia E. Weppner were remembered in separately sung Masses. On this occasion, in the absence of the bishop, the trustees received approval for this Foundation from Rt. Rev. Nelson H. Baker, vicar general, on May 9, 1911.

*T*hree pastors at St. Louis Church requested Foundations from the trustees. Father Joseph Sorg died on September 15, 1888. His Mass requests were based upon the contents of his will which allowed St. Louis Church to inherit a piece of land which bordered on the eastern line of the church's property and on Franklin Street on the western side. This land was adjacent to the school building. Monsignor Paul Hoelscher, in his last will and testament, bequeathed to St. Louis Church $5,000. On December 27 each year the church faithfully offered a Requiem Mass for the repose of his soul. Father Henry B. Laudenbach died on December 29, 1943. His executors, Fathers Edward S. Schwegler and Henry W. Keitzel delivered to the trustees a paid up Life Insurance Policy for $2,000 that had been taken out by Laudenbach on November 19, 1941. The Foundation then provided the proper amount of spiritual benefits for both the Laudenbach and Keitzel families.

*I*n 1938 the trustees changed the rules governing Foundations. After that year, before a Foundation was made, previous consent had to be obtained from the bishop, copies of the contract had to be filed in the chancellor's office and registered in the vestry of the church, no further perpetual Foundations were acceptable, and new annual fees were established. Altogether there were five Foundation books in which the records were kept. On April 30, 1964, Father Clarence Ott, then pastor of St. Louis Church, meticulously reviewed Book I. His audit showed that all Masses up to that time had been faithfully executed except for one-hundred and five. Immediately he sent twenty-five Mass requests to Monsignor Eberz, twenty-five to Father Clarence Dye, and fifty-five to Father

Pius Benincasa. They sang all the required Masses for the proper intentions thus completing all of the unfulfilled bequests. With this degree of care for executing the proper spiritual benefits attached to these Foundations, the Society of St. Louis Church showed its deep faith in the doctrine of the Communion of Saints. [7]

REFERENCES AND NOTES ✠ CHAPTER SEVEN

1. Information concerning the details of the end of the Civil War see: Mark M. Boatner III, *The Civil War Dictionary*, Vantage Books, New York, 1988, pps. 22, 299, 822; Participation of the Turnverein in antebellum period and in the War see: op. cit., *History of Germans of Buffalo and Erie County*, pps. 149-58; The Buffalo Germans' attitude toward slavery see: op. cit., *Der Turner Soldat*, p. 45; Buffalo during the time of the Civil War see: op. cit., *High Hopes*, pp. 92-4, 121-23; Colonel Daniel Bidwell, for whom Bidwell Parkway, Buffalo, is named commanded the 49th New York Infantry Regiment.

2. Catholicism and the Black population of Buffalo see: op. cit. *Celebrating God's Life in Us, The Catholic Diocese of Buffalo, 1847-1997*, pps. 127-8; For biographical material of Sergius Schoulepnikoff see: op. cit. *Good Shepherd: The Church on the Canal*, p.7; For the story of the funeral of Mathias Hausle see: Leo H. Hausle, *Hausle family and Biographical Sketches*, Buffalo, New York, 1905, a copy is in the St. Louis Church Archives.

3. For the concern which Catholicism has for the departed see: Rev. F.J. Shadler, *The Beauties of the Catholic Church*, Frederick Puset and Co., New York, New York, 26th ed., 1881, 268-89

4. For description and position of cemeteries in Buffalo see: Notes by Patrick Kavanaugh, Buffalo, New York, 2001, presented to the editors, copy in the St. Louis Church Archives; also see: William Hodge, *Buffalo Cemeteries*, a paper read before the Cemetery Society, Buffalo, New York, February 4, 1879; further see: H. Perry Smith, *History of the City of Buffalo and Erie County, 1620-1884*, D. Mason and Co., Syracuse, New York, 1882, vol. 2., pp. 64-67, 90-91, 502-511; For a description of Catholic cemeteries see: Rev. Thomas Donohue D.D., *History of the Diocese of Buffalo*, The Buffalo Catholic Publication Co., Buffalo, New York, 1929, p.391, and Pamphlet, *Louis Etienne Le Couteulx de Chaumont, 1756-1840, Pioneer Philanthropist, Financier, Druggist, First Clerk of Niagara County*, Mount Calvary Cemetery Inc., Heritage Blvd, 800 Pine Ridge Road, Cheektowaga, New York, June 2001; For background on Captain William Johnston see: Chrisfield Johnson, *Centennial, History of Erie County, New York*, Printing House of Matthews and Warren, Office of the *Buffalo Commercial Advertiser*, 1876,

pp. 64-91; Further, according to Ronald Pazek, superintendent of Holy Cross Cemetery, in an interview with the author/editor, Nov. 1, 1996, Bishop Timon had purchased five acres of land at Limestone Hill in Lackawanna for a cemetery which became known as the "Bishop's Cemetery." Today it is known as Holy Cross Cemetery. Limestone Hill was so called because much limestone was found there at the highest point of West Seneca, New York. The cemetery was prepared for the Irish only because they would not have been accepted in the New St. Louis Cemetery or later at the United German and French Roman Catholic Cemetery. Father William Kettner, a Jesuit, who came to Buffalo with Caveng and other Jesuits so as to break the deadlock with the trustees of St. Louis Church, was first buried in Section D. He died on March 23, 1854. His remains were next to those of Father Nelson Baker, prior to Baker's remains being brought inside of the Basilica of Our Lady of Victory. Kettner's remains were moved to Section O, Lot 125, which is in front of the chapel. For a description of cholera and its epidemic in Buffalo see: op. cit. *Illustrated World's Encyclopedia*, under definition of cholera; For facts concerning the development of police force, water works, and railroads in Buffalo see: In preparation for the Buffalo Pan American Expo. In 1901, *Buffalo of Today, Queen City of the Lakes*, Interstate Publishing Co., Buffalo, New York, 1898, pp. 33-78; The Old and New St. Louis Cemetery, North Street Cemetery, and German and French Cemetery see: Notes by Molly Hauck, Historian for Mt. Calvary Cemetery, Buffalo, New York, 2001, presented to the editors, copies in the St. Louis Archives. She includes the Minutes of the United German and French Roman Catholic Cemetery. It has also been stated that as early as February 19, 1848, William Le Couteulx spoke of his intentions of taking legal action to prevent Catholics from other parishes from using the cemetery. It was at this time, however, that Bishop Timon temporally persuaded the trustees not to petition the mayor and the city council; he contended that Louis Le Couteulx had intended the new cemetery, a replacement of the old, to be for the use of all Catholics. It was pointed out that when this beloved donor died in 1840, he was buried in the New St. Louis Cemetery although in his deed he had requested a plot reserved for himself in the original cemetery, the Old St. Louis Cemetery, bounded by Edward Street, see: op. cit. *Lay Trusteeism at St. Louis Church*, p.69.

5. For the discussion on the controversy between William Le Couteulx, the St. Louis Church Trustees, and Bishop Timon over the administration of the New St. Louis Cemetery on North Street see: op. cit. *Lay Trusteeism at St. Louis Church*, pps. 68-71; for the financial preparation for the *Founder's Commemoration Day* see: *Mass Foundations, Mass Bequests Book*, St. Louis Church Archives, Book 1., pp. 23-5. For the organization of the United German and French Roman Catholic Cemetery see: *Minutes, United German and French Roman Catholic Cemetery, organizational meeting at St. Mary's School House, February 21, 1859*, copies of the minutes are in the Mount Calvary Cemetery Archives. Information concerning the Le Couteulx monument is contained in ibid., 1879. The following is an alphabetical list of those

parishioners at St. Louis Church who contributed five dollars or more toward financing the *Uebertragung* of Louis Le Couteulx and his family: Bacher, Celestin; Born, Maria Anna; Brennan, George; Brunner, Joseph; Davis, Jacob; Deck, Jacob N.; Diebolt, Bernhard; Dietsche, Xavier, Feldmann, Anton; Feldmann, George; Fornes, Carl V., Foster, Joseph; Garono, Heinrich; Garono, Lorenz; Haberstro, Joseph Lambert; Hack, George; Hausle, Mathias; Hausle, Paul; Henry, F.J.; Jacobs, J.L.; Kieffer, Friedrich; Kraft, F.J.; Kretz, Edward; Land, Paul; Lang, Gehard; Lautz, Adam; Martin, Alexander; Martin, Mrs. Maria; Mergenhagen, Peter; Muehlbach, Andreas; Ordner, Mrs. John; Ottenot, Nicholas; Pfohl, Mrs. Emma; Rinck, Mrs. Maria Anna; Rosar, Peter; Rose, Joseph; Roth, Mrs. Martin; Schindler, John; Sorg, Father Joseph M; Spoere, Franz; Stadelmeyer, Michael; Steffan, Family; Vogt, Peter A.; Welker, John; Weppner, Arnold; Weppner, Jacob; Weppner, Mrs. Jacob; Werich, Heinrich; Werich, Joseph; Weyand, Christian; Zinns, Friedrich.

6. For a description of All Saints Day and All Souls Day see: op. cit. *The Beauties of the Catholic Church*, pp. 259-67; For the scandals in re-interring the dead when cemetery locations were changed see: *Express*, May 12, 1901, May 14, 1902, Nov. 20, 1902, Jan. 5, 1903, Feb. 26, 1903, Mar. 3, 1903; the *Commercial*, July 22, 1899; *Buffalo Evening News*, Jan. 4, 1906, Jan 6, 1906, Mar. 12, 1906, Mar. 13, 1906, Mar. 14, 1906, Mar. 16, 1906, Mar. 17, 1906, Mar 21, 1906, Mar. 28, 1906, July 25, 1906, Aug. 12, 1906, Nov. 12, 1906, Nov 13, 1906, Nov. 12, 1907.

7. In the op. cit. *Mass Foundations, Mass Bequests Book*, one finds the following small papers on the inside front cover. Apparently these Foundations were placed in Books II, III, IV, and V. The name is followed by the date of the foundation, the number of Masses requested, and the volume and page number in which one finds the details of the bequest. They are: John Hoffman Family, May 2, 1925, 100, V-61; Joseph and Ottilia Kam, April 1, 1958, 20, IV-122; Katherine Kraus, July 1, 1962, 100, IV-49; Max and Metz Fam., March 3, 1964, 15, V-65; Jacob E. Mueller, April 1, 1961, 40, V-I; Mary G. Miller, January 1, 1961, 40, IV-100; Harvey M. Radcliffe, September 1, 1961, 20, V-43; Joseph Reade, September 1, 1955, 400, V-11; Joseph Reinlander, December 12, 1923, 50, V-22; Thomas Ring, May 10, 1947, 20, I-257; Frank A. Schwegler, July 20, 1959, 200, IV-105; William and Eleanor Hauser, May 5, 1962, 40, IV-120; Rev. Robert T. Bapst, January 1, 1962, 50, V-46; Louise M. Bauer, November 29, 1961, 22, IV-124; Mary F. Bernhardt, January 1, 1961, 40, IV-117; Francisco Bidegain, August 18, 1959, 20, III-84; Charles and Caroline Bohn, February 1, 1960, 50, V-40; Bertha Breithecker, March 1, 1959, 200, V-22; Theresa G. Daly, March 31, 1964, 100, V-65; William and Agnes Dickinson, May 1, 1964, 20, V-67; Valentine and Louise Doerfler, October 10, 1952, 40, V-4; Ida E. Ess, April 2, 1958, 60, IV-101; Edward Garono and Family, July 1, 1959, 20, IV-175; Christian Gerhard Family, November 11, 1951, 200, V-2; George J. Hager, February 1, 1954, 200, V-6; Frank Simon, May 1, 1962, 20, V-47; Leon Skier and Family, June 30, 1961, 51, V-42; John H. Smith,

June 11, 1958, 20, V-28; Mary J. Swang, November 25, 1958, 20, V-21; Joseph Troidl, January 1, 1960, 100, V-37; George Vogelsang, 1934, 30; John and Theresa Schmauss, 1954, 20; John and Anna May, 1950, 35; John and Elizabeth Steffan, 1954, 25; Fred and Wilhelmina Zorn, October 1, 1963, 40, V-44; Mr. and Mrs. Alphonse Steinman, May 25, 1963, 100, V-53; Charles Steinman, May 25, 1963, 100, V-57. Below is listed the names in the *Mass Foundations*, Book I, as they are given Chronologically. In order they appear as the names, dates of the commencement, sums of money donated, numbers of Masses requested (usually one each year for a determined number of years), and the page numbers in Book I: Elizabeth Flexing, 1868, $139.56, 10, p.2; Catherine Theresa Jungmann, 1874, $300, 10, p.4; Doll Family, 1874, $50, 10, p.6; Francis Louis Schreck, 1869, $200, perpetuity, p.7; Joseph Bersch, 1876, $100, 10, p.10; Charles Brossard, $100, 10, p.12; Julianna Stasser, 1875, $50, 5, p.14; Joseph Zimmermann, 1876, $200 (stipulation that money used for education of poor children); George Doppel, 1877, $100, 10, p.18; Maria Anna Doll, 1879, $50, 10, p.20; Rosina Sprissler, 1880, $100, 10, p.22; Anton and Barbara Feldmann, 1882, $100, 10, p.28; Anna Maria Hittler, 1888, $50, 10, p.30; Bensler Family, 1886, $100, 13, p.32; Carrie Fix, 1886, $100, 10, p.34; Nunold Family, 1888, $75, 10, p.36; Georg Hack, 1889, $100, 13, p.38; Gleeson Family, 1889, $500, 7, p.40; Apollonia Motsch, 1889, $100, 13, p.42; Joanna Kampleshofer, 1889, $800, 5, p.44; Rosalia Kurtzman, 1893, $1200, (as long as the church should exist for Rosalia and her husband, a Protestant and 50 years for the family), p.45; Teresa Hack, 1893, $100, 13, p.48; Philip Zechmann, 1893, $100, 13, p.50; Gerhard Lang and Charles Lautz, 1894, $5000, (as long as St. Louis Church exists), p.51; Joseph Doll, Charles Doll, George Doll, and Mrs. Arnold Weppner, 1895, $200, 35, p.56; All deceased pastors, 1895, (money from the church treasury, Masses said one every year in perpetuity, in November), p.57; Mrs. Rosalia Bortzmeier, 1895, $1000, (one Mass said every year in November for Rosalia and Andrew Bortzmeier, money was assigned to the altar fund), p.61; Rev. Joseph Sorg, 1888, deeded the land bordering on Franklin Street to St. Louis Church; one Mass sung annually), p.65; Johann Zahm, 1896, $150, 25, p.70; G.F. Deck, 1897, $100, 13, p.70; Regina Pfluger, 1897, $100, 13, p.74; Anna Maria Rinck, 1897, 30, p.76; Peter Wex, 1899, $200, 20, p.78; Margaret Motsch, 1888, $200, 13, p. 80; Catherine Neunder, 1902, $1000, (as long as St. Louis Church exists), p.81; Catherine Neunder, 1903, $20,000, (as long as St. Louis Church should exist), p.83; Emma Lang, 1898, $35,000, (for the duration of St. Louis parish), p.87; Emma Weppner, 1903, $6000, (annual Mass for Emma and Jacob Weppner), p.91; Charles Lautz, 1903, $1000, (annually on anniversary of his death), p.93; Charles Lautz, 1903, $200, 38, p.98; Fransika Bensler, 1904, $200, 40, p.100; Magdalena Williams, 1906, $100, 13, p.102; Catherine Feist, 1908, $3500, (in perpetuity), p.103; Frank T. Hartmann, 1909, $4000, (in perpetuity), p.107; Edward M. Hager, 1909, $4000, (annual for himself and wife Ottilia), p.111; Domedion Family, 1909, $500, 25, p.116; Catherina Didley, 1909, $200, 25, p.118; Margaret Tuell, 1909, $100, 10, p.120; John Kraus, 1910, $2500, (annual Masses),

p.124; Mrs. Mary Schimpf, 1912, $100, 13, p. 128; Augusta Ottenot, 1912, $300, 25, p.130; Catherina Didley, 1913, $150, 25, p.132; John Fornes, 1913, $75, 10, p.134; Emma Weppner, 1914, $300, 26, p.136; Maria Bensler, 1915, $200, 39, p.138; Miss Romana Beer, 1916, $1000, 25, p.140; Carolina Kohlbrenner, 1917, $200, 35, p.141; William Guenther, 1917, $300, 50, p.143; Frederica Muschall, 1917, $200, 35, p.149; Rt. Rev. Paul Hoelscher, 1917, $5000, (annual on day of death), p.153; Catherina Feist, 1916, $500, 100, p.159; Carolina Kohlbrenner, 1917, $200, 35, p.163; Josephine M. Steffan, 1917, $1000, 150, p.165; Mary Garono, 1919, $1000, 150, p.169; John A. Werich, 1919, $100, 15, p.173; Lawrence Wex, 1919, $250, 50, p.175; Mrs. Catherine Lorenz, 1921, $600, 36, p.179; Charles Augustine Miller and Catherine Miller, nee Grimm, 1922, $300, 50, p.181; Adam Lautz, 1924, $100, 15, p.185; Henry and Mary Garono, 1924, $1800, 300, p.187; Catherine Garono, 1924, $150, 25, p.189; Charles and Suzanna Lautz, 1924, $500, 75, p.191; Suzanna Lautz, 1925, $1000, (one annually in perpetuity), p.195; Nicholas Scherer, 1925, $100, 13, p.199; Luise Zechman, 1925, (25 Masses due to a vote taken by the trustees in gratitude for the donation given by Luise Zechman in 1914), p.201; Magdalene Becker, 1926, $200, 25, p.203; Elizabeth Berbeisch, 1928, $100, 13, p.205; Magdalen Ely, 1929, $70, 14, p.207; Barbara Mingen, 1930, $150, 25, p.210; Joseph M. Zahm, 1930, $100, 12, p.211; Adam and Mary Miller, 1931, $150, 10, p.213; Charles X. DeShou, 1934, $200, 25, p.215; Bertha Jerge, 1934, $500, 63, p.217; Elizabeth B. Eagan, 1934, $4000, 465, p.219; Clemens Neunder and John Schetter, 1934, $200, 25, p.220; William Mittling, 1935, $400, 50, p.227; Wallis Schnell, 1937, $200, 24, p.230; Sylvester B. Eagan, 1938, $1000, 120, p.233; George and Mary Vogelsang, $300, 60, p.235; Ida Dearing, 1939, $1000, 125, p.237; Frances Didley, 1939, $50, 10, p.239; Starck Family, 1940, $200, 25, p.241; Charles J.J. Miller, 1940, $100, 10, p.243; William R. and Rose Grant, 1941, $3537.90, 100, p.244; Otto F. Welker, 1942, $200, 80, p.248; Barbara Kleber, 1942, $400, (number as set by the diocese for this amt. of money), p.251; Henry Laudenbach, 1941, (for Laudenbach and Keitzel families), $2000, p.252; Howard W. Georger, 1943, $25, 5, p.253; Edward M. Hagar, 1945, $400, 50, p.254; Josephine Hinterleitner, 1945, $200, 25, p.254; Michael Callahan, 1945, $1000, 125, p.255; Anna May, 1946, $75, 14, p.256; Kathyrn Keating, 1947, $200, 40, p.256; Thomas Ring, 1947, $100, 20, p.257; Adele C. Garono, 1947, $600, 20, p.257; Margaret Koehler, 1947, $100, (approved number of Masses), p.258; Genevieve Georger, 1948, $100, 20, p.259; Frederick J. Burke, 1948, $60, 12, p.258; Jacob E. Meuller, 1949, $200, 20, p.260; Frank Huth, 1948, $100, 20, p.260. After 1938 no more "in perpetuity" Masses were accepted. Also it should be noted that up to 1938 the donation for each Mass varied and each amount and number of Masses was decided on a "one-on-one" basis. After 1938 a set amount was perscribed: One annual Mass for 25 years (High Mass $200; Low Mass $100); One annual Mass for 10 years (High Mass $100; Low Mass $50). John Kraus' family plot is Lot 152, Section C. His father's grave is Lot 12, Section B. John Kraus' pew at St. Louis Church was #177. Today there are no Foundation Masses offered in the Diocese. After Vatican II all Foundation

At the German and French Roman Catholic Cemetery, the gravesite of Louis Etienne LeCouteulx de Chaumont, his wife Jane Eliza, and his son William Benedict. Their burial ceremony took place on August 3, 1879. On November 2, 1894, the thirty-ton granite cross, twenty-six feet high, sculptured by James Gilbert Hamilton at Empire Granite Company in Barre, Vermont, was erected.

Masses still activated were satisfied by a $10 offering for the Mass according to the new rite being conducted by the priest in the ethnic language, facing the congregation, and with the lay attendants participating in the conduct of the Mass, singing and responding. Before Vatican II all Catholics were required to *attend* Mass on Sundays and Holy Days of Obligation under the penalty of *mortal* sin; today the rule reads, see *Codex Iuris Canonici*, canons 1245, 1247 and op. cit. *Catechism of the Catholic Church*, numbers 1389, 2180ff: "All Catholics will *participate* at Mass on Sundays and Holy Days of Obligation under the penalty of *grave*

sin. Father Ott, in 1964, sent unfulfilled Mass requests to Monsignor Eberz who has since died; Father Clarence Dye who has been secularized; and Father Pius Benincasa who became a bishop and has since died. The follow-up information on these priests was obtained in an interview of the editors with Monsignor George B. Yiengst, pastor of Pius X Church, Amherst, New York. John Kraus' family gravesite in the United German and French Roman Catholic Cemetery is Lot 152, Section C. His fathers gravesite there is Lot 12, Section B.

CHAPTER EIGHT

Sorg Fashions a Truly German Church

In the period between the American Civil War and the United States' entry into World War I, the war to end all wars, the parish of St. Louis Church moved from the dawn of a new era of peace and good will, through tragedy, consolidation, construction, indebtedness, and ending with a newly decorated Gothic Church whose architecture bore a striking resemblance to the Cathedral in Cologne, Germany. The era covered twenty-one years of pastorship by Reverend Joseph M. Sorg and twenty-eight years by Reverend Paul Hoelscher. It had three phases: the eighteen years before its brick church was burned beyond recognition, the years of creation of a larger one to replace it, and the years during which it was beautifully decorated. Through all three phases German Catholics flocked to its aid and continued to worship within its spiritual community with vigor and enthusiasm.

As Father Sorg began his pastorship, the Republican Congress in Washington D.C. began undoing the reconstruction policies of President Andrew Johnson; the South was to be punished for its secession and bloodletting on many battlefields. The Ku Klux Klan ran roughshod over freed blacks and carpetbaggers corrupted the Southern States. By 1868, Congress readmitted seven former Confederate States to the Union; these had been reorganized under the Federal Reconstruction Act. In 1869, Ulysses Simpson Grant was inaugurated as the eighteenth president of the United States. He held the office for two terms and was followed by another Republican, Rutherford Birchard Hayes, who ran an election campaign against

Samuel Jones Tilden, governor of New York State; it ended in an inconclusive deadlock. Tilden won a victory of the popular vote, but was unable to muster sufficient electoral votes to be named the victor. Florida, Louisiana, South Carolina, and Oregon claimed no majority of vote in their States. An Electoral Commission of fifteen members was created to determine the outcome of the election. When it cast its ballots, Hayes won by a margin of one vote. Upon taking office on April 24, 1877, he removed Union troops from Louisiana, the last State governed by Northern support. The Civil War had finally ended. [1]

In Buffalo, eight years later, the city experienced the largest fire of its history. A conflagration as shocking as the burning of the village of Buffalo in 1813 by the British supported by Indians. When all the flames had been extinguished the Great German-American Music Hall and proud St. Louis Church, once the largest Catholic church in America, were completely doomed. Men, women, and children wept! It was so tremendous that it was impossible for a fire department of more than eight companies, which had evolved effectively over sixty-two years, called out on a general alarm, to extinguish the blaze. Fire fighting in Buffalo began in 1817. For the first seven years the task of extinguishing fires in the city was the responsibility of an unorganized group of men who had made themselves self-appointed firemen, and operated under conditions established in the village since 1816. Twenty-five ladders had been procured with money from the village treasury for use by these volunteers, every house

135

was required to provide one good leather bucket to them on the occasion of a fire, and chimneys were required to be swept and wide enough for the sweepers to go through. The first of several organized volunteer fire companies, however, was founded on December 16, 1824. During the years of their development, many Germans served as volunteers, and several were members of St. Louis Church. John Lorenz and John Davis served at Jefferson Engine Company Twelve, which was located on Batavia Street, later called Broadway. Philip Beyer and Philip Pfeifer were prominent members of Engine Company Four at Huron and Washington Streets. In 1856, Lorenz served as the Volunteer Fire Department's Chief Engineer.

By 1826, the sum of $100 had been levied on village property in order to provide for the construction of an engine house. In 1831, a tax was levied on the entire village in the amount of $3,000 in order to construct wells and reservoirs to provide sufficient amounts of water for fire fighting needs. Some money was diverted to purchase an engine and two hundred feet of hose. When the Water-Works was completed in 1850 the purchase of more wells was not required. On February 3, 1859, the first steam fire engine was proudly unveiled and paraded up Main Street. In 1865, the Gainewell Fire Alarm System was installed. Finally, in 1880, the City Council decided to take control of the volunteers and organize a department of paid fire fighters under the authority of commissioners appointed by the mayor. It was this newly formed City Fire Department which, in its fifth year of existence, was called to attempt a rescue of the famed German-American Music Hall and St. Louis Church. [2]

On March 25, 1885, McCaul Opera Company was prepared to perform the comic opera *Falka* on the large stage of the German-American Music Hall, located on the south side of Edward Street with its front entrance facing Main Street. This was a magnificent building.

Two tremendous towers separated the main entrance from two side sections of the building. Seven very large wooden doors graced the entrance. They rested on a flat platform seven steps above street level. A large patio-like floor separated the bottom stair from the street. Those attending the opera could congregate on it, and greet friends before entering the hall. Eighty-three windows acted as adorned eyes looking from the hall out onto Main Street. Seven of these were placed over the doors such that a large rectangular window topped each door with a semi-circle at the top. The north and south sides of the building ran from Main Street to Franklin Street. At the rear of the building was a large chimney projecting into the sky. From the top of the two towers flew two flags that expressed the deep feelings of the German immigrants and their descendants. Over the right tower flew the Stars and Stripes, red, white, and blue, the flag of the United States, their adopted country. Over the left tower flew the black, red, and gold, the flag of the *Achtundvierziger*, the freedom flag of the revolutionaries who had fought the Prussians in 1848 in the southwestern German States. These colors symbolized the coming out of the black night of slavery, being soaked in the bloody strife of revolution, and rising into the golden dawn of freedom.

This magnificent structure was the pride of the German Young Men's Association. In the summer of 1883 the Saengerfest of the German Saengerbund of North America was scheduled to be held in Buffalo. To host this great festivity a large hall was required. Jacob F. Schoellkopff and Philip Becker promoted the idea of purchasing land from Judge Ebenezer Walden, a lot three hundred and thirteen feet by five hundred and thirty-eight feet between Main and Franklin Streets running parallel to Edward Street. On this land these gentlemen, Albert Ziegele, and the German Young Men's Association, whose membership in 1882 was one hundred and eighty-five, decided to construct a Music Hall. It would contain an assembly hall for the Saengerfest. Later it would be used for plays, concerts, and operas. It would also be a center for all German social events and serve as a home for German Labor Unions that were being formed in Buffalo. A council of five directors was established: J. Adam Lautz, F.G. Georger, Alexander Cordes, Dr. John Hauenstein, and Edward Warner. Renowned architects presented twelve plans. The plan of August Esenwein was accepted. Money through a collecting fund had to be raised; $75,000 was needed to purchase the lot and $160,000 was needed for the building. Rich Germans supported the fund lavishly, and thirty-year bonds were floated at an interest rate of five percent.

*S*ufficient funds were in hand by March 5, 1883, and the corner stone was laid. Work proceeded immediately; the building was a giant with two hundred feet on Main Street and a depth of two hundred and thirty-four feet on Edward Street. A banquet hall and parlors for social affairs were on the second floor toward Main and Edward Streets. Although the interior was not quite finished by July 16, 1883, the first day of the Saengerfest, it was, nonetheless, held in the great hall of the building with success. The entire building was completed by December 7, 1883. A grand banquet was held and a profit of $170 was devoted to the library fund. In February 1884, a fair, called the *Carnival of Nations*, was held. It netted $5,000 to help pay down the debt. In February 1885, another fair titled *Carnival of Authors*, netted $2,750. By this time the building was able to pay for itself; two halls were being rented during the winter, and the library had reached seven thousand four hundred and fifty-one volumes. As the pages of the calendar flipped away during March no one would have believed that disaster was just around the corner. [3]

*W*hile a very gusty March wind whipped its way up Main Street on the evening of March 25, 1885, horse drawn street-cars and open and closed carriages brought the audience to the front patio and doors of the Music Hall to attend the opening night of the opera, *Falka*.

The cast was inside dressed in their wardrobes. Approximately fifty people were already in their seats. Suddenly someone screamed, fire! Gas had escaped from a leaky pipe and mysteriously became ignited. Flames immediately spread to the painted scenery that was suspended from the ceiling; and, on stage, to that which had already been placed in position for the first act. Within an extremely short time the entire stage was incredibly a mass of flames. Those in their seats ran for the exits. The first alarm was sounded at 7:50 P.M. Three minutes later the second alarm went out, and finally ten minutes after the second alarm the general alarm was broadcast. First three steam operated engines appeared coming up Main Street. Arriving, these found that the hydrants near the Music Hall were frozen. No water was available. One fireman, however, found that the hydrant at the corner of Goodell and Main Street, east of St. Louis Church was operable. Quickly, one engine crew attached three hoses. Simultaneously, two other hydrants were found acceptable. By this time, however, the entire Buffalo Fire Department was at the scene. Captain Hornung was in charge of the operation. At his disposal he had sixteen steam-operated engines, four hose and chemical apparatus, four hook-and-ladder units, and two hundred men. Although as much water as could be mustered was sprayed upon the Music Hall, Hornung was convinced that it could not be saved. He turned his attention to protecting St. Louis Church on the north side of Edward Street.

*F*iremen fought in vain to save the Music Hall. The raging of the destructive element produced dense clouds of smoke under the roof above the stage where the fire first started. Suddenly the wall fell outwards and a large draught of air drove flames forward into the large hall. Before the general alarm was sounded the magnificent building was a fiery sea of flames. They crept up the two towers and leaped high into the air gnarling their way between thick black clouds of smoke. Millions of sparks and firebrands were driven northward by the fierce south wind of March. An enormous crowd of terrified spectators surrounded the place of fire and witnessed how one of the most beautiful buildings of the city, a monument to German enterprise, fell prey to the fiery demon. At 8:00 P.M. the upper wall collapsed with such a terrible crash that the sound could be heard many blocks away. It fell outwards upon the great entrance facing Main Street; the rubble of stones descended down upon the vast entrance-stairs and covered them completely. One would have thought that a gigantic bomb had exploded within the building and let fly a bursting charge of shrapnel. At first the southern wing seemed to be untouched; but, after the wall fell, it too was attacked by flames. The streams of water thrown onto the crumbling mass made a weak impression in abating the conflagration. High columns of flames rose from the center of the building into the night sky filled with sparks. When the main roof of the hall collapsed, the entire interior was a roaring crater. Through the open doors of the front main entrance the crowd could see only a furious mass of fire and flames. Soon the cupola of the southern tower sank. All was lost! [4]

While the second alarm was sounding, Father Joseph M. Sorg was in the pulpit of St. Louis Church preaching. It was a Wednesday evening during Lent. A large group of parishioners had gathered. Through the stained-glass windows they witnessed a very vivid and eerie reflection on the Edward Street side of the church. Quickly they realized that some building in the neighborhood had to be on fire. The discovery was first made by some of the members in the choir loft, whose elevated position gave them the best place to detect such an alarming visitation. Immediately the reflection became brighter. It was then manifest to them that the neighboring building, the Music Hall, was on fire. They became uneasy, bestirred themselves, and made a hasty exit from the loft down the stairs. They created quite a noise in their hurry to leave. Frightened, members of the congregation turned in their seats to learn the cause of commotion. Naturally they too became more excited when they saw the increased brightness of the

reflection in the windows.

Sorg, who was still in the pulpit, and in the midst of his sermon, had foreboding not of the pleasantest. He saw the danger of the situation at once. With extraordinary coolness and self-possession he asked those present to stay in their pews and be perfectly calm while he went out and checked to see what the matter was. Quickly returning, he said that there was a fire a short distance down the street, and any of the congregation who wished to go out and see for themselves were free to do so. A large number began to leave at once; Frank X. Burkhard and Peter Paul, two trustees who attended the services, hurriedly opened all the doors, allowing the people to get out as rapidly as possible. Although the people behaved remarkably well under the trying circumstances, a considerable scramble did take place. The two gentlemen, however, testified later that anxious members of the congregation carried them along in the surging crowd for quite a distance, but no real panic occurred. No one suffered any injury. Steps were further taken under the direction of Father Sorg's masterly hand, to remove the Eucharist in the tabernacle, vestments, chalices, stations of the cross, and many other valuable articles in the church. Before this could be fully accomplished, however, everyone assisting in the removal operation was required to flee the church. So many small patches of fire were seen in a number of places and Captain Hornung knew, that anyone present inside would be in extreme danger. He ordered everyone out, and shouted to them as they left, " This is a hard Blow!"

Before the last one had left, all the trustees, even those who had not attended the service, were on hand directing their full attention to protecting the church. More than a quarter of a million dollars was at stake if it was lost. When they arrived, however, they could see nothing but a red glare through every door and window. Somehow the patches of flame turned into a burning mass. Once they got among the rafters, the flames seemed to be laughing at the deception they had practiced on the onlookers. It appeared that they were in high glee at the destruction they were about to cause, and scoffing at the pigmy-like streams of water playing around and about them with little effect. Great efforts were made to overcome the ravages of the fire. Several parishioners risked their lives in trying to aid the firemen in their task. They were Joseph Ramsperger, William Crowley, Edward Ford, Peter Southwick, and Joseph Grimm. After attempting to bring hoses up through the tower in hopes to wet down the church from the top, Grimm was isolated as the flames and smoke pushed their way up through the belfry. Everyone in the street saw his dreadful position. Was it possible to save him? Not through the inside of the tower which was completely inundated with smoke and fire. All hope was cut off, as the flames were seen through the stained glass windows. At times he could be seen; but, then, he would disappear in the cloud of smoke. On the ground, willing and stout hands stretched heavy tarpaulins ready to catch him if he should leap from the tower. In loud voices they shouted, "Jump! Jump! Jump!"

He was seen by some Jesuits watching the fire from the belfry at St. Michael's Church on Washington Street. They watched the stranger's hopeless fight for life. They saw extension ladders run up to save him but they were too short. Soon they realized that his choice remained between two deaths, by jumping or smothering. Every moment seemed an era of time. Suddenly the stranger, who to those close to the church knew was their friend, Grimm, had but one choice. Jump! The tarpaulin was stretched out below. He ventured over the coping, once, twice, three times, always shrinking again. The fourth time he mustered the courage necessary, and fell feet first. Half way down his foot caught the cornice, turning him over, and he fell the remainder of the distance headfirst. Nearing the tarpaulin his foot barely touched the edge of it; his head struck the stone steps. It was instant death! At that moment, as if to hail a victory, the flames burst out in all their fury; the east face of the clock fell out, falling to the ground, and

joining the broken and half-melted bell which had already smashed into the earth after ringing out its last toll. It was later reported that as Grimm had made his descent from such a giddy height, the Jesuits watching from the bell tower of St. Michael's Church raised their arms and hands, and gave him absolution. One of those present on that fatal night was Father Joseph Kreusch, S.J., who had been appointed pastor in 1873. It was he who commissioned the construction of the tower at St. Michael's Church.

All the details of the attempt to save the church by bringing hoses to the tower were reported by Joseph Ramsperger. To the editors of the *Buffalo Volksfreund,* he related his experiences while the fire was raging. He said, "I had assisted in removing the stations of the cross, church vestments, and altar articles to a place of safety. In passing out of the sacristy I noticed some sparks dropping on the roof of the church. I approached several men prominent in church affairs and told them it looked very dangerous. It was suggested at once that firemen place a stream from street level onto the roof, but the pressure proved inadequate. I ventured the idea of carrying a line of hose into the tower, being very familiar with the building, and would assist and lead the way. On entering the church grounds Joseph Grimm came along and offered me his assistance. In order to get to the roof, it necessitated the removing of a window at the rear of the tower. It so happened that earlier Mr. Duffner and I had been employed in repairing the organ, so my tools used in the afternoon were in the organ loft. I hastened to get my hammer; and, with it, forced the window open, so that the firemen could get the hoses out on the roof."

Excitedly, Ramsperger continued, "I then hurried up into the belfry to see if everything was safe there, taking my hammer. As there seemed no danger, I retraced my steps, and on my way down, as the clock room was reached, I was met by Grimm. He told me that all escape was cut off. Naturally I was terribly shocked and unnerved, but after collecting my thoughts for a moment, I said to him, 'We must go down, going up is sure death.' I went ahead because I knew the way. We went but a short distance, when we were driven back by dense clouds of smoke. Twice we tried it, on hands and knees groping along, but we were driven back at every attempt. When all efforts failed we intended to open the scuttle, a small hatch in the wall, which we had originally closed while rising into the belfry. We concluded that if it were not opened we would die from suffocation, inhaling smoke. Leaping from that height would have been sure death. At this time Grimm said, 'Oh, my poor wife and child! Is there no hope?' I then tolled the bell used at funerals. I made the remark to Grimm, as he knelt and prayed, 'Here goes three bells for the poor souls in purgatory and within a short time we will be there.'"

Ramsperger then described Grimm's reaction, "He said to me, 'For God's sake, must we die like this?' By then the smoke was pouring into the tower and we were both at the point of suffocating; Grimm became hysterical. I endeavored to console him and told him, 'If we die we will die together.' I never thought that I alone would be saved. I rang the bell to let those below know that we were in the tower, when Grimm said, 'I am dying from smoke,' I gave him my hammer and asked him to break the slats in the belfry. He tried with all his strength, but no slat would give way. Grimm was becoming weaker, and I took the hammer to see what I could do. I did no better; they seemed to be made of something stronger than wood. In groping around in darkness and smoke, I got hold of a piece of timber, which I promptly thrust between the slats and called on Grimm to help me pry them apart. The slats would not bulge a particle. Grimm said, 'I cannot hold out any longer.' I had him step aside and with superhuman effort I got the timber in between the slats and broke them into kindling. I lifted Grimm into the opening for air, and stepped out onto the cornice, waving my hat, calling for help."

Ramsperger continued, "Whilst I was on the outside of the tower, Grimm asked if a telegraph wire was near the building. On the north side there was one, but too far down; he intended to jump and catch it. I prevented him, and as I was still calling for help a cloud of smoke enveloped the tower and drove me to its rear; when I regained my balance, I saw that the entire south roof of the church was ablaze. I took in the situation, not knowing what to do, when a terrible crash told me that the walls of the Music Hall had fallen. I was covered with sparks; the roof below was on fire. Now frantic, driven to my wits ends, I wondered what to do. Finally I called to Grimm; 'I shall try to jump.' He said, 'You will never get out of it alive.' I put my hand through the slats and bid Grimm good-bye, he saying, 'we will never see earth together; this is my last day.' I replied to him, 'I am afraid it is, but where there is life there is hope.' At that Grimm said, 'Joe, are you going to leave me alone up here?'"

Ramsperger then told the editors, "He never heard my reply because another burst of smoke and sparks drove me away to where the lightning rod was. Here was my only chance of escape. I hesitated a moment, but realizing this was my only means to save myself, I grappled the lightning rod and made the descent, and when about twelve feet from the roof I was obliged to let go my hold. In doing so I dropped to the roof, hitting it hard. After turning several somersaults I managed to catch hold of the rod once more, which helped me along the roof, amid the smoke. Greatly excited, I reached the edge. Looking down, I saw some firemen ready to save me. They had a blanket stretched and called on me to drop. I refused and shouted to them to bring a ladder, which was brought, but was too short. I sized up the distance from myself to the top of the ladder, jumped, and caught the top rung. Catching my breath and knowing that I had firmly embraced it, I went down to *terra firma*, where I was received by a dozen hands ready to care for me. In falling from the rod to the roof I had injured my side, which I did not notice at the time. I asked to be allowed to go back, and show the firemen how to save Grimm. They praised my generosity but told me that the effort would be useless. Grimm had somehow managed to get himself out from the broken slats in the tower, and leaped to the ground. He was picked up dead with all his limbs broken. The only other fatality was that of George J. Roth, a fireman. His charred corpse was found in the ruins after the fire had been completely extinguished." [5]

While Ramsperger and Grimm were trapped in the tower by flames and smoke, they discussed their fate in terms of meeting that night in purgatory. According to their understanding of the teaching of the Catholic Church, both had profound belief that Jesus Christ by his death on the cross had saved all from their sins. In a life beyond the grave, they knew that eventually they would see the Beatific Vision of God. They also understood, however, that they were not perfect men, and reasonably some retribution would be needed to make them perfectly pure before they saw the eyes of God. In their catechism, they had been instructed that this could be done after death only in a place called Purgatory. Both were men of strong convictions, but they were men whose consciences had not been anesthetized by personal insensitivity to proper moral codes. They knew right from wrong; they knew when an evil act of theirs was mortal or venial. Mortal if it was a transgression which separated them from God, depriving them of His love and friendship. Venial if it was an offense against God; but one which only weakened their fear and love of God. They also had the assurance of their faith in the Church that upon confessing their sins to a priest, for which they were truly sorry for having committed, and a firm resolution to commit them no more, the priest had the power to offer them absolution. In that act they were assured that God no longer saw them as evil; He promised forgiveness of their sins.

On that fatal night as Grimm hurtled through the air, plunging down to the concrete below, the Jesuits, watching from the belfry of St. Michael's Church, raised their hands and assigned to him absolution using the words, "May the Almighty and Merciful Lord grant thee pardon, absolution, and remission of sins. Our Lord Jesus Christ absolve thee; and we, by his authority, absolve thee; in the first place, we absolve thee from every bond of excommunication or interdict, as far as we have the power and thou standeth in need; in the next place, we absolve thee from all sins, in the name of the Father and of the Son and of the Holy Ghost. Amen." The Jesuits assumed that before his fall, while hesitating, or during the fall, Grimm had made an act of contrition, which included a firm resolution to sin no more. Although his descent was so rapid that they could not complete the concluding prayer, the Sacrament of Penance had been properly performed.

Neither the spectator at the fire on that fatal night nor the historian who writes about it more than a century later, can verify if Grimm was contrite and asked for forgiveness, and if the Jesuits, who because of distance, could neither hear his voice nor see his expression, responded with acceptable absolution. It is not necessary that they do. Only God can be the true judge. It is possible, however, that both actions, which allegedly took place simultaneously, were achieved, and the Sacrament of Penance was properly invoked. In the theological teachings as put forth by St. Thomas Aquinas the *matter* of the sacrament was there. It was the action of the penitent and the priests. The *form* was there in the words uttered by the priests, "We absolve you from your sins." These words signified the hidden reality of Divine forgiveness. It was an action of an outward sign giving inward grace, as it was intended to be as instituted by Christ himself. He had told the Chosen Twelve, "Whose sins you shall forgive, they are forgiven them; and whose sins you shall retain they are retained." The Jesuits used their power, not according to their own caprice, but exercised it according to the merits of the penitent. [6]

Forty-one days after the great fire, Joseph C. Ramsperger was prepared to celebrate his thirty-second birthday. He was born in Hechingen, Wuerttemberg, a town situated in Swabian country surrounded by beautiful green mountains in the summertime. To the immediate south rises the Hausterberg, a mountain over two thousand feet. Further south lies the famous Hohenzoller Berg that rises above the Hausterberg by nearly five hundred feet. To the northeast one views the Deifuerstenstein, a mountain equal in height to the Hohenzoller. Ramsperger never saw this beautiful country with sheep grazing in the green pastures, beautiful castles dotting the landscape, and the towers of churches rising above the treetops. He was born on May 5, 1853; his parents were in the process of emigrating from this beautiful land because his father, who had failed to finish his *Wanderjahre*, was not able find work without his mastercraftsman's license.

The family arrived in Buffalo on October 30, 1853. At the age of six, Joseph Ramsperger began his education at St. Louis' parochial school. From his years in third grade until his fifth grade he was a member of the church choir. In 1867, he graduated and entered the apothecary of Walker and Company. Later another pharmacist, Julius E. Francis, hired him. In 1870, he choose the business of carpenter and builder. He was so adept at his work that in 1889, he was appointed inspector of buildings for the city of Buffalo. Colonel John Feist, who was the superintendent of buildings, chose Ramsperger to be his assistant. In 1882, Ramsperger remodeled the old tower of St. Louis Church, requiring some daring work, which was accomplished without mishap. In 1900, he erected the building in which the St. Louis Church Bazaar was held. It became a cafe and was well patronized. He was an excellent photographer, and he took many interior views of the St. Louis Gothic Church built in 1888.

Colonel John Feist, who appointed Ramsperger as his assistant superintendent of buildings in Buffalo, was a native of the city, born in 1843. He was baptized in the Lamb of God Church while it stood within the walls of the brick church that the fire destroyed. He received his primary education at St. Mary's parochial school. His family was among those who left St. Louis Church and joined St. Mary's Church during the interdiction imposed by Bishop Hughes. Its formation took place when John Feist was only one year old. Subsequently, however, he again became a faithful member of the congregation at St. Louis Church and an honorable citizen of the city. He was secretary of the St. Alphonsus Society, a life member of the Buffalo Catholic Institute, at which he served a term as president, and of the Catholic Mutual Benefit Association. He also was a member and first president of the Builders' Exchange, member of the Board of Directors of the Orpheus Singing Society, and for three years he was a member of the Board of Trustees of St. Louis Church. For many years he was a prominent contractor in Buffalo. Two of the buildings of which he was very proud were the Post Office and the Temple of Music, constructed for the Pan American Exposition in 1901.

Ever since the American Civil War, he always had a yen for the discipline of the military. In that war he had served in the Quartermaster's Department for the Army of Tennessee, which was commanded by General George Henry Thomas, *The Rock of Chickamauga*. In the latter half of the nineteenth century, he became a member of the Knights of St. John, Commandery 14 and a member of the Knights of Columbus. He was also a member of the Knights of St. George where he increased in rank until he achieved the honor of colonel. In 1900 he served as Judge Advocate on the staff of Colonel John L. Schwartz. On Sunday, January 6, 1907, he died at his home on Ellicott Street. His wife, Catherine, two daughters, Mrs. Rose Hoefner and Mrs. Minnie Liddle, and three sons, Joseph J., Henry M., and Charles G. Feist survived him. All three boys had been associated with their father in the contracting and building business.

The Buffalo Catholic Institute of which Feist was a life member was an outgrowth of an organization of youthful German Catholic men connected with St. Michael's Church. It was formed in the year 1866, and was intended to be a literary and social society. In 1869, Fiest and the other directors of it secured a larger site in the American Block on Main Street. Five years later they purchased another site at Main and Chippewa Streets. Here, on three floors, they maintained a fine library, reading rooms, and an amusement center. Gradually young men from English speaking parishes, who had always met at St. Stephen's Hall, became part of the Catholic Institute. In 1893, a prominent site was secured on the corner of Main and Virginia Streets, near St. Louis Church. A few years later a magnificent building was erected.

Many other men who had become prominent in the St. Louis Church community and were witnesses of the great fire were: Frank J. Abel, Otto Andrle, Christian Bauer, Charles S. Burkhardt, Charles Dearing, Charles Doll, Charles Fix, Edward M. Hager, Charles Huck, John Kam Jr., Joseph Kam, John A. Kerker, Charles Lautz, Edward Metzger, Gregory Strootman, Charles Weyand, and Charles Williams. Frank J. Abel was born at Buffalo Plains, which today is the area around the University of Buffalo, South Campus. Near his birthplace was St. Joseph's Church that was founded in 1850. It was there that he attended parochial school. At the age of eleven he entered St. Joseph's College, located adjacent to St. Joseph's Cathedral; after which in 1879, he went into the employment of the Lake Shore and Michigan Southern Railway. In 1884, however, W. Perry Taylor, general manager of the Canadian Southern Railway, weaned him away from his position so as Abel could take a prominent position in his company. Abel was twenty years old when he witnessed the fatal fire at the Music Hall and St. Louis Church. In 1888, at the age of twenty-three, after he married Miss May Weppner, he worked as cashier at the Buffalo Storage and Carting Company. In the last four years of the nineteenth century, he was secretary and treasurer

for the Citizens' Ice Company.

Otto Andrle another member of St. Louis Church who witnessed the fire in 1885 at the age of twenty was born in Buffalo on January 1, 1865. His ancestors were among the organizers of the Lamb of God Church in 1832. He received his early education in St. Louis' parochial school under the direction of Henry Hemmerlein who also was a member of the parish. For several years Andrle was a student of G.R.W. Berger, artist and member of the Buffalo Art School. Besides art, Andrle was fond of elocution and studied with Professor Beers. Andrle's father, who was twenty-two years in the Academy of Music Orchestra, taught him music. For eight years Otto was a designer at the Buffalo Stained Glass Institute owned by Riester and Frohe. Always ready to dabble, but seeking perfection, he tried wandering into new avenues of art. For a few years he obtained roles in stage productions with different companies; with the Booth-Barrett production of *Julius Caesar*, he played Cassius; with Frank Mayo's production, he played Prince Leo; with Ada Grey he performed as Levison; and with James O'Neill he had the role of Marcellus. For twelve years he was a member of the Orpheus and for sixteen years a member of the St. Louis Church choir. He was always a bundle of energy; his activities read like a litany: St. Louis Church Dramatic Circle, the Catholic Institute, member of the 74th New York Regiment, and member of the Catholic Mutual Benefit Association. While participating in these extracurricular activities he was always the artist. After leaving Riester and Frohe, he established himself in the painting and decorating business; and, in 1900, he completed the interior adornment of the Teck Theater.

Christian Bauer was a young man of twenty-nine when he stood before the tower and saw Joseph Grimm leap to his death. He was born in Buffalo on March 14, 1856. He received his education at St. Boniface's parochial school, but joined the congregation of St.

Louis Church as an adult in 1870. He took an active interest in the German Roman Catholic Orphan Asylum, for which he acted as one of the district collectors and afterwards served as a member of its Board of Directors. The orphanage had been incorporated in 1873. On June 1, 1875, the children were given to the care of the Sisters of the Third Order of St. Francis, who had come to Buffalo in 1861 from Philadelphia. They came at the mediation of Father Kleineidam C.SS.R. The orphanage had had its origin in the cholera epidemic of 1832. Its first establishment was at Broadway and Pine and the children were under the care of the Sisters of Notre Dame. On October 1, 1864, a new building was opened on Dodge Street. Nine parishes with large German populations supported it. After World War I it became known as the Dodge Street Home. Bauer always took a lively interest in the Catholic Mutual Benefit Association Branch Fifteen, since 1883. He served a term as Chairman of its Board of Directors. In business, until 1881, he was associated with Weller, Brown, and Messmer; a firm devoted to excellent refinishing of hardwood floors. In that year he took a position with A. Cutler and Son, manufacturers of roll-top desks; he was their shipping clerk and stock-keeper. At work he was well appreciated because he had the quality of faithfulness; a promise once made by him was carried out in the most exacting manner. He always enjoyed his task at St. Louis Church as being usher for Sunday Mass, bringing to the service his best attention and lending his every aid, especially to older ladies who had difficulty navigating the long aisle of the church.

Charles J. Fix, who was the same age as Christian Bauer on the night of the great fire, was born on July 11, 1856 at Buffalo. After receiving his early education at St. Louis' parochial school he entered the printing business, at which he developed his many talents until 1882. He went into the employ of Henry Garono, who had made a success in the hardware business, and had joined St. Louis Church in 1843. Ten years later Garono died and Fix opened his own hardware business in a building on Main Street just north of the church. Those who stocked his store with gas ranges and heating stoves knew that he was an honest man; his word was his bond. On March 17, 1900, Mr. M. Strauss wrote a letter to Fix. In it he said, " With pleasure, I herewith wish to state, that I bought a Dockash Range from the late Henry Garono on August 19, 1887. You were the salesman who sold it to me. I have used the range ever since and it is satisfactory in every respect. I would recommend the Dockash to anybody; it's the best on the market." The clubs which Fix belonged to could be enrolled: the Amicus Club, the Union Club, the Catholic Mutual Benefit Association, Catholic Institute, and Knights of Columbus. He was a member of the Board of Trustees of St. Louis Church and Director of the German Roman Catholic Orphanage.

Charles S. Burkhardt was a young man of twenty-five when he heard the general alarm of the fire department on March 25, 1885. With all the commotion that was going on he went immediately to the church. He was born on October 12, 1860 at Lower Black Rock near Amherst Street. He received his early education at St. Francis Xavier's parochial school. The church had been founded in 1849. He graduated in 1874, took various odd jobs until he was able to engage himself in the stationary business in Black Rock. He had a good personality and loved people. These attributes fostered his election in 1885 and again in 1886 as a member of the Board of Supervisors, Twelfth Ward. In 1878, he and his brother entered into the real estate and insurance business, at which they were very successful. He also devoted his time to charitable and social activities being a member of the Catholic Institute, Catholic Mutual Benefit Association Branch Fifteen, and the Knights of Columbus.

Charles J. Dearing was in attendance at Lenten services when the congregation saw the reflection of flames emanating from the Music Hall in St. Louis Church's windows. He was thirty-two years old. He was only two years old when he came to America in 1852, with his parents whom had emigrated from Hesse-Darmstadt. He received his early education in the Buffalo public school system, but later completed it at St. Louis' parochial school. After graduation, he learned his trade as a wood-carver. By 1873, however, he found this work to be dull, with little physical exercise. He took a position as a letter carrier with the United States Post Office, and remained in its employ until 1883. Again he was not happy; he began to feel this work irksome. Leaving the postal service he bought a building on Allen Street and became a self-trained butcher. In the spring of 1893, he retired from the business and rented the premises to Arnold Weppner's sons. He was a member of the Buffalo Butcher's Association, serving as its president for six years. He was a member of Catholic Mutual Benefit Association Branch Fifteen, Catholic Institute, and the Board of Trustees of St. Louis Church. For five years he served the board as its treasurer.

*O*ne who was very eager to see a new church replace the old one after a night of terror was Charles F. Doll. He was born in Buffalo in 1842 and attended School twenty-four. From the age of thirteen until he was twenty-one years old he labored in the grocery business. In 1871 he went into partnership with John B. Schlund and established the furniture business known as Schlund and Doll. Schlund died in 1890 and Doll became sole owner, buying out his partner's interest from the estate. Doll's parents were among the original families of the Lamb of God Church. Three times in St. Louis Church's history, Doll served as a member of the Board of Trustees. For one period he was its treasurer. Like many of his business associates and parishioners, he was a member of Catholic Mutual Benefit Association, Knights of Columbus, and Catholic Institute.

*A*lthough he saw much suffering as a veteran in the Union Army during the Civil War, Edward M. Hager admitted how shocked he was when he saw the devastation of the fire on the day following the blaze. It was comparable to the destruction of the cities, towns, and villages that he saw while accompanying General William T. Sherman in his march through Georgia. Hager was born at Blieskastel, Germany, on April 18, 1842, and came to America in 1852. Immediately upon arriving, he set to work as a carpenter, contractor, and builder. He was a very outspoken man, and at times, emphatic, but underlying it all, a man with a congenial heart, very energetic, and always reliable. As a veteran he was a member of the Grand Army of the Republic. It was a patriotic association made up of surviving soldiers and sailors of the Civil War. Dr. B.F. Stephenson and Reverend R.W.J. Rudolph of the 14th Illinois Regiment organized it in Chicago during the winter of 1865-66. Its main purpose was to help families of dead comrades, care for their orphans, establish soldiers' homes, and secure proper pensions for widows. By 1931, because of natural demise, its membership was reduced to fifty thousand. Hager also was a member of the Catholic Mutual Benefit Association Branch Fifteen, Knights of Columbus, Catholic Institute, and a trustee of the United German and French Roman Catholic Cemetery Association.

*C*harles M. Weyand was just sixteen years old while he watched the sparks and firebrands leap into the sky from the Music Hall. He had been born in Buffalo on March 1, 1869. Like others of his age he received his primary education at St. Louis' parochial school. Immediately after graduation he went to work for his father in the brewing business in 1882. It seems that the fathers of the German families had the attitude that their male children would follow them in the family business and thirteen was the age at which they should begin their apprenticeship. In 1900, he was the secretary and treasurer of the Weyand Brewing Company located at the corner of Goodell and Main Streets. It was noted for its Lager and Dunkel Bier.

On the night of the fire, John Kam Jr. was another teenager and a friend of Charles Weyand. Together they watched in awe. Kam was born in Buffalo on April 15, 1871. He first attended St. Mary's parochial school and later studied at Canisius College located on Washington Street. Upon his graduation, he accepted a position as an apprentice from his father, John Kam Sr., at the John Kam Malting Company that had begun in 1869 on Genesee Street. He worked his way up the business ladder; and, with newfound knowledge and technique, he became bookkeeper. Finally in 1889, he was admitted to a partnership. John Kam Sr. had been a native of Bavaria who, as an accomplished brewer and maltster apprentice, came to Buffalo in 1855. Before devoting full time to malting, however, he busied himself with the bakery business. Not being successful he went to work as a brewer with Jacob Scheu. Three years after founding his company, John Kam Sr. erected a malt house on Pratt Street near Genesee Street. It had three stories in height having dimensions of forty by one hundred and fifty feet. He erected a much larger, building on the same street in 1879. Year after year the company grew larger and larger until in 1889, it was incorporated with a capital of $200,000. In 1900, the oldest son of John Kam Sr., Joseph, was made president and John Kam Jr., seven years younger than his brother, was placed in charge of the head office. A third son, Henry J. Kam, was the chief engineer and superintendent of shipments. Their malt houses then had the capacity of processing two hundred and fifty thousand bushels annually, and a storage capacity of one hundred and fifty thousand.

Joseph Kam was born on October 13, 1864 in Buffalo. He attended St. Boniface's parochial school, graduated at the age of thirteen, and later took a commercial course at Canisius College. One year after completion of his studies, he joined his father at the John Kam Malting Company. He grew with it, and became its president. In 1889, four years after he saw the fire accompanied by his parents, he became a member of St. Louis Church. He wanted to be in the congregation of the new gothic church, which like a phoenix grew out of the ashes of the old brick one. Like other members of the parish he too was gracious with his time and energy in activities of generosity. He was a member of the Buffalo Catholic Institute, Catholic Mutual Benefit Association Branch Fifteen, and the Orpheus Singing Society. He was also Director of the German-American Bank and the Metropolitan Bank.

John A. Kerker, the youngest of this distinguished group of gentlemen whose lives are being briefly explored had to wait for news of it until his father Henry Kerker returned home after seeing the fire. John was but eleven years old being born in Buffalo on April 12, 1874. He was the grandson of Anthony Feldman, who had come to Buffalo in 1827, and was in the first Catholic community organized by Louis Le Couteulx. Anthony had heard Mass said by Stephen Baden when he came to visit the city in 1828. John Kerker was a very prominent lawyer in Buffalo. After being first educated at St. Louis' parochial school, he went on to Canisius College, Buffalo Law School, and was admitted to the bar in 1897. He had preaxial training in the law firms of Charles F. Feldman and Roberts, Becker, Messer, and Groat. In 1900 he was independently practicing law from his offices in the Erie County Savings Bank Building.

Attending the Lenten service at St. Louis Church on March 25, 1888 was Charles Lautz. He was born in Hesse-Darmstadt in 1842, and immigrated with his mother, father, and family to America in 1853. Whenever someone living in Buffalo at the dawn of the twentieth century would mention the name Lautz, others would invariably equate it to Acme soap. Besides being part of that industry, he also was a leading hand in the Lautz Marble Works, the Niagara Tool and Machine Company, the Niagara Starch Company, Niagara Heights Land Company, and the Williamsville Electric Railway. His Marble and Onyx Company, whose office was on Main Street with the factory on Washington Street, specialized in altars, altar rails, and baptismal and holy water fonts. He was president of the Buffalo Catholic Institute for four years, president of the Board of Trustees of St. Louis Church for several years, and a benefactor of the German Roman Catholic Orphanage.

After he left the Lenten service at St. Louis Church on that cold and windy night in March, Edward Metzger watched the firemen at work while he stood at a spot east of the church on Goodell Street He was twenty-one years old being born on May 10, 1864 in Buffalo. Educated at St. Louis' parochial school in his early years, he went on to attend public schools and Central High School from which he graduated in 1881. He then studied architecture for eight years and began the practice of that profession in 1889. Many public and private buildings in Buffalo were planned and erected by him. The Buffalo Catholic Institute, Main and Virginia Streets, was a monument to his ability. Like many of his fellow church members, he was a member of the Catholic Business League, Union Club, Buffalo Catholic Institute, Catholic Mutual Benefit Association, and the Knights of Columbus. In 1888 he was chosen to be the chairman of the *Bazar Chronicle* Committee; and, again in 1900, he assumed the same position for the *Bazaar Herald*. Others associated with the production of these two journals were: M.F. Boechat, Peter P. Seereiter, Charles J. Fix, Peter Paul, Nicholas Scherer, Francis J. Rohr, and J. Henry Wallenhorst.

On the night of the fire, at twenty-six years of age, a second generation member of the German-speaking population of Buffalo, and a Catholic in good standing, Gregory Strootman, stood paralyzed while he watched the clock works fall from the tower; time had seemingly run out for the glorious reign of St. Louis Church. He was born in Buffalo on July 14, 1859, attended St. Mary's parochial school beginning at the age of seven, began commercial courses at Buffalo Practical School at age fifteen, and graduated in 1878

at age nineteen. During his lifetime he was interested in labor relations, and had great concern for the poor working class. He was one of the organizers and later a director of the Freehold Savings and Loan Association. He was an excellent banker and financial advisor. He accepted temporarily the presidency of the Buffalo Catholic Institute on the death of Frederic W. Domedion; and, later, was elected to that office for three consecutive years beginning in 1890. It was in his final year that the Institute purchased the land on the corner of Main and Virginia Streets from the University of Buffalo so as to begin construction of its new home. Strootman was a member of its building committee, and served as secretary. He was a member of the Knights of Columbus, and an officer of Catholic Mutual Benefit Association Branch Fifteen.

He had been made aware that his church was burning. He could not stay at home. He had to go and see for himself the ravages of the conflagration. So it was with Charles J. Williams on that fatal night. He was born in Buffalo on January 23, 1849, received his education in the parochial schools of St. Michael's and St. Louis Churches. For twenty-one years he was bookkeeper for Lautz Brothers Company; makers of Acme soap; as advertised, the best bar of soap ever made. According to company propaganda, the reasons that a housewife had to use Acme soap was because it was made of the very best material, was clean and pure, and did not shrivel their hands or make them sore. In 1900, Williams was Captain of the Knights of St. John, Commandery 15 at St. Michael's Church; he had served in it since 1875. Commandery 204 at St. Louis Church had not as yet been founded; it came into existence in 1913. He was also a member of the Catholic Mutual Benefit Association Branch Eighteen, the Catholic Business League, the Catholic Institute, and a Trustee of St. Louis Church, having served nine years of which eight was in the capacity of its secretary.

Charles Williams and Charles Huck were the same

age and very good friends. On the night of March 25, 1885, they stood together before the flames. Huck was born in Buffalo on September 21, 1849; Williams was older than he by ten months. At the age of four years, Huck began his education at Public School Twelve. When he was seven years old he began attending classes at St. Louis' parochial school. It has been related that his years at school were filled with experiences that are laugh provoking. Details, however, are lacking. At the age of thirteen, he considered himself a graduate who could be a self-made man. He took his first job as bundle boy at Sherman and Barnes' dry goods house for a dollar a week. As time went by, he rose to being a prominent plumber. He was vice president of the Master Plumber's Association for the State of New York, a three term member of the Examining and Supervisory Board of Plumbers and Plumbing in Buffalo; a position he received by appointment from three mayors, C.F. Bishop, E.B. Jewett, and Conrad Diehl. He was a workingman's man, who was a member of the Board of Directors of the Freehold Savings and Loan Association. It was there with his assistance that a hardworking laborer found funds to tide him over in trying times. Huck was also a member of the Board of Trustees for St. Louis Church. At its meetings all relished his inexhaustible humor, outspoken and frank opinions, and all around good cheer. [7]

By Friday, March 27, 1885, when the *Buffalo Volksfreund* published Ramsperger's eyewitness account, the lashing winds had subsided. Beautiful warm weather during the day, with a high of fifty-two degrees, brought many curious spectators, from far and wide into the city, to see the gutted and charred remains of the twin sisters of disaster. As they stood there, their minds focused back on the glorious event that took place on January 5, 1879. It was the fiftieth anniversary of the founding of St. Louis Church. On that occasion speeches were given which included vignettes of the beginnings of the church which had just been destroyed. It was a large brick church with nine stained glass

windows on each side. Its entrance faced Main Street. Three large wooden doors, nine steps up from the street level greeted the congregation every Sunday. They usually gathered in front of the church and walked into it together in procession to take their pews that they had rented. Nine beautiful stained glass windows adorned each side. In the front, facing Main Street, three stained glass windows hovered over the wooden doors, and a large full-length window graced each side of the frontage adjacent to them.

The roof was slanted, running the full length of the nave of the church, with an angular slope of five degrees with the horizontal. As one ascended a very tall tower that pierced the sky above the front, one first passed a glass window just below the clock room. The clock had three faces; one on the front and the other two on the sides. It kept perfect time and could be seen clearly from the ground. Many a passerby stopped, looked up, and checked his pocket watch, resetting it if it was not in agreement. On the very top of the steeple was a cupola separated from the clock room by a hexagonal tubular structure containing a series of slats allowing air which rose in the tower to escape into the atmosphere. It allowed the tower to act as a chimney; constant moving of the air kept the inside fresh, preventing moisture and mildew buildup. Above the cupola was a large cross, which symbolized that this was a church of Jesus Christ, a Catholic Church. It had been dedicated in 1840. Many in the crowd of curious spectators, viewing the devastation of this gorgeous edifice, recalled that its builder was Peter Kramer and that the first wagon load of stones was brought to the building site by Joseph Armbruster. While recalling these names they bowed their heads and whispered a *requiescat in pace* for the repose of their souls. [8]

That fiftieth anniversary celebration had begun in the morning hour with a Pontifical High Mass celebrated by Reverend A. Heiter, D.D., assisted by Reverend Joseph M. Sorg, pastor of the church, as deacon, and

Reverend Father Gull, a priest from West Virginia, as subdeacon. Before the Mass, while the congregation was gathering on the patio in front of the church on Main Street, the three priests were in the sacristy adorning themselves in their vestments. Each priest clothed himself with the amice, alb, cincture, and maniple. The celebrant wore the stole crossed over his breast, the deacon wore his stole over his shoulder and crossed under his right arm, and the subdeacon did not wear one. All the vestments were modeled after the robes of state used in the Roman Empire. The amice was a type of kerchief or shawl placed over the shoulder and tied about the neck. The alb was a long white garment that ran the full length of the body from shoulders to the feet. It went on over the amice. It was held in place by a tasseled cincture. The stole was a long narrow band made of the same material as the chasuble and carried the same color. The maniple, likewise of the same color and material, was a long narrow strip placed over the left arm. In ancient times it was used as a handkerchief.

Heiter, the celebrant, placed the chasuble over his head. It was representative of the ancient Roman *trabea*, heavily embroidered in golden thread of fine texture. It slipped over his head, rested on his shoulders, and hung down on every side flowing even to the ground. The attendants helping to vest Heiter gathered up the material on the sides of the chasuble, producing folds that were fastened to his shoulders by chords. When thus looped his vesture had, in front and back, the appearance of rich garlands hanging in a curve. Sorg, acting as deacon, donned a dalmatic, shorter than the Roman *trabea* having a square edging, open at the sides, and furnished with wide moderately long sleeves. Gull, acting as subdeacon wore a similar vestment as Sorg, but it was called a tunic. Chasuble, dalmatic, and tunic were all of gold because, although the fifth day of January was the feast day of St. Telesphorus, a Pope and martyr, the anniversary day called for the text of the Mass to be taken from the Mass of Dedication of a Church. For this Mass either white or gold was the assigned color.

After the priests were attired they moved with the cross bearer and acolytes to the front of the church where the congregation was fully assembled. Members of the choir were already in the loft and the organ was ready for its introductory piece. The great procession of entering the church was arranged. First into the front doors passed the cross bearer and acolytes, followed in order by children, women, men, trustees, and subdeacon, deacon, and celebrant. As they came down the long aisle, the organ filled the entire church with a sound that excited all with joyful and spirit moving emotion. After the children and congregation had filled the pews, the priests proceeded to the altar. On that day with all hearts filled with gladness, the Mass began. All in attendance had learned the meaning of the word Mass from their catechisms. It was taken from *missach*, a Hebrew word which meant free gift offering, from *dimisses*, a Latin word meaning to dismiss as heard in the closing phrase, *Ite Missa est*, the Mass is ended, and from *mittere* a Latin verb which means to send an ambassador.

Mass, therefore, was considered as a sacrifice, an offering of a sensible object made to God the Father by a lawful minister. The object was destroyed or changed so as to acknowledge the sovereign power of God and render Him homage due to His supreme power. The first part was called the Mass of the Catechumens, which included prayers at the foot of the altar, confession and absolution of sins, Introit prayer, recitation of the Kyrie and Gloria, reading of the Epistle, Gradual, and Tract, and reading the Gospel followed by a sermon. In the early days of the church pagans preparing for baptism, were present at this part, but were dismissed following the sermon which came after the reading of the Gospel. On this day of celebration, Sorg preached an interesting sermon. He began by saying that to many Catholics who had European origins it might seem strange to have a formal observance of a church after only fifty years. In the old country many had been identified with churches which were one hundred, five hundred, and a thousand or more years old. Continuing, he explained that in Rome there were religious edifices erected during the days of paganism, long before the Christian era. He then related a complete history of the Catholic Missionary Church in North and South America. Finally he reviewed the early days of Catholicism in Buffalo praising men such as Louis Le Couteulx, John Nicholas Mertz, Alexander Pax, and Francis Guth. He briefly dwelt upon what he called the rotational priestly service at St. Louis Church that involved Reverend Fathers Wenninger, Disters, Meshall, and Schoulepnikoff. With a remark which brought quite a bit of jovial laughter from the congregation he concluded, "And now lastly Father Sorg."

The second part of the Mass, which was to be witnessed only by those in communion with the Church, was called the *disciplina Arcani*, the discipline of the Secret. It contained the Nicene Creed, the Offertory, the Canon, the Communion, and the Final Prayers. During the Canon, the celebrant was the ambassador of Christ who offered and transmitted the unbloody sacrifice to the Heavenly Father. At the Last Supper, Jesus Christ acted as an ambassador offering himself to the Father for the redemption of all mankind. The first man Adam had sinned, all sons of Adam and their sons shared in their father's sin. Humankind needed a member of their race to make an offering to God the Father to redeem it, but that sacrifice was only acceptable when that member was the Son of God, Jesus Christ. He, therefore, conducted the first Mass when, taking bread into His hands, He said, "This is my Body," and again taking the cup, He said, "This is the cup of my blood of the new and eternal covenant: the mystery of faith: which shall be shed for you and for many unto the forgiveness of sins." Replacing the cup onto the table, He said, "As often as you shall do these things, in memory of me shall you do them."

When Heiter, Sorg, and Gull approached the foot of the altar at the beginning of the Mass with their backs to the congregation, they genuflected, bowed their heads, and recited the *Confiteor*, the confession of sins. After the absolution had been given, Heiter incensed the altar and Sorg, his deacon. Heiter then went to the right side of the altar and intoned the Introit, a prayer of introduction. Following this the choir sang the triad of *Kyrie eleison; Christe eleison*. Heiter intoned the Gloria, and the choir burst forth in song praising the Trinity. Gull then proceeded to chant the Epistle following the completion of some prayers said by Heiter. Sorg then moved the Missal Book to the left side of the altar and held it while Heiter blessed it. Sorg then chanted the Gospel. When finished, he returned the book to Heiter, who kissed it. Once Sorg had finished his sermon, he gave the paten holding the host to Heiter, who uncovered the chalice. Heiter then placed the host upon the paten, raised it, and offered this gift of bread to God. Sorg poured wine into the chalice and Gull added a bit of water; both gifts were blessed by Heiter who again offered the contents to God, the Father. Following these offerings, Gull received the paten from the deacon, covered it with the ends of a veil worn over his shoulders, held it before his eyes and took his place at the foot of the altar where he remained until the conclusion of the *Pater Noster*, the Lord's Prayer.

Heiter then incensed the bread and wine with the assistance of Sorg, who lifted Heiter's chasuble so as to give him freedom of movement. Upon completion, Heiter washed his fingers, kissed the altar, prayed, and intoned the *Preface* to the Canon, in which, like Christ before him, Heiter repeated Christ's words at the Last Supper. After each consecration, Heiter raised each species high over his head while bells rang out. Following the remaining prayers of the Canon, the Lord's Prayer was intoned, the bread and wine, which had been changed to the Body and Blood of Christ, were consumed by Heiter, Sorg, and Gull. Following the singing of the *Agnus Dei*, only the Body of Christ, the communion bread, was distributed to the congregation.

All, who had received it, including the priests, had been fasting from food and drink since midnight. Once the instruments of the celebration had been washed and covered, a set of prayers were said, and the last Gospel read. Then Heiter turned to the congregation, and gave it his final blessing. At this point Sorg intoned the *ite Missa est*. Heiter, Sorg, and Gull filed out in procession with acolytes carrying candles, following the crossbearer. Behind the priests, the congregation joined in the procession while the choir sang a resounding hymn of glorious praise.

The evening was set apart for a banquet, which was held in the school at the rear of the church building. In some respects the affair was a good deal like an old folks reception and tea party. The third floor was transformed into a banquet hall and presented a picturesque and attractive appearance. The ceiling was festooned with bunting, and the walls were trimmed with monstrous American flags and papal banners. At the south end was a large Roman tiara with pontifical keys composed of bright garlands. At the north end was a frame of evergreens in which appeared the word *Willkommen*. Above it in crimson paper garland was an inscription which contained the date of the church's founding, January 5, 1829 and the fiftieth anniversary date, 1879, held on the same day and month of the year. Service had been prepared for two hundred and fifty guests, a very large majority of which were members of the church. The company sat down shortly after eight o'clock, and was served a fine supper; and, when all had eaten heartily, Sorg addressed those present. He had titled his talk, "*The Day We Celebrate*." Following his speech, the congregation was led by the trustees in a double toast, one to the Holy Father, Pope Leo XIII, and the other to the Bishop of Buffalo, Stephen Vincent Ryan. Then the Reverend Heiter rose to his feet and admirably responded, praising the laity of the church in a speech titled, "*The St. Louis Congregation and Memory of Our Departed Members*." Needless to say the press was on hand, taking it all in, ready to report it the next day. One of the distinguished guests invited was Mr. Mathias Rohr, editor of the *Volksfreund*.

Music was provided by a double male quintet from the church choir, composed of Charles Roth, Celestine Baecher, A.J. Klug, G. Frank Deck, Jacob Glass, William J. Weigel, Andrew Fuller, Frank Hein, Jacob A. Gittere, and John Dossert. Officiating as director was Henry Hemmerlein. Peter Paul handsomely complimented the young ladies who had so diligently expended their energy and good taste in preparing for the festivities. With one great rousing medley of vocal renditions the program was brought to a close. Ladies and gentlemen then distributed themselves about the building, whiling away the time in social intercourse until a late hour. Old people compared notes on incidents and occurrences of times long gone by. In conversation with some of the oldest members of the congregations, the newly arrived members of the church learned that the contractor for the erection of the Lamb of God Church was George Schneider, long since dead, and the contract for the new edifice had been obtained by Peter Kramer who was still living. Joseph Armbruster, Sr, had brought the first load of bricks. Both of these men were in attendance that evening. In one conversation, Kramer mentioned that the first Board of Trustees elected in 1838 after the charter of incorporation had been drawn up and accepted were: Michael Wehrle, Peter Kramer, Peter Eslinger, George Zahm, George Bemgesser, John Dingens, and Peter Zinns. Eslinger, who resided in Manitowoc, Wisconsin, but was at the party that night mentioned that only Kramer, and Wehrle, both of whom had homes in Buffalo, were alive. Every one in attendance that evening was asked to sign a register stating their name, place of origin, and date on which they became members of St. Louis Church. [9]

No one could have been prouder and more satisfied that evening than was the pastor, Father Sorg. To him it was the successful completion of twelve years that he had spent at St. Louis Church since he replaced

Sergius Schoulepnikoff in 1867. He had become the first native pastor of the church since its founding. His coming, however, had not been without incident. During the funeral services for Mathias Hausle on August 16, 1867, Schoulepnikoff had been literally beaten out of town by a few arrogant parishioners. The trustees, who were the instigators of this uncontrollable riot, would never have gone unpunished if Bishop Timon had been alive; he had died after a long illness on April 16, 1867. His successor, Stephen Vincent Ryan, was not consecrated the second bishop of Buffalo until November 8, 1868; the Catholics in Buffalo were without a resident bishop. Reverend William Gleason, however, had been the vicar general of the diocese and rector of St. Joseph's Cathedral since 1864. The daily operation of the diocese had fallen into his hands upon Timon's death. Although he ignored the riot and the untimely departure of Schoulepnikoff, he set about to fulfill one of Timon's wishes. On the feast day of St. Louis, King of France, August 25, 1867, nine days after the riot, Gleason assigned Sorg as the pastor of St. Louis Church. Surprisingly, the trustees not only accepted Sorg with open arms, but they made a special mention to the congregation praising his qualities.

*I*n 1838, although Sorg was born in Lancaster, a town approximately ten miles due east of Buffalo via travel along Broadway, he was baptized at St. Louis Church. Although Nicholas Mertz had conducted some divine services in a small frame building in Lancaster in 1835, one could not truly call it a church. John Neumann continued this practice when he arrived in Western New York in 1836. Sorg was taught his first catechism lessons in that frame building, but attended classes to learn the rudiments of secular knowledge at the district school. His parents, however, frequently attended Mass at St. Louis Church, to which they had a strong lifelong attachment. They, as immigrants, had been parishioners there when they first arrived in Western New York.

*A*fter his primary education, his parents sent Sorg to St. Mary's College in Montreal, where he studied the classics and received a call from God to consider entering the ecclesiastical life. He completed his studies in philosophy and theology at St. Bonaventure's College at Olean in the Allegany region of New York State. Prior to his ordination he spent much time as a deacon working among the parishes in Buffalo. After his ordination by Bishop Timon, on September 8, 1863, he was stationed at St. Joseph's Cathedral in Buffalo. One of his special duties while being active there was to accompany Timon on episcopal visitations throughout the diocese and act as his secretary. While making many arduous journeys together, Sorg and the bishop became very close friends and shared many ideas concerning the future of the diocese. At one point the bishop asked Sorg to be responsible for founding St. Vincent de Paul's Church in a small frame building at Main and Eastwood Streets. At another time he was asked by the bishop to administrate at St. Peter's Church and at St. Boniface's Church.

*O*n June 10, 1864, two days after President Abraham Lincoln was nominated to run for the presidency by the National Convention in Baltimore, Sorg received a draft notice from the Provost Marshal's Office in Buffalo. It was only nine months after the date of his ordination. By this time, he had won the affections of Bishop Timon and all those with whom he had come in contact. Sorg's draft situation was announced from the pulpit of the Cathedral on the Sunday following his notice. The draft law during the Civil war had an escape clause written into it. If a person felt that his position in life required that he should be exempted, the draftee had to find a person whom, not being drafted, would be his substitute. Further, the sum of $300 was to be paid to the government to seal the transaction. Following the announcement at the pulpit more than enough money was raised by a voluntary and unsolicited subscription. On June 27, 1864, a substitute responded and was inducted into the United States Navy in his place.

For the next three years Sorg continued to work closely with Timon. In him, Timon knew that he had a man he could trust and a clergyman who could cajole the laity. From Timon, Sorg learned the ecclesiastical side of the history of St. Louis Church, as he had learned the laity's side of that history from his parents. Sorg was ready to handle the pastorship of the parish as the summer of 1867 approached. He took the position with a prayerful heart and a profound determination to bring peace into the parish. During his first twelve years, he worked smoothly with the trustees; and, together, they renovated the interior of the church, erected a splendid parish schoolhouse, an enlargement of the older one, and constructed a fine and commodious pastoral residence. Although of German rather than of Alsatian descent, he was a true type of American, a man who idolized the flag of freedom, the Stars and Stripes. In mind, feeling, and culture, he was truly cosmopolitan, a veritable citizen of the world. He was as much at home in Cork, Ireland, as in Berlin, Paris, or Vienna. He was, likewise, equally at ease in the company of non-Catholics as among his own co-religionists. Lofty of stature and graceful of carriage, a person of dignified comportment and polished manners; one saw in him the person of the "ideal gentleman." He mingled into his nature ease and gravity, sweetness and determination. He was neither dull nor stupid in his composition. He had always on hand a fund of humor rich and rare, spiced with attic salt.

In addition to these personal characteristics and charms, he was noted for independence in the exercise of thought and for a vigorous and keen judgment; he never lost his head in the most critical emergencies. He did his own thinking, marked out a course that was *sui generis* and with the courage and convictions pursued it constantly to the end. There was no smallness in his soul; he took broad views of everything; he understood human nature, and hence knew how to win and lead humankind; and hence, also, he always enjoyed the allegiance and respect of his congregation. He was well aware that in his parish and among civic leaders there were those who could be considered gossips, slanderers, and liars. To these he had the ability to use a heavy hand covered with a velvet glove; he could make a few hypodermic injections with wonderful skill but with terrible force. He was patient, forbearing, resigned and filled with philosophical as well as moral principles. If he had enemies no one knew it, for he was ever friendly to all with which he came in contact. No one ever saw suspicion or resentment in his countenance, or heard a bitter or mean allusion in his conversation.

It was Sorg's delightful experience to see St. Louis Church truly become a German parish. It had always been German-speaking; but, on the Sunday after May 10, 1871, as the congregation met outside the church doors, Alsatians, Lorrainers, Bavarians, Hessians, Prussians, Badeners, Wuerttembergers, Swabians, and Franconians could embrace and shake hands with each other as Germans. The Franco-Prussian War had come to an end and a treaty between France and Prussia had been signed. The war had begun during the fading days of summer in 1870. The French army was devastated at the battle of Sedan on September 2; and, from that time, Paris had been under siege by the Prussian army. On January 18, 1871, in the Hall of Mirrors, within the chateau of Versailles, Otto von Bismark caused the German Empire to be proclaimed and the King of Prussia received the hereditary title of Emperor. Ten days later the people of Paris, shivering, hungry, and helpless, opened their gates to the enemy, but no treaty could be signed because France had no government. Europe had to wait until spring for a final outcome. When it came, all Germans except those in Austria, Bohemia, and the Danubian domain were under Prussian rule. France had to pay the German Empire an indemnity of five million gold francs and cede to it the border region of Alsace and Lorraine. The German newspapers in Buffalo ran large printed headlines; the German-speaking population was ecstatic. Now the parishioners at St. Louis Church could stick out their chests and say, "Wir sind alles eins; wir sind ein und derselbe!" From that day forward they were one people.

Of the many things which Sorg did while pastor of St. Louis Church, one activity is outstanding. On February 5, 1875, *Die Christliche Woche* made its first appearance in Buffalo. This was to become the elite German Catholic Newspaper that was to be a welcome guest in thousands of Catholic families in Western New York and other parts of the State. When it came into existence it became one of three German Catholic papers being read in homes weekly. When it came out someone asked, "Why do we need another Catholic paper in the German language?" It was Sorg who answered this question to the satisfaction of all. For four years he carried on at his own expense, without compensation so justly due to incessant labor, writing many columns for the paper. During these years it carried on, at a loss to him; but, with continued push and determination, he finally established it on a paying basis. He then presented it as a lasting legacy for the benefit of the German Roman Catholic Orphanage. The circulation increased by leaps and bounds and it secured for the asylum an annual income of $1,000. Not only did the paper appear locally but also many copies were sold in cities and towns in Europe. Although Sorg received no income from his endeavors, he remained for a long time as the president of its board of directors.

Sorg's pastorship at St. Louis Church prior the fiftieth anniversary of the parish parallels the materialistic, educational, and spiritual activities that were generated in the diocese by Bishop Ryan. Born in Ottawa, Canada, January 1, 1825, Ryan, while he was still very young, was brought to the United States by his parents who settled in Pottsville, Pennsylvania. In 1840, he was sent to the Seminary of St. Charles Borromeo, Philadelphia, where he began his studies for the priesthood. In 1844, he went to Missouri and joined the Vincentian community, and finished his studies at Cape Girardeau and at the Barrens. In 1849, he was ordained at St. Louis, Missouri, by Bishop Kenrick. Immediately he was appointed president of St. Vincent's College at Cape Girardeau Mission, Missouri, where he had done his studies. When the Superior of the Vincentian Order in the United States was called to Rome, Ryan was chosen to fill his office. He continued to hold it until he was consecrated Bishop of Buffalo.

While bishop, Ryan concentrated on developing new churches in the city and in the rural areas of the diocese; and, in each of the old and new parishes, he pursued a policy of integrating parochial schools into each of them. He defended the papacy against Protestant critics in America, fought the Episcopal Bishop of Buffalo, who cast aspersions on Rome, and in 1872 founded the *Catholic Union and Times,* the predecessor of the *Magnificat* and the *Western New York Catholic*. His major legacy, however, was his devotion to education in the diocese. He developed a board of examiners, made frequent visits to the parish schools, recommended improvements in instruction standards, and initiated a uniform grading system. His endeavor to establish parochial schools grew to a high pitch after he returned from the Third Plenary Council of the Catholic Church in the United States held in Baltimore in 1884. The Council had mandated that each parish open a school within two years and set the ideal that every Catholic child be in a Catholic school. Although Ryan was highly intent on achieving this ideal his technique sometimes lacked rationality.

As Ryan returned from the Council, he discovered that he had received some anonymous letters from parishioners at Good Shepherd Parish in Pendleton, New York. They claimed that, Jacob Blum, the headmaster who had been hired at the parish school in 1868 by the pastor, Father John Soemer, and had served faithfully for sixteen years, was now too old to teach, and did not properly prepare the children to receive the Sacrament of Confirmation. Ryan immediately called upon Francis Stephen Uhrich, then the reigning pastor at Good Shepherd. Ryan demanded Uhrich to fire Blum, who had gained a very good professional reputation in Pendleton's public educational system besides donating his time and talents to the children of Good Shepherd. Uhrich pointed out to Ryan that Blum had successfully prepared students for Confirmation in 1869, 1873, 1876, and 1881 without any complaint from the congregation. Uhrich concluded, "Even Your Excellency, yourself, found no fault in this man during these years of your reign." When Ryan received Uhrich's rebuttal he refused to accept it; but, in fact, he reddened in rage. He ordered Uhrich to assemble the children who were to receive the sacrament for an ecclesiastical interrogation, which he would personally conduct. He demanded that the children be orally tested on the articles of their catechism. Besides the bishop, present at the interrogation were several priests of the diocese, including Uhrich, and many adults from the congregation. Either because of anxiety, fear, inability, or ignorance, the children performed poorly before this elite group of observers. Ryan concluded that they were ignorant in knowledge of their catechism, and refused to allow them to receive the Sacrament of Confirmation on August 5, 1884.

Ryan then sermonized and said, "A christian school must be ready to take the child from the threshold of a christian home and fit the young boy or girl to be consistent, instructed, and faithful members of the Christian Church. This will be done in parochial schools, our Catholic schools. The Catholic Church is fed from the Catholic School!" He did not simply sermonize and refuse confirmation; he exercised his ecclesiastical authority with a vengeance. He was bound to make this little parish, far away from the city, and unknown to even the city's press, an example to all the priests and parishes of the diocese. He deposed Blum, forbade him to teach in any church school in the future, and discharged Uhrich as pastor of the parish. Immediately he appointed Father Chrysostom Wagner as the new pastor. Immediately, Wagner encouraged the Sisters of St. Joseph, whose convent was in Buffalo, to provide three nuns so as to open a parochial school at Good Shepherd Church. They arrived and opened

classes on September 7, 1885. Only fifteen children were in attendance. Ironically, however, on September 15, 1885, Ryan came to Pendleton and confirmed fifty-four children.

Sorg had little interaction with Ryan concerning the school at St. Louis Church; it was, in conjunction with the vigilance of the trustees, well established, and fulfilled the spirit and mandate of the Council of Baltimore. Sorg was, however, much aware of the growth of Catholicism in the city. From 1868 until he died on September 15, 1888, Sorg had seen eight new churches opened extending convenient access to the Catholic faith into a circular arc with a radius of some four miles around St. Louis Church. It moved east out Clinton Street to Fillmore some three miles, then northeast to Bailey and East Ferry area, west again to Utica and Jefferson Streets, and northwest to Amherst-Elmwood region, and even as far as Hertel Avenue adjacent to the Niagara River.

When Sorg died he was replaced by Reverend Paul Hoelscher D.D. He was born June 29, 1852, at Muenster in Westphalia. After graduating from the gymnasium of his native city, in the year 1870, he studied theology at the University of Innsbruck, Tyrol, where on July 3, 1875, he was awarded the degree of Doctor of Divinity. On July 15, Bishop Stephen Vincent Ryan received him into the Diocese of Buffalo. At the time of his incardination he was still at Tyrol. Ryan gave direction that he be ordained there by his authority. Right Reverend Bishop Vincent Gassner performed the ordination in the Cathedral of Brixen, South Tyrol, on July 25. Hoelscher came to Buffalo on June 4, 1876, and was appointed chancellor of the diocese and secretary to Bishop Ryan in October 1877. On September 20, 1888, he was appointed pastor of St. Louis Church, fulfilling a promise made by Ryan to the trustees that he would send only a German priest to the parish. [10]

The rubble of destruction in the aftermath of the great fire of March 25, 1885 remained visible for only a short time. Two days after the conflagration the German Young Men's Association decided to build another Music Hall. Immediately, a subscription committee was appointed; twenty-five members rallied the cry of cooperation; and, at the first meeting $20,000 was subscribed. Frank Georger and Heinrich Schmidt were most vocal in this effort. Philip Becker and Jacob F. Schoellkoff each gave donations of $5,000. The firm of Barnes and Hengerer was most generous, as was Grover Cleveland, former mayor of Buffalo, who became president of the United States. The Association moved forward quickly and the architect, Richard A. Waite, had the building finished by November 7, 1887. It opened with a ball, a banquet, and a grand promenade concert. The total cost of the building was $246,000. The German Young Men's Association, however, carried a gargantuan debt. The building had cost $90,000 more than expected. Because of the effort of Judge Jacob Stern and an army of helpers, a Grand Prize Fair was held in April 1889; The most unexpected sum of $43,539 was netted as clear profit. The property, the building, and the future of the organization were then on fiscal stability. On May 11, 1891, the fiftieth anniversary of the German Young Men's Association was held in the new Music Hall. At the banquet, President Grover Cleveland spoke in English and Dr. Senner, editor of the *New Yorker Staatszeitung* and Commissioner of Immigration for New York City, spoke in German. Both men were eloquent and filled the German heart to overflowing. Several officers of the organization who were present for the occasion were also members of the congregation of St. Louis Church.

Like the German Young Men's Association, the trustees of St. Louis Church were dismayed and sorely tried by the disaster of March 25, 1885. They were, however, not discouraged and within four days had determined on the erection of a church that would exceed in dimensions and beauty any structure of its kind in Western New York. In order to accomplish this great work, however, Sorg and the experienced leaders of the congregation clearly foresaw that several years would be consumed, and in the meantime the congregation would be exposed to the risk of losing many members to other churches if a suitable edifice of worship was not offered to them at Main and Edward Streets. To avoid this danger a suggestion was made that a temporary church be erected at an estimated cost of $5,000. Though this proposition, at first thought, seemed extravagant at a time when funds were so necessary to carry out the great work projected, on mature reflection it became evident to all that the plan would result in the ultimate good of the congregation, and it was finally adopted by the trustees, the pastor, and the bishop. When the decision was announced to the entire congregation there was not one dissenting vote. Next to the unbounded confidence in the liberality of the congregation exhibited in these proceedings, the most remarkable feature was the promptness and decision with which all questions were determined and the energy with which they were executed.

On the fourth day after the destruction of the old church, orders were given for the plans of the temporary building. The plans and specification were completed in three days, and work on the building was begun on April 1, 1885, just six days after the fire. The entire building was completed in sixteen and one-half days, including painting, gas-piping, and necessary appurtenances. On Sunday, April 19, 1885, the church was formally dedicated. It was a one story, rectangular building with a sloping roof of twenty degrees with the horizontal, three doorways facing Edward Street, seven windows on each side, one window over each doorway on the front, and one at the proposed sacristy entrance in the rear. It was placed onto the property so that the new church could be constructed while services continued uninterruptedly. Likewise the position of the temporary church did not interfere with the progress of the builders of the new church. In order to give it a sense of beauty, a fence was constructed about it and young trees planted. It remained there until the new edifice of Great Gothic Grandeur was completed.

The cornerstone for the new edifice was laid on May 29, 1886. Three years later the designs, drawings, and engineering specifications of the architectural firm of Schickel and Ditmar became a physical reality. It was and still is a church built in the continental Gothic style of the fourteenth century. It bears a striking resemblance to the great Gothic Cathedral in Cologne, Germany. The exterior is of Medina Red Sandstone. The ground plan is cruciform with naves, sanctuary, and transepts. Magnificent columns of polished granite with richly carved stone capitals divide the nave. The dimensions are: exterior length, two hundred and thirty-four feet; exterior width, one hundred and thirty-four feet; height from ground to ridge of roof, one hundred and five feet; length of transept, one hundred and twenty feet; width and height of the nave, forty-two and seventy-five feet; width and height of the side aisles, nineteen and thirty-six feet. There is a clear height at the intersection of the nave and transept of seventy-six feet. The vaulted ceiling is richly groined with ribbing having bosses of foliage of various designs at their intersection. The principal front on Main Street is designed on grand proportions. The chief tower, which is without doubt one of the most artistic and elegant in the country, rises to a height of two hundred and forty-five feet. The clock in the steeple was a gift of E.G. Spaulding, who during the Civil War was known to Americans as the Father of the Greenback. There are two side towers each one hundred and twenty-eight feet high. With two hundred and seventy-five pews, the seating capacity is one thousand nine hundred, however, using standing room and access to the choir loft two thousand people can be accommodated. Exclusive of all movable furnishings, the construction cost was $265,000, a price tag of $19,000 more than the new Music Hall, its next door German neighbor.

Here, one does not have to dwell further on the details of its construction since today it can be viewed as it was upon completion one hundred and fifteen years ago. One should reflect on it, however, as the crystallized embodiment of the charity and devotion of its nineteenth century parishioners and friends who have gone to join the Church Triumphant in the bosom of their God. A more glorious memorial to their love and generosity could never be conceived because in it everything has been united that could please the eye, elevate and inspire the soul, and in a befitting manner point to the glory and dominion of God. When one considers its relations with the surroundings of nature, when nature paints an effective background to its beautiful symmetry, it is then that one's romantic imagination can be titillated. Coming up Goodell Street, on a quiet autumn evening, when the sun is painting the sky with its most variegated colors, one views the spire, pointing with its finger to heaven. The beauty of this picture is indescribable. So also is the view of it in the moonlight, when it rises strongly and boldly against a sky lit up by the moon and flecked with myriads of fleeting clouds. The massive gloom and almost frowning, forbidding stateliness of the whole church awes the casual traveler and seems to speak of the fear of the Lord.

In the very late years of the nineteenth century, strollers on Main Street, moving past the church, caught snatches of the musical voices chanting Sunday Vespers. Looking up, they saw those windows, wonderfully gleaming with a soft and somber harmony of color; each one was an ornate transparency framed into the dark mass of that gothic structure. It was then that their hearts beat with exalted delight; they experienced the beautiful and the true. Their mythical sensation became the common denominator between poetry and religion. For those who entered the church, their souls were carried to higher spheres of thought and feeling. Its grand and graceful moving lines, its spacious and lofty nave and transept, its light and airy arches, drew them up into the very skies. Those who attended High Mass, when the sun was shining from the side, forgot that humanity was all about them. They let the strain of the beautiful Mass and the music of the organ thrill their soul. The entire atmosphere of the church and the liturgy seized them and swept them away into the awful and overwhelming contemplation of the Almighty. They sat in ecstasy while their eyes wandered along those stately pillars, speckled and flashing with all conceivable hues and tints, thrown upon them by the kaleidoscopic effect of the morning sun shining through the stained glass windows. It was those surroundings that were so inducive to pure and exalted prayer to God.

*W*hen they sat there in the evening at the end of a summer day, in restful and dreamy repose, they saw the church as most entrancing. At this time, nature painted her most beautiful pictures to remind them of the glories of eternal peace. The air was cool and light. The soul was enraptured by the beautiful coloring of the sanctuary windows. The departing sun shot wonderfully tinted rays through the stained pictures, heightening the effect of their composition, and making the noble and saintly figure of King Louis float and waver, as it were, like some gorgeous vision in the brilliant but yet mellow clouds of color. Below these windows, the meditative people sat, almost in darkness, forgetting their surroundings, and lost in an indescribable symposium of joy. Those who remained in a trance too long were suddenly awakened by the loud closing of the doors behind them; the sexton was locking the church for the night. Quickly they left but reflected on how the church would look when the new high altar would be in place, the walls ornamented with artistic decorations and chandeliers, and when the new mammoth organ would peal out its thrilling notes, reverberating thunder to the glory of the Lord. Father Joseph Sorg would have been so enthralled to see these wondrous decorations fill the church that he so ardently worked to build. Like Moses, upon entering the Promised Land, however, this was not to be his lot. He died on September 15, 1888; but a room adjacent to the great hall, beneath the nave of the church, was his final resting-place. On the last day his body can come forth from his tomb into the church he devoted his life to build. [11]

REFERENCES AND NOTES ✤ CHAPTER EIGHT

1. This chapter concludes just before the pastorship of Rev. Dr. Paul Hoelscher who had become pastor on September 18, 1888. Working backward the following is the list of pastors at St. Louis Church who preceded him. Rev. Joseph M. Sorg, August 25, 1867 to Sept. 15, 1888. Rev. Serge de Schoulepnikoff (after a vacancy during which the church was attended to by the Fathers of St. Michael's Church), from January 12, 1864 to August, 1867. Rev. Francis Anthony Gerber, Feb. 2, 1862 to Nov. 27, 1863. Rev. James Aegidius Meshall, (after a vacancy during which the church was attended to by the clergy of St. Michael's Church and St. Mary's Church), from Sept. 1, 1861 to Feb. 2, 1862. Rev. William Disters from Sept. 16, 1855 to June 11, 1861. Rev. Francis X. Wenninger, S.J., from the beginning of June, 1855 to about September 15, 1855. Rev. Francis Stephen Uhrich, (the assistant of Rev. J. Raffeiner), continued together with Rev. Lucas Caveng, S.J., to the end of April 1851. Rev. J Raffeiner, (who had been assistant to Francis Guth), from April 1, 1850 to April 13, 1851. Rev. Francis Guth, from Sept. 1, 1844 to April 1, 1850. Rev. Alexander Pax, from the beginning of August, 1835 (with Mertz) to March 19, 1843. Rev. John Nicholas Mertz, from Nov. 1829 to middle of June 1836. (technically he was pastor even though Pax was administrating). The original lot given by Le Couteulx upon which the first church was built was valued at $1,000. The events in America which take place as Sorg becomes pastor see: John S. Bowman, *Civil War Almanac*, Bison Book, New York, 1982, pps. 273-77.

2. For Buffalo Fire Department see: op. cit. *History of Germans of Buffalo and Erie County*, pps.81-5, and op. cit. *Buffalo of Today*, p.58.

3. For a description and history of the first Music Hall and the German Young Men's Association see: op. cit. *History of Germans of Buffalo and Erie County*, p.92, 109. Description of the construction of the New Music Hall see: Ibid, p.112. For a discussion of the Saengerfest held at the Music Hall in Buffalo in the summer of 1883 see: *Fest Zeitung fuer das 23ste Nord Amerikanische Saengerfest*, Buffalo, August 23, 1883, no. 20, the entire magazine was devoted to the event.

4. Description of the Music Hall Fire on March 25, 1885 see: *Buffalo Volksfreund*, Friday March 27, 1885, Jahrgang 17, No.202, and op. cit. *History of Germans of Buffalo and Erie County*, pps. 85-7. Also for the fire at St. Louis Church see: Ibid. Other descriptions of the fire were addressed in the following newspapers: *Der Weltbuerger und Buffalo Demokrat*, Thursday, April 2, 1885; *Sunday Express*, March 29, 1885. Fire Chief Hornung had been criticized by an insurance agent who said that during the fire he was stationed at the Tift House on Main Street. The agent claimed that he had seen the light of the fire in the Music Hall fifteen minutes before any fire engine passed him. Hornung retaliated saying, "There would have been only two engines which could have passed the Tift House—No. 8 of Chicago Street and No. 10 of Perry Street. The first alarm went off

at 7:50 PM. Thirteen minutes later at 8:03 the general alarm went off; and. after ten minutes passed from thence, the engines passed the Tift House. The Chicago Street engine passed the Tift House on the general alarm. The others did not go up Main Street because they wanted to avoid the tracks. So they took a side street." Hornung also said that when the firemen saw Grimm appear in the Tower they raised their Hayes truck-ladder to full length which was 85 feet, but it was not sufficient to reach him. He also, with much emotion, said that he worked harder to save the church than he had in any other fire he had experienced in his lifetime. Actually, however, Grimm and Ramsperger wanted ladders to be placed on the side of the tower hoping to be able to reach them. The firemen, however, misunderstood them and brought the ladders around to the front of the church. It was not reported in Ramsperger's story, but he did cut his hands painfully as he slid down the lightning rod. His leap to the top of the firemen's ladder was made from the cap which surmounted a pillar formed by the brick work of the walls near the eaves.

5. For the extended version of the St. Louis Church Fire and the eyewitness report of Ramsperger see: op. cit. *St. Louis Bazaar Herald*, Sept. 27, 1900, vol. 1, no.10; Sept. 28, 1900, vol. 1, no. 11; Sept. 29, 1900, vol. 1, no. 12; Dec. 8, 1900, vol. 1, no. 13, which is an English translation of the German text found in the *Buffalo Volksfreund*, March 27, 1885. The sketch of the fire which is presented in this book first appeared in the *Buffalo Express*, Friday, March 27, 1885. It was drawn by Mr. Joseph Fleming, chief of the art department of Matthews, Northrup, and Company, at the exact moment of the fall of the south tower of the Music Hall. He was perched on the ledge of a building nearly opposite St. Louis Church. He took ten minutes to make the sketch. Next morning at 9:00 AM, on a glass plate, Fleming sketched the picture and put it into the hands of Charles Chetham who did the engraving for the illustration which was to appear in the newspaper that day. See: *Buffalo Express*, Sunday, March 29, 1885. Also in this paper are other pieces of information pertinent to the fire: George Roth was a man held in high esteem by his comrades in the Fire Department. He was duly mourned by them as a brave man who died in the discharge of his duty. Roth left behind a wife and six children from one to thirteen years old. Of his body only three or four small bones were found in the middle part of the tower. These were gathered, placed in a box, and given to Mr. Kraft, the undertaker. Roth was a member of St. Louis Church but under the circumstances his funeral was held at St. Michael's Church on Washington Street on Saturday, March 28, 1885. The newspaper had an illustration of Joseph Grimm, the laborer who leaped to his death. It was sketched from a picture which was in the possession of one of his friends. An article also discussed the argumentation between the Water Department and the Fire Department concerning frozen water hydrants. Reichert and Miller who were commissioners for the Water Department claimed that the hazard was not as drastic as published in the newspapers. They described how Buffalo had 12 large reservoirs in the city ready to fight fires. The nearest one to the Music Hall and the church was on Goodell Street near Washington Street. It held 1,100 barrels of water and its supply was well sufficient for four engine pumpers. They also said that the Fire Department should have had a mortar which could

have shot a line to Grimm when he was caught in the tower. Captain Williams of the Life Station on the River was adept at doing this kind of life saving operation. He said that if it had been done at the church tower, Grimm would have been down safely in five minutes. Joseph Grimm, who fell from the tower during the fire, married Mary Elizabeth Miller on February 17, 1883 at St. Michael's Church. Mary Elizabeth was a daughter of Nicholas Miller Jr., who we have referred to in Chapter Five. She was the older sister of Charles Augustus Miller who is the grandfather of the author/editor of this text, Carl Anthony Miller, aka C. Eugene Miller. During the fire Charles Miller was 23 years old and Mary Elizabeth Miller Grimm was 30 years of age.

6. For the discussion of the sacrament of penance as applied to the case of the St. Louis Church fire see: op. cit. *The Beauties of the Catholic Church*, pps. 387-99. Also for the discussion of the Celebration of a Pontifical High Mass see: Ibid, 324-44 and Rev. Hugo H. Hoever, *St. Joseph's Daily Missal*, Catholic Book Co., New York, 1957, pps. 3-15. The poem and the song, concerning the fire, are on cards with unidentified authorship; these cards are preserved in the St. Louis Church Archives. The song is titled: Song, Music Hall Fire; The poem appears to be taken from the same journal as the song, but has attached to it a picture of the temporary church, built after the fire. The title under this picture is,"Die Nothkirche der St. Louis Gemeinde." The poem reads:

When the fire had reached its utmost strength
A Human form was seeen
Clinging to the tall church tower:
It caused strong men to scream.
Twice he tried to reach the ladders,
But climbed back to his place:
A rush of smoke; an awful scream,
And his body shot through space,
And then a sickening thud was heard
For many yards around:
A Fellow-being there lay crushed
And dying on the ground.
Let us pray peace to his ashes,
As we think of that fall,
That robbed poor Joe Grimm of his life,
Through the fire at Music Hall

Another life was also lost,
Yet we cannot tell how;
His remains were found next morning;
He's before his maker now.
As good a fireman as we had,
While on duty lost his life
And now something ought to be done
For his grief-stricken wife.
A good man while on duty,
He was considered brave,
And many a time has risked his life
Another one to save.
Poor Roth met an untimely death—
That alarm was his last call;

He went and found his funeral pyre,
Through the fire at Music Hall.

The song is as follows:
At half-past seven, March the twenty-fifth
Excitement pervailed around;
The fire king had taken hold,
And was burning to the ground,
The finest building in our town:
Beneath his touch must fall;
A heap of ruins now fills the place
Of the far-famed Music Hall.

The well-known McCaul Opera Troupe
Was to play there that night;
They were all ready to proceed
When flames burst on the sight.
It caused a panic there and then
With the company one and all;
They lost most everything they had
In the ill-fated Music Hall.

St. Louis Church, it was filled
With people young and old,
Who saw the flames, but did not move,
But knelt down as they were told;
For their priest with wondrous presence of mind
Cried, do not be afraid,
And many ought to thank their God
That they took his advice and stayed.

For many lives would have been lost
In the panic stricken rush,
And have been trampled down:
It would have been an awful crush.
To the priest they ought to give their thank
By his coolness he did save
Many a precious human soul,
From a dreadful fiery grave.

7. For the biographies of the men listed as witnesses of the fire see: op. cit. *St. Louis Church Herald*, according to the names, dates, and numbers given below. All come from year 1900 and vol. 1. They are: Ramsperger (Sept 29, no.12); Feist (Sept. 19, no. 3), for Feist also see obituary *The Buffalo Courier*, Monday, January 7, 1907; Metzger (Sept 29, no. 12); Hager (Sept. 29, no. 12); Doll (Sept. 28, no. 11); Fix (Sept. 28. no. 11); Kam Jr. (Sept. 28, no. 11); Weyand (Sept. 19, no. 3); Huck (Sept. 27, no. 10); Williams (Sept. 26, no. 9); Bauer (Sept. 26, no. 9); Dearing (Sept. 25, no. 8); Andrle (Sept. 25, no. 8); Burkhardt (Sept. 22, no. 6); Kam (Sept. 22, no. 6); Abel (Sept. 21, no. 5); Lautz (Sept. 21, no. 5); Strootman (Sept. 20, no. 4); Kerker (Sept. 20, no. 4). In the *Sunday Buffalo Express*, March 29, 1885, an article described the destruction of the remnants of the St. Louis Church Tower on Sunday morning, March 29, 1885. Between 3:00 AM and 4 :00 AM on that Sunday morning explosives were put in place by John McGuire so as to demolish the tower which in its state of destruction was a hazard.

Sergeant Nathan of the police department put ropes across all the streets surrounding the church about 300 to 400 feet from the ruins. This was to keep back the crowd which had gathered; it numbered about 100 people. When the sky was in full light at about 6:00 AM the wires attached to the cartridges were brought to the corner of Main and Virginia Streets; this was the firing point. At 6:10 AM the blast went off with flying bricks going into doorways and behind trees. The tower crashed to the ground with a roaring sound beyond description. A dense cloud of mortar dust rose into the air up to 150 feet and then settled as all stood in awe.

8. For a description of the second St. Louis Church, the brick church which burned in the fire see: op. cit. *History of Germans of Buffalo and Erie County*, p.38. Accordingly see: *Sunday Buffalo Express*, March 29, 1885. St. Louis Church was insured to the extent of $27,700. The companies involved in this insurance program were: Rochester German Insurance Co.; Buffalo German Insurance; Hanover; Connecticut of Hartford; Phoenix of Brooklyn; Germania of New York; Connecticut of Hartford; and Union of Buffalo. The church was considered to have a good risk factor, charging fifty-five cents per $100 value, and paid for the damages without complaint.

9. For a discussion of the Fiftieth Anniversary Celebration which took place at St. Louis Church in 1879 see: op. cit. *St. Louis Church Herald*, all are vol. 1, Sept. 18, 19, 20, 21, nos. 2,3,4,5. This reference includes the names of all those who were present at the banquet with their place of origin and the date on which they joined St. Louis Church. They are: Addler, Anna Mary, Empfingen, Baden, 1834; Aeldman, Anthony F., Buffalo, 1833; Ailinger, Carrie, Buffalo, 1860; Ambs, Hiram, Armbruster, Joseph, Mr.&Mrs., Buffalo, 1845; Heidendorf, France, 1836; Baker, Henry, Oberhausen, Baden, 1852; Barth, Mary S., Cheektowaga; Bauer, Christian, Buffalo, 1858; Bauman, Regina, Strasburg, 1837; Becher, Celestin, Tirschnitz, Bavaria, 1855; Beiler, Magdalina, Niedermohr, Rheinpfalz, 1832; Biesinger, Catherina, Reidsch, Alsace, 1833; Bork, Joseph, Gaubikalheim, Hesse-Darmstadt, 1840; Bork, Mrs. Joseph, Rottenburg, Wuerttemburg, 1840; Breis, Caroline, Wittingen, Switzerland, 1863; Breis, David, Tyrol, Austria, 1857; Brunner, Louis, Buffalo, 1849; Buchheit, Charles F., Buffalo, 1841; Buchheit, Magdeline, Buffalo, 1845; Busher, P., Mrs., Buffalo, 1836;Deck, Frank G., Grossfishlingen, Rhein, Bavaria, 1847; Deck, Jacob N., Grossfishlingen, Rhein Bavaria, 1847; Deck, Josephine, Buffalo, 1840; Deck, Louisa Mrs., Buffalo, 1838; Deck, Magdalena, Buffalo, 1851; Degenfiter, Mary, Buffalo, 1840; Deitsche, Xavier, Baden, 1860; Densinger, Elizabeth, Buffalo, 1860; Densinger, William, Phanbosen, 1855; Diebold, Anthony, Alsace, France, 1838; Diebold, Anthony, Alsace, France, 1839; Diebold, Mrs. Anthony, Alsace, France, 1839; Diebold, Catherine, Alsace, 1843; Diebold, George, Alsace, 1843; Diebold, Josephine, Buffalo, 1851; Dole, Charles F., Buffalo, 1842; Domedion, F.W., Buffalo, 1854; Domedian, G.A., Buffalo, 1860; Domedion, Mrs. Jacob, Brechtholzhein, Hesse-Darmstadt, 1847; Dossert, G.B., Nancy, France, 1848; Eger, Mrs. A., Buffalo, 1854; Erb, Henry, Weidenthal, Bavaria, 1834; Erb, Mary E., Buffalo, 1831; Erisman, Magdalena, Alsace, 1838; Erisman, Martin, Buffalo, 1833; Eubelhoer, John C., Louisville, Kentucky, 1870; Feldman, John, Buffalo, 1846; Feldman, Mary A., Buffalo, 1871; Fell, Joseph, Philadelphia, 1856; Fertig, J.V., Bucha, Baden, 1852; Fiegel, John, Ebendorf, Bavaria, 1851; Fix, Caroline, Buffalo, 1862; Forster, Julia, Buffalo, 1873; Fougeron, Augusta, Buffalo, 1859; Fougeron, Francis M., Buffalo, 1870; Franz, Michael, Lobsend, Alsace, 1845; Fuller, Andrew, Bavaria, 1846; Garono, A., Buffalo, 1844; Garono, Henry, Buffalo, 1843; Garono, Lorenz, Mr.&Mrs., Wellstein, Germany, 1840; Garono, Mary, Buffalo, 1840; Gattie, Mrs. Mary, Willsburg, Alsace, 1836; Gattie, Joseph, Reinheim, Alsace, 1831; Gerhard, Anna, Walzhud, Baden, 1855; Gerhard, Joseph, Hamburg, Rhein, Bavaria, 1857; Gerber, Antonia, Diengeldorf, Baden, 1850; Gerber, Emil, Forchheim, Baden, 1849; Gerber, Louisa, Buffalo, 1861; Gittere, Jacob A., Buffalo, 1837; Glass, Lizzie, Buffalo, 1855; Glass, Mary, Buffalo, 1847; Glass, Jacob J., Buffalo, 1847; Jacobs, Mary, Mergenhagen, 1851; Glass, Sophia, Buffalo, 1857; Hack, George, Kirchenbach, Bavaria, 1855; Hack, Theresa, Kirchenbach, Bavaria, 1855; Hasenfratz, Frank, Reichschafen, Alsace, 1851; Hausle, Louise, Buffalo, 1853; Hausle, Magdalena, Metz, Lorraine, 1836; Hausle, Magdalina, Buffalo, 1843; Hausle, Mary Ann, West Flamboss, 1862; Hausle, Paul, Buffalo, 1835; Hausle, Rosa M., Buffalo, 1857; Heffon, Josephine M., Buffalo, 1852. Heisle, Julia B.S., Buffalo, 1855; Hemmerlein, Henry, Oesfeld, Bavaria, 1861; Hemmerlein, Lizzie M., Hamilton, Ontario, 1851; Hemmerlein, Wilhelmina, Oesfeld, Bavaria, 1861; Hibsch, Agnes, Geschweir, Baden, 1863; Hibsch, Jacob, Buffalo, 1840; Hitchler, Mrs. Magdalina, 1864; Jacob, Joseph F., Buffalo, 1854; Jacobs, Emma, Buffalo, 1861; Jehle, Fred, Baden, 1866; Jehle, Henrietta, Buffalo, 1848; Kerker, Mary, Buffalo, 1838; Kerker, Mary, Buffalo, 1861; Kiefer, Elizabeth, Riedselz, Alsace, 1831; Kiefer, Simon, Susenheim, Alsace, 1830; Killinger, Anthony, Tirnbach, France, 1857; Kirn, Louisa, Buffalo, 1858; Kleber, Cecilia, Entschbach, Baden, 1834; Klug, Alois J., Baden, 1846; Kolb, Mary, Buffalo, 1861; Koch, Catherine, Sulzheim, Alsace, 1855; Kost, Philip, Plaing, Hesse-Darmstadt, 1854; Kraus, Andrew, Buffalo, 1870; Kraus, Andrew, Hakenheim, 1855; Kraus, Caroline, Mrs., Buffalo, 1857; Kraus, John Jr., Buffalo, 1841; Kraus, Katie, Buffalo, 1862; Kraus, Mary R., Buffalo, 1847; Kung, Theresa, Buffalo, 1862; Lautz, J. Adam, Dieburg, Hesse-Darmstadt, 1873; Lederle, Bertha, Hamilton, Ontario, 1862; Leitzenstatter, Carone, Vienna, 1875; Lenhard, Kittie E., New York City, 1861; Lettau, Michael, Eierhausen, Bavaria, 1840; Lienert, J.B., Buffalo, 1833; Lienert, Mary B., Traumfeld, Bavaria, 1855; Loesch, Anna, Ashbach, Alsace, 1830; Loesch, C.F., Buffalo, 1857; Loesch, Frank, Forchheim, Baden, 1846; Losson, George, Buffalo, 1853; Lutz, Mathias, Entendorf, Alsace, 1833; Martin, Mrs. Alexander, Buffalo, 1860; Memmelshofen, Barbara, Buffalo, 1844; Mergenhagen, Celia, New York City, 1870; Mergenhagen, Frank, Buffalo, 1862; Messmer, Mrs. Michael, Rechtebach, Rheinpfalz, Bavaria, 1828; Metzger, Frank, Metzger, Josie E., Buffalo, 1862; Eiserthal, Rhein, Bavaria, 1844; Metzger, Mrs. Frank, Mundesheim, Bavaria, 1839; Meyer, Barbara Williams, Buffalo, 1841; Meyer, Catherine, Weisenburg, Alsace, 1831; Meyer, John B., Altkish, Alsace, 1855; Meyer, Mrs. Mary Ann, Riedselz, Alsace, 1831; Miller, Mary, Hohenrechterburg, Wuerttemburg, 1849; Moesinger, Adam, Kickheim, Bavaria, 1870; Motsch, Louis, Adelhausen, Baden, 1846; Motsch, Margaretta, Weisenthar, Bavaria, 1846; Muth, Jacob, Nassau, 1854; Muth, Magdalena, Buffalo, 1838; Muth,

Rosa E., Buffalo, 1861; Ordner, F.H., Buffalo, 1859; Ottenot, Augusta, Schusenreid, Wuerttemburg, 1841; Ottenot, Emma, Buffalo, 1862; Ottenot, Nicholas, La Petite, France, 1835; Paul, Caroline, Buffalo, Paul, Mary, M., Buffalo, 1855; Paul, Joseph, Buffalo, 1853; Mrs. Jos. Paul, Cheektowaga, 1853; Ramsperger, Elizabeth, Buffalo, 1834; Ramsperger, Joseph C., Germany, 1853; Reinnagle, Katie, Buffalo, 1871; Reisterer, Christian, Baden, Richert, Christina, Kalbsheim, 1846; Richert, Louisa, Buffalo, 1857; Rink, Maria, A., Roschwoog, Alsace, 1834; Roch, Louisa M., Buffalo, 1856; Rohr, Mathias, Reinish, Prussia, 1868; Rohr, Sophia, Buffalo, 1868; Rose, Joseph, Buffalo, 1834; Rose, Mrs. Joseph, Buffalo, 1836; Ruble, Mary A., Buffalo, 1841; Sand, Catherine, Genheim, Bavaria, 1846; Sand, Paul, Ormesheim, Bavaria, 1833; Schennon, Clara, Bermersheim, Hesse-Darmstadt, 1849; Scherer, A., Prussia, 1855; Scherf, Rosa, Buffalo, 1861; Schildknecht, Constantine, Buffalo, 1858; Schildknecht, Lydia, Riedern, 1832; Schillo, Katie, Buffalo, 1860; Schmidt, Anthony S., Baden 1856; Schmit, Anthony, Coblenz, Prussia, 1839; Schneidewind, A., Buffalo, 1843; Schonacker, A., Hildenhausen, Lorraine, 1836; Schum, Frank, Bartenstein, 1849; Schwanz, Fanny, Buffalo, 1861; Schwanz, Vincent, Buffalo, 1847; Schweizer, Joseph, Wallengen, Switzerland, 1868; Smith, Alexander, Buffalo, 1842; Smith, Bernard Jr., Buffalo, 1835; Smith, Bernard, Sr., Buffalo, 1833; Smith, Franuska, Altbreisach, Baden, 1872; Smith, Matilda, Buffalo, 1862; Smith, Sophia, Eden, 1840; Sonnick, Amelia, Buffalo, 1872; Spoeri, Anna, Bavaria, 1855; Spoeri, Francis, Switzerland, 1855; Stabel. Bernard, Stundweiler, Lower Alsace, 1847; Stabel, Frank, Stundweiler, Lower Alsace, 1846; Stadel, Mary M., Buffalo, 1850; Stadel, Wendle, Hagenau, Alsace, 1837; Steffan, A.C., Buffalo, 1850; Steffan, Barbara, Buffalo, 1841, Steffan, Martin, Buffalo, 1834; Steffan, Michael, Oensbach, Baden, 1830; Steffan, Rosina F., Rochester, 1876; Stemler, Anna M., Buffalo, 1835; Urban, Josephine, Pendleton, New York, 1873; Vogt, Brigita, Buffalo, 1840; Vogt, Peter A., Buffalo, 1840; Weber, Carrie, Buffalo, 1854; Weber, Louise, Vasseline, Rhein, Bavaria, 1832; Weber, Mary A., Hildenhausen, Lorraine, 1836; Wechter, Joseph, Kendwiller, 1828; Wechter, Mary A., Erldendorf, Bavaria, 1831; Weigel, William J., Buffalo, 1851; Weppner, Arnold, Rheinpfalz, Bavaria, 1834; Wehrle, Anthony, Eschlerg, Alsace, 1831; Wehrle, Michael, Eschlerg, Alsace, 1828; Werrich, Henry, Flamenshein, 1836; Werrich, Joseph, Flomershein, Bavaria, 1840; Werrich, Mrs. Jos., Gumbrechthofen, Alsace, 1828; Werrich, Veronica, Buffalo, 1838; Wex, Lorenz, Niedermorlen, Hesse-Darmstadt, 1856; Weyand, Christ, Auchen, Lorrain, 1847; Weyand, Emma, Buffalo, 1854; Wilhelm, Mrs. Jacob, Brumah, Alsace, 1830; Willman, Anthony, Baden, 1838; Young, Victoria M., Buffalo, 1847; Zahm, John, Bliesbruken, Lorraine, 1832; Zechman, Philip, Buffalo, 1842; Zeller, Mary M., Buffalo, 1838; Zeller, Rosa M., Buffalo, 1860; Zinns, Frederick, Aldenstadt, Alsace, 1838. Also for the discussion of the Celebration of a Pontifical High Mass see: Ibid, 324-44 and Rev. Hugo H. Hoever, St. Joseph's Daily Missal, Catholic Book Co., New York, 1957, pps. 3-15.

10. Information about Bishop Stephen Vincent Ryan was taken from the following sources: op. cit. Celebration of God's Life in Us, pps. 34-9, 151-2; op. cit. St. Louis Bazar Chronical, Oct. 22, 1888, vol. 1, no. 1. For a discussion of Ryan's conflict with Uhrich at Good Shepherd Church, Pendleton, New York, see: op. cit. Good Shepherd: The Church on the Canal, pps. 27-9. For a description of the construction of the temporary church at St. Louis Church see: op. cit. St. Louis Bazaar Herald, Dec. 29, 1888, vol. 1. no. 13. The source reference for the life and activities of Father Joseph Sorg see: op.cit. St. Louis Bazar Chronicle, Nov. 1, 1888, vol. 1, no. 10. For the Franco-Prussian War see: Palmer and Colten, History of the Modern World, Alfred A. Knopf, New York, 178, pps. 516-19. The churches in the increased arc of Catholicism their addresses, and their dates of foundation were: Assumption, 436 Amherst, 1888; Holy Name of Jesus, 1947 Bailey Avenue, 1887; Sacred Heart, 200 Emslie, 1875; At Adalbert Basilica, 212 St. Stanislaus Street, 1886; St. Agnes, 194 Ludington Street, 1883; St. Columba, Eagle and Hickory Streets, 1888; St. John the Baptist, 60 Hertel Avenue, 1867; St. Nicholas, 286, East Utica at Welker Street, 1874.

11. For description of the construction of the New Music Hall see: see: op. cit. History of Germans of Buffalo and Erie County, p.112. For a discussion of the Saengerfest held at the Music Hall in Buffalo in the summer of 1883 see: Fest Zeitung fuer das 23ste Nord Amerikanische Saengerfest, Buffalo, August 23, 1883, no. 20, the entire magazine was devoted to the event. For source material on the new Gothic Church at St. Louis Church opened in 1889 see: One Hundred and Twenty-Fifth Anniversary: 1829-1954, St. Louis Church Souvenir Book, October 3-6, 1954, pps. 21-2; Also consult op. cit. St. Louis Bazaar Herald, Dec. 8, vol. 1, no. 13. On September 17, 1888, The Buffalo Health Department located in the City and County Hall penned a letter from William Summus, president of the Board of Health, to the trustees of St. Louis Church. It reads: "You are hereby notified that permission is given you to deposit the remains of Very Rev. Father Sorg in a vault under St. Louis Church providing that the construction of such vault shall be approved by the Health Physician." The original of the letter is in the archives of St. Louis Church. In chapter eight, some details of the new gothic church structure were given, however, it seems that this history should present the description of it as given by the editors of the St. Louis Bazar Chronicle, Thursday, November 1, 1888, vol. 1., no. 10, pps. 8-9. "The soil upon which the building stands may be described as sandy loam. The footing-courses of the foundation-walls are of very large blocks of Yammerthal stone; no stone having less than twenty-square feet bed-area. Those under the main walls being twelve inches thick, and all others at least nine inches thick. The base-courses were bedded in cement on a layer of concrete, the full width of the course, and two feet under the front wall, walls of the sanctuary and transept piers; and twelve inches thick under the side walls. The walls are laid in cement mortar up to the level of the ground. Above the grade line the whole exterior building is faced with Medina sandstone of excellent quality, being extremely hard and uniform color. The stone is rock faced on the walls, and tooled in moulded courses, door and window jams, etc. The stone facing is backed up solid with brick masonry in the most substantial manner; and every course of brick in the tower has been thoroughly grouted with liquid water lime. The tower walls are isolated from the remainder of the building, so that the greater settlement caused by the immense weight upon them will not crack, or in any way effect the adjoining walls.

The style of the building is that known as continental gothic of the fourteenth century, which was contemporaneous with and similar to the English decorated. Though conforming to all the requirements of this style, the design is original and distinct, and possesses an individuality of detail which places it on the level with many of the finest cathedrals of the old world. The ground plan of the building is in the form of a latin cross with nave, sanctuary, and transepts. The nave is divided into a centre aisle with clerestory, and two side aisles, by fourteen magnificent columns of polished granite, with richly carved stone capitals. The dimensions of the church are as follows: Exterior length, 234 feet; exterior width, 134 feet; height from the ground to the ridge of the roof, 105 feet; length of transept, 120 feet. The nave is forty-two feet wide and seventy-two feet high in the clear; the side aisles are nineteen feet in height; and the clear height at the intersection of the nave with transept is sixty-six feet. The vaulted ceiling is richly groined with ribbing, having bosses of rich foliage of various designs at their intersection. The principal front on Main Street is designed on grand proportions, with a large centre tower reaching the considerable height of 245 feet, and two similar side towers, each 128 feet high. The grand portal in the main tower is divided by a mullion into two door-ways, each five feet wide, with jambs richly decorated with columns, having foliage capitals and clustered mouldings; the whole being surmounted with a tympanum, which will be richly carved with a sculptured figure in the centre. The high window in the gable over the main portal, has moulded stone mullions, and tracery of a beautiful and original design. The door is flanked on either side by buttresses, enriched by graceful pinnacles, with gablets and foliated finials. The centre gable terminates with a finial of rich foliage just underneath the clock dial and the point where the tower changes from the square to the octagonal form. The dial is of stone, with the figures carved on the rim, and a quatre-foil in the centre, and is 101 feet above the sidewalk. The tower retains the square form to the height of ninety-six feet, where it off-sets with graduated weatherings to the octagonal, having windows on each of the eight sides, with fine tracery, and each surmounted with a gablet springing from the buttresses and terminating with a foliated finial. The buttresses, continuing up, are finished with pinnacles. The spire will be octagonal. The angles will have rich moldings, ornamented with foliage crockets, and the faces will be paneled with tracery, the whole terminating in a magnificent finial eleven feet high. The side portals are each seven feet wide in the clear. The jambs are ornamented with columns, and the tympanum is filled with tracery of a beautiful pattern. Above the arch is a gablet terminating in a finial, and above this is a traceried window, with a richly molded label. Circular iron stair-ways are carried up in the side towers, which will communicate with the organ galleries and upper stories of the tower. The side aisles of the nave, behind the towers, are divided by buttresses with pinnacles in six bays. Each bay is pierced by a window five feet six inches wide and eighteen feet six inches in height, having the arch filled with traceries of varied designs. The main feature of the transept fronts is the magnificent rosewindows, twenty-two feet in diameter, which, for beauty and richness of design, may safely be said to equal any in this country. The labels above these windows terminate in handsome bosses. The molded and corbeled cornice of the clerestory roof extends across the transept fronts, and a triple window above it relieves the solid appearance of the gables. The side aisles of the sanctuary have one bay similar to those of the nave. The sacristy has seven bays. The clerestory, which rises twenty-seven feet above the roof of the side aisles, is divided into seven bays in the nave, two bays in the transept, one bay in the sanctuary to the apsis which has seven bays, being a half decagon. Each bay in the nave and transepts is pierced by a window eight feet wide and nineteen feet high; and five bays of the sanctuary , each contain a window, six feet wide and twenty-eight feet in height. The intersection of the roofs of the transept and nave is marked by a lofty spire bearing a cross. The windows will be glazed with two thicknesses of sash and glass, set several inches apart in order to produce an even temperature and avoid injury to the costly stained glass. The exterior sashes are glazed with plain glass; and the interior sash will contain stained glass of the most beautiful designs, which will give the soft, mellow light so much admired in the cathedrals of Europe. The seating capacity of the church will be sufficient for about 2,000 people, still leaving abundant space for the aisles and sanctuary. The boiler-room is absolutely fire-proof, the floor above it being constructed with iron beams and brick arches filled in with concrete; and the doors covered with tin. All the interior wood-work and finish in the body of the church is to be quarter-cut oak, stained semi-antique, and rubbed down to a dead polish. The gallery front will be richly ornamented with traced panels. The wainscoting in the vestibules is to be four feet high, of Tennessee marble, enriched with Glen's Falls black marble base and cap-moldings. The floors of the vestibules are to be tiled with red tiles, set off by a variegated border in regular geometric patterns. The outside doors will be hung with large brass hinges of gothic design. Beautiful altars are to adorn the sanctuary and a canopied pulpit is to be placed at the transept column. These together with the chimes of the tower, and all the necessary articles of church furniture, will afford ample opportunity for the congregation of St. Louis church to show still further its liberality in aiding this great and nobel work. The plans were drawn by Mr. Schickel, Architect, of New York, and the construction is being superintended by Mr. Geo. J. Metzger, Architect, of this city. The various contractors employed on the work are: John Druar, foundations; Wm. D. Collingwood, cut stone facing, bases, and capitals of columns; Chas. Berrick, mason-work of superstructure; Hager and Feist, carpentry and finishing; Machwirth Bros., slating and metal work; Byrne and Bannister, plastering; and Irlbacker and Davis, gas piping. The building committee: Rev. Dr. Paul Hoelscher, J. Adam Lautz, Chairman; Gerhard Lang, Jacob Davis, Peter A. Vogt, Charles Lautz, Wm. J. Weigel, Peter Paul, G. Frank Deck, Fred Jehle, Lawrence Wex, Xavier Dietsche, Jacob Gittere, F.X. Burkhard."

The Temporary Church 1885-1889

The German Music Hall and St. Louis Church destroyed by fire March 25, 1885

St. Louis Church dedicated August 25, 1889

Left to right starting at top: In 1896 the seven trustees of St. Louis Church were: Charles Burkhardt, Charles Dearing, John Feist, Charles Lautz, Peter Seereiter, J.H. Ullenbruch and Charles Williams. **Bottom row left to right are:** Charles Doll, Charles Fix, Charles Huck and John Kamm, Jr. who replaced Burkhardt, Feist, Lautz and Ullenbruch in 1900.

CHAPTER NINE

Into the Twentieth Century with Hoelscher

The Reverend Paul Hoelscher had arrived in Buffalo on June 4, 1876. Sixteen months later this native of Muenster, Westphalia, clothed with the robes of an earned academic degree of Doctor of Divinity from the University of Innsbruck and ordained a priest at the hands of Bishop Vincent Gassner at Brixen, both in Tyrol, Austria, was incardinated into the Diocese of Buffalo by Bishop Stephen Vincent Ryan, and appointed its first chancellor. For the next eleven years, he served the diocese as the bishop's right-hand man. As chancellor, he was not only his secretary and his confidant, but he was also pastor of St. Joseph Cathedral's parish. Although he gained renown as a Doctor of Divinity, he was humble enough to establish and minister to a mission church on the seawall strip of lower Buffalo. The small chapel, which he erected there, remained viable until after his death in 1916. He also established St. Agnes' Church on Benzinger Street, Buffalo, in 1883. With the sudden death of Joseph Sorg, Bishop Ryan could not think of a worthier candidate to inherit the pastorship of St. Louis Church. On September 18, 1888, Hoelscher moved into the church's rectory only three days after Sorg died. Into Hoelscher's hands was laid the task of completing the work of gothic grandeur that Sorg had begun.

On the very day of the fire, it had been Sorg who suggested that the new church should be immediately designed; he offered the first $100 donation to a fund drive which lasted for ten months, achieved a grand sum of $26,031, which then was added to $27,700 paid by the insurance companies. Achieving this amount of money was not an easy task. Six months after the drive began, the trustees thought that it was lagging. Although the total amount banked to that point had been $11,919, they considered this less than one-half of what they hoped to achieve by the end of ten months. They discussed the matter with Sorg, who said, "I believe it is time that I make a special visit to Gerhard Lang's home." He did so, taking Fred Kiefer with him. After a very long social evening, speaking of many other things besides money, Lang said, "It's getting late, Father, and we do have a full day of work ahead of us tomorrow. Before you arrived, however, I guessed that you and Fred were not simply coming tonight for a social visit. So I prepared. Over there on the mantel of the fireplace lies a check for $1,000!"

In 1848, Gerhard Lang, a very poor boy, had arrived in Buffalo without fanfare, but at his funeral at St. Louis Church forty-four years later, following his death on July 14, 1892, thousands crowded the church; every pew was filled to capacity. He had made an indelible mark on the history and the community of Buffalo. Although he was primarily a man of business, undertaking large enterprises, he was a very private person who had interesting and admirable characteristics. Lang was born at Flersheim, Germany, November 24, 1834. When he was only fourteen years old his father, Jacob Lang, a butcher by trade, brought him to Buffalo. For twelve years Gerhard worked for his father, who did not believe in paying him a salary. His father, following the custom of German immigrants, assumed that giving his son the opportunity to learn the art of butchering, meat sales, and the English language was a sufficient reward without indulging him in financial retribution. Always offered to young Gerhard, however, were sufficient board and room with family love and respect. In 1860, Gerhard left his father's business and took a position with Philip Born, who owned and operated one of the largest breweries in the city, located on the corner of Genesee and Jefferson Streets. Having great admiration for his new employee, Born sent him to Dr. Wyatt's School of Technical Brewing in New York City so as to learn more about the art of making beer. In 1860, Born approved of Gerhard's marriage to his daughter, Barbara, at St. Louis Church.

Shortly after the wedding, Philip Born died and, his widow went into partnership with Lang. By 1874, they had erected another brewery, the largest one in Buffalo, located on the corner of Best and Jefferson Streets. It was known as the Park Avenue Brewery, which produced thirty thousand barrels of beer a year. Most of it was sold in Buffalo but like other local beers, brewed by Philip Schaefer, William Simon, and Magnus Beck, theirs was well known throughout the Northeast and Midwest. To the casual passerby on Jefferson Street, the Park Avenue Brewery was known as the *Palace of Fine Beer*. Besides being manager of their brewery, Lang was director of the Western Savings Bank, the German-American Bank, the People's Bank, and president of the Erie County Natural Gas Company. Although mostly engrossed in his work, he found time for outside interests and political affairs. Having a fine voice, he enjoyed singing with the members of the Orpheus, Liedertafel, and Saengerbund. He was also a member of the German Young Men's Association; and, on many nights, he could be found participating in their activities at the German-American Music Hall. He was a devout and generous Catholic, a faithful benefactor of St. Louis Church and a member of the Catholic Mutual Benefit Association.

Barbara Born bore Gerhard seven children Annie E., Catherine, Emma, Bertha, Jacob, Mary, and Ludwina. All grew to maturity. Annie married Edwin G.S. Miller who in 1884 became manager of Lang's Brewery at Best and Jefferson Streets. Gerhard was an earnest advocate of the Democratic Party and represented the old Sixth Ward in the Common Council, being elected twice, first in 1877 and again in 1879. He was a friend of both Grover Cleveland and Jonathan Scoville, for whom he campaigned and successfully saw elected as consecutive mayors of Buffalo in 1881 and 1883. During Scoville's campaign in 1883, Lang's wife, Barbara, died. Some years later, Lang was offered the nomination of his party for mayor, but he declined. In 1890, he married Augusta Gerhardt. Their life together was quite short. In May of 1892, he was diagnosed with a serious condition of stomach cancer. His doctors gave him no hope of survival but sent him to New York City for treatment. It, however, was not productive; and, on Sunday, July 10, 1892, he returned to Buffalo. By Wednesday, he was sinking rapidly; and, on Thursday, at 8:20 A.M., he met his demise at his beautiful home on the corner of Main and Tupper Streets. At his funeral from St. Louis Church which took place on Saturday, Bishop Stephen Vincent Ryan ended his eulogy of him saying, "His genial countenance, which bespoke the generosity of his soul, will no more be seen by his dear friends, but I am sure he will look down from heaven upon earth where he was so long engaged, and where he lived so well and so generously. The Holy Scriptures give us in a few words a description of his character, 'A man simple, upright, and fearing the Lord.'"

One month before the first bazaar, which raised a net value of $14,853, Lang was very much alive and active at St. Louis Church. Sorg, however, had died, and Hoelscher was given the task to be the spiritual advisor and pastor to the trustees and parishioners. Together they would labor not only at this one bazaar; but also, through the years of giving, accepting gifts from well-to-do patrons, and planning a second bazaar, they would see that church, whose structure had been nearly completed before Sorg's death, furnished and consecrated. The consecration, however, did not happen until 1913. In that year Hoelscher was made a monsignor by Pope Pius X and dean of German priests in the Diocese of Buffalo. During his years at St. Louis Church, he had grown in such stature that priests throughout his diocese and other parts of the United States sought his counsel in theological and ecclesiastical matters. He sat on the Board of Trustees of the German Roman Catholic Orphanage, promoted the development of the Catholic diocesan newspaper, *The Echo*, established himself as the moderator of the Catholic Institute, and kept a keen interest in the Knights of Saint George. He was also *denfensor vinculi* in matrimonial cases and a notary in the court disposing clerical discipline. Although he influentially served under four bishops in the Diocese of Buffalo, he was not pompous; and, as a humble priest and pastor, he spent long hours regularly hearing confessions.

After a two-week illness Hoelscher died in the rectory at 2:45 P.M. on Wednesday, December 27, 1916. At his bedside were Father Ferdinand Kolb, pastor of Saint Boniface Church, and Fathers Albert Rung and Albert Hoffmeyer who were assistants at St. Louis Church. His body was brought into the church on Friday afternoon by the Knights of St. John so that it could lie in state, and be viewed by the public. Early on Saturday morning the diocesan priests, led by Monsignor Nelson Baker, Vicar General, chanted the Office of the Dead. Immediately following, a solemn requiem Mass was celebrated by Denis Dougherty, bishop of Buffalo. Right Reverend Bishop Thomas F. Hickey, bishop of Rochester, occupied a seat in the sanctuary while more than two hundred priests occupied the front pews in the church. At Mass, Reverend J.J. Nash D.D. acted as the deacon with Reverend George J. Weber as subdeacon. Fathers Thomas A. Donohue and Alexander Pitass, were honorary deacons. Fathers B. Cohausz, S.J. and Laurenzis were assistants to Bishop Hickey. The

chancellor of the Buffalo Diocese, Reverend Thomas J. Walsh, D.D., and Reverend William J. Schreck acted as masters of ceremony. Father Henry Laudenbach, former assistant at St. Louis Church, who at the time of Hoelscher's death was pastor at Sacred Heart Church in Dunkirk, New York, delivered the eulogy.

Laudenbach said of Father Hoelscher, "His life was always an open book. Its span was allotted by the Providence of the Most High to well-defined, sharply limited spheres of activity which he strove to fill to the best of his ability. The Kulturkampf of Germany brought him to the Western World after an honorable doctorate had been earned in Tyrol. He was a good shepherd who never omitted Mass or a good preparation for it. His many assistants can testify to the fact that Dr. Hoelscher was to them a father of spiritualism, a sure guide, a shining exemplar of the priest. How many people who heard him preach, who came to him with troubles big and small, left his presence consoled, cheered, and fixed to better endeavor? His instructions were solid and well thought out, to the point, and methodical. He did not fail in his capacity as shepherd, guide, doctor, and friend. You, his people know more than any others that his watchword was service first to God and next to you. He visited the sick, brought communion to his parishioners, and consoled the dying."

Laudenbach continued touching on Hoelscher's human side saying, "No man is a hero to his valet, but Monsignor Hoelscher was the ideal to his friends who really knew him. And he was easy to know! His life so blameless in its loyal devotion will be better appreciated and better followed now that he is dead. For it seems to be the lot of men to appreciate their best characters more in their loss than in their actual presence. Monsignor Hoelscher was above all, a true friend. You saw candor and uprightness in him and felt it in his looks, words, and actions. How kindly he tried to make you feel at home, how hospitable to all! He never tired seemingly, when the laws of charity spoke.

He was never found wanting when justice claimed her share."

Turning then to the priests in the church, Laudenbach said, "He was a wise counselor. You his fellow priests will bear me out that his word was law, because we knew that he knew his matter. As master of conferences we might have tried to puzzle him, but we did not succeed in confounding him when he knew his path was right. He saw and thought quickly, with a mind sharpened to a keen edge by all those years of incessant study and careful meditation: he was mellowed by the never-ending and ceaseless sorrow of mankind to take a fatherly interest in our little troubles and make them his own. His bishops respected his counsel. As secretary of the diocese, as its chancellor, as synodal examiner, as superior of religious communities, he was *facile princeps* and unswervingly loyal to everyone whom God placed over him. Yes, loyalty was in his blood: *noblesse oblige* was his motto, and as he held that true aristocracy in the soul, he was an aristocrat in the right sense of the word: a gentleman in his outer bearing, a truly humble soul in his every fiber, a model priest."

Hoelscher had no relatives in America. Only his elder brother, Herman, survived him and served as parish priest at Engberg, Germany. In his will, Hoelscher bequeathed $5,000 to St. Louis Church. To each of the following institutions he gave $500: St. Agnes Training School for Girls, German Roman Catholic Orphanage, and St. Mary's Infant Asylum and Maternity Hospital. After making a foundation of $500 for Masses to be said for the repose of his soul, he made a bequest of the remainder of his estate to the Society for the Propagation of the Faith and the Catholic Church Extension Society of the United States of America. After Mass, his body was escorted to the United German and French Roman Catholic Cemetery where Father Albert Rung performed the last rites at the grave. Following the announcement of Hoelscher's death,

letters of condolence reached the offices of the *Aurora* and the *Echo*. Among the many writers were: Joseph Frey, president of the Central Verein for the Knights of St. George and Charles Korz, president of the New York *Staatsverband*. [1]

In 1888, during the brief period of a month and one-half which preceded the St. Louis Church Bazaar, a time when the sadness of Sorg's demise still lingered, Hoelscher, in his new role as pastor, won the hearts of his parishioners by his hearty sympathy and earnest cooperation with them in the great work which they had undertaken. The church, a great gothic structure had been completed, but it was unadorned. There was only open space beneath its vaulted ceiling; there were no altars, pews, statues, stations of the cross, or fancy candelabras. These items would only arrive as the debt on the church was paid. The most ambitious bazaar of 1888 was about to begin; it was to be a giant step on the road to bringing this goal to fruition.

Finally all preparations had been made, and it was opening night, October 22, 1888. Early in the evening admiring crowds began sight-seeing among the magnificently decked booths; and, gazing at everything so attractively arranged, the viewers were first at a loss whether to admire mostly the pretty articles, their happy arrangement, or the bright and winning attendants. As a compromise they divided their attention among them and all were shared alike. At 8:00 P.M. Kuhn's orchestra added sensibly to the enjoyment of the occasion, and a little later Bishop Ryan with a happy address formally opened the bazaar. His estimate of the possible financial result of the fair evidently pleased his hearers, and why not? He hoped that the organizers of the event would clear $25,000 in two weeks. He then said, "Now let every one keep this sum before their eyes, and who knows; perhaps we may clear that amount. But that means work, work, and more work all the time for everyone." The attendance was most gratifying; more than one thousand people were present to hear the bishop's address. His engraved picture had appeared in the *Buffalo Morning Express* on the day before opening night, announcing his presence at the ceremony. The bishop commented on this advertisement. He said, "Using the press to announce the presence of a prestigious guest is always a good way to encourage attendance."

One of the strongest attractions at the bazaar was the new church itself. On all sides words of praise were expressed at the sight of the magnificent interior. Although the booth attractions were wonderful that evening, everyone admitted the unqualified success of opening night was the grandeur of the church. With such substantial encouragement as the visitors gave that night the managers of the fair expressed themselves as being perfectly satisfied. They said, "Everything now points to an unparalleled success in the history of church bazaars in Buffalo; the enthusiasm of the patrons this evening seems to say that it will." On that first evening Reverends Dr. Quigley, Buchholz, Dr. Hoelscher, McGloin, Kamp, and Trautlein attended with Bishop Ryan who, upon entering, said, "It is the grandest and most superb edifice; it is one for which our city can boast."

The following afternoon, the doors of the bazaar were thrown open to the children who were admitted free of charge. The church was thronged for more than three hours starting at 3:00 P.M. They never seemed to tire viewing and admiring the pretty booths. Hoelscher entertained the little ones in royal style at the fishing pond, the place that seemed most to delight the venturesome little fish-men and maidens. Very disagreeable weather accompanied the opening for the adults that evening; but the crowd was quite respectable. As the people came into the church, they had the opportunity to look intently at the layout of the many booths displaying gifts and prizes as well as at those that offered food and drink.

As the people entered through the Main Street doors, the ushers who gave them directions first greeted them; and, who upon receiving their money for admission presented them with a pass. Proceeding into the nave, the patrons came upon the *Bazar Chronicle* booth. It was located on the left-hand side of what eventually became the center aisle of the church. The *Bazar Chronicle* was an eight-page magazine that had thirteen issues, one published each night of the fair except Sundays and a final summary issue, published on December 29, 1888. The publication committee was D. Edward Metzger, M.F. Boechat, Peter P. Seereiter, Charles J. Fix, and Peter Paul. Individual copies cost five cents and an entire set of issues was sold at fifty cents. When the fair's visitors approached the booth they were greeted by the cheerful personalities of Miss Theresa Gundelfinger, Miss Margaret Fell, and Miss Clara Beutter. Their winning smiles and persuasive solicitations secured many subscribers and sold many copies of the paper.

Visitors who could not get near the booth immediately, and decided to travel around it to other areas which seemed less crowded, did not escape the merry band of little *Chronicle* workers who darted in and out of the many groups standing and chatting. Every patron of the bazaar will remember with pleasure their bright faces underneath the ribboned caps and their clear voices crying, "Here's your *Chronicle*; it's only five cents!" These boys were: Edward Paul, Lawrence Wex, Albert Hausle, Charles Bott, Edwin Voltz, Edward Smith, Joseph Voltz, Frank Cullen, William Smith, and Albert Wagner. During the course of two weeks, this determined little band secured three hundred and eighty-nine complete subscriptions and sold more than five hundred single copies. At the end of the bazaar, Edward Paul won first prize for selling the most subscriptions; he received a pair of nickel-plated skates. Second and third place prizes were awarded to Lawrence Wex and Albert Hausle. *The Bazar Chronicle*, besides making a running-commentary on the events of the fair, provided a wealth of historical facts concerning the development of St. Louis Church in Buffalo. It netted $565.00 over the entire period of the fair.

Across from the *Chronicle* was St. Joseph's booth. The ladies in charge of its display were Louisa A. Weppner and M. Amelia Davis. Those who came to it on that Tuesday night saw numerous and valuable donations. Among them were: a Portland cutter, a nickeled Dockash Range, a handsome painted sconce, a fine tapestry featuring painted soap bubbles, and a blond doll who asked the onlookers to guess her name at five cents a chance. Sometime late that evening after many nickels had been collected the name Susie was proclaimed; the booth had its winner. The donors of these fine gifts were Henry Garono, Miss Della E. Kraus, and Miss May Weppner. As in all the other booths many people who could not donate quality items gave the ladies cash donations. St. Joseph's netted $1,434.61. One of the cash donors was William Schickel, the architect who designed the gothic church. He gave a gift of $50.00.

Moving down the aisle, next to St. Joseph's, was St. Louis' booth. The matrons on duty were Mrs. John Coon, Mrs. Joseph Paul, Mrs. John Dingens, and Mrs. William Chretien. Viewers gazed upon a fine cherry mantel, a granite set of figurines, a beautiful painting of the Madonna by Schnur, an elegant Indian couch, a parlor suite, and a hall rack. J. Uebelhoer, Henry Garono, Mrs. John Lorenz, Rung Brothers, and A. Cutler and Son had donated these items. Each night more gifts were added; but none drew more attention and unanimous admiration than the handsome life-like oil portrait of Father Sorg. The father of the "Greenback," E.G. Spaulding, donated $100.00, and Devoe Paint Company of Buffalo and Collins Downing Company of New York City each gave cash donations of $25.00. The Devoe family was a member of St. Louis Church. By the end of the fair the booth had netted $1,760.24.

Across from St. Louis', the visitors found St. Anne's booth. The ladies at this booth were the recipients of some of the finest and most valuable presents donated. In the display some items were: a fine upright piano, a pair of statues, a clock, a sofa cushion, a plush rocker, a dozen knives and forks, fine paintings, parlor lamps, prie-dieus, and sanctuary veils. Although there were many more items, too numerous to list and evaluate, they, brought great revenue to the fair. Those who were responsible for gathering all the items and putting them so artistically on display were Mrs. Peter Mergenhagen, Mrs. Frank Deck, Mrs. J. Armbruster, and Mrs. J. Ordner. Prior to the bazaar, Miss Josie Mergenhagen, who had donated her hand-painted mirror to the booth, had written a letter to Grover Cleveland, president of the United States, requesting his financial support for the bazaar. On October 14, 1888, he responded to her, he wrote, "I have received your letter in which you tell that you are trying to help in the rebuilding and refurbishing of St. Louis Church. Many times I am called upon from every quarter to aid such efforts, and I am not always able to do what I would like to in those cases. But this is such a good cause, and I remember your father and mother so well that when their daughter asks me, I feel that I should do something to help. I send you a small gift for the purpose of adding a little to the receipts of the fair. Please give my regards to your father and mother." The letter was signed Grover Cleveland. Although the sum donated by the president was not mentioned in the letter, deposits of more than $254.00 were made in the bank by the fair's treasurer on October 17 and 19. It is very possible that Cleveland's receipt was part of that deposit. The booth also had the largest number of cash donations amounting to $230.65 from nineteen contributors. Its total net for the bazaar was $3,655.60.

Moving toward the sanctuary of the church and adjacent to St. Ann's was St. Mary's booth. It was a most handsome one whose officers were Mrs. J. Rose, Mrs. F. Kiefer, Mrs. M. Zeller, and Mrs. Philip Schreck. Their assistants were Louisa Williams, Louise Rose, and Fannie Kiefer. Visitors were greeted by a view of choice objects artistically assembled. Included were an elegant large bookcase, a library and parlor table, gold watches, and sets of dishes. One item drew a great deal of comment; it was a fifty-pound can of lard donated by Mrs. Xavier Dietsche. These gifts and many others were given by: L. Granacher and Co., George Rudolph, Mrs. F. Kiefer, Mrs. P. Schreck, Jacob Christ, Joseph Rothballer, Mrs. J.M. Prozeller, Mrs. Barbara Zahm, Mrs. L. Williams, and Fred Breithecker. The net proceeds at St. Mary's booth were $2,610.78.

Across from St. Mary's was the cafe, at which Edward Wilhelm and Augustus F. Weppner showered their genial smiles on all that entered. Mr. E.A. Weppner, employee of the German American Bank did cashier's duty at the cafe, and the ladies in attendance were: Miss Denzinger, Mrs. Aman, Miss Gebhard, and Miss Bierman. Moderate prices made this booth quite a popular attraction. It was entered through three beautifully decorated arches constructed across the chancel floor, which was in that part of the church east of the nave. Later, when services were eventually conducted in the church, this area formed part of the sanctuary. A running fountain added an Arabian effect to the attractions contained therein. Good eatables were on hand, the cuisine was superb, the chef was a genius, and handsome young ladies did the serving. There were matinees at the bazaar on Tuesdays and Thursdays. Good meals were served in the afternoon as well as in the evening, but the evening ones were considered more delicious.

On the west side of the nave, complimenting the cafe was the smoking-room. Although this was not considered a booth, it was a draw for the men who congregated there in large numbers. Puffing on their cigars, they recollected on the fact that this would be the last time that they would ever smoke in a church. It was also a good thing that the ceiling was very high; the smoke could rise well into the air. Keeping the

patrons aware of the devastation of fire that destroyed the old church, signs directed butts to be well extinguished. The trustees were on hand to make sure the regulation was seriously heeded.

Next to St. Mary's on the same side of the aisle but next to the sanctuary was St. Cecilia's booth. It was divided into two compartments. One was filled with a clock, footrest, oil painting, rocker, set of carvers, a horn footrest, a pincushion, a knitted bedspread by Magdalena Buchheit, and many books. One of those books was *Our Saviour's Life*, authored by Father Francois de Ligny and translated into English by John Gilmary Shea. McDavitt and Co., New York City, published his translation in 1875. Mrs. George Brennan donated it. The other section contained a fishpond, candy store, and soda fountain. During the two weeks of the bazaar, confections from a sweet-meat table at the candy store were put in Japanese bags, and sold to parents of anxiously awaiting children by Lizzie Zoll, Clara Wehrle, Anna Wehrle, Minnie Schindler, Mary Deck, Augusta Haas, Louisa Deck, Rosa Meyers, Louisa Kern, and Katie Biesinger. At the soda fountain yummies of vanilla, lemon, sarsaparilla, hard cider, and sweet cider were purchased from Misses Smith, Wehrle, Metz, Ducro, and Wagner. With each delectable item sold, the patron received a complementary red posy. The fishpond netted $254.32; candy and soda sales netted $349.94.

Overall, the St. Cecilia booth gave to the treasury a net of $2,617.01. Miss Tina Schildknecht, an attentive lady, presided constantly over the activities always trying to increase the booth's total receipts. She encouraged cash donations. They were obtained from: Mrs. J. Muth, A. Didley, Barbara Rosar, Mrs. F.J. Snyder, Christ Bauer, Mrs. E. Rebstock, Mrs. Anna Bardoll, Miss Braumstarck, C.B. Huck, Miss M. Kitzen, Louisa Garono, J.A. Ullenbruch, B. Stapel, Mary Langenfeld, and Mrs. Heier. In order to make the booth more attractive, Schildknecht featured specialties in her art gallery. Out of town publishers had donated to her some of their finest works in book-craft. Everything on display had magnificence, wealth, luxury, and beauty. Among the paintings and prints were Pope Leo XIII, Lord's Supper, Christ before Pilate, Pope addressing Cardinals, and Raphael's Grand Duca Madonna. Each item carried a tag naming its donor of which several were prestigious: Hersee and Company; Bettinger and Co.; Benziger Brothers; Roberts Brothers of Boston; Dahlman, Spiegel and Weil; Art Industry and Manufacturers' Centennial; and Smith and Sherman. The gallery's matrons were Mrs. Coon, Mrs. Joseph Paul, and Mrs. John Dingens. They were graciously assisted by Misses L. Kiener, Sonnick, Vogt, Haberstro, Stainton, McManus, Weppner, Stover, Fries, Young, Chretien, Friedman, Rieman, and Reese.

In the sanctuary, which had not yet been adorned with altars and sacerdotal accessories, the men attending the fair found their home for conversation over a libation of their favorite elixir, beer! There, well supplied by Gerhard Lang, Adam Lautz, Peter P. Seereiter, Peter Vogt, and Andrew Kraus, stood the refreshment booth. On the counter of a temporary bar stood mugs constantly being filled while dishes of meats, cheese, and crackers, from Charles Dearing, Augustus F. Weppner, and Xavier Dietsche, were endlessly refilled. While the women labored in the vineyards of booths surrounding the high rising pillars of the nave, the men were in their glory in the sanctuary discussing the affairs of state. One can understand the success of the refreshment booth when one observes its net profit of $518.47. Among those who mingled among its many patrons were the officers and committee chairmen of the bazaar: They were: Henry Garono, Andrew Kraus, Otto Andrle, Mathias Smith, Peter P. Seereiter, Charles B. Hauck, Joseph Paul, Edward M. Hager, William C. Chretien, Jacob J. Glass, Edward M. Wilhelm, Louis Pfohl, William Wilhelm, D. Edward Metzger, and Matthias F. Hausle.

Henry Garono was the president of the bazaar. He had had fourteen years of business life with Sidney, Shepard, and Company. The vice-president was Andrew Kraus. He was born in Buffalo on December 10, 1846. Essentially, he was a society man, being a member of the Catholic Mutual Benefit Association, the Orpheus, German Young Men's Association, and the incorporator of the Buffalo Cooperative Brewing Company. The man who looked after all the receipts as treasurer was Peter P. Seereiter. He was born July 15, 1854 and educated at St. Mary's parochial school. For ten years he had been an accountant with Peter Paul and Brothers. At the time of the bazaar, however, he was treasurer of the Ziegele Brewing Company. Secretary of the fair was Mathias Smith. For nine years, he had served on the board of trustees at St. Louis Church. He was born in Prussia in 1833 and immigrated into America in 1847. The parents of Jacob Davis, a member of the church's building committee, were married at St. Louis Church in October 1836. He was born to them on September 19, 1837; first attended public school and later studied at St. Louis' parochial school. He served as president of the St. Louis Society for two years and as a member of the board of trustees for nine years. At the time of the bazaar he was a partner in the firm Irlbacker and Davis.

Mr. Peter Vogt, a most influential supporter of St. Louis Church, was born in Buffalo on December 25, 1840, first received his education at St. Mary's parochial school, and later attended St. Junius school which became known as St. Boniface's parochial school. He was a member of the Catholic Institute, German Young Men's Association, and vice president of the board of directors for the United German and French Roman Catholic Cemetery Association. At the time of the bazaar he was president of the Empire Brewing Company. The youngest member of the church's building committee was William Weigel, born on September 15, 1851. He was educated first in public schools and later at St. Louis' parochial school. In 1864 he began twelve years of employment with Pardridge

Dry Goods. He then accepted a four-year appointment as clearance clerk in the collectors' office associated with the Erie Canal. In 1880 the firm of C.W. Miller hired him as a full time accountant. At the time of the bazaar he was a partner at the Weyand and Weigel Bottling Works on Main Street as well as president of the Buffalo Beer Bottling Association. [2]

When the bazaar was finally over and the church was cleared of all the structures that went into making booths, the officers of the fair issued their final financial statement. It had been a brilliant achievement in church fairs; better than any ever held in Buffalo. Thousands of people attended. There were twelve thousand one hundred and fifty one paid admissions, exclusive of workers and providers. The final net profit was $14,582.82. The expenses incurred by the various committees were quite small; they accounted for less than seven percent of the gross income. This resulted because those employed by the bazaar committee provided their services for inexpensive prices. The music, for example, was rendered each evening by Kuhn's band for a total of $335.00. Counting the number of instruments played in his orchestra, each member received a nightly salary of $1.20 that translates into twenty-four cents per hour. Not only did the band members do their work cheerfully; they also volunteered to play for no cost at the victory banquet that was held in the church on Sunday evening, November 18, 1888. Over eight hundred people attended; it netted $343.80. M. Louis Goetz catered it pro gratis. He provided enough food for a "million," and his waiters served it with great brilliancy of achievement greeted by acclaim from all present.

Mr. J. Adam Lautz was the toastmaster who introduced Father Hoelscher saying, "and now let us hear from our pastor, the Reverend Hoelscher. This entire parish is so proud not only to have a priest, but a priest who is a Doctor of Divinity. Not many churches can boast of this privilege." Hoelscher then officially addressed his congregation for the first time. His remarks were very touching. When he finished, he received a thunderous applause. Several other speakers who met with varied success in overcoming the acoustical properties of the unadorned church followed him. One speaker, humorously remarked, "It is so difficult to be heard in here that I wonder how Jesus Christ could have been heard by five thousand people when he gave his sermon on the mount?" The vast vaulted roof and the length of the church made it almost impossible for the speakers to be heard by one-half the audience. That night, however, the entire assemblage was one large family; it was not a time to be critical, and no kindlier mutual regards could have been exchanged.

For many months after the bazaar one could hear the parishioners praising the musical renditions offered by members of Kuhn's family. On July 4, 1847, Franz Anton Kuhn married Maria Katharina Gramm at St. Louis Church. Each had come separately from Europe. He came from Schneeberg, Rheinpfalz, where he had been born on September 2, 1823; and she, born on December 25, 1824, came from Amorbach, a village in the same kingdom. Together, they raised six children to maturity, Joseph, Karl, Henry, William, Frank, and Josephine. After a long illness, Maria died; she received a long and beautiful memorial written by Hermann Hoffmann in the *Buffalo Sontagspost*. Franz Anton had arrived in Buffalo on June 26, 1847 while Maria Katharina came eight days later. Before coming to America, Franz Anton, who had learned the trade of tailoring, traveled extensively through Bavaria seeking work. He was most successful in both Munich and Bamberg, but he felt insecure about the future. At the age of twenty-four he came to New York City from which he took the steamship to Albany and the railroad to Buffalo. After marriage he and his wife settled in a house on Goodell Street near Michigan. He gave up his craft of tailoring, and went into the inn-keeping business. At first he opened a small restaurant similar to a Gasthaus in Europe. Between 1849 and 1868 he ran the *Apollo*, a grand building which was a combination of restaurant, theater, and concert hall. His love for music was instilled into his five sons.

Joseph Anton Kuhn was born on September 1, 1850; he attended parochial school at St. Louis Church, but later enrolled at School Fifteen. From an early age he was captivated by music. He learned violin from Carl Graefe, studied musical theory under the direction of C. F. Baum, and developed expertise with the clarinet under the tutelage of Leitung von A. Schwiedop. From 1870 to 1895, with only short breaks, he was the conductor of the orchestra of the Academy of Music on Main Street. With an orchestra of forty musicians, he conducted a seasonal concert in St. James Hall. In 1890, he organized an orchestra at the Iroquois Hotel that was in great demand for dinners and banquets. He also developed the Beethoven Quartet, the first string quartet in Buffalo. In the 1880's, while in residence on Prospect Avenue, he was the bandmaster for the seventy-fourth regiment.

His brother Frank, who was born on June 18, 1852, had also been a student at St. Louis' parochial school, School Fifteen, and studied music under Graefe, Baum, and Schwiedop. He further, however, specialized in playing piano, learning the basics from Theodore Moelling. In 1881, Frank married Mathelde A. Fuchs, the daughter of August Fuchs. While living on Ellicott Street, she and Frank had four children, three boys and a girl. As they grew to maturity, Frank supported his family from the income obtained by his orchestra as it played at balls, concerts, social gatherings, and weddings throughout Buffalo. At the same time he was a private teacher of violin, piano, and flute.

Two other brothers, Karl and Henry, also attended St. Louis' parochial school and went on to study and become proficient musicians. In the 1870's, Karl was a music instructor at Canisius College and participated in Joseph Anton's Beethoven Quartet. Also, he was a member of the Buffalo Symphony Orchestra and music director in the Star theaters in Buffalo. His wife of eighteen years, Caroline Reigelmann, with whom he had six children, died on December 31, 1895. Afterwards he remarried; his second wife was Louise Hailer who had been born in Berlin, Canada. Like Karl, Henry also attended St. Louis' parochial school; but, although he failed to be enthusiastic about music at a young age, he satisfied his parents' wishes by learning to play the violin, clarinet, and piano. As he matured, instead of staying with music, he tried his hand at being a cigar-maker, and started a small business. His older brother, Frank, however, constantly begged Henry to play as a substitute in his band at various engagements such as social gatherings and weddings. Soon Henry realized that he was being pressed for time. He gave up his cigar business, and gave full attention to music. Although, the fifth brother, William also played in his brothers' bands and orchestras, and made a good financial living doing so, he never appeared as committed to music as they were. He lived with his wife Emma Huber at his parents' home at Huron and Ellicott Streets. His sister, Josephine, also lived there with her husband Louis Schultes. Both William and Josephine received their early education at St. Michael's parochial school because their mother and father had joined that church in 1866. [3]

The year following the bazaar brought together a cast of characters who played a very decisive roll in the payment of the debt which was incurred in building the magnificent gothic structure known as St. Louis Church. These were Stephen Vincent Ryan, Bishop of the Diocese of Buffalo, Michael Augustine Corrigan, Archbishop of New York City, Jonathan Scoville, a rich industrialist who had been elected mayor of Buffalo in 1881, James O. Putnam, who after a long political career was appointed the chancellor of the University of Buffalo, and the seven trustees of St. Louis Church. Bishop Ryan had become a good friend of Jonathan Scoville. In 1889, Scoville, who had been diagnosed with heart disease, fell victim to typhoid pneumonia. Ryan, who was most concerned about his health, often visited him, and was very happy when Dr. L.P. Dayton, who was Scoville's personal physician, announced that he would substantially improve. It was at this time that Ryan discussed the financial situation of St. Louis Church. Scoville agreed that the great gothic structure was a boon to the beautification of Buffalo and eventually would be an historical landmark.

Ryan wondered if Scoville could help the trustees of the church reduce the principal on its debt. Scoville thought that his loan of $60,000 would do so. In the discussion, however, there arose the subject of collateral and the conditions of ownership of the property. Scoville knew that James O. Putnam, when he was Senator of New York State, had the Putnam Bill voted into law in 1855. This was a ruling that confirmed the ownership and control of the property by the trustees of St. Louis Church. Scoville wanted to know, however, if this law was still valid or had Bishop Ryan become owner of the property. Ryan explained that the land was given to Bishop Dubois and his successors in 1829 and that a deed could be made to himself by the present Archbishop of New York, Michael Corrigan, a successor of Dubois. It could then be registered in the County Clerk's Office in Buffalo. Accepting Ryan's opinion, Franklin D. Locke, legal advisor to Scoville, without further investigation, drew up a mortgage between Ryan and Scoville for $60,000. This sum was then given by Ryan to the trustees to reduce the principal of the loan that they had previously negotiated elsewhere.

It was at this point that the trustees also decided to seek legal advice, and they chose to go to their friend, James O. Putnam, who had become Vice Chancellor at the University of Buffalo. He was born at Attica, New York, on July 4, 1818, and studied at Hamilton and Yale Colleges. In 1842, he was admitted to the bar, married Harriet Palmer of Buffalo, and began his practice in

that city. She died while he was at the height of his political career defending the property rights of the trustees of St. Louis Church in Buffalo. On March 15, 1855, he married Kate F. Wright of Vermont. His political achievements were Postmaster of Buffalo, 1851-53; State Senator, 1854-55; United States Counsel at Le Havre, France, 1861-66; United States Minister to Belgium, 1880-81; and Vice Chancellor of the University of Buffalo, 1882-96. With pride he accepted the university's offer of chancellorship in 1896.

Jonathan Scoville was born in the small town of Salisbury, Litchfield County, Connecticut, on July 14, 1834. He was the eldest of six children. His father was Samuel C. Scoville, farmer and manufacturer of pig iron, the ore for which came from the mines near his farm. Jonathan remained at the local school until he was sixteen years of age. It was then that his father found him a position in the local country store where Jonathan learned how to understand mercantile pursuits by being an errand boy who opened the store at 6:00 A.M. and closed it at 9:00 P.M. His day was not finished until he had properly swept, dusted, and put in order its counters and shelves. After two years of this basic learning, he was sent to the scientific department of Harvard University where he studied engineering, chemistry, geology, physics, and mathematics. Returning home upon graduation, he took care of his father's furnaces at the iron mill and went on the road as a salesman of car wheel iron. He first made sales in Buffalo in 1856. After reviewing business possibilities with his father, he took up permanent residence in Buffalo in 1860, and established a foundry for the manufacture of car wheels. Eventually his brother, Nathaniel C. Scoville joined him; and, together, they opened other blast furnaces in Toronto, Ontario, and Chenango, New York. In 1880 Jonathan joined the Democratic Party and was elected United States Congressman from Erie County. Later, he followed Grover Cleveland as mayor of Buffalo. He never married, and his brother, whom he loved deeply, died in November 1890. Before his brother died, however, he moved to New York City and resided with him at the Windsor Hotel. Jonathan spent the last four years of his life ailing. Returning to Buffalo, he died on March 4, 1891. His estate was estimated to be between eight and ten million dollars.

*M*ichael Augustine Corrigan was born in Newark, New Jersey, in 1839. He was educated at Mount St. Mary's College, Emmitsburg, Maryland. This was the college that Bishop Dubois had established before he became bishop of New York. Later Corrigan attended Roman Urban College. After ordination as priest, he became director of the seminary at Seton Hall College, South Orange, New Jersey. From 1873-1880, he was Bishop of Newark, New Jersey. He was then chosen to be coadjutor bishop to Cardinal McCloskey of New York City. After five years, upon the death of McCloskey, he replaced him as archbishop. His service there was a profound one and lasted from 1885 to 1902. He was a great opposer of the philosophy and theology of *Americanism* that was prevalent during his reign.

*I*n 1889, the trustees at St. Louis Church were: Peter Paul, president; G. Frank Deck, secretary; Fred Jehle, treasurer; Lawrence Wex; Xavier Dietsche; Frank X. Burkhard; and Jacob Alexander Gittere. Peter Paul, president of the trustees, was born in Buffalo on August 19, 1849. He received his education in the private school of Mr. Franz L. Schreck and later at St. Louis' parochial school. In 1862, E.S. Brooks employed him as an errand boy in his bookstore. Peter Paul worked there for three years. For the following nine years Breed and Lent Company employed him. In 1874, he formed a co-partnership with his brother Joseph; they titled their business as Peter Paul and Brother, Booksellers and Stationers. He served as a trustee for seven years, and was a member of its building committee.

*F*rank Deck, secretary of the trustees, was born in Rheinpfalz at Gross Fistlinger, November 18, 1839. He came to America in 1847, attended St. Louis' parochial school and later took classes at a night school. For twenty-two years he was a partner in the firm operated by the Deck Brothers. Fred Jehle, treasurer of the trustees, was born in Baden March 17, 1846. When he was six years old he was brought to America and was left an orphan immediately after arrival. He was raised in the Broadway Orphan Asylum, and later adopted by Mr. Sippel of Collins, New York. He spent ten years as clerk for D. Holzborn and then began business on his own account. Jehle was a member of the Catholic Institute, and the Catholic Mutual Benefit Association.

*L*awrence Wex was born at Niedermoehlen, Frankfurt am Main, December 24, 1839. At age thirteen, he came to America with his parents in 1852. His early education was in Germany; but, in Buffalo, he attended public school. In 1862, he went to Brooklyn, New York, where for ten years he involved himself in the manufacture of furniture. Returning to Buffalo in 1872, he set himself up in the wholesale paper business at which he was very successful. He was a man who liked to belong to influential groups, and joined many associations. These were: Catholic Mutual Benefit Association, Catholic Institute, St. Louis Society, American Land Association, and the Union Land Association. He too served as a trustee at St. Louis Church, and was a member of its building committee.

*X*avier Dietsche was born at Amt Waldshut, Baden in 1836. He came to America in the spring of 1857 after he had received his primary education at his village school in Waldshut. For twenty years he operated one of the best meat markets in the City of Buffalo located on the East Side. Like Wex, he too, was active in several associations: St. Nicholas Society, Saving and Aid Society located on the corner of Elm and Burton Alley, and the Goodell Permanent Loan Association. He served as a trustee at St. Louis Church, and was a member of its building committee. Frank X. Burkard was born in Baden on July 12, 1826. He learned his trade as a machinist in Europe and immigrated to America in 1847, and came directly to Buffalo. He worked many years for others; but, in 1873, he began his own business. He was treasurer of the St. Nicholas Society and, for five years, a trustee at St. Louis Church.

Jacob Alexander Gittere was born on June 19, 1837, the eldest son of Jacob Gittere who had immigrated to Buffalo in 1830. Jacob Alexander had the distinction to be baptized by Father Alexander Pax in the Lamb of God Church. He received his First Holy Communion from the hands of Father Francis Guth; and, in 1847, he served Bishop Timon's first Mass at Buffalo, which the bishop said at St. Louis Church. Later he was confirmed there. Until 1850, his occupation, like his father's, was as a stonemason. In that year, however, he went into apprenticeship with S.V.R. Watson, the builder of the first horse drawn street car line on Main Street which operated from the docks to Edward Street. On August 28, 1861, he purchased property from Watson at Swan and Ellicott Streets. The following year he was able to buy his father's house on Sycamore Street, the one in which he had been born. Again in 1863, he purchased another house in the three hundred block of Watson Street and set himself up in his own business as a land agent. For the next ten years he served in many different capacities: Commissioner of Deeds for the Central Wharf Insurance Agent, Director of the Union Fire Insurance Company, and City Treasurer.

On June 19, 1867 Jacob Alexander Gittere married Elizabeth Dietz in the rectory of St. Louis Church. She was a member of St. John's Lutheran Church; and, although there is no record of their marriage at St. Louis Church, the *Buffalo Daily Courier* announced their nuptials given by Father Joseph Sorg. One year later their first child was born, Alexander Jacob, who was baptized by Sorg. Alexander Jacob was the first of ten children, seven girls and three boys. On November 8, 1869 Jacob Alexander purchased a home for his new family in the one hundred block of

Park Street from Joseph Churchyard, president of the Union Fire Insurance Company. On June 3, 1885, Elizabeth died from medical complications resulting while giving birth. On her deathbed, she received her baptism, *sub conditione*, from Father Hoelscher, pastor of St. Louis Church. Jacob Alexander was so sad that he returned to Europe for a time so as to visit the place of his family origin at Dabo, Lorraine. In 1892, he remarried; his spouse was Magdalena Druco, nee Demerle. Her husband, Gregory, had died on February 18, 1888, prior to the grand bazaar at St. Louis Church. Jacob Alexander died on July 31, 1897. He sang with the choir at St. Louis Church under the direction of Dossert and Hemmerlein; and, for five years, had been a member of its board of trustees.

At the beginning of August, 1889, these seven trustees sent a series of questions to James O. Putnam at the University of Buffalo, soliciting his opinion of their present relationship as the Corporation of the St. Louis Church Society with the real estate which was conveyed by Louis Le Couteulx to Bishop John Dubois and his successors in the deed of January 1, 1829. Specifically they wished to know what was the effect made on that relationship by the deed that Archbishop Corrigan had sent to Bishop Ryan? Further they wanted Putnam to clarify the effect which the mortgage executed by Bishop Ryan to Jonathan Scoville would have on them? Would Bishop Ryan have any legal claim to the title or interest in the church property because of the execution of such a mortgage? With Corrigan's deed adrift, who then held the legal title to the church property? Was the object of the deed to Bishop Ryan from Archbishop Corrigan a ploy to give Ryan control of it and its temporalities? If such a mortgage or loan would be executed who would become the creditor? Finally, in what relation would Jonathan Scoville stand to their society when they would receive $60,000 from Bishop Ryan? It was to these questions that Putnam gave serious consideration and conveyed his answers not only to the trustees, but published his decisions in *The Buffalo Commercial Advertiser*.

Clearly, Putnam answered the questions. He said that the deed, which Corrigan had sent to Ryan, was null. Since Corrigan did not own the property he could not take a mortgage on it. If a mortgage were made by Ryan with Scoville, it too would be a void instrument. In executing the void mortgage Ryan would have no claim on the St. Louis Church property. If Ryan received $60,000 from Scoville and in turn gave the money to the trustees, then Ryan would become the creditor of the trustees; but, Scoville in turn, would become the creditor of Ryan. If the money was not paid back, Scoville could sue Ryan in the ordinary way and Ryan could sue the trustees in an ordinary way. The suits, however, would not be the result of default on a mortgage because no mortgage would have been possible in the first place. Scoville could not sue the trustees directly. If such a suit were activated by Scoville against Bishop Ryan, the bishop could assign his claim against the trustees to Scoville, and then Scoville could sue the trustees. In any case it would stand that the mortgage is a nullity and the title of the church property in the trustees can in no way be affected by the suit. The trustees were legally allowed to take the $60,000 from Ryan if Scoville was content with the security he got, but that security was not any interest or title in the church property.

Putnam concluded his remarks both to the trustees and to the *Commercial Advertiser*; saying that he did not think that Bishop Ryan had any thought of interfering with the temporalities of St. Louis Church, or did he believe any litigation would arise out of the transaction of the $60,000. Putnam further praised Ryan as a man of great good sense; a man who understood the situation perfectly. There is no historical evidence that Franklin D. Locke pursued any legal action to recover the $60,000 given to Ryan, which had been transferred to the trustees. Scoville was a man of ill health, slowly dying, who in 1890 lost his brother with whom he shared all his finances equally, and knew that in his own death $60,000 would represent only six tenths of one percent of his estate. After his death it would

have been wise and reasonable for Locke, therefore, to avoid unwanted publicity and to carefully terminate the loan. Furthermore, there was a precedent for assuming that a favorable expiration of the loan, if it were not repaid, would result because of Jonathan Scoville's former generosity to St. Louis Church. In the initial fund drive of 1885-86 initiated by Father Sorg, he donated $500. The only larger gift was that of Gerhard Lang who gave $1,000. Besides being very friendly with Bishop Ryan, Scoville was also a very good friend of Louis Bapst, a very generous member of St. Louis Church, whose home was on the corner of Franklin and Edward Streets. In that initial fund drive Bapst's personal gift was $250, and it was through him that Scoville gave his $500 donation. Bapst was the father of Reverend Robert T. Bapst who wrote a history of St. Louis Church for its one hundred and twenty-fifth anniversary celebration.

The indication that the loan of $60,000 was given to Ryan and that he in turn gave the same to the trustees rests in the statements made by Hoelscher in his Christmas message to the congregation in 1898 and again in 1909. In 1898, Hoelscher told the congregation that the church's debt was $116,000. This meant that from the end of the first bazaar until 1898 there had to have been a debt reduction of $90,416. Reducing the principal and paying the interest at slightly less than two per-cent over a ten year period would have required the parish to have made an annual donation of $12,668. This would have been impossible in light of the fact that after Hoelscher's Christmas letter of 1909, when he asked the congregation to reduce the remaining debt from $42,500 to $32,000, it took four years at an annual giving rate of $2,625 to accomplish the task. If one assumes that the Ryan-Scoville deal was accomplished and the trustees immediately reduced the debt at that time by $60,000, then the annual giving necessary to reach Hoelscher's stated debt of $116,000 by 1898 would have been $2,542; very similar to what it was between 1909 and 1913.

Between 1898 and 1909, the trustees knew that they might not reach the reduction of the debt to $42,500, as later stated by Hoelscher, unless they ran a second bazaar. Thus they did so in 1900, within a building established behind the church in the area where the temporary church stood while the great gothic church was being built. That bazaar was very similar to the one run in 1888. The daily magazine, however, was called *The St. Louis Bazaar Herald*. The spelling of the word bazaar in its title indicated that the parish had become more Anglicized. The names of the booths also reflected changes in its structure of the spiritual and social societies that had come into existence since 1888. They were named: Christian Mothers, Dramatic Circle, Ladies Catholic Benevolent Association, St. Louis, St. Cecilia, Children of Mary, Catholic Mutual Benefit Association, and St. Anthony. In 1900, the fair ran from Monday, September 17 to Saturday September 29. The final summary issue of the *St. Louis Bazaar Herald* appeared on Saturday, December 8. In giving its farewell to the congregation, the Journal reminded the congregation that the seventy-fifth anniversary of the beginning of the church was to be celebrated on January 5, 1904. The bazaar netted a grand total of $16,626.50 with an expense rate of eight per-cent.[4]

During the fair, *The St. Louis Bazaar Herald* published two photographs of the interior of St. Louis' gothic-style church. One recalls that in 1888, when the fair was held inside the church there were no interior decorations. The photographs show that by 1900 the pews had been installed, the stained glass windows over the main altar depicting the life of St. Louis, King of France, were in place, a small high altar in the center of the sanctuary the width of one of the windows above the altar had been constructed, and the two side altars, gifts of Lang and Lautz in 1893 and refurbished in 1895, were positioned. Also, a small altar rail, the width of the central sanctuary, had been installed; a wooden pulpit had been constructed in the nave at a position approximately one-third the total distance of its length forward from the sanctuary; the stained glass windows

on the lower half of both sides of the nave depicted the lives of various saints and occasions in the life of Christ; and the windows in the upper sides of the nave were made of a less ornamented-type of glass. Soon after 1900, Edward M. Hager's Company in Buffalo began construction of the new wood-carved pulpit; it was completed in 1909 and represented a cost of $4,000.

Between 1903 and 1904 sufficient funds were donated by Emma and Jacob G. Lang, children of Gerhard Lang, so that the new marble high altar with the statue of St. Louis, King of France, could adorn the large section of the sanctuary. The Lautz Marble Works, whose factory was on Washington Street with its office located on Main Street, supervised its design, fabrication, and installation. The gift amounted to $25,000. In the same year Mrs. Emma Weppner gave $6,000 to the trustees so that they could install a new marble communion rail separating the nave from the sanctuary, which extended the full length of the main sanctuary and moved across the two side altars. Hinged gateways were put in place, one before each side altar and one before the main altar. Between 1908 and 1909, Catherine Feist and Elizabeth Hartman gave a total of $7,500 which was used to construct the marble altars in the transepts of the church. One was given in honor of St. Joseph and the other in honor of the Sorrowful Mother of Jesus. In 1902, Charles Lautz and Catherine Neunder, each with gifts of $1,000, began an organ fund. In 1918 Catherine Feist increased the value of the fund by $20,000. With the exception of Catherine's gift, all other adornments took place during the pastorship of Dr. Paul Hoelscher and the tenure of the trustees: Peter P. Seereiter, Charles J. Dearing, Charles J. Williams, Charles F. Doll, Charles J. Fix, Charles B. Huck, and John Kam Jr.

In the evening of Friday, April 10, 1896, Hoelscher informed the trustees that Bishop Ryan had died that morning at his residence on Delaware Avenue, and that his body would be taken to the cathedral on Sunday, so as to lie in state until the funeral services could be conducted on Tuesday. On Sunday evening a massive meeting of Protestants and Catholics was held at the Music Hall adjacent to St. Louis Church for the purpose of paying tribute to this priest and bishop who to them in life had been simple, honest, strenuous, and noble. The congregation at St. Louis Church had found a friend in him; and, he having helped so much with fund raising and paying off the debt on their church was considered as a man of charity, patience, justice, honor, and gratitude. As bishop, he had left a large liberality of conscience to his priests and laymen. This was a virtue most appreciated by the trustees. When Ryan had authoritative problems with one of the Polish congregations, the trustees at St. Louis Church could only reflect upon their own problems that had generated their interdiction under Timon. In the case of the Poles, however, they became schismatic, and opened their own national church under the leadership of renegade Polish priests who told them that their church was still Catholic as it had been in Europe, but that it no longer had to have allegiance to an Irish bishop. The year before Ryan died, William Gleason, his vicar general for the diocese who had served under Ryan for his entire episcopate, had also died. Father James Lanigan who had replaced Gleason was chosen as administrator of the Buffalo Diocese until the Pope appointed a new bishop.

The appointment came quickly; and, on February 24, 1897, Archbishop Corrigan consecrated James E. Quigley, at St. Joseph's Cathedral in Buffalo. In 1855, Quigley had been born in Ontario, Canada, but with his parents he came into Western New York while he was very young. When he was ten years old, he came to Buffalo and resided with his uncle, Father Edward Quigley, who was pastor of Immaculate Conception Church. James Quigley was educated by the Brothers of the Christian Schools, whose order was originally founded in France by Jean Baptiste de La Salle in 1691. The Brothers taught him at St. Joseph's College built on the property surrounding the St. Joseph's Cathedral.

During his tenure as Bishop of Buffalo, he was entrenched in his struggle with militant atheism and socialism, twin evils, which spread like a contagious disease throughout the working class of the city. He issued a pastoral letter to the German pastors of the diocese, advising them to warn their people of the danger of the theories advocated by the socialists through means of labor unions. By their profound and dramatic exhortations, he, Father Anthony Heiter, pastor of Seven Dolors Church, and Father John Pfluger, a delegate to the National Convention of Catholic Societies in America, denounced the evils of socialism at a massive meeting at St. Ann's Hall, in Buffalo, on Sunday, March 2, 1902.

The attendance by Germans living in the city was legion. They learned in their own native language that Herr Ferdinand August Bebel, who had come to America to spread his brand of anti-Catholicism, was wrong. He was a German socialist, a student of the teachings of Karl Marx, a member of the Reichstag in Berlin, and a most important member of the German Social Democrat Party. These credentials did not phase Father John Pfluger who said, "The Catholic Church and democracy are reconcilable. Neither one is the slave of the barons of capitalism." Quigley firmly told the crowd, "The Catholic Church is a beacon directing the ships of the working man to their safe and fruitful harbors." At that time, the largest city in America facing labor unrest was Chicago. It was a hotbed of socialism and a thorn in the side of an ailing Pope, Leo XIII. In 1903, the Pope wanted someone who could counteract the Chicago crisis; and, hearing of the success of Quigley in his meeting at St. Ann's Church appointed him Archbishop of Chicago. When Quigley left Buffalo, Reverend M.P. Connery was appointed administrator of the diocese. He organized electors to select a replacement for the departed bishop. Eventually Charles Henry Colton was chosen; he had been chancellor of the Archdiocese of New York City and rector of its St. Stephen's Church. Pope Pius the X, who had replaced Leo XIII, approved of his selection; and, on August 24,

1903, Archbishop Farley consecrated Colton at St. Patrick's Cathedral in New York City. He became the fourth Bishop of the Diocese of Buffalo. During his reign, he began construction on the new St. Joseph's Cathedral on Delaware Avenue. His time in office, however, was short; he died in 1915, and his funeral was the first service conducted in the new cathedral. [5]

While in office, Colton was dramatically hurled into a battle in 1909 alongside the trustees and parishioners of St. Louis Church. It was like a foreign invasion on American soil. The property upon which their great gothic-styled church stood was placed in jeopardy. Unexpectedly, Colton was notified that Henry Le Couteulx de Chaumont, Louis Le Couteulx de Chaumont, and Emmanuel Baron de Bizi, descendants of St Louis Church's original donor, sought to reclaim the property and assets of the church. The three traced their decendancy directly to Pierre Alphonse Le Couteulx, the younger son of Louis Stephen Le Couteulx and the brother of William Le Couteulx. Coming to America, the trio began a lawsuit that involved the clarification of the facts surrounding the original deed of the property to Bishop Dubois and his successors. The newspapers referred to it as a revival of a lost legend! These heirs claimed that because the church had sold certain parcels of the land for purposes other than those articulated in the original deed, the property had reverted to the family. These claimants argued further that the gift of Louis Le Couteulx was a limited one, being invalidated upon the death of Bishop Dubois in 1842. They further contended that the property was not being used as a cemetery, a condition that was one of the stipulations of the original deed.

Attorney Edward Randall, in defense of Bishop Colton and the trustees, argued that the deed had been clearly made out to Bishop Dubois and his successors. Ironically, Randall built his case on the fact that the trustees had incorporated in 1838 and in doing so took legal possession of the property. The very act of

incorporation that Bishop Timon fought so desperately to break became the church's strongest defense. Randall further added to his arguments saying, "Even if the title of the property could be found to be invalid, which is most unlikely, the construction of subsequent church buildings on the site entitled the trustees to the control of the property on the grounds of adverse possession." In order to clarify his position to the court Randall made quite a lengthy observation. He said, "It is obvious that Louis Le Couteulx intended to convey the premises for the use and benefit of a Roman Catholic Church. The subsequent formation of the corporation, the erection of the brick church in which he continued as a member until his death in 1840, and the use of the cemetery for burial purposes until legally prohibited, would manifest his acquiescence in the method followed in carrying out his conditions as expressed in the deed. These have been followed to the present day, so that the sole question of this branch of the case is whether or not the deed was valid to pass the title. If it was not, then we are met with the fact of continuous possession, certainly from 1832 when the first church was erected to the present time, and the necessity of a determination whether or not such possession defeats the claims of the plaintiffs."

Randall continued by defending the rightful administration and possession of the property by the trustees. In order to demonstrate the continuous ownership of the property for the purpose of a Catholic church and cemetery, he defended the incorporation of the trustees as fulfilling the wishes of the original donor. He said, "The corporation is a legal body under the Laws of the State of New York, with ample powers conferred by the State and exercised through its trustees, for the very purpose of taking over the property as in this case, and when it met the requirements of the statute and also fulfilled the conditions of the gift, the property passed by operation of the statute, to the corporation. It therefore seems to me that the title became absolutely fixed in that corporation, as if the donor had retained it until the accomplishment of these things, and then had deeded it absolutely to that corporation." Randall also proposed the argument that since Father Sorg, pastor, during the construction of the gothic-like building, had been buried in the basement of the church with the permission of the Health Department on September 17, 1888, the property could still be considered as a cemetery according to the original stipulation of the deed. All arguments on both sides were reviewed by the New York State Supreme Court which decided in favor of the corporation titled *The Trustees of the Roman Catholic Church of St. Louis, Buffalo, New York.* The relatives had the case appealed; but, in 1914, the Appellate Division and the Court of Appeals upheld the Supreme Court's decision. The relatives had to return to France empty handed. Another crisis for St. Louis Church had passed into history. [6]

One of Hoelscher's fondest spiritual activities was his organization of weddings at St. Louis Church. He would often recall the thrill which he experienced while standing at the massive marble altar rail, looking down the long almost endless aisle originating inside the Main Street entrance doors, and hearing the organ play the processional song of the bride as she began her long promenade toward her groom waiting at the pew nearest to the altar. This was the climactic event following months of consideration, engagement, and public proclamation by and for the couple who were about to receive the Sacrament of Matrimony. Being a Doctor of Divinity, Hoelscher, as he stood waiting, recalled the words of Thomas Aquinas who said, "the matter in the Sacrament of Matrimony is a social and divine institution, an agreement between persons, an intimate partnership, a union in love, a community, and a covenant." Hoelscher knew that marriage, like the doors of his beautiful St. Louis Church, was the portal to the sacred! It symbolized the union between one head, Christ, and one body, the Church. He then reflected on the Thomistic view of the form of the sacrament; these are the words of consent that would soon be pronounced by the advancing bride after meeting her groom. Words

that signified for them the same enduring fidelity which Christ had for his Church. Although he knew that the minds of the couple approaching this climax would not be dabbling in theology as he was, he felt that their emotion after their serious engagement was grounded in sincere spirituality.

One such wedding performed by Hoelscher was that of Kathryn E. Eggleston to Jacob P. Steffan on April 29, 1902. Kathryn became Jacob's second wife, his first, Catherine Almeter, died on July 24, 1899. Jacob's older brother, Father John Steffan, who was a member of the Resurrectionist Order, also had married them at St. Louis Church on September 9, 1891. Jacob had been the youngest of ten children born to Michael Steffan and Mary Frances Kloepfer, who saw St. Louis Church grow from its infancy as the Lamb of God Church to a few years before the great destructive fire of the second church. In 1877, they had purchased the building that was the Sisters of Charity Hospital on a block of land facing both Pearl Place and Virginia Street. Before the Sisters had arrived, it was the Literary and Scientific Academy, Buffalo's first secondary school. At number six Pearl Place was a small frame cottage, containing a living room, kitchen, combination bedroom and sitting room, and a bath. The cottage was built in 1828 and the school came into existence in 1831. After the school began, the cottage was used as the home of its principal. Mary Frances Kloepfer worked for him as a cook and servant girl for four years beginning with 1835.

In 1847, the academy ceased operation, and Bishop Timon purchased both the school and the cottage. In the following year he gave the property and the buildings to the Sisters of Charity who used the cottage as a convent. In 1849, when the worst of the four cholera epidemics struck Buffalo, nine hundred out of a population of thirty thousand died within a short time. The Sisters moved out of the cottage; and, although it was only thirteen feet wide and forty feet deep, it was turned into a morgue. Further, the hospital was overwhelmed with patients. It was not until 1873 that the street known as Pearl Place was constructed and paved up to the brick wall on St. Louis Church's property. After purchasing the hospital and cottage, Michael and Frances Steffan divided the rooms into apartments so that each of their married children would have a home to begin the propagation and procreation of their families as well as a home for the unmarried children; their family totaled ten. One of their daughters, Barbara Steffan, had married Charles Buchheit in 1869. They and their two children, Francis Michael and Charles John Michael, immediately took up residence in one of the apartments. During the next eight years three more children were added to their family.

*I*n 1880 Mary Frances Kloepfer Steffan died, followed by her husband three years later. Prior to his death, however, he had divided his estate into ten parts, each child receiving an equal share. Although the apartments and cottage remained in possession of the family, several of the children moved elsewhere. Barbara and Charles Buchheit occupied number twenty-one Pearl Place across the street opposite the apartment building. In 1889, another boy was born to them making the number of their children six. One child was Rosina Maria who had been born in 1883. By 1912, she was twenty-nine years old and a very active member of St. Louis Church especially contributing her beautiful voice to the choir and being vivacious in the St. Cecilia Society, which was an outgrowth of the Children of Mary. The Society was composed of young single ladies who gathered together so as to develop and express their own personal piety. They conducted conferences, set up regular days for group attendance at Mass, and mutual reception of Holy Communion followed by a breakfast in common. They also ran social events such as card parties and entertainment to which young single men who were members of the St. Joseph Society were invited to attend. This society was the male counterpart of the St. Cecilia Society that followed a schedule of activities and events much like

those of the young girls. In this manner, the two societies acted as a complimentary dating service with a spiritual flavor. In the St. Cecilia Society, Rose Buchheit and Mary Frances Futterer, who lived on Elmwood Avenue between Allen and North Streets, were very close friends having known each other since they were pupils in St. Louis' school. By 1912, being very good friends, they exchanged visits to their homes and met the members of each other's families.

*M*ary Frances Futterer was the daughter of Erhard Futterer and Magdalena Rehm; she was the youngest of their eleven children, six of whom died at a very young age. Erhard and Magdalena had been married in New York City in St. Francis of Assisi Church on Thirty-First Street on March 28, 1864. Erhard had emigrated from Forchheim, Baden, in 1855, joined the New York Turnverein upon arrival, enlisted in the Turner's regiment, the 20th New York, at the beginning of the Civil War, was seriously wounded at the Battle of Antietam, survived, and continued his craft of fresco painting, gold leafing, and interior decorating in New York City until 1865. He and Magdalena decided to leave New York City and move to Buffalo following the death of their first child. Her parents had emigrated from Landau, Germany, some years before, moved to Buffalo, but had left her in New York City to work as a maid in the Grand Fifth Avenue Hotel. Upon arrival in Buffalo, Erhard and Magdalena resided with her parents for awhile, but later purchased a house on Mulberry Street.

*I*n 1872, Erhard's sister, Francisca, who had accompanied him when he first immigrated to America, and married George Zell, a wholesale and retail storeowner in Philadelphia, was killed with her husband in an unfortunate accident. Their two boys came to live with Erhard and Magdelena, but George's sister living in Philadelphia cared for their daughter, Louise. While doing his fresco painting in Buffalo, Erhard was especially familiar with John Lorenz and the Chretien Brothers. On Sundays, the Futterer's would meet their families at St. Louis Church where all were parishioners. During the week their mutual activities in artistic painting intermingled their professional lives. After Erhard died in 1889, Magdalena moved into one of two houses that she owned on Elmwood Avenue. She was a very enterprising lady; she was an expert seamstress who wore out eleven sewing machines in her lifetime. While her family lived on Mulberry Street she operated a notions store. She did beautiful lace work for the priest's surplices and other sacerdotal finery. She had many friends among the clergy and for a time was a housekeeper for Father E.J. Rengel who had been pastor of Immaculate Conception Church in East Aurora.

While Mary Futterer was visiting Rose Buchheit at her home one evening, Charles John Michael Buchheit, Rose's older brother, felt a bit of chemistry in his system as he gazed upon Mary while she was discussing trivialities with his sister. He engaged her in conversation and mentioned that he was a member of the St. Joseph's Society. Before she left, he offered to walk her home. She accepted that offer; but, upon arrival on Elmwood Avenue, she refused to accept his invitation to attend a dance that his society was soon to have at the church. In their conversation during the walk, she realized that he was six years older than she was. Some days later, after long intimate talks with Rose, Mary decided to accept Charles' offer. After this first date, there were others until their relationship developed into a proposal of marriage by Charles. In early May, he knew that he wanted to give her a beautiful ring. He went to King and Eisele, Jewelers, who had a store on Washington Street. He discussed his intentions and his desire for a ring; five different diamonds were laid out on the counter before him. He could not make the choice. Which one would please Mary? He could not decide! Charles F. Smith, one of the proprietors said to him, "I'll wrap these five diamonds in a tissue. You take them to Mary and let her decide. Bring them back with your choice and I will

put the victor in its setting." Promptly Charles accepted the offer and as fast as his legs could carry him he found Mary at home. Diamonds are judged in value for the number of carats and by color and clarity. Mary was not an expert; but, looking at all five, she said to Charles, "I do not want the largest one, I would like the prettiest one." She made her choice and the day of the wedding, June 25, 1912, was set in their minds.

Much had to be done before the event. Father Hoelscher had to be informed; he had to have sufficient time to determine their seriousness and their obligations to marriage as a sacrament. On three Sundays preceding the wedding, the banns, the announcements of their intended marriage, were placed before the congregation. Mary had to discuss her dress with her mother, Magdalena, while Charles concerned himself with purchasing a Prince Albert coat and pin striped trousers as well as cuff links, tie pin and clasp for himself, a gift for his best-man, and a beautiful brooch for his bride. Soon the day arrived when Mary Frances stood at the far end of the long aisle of St. Louis Church. It was 9:00 A.M. Far in front of her, stood the leader of her bridal procession, the flower girl, Miss Marie Rick, the five-year-old daughter of Otto and Frances Rick, who lived on Highland Avenue. Frances was Mary Futterer's sister. Miss Marie Rick wore a frock of chiffon and shadow lace over pink silk. The bridesmaid, Helen Czerwinski, was gowned in white voile with embroidered net over yellow taffeta, wearing a large white hat, and carrying a bouquet of tea roses. The maid of honor, Miss Rose M. Buchheit, wore white voile with Venetian lace, made over yellow messaline, a white lace hat; she too carried tea roses. Finally, the bride appeared, dressed in ivory charmeuse satin-trimmed with princess lace, with court train, and a full-length veil fastened with orange blossoms.

Carrying a shower of bridal roses and lilies-of-the-valley, with the processional music filling the air, Mary Frances was ready to walk down the aisle. Usually the father of the bride escorted his daughter and gave her away to the groom, but her father had died and had joined the membership of the Church Triumphant in heaven. Her brother, Edward Futterer, an artist, was supposed to be his substitute, but he had just been offered a new job, and was afraid that if he were not present for his first day of work, he would be fired. Bravely, Mary made the long promenade unescorted, following the ladies leading her, until she found her groom, Charles John Michael, at the altar waiting for her. At his side were his youngest brother and best man, Louis Buchheit. With Louis were the two ushers, George W. Buchheit, another brother of the groom, and Joseph Reade, a long-time friend of Rose Buchheit. Waiting inside the sanctuary to greet the couple were Father Walter Fornes, the celebrant of the Mass and ecclesiastical witness of their marriage, Father Albert Rung, deacon, who had sung his first Mass at St. Louis Church, and was presently assistant to the pastor, Hoelscher, Father F. A. Bank, subdeacon, and Fathers J. Jones, and Andrew Haberstro, friends of the families.

*F*ather Walter Fornes gave a short address to the couple before him. He admonished them on the sanctity of the state of life they were about to enter. He reviewed their duties and responsibilities in that state. Then he questioned, "Charles John Michael will you take Mary Frances, here present, for your lawful wife according to the rite of our Holy Mother, the Church?" Charles replied, "I will!" Fornes then turned to the bride and asked, "Mary Frances will you take Charles John Michael, here present, for your lawful husband according to the rite of our Holy Mother, the Church?" She replied, "I will!" Fornes then asked them to join their right hands as a symbol of their union. Prompting them, he had each of them, in turn with the groom going first, say to the other, using the other's name as they spoke, saying, "I will take you for my lawful spouse, to have and to hold, from this day forward, for better, for worse, for richer, for poorer, in sickness and in health, until death do us part." Then Fornes placed

the end of his stole upon their joined hands and said, "I now join you in matrimony. In the name of the Father, and of the Son, and of the Holy Ghost. Amen" As he said those words he made the sign of the cross over their hands to express that the grace of the sacrament, like every other grace, was derived from the crucified Redeemer. He sprinkled the couple with Holy Water, symbolizing that the heavenly blessing, just received, had descended upon them like morning dew upon the grass.

*F*ornes then asked to receive the wedding ring. Blessing it, he prayed, "Our help is in the name of the Lord, Who made heaven and earth. O Lord! this ring we bless in Thy name, that she who shall wear it, keeping inviolable fidelity to her spouse, may ever remain in peace in Thy will, and always live in mutual charity, through Christ our Lord. Amen." He then sprinkled it with Holy Water. Charles then took the ring and slowly placed it on Mary's fourth finger of her left hand. While he did so, he said, "With this ring, I thee wed, and pledge unto thee my troth." Making the sign of the cross over Charles' action, Fornes said, "In the name of the Father, and of the Son, and of the Holy Ghost. Amen." Rung, standing beside Fornes then said, "Confirm, O God! this which Thou hast wrought on us, from Thy temple, which is Jerusalem. Lord have mercy on us, Christ have mercy on us, Lord have mercy on us." All those who were surrounding the couple then said, "Our Father, Who art in Heaven, hallowed be Thy name. Thy kingdom come, Thy will be done on earth as it is in heaven. Give us this day our daily bread, and forgive us our trespasses as we forgive those who trespass against us. And lead us not into temptation but deliver us from evil. Amen," When they finished, Fornes continued, "Save Thy servants, trusting in Thee, O my God! Send them help, O Lord! from Thy sanctuary, and defend them from Zion. Be to them, O Lord! a tower of strength against the face of the enemy. O Lord! hear my prayer, and let my cry come unto Thee." As a preface to his next prayer he said, "The Lord be with you." The deacon and subdeacon replied, "And with your Spirit." Fornes then added, "Let us pray: Look down, O Lord! we beseech Thee, upon these Thy servants, and afford Thy favorable assistance to Thy own institutions, by which Thou hast ordained the propagation of mankind, that those who are joined together by Thy authority may be preserved by Thy aid. Through Christ our Lord! Amen."

When the above nuptial benediction was terminated, Fornes began the Mass with the sign of the cross. The couple knelt on a double prie-dieu provided for them before the altar. After singing the "Pater Noster" Fornes turned to the newly wed couple and prayed, "Mercifully give ear, O Lord! to our prayers, and let Thy grace accompany this institution which Thou hast ordained for the propagation of mankind so that this tie which is made by Thy authority may be preserved by grace. O God! Who by Thy omnipotent hand didst create all things; Who at the first forming of the world, having made man to the likeness of God, didst out of his flesh make women, and give her to him for help, and by this didst inform us that what in the beginning was one, ought never to be separated; O God! Who by so excellent a mystery hast consecrated this union of both sexes, that Thou wouldst have it to be a type of that great sacrament which is between Christ and his Church; O God! by Whom this contract and mutual commerce has been ordained, and privileged with a blessing which alone has not been recalled, either in punishment of original sin, or by the sentence of the flood, mercifully look on this Thy servant the bride, who, now given in marriage, earnestly desires to be received under Thy protection. May love and peace abound in her; may she marry in Christ, faithful and chaste; may she ever imitate the holy women of former times; may she be acceptable to her husband as Rachel, and as discreet as Rebecca; may she in her years and fidelity be like Sarah, and may the author of evil at no time have any share in her actions; may she be steady in faith and the commandments; may she be true in her engagements and flee all unlawful addresses; may she fortify her infirmity by thy discipline; may she be

gravely bashful, venerably modest, and well learned in the doctrine of heaven; may she be fruitful in her offspring; may she be approved and innocent, and may her happy lot be to arrive at length to the rest of the blessed in the kingdom of heaven; may they both see their children's children to the third and fourth generation, and live to a happy old age; through our Lord Jesus Christ."

Following this prayer, Fornes continued with the Mass to Communion. After he, the deacon, and subdeacon had received the Eucharist, Fornes distributed it to Charles and Mary. Communion was then distributed to those who wished to receive. At the end of Mass before the usual blessing of the people, Fornes turned to Charles and Mary and pronounced over them their final blessing. He prayed, "The God of Abraham, the God of Isaac, and the God of Jacob be with you; and may He fulfill His blessing in you, that you may see your children's children to the third and fourth generation; and afterwards enter into the possession of everlasting life, by the help of our Lord Jesus Christ, Who, with the Father and the Holy Ghost, liveth and reigneth God forever and ever. Amen." Fornes then proclaimed, "Ite Missa Est," and Charles and Mary walked down the long aisle to the exit of the church onto Main Street. They were greeted with a hail of rice. From the church all that had been invited came to Magdalena Futterer's home on Elmwood Avenue for a breakfast. Covers had been laid for twelve at the bride's table that was decorated in pink and white. After the breakfast, the newly wedded couple prepared for their honeymoon which took them to Chicago, Illinois, where they were able to meet with Mary's oldest brother William, who to her was the best butcher Chicago ever had. Charles and Mary made quite a stay of being away; they did not return to Buffalo until September 1, 1912. By Thanksgiving Day in November they were able to entertain family and friends in their new home which they had purchased at forty-two Park Street. One of their first guests was Father Walter Fornes.

*B*esides being the resident assistant to Monsignor Paul Hoelscher, Walter Fornes, had had strong ties with St. Louis Church which extended back to his birth. He was born in Buffalo on March 6, 1883 to John Fornes Jr. and Amelia Frances Doll, who also had eight other children; Clara, Frederick, Joseph, John N., Edward G., Irene, Robert V., and Gerard L. John Fornes Jr. had been in the woolens and tailors' trimmings business with his brother Charles Victor Fornes since 1876. Although the main office of the business was moved to New York City, a branch office in Buffalo, a large structure on the corner of Court and Pearl Streets, was managed by John Fornes Jr., who had been born to John Fornes and Rosina Krumholz. Besides John Jr. and Charles Victor, they also bore Anthony, Peter, Michael Anthony, Sarah, and Amelia. Michael Anthony married Blondina Steffan and had two sons, John M. and Michael J. Fornes. They operated John M. Fornes and Company, leather goods and trimmings business. All the marriages between the Fornes, Steffan, and Krumholz families were performed at St. Louis Church. Since Charles John Michael Buchheit's mother had been Barbara Steffan prior to her marriage, it seemed quite an honor that Walter Fornes would perform the marriage of Charles and Mary Buchheit at St. Louis Church during his assistantship in the parish.

*A*fter Walter Fornes was baptized at St. Louis Church, his parents moved to Brooklyn, New York, for a few years, but returned when Walter was six years old. He attended St. Louis' parochial school, and graduated in 1897. He continued his studies in high school and college at the Jesuit institution of St. Peter Canisius, then situated on Washington Street. In 1904, he left Buffalo with several of his classmates so as to attend courses in theology at the Canisianum of the University of Innsbruck, Tyrol, Austria, conducted by the Jesuits. After receiving the sub-diaconate from the Prince-Bishop of Brixen he returned to Buffalo, escorting a slowly dying fellow seminarian. Once at home, Fornes was ordained deacon, and immediately elevated to the sacred priesthood by Bishop Henry

Colton on July 18, 1908. He then returned to the parish of his birth as an assistant to the pastor, Paul Hoelscher. While serving in this capacity he also accepted the chaplaincy of the 65th New York Infantry Regiment, a militia organization stationed in Buffalo.

*I*n early spring of 1916, he was transferred to Our Lady of Good Counsel at Darien, New York; but, in June, he was called into military service when Major General Leonard Wood, head of the Department of the East, was ordered by the Secretary of War, Newton Diehl Baker, to commit Troop I, a cavalry regiment, and the 65th and 74th New York Infantry Regiments to activity along the Mexican border. Fornes was chaplain of the 65th New York. Six months later, after the Mexican conflict had subsided, he was required to accompany his regiment to a training camp at Spartansburg, South Carolina. The United States had joined the Allies in World War I. By the summer of 1918, he with his 65th Regiment was in France; and, until the armistice was signed, he was actively engaged in spiritually caring for it while undergoing shell-fire by doing the gruesome work of comforting the wounded, burying the horribly mangled dead, and making trips across exposed areas for the purpose of bringing the sacraments to the troops. In the last two months of the war he survived the horrors of the Meuse-Argonne offensive. On returning home in the spring of 1919, he was given the post of administrator of Sts. Peter and Paul Church in Williamsville during the final days of Monsignor Anthony Adolph's pastorship. When Adolph retired, Fornes replaced him. For the next quarter of a century, he guided the church through a series of developments that brought it an increase in parishioners, spiritual activities, and educational benefits. Suddenly stricken with a coronary thrombosis, he died at the rectory on February 19, 1945. Four days later funeral services were held at Sts. Peter and Paul Church with Bishop Joseph A. Burke officiating at a Solemn Pontifical Requiem Mass. Charles and Mary Buchheit were among the more than six hundred persons who crowded into the church for

Mass and were with those who accompanied his remains to Mount Calvary Cemetery. [7]

REFERENCES AND NOTES ❖ CHAPTER NINE

1. Biography of Father Paul Hoelscher was derived from *The Echo*, Buffalo, New York, Thursday, December 28, 1916. Also see: "Pay last tribute to Msgr. Paul Hoelscher," *The Echo*, Buffalo, New York, Thursday, January 4, 1917. Rev. F. J. Trautlein was an assistant of St. Louis Church during the bazaar of 1888. He was born in Buffalo on October 1, 1863. His early education was obtained at St. Michael's parochial school and Canisius College, where he received a bachelor's of arts degree. He then went to Europe and entered the University of Innsbruck, Austria, from which he was graduated with honors. Returning to America and having been ordained, he was appointed pastor of St. Mary's, Queen of the Rosary, Church at Strykersville, Wyoming County, New York. He remained there until he was appointed assistant to Father Sorg at St. Louis Church in July 1888. Sorg, just prior to his death on September 15, 1888, had his name sent to Rome to be considered for the position of Bishop of Bellville, Illinois. see: *Catholic Union and Times*, October 4, 1888. For the biography of Gerhard Lang see: op. cit. *The Men of New York*, section D, p-38-9; and also see: op. cit. *High Hopes*, p.144. An obituary of Gerhard Lang is found in *The Buffalo Courier*, July 15, 1892. In the initial fund drive from March 25, 1885 to January 31, 1886, subscriptions numbering 1,102 were made, see: *Cash, St. Louis Church Building Fund, 1885-1886*, pps. 1-54, contained in a journal in the St. Louis Church Archives. The following people or companies donated $100 or more. They are: Joseph Sorg, Gerhard Lang, Louis Bapst, Jonathan Scoville, Louis Goetz, Altman & Co., Andrew Driskel, John Doll, Peter Hasenfratz, Franz Hacker, Joseph Brunner, Augustus F. Weppner, Philip Zechman, C.M.B.A. Branch No. 15., Josiah Jewett, E&B Holmes, John B. Meyer, Augustine Gerhardt, Christ Klinck, Anthony Neupert, Thomas Robinson & Co., Gerhard Lang, Barnes Hengerer & Co., Jacob Ubelhoer, Michael A. Fornes, Charles Lautz, Charles J. Dearing, Mrs. A.M. Born, Michael Messmer, Jacob Manhart, John Kraus, Edward M. Hager, Frank Metzger, J.L. Frank, G. Frank Deck, Hausle Family, Peter A. Vogt, Arnold Weppner, Jacob Weppner, *Buffalo Commercial Advertiser*, E.G.S. Miller, Christ Weyand, F.J. Henry, Rung Bros., Henry Garono, Frank Handel, Henry Garono, Frank Handel, Peter Mergenhagen, John Lorenz, Louis Wagner, J.M. Richmond, John Kuhn, W.H. Henny & Sons, Corinir Company, German-American Bank, and Charles Fuller. The following named people donated $50.00 or more to the drive; it will be noted that some of the names who gave $100 or more are repeated here because these sums were added to the $100 or more gifts on other days: Rummell & Rupp, Mrs. Vincent Schwanz, A.M. Hausle, A. Friend, Louis L. Pfohl, Catherine Herman Meyer, Franz Hassenfratz, E.G. Grey, Charles Lautz, Albert Stover, Charles Person, Mrs. Catherine Rebstock, Peter Mergenhagen, Louis Motsch, W. Band, Hon. Robert C. Titus, John B. Weber, Lorenz Schmidt, George Brennan, Frank X. Burkhard, Hansman&Schweigert, John Schaefer, Alois Zehnle, Julius Haas, James P. White, Elijah Ambrose, Adam M. Kochemb, Joseph Doll, Joseph Argus, John Fertig, George Diebold, Albert Hofschmitt, Henry Striegel, Bernard Diebold, Anton Willmann, Louis J. Ernst, Andreas Muchlbach, George Hack, John Zahm, Fred Kiefer, John Schaff, Mathias Becker, Fred Jehle, Lorenz Granacher, C. Kurtzmann, Farrar&Tifts, Mrs. M. Rieter, Jacob Rosskopf, Dahlman Spiegel, Mrs. Barbara Kleinschmidt, Anton Batt, Frank Spoeri, Frank J. Miller, Booth & Riester, A.F. Weppner, Joseph Stopf, Fisher Bros. & Co., Christopher Cullen, Otto Kiener, Edward Heron, Hausle Family, Mathias Wagner, Andrew Kraus, Charles Kamper, A.F. Weppner, Charles B. Huck, Lorenz Wex, Xavier Schoenberger, Anthony S. Schmidt, J. Rung, George Zimmerman, August Koepke, Albert Ziegele, M. Rohr, Michael Nellann, Louis Pohl, C.G. Voltz, Joseph Philips, and John Feist. The remainder of the names of those who gave less are too numerable to mention here but can be found in the journal in the archives. C.M.B.A. is abbreviation for Catholic Mutual Benefit Association.

2. It must be made clear that there was no misspelling of the word bazaar in relation to the journal titled *Bazar Chronicle*. The word bazaar in German is "Der Bazar." It is a Verkauftshalle, a Warenmarkt, or a Wohltaetigkeits, which means in English a beneficient or charitable market or fair. In the writing of this book the editors have tried to use the word bazaar as so spelled for all situations except for the name of the *Chronicle*. It should be known, however, that this was the spelling used by the Germans of St. Louis Church in any reference which they made of the bazaar in 1888. The letter of Grover Cleveland to Miss Josie Mergenhagen is part of the collection in the archives of St. Louis Church. The purchaser of the *Life of Our Saviour* was Mrs. Magdalena Futterer who is the maternal grandmother of Marie Buchheit Miller referred to in chapter five, "Immigrant Catholics in Antebellum Buffalo." The book is in the posession of Mrs. Miller, Pendleton, NY. Following are parishioners and friends who won prizes at the St. Louis Church bazaar in 1888. These names are given with their addresses so that one can understand the area of Buffalo where they lived. See: *The St. Louis Bazar Chronicle*, December 29, 1888, vol.1., no. 13. Mrs. Chretien, 594 Oak St.; Albert Young, 1053 Michigan St.; Roas Hoelfelder, 1056 Michigan St.; Mrs. Miller, 256 Sycamore St.; Lizzie Hoelscher, 209 Locust St.; Sophie Bichman, 191 Lemon St.; Mary Coon, 19 N. Pearl St.; Charles Kiefer, 514 Washington St.; Miss Biesinger, 470 Elm St; John C. Rush, 226 Carlton St.; Elizabeth Keim, 149 York St.; Pauline Daniels, Williamsville, NY; Anna Hoelscher, 24 Weaver Alley; Mrs. C.L. Feldman, 170 Maple St.; Louise Baecher, 797 Main St.; Florian Feyl, Main St.; Lizzie Dorschell, 75 Tupper St.; Huntington, 50 W. Eagle St.; Mary Friedman, 187 High St.; Miss Schwiegler, 382

Maple St,; Joseph M. Zahm, 308 Virginia St.; Mary Scherer, 16 E. North St.; John Siegel, 537 Monroe St.; Catherine Miller, 69 Mulberry St.; Elizabeth Koepke, 64 Huron St.; Miss Schlenker, Eagle St.; C.M. Weyand, 793 Main St.; Mrs. Szen, 954 Washington St.; William J. Weigel, 814 Main St.; Franz Stabel, 600 S. Division; Mrs. Wilhelm, 64 Howard Avenue; Mrs. Irlbacker, 704 Ellicott St.; Peter Paul,136 N. Pearl St.; Mrs. G.F. Deck, 50 Mariner St.; Mrs. F. Driskel, 106 Burton St.; Mary Spies, 526 Genesee St.; Mrs. Schoeman, 269 Sycamore St.; John C. Dingens, 34 N. Pearl St.; R. Huber; Charles Baecher, 797 Main St.; Anthony Batt, 86 Maple St.; T. Hoffman, Broadway; A. Willmann, 586 Washington St.; H. Kramer Jr., 851 Michigan; Theresa Hoffman, 44 Mulberry St.; Henry Strot, 461 Broadway; Mrs. Hassenfratz, 468 Elm St.; M. Pollar, 156 S. Hampton; Mrs. M. Fisher, 51 Elmwood Ave.; Lizzie Strigel, 453 Elm St.; W.O. Ottenot, 536 Ellicott St.; Susan Lorenz, 666 Ellicott St.; Mrs. John Coon , 19 N. Pearl St.; Joseph Casper, Grider Street; Emily J. Huber, 42 Mulberry St.; Mrs. Hausle, 19 Allen St.; J.J. Polichke, 652 Michigan Ave.; J.A. Weyand, 793 Main St.; Robert H. Crosby, 143 Washington St.; Mrs. Roth, 453 Oak St.; Charles Gillig, 546 Oak St.; E.A. Vogt, 81 Broadway; Henry Garono, Main St.; Gregory Strootman, 154 Genesee St.; Dr. Lothrop, Pearl St.; E.M. Adams, 490 Jefferson St.; S. Elser, Broadway; Henry Wagner, 85 Mulberry; Mrs. Steker, 106 West Ave.; Mary Batt, 205 Maple St.; Mrs. B. Koepke, Dunkirk, NY; Mrs. Reino, Michigan St.; Mrs. F. Hacker, 116 E. Tupper; John Zoll, 72 Howard Ave.; Joseph Kam, 377 Genesee St.; W.J. Tuttle, Rochester, NY; Miss Adams, Bradford, PA; Mrs. J. Henry, 900 Main St.; Louise Zechman, 64 Burton Alley; Mr. G. Laub Jr., Ellicott St.; F.S. Fries; Walter Caddell, 36 Oak St.; Henry Garono, Ellicott St.; Mrs. L. Lienert, 1053 Michigan; Frank Scherf, 238 Boston St.; Rose Mettling, 111 William St.; Catherine Bingeman, 135 Best St.; Mary Smith, 166 Clinton St.; Charles J. Fix, Ellicott St.; Charles S. Diebold, 107 E. Genesee St.; Kate Freiburger, 365 Walnut St.; Maggie Strigel, 453 Elm St.; Adam Schoell, 513 Broadway; Mary Schuts, 90 Best St.; Xavier Dietsche, Elm St.; Maggie Kreckel, Rochester, NY; Ed Hager, Oak St.; Mrs. Bingeman, 423 Oak St.; George L. Abel, 105 Delaware Place; Miss Vetter; J. Siegrist, 119 W. Huron St.; A.W. Voltz, 129 W. Huron St.; E.S.F. Bradish, 50 E. Genesee St.; Mrs. Heier, Oak St.; Miss Prozeller, Lancaster, NY; A. McGlasken, 197 W. Huron St.; Louisa Goetz, 62 N. Pearl St.; Joseph Hauck, 31 Milnor St.; Thomas Cronyn, 55 W. Swan St.; Bertha Lang, 704 Main St.; Ed. Hager, Oak St.; Mrs. Meyers, 207 Riley St.; Alex Weppner, 1336 Main St.; C. Zimmerman, 845 Michigan; Philip Bachert, 353 Oak St.; Mrs. Domedion, 28 Sycamore; Maggie Roth, Michigan; John A. Weyand, 793 Main St.; Otto R. Rick, 86 North St.; Henry Weyand, 812 Main St.; Miss Murphy, Goodrich St.; Catherine Schirman, 108 Sycamore; Mrs. W.A. Rix, 350 Franklin; Philip Houck and Co., 141 Genesee St.; K. Lang, 704 Main St.; Cecilia Gleber, 421 Oak; Mrs. L. Krieg, 963 Ellicott; Frank Weimann, 594 Oak; A. Verstratten, Spring St.; Mrs. Messing, 88 16th St.; Emma C, Kirn, 57 Delaware Place; Miss Feldman, 559 Ellicott; John Zahm, 308 Virginia; M. Schneidewind, 123 Ash; Jacob P. Steffan, 811 Main St.; Mrs Willesucker, 393 N. Hampton

St.; Mrs Wagner, 58 N. Pearl St.; Dr. Hoelscher, Edward St.; Ada Diebold, 665 Ellicott; Ge. E. Taylor, 105 E. North St.; Anna Jessel, 2339 Oak St.; H.C. Smith, 194 Amherst St.; Ed M. Roop, 38 Keil St.; Mrs F. J. Kraft, E. Huron St.; Eugene Klein, Klein & Co.; Tony Haas, 59 Oak; Louisa Stabel, 600 Elm St.; Mrs. M. Luke, 85 Goodrich St.; Emil Gerber, Jr., 70 E. North St.; Mike Hubuch, 511 Ave. A.; Joseph Paul, 152 Park St.; Louise Richert, 311 Bryant; Fred Simon, 436 Broadway; John Thurn, 461 Broadway; Henry Weyand, 812 Main St.; L. Rahmmacher, 810 Seneca St.; J. Teckmeyer, 228 High St.; Mathias Meyer, 63 Orange; Charles B. Huck, 262 Summer; Mrs. Pfeffer, 70 Dodge; Lizzie Leftler, 49 Boston St.; Fred Heeman, 919 Michigan St.; John Carroll, 11 Preston; Miss Miller 256 Sycamore; Mrs Sponlop, 344 Genesee St.; Lillie Welker, 596 Genesee St.; Mrs. G. Riester, 245 Allen St.; Mrs. Kerling, 240 Elm St.; Ed Hager, Oak St.; Charles J. Fix, 563 Ellicott; Mrs. K. Weber, 322 Pratt St.; Lena Glass, 654 Elm St.; Ed. Jehle, 28 12th St.; John Mumm, 168 Best St.; Clara S. Person, 390 Elm St.; George J. Schwartz, 637 Virginia; Frank Metzger, 674 Ellicott; Margaret Heinz, 591 Oak; William Weber, 353 North St.; Tony Schwartz, 8 Goodell; Mr. Schwert, Seneca St.; Annie Endes, 347 Adam St.; W.J. Hanraham, 112 E. North St.; Louisa Richert, 311 Bryant, S. Illig, 451 William St.; Peter Zahm, 122 Main St.; George L. Steffan, 813 Main St.; E.A. Diebold, Broadway; F. Gebhard, 607 Michigan; Leo Kessel, 107 Carlton St.; Lena Diebolt, 729 Washington St.; Rosa Seitz, 19 Bremen St.; F.E. Beilman, 468 Ashland Ave.; John Mumm, 168 Best St.; Leonard Miller, 1477 Main St.; W. Wilhelm, Howard Ave.; P. Schweigert, 84 Goodrich; Fred Rabst, 500 Fargo Ave.; Nicholas Smith, 222 Cherry St.; Mrs. F.J. Smith, 164 Dodge; Catherine Gunther, 194 North St.; Johanna Curier, 82 N. Pearl; Mrs J. Kreuzer, 917 Michigan St.; Mrs. F.J. Henry, 900 Main St.; Estella Pollett, 22 E. North St.; Tillie Unger, 655 Elm St.; Tillie Jupp, 64 Riley St.; Mary Born, 1004 Main St.; H,W. Moore, Tremont House; R.W. Grills, 421 Pearl St.; Clara Wehrle, 605 Main St.; John Lorenz Sr., 540 Washington St.; Otto R. Rick, 86 E. North; J.V. Brennan, 2064 Main St.; G.F. Deck, Mariner St.; Louis Smith, 72 Goodell; Mrs Gollwitzer, 655 Ellicott; Rev. G. Weber, Heart of Jesus Church; Mrs. F. Kleber, 514 Ellicott; Joseph Schwitzer, 18 Pearl Place; E.B. Griffith, 217 Dearborn St.; Mrs. M. Rohr, 126 Edward; Florence Zeller, 1196 Main St.; Rosa Phillips, 867 Washington; Henry Garono, Ellicott; Eddie Welter, 803 Elm St.; N. Scherer, 16 E. North St.; Florence Wild, 42 Potter St.; Frank Diebold, 73 Mulberry; Frances Lutz, 353 Howard; Peter Frank, Broadway; Frank J. Siefert, 82 Goodrich; James J. Milne, 33 Oak; Clara Gentsch, 509 Linwood Ave.; Breitecker, 120 Genesee; N.S. Roseman, 72 N. Pearl St.; Mrs. Kurtman, 168 Hickory; J.A. Lautz, Ferry St.; Frank Rung, 582 Broadway; Mrs. Killinger, 30 Delaware Place; Mrs. Reimann, 42 Mulberry St.; Emelia Duquir, 27 St. Paul St.; M. Hausauer, 190 Franklin St.; Joseph Schwelle, 114 Orange; Miss Branner, Oak St.; G. Stevens, 113 E. Tupper; Mrs. Smith, 150 Tupper; Charles J. Fix, 563 Ellicott; M. Koerner, 24 Goodell; H. Meyer, 63 Orange; John Christ, 220 Mulberry; Josie Deck, 50 Mariner St.; Mary Eisel, 178 North St.; Miss Roth, 453 Oak; E. Huskissver, 947 Ellicott; M. Engel, 7 Washington Market; Tuty Pearls, 171 18th St.;

Kirchgaessner, 233 William St.; H.J. Sturmer, 730 Main St.; John Miller, 348 Pratt; Mrs. Wieckman, 129 Broadway; Henry Meyer, 63 Orange; Mrs. A. Rix, 350 Franklin St.; J. Schmidmeyer, 254 High St.; Rev. J. McGloin, St. Joseph's Cathedral; J. Erisman Jr., 227 Sycamore; F.J. Henry, 900 Main St.; B. Lang, 704 Main St.; Edith Armbruster, 314 Broadway; George Steffan, 813 Main St.; L. Wex, 601 Oak St.; H. Wolf, 356 Franklin; Rev. Trautlein, St. Louis Church, Edward St.; George J. Doll, 239 Allen St.; John L. Peters, 893 Michigan; John B. Meyer, 286 Prospect Ave.; Mrs C. Shaefer, 578 Elm St.; Miss Thed, 197 E. Genesee; Elizabeth Koepke, 64 Huron; Anthony Zimmermann, 116 Pine St.; Mr. Ducro, 70 Edward St.; Rosa M. Hausle, 661 Elm St.; Albert Groben, Spring St.; C.J. Williams, 18 Best St.; Bertha Lang, 704 Main St.; Julius Haas, 34 Potter St.; John Thurn, 314 Sycamore; Henry Werick, 427 Oak St.; Julia Hitcher, 426 Genesee; Martin Stephan, 520 Elm St.; Mrs. J. Reimann, 77 Bennett St.; Carrie Stark, 574 Elm St.; Joseph Matter, 133 Goodell; Joseph Gremmel, 400 Madison St.; A.C. Schaefer, 348 Maryland St.; Alois Walser, 590 Ellicott; F.J. Freiburger, 365 Walnut St.; Mrs. Zehnder, 19 State St.; Joseph Paul, 152 Park St.; Louis Lienert, 1053 Michigan; Mary Faxlanger, 433 Ellicott; John Schindler, Goodell St.; F.J. Kraft, 27 E. Huron St.; Charles Lautz, 81 Linwood Ave.; John M. Hartinger, 255 Sherman St.; J.G. Marchand, 757 Michigan; John Nold, 881 Washington; Annie Stanton, 341 Virginia; Mrs. George Rung, 135 Spruce St.; Rev. F.X. Kofler, Black Rock; Mrs. J. Wagner, 1209 Michigan; Jacob Crowder, Overseer of the Poor; George Miller, 264 Genesee St.; Mamie Nolan, 352 7th St.; Miss Schmidt, 233 Genesee St. Companies which advertised in the *St. Louis Bazar Chronicle* in 1888 are: Peter Paul and Brothers, Printers, 420 Main St.; Adam, Meldrum & Anderson, Dry Goods, 396-402 Main St.; Charles S. Dieboldt, Shoes, 107 E. Genesee St.; Ullenbruch, Optician, 274 Main St.; George E. Moore, Clothes, 327 Main St.; Mayer & Co., Stained Glass, Ecclesiastical Art, 124 West 23rd St., New York City; Irlbacker & Davis, Chandeliers and Gas Fixtures, 529-33 Main St., Charles J. Dearing, Butcher, 229 Allen St.; King and Son, Jewelers, 452 Main St.; Mathias Smith, Tailor, 190 Main St.; John Kraus, Garments, 440 Main St.; Dr. E.C. Longnecker, Dentist, 85-9 East Genesee St.; Miller Brothers, Carriages & Phaetons, 319-21 Ellicott St.; Fred Jehle, Groceries, 311 Bryant St.; George J. Lutz, Wall Paper, 71 Genesee St.; Augustus Weppner, Butcher, Michigan at Northampton; L. Granacher & Co., Furniture, 215-17 Genesee St.; Schlund and Doll, Furniture, 460-66 Main St.; Deck & Emerling, Photographers, 458 Main St.; Weyand & Weigel, Bottling Works, 814 Main St.; C. Kurtzmann & Co., Pianos, 106-110 Broadway; Chretien Brothers, Fresco Artists, 601-03 Main St.; Kessel & Richert, Shirts, 511-13 Main St.; Wagner's Tobacco, Fred. H. Kaiser, Millinery, 207-09 Genesee St and 528 William St.; A. Snyder's, Shoes, 187 Genesee St.; Xavier Dietsche, Butcher, 528 Elm at Burton Alley; Cyclorama, On German Music Hall Grounds opposite St. Louis Church, featured Jerusalem on the day of the Crucifixion; Gerhard Lang, Brewery; Ziegele Brewing Co., Phoenix Beer, J. Adam Lautz, Pres., The Parsons & Co., Printers, 351 Main St.; Ivo & Wagenaar, Monuments, 502 Washington St.; Alphons J. Roehner, Real Estate & Insurance, 295 Broadway and

360 Main St.; Frank J. Miller, Tailor, 189 E. Genesee St.; Val Hoffman, Oysters and Clams, 204-06 Genesee St.; C. Schirra and Son, Tailor, 203 Main St.; Alexander Martin, Insurance, 426 Main St.; George Feldman, Undertaker, 322 Broadway; Henry Garono, Dockash Ranges and other Stoves, 563 Main St.; L.H. Loepere, 807 Main St.; Hausle and Kraus, Toys & Holiday Goods, 476 Main St.; George J. Rudolph, Artist, 15 German Insurance Building; Lautz Brothers, Soap, Acme Soap; J. L. Hudson, Suits, 392-94 Main St.; A. Neupert & Co., Wallpaper, 464-66 Main St.; Boechat Brothers, Shoes, 512 Main St.; German-American Bank of Buffalo; Paul Hausle, Dry Goods, 525-27 Main St.; John L. Schwartz, Coal, 330 East Genesee St.; M. A. Fornes, Wines & Liquors, 533 Washington St.; F.J. Riester, Buffalo Stained Glass Works, 29 Pearl St.; Frank G. Phillips, Trunks and Traveling Bags, 352 Main St.; Fred Breithecker, Parlor and Chamber suits and Carpets, 120 Genesee St.; D.E. Morgan & Son, Carpets and Drapery, 259 Main St.; Lawrence Wex, Stationary, 139-141 Washington St.; John Lorenz, Paints, Oils, and Glass, 540-42 Washington St.; Boutin's Department Store, Wholesale and Retail, 347-351 Main St.; Chicago Hardware Mfg. Co., Chicago, Illinois, Henry Garono, Buffalo Distributor, 563 Main St.; J. Ginther, Washington Iron Works, Broadway and Pratt Sts. The short biographies of distinguished men at the bazaar were taken from the thirteen issues of the *Bazar Chronicle*. One of the advertisements in the *Chronicle* was concerned with the German-American Bank in Buffalo. Members of St. Louis Church dominated the board of officers for the bank. They were: Gerhard Lang, Judge L.L. Lewis, Michael Nellany, Jacob Reimann, George Sandrock, Jacob W. Diehl, Francis Handel, August Baetzhold, and Jacob B. Schlund.

3. *The St. Louis Bazar Chronicle*, Saturday, December 29, 1888, Buffalo, New York, vol.1., no.13, p.2. Biographies of the Kuhns were taken from op. cit. *History of the Germans of Buffalo and Erie County*, p. 38 and biography section pps. 1-121. Translation from the German was done by the author/editor.

4. Although the narration given in the text concerning the payment on the debt of the St. Louis Church, which replaced the one destroyed in the fire of March 25, 1885, is speculative, it is, however, deductive and based upon several sources. Over a period of twenty-eight years the pastors, Sorg and Hoelscher, the trustees, and the parishioners struggled financially to pay the debt incurred on the church whose initial cost was $265,000 plus the $5,000 which was paid for the construction of a temporary church to be used while the great gothic church was being established. The insurance companies had paid $27,700 to the church following the fire. As reported op. cit., these companies were Rochester German, Buffalo German, Hanover, Connecticut of Hartford, Phoenix of Brooklyn, Germania of New York, and Union of Buffalo, see: *The Buffalo Express*, Friday, March 27, 1885. Starting on the day of the fire, Sorg initiated a fund drive which ran from that day until January 31, 1886. He made the first contribution of $100.00. By the end of the drive the trustees had collected and banked $26,031.00, see: *Cash, St. Louis Church*

Building Fund, 1885, pps. 1-54, contained in a journal in the St. Louis Church Archives, in which all the names and amounts of the donors are listed. In the fall of 1888, the parish ran the great bazaar and netted $14,853, see: *The Bazar Chronicle*, December 29, 1888, vol.1., no.13. By Christmas, 1888, the debt had been reduced to $201,416. Ten years later in his Christmas message of 1898, Hoelscher told the congregation that the debt on the church was $111,000, see: *Christmas Message of Rev. Hoelscher*, December 12, 1898, published both in German and in English. A copy is in the St. Louis Church Archives. This is a reduction of $90,416 which means that in ten years the congregation would have had to donate this amount of money over and above their regular collections. In that same message, Hoelscher also stated, "Owing to the large amount of interest to be paid, its regular annual income is by $2000 smaller than its regular annual expenses." If the interest rate was 1.8 percent as reasoned below, the congregation would have paid $3,626 annually in interest. In order to have had a reduction of $90,416 in the debt over a ten year period they would have had to contribute an additional $9,042 per year to meet Hoelscher's announced amount of $111,000. This appears to be an unreasonable conclusion; the parish could not afford to donate $12,668 annually. If, however, as seen below that the parish could afford $2,625 per year, then the remaining $10,063 annually would have had to come from another source or some bulk sum was paid off the debt in 1889. One such payment appears possible in an arrangement between Bishop Ryan, the trustees, and Jonathan Scoville on August 3, 1889. This speculation is expanded below. In 1900, however, the parish ran a second bazaar in a building which was constructed on the property between the church and the school. It netted $16,627. This was of course 12 years after the first bazaar, during which time we know that many donations were made to the church as Foundations and also as regular church fund donations. By Christmas of 1900, and subtracting this $16,500 from $111,000 one finds a debt of $94,500, see: *The St. Louis Bazaar Herald*, December, 8, 1900, vol.1., no.13. In a bulletin, a copy of which is in the St. Louis Church Archives, issued on September 3, 1909, St. Louis Church announced that the gothic church with all of its furnishings cost $350,000. The interest over 24 years incurred on the debt was $116,000. According to our initial estimate the furnishings must have been $80,000 of which much of it was paid for by large Foundation donations. Hence, based on an initial debt of $270,000, it can be concluded that the interest rate was 1.8 percent. Hoelscher also stated that the debt in 1909 was $42,500. He requested that the debt be reduced to $32,000 which was the appraised valuation of the church's property on Delaware Avenue. If this were done, he contended that the church could be consecrated. The ceremony took place on September 11, 1913. Hence there was a reduction in debt of $10,500 in four years at an annual rate of $2,625 per year. Hoelscher mentioned that he had 248 pew-holders from whom he faithfully received subscription. If this was paid by them it seems that each would have donated $10.58 each year during this period. Assuming that the same number of pew-holders existed between 1888 and 1898 one can propose as a thesis that $60,000 had been paid off the debt to the

banks in 1889. If so it would have become $141,416 which was further reduced to $116,000 by 1898. The interest paid from 1888 to 1898 would have been $2,088 annually. For the reduction of the principal the parish would have had to donate $2,542 annually. It appears from Hoelscher's 1898 Christmas message that the parish was absorbing the interest payments by not meeting expenses. It is of interest, under this scenario involving a lump sum payment of $60,000, that the resulting pay-down of principal from 1888 to 1898 is nearly the same amount as was the pay-down from 1909 to 1913. Although there is, at this time, no positive proof, this mathematical interpretation gives some credulity to the fact that it was possible that the proposition negotiated between Bishop Ryan, the Trustees, and Jonathan Scoville resulted in a gift or an uncollected loan, see: *Letter from James O. Putnam to Peter Paul Esq. and Others, Trustees of the St. Louis Catholic Church in Buffalo*, August 13, 1889. Also see: Hon. James O. Putnam, "The Title of the Church Property Absolute in the Trustees: The Question Thoroughly Explained," *Commercial Advertiser*, August 8, 1889. From documents in the Archives of St. Louis Church, other facts which are known are: The Bond between Bishop Ryan and Jonathan Scoville for $60,000 was made on August 3, 1889 and had a due date of August 3, 1909. If it was not paid by that time an extra $60,000 payment was to be added as a penalty. It is known that $40,000 was paid off that principal between February 3, 1904 and February 4, 1908. It is also known that on May 23, 1891, following Jonathan Scoville's death the bond was transferred by Franklin D. Locke and Associates, as Executors of Scoville's will, to Frances Wasson Scoville and the Farmers' Loan and Trust Company. No further action on the part of these two parties was known. Also the following members of St. Louis Church made a bond with Bishop Ryan to give $120,000 to him if the $60,000 could not be paid by 1909. This bond was made on August 19, 1889. Those so bonded were: Gerhard Lang, Peter Paul, G. Frank Deck, Fred Jehle, Lawrence Wex, Xavier Dietsche, Jacob A. Gittere, Frank X. Burkhard, Jacob Davis, Lorenze Granacher, Peter A. Vogt, George J. Metzger, Matthias Rohr, Anthony Neupert, William J. Weigel, Matthias F. Hausle, Celestine Baecher, William Wilhelm, J. Adam Lautz, and Charles Lautz. On April 24, 1894 the names of Charles Dearing and Edwin G.S. Miller replaced the names of William J. Weigel and Gerhard Lang on the bond because the latter had died. Gerhard Lang had been bonded for $20,000 and each of the others for $5,000. Credit and gratitude is extended to G. Peter Higgins, Real Estate Attorney, Pendleton, New York for helping the author/editor make the above scenario. For a biography of Hon. Jonathan Scoville see: *Men of the Time*, Buffalo and Erie County Public Library, Scrapbook Collection, Buffalo, New York, an article reprinted from the *Buffalo Sunday Times*. For an obituary of Jonathan Scoville see: *Buffalo Courier*, March 5, 1891, part of the Scrapbook Collection at the Buffalo and Erie County Public Library. Also see: Album and Yearbook, A Record of Buffalo's Local Events for the Year 1891, *Buffalo Express*, January 1, 1892, Buffalo, New York, copies at the Buffalo and Erie County Public Library. These articles were researched and supplied to the author/editor by Christopher Andrle. Gratitude to him is in order. For a biography of Michael Augustus Corrigan see: op. cit. *Encyclopedia of Catholicism*, p.370. For short biographies of members of the Board of Trustees of St. Louis Church see: op. cit. *The Bazar Chronicle*, vol.1., nos. 8, 9, 12. Short biography of James O. Putnam see: *The Men of New York*, A Collection of Biographies and Portraits of Citizens of the Empire State prominent in business, professional, social and political life during the last decade of the nineteenth century, George E. Matthews and Company, Buffalo, New York, 1898, Vol. II, synoptical index, p.53. For a more extended biography of Jacob Alexander Gittere see: op. cit. *The Gitteres of Lorraine*, 49-58. In this text, the author Edward Zimmermann assumes that Jacob Alexander Gittere and Elizabeth Dietz were married on June 19, 1867 at St. Louis Church even though no record there indicates it. Sorg was not pastor at the church at that time. He became pastor after Schoulepnikoff left in August, 1867. Furthermore, although Bishop Timon had died in the Spring of 1867, Sorg was still secretary to Gleason, the vicar general of the diocese, and rector of St. Joseph's Cathedral. Hence since the *Buffalo Daily Courier* acclaimed the wedding to be performed by Sorg it must have been so done at St. Joseph's Cathedral.

5. For the record of donations given to the St. Louis Church so as to provide funds for the adornments mentioned in the text see: op. cit., *The Foundations Book*, Vol 1. This book which is in the St. Louis Church Archives was also referred to in this book, G*othic Grandeur: a Rare Tradition in American Catholicism*, see "Gather Our Relics, We Rise Eternally. For information concerning what the interior of the church looked like in 1900 see: op. cit. *The St. Louis Bazaar Herald*, vol. 1., no.13, copy of which is in the St. Louis Church Archives. For details of the bishops of Buffalo who succeeded Bishop Timon and progressed through history until 1916 see: op. cit. *Celebrating God's Life in Us*, pps. 34-44. Also see: op. cit. *History of the Catholic Church in Western New York*, pps. 230-35. In these texts it was stated that Ryan said his last Mass on the feast of the Annunciation in 1896. Normally the feast of the Annunciation is celebrated on March 25, however, if the feast falls on a day during Holy Week then it would be transferred to the Monday following Low Sunday which is the Sunday following Easter Sunday. It would seem reasonable that Ryan said his last Mass on April 6, 1896. For which Pope appointed Quigley as archbishop of Chicago and which Pope appointed Colton as bishop of Buffalo see: op. cit. *Encyclopedia of Catholicism*, p. 1032. Pope Leo XIII died on July 20, 1903. During his reign he wrote the Encyclical, *Rerum Novarum*, which, in English is *Of New Things*, promoted social justice and the rights of the workers. Pope Pius X succeeded Leo XIII on August 4, 1903. Colton was consecrated on August 24, 1903.

6. For a review of the court case see: op. cit. *Lay Trusteeism at St. Louis Roman Catholic Church, Buffalo, New York*, pps. 85-6. Further see: An unidentified newsclipping from the year 1919 held in the archives of the St. Louis Church. The clipping states that land bought by Louis Le Couteulx from the Holland Land Company in 1812 for $180 was then worth $1,000,000. It was over this land that the court case was being decided. also see: *The Buffalo Times*, *The Buffalo Express*, June 30, 1909; *Buffalo Express*, August 12, 1914. The case was also dwelt upon in the Minutes of the Board of Trustees of the St. Louis Church, see: *Henry Le Couteulx de Chaumont, Louis Le Couteulx de Chaumont, and Emmanuel Baron de Bizi vs. The Trustees of the Roman Catholic Church of St. Louis*, Superior Court. N.Y., 1914, copy found in the archives of the Diocese of Buffalo, Diocesan Center, Main and Goodell Streets, Buffalo, NY.

7. For the history of the impediments to marriage see: op. cit. *The Beauties of the Catholic Church*, pps. 476-78 and op. cit. *Doors to the Sacred*, pps. 360-72. Some of these are: In 314, at the Council of Neocaesarea, it was determined that a woman could not marry her brother-in-law. If she did she was excommunicated. Pope Siricius (385-398) claimed the vow of virginity as an impediment. Pope Gregory the Great, 601, forbade marriage in the second degree of consanguinity. At the Fourth Lateran Council, 1215, it was stated that marriage had to be publicly stated in advance. The Council of Trent in 1542 and 1564 stated that marriage had to be performed before the pastor of either party and in the presence of two other witnesses. According to the theology of the Scholastics as led by Thomas Aquinas, it was claimed that in the early centuries of the Church, marriage as a sacred reality *should* not be dissolved, but in the middle ages the dissolution of marriage was not permissible because it was not *possible*. To Aquinas, the bond between spouses was unbreakable because it was a metaphysical bond which was the sign of the equally unbreakable bond between Christ and his Church. To John Duns Scotus, another theologian of the Middle Ages, intercourse in marriage was legitimate not only for begetting children but also for protecting the marriage bond. Married people could ask each other for sex without blame, provided they did so not out of lust but to relieve their natural needs. All impediments were divided into those which made the marriage *unlawful* and those which made the marriage *invalid or null*. The first group resulted from the prohibition of the Church. They were: No marriage can be had outside the forbidden time. Those times were between the First Sunday of Advent and Christmas inclusive. From Ash Wednesday to Easter Sunday inclusive. No marriage was allowed with non-Catholics. No marriage was allowed without previous proclamation. No marriage was allowed if one party had taken the vow of chastity. No marriage was allowed if a promise of marriage to another party had not been properly dissolved. Those impediments which made a marriage *invalid or null* were: Marriage to the wrong person or unintended person. Marriage by force or violence. Marriage with a disregard for the decrees of the Council of Trent. Marriage where one or both parties had hidden their impotency. Marriage between baptized and non-baptized persons. Marriage of public indecency or impropriety. A man who had promised a marriage to a woman, even if the engagement was broken, could not marry the woman's sister, mother, or daughter. This was similar for the woman; she could not marry his brother, father, or son. Marriage was not

allowed when one or both of the parties had taken solemn vows. Marriage was not allowed when a crime would have been committed such as adultery, murder, conspiracy to murder. Marriage was not allowed between blood relatives up to and inclusive with the fourth degree. Marriage was not allowed between those having improper spiritual affinity. Affinity of baptismal and confirmation sponsors with those receiving the sacraments. There is no affinity, however, between sponsors. Marriages of improper legal affinity were not allowed. Likewise, situations involving relationships of those adopted and the adoptees. For the personal details of Charles Buchheit and Mary Futterer being engaged, married, purchase of rings and other gifts, the author/editor had interviewed Marie Buchheit Miller at her residence on September 17, 2001, and copied notes from memorabilia which she has in her personal archives concerning the Futterer and Buchheit families. The Steffan family, Buchheit family, and the old Sister's Hospital referred to in the text was located on Pearl Place. Today this short street is known as St. Louis Place. Historical aspects of the Futterer family can be found in Carl Anthony Miller aka C. Eugene Miller, *One Man's Life*, copyright, Buffalo, New York, 1982; and also op. cit. *Der Turner Soldat*. For sodalities at St. Louis Church, see: *Solemn Commemoration of the Centenary of the Founding of St. Louis Church, Buffalo, New York*, Published by the Centennial Committee, Buffalo, New York, 1929. A copy is in the archives of the St. Louis Church. For biographical material on Father Walter Fornes see: *Union and Echo*, Buffalo, NY, February 25, 1945; *Buffalo News*, Buffalo, NY, February 23, 1945; *Amherst Bee*, Amherst, NY, February 22, 1945; Rev. George Zimpfer, *History of SS. Peter and Paul Church, 1836-1936*, Williamsville, NY, 1936, pps. 51-8. For family histories of the Fornes and Steffan families consult with the archives of Mrs. Cathy Steffan, Buffalo, NY. The source of the material for the paragraph on the hospital and cottage on Pearl Place see: The Archives of the Steffan Family in the possession of Cathy Grupp Steffan in a newspaper clipping, *Courier Express*, June 26, 1966. At the time the article was written George Steffan was responsible for renting the Steffan properties on Pearl Place which had become known as St. Louis Place. He rented the cottage to Mrs. Elizabeth S. Ward, who kept a tiny but well cared-for lawn in the front of the house. The lot was 30 feet by 138 feet and partially paved in the rear with large squares of sandstone. Bishop Timon bought the hospital building and the cottage in 1847 for $1,000.

The seven trustees were beneficiaries of the loan of $60,000 made to St Louis Church in 1889. Top row, left to right are Trustees Francis S. Burkard, G. Frank Deck, Xavier Dietsche, Jacob A. Gittere and Fred Jehle. Bottom row, left to right are Bishop Stephen Vincent Ryan, Trustees Peter Paul and Lawrence Wex and Jonathan Scoville, the donor of the loan.

Interior of St. Louis Church 1954

CHAPTER TEN

Catholicism in Art and Music

Catholicism is the faith and practice that proclaims universality. By such a definition Anglican, Protestant, Orthodox, and Oriental Christians as well as Roman Catholics can identify themselves with Catholicism. Of this group, however, only Roman Catholics recognize the Bishop of Rome, the Pope, as the perpetual and visible source and foundation of the unity of the bishops and the multitude of the faithful. After Jesus Christ's death, resurrection, and ascension into heaven, the first leader of the Christian community was Peter, the Apostle; he was the first primate of the Catholic Church. Because he moved his place of residence from Jerusalem, where Christianity was founded, to Rome, and remained there until his death during the persecution of Nero sometime between 64-68 AD, the expression Roman Catholicism refers to the diocese over which he spiritually ruled rather than to his primacy as the first head of the Catholic Church. If an adjective were needed to define Catholicism as a qualification of Christianity it would be Petrine Catholicism rather than Roman Catholicism because it was not until the end of the second century that tradition in the Church identified Peter as the first bishop of Rome.

Although Catholicism in art and music as an expression of Christianity might be considered more universal because it applies equally to Anglican, Protestant, Orthodox, and Oriental Christian Churches as well as to Petrine or Roman Catholic Churches, here one uses it as a means to recognize how art and music displayed in Roman Catholic Churches signifies

Christian tradition, community, and a way of life that emphasizes a belief in a triune God, redemption of humankind by Jesus Christ, and the theological principles of sacramentality, mediation, and communion. In its art and music, Roman Catholicism connotes the sacrament of Christ mediating salvation within a worldwide community of faith. In a particular way of demonstrating this concept, the art and music operative during the one hundred and seventy-five years of the history of St. Louis Church are vehicles by which these lofty concepts are given practical expression through media such as architecture, icons and paintings, statuary, furnishings and appointments, vesture and textiles, musical instrumentation, execution of musical opera, and choral endeavors.

In style, the architecture of the present St. Louis Church is continental gothic of the fourteenth century, which is contemporaneous with and similar to the English decorated gothic. Both of these art forms were outgrowths of the Romanesque style of architecture that developed in Western Europe with the spread of Christianity. The general design of later churches was nearly the same as the Roman basilicas but semi-circular arches were substituted in place of the architraves, the ponderous beams acting as tie rods from one pillar to another. As an art form it spread from Sicily to northern Italy. Most arches were rounded but in Sicily, where the followers of Mohammed ruled for two centuries, the architects introduced the Arabic pointed arch into the design. More of the Byzantine influence crept into structures built in southern France

197

owing to the considerable trade carried on with Venice and the East. Soon the churches there were built with long naves with vaulted roofs, aisles, transepts, apses at the eastern ends, and a central tower. Buttresses counteracted the lateral thrust of the stone vaulting of the nave — a difficulty that the Romans avoided by building vaulted roofs in solid concrete, which simply rested upon the walls like a lid. In northern France the gothic style was based upon the German Romanesque architecture which was closely modeled upon the northern Italian designs. The gothic style absorbed into England was taken from France, particularly that of St. Etienne at Caen, and from Germany, that of the Cathedral at Aix-la-Chapelle, built in the beginning of the ninth century. Within a century after the Norman Conquest of England in 1066, the Romanesque architecture with its added Byzantine influence was entrenched in that country. Among the many examples which today's tourists stand before in awe are the Durham Cathedral, Ely Cathedral, the crypt of Canterbury Cathedral, and Kelso and Jedburgh Abbeys.

*I*n gothic architecture, although the pointed arch was adopted from the Romanesque, the churches, because they became oblong instead of circular or square, used ribbed vaulting for the ceilings. Skeletons of ribs going transversely and diagonally across the nave made a framework which was filled in with lighter masonry, and the thrust was brought to bear on separate points, the wall being strengthened at those points by buttresses. Thus in the gothic style the massive walls of the Romanesque disappeared, and the spaces between the buttresses were filled with great windows, making the interior light and airy. With the invention of painted glass these windows became one of the chief glories of the gothic style. From France, gothic architecture was introduced into England at the time of the rebuilding of the Canterbury Cathedral in the twelfth century. Toward the end of the thirteenth century, a transition took place in English gothic. Its style was named *Middle Pointed* or *Decorated*. Windows were widened and divided by mullions. Traceries were introduced which went from the geometrical at first to the wavy and variated type later. Buttresses were more decorated and the ornamentation and capitals of the columns were more richly carved. This was considered the finest period of the gothic style and tourists today see its grandeur exemplified in the naves of the York Minster and Melrose Abbeys.

*T*he gothic architecture of St. Louis Church has many of the features of the English Decorated Gothic as well as the features of medieval gothic churches in France and Germany. Although its tower is considered modeled after the traceried towers and spires of the Cologne Cathedral, Germany, which is little more than an enlargement of the cathedrals at Amiens, Chartres, Paris, Rheims, and Strasbourg, St. Louis Church's interior nave is constructed more along the lines of Westminster, York Minster, and Melrose Abbeys in England. The ground plan of the building is in the form of a Latin cross with its nave and clerestory representing the shaft upon which the body of the crucified Christ was positioned with his feet nailed into place. The transept and its clerestory, meeting the nave at a right angle, represents the cross-beam upon which the arms of Christ were stretched so that his hands or wrists could be firmly attached by nails. The greater portion of the nave, flanked by five magnificent columns of polished granite on each side of an aisle forty-two feet wide and seventy-two feet high into the clear, runs from the narthex, a portico or vestibule just inside the door from the tower, to the transept. The lesser portion of the nave runs from the communion rail at the foot of the sanctuary to the beginning of the apse, the half of decagon surrounding the permanent altar. On this portion of the original cross hung the plaque ordered to be placed there by Pontius Pilate, which carried the letters INRI, Jesus of Nazareth, King of the Jews. This section of the nave is completely within the confines of the sanctuary and is flanked on each side by two pillars that are the same as those in the greater portion of the nave both in material, size, and design. On each side of the greater portion of the nave are side aisles that are nineteen feet wide and thirty-six feet in height. These represent the place before the cross where the Roman soldiers cast lots for ownership of Christ's seamless tunic, and the mourners, including Mary, the Mother of Jesus, Mary of Cleophas, Mary Magdalen, and John, the beloved Apostle, stood.

The gothic cruciform architecture of St. Louis Church with an exterior length of two hundred and thirty-four feet and exterior width of one hundred and thirty-four feet is an example of the style of art that from 1150 to 1500 symbolically and allegorically emphasized the humanity of Jesus especially in his suffering and crucifixion. It is an example of gothic spirituality. In the clerestory of the nave, the weightlessness, harmony, and unity of its architecture and the translucency of its glass windows expresses the ineffable presence of God, the immaterial True Light to which all who attend services there are aspired to ascend. The clerestory rises twenty-seven feet above the roof of the side aisle. On each of its sides there are seven stained glass windows with run-on designs of differing patterns, each eight feet wide and nineteen feet high. Six windows are in the longer section of the nave and one window is in the small portion of it above the sanctuary. In the transept there are four windows of the same art form and dimensions on each side. All of these windows appear high in the clerestory above the triforium, the plastered wall between the capitals of the pillars and the lower framing of the windows. Another name sometimes given to the triforium is the gallery because upon it are painted symbolic decorative insignias. Also at each end of the transept, at the same height as the clerestory, is a most beautifully designed Rose Window, a circle of stained glass, twenty-two feet in diameter, with divided compartments and tracery radiating from the center. Through these windows a copious amount of light brightens and radiates the central aisle of the nave giving the faithful a sense of Divine Grace freely flowing into their souls. The windows are most appreciated when shafts of sunlight play upon their rich coloring to the fullest. It was this

emotion, this touch of the divine with the human, which the English designers instilled into their art of Decorated Gothic Architecture.

Within the walls of the side aisles of the greater portion of the nave, stained glass rectangular windows pierce six bays on each side, each containing a mullion in the center and a pointed arch at the top. They are five feet six inches wide and eighteen feet six inches in height. The arch of each window is filled with traceries of varied designs, and the rectangular section exhibits a scene illustrating an aspect of biblical or church history. A seventh bay and window, the same as the other six, is located in the chancel inside the sanctuary. Starting in the chancel on the south side of the sanctuary, going across the transept, and moving down the south aisle of the nave one finds, in order, the following depictions: The Baptism of Jesus, donated by Charles Lautz; Conferral of the Keys on St. Peter, in memory of Nicholas Ottenot; St. Boniface, the Apostle of Germany (680-754), donated by Joseph and Anna M. Krumholz; St. Augustine, Bishop and Doctor (354-430) and St. Gregory the Great, Doctor (540-604), donated by Mr. and Mrs. Charles J. Dearing; St. Dominic, Founder of the Dominicans (1170-1221), in memory of Joanna Hampelshofer; St. Anthony, An Egyptian Hermit (251-356), donated by Anthony Neupert; and St. Rose of Lima (1586-1617), and St. Genevieve of Paris (422-500), in memory of Genevieve Kraft. Beginning in the chancel on the north side of the sanctuary, going across the transept, and moving down the north aisle of the nave one finds, in order, the following depictions: The Annunciation, donated by Jacob Davis; The conversion of St. Paul, donated by Barbara Kleinschmidt; St. Francis Xavier, Jesuit Missionary (1506-1552), donated by Xavier Dietsche; St Francis de Sales (1567-1622) and St. Bernard of Clairvaux (1090-1153), donated by Michael and Blondina Fornes; St. Margaret Mary Alacoque, Visitation Nun (1647-1690), donated by John Irlbacker; Mary of Bethany, sister of Martha, donated by Christian Weyand; St. Odilia, Patroness of Alsace (died circa 720) and St. Elizabeth of Hungary (1207-1231), in memory of Elizabeth Lautz.

*I*n seven bays in the sanctuary surrounding the main altar one finds seven large stained glass windows each depicting an event in the life of St. Louis, King of France (1214-1270). Technically two of these are in the smaller section of the nave while the other five are in the apse forming a half decagon. They run, however, contiguously presenting snippets in the life of the saint. From left to right facing the apse one observes, in order, Louis carefully reared by his saintly mother, donated by Clemens Neunder; Louis arbitrating one of the many feuds of the age in which he lived, donated by the ten children of Michael Steffan; Louis, true to his vow, leading a crusade, donated by Edward Hager and John Feist; Louis carrying the Savior's crown of thorns to the church of Sainte Chapelle in Paris, donated by the St. Louis Church congregation in memory of Father Joseph Sorg, D.D.; Louis feeding the poor and comforting the oppressed, donated by Gerhard Lang; Louis, a man of great piety, deeply conversing with God in prayer, donated by Jacob Weppner; and Louis, on his death bed, a victim of the plague receiving communion, donated by Jacob Davis.

A century ago, pictures and reproductions served as the poor man's prayer book and catechism. Unable to read, he could spell out his lesson from the pictures before him. When he had become educated and more sophisticated, he could still stand before these images and prayerfully contemplate their meaning. As a teacher, presenting these images to his students, he could excite them by exposing the hidden meanings in the windows. Looking at the window of St. Dominic he could explain that the dog with a burning torch it its mouth symbolized the dream of Dominic's mother who had an omen that her son would be a *Dog of the Lord* and carry a burning torch in his mouth. So it was! Dominic extirpated the big heresies of his day, such as Albigensianism, and carried the burning torch of faith to every part of the world. In the window featuring St. Boniface, one sees the saint chopping down an oak tree. This was the mighty oak, the idyllic god of the Germans to whom Boniface was sent to convert to Christianity. Although he and several of his companions died as martyrs, he succeeded in establishing Catholicism in northern Europe. In the scene where St. Anthony, the Hermit, is at prayer in his cave in the desert, a pig stands beside him. The pig typifies the heavy temptations that assailed him throughout his whole life. The teacher can tell his children that, like Anthony, we all have pigs in our lives, but we all can be saints too!

*T*he principal front on Main Street is designed on grand proportions, with a large center tower reaching the considerable height of two hundred and forty-five feet, and two similar towers, each one hundred and twenty-eight feet high. The grand portal in the main tower is divided by a mullion into two door-ways, each five feet wide with jambs richly decorated with columns, having foliage capitals and clustered moldings; the whole being surmounted with a tympanum, richly carved with a sculptured figure in the center. The high window in the gable over the main portal has molded stone mullions and an original beautifully designed tracery. The doorway is flanked on either side by buttresses, enriched by graceful pinnacles with gablets and foliated finials. The center of the gable terminates with a finial of rich foliage just underneath the clock dial and the point where the tower changes from a square to an octagonal form. The dial, one hundred and one feet above the sidewalk, is made of stone with figures carved on the rim and a quarter-foil in the center. The tower retains its square form to a height of ninety-six feet, where it off-sets with graduated weatherings to octagonal, having louvered windows on each of the eight sides with fine tracery, and each surmounted with a gablet springing from the buttresses and terminating with a foliated finial.

The buttresses rising upward are finished with pinnacles. The spire is octagonal. The angles have rich moldings, ornamented with foliaged crockets and the faces are paneled with tracery, the whole terminating in a magnificent finial eleven feet high. The clock was a gift from Elbridge Gerry Spaulding, who lived in a grand building diagonally across from the church on the East Side of Main Street. He was born in Cayuga County, New York, on February 24, 1809. He resided in Buffalo for sixty-three years, developed Spaulding's Exchange on Main Street and the Terrace intersecting Commercial Street, served one term as mayor in 1847, was elected a member of the United States House of Representatives in 1861, became Chairman of the House Ways and Means Committee, wrote legislation which led to the issuance of legal tender treasury notes, accepted the title of the *Father of the Greenback*, achieved the presidency of the Farmers and Mechanics Bank, and was known as the financial savior of the Union during the Civil War. He contended that the clock in the St. Louis Church tower was so accurate that he set his own pocket watch by it every day as he paused before the entrance on his way to the Exchange. He died in Buffalo on May 5, 1897.

The side portals built into the side towers and imitative of the main portal, are each seven feet wide in the clear. The jambs are ornamented with columns and the tympanum is filled with tracery of a beautiful pattern. Above the arch is a gablet terminating in a finial, and above this is a traceried window, with a richly molded label. Inside each of the two side towers is a circular iron staircase that rises from the main floor and communicates with the organ galleries and the upper stories in the main tower. In order that the main tower and the side towers had safe and adequate stability, they were mounted on stone foundation walls that are sixty-six inches thick. The walls are embedded into the sandy loam soil under the church and rise from that ground level to the floor of the main entrance to the church. The floor of the tower sits on a series of arched brickwork with each arch keystoned by a steel beam.

These beams were among the first to be produced by Andrew Carnegie who began operation in 1885.

Above the grade line the whole exterior of the building is faced with Medina red sandstone. It is rock faced on the walls, which up to the roof level of the side aisles, has a two and one-half brick thickness. The sandstone is tooled in the molded courses, doors, and window jambs. Buttresses are strategically placed along the outside of the building so as to carry the entire horizontal load activated by the roof and the arch formation inside the structure. Their base width and weight was so designed that vertical reaction force and moments of force were sufficient to keep the walls in equilibrium. All the vertical loads of the structure are carried by the pillars that are built on solid stone footings of octagonal shape that could be inscribed in a circle with a diameter of five feet. The tower walls were purposefully isolated from the remainder of the building so that the greater settlement caused by the immense weight upon them did not crack or in any way effect the adjoining walls. That tower, with its twin ones by its side, and from whose walls the church is isolated, after all the vicissitudes of one hundred and seventy-five years, stands physically, spiritually, and inspirationally as a Spire in the City, a Steeple in the City, and a Tower in the City. It has ascension, aspiration, and surge; and, as such, it has grandeur to lift to great heights the devotion of its parishioners and be an inspiration to the visitor and the casual passerby. [1]

All gothic churches such as St. Louis Church contain a series of icons and paintings. Under this title one includes all art representations by pictures or images whether these are on walls or in windows. As such, attention is brought to bear on the Catholicism being displayed in the church by the two dimensional arts of iconography, painting, stained glass imagery, and mosaic. Serious consideration should be given to the fourteen windows that run along the sidewalls of the church. They are exquisite in conception, color, and form, and are an inspiration and a silent sermon to the passerby whether in church for attendance at morning or evening services or simply there as an observing tourist. Beginning at the first window in the wall of the left side-aisle, as one faces the sanctuary, is the window whose title is *Conferral of the Keys on St. Peter*. Its artwork was inspired by the words of chapter sixteen of St. Matthew's gospel. Jesus had just come into the quarters of Cesarea Philippi and paused to ask his disciples, "Who do you say that the Son of Man is?" The scene depicts the disciples standing about Jesus, their boat with the sail aloft, is in harbor behind them. After several had offered their answers Peter finally spoke and said, " Thou art Christ, the Son of the living God." Jesus praised him for his answer, told him that he was the rock upon which the Christ would build His church. Then Jesus said, "And I will give thee, Peter, the keys of the kingdom of heaven, and whatsoever you shall bind on earth shall be bound in heaven: whatsoever you shall loose on earth shall be loosed in heaven." In the portrait Jesus holds the keys which He presents to Peter who is on one knee before him. Pius IX proclaimed the doctrine of papal infallibility in 1870. To the parishioners of the late nineteenth century, when these windows were installed in the church, the scene was a silent reminder that their Catholicism was entrusted to Peter and his successors after Christ's death. It is ironic but also enlightening that this window was donated in memory of Nicholas Ottenot, who had been one of the trustees during the days of interdict and excommunication when the members of St. Louis Church had established a Rare Tradition in American Catholicism.

The adjacent window features St. Boniface, fully dressed in his hierarchical robes, wearing his miter and carrying his crosier. His right foot stands on the stump of a mighty oak tree which, as it is claimed, he, miraculously and without axe, chopped down in the forest without danger or harm to himself. Three of the leaders of the German Teutonic tribe akin to the Angles and Saxons, two kneeling and one standing, offer their fealty to him. They represent the three provinces in which he did his greatest preaching, Thuringia, Frisia, and Hesse. On the occasion of the felling of the oak, which the barbarians held to be their heathen deity, he said, "There is only one God and it is not this tree." The vestments that he wears are colored red because on his last mission to Frisia in 754, he and thirty of his companions were massacred at Dokkum, Holland, now covered by the Zuider Zee. His tomb is honored in the abbey at Fulda. Boniface was born in Devonshire, England, attended the Benedictine seminary in Winchester for which later he became the director after being ordained in 715. Pope Gregory II sent him to the missions as an assistant of St. Willobrord, who at the time was archbishop at the cathedral of Utrecht, Frisia. While on his early missions, Boniface was under the protection of Charles Martel, the grandfather of Charlemagne, named *The Hammer* because he was in 732 the victor at the battle of Poitiers, halting the advance of the Muslims into Europe. In the same year, Boniface, whose family name was Wynfrith, was consecrated archbishop by Gregory III. Joseph and Anna Krumholz donated this window as a reminder to the congregation that Boniface was the Apostle to the Germans and was to be considered as their patron saint. His feast day is held on June 5, each year.

The next window to be observed is that of St. Augustine and St. Gregory the Great. Both saints were bishops, and doctors of the church. Whereas in the first two windows, the mullion in the center separates a single scene, here it divides the two persons as if each stands complete in his own niche. On the left is Pope Gregory I, who is considered as one of the most influential popes in the history of the Roman Catholic Church. He is called Gregory the Great because of the guidelines he set down for the papal ministry of bishops, his liturgical reforms, and the development of Gregorian chant. It was against the dark background of invasions into Italy and Spain by Vandals, Arian Ostrogoths and Visigoths, and Lombards which brought a final blow to Roman civilization that Gregory accepted the tiara as

Pope in Rome. He was a man of true genius, profound spirituality, and unflagging energy. He set the course for the papacy to follow throughout the Middle Ages of Europe. In the portrait, he stands clothed in papal vestments, wearing the tiara, carrying his papal crosier, holding a book into which he is composing, and listening to the dove representing the Holy Spirit.

The artist may have been a bit unhistorical by representing the tiara as a beehive shape that did not take this form until the fifteenth century. In the Middle ages it was simply a cap which first evolved into a single coronet, then double, and finally a triple coronet with two cloth strips or lappets hanging behind. His vestments are white because white is the color used at Mass on all feasts of the joyful and glorious mysteries of Jesus Christ's life such as Christmas, Easter, feasts of the Blessed Virgin Mary, angels, and all saints who were not martyrs. He carries the book and pen representing that he was a voluminous writer of theses on exegetical topics, compendiums on spirituality, texts of homilies on the gospels, and written discourses on pastoral rule. He sent Augustine the Abbot to England to evangelize and establish Christianity on the island. In doing so he began the long train of events which brought Boniface to the Germans and the Christianizing of the barbarians whom had thrown Europe into the dark ages.

On the right side of the mullion, next to Gregory stands St. Augustine, Bishop of Hippo. He too is dressed in his bishop's liturgical robes and carries the crosier. He wears only the simple miter of his historic period. He was not a martyr and should be wearing the white vestments according to the usual liturgical color code. The artist, however, chose the color purple because he wished to represent the penitential aspect of Augustine's life. He was born in Tagaste in Numidia, North Africa on November 13, 354. Although extremely intelligent, he was quite risky with his sexual morality. He took a mistress and fathered a child. He joined with the Manicheans who shared his abhorrence of the Old Testament. Following them, he wished to rely upon reason, not authority, and indulged in an absolute cosmic duality which seemed to be a satisfying explanation of the problem of evil. He taught rhetoric for many years in Africa, Rome, and Milan. His mother Monica never ceased to pray for his conversion; he then came under the influence of Ambrose, bishop of Milan, was converted, and baptized in 387. He was later ordained at Hippo, North Africa, remained there writing, teaching, and preaching. In 395, he was consecrated its bishop. There he ecclesiastically presided, adjudicating cases referred to the bishop's tribunal, combating controversies and heresies, and living in community with his clergy, until his death during the siege of Hippo by the Vandals in 430. The artist portrayed Augustine holding a heart in his left hand; an arrow is piercing it. It symbolizes one deeply in love. One of his most read books is his *Confessions*. In it he writes, "Thou has made us for thyself O' Lord, and our hearts will ever be restless until they rest in Thee." This window was a gift to St. Louis Church by Charles J. Dearing who in 1900 was a trustee and treasurer of the church corporation. In 1893, he retired from the meat business, sold his store on Allen Street to Arnold Weppner, but continued to be a member of the Buffalo Butcher's association.

Moving on to the next window one finds an artist's display of St. Dominic kneeling before an elevated throne upon which sits Mary, the Mother of Jesus, holding her child on her lap supported by her left arm, and a staff in her right hand. Jesus is presenting a garland of roses in the traditional form of the rosary of five decades for the recital of *Hail Marys*, beads of introduction, *Our Fathers* to each decade, and the triple set of beads capped by the crucifix. Dominic's special love of Mary is demonstrated in this artistic rendition of the legend that it was he who established the devotion of the Rosary that has been faithfully followed by Catholics for over four centuries. The artist presents Dominic in the traditional robes of the

Order of Preachers, which he founded and received full approbation from Pope Honorius in 1216. On his head, Dominic wears the full tonsure of a monk, a distinct practice as an admission to ordination beginning in the sixth century. The faces of three angels appear at the feet of Mary indicating that even the angels of heaven honor the Mother of God. The vase of flowers is a nice artistic touch showing that life is continually blossoming.

*I*n the forefront is a dog carrying a burning torch. The Latin word for Dominican is *dominicanis*, meaning Dog of God. The Dominican logo is *deliverers of the burning truth*. The Order of *Preachers* filled a great need for intellectual teachers who clearly gave instruction in the dogmas of faith, but lived in utter poverty in contrast to the rich clergy of the era. The Saint was born Dominic Guzman at Carla Ruega, Spain in 1170. He studied at Palencia, was ordained priest and became a canon of the newly reformed cathedral chapter of Osma in 1199. The window was donated in memory of Joanna Hampelshofer who had a strong devotion to the Blessed Virgin Mary and enjoyed moving her fingers along the decades of her rosary beads while she meditated on the joyful, sorrowful, and glorious mysteries so as to motivate herself to imitate what they contained, and develop the virtue of hope so as to obtain what they promised.

*T*he next window, a gift of Anthony Neupert, portrays St. Anthony, the Hermit, who is the classic representative of the solitary version of early monasticism in Lower Egypt, the *father of monks*. The theologian Athanasius of Alexandria turned the recluse into a hero throughout all northern Africa by publishing his biography, *Life of Antony*, circa 357. In it is recorded that after Anthony's parents had died, and while he was living and caring for his younger sister, he was, one Sunday, late for Mass and entered church during the Gospel. Looking for a place to stand among the community, he heard the priest read the words of

Jesus, "If thou wouldst be perfect, sell what thou hast, give to the poor, and come follow Me." He was so struck by these words that, after returning home, sold everything he had, placed his sister in a convent, and retreated to a graveyard in a desert cemetery to live in solitude for many years, enduring many fierce temptations. Although his life was extremely austere, he inspired many other young men to come out into the desert; and, like John the Baptist, be accessible to each other and to visitors especially pilgrims seeking solitude and peace.

*I*n the scene, the artist has Anthony clothed in a brown robe, more symbolic of the Franciscan monks of the eleventh century than those hermits of the early church. He wears a long white beard to indicate that he spent his whole life in the desert; he only visited the city of Alexandria twice. His hands are clasped in prayer as he reads from the Scriptures, the source of Divine Revelation. Before him rests a skull and coffin at the base of a cross. Like Jesus, he too must die, but he knows neither the day nor the hour. Although looking out the window in front of him he sees the vast desert of nothingness, this world, to his side is the Garden of Eden, containing the fruits he will enjoy in the next world. Neupert chose this window as his gift not only because he held Anthony, the Hermit, as his patron saint, but also because he had a strong belief that the consecrations he had received in Baptism and Confirmation, would sustain his courage to live a faithful and moral Christian life.

*T*he last window of this side aisle depicts St. Rose of Lima and St. Genevieve of Paris. Here again the mullion divides the scene into two equal parts, both subjects, however, having the same background as if, although separated in time by sixteen centuries, they complement each other. Both were women, both never married, both never became nuns. On the left, Rose of Lima, the first saint from the Western Hemisphere canonized by the Roman Catholic Church, stands clothed in garments resembling those worn by the Dominican Order of women. Although she was a member of their Third Order, she never was a nun. If the artist wished to be consistent in having her dressed as a member of the Order, he would have had her draped in a black mantle rather than a blue one. In designing and producing stained glass, black being undesirable and non-functional, another color is always used. The white habit and the veil, however, are consistent with those worn by the Dominicans. Rose had a strong admiration for St. Catherine of Siena. One day Rose had a vision of the Blessed Virgin Mary flanked by two members of the Dominican Order, Catherine of Siena and Agnes of Montepulciano. In that vision Agnes held the baby Jesus while Catherine held a large cross. It was for this reason that the artist placed a cross in Rose's hand. She, like Catherine, led a life as a recluse, wore a crown of sharp spikes beneath her veil, and meditated constantly on the sufferings of Christ crucified.

Genevieve, on the other hand, was a member of the Old World; and, in this way, complimented Rose who was of the New World. Genevieve was born in Paris, lived there as a virgin, and has been distinguished as the shepherdess and patron saint of that city. She earned that honor because she averted Attila II and his Huns from sacking it in 451. The artist portrays her holding a lamb and carrying a staff. The window is not only appropriate as representing the patroness of Genevieve Kraft for whom it was given as a memorial, but it shows that in St. Louis Church by the turn of the century, the New World and the Old World were solidly bound together in the parishioners who occupied its pews each Sunday.

If one would begin a tour of the stained glass windows on the wall of the north side aisle outside the sanctuary beginning with the one closest to the communion rail, a scene depicting the conversion of St. Paul would be appealing to the eye. Placing this artistic rendition at this spot gives balance to the window displaying the conferral of the keys of the kingdom to Peter shown on the opposite side of the church. The artist drew upon the text in the Acts of the Apostles, chapter nine, in which Paul, who was then known as Saul, made a journey to Damascus after the martyrdom of Stephen, the deacon, at which Saul played a role of antagonism. Following that event, he obtained permission from the high priest of Jerusalem to go off to Syria, present himself at its synagogue, seek out all those Jews who had come to believe in the new Christian heresies, and drag them back to Jerusalem in chains for prosecution. He was dressed in his military regalia and was accompanied by his band of loyal military activists. Suddenly while on the road to Damascus, a light from heaven shone round about him, and a voice from the sky said, "Saul, Saul, why persecutest Me?" Falling to the ground Saul replied, "Who art thou?" Then came the reply, "I am Jesus who thou persecutest. It is hard for thee to kick against the goad!" On that day Saul was left blinded, had to be led by his followers into Damascus, and subsequently received back his sight by Ananias who witnessed his conversion. At his baptism, Saul took the name Paul. From that time, he became a fiery apostle of the risen Christ. The artist has faithfully represented this vignette in the glass of the window. Paul is on the ground facing up to heaven where a very moody sky has opened, and the Christ is seen in the clouds holding out his arms. Saul's sword lies limp upon the ground, a sign of surrender. His followers are shown gravely distressed; fear can be seen in their eyes. The entire scene captures the rumbling of the heavens and the power of the supernatural. Barbara Kleinschmidt the donor of this artwork had great devotion to Peter and Paul, Apostles, founders of the Church at Rome. The Roman Catholic Church celebrates their feast day each year on June 29.

Next, one sees the window featuring St. Francis Xavier, patron saint of its donor, Xavier Dietsche. The saint was born in Spain, attended the Sorbonne University in Paris with St. Ignatius Loyola, and became one of the first seven Jesuits to take vows at

Monmartre in 1534. Francis was ordained at Venice in 1537 and went to the province of Goa, India, in 1542, where he spent a considerable amount of time preaching, evangelizing, and baptizing those of the lower caste; he was unsuccessful at gaining a hearing among the Brahmins who were the upper caste. He also preached at Malacca, on the southwest coast of Malaya. Later, he spent two successful years bringing Catholicism to Japan, returned to Malaya, and then decided to go to China, but he prematurely died on the island of Sancian off of its coast. Francis Xavier is known in the liturgy as the *Apostle to India and Japan.* He was canonized in 1622, and later Pope Pius X proclaimed him as patron of the missions. The artist displays Francis dressed in his cassock and surplice, wearing his stole, and holding a crucifix in his left hand, while he pours water from an earthenware vessel over the head of the father of a family using his right hand. Seated to the left is the wife holding a baby with a young daughter clutching at her dress. Apparently they also are waiting their turn to be likewise baptized. In the background three native hunters and warriors, standing by equatorial foliage, look upon the reception of this sacrament in awe. Two grass-roofed huts and a bright sky filled with white clouds complete the scene. Although the warriors wear a type of turban indicative of Indian origin, the natives are dark skinned and have complexions differing from Indians or Orientals. An art critic would have to conclude that the scene is set in Malaya rather than India or Japan.

The next window, donated by Michael A. Fornes and his wife Blondina Steffan Fornes, features St. Francis de Sales and St. Bernard of Clarivaux. Both men were intellectuals, both were mystical writers, both were Doctors of the Church, both were founders of Religious Communities, and both were Ordinaries, one a bishop, the other an Abbot. Their window rests directly across from that of St. Augustine and St. Gregory the Great who were intellectuals and powerful preachers of the first millennium whereas Francis and Bernard were the spiritual powers of the second

millennium. Looking at this window the observer suddenly sees the balance and harmony, the symmetry and equivalency in the choice of subject matter for the artistic display of all the stained-glass windows of the side aisles of St. Louis Church. They blossom into an art form of order and equality so appreciated in gothic art. One observes the relation between the positioning of the window featuring St. Peter with that of St. Paul. In life Paul, the Apostle to the Gentiles complimented Peter, the leading evangelist of the Jews. Then the window featuring Francis Xavier, missionary to Asia balances that of Boniface, missionary to the Germans in Europe. Here one sees the symmetry between Frances de Sales and Bernard of Clarivaux with their opposite, Augustine and Gregory. Three more windows remain to be discussed, but the equality and order will remain. Margaret Mary Alacoque in vision with the Sacred Heart of Jesus will balance Dominic with his vision of the Blessed Virgin Mary. Next the legend of Mary of Bethany in a penitential act of washing the feet of Jesus appears symmetrical with the opposite penitent scene of Anthony, the Hermit. Finally, the display of Odilia of Alsace and Elizabeth of Hungary are perfectly in balance with the window facing them featuring Rose of Lima and Genevieve of Paris.

Francis de Sales was born at Savoy, France and educated at Paris and Padua. He was ordained a priest in 1593 and won thousands back to Catholicism with his kindness and understanding. In 1602 he was consecrated bishop of Geneva, Switzerland, whose cathedral had been seized by the Calvinists and made headquarters of the present Presbyterian Church. He was a writer and journalist in defense of the Catholic Church and co-founder of the Visitation Nuns with St. Jane Frances de Chantel. He died at Lyons, France, on December 28, 1622. He was pronounced a Doctor of the Church by Pope Pius IX in 1877, and is the patron of the Catholic Press. Bernard of Clarivaux was born at Dijon, Burgundy, France, in 1090. At the age of twenty-one he entered the Cistercian Abbey of Citeaux which was only a few miles south of his family's estate.

Because of his influence thirty-one of his relatives and friends joined him there in the monastic life. He, however, went away and founded a new Abbey at Clarivaux from which sixty-eight other Abbeys sprang up during his lifetime. Throughout all of northern Europe by order of Pope Eugenius III, Bernard preached and promoted the Second Crusade to the Holy Land. It was led by the French King, Louis VII, grandfather of Louis IX, King and Saint, for whom this magnificent gothic structure is named.

Continuing on, one observes the window donated by John Irlbacker, featuring St. Margaret Mary Alacoque, a visionary, kneeling before the Sacred Heart of Jesus. John Irlbacker with his friend and business partner, Jacob Davis, were responsible for the installation of the gas piping and hot steam heating system in this gothic structure. They operated two establishments, one on Main Street the other on Washington Street. Ironically someone might say that they were men of light and heat. Was the burning heart of Jesus always ready to light the way to salvation and give the fire of courage to follow that way uppermost in their minds when Irlbacker decided to give this window as a gift to the church? Is this why Davis complimented his gift by donating the window display of the Annunciation of the Blessed Virgin Mary which is located in the chancel?

St. Margaret Mary Alacoque was born at Burgundy, France. She became a nun of the Visitation Order, founded by St. Francis de Sales and St. Jane Frances de Chantal. One day while adoring the Blessed Sacrament, exposed on the altar of her convent chapel at Paray-le Monial, she had a vision of Jesus in which He exposed His Sacred Heart. He urged her to spread, throughout France and beyond the oceans, a devotion to His Heart always full of warm love for all humanity. Jesus promised His blessings wherever His picture with His heart so exposed was honored. Specifically, He offered peace to families, refuge and mercy to sinners, increased

fervor to the devout, and grace of final repentance to those who would go to confession and receive communion on the first Fridays of each month for nine consecutive months. The artist displays Margaret before the monstrance, the vessel used to expose for adoration the consecrated eucharistic bread, the body and blood of Christ. It is made of precious metal as the artist describes. He captures the sudden vision of Jesus by placing Him upon a cloud directly in front of the vessel. The tilt of Margaret's head and her outstretched arms indicate her surprise at what she sees. The comparison between the theme of this window with that of Dominic's vision of Mary shown on the opposite side of the church finds another balance and counterbalance between the two side chapels and these two windows. The altar of Sacred Heart is on the left with the window containing Mary and Dominic while the altar of the Immaculate Heart of Mary on the right provides balance with the window of St. Margaret Mary with her vision of the Sacred Heart of Jesus.

Next, one observes the window featuring Christ having His feet washed and anointed at Bethany prior to His last visit to Jerusalem, where He underwent His crucifixion and death on the cross. It was donated by Christian Weyand, the owner of Weyand's brewery which was located at Main and Goodell Streets. Today the Catholic Center of the Diocese of Buffalo occupies the property upon which the brewery was built. The theme of the window is based on chapter twenty-six of the Gospel of St. Matthew where the author contends that the event took place at the house of Simon the Leper. In this account an unnamed woman arrived with an alabaster box, made of white translucent marble, and filled with precious but undefined ointment. She poured it upon Jesus' head while He was seated at the table. In chapter twelve of the Gospel of St. John the same event is recorded as occurring at the home of the siblings, Martha, Mary, and Lazarus, the man Jesus had raised from the dead after being four days in the tomb. In this account, it was Mary who anointed the feet of Jesus with spikenard, derived from the valerian family of plants, used for medicinal purposes, and being of East Indian origin. As the gospel infers, it was very expensive and so powerful that the aroma filled the room. John's account continues with Mary wiping Jesus' feet with her hair. It appears that the artist had relied on the account given by John rather than that of Matthew. Both evangelists, however, underline the disapproval, by the apostles who were present, of the woman wasting her precious ointment in such a manner when it could have been sold and the profit given to the poor.

The artist shows Jesus at the table with Mary at his feet while across from him are four men. If one accepts John's account, the man wearing the blue cap was Judas Iscariot who was the primary accuser of Jesus for allowing this woman to do such a foolish act. Judas' finger points at Jesus with a profound, "I accuse!" The apostle seated, wearing a gold turban, has his hand clenched so as to say, "Do you mean the Lord is wrong?" The balding white haired apostle standing in the rear seems to give the indication of approval of Judas' accusation because his finger points away from the house to a place where one would find the poor. Across from Jesus sits Lazarus, the head of the household; John distinctly claims that Lazarus was present for the occasion. As John describes, Martha is in the background doing the serving. One might ask, "Who is the woman in the window, washing Jesus' feet and wiping them with her hair?" Is it Mary Magdalene, Mary of Bethany, or the woman taken in adultery that Jesus forgave in chapter eight of the Gospel of St. John? Are these three the same Mary? For the artist to retain his symmetry having a compliment with St. Anthony, the Hermit, on the opposite side of the church, he might have considered her to be the woman taken in adultery. By staging the event at the house of Lazarus, however, he appears to depict a different woman, Mary of Bethany, who most likely was not the penitent woman. The only reason one might consider the penitent woman to be Mary Magdalene is because, in the eighth chapter of the Gospel of St. Luke, it is recorded that Jesus drove

seven devils out of her while he was in Galilee, which, however, was some ninety miles from Bethany and at least a year before the event of the adulterous woman takes place. Details in the Gospels of Matthew, Mark, and John, however, do place Mary Magdalene at the foot of the cross during Jesus' crucifixion and at the tomb of Jesus on the morning of His resurrection which is but a week after the visit of Jesus depicted in the window. Which Mary, therefore, did the artist have in mind? The solution to the dilemma lies in the eyes of the beholder.

The final window on the side aisle illustrates two saintly women for whom Elizabeth Lautz, in whose memory it was donated, had great devotion. They are St. Odilia, Patroness of Alsace and St. Elizabeth of Hungary. Like the window on the opposite side of the church this one features two female saints, one from the first millennium and another from the second. Rose of Lima was a member of the Third Order of St. Dominic whereas Elizabeth was a member of the Third Order of St. Francis. Odilia is considered the patroness of Alsace in southern France while Genevieve is the patroness of Paris, France. Both sets of ladies were known for their care of the poor. Odilia was born blind; her father ordered her to be put to death. Her mother pleaded for her life, raised the child in a place where the family was not known, and at the age of twelve placed her in a convent near the city of Besancon, France. While Bishop Erhard was then baptizing her at the Benedictine convent, the Holy Chrism touched her eyes; immediately she was able to see. Her father, hearing the news, was infuriated and killed his own son who went off to the convent to bring his sister home. Going to confession, he repented his heinous sin, and asked Odilia to come home and marry a German Duke. She refused; and, although her father's rage once again flared, it again subsided. He gave her a castle at Hohenburg, now called Odiliensburg, for a convent. She died at Niedermunster; her shrine is a place of great pilgrimage. Her feast is held on December 13, each year.

Two stained glass windows. Left: A window in the right chancel features the Annunciation. Right: A window depicting the Conversion of St. Paul can be found on the north side aisle outside the sanctuary.

Elizabeth was the daughter of Andrew II, King of Hungary, and a pious but reckless and spendthrift man. At a very young age he sent her to Wartburg Castle, Thuringia, where she married Louis IV, son of Hermann I, count of Thuringia; they had three children. In 1227, when the first child was five years old, Louis went on a crusade to the Holy Land with Frederick II, Emperor of the Holy Roman Empire. Louis, however, never saw Jerusalem; he died in Italy before the ships sailed. Upon hearing of his death, Elizabeth who had become queen, was dethroned, and forced out of the castle with her children. She found refuge among the many poor peasants for whom she had so faithfully cared for while she reigned. She joined the Third Order of St. Francis at Marburg and continued looking after the poor and the sick. The artist has placed a large bouquet of roses in her mantle. It was a legend in Thuringia that while she was walking down the street one day, carrying loaves of bread to the poor, as was her daily custom, she was accosted and asked to expose what she had hidden in her mantle. Opening it, a bouquet of roses fell to the ground. She continued on, unharmed. During her stay at Marburg she was tormented by an ecclesiastic called Conrad, who acted as her spiritual director. He was also a papal inquisitor and shortened Elizabeth's life by continuing to overburden it with work and meager compensation. Her feast day is November 17, each year.

Two other stained glass windows, one in the left chancel and the other in the right are to be considered. A chancel is that area in the sanctuary that in history was reserved for the clergy. In St. Louis Church they are the areas in proximity to the side altars. The stained glass windows at the ends of each are a continuation of the artwork in the walls along the side aisles of the church. In the left chancel, while facing the altar, one sees the scene depicting the Baptism of Jesus Christ by John the Baptist in the Jordan River at the beginning of Jesus' public life, donated by Charles Lautz who was the owner of the Lautz Company, importers and dealers in marble and onyx for altars, altar rails,

baptismal and holy water fonts. Its office was at 861 Main Street. Opposite this window, at the end of the right chancel, one observes the Annunciation of the birth of Jesus Christ to the Blessed Virgin Mary by the Angel Gabriel, donated by Jacob Davis who was a graduate of St. Louis' school, President of the St. Louis Society for two years, and a member of the church's board of trustees for nine years.

In these spectacles the artist has continued to carry out his complimentary, balanced theme; manifestation of Jesus Christ's human birth with His Divine birth. In the *Annunciation* the angel speaks to Mary, "Hail full of grace, the Lord is with thee; blessed art thou among women. Behold, you shall conceive in your womb and shall bring forth a Son; and you shall call His name Jesus. He shall be called the Son of the Most High. The Holy Spirit shall come upon you and the power of the Most High shall overshadow you; and therefore the Holy One to be born shall be called the Son of God." This same manifestation is continued in the window showing *Baptism of Jesus*. John the Baptist says, "Behold the Lamb of God, Who takes away the sin of the world! While I was baptizing, I saw the Spirit descending as a dove from heaven, and it abode upon Him." Both pictures feature the presence of God, the Holy Spirit, and the two natures, Divine and human, of Jesus Christ. [2]

The twelve stained glass windows along the side aisles of the nave which have been described above were designed and installed by the Buffalo Stained Glass Works, which until 1900 was located at 29 Pearl Street, Buffalo, New York. After 1900, it was known as Art Stained Glass for Churches and Dwellings, owned and operated by Leo P. Frohe and located on Broadway. William G. Miller who was succeeded by J. Thurston, however, originally established the business, in 1845. In 1864 it came under the management of Booth and Riester; but not long after, Booth left the organization and Ferdinand J. Riester took on Godfrey Frohe as a partner. Riester was born in Granheim, Germany, brought up in France, and immigrated to America about 1840. Frohe was a native of Holland. Both men had been trained in Europe as fresco painters, gold leafers, and interior decorators. After arriving in America, however, they self-trained themselves to the art of making stained glass windows. In 1888, Leo P. Frohe, son of Godfrey, entered the business and developed a new style of staining glass. He hired Otto F. Andrle, a flamboyant, twenty-three year old, who had been born in Buffalo of parents who were organizers of the original St. Louis Church. Upon entering the business Andrle became an instant success; and, by 1896, he was considered to be a designer in glass equal to renowned artists such as John Comfort Tiffany and John LaFarge. By 1900, Andrle had left the Buffalo Stained Glass Works, also known by then as the Stained Glass Institute, and opened his own business called Artist in Fresco, which was located on Genesee Street near Michigan Avenue.

The aisle windows in St. Louis Church were designed and installed sometime between the years 1890 and 1894. Leo Frohe and Otto Andrle designed them in the shop on Pearl Street which was a large three story brick building eighty by sixty feet. It had two large kilns with a capacity of one thousand feet of glass daily. Twenty-two skilled workmen were employed. From 1865 to 1896, it furnished windows for over twelve hundred churches in all parts of the continent. It was one of the largest companies of its type in the United States. About 1891, Frohe began to interview the prospective donors of the windows. Andrle proposed the idea of complimentary symmetry in the choice of design so as to blend in with the gothic nature of the church. The donors suggested the topics for each window so as to fulfill their reasons for a choice and to satisfy Andrle's artistic imagination corresponding to his basic plan. By the end of the year the choices were made and the price per window was set at $527.15 per window. The donors made a fifty-percent down payment and the program was initiated. The windows

in the clerestory were also made at this time by a less expensive process such that each cost $225. At approximately the same time the two windows in the chancel area of the sanctuary and the seven large windows, high above the main altar in the apse were installed. The Royal Munich Art Institute in Bavaria had made these. Each of these windows cost the donors $750 each. [3]

The Buffalo Stained Glass Works immediately began its art. It chose glass composed of silica sand with approximately one-percent iron, soda, ash, limestone, and some borax. It was careful not to add too much iron that would have given too dense a greenish cast to the glass. For colors it used various metallic oxides. The blues were developed from copper oxides or cobalt. Reds, rubies, oranges, and yellows came from selenium and gold salts. A bright type of yellow was produced by the addition of cadmium. A dichromatic process of mixing the salts and oxides that blended blues and yellows produced green; amber resulted from a mixture of sugar and sulfur. Riester and Frohe were noted for their grade of opalescent glass. It was never of one color except when it was pure white or pure black. It was almost opaque to light but spread the light within itself. To make some windows less expensive they used flash glass, granite backed glass, hammered glass, crackle glass, Flemish glass, or slate glass. Flashed glass was one color such as blue flashed on yellow, red on white, red on yellow, or blue on orange. With the equipment in order the Buffalo Stained Glass Works meticulously set out on a well-defined procedure to produce artistic windows for St. Louis Church. Their craftsmen made sketches, put together a template and came up with a final cartoon. On it they drew lines and cut out patterns. Then they selected the glass and cut it with a three bladed scissors. Finally the glass was painted, fired, and glazed which was the art of fixing it into the lead cames. By 1894 the work was completed, and the windows were installed.

The set of seven windows in the apse is a kaleidoscopic scenario of the highlights in the life of Louis IX, king of France during his reign of twenty-two years in the thirteenth century. Starting from the left while facing the altar, one begins to see the story unfold. In the first window, Blanche of Castille, mother of Louis, carefully attends to her son the future king. She was indeed a saintly woman. The year of the birth of her son was 1214. Early in his life, Louis heard and forever heeded his mother's words, "I would rather see you dead than living in sin." Taking his mother's words to heart he lived a life which was a model of virtue. Upon the death of his father, Louis VIII, young Louis became king at the age of twelve. His mother acted as regent during his minority and through a period of illness in his early years of maturity. After gaining great confidence, Louis set about dealing wisely with unruly vassals and reforming France's judicial system. The artist captures this theme in the second window. Louis had become widely known throughout Europe. The high regard, in which he was universally held, caused him to be chosen as an arbitrator during many feuds of the age in which he lived. He was in the forefront of settling controversies between King Henry III of England with the English barons, and between the Pope and the Holy Roman Emperor, Frederick II, who was a persistent thorn in the side of the papacy.

These arbitrations and the various treaties that France had entered into, proved that Louis was, above all, a great lover of peace. He was dominated by only one ambition, namely, to put an end to all existing conflicts, by force if necessary; and, by doing so, remove the causes of future petty disputes resulting in open warfare. In the third window, the artist shows Louis on his white horse leading his troops, under the banner of the Christian cross, on the seventh crusade. Jerusalem had been stormed by the Islamic infidels, as the Europeans called them, and a brief respite that had lasted for fifteen years following the sixth crusade was at an end. Churches in Palestine were being destroyed, public worship was forbidden and Christian blood flowed in the streets. Pilgrims who had left their homes in Europe by the thousands found their numbers cut down to hundreds. In 1244, calling for a crucifix, Louis vowed to lead a crusade himself. Gathering an army of fifty thousand men under his leadership, together with a large fleet of vessels, he set out for Egypt. There, reinforced by another fleet of English crusaders, his expedition advanced on to the Holy Land, where it met disaster in 1250. Louis, along with the greater part of the army was captured. For four years he remained a captive in Syria; but, after a large sum of ransom money was paid to the Saracens, he and the remnants of his army were released. After spending some time in Palestine caring for the poor, he returned to France upon receiving word that his mother, who had been acting as regent in his absence, had died.

The middle window is the artistic and historic jewel of the set. It features King Louis as the center attraction walking through the streets of Paris, carrying the crown of thorns which allegedly was fashioned by the Roman soldiers and placed upon the Christ's head after his violent scourging. The scene features Louis being accompanied by clergy, young lads playing musical instruments, soldiers on horseback, and crowds of people peering from windows or kneeling in the street. In the background is the grand gothic cathedral of Notre Dame. The entourage is on its way to Sainte Chapelle, a church which Louis caused to be constructed in 1245, a year after he departed on his crusade. It was destined to be the resting-place for the sacred relic he was now carrying. To appreciate the emotion that this painting in glass stirs in the hearts and minds of the Catholic, one must understand the spiritual side of Louis' era that commands profound respect. It was the maturing years of the Middle Ages. St. Francis of Assisi and St. Dominic Guzman had organized two of the greatest religious orders in the Catholic Church. Great universities sprang up at this time, and they drew their students, by the thousands, from every quarter of the known civilized world. Notables among the many were at Oxford, Bologna, Padua, Rome, and Paris. Philosophy,

Louis IX, King of France and Saint, bearing the crown of thorns to Sainte Chapelle in Paris.

theology, poetry, and drama attained a rich flowering in the writings of such masters as St. Thomas Aquinas, St. Bonaventure, Duns Scotus, and Dante. Finally it was the era of Gothic styled architecture that had originated in France and spread to England and Germany.

In the fifth window the artist has brought to life the humble side of the King. Although deeply occupied with the affairs of state, Louis was a man of great almsgiving. He built numerous monasteries, hospitals, and asylums throughout his kingdom. The poor, the weak, and the oppressed were some of his great concerns. In the window, Louis is distributing bread among the destitute of the land. Although a king, his raiment was plain. He visited the sick regularly and was reputed to have, in necessity, waited on them personally. In humble action, he was the Father of his people. The sixth window carries this theme of humility into his personal life. He was a man of great piety. Fasting and prayer were a fixed part of his life. It was assumed by many that he was a perpetual wearer of a hair shirt, the discomfort of which he bore with profound patience. In his royal estate he had a small room where he kept a private chapel, where he could retreat and lose himself in meditation. As rays of the morning sun flood light into this window, a viewer below can easily project one's own consciousness into Louis' fervor while he is kneeling at his prie-dieu.

Finally the seventh and last window comes into focus. It was towards the close of the century when word was brought to Louis that the last remnant of Christian holdings in the Holy Land was doomed. The reports graphically described how the great churches of Nazareth, Bethlehem, and Tabor lay in ruins. The Pope appealed to Louis, "Please carry out an eighth crusade!" In 1270, accepting the Pope's challenge, he set out at the head of his men, only to meet misfortune again. Arriving at Tunis in North Africa, he and his army fell victims to the plague. After being infected, Louis fell hopelessly ill. In the scene of the seventh window, he is

upon his deathbed receiving the last rites. With these words, "Into Thy hands, O Lord, I commend my spirit," he breathed his last. Thus died one of God's noblemen. Precious in the sight of the Lord is the death of one of his saints! His feast day is held August 25, each year. [4]

In modern living, as through history, every house, hotel, and office has furnishings and appointments. Within these establishments, each piece of furniture, fixture, or fitting has a functional purpose, but man has seen fit to perform whatever art or craft is necessary to make them ornate. In a home one finds furnishings such as beds, sinks, tables, chairs, dressers, dinner plates, and cookingware. In an office one finds appointments such as desks, chairs, lounges, pen and pencil holders, and copying machines. Each of these items is made as ornate as possible so as to have a comfortable style of living. The church is the house of God and the spiritual home for those who worship there. It deserves no less attention from the fields of arts and crafts than that given to the homes, offices, theaters, and banquet halls of the world. The functions performed in a Catholic Church are the application and reception of the sacraments, the celebration of the sacrifice of the Mass, and the exercise of private and public devotions. Therefore, within the walls of a church one needs to find the appointments for the exercise of Baptism, Confirmation, Penance, now called Reconciliation, Matrimony, Ordination, Eucharist, and Extreme Unction, now called the Sacrament of the Sick. All the furnishings and appointments are needed to carry out all the phases of the Holy Sacrifice of the Mass and to provide an atmosphere for meditation, stirring of emotions, and public and private prayer. Because of the sacredness of these activities the furnishings and appointments should not be banal but elaborate in artistic taste, design, and construction.

For the exercise of Mass one finds that the following items are needed: altar for Mass, tabernacle, chalice, paten, ciborium, presidential chair, ambo or lectern, pews, kneelers, pulpit, communion rail, thurible, incense stand and boat, candle holder and candles. For the administration of the sacraments one looks for baptismal font, holy water fonts, confessionals, monstrance, and chapel-like cache for the holy oils. For a devotional atmosphere one finds: Rood screens, sconces with lights or candles, vases and flowers, a red sanctuary vigil light, votive candles, statues, paintings, wall inscriptions, devotional altars, stations of the cross, and plaques. The main altar in a church building is considered the locus of the sacramental presence of Christ. Attending service at St. Louis Church, one might say, "I see two altars, a large beautiful marble structure in the apse of the sanctuary, and a smaller table-like structure, also in the sanctuary, but nearer to the congregation. Which one should be the locus of my devotion?" Historically, the altar in the apse is your locus of devotion, however, around the altar nearer the congregation you will gather to participate in the Holy Sacrifice of the Mass, led by the priest who will be facing the faithful who kneel, stand, and sit in their pews. Much Christian typology of the altar derives from the Book of Revelation whose authorship is attributed to John the Apostle. Words from that text lead the faithful to believe that the altar of the heavenly liturgy symbolizes the place of the sacrifice of the Lamb.

The high altar in the apse of St. Louis Church is a product of the early twentieth century, a period during which Catholics held their altars in such high esteem that artistic elaboration was to be carried out without quibbling over the cost. Charles Lautz, director of the Lautz Company, importers and dealers in marble and onyx, supervised its installation. He was a most energetic leader of industry and business on the Niagara Frontier. Besides his marble company, his influence was very prominent with the Niagara Machine and Tool Company, the Niagara Starch Company, Niagara Heights Land Company, Williamsville Electric Railway, and Lautz Brothers, manufacturers of fine soap. This beautiful marble altar was a gift to St. Louis Church from Miss Emma Lang, daughter of Gerhard Lang. A

life size marble statue of St. Louis surmounts it. He holds his sword at his side as a memento of a valiant knight who led two crusades, and he carries a crown of thorns that he brought back to Europe from his first crusade and made a place for it in his church, Sainte Chapelle, at Paris. In the center of the altar is the tabernacle, the temple of God, the repository for the consecrated living Christ, the Real Presence. A large mosaic is on each side of it; the one on the left represents Abraham about to sacrifice his son Isaac, and the other, on the right, represents the offering of the bread and wine by the Jewish priest, Melchizedek. The bronze tabernacle door depicts a Lamb, the symbol of Jesus Christ, the true Lamb of God, whose image in crucifixion stands in its niche above it. While looking at the door one might reminisce about Mertz's donation of his bronze tabernacle door installed in the Lamb of God Church.

For the execution of the eucharistic liturgy one observes the use of several sacred vessels: chalice, paten, ciborium, and monstrance. The chalice is the cup used for the wine which is transformed by transubstantiation into the Precious Blood at Mass. Historically *the cup* traces its initiation to the Last Supper which Jesus Christ ate with his disciples in Jerusalem preceding his death on the cross and his resurrection on the third day. In 1929, the one hundredth anniversary of the beginning of St. Louis Church in Buffalo, a new gothic chalice was presented to Father Laudenbach, pastor. It was ordered for the centenary and donated anonymously. It was made by a firm of silversmiths in Mainz on the Rhine, Germany. It is almost one foot in height made of solid silver and gold plated. There are one hundred and eight precious stones scattered on its surface and no less than forty-two pictures and medallions, done in silver and etched metal-work. These include the twelve Apostles, St. Louis, St. Joseph, St. Paul, and St. Henry. It is a work of art that took months to complete, original in design, and matches the famous gothic monstrance owned by the Church.

The monstrance is a sacred vessel used to expose to view the eucharistic bread. It has a broad base, a stem with a node, and a round opening surrounded by a design. A round flat window called lunette encases the consecrated host. The monstrance is placed on the altar during the rite of exposition and benediction of the Blessed Sacrament. In past history it was always carried in a distinguished manner in processions around the interior and exterior of the church. The use of the monstrance originated in France and Germany in the fourteenth century when eucharistic devotion outside of Mass flourished. The paten is a small, circular, flat dish that holds the celebrant's host at Mass. It was originally made of glass but through history it evolved as a gold-plated metal dish. Before the ninth century it was so large that it contained sufficient bread for the entire congregation which had come to Mass and received communion. Later, the ciborium was used to carry the hosts that were distributed to the faithful at communion. It is an ornate metal cup, the interior of which is required by rubric to be gold-plated. When it is placed in reserve in the tabernacle, a metal canopy covers it.

All through history the priest or bishop, in carrying out the exercises of the eucharistic liturgy, donned himself with unique vesture of amice, alb, cincture, maniple, stole, chasuble, and dalmatic. The chasubles and dalmatics used at Mass were colorful works of art, filled with symbolism. Red, the color of blood was used on all feasts of the Lord's Cross and Passion, feasts of the Apostles and Martyrs, and at Masses relating to the Holy Spirit. Purple symbolizing penance and expiation were worn during Advent, Septuagesima, Lent, and on other days of fast. Green, the color of budding and living vegetation, a symbol of hope brightened the altar on Sundays after Epiphany and Pentecost. Old Rose was used only on two Sundays during the year, *Gaudete and Laetare Sundays*. The first came in the middle of Advent and the second graced the middle of Lent. On these days the priest wore these vestments to temper the sadness of the penitential seasons. Until the end of the Second Vatican Council, Black was called for on Good Friday and for Masses for the Faithful Departed. Gold vestments were permitted in place of white, red, or green. In their use both clergy and laity wished to express an extreme joy on some very special occasion for which the Mass was being conducted. On the one-hundredth anniversary of the existence of St. Louis Church a magnificent set of gold brocade vestments was used for the first time. They were made in Crefeld and Munich, Germany, and gifted to the church by an anonymous donor. The set contained two chasubles different in design; one was Roman and the other Gothic. There were also two copes, four dalmatics, a veil, and a special gold cloth preaching stole.

In these vestments, all materials, such as brocade and borders, were genuine fire gold, woven to order. The metal used had been interlaced with the finest silk and all other ornamentation had been created of the same combination. Twenty-eight figures in the vestments are of the most delicate *needle painting*. The ornaments outside the *paintings* are done in *Email-work*, a specialty of the firm of Joerres at Munich. All garments are lined with very heavy pure *Gros de Naples* silk in a rose-color effect. One hundred and fifty-two yards of gold-brocade were used for the set, and this material bears the Crown of St. Louis and the *fleur-de-lis* of Imperial France. The chasubles bear figures of St. Louis as King and Crusader and Saints Peter and Paul. The copes are ornamented with the Holy Trinity and Christ the King, while their sides bear Fra Angelico angels with the proper gold background and are made more effective by the addition of heavy solid gold pendants on each garment. The shoulder-veil used by the subdeacon during a solemn high mass is graced by a group of Beuron angels in a blue background with the chalice and the sacred host being adored. The set was ordered through Mr. Theodore Kluth of New York, who was an authority on ecclesiastical art. In Europe the cost of making the set was $5,000, but it was valued at $10,000 in the United States in 1929.

The use of incense is a common practice during ecclesiastical functions. Aromatic gums of resinous trees are burned upon hot charcoal bricks in a brazier or thurible. Incense is used during processions, to honor sacred objects such as the altar, the gospel book, the eucharistic bread and wine, and the bodies of Christians both living and dead. It is a sign of prayer and a sign of sacrificial praise. Because of the sacred symbolism in the act of incensing, the thurible, the stand, and the incense boat are molded from precious metals with artistic carvings. Likewise other symbolic objects artistically adorn the church. A vigil light burns perpetually before the tabernacle signaling the eucharistic presence, votive candles, lit by members of the congregation, prolong prayers of petition, and the stations of the cross provide visual reenactment of Jesus Christ's final hours culminating in his death on the cross and burial. Devotion to Christ's passion began in patristic antiquity and continued throughout the Middle Ages. Since all Christians were not able to make a pilgrimage to the Holy Land, the erection of shrines, featuring Christ condemned, tortured, and crucified, became commonplace throughout Europe. The current number of fourteen stations of the *Way of the Cross* first appeared in Holland and Belgium in the sixteenth century. Because of the promotional insistence of Leonard of Port Maurice, a Franciscan, the papacy made the fourteen Stations of the Cross standard practice in the eighteenth century.

The interior of a large Catholic Church in America not only accommodates but also educates with the installation and use of its furniture and appointments. As one stands in the center aisle of St. Louis Church, a panorama fills one's eyes. Besides those items which have already been described, the view shows two hundred and seventy-five wooden pews, four decorative chapels, a vast marble communion rail, wooden and marble statuary, a towering hand carved pulpit, artistic symbolic paintings on the walls of the triforium, beautiful rood screens, confessional boxes, and a baptismal font. In cathedrals and basilicas one finds radiating chapels around the rear of the main altar accessed by an ambulatory pathway. In each of these places of worship is a separate altar. According to Canon Law a chapel or an oratory is reserved for the benefit of some particular assembly of the faithful whereas the church itself is open to the gathering of all worshippers. In imitation of a cathedral or basilica, St. Louis Church provides its congregation with four chapels, called side altars, for specific forms of devotion. In the naves one finds the chapel of St. Joseph on the left and the chapel of the Pieta on the right. Again the artists show balance. Joseph is the non-biological father of Jesus and Mary is the mother conceived by the Holy Spirit. The concept of the Pieta, the Blessed Virgin Mary holding her son, Jesus Christ, in her arms as he was brought down from the cross, is attributed to a Rheinland Dominican mystic, Henry Suso, about 1323. It was Michaelangelo, however, who gave the Pieta universal attention by his marble sculpture of Mary cradling the crucified body of her Son which is on display in St. Peter's Basilica in the Vatican at Rome.

The two chapels flanking the main altar display artistic balance. That of the Sacred Heart of Jesus is on the left and that of the Immaculate Heart of Mary is on the right. Both altars are identical in background screening, gothic rib-work, tri-pinnacle niches, angeled gablets, and electrical sconces. Statuary of the Sacred Heart is flanked by St. Thomas Aquinas on the left and St. Aloysius Gonzaga on the right while that of the Immaculate Heart is flanked by St. Charles Borromeo on the left and St. John, the Apostle, on the right. Across both of these altars and the main altar, distinguishing the sanctuary from the body of the church is a beautiful marble communion rail, the concept of which has vast historical significance. From the time of St. Paul, Christians understood that to share in the bread and the cup of the Lord's supper was to share in his body and blood. Through the Eucharist they had communion with the Lord and with each other. These were likewise the theological teachings of Saints Ambrose and

Augustine in the second century and continued as long as the Roman Empire existed. The barbarian invasions, however, devastated the religious, cultural, and sociopolitical world known to them. Theological controversies of the Middle Ages brought an attitude of extreme realism regarding the elements of bread and wine. As a consequence, the laity, being unable to understand the philosophy behind the controversies and not being well taught by the clergy, brought great adoration to the Real Presence of Jesus in these elements but developed a deep sense of unworthiness to receive the Eucharist. At the Fourth Lateran Council in 1215, Pope Innocent III, demanded that all Catholics receive Communion at least once a year during the Easter season; and, that since Christ is present in the entirety of his being under each form of the Eucharist, bread or wine, Catholics were required to receive only the host at communion. The Council of Trent (1545-63) reaffirmed this commandment of the Church.

Catholics henceforth, rarely met at the communion rail, and when they did it was in fear and trepidation. They, however, piously and multitudinously attended processions and Benediction of the Blessed Sacrament, but their ignorance and superstition became a constant pastoral problem for the clergy. Along with the decrease in reception, stories of the existence of miraculous hosts and wine flourished. People ran from church to church to be there when the host was raised at the consecration while at the same time failing to understand the Mass as a sacrifice. They believed that looking upon the elevated host preserved their youthfulness. The clergy built huge tabernacles to house hosts needed for distribution to the sick because only at death was communion gravely desired. Renewal and a change in attitude began to prevail late in the nineteenth and early in the twentieth centuries.

Pope Pius X encouraged early and more frequent communion and modified the liturgy. First Communion was allowed for children who had attained six years of age rather than waiting until they were at least thirteen. Fasting from midnight before the reception of communion on the same day, a rule in effect since the fourth century, resulted in attendance at Mass at an early hour. To foster education in the reception of communion children in Catholic schools, accompanied by their teachers, attended as a body at a specified Mass on Sundays. They formed a communion procession and went in an orderly fashion to the altar rail where they received the host on their tongues. The faithful attending the same Mass followed in suit. Although each parish had several fraternal societies which required their members to attend annual or monthly communions followed by an elaborate breakfast, the general congregation was more enthusiastic with participating in adoration of the host at Holy Hours, Benediction, First Fridays, and Holy Thursday's church visitations. Until the end of the Second Vatican Council (1962-1965), however, the communion rail was not only the barrier between the sacred and the banal, it was the place where, for more than four hundred years, the twain reluctantly met.

The confessional is an ornate place where the priest and penitent celebrate the Sacrament of Penance, which since the Second Vatican council has been named the Sacrament of Reconciliation. Confessionals as they are seen at St. Louis Church began in Milan in the sixteenth century initiated by Charles Borromeo. The Council of Trent mandated them. Two confessionals are found in the left side of the transept and two more are found in its right side. They are of gothic styled pinnacles with spires covered with crockets. Edward M. Hager and Sons created all four at a cost of $1,257. High above the confessionals, below the rose windows in the transept are four fresco paintings of the evangelists, Matthew, Mark, Luke and John. In other sections of the triforium of the transept and the nave symbolic paintings of a repetitive nature are systematically placed below the windows of the clerestory. Objects such as chalices, angels, crosses, banners, ciboriums, commandments, flowers, candles, and tabernacles are representative of rituals and rites of the Old and New Testaments. Below the windows in the apse, one finds a series of seven painted eucharistic emblems. From left to right they are The Lamb of God, The Cross and Crown, The Cross and Wheat, The Cross and IHS, the Cross and Grapes, The Cross and the Ten Commandments, and a large Pelican with its young. The series is pregnant with educational ramifications. IHS, for example, is a Christian inscription found frequently in art. The initials are a compression of the Greek word for Jesus; Iota, Eta, and Sigma. The Sigma, Omicron, and Psi of the SU in Jesus are omitted in the symbolic art. The church also has a most ornate baptismal font located in the left transept in front of the larger than life statues of St. Anthony of Padua and St. Francis of Assisi. This bapistry is situated within the church, can easily be seen by the faithful, is large enough to accommodate the faithful, and holds an honored place where one can be conveniently reborn with water and the Holy Spirit.

*I*n St. Louis Church, the pulpit, placed one-third the distance into the nave from the sanctuary, is a huge structure made in wood and contains beautiful carvings of Matthew, Mark, Luke, and John along with the imagery of the Book of Revelations which symbolizes each of them in terms of the four living beings: the lion, the ox, the man, and the eagle. In between the seated evangelists are carved niches that feature small standing figures of the Fathers and Doctors of the Church. In the early days of the church in the Mediterranean World, the pulpit was a place from which litanies were sung, the scriptures proclaimed, and diptychs read. Diptychs were panels of wood from which were read the names of Christians, dead or alive, who were to be included in the eucharistic prayer. Each year from the pulpit, the *Exultet*, the Easter proclamation that Christ had risen and he would die no more, was proclaimed. Each Sunday from the pulpit, the gospels were read in the vernacular followed by a sermon given by the priest, who was either the celebrant of the Mass, a visiting clerical missionary, or an

ecclesiastical dignitary.

*T*he pulpit at St. Louis Church was one of the many artistic accomplishments which came from a planing mill located at Elm and Clinton Streets, whose artistic productions had adorned a vast number of churches, theaters, and homes in Buffalo and throughout the United States. It was owned and operated by Edward M. Hager and his sons, and had begun in 1883 when he formed a partnership with John Feist and Ralph Clark. Before these three joined hands in business, Hager had been in the carpenter-construction business on Mortimer Street since 1868. He was born at Blieskastel, Alsace, April 18, 1842 and immigrated to America in 1854 with his brother, August John Hager. Edward M. Hager enlisted as a private in the 68th New York Regiment, at Hudson, New York, on August 14, 1861, four months after Fort Sumter surrendered to the Confederates initiating the Civil War. After four years of service, he was discharged with the rank of sergeant. Clark retired from the partnership in 1887; it then became known as Hager and Feist. Both men were members of St. Louis Church, but Feist, unlike Hager, was born in Buffalo in 1843. In 1894, Feist sold his interest in the business to Hager, whose sons had become of age, had fulfilled their apprenticeship, and were ready to become his partners. When the pulpit was completed it was donated to St. Louis Church by Hager and his sons. In the meantime, Feist had set up his own planing mill on Ash Street, and continued with his profession as a contractor and builder. Both Feist and Hager, operating from their separate companies, contributed to the construction of many of the palatial buildings of the Pan American Exposition. These were made of wood and then sculptured in plaster to resemble stone edifices.

*B*efore Hager constructed and hand carved the pulpit he approached Schickel and Ditmar to obtain a set of plans which would be architecturally sound but fashioned on Old World models. After his company manufactured this masterpiece, he presented it to the church as a permanent memorial to his family. The trustees of St. Louis Church were so pleased with the gift that they donated the hand carved pulpit that was in the church since 1890, and was a thing of beauty unto itself, to Corpus Christi Church at 189 Clark Street. In 1968, in celebration of E.M. Hager and Sons Company's one hundredth anniversary, brochures were published lauding its past works and stating that such work was done by employees who had been hired because they were craftsmen and artisans of the highest skill. In the early 1900's one of those craftsmen was Leopold Schneggenburger who was born in 1878 in the Schwarzwald of Wuerttemberg, Germany, and came to the United States in 1895. He was a master carver who had done his apprenticeship in Wuerttemberg and had learned well the art of designing and carving in maple, ash, oak, and cherry. Although he owned a small studio on Pine Street, he found excellent financial opportunities working at E.M. Hager and Sons and at Schmitt's Buffalo Sculptures. As such, he did much of the carving on the pulpit donated by the Hager family to St. Louis Church and on the two statues of St. Anthony and St. Francis of Assisi. He also was responsible for the large Boar carved for the Pan American Exposition. Throughout Europe, young artisans and apprentices, such as the twenty-four year old Leopold, did their work carefully and with great heart, but received little credit for doing it. Several, however, carved surreptitiously a symbol of themselves in their work so that future generations might find it, and know what they had achieved. Maybe if one does some investigative work on the pulpit at St. Louis Church, they may find LSCH inscribed somewhere on it. This is how Leopold Schneggenburger signed his work.

On the lower right side of the chapel of the Immaculate Heart of Mary, one observes a most beautiful painting on cloth. It is a replica of Our Lady of Aglona, Latvia. It was donated and installed by the Latvian refugees who were brought to the United States and to Buffalo, New York, by the Catholic Charities of the diocese. These refugees were taken under the wing of Father Howard J. Schwartz who was pastor of St. Louis Church from 1948 until 1964. He and the trustees sponsored them and gave them succor. Father Albert J. Bosack, then an assistant to Schwartz and now retired, fondly remembers the devotion of refugees such as Anthony and Marion Jubulis, Maria Kudins, and Anthony Ozolins, and several others who after enjoying their first taste of freedom in America donated the replica of Mary holding her child, Jesus, in her arms. Schwartz dedicated the painting and installed it in St. Louis Church in the presence of the Latvian congregation on August 12, 1962. The original painting which is on display in the church of Aglona, Latvia, came from the Orient in 50 AD. It was painted on the back of oak panels. The subjects' clothes were carved in silver and covered with gold; real jewels were in the crowns of the Madonna and her Child. The Latvians carried the icon into battle and for four hundred years it was claimed to have protected the land. Outside the church in which the icon rested was a spring in which many of those who washed were allegedly cured.

The Latvian Catholics, however, had a hard life. Christianity came to the country with the invasion and domination of the Teutonic Knights, who were veterans of the crusades, late in the twelfth century. In 1795 Russia conquered the country. By the end of World War I, while the nation enjoyed freedom, twenty-four percent of the country was Catholic, and a concordat was signed with the Holy See in 1922. In 1940, however, the Soviets occupied Latvia, Lithuania, and Estonia, bringing an atheistic motif to the country. Churches were closed, public prayer was forbidden, and icons were destroyed. The German Nazis took the territory away from the Soviets in 1941. The Soviets, however, returned in 1944; one-third of the number of priests were deported or killed, and again a campaign against religious freedom flared up. Once more, churches were closed and Christian feasts were replaced by secular holidays. Many Latvians seized any opportunity to leave. First they escaped to Dresden, Germany, from which they entered into West Germany which was under the supervision of France, England, and the United States. The remnants of this band of freedom seekers and their descendants are still parishioners of St. Louis Church even though their residences are scattered far and wide.

*T*here are two hundred and seventy-five pews in St. Louis Church sufficient to seat one thousand six hundred and fifty people. It is estimated, however, that approximately two thousand could be accommodated for Mass on a special occasion with standing room only as a last recourse. Every pew has a kneeler upon which one assumes a posture for prayer that emphasizes adoration of God and the presence of Christ in the Eucharist. Attitudes of penitence and humiliation are also associated with kneeling. All humble adorers, however, need a soft landing. In St. Louis Church, sponge material covered with red fabric forms a soft landing place for the knees of the members of the congregation. At present these are the same cushions which were installed more than fifty years ago. Although they show their age, they are still functional and are a credit to the artisan who made them.

*E*ugene W. Miller Sr. designed and constructed them in his shop, Niagara Trailer, at 682 Genesee Street. Miller used materials and equipment that were used in the fabrication of seats for wagons, trucks, and trailers. He had been in this line of work since he graduated from St. Louis School in 1917 after finishing two years of post grammar school under the tutelage of the Brothers of the Christian Schools. After graduation, he immediately went to work for Anthony Zimmermann who owned a wagon shop at 136-38 Northampton Street. In 1928, Miller became a partner of Zimmermann. Together they were well known as the producers of Hall Bakery's, yellow painted, horse driven, low centered wagons. One of their wagons was

the first to cross the newly opened Peace Bridge in 1927. On its rear panel it carried the logo *Gold Prize Bread* because in 1922 the bakery had won first prize in national competition for the best baked bread in America. In 1947, Ernie Gross, a reporter for the *Buffalo Evening News*, concerning the horse-and-buggy days of bygone memories, interviewed Miller. Besides discussing the wagons made for Hall Bakery, Miller boasted of the wagons sold to others in Albany, Cleveland, Detroit, and Denver in the United States as well as to the Neal's Baking Company in Windsor and St. Thomas, Ontario, Canada. Eugene W. Miller Sr. was a direct descendant of Nicholas Miller Sr., his great-grandfather, who was one of the original parishioners of the Lamb of God Church. [5]

*S*ince the completion of the new gothic structure in 1889, St. Louis Church has taken great pride in its ability to fill the space between its walls with colorful, emotional, and broad timbre of mellow and warm music both instrumental and vocal during its ecclesiastical exercises. During the past one hundred and seventy-five years, the history of the church's organ and choir have been intricately interwoven. As a first step in reviewing this history, one needs to confront the circulation of the mythical legend that the organ in the present church is the same one that entertained thousands of attendees of the Temple of Music at the Pan American Exposition at Buffalo, New York, in 1901. The legend began with the authors of *The St. Louis Bazaar Herald* in 1900. The huge organ scheduled to be played in the Temple of Music was in construction by the company of Emmons Howard and Sons, Westfield, Massachusetts. It was a mammoth organ of tubular pneumatic action with four manuals or keyboards for the hands and pedals for the feet, blown by five different wind pressures, carried four miles of tubing, and operated by three of the largest sized Spencer water engines. It was thirty-four feet wide, eighteen feet deep, and thirty-two feet high, and assembled in Buffalo with a starting date of May 2, 1901.

On the dedication day of the Exposition, May 20, 1901, it was to be first played in concert by a world celebrated organist at the turn of the century, Frederic K. Archer. During the duration of yearlong festivities, besides Archer, nearly two hundred other musical artists from Maine to California and from Florida to Oregon, made applications to have the privilege of playing the majestic instrument. On September 24, 1900, however, *The St. Louis Bazaar Herald* congratulated the congregation of their church for having purchased the organ, a drawing of which appeared in the *Catholic Union and Times* with an article about it on the same day. Through the encouragement and efforts of Father John J. Sheahan, the organ, following the close of the Exposition, was to be installed in the choir loft of St. Louis Church. This never happened. Mr. J.N. Adam, of J.N. Adams Company, became the owner of the organ and donated it to the City of Buffalo provided that a suitable home for it could be found. It was so large that it would never have fit into St. Louis Church's choir loft. Simon Fleischman of the City Council announced on November 4, 1901 that, if Convention Music Hall on Virginia Street could be prepared, the organ would be installed there.

In early February, 1901, after Mr. Emmons Howard came to Buffalo from Massachusetts and visited with the trustees and Father Hoelscher, the trustees knew that it was impossible to provide the required thirty-four feet nine inches width and twelve foot depth in the organ loft with an added six square foot area for the console, pedals, and organ seat so as to accommodate the mammoth organ. They then decided, however, to replace the Garret House organ which had been first played in the church on August 25, 1889, and was still intact. They first made a study of the history of organs in St. Louis Church following the demise of the reed organ that Father Mertz reluctantly allowed in the Lamb of God Church. They discovered that for twenty years beginning in 1843, the second church used an old pipe organ. In 1863, it was sold and installed in St. Paul's

Church, Rochester, New York. In 1903, when a new St. Paul's Church was built, it was once again sold and reinstalled in Holy Trinity Church, Webster, New York. Looking further into their records, the trustees found that on February 2, 1863, St. Louis Church had asked for bids on another organ from the firms of Schwab, Koehnken, and Company and from Wilhelm Mohr Company. Although Mohr's bid was lower than Koehnken's, a purchase was made with the latter. Koehnken, a company that had been in existence from 1861 until 1890, had its office and factory in Cincinnati, Ohio. The music director, Mr. Kemmer, first played the organ in the church; it perished in the great conflagration of 1885. Following that disaster, the trustees provided the church with an interim organ purchased from a Buffalo firm, Garret House. Since the church could not accommodate the Temple of Music organ, the trustees looked for an alternative.

In March 1901, the trustees called upon Schickel and Ditmar, the architects of the gothic church, at their New York City offices. The trustees asked them to design the choir loft so that an organ properly sized for the acoustics of the church would have sufficient room to fit within the space. The trustees then asked Father Hoelscher to communicate directly with Schickel and Ditmar; and, whatever they agreed upon, it would be automatically acceptable to and approved by the trustees. On March 11, the trustees met again and appointed their attorney, Anthony Roty, to contact Emmons Howard and inform him that the church wished to be released from accepting the mammoth organ scheduled for the Temple of Music once the Exposition was over. One year later the trustees made negotiations with Mueller and Abel, organ builders in New York City, to fill the floor plan devised by Schickel and Ditmar, but did not wish the price to exceed $6,000 while including a wind power supply operated by electricity. Negotiations between the trustees and Mueller and Abel broke down during the summer because the company was in the throes of completing an organ, called opus fifty-six, which survives today at the German Zion

Evangelical Church at 125 Henry Street, Brooklyn, New York.

*N*ext the trustees approached the W.W. Kimball Company, Chicago, Illinois. It began building reed organs in 1880 and expanded to pipe organs about 1894. It continued to manufacture church and theater organs until 1942, when wartime shortages of materials forced them to close. Frank T. Milner, representative of the company wrote to Father Hoelscher on November 3, 1902, informing him that the company's offer would be to build and install a complete organ, to specifications agreed upon by all parties concerned and completed within six months, for the set blanket price of $7,000. It was to contain thirty stops with thirty-three ranks containing one thousand eight hundred and ten pipes, three manuals, and pedals. On November 12, the Board of Trustees of St. Louis Church met; and, with the consultation of John B. Singenberger, unanimously approved the contract. He had been Musikprofessor at the teacher's seminary at St. Francis, Wisconsin, and the founder of the *Caecilia Magazine* for priests, sisters, choirmasters, organists, singers, and school music supervisors in 1874.

*U*nder his watchful eyes and ears on the evening of November 24, 1903, the music from Kimball's organ was first heard resounding within the walls of St. Louis Church. The *Courier* reported the event on the following day. It read, "A local musical event of more than usual interest and importance took place last evening when a recital was given upon the new organ in St. Louis Church by Gaston M. Dethier of New York City. A large audience was present and the fine acoustics and beautiful interior added to the delight of the musical program. The instrument is a three manual one with thirty stops and many mechanical conveniences. Its voicing is most pleasing. The reeds are telling without being in the least rasping. The diapasons have the pure organ quality and the flutes are lovely and mellow in character. There is much

variety in the selection of stops and there is, therefore, chance for great diversity of combination. The action is excellent. The response of the organ is perfect, even in the most rapid work, and there is no blurring of tone."

*F*ollowing the concert, the participants and the members of audience mingled among each other. Mr. Dethier was praised for his work; it was most admirable in every point. With a technique of manual and pedal which was invariably clean, smooth, and facile; and, with a musicianly conception and inventive fancy that secured the most variegated and charming effects in tone color, his playing was absolutely satisfying. Besides playing several of the classics, Dethier played three of his own compositions, a barcarole, a scherzo, and a three-movement fantasy titled *Christmas*. The St. Louis Church choir under the direction of Ignatz P. Czerwinski, sang five numbers, the first one an unaccompanied anthem by Reverend L. Bonvin. It was written in excellent polyphonic style and it was well sung with good balance of voices and clean attacks. The male chorus sang an *O Salutaris*. The Postlude was Gounod's impressive *Marche Romaine*, played by Czerwinski. [6]

*I*n 1952, the Tellers Organ Company of Erie, Pennsylvania was contracted by the trustees through Stephen Po-Chedley and Son, its Buffalo office, to rebuild the Kimball organ. In its original construction it had tubular pneumatic actions; these were converted to electro-pneumatic action, the windchest pneumatic actions were recovered with leather, and a new console was installed. The organ was enlarged by eight ranks of pipes, giving it a new total of thirty-five stops. Once it was finished it contained two thousand two hundred and thirty pipes. For this work including parts, labor, and installation the cost was $10,500. On October 29, 1952, Louis H. Huybrechts, St. Louis Church's organist, played the rededication recital. He had become resident organist upon the resignation of Mary M. Zeinz, who replaced her father, Henry J. Zeinz, who had served in that capacity for thirty-three years beginning in 1911. Otto A. Singenberger had preceded him for one year following the tenure of Professor Ignatz Czerwinski whom had played the organ and directed the choir from 1889 until his death in 1910.

*I*gnatz Czerwinski was born at Strelnau, a province of Posen, Prussia, on January 31, 1859. He attended primary school at Strelnau; and, upon completion, he went to Warsaw, Poland, where he began study in piano, violin, and organ. On September 29, 1876, he came to America, proceeded to Cincinnati, Ohio, where he received instructions in musical theory and directing from the noted maestro, Carl Barus. Upon finishing his instructions, Czerwinski spent four years teaching music at Portsmouth, Ohio. While teaching there, he acted as organist at St. Mary's Church and was director of the Saengerbund Maennerchor and the Opera House. Returning to

Cincinnati, he courted and married Carrie K. Merkel on May 27, 1884. Together they had four children, but unfortunately one, a son, died at childbirth. The three girls who grew to maturity were Elizabeth K., Helen J., and Antoinette. Each one found the deep musical trait of their father in their souls.

*O*n January 1, 1886 he and his family came to Buffalo where three years later he became the organist and choir master of St. Louis Church. Besides his musical activities at church, he was a member of the Buffalo Symphony Orchestra, a member of the Davidson Stringed Quartet, taught classes in piano, organ, and violin at Canisius College, and composed many musical works. While at St. Louis Church, his record was enviable; he missed only three Sundays at the organ in twenty-one years of service. He died May 5, 1910 and is buried in the United German and French Roman Catholic Cemetery, Lot forty-two, Section D.

The 1903 Kimball Organ

Antoinette Czerwinski, who was born at Portsmouth, Ohio, in 1885, graduated from St. Louis' school on June 27, 1900 with highest honors. While she was in her teens, she performed excellently at the piano during concerts given at the Catholic Institute. On July 4, 1909, she married Paul J. Batt, a young lawyer who later became a Supreme Court Judge. Together they had thirteen children. Following her father's death, she acted, for a short time as co-organist with Otto A. Singenberger at St. Louis Church. During this period, she was also the organist and music director at the Church of Our Lady of Perpetual Help at 115 O'Connell Street. In the late 1920's Mrs. Antoinette Czerwinski Batt organized the Canisius College choir. Elizabeth Czerwinski married John Steffan and had ten children. Helen Czerwinski married Joseph Clody. Family members have told that Helen held her wedding with Joseph very early in the morning at St. Louis Church because she did not want her young friends to know what an elderly man she was marrying. Although the couple enjoyed a beautiful life together, they had no children. Following his short stay at St. Louis Church, Otto A. Singenberger was editor of the *Caecilia Magazine* and professor of Gregorian Chant at St. Mary of the Lake Seminary, Munderlein, Illinois; Supervisor of Music, Milwaukee Parochial Schools; and Director of a choir composed of thousands of children at the Eucharistic Congress in 1929.

Louis H. Huybrechts was born near Antwerp in Belgium on August 18, 1911. His father was a church organist and choirmaster who allowed him to play his first concert at the church at the age of nine. Louis Huybrechts began his musical career at the Lemmens Institute of Liturgical Music in Malines, where he studied piano, organ, counterpoint, fugue, Gregorian chant, and composition. He graduated with the school's highest honor, the Lemmens Tinnel prize. Malines was a small area adjacent to Antwerp, Belgium, on the Dyle River. It was the cardinal primate seat of the country. In 1930, at the age of nineteen, he was chosen to play, before thousands of people, the new organ installed in the Antwep cathedral for the occasion of the World's Fair held there that year. He did post graduate study with Flor Peeters, a renowned Belgium composer in the early twentieth century. Huybrechts died at Pittsburgh, Pennsylvania, on January 3, 1973. His loss to the musical world as an organist, choral director, and composer brought many tears to the eyes of those who had enjoyed his concerts.

Leaving Peeters, he continued more advanced studies at the Royal Conservatory of music at Antwerp, where he earned first prize for his ability at the piano. During that time he was also organist of Christ the King Church in Antwerp, and performed regularly for the National Institute of Radio in Brussels. In 1951, he came to the United States. Before coming to St. Louis Church in 1952, he was organist and choirmaster at St. Francis Church, Petoskey, Michigan, where he met Mrs. Cecilia Gordon a resident of Buffalo who was visiting in Michigan. Through her he made the contacts which led to his position at St. Louis Church. He left Buffalo in 1954, prior to the one hundred and twenty-fifth anniversary of the birth of the parish, because he was dissatisfied with the operation of the revised Kimball Organ and its use in the church. His recommended alterations, which he discussed at length with the trustees, fell on deaf ears. They felt that the cost of carrying out his suggestions was excessive. From Buffalo, Huybrechts went on to Sacred Heart Cathedral in Rochester, New York, but subsequently moved his talents to Duquesne University and Sacred Heart Church, Pittsburgh, Pennsylvania, where he stayed, composing works for organ used in liturgical services until his death.

When he left, Joseph Kurzdorfer, who quickly reorganized the choir replaced him. On September 1, 1954, the choir bound itself together under the title of St. Louis Church Choir Society. Its mission was to perform the solemn services according to the rubrics of the Catholic Church. In order to sing in the choir one had to be a member and conform to the rules of membership, which were principally mandatory presence at all High Masses on Sundays and at all rehearsals called by the choirmaster. If a member could not attend because of very pressing life interruptions, prior permission to be absent was required. As was the custom with societies, officers were elected by the members and approved by the choirmaster. In 1954 Joseph Koch was president, Louis Haas was vice-president, Gertrude Zeinz was secretary, and Fred Hardick was treasurer. There were thirty-eight active members who were musical lovers, devoted achievers in true pitch and harmony, and desirous to emotionally move themselves and the congregation by rendering as perfectly as possible a liturgical composition. All through history some form of vocal music was integrated into the liturgy. Before he died in 1914, Pope Pius X issued various instructions that, in principle, held music as an integral part of worship and urged the participation of the people in the liturgy. He reiterated, however, the ban against use of the vernacular in the liturgy but allowed it for devotional activities. At Midnight Mass on Christmas Eve, as the statue of the baby Jesus was brought forth in procession to be placed into the crib, prior to Mass, the choir traditionally sang *Silent Night, Holy Night* in German.

Following the instructions of Pius X, the St. Louis Church choir regularly prepared and practiced singing in four part harmony the triform *Kyrie-Christe Eleison* sequence, the *Gloria in Excelsis Deo, Sanctus, Sanctus, Sanctus*, the Great *Amen*, the triform *Agnus Dei*, and various interim responses to the priest throughout the Mass. In order to achieve their goal the choir utilized sopranos, altos, tenors, and basses. The sopranos in the St. Louis Church choir were all women, their treble voices covered two or more octaves above middle C. In 1954 they were: Teresa Abel, Ruta Abrickis, Diane Bradford, Anna Buchheit, Dorothy Gentsch, Marguerite Haas, Ruth Kolb, Betty Lochner, Loretta Meisreimer, Marie Meisreimer, Joan Rott, Lucy Spogis, and Anne Strigl. In choirs associated with concert performances alto voices can reach the high accented octave and belong to some male voices, but can also be achieved by female voices that are in a range lower than the sopranos. Church choirs, which have more women than men, usually rely upon females for the alto section. This practice was followed at St. Louis Church.

Joining the sopranos, the altos were: Brijita Abrickis, Rose Buchheit, Louise Haas, Frances Heitzman, Marian LaBarge, Noreen Lesile, Berta Michel, Mary Strigl, and Gertrude Zeinz. A tenor is the highest male voice, except falsetto, having a compass between the first C below middle C and the first C above middle C. The men who accompanied the above group of women as tenors were: Frank Delgado, Anthony Kaiser, Joseph Koch, Antons Mikulis, and John Piscitello. Finally to complete the choir, the group needed the bass voice, which is the lowest one in harmonic or polyphonic music. A good bass has a compass from E to e´ on the scale of pitch which is audible to the ear. Joining the others this group was Paul Buchheit, Fred Hardick, Howard Lamm, and Edward Simon. Besides these members listed above, the choir listed seven passive members: Olive Doll, May Graney, Sophia Hoffman, Mary Koch, Catherine Maguire, Edward Stratameyer, and Helen Wynn. This group continued intact throughout the 1950's and early 1960's; and they together with the proficiently played Kimball Organ, filled the nave, transept, and sanctuary of the church with the language of sound which expressed deep feelings. The words of their music were tones and chords, the sentences were melodies and harmonic sequences, the stories were songs, hymns, psalms, dances, and fugues, and the books and essays were suites, sonatas, arias, toccatas, and choral preludes. All of which were performed with indescribable grandeur and brilliance.

On March 1, 1954, Father Howard Schwartz, pastor of St. Louis Church, announced that the Board of Trustees had accepted the application of Joseph

Kurzdorfer to succeed Louis Huybrechts as organist and choirmaster at the church. Before coming to St. Louis Church, Kurzdorfer had studied organ and piano under Leon Trick, respected pianist in Buffalo, developed the ability to direct choir voices from John J. Ball, a well known operatic teacher in New York City, and learned harmony, theory, and composition of music at the University of Chicago. For thirteen years, prior to making his application to the trustees, Kurzdorfer had been organist and choirmaster at St. Boniface Church located at 124 Locust Street in Buffalo. He loved music so much that he made it his profession, hobby, recreation, and relaxation. He was an excellent choice to replace Huybrechts who was not a happy man playing and directing in the choir loft of the church. Huybrechts' good friend and admirer, Hans Vigeland, described him as a brilliant organ player but a total misfit in Buffalo. Vigeland was his contemporary in Buffalo as the organist and choirmaster at Westminster Presbyterian Church from 1949 to 1976. While fulfilling his obligations at the church he was also director of music at the Buffalo Seminary from 1954 to 1970.

The W.W. Kimball organ has been made ready for its debut into the twenty-first century and for the one hundred and seventy-fifth anniversary celebration of the founding of St. Louis Church and the beginning of Catholicism in Buffalo by the hands, mind, heart, and soul of William Kurzdorfer, organ specialist and curator. He was born in Buffalo in 1944, the son of Vincent Kurzdorfer and Florence Stephen. Florence's family members were residents of Lancaster, New York, and Vincent's family members were parishioners of St. Mary Magdalene's Church, founded in 1899 at 1327 Fillmore Avenue. Vincent's brother was Joseph Kurzdorfer who was organist at St. Boniface's Church in the Fruit Belt for thirteen years before replacing Louis Huybrechts at St. Louis Church in 1954. When William Kurzdorfer was thirteen years old, he studied music and the art of playing the organ under the tutelage of his uncle, Joseph Kurzdorfer, whom allowed

him at a very early age to play the Kimball organ. In 1962, William took a position with Po-Chedley and Son as a pipe organ technician. This company had been the local representative of the Tellers Organ Company of Erie, Pennsylvania, which updated the Kimball Organ in 1952. He worked there until 1969, during which time he had attended electrician adult education classes in Buffalo's public school system. In 1967, while still working for Po-Chedley, he became an organist with St. Boniface's Church and voluntarily rebuilt its organ. News of his success at revitalizing that organ spread by word-of-mouth throughout the city's church population.

From 1969 until 1974 he was in demand by several others for organ repair. In this latter year he received his Master Electrician's license and took a permanent job as electrician at the University of Buffalo, mainly working at the present south campus. He remained there until he retired in 1999. In 1971, he took over the maintenance of the Kimball Organ at St. Louis Church. For him it was an opportunity to fulfill a life-long desire, but it came by default because the trustees did not feel that they had sufficient funds to hire a full time person. William served pro-gratis for the next ten years. In 1981, he was able to convince the pastor, Father William A. Schwinger, that the church needed to spend some money to repair the bellows. Schwinger followed his suggestion and paid a contractor $5,800 to re-leather the bellows; the job, however, was not satisfactory. The organ needed much more attention; and, although still working full time at the University of Buffalo, William began to rebuild and update it. His labor of love consumed all his spare moments from 1987 until 1992. When he felt that he had satisfied himself as to what the final state of the organ should be with added stops and ranks, it had a total of two thousand six hundred pipes. From that time on, as a volunteer, he assumed the position of curator of the organ and organist at some of the Masses on weekends. Once he was asked, "Why do you donate your services like this to the church?" He replied, "For me this is a labor-of-love because I was only thirteen years old when I first played this

Kimball Organ. My uncle taught me my music in this church. To me the organ is one of its kind, it is one of the very few operating organs left in the city since the time of my youth." [7]

St. Louis Church Choir 1929. Left to right, 1st row: D. Stressinger, H. Reisch, E. Mischka, Henry Zeinz (Director and Organist), F. Mingen, F. Mayer, V. Blassser, M. Dehlinger. 2nd row: E. Albert, D. Didley, M. Jerge, I. Zeder, M. Zeinz, F. Steffan, M. Steffan, J. Baecher, A. Strig, A. Dentinger, M. Maguire, P. Albert. 3rd row: J. Steffan, L. Meisreimer, G. Steffan, B. Warner, M.J. Steffan, M.H. Zeinz, M. Strigl, M. Gottstein, B. Lochner, M.G. Buchheit. 4th frow: J. Bruss, H.Hacker, R. Kolb, M. Meisreimer, M. Shannon, G. Jordan, M.G. Smith, M. Koch, R. Buchheit. 5th row: P. Buchheit, J. Juenker, E. Huber, E. Biesinger, E. Simon. A. Sherer, J. Steggan, F. Ernewein.

REFERENCES AND NOTES ✤ CHAPTER TEN

1. This section opens with concepts from the *Dogmatic Constitution of the Church, no. 23.* In order, for definitions of Catholicism, Catholicism and culture, Catholicism and architecture, gothic style, and gothic spirituality see: op. cit. *Encyclopedia of Catholicism*, pps., 993, 256-57, 261-62, 258-261, 575-6. For an extended account of Romanesque and gothic architecture see: op. cit., *World's Popular Encyclopedia*, vol. 1. Architecture is the art of building and the planning of a structure with its harmonious arrangement and ornamentation according to definite principles. It is a work of beauty and grandeur. With a choice of materials taken from the earth such as wood, stone, clay, and iron, one begins the art and application of these principles. Beginnings of known periods of architecture are: Egyptian (3000BC), Assyrian (800BC), Persian (500BC), Ionic, Doric, and Corinthian styles of the Greek (400BC), Etruscan and Roman (200 BC), Byzantine (500AD), Christian and Romanesque (800AD), Mohammedan (900AD), Indian (1000AD), Gothic (1150 AD), and Modern (1800AD). A building is essentially a structure of walls with a roof. It has to be built upon soil known as loam that consists of a friable mixture of varying proportions of clay, sand, and organic matter. St. Louis Church is constructed upon a sandy loam. Its foundations and walls are made of stone and brick. Natural dimensional stone has been used in the construction of St. Louis Church. The forms of natural stone are granite, marble, limestone, sandstone, and slate. The footings and foundations in the St. Louis Church are of Yammerthal stone (or Jammerthal; this term is explained elsewhere), a form of granite with a very high compressive strength. The outside walls of the church are faced with Medina sandstone. They are bearing walls and support a vertical load as well as their own weight. St. Louis Church being a form of gothic architecture has within its design the use of structural and artistic terminologies which are: buttress, clerestory, triforium, gallery, bay, mullion, jamb, tympanum, capital, pillar, cornice, entablature, arches which are rounded, pointed, or trefoiled, aisle, transept, foliage, gable, pinnacle, gablet, finial, tracery, crockets, corbeled cornice, apse and apsis, wainscoting, frieze, architrave, and chancel. *Buttress* is a structure of masonry projecting from the face of a wall, either to strengthen it or to resist the thrust of an arch, roof, or wall against which it abuts. St. Louis Church has buttresses that are of the *Orton-on-the-Hill* type that came into existence in England about 1330; *clerestory* is the upper wall of the nave or gallery of a room. In a gothic structure such as St. Louis Church the gallery is mainly open space between the pillars. Although open, however, the area between the pillars is called the nave and it contains stained glass windows; *triforium* is the plastered wall that remains in the gallery above the pier arches but below the clerestory. It carries designs painted upon it; *bay* is a term used for a space for a window with its usual setting of framing and jambs; *mullion* is the main upright and horizontal member separating sections of a window or screen, usually of decorative design, and it sometimes forms an arch-like division; *jamb* is a term used for the upright piece forming the side of an opening such as a door or window; *tympanum* is a space within an arch, and above a lintel or a subordinate arch, usually recessed; *capital* is a separate stone piece forming the uppermost part of a column. In Greek architecture an *architrave*, is a heavy beam placed on top of the *capital* connecting a set of pillars. In gothic architecture the *architrave* is replaced by archwork; *cornice* is a projection from the face of the wall. It is a load bearing structure usually very ornate. Outside the building one usually finds a *buttress* which will carry the horizontal load placed on the wall at the *cornice*. The vertical load is distributed down a set of stone moldings know as *friezes* which terminate at the *capital* of a pillar; *entablature* is the three part ribbing which carries the weight of the roof to the *cornice*; *arches* in a gothic church are usually roof arches and are of the pointed type; an *aisle* in a gothic church refers to the space in the *nave* between the pillars known as the center aisle or to the space in the sections outside the *nave* known as the *side aisles*; *transept* is the open space of the gothic cruciform church which intersects the nave at a right angle and is the same height as the nave; *foliage* is the art work of fruit or leaves carved in stone or wood; *gable* is a decorative member having the shape of a triangle usually above an arch or doorway; *pinnacle* is a member made of stone or wood usually ending in a small spire on a buttress or a pier; *gablet* is a small gable springing from a buttress and terminating in a foliage finial; *finial* is the ornament that forms the upper extremity of a pinnacle or gable; *tracery* is any artistic scrolling found within the windows, gables, doors, or vaulting; *corbel* is a projection from the face of a wall supporting a weight usually associated with a type of cornice called a *corbled cornice*; *crocket* is an ornamental swirl of foliage usually located on the sloping edge of a gable or spire; *apse* is the name given to the polygonal section of the sanctuary with an *apsis* which is the point at which the distance from the center of the apse is the greatest. St. Louis Church has an apse which is half of a decagon with the main marble altar located at its center; *wainscoting* refers to the fine grade of oak used for the woodwork lining of an interior wall usually at the lower section of the wall separated from the top by decorative molding. In St. Louis Church wainscoting is prominent in the walls of the side aisles and in the vestibules of the three towers leading to the portals on Main Street. The *chancel* in St. Louis Church includes the two areas flanking the arches of the nave that is part of the sanctuary. These areas could be considered as vestibules of the sanctuary; and, historically, were reserved for the use of the clergy. In some churches the chancel includes the choir and the sanctuary. The following is a summary of the contracts given out between 1885 and 1889 for construction and decorating of St. Louis' gothic church as presented in op. cit. *St. Louis Commandery 204*, Elmwood Music Hall, October 27, 1925. "William Schickel, 2.5% commission on all contracts, $6,642.00; George J. Metzger, 1.5% for superintending the construction of the building, $3,964. 46; Edward M. Hager, building the temporary church, $5,068,58; George Nachtreib, for tearing down the old church, clearing the site, $2,150.00; John Druar, for constructing the foundation, $15,186.00; William D. Collingwood, $127,938.54; New England Granite Co., for granite columns,

$6,308.00; Jacob Ginther, for 16 cast iron columns in basement, $325.00; H.C. Harrower, for wrought iron beams and girders in basement of the church, extra channels, winding stairs, railings and accessories in towers of the church, wire grates and tower guards, ladders, crane, and changes in railing, $3,245.35; J.J. Spurr, for brown stone windows in transept, tower, and interior bases and for granite columns, $6,009.00; Edward M. Hager, for furnishing all joists, timber, and flooring in the auditorium of new church, $1,848.50; Clark, Hager, and Feist, for furnishing good window frames in body of the church, $2,434.00; Edward M. Hager, for roof, gallery, slating complete, $13,850.00; Hager and Feist, for all wood forming and groining preparatory to plastering, 53 bevel guards on window frames, laying floor and setting temporary doors and steps and windows in basement, towers, roof; and, elsewhere, for screens and extra on groining, $13,168.21; John Gisel, to lay tile sewer in churchyard with connections, $400.00; Machwirth Brothers, to set copper gutters and all other trim needs, $626.21; Joseph Foerster of New York City, for furnishing ten copper conductor heads, $340.00; Charles Berrick, for work on the walls and tower of the church, setting brown stone bases, two brick piers, cutting bases, setting rose windows, interest on notes with extra on tower and foundation of rear steps, $32,995.21; Byrne and Bannister, contract to plaster, to furnish all ornaments and stucco work, remove brick wall, and other masonry, change niches, change main hall, and thirty days modeler's service, $6,222.96; Ferdinand J. Riester, contract to furnish and set all the plain glass and architectural glass, and 24 ventilators, $8,513.00; Charles F. Chretien and Brothers, contract to tint and gilt entire inside of church, painting window frames, repairs, painting, and tinting, $2,325.52; Nason and Hay, contract to furnish and lay tiling in vestibule, $352.00; Lautz and Co., for marble wainscoting, and two marble platforms, $1,393.00; Granacher and Co., for pews, extra for partitions, extra for pew ends, interest on note, and repairs, $4,257.00; Irlbacker and Davis, hot water heating apparatus, gas pipe and fitting, and plumbing, $5,565.74; Metz and Meyer, for quarter-cut white oak wainscoting for gallery front doors, transoms over doors, interest on note, contract for two doors, jambs and casings, $7,357.40. The final sum of all the contracts was $278,485.68." For biographical material concerning Elbridge Gerry Spaulding see: *Western New York Heritage*, Buffalo, New York, Spring 2002, Vol. 5., No.2, pp. 32-5.

2. In St. Louis Church there are forty-six full-length windows and two large rose windows, one of the latter at each end of the transept. The tall windows are apportioned as follows: seven in the apse of the sanctuary, far above the high altar; six are in each side aisle's wall at an elevation above eye level with two more in the chancel; seven on each side of the clerestory in the nave; eight in the transept; and three on the Main Street side at the rear of the organ loft. The rose windows are exquisitely beautiful circular windows, filled with rich tracery. Their beauty derives from the intricacy of that tracery and the richness of color effects, heightened by an ingenious blending of harmony and contrast. The stained glass in the clerestory has a run-on design, the pattern

differing with each window. Like most clerestory windows, their purpose is functional rather than decorative; the purpose being to introduce more light into the upper part of the church. Yet these windows, in achieving their purpose, have lost none of their beauty. They are seen at their best when shafts of sunlight from an unobstructed exterior play upon their rich coloring to the fullest. For a description of the twelve side aisle windows, with colored photographs of them see: *St. Louis Roman Catholic Church, Buffalo, New York, The Mother Church of the Diocese, Founded in 1829*, a pictorial of the church and a directory of the parishioners given in alphabetical order; published by St. Louis Church, Buffalo, New York, 2000. Notes pertaining to the stained glass windows along the side aisles are as follows: Some books give Boniface's name as Winfrid. Since Vatican II we would refer to Holy Ghost as Holy Spirit. The symbolism of the tiara was closely associated with both sacred and secular power. With the Second Vatican Council (1962-65), however, the symbolism, plus its increasingly ornate and costly character, came to be regarded as inappropriate. The use of the tiara, and any *crowning* with it for new popes, was ended by Pope Paul VI after the Second Vatican Council, and no pope has used it or been crowned with it ever since. Paul VI sold his tiara and gave the proceeds to the poor. Since then, the popes have chosen to be *installed* rather than *crowned* in order to emphasize the essentially spiritual role of the papacy today. See: op. cit. *Encyclopedia of Catholicism*, pps. 369, 1256. In the center of Augustine's miter is the symbol of the cross. Other artists have depicted his miter with an erect figure of Christ carrying his cross as a staff. Some of Augustine's literary works are: *Confessions*, a masterpiece of introspective autobiography; *The City of God*, breathes the atmosphere of Goetterdaemmerung that pervaded the world as the Roman Empire began to crumble. There are two cities, The City of God and the City of Man. The latter finds its fitting symbol in the Roman Empire that was in the first stage of decay. The former embraces all souls who live only as pilgrims in the midst of the world and have placed their hopes only in God. In the window featuring St. Dominic one sees that he wears the full tonsure. Originally a monastic practice, tonsure later emerged as a distinct rite of admission to the clerical state. In 1972 Pope Paul VI eliminated tonsure and all minor orders and the subdeaconate. The liturgical functions of the subdeacon were transferred to the lay ministries of reader and acolyte, but reserved for men. Admission to the clerical state now occurs at ordination to the diaconate. Dominic's reception of the rosary is legend. It can no longer be historically sustained; the rosary as we know it today received its present form in the sixteenth century rather than the tenth century. Also the use of beads for prayer extends back to patristic antiquity. It was the Dominican Pope, Pius V, who strongly fostered the use of the rosary and its devotion in 1572 by establishing an annual celebration giving thanks to the Blessed Virgin for having delivered Christendom from the invasion of the Turks by the decisive sea battle of Lepanto in 1571. The feast day is October 7, each year. A beautiful fresco of the vision seen by Rose of Lima can be viewed as an eighteenth century painting by Tiepolo in the Church of St. Mary of the Rosary in Venice. For details concerning the window of St. Francis Xavier see: op. cit. *Encyclopedia of Catholicism*, pps. 543-44 and *Premier World Atlas*, Rand McNally, New York, 1952, p. 36. The window featuring Jesus' visit to the home of the siblings Martha, Mary, and Lazarus at Bethany prior to His death and resurrection, has its roots in the Gospels of the evangelists; see: Matt. 26: 6-12; John 12: 1-8; John 11: 1-46; John 8: 1-11; Luke 10: 38-42; Luke 8: 1-3; Matt. 27: 56; Mark 15: 40; John 19: 25; Matt. 28: 1; Mark 16: 1; John 20: 1; Matt. 28: 9-10; John 20: 14-18. An Italian artist, Michelangelo Merisi da Caravaggio, which can be viewed at the Vatican, did a beautiful painting of Mary Magdalene. His greatest masterpiece was *The Burial of Christ*. He was a master of realism. There is an Apocryphal Gospel titled *Gospel of Mary*, supposedly written by Mary Magdalene reporting the secret teaching she had received including the soul's journey past hostile powers. Mary Magdalene is Mary of Magdala, a rich woman from this cosmopolitan city on the Sea of Galilee, on the caravan trade route between Egypt and Damascus, Syria. She was the first person to receive a vision from Jesus following His death. Also there is no mention in the gospels of Mary of Bethany kissing the feet of Jesus as depicted in the stained glass window. In the last window on the aisle, St. Odilia is considered as an Abbess of her convent at Niedermunster. She is also known as the patroness of the blind. The nunnery Odilienberg is in the Vosges Mountains. From 1815, Thuringia was in the hands of the Prussians, but in 1919, after World War I, it became known as the Weimar Republic. It includes Saxe-Weimar-Eisenach, Saxe-Meiningen, Gotha, Saxe-Altenburg, Reuss, Schwarzburg-Rudolstadt, and Schwarzburg-Sonderhausen. Its capital is Weimar, Germany. One third of Thuringia is forest and the highest point is Grosser Beerberg at 3225 feet. Louis IV and Hermann I were actually known as *landgraves*, which is a specific name for a count. Hermann I died in 1217 AD. In op. cit. *World's Popular Encyclopedia* Louis IV is written as Lewis IV. In op. cit. *St. Joseph's Daily Missal* it is written as Louis IV. As the wife of Louis IV, Elizabeth was Queen of Thuringia until 1227. Frederick II (1194-1250) was the Holy Roman Emperor who carried the crowns of Sicily, German States, Jerusalem, and the Empire. King Otto I founded the Holy Roman Empire in 962 AD as a successor to the Empire of Charlemagne and it included Austria, Bohemia, parts of Italy, and the Netherlands. The crowning of the emperors by the Popes ended in 1562 AD. After the 15th century almost all the emperors were from the Hapsburg dynasty. Francis II dissolved the Empire in 1806. The two stained glass windows in the chancel, which were made at the Royal Munich Art Institute in Bavaria, are the *Annunciation* and *The Baptism of Jesus*. The biblical texts upon which these are based are Luke 1: 26-38 and John 1: 29-34.

3. The cost of the windows in the apse, featuring Louis IX, was obtained from the genealogical study of the life of Michael Steffan by his son Jacob Steffan. Michael had 10 children. When Michael's property adjacent to the Erie Canal was sold, the money was divided among the 10 children. Each child donated $75 toward the cost of the second window from the left in the apse featuring Louis IX haggling with the aristocrats and barons of his kingdom. Each

of these seven windows, of which this is one of the sets, cost $750 paid to the Royal Munich Art Institute in Bavaria. This same amount was also paid to this Institute for each of the two windows in the chancel which were mentioned above. To determine the cost of the six windows in the aisles of the nave, which were supplied by Riester and Frohe, one looks elsewhere. Otto Andrle designed the two beautiful stained glass windows near the altar in Good Shepherd Church, Pendleton, New York, when he worked for Riester and Frohe. His process was also used in creating the windows on the aisle walls for St. Louis Church. The donors at Good Shepherd paid Riester and Frohe $1,054.30 for their two windows. It is assumed that the twelve aisle windows in St. Louis Church would have been the same price because both sets were installed at approximately the same time. Therefore each window in St. Louis Church would have cost $527.15. Also, the lesser grade windows in Good Shepherd Church cost the donors $225 per window. These are equivalent to the grade of window in the clerestory of St. Louis Church for which the trustees paid the same price. See: *Financial Reports of the Trustees of Good Shepherd Church, 1899-1972* and *History of the Pendleton Mission*, pps. 14-16; Archives of Good Shepherd Church, Pendleton, NY. For a description of the Buffalo Stained Glass Works see: *Buffalo of Today; the Queen City of the Lakes*, Interstate Publishing Company, New York, 1896, p. 104. This book was prepared by the Buffalo Chamber of Commerce to promote the City of Buffalo in the competition for hosting the Pan American Exposition, which took place in Buffalo in 1901. The exposition celebrated the progress of civilization in the Western Hemisphere during the 19th century. The exhibition's success was marred by the assassination of President McKinley. A biography of Otto Andrle appears in the chapter of this book devoted to the Dramatic Circle that was in existence at St. Louis Church from 1886 until 1960. In dealing with the creation of stained glass windows some expressions need clarification. A cartoon is a full sized design of a figure or scene that is to be interwoven into the final stained glass window. See: Metcalf, Robert, and Metcalf, Gertrude, *Making Stained Glass*, McGraw-Hill Book Company, New York, 1972, p.253. Stained glass is a fabric composed of many small pieces of colored glass, painted with monochrome enamel, fastened together with narrow strips of lead called cames, and held in place by crossbars. The glass is not stained — the color is in the glass. Monochrome brown enamel is applied to colored glass in order to add details such as hands, feet, drapery, and add tones for the modification of forms. See: ibid, *Making Stained Glass*, pps. 19-20. For a discussion of flashed glass see: Isenberg, Anita and Seymour, *How to Work in Stained Glass*, Chilton Book Company, Philadelphia, Pennsylvania, 1972, pps. 1-4. For tools and equipment for fitting glass into cames: glazing bench, a lathykin, a tool to open flanges of cames, a stopping knife, a lead cutting knife, a lead stretcher, glazing hammer, and lengths of cames see: op. cit. *Making Stained Glass*, p.116. Ferdinand Riester, partner of Godfrey Frohe, is buried in the United German and French Roman Catholic Cemetery, Pine Ridge Road, Buffalo, NY. For a description of the Riester's and Frohe's workshop on Pearl Street see: op. cit. *Good*

Shepherd, the Church on the Canal, pps. 61-2.

4. Material for the discussion of the subject matter displayed in these windows was taken from: Father Robert Bapst, *125th Anniversary of St. Louis Church, 1829-1954*, Buffalo, NY, 1954, pps. 35-41. Bapst was an assistant at St. Louis Church at this time. A copy of the anniversary booklet is in the Archives of St. Louis Church. For information concerning St. Louis, King of France, Crusades, and Sainte Chapelle see: op. cit., *Encyclopedia of Catholicism*, pps. 384, 795, 1153. Louis VIII and Blanche of Castille were the parents of Louis IX. She was regent until 1236. She, with the aid of poet Conrad Thibaut of Champagne, repressed the nobles. She prepared the union of several provinces to the crown and carefully educated Louis IX. The rebellious English barons asked Louis VIII to invade England in 1216. He, however, was defeated at Fair of Lincoln in 1217, recovered Poitou from Henry III of England in 1224, and led a crusade against the Albigenses in 1226. Henry III of England took the throne from his father King John in 1216. Henry aroused the hostility of the barons. He engaged in the "Baron's War" and was defeated at Lewes in 1264. Frederick II (1194-1250) was the emperor of the Holy Roman Empire, but was in bitter opposition to the papacy under Innocent III.

5. Quotes from *Revelations* concerning the symbolism of the altar are: "When the angel offers incense upon the altar, the prayers of God's people are said to ascend. (Rev. 8:3); I saw under the altar the souls of those who had been slaughtered for the word of God. (Rev. 6:9)." In the early church the altar was a simple wooden *mensa*, table. From the third century Christians built altars over the burial places of the martyrs. This brought about the sealing of relics of martyrs in modern altars and the erection of whole churches over the tombs of the martyrs. During the Reformation, the cultic significance of the altar was challenged; reformers called for the destruction of stone altars, replacing them with simple wooden communion tables. Catholic response to the Protestants was to build more elaborate altars with greater artwork. The elaboration of the 17th and 18th centuries have given way to reverent but simple forms since the Second Vatican Council. Typology refers to interpreting older realities or types as foreshadowing, according to God's plan of salvation, future realities or antitypes. One clear example of typology is in Romans 5:14, where St. Paul identifies Adam as a type of the one who is to come, that is, the Christ. For a discussion of the altar at St. Louis Church see: op. cit. *The 125th anniversary of St. Louis Church*, p. 29. For a biblical description of the scenes portrayed in the mosaics in the altar see: Genesis 22:1-18 and Genesis 14:18-20. In a niche over the exterior of the main entrance of the church, one finds a fine piece of oversized statuary, representing Louis IX, similar to the one over the tabernacle of the altar. It cost $550 when it was installed in 1896, an expense defrayed by Christian Weyand. It should be noted that over the altar, Louis IX holds his sword in his right hand while in the niche over the main entrance he holds it in his left hand. See: *Anniversary Souvenir and Program of St. Louis Dramatic Circle*, Music Hall, January 7, 1896, p. 37. For information concerning

the donation of the pulpit see: Chapter Seven of this text, "Gather Our Relics, We Rise Eternally." Information concerning the construction and carving of the pulpit was obtained from interviews with Roy Schneggenburger, grandson of Leopold Schneggenburger, and from Theodore Fink, great-grandson of Edward M. Hager. Also see: *Minutes of the St. Louis Board of Trustees' Meetings, 1909*, Theodore Schneggenburger sent a bill for $900 to the trustees requesting compensation for the work he had done in carving the evangelists on the pulpit. Also see: Anne Matthews, *Buffalo Courier Express*, Sunday, May 26, 1968; *Courier Express*, May 29, 1968; *A Century of Service in the Woodworking Business*, E.M. Hager and Sons, 141 Elm Street, Buffalo, New York, 1968. For chalice see: op. cit. *Encyclopedia of Catholicism*, pps. 296, 876, 1290. The ancient Armenian custom was to consecrate pure wine unmixed with water. In the Roman custom or rubrics a little water is mixed with the pure wine before consecration. Allegorically, the water is the baptized people who's sins are absorbed into the saving blood of Christ; both water and blood flowed from the heart of Jesus when it was pierced by the soldiers sword at the crucifixion; water and wine represent the human and divine natures in Christ. Some reformed Catholic churches have rejected this practice. Transubstantiation is the teaching of the Catholic Church whereby the substance of bread and wine offered at the Eucharist is changed into the body and blood of Jesus Christ. According to St. Thomas Aquinas and the Scholastic theologians all things have matter and form. The form is the soul of the thing, its substance. So the substance or soul of bread and wine becomes the substance of the body and blood of Christ while the matter or the accidents such as weight, texture, color, and taste, remain as they were before the consecration and the change of the substance. Transubstantiation is a term found in the 12th century and used at the Fourth Lateran Council in 1215. A picture and description of the 100th anniversary chalice can be found in *St. Louis Centennial Celebration*, p.19. In the description one finds that the chalice was made at Mayence, Germany. Today, there is no Mayence listed on maps of Germany. It appears, however, that these silversmiths would have been from Mainz, which is a modern day spelling of Mayence. The St. Henry (973-1024) featured on the chalice was a German King and emperor of the Holy Roman Empire, crowned in 1014. He founded the See of Bamberg, Bavaria, as a center for missions to Slavic nations. His feast is July 13, each year. The significance of the monstrance is derived from its synonym that is *ostensorium* that means to display. In early Church history the entire body of a martyr was exposed within a glass cylinder. Here Jesus the prime martyr is exposed in the host. For explanations of chalice, paten, monstrance, and ciborium see: op. cit. *Encyclopedia of Catholicism*, pps. 296, 317-18, 890. Information concerning the vestments used for the first time in 1929 see: op. cit. *St. Louis Centennial Celebration*, "Gold Brocade Vestments," Monsignor Richard J. Hofmann of Munich superintended the making of the vestments and had them delivered to Father Henry Laudenbach, who was thankful for receiving such a gift of lasting value and artistic utility. For further information on Stations of the Cross, chapels and side altars, the

Pieta, Henry Suso, St. Aloysius Gonzaga, St. Charles Borremeo, communion rail, Real Presence, eucharistic adoration, confessional, and pulpit see: ibid, using the appropriate given word description. For information concerning Our Lady of Aglona, Latvia, see: article attached to the reverse side of the painting of her, located in the chapel of the Immaculate Heart of Mary in St. Louis Church; it was placed there during the dedication of the painting on August 12, 1962. For information concerning Howard Schwartz and Albert Bosack in regards to the Latvians see: op. cit. *125th Anniversary of St. Louis Church*, a copy is in the church's archives. Information concerning the Latvians coming to America and persecution by the Soviets and the Nazis was obtained from Hedwig Gertmanis, Wilhelmina Pusmuscans, Anthony Jubulis, Anthony Ozolins, and Maria Kudins through the cooperation of Father Albert Bosack with whom the editors had an interview in September 2000. Information pertaining to Eugene W. Miller Sr. was obtained from his son, Carl Anthony Miller, aka C. Eugene Miller, the author/editor of this text, and C.E. Miller and John E. Miller, "Hall Bakery," *Buffalo Magazine*, March/April, 2000, pps. 20-22, 98. Hall Bakery was founded by Frank L. Hall in 1915 at 2381 Fillmore Street at the corner of Main Street in Buffalo, New York. In 1922, the bakery won the first place prize for the best baked bread in America at the National Baking Exposition held at Chicago, Illinois. Although purchased by the Continental Baking Company in 1925, it retained its original name until it was sold to Kaufmann's bakery in 1967. It was a home-to-home delivery bakery and reached its peak of sales in 1949 with 500 employees and 250 delivery routes within the city limits of Buffalo and others in rural areas of Erie and Niagara Counties.

6. For installation of the mammoth organ in the Temple of Music see: *Buffalo Evening News*, May 2, 1901. For a description of the mammoth organ and its purchase by St. Louis Church see: *The St. Louis Bazaar Herald*, September 24, 1900. For discussions of the contacts made by St. Louis Church to find a suitable substitute for the mammoth organ which it rejected see: *Minutes of the St. Louis Church Trustees, January 1901 to October 1904*, copy is held in the Archives of St. Louis Church. The Convention Hall was also known as the Elmwood Music Hall. See: *Buffalo Evening News*, November 4, 1901 and an anonymously written article retained in the St. Louis Church Archives which states that the organ in the Temple of Music was installed in the Elmwood Music Hall. It remained there until the Hall's demolition in 1938. It was saved, removed, and stored in an old city horse barn, where it deteriorated beyond repair. It was finally sold for scrap in 1942. Mr. Garret House built the earliest known organ for St. Louis' gothic church in 1886. He was in business from 1845 to 1899. The organ was installed in 1889 and remained there until it was replaced in 1903. Articles concerning the organ built by Emmons Howard and Sons are found in *Buffalo Commercial*, June 6, 1900 and in *The Courier*, September 9, 1900. The facts concerning the pipe organ used in the second St. Louis Church, the brick church, from 1843 to 1863 was obtained from Robert Vogt, historian for the Diocese of Rochester. He was in communication with Bill Kurzdorfer

during the month of November 2001. For information concerning the purchase of the Schwab, Koehnken & Co. organ over the other bid by Wilhelm Mohr Company see *Minutes of the Board of Trustees of St. Louis Church, February 2, 1863*, it is written in German script. For the source concerning the Mueller and Abel organ made for the German Zion Evangelical Church in Brooklyn, New York, see: *The Tracker*, 14:2 (Winter 1970), pps.27-8. For a description of the original Kimball organ see: *Specifications,Details of Construction, Contract*, W.W. Kimball Company, Chicago, Ill., with cover letter from Frank T. Milner, Buffalo representative of the company, to Father Hoelscher, Nov. 5, 1902. A copy is in the St. Louis Church Archives. For the details of the Kimball Organ subsequent to the refurbishing see: *Tellers Organ Company Contract for Tellers' opus 781*, copy in St. Louis Church Archives. Information concerning Ignatz and Antoinette Czerwinski was obtained from genealogy studies made by the Batt family descending from Paul Batt, former Supreme Court Judge. See: St. Louis Church Archives. Information concerning Elizabeth Czerwinski, or Lill as she was also called, and Helen Czerwinski was supplied to the author/editor by Marie Buchheit Miller.

7. The list of organists and choir directors of St. Louis Church since 1889 to the present are: Ignatz Czerwinski (1889-1910); Otto A. Singenberger and Antoinette Czerwinski (1910-1911); Henry J. Zeinz (1911-1944); Mary M. Zeinz (1944-1952); Louis H. Huybrechts (1952-1954); Joseph Kurzdorfer (1954-1963); David Wagner (1963-1968); Leonard Wiegand (1968-1971); James Kosnik (1971); Susie Swinnich (1971-1972); Dona Vasey (1972—). Mischka, who taught music at Canisius College, was choir director during a period when Zeinz was the organist. These data were provided to the author/editor by William Kurzdorfer, an organ specialist, nephew to former organist, Joseph Kurzdorfer, has been curator of the 1903 Kimball organ since 1971, has continuously upgraded the organ since 1987, and presently is assistant organist with Dona Vasey. For information concerning Henry J. Zeinz one can contact Angie Nowak, his daughter, and Catherine Berger, one of his former students. A biography of Zeinz appears in a later chapter of this text. In the church tower a clock known as the Seth Thomas Clock built in 1889 was intact until the pastorship of Father William A. Schwinger. He sold the inner works but the hands and dials have been retained. The tower also boasts of an enormous bell 53" in diameter weighing 3,000 lbs. It was cast in Troy, New York, at the Meneeley Bell Foundry in 1889. The history of organ emplacements at St. Louis Church is as follows: Father Nicholas Mertz reluctantly allowed a reed organ to be played in the Lamb of God Church. It is doubtful that this organ was used in the brick church of 1843 because the church was too large for it. According to William Kurzdorfer, a pipe organ was installed in the brick church from 1843-1863; it was then sold to St. Paul's Church in Rochester, New York. In 1863 a Schwab, Koehnken and Co. organ was installed and used until the fire in 1885. Then used was a Garret House organ from 1889 to 1903. Although there is no proof, this organ may have been sold for scrap because Garret House was a Buffalo firm that dealt only in start-up organs for churches.

They were never meant to have long life. Then came the Kimball Organ (1903-1952); it was in place after being repaired and updated by Teller Organ Company (1952-1988); This Kimball-Teller organ was later repaired, and again updated by William Kurzdorfer. It now contains 44 stops, 49 ranks, 2,600 pipes ranging from one-half inch to sixteen feet in length and three-sixteenths to eighteen inches in width, and has two blowers with a capacity of 3,000 cubic feet per minute. For a description of the members of the choir in 1954 see: op. cit. *125th Anniversary of St. Louis Church*, p.50. A biography of Louis H. Huybrechts was obtained from an article in *The Diapason* presented to the author/editor by William Kurzdorfer. Also see: *Buffalo Evening News*, Section III, October 30, 1952, and p.42. For more biographical information on Huybrechts, and his first concert with the rebuilt and electrified Kimball organ on Easter Sunday 1952 see: *Buffalo Courier Express*, Sunday April 13, 1952. A biography of Ignatz Czerwinski was obtained from genealogical material obtained from Ronald Batt handed down from Paul Batt, husband of Antoinette Czerwinski. The names of the parishioners who donated money for the updating of the Kimball organ by the Tellers Organ Company are listed on a plaque in St. Louis Church adjacent to the rood screen in the right side of the transept. Information for the biography of William Kurzdorfer was obtained in an interview with him by the author/editor on December 11, 2001. In this interview, he mentioned some facts concerning Huybrechts obtained from Hans Vigeland. While waiting at the New York Central Railroad Station in Albany, Vigeland wrote a letter to Bill Kurzdorfer on December 20, 1977 describing Louis Hybrecht's tenure in Buffalo. He added, "Of course, St. Louis Church is the most beautifully proportioned gothic "cathedral" in Buffalo. I guess, however, that the parish is now a shadow of its heyday; those days of the Pan American Exposition when it was pictured in many brochures as one of the great sights of the city. Of course a church of that size could take an organ twice as big as the Kimball; and what superb acoustics!" Hans Vigeland left Buffalo in 1976 to become the organist and choirmaster of the First Congregational Church in Great Barrington, Massachusetts. He moved to Tyron, North Carolina in 1979. He died there on August 17, 1982 at the age of 64 years. John E. Miller, youngest son of Eugene W. Miller Sr., the maker of the kneeling pads in the church, was a member of the St. Louis Church choir during Louis Huybrecht's tenure. In communication with the author/editor on January 1, 2002, he told how Huybrechts was very unhappy at St. Louis Church, and upset with the attitude of the trustees' unwillingness to spend the funds needed to put the organ in a proper condition. John E. Miller also gave credence to what others had said concerning Huybrechts' professionalism and devotion to music. References to the physics of music, pitch, quality, overtones, and acoustics were taken from: Irwin, Stevens, *Dictionary of Pipe Organ Stops*, G. Schirmer, Inc., New York, New York, 1962, and Barnes, William Harrison, *The Contemporary American Organ*, J. Fisher & Bros., Harrison Road, Glen Rock, New Jersey, 1959.

CHAPTER ELEVEN

The Dramatic Circle

After the great fire of 1885 that totally consumed both the German Music Hall and St. Louis Church, the German Young Men's Association and the parishioners of St. Louis Church decided to immediately rebuild their respective establishments. Besides the fund drive initiated by Father Joseph Sorg, which achieved much success in one year, about sixteen young men of the parish decided to initiate an organization of male members of the congregation which had two productive and connective goals. Through the creation of an amateur dramatic society, they decided to present stage productions which would be profitable. In this manner they assumed that their talent and effort would act as a fund raising vehicle to help defray the expense of constructing the new church.

A concept of a dramatic society was not new to the German community in Buffalo. The German Young Men's Association had established one in the city before 1850. Performances, although they met with much artistic and financial success, were limited, however, to members of the association rather than to the general public. On February 25, 1850, a group of people, who imagined themselves to possess great talent but were still amateurs, organized the *Theater Company* and produced a well attended production, *William Tell*, at the Eagle Street Theater. On January 21, 1851, an organization called the *Union* performed dramatic and musical entertainment in the Barnum Museum on Washington Street. A traveling German Theater Company came to Buffalo on May 24, 1851 and performed in McArthur's Garden Salon, on the

corner of Main and Eagle Streets. On March 8, 1852, *The Harmonie Society* was founded. In 1854 the German Workingmen's Union formed a Dramatic Circle called the *Thalia Theater*. They gave productions at the Eagle Street Theater and later at Geyer's Hall on Court Street. The Turnverein also developed its own dramatic company and held its renditions at Gillig's Hall at the corner of Genesee and Ash Streets. By 1858, productions by the Turners were being performed to crowded houses; theater and drama had become very popular among the German population of Buffalo.

Although people loved the productions and supported them with their attendance, many of the Dramatic Circles were too greedy and overextended themselves. Expenses became greater than profits. The young thespians at St. Louis Church, however, had learned of the successes and failures of these Circles, such as that of the Turnverein, and wished to glean for themselves the best and avoid the worst. In forming their organization they had high ideals; the improvement of their members in the arts of reading and elocution, the cultivation of a taste for drama and other literature, and the promotion of social enjoyment. Whatever their success, they pledged their profits to be donated to the building fund of their proposed gothic church. Although membership in the society was limited to males, women were expected to be used in female roles in the plays. The officers elected to the initial society in June, 1885 were: Otto F. Andrle, president; Edward F. Mischka, vice president; Charles M. Weyand, secretary; and Adolph Zeller, treasurer. The other charter members were: Adam Dory, Albert J. Zahm, Alois P. Andrle, Albert Rose, Fred A. Zorn, Charles Deck, Edward J. White, William J. Schreck, John C. Hazenzahl, John L. Wex, Louis J. Roth, and Charles Biesinger. They called themselves the St. Louis Dramatic Circle. Immediately, Andrle and Mischka were assigned the management of developing a theatrical performance that was to be given in the school auditorium in the late summer. It had a seating capacity of four hundred. They were to select a play, assign the roles to be played, call rehearsals, and provide for wardrobe and scenery. On August 11, 1885, however, the society was depleted by one charter member; Albert J. Zahm had resigned.

Although amateurs, the sixteen charter members of the St. Louis Dramatic Circle did not suffer from any theatrical inferiority complex. They chose the fine old classic comedy, *Legend of the Catskills*, for their debut production. It was based upon one of the stories by Washington Irving found in his *Sketch Book, 1819-20*. Irving told his readers that he found the tale amid the papers of Diedrich Knickerbocker, who was an old gentleman from New York curious about Dutch history during the time of the governorship of Peter Stuyvesant. The staging for the Dramatic Circle's production was set in a small village of Dutch colonists along the Hudson River some eighty miles north of New York City. The first Act was set in 1763 while the second Act retold events twenty years later. The opening scene featured the village inn in the forefront with a background illustrating the Catskill Mountains in the west, swelling up to a noble height and lording over the surrounding country. The stage painting, lighting, and sound were so unique that every change of season, every change of weather, indeed every hour of the day which produced changes in the magical hues and shapes of that magnificent barrier in the west were ingeniously captured.

The version of the play was based upon that of Joseph Jefferson, born in Philadelphia in 1829. Throughout his career, he was well known for his acting and playwriting in Mexico, Europe, and the United States. His performances as Rip Van Winkle made the play a classic of the American stage. He died in 1905. In the Dramatic Circle's production, arranged from Jefferson's work by Charles Burke in two acts and nine scenes, Edward F. Mischka played Rip Van Winkle. Edward was the youngest sibling of the popular musical family of Joseph, Carl, August, Emily, and himself. Joseph, the oldest, was born at Hermanmestec, Austria on May 8, 1846. He, with his siblings, came to America in 1852 and settled in Buffalo. He was choirmaster for the Buffalo Opera Troupe, engaged in business as a music dealer and publisher; teacher of music, church organist, and for seven years was the director of the Buffalo Liedertafel. Edward easily followed in his brother's footsteps; and, during Zeinz's reign as organist at St. Louis Church, he was director of the choir.

On the opening night of *Legend of the Catskills*, September 13, 1885, produced in the school auditorium of St. Louis Church, Edward was a smash hit with his impersonation of the rollicking and ne'er do well Rip Van Winkle both as the young man of the village and as the white bearded tottering old man descending from the mountain twenty years later. Shortly before curtain time, however, he had disappeared. A frantic search for him was on by the other members of the cast. When he was found, all still seemed lost, for he had been celebrating and had imbibed a bit too much. His loyal club-members, however, half-dragged him to the theater and shoved him on to the stage. He was so real in his role that at the end of Act One he did not need acting ability to fall asleep as required by the script as the curtain fell. During the break, with several quaffs of coffee, he was able to return to the stage for Act Two, feeling mighty poorly and really experiencing his required agedness. Next day the critics, not knowing his true condition, acclaimed that no actor had ever so captured the spirit of Rip Van Winkle. Sober on the next evening for the second performance, he did just as well. Although unfortified, his great acting ability scored a second round of rave notices.

Charles W. Deck played Diedrich Knickerbocker, the storyteller and schoolmaster. In the first Act, the set of male sages who frequented the inn for noxious liqueurs, morsels of pastries, and increasingly loud conversation were portrayed by Adam Dory, John C. Hazenzahl, Edward J. White, and Fred A. Zorn. Charles M. Weyand, who took the part of Nicholas Vedder, the owner of the inn and controller of the opinions of this junto was excellent. The young ladies who played the female roles were: Miss Mila Andrle, Miss Emma Phillips, and Mrs. Emily O'Neil, who made a most convincing nag of a wife as Dame Van Winkle. Alois P. Andrle, John L. Wex, Fred A. Zorn, and Charles Biesinger played the Spirits of the Catskills. They were the personages, dressed in quaint outlandish fashion, which Winkle met high on the mountainside. Some wore short doublets, others jerkins, with long knives in their belts, and most of them had enormous breeches. Their visages, too, were peculiar; one had a large beard, broad face, and small piggish eyes, the face of another seemed to consist entirely of nose, and was surmounted by a white sugar-loaf hat, set off with a little red cock's tail. All had beards of various shapes and colors. For the second Act which took place in 1783, a few new characters were added: Louis J. Roth as Seth Slough, Adam Dory as the judge, Adolf Zeller as Gustaff, Alois P. Andrle and Edward J. White as villagers. Miss Mila Andrle portrayed Alice, Rip Van Winkle's sister, who as a young lady appeared in Act One. She, however, was made up to have aged considerably in her role as Alice in Act Two, where she was about to marry Knickerbocker. Miss Emma Phillips, a very young girl, played Rip Van Winkle's daughter, Lorenna, in Act One, however, in Act Two, an older women, Miss Emma Kern, played the part.

The plot of the play revolved around the life of Rip Van Winkle, a henpecked husband. His wife, Dame Winkle, was a brawling, boisterous, turbulent, scolding woman who drove Rip to seek consolation among his male friends at the village inn. Rip's decision to leave home and find peace and solace in the mountains came to a head when his wife descended into his stronghold at the inn demanding that he sign a contract. She suddenly broke upon the tranquillity of the assemblage and called the members all to naught. She, especially, gave Nicholas Vedder a piece of her mind. He was not spared from the daring tongue of this terrible virago; she charged him outright of encouraging her husband in habits of idleness. In despair, Rip decided to escape the labor of his farm and the clamor of his wife. In frustration he signed the contract. Then with rifle in hand and his faithful dog, Wolf, by his side, he took off for one of the highest parts of the Catskill Mountains. There he found odd looking personages playing nine pins. The rolling of the balls and the crack of the pins seemed like the sight and sounds of thunder and lightning to Rip's ears and eyes. One of the strangers, Hendricks, was a short square-built old fellow, with thick bushy hair, and a grizzled beard. He toted on his shoulder a stout keg, full of liquor, and made signs to Rip to give him assistance with his load. Soon the contents of the keg were emptied into large flagons, and quaffed by the assemblage that then went on with their bowling. When no eye was fixed upon Rip, he, too, tasted the beverage that he found to have much of the flavor of a most excellent Holland vintage. One taste provoked another; soon his senses were overpowered, his eyes swam in his head, which gradually declined, and he fell into a deep sleep. At this point the curtain came down on Act One while a musical refrain rang out expressing that "This day is done!"

As the curtain rose on the Act Two, Rip found himself awake on the green knoll whence he had been drinking from his flagon. He looked around for his gun, but in place of the well-oiled fowling piece, he found an old firelock lying by him, the barrel incrusted with rust, the lock falling off, and the stock worm-eaten. Wolf, too, had disappeared. Everything around him seemed different than before he went to sleep. Although he hated to think of meeting with his wife again, he decided to go back to his village that he had left, but as he arrived he did not see anyone that he knew. Suddenly he found his house; it had gone to decay with the roof fallen in, the windows shattered, and the doors off the hinges. He hurried to the inn; it too was gone, and in its place he found a poorly rebuilt tavern. The face of what used to be King George painted on a wooden poster had been done over to represent General George Washington. He could not find Nicholas Vedder or any of his old cronies. Instead he saw a lean, bilious-looking fellow haranguing vehemently about rights of citizens, elections, members of congress, liberty, Bunker Hill, and heroes of seventy-six. The appearance of Rip, with his long white beard, his rusty fowling piece, his uncouth dress, and an army of women and children at his heels, soon attracted the attention of the tavern-politicians. Rip, however, soon left their company because he realized that they thought of him as a spy. Once out of reach he met a young girl. Upon questioning her, he found her to be his daughter, Lorenna, now in her late twenties. She was played by Miss Emma Kern. He then understood that he had been asleep for a long time, his wife had died, and no one, but his daughter seemed to know poor Rip Van Winkle.

Soon, however, appeared Alice, his sister, and Sophia, a servant girl. Sophia was played by Miss Christine Zehnle, Although all had aged, they, after a moment of hesitation recognized him. They said, "Sure enough it is Rip Van Winkle. Welcome home old neighbor; where have you been for twenty years?" Rips's daughter took him home to live with her and her husband and children. Now free of the tyranny of Dame Winkle and the outmoded contract that he had signed, Rip roamed the streets telling of his experiences in the Catskills. From that day forward, the villagers would remark, when a thunder-storm of summer invaded the mountains, that Hendrick Hudson and his crew were engaged in a game of ninepins, and all henpecked husbands thought that it was time for them to take a quieting draft out of Rip Van Winkle's flagon. So ended the Second Act, on the first night of the production, to the thundering applause of the audience. In the newspapers the following day, the critics expressed their opinions. They said, "It was a worthy production and the principals, aye even the humble roles assigned to the sprites, hobgoblins, and villagers, acted their various parts exceedingly well. The performance was repeated the following night and many of the most skeptical were forced to admit that this pretentious first play by the St. Louis Dramatic Circle was creditable alike to the members of the society, to the church, and to the City."

Soon after the two-night run of the play, Otto R. Rick and many other men joined the group. He and John C. Hazenzahl, Charles M. Weyand, Otto F. Andrle, and Edward F. Mischka were designated to form a committee so as to draw up the rules and regulations by which the organization would be guided. The committee elected Edward F. Mischka as their chairman and quickly settled down to write their Constitution. The title of the organization was chosen as the *St. Louis Dramatic Circle*. The mission of the society was spelled out: "the stated object of this society is the diffusion of knowledge and mutual advancement in acting among its members." The articles of conduct that followed provided for the election of officers, duties of officers, and the establishment of a standing Membership Committee of three. Membership was limited to twenty-five and each was to pay an entrance fee of one dollar and a monthly subscription. Each member was required to be a practicing Catholic and a member of St. Louis Church. Members were elected by ballot and a negative vote of three prevented a person from being accepted. All members were expected to play the roles which the managers assigned to them, and they were responsible for purchasing their own playbooks.

The Dramatic Circle

Some time after these articles were accepted by a vote of the entire membership, they were amended. To the original mission statement was added an amended objective: "the preparation of moral entertainment for the church and charitable benefits." Membership was increased to thirty including up to five honorary members who were not entitled to vote or hold office and were exempt from dues. They were persons who, in the judgment of the voting body, had performed meritorious service but were unable to take active part in the Circle. Their election had to be a unanimous decision on the part of the total active membership. In an other amendment, a Dramatic Committee of three was created so as to select plays, assign character roles, and have all dramatic affairs under their control; their decision binding on all participants. Further, an Entertainment and House Committee of three was appointed to arrange activities, initiate functions for the members, and provide the space in which meetings could be held. When the constitution was approved and signed, the membership had swelled to the following: Otto F. Andrle, John C. Hazenzahl, George A. Hartmann, Edward F. Doll, Charles M. Schmidt, George J. Schwartz, Fred A. Zorn, Otto R. Rick, Charles Biesinger, William J. Schreck, John L. Wex, Edward J. White, Louis J. Roth, Charles M. Weyand, Frank L. Mayer, Alois P. Andrle, Charles E. Baecher, Henry J. Swanz, John P. Mayer, Joseph Bielstein, Henry J. Schmidt, Jacob Alex Gittere, Frederick J. Beutter, Joseph S. Schmidt, Frank L. Diebold, Edward F. Mischka, Albert Rose, Adam Dory, and Charles Deck.

Meetings were held on the first Monday of each month with a gathering at 7:45 P.M., and business commencing promptly at 8:00. Rules concerning absenteeism and tardiness were strictly enforced. Members were required to attend all meetings and rehearsals or give previous notice to the secretary; if they did not do so they were fined ten cents. If a member was not present when the meeting was called to order, he was fined five cents for his tardiness. A most serious infraction was missing a rehearsal without prior notification; this resulted in a fifteen cent fine for each offense. Members who failed to pay dues, missed three consecutive meetings or two consecutive rehearsals, or were guilty of improper conduct, were expelled from the Circle at the decision of the officers or by a two-thirds vote of the members present at any regular meeting. The officers, however, took no action, until the wayward one was allowed to present a defense.

Any amendments to the Constitution were permitted after written notice and a vote of three-fourths of the members present at any regular meeting. The monthly meetings began with a call to order, roll call, reading of the past minutes, collection of fines and dues, applications of prospective members, committee reports, miscellaneous unfinished business, and adjournment. The verbalization carried on during each of these phases of the meeting was carefully recorded by the secretary in neatly handwritten minute books. The meetings were always held in the school building, at first in St. Louis Hall, and later in rooms on the third floor set aside for the Dramatic Circle. Following the conclusion of business, no recess was ever taken until beer and snacks had been consumed by the members while they enjoyed the camaraderie of good-fellowship over several hands of poker. It was during these games that Edward Joseph White was nicknamed "tap." He was a giant of a man but gentle as a lamb. Whenever he had a full house or a royal flush, he would tap his hand on the table. All present knew that it was time to call for his cards. He was a winner more times than he was a loser.

The first twenty-five years of the Dramatic Circle were hectic ones. Some members resigned and later joined again, several resigned and did not rejoin; others joined but soon resigned. There always was, however, a large group of the membership attending monthly meetings and accepting roles for plays that were produced. As early as August 11, 1885, prior to the production of *Legend of the Catskills*, Albert J. Zahm

239

resigned. Between 1887 and 1897, several others followed in Zahm's footsteps. They were: John C. Hazenzahl, Henry J. Swanz, Fred J. Beutter, Jacob Alexander Gittere, Frank J. Haberstro, Louis F. Jansen, and Joseph Muth. In 1886, Adolph Zeller, the charter treasurer of the Circle was not able to fulfill all the rules concerning monthly meetings, but instead of accepting his resignation, the society proclaimed him to be an honorary member who was not required to pay dues or attend meetings. John C. Hazenzahl, who had resigned in 1887, rejoined the group in 1895 along with others such as H. William Haas, Louis F. Jansen, William Sanders, Joseph E. Voltz, Otto R. Rick, George F. Neunder, John P. Mayer, John A. Kerker, Frank L. Mayer, Edward Mischka, Edward M. Ottenot, Charles M. Schmidt, and George J. Schwartz. Louis F. Jansen was related to the Jansen Brothers who established a Harness and Saddlery Business on Broadway. Rick and Mischka had been members, resigned, and rejoined. Haas, Jansen, Voltz, and Muth only remained in the society for two years.

*I*n those twenty-five years the following actively participated in one or more of the plays produced by the Circle: Adelbert W. Andrle, Aloysius P. Andrle, Otto F. Andrle, Leon J. Armbruster, Frank P. Batt, Charles Biesinger, Herbert H. Churchill, Edward J. Dearing, Charles M. Deck, Eugene L. Diebold, Frank L. Diebold, Karl J. Dietsche, Edward F. Doll, Adam Dory, Thomas G. Dunphy, Michael J. Fornes, Lucien Haas, Joseph K. Hartfuer, John C. Hazenzahl, August Hettrich, Edward Jacobs, John A. Kerker, Fred Kessel, Louis Ludaescher, Joseph J. Lux, Bernard F. Mayer, Frank L. Mayer, John P. Mayer, Carl Mischka, Edward F. Mischka, Joseph O'Neil, Otto R. Rick, Louis J. Roth, Charles M. Schmidt, Joseph S. Schmidt, William J. Schreck, Fred C. Schweigert, Harry Schweigert, John A. Schweigert, John L. Wex, Charles M. Weyand, Norman P. Weyand, Edward J. White, Adolph Zeller, Andrew Zillig, Edward L. Zimpfer, and Fred A. Zorn. Although women were not allowed to be members of the Circle, participate in the monthly meetings, or cast votes on

proposals and decisions, they did take all the female roles in the plays. Those for whom note should be made were: Bohumila Andrle, Anna W. Beutter, Olive Coveny, Alla O. DeBock, Marie A. Delahunt, Elenor Feldman, Martha M. Gottstein, Carrie Hager, Lizzie M. Hazenzahl, Loreen Hausle, Emma Kern, Genevieve Lux, Amelia Max, Gertrude Murphy, Emily O'Neil, Emma Phillips, Anna E. Ryan, Elizabeth Schwartz, Clara M. Sendker, Terry Strauss, Anna Strigl, Margaret Swanz, Della Taylor, Alice Winter, Loretta Zahm, and Christine Zehnle.

*T*hose members who were the bulwark and the greatest enthusiasts of the Circle were: Aloysius Andrle, Otto F. Andrle, Frank L. Diebold, John C. Hazenzahl, Frank L. Mayer, Edward F. Mischka, Charles M. Weyand, Edward J. White, and Fred Zorn. As one goes through the records of the Circle, it is these names which appear the most as actors, as managers, or as assistant managers of stage properties, costumes, scenery, and lighting. They also appear most often in the columns of those who were directors of the business committee or membership committee, who held office of president, vice-president, secretary, or treasurer, and those who chose and directed plays or arranged the music.

*O*f this group, Otto F. Andrle could be considered as the igniter of enthusiasm. He was born in Buffalo on January 1, 1865. His ancestors were among the organizers of St. Louis Church, and he received his early education in the church's parochial school under the directorship of Henry Hemmerlein. Later he was for several years a pupil of G.R.W. Berger, artist and member of the Buffalo Art School. Andrle also took elocution lessons under the tutelage of Professor Beers, but he received his musical education under the direction of his father who for twenty-two years was active in the Academy of Music Orchestra. For eight years, Andrle was a designer in the Buffalo Stained Glass Works that was owned and operated by Ferdinand Riester and Leo P. Frohe. While with them, he designed the stained glass windows for the side aisles in St. Louis Church. After leaving them, he went into the painting and decorating business for himself. On November 2, 1899, he tendered his resignation as manager of the St. Louis Dramatic Circle. At that time he wrote with great displeasure, "The boyish annoyances, which have taken place of late in the Circle, are sufficient inducement for me doing so!" In 1900 he completed the interior of the Teck Theater. For several years he was on stage with several companies; with the Booth-Barrett production of *Julius Caesar* as *Casca*; with Frank Mayo productions as *Prince Leo*; with Ada Grey as *Levison*; and with James O'Neill as *Marcellus*.

He was a member of the Orpheus for twelve years and of the St. Louis Choir for sixteen years beginning in 1884. He served for six years in the 74th New York Regiment as corporal, sergeant, and was honorably discharged with the rank of lieutenant. He was second vice-president of the Catholic Mutual Benefit Association, member of the Catholic Institute, organized the St. Louis Dramatic Circle in 1885, was its president from 1885 to 1889, and its production manager from 1885 to 1900. He was chairman of the Entertainment and Decoration Committee for the St. Louis Bazaar held in 1900; it raised funds to decrease the debt on the present day gothic church. Tragically, after making his debut with Frank Mayo of New York City in 1895, Otto Andrle was expelled from the St. Louis Dramatic Circle for violating the constitution by missing too many meetings. He and his brother Adelbert Andrle, however, continued to have a good relationship with the Circle. Otto was often hired to design and build stage sets and scenery while Adelbert provided the music for the productions. On one occasion Edward A. Rick recalled that Otto was paid $50.00 to act as the manager. He was so enthusiastic that he was found lying on the floor at the front of the stage with a book in his hand and prompting the actors when they forgot their lines. Otto married Anna W. Beutter, sister of Frederick J. Beutter; she played Queen Gertrude in the Dramatic Circle's production of Hamlet in 1887. Charles M. Weyand, son of the brewer, Christian Weyand, married Mila Andrle, sister of Otto Andrle, in 1892.

January and February of 1893 were not very enjoyable months for holding meetings in the school building at St. Louis Church. During January, Joseph S. Schmidt, John P. Mayer, George J. Schwartz, Fred Kiefer, and Charles M. Schmidt wrote to Frank L. Diebold, who was the Circle's secretary, requesting that they be excused from attending all meetings during the year. This rash of requests was the result of experiencing little or no heat in the building on meeting nights. Although the Circle never missed a meeting during its entire history, they were sometimes sparsely attended. Diebold, knowing that the members were uncomfortable, wrote to Charles Lautz who was president of the Board of Trustees for St. Louis Church. He said, "I kindly ask that the steam heat be left on in the building so that we will be comfortably warm at our meetings. The reason we make this singular request is because we have repeatedly asked the janitor for steam heat, and he has failed to provide the same. It has not been an infrequent thing, on nights of our winter meetings, for members to be compelled to keep their overcoats and hats on, and walk up and down the floor in order to keep warm."

Upon receiving this request Lautz replied, "I can assure you that the trustees were not aware that the St. Louis Hall was cold, and not heated. Positive instructions have been given to the janitor to keep the furnace going day and night. The hall should be heated on the night you have your meetings, and we would have acted sooner, as we do now, if we had known that this was not the case." The situation was only partially corrected and Diebold had to continuously write to the trustees, each time varying what the members of the Circle thought about the cause of the heat problem. On another occasion, he told John Feist, chairman of the Board of Trustees' Real Estate Committee, that the janitor turned the steam on about 8:00 P.M., used only two radiators, and shut it off at 9:00 P.M. He ended by saying, "The hall never got hot enough and whatever heat did get into the room disappeared in a flash after the radiators were turned off." Although some progress was made after each complaint, it was never solved. Letters were still flying back and forth between the Circle and the trustees even into the year that the new century was born.

During the period set aside for business, besides being displeased with the heating conditions, many other topics were taken under consideration at the monthly meetings. Among these were discussions of details concerning the types of plays to be staged and the sale of tickets for theatrical productions, requests by members to be excused from attendance at meetings, discussion of reasons for not being able to be present, requests by other dramatic circles soliciting patronage from the St. Louis Dramatic Circle, consideration of the election of members, determination of the status of members whose dues were in arrears, acceptance or non-acceptance of resignations from members, officers and chairmen of committees, requests for members to help in church functions such as acting as ushers, accepting invitations to attend social functions in the city, requests for money to have Masses said for deceased members, and determining times when the Circle as a body would attend Sunday Mass and receive Communion.

Primary, however, was the status of membership, dues, and the ability to attend meetings. On October 5, 1894, Frank L. Diebold, secretary, was required to inform John L. Wex that his failure to attend meetings regularly was a severe violation of the constitution. Wex was warned that continued violation would result in his expulsion. Few indeed, were members who did not receive a similar notification at one time or another. Even charter members and the great theatrical enthusiast, Otto F. Andrle, suffered being taken to task for absenteeism. Although a letter sent to him by Frank L. Diebold on October 31, 1894 was courteous, it was

also condescending. It read, "The last meeting you attended was on February 19, 1894, since which time you have missed more than three consecutive meetings. I will not say that you have done this intentionally. I am aware of the fact that you are a very busy man, and can't always favor us with your presence, but you will readily agree that the missing of three consecutive meetings means a violation of the constitution, which I understand you assisted in framing." Others who came under the axe and were suspended or dismissed were: Frank L. Diebold, himself, Jacob Alexander Gittere, Frank J. Haberstro, John C. Hazenzahl, Henry Schmidt, Henry J. Swanz, John L. Wex, and Al Weppner.

After producing *Legend of the Catskills*, the Dramatic Circle entertained again during Christmas week of 1885 in the school auditorium with a short play titled *Joseph in Egypt*. When it was produced, preparations were made with great fanfare. Programs advertised products such as chandeliers and gas fixtures, red-hot peanuts, livery stables, harnesses, and elegant gold papers. The play was staged, as was the *Legend of the Catskills*, in the auditorium on the third floor of the school building. All went well until the performers tried to get a live donkey up three flights of stairs. For a while it looked as if Mary, the mother of Jesus, would have to make the flight into Egypt on foot, but perseverance of the thespians won over the obstinacy of the jackass. Next, using the same hall, the Circle rendered *Paul Pry* in September 1886, *Companions* in September 1887, and then decided to stage Shakespeare's *Hamlet* on three nights, December 27, 28, and 29, 1887. It was a bold undertaking for amateurs to attempt a performance such as *Hamlet*. The Circle, however, placed advertisements in the Buffalo newspapers. They read, "The St. Louis Dramatic Circle, in Shakespeare's masterpiece, in three Acts, *Hamlet*, with new scenery, elegant costumes, and stage effects. General Admission, twenty-five cents. Reserved seats, thirty-five cents. Seats now on sale at Peter Paul and Brothers' Printing Office, 490 Main Street." Otto F. Andrle assisted by Edward F. Mischka managed the production. The business manager was

Charles M. Weyand. Adelbert W. Andrle directed music while Fred A. Zorn and Alois P. Andrle arranged properties. Besides the choice of extras for roles as lords, ladies, officers, soldiers, messengers, ambassadors, and attendants, the sixteen principal actors and actresses assigned by the manager and his assistant were:

Hamlet .... Otto F. Andrle
Laertes .... Edward F. Mischka
King Claudius .... John P. Mayer
Polonius .... Charles M. Weyand
Horatio .... Otto R. Rick
Ghost .... Frank L. Mayer
Rosencrantz .... Charles M. Schmidt
Guildenstern .... William J. Schreck
Osric .... Alois P. Andrle
Marcellus .... John C. Hazenzahl
Bernardo .... Fred A. Zorn
First Gravedigger .... Edward J. White
Second Gravedigger .... John L. Wex
Queen Gertrude .... Miss Annie Beutter
Ophelia .... Mrs. Emily O'Neil
Player Queen................... Miss Bohumila Andrle

*H*amlet, one of the greatest tragedies, written by Shakespeare in 1602, was founded upon a legend in *Historia Dancia*, a history of Denmark and its dependencies from their beginning down to the year 1186. Saxo Grammaticus, a grammarian known as the "Learned One," wrote it. Shakespeare, however, owed little but the outline of his plot to Saxo, whose hero, Amleth, only feigned his madness and plotted deliberate vengeance a year before carrying it out. For a small group, such as the St. Louis Dramatic Circle, an undertaking of this magnitude needed some arrangements in composition and adaptation to a small stage. Besides devising appropriate costumes, lighting, and sound effects, the managers provided for a reduction of the size of the cast. Only three courtiers were used in the Circle's production; the roles of Voltimand and Cornelius of Shakespeare's original play were incorporated into the characters of Rosencrantz

and Guildenstern. The role of Osric, who appears in the last Act, was produced intact. Lines for Reynaldo, a servant to Polonius and Fortinbras, prince of Norway, were interwoven into other characters, introduced by inference, or dropped when unnecessary for the substance of the play. No changes were made in the characterizations of Claudius, King of Denmark; Hamlet, son of the late King, known as Amleth, and nephew to Claudius; Polonius, the lord chamberlain; Horatio, a friend and schoolmate of Hamlet; Laertes, son of Polonius, Gertrude, queen of Denmark and mother to Hamlet; Ophelia, daughter of Polonius. The role of Francisco was incorporated into those of the principal officers, Marcellus and Bernardo, and the two gravediggers were given the same prominence as in the original play. Several non-speaking or limited-speaking parts as lords, ladies, officers, soldiers, sailors, messengers, attendants, and minor actors and actresses for the play within a play were performed by members of the society or chosen from the general parish population without credits.

*A*s in all of Shakespeare's tragedies, a single flaw in the principal character caused his downfall and that of many around him. Within Hamlet that flaw was indecision and procrastination. Although he learned, early in the play from the Ghost of his father, that King Claudius, his uncle, had poisoned his father and married his mother, the queen, an act of incest, he, through vacillation and irresolution, postponed and deferred open accusations. He advocated devious activities, such as "a play within a play," exposing their crimes while performing before the court so as to bring the king and queen to realize their sins and elicit their confession. The story continued to unfold with one disaster after another, inflicting pain and death upon the principals in the cast, until the last Act ended with all but Horatio dead. It was then that he, whose role was near flawlessly played by Otto R. Rick, expressed the disaster resulting from Hamlet's want of firmness. Horatio said, "And let me speak to the unknowing world of carnal, bloody, and unnatural acts, of accidental judgments, casual slaughters, of deaths put on by cunning and forced cause, and, in this upshot, purposes mistook fall'n on the inventors' heads: all this I can truly deliver."

The entire play was staged at Elsinore Castle in Denmark. In the leading role, Otto F. Andrle gave a marvelous impersonation of Hamlet, the melancholy Dane. He was most convincing in his rendition of Hamlet's soliloquies. With deep emotion he bewildered himself as to how his mother could mourn the death of Amleth, her husband, while sharing her bed with his brother, Claudius. After a group of players had performed at the castle, Hamlet decided to employ them to present a play in which the actors would blatantly express the sins of his uncle and mother. In a soliloquy at this point, Andrle was most impressive in expressing Hamlet's inability to act in vengeance. He says, "But I am pigeon-liver'd and lack gall to make oppression bitter, or ere this I should have fatted all the region kites with this slaves offal: bloody, bawdy villain! Remorseless, treacherous, lecherous, kindless villain! O, vengeance! Why, what an ass am I! This is most brave, that I, the son of a dear father murder'd, must like a whore, unpack my heart with words, and fall a-cursing, like a very drab, a scullion! Fie upon 't! About my brain! Hum, I have heard that guilty creatures, sitting at a play, have by the very cunning of the scene been struck so to the soul that presently they have proclaimed their malefactions. The play's the thing wherein I'll catch the conscience of the king."

Andrle was most convincing of Hamlet's ability at indecision while he expounded those most oft quoted words, "To be or not to be that is the question: Whether 'tis nobler in the mind to suffer the slings and arrows of outrageous fortune, or to take arms against a sea of troubles, and by opposing end them!" The review of the play in the *Buffalo Times* praised Andrle's talent saying, "he has unmistakable talent, a strong dramatic face and a good stage presence. With proper training he might attain to more than ordinary success as an actor." The *Commercial Advertiser* said, "Andrle was excellent and at times showed true dramatic fire and inspiration. He surprised his many friends by his fine interpretation of so difficult a role." Andrle, who was a twenty-two year old amateur, was most pleased with the critics' remarks.

The casual slaughters and deaths by cunning or forced causes that Horatio spoke of in the last Act began with the accidental death of Polonius in Queen Gertrude's chambers. Hamlet, who had come to confront her with her incest with Claudius, following the "play within a play," saw a motion behind the hanging drapery. He thought it was a rat, pulled forth his rapier, and slashed down on the curtain. Polonius, who had been speaking to the queen before Hamlet entered, had hidden himself behind the cloth. The swish of the drape was not the motion of a rat; it was Polonius, and Hamlet mortally wounded him! Hamlet feigned madness, Polonius' body was conveniently and privately buried, and the king ordered Rosencrantz and Guildenstern, two faithful courtiers, to sail with Hamlet to England. Laertes, son of Polonius, who had gone to Paris earlier in the play, returned to Denmark seeking the murderer of his father. His sister Ophelia, who had fallen in love with Hamlet, had flights of insanity when she found out that her father had been murdered and that Hamlet had departed for England. In her despair she committed suicide by drowning. Pirates attacked the ship upon which Hamlet and the courtiers had sailed, and Hamlet was saved by them. Rosencrantz and Guildenstern, however, went on to England but only found death at the end of their adventure.

Upon returning to Denmark, Hamlet met with Laertes, who, believing Hamlet had killed his father, challenged him to a duel. Before this gentleman's deadly combat began, King Claudius devised a plan to rid the world of Hamlet. He placed a cup of poisoned wine at the table set at the scene of action. Laertes' foil was dipped by the king into the poison but Hamlet's was not. The game began and Hamlet struck first and cut Laertes. Sweat fell from Hamlet's brow; his mother, the queen, wiped his forehead; and, in her thirst, she drank from the poisoned cup. She died! Hamlet and Laertes continued on with the bout and Hamlet was struck and bled. The poison took time to travel through his blood stream so the fight went on. In a series of parries and thrusts, the foils were dislodged from their hands and exchanged. In the immediate renewal of combat, Laertes was cut and blood came forth. The fight stopped. Laertes told Hamlet how the king, with tongue in his cheek, had devised this mortal farce. With violence, Hamlet stabbed the king; he died! Laertes died! Hamlet died! In the end four bodies lay crumpled upon the stage, and in military fashion were withdrawn with rueful music playing amidst a drum roll and a peal of canon ordnance.

*O*tto Richard Rick, who at the age of twenty-two played magnificently the role of Horatio, was born in Buffalo, August 26, 1865. He was the son of John Rick and Elizabeth Catherine Motsch. Otto's grandparents, John Adam Rick and Teresa Fromweiler, who were emigrants from Germany, first settled in New York City, then came to Buffalo in 1841. They and their families were early members of St. Louis Church. Otto received his education in St. Louis' parochial school and in Public School Sixteen. At the age of thirteen, he became associated with the firm of Adam, Meldrum, and Anderson Company. His first position was as sweeper of the street in front of the store and cash boy. When he was twenty years old, after moving up the ladder of responsibility, he became a buyer. He was one of the youngest buyers to visit New York City from the large mercantile firm. He made numerous trips abroad, visiting foreign markets; he was most fond of his visits to Paris. From 1920 to 1930, he was a department manager and a stockholder in the company. He also was joint owner, with his brother, Frederick F. Rick, in the firm of F.F. Rick, dealers in bicycle supplies on Main

Street. They also operated a factory on Oak Street were they manufactured artistic designs and pictures on leather and wood by burning the material with hot instruments. This art form was known as pyrography. For three years Otto Rick was president of the National Wholesale Notion Buyers Association. On February 6, 1895, he married Frances Barbara Futterer, daughter of Erhard Futterer and Magdalena Rehm, at St. Louis Church. Frances had been born in Buffalo in 1866, and received her education at St. Louis parochial school and at D'Youville College. When they made their family residence on Highland Avenue, they became members of Cathedral Parish on Delaware Avenue. Otto was one of the early members of the St. Louis Dramatic Circle but offered his resignation on January 13, 1896 because his work took him away from Buffalo for extended periods of time. Besides having the role of Horatio in Hamlet, he also played Jacques Strop in *Robert Macaire* in 1894. He died in Buffalo at the age of seventy-three in 1938. [1]

*E*ach of the three performances of *Hamlet*, Shakespeare's masterpiece, was given before "a full house;" it was standing room only! For the three nights, the box office told a flattering tale of admission of more than fifteen hundred with a gross profit of $450.00. After *Hamlet*, the Circle turned to comedy. On May 8, and 9, 1888, it produced two one-act, truly belly-tickler comedies, *The Good for Nothing* and *Slasher and Crasher*. Again the school auditorium was filled to capacity. A year later, on September 25, and 26, 1889, the auditorium was again the scene of hilarious laughter as the Circle presented *Lucky Sixpence* and *Declined with Thanks*. In 1890 plays were given in April and in November. Even ten years later many parishioners and friends of St. Louis Church who had come in from the countryside remembered seeing and enjoying the acting of *The Bells, Cool as a Cucumber,* and *A Day's Fishing*. Of the three, only *The Bells* was produced in St. Louis Church's schoolhall. Following this production in April, the Circle's response to its advertising for the next set of plays to be offered on

Thanksgiving night was so overwhelming that a larger theater was employed. When ticket sales for a single performance reached one thousand two hundred, the officers of the Circle knew that only the Concert Hall, also known as the Elmwood Music Hall, would accommodate such a vast audience. On opening night the placard reading "standing room only" was hung out before the curtain rose. For the next five years the Concert Hall was the home to the St. Louis Dramatic Circle. Among the several plays presented there, one parishioner remembered with delight *The Charcoal Burner*, a romantic drama in two acts by George Almar, and *Robert Macaire*, a melodrama, in two acts by Charles Sellig. In 1896, the Music Hall was again used to present, *The Signal*, a drama in three acts written by Sterling Coyne that had been first produced at the Royal Olympic Theater.

On the tenth anniversary of the founding of the Dramatic Circle, the society held a banquet in St. Louis' school hall on August 12, 1895. It titled the entertainment that evening, *The Tin Wedding*. It was not a play, but the hall was decorated with artistic taste and skill; it presented a very attractive appearance. Above the proscenium, the framework of the stage above the curtain was an emblem suggested by scenes from the upcoming play, *The Signal*. These included the chateau in the Tyrol, Klaus Gottstein's mill, St. Basil's chapel, the village of St. Michele, and the Rock of Salurn. Also placed there was a shield formed of smilax, woody vines having leaves with several parallel veins, dioecious flowers, and globose berries. Embedded in the smilax were torches, weapons, and masks; on either side of the shield was an American flag. Throughout the hall statues of Shakespeare, Othello, Joseph Jefferson, and other famous people from the fields of music and drama were delicately placed. Upon opening the curtain, the dinner guests saw the stage set as the ravine scene in *Legend of the Catskills*, the first play produced by the Dramatic Circle. Around the walls of the hall were ornamental placards, bearing the titles of the plays presented by this amateur society

during the ten years of its existence. One would have likened the general aspect of the hall to that of a conservatory filled with palms and beautiful flowers.

A huge table set in the form of a "T" was profusely and elegantly decked. The menu card provided for the guests was a decidedly unique and original affair, consisting of two heavy pieces of American tin, hand-painted, with a silver-mounted card between, on which was printed the "bill of fare," and the names of officers and members of the Circle. On the reverse side was inscribed, *Our Tin Wedding*, with a note of appreciation to all the parishioners attending plus the many prominent citizens of the city who were accompanied by their wives. In the center of the crossbar of the "T" sat the pastor, Father Paul Hoelscher, and his assistant, Father Fuchs. On the wings, next to them, with their wives, sat the officers of the Dramatic Circle. On the right were: Charles M. Weyand, president; Otto F. Andrle, honorary president and manager; Louis J. Roth, vice-president; Frank L. Diebold, secretary. On the left, with their wives sat: Fred J. Kiefer Jr., treasurer; Fred A. Zorn, business manager; Edward J. White, properties; and Frank J. Haberstro, chairman of the membership committee. In the first places, in the stem of the "T", sitting with their wives, were the remaining members of the society: Frank P. Batt, John C. Hazenzahl, John P. Mayer, Edward F. Mischka, Otto R. Rick, Charles M. Schmidt, William Sanders, Edward M. Ottenot, Thomas G. Dunphy, Frank L. Mayer, George F. Neunder, Joseph S. Schmidt, Louis F. Jansen, John A. Kerker, George J. Schwartz, and Jacob Muth.

Edward F. Mischka acted as the toastmaster and chairman of the banquet committee. Following the consumption of a most delicious and expertly served dinner by caterer Brown, he opened the entertainment by introducing Charles M. Weyand, president of the St. Louis Dramatic Circle, who delivered a brief, but pleasing address, in the course of which he gave many interesting facts concerning the amateur organization. When he had finished, Reverend Paul Hoelscher, pastor of St. Louis Church, was called upon; he made flattering mention of the good works accomplished by the Circle since its formation. He spoke of the substantial aid it had made in diminishing the debt of the church, and declared that its management must have been in the hands of good and able pilots, to have gone on so harmoniously and prosperously for a period of ten years. Father Fuchs, assistant to the pastor, took to the podium and said that the society had done much to elevate the moral drama, which was a necessity of the time. Following up on Hoelscher's remarks, he stressed that the entire net proceeds of each and every performance had gone toward extinguishing the debt on the church. Speaking of the members of the society he said, "Not one of them was ever personally benefited to the amount of a single penny. On the contrary, all gave their time and services gratuitously and cheerfully; and in many instances this was done at greater or less sacrifice of their own business interests which in most cases were legion." Edward J. White then recalled how in 1885, following the great fire, that the Dramatic Circle was formed for the purpose of obtaining the necessary funds to rebuild the church. It was at this point that he gave his recollections of events on that tragic night. He said, "I saw two young men going up into the steeple ahead of one of the firemen who was carrying a hose. Later I learned that the young men were Ramsperger and Grimm; the fireman was Roth. I was only fourteen years old, but I thought I could be of some help, so I began to follow them. Suddenly I saw a mass of flames bust from the steeple, the lads were trapped, and Roth fell through a gaping hole in the roof. I ran down the stairs as fast as I could."

*B*efore Mischka introduced the next series of songs and sayings, he too followed up on Fuch's comments. He said, "The sums realized from these performances, during the past ten years, have increased with each succeeding entertainment, and the aggregate amount realized and handed over to the trustees of the church was far from insignificant." He then proceeded to speak from his heart about the members' devotion, talent, and reward. He said, "Amateur dramatic performances, as a rule, may not be written down as unqualified successes. While some amateur actors and actresses have shown very decided histrionic ability, others have proved lamentable failures; but these latter have been let down easy, as not being amenable to strict and rigid criticism because they were doing their level best for the benefit of a worthy cause. Now we, the St. Louis Dramatic Circle, while we would not, like the lady in the play, 'protest too much,' claim with due and beseeming modesty, that the entertainments we have thus far given, have been such as to win the favor of our audiences and to call forth encouraging comment from those competent to judge. Therefore we ask no exemption from censure when such is merited, at the hands of the critics. We shall always labor zealously and conscientiously to please, and will never be discouraged or consider ourselves ill-treated by the candid setting forth of failures or shortcomings on our part. It is no boast for us to say, that the dramatic representations hitherto given by the Circle have been highly successful from a financial point of view; and we might perhaps go a little further, without laying ourselves liable to the charge of 'blowing our own horn' and state our belief that the patrons of the Circle have been pleasantly entertained by our efforts. For your encouragement and support, hitherto extended to us, we return our most sincere thanks. Further, we promise that, in the future, as in the past, we will use our best exertions to merit the approval and favor of our friends, patrons, and the general public."

*W*hen Mischka had finished, John A. Kerker, one of the youngest members of the society, asked the toastmaster if he could make a comment. Mischka replied in the affirmative. Kerker then rose from his place at the table and said, "While I was listening to Ed White recall his experience during the fire of 1885, my memory also went back to the events that I experienced that evening. I was three years younger than White and was at home during the conflagration. I had to wait to hear of the events from my father, Henry, who was an observer of the fire. He told how Mr. Louis H. Plogsted, well known cornet player and leader of the Buffalo's celebrated 65th Regiment Band, had just taken his seat in the orchestra pit of the German-American Music Hall, to arrange his instrument, when Mr. Tischendorf, a trombone player, rushed in and shouted that there was a fire on the stage. Plogsted looked up and saw the blazing scenery. He rushed back to get his overcoat; and, by the time he got back out front to retrieve his cornet, the heat and smoke were so intense that he had to crawl out through the auditorium without a moment to spare. While he was making his escape, performers were exiting through the stage door in their costumes, each grabbing whatever they could save. Manager John H. Meech and the doorkeepers were in hot pursuit of them. Luckily, only a few of the audience had assembled; they were able to exit, very frightened, but without being harmed."

Like a true Toastmaster, one always ready for a comment that would bring laughter to a rather serious topic, Mischka said, "Thank you, John, for those memories. I understand that your father also told you that the performers, who had escaped in their costumes, made quite a spectacular entrance into Schenkelberger's beer garden on Main and Virginia Streets following their escape. Good German beer always has that effect of washing away fears and tears!" Following these speeches, comments, and subsequent toasts Otto F. Andrle and Miss Murphy gave a vocal music rendition which, upon completion, was greeted with hearty applause. Mrs. Edward F. Mischka who contributed a series of humorous stories that brought much laughter into the room followed them. When it seemed that the entertainment had run its course and there were no more performers waiting in the wings, the guests responded with loud cries of encore, encore, encore! At this point Otto F. Andrle, always the flamboyant eccentric, the perpetual thespian who in daily life dressed in black and wore a cloak and hat, rose to the occasion and gave

Mark Antony's Oration from Shakespeare's play *Julius Caesar*. Immediately applause went up with his introduction, "I come not to bury Caesar, but to praise him." After he finished the full oration, he received a standing ovation. Informal proceedings and mingling continued until a late hour when the guests dispersed with all conceding that they had had a right good jolly time!

During the next thirty years, the St. Louis Dramatic Circle was very faithful to produce at least one extraordinary play on each anniversary year of its founding. In 1905 it rendered *Paul Revere*, held at the Teck Theater. In 1925, *To the Ladies* was produced at the Majestic Theater, and on May 12, 1935, *The Dictator*, written by Richard Harding Davis and presented at the Teck Theater, was the Circle's offering for its Golden Jubilee. The play was a situation-comedy, a farce filled with trenchant wit, irony, and sarcasm. It exposed and discredited the vice and folly of the United States' intervention in the internal affairs of the Banana Republics of Central America; the instability of these Republics, where dictators reigned supreme under the guise of presidents allegedly elected by the people; and a social attitude whereby all peace was to be achieved when sufficient amounts of wealth were dispersed into the most influential pockets. The Dramatic Committee, composed of Edward M. Simon, Louis Ludaescher, and Carl A. Albert, chose the script as it was presented by Charles Frohman at the Criterion Theater in New York City in 1904. That year saw the election of Theodore Roosevelt as President of the United States, who, while vice-president, first took the oath as president in Buffalo, New York, upon the death of William Mckinley at the Pan American Exposition in 1901. Roosevelt had been the hero of San Juan Hill, near Santiago de Cuba, in 1898 during the Spanish-American War. His policy in the Caribbean and Central America was to "speak softly and carry a big stick!" He arrogated the sole right of intervention in Latin America to the United States. In 1935, however, the Dramatic Committee chose the play because they believed that it ridiculed indirectly the dictatorial powers which had been given to Benito Mussolini of Italy in 1922, and to Adolph Hitler of Germany in 1933. In 1935, both Mussolini with his Facist Party and Hitler with his Nazi Party were strongly affecting world politics.

The story line of the play revolved around a fictitious Republic of Central America known as San Manana whose major port and capital was located at Porto Banos. It was situated somewhere near the Republic of Panama and within easy reach of Jamaica, an island paradise in the West Indies governed by Britain. There were three acts to the play; the first was a scene aboard the *Bolivar*, a cruise ship of the Red "C" Line, which came to anchor in the harbor of Porto Banos before discharging its passengers at 5:00 A.M. The next two acts took place ashore at the United States Consulate. The first at 7:00 A.M. and the second at 10:00 A.M. True to comic opera, much action took place in a short time. Arriving at Porto Banos on the *Bolivar* were Brooke Travers, played by John P. Mayer Jr. and his valet, Jim Simpson, played by H. Edward Albert. With them were Colonel John T. Bowie, United States Consul to San Manana, played by Louis Ludaescher and Bowie's wife, Julia, played by Mary I. Kammerer. Another principal character was Duffy, a New York City detective, played by Emmanuel F. Gollwitzer. Also aboard was Lucy Sheridan, played by Mary Frances O'Neil, who had come to Porto Banos to seek out her betrothed, Arthur Bostick, a missionary whose parish was in the hills surrounding the city. Gerard Ernewein played his role. Edward A. Rick, played Samuel Codman, the ship's captain; Walter J. Rick, played Charley Hyne, the wireless operator, and Carl A. Albert, played Doctor Vasquez, the health officer of Porto Banos.

Travers and Simpson were traveling under assumed aliases. They had left New York in a rush after having a fight with a con-man cabby who overcharged them. In the tussle the cabby fell down and cracked his skull against the curb and was assumed dead. A crowd of ruffians accused Travers and Simpson of murder. In desperation the two had stolen the cab, drove to Twenty-Third Street; and, at midnight, boarded the *Bolivar*, not knowing for whence it was bound. Hearing those two suspects of the crime had boarded the Red "C" Line, but not knowing who they were, Duffy decided to go along and follow the clue. Bowie and his wife, Julia, were already on board. Bowie had been United States Consul in all but one Central American Republic, San Manana. It was his new assignment and he carried his credentials with him. He also had sent ahead of him to Porto Banos, Senor Rigas, for whom he had purchased the right to be president of the Republic with $1,500 placed in selected hands of the nation's military. With his pawn and dupe, Rigas, as president, Bowie imagined himself, upon arrival, to be the future dictator of San Manana with Julia as the first lady of the land. Travers tried to find out if Bowie, when he became the Consul would have an extradition policy favorable to himself and Simpson; one which would prevent them from being sent back to New York where they feared conviction and hanging.

Duffy thought that he could arrest the two men responsible for the dastardly act of murder when he saw the ship's passengers disembark. Lucy Sheridan hoped that Arthur Bostick would be waiting for her at the dock. Bowie, however, was unaware that at the hotel in Porto Banos, Senora Juanita Arquilla, who had known him in Panama, was present. She would have married him; but instead of doing so, he went north and married Julia. Because of this, Juanita now hated Bowie and wanted only to carve out his heart with her ever-ready dagger. Suddenly, Vasques, the health officer, boarded the ship so as to approve the passengers for disembarkment. He announced that a revolution had taken place in Porto Banos, Rigas had been put in a dungeon as a prisoner, and General Santos Campos was now the president and dictator of all San Manana. Bowie was shocked and frightened because he knew that he would be recognized at the dock and killed before he reached the Consulate. He accepted Travers' offer to exchange identities, stay on board, and allow Travers to assume the role of Consul with his credentials. The curtain fell on Act One as Travers exited the deck of the ship. With Duffy watching everyone intently, Travers, making-believe that he was Bowie, pulled Julia into his arms and cried, "Goodbye, Julia, I'm going ashore, be back in a minute."

As the curtain rose on Act Two, Travers, Simpson, and Hyne were at the Consulate. They had arrived there safely because Campos' soldiers had not recognized them at the dock. Although they knew that Campos would not kill them once they were inside the Consulate, they realized that they were essentially his prisoners and had to play for time. First, they had to get Duffy to arrest Bostick, claiming him to be the murderer of the cabby, and take him back to the ship which would return to New York. Juanita, however, came to the Consulate and learned that Travers had made a switch of identity with Bowie. Travers, in turn, learned that she was in love with Bostick and wanted to marry him. She told Travers that she would not spill the beans to Campos if Travers, acting as the Consul, would refuse to extradite Bostick, who had been arrested by Duffy. Lucy, however, arrived and said that she wanted to marry Bostick. Travers, who had become infatuated with Lucy, did not want this to happen, refused to let Bostick go free, sent Duffy, Juanita, and Bostick back to the ship to be taken to New York. Campos arrived with his men, thought Travers was Bowie, but told Travers that he would kill him if he went outside the door. Travers showed Campos how Hyne had set up the wireless and could contact the United States as he wished. Campos took this news lightly and left. His aide, Corporal Manuel, played by Frank L. Diebold, remained behind. Travers, who had brought $25,000 with him from New York, asked the corporal how much it would cost to buy an army. Manuel said that he could rent two thousand good men, all belonging to Campos, for twenty cents a man per day. He said, "Campos only pays each

cents a day." Travers thought that it would be a good deal to buy an army for eight days for only $3,200. All the other soldiers in the room with Manuel agreed. They said, "It's a good deal; the new revolution will begin at 11:00 A.M." Travers jumped to the top of the table, raised his glass of rum and proposed a toast to the assemblage, he said, "We start a revolution. I am going to make myself president. Before lunch, I will be dictator of San Manana!" With this cry the curtain fell.

Act Three opened at the Consulate on a sad note. People from Bostick's mission in the mountains had come down and liberated Bostick and Juanita from Duffy. Duffy all dirty and bruised, entered the room and told his sad story. Travers asked Duffy to forget Bostick, but to go back on board the *Bolivar*, and arrest Bowie as the murderer he was seeking. All seemed to go well; Julia had her Bowie on board, Duffy thought he could arrest Bowie, Juanita was off in the mountains with Bostick, and Lucy, who did not have to marry Bostick, looked with favor upon Travers who liked her very much. Hyne who had set up the wireless made contact with the *U.S.S. Oregon*, a cruiser heading into the harbor of Porto Banos. Colonel Garcia, aide to Campos and played by Norman L. Kolb, suddenly arrived with his men and surrounded the Consulate. Campos came into the room and announced that Travers would be thrown into a dungeon. Suddenly, however, the clock struck eleven and the revolution began.

Next the United States Marines from the *Oregon* burst into the room and took Campos prisoner. They were played by members of the Knights of St. John, Commandery 204. They were: Joseph F. Lux, Paul Hardick, Albert Egar, Eugene W. Miller Sr., Frank Ross, Richard Ball, Charles Schifferle Jr., and Clarence Bork. With them was Lieutenant Victor Perry, played by Paul A. Albert. Perry informed Travers of what had happened since the *Oregon* received the message of the problem in San Manana. He said that Duffy was really assigned to come to Porto Banos, not to arrest anyone, but to find out whom the two men were who left from New York on the *Bolivar*. He said that no one was murdered in New York, but that some ruffians had been rounded up and accused of hurting two men who had quite a bit of money with them. Travers confessed that he was not Bowie and told Simpson and Lucy that everyone could go home now because there was no crime and no one would be hanged for murder. As Travers and Lucy were leaving the room, Travers said to her, "Lucy I will go home now; and, if I must be dictator, I prefer to do my dictating to a stenographer in little ole New York!" The curtain fell. The play ended.

After 1913, the Circle began to produce a lesser number of plays because the first objective of the society had been fulfilled. With the generosity of all parishioners the debt on the great gothic structure had been reduced to zero. The mortgage was burned, and the Circle had been extremely helpful in gradually reducing that debt. From profit on the plays it gave $11,000 to the building fund. In 1900, during the second bazaar, it gave another $3,230.61 to the trustees. This amount was nineteen and one-half percent of the net profit of the entire group of societies working for the reduction of the debt in that year. Another societal change affected the second objective of the society. The legitimate theater, so popular at the turn of the twentieth century, was endangered by the fledgling motion picture industry. The production of plays became prohibitive in cost with little net return. The last play, *Room Service*, which the Circle staged at the Knights of Columbus Hall, was produced just prior to World War II. After this performance, the members retained their affiliation with each other, but only as a social organization. In 1960, eighteen members held a dinner celebrating the Circle's seventy-fifth anniversary. In 1978, four surviving members were still using funds from their treasury of petty cash as bequests of Masses to be said at St. Louis Church for their deceased members. Formerly, when the membership had been in its prime, this money was used to purchase beer and snacks for each of the monthly meetings. (2)

The Dramatic Circle membership rarely missed an opportunity to get together and celebrate, and the long-lived organization had many anniversaries to honor. It held the distinction of being the oldest amateur dramatic society in continuous existence in the United States. The members enjoyed many dinners together, and joined with the Knights of St. John Commandery 204 on river parties aboard a barge whose home base was Grand Island, smack in the middle of Niagara River. During a daylong cruise it stopped at the Bedell House and the amusement park where everyone enjoyed a ride on the Ferris wheel. On other occasions the two groups went to Crystal Beach in Canada. Norman White, whose father was Edward Joseph White, one of the founders of the Circle, recalled, "Going to Crystal Beach, we always teamed up with members of the Fornes and Schifferle families. Charlie Schifferle was the mechanic at Rick's bicycle shop on Main Street. He was an expert at putting monogram name plates on bikes."

On the twenty-fifth anniversary celebration in 1910, a grand affair was held at the German-American Cafe in Buffalo. Twenty-five members and their wives enjoyed a menu featuring oyster cocktail, green turtle soup a la American, devilled crabs, filet mignon with mushrooms, broiled squab, café parfait, coffee, and cigars. After dinner a songfest was held, featuring old favorites such as *America, A Stein Song, Swanee River, By the Light of the Silvery Moon, Dixie Land, Grand Old Flag, Has Anybody Here Seen Kelly, Old Black Joe, My Old Kentucky Home, Star Spangled Banner,* and *Auld Lang Syne*. The same type of banquet was held on the fortieth anniversary on October 19, 1925, with twenty-nine members and their wives and again on the fiftieth anniversary on October 21, 1935. On Thursday evening, October 20, 1960, eighteen members and their wives met at the American Legion Post Troop I in the Hamlin House on Franklin Street one block north of the church. They celebrated their seventy-fifth anniversary with a dinner, toasts, and good song. Walter J. Rick was the toastmaster. Among the many songs sung that night it seemed as if the *Stein Song* was the one most deeply embedded in their hearts. The words rolled off their tongues, " Give a rouse, then in the May-time for a life that knows no fear! Turn the nighttime into daytime with the sunlight of good cheer! For it's always fair weather when good fellows get together, with a stein on the table and a good song ringing clear." One might consider this party as the ringing down of the final curtain on the last Act in the Dramatic Circle's life.

*I*n theatrical compositions, however, the score writers sometimes like to have a denouement, the final revelation. Each Sunday when one sees Robert Paul Albert and his wife Patricia, nee Riley, greeting people arriving at the 10:30 A.M. Mass and listening to her beautiful voice in the choir, one can reflect on this final revelation. Robert Albert could claim himself to be the last living member of the Dramatic Circle; he joined in 1950; he was one of the eighteen members who celebrated the seventy-fifth anniversary with the group at Troop I. With him at the banquet that evening was his father, Carl A. Albert, the vice-president of the Circle. The others were: Louis Ludaescher, Edward A. Rick Sr., Edwin H. Kolb, William A. Breitweiser, Raymond M. Didley, Raymond J. Hoffman, Frank M. Keller, Raymond G. Kessel, Raymond P. Lux, Charles S. Mergenhagen, Edward A. Rick Jr., Walter J. Rick, Frank S. Ross, Karl I. Schirra, Edward M. Simon, and William P. Walters. Five years later, the Dramatic Circle wanted to celebrate the eightieth anniversary with a dinner in the Church Hall for its remaining thirteen members. It never came to pass. At the time, Louis Ludaescher, the oldest member who had joined in 1903, was eighty-nine years old, president of the Circle, and living on Northampton Street. Edward J. Rick Jr., who with Robert Albert joined in 1950, was forty-one years old and lived on Dalton Drive in the Town of Tonawanda. Edward A. Rick Sr. was still in good health and held the office of Secretary-treasurer; he died in 1979. The other two officers present were Carl Albert, treasurer, and Edwin H. Kolb, business manager.

Edward A. Rick Jr. died on July 29, 1991 at the age of sixty-seven. Now only Robert Albert is alive.

A predominance of the family name "Rick" appears in the programs for plays and banquets of the Dramatic Circle. One finds Otto Richard Rick, Edward Anthony Rick Sr., Edward Anthony Rick Jr., and Walter Joseph Rick, all associated, life-long, with St. Louis Church, as were all their ancestors. These men trace their roots to John Adam Rick, born in Germany in 1813, married Theresa Fromweiler in 1836, and died in Buffalo in 1889. Two years before he died, while in the employ of Holmes Manufacturing Company, he had the opportunity to see his grandson, Otto Richard Rick, play the role of Horatio in Shakespeare's drama *Hamlet* produced by the Dramatic Circle. His own son, John Rick, who had been born in Buffalo in 1841 and married Elizabeth Catherine Motsch at St. Louis Church in 1862, had five other children, all boys, besides Otto Richard. They were Edward John, Julius Anton, Julius Michael, Frederick Francis, and Thomas Anton. Edward John married Mary Elizabeth Neupert at St. Louis Church in 1889, the same year his grandfather died. They had five children: Edith Mary, Edward Anthony, Walter Joseph, Leo Frederick, and Mary Frances. Edward Anthony, being born in 1892, was two years older than Walter Joseph, who died one year before the seventy-fifth anniversary banquet was held.

*E*dward Anthony, like his uncle, Otto Richard Rick who was a successful employee of Adam Meldrum and Anderson Company, humbly started out as mail boy, promoted to office boy, moved on to approval clerk, assigned as a bookkeeper, raised to a secretary, and finally chosen to be cashier and director of the Adam Meldrum and Anderson State Bank. Besides being a member of the St. Louis Dramatic Circle, he was active in the Democratic Party, served as a trustee at St. Louis Church where he was a member in good standing, achieved the fourth degree in the Knights of Columbus, kept his membership in the Buffalo

Automobile Club, and continued as a member of the 74th Regiment, New York National Guard, for seven years, from which he was discharged with the rank of sergeant. On June 6, 1917, he married Charlotte B. Wischerath, daughter of Henry Wischerath, who was associated with the Buffalo Forge Company, and his wife Lottie, nee Kern. Lottie Kern was a student at St. Louis' parochial school but transferred to a public school before graduation. Together, Edward A. Rick and Charlotte had four children: Dorothy Edith, Lucile Esther, Edward A. Jr., and Charlotte Mae. They had their residence on Ellicott Street during World War II from whence Edward A. Jr. entered and served in the military until its conclusion.

Dorothy Edith married Michael John Zobel at St. Louis Church in 1943. Their only child was a son, Michael John Zobel Jr. In July 1975, four years before he died, Edward A. Rick Sr. returned to the room on the third floor of the school, which the Dramatic Circle had used as an office. The room had been collecting only dust on the various memorabilia which had decorated the walls or were filed away in the cabinets since 1970 when the last thirteen members discussed having one last dinner together. On that day Michael John Zobel Jr., his grandson, accompanied him. It was with heavy heart that they began to sort out old pictures, programs, tickets, receipts for program ads, and banquet menus. Tears came to the eyes of Edward A. Rick Sr., a man who had turned eighty-three on his birthday, March 26, 1975. Collecting this material, which his grandson called treasures, brought back many memories, some serious, some comical.

When all the material was gathered, Michael Zobel took it home. His own words express the drama of the occasion. He wrote, "As a youth, I delighted in my grandfather's recollections of 'ancient history' and his uncanny ability to still recite his lines of several plays verbatim with much exuberance! In 1975, the few remaining members realized that all good things had to come to an end. Luckily I was available one evening to help my grandfather close the Dramatic Circle Room in the old schoolhouse. I finally got to see first hand the St. Louis Hall that I had heard so much about. I was awestruck. Recently I found myself comparing it to seeing photographs of the sunken Titanic. We loaded all the material into the car and that was it. I, however, have never forgotten the experience! My Mother and I had always planned that one-day we would put all these treasures in chronological order. Years later, I became the self-appointed guardian of the Dramatic Circle memorabilia. To display the collection as much as is practical, while protecting its integrity for future generations was my chief concern. I did so in two large volumes that contain programs which, although some are quite deteriorated, have both entertainment and educational value, and paid advertisements which are treasures in themselves. They promote products and services that uniquely reflect the every day business scene in Buffalo during the latter nineteenth century and nearly one-half of the twentieth century. It is a collection and a display which shows that the Dramatic Circle played an important role in the history of St. Louis Church and the City of Buffalo."

Catholics believe in the resurrection and the life; it is the basis of their faith to believe in life everlasting. One can then say that old thespians of the St. Louis Dramatic Circle never die; they just fade away. They wait to take the last curtain call, and when they do one shall see: Otto Andrle, Louis Roth, Adam Dory, Albert Zahm, Albert Rose, Adolph Zeller, Alois P. Andrle, Charles Deck, John L. Wex, John C. Hasenzahl, Reverend William J. Schreck, Charles Biesinger, Otto Richard Rick, Charles M. Schmidt, William Sanders, Edward M. Ottenot, Thomas G. Dunphy, George F. Neunder, Joseph S. Schmidt, Louis F. Jansen, George E. Schwartz, Jacob Muth, William Breitweiser, Frank J. Haberstro, Raymond M. Didley, Raymond J. Hoffman, Frank M. Kellner, Raymond G. Kessel, Raymond P. Lux, Charles S. Mergenhagen, Edward A. Rick Sr., Walter J. Rick, Frank S. Ross, Karl I. Schirra,

Edward M. Simon, William P. Walters, Charles M. Weyand, Joseph J. Lux, John A. Kerker, Frederick Schweigert, John Kam, Frederick Kiefer, Charles Scherf, Edward F. Mischka, Fred A. Zorn, Frank P. Batt, Edward J. White, John M. Fornes, Michael J. Fornes, John P. Mayer Sr., John P. Mayer Jr., Frank J. Mingen, Frank L. Mayer, Frank L. Diebold, William H. Kiefer, James Ogden, John A. Bralla, Frederick J. Kessel, Karl A. Kiefer, Frank Schoenberger, William Ramsperger, Bernard F. Mayer, Lucian Haas, August Hettrick, Norman Kolb, Raymond Kopp, Harry A. Schweigert, and Henry Hecht.

*B*efore the curtain comes down after their last bow, one member, Charles Weyand will step forward and repeat his written invitation which he wrote prior to the production of *The Ticket of Leave Man* produced by the Circle in 1902. In that invitation he managed to include every play which had been produced from the founding of the organization to the play he was promoting. He wrote, "This is aimed at you! Keep *Cool as a Cucumber*, and do not act as if you were *Flying From Justice*. This is merely a *Signal* to you to assist in making Saturday, March 1, 1902, *A Red Letter Day* on Dodge Street, situated on the north side of a *Hamlet* bounded by Main and Ellicott Streets. Bear date in mind and do not arrange for *A Day's Fishing*. The *Bells* will ring at 8:30 PM sharp, and the undersigned hopes this invitation will not be *Declined With Thanks*. This invitation is given *Advice Gratis*. Oh dear me and P.S.! *The Charcoal Burner*, that *Good For Nothing*, while *In Search of His Dad* found *A Lucky Sixpence* and with his *Companions, Rip Van Winkle, Bummelfritze, Paul Pry, Robert Macaire, Slasher and Crasher*, and others went to spend it with *Joseph in Egypt*, so they are excused for that evening, but not you!" Then as the curtain falls for the last time, the thespians will bid Adieu, Adieu, Adieu! [3]

REFERENCES AND NOTES ❧ CHAPTER ELEVEN

1. The introductory material for this chapter was gleaned from op. cit. *History of Germans of Buffalo and Erie County*, pps. 144-60. That which followed the introduction was researched by Christopher Andrle, 5554 Juno Drive, Lake View, New York 14085-9724. He listed his sources of information as: *St. Louis Dramatic Circle Constitution Book, St. Louis Dramatic Circle Minutes*, and *St. Louis Dramatic Circle Correspondence*, which are preserved in the St. Louis Church Archives, Main and Edward Streets. He found other materials at the Buffalo and Erie County Public Library, *Special Collections File*, and at the Buffalo and Erie County Historical Research Library. He also found articles in several Buffalo newspapers: *The Buffalo Times, The Buffalo Courier Express*, and *The Buffalo Commercial Advertiser*. From the *Buffalo Courier Express*, Buffalo, New York, January 15, 1950, p.28, Andrle found the article, "Drama Circle Began As Fund Raiser in '85." This article supplied this chapter with information on the early history of the society, what its objectives were, vignettes concerning some of those who participated in productions, how the plays became infrequent in the twentieth century, and how the members, after World War II, bound themselves together as a social group. From its inception, members of the Dramatic Circle met every month in the same room on the third floor of the school behind the church for 65 years. Only when the school was closed as a fire hazard did the society change its meeting place. In 1950 Carl A. Albert, who had been secretary of the circle since 1911, said, "To my knowledge we've never skipped a meeting." Albert himself belonged to three generations of thespians. His mother, the former Miss Emma Kern, played Lorenna, daughter of Rip Van Winkle in Act II of *Legend of the Catskills* in 1885; Carl A. Albert's son, Robert P. Albert, became a member in 1950. It was the article in the *Buffalo Courier Express* which exposed the antics of tipsy Mischka as he played Rip Van Winkle. William J. Schreck, who had played Guildenstern in *Hamlet*, later joined the priesthood and by 1950 was known as Monsignor William A. Schreck, pastor of St. Gerard's Church on Delavan and Bailey Avenues. Charles M. Weyand, who was the business manager and played Nicholas Vedder in the 1885 production of *Legend of the Catskills*, and played Polonius in the 1887 and 1905 productions of *Hamlet,* was owner of a brewery and restaurant on the site which in 1950 was the Courier Express building and today is the Center for the Catholic Diocese of Buffalo. Miss Clara M. Sendker, who played Martha Giddens in *Old Jed Prouty*, in 1910, was sister to Lieutenant Alfred J. Sendker of the Buffalo Police Department. He was a member of Blessed Trinity Church and belonged to its commandery of the Knights of St. John. Her other brother was Raymond Sendker, who was a surgeon employed at Deaconess Hospital. They could trace their genealogy back to Alfred H. Sendker who was a brother of Frank P. Sendker, who in turn was in partnership with his brother, William W. Sendker. They operated a grocery store on William Street at the corner of Stanton, and were large holders of realty through their brokerage business. The grocery store was located

Fortieth Anniverary of the Dramatic Circle, 1885-1925. Center: John M. Fornes, president. From the bottom, left to right, 1st row: Irving Batt, Karl Kiefer, Edward J. Biesinger, Edward J. White, Edward F. Mischka Sr., Phillip Wagner, Emanuel F. Gollwitzer, Norman L. Kolb. 2nd row: John P. Mayer Sr., Frank J. Mingen, Fred Kiefer Jr., Frank L. Diebold, Edward M. Simon, Walter J. Rick. 3rd row: Carl Albert, Frank Batt, Edward A. Rick, Bernard F. Mayer, Louis Ludaescher, John P. Mayer Jr. 4th row: Michael J. Fornes, H. Edward Albert, Carl A. Albert, Frank L. Mayer, August Hettrick, Fred A. Zorn, Joseph Steinwachs, Eugene B. Ebner.

next door to Rudolf Frey's meat market. Today Rudolf Frey Inc., noted for its German sausage, has its establishment at 678 William Street. Clara, Alfred, and Raymond Sendker were cousins to Edmond Sendker, who lives at present in Pendleton, New York. He supplied the author/editors with information concerning the Sendker family. His great grandfather was William W. Sendker, who, after marrying a protestant girl changed his religion from the Catholicism practiced by his brothers, Frank P. Sendker and Alfred H. Sendker. In the early days, Frank, Alfred, and their families were members of St. Louis Church. Information concerning the grocery store was found in op. cit. *Buffalo of Today, The Queen City of the Lakes*. In 1929, Clara Sendker, who had played in many productions of the St. Louis Dramatic Circle, married John Fisher who also had acting abilities. Karl Kiefer who had acted in *To the Ladies*, in 1925, had performed as a small boy in *Down in Maine*, in 1906. Carl A. Albert, who played Lige Prouty in the 1910 production of *Old Jed Prouty*, went on to become comptroller for the Buffalo School Department. There were several Father and son combinations in the Circle. Fred J. Kieffer Jr. was treasurer for thirty years; when he died his son William Kieffer took over the job and kept it until his death; William's son Karl Kieffer joined the society in 1950. Joseph J. Lux became a member in 1905; his son, Raymond Lux, joined in 1950. Other combinations were: Henry Hecht and his son Robert; Edward A. Rick and his son Edward A. Rick Jr; William Walters and his son Kenneth Walters. Christopher Andrle also found an article in *The Buffalo Times*, Buffalo, New York, May 26, 1929, titled "St. Louis Dramatic Circle Formed 1885, Plays *The County Chairman* Tonight at the Teck Theater, Directed by Otto F. Andrle." The newspaper article was written by Johnny Oldboy. The play marked the forty-fourth year of the existence of the Dramatic Circle. The article included the names of the charter members which have been included in this chapter. It was also from this article that the material in the text concerning *Legend of the Catskills* and *Hamlet* were gleaned. Much of this same material had been given earlier in *Anniversary Souvenir and Programme of St. Louis Dramatic Circle*, Music Hall, January 7, 1896, pps. 70-4. The newspaper article, however, verifies that Otto F. Andrle married Miss Annie Beutter, who played Gertrude, the Queen, in *Hamlet*. Also Charles M. Weyand married Miss Bohumila Andrle, sister of the Andrle boys. Mrs. Emily O'Neil was a sister to Edward Mischka. Two steadfast patrons of the Dramatic Circle's productions were Miss Katherine Boyle and Miss Katherine Wierling. Miss Katherine Boyle wedded Edward Mischka while Otto F. Andrle and Johnny Oldboy, the writer of the newspaper article, were the only attendants at their marriage. Johnny Oldboy would have liked to have been a member of the Circle, but he felt that he had no acting ability. He married Miss Katherine Wierling. Charles Weyand, was the son of Christian Weyand. Christian donated one of the stained glass windows in St. Louis Church. Charles died in 1905 at the untimely age of 36 years. Charles' wife died in 1929. By 1929, the early members of the Circle who had died were: John L. Wex, Louis J. Roth, Frederick Schweigert, Charles M. Schmidt, John Kam, Thomas Dunphy, John A. Kerker, Frank J. Haberstro, William Sanders, Frank

Schoenberger, and actress, Mrs. Emily O'Neil. In the 1929 article by Oldboy, Otto F. Andrle was listed as being the head of Buffalo's Stained Glass Works and had painted many artistic glass works in churches throughout the United States. Around the beginning of the twentieth century, he was in equal competition with renowned artists such as John Comfort Tiffany and John LaFarge. He also took up a theatrical career. Besides those productions mentioned in this chapter, he also appeared in the Frohman's staging of *Prisoner of Zenda* in the role of Rupert alongside Robert B. Mantell, and he had leading roles with H. Beresford's Company which in 1929 was playing in England. Andrle was with James O'Neil in various roles. He was in classic roles with Charles B. Hanford, and had a leading role with E.S. Willard in *The Cardinal*. Also he had leading roles with Louis James. After the first production of *Hamlet* by the Dramatic Circle, Hannibal Williams, eminent Shakespearean critic of New York City wrote, "Mr. Otto F. Andrle gave a performance of *Hamlet* worthy of more pretentious artists. The reflective, vacillating Dane was strongly outlined by Mr. Andrle without rant or miasmatic mannerisms." The biography of Otto F. Andrle was developed from material supplied by Christopher Andrle and op. cit. *St. Louis Bazaar Herald*, September 25, 1900, p.5. Biographical material for Otto R. Rick was supplied by Marie Buchheit Miller from her genealogical studies and from *History of Niagara Frontier*, p.540-43. Otto Rick and Frances Futterer had four children: Maurice, Richard Thomas, Marie Elizabeth, and Agnes Elizabeth. Maurice died at the age of two years. Richard Thomas graduated from West Point and served in the Panama Canal Zone as a First Lieutenant. Marie Elizabeth attended Nardin Academy; and, following graduation, married George T. Ganey. Together they had ten children of which George T. Ganey Jr. and his wife Jane are presently members of St. Louis Church. Before marriage, Marie Rick Ganey taught Kindergarten in the Buffalo Public School system. Agnes Elizabeth also attended Nardin Academy and later graduated as a nurse from Children's and General hospitals. The first production of *Legend of the Catskills* was performed in September 1885. On February 9, 1889, it was repeated with some variations and the title was changed to, *Rip Van Winkle, the Vagabond of the Catskills*. The players in the second production were: Edward F. Mischka, Theodore A. Huck, Frank L. Mayer, John C. Hazenzahl, Edward J. White, Frank P. Batt, John A. Kerker, Thomas G. Dunphy, William Ramsperger, George F. Neunder, Louis J. Roth, Mrs. Otto F. Andrle, Miss M. Caroline Rose, Little Bessie Chretien, Fred A. Zorn, Frank L. Diebold, Bernard F. Mayer, George J. Schwartz, William Sanders, Miss Amanda Windrath, Miss Kitty Ramsperger.

2. These paragraphs were formulated from research material found in op. cit. *Anniversary Souvenir and Programme of St. Louis Dramatic Circle*, pps. 60-8; 70-6. For the appearance of Otto F. Andrle, as he might have looked at the banquet see: op. cit. *Good Shepherd, The Church on the Canal, 1847-1997*, p. 62. For topics such as: The Fire, The Organization, First Production, Hamlet, Additional Productions, Halls, Constitution, Monthly Meetings, Family Connections, River Parties, Anniversaries, and Sources see:

The Dramatic Circle

Christopher Andrle, *The History of the St. Louis Dramatic Circle*, Draft, unpublished, given to the author/editor in November 2001, pps. 1-18. For his work Andrle took excerpts from *The Buffalo Times*, Buffalo, New York, November 4, 1934, "St. Louis Circle, Born in Fatal Fire, Dedicated To Building New Church, Its Membership Continues On," written by Robert Burlingham, *The Times* Staff Writer. The article was written at the time of the Circle's fiftieth anniversary. Dates and places where productions were staged: Elmwood Music Hall, simply called the Concert Hall or Music Hall, Majestic Theater, Teck Theater, and Shea's Theater. *To the Ladies*, was staged at the Majestic Theater on May 17, 1925. After this the Circle staged comedies: *Turn To the Right, Easy Payments*, and *The County Chairman*. The last named was given at the Teck Theater on May 26, 1929. In the Spring of 1935, the Dramatic Circle produced *The Dictator*, written by Richard Harding Davis. Although never a member of the Circle, City Court Judge Hager directed several plays for the Circle. Burlingham mentions that beer helped to provide conviviality at the Circle's meetings. He also mentioned that in 1934, Edward J. White, who as caretaker of the St. Louis Church, was in closest touch with the Circle and with members who dropped in to chat about the old days. White was sixty-six years old in 1934, hale and hearty, picked up hefty boards, and tossed them about like matchsticks. Frank Diebold, who joined the society shortly after its founding, was working for the Erie Railroad and still acted in plays in 1934. The year 1960 was the seventy-fifth anniversary of the beginning of the Dramatic Circle. Another reference concerning Otto Andrle is: March 14, 1885, Otto F. Andrle elected president of SLDC, *Buffalo Times*, March 13, 1910; The story line for the play *The Dictator* was taken from the play book which was included in the publication: Richard Harding Davis, *Farces: The Dictator etal*, Charles Scribner and Sons, New York City, 1906, pp. 2-133. It was produced by Charles Frohman at the Criterion Theater, New York, on April 4, 1904. The remainder of the cast not mentioned in the text are: Paul A. Albert as Lieutenant Victor Perry, William H. Kiefer as General Santos Campos, Frank L. Diebold as Corporal Manuel, Norman L. Kolb as Colonel Garcia, Nicholas Funk as the Smoking Room Steward, and Grace Kelly as Senora Juanita Arquilla. In 1935, the members of the St. Louis Dramatic circle were: Frank J. Mingen (president); William H. Kiefer (treasurer); Raymond J. Hoffman (business manager); Walter J. Rick (vice president); H. Edward Albert (secretary); Frank L. Diebold (librarian); Father Henry B. Laudenbach (moderator); Carl A. Albert; Paul A. Albert; John A. Bralla; Eugene B. Ebner; Gerard Ernewein; John G. Fisher (he had married Clara Sendker); John M. Fornes; Michael J. Fornes; Nicholas Funk; Emanuel F. Gollwitzer; Frank Kellner; Norman L. Kolb; Louis Ludaescher; Raymond Lux; John P. Mayer Jr.; Edward A. Rick; Edward M. Simon; William Walters; Edward J. White; Fred Zorn; Frank Batt; Frank L. Mayer; and John P. Mayer Sr. Those who had behind the scenes duties for the production *The Dictator*, were: Margaret Ryan, stage director; Raymond J. Hoffman, business manager; Gerard Ernewein, assistant business manager; Edward A. Rick, master of properties; Frank Kellner, assistant master of properties; and Hal Mordaunt, make-up artist. The musical score for the play under the direction of George J. Fuller was as follows: *Panamericana* by Victor Herbert; *The Dream Tango:La Conchita* by Uriel Davis; *Marcheta* by V.L. Schertzinger; *L'Estudiantina* by Waldteufel; *Chinchilita* by B. Bartz; and *Folies Bergere*, a march, by Paul Lincke.

3. At the twenty-fifth anniversary celebration of the Dramatic Circle, one of the songs sung by the attendants contained the words *Swanee River*. It was written by Stephen Foster, who used the name of the Suwanee River which flows through Florida and Georgia, but misspelled it in his song which is known as either *Old Folks at Home* or *Swanee River*. Michael J. Zobel Jr. supplied the author/editor with a compilation in outline form of the productions produced by the Dramatic Circle from 1885 to 1940. He supplied titles of plays, dates of production, authors of the scores, places at which they were performed, and the cast members of each play. His maternal grandfather was Edward A. Rick Sr. who joined the Dramatic Circle about 1916. In 1975, Zobel helped his grandfather in cleaning out the room in the St. Louis School which acted as an office for the Dramatic Circle. Michael Zobel Jr. expressed his feelings, he said, "We loaded these programs, news articles, and pictures into the car and that was it...but, I have never forgotten the experience. We had always planned to one day put all these treasures in chronological order. Years later I became the self-appointed guardian of the Dramatic Circle memorabilia. It is hoped that this collection will be a valuable addition to the material being assembled in celebration of the 175th Anniversary of St. Louis Church." So it has been, and that is why the author/editor has incorporated his material into the book, *Gothic Grandeur: A Rare Tradition in American Catholicism*. In the following, SLDC denotes St. Louis Dramatic Circle and pertinent references are given when they apply. The outline is as follows: September 13, 14, 1885, SLDC *Legend of the Catskills*, score by Charles Burke, first production with 400 seating capacity at St. Louis School Hall; December, 27, 28, 1885, SLDC *Joseph of Egypt*, St. Louis School Hall. Also during this week the SLDC assisted Father Joseph Sorg in presenting a cantata titled, *The Birth of Christ*; June 28, 29, 30, 1886, SLDC *Paul Pry*, score by John Poole, St. Louis School Hall; September 28, 29, 1887, SLDC *Companions*, St. Louis School Hall; December 27, 28, 29, 1887, SLDC *Hamlet*, score by Otto Andrle based on play by William Shakespeare, St. Louis School Hall, *Buffalo Express*, December 28, 1887, *Buffalo Daily Courier*, December 27, 1887, *Buffalo Daily Courier*, December 28, 1887, *Commercial Advertiser*, December 28, 1887, *Buffalo Times*, December 28, 1887, *Sunday Truth*, January 1, 1888, *Albany Daily Press and Knickerboker*; May 8, 9, 1888, SLDC *Good for Nothing*, and *Slasher and Crasher*, St. Louis School Hall; September 25, 26, 1889, SLDC *Lucky Sixpence*, and *Declined With Thanks*, St. Louis School Hall; April 23, 24, 1890, SLDC *The Bells*, sub titled, *The Polish Jew*, a grand romantic psychological moral drama, score by Leopold Lewis, final production at St. Louis School Hall; November 27, 1890, SLDC *Cool as a Cucumber* and *A Day's Fishing*, first production with 1200 seating capacity at the Elmwood

The Dramatic Circle

Music Hall; December 29, 1891, SLDC *Advice Gratis*, and *In Search of His Dad*, score by Charles Dance, Elmwood Music Hall; May 26, 1892, SLDC *The Charcoal Burner*, score by George Almar, Music Hall; November 24, 1892, SLDC *A Days Fishing*, and *Cool as a Cucumber*, repeats, scores by John Maddison Morton, Music Hall; February 24, 1894, SLDC *Robert Macaire*, score by Charles Selby, Music Hall, *Buffalo Express*, January 28, 1894; January 7, 1896, SLDC *The Signal*, the 10th anniversary production, score by J. Sterling Coyne, Music Hall; February 22, 1898, SLDC *A Red Letter Day*, score by Horace W. Fuller, Music Hall; February 9, 1899, SLDC *Rip Van Winkle: The Vagabond of the Catskills*, a variation on *Legend of the Catskills*, score by Charles Burke, last production at the Music Hall; There were no productions in 1900 or 1901; April 27, 30, 1902, SLDC *The Ticket of Leave Man*, a who-done-it set in London, England, Teck Theater; April 26, 1903, SLDC *The Pride of Virginia*, a Civil War Theme, Teck Theater; May 9, 1904, SLDC *Paul Pry*, repeat, Teck Theater; May 14, 1905, SLDC *Paul Revere*, the 20th anniversary production, a colonial period melodrama, score by Dodson Mitchell, Teck Theater, *Buffalo Courier*, May 14, 1905, p.37; May 6, 1906, SLDC *Down in Maine*, about events on Hardscrabble's farm in the State of Maine, Shea's Theater, *Buffalo Courier*, May 6, 1906, p.53; May 8, 1907, SLDC *Nathan Hale*, Teck Theater; December 29,30, 1907, SLDC *Hamlet*, a replay of the 1887 production but the theater was not stipulated; May 27, 1908, SLDC *Bummelfritze* and *Flying From Justice*, Teck Theater; May 17, 1909, SLDC *May Blossom*, score by David Belasco, Teck Theater; May 29, 1910, SLDC *Old Jed Prouty*, the 25th anniversry production, general admission 25 cents, Shea's Theater, *Buffalo Courier*, May 30, 1910, p.7; April 21, 1912, SLDC *Held By The Enemy*, score by William Gillette, Teck Theater; May 21, 1914, SLDC *At the Picket Line*, Civil War Drama, score by Justin Adams, Majestic Theater; April 30, 1916, SLDC *The Fortune Hunter*, score by Winchell Smith, Majestic Theater; November 25, 1917, SLDC *The Traveling Salesman*, comedy, score by James Forbes, Sheas Theater; no productions in 1918 or 1919; May 23, 1920, SLDC *Down in Maine*, repeat, score by Charles Townsend, Majestic Theater; May 8, 1921, SLDC *Rolling Stones*, comedy score by Edgar Selwyn, Teck Theater; November 26, 1922, SLDC *It Payes To Advertize*, a Farcical Fact by Roi Cooper Megrue and Walter Hackett, Majestic Theater; May 18, 1924, SLDC *Keep Her Smiling*, comedy by John Hunter Booth, Majestic Theater; May 17, 1925, SLDC *To the Ladies*, the 40th anniversary production, comedy by George S. Kaufman and Marc Connelly, Majestic Theater; May 16, 1926, SLDC *Turn to the Right*, a comedy by Winchell Smith and John E. Hazzard, Majestic Theater; no production in 1927; April 22, 1928, SLDC *Easy Payments*, comedy by George V. Hobart, Teck Theater; May 25, 1929, SLDC *The County Chairman*, comedy-drama by George Ade, Teck Theater, *Buffalo Times*, May 26, 1929; November 20, 1932, SLDC *The Bride*, mystery comedy by Stuart Oliver and George Middleton, Teck Theater; May 12, 1935, SLDC *The Dictator*, comedy-drama by Richard Harding Davis, 50th anniversary production, Teck Theater; no productions in 1936, 1937, 1938, 1939, unless there were repeats of SLDC *Traveling Salesman* and, *Rolling Stones*;

April 14, 1940, SLDC *Room Service*, comedy by John Murray and Allen Boretz, the last play given by SLDC before World War II at the Knights of Columbus Auditorium, Delaware Avenue. The author/editor in conversation with John E. Miller, son of Eugene W. Miller Sr., came to understand that theatrical productions, given by some organization from St. Louis Church, between the years 1936 and 1939, may have been presented at either the Erlanger Theater at Delaware and Mohawk, or at the Court Street Theater. John E. Miller knew that his father acted, as a representative of St. Louis Church, in one or more of these plays but did not know what role he took. These facts were also substantiated to the author/editor by Sylvina Miller, wife of the late Eugene W. Miller Jr., oldest son of Eugene W. Miller Sr.; There appears to be no productions from any St. Louis Church organizations after World War II, with the exception of those produced in house by the CYO or as school related events such at graduation; On October 20, 1960, although no play by SLDC was produced, a 75th anniversary dinner was held at the American Legion Troop I, Hamlin House, Franklin Street, Buffalo, New York. Michael J. Zobel Jr. supplied the author/editor with programs listing members and actors. From this source the author/editor drew up the following list of members and performers. It should also be understood that some names may not have been members but only acted in some plays. The Dramatic Circle had the policy to limit membership to no more than thirty. Date after a name is the year in which the individual took membership or acted in a play. Able, Walter, 1912; Albert, Carl A., 1910, 1912, 1914, 1916, 1917, 1920, 1921, 1924, 1925, 1926, 1928, 1929, 1935, 1940; Albert, H. Edward, 1920, 1921, 1924, 1925, 1926, 1928, 1929, 1935, 1940; Albert, Paul A., 1924, 1925, 1929, 1935, 1940; Albert, Robert P., 1950; Andrle, Adelbert W., 1885, dismissed 1889; Andrle, Aloysious P., 1885, 1887, 1892; Andrle, Otto F., 1885, 1887, 1888, 1895, 1902; Armbruster, Leon J., 1902, 1905, 1906; Baecher, Charles E., 1886, 1892; Ball, Richard, 1935; Batt, Frank P., 1895, 1899; Batt, Irving P., 1916, 1922; Paul J. Batt, no date known; Beutter, Fred J., 1886; Bielstein, Joseph, 1886; Biesinger, Charles, 1885, 1912; Biesinger, Edward J., 1925; Bork, Clarence, 1935; Bott, Charles M., 1902, 1904, 1905; Bralla, John A., 1929, 1932, 1940; Churchill, Herbert H., 1910; Dearing Edward J., 1904, 1905, 1907, 1909; Deck, Charles M., 1885; Didley, Eugene, 1912; Diebold, Eugene L., 1907, 1910; Diebold, Frank L., 1890, 1892, 1894, 1899, 1902, 1903, 1904, 1906, 1907, 1909, 1910, 1912, 1914, 1917, 1920, 1921, 1922, 1924, 1925, 1929, 1935, 1940; Diebold, Joseph, J., 1907; Dietsche, Karl J., 1910; Doll, Edward F., 1885; Dory Adam, J., 1885; Dunphy, Thomas G., 1895, 1895, 1899; Eager, Albert, 1935; Ebner, Eugene, 1912, 1921, 1924, 1925, 1926, 1928; Eger, Joseph, 1916; Ellis, George T., 1909; Ernewein, Gerard, 1935; Fornes, John M., 1902, 1905; Fornes, Michael J., 1910; Fornes, William, 1903; Funk, Arthur, 1902; Funk, Nicholas, 1925, 1928, 1929, 1935; Gittere, Alex J., 1886, Gollwitzer, Emmanuel F., 1907, 1909, 1912, 1914, 1920, 1935; Haas, Lucian, 1903, 1904, 1905, 1906, 1907, 1910, 1917; Haas, William, 1895; Haberstro, Frank J., 1895, Hardick, Paul, 1935; Hautfuer, Joseph K., musical director, 1905; Hazenzahl, John C., 1885, 1887, 1895, 1899, 1902; Hecht, Henry, unknown

BUFFALO, N. Y., TUESDAY EVENING, DEC., 29, 1891.

TUESDAY EVENING DEC. 29, 1891.

THE

St. Louis Dramatic Circle

IN A DOUBLE BILL.

THE PROGRAMME WILL COMMENCE WITH AN AMUSING FARCE IN ONE ACT,

BY

Charles Dance, Esq.,

ENTITLED

Advice Gratis.

CAST OF CHARACTERS.

ODBODY	MR. ED. F. MISCHKA
EVENTIDE	MR. FRANK L. MAYER
EDMUND	MR. OTTO RICHARD RICK
GRIMES	MR. ED. J. WHITE
MRS. EVENTIDE	MISS LOUISE HALWEIS
ELLEN	MISS EMMA PHILLIPS

DURING THE INTERVAL THERE WILL BE RENDERED VOCAL SELECTIONS BY . . . . MR. LOUIS J. ROTH

AND

VIOLIN SOLOS, BY . . . . MISS LIBBIE FRIES

date; Hecht, Robert, unknown date; Hettrich, August, 1905, 1906, 1907, 1909, 1910, 1912, 1914, 1916, 1917, 1921, 1924, 1929; Hoffman, Raymond, 1929; Huber, Henry, 1912; Huck, Theodore A., 1899; Jacobs, Edward, 1904, 1905; Jansen, Louis F., 1895; Kaiser, Anthony, 1940; Kam, John Jr., 1905; Kellner, Frank M., 1940; Kent, Irving, 1907; Kerker, John A., 1894, 1895, 1899, 1903, 1904; Kessel, Fred, 1910; Kiefer, Fred J. Jr., 1895, 1917; Kieffer, Karl, 1906, 1950; Kieffer, William, 1926, 1928, 1929, 1935, 1940; Koch, Joseph; Kolb, Norman L., 1924, 1929, 1932, 1935; Kopp, Ray, 1890, 1892; 1912; Lehner, Andrew, 1929; Ludaescher, Louis, 1904, 1905, 1906, 1907, 1909, 1910, 1912, 1914, 1917, 1920, 1922, 1924, 1925, 1926, 1928, 1935, 1940; Lux, Joseph F., 1935; Lux, Joseph J., 1902, 1903, 1904, 1905, 1906, 1907, 1909; Lux, Raymond, 1950; Marnell, Earl J.F., 1922; Mayer, Bernard F., 1899, 1902, 1903, 1904, 1905, 1906, 1907, 1909, 1910, 1912, 1917, 1924; Mayer, Frank L., 1887, 1891, 1892, 1894, 1895, 1899, 1902, 1903, 1905, 1907, 1912; Mayer, John P., 1887, 1888, 1890, 1892, 1894, 1895, 1925; Mayer, John P. Jr,. 1920, 1921, 1922, 1924, 1926, 1928, 1929, 1932, 1935; Mingen, Frank J., 1912, 1914, 1916, 1920, 1921, 1924, 1925, 1926, 1928; Miller Eugene W., 1935; Mischka, Carl, 1910; Mischka, Edward F., 1885, 1887, 1888, 1890, 1891, 1892, 1894, 1899, 1916, 1924, 1925; Murray, M.H., 1890; Muth, Jacob, 1895; Muth, Paul, 1912; Neunder, George F., 1895, 1899; O'Neil, Joseph, 1890, 1895, 1896; Ottenot, Edward M., 1895; Ramsperger, William C., 1899; Rick, Edward A., 1917, 1920, 1922, 1925, 1928, 1929, 1932, 1935, 1940; Rick, Edward A. Jr., 1950; Rick, Otto R., 1886, 1887, 1888, 1890, 1891, 1892, 1894; Rick, Walter J., 1921, 1922, 1924, 1925, 1926, 1928, 1929, 1932, 1935, 1940; Rose, Albert, 1885; Ross, Frank, 1935; Roth, Louis J., 1885, 1890, 1892, 1895, 1899, 1902, 1907; Sanders, William, 1899, 1902; Schaefer, Joseph, 1929; Schifferle, Charles Jr., 1935; Schmidt, Charles M., 1887; Schmidt, Henry, before 1889; Schmidt, Joseph S., 1895, 1890, 1892; Schreck, William J., 1885, 1887; Schwartz, George J., 1895, 1899; Schweigert, Fred C., 1905, 1910, 1912, 1914; Schweigert, Harry A., 1902, 1903, 1904, 1905, 1906, 1910; Schweigert, John A., 1903, 1904, 1905, 1907, 1910, 1912, 1914, 1916, 1917; Simon, Edward M., 1912, 1914, 1917, 1924, 1925, 1926, 1928, 1932, 1935, 1940; Spoeri, Frank Jr., 1929; Steffan, Jacob P., 1924; Steinwacks, Joseph, 1914, 1917; Swanz, Henry J., 1886, 1888; Vincent, Lawrence, 1912; Voltz, Joseph E., 1895; Walters, William, unknown date; Wagner, Matthew, 1909; Walters, Kenneth, unknown date; Warner, Philip, 1922; Welding, George, 1912; Wex, John L., 1885, 1887, 1888; Weppner, Albert, before 1889; Weyand, Charles M., 1885, 1887; Weyand, Norman P., actor 1905; White, Edward J., 1885, 1888, 1887, 1890, 1891, 1892, 1894, 1899, 1902, 1903, 1921; Winter, Harold, 1912; Zeller, Adolph, 1885; Zillig, Andrew, actor 1905; Zimpfer, Edward L., 1910; Zorn, Fred A., 1885, 1887, 1888, 1891, 1892, 1894, 1899, 1902, 1903, 1910. Included in Michael J. Zobel's programs were the names of women involved. Although they could not be members of SLDC, they were allowed to act in the plays as were many male cast members. Listed below are these ladies' names and the years in which they performed: Andrle,

Bohumila, 1885, 1887, 1888, 1907; Barrett, Mary, 1929, 1932; Bauers, Florence, 1892; Beisinger, Catherine M., 1917; Beutter, Anna W., 1887, 1888, 1907; Beutter, Clara, 1888, 1890; Buchheit, Georgianna, 1929; Carlin, Anna, 1926; Chretien, Bessie, 1899; Coveny, Olive, 1910; D'Anne, Dorothy, 1940; DeBock, Alla O., 1905; Deck, Emma, 1916; Delahunt, Marie A., 1895, 1896; Feldman, Eleanor, 1910; Fornes, Marcella M., 1924, 1925; Gottstein, Martha M., 1910; Hacker, Henrietta, 1929; Hagar, Carrie, 1892, 1895, 1896; Halweis, Louise, 1891, 1892; Hazenzahl, Lizzie M., 1895, 1896; Hausle, Loreen, 1910; Hayn, Eva, 1917; Hennesey, Mary, 1928; Hertzog, Lillian, 1907; Howard, Matie, 1890; Jackson, Marion E., 1907; Kammerer, Mary I., 1935; Kennedy, Grace, 1935; Kern, Emma, 1885; Knoll, Josephine Marie, 1904; Kreuzer, Carrie, 1890, 1891, 1892; Kreuzer, May, 1890; Lamb, Gertrude, 1902; Lehner, Belle, 1921; Lienert, Clara, 1907; Lux, Genevieve, 1910; Maser, Celia, 1925, 1926; Max, Armella, 1910, 1920, 1921, 1924, 1925; Mayer, Mary Ann, 1917; McDonnell, Catherine, 1914; McNeil, Anne, 1914; Mischka, Frances, 1892; Morrison, Betty Jane, 1940; Murphy, Gertrude A., 1895, 1896; Noonan, Mary M., 1925, 1926; O'Brien, Genevieve, 1929; O'Brien Patricia, 1929; O'Neil, Emily, 1885, 1887, 1907; O'Neil, Mary Frances, 1935; Ortner, May, 1902; Phillips, Emma, 1885, 1890, 1891, 1894; Prost, Minnie, 1904, 1906; Ramsperger, Kitty, 1899; Regan, Margaret M., 1928; Reisch, Helen, 1928; Riester, Bertha, 1907; Roberts, Elizabeth, 1916, 1917, 1920, 1921, 1922, 1924, 1928, 1929; Roberts, Margaret M., 1917; Rose, Caroline, 1899; Ryan, Anna E., 1905; St. James, Henrietta, 1904, 1906; Schumacher, Loretta, 1909; Schwartz, Elizabeth, 1910; Seereiter, Helen, 1922; Seereiter, Mary L., 1926; Sendker, Clara M., 1909, 1910, 1912, 1914, 1916, 1920, 1921, 1922, 1924, 1925, 1926, 1929, 1932; Sendker, Rose M., 1920, 1921, 1922, 1924, 1925; Strauss, Mamie, 1906; Strauss, Terry, 1902, 1904, 1905, 1906; Stressinger, Dorothy, 1928; Strigl, Anna, 1909, 1910; Swanz, Margaret, 1910, 1912; Taylor, Della, 1894; Wanenmacher, Lilian, 1912; Warren, Ella, 1890; Williams, Minnie, 1909; Windrath, Amanda, 1899; Winter, Alice, 1910; Zahm, Loretta, 1910; and Zehnle, Christine, 1885. The author/editor received information concerning Robert P. Albert from him in a telephone conversation on March 20, 2002. Information concerning the genealogy of the Rick Family, partictularly the biography of Edward A. Rick Sr., was supplied by Thomas J. McKeon Jr., 131 Kingsland Circle, Monmouth Jct., NJ 08852-2533. McKeon is a cousin of Michael J. Zobel Jr. Edward A. Rick married Charlotte B. Wischerath. They had four children: Dorothy Edith, Lucile Esther, Edward A. Rick Jr., and Charlotte Mae. Dorothy Edith married Michael J. Zobel Sr. with whom she bore Michael J. Zobel Jr. Charlotte Mae married Thomas J. McKeon Sr. with whom she bore Thomas J. McKeon Jr. Walter J. Rick is Edward A. Rick Sr.'s brother and therefore an uncle to Dorothy Edith, Michael J. Zobel Jr.'s mother. Karen, the great grand-daughter of Edward A. Rick Sr. is the daughter of Michael J. Zobel and Carol, nee Naber. Karen married Devin L. Palmer in St. Louis Church on October 27, 2001.

CHAPTER TWELVE

Do You Know Where Your Children Are?

Each evening prior to witnessing the 11:00 P.M. local newscast by Keith Radford and Susan Banks aired on Buffalo's WKBW-TV, the viewers hear a voice anxiously questioning, "Do You Know Where Your Children Are?" It is an appeal for vigilance, guidance, and education. Would a newscast that describes the youth as gambling on street corners, conning others in the latest swindle, perpetrating petty thievery, fighting and bullying, lurking in dark areas slovenly dressed and reeking with odors of uncleanness, and engaging in fierce rivalries, murders, orgies, and opium parties, be an accurate representation of their actions in modern neighborhoods? One might say that the phrase expresses similarities to modern crime on the streets and exploitation of children by drug barons; but, as it is expressed, it is melodramatic, exaggerated, and dated. The historian would agree with this observation because the phrase was not issued in modern times, but is a description of that which took place on the streets of Paris, Rouen, Lyons, Rheims, Marseilles, and Bordeaux, France, in 1684. It was then that Jean Baptiste de La Salle founded the Brothers of the Christian Schools so as to take the ruffians and hoodlums off the streets, put them in classrooms, and give them a character changing education. It was a time when there were no free elementary schools for poor boys and very few of them for poor girls.

There were, however, Little Schools, Writing Masters' Establishments, Parish Charity Schools, and Religious Congregational Schools. The Little Schools and the Writing Masters charged tuition. Congregational Schools were operated by nuns for girls. Only the Parish Charity Schools were free and admitted boys. They were, however, haphazardly established, and their success depended entirely upon the piety and devotion of the parish curate who may or may not have been well educated himself, and who was often drowned in other more demanding ecclesiastical duties. The Charity School of his parish was not his top priority. Throughout the major cities of France, when de La Salle died on April 6, 1719, there were twenty-two Lasallian Schools teaching gratuitously the children of poor families where both father and mother were working, sometimes as long as fourteen hours per day with no Saturdays free, no paid holidays, and no summer breaks. The curriculums followed by the students were taught by two of de La Salle's educational innovations: the use of the vernacular in the classroom in place of Latin, and the simultaneous method of teaching, for which the French government later gave official recognition.

Almost wiped out by the horrors of the French Revolution, the Order of the Brothers of the Christian Schools rebounded and rose like a phoenix during the reign of Napoleon Bonaparte. By 1810, thirty-two communities had been reconstructed in France. In 1837, the Brothers arrived for the first time in America and set up a school in Montreal, Canada. In 1845, the French-Canadian Brothers, having increased in numbers, opened Calvert Hall College in Baltimore, Maryland. By 1861, there were three hundred and sixty-eight Brothers, seventy-four novices, seventy-eight schools, and more than twenty-four thousand pupils in elementary free schools in the United States and Canada. Bishop Timon requested these Brothers to come to Buffalo in the fall of 1861. He placed St. Joseph's College and the Cathedral's parochial school in their charge. Both establishments had been constructed on the site of Webster's Gardens at Swan and Franklin Streets. By 1872, the college was moved to Delaware Avenue. In 1892, owing to the growth of the city and the encroachments of the railroad and manufacturing interests, it became necessary to transfer it again. Temporarily it was established at Prospect Avenue and Jersey Street, but in 1897 it was moved to its permanent site on Main Street near Bryant. By 1904, the Brothers were not only teaching at St. Joseph's College but were also responsible for the educational conduct of boys at the parochial schools at the St. Joseph's Cathedral, and St. Bridget's, St. Stephen's, and St. Louis' Churches.

This was but one of the French connections, dating back to the seventeenth century, which St. Louis' school experienced. The other was the Religious Order of nuns known as the Sisters of St. Joseph, which had been founded in the mid seventeenth century at Le Puy, France. Inspired by the preaching of Father Jean Pierre Medaille, five women gathered together to form a community and asked him to draw up a constitution and a set of rules for their budding congregation. On March 10, 1661, twenty-three years before Jean Baptiste de La Salle created his first community of Brothers, these women led by Francoise Eyraud won an official approbation of their existence from Bishop Henri de Maupas du Tour. Quickly more women were attracted to them, and they spread out, living in small communities and administering in hospitals, reformatories, and schools. Like the Brothers, experience with the French Revolution and its anticlerical decrees, disrupted their religious life. By 1792, all of the Sisters had returned to their families; but, after Napoleon's concordat with Rome in 1801, their communities were restored. The congregation was reactivated under the direction of Mother St. John

Fontbonne, on July 14, 1808, nineteen years after the Bastille was stormed, opening the French Revolution.

On March 25, 1836, the Bishop of St. Louis, Missouri, Joseph Rosati, welcomed Mother Fontbonne's two nieces, Sisters Febronie Fontbonne and Delphine Fontbonne, plus four other Sisters to his diocese. These were the first Sisters of St. Joseph to come to the United States. As years turned into decades all other communities of St. Joseph Sisters in the United States and Canada sprang forth from this center. They were Philadelphia, Pennsylvania; Toronto, Canada; Brooklyn, New York; Baden, Pennsylvania; Rutland, Vermont; Boston and Springfield, Massachusetts; and Canandaigua and Buffalo, New York. In December 1854, Bishop Timon secured the Sisters of St. Joseph directly from St. Louis, Missouri, for the purpose of operating the parochial school in Canandaigua at a parish that was pastored by Reverend Edward O'Connor. The first Sisters to arrive were Mother Agnes Spencer, Sister Francis Joseph, and Sister Patronella. When more Sisters were available in Missouri, Timon brought them directly into Buffalo where they established a novitiate for postulants and a school for the Deaf in three small cottages on Edward Street, west of St. Louis Church. Louis Le Couteulx de Chaumont had originally donated the property to the diocese.

In 1858, while Father William Disters was pastor of St. Louis Church, Timon again procured four more Sisters from Missouri, who took over the conduct of elementary education at St. Louis Church. A frame building, erected in 1850 behind the church and adjacent to the rectory, was first used as the schoolhouse, but it was soon torn down and replaced by a brick building with a French styled motif. Among this group of teachers were Sister Mary Antoinette and Sister Mary Julia, who acted as superior. They opened three classrooms in the building; all were soon crowded with three hundred and sixty-eight pupils. The Sisters, however, were recalled back to Missouri in 1861, but

Timon replaced them with Sisters Mary Stephen, Alphonse, Joseph Theresa, Mary John, and Mother Magdalena who had been originally assigned to Philadelphia in 1847. When Sister Mary John left Buffalo in 1862, Sister Mary Antoinette replaced her, and after 1864 Sisters De Pazzi and Martha joined the group.

By 1850, because of a major influx of Catholic immigrants from Europe, the Catholic population in the United States had risen to six million. Catholic bishops began to challenge Protestant control of curriculum in common schools and favored a truly public school system; Horace Mann who advocated a nonsectarian school system supported by the public aided them. This secularization of schools, however, met with stiff opposition from influential Protestants. Although not interested in supporting Mann's nonsectarian schools, they and nativist groups, such as the Know-Nothing Society, did everything to eradicate any taint of Catholicism associated with common school education. The bishops, therefore, decided to go-it-alone. The First Plenary Council of Baltimore in 1852 urged that every parish build a parochial school. This plea was reiterated at the Second Plenary Council in 1866. At the Third Plenary Council in 1884, the bishops legislatively decreed that, within two years following the council, every parish, if it did not already have one, would have a school building near or adjacent to the church. It also indicated that it would be a grave error in judgment for Catholic parents not to send their children to these parochial schools. The school at St. Louis Church, however, was already in conformity prior to the First Plenary Council.

In 1829, Father John Nicholas Mertz had secured a little log house on the west side of Pearl Street between Court and Eagle Streets, where he dwelt for several years. Nearby he rented a small frame building in which he said Mass in the mornings, and in the afternoons, he invited children from the neighborhood, mainly those speaking German, to come and learn to read, write, and spell. He had small prayer books and catechisms written in German for their use. One might call this building the first St. Louis School. By 1831, Mertz was fortunate to be assisted by Professor Henry Hemmerlein; he seemed to have fallen from the sky, but his stay was for more than thirty years. In 1896, the members of the Dramatic Circle praised his memory as the old *Schulmeister*. They claimed him to be the principal of the parochial school for a period embracing more than thirty years while also serving as organist and vestryman with fidelity and efficiency. They claimed that many enterprising and successful businessmen of Buffalo owed their early training to his talent and devotion. They advocated that if he ever had what might be called a fault, it was his disbelief in the efficacy of the rod as the sole and chief incentive to application and obedience on the part of his pupils. His rule was that of kindness, and he had been looked upon with respect and affection by all that sat beneath his teaching. When these compliments were given, Hemmerlein was, although retired, still present among them because these members ended their remarks by saying, "Although his head is silvered o'er the years, his services are still in constant requisition, in one form or another, about the church." He had been there in 1848 when Timon asked the Sisters of Charity to take over the school and the trustees dismissed them without the bishop's permission. He had been there to help the Sisters of St. Joseph get started in the new building in 1858. He had been there when, in 1864, Father Sergius Schoulepnikoff entered his name in the parish log, and recorded his October salary as $9.83. By 1868, however, his name disappeared from the ledger.

St. Louis' school as operated by Mertz, Pax, Guth, Disters, and Hemmerlein was much like the Charity Schools in France in the seventeenth century; schools not necessarily to be criticized, but to be improved. Jean Baptiste de La Salle and the Sisters of St. Joseph, however, blazed a new trail. They raised the task of teaching the children of the poor to the dignity of a vocation; they created religious communities whose members taught, together and by association, in gratuitous schools. It was to the genius of de La Salle that he was able to weave French Sulpician spirituality into the fabric of this vocation and develop within the religious teachers the virtues of good masters and produce the methods by which they would conduct good schools. Because of his own spiritual life, his sacrifice and his holiness, he was canonized on May 25, 1900 and pronounced the Patron of all Teachers. His educational concepts and directives became the fundamentals followed by both Sisters and Brothers who taught at St. Louis' parochial school.

Accordingly, Christian education was a necessity because the working classes and the poor, being little instructed and ever occupied with earning their living and supporting their families, were unable to give their children the Christian and moral education that they required. All disorders, especially among the working classes and the poor, ordinarily proceeded from the fact that the children, at an early age, were left to their own resources and were badly brought up. Instruction in the elements of profane knowledge, however useful and even necessary they might be, were considered entirely subordinate to instruction in religious matters and education in Christian behavior. Throughout the whole day, the pupils were constantly reminded of their religion by pictures in the classroom, by special textbooks that they used, and by the teacher who wore a religious habit and gave good example. The children were taught that man's life on earth was something far higher than the vulgar pursuit of wealth and power. They were taught respect and obedience not from a motive of fear or servility, but for the reason that all authority came from God; and, as a consequence, obedience was a Christian virtue. It was the aim of the good teacher to reduce corporal punishment as much as possible. Children were punished but rarely; the good teacher, however, was ever vigilant. Silence was regarded as a cardinal factor in school management.

In his text titled *School Management*, de La Salle, instructing his teachers, wrote, "The first thing you owe to your pupils is edification and good example. Do you teach your students anything that you do not practice yourself? It is important that your example should speak louder than your words." He then cited twelve particular virtues as especially appropriate for a good teacher: gravity, or seriousness without gloom that would provide a distinctive air; silence, or a calm demeanor that commands attention; humility, or simplicity that does not overwhelm the child with heavy-handed authority; prudence, or the ability to adapt to the level of the child; wisdom, or the common sense that knows what is practical and not just theoretical; patience, or the toleration of imperfection in others; restraint, or self-control; mildness, or the goodness that engenders affection; zeal, or devotedness in action; vigilance, or constant attention to guard against anything that could cause physical or moral harm to the student; piety, or the recourse to God for oneself or for others; and generosity, or an unselfish spirit that never counts the cost. For de La Salle, what mattered most was not what the teacher said or did, but what sort of a person the teacher was. In practicing these virtues, in front of the pupils, day in and day out, he contended that the teacher would express the qualities of love for the poor, detachment from worldly possessions, concern for the disadvantaged, energy, constancy, fidelity to one's promised word, and obedience to the Church. It was these qualities which the students and their parents recognized in the religious Sisters and Brothers who taught at St. Louis' parochial school. Some aspects of each of these qualities have been touched upon by former students when they were interviewed by Robert McCarthy, a political staff writer for the *Buffalo News*, and Marie Buchheit Miller.

As an introduction, McCarthy wrote, "Meet Bob and Pat Albert; they grew up in St. Louis' parish. Bob graduated in 1936 and Pat, nee Riley, in 1943, from the three story brick structure, with the French styled architectural cupola and roofing similar to that developed by Francois Mansart in the seventeenth century. It was constructed behind the church in 1858, but experienced the blows of the wrecker's ball in 1986. Bob and Pat were married in St. Louis Church, and they have since continued to be devoted workers at a vast number of parish functions. They recalled the boys playing baseball and the girls jumping rope in the school yard." After speaking with several students, Marie Buchheit Miller summarized their observations concerning a nun's habit as they remembered it. She wrote, "A combined hood-like headpiece and white starched scapular not only covered their shoulders but encased their cheeks, ears, and foreheads. Only the most central part of their faces could be seen. Many children wondered how the nuns could hear so well without ears? The scapular was a large, highly starched neck apron; students called it a bib. They wore a long black robe that fell down to their ankles, where it met their polished black laced shoes. Their sleeves came down to their wrists where, in order not to expose even these, a white cuff protruded from under the black material. It was noted, however, that the hands did have veins, and it was assumed that blood did run through them. A crucifix hung squarely over the center of their chest underneath the bib; it was attached to a cord that encircled the neck. They wore a graduation-like mortarboard cap, without the tassel, over which was draped a black silk veil. A prominent gesture of most Sisters in the classroom was the fling of that veil over their shoulders as they turned toward the pupils subsequent to writing on the blackboard. A set of large Rosary beads hung from the cincture around their waist, and what big pockets the nuns had! No one could really tell how much a nun weighed; the tall ones were always considered skinny and the short ones were said to be fat. To the children this was the uniform of God; it set the nuns aside as something special."

*B*ecause the method of administration of St. Louis Church, a triune operation between pastor, trustees, and bishop, was a Rare Tradition in American Catholicism,

McCarthy asked some of the former nuns to comment on how this method concerned them in their teaching. Sisters Rita Kane, Cecile Ferland, and Mary Ann Kolb were quick to respond. They pointed out that the nuns had excellent relations with the priests and trustees. While they were active in the school Father Howard Schwartz was the pastor and Father James P. Cahill was one of his assistants. Sister Cecile, a rookie teacher in 1947, recalled attending the noon Mass. "The priests gave two minute sermons and they were just wonderful," she said. Also, she had no adverse opinion of the priests interfering in the activities of the school. She said that the Sisters had the obligation to teach classes according to the traditions of their Order and that this never seemed to bother the trustees who ran everything. Sister Rita said, "If the priests or trustees did come to the classroom, it was usually a social visit or one which each teacher had knowledge of beforehand." One day, in 1949 when Mary Ann Kolb was in eighth grade, Father Howard Schwartz visited the fourth grade. Barbara Tonte asked him, "Why do we have Purgatory?" Schwartz replied, "Purgatory is for souls who have been good, but have a few small stains on them. It's like, when you come into the house, your mother commands you to wipe your feet before you come in!" Then he asked, "Has anyone ever heard your mother say that?" At that moment all eleven boys in the class raised their hands simultaneously!

*W*henever the trustees had to interview a nun it was always with courtesy; they were considered by the nuns as decent men who respected the teachers. Sister Cecile recalled Mr. Edwin H. Kolb, one of the long-standing trustees. She said, "I remember him well. If we had needs as teachers, he took care of them." Sister Mary Ann Kolb, Edwin's daughter, who graduated from St. Louis' school in 1949, recalled similar instances of her father's kindness towards the nuns. She said, " He was always driving the nuns all over God's creation. My father was forever their taxi driver." She then added, "If there was any conflict between the priests, or trustees, and ourselves, we understood who was the boss. Back in those days, women were a little more docile than in these days of liberation." She added a note of interest, "My class was very small, we had only seven graduate in 1949. That year, however, Evelyn M. Foegen graduated with me; she, like myself, attended Mount St. Joseph's Academy on Main Street." Sister Mary of the Sacred Heart, who published a book about the Sisters of St. Joseph, wrote about the praise which Father Laudenbach in 1934 had given to the work being done at St. Louis Church by the Sisters. She quoted him as saying, "We again must confess that the Sisters here and elsewhere have been the backbone of our Catholic school system. Without their help, cooperation, and sacrifice, there would be no parochial schools. How many priests must testify to the fact that the coming of the Sisters into a parish spells new life and vigor for everyone connected with it! The roles of Martha and Mary have been in their hands; the life of these consecrated women has been the greatest influence in shaping and keeping intact the decencies to which the Catholic Church is committed by her divine mission."

After interviewing Catherine Almeter, nee Berger, who in February 2002 celebrated her one-hundredth birthday, McCarthy wrote, "She claims to recall the history of St. Louis Church and its school further back than anyone else who may be alive. She says that she entered the school while her parents were living on Lemon Street in 1907. She remembered how apprehensive she was on her first day, being escorted by her mother Anna, who was a seamstress. It was a walk of nine blocks, a little more than a half mile. The entire family had always been parishioners of St. Louis Church. When she graduated in 1916 there were twenty-two students in her class with Sister Christina as the teacher, and Veronica T. Beck was her best class friend. They learned German, English, Elementary Representation and Design, Business Writing, Algebra, Bookkeeping, Physiology, Music, and Chorus Singing. The Brothers of the Christian Schools taught the boys. Catherine said, 'Although we were scared when we first

entered class, we were soon put at ease, the nuns made it easy. They were kindly, protective, nurturing people who were good at heart.' She still remembered Sister Anselm, her fifth grade teacher, as being a big, jolly lady who was lots of fun; tops as a human being. To her, Sister was fun because she made learning fun. She devised competitions for everything, transforming ordinary book learning into something more. Joe LaFalce was Almeter's partner and together they worked like mad to win. Almeter didn't know whatever happened to Joe; he didn't graduate with the class. She also recalled another little boy who was called a neglected child—always dirty and a mess. Sister would take him to the washroom, and he would come out with his face shining. She remembered Sister Beatrice, her first grade teacher as well as Sister Mount Carmel and Sister Expedite. With Sister Mount Carmel, the pupils had to put their hands out so that she could slap them as a form of disciplinary action. Almeter thought that it hurt Sister more than it did the pupils because the look in her face especially her eyes indicated her unhappiness in carrying out the task. To Almeter, Sister was such a softy."

Marie Buchheit Miller spoke freely with McCarthy telling him of her fear, reverence, and affection that she had had in her relations with the nuns. Marie started in first grade at St. Louis' parochial school in 1928; her teacher was Sister Rosalia. Marie said, "I didn't like her very much; things were a bit scary getting started. My favorite teacher was Sister Marguerite in seventh grade, but I also admired Sister Gregory in eighth grade. Sister Marguerite was always available for help and Sister Gregory was full of fun and funny too." Marie lived at 42 Park Street, which was about a quarter of a mile from school. She could trace her family back to the days when Father Nicholas Mertz was the pastor. Through her father, Charles J.M. Buchheit, she could trace her beginnings to her great-grandfather Francis Buchheit who had arrived in Buffalo in 1835. Her grandfather, Charles Buchheit, had married Barbara Steffan, whose ancestors owned the leather shop and livery stable on Main Street across from St. Louis Church at a time when the farmers used to come into church on Sunday from Williamsville. Then it was the only church in Western New York. Before marriage, Marie's mother was Mary Frances Futterer, whose father was Erhard Futterer, who immigrated to America from Forchheim, Baden, in 1855. His wife, Magdelena Futterer, nee Rhem, came with her parents from the Rheinpfalz. All were parishioners of St. Louis Church. Like Catherine Berger Almeter, who remembered the disciplinary action of the Sisters, Marie recalled the time when her brother, Richard, came home from school and told his mother that Sister Dionysia had disciplined him by hitting him on the knuckles with her ruler. His mother went over to school and asked Sister not to do that again because some day he would be making a living with his hands, and so he did as an artist and a designer. He was in the graduating class of 1931 with his cousin Georgianna Buchheit, who was the sister of Father Robert Buchheit the founder of St. Gregory the Great Church in Amherst. Georgianna married Charles Besch and their daughter is Carolann Besch, one of the members of the Parish Council at St. Louis Church.

*M*any other students also admired Sisters Marguerite and Gregory. After all, both had long terms as teachers at St. Louis' school. Sister Marguerite was first assigned there in 1920 and Sister Gregory arrived again in 1931, after having been first assigned in 1896. Both were elderly when they finished their careers two decades later; but, even to the end, they still proved success in their ability to connect with young people. Marie's cousin, Louis Buchheit, who graduated from St. Louis' parochial school in 1939, had the fondest memories of Sister Gregory; he acclaimed her as his favorite. He said, "From her, you didn't expect any more than you deserved." He was the son of Louis Buchheit Sr. and Jeannette Hatten. While Louis Jr. attended school he lived with his parents at 20 Pearl Place. He felt that he was so close to the church that if he rolled out of bed he could with ease roll right into the sacristy. He

always fulfilled his assigned times of serving Mass, and Father Laudenbach thought of no one more appropriate to call upon when another server could not fulfill his duty than Louis Buchheit. Louis was so faithful to Laudenbach's requests, which in the winter months were legion, that on his eighteenth birthday he received an autographed picture of Laudenbach with a note saying, "Happy birthday; to my boy, Louis." Not long after that Louis donned his military uniform and was off to fight for Uncle Sam in World War II. Today he lives in Naples, Florida, with his wife Carmene, nee Didio, who he met for the first time when they were in the same Confirmation class at St. Louis Church. Another example of Father Laudenbach's appreciation of his servers was on the occasion of Christmas recess in 1930. Just before the holiday break, he came into Sister Dionysia's eighth grade class, the same class in which Richard and Georgianna Buchheit were in attendance, and gave two boys beautiful watches. They were Richard and Robert Stedler, twins, who had served Laudenbach's early morning Mass every day, never missing a one, during the previous summer months.

*B*oth Pat Riley Albert and Sister Rita Kane recalled some vignettes in regards to Sister Gregory. Pat, remembering her to be quite feisty, said, "She was more than capable of looking askance at those on the other side of the room while teaching. She was eternally vigilant and she was an activist. Back in those days, I would always get the job to accompany her downtown. When we would see those Jehovah's Witnesses giving out Watchtower booklets, Sister would sneer at them. Many times I was afraid that she would punch them out!" Sister Rita Kane remembers Sister Gregory not only as a committed nun but also as a top-notch teacher. Sister Rita said, "She had those eighth graders finished with high school stuff before they left St. Louis. She taught them Latin, algebra, the rudiments of good writing, and a loving appreciation of great literature." When Sister Rita Kane arrived at St. Louis' parochial school in 1945, she was twenty-two years of age. She was then known as Sister Aloysius John, a name assigned to her by the Order. After the Second Vatican Council, the Sisters were allowed to keep their given name or use their family name; as can be seen, Rita chose the latter. Her residence was with the nuns at the convent on Elmwood and Edward Streets. It was there that she first came in contact with Sisters Marguerite and Gregory. Being as young as she was she thought all the nuns in the house were old, but they became great role models for her. "Of course I would be the butt of some of Sister Gregory's humor," Sister Rita said. "When Sister Gregory would go down to the jail and do a bit of prison ministry, she would return and tell the community how well some of my former pupils had made it!" Then Rita concluded her remarks saying, "But those two nuns were really into peoples' lives, and I mean that in a good sense; they truly cared about people."

*M*arie Buchheit Miller requested Dorothy Ball, sister of Richard Ball and Rita Ball Foegen, and wife of Allen Joseph Schneggenburger, to provide some vignettes concerning her and her husband's attendance at classes at St. Louis' parochial school. Both had been baptized, made First Holy Communion, were confirmed, married, and persevered as life long members at St. Louis Church. Dorothy recalled that, each year Father Henry B. Laudenbach was pastor, he would enter the classes just before Christmas break, and present each student with a gift such as a rosary, medal, or statue. Each class received something different. After Christmas, on January 6, the Epiphany of Jesus Christ, or more familiarly referred to as the Feast of the Three Kings, he would again enter the classes. He would say to the children, "Today Jesus was visited by three kings, the Magi. One of those kings was called Balthazar. Did you know "B", the middle initial in my name, means Balthazar? Because, therefore, I am Henry Balthazar Laudenbach you may all have the rest of the day off; this is my gift to you!" After that announcement, one would think that the children would never stop clapping.

*D*orothy spoke about the children's attention to prayer, sacraments, and devotions. She said, "Every Thursday each class had a certain time of the day to go over to the church for confession and pray the stations of the cross. On First Friday all classes would attend Mass and receive Communion. School instruction would start later so as all could eat breakfast. Every Sunday afternoon all the children were expected to be at Vespers at three o'clock so as to attend a catechism class. The children of the four grades, five to eight, would sing in the choir during the week at eight o'clock morning Mass and at the nine o'clock morning Mass on Sundays. On every Corpus Christi Day, which was the Thursday after Trinity Sunday, the children looked forward to being in the procession which went around the church and came into the schoolyard, where Benediction of the Blessed Sacrament took place. The girls carried flowers and dropped petals on the way to the altar that was set up under a tent in front of the school. At the end of eighth grade all girls were expected to join the Ladies Sodality of Mary. They enjoyed mostly the roller skating parties which annually took place in the church basement."

*T*he record book of St. Louis' school, which lists the names of the graduates from 1893 to the closing of the school in August 1959, contains many names of boys and girls who followed a priestly or religious vocation. Marie Buchheit Miller brought one class in particular to the attention of the author/editor. It was the class in which her brother, Edward Buchheit, graduated in 1928. It was also the class that Allen Joseph Schneggenburger, who graduated one year later, called the "Holy Class." Although Marie's brother Edward grew to adulthood to be a good and honest man, he would not have fit the definition indicated by Schneggenburger who said, "Four boys in that class became priests. They were Robert Buchheit, Marie Buchheit Miller's cousin, and three others: Edmund Dietzel, Eugene Wagner, and James Malone." Schneggenburger also pointed out that Florence Steffan, another member of the class, became a nun. Robert Buchheit attended the Diocesan

Preparatory Seminary and Christ the King Seminary at St. Bonaventure University. He was ordained in 1939 and was immediately assigned as assistant pastor to Father Edward J. Rengel at St. Mary of the Angels, Olean, New York. After almost twenty years there, Buchheit was given the pastorship of a fledgling parish in Amherst in 1958; a parish which he built into the thriving complex known as St. Gregory the Great. In 1974, he asked the bishop for a more modest location in a rural part of Western New York; the bishop responded and gave him the pastorship of St. Mary Queen of the Rosary at Strykersville, New York. From there he retired in 1986; he died in 1995.

℮dmund Dietzel was born in Buffalo in 1915, the son of William J. and Christina Dietzel. He attended St. Louis' school for eight years, starting in the year that the Brothers of the Christian Schools departed. The nuns had taken over teaching both the boys and the girls for the entire set of grammar grades. After graduation he attended the Little Seminary in Buffalo followed by matriculation at Our Lady of the Angels Seminary at Niagara University. He was ordained to the priesthood by Bishop James A. Duffy at St. Joseph's Cathedral on June 3, 1939. His assignments as assistant pastor were at St. Rose of Lima, 1939; St. Agnes' Church, 1941; St. Matthew's Church, 1946; Blessed Trinity, 1947; St. Nicholas, 1950; and St. Anthony's, Batavia, 1951. In 1958, the bishop gave him his greatest challenge. With only a wooden altar set up in a dirt parking lot to say Mass and the use of a car for a confessional, Father Dietzel began St. John Vianney parish in Orchard Park, New York. By the time he established a gymnasium, which doubled as his church, he had a flock of three hundred families. From these humble beginnings, he, like Father Robert Buchheit, created a behemoth of a parish of over one thousand families. He was its founding pastor and resided there for thirty-one years until his death on April 19, 1989 at the age of seventy-four. During his priestly career, besides his pastorships, he was chaplain for the Knights of St. John, Commandery 387, assistant chaplain of the Knight's

Second Regiment with the rank of colonel, and a military chaplain in World War II. He was also a member of the Catholic Chaplain's Association, a holder of the fourth degree in the Knights of Columbus, and raised to the dignity of monsignor on October 15, 1988. At the ceremony of his induction to this distinguished honor, over which Bishop Edward Head presided, Dietzel, in responding to the bishop, said, "What took you so long?"

℮ugene Wagner was born to Lawrence Wagner Sr. and Loretta Weibert on November 8, 1915. His younger brother Lawrence Wagner Jr. also graduated from St. Louis' school, however, he did so ten years later. Although the family lived on Lemon Street, in close proximity to St. Boniface Church, the family attended the liturgy at St. Louis Church and contributed to its upkeep. Lawrence Wagner Sr. was a proud and faithful member of the Knights of St. John, Commandery 204. After graduation in 1928 from St. Louis' school, Eugene Wagner entered Canisius High School and graduated in 1932. From there he began taking classes at Canisius College, but only stayed two years. He strongly felt the urge to accept his calling to the priesthood. He, therefore, entered Holy Angels Seminary at Niagara University in order to learn Latin and Greek so as to prepare for studies at a major seminary. In 1936, his opportunity came, and he went to Innsbruck, Austria. In 1938, however, when Adolph Hitler succeeded in executing the Anschluss against Austria, he had to go to Switzerland. German troops occupied the seminary at Innsbruck and discharged the clergy. The bishop of Sion, in the French sector of Switzerland, offered an abandoned hospital as a seminary for the young aspirants to the priesthood who had been ousted from Austria. It was for this seminary that Father Henry B. Laudenbach faithfully raised funds in America during World War II. Eugene Wagner finished his studies in 1940 and was ordained the same year at Sion, after which he returned to Western New York. While crossing the Atlantic on the steamer *Washington*, he was struck with fear when a German submarine rose above the surface and commanded the steamer to halt. After a period of delay, the *Washington* was allowed to proceed unharmed.

*A*lthough Wagner had said several Low Masses before returning to America, he was privileged to sing his first Solemn High Mass at St. Louis Church on June 30, 1940. Following which he was immediately sent to Frewsburg, New York, in the Southern Tier, where Bishop John Duffy had initiated a new missionary apostolate. It was Wagner's charge by the bishop to get a parish activated in this area where the Catholic population was a minority. By the end of 1941, having had some success, he was replaced by other priests, and was sent to be an assistant pastor at St. Matthew's Church in Buffalo. His stay, however, was short. After only three months, the bishop had Wagner and Father Zeitz, who was assistant pastor at St. Gerard's parish, swap positions. Wagner's following stay of twenty-one years at St. Gerard's Church saw him through the remainder of Duffy's tenure as bishop and continuous through the reigns of Bishops John O'Hara and Joseph Burke. Besides these bishops, he served at St. Gerard's under two pastors who had been former graduates of St. Louis' school: Monsignors William J. Schreck and Eugene H. Selbert. Schreck graduated about 1881 and Selbert graduated in 1912. In 1887, Schreck played the role of Guildenstern in *Hamlet*, the fifth production of the St. Louis Dramatic Circle, an amateur group of thespians first organized in 1885. In 1962, Bishop Burke assigned Father Eugene Wagner as pastor at St. Charles Borromeo Church at Olcott, New York. In 1990, he retired but retained his residency at Olcott. At present he assists Father Hassett who has the pastorship of the combined parishes of St. Patrick's in Barker, New York, and St. Charles Borromeo.

*U*nlike his three classmates who chose to be diocesan priests, Father James Malone wanted to be a priestly teacher and entered the Society of Jesus, the Jesuits. After leaving St. Louis' school at the age of thirteen, he attended classes at Canisius High School. After graduating in 1932, he entered the Jesuit Order at Wernersville, Pennsylvania, pursued, for thirteen years, a course of study and teaching which led to his ordination at Woodstock College, Maryland, in 1945. As a priest, Malone taught English, Latin, and religious studies at St. Peter's Prep, Jersey City, New Jersey, and at McQuaid High School, Rochester, New York. McQuaid was named for Right Reverend Bernard J. McQuaid, who was Bishop of Rochester in 1901. He was the preacher at the Solemn Vespers, during the tridium, that year, held at St. Joseph's Cathedral, Buffalo, in honor of the canonization of St. Jean Baptiste de La Salle, founder of the Brothers of the Christian Schools and patron of all teachers. Malone was also guidance counselor at Regis High School, New York City, and teacher-counselor at Our Lady of Lourdes School, Brighton, New York, a suburb of Rochester. While in the vicinity of Rochester, which comprised forty-five years beginning in 1955, he was a member of the Jesuit Community at McQuaid. For nine of those, he was the school's administrator. Even in the years of his retirement, which began in 1990, he did not stop teaching and counseling. He was continually involved in priestly ministry, lay and clerical spiritual advisement and director of parish retreats. At the time of his death, John Roselli, McQuaid's assistant principal for student affairs, said, "Father Malone was well loved. He was known for his gentleness, kindness, and sensitivity to others. He was open and never guarded. Even if he did not have a solution to a person's problems, he always made the individual who confided in him feel better." Father Francis McNamara S.J., McQuaid's alumni moderator and a longtime friend of Malone, said of him, "He was a good, humble, genuine person."

*F*lorence Steffan entered the Order of the Sisters of St. Joseph, and for many years was known as Sister Luke. Like Sister Rita Kane, she changed her name after the Second Vatican Council to her family name; and, until her death on August 26, 1982, was known as

Sister Florence Mary Steffan. She had been born in Buffalo in 1913; and, after graduating from St. Louis' school, she attended Nardin Academy until her graduation in 1932. From there she matriculated at State University of Buffalo and earned a degree in nursing. After completing her internship at Our Lady of Victory Hospital, she worked in many Buffalo hospitals as a surgical nurse. Later she became the night supervisor at the Marine Hospital on Main Street. In 1942, she entered the novitiate of the Sisters of St. Joseph at Main Street and Humboldt Parkway. Although she had donned the nun's habit, she continued her medical studies in obstetrics and pediatrics at Marquette University. Upon completion of her studies, she returned to Buffalo, where for many years, she applied her skills at Our Lady of Victory Hospital. She also nursed at St. Mary's School for the Deaf and St. Joseph's Orphanage. One has to admire Sister Florence who, although following a nursing career, humbly accepted teaching assignments in parochial schools such as Good Shepherd, Pendleton, St. Joseph's, Dunkirk, and St. Boniface, Buffalo.

One year before the one hundred and fiftieth anniversary of the beginning of St. Louis Church, the class of 1928 held its fiftieth anniversary reunion. Twenty-two out of thirty-five were able to attend. It was held on June 25, 1978, fifty years plus one day following the exciting graduation exercises at St. Louis' school. The liturgical ceremony was held in St. Louis Church at 4:30 P.M. with a Mass concelebrated by the Most Reverend Bernard J. McLaughlin, Auxiliary Bishop of Buffalo, and the four priestly classmates: Robert Buchheit, Edmund Dietzel, Eugene Wagner, and James Malone S.J. Following the Mass, cocktails and dinner were served at the Lenox Hotel at 140 North Street. Florence Steffan, who was nursing at Our Lady of Victory, and her twin sister Marian Steffan, who had married Frank Metzger, from Wanakah, New York, were honored at the dinner. Several other girls had married and raised families. Their new titles were: Mary Bert, Mrs. Earl Young; Ruth Bork, Mrs. Leo Volk; Marion Chandler, Mrs. Joseph Dundon; Dolores Herr, Mrs.

Thomas McKenna; Mildred Klemp, Mrs. Martin Salers; Elizabeth McCue, Mrs. Robert Dundon; and Adele Michaels, Mrs. William Mitchell. Several of the other girls remained single: Marjorie Ludaescher, Vera Nebrich, and Mary Zeinz. The boys at the party had all married. They were Edward Buchheit, Herbert Hettrick, Willis Houghtling, Peter Parisi, Frank Stelley, and John Turski. The one who lived closest to St. Louis Church was Mary Zeinz, residing on Chelsea Place near the Erie County Medical Center. Vera Nebrich was in residence in North Buffalo and Elizabeth McCue lived near Municipal Park in Kenmore. The remainder were scattered into Tonawanda, Williamsville, Cheektowaga, Kenmore, Orchard Park, East Aurora, and Niagara Falls. Adele Michaels and her husband William Mitchell lived in Welland, Ontario, Canada, and Dolores Herr and her husband Thomas McKenna had come to the reunion from Gaithersburg, Maryland. One can understand why, by 1978, participation at Mass at St. Louis Church on a Sunday morning was limited to a very few number of downtowners, several from suburbia, and a splash of tourists.

Thirty years earlier, in 1948, another fiftieth graduation anniversary took place at the Westbrook Hotel at 675 Delaware Avenue. Rosina M. Buchheit organized a reunion of the class of 1898. In that year only five had graduated: Anna Strigl, Rose Knopf, Rosina Buchheit, Amelia Dentinger, and Martha Gottstein, who had married Henry Zeinz, organist at St. Louis Church. All five were invited to come with guests of their choice; but, because of illness, Rose Knopf could not attend. Among the others who enjoyed the festivities were Isabelle Dewitt, Rose B. Miller, and Mary Haberstro, who graduated in 1899. Although they were all sixty-five years of age, they spoke about their life at school as if they were still fifteen. They recalled the kindness of their teachers, Sisters Lucy, Hildegarde, and Gregory. They were concerned about the health of both Anna Smith and Elizabeth Hazenzahl, who had graduated the year before them. They recalled the fun days before 1912 when they were all active in the St.

Cecilia Singer Circle, an outgrowth of the *Children of Mary*, a form of sodality which rebuilt genuine piety and religion in the hearts of girls and young women. The group held meetings on the second Wednesday of each month at the church.

Besides the five graduates of 1898, also in attendance were Mary Frances Futterer, Helen Czerwinski, and May Strigl. Helen Czerwinski, the youngest, had graduated from St. Louis' school in 1905. Together, these ladies had also been members of the Ladies Catholic Benevolent Association, known as the LCBA, and the Confraternity of Christian Mothers. The LCBA was essentially an insurance group which by paying dues and contributing assessments the members would then receive funds for a beneficiary should they have the misfortune to die during a period of enrollment. Members of St. Louis Church belonged to Branch No. 368 with quarterly dues of fifty cents and monthly assessments of thirty-eight cents, during the period of the twentieth century preceding World War I. The Archconfraternity of Christian Mothers was a pious association joined together under the special blessing of the Holy Father, the Pope. Their purpose was to, more easily and successfully, fulfill their duties as Christian and Catholic mothers toward their children. Mary Frances Futterer, who had married Charles John M. Buchheit in 1912, was received into the confraternity by Father Paul Hoelscher on December 19, 1915. She had graduated from St. Louis' parochial school in 1892.

Speaking with Dorothy B. Reuvain, nee Dziwuski, Marie Buchheit Miller learned that Dorothy and her husband, Francis, were married at St. Louis Church on July 8, 1950. He graduated from St. Louis' school in the class of 1938. Although Dorothy had been a member of the parish, she did not attend the school, but received religious instruction at the church. She and Francis had met at the church socials. Dorothy had been a member of the parish's Catholic Youth Organization and did secretarial work for Father James Cahill who was the assistant pastor. When they celebrated their fiftieth wedding anniversary at their daughter's home in Derby, New York with her and their son's families in the year 2000, Francis had been retired from Bethlehem Steel Corporation, Lackawanna, for some years, and Dorothy was a retired secretary from St. Barbara's Catholic Church. After Francis told Marie that he had received all his sacraments; Baptism, Holy Communion, Confirmation, and Matrimony at St. Louis Church, he said, concerning his teachers, "I can remember Sister Marguerite, the principal, who taught seventh grade. She was easy going and a very pleasant lady. Sister Gregory, our eighth grade teacher was very old. We heard that she had been there since the last decade of the nineteenth century. With her quiet pussyfooting around the room, we didn't know where she was until she appeared in front of us. The kids all said, "You better not shout, you better not pout, Sister Gregory's all about!"

It was then that Marie realized the truth of the statement, "When an interviewer passes from one person to another, and relates to the second person how kudos were passed out by the first claiming a certain class as being the greatest, one can be sure that the second will top it." So it was with the kudos of Allen Joseph Schneggenburger's remark about his defined "Holy Class" of 1928. When Francis finished telling Marie how he faithfully served Father Laudenbach as an altar boy, he was so happy to announce that his class could boast of generating five vocations to the priesthood, one more than the 1928 class. The five priests he mentioned were Anthony Caligiuri, Theodore Caffarelli, William Crumlish, Ralph Gibson, and Joseph Hassler. Only Monsignor Caligiuri is alive, retired, and residing at the Cardinal O'Hara Residence in Tonawanda. He offered some insights into lives of his four other classmates. William Crumlish had joined the Franciscan Capuchin Friars and for some time did ecclesiastical work around Seneca Lake, New York. Theodore Caffarelli had joined the Columban Fathers and served on the missions in the Philippine Islands. Ralph Gibson and Joseph Hassler had been diocesan priests who served in Western New York.

*I*n an interview with Lawrence Wagner, younger brother of Father Eugene Wagner and classmate of Francis Ruvain, Marie discovered that Richard Nason was also in the 1938 graduating class. For several years his classmates wondered whatever had happened to him because he never came to any of the reunions of the class. Richard was the son of Warren Nason and Cecilia Miller, who had graduated in 1918 receiving the diligence medal. They lived on Neptune Place in a house owned by Charles Augustine and Catherine Miller, Cecilia's parents. In World War II, Richard's military unit was in the first wave that attacked Omaha Beach on June 6, 1944. His unit managed to make it to the shoreline, but, before it could set up machine guns, a shell burst overhead. Richard and his entire unit were killed instantly. He was buried in Europe during the war. Following the surrender of Germany, Richard's parents went to Europe, retrieved his body and buried him with honor in a military cemetery on Long Island, New York.

*S*alvatore Mistretta, another member of the class, who makes arrangements for some of the class reunions, appreciatively welcomed this information. Another 1938 graduate, who only spent his eighth grade there, was Paul Frohe; one of the owners of Frohe Glass Works on Harlem Road, whose grandfather, Godfrey Frohe, along with Ferdinand Riester installed the stained glass windows along the side aisles of St. Louis Church. Through his mother, Paul Frohe is a descendant of Colonel John L. Schwartz, distinguished leader of the Second Regiment, Knights of St. John, former brewer, and Commissioner of Buffalo's Streets appointed by Mayor Francis X. Schwab. Paul's family, having been financially solvent prior to the Depression, suffered greatly in the Stock Market crash of 1929. After struggling to keep their home for seven years, his

parents had to move from Snyder, New York, back into the City of Buffalo, to live with Grandma Frohe on Ellicott Street. He had spent seven years at Christ the King parochial school and had to finish at St. Louis' school. He said, "At St. Louis during my last year, I was not a happy-camper. It was not easy for me to leave my old school chums behind and make new friends."

*W*hile being interviewed, Monsignor Anthony Caligiuri noted that the 1938 class was thirty-eight percent Italian. The records of the graduating classes show that from 1928, when the number of Italians represented only ten per-cent, they peaked to forty per-cent by 1940. From then their number leveled off to thirty-five per-cent and remained so almost until the school closed in 1959. In the meantime, the number of Germans in the eighth grade decreased from a high of sixty per-cent in 1928 to less than thirty per-cent by the end of World War II, and continued to fall drastically so that by 1950 there were less than twenty per-cent on the roster. Besides Italians and Germans registered at St. Louis' school during these same years there was a representative mixture of Irish, Polish, French, and Latvians. When asked the reason for the increase of Italians at the school, Caligiuri replied, "After 1900, the Italian immigrants began to flow into Buffalo and took up residence on the lower West Side of the city. Streets such as Seventh, Maryland, Fifteenth, Hudson, Virginia, Tenth, Jersey, and Rhode Island were collectively called Little Italy."

*I*t was true that the lower West Side near the Erie Canal was filled with venders, peddlers, and shopkeepers, all in the vintage of the old country not unlike Roma, Siena, or Sicily. These immigrants had come to Buffalo in search of a more assured livelihood and means of prosperity. Those who had clustered around Holy Cross Church soon found that there was no Catholic school available to them. Father Joseph Gambino, pastor, did not have one and could not afford to build one. He, however, wanted his children to attend a parochial school; what better one could he find than St. Louis' school even though it would require a mile walk for the children. Gambino quipped, " It will do them good and make room for the pasta!" Caligiuri said, "Father Gambino was so sure that many of his boys would have vocations to the priesthood and the religious life that he not only sent them there but paid their tuition." Not only from Holy Cross Church did students come, but also from St. Anthony's Church on Court Street and from Our Lady of Loretto on Fifteenth Street.

Not all of the Italian students who came to St. Louis' parochial school from other parishes were completely happy and satisfied with the excellent academic achievements that they experienced upon arrival. They studied hard and held their own, but some of them looked for excellence in sports. St. Louis' school's children were intellectuals. They won debate contests and excelled artistically in drama and comedy stage productions, but in baseball and basketball they were considered as the bottom of the barrel. One student, who complained bitterly later in life, was Francis V. Tonello. He had come to St. Louis' parochial school from Our Lady of Loretto, a new parish that was being formed in 1939 on Fifteenth Street. It, like Holy Cross Church, had no grammar school and the children were required to attend the nearby public school. In September 1939, the pastor of Our Lady of Lorretto, requested Tonello and James Ralabate to leave public school and attend classes at St. Louis' parochial school.

Ralabate was a year older than Tonello and entered sixth grade while Tonello was placed in fifth grade. James' brother, John Ralabate, had graduated in 1939. Being on the school grounds for only a short time, Tonello ran amok with Father Laudenbach and his sister, Anna. While tossing a softball back and forth outside the rectory window with Ralabate on a cool fall day, Anna shouted from the window, "If you boys don't stop disturbing us, I will send Father out to chastise

you." They didn't know what chastise meant, but they soon found out. Laudenbach appeared on the scene and took Tonello's ball away from him and told him and Ralabate to get inside the school building. Tonello later said, "He was a bastard. He stopped me, took my ball, and never gave it back to me. When I entered the school I complained to Sister Marguerite. I told her that Father Laudenbach wouldn't let us practice outdoors. If we couldn't do so there, where were we supposed to play?"

Marguerite came to the rescue. She helped the boys to jerry-build a basketball court in the small U-shaped courtyard of the school building on the Franklin Street side. It was an area isolated from the rectory, out of the range of the sharp ears of Anna Laudenbach, and could be put together with junkyard materials at no cost. Tonello said, "Circuitously away from the pastor, and his beloved little sister peeking out the window, we got our basketball court. Sister Marguerite, the principal, knew that Laudenbach was not going to give any money to support us. She said that when it came to sports we had to live on a shoestring. We were considered as a disgruntled group of immigrant Italians from the West Side, shady characters from School Ten, delinquents, and rejects playing choose-up basketball and dreaming that we could become a successful team." Tonello was able to get through the sixth and seventh grades without getting into deeper trouble by avoiding any further confrontation with Laudenbach.

The episode of losing his ball, however, tainted Tonello's attitudes for the rest of his life. From that day on he was not a happy-camper at school. He considered it a dinky little educational establishment fit for the birds! In eighth grade Sister Gregory taught him. He said of her, "She favored the group that could achieve ninety or above in Reading, English, History, and Writing. Those in that category were asked to sit next to her, and she would smile upon them. For the many of 'not so gooders,' as I was, she scowled, she scorned, and she stared silently and endlessly. When I went home and told my parents that I received a rap on the knuckles from her, the only sympathy I received was an inquisition as to why Sister was angry with me. Any explanation I gave only resulted in my receiving a whack on my behind from either my mother or father." In the regents examinations that year Tonello received grades above average: Geography 87; Arithmetic 99; Spelling 96; Reading 86; English 87; History 86; Writing 80. His recollections of Sister Gregory complimented those of John Marciano, an Italian boy from St. Anthony's Church who graduated in 1937. Marciano said, "I bet she could have stared down a big black bear on any occasion. Whenever someone asked her something she couldn't answer she would say, 'Why is an onion? Why is an onion!' Since we couldn't understand what she meant, we just walked away."

A decade later, the athletic program at St. Louis' school was much more successful than the gloomy picture painted by Tonello. Ronald Foegen, son of Joseph and Evelyn Foegen, graduated in 1955. Today, Ronald and his wife Margaret, nee Rooney, are staunch parishioners of St. Louis Church who, driving into the city from Hamburg, attend Mass there each weekend. Ronald, like Tonello, was a lover of sports; but, unlike him, had an upbeat attitude toward the school's athletic abilities. Ronald said, "Father Albert J. Bosack was the coach of our basketball, baseball, and track teams. We played in the Buffalo Catholic Grammar School League that was directed by Monsignor William J. Martin. Bessi Boller, a parishioner at St. Louis Church, worked for him and helped give out the trophies. I can remember the exciting games we had with Blessed Trinity, Our Lady of Lourdes, Holy Angels, and St. Joseph's Cathedral. Even though we lost by a score of four to three in the championship baseball game with Holy Angels in 1955, I was extremely proud to be part of that team." There was no distinction among large or small schools for basketball and baseball events; but, for track, the schools were divided into programs listed as large, medium, and small. St. Louis' parochial school

was always in the small division. Outdoor meets were held at Delaware Park and indoor meets took place at the armory of the seventy-fourth infantry located at Connecticut and Niagara Streets. Father Bosack said, "Our students participated in all the track events such as mile and quarter mile runs, relays, broad jumps, and dashes. The girls were very good in the relay. They were not the fastest young ladies alive, but they sure knew how to pass the baton. We always had a good runner for the last leg of the event; and, when she kicked it in coming down the stretch, we knew we had a winner." In 1955, St. Louis' school entered all the events in the annual Outdoor Spring Meet. The boys missed the first place trophy by only one point and the girls missed their first place by two points. Ronald said, "Although they didn't come home with top grade bacon, no one could accuse the second place winners as being at the bottom of the barrel."

*N*ot every Italian immigrant who came to Buffalo wished to reside in Little Italy on the West Side. One such family was that of Allesandro Didio who came to America in 1901. Like other Italian families who came at the same time, he settled with his flock on Dante Place near Canal Street. In 1915, however, he moved the family to North Division Street on the East Side. He refused to register either in St. Anthony's parish or in the newly formed parish of Holy Cross. Instead, his family mingled with the Germans who attended St. Mary's Church at Broadway and Pine Streets. With his sons he opened his business, in 1918, on North Division known as Didio Brothers Cut Glass Works. One of those sons was John Didio who, that same year, met and dated Clara Vitale who had arrived in America with her parents in 1908. They were married in 1919 at St. Lucy's Church located at Swan and Chicago Streets. On May 14, 1924, they were blessed with the birth of a daughter, Carmene, at their residence on Carlton Street near the west side of Elm Street. At the time, they were attending religious services at St. Boniface Church where Carmene was baptized. After her baptism, however, her father and mother registered the family at

St. Michael's Church where, at the age of six years, Carmene received her first Holy Communion. She did not go to Catholic school, however, but attended School 15 for Kindergarten and first grade. Following her reception of the Eucharistic Sacrament for the first time, her parents fell in love with St. Louis Church and registered there while she began attending elementary classes at School 48.

As Carmene advanced in age, she discovered that she was required to attend classes of religious instruction at St. Louis Church in preparation for the reception of the Sacrament of Confirmation. After her classes at public school she, with students from various other public schools, came to St. Louis' school building where the Sisters of St. Joseph instructed the children in the rudiments of their faith through the use of the catechism. These classes were not attended by the students who regularly attended the parochial school at St. Louis Church until the last few weeks prior to the reception of Confirmation, at which time they all made preparation together. It was during these final weeks that Carmene, for the first time, met Louis Buchheit who was a resident on Pearl Place, a regular altar boy at St. Louis Church, and a student at the church's parochial school. Confirmation took place in June of 1936.

In an interview, Carmene said, "As I reflect back on those years, I think that quite a bit of discrimination was shown toward us public school scholars. During the Confirmation service the bishop received all the parochial school kids, boys and girls, before he confirmed us. We got the feeling that we were not their equals." Carmene graduated from School 48 in 1938, and Louis Buchheit graduated from St. Louis' parochial school in 1939. Both went to high school; Carmene attended Fosdick-Masten High and Lou went to St. Joseph's Collegiate Institute. After attending high school, Carmene and Lou began dating, but had to put off their wedding because World War II interrupted

them. They were, however, married on June 11, 1949 at St. Louis Church. In 1940, Carmene went to work for thirty cents per hour at the Didio Glass Works and remained an employee there until 1965. In 1954, her family house on Carlton Street was razed to make room for the expansion of Roswell Park Memorial Institute. John and Clara Didio moved the family to Mona Drive in Eggertsville behind the present Veteran's Hospital. They then changed their religious affiliation to St. Benedict's Church. Later, Carmene and Louis Buchheit had three children, Clara Suzanne, who chose teaching as a career; and Louis John Jr., who is a TV News Director with WKBW, Buffalo; and Kimberly Ann who is a successful professional surveyor.

The dawn of the twentieth century was a long way down the road from 1684 when Jean Baptiste de La Salle introduced teaching in the vernacular. After two hundred years of experiencing education in a parish school system, people probably have forgotten where the idea began. At St. Louis' parochial school, however, teaching in the vernacular meant something a little different. Which vernacular would be the vehicle of teaching: English or German? Although English was the language of the land, the parish was dominated by a German influence. German was the language of the people. When she attended school, Catherine Berger Almeter recalls that all students prayed in German in the morning and in English in the afternoon. When interviewed, John E. Miller remembered that his father, Eugene W. Miller Sr., who was in the graduating class of 1917, had learned all his morning subjects in German and the afternoon subjects in English. Every other day the curriculum topics were reversed from morning to afternoon. One of the official guidelines for education at St. Louis' parochial school published in 1896 bears out what Catherine and Eugene had said. It stated, "The philosophy of education was a bilingual one. Two languages are taught: English and German. The school is well graded. Every facility is offered for enabling pupils to acquire a thorough knowledge of the German language. German forms a part of the daily curriculum of studies, in all the grades, thereby, students acquire a sufficient knowledge of it to fit them to take up the examination of the Regents' Advanced German, when they have reached the end of the grammar grades. Because a thorough knowledge of English, the language of their country, is of great importance to the pupils, special attention is also paid to all branches of it." Eugene W. Miller Sr. also pointed out that while he attended St. Louis' parochial school graduation came after ten years of study; two years of advanced training for boys and girls beyond eighth grade. During those extra two years, the Brothers of the Christian Schools taught him. He said, "Because World War I had not yet begun, bringing about a situation where being American came into conflict with one's German culture, we still integrated the German language into our extra two years with the Brothers."

For antebellum World War I, German influence in the enrollment at St. Louis' school was profound. During the period from 1900 to 1919, the official school record of graduates listed only eight family names that appeared to represent English or Irish ancestry. In Catherine Berger Almeter's class of 1916, however, it was very obvious that her friend Evelyn Duffy was one, as was Francis Kennedy who graduated in 1918. The total number of English-speaking scholars, however, only represented two percent of the total number who graduated during this nineteen-year period. As more German Catholic immigrants poured into the Fruit Belt, the neighborhood bounded by Genesee Street in the south, North Street in the north, Jefferson Street in the east, and Main Street in the west, the Germans clustered together and relied on their church for identity and a sense of security. Fortunately they had no problem finding it in the churches within walking distance from their homes. St. Mary's, St. Boniface, St. Michael's, and St. Louis surrounded them. These also had free schools that were available for the religious and secular education of their children staffed by priests and religious. For the parents, their heavy guttural language was looked upon, by every-day business associates, as an impediment. They needed to shed that remnant of the Old Country as soon as possible to be able to compete in modern America, however, their German language and customs formed the basis of their commonality. St. Louis' school, as did other parochial schools across the nation, played a huge roll in their assimilation. Catholic Germans really felt the need for having their own religious schools. By 1914, ninety-five percent of the German parishes in the United States had established one.

Catholicism was not the dominant religion of the totality of the German community. No more than thirty percent of the German immigrant population was Catholic. Members of St. Louis Church and of the other German Catholic Churches in Buffalo had to compete with rival beliefs and allegiances. These were not only those of Anglo-Saxon Protestants, but included German Protestants, free thinkers, gymnasts, and radicals who had flooded the immigrant population. To ward off their philosophical threats, German Catholics gathered around the parish and closely identified with it. As a result, the parish became much more than a religious center; it was a social center as well. In addition to the devotional societies in the parish, it organized insurance companies, music and choral societies, libraries, military groups, and social activities such as parades, picnics, and public displays. World War I, however, sharply changed the ethnic nature of these organizations. The year 1918, with America's generated hatred of Kaiser Wilhelm, brought a negative reaction to anything German. Hamburgers became known as Salisbury steaks, daschunds, if not shot in the parks, became known as liberty pups, and the German-American Bank took the new name of Liberty Bank. Instruction in the German language, by legislative decree, was dropped from the public school curriculum. Voluntarily, after 1918, German I and II were dropped from the curriculum of St. Louis' parochial school. Following the war, all grammar school classes were taught in English; study of the German language became part of the modern language curriculums in high schools.

American doughboys that had been members of St. Louis Church returned home, married, and began their own families. Others who were slightly younger and were not militarily involved in the war also married and had families. While many of these who had parents living in the Fruit Belt and in the area of the West Side tucked into the neighborhood which today is known as Allentown, they took their families elsewhere, such as into the vicinities surrounding the churches of St. Vincent de Paul and St. Nicholas. Although they did not take the German language with them as a daily household medium of conversation, many a boy knew he was of German heritage when in doing wrong he heard his father say, "Du bist ein Dummkopf! Was bist du, ein Esel?" The young ones also learned that they were very much German when they attended summer picnics of the Knights of St. John or were involved with their parents in social activities of the Dramatic Circle. The sounds of the German Ompah-pah bands and the dances with girls and boys dressed in costumes stirred the flow of German blood in their ethnic arteries and veins. Finally, they really knew they were still German when the party ended with the lifting of the Bier Seidel and singing the rousing refrain, "Ein Prosit, Ein Prosit, Gemuetlichkeit!"

*M*any post war parents and their children remained parishioners at St. Louis Church through the Roaring Twenties and the Dark Years of the Depression, but the children attended parochial schools within the geographical boundaries carved out by the bishop of the diocese for church and educational participation. Although the rosters of students attending St. Louis' parochial school began to include names that represented the influx of Irish and Italians into the parish, the numbers of Germans still remained high. For the eight years between 1925 and 1933, the school registered per year nearly two hundred students of German descent. For the same period between 1933 and 1940 the number was only

about fifteen less per year. In McCarthy's interview with Carlos Carballada, a graduate of St. Louis' school in 1948, chairman of the Rochester Fund, Director of the M&T Bank, a member of the Board of Regents for New York State, and a resident of Pittsford, New York, Carlos said, "By the end of World War II we had gone through the German period, and in 1948 we were going through typical changes in a neighborhood where one population went through the low end of the social strata, but there certainly were still strong indications of German culture and tradition being evident." By the time St. Louis' school closed in 1959, however, change was rampant throughout Buffalo, and German assimilation was among the most profound. Because of the impact of two World Wars involving the United States, many Germans not only shed their language and customs, but their sense of cohesiveness too. Although they remained the largest ethnic group in Erie County, most experts said they were never counted among the various ethnic blocs that politicians counted. Today, St. Louis Church has no school and the church has reverted to a multi-ethnic character, but beautiful German names still grace the stained glass windows and the singing of *Stille Nacht, Heilige Nacht* still fills the air at Midnight Mass on Christmas Eve.

*T*he school building, designed in 1858, replaced the frame building constructed in 1850. It was similar in style to the lay buildings, chateaux, country houses, and hotels that sprang up in France about the middle of the seventeenth century. Upon their arrival at the school for the first time, the Sisters of St. Joseph recognized the style. The three story building reminded them of the their historic convent at LePuy, France. The roof of the school and its cupola were like those of the buildings designed by Francois Mansart who, in 1840, was the architect for the Chateau de Masions-Laffitte and the Church of the Val-de-Grace in Paris. During the pastorship of Joseph Sorg the schoolhouse took on the physical characteristics by which most graduates, still alive today, remember it. Sorg and the trustees knew that the growing numbers of students necessitated an expansion of the building. Accordingly, plans were devised and funds raised so as to replace the two wings on the north and south sides of the building following the dismantling of those that had been there since 1858.

These new wings were more spacious so as to accommodate more classrooms, offices for the trustees, a faculty room for the Sisters and Brothers, and living quarters for the family of the parish custodian. Once completed the school was absolutely symmetrical on either side of the cupola situated in the center of the mansard roof. Three dormer type windows graced the roof symmetrically on either side of it facing the schoolyard, and two of the same type windows on the roof faced north and south. One of the same type dormer windows was in the center of the roof at the base of the cupola. Four large air vents protruded from the center of the rooftop. The four sides of the cupola were louvered so that a continual airflow was maintained but rainwater could not enter. A cross had been erected at the very peak of the cupola. If the building had been seen on any of the streets of Rouen, Paris, or Rheims in the nineteenth century, it would have gone unnoticed by the citizenry because it would have been a perfect fit in their culture. It was le Hotel Francais par Excellence!

On the front side of the building, facing the schoolyard, a fire escape from the ground to the second floor formed a trapezoidal structure of two stairways leading to a platform outside the three center windows of the second floor. From that platform a single stairway rose to a platform outside the window adjacent to the center protrusion of the roof underneath the cupola, which contained the school bell. A screened railing guarded the sides of the stairways so that the children and adults hurriedly fleeing from the building during a fire could not be hurled traversely off the stairway. In the south wing there were two large windows on each of the first two floors facing the school yard and six windows on each floor facing south

toward the rectory. A complimentary set of windows was in the north wing. In the central section of the building a single doorway gave entrance to each of the wings on the first floor and double doorways adjacent to each of them gave access to the school proper. Over each of these doorways was a window on the second floor. Between the double doors there were eight windows on the first floor and a complimentary set on the second floor.

In one of his interviews, McCarthy asked Marie Buchheit Miller to describe the building as she remembered it as a student. Marie said, "When you went into the double doors on the south side of the building you faced a large stairway going to the second floor. On the first floor, to the right of the stairs, was a hallway that led to the back of the building. In the rear was a door that led to the outside. Next to it was the boys' bathroom. At the top of these stairs on the second floor, over the boys' bathroom, was the girls' bathroom. Left of the stairs on the first floor was a divided room. In the front, with an entrance inside the building, was a room reserved for the trustees. In the rear was a lounge used by the teachers. To the right of the hallway was a large room occupied by the first and second grades. Sister Rosalia taught these classes. When you went into the double doors on the north side of the building you met a complimentary stairway, hallway, and classroom, with the hallway and room to the left of the stairs. On the first floor the room was for the third and fourth grades. Miss Rung, a lay teacher, taught there. On the second floor, above her classroom, was a room for the fifth and sixth grades; I cannot remember who taught these grades. To the right of the stairs, in the north wing, was an apartment, with a separate doorway, for the family of the custodian, Mr. Edward White; he was a very industrious man, always working somewhere on the property. On the second floor of the building, on the south side near the girls' bathroom, a set of stairs led to the auditorium on the third floor. To the left of the landing on the second floor was a doorway that led into the eighth grade that was directly over the trustees' room and the faculty lounge. Sister Gregory taught it. To the right of the landing was an entrance into the seventh grade, a room that ran the full width of the building. Sister Marguerite, the principal, taught there."

*B*ecause there were no bathrooms on the north side of the building and no apparent hallway connecting the north side with the south side on either the first or second floor, one might ask, "What was the procedure of obtaining access to the bathrooms during class sessions by the students of grades three to five?" Robert Albert clarified the mystery. He said, "On nice days students on the north-side walked out of the building, came around the outside, entered the south side doors and used the bathrooms. On rainy and snowy days, the teachers allowed the pupils of the north side to go through connecting doors in the classrooms to the south side on both floors so as to have access to the bathrooms." The school had no facilities for serving lunch; and, as was the custom in most Catholic parochial schools of the time, the generality of pupils went home for lunch. Marie Buchheit Miller said, "I had to walk to school every day, about a quarter of a mile one way. That meant I walked a whole mile every day. One day while I was in first grade, I got home for lunch and my mother asked what I would like to eat. Standing between the sofa and the armchair in the parlor, while swinging my feet, I told her that I would like a baloney sandwich. She told me I couldn't have it because it was Friday and a fast day. Undaunted, I was quick to respond, 'that's OK, I'll eat it fast!'"

*T*he trustees' room was considered sacred; it was a place where even adults entered by invitation only. Robert Albert recalled that families paid their pew rent to the trustees in that room. Another room that loomed large in the memories of St. Louis' grads was the auditorium on the third floor. It was a large, all-purpose hall, which served as the gathering place for many school and parish functions. It was a place for Christmas pageants, spring plays, graduation exercises,

ceremonies marking the end of first and second grades, concerts, and productions by the Dramatic Circle. It was a hall that could seat about four hundred people. Robert Albert said, "It was an auditorium with a stage; it had old-fashioned embossed metal walls and wainscoting. The ceiling had metal too." Several students recalled the bell that was in the cupola. Each day it rang at twelve o'clock noon for the recitation of the *Angelus*, a prayer honoring the Blessed Virgin Mary. It also rang to summon the students to the classroom. Robert Albert explained that the bell is on display in the museum in the basement of the church. As Marie Buchheit Miller has pointed out, Ed White and his family lived in the school building. They had been there in residence more than forty years. He served as the all-around superintendent of the vast physical plant—church, school, rectory, and grounds. White's son Norman, who is over eighty years of age, described to Michael Riester, the church historian, some interesting details concerning the school, his father's devotion to caring for it and the church, the family's living quarters, and life around the neighborhood.

*N*orman White, who began parochial school at St. Louis Church in 1924, said, "At the north end of the school building the trustees had made an apartment for my family. One would neither have called it large nor lavish. It was more like a one-bedroom apartment. There my father and mother, my three brothers and I lived. My mother and father slept in the bedroom, two brothers and I slept in the hallway, and my oldest brother slept in a closet. The school had fourteen-foot ceilings, long windows, and the furnace heated both the school and the rectory. The trustees had a room on the first floor on the south end of the building. Adjacent to their meeting area they had a room that served as the nuns' lunch room. I'm not sure if it had a sink, but it did have a table, chairs, and a stove. They could eat and make coffee, but a school day never went by that we did not have one or two nuns joining us at our table in the apartment."

Do You Know Where Your Children Are?

John Marciano, a fellow classmate of Marie Buchheit Miller who graduated in 1937, recalled that Sister Gregory would allow him to leave class early each day so that he could go to the Sisters' convent on Edward Street and fetch their lunch basket. He would bring it to the room described by White; and, on rainy days, they would invite him to eat with them. Usually Marciano preferred to eat with the other boys who did not go home for lunch. He was from St. Anthony's parish, lived on Whitney Place near Georgia Street, and came to St. Louis' school with several other Italian boys. White recalled his tardiness in getting to his classes. He said, "Rita Mayer, who sat next to me in eighth grade and lived on Grand Island, took the ferry and streetcar to get to school each day; she was always on time. I lived right in the school building and was late! We had twenty-three students in my class, fifteen boys and eight girls. Dorothy Ball, who later married Allen Joseph Schneggenburger, was another classmate of mine. My brother, Elmer, graduated five years before me, and my two oldest brothers were taught by Brothers Azarias Raphael and Bonaventure John. They graduated in 1921. The Brothers had a residence on Cottage Street and said their rosary as they walked to school each day wearing their robes. When Brother Azarias Raphael would be with us in the yard, he would reach down through a slit on the inside of his robe's pocket and pull the bottom of the robe up through it. This allowed him to run around freely while playing ball with us."

Norman described his antics about the church and school during his leisure time. He said, "There was one work room underneath the school nearly in the middle. Another workroom was underneath the apartment with a laundry room attached. One part of that room was used as a fruit cellar; the other part I made into a clubroom. I stapled a large American flag, which had been flown over the church during World War I, to the ceiling of my clubroom. At the other end of the basement was a huge coal bin. Before the first snowfall of November, my father had that bin filled with hard coal that reached right up to the floor joists. My brothers and I would have lots of fun playing and getting dirty with it on those days when it was delivered. We had a big hall on the third floor of the school and another underneath the church. In the church hall my brothers and I would roller skate, ride bicycles, and play with our toys. In the school hall we would get into the stuff stored there by the Dramatic Circle. What great stuff: props, books, old time flintlock rifles, and costumes. In winter with ice and snow on the roof, we would crawl out of the third floor window, and play chase down an eighteen inch wide eave trough like a group of nuts."

Norman continued, "Next to our apartment we had three beautiful pear trees. Every year they would give us three or four bushels of pears that we distributed throughout the neighborhood. My oldest brother was a real nutty daredevil. One day he tied a rope up in one of the trees as high as he could, pulled it tight and secured the other end around the bottom of another tree. With a rope and pulley he pulled one of the teacher's chairs, a docent chair, to the top of the first tree, balanced it on the rope with himself sitting in it, slid down the taut rope, and smashed into the base of the second tree with such a force that he nearly knocked himself out. Needless to say once was enough for this kind of adventure. One day I got up into the organ loft and began playing it so loudly that Anna Laudenbach, the pastor's sister who was his housekeeper, called my father and questioned ' Ist somvun in Kirche practicing on der ogen Herr Vite? Ist pretty Laut!' I received a good lacing down from him for this musical achievement. Sometimes we got into a storage room off in the basement of the church where, among many other things, my father stored the Christmas crib set. For many years I really thought it was a storage room; but, in fact, it was the vault room for Father Sorg's body. It was a burial site; but, in my estimation, a helluva place for a priest to be buried."

Norman described some historic highlights and

gave his views about the neighborhood. He said, "In 1921, the year my oldest brother graduated from school, the church was struck by lightning and the rear tower was set on fire. My father helped the firemen up the circular staircase; because of the dense smoke they were unable to effectively get their hoses in place. It was a good thing that the cross beams, which were on fire, were extremely large. They were really only charred and are still that way. New ones were never put in. Once when I was very small, I watched my father ringing the church bell during the prayer time called *The Angelus*. While he rang the bell he would say his prayers in German. I said, 'Dad, what are you saying?' He replied, 'Son, I'm saying my prayers in German. I responded, 'Don't you know them in English?' There were lots of real wealthy people who lived around the church on Edward, Franklin, North Pearl, and Linwood Streets and on Delaware and Elmwood Avenues. Many of them donated diamonds, pearls, and rubies to the church to be embedded in the chalice and the monstrance. The backyard of the school would have made an excellent playground for the school kids but it was overgrown with weeds. One day I came in to tell my mother that an Italian woman from the West Side was in the weed patch; she was picking flowers that I called burdocks and believed to be poison. I said that if the woman eats those she would die. My father went out to see her and when he returned he told us that she knew what she was doing. Those aster-like flowers were called cardoons by the Italians and were considered by them to be a great delicacy."

*N*orman rambled on, "Around the church especially on Main Street there was a lot of business activity. The Steffan Brothers leather goods store was there along with Barclay and Sons, the former site of Weyand's Brewery and later the home of the *Courier Express* building. The brewery had had enormous underground storage rooms below Main Street for the purpose of keeping beer cool. There was an IRC power station on Virginia that supplied the electric for the streetcars. Scotts Roller Rink and Floss's Bowling Drome were at Burton Alley. Across the alley was Ray Flynn's Golden Dollar, a well-attended watering hole for men who wished to quench their thirst with a tasty brew. I liked Ray very much especially after my father died. The younger crowd called him "Pops" or "Uncle Ray." As I grew older Fathers Kasprzak and Galbraith joined the church as assistants to the pastor. They always wore their Roman Collars in public even when they sometimes slipped over to Ray Flynn's to enjoy a nightcap. One night while they were sitting at the bar, one of the patrons let go some miserable slang and swear words. In a loud voice Flynn admonished the man saying, 'Do you know that you have a priest sitting next to you?' Kasprzak responded, 'Hush, Ray, keep it quiet before the word gets out!' It was also rumored that during Prohibition several brands of spirits donated by Ray were stored in St. Louis' school basement under the close supervision of Father Laudenbach who liked the Cadillac he received new each year from the trustees. Laudenbach kept the car in the Edward Street Garage. One day my brother, Marvin, decided to take it for a ride around the block just when Laudenbach came over to take it on a sick call. Finding the car gone, and knowing from the attendant at the garage that Marvin had taken a little spin around the corner, he waited. Marvin, upon his return and while he was taken bodily by Laudenbach to see my father, heard a sermon he would never forget. My father was furious and told Marvin to apologize to Laudenbach. Poor Marvin! He only exacerbated his situation by saying, 'I will not apologize to him, he swears!' Needless to say Marvin did eventually say that he was sorry."

*N*orman finished his remarks by reminiscing, "My dad dedicated his whole life to St. Louis Church. It was his whole life; he worked seven days a week, sometimes from 5:30 A.M. until 2:00 A.M. Besides all the indoor and outdoor maintenance, he took care of clubs that had parties. Many times my mother and us boys pitched in to help. When we got married our wives helped also on various occasions and at different functions. When dad died the church was packed for the funeral service. He had been a member of the Knights of St. Gregory at St. Michael's Church. They carried his casket from the apartment in school down Pearl Place to Main Street and then into St. Louis Church. Father Laudenbach said to my mother, 'This man had a funeral fit for a general.' My father was loved by so many men because of his honesty, devotion, and generosity. Oshei, who was the head of Trico and previously manager of the Teck Theater, recalled how he came to my dad one day and asked, 'Do you know of anybody who rents furniture? We need some for a play to be used as stage props. Things like a divan, table, chairs are needed.' Without hesitation, my dad said, 'Send your men over to my house and take whatever you need.' Oshei said, 'No! No!' My dad, however, insisted that they come but to be careful. On the night of the production our whole family, at the invitation of Oshei, were able to see our furniture in action. One also has to have a strong wonderful feeling of appreciation for my mother, who before marriage was Julia Scholastica Batt. She understood that my father could never say no to a man in need, and graciously put up with any inconvenience. It is through her that I am able to trace my ancestry back to Franz Joseph Batt, the man who built Our Lady Help of Christians Church."

Like the Buchheits, Millers, Alberts, Steffans, Diebolds, and many other families whose children attended St. Louis' school in large numbers, the Batt family also contributed young scholars even though the core of the family resided in Williamsville. During the first two decades of the twentieth century, three children born to Robert Charles Batt and Katherine M. Dentinger graduated. They were Robert Nicholas, Hildegarde Louise and Norman Peter. Robert Charles Batt, their father, traced his ancestry directly back to Franz Joseph Batt through his father, Nicholas Batt, and his grandfather, Franz Joseph Batt Jr. Nicholas Batt had served with the Union Army in the Civil War and at its end married a Southerner, Rosina Voelker, in New Orleans, Louisiana, in 1865. They moved back to Buffalo, bought a house on Humboldt Parkway, and

registered at St. Louis Church. In September 1906, Robert Nicholas Batt entered first grade. He graduated in 1916 after attending classes for nine years including his last year in which advanced subjects were taught by the Brothers of the Christian Schools. His sister, Hildegarde Louise, was the next in line to enter school in 1910. She likewise attended for nine years being taught her advanced subjects by the Sisters of St. Joseph. In 1919, the same year Hildegarde graduated, her brother, Norman Peter Batt, also did so but only after attending for eight years. By this time, the new brick building of St. Joseph's Collegiate Institute at Main and Northampton Streets had been completed and he attended classes there for the next four years. Upon graduation from high school he joined the Catholic Foreign Mission Society known as the Maryknoll Mission. He was ordained on January 26, 1930 and spent his life as a missionary until his death on November 5, 1975. He is buried at Maryknoll on the Hudson River.

Although baptized at St. Louis Church in 1931, William Edward Batt was never a student at the school. As a Brother of the Christian Schools, he was a professor and an administrative director at Manhattan College, New York City, and is now President of St. Joseph's Collegiate Institute based in Kenmore. William also traces his ancestry directly to Franz Joseph Batt through his father Clarence Charles Batt who had married Florence Catherine Cummings, joined St. Louis Church, and ran a carpenter shop on Northampton near Ellicott Street. Clarence Charles Batt advertised many times in the program journals distributed by the Knights of St. John, Commandery 204.

When Ronald Foegen was interviewed about the school he mentioned that the third floor had been condemned to activities by 1954. He said, "We had to have gym class in the school yard because the third floor was off limits. We would sneak up there, however, to play some pick-up basketball illegally and at our own risk. To prepare for dashes in school track meets we would use Pearl Place, now known as St. Louis Place. We would run from half way to three-quarter way down toward Virigina Street up to the gate entering the St. Louis' churchyard. Father Bosack would time us and the best runners became dash-men! We were also required to hold all of our Catholic Youth Council dances in the basement of the church; and, by the end of 1958 even though the group at St. Michael's had joined ours, we could not make a go of it." Father Schwartz closed the entire school to classes on August 3, 1959 because it was considered a fire hazard and could no longer be used as a school unless the building could be greatly improved. The trustees did not feel that they could financially support the estimated $25,000 in improvements necessary to make the building into a modern schoolhouse.

*B*ishop Joseph A. Burke agreed and asked that the school be closed because of its obsolescence. It was felt that St. Louis Church could support pupils in nearby parochial schools for less money than it would cost them to finance a proper revamping program. Subsequent to the closing, children from the parish attended schools at either Immaculate Conception, Elmwood and Edward Streets; Our Lady of Lourdes, Best and Main Streets; or at St. Boniface, Locust and Mulberry Streets. When Donna Ball completed seventh grade in 1959, there were one hundred and eighty-nine pupils enrolled at St. Louis' parochial school. She graduated the following year from St. Boniface's parochial school. One singles out Donna, from among the twelve who were in her class, because of her interesting family ties with St. Louis Church. Her father was Richard Ball, a Knight of St. John, who had graduated in 1927; his brother was Art Ball, a trustee of the church who died October 19, 1983. Donna's mother was Doris Dietzel, sister to Father Edmund Dietzel who had graduated in 1928. The other siblings in the Ball family were: Edward Ball; Dorothy Ball, class of 1932, who married Allen Joseph Schneggenburger, class of 1929; Rita and Evelyn Ball, both graduates who married into the Foegen family. Besides Donna, seventy-one other enrolled students at

St. Louis, whose parents were members of St. Michael's parish, also had to find another school to attend and gain their graduation.

*O*n May 26, 1961, Matthew X. Wagner wrote to Edwin H. Kolb, trustee, who was instrumental in starting the museum of artifacts at St. Louis Church so as to preserve its history. Wagner was saddened to know that the school had been closed, however, he was happy that the parishioners were contributing old documents and stories. His family ties to the church went back to his great-grandparents who lived on Franklin Street and attended Mass said by Father John Nicholas Mertz at the Lamb of God Church. His grandparents lived on Elk Street near Louisiana and each Sunday they walked two miles to hear Mass at St. Louis Church. Matthew's maternal grandfather was Xavier Dietsche, a famous butcher, who had served five years as a trustee at St. Louis Church before it burned, and was a member of the building committee for the construction of the Gothic church. Matthew recalled his years at St. Louis School between 1905 and 1913. During that time he was an altar boy who had a disastrous experience. Although Mrs. Kleber and Mrs. Garono would do the sewing which would raise and lower the black cassock hems for the boys, sometimes they did not fit well, some were too long, others too short. One day Matthew donned a long one by mistake. While changing the Missal from the Epistle side of the altar to the Gospel side, he caught his foot in his cassock, and rolled down the full length of the altar steps with Missal in hand. Needless to say Father Hoelscher may have been shocked, but Matthew said that he thought a small smile appeared on his face. From 1911 to 1922, Matthew's father was a trustee at the church. In 1961, Matthew and his own son Matthew Wagner Jr. were attorneys at law with offices in the Crosby Building. Their contribution to the museum was the *Record of Appeal*, the legal action that was brought by the Le Couteulx heirs to recover the church property which had been donated by their ancestor, Louis Le Couteulx, to Bishop Dubois in 1829.

Although the school was closed, the trustees still used their room as did the members of the Dramatic Circle, but all other activity in the building was curtailed. Destruction of the building was out of the question because the Historic Preservation Coalition and the Buffalo Landmark and Preservation Board claimed that it had to be preserved. In 1984, the trustees considered allowing Daniel and Stephen Krasinski, developers, to remodel the building into eighteen luxury apartments. Daniel Krasinski was the finance officer for the Niagara Frontier Vocational Rehabilitation Center, and Stephen Krasinski operated a business, Buffalo Maid Cabinets, located at 1247 Broadway. They chose Steven J. Carmina, an architect with John Edward Kloch, Associates of Tonawanda, to draw up the plans of the restoration project that was estimated to cost $900,000. This adventure, however, met with opposition because the original deed of the property from Louis Le Couteulx to Bishop Dubois stated that the property was to be used only for a Catholic Church, Catholic school, and Catholic cemetery.

Hence the building stood, eroding for two more decades. Father Schwinger had become pastor when the roof had so deteriorated that large holes let rain, snow, leaves, and pigeons into the interior. Pigeon dung created an odor of disgust most noticeable on warm humid days. Then came the cats, large destructive alley cats. In an interview with Father Schwinger, he said, "Up there, on the third floor of the school, the cats had Thanksgiving Day every day!" Finally, endeavors to rid himself of the responsibility of the school arrived unexpectedly in 1986. Robert Albert rushed into the sacristy one day, just before Mass, and told Schwinger that the back wall of the school had collapsed. Schwinger said, "My prayers have been answered." The City gave an emergency condemnation ruling and the school was ready for demolition. Marie Buchheit Miller, who was living in Kentucky at the time, recalled coming to Buffalo, to find a large pile of bricks, which used to be her school, lying grotesquely in a heap in the parking lot. Father Schwinger told her to pick out a brick

of her choice as a memento; she took one with a small chip in it. The brick is on display in her garage but the memory of the school is in her heart. [1]

Marie's brother, Richard, who graduated in 1931, often spoke of the one textbook that he always kept after graduating from St. Louis' school — it was his catechism. Although he had taken and passed the Regents Examinations in Geography, Reading, Writing, Spelling, Elementary English, Arithmetic, and History, he did not keep any texts in these subjects, but his catechism was a treasure. It was a small book, four and one-half inches wide, seven inches high, and one-fourth inch thick. It was originally written in German by Joseph Dehabre, S.J. of the province of Missouri and used in many German parishes in the United States. It was translated into English by the Jesuit Fathers and given an imprimatur by John Cardinal McCloskey, Archbishop of New York, on May 26, 1882. After thirty-nine years, it was revised and republished by Benziger Brothers under the imprimatur of Patrick J. Hayes, Archbishop of New York on June 29, 1921. During the students' eight years of grammar school they were expected to go through the entire book at least three times. Beginners learned the simplest details in the text, the second-timers went into each question and answer in more detail, and on the third run-through the pupils learned literally or in substance all the scriptural passages associated with the questions and answers.

The *Answers* in the catechism could only have been understood in connection with the *Questions*. The *Answers*, therefore, repeated or embodied the *Questions* thus forming sentences complete in themselves. The *Applications* at the close of each paragraph embodied the chief points that were impressed on the minds and hearts of the students. Father Dehabre's educational philosophy was that while the training in Christian Doctrine using the catechism was to be sufficiently comprehensive, it also had to be as plain as possible. No matter how progressively detailed the teaching became, the six basic points of Faith were reviewed over and over. These were: There is but One God who created and who governs all; God is a just judge who rewards good and punishes the wicked; There are three Persons in One God, Father, Son, and Holy Ghost; The Second Person, Jesus Christ, became man, and died on a cross to save all; The soul is immortal; and The Grace of God is necessary for salvation. So the catechism was divided into three parts: Faith with all the articles of the Apostles Creed; the Ten Commandments of God and the Commandments of the Church; and the types and vehicles of Grace: actual, sanctifying, sacraments, sacramentals, and prayer. Upon graduating, each pupil had a motivation to say morning prayers, evening prayers, and prayers before meals. Each was aware of the chief feasts of Jesus Christ, the Blessed Virgin Mary, and important saints. Each knew the nature of the Holy Seasons of Advent, Christmas, Lent, Holy Week, Easter, Ember Weeks, and Rogation Days. The boys knew the prayers, in Latin, and the movements and duties on the altar required of those who would serve the priest at Mass. No wonder the book was a treasure.

The Brothers of the Christian Schools, whose educational innovations of Jean Baptiste de La Salle, their founder, graced the beginning of this chapter, first came to Buffalo in 1861. Accepting the invitation of Bishop Timon, six Brothers took over the obligation of teaching young boys at St. Joseph's Academy and St. Joseph's Free Parish School on the property associated with St. Joseph's Cathedral. Brother Crispian was the director of the Brothers' community and Brother Pompian was the subdirector. By the end of the first year, the Brothers were teaching two hundred and eighty pupils. Five years later, the school had the name of St. Joseph's College and the number of students had increased to five hundred and forty. In 1874, the college was moved to Delaware Avenue; and, by 1888, it was not only the residence of the Brothers who taught there, but also for those who had taken over teaching the boys in the upper grades at the parochial schools of St. Louis, Main and Edward Streets; St. Bridget, Fulton and Louisiana Streets; and St. Joseph's Cathedral, 50

Franklin Street. One year later, other assigned Brothers residing in the community were teaching at St. Stephen's parochial school at 193 Elk Street. At first, the positions of Brothers at St. Louis' school were not permanent; five different Brothers taught over a two-year period. Brothers Agapas of Mary and Imbert Victorinus, however, were well entrenched at the school by September 1890.

They were fortunate that the electric streetcar had been installed on Main Street. Before 1885, there were no electric streetcars on Buffalo's streets. By 1900, there were twenty-five routes in operation with eighty-seven miles of track. From the college to St. Louis' school the distance was approximately one mile. Although this was not an extraordinary walk for the Brothers, the streetcar made the trip in a much shorter time provided that the arrivals and departures had been well researched. The streetcar was also very helpful when they had several heavy items to carry to and from school. Whether they took the streetcar or walked to school, they presented quite a spectacle to those folks who were on their way to work or waiting for transportation. The two Brothers wore their traditional habit whose most distinguishing features were the long black soutane which reached to the calf of the leg, the white rebato, a starched cloth acting as a seventeenth century cravat, and a black calotte, a plain skullcap. Inside his robe that had two large pockets in the sides and a small vest pocket, each Brother wore his crucifix, and carried his rosary and New Testament that he received on the day he was first invested. He was quite comfortable walking in his heavy black leather shoes with laces. As they walked, the two Brothers were silent companions going through the streets saying their rosary. Brother Imbert Victorinus was a real anchor at St. Louis' parochial school, as the principal and the eighth grade teacher for five consecutive years. Before becoming a Brother his family name was Joseph Vogt, descending from a family which traced its roots back to Baden where Vogt was the name given to the village caretaker. Later in history a Vogt became known as

286

Buergermeister.

*D*uring those five years, two hundred and thirty three boys under their tutelage graduated from St. Louis' school. While they had attended school, they heard, for the first time in their lives, the Brother start each class with the invocation, "Let us remember that we are in the holy presence of God!" After a short, silent reflection and a prayer to St. Jean Baptist de La Salle, the Brother said, "Live Jesus in our hearts!" All in the classroom responded, "Forever!" With Brother Imbert's departure by reassignment, Brother Felan of Jesus became the anchor in the school for the next four years, during which time one hundred and eighty-eight more boys graduated. Starting in 1897, the Brothers began teaching a ninth grade as well as seventh and eighth. The ninth grade became a year of post-graduate study which gave credits toward going to St. Joseph's College, which had been moved from Delaware Avenue and reopened on Main Street near Bryant after a period of being temporally located at Prospect Avenue and Jersey Street. At the college, students were provided with instructions in academic, commercial, and collegiate branches, with a preparatory course for boys not yet ready to take up the higher studies. In age, the scholars ranged from eight to twenty-two years.

*W*ith the arrival of Brother Agatho, starting in September 1899, a faculty of three Brothers taught the boys at St. Louis' school in the eighth grade and in two upper grades, in which the subjects taught were equivalent to the preparatory course given at St. Joseph's College. The Sisters of St. Joseph, likewise, extended the education of the girls to two years beyond the eighth grade. Thus, from 1899 until the Brothers left St. Louis' school in 1921, both boys and girls attended classes for ten years starting with first grade. During the years of advanced instruction the Sisters taught First and Second Year German, Advanced English, Elementary Representation and Design, Drawing, Business Writing, Algebra, Bookkeeping, Physiology, and

Rudiments of Music and Chorus Singing. The Brothers taught their boys First and Second Year German, Bookkeeping, Business Writing, Business Mathematics, Job Estimation, and Elementary Engineering. From 1900 to 1905, Brother Claudius Anthony was the principal of the boys division at St. Louis' school.

*I*n 1901, St. Joseph's College officially became known as St. Joseph's Collegiate Institute. For the next twenty years, the Brother's community house on its campus became the residence of the three Brothers who annually taught at St. Louis' school. The distance from their residence to the school was approximately one mile. The Brothers taught three classes until September 1907, when the principal, Brother Conrad Ernest, decided that the Brothers would cease teaching in the eighth grade and concentrate on teaching only the upper grades as a pre-college program of two years. This also meant that St. Louis' school would be assigned only two Brothers instead of three. The Sisters of St. Joseph assumed the teaching responsibilities of both boys and girls for the eight grammar grades. Sister Hildegarde was the principal in that year.

*F*ourteen boys entered this new program from eighth grade and graduated in 1909. They were: Paul Abel, Herbert Abel, George Bielmann, Edward Biesinger, Eugene Didley, Raymond Kessel, Karl Kiefer, Edward Kohlbrenner, Cornelius F. Miller Sr., Harold Mueller, Walter Rick, Rudolph Schwartz, James Schields, and Harold Winter. Eugene Didley served in the navy during World War I, Walter Rick became a member of the St. Louis Dramatic Circle, and Cornelius F. Miller Sr. held many offices with the Knights of St. John, Commandery 204, and also served in the army in World War I. He was born on January 7, 1894, the son of Charles Augustus Miller and Catherine Grimm. His older brother Lawrence Miller had graduated from St. Louis' parochial school in 1904. Cornelius attended Fosdick-Masten High School following his education with the Brothers. Upon graduation, he immediately went to work for Buffalo Fire Door Company. Upon leaving work there he spent fifteen years from 1930 in the employ of John W. Cowper Company as their head accountant. From 1945 until his retirement in 1965, he was comptroller at International Chimney. Although a member of St. Louis Church, he married Genevieve Mary Butterworth at Holy Angels Church on February 10, 1920. They had five children: Edward C. Miller who married Alice Grupp; Helen M. Miller who married James Roche; Loretta R. Miller, Cornelius F. Miller Jr., and Charles A. Miller. Cornelius F. Miller Sr. died on May 2, 1971, and was buried from St. Benedict's Church in Eggertsville.

From 1915 until 1917, the three Brothers who taught the two advanced classes at St. Louis' parochial school were Brothers Bonaventure John, Amandus Henry, and Celestine Faber. Only five boys graduated in 1917: Raymond J. Hoffman, Joseph M. Lienert, Eugene W. Miller Sr., Arthur J. Schemel, and Elmer W. Nebrich. Eugene W. Miller Sr. was the younger brother of Cornelius F. Miller Sr. and the older brother to Cecilia M. Miller, who graduated, earning the diligence medal, the following year. When Cecilia graduated, Sister Claudia was the principal of the grammar school. Upon graduation from the Brothers' department, Eugene W. Miller Sr. immediately went to work in the employ of Anthony Zimmermann, wagon maker, whose shop was at Northampton and Michigan, less than one-fifth of a mile from St. Joseph's Collegiate Institute. Miller, who in 1935, had become sole owner of Zimmermann's Body Shop, so admired the Brothers and was so pleased with his education that, besides his many other generous gifts to them, he gifted a case of beer to the Brother's community each week, a practice which he continued until he moved his shop to Genesee Street in 1949. By that time the Christian Brothers had made plans to move St. Joseph's Collegiate and the community to a new school to be built in Kenmore, New York.

Miller had also insisted that his three sons, Eugene W. Miller Jr., Carl A. Miller, and John E. Miller attend St. Joseph's Collegiate Institute. All did go there, but only Eugene W. Miller Jr. graduated. Following World War II, he married Sylvina Godfrey, from St. Vincent de Paul's parish. They had four children, two boys and two girls. Following his father's devotion to the Brothers, he had his two boys, Mark and William, attend St. Joseph's Collegiate Institute in Kenmore. Carl A. Miller did not graduate, but left at the end of his sophomore year to complete his high school at St. Joseph's Normal Institute at Barrytown, New York. John E. Miller left after his first year and finished his education at a local business school. All the Millers, however, continued their relationship with St. Louis Church. Eugene W. Miller Jr., having been a Knight of St. John at St. Louis Church, joining after World War II, and realizing that his ancestry could be traced back to Nicholas Miller Jr., John Miller, and Peter Miller, all masons, who were involved with the committee to construct the Lamb of God Church, wished to have his children baptized in the church. Three of his four children, Mark, William, and Susan were baptized at St. Louis Church. The fourth child, Barbara, was baptized elsewhere. Later Susan and Barbara extended the tradition; Susan and her husband, James Kolbe, were married at St. Louis Church on September 2, 1972 in the presence of Father Michael O'Hara, assistant to Father Mosack, the pastor. Barbara married William Rash there on July 9, 1976. Susan and James Kolbe's two boys, Christian and Karl, were both baptized during Mosack's tenure as pastor. This chain of participation in the sacraments at St. Louis Church brought the continuous connection of the Millers with the church through one hundred and fifty years; the full extent of time through which the church experienced the devotion of the trustees to its temporal affairs and the fulfillment of a Rare Tradition In American Catholicism.

From 1918 until 1921, when the Brothers retired from St. Louis' school, Brother Celestine Faber served as director for two years, followed by Brother Austin William who closed the Brothers' department in 1921. From then on, all boys graduating from eighth grade could choose which high school in the city they wished to attend. In 1927, thirty-percent of the boys in the graduating class entered St. Joseph's Collegiate Institute. One of those boys was Charles Buchheit, brother to Marie Buchheit Miller, who has described the classroom sequence, as it was when she graduated in 1937. Graduating with Charles Buchheit was Joseph Shields who went directly to the Catholic Seminary. Richard Ball who also was in that class, and later became a prominent Knight of St. John at St. Louis Church, went to Seneca Vocational High School. The female graduates, who no longer had a postgraduate program, choose local high schools to attend. More than fifty percent chose Buffalo Academy of the Sacred Heart, which was founded by the Sisters of St. Francis in 1874. Many others attended Nardin Academy on Cleveland Avenue. As the years passed the two Catholic high schools which became the favorites of the boys graduating from St. Louis' parochial school were St. Joseph's Collegiate Institute at Main and Northampton Streets and Canisius High School on Washington Street. The trustees at St. Louis Church were so pleased with the students' decisions to do so that they subsidized their tuition at these two schools. For this purpose, during the first five years of the Depression, they allocated $2,543.00 The practice, however, was discontinued in 1935; the financial burden became too heavy.

To conclude the history of St. Louis Church Parochial School, one must discuss the career of a most distinguished student who was a descendant of one of the earliest families to join St. Louis Church. Professor Henry Hemmerlein and the Sisters of St. Joseph taught him there. Later he was taught by the Brothers of the Christian Schools at St. Joseph's College on Franklin Street, reached the highest academic levels in education earning degrees of Doctor of Divinity and Doctor of Philosophy, was ordained to the priesthood, became president of St. Mary's College, Kentucky, and fostered new techniques in the teaching of the Deaf. He was John L. Steffan, born in Buffalo on February 20, 1854, son of Michael Steffan and Frances Mary Kloepfer, He attended St. Louis' school from 1860 to 1868 after which he attended preparatory college classes at St. Joseph's College in Buffalo. In 1870, he entered St. Jerome's College in Berlin, Ontario, Canada. His mother's family owned farms throughout the area, and John's cousin, Reverend Willliam Kloepfer, a member of the Order of Resurrectionist Fathers that operated the college, was in attendance there. In 1875, having completed all academic courses required for a Bachelor of Arts Degree, he traveled to Rome, Italy, where he spent twelve years studying philosophy, theology, Greek, Latin, modern languages, and science at the College of the Order of the Resurrection.

John L. Steffan was accepted into the Order and to the priesthood, being ordained on March 19, 1883, and he was awarded the degrees of Doctor of Philosophy and Doctor of Divinity in 1887. He returned to Canada, taught at St. Jerome's College for three years, and was assigned to teach at St. Mary's College, Kentucky, owned and operated by the Resurrectionist Fathers. While teaching there, he developed successful techniques in teaching the Deaf and was appointed president in 1893. Three years later, returning from his circuit of instructing deaf children who lived on the local farms near St. Mary's, he was awaiting the passing of a train at the New Hope railroad crossing about six miles from the college. The sudden shriek of the train whistle so frightened his horse that it threw him, from his carriage, violently against a tree. As he lay unconscious, Edward L. Miles, owner of a bourbon distillery in New Hope, came upon him and revived him. Father John Steffan seemed to recover from the tragedy, but after he returned to the college, he suddenly suffered a paralytic stroke. His brother, George, and his sister, Josephine, were summoned from

Buffalo. They were with him at his bedside when he died after slipping into a coma. It was November 6, 1896. His remains were transported back to Buffalo; and, on November 10, a Solemn Requiem Mass was sung at St. Louis Church after which his casket was taken to the United German and French Roman Catholic Cemetery where he was interred. Father John Steffan had always been a great advocate of Catholic education. Often he would say, "Catholic Schools keep up the Church, and Public Schools will be a ruination of the Country." [2]

Above: **St Louis School in 1954**. Opposite, top: **The graduating class of 1928**. Robert Buchheit, James Malone, Edmund Dietzel and Eugene Wagner entered the priesthood; Florence Steffan joined the Sisters of St. Joseph. Bottom: **The Class of 1928 celebrating its 50th anniversary in 1978**. Robert Buchheit is not present. The priest wearing glasses is Monsignor Alfred Mosack, pastor of St. Louis Church.

REFERENCES AND NOTES ✤ CHAPTER TWELVE

1. Source material concerning education in France in the late seventeenth century was taken from Leon Aroz F.S.C., etal, with an English translation by Luke Salm F.S.C., *Beginnings: De La Salle and His Brothers*, Christian Brothers National Office, Romeoville, Illinois, 1980, pp. 55-80; for the virtues of a good master see: 87-8. For contributions of St. John Baptiste de La Salle to Catholic education in France in the late seventeenth century see: Battersby, W.J., *De La Salle: A Pioneer of Modern Education*, Longmans, Green and Co., London, pp. 79-102. These pages cover the Simultaneous Method of Teaching, Teaching in the Vernacular, and a discussion of the two books written by De La Salle, The *Conduct of Schools*, and *School Management*. For a background history of the Sisters of St. Joseph see: op. cit. *Good Shepherd: The Church on the Canal: 1847-1997*, pp. 30-31; M. Immaculata S.S.J., *Like a Swarm of Bees*, Society of St. Paul, Derby, New York, 1957, p. 188; Dunne, M.A. S.S.J., (Sister Mary of the Sacred Heart), *A Brief Account of Its Origin and Work: The Congregation of St. Joseph of the Diocese of Buffalo*, Holling Press, Buffalo, New York, 1934. For other sources concerning Catholic education in America see: Martin E. Marty, *Short History of American Catholicism* and Charles Morris, *American Catholic*. Also a document submitted from the Sisters of St. Joseph, Mother House at Mount St. Joseph, 2064 Main Street, Buffalo, New York, March 12, 1956, contains a list of 57 nuns who taught at St. Louis Church School from 1899 to 1959. This document is in the Archives of St. Louis Church. For reference to Henry Hemmerlein, the Schulmeister, see op. cit. *Anniversary Souvenir and Programme of St. Louis Dramatic Circle: January 7, 1896*, p. 52. Interspersed throughout this chapter are the informational results of interviews carried out by Robert McCarthy, political writer for the *Buffalo News,* and Marie Buchheit Miller. They submitted a series of notes to the author/editor and from these notes several paragraphs were constructed. The author/editor took the liberty of weaving into some of the story line of their interview material that he had already gathered and was pertinent to the topic. One such noteworthy reconstruction was a description of the nun's habit that was taken from op. cit., *Good Shepherd: The Church on the Canal*, p. 100. The Biographies for the priests of the "Holy Class" were obtained from interviews conducted by the author/editor. The biography of Father Robert Buchheit was from the interview with Blanche Buchheit, a lady in her nineties, widow of Paul Buchheit, brother to Father Robert Buchheit. The biography of Monsignor Dietzel was gleaned from obituaries sent to the author/editor by Donna Ball, niece of Father Dietzel. She attended St. Louis' school from the first to the seventh grade. Because the school was closed in 1959 she had to attend eighth grade at St. Boniface's school. Then she attended Bishop McMahon High School, 1960-1964. She was secretary at St. Louis Church, 1964-1968, working for Fathers Clarence Ott, Alfred Mosack, Francis Baratto, and Leonard Wojcinski. Francis B. Baratto was born in Buffalo, March 13, 1929; ordained on May 30, 1953 in St. Joseph's New Cathedral, after finishing his seminary at Christ the King, St. Bonaventure College. He was

associate pastor at St. Francis of Assisi, Tonawanda; St. Gregory the Great, Amherst; St. Louis Church, Buffalo; and pastor at Our Lady of Lourdes, Buffalo; St. Andrews, Kenmore-Tonawanda. He died September 6, 1992 and is buried at Mt. Calvary Cemetery. For obituaries on Dietzel see: *Island Dispatch*, April 28, 1989; *Western New York Catholic*, June 1989. Biographical material on Father Eugene Wagner was obtained directly from him to Marie Buchheit Miller in a telephone conversation on April 15, 2002. Wagner is retired and living at St. Charles Borremeo Church Rectory in Olcott, New York. Biographical information concerning Father James Malone S.J. was sent to the author/editor on April 18, 2002, by Father Philip G. Judge S.J., principal of McQuaid Jesuit High School, Rochester, New York. He sent an obituary of Father Malone that appeared in the School's Alumni News Magazine. The biography of Florence Steffan was one of the obituaries presented to the author/editor by Sister Mary Anne Butler, archivist at the Mother House and Retirement Home of the Sisters of St. Joseph, Strickler Road, Clarence, New York. Marie Buchheit Miller had solicited a series of notes from Dorothy Ball, wife of Allen Joseph Schneggenburger, and from Rita Ball Foegen, sister of Richard Ball. These notes gave enlightenment to school activities surrounding the Ladies Sodality of Mary, skating parties, class attendance at weekday and Sunday Masses, Corpus Christi Celebration, and Christmas gifts given by Father Laudenbach. The information concerning the class reunion of 1928 in the year 1978 was obtained from the collection in the archives of Cathy Steffan, family genealogist. Source material for the style of architecture of the St. Louis' school building was a contribution from Barbara La Vigne Braun, who provided the text: Germain Bazin, *A History of Art: From Prehistoric Times to the Present*, Bonanza Books, New York, pp. 342-48. The name of the French style roof on the school is spelled Mansard. The name of the architect who designed that style is Francois Mansart. Both spellings are correct as given. The archives of St. Louis Church contains a book titled *Specimen Works, 1896*. In it are examples of classroom work done in the secular subjects by the students of that time. They cover topics in sentence diagramming, English literature, foreign language, grammar, mathematics, science, geography, physiology, and history. The introduction of the work provided a mission statement of the school: "The method of instruction pursued is the same as that in the city schools, thereby, enabling pupils who attend our school, to take the examination issued by the Board of Regents. Gold medals are awarded by friends of the school to those who successfully pass the Regents' examination. It is gratifying to note that many of the parents appreciate the work of the school, and allow their children to remain until they have finished the course of study prescribed, thus preparing them to pass the examination with credit to themselves and their teachers." In the text, Rev. Paul Hoelscher, pastor, is listed as the superintendent of the school, assisted by Reverends J. Schaus and J. Franz. At the time of the writing of the text (1896), the Christian Brothers teaching there were: Brothers Imbert and Henry. The Sisters of St. Joseph were: Sisters Lucy, Francis Regis, Christina, Regina, Ligouri, Hildegarde, Anselm, and Gregory. The ten teachers taught 500 students annually. Not all, however, graduated; some left school early as was the case also in public school. What was different about St. Louis' school from the public schools was that the children began and ended each day with prayers, and the catechism of Catholic faith provided a key part of the curriculum. In the Brothers' classes, before each period the Brother announced, "Let us remember that we are in the Holy Presence of God." Then after a short period of reflection he said, "Live Jesus in our hearts," and the boys responded, "forever!" In the first four decades of the 20th century the catechism used by the pupils was: Deharbe's *Large Catechism*, Benziger Brothers, New York. During the first two decades the book was in German but after World War I the translation of the book into English, for use in the United States, was the one used at St. Louis' school. The first American edition was published in 1882. The second edition was published in 1921. It carried the Imprimaturs of John Cardinal McCloskey, 1882, and Patrick Hayes D.D., 1921, both Archbishops of New York. The Order of the Sisters of St. Joseph received an annual salary for each Sister. In the first two decades of the 20th century this amounted to $200 per nun per year. The bishop set the rate. No individual nun received any money; however, each had taken the vows of poverty, chastity, and obedience. Although the nuns were religious, they were only lay persons and did not enjoy any of the privileges of the ecclesiastical state. The Christian Brothers were the male counterpart of the nuns, having the same vows and lay status. During the depression the salaries were increased by $5.00 per month per teacher. Besides classroom work there was also extracurricular activity. One such activity was scouting. Boys from St. Louis' school belonged to Troop 153 organized by Frank and Bill Breitweiser. They had campsites in Cattaraugus County and Frenchman's Creek, Canada. Some of those involved in the Scouts were: Robert Albert, Louis Buchheit, Bob Foegen, Dave Kelso, Norm Schaefer, Paul Kolb, and Eugene Kolb. The closing of the school was described in the *Courier Express*, August 3, 1959. The planned restoration of the school building in 1984, which if had it been carried out would have restored the exterior of the building to its original state, was described in *The Buffalo News*, Friday, March 9, 1984. The following genealogical information was taken from: op. cit. *Batt Genealogy*, p.30-31: Edward Joseph White, the father of Norman Alphonse White, was born in Buffalo on October 14, 1868. He was the son of Adam White and Elizabeth Zimmermann, and was caretaker of St. Louis Church for forty years, faithful parishioner, and one of the founders of the St. Louis Dramatic Circle. He married Julia Scholastica Batt, born at Lancaster on December 5, 1873, the daughter of George Batt and Christina Mayer. George Batt was the son of Franz Joseph Batt Jr. whose father was Franz Joseph Batt Sr. who came to America and built Our Lady Help of Christians Church. Therefore Norman was the great-great grandson of the patriarch of the Batt family which emigrated from Morschweiler, Alsace, on October 20, 1836. Norman's brothers were: Edward Joseph White Jr., Marvin George White, and Elmer John White. Norman was born August 14, 1917, attended St. Louis School, graduated in 1932, and married Rose Millace on October

1, 1949. They had four children: Patrick Gerard, David Samuel, Gregory James, and Mary Ellen. Norman White provided Michael Riester with the oral history concerning his family and the school. For the material concerning members of the Batt family being associated with St. Louis' church and school see: op. cit. *Batt Genealogy*, pp. 13-14, 51, and op. cit. *Our Graduates, St. Louis School*, for graduating years 1916, 1919. The information concerning the Didio family settling in Buffalo, Carmene Didio and her family, and Louis Buchheit's association with the Didio family was taken from an interview conducted by the author/editor and Marie Buchheit Miller with Carmene Didio and Louis Buchheit at their summer residence at Ellicottville, New York, July 11, 2002.

2. Information concerning the Brothers of the Christian Schools who taught at St. Louis' school was obtained by Carl J. Albert from Brother Luke Salm F.S.C., Archivist, New York District Archives, Manhattan College, Bronx, New York, 10471. Albert requested the information on October 1, 2000; received and answer in a letter dated October 23, 2000, and he made a reply of gratitude on October 27, 2000. The material obtained by Carl Albert was verified by Brother Edward Martin F.S.C., local historian, St. Joseph's Collegiate Institute, 845 Kenmore Avenue, Kenmore, New York, 14223. The following sources were included in Luke Salm's reply: *The Community Register of St. Joseph's Collegiate Institute*, Buffalo, New York; *Etat nominatif & statistique forms*. These are annual reports, statistical in nature that each community of the Institute sent to the Motherhouse at the end of each calendar year. They are preserved in the archives of the Brothers in the Motherhouse in Rome, Italy; Personnel cards of individual Brothers. These cards are in the provincial headquarters of the New York District in Lincroft, New Jersey. In April 1991, Brother Eugene O'Gara, F.S.C., prepared the following listing of Brothers who taught at St. Louis' school In the list, the school year is given followed by the Brothers present that year. The number in parenthesis indicates the number of classes taught that year. Not all Brothers listed in a particular year were there for the whole year; some were reassigned, some became ill, and some died. Names in parenthesis are the Brothers' family names. 1888-1889, (2), Brothers Basilian of Mary (Henry Wehage), Agapas of Mary (Jacob Theis), Amelian of Mary (Joseph Feineis), Imbert Victorinus (Joseph Vogt); 1889-1890, (2), Brothers Imbert Victorinus (Joseph Vogt), Alpinian John (Joseph Gruenfeider); 1890-1891, (2), Brothers Imbert Victorinus (Joseph Vogt), Adelphian (Vincent Lux); 1891-1892, (2), Brothers Imbert Victorinus (Joseph Vogt), Adelphian (Vincent Lux); 1892-1893, (2), Brothers Imbert Victorinus (Joseph Vogt), Azadan Henry (August Stahl); 1893-1894, (2), Brothers Aubert of Mary (Ferdinand Merkens), Azadan Henry (August Stahl), Felan of Jesus (Sebastian Kempter); 1894-1895, (2), Brothers Felan of Jesus (Sebastian Kempter), Arthemian Peter (William Grossjung); 1895-1896, (2), Brothers Felan of Jesus (Sebastian Kempter), Arthemian Peter (William Grossjung), Carthagh of Jesus (Francis Berschbach); 1896-1897, (2), Brothers Felan of Jesus (Sebastian Kempter), Cyprian (Henry Grewe); 1897-

Do You Know Where Your Children Are?

1898, (3) Brothers Damian (Johann Diefenbach), Lamand (Adolph Gebhardt), Cyprian (Henry Grewe), Claudius Anthony (William Eiermann); 1898-1899, (3), Brothers Lamand (Adolph Gebhardt), Cyprian (Henry Grewe), Claudius Anthony (William Eiermann); 1899-1900, (3), Brothers Lamand (Adolph Gebhardt), Agatho (Michael Day), Claudius Anthony (William Eiermann), Conrad Ernest (Gustav Hoffman); 1900-1901, (3), Brothers Agatho, (Michael Day), Claudius Anthony, (William Eiermann), Conrad Ernest (Gustav Hoffman); 1901-1902, (3), Brothers Claudius Anthony, (William Eiermann), Dagan Nicholas, (Philip Bitner), Basilian Joseph (Joseph Betz), Boniface Hubert (Simon Eichert), Edmund Francis (Joseph Hinssen); 1902-1903, (3), Brothers Claudius Anthony (William Eiermann), Alexius Austin (Nicholas Schumann), Edmund Francis (Joseph Hinssen); 1903-1904, (3), Brothers Claudius Anthony (William Eiermann), Edmund Francis (Joseph Hinssen), Amandus Henry (George Kargl); 1904-1905, (3), Brothers Claudius Anthony (William Eiermann), Edmund Francis (Joseph Hinssen), Amandus Henry (George Kargl); 1906-1907, (3), Brothers Conrad Ernest (Gustav Hoffman), Amandus Henry (George Kargl), Clement Gregory (Joseph Welber); 1907-1908, (3), Brothers Conrad Ernest (Gustav Hoffman), Amandus Henry (George Kargl), Arthur Berchmans (Emil Biller); 1908-1909, (2), Brothers Conrad Ernest (Gustav Hoffman), Basil Gregory (Joseph Kapp); 1909-1910, (2), Brothers Conrad Ernest (Gustav Hoffman), Adolophus of Mary (James Casey), Basilian Joseph (Joseph Betz); 1910-1911, (2), Brothers Anthony Francis (Peter Wolf), Basilian Joseph (Joseph Betz); 1911-1912, (2), Brothers Anthony Francis (Peter Wolf), Basilian Joseph (Joseph Betz); 1912-1913, (2), Brothers Anthony Francis (Peter Wolf), Charles Henry (George Beaudoin); 1913-1914, (2), Brothers Charles Alfred (Peter Schreiber), Charles Henry (George Beaudoin); 1914-1915, (2), Brothers Charles Alfred (Peter Schreiber), Charles Henry (George Beaudoin); 1915-1916, (2), Brothers Bonaventure John (Leonard Droste), Celestine Faber (John Peters); 1916-1917, (2), Brothers Amandus Henry (George Kargl), Celestine Faber (John Peters); 1917-1918, (2), Brothers Charisius Albert (John Grimston), Celestine Faber (John Peters), Bertin Philip (Anthony Ulenberg); 1918-1919, (2), Brothers Celestine Faber (John Peters), Bertrand Julius (Otto Schmidhauser); 1919-1920, (2), Brothers Celestine Faber (John Peters), Azarias Raphael (Robert Cleary); 1920-1921, (2), Brothers Austin William (John Flanagan), Bonaventure John (Leonard Droste), Azarias Raphael (Robert Cleary). Brothers do not return to St. Louis' school in September 1921. Newspaper articles referring to the Brothers of the Christian Schools in Buffalo are: *Courier Express*, August 3, 1959; *The Express*, February 27, 1897; *Buffalo News*, January 20, 1950; *Buffalo News*, November 12, 1947; *Buffalo News*, October 12, 1946. Also see: op. cit. *History of the Catholic Church in Western New York*, pp. 320-21. The biography of Cornelius F. Miller Sr. was taken from notes given to the author/editor from Helen Miller Roche, daughter of Cornelius F. Miller and Genevieve Butterworth. Her information was sent on October 16, 2001 from 20 Rosedale Blvd., Amherst; For a biography of John L. Steffan see: op. cit. *Michael Steffan History*, a copy is in the St. Louis Church Archives. In the biography of Father John Steffan mention is made of Berlin, Ontario, Canada. During World War I, the name of the city of Berlin, Ontario, Canada, was changed to Kitchener, Ontario, Canada, because of the reactionary phobia to anything German. From a document held at the St. Louis Church Archives the following information is pertinant to the names of the Sisters of St. Joseph who taught at St. Louis' school and dates of arrival. There is no information as to how long each nun stayed except to say that no more than eight were on hand at any one time except for the years between 1897 and 1921 when there may have been ten years of education prior to graduation. (1858) Sister M. Julia and three other unidentified; (1861) Sisters Magdalene and M. Julia; (1862) Sisters Stephen, Alphonse, Joseph Theresa, Mary John; (1864) Sisters Alphonse, De Pazzi, Martha, Antoinette; (1896) Sister Gregory and other unidentified Sisters; (1899) Sisters Hildegarde, Anselm, Justina, Philomena, Francis Clare, St. Luke, St. Felix, Hedwige; (1900) Sisters Hilary, Beatrice, Bernadette; (1916) Sister Christina; (1919) Sisters Angela, Dionysia, Claudia, Rita, Rosalia, Lucia; (1920) Sisters Ludwina, Marguerite; (1923) Sisters Paula, Charles; (1924) Sister Expedite; (1927) Sister Flora; (1928) Sister Louise; (1929) Sister Ferdinand; (1931) Sisters Gregory, Cyprian, De Pazzi; (1933) Sister Rosarii; (1934) Sisters Elizabeth, Kevin, Bartholemew; (1936) Sisters Davida, Anthony, Agnes Teresa; (1937) Sister Alphonse Marie; (1938) Sister Anne Patrice; (1941) Sisters Hieronyme, Annette; (1943) Sisters Joseph Damien, John Aloysius; (1945) Sister Thomas; (1946) Sister Carlotta; (1947) Sisters Edwarda, Marie Clarice; (1949) Sisters Crescentia, Rose Anthony; (1950) Sisters Joan of Arc, Joseph Marie; (1951) Sisters James Edward, Mary Terence; (1952) Sisters Cecilia, Francis Gabriel; (1953) Sister Tarcisius; (1954) Sister Guardian Angel; (1955) Sister Teresita. The Sisters of St. Joseph began keeping a record of the graduates beginning with 1893 in a book, *Our Graduates, St. Louis School, Buffalo, New York*; it is kept on file in the St. Louis Church Archives. From 1893 to 1921, it lists the names of the graduates, their ages, residence addresses, and advanced subjects taken. The girls appear to attend school for at least nine years, some ten. The boys whose advanced subjects are not shown in the book were taught by the Brothers of the Christian Schools. Each boy attended for ten years. From 1925 to 1955 the book becomes a regents report of the grades received by the graduates of the partictular year of graduation which is signed by a teacher. From 1955 to 1959, the book simply offers the students grades but unsigned by a teacher. The signers of the book by years are as follows: (1893-1894) Sister M. Lucy; (1898-1908) Sister Hildegarde; (1909) Sister Expedite; (1910-1913) Sister Hildegarde; (1914-1917) Sister Christina; (1918-1920) Sister Claudia; (1921-1925) Sisters Ludwina and Expedite; (1926-1929) Sister Marguerite; (1930) Sister Ferdinand; (1931) Sister Dionysia; (1932-1933) Sister Cyprian; (1934-1945) Sister Gregory; (1946-1947) Sister Charles; (1948-1949) Sister Edwarda; (1950-1953) Sister Crescentia; (1954-1959) no signees. The list of graduates from St. Louis Parochial School, beginning with 1893 are: (1893) Louisa Domedion; (1894) Anna Smith, Elizabeth Hasenzahl; (1898) Anna Strigl, Rose Knopf, Rosina Buchheit, Amelia Dentinger, Martha

Do You Know Where Your Children Are?

Gottstein; (1899) Mary Glass, Anna Winter, Lavina Abel, Mary Haberstro, Elizabeth Sidon, Clara Schmitz, Emmanuel Golwitzer, Francis Rung, Albert Rung, Stanley Schwornn, William Kuhn (died Jan. 22, 1907), Philip Dentinger, Walter Hausle (died June 20, 1905); (1900) Julia Noe, Gertrude Gottschall, Angelina Warner, Mary Staffinger, Anna Schifferle, Florence Bork, Frederick Hardick, Clarence Abel, Albert Weber, Charles Mayer, John Hassler, Herbert Wechter; (1901) Florence Leonard, Mary Strigl, Frances Fuesel, Elizabeth Hardick, Clara Stabel, Mary Miller, Gertrude Weber, Anna Bauer, Bertha Keim, Louise Goetz, Edward Dearing, Paul Hoffman, Frank Keppner, George Steffan, George Winter, Louis Rung, Harry Rung; (1902) Olive Doll, Mary Koch, Mary Heid, Antoinette Flavin, Bertha Warner, Susanna Winter, Florence Rudolph (died 1908), Jeannette Goettelman, Joanna Stoll, Catherine Michel, Charles Borneman, Jerome Werich, Lawrence Paul, John Drexelius, Clarence Hammer, Howard Warner; (1903) Oliva Zell, Julia Strigl, Marie Winter, Elizabeth Czerwinski, Eleanor Rung, Agnes Walski, Florence Stabel, Clara Fath, Albert Bauer, Howard Georger, Otto Grupp, Raymond J. Howard, Joseph F. Hacker, Leo R. Keppner, Albert Steffan, Frank Schreck, William M. Voltz (died 1909), Arthur Kolb; (1904) Julia L. Steffan, Emma R. Batt, Josephine M. Kiene, Frances E. Hertel, Rose D. Rung, Florence B. Emert, Arthur Rung, John Fisher, Eugene Bauer, Anthony Didley (died WWI), Lawrence Miller, Emil Huber, Leon Walski, William Bauer, Frank Hacker, Charles Knoll, Harvey Bruder, Andrew Diehl; (1905) Stella Leonard, Angeline Rung, Margaret Gottschall, Genevieve Doll, Helen Swanz, Helen Czerwinski, Dorothy Steffan, Bertha Pfeiffer, Louise Stoll, Martha Weltzer, Florence Fath, Clara Rung, Jerome Hausle, Philip Warner, Adam Schmitz, Edwin Georger, Louis Buchheit; (1906) Mary Abel, Elizabeth Hoelscher, Stella Weber, Edith Rick, Adelaide Armachen, Mary Swanz, Martha Heid, Agnes Heid, Amelia Bauer, Anna Bielman, Olive Donnelly, Marie Drexelius, Cornelia Rudolph, William Davenport, Carl Albert, Joseph Lettau, Walter Abel, Edward Gueth, Stephen Stoll, Elmer Weigel, Carl Hacker, Henry Huber, Robert Rung, Oliver Schweigert, Herbert Fath, Joseph Argus, Edwin Leonard, Edward Rick; (1907) Anna Hartmann, Bertha Berberich, Gertrude Knickenberg, Eleanor Lazarus, Madelein Steffan, Catherine Clain, Edward Hoffmann, Walter Mueller, Henry Nebrich, Joseph Didley, Joseph Grunneisen; (1908) Henrietta Schworm, Florence Voltz, Catherine Steffan, Antoinette Schwartz, Loretta Selman, Teresa Luber, Louise Blaser, Catherine Paulus, Florence Rief, Charles Biesinger, Frank Drexelius, Rudolph Rung, Louis Koch, Clarence Bauer, August Stoerr, Oliver Weppner, Raymond Williams, George Wendling; (1909) Margaret Birrer, Clara Deck, Eleanor Fath, Clara Hacker, Teresa Hartmann, Esther Latshaw, Marguerite Welker, Julia Weltzer, Ruth Weppner, Paul Abel, Herbert Abel, George Bielmann, Edward Biesinger, Eugene Didley, Raymond Kessel, Karl Kiefer, Edward Kohlbrenner, Cornelius Frank Miller, Harold Mueller, Walter Rick, Rudolph Schwartz, James Schields, Harold Winter; (1910) Louise Auer, Alma Bolton, Bertha Birrer, Emma Deck, Irene Doll, Henrietta Huber, Louise F. Kolb, Adella Keim, Genevieve Rohr, Freda Schoenberger, Antoinette Zahm, Frank Dietsche, Norbert Berger, Joseph Drexelius, Herbert Doll, Norman Fath,

Howard Hess, Paul Muth, Clarence Rung, William Schwing, George Schwarzott, Francis Williams (1911) Catherine Hogg, Mary Meier, Marie Mayer, Clara (Catherine) Sweigert, Vera Seitz, Margaret Uebelhoer, Genevieve Zahm, Jeannette Zimmerman, Norbert Berberich, Edwinn Churchill, Alphonse Gueth, Andrew Hoffman, Sidney Hughes, William Martin, Carl Rieman, John Smith, John Steffan, Alexander Steinwachs, George Zimpfer, Norman Vance; (1912) Edward E. Bauer, Herbert H. Churchill, Karl H. Dietsche, John H. Mowrey, Albert F. Hardick, Leo A. Koch, Albert J. Ross, Herbert P. Rung, Eugene H. Selbert, Herbert A. Werich, Cecilia M. Ball, Catherine M. Biesinger, Marcella R. Didley, Eleanor M. Feldmann, Catherine Hacker, Marion H. Lienert, Mildred S. Lewis, Evelyn M. Schwing, Loretta F. Weltzer; (1913) Leroy Diebold, Henry Erb, Emory Fath, Frank Hauger, Howard Johnson, Harold Kolb, Arthur Lewis, Alphonse Steinwachs, Matthew Wagner, Edward Zimpfer, Helen Hacker, Loreen Hausle, Margaret Huber, Agnes Senn, Blanche Sindecuse, Esther Spahn, Alice Winter, Valencia Zaepfel; (1914) Helvetia Bianchi, Loretta Doerrler, Marian Gueth, Mildred Haas, Emily Hatten, Marie Huber, Hilda Schmauss, Margaret Selbert, Marie Welker, Loretta Zahm, Edward H. Albert, Charles J. Bassett, John J. Bauer, Charles J. Berger, Robert Blum, Norman Bolton, John Feist, Raymond H. Feldman, William A. Hauger, Edward P. Hess, Bernard H. Martin, Carl R. Nebrich, Jacob Steffan, Edgar W. Weigel; (1915) Anna M. Beck, Marian M. Fleiner, Kathryn M. Jones, Helen M. Klipfel, Helen S. Reisch, Martha M. Sweigert, Emily M. Senn, George Brose, Alfred W. Gangloff, Arthur W. Hartke, William H. Kiefer, Edwin E. Koch, Joseph H. Olds, Carl I. Schirra; (1916) Evelyn A. Batt, Veronica T. Beck, Catherine M. Berger, Florence Crosman, Evelyn M. Duffy, Helen R. Ecker, Mary F. Rick, Veronica L. Schlager, Beatrice C. Schoenberger, Loretta M. Schumacker, Hilda M. Sidon, Eleanor M. Thorn, Marcella E. Zaepfel, Catherine E. Zimpfer, Carl F. Argus, Robert N. Batt, Raymond E. Didley, Walter C. Kinskey, Harold J. Latshaw, Carl F. Schmauss, Franklin T. Smith, Joseph W. Zahm; (1917) Virginia L. Fath, Grace M. Fleiner, Anna C. Koch, Antoinette M. Kolb, Elizabeth M. Michels, Mary Mockers, Harry B. Gueth, Raymond J. Hoffman, Joseph M. Lienert, Eugene W. Miller, Arthur J. Schemel, Elmer W. Nebrich; (1918) Lenore K. Cassube, Bertha M. Feldmann, Evelyn F. Haas, Ada O. Hatten, Josephine S. Koch, Catherine M. McGavis, Cecilia M. Miller (diligence medal), Catherine M. Muth (excellence medal), Genevieve M. Scherf, Cecilia G. Schneeberger, Edna M. Schumaker, Catherine M. Senn, Dorothy J. Stressinger, Albert A. Paul, John E. Feuerstein, Francis J. Kennedy, Peter C. Kiefer, Norman L. Kolb, Franklin J. Stapf, Thomas M. Steffan, Amos Jon Waechter, Albert E. Wagner, Frederic C. Wagner; (1919) Louise E. Bassett, Hildegarde L. Batt, Dorothy C. Bowser, Mildred M. Cassube, Dorothy F. Didley, Adele M. Hausle (excellence), Hilda M. Kirchgessner, Teresa C. Kreppel, Elizabeth M. McGavis, Loretta F. Meisriemer (diligence), Irene G. Nebrich (christian doctrine), Marian B. Olds, Helen A. Rohr, Lillian A. Seelbach, Norman P. Batt (excellence), Raymond E. Bauer, James E. Burke, Arthur F. Diebold (christian doctrine), Eugene C. Ludaescher (diligence), Charles J. Missert (excellence), William Edward Steffan, William

Do You Know Where Your Children Are?

F. Stressinger; (1920) Louise Marie Bittermann, Anna Catherine Durnein, Marcella Marie Fornes, Helen Christina Helbringer, Ruth Antoinette Kolb, Marie Margaret Malone, Gertrude Agnes Moran, Helen Marie Rohwer, Eleanor Elizabeth Smith, Evelyn Regina Ziewers, Elmer Peter Bergem, Eugene Henry Feldman, Henry John Kohlbrenner, Charles Edward Rung, Charles Francis Scherf; (1926) Irving Bauer, Francis Bork, William Bork, Phyllis Coughlin, Charles Deckop, Frances Dorscheid, Georger Feldmann, Alice Graber, Catherine Harvey, Robert Hecht, Joseph Howard, Gerard Kistner, Joseph Huntz, Thomas Ketter, Alfred Lang, Marie Luber, Irene Mazenauer, Thomas Meers, Joseph Metzger, Bernice Michels, Robert Nebrich, Betty Neucomb, James Ogden, Joseph Peters, Ida Peters, Marie Rodden, Geraldine Weitz, John Zoll, Katherine Zwelling; (1927) Margaret Aumiller, Richard Ball, John Bianchi, Elmer Bork, Charles Buchheit, Nicholas Cecchine, Frances Collins, Robert Corrigan, Caroline Duffy, Clarence Feuerstein, Helen Koch, Victoria Metzger, James Sarra, Clara Schiesl, Joseph Shields, John States, Robert Stelley, George Ward, Kathyrn Weigand, Elmer White; (1928) Charles Beck, Mary Berst, Ruth Bork, Edward Buchheit, Robert Buchheit, Paul Cecchine, Marian Chandler, Francis Costello, Edmund Dietzel, Mabel Eddy (left, March 1928), Marie Feldmann, Marian Graber, Dolores Herr, Herbert Hettrick, Willis Houghtling, Marian Kennedy, Madeline Ketter, Mildred Klemp, Anna Longo, Margorie Ludaescher, William Ludaescher, James Malone, Gertrude McCue, Adele Michels, Vera Nebrich, Peter Parisi, Martha Perreault, Florence Steffan, Francis Stelley (left, May 1938), Teresa States, John Turski, Eugene Wagner, Mary Zeinz, Gladys Schimpf; (1929) Alice Brown, Louis Corrigan, Bernard Crellian, Lillian Cole, Harold Hacker, Arthur Legg, Daniel McCue, Marian Miller, Walter Nebrich, Martin Schiesl, Allen Joseph Schneggenburger, Louis Schwing, James Shields, Walter Steffan, Jennie Terranova; (1930) Martha Aumiller, John Beaser, Loretta Collins, Doris Dietzel, Bernard Duffy, Gervase Ernewein, George Herr, Robert Hebschweiler, Gerhard Lang, Kenneth Lauer, Robert Meers, Theodore Nebrich, Herbert Rieman, Theodore Turski, Martha Zeinz, Raymond Zwelling, Arnold Barill, William Holch, Gordon Wilson, Merle Montclair, George Beck; (1931) Bernice Breitweiser, Richard Brown, Robert Brown, Georgianna Buchheit, Richard Buchheit, Irene Crellian, Catherine Ernewein, Albert Feldmann, Richard Hughes, Arlene McHugh, Bernadette Miller, Thomas Morris, Albert Parisi, Richard Pfeffer, Edward Quinlan, Doris Schiesel, Patricia Smith, Richard Stedler, Robert Stedler, Ruth Steffan, Dolores McGinley, John Simmons, Quentin Kalick; (1932) George Annis, Dorothy Ball, John Barrill, Dorothy Betz, August Cusimano, William Hock, William Kaser, Norbert Kolb, Rose Marie Lang, Frances Marie Longo, Rita Mayer, Norbert Metzger, Rita J. Mullen, Joseph Naples, Rita Nebrich, John J. Page, Richard Schafer, Elizabeth Steffan, Theodore Wainer, Norman White, Paul Aronnia, Emanuel Morwich, Salvator Costello; (1933) Francis Auer, Albert Beaser, Raymond Blair, Anthony Caffarelli, Anthony Colucci, Salvator Digati, Jeanette Graber, John Harvey, Carl Hettrick, Betty Rose Kahle, Meldard Kalick, Paul Manall, Francis Metzger, Dorothy Miller, Geraldine Miller, Frances Parisi, Louis Privitera, Anthony Roth, Howard Schattner, Dolores Shields,

Philip Terranova, Martha Toczek, Robert Turski, Charles Valvo, Emma Vlasich, Gertrude Wagner, Gertrude Zeinz, Evelyn Annis (moved to Canada), Joseph Fitzpatrick (moved to Holy Redeemer), Jean Lackin (Public School), John Lee (moved to Holy Angels); (1934) Rita Ball, Joseph Battaglia, Roy Brown, Frank Christopher, Francis Corrigan, Jerry Curran, Lorraine Freyburger, Robert Hughes, Edward Kohlbrenner, Ruth Manall, Catherine McDonald, Bernard Metzger, Harry Pelleteri, Robert Schleg, Robert Steffan, Rosalia Tripi, Erwin Schattner; (1935) Joseph Colucci, Francis English, Frank Fasco, Marvin Ford, Santo Marciano, Mary McDonald, Mildred Pelleteri, Daniel Rinaldo, Irwin Schattner, Harold Schleg, Thelma Schiesel, Anna Sutherland, Keneth Walters, Helen Zeinz, Joseph Costello; (1936) Robert Albert, Sebastian Caffarelli, Margaret English, Norma Fulton, Alice Freyburger, James Garvey, Michael Giovina, Rita Godert, Marion Holmes, Gertrude Hughes, John Metzger, Catherine Nason, Paul Reisch, William Schifferle, Irene Schwam, Geraldine Steffan, Margaret Stelley, Salvatore Terranova, William Vlasich, Nancy O'Rourke, Edison Koerner; (1937) Marie Buchheit, Norma Burke, Nicholas Costello, Catherine Field, Carl Godert, Donald Hettrich, John Marciano, Florence McDonald, Jack O'Brien, Russell Pillettere, Eleanor Rieman, Betty Schifferle, Jean Schmidt, Anthony Sciolino, Frank Spano, Georgiana Stuart, Roy Tierney, Minnie Chtheroe, Vitalina Costello; (1938) Mario Caffarelli, Theodore Caffarelli, Anthony Caligiuri, Edna Chtheroe, Genevieve Conlin, William Crumlish, Raymond Earsing, Marie English, Ralph Gibson, Claire Graber, Joseph Hassler, Pearl Kvasnak, Irwin Kranse, Francis Lambrix, Salvatore Mistretta, Donald Mullen, Richard Nason, Kathleen O'Rourke, Francis Reuvain, George Schifferle, Frances Thomas, Lawrence Wagner, Dorothy Watson, Angela Zeinz, William Miller, Paul Frohe; (1939) Joseph Ralabate, Louis Buchheit, William Burke, Michael Caligiuri, Vincent Carbone, Genevieve Conlin, Thomas Crumlish, Joseph Danna, Salvatore Giovino, Fred Godert, Margorie Goodrow, Raymond Hassler, James Hock, Eugene Kolb, Anne Metzger, John Miller, Frank Nappo, Shirley O'Brien, Doris Peterson, Rosalia Puleo, Joseph Sceusa, Nicholas Vacca, Joseph Campagna, June Hamilton, James Howard, Robert Maher, Lawrence O'Byrne; (1940) Joan Albert, Gordon Day, Rose Mary English, Peter Fasanello, Herlein Ford, Joseph Giovino, Henry Godert, Kenneth Hines, Irene Kennedy, Paul Kolb, Irene Komrek, Cora La Marco, Raymond Lang, Mary Ann Mathers, Vincent Merlino, Frances Mistretta, Donald Murphy, Vincent Nebrich, Carmelo Parlano, Charles Palmeri, Joseph Parisi, Salvatore Raimondo, Christopher Ross, Andrey Jehle, Wayne Bowen, Stephen Rine, Ann Varco; (1941) Charles Amico, Joseph Amico, Robert Beechler, Richard Crumlish, Vito Gennaro, Arthur Koch, Nicholas Lagattuta, Joseph La Porte, Gloria Maly, Anatole M. Pelezos, Mildred Nenno, Evelyn Peterson, James Ralabate, George Ricotta, Francis Vetter, Norfie Zarbo, Daniel Robert Dwyer, Robert Patton; (1942) Richard Carballada (Rick Azar), Jean Costello, Betty Grady, Joan Howard, Rose Mary Johnson, Gloria Jordan, Richard Komrik, Betty McGarel, George Metzger, Victor Mistretta, Nicholas Puleo, Carol Schmidt, Louis Vasquez, Thelma Jordan, Harry Miller, James Clunie, Eugene Liakas; (1943) Joseph

Do You Know Where Your Children Are?

Birkemeier, Charles Carlson, John Carr, Joseph Cosmano, Donald Gibson, James Hines, Joan Kennedy, Patricia Murphy, Patricia Riley, Daniel Skubinski, Francis Tonello, Henry Carlson, Rose Constantino, Vincent Mule, Frank Randolfino, Nola Richardson, Andrew Sciolino, Rose Varco; (1944) Bernaed Birkemeier, Anna Carlson, Anthony Costello, Louis Chilelli, Lois Dillon, Shirley Hogg, Marion La Porte, Edwin Kolb, Edward Norton, Anna Scoma, Lorraine Ulrich, Shirley Zeis, Rosalie Marchese, Eleanor Kashube, Margaret Puleo, John Talley; (1945) Richard Battaglia, Dolores Campbell, Lois Ford, Alfred Herod, Charles Hock, Gloria Lopez, Doris Miller, Paul O'Rouke, Marie Pierro, Thomas Powers, Richard Randall, Anthony Rine, Gerald Thomas, George Washer, Margaret McCoy; (1946) Peter Allen, Donald Beechler, Joseph Carbone, Francis Fultz, John Hassler, Alfred Herod, Eugene Howell, Marian Lojacono, Robert Marshall, Anthony Mistretta, Anna Mule, Felix Pecorao, William Jame Radig, Norman Schaefer, Joan Sutchiffe, Thomas Walters, Gary Seiler; (1947) Carol Albert, Kenneth Bardol, Maurice W. Bolinger, John Brennan, Robert Foegen, Nacy Harrington, Elaine Liakas, Ellen Myers, John Ryan, Florence Scomo, Charles Sutcliffe, James Walters; (1948) Carlos Carballada, Michaeline Cosmano, Charles Gass, Susan Herod, James Kelly, Arthur Liaksa, Andre Martel, Dorothy McNaney, Philip Mule, Marie Powers, Nancy Rine, Rose Ritter, Joan Smith; (1949) John H. Bauer, Eugene C. Brown, Evelyn M. Foegen, John W. Hamilton, Mary Ann Kolb, Dolores M. Komrek, Patricia M. McNaney; (1950) Libby Bellitter, James B. Birch, Catherine Brennan, Barbara Brown, Joyce Carson, Marie Caruso, Thomas Cheney, Donald Figliola, Hilda Gessner, Carol J. Gruber, Florence Guest (Burke), Robert Hanrahan, George Karcher, Mary Lou Licata, Jo Ann Marsh, Lucy Agnes McCafferty, Elizabeth Mitchell, Marie Therese Pares, Angela Raimonde, James Staveski, Robert Van Ghle, Charles Vrenna; (1951) Margaret M. Broderick, Janet Bratz, Robert Boling, Rose Marie Campbell, Patricia Dustin, Helen Foegen, Andrew Fuetterer, Suzanna Hassler, Richard Hibschweilder, Robert Komrek, Joan Ligouri, Michael Ormand, Shirley Rhol, Dolores Sarama, James Special, Charles Syracuse, Daniel Tronolone, Paula Volpe, Mary Jane Lorefrice; (1952) Richard C. Borcik, James Brennan, Michael Broderick, Mary Louise Continelli, Joseph Gaglione, Robert Hayhurst, Janina Jubulus, Mary Ann Liakos, Marietta Marshall, Evalds Pundruss, Dianna C. Sharp, Patricia A. Slark, Theodore Strachura, Salvatore Valvo, Donna A. Wells, Lilya Zeile; (1953) Brigita Abrickis, John Book, Ida Barsotti, Katherine Brugnone, Gerald Cheney, Paul Cheney, Dolores DeLuca, Anthony Dombrowski, Dawn Fraser, Donald Gavin, Patricia Gavin, Elaine Gebler, Anthony Jacono, Francis Locastro, John Leddick, Martha Mohler, Michael Montour, JoAnn Perna, Russell Rhoe, Lucy Spogis, Olga Stachura, Barbara Tonte, Joseph Volvo, Carol Ann Weber; (1954-1955) missing; (1956) Bruno Blavescuinas, Catherine Chavel, David Drumsta, Michael Drumsta, Elizabeth English, Edmund Jaskulski, Joann Lacastro, Fulgencia Medina, Patrick Murray, Donald Naughton, Peter Nugent, Annette Paternite, Ruth Prizel, Rose Purpura, Leone Salamone, Joan Schick, George Schieferstein; (1957) Joseph Abello, Roger De Vito, Dennis Dowser, Roger Gyhra, Paul McCarville, Thomas Pares, Beverly Rassler, Robert Zeis; (1958) Frank Andrzyiwski, Carol Birkaski, Roderick Buchanan, Helen M. Cheney, Winifred Cole, Catherine Conklin, Sharon A. Fraelich, John Jubulis, Geraldine Kuligawski, Michael Reid, Joyce Sharpe, Linda Szymanski, Jeanne Weber; (1959) Donna Colatasti, Marcia De Vito, Elfriede Hudolin, Bernice Hudson, Paul Indelicato, Florence Jaskulski, John Mercurio, Alice Ann Mortimer, Charles Nigro, John Pares, Valentine Pierotti, Gloria Rush, Mary Ann Slagar, Patricia Smith. (school closed August 1959 by order of Reverend Howard J. Schwartz, Pastor).

The St. Louis School Building, under an emergency demolition permit issued to the Diocese of Buffalo by the City of Buffalo, was razed on June 18, 1986. The photo was taken by Robert L. Smith / *Buffalo News*

CHAPTER THIRTEEN

First World War and the Roaring Twenties

On September 14, 1913, the Right Reverend Doctor Messmer, Archbishop of Milwaukee, dedicated the new St. Louis Church. On this beautiful Sunday, the archbishop, his train of clergy acting as deacon, subdeacon, and assistants, and the altar boys, gathered in the church yard in front of the school accompanied by the trustees, the Sisters of St. Joseph, the Brothers of the Christian Schools, members of the Dramatic Circle, organizational officers and men of the proposed Knights of St. John Commandery 204, members of the Catholic Mutual Benefit Association, members of the Ladies Catholic Benevolent Association, the Choir, members of the Young Men's Society, ladies of St. Cecilia and St. Agnes Sodalities, men of St. Joseph and Holy Name Sodalities, and members of St. Louis' Chapter of the Third Order of St. Francis. Many of those in the parish who were not actively involved in one of these structured groups were also present acting as witnesses to this most wonderful occasion. Since 1885, the entire parish had worked hard and donated much in time, talent, and treasure to see the events of this day and feel with pride the words so well voiced by Father Hoelscher, "When St. Louis Church says, 'yes,' there must be no failure!" From the very first fund drive put in motion by Father Sorg on the day following the great conflagration, followed through by the efforts of the parish in two grand bazaars, through the endeavors of the Dramatic Circle, and the continued donations of the faithful, the debt on the church had been brought to zero! The mortgage was burned and the church dedicated.

The rite of dedication of St. Louis Church began several years before this climactic day. It began before the church was built; it began in 1829 when the site was blessed by Bishop Dubois and again when the foundation stone for this new gothic church was blessed on May 29, 1886 by Bishop Stephen Vincent Ryan. Now on September 14, 1913, during the bishopric of Charles H. Colton, Archbishop Messmer of Milwaukee preformed the four part ceremony of solemn blessing called the Rite of Dedication of a church and altar as found in the Roman Pontifical, a book of ceremonies reserved for bishops. The archbishop was most distinguished walking under the great canopy whose four poles were supported by the trustees. The vast crowd of people stood in awe as they saw him displaying his long white beard, large ears, and squared spectacles, wearing his chasuble and white gloves, carrying his crosier with the gold spiraled handle, being flanked by deacon and subdeacon, and preceded by other clergy, altar boys, and marching members of the societies. As the procession turned on to Main Street, a host of spectators, parishioners and friends of St. Louis Church, who were Protestants as well as Catholics, met the entourage.

Among them were men wearing bowler, boater, and panama hats, men with bald heads, bearded or clean shaven, hands at their sides or folded at their backs, ladies dressed in their finest long flowing dresses and exquisite bonnets, and little children running along the sidewalk dressed in long stockings, buckled shoes, and long coats. The ceremonious entrance into the church was the first of the four-part rite after which the archbishop sprinkled holy water on the people, walls, and altar. Once the clergy had reached the altar and the parishioners were seated, they heard the readings from the Scriptures. This was followed by the formal prayer of dedication, the anointing of the walls and altar of the church with holy chrism, the incensing of the altar, covering it with the fresh linens, and lighting the candles. Following these rites the archbishop celebrated Mass and all were invited to receive Communion.

*N*ine months later on June 28, 1914, the archduke and heir to the dual empire Austria-Hungary, Francis Ferdinand, and his wife Sophia were murdered on the streets of Serajevo in Bosnia-Herzegovina. It was this act which served as an excellent pretext for a war which had already been planned in 1913 so as to commence in the summer of 1915. Before it was over with an armistice on November 11, 1918, the whole world had been placed into chaos. It was World War I, a war to end all wars! When it ended the toll was gargantuan in death and debt. Over forty million men had been put under arms; the total world stretching across the Atlantic and Pacific Oceans was affected. More than nine million soldiers died in action and the total death including civilians reached thirty million. In Eastern Europe those who died of disease and privation amongst the populations were incalculable. The United States placed four million eight hundred thousand men under arms; its casualties, of killed, wounded, and missing in action reached two hundred sixty eight thousand. The total financial cost of the war to the world was two hundred and fifty billion dollars. On the vestibule wall, Main Street exit of St. Louis Church, a brass plaque proudly displays the names of those members of the parish who participated in the Army and Navy Corps of the United States Armed Forces. The military units for thirty-four names could not be identified. Forty-one were identified serving with the Army and eleven were active with the Navy. Of these Anthony Didley and

Clayton J. Souter were killed in action. Frank Bauer, Louis A. Buchheit, and Richard Eger were severely wounded but survived. Reverend Walter Fornes served as chaplain of the 65th New York Regiment at Camp Wadsworth, South Carolina, which later was referred to as the 106th Field Artillery while attached to the American Expeditionary Force in Europe.

*T*he United States declared war against Germany and joined the Allied endeavor in Europe on April 6, 1917. During that year, the first major engagement of the enemy in which American troops participated was at the battle of Cambrai. Their involvement was minuscule and they sustained no casualties. This was not the case, however, when the campaign of 1918 was initiated and the Germans went on the offensive. In the north the Germans approached Kimmel Hill and Ypres, within striking distance of the port cities of Calais, Dunkerque, and Oostende. In the west they stretched down across the old battlefield of the Somme River with an anchoring point at Armentieres. They were in control of all the territory through France to Metz, north of Nancy, and dug in along the Baccarat line between Luneville and St. Die. Likewise they were solidly entrenched in Belgium and Alsace-Lorraine. Although Hindenburg was the chief of the German general staff, Eric Von Ludendorff shared in his command on the Western Front. Ludendorff opened his offensive campaign on March 21, 1918 from the north; and, within seventeen days, he had advanced beyond Noyon and Montdidier; his troops were only twelve miles from the important railroad center of Amiens. Next he moved against the British and Americans in the Armenteries sector and advanced seventeen miles up the Lys River Valley. On May 27, he attacked the French Front along the Chemins-des-Dames River north of Aisne. The French line from Rheims to Noyon was forced back and Soissons fell into his hands. By May 31, his forces had reached the Marne Valley through which he continued advancing toward Paris. At Chateau-Thierry, however, he was blocked by the 2nd, 3rd, and 28th Divisions of the United States Army and thrown back from his tactical strongholds at Bouresches, Belleau Wood, and Vaux.

Although stopped, the German army had established two salients threatening Paris. Ludendorff immediately rendered a terrific blow to the Allies along a twenty-two mile front between Montdidier and Noyon. The French, however, resisted valiantly. Once again, however, Ludendorff sought victory and an end to the war. On June 15, he struck simultaneously on both sides of Rheims, the eastern corner of the salient that he had created in the Aisne drive. To the east of the city he gained little. On the west he crossed the Marne River, but made slight progress. A force that included eighty-five thousand Americans, however, blocked his path; their 42nd Division was in the extreme east anchored at Champagne, and their 3rd and 28th Divisions in the west were near Chateau-Thierry. The turning point of the war had come. The great German offensive had been stopped. The initiative, which had been enjoyed by Ludendorff now, passed to Marshal Ferdinand Foch, who, in March 1918, had been appointed to the distinguished command of all allied armies in France and Flanders. Physically he was a man of medium height with a large head, deep bass voice, and gray-blue eyes, with a typical French military moustache.

Many of the Buffalonians who served in the army at that time were parishioners at St. Louis Church; they were scattered among the various regiments making up the 77th and 78th Divisions which had established their presence in Europe early in the spring of 1918. Edward Bauer recalled how his 302nd Engineer Regiment, including his two buddies, Edward G. Dearing and Frank Dietzel, had sailed from New York harbor on the Cunard Line's *S.S. Carmania* on the morning of March 27, 1918 and joined the overseas convoy at Halifax that evening. As they were boarding the ship at New York, they heard the large crowd, which had gathered to see them off, shouting, "Take Berlin, bring back the Kaiser's whiskers!" They landed in Liverpool, England,

on April 12, and were immediately put on smaller vessels that reached Calais, France, on April 15. They were in the first American Division to reach Calais for training with the British, who were under the command of Douglas Haig. In a few days they were at Ruminghem in Pas-de-Calais and assumed that they would be thrown-in as human fodder to halt the German drive against Kemmel Hill and Ypres by exhausting the enemy's ammunition. Their main objective in their first engagement, however, was the recapture of a Canadian aerodrome about one-half mile from where they were in billet; they were very fortunate that their casualties were few. On June 7th the 302nd Engineers moved by train to a railhead near St. Pol back of the Arras front. It was from there that they left the British sector to join other American outfits at Thaon-les-Vosges. After seven days they relieved the 117th Engineers of the Rainbow Division at Baccarat south of Nancy. Soon after their arrival other units of the 77th Division joined them. It was supposedly to be a quiet front; most of the German offensive was considered to be north and west of them.

Also approaching the Baccarat front were the division's' 306th and 307th Infantries and the Sanitary Squad. These three units are mentioned because they contained Louis A. Buchheit, Richard Eger, Frank McGavis, John Hatten, and Paul Muth who had been fellow parishioners with Bauer, Dearing, and Dietzel at St. Louis Church. On June 19, the 77th Division had almost completely replaced the Rainbow Division on a line between Luneville in the north to St. Die in the south running through a line that had its center at Baccarat. The intelligence department of the German army had knowledge of the lack of training in this new division which was taking up the line. The Germans decided, therefore, to give the newcomers a welcoming that they would never forget. On June 24, 1918 at 4:00 A.M., they sent over the American lines a shower of gas composed of a mixture of phosgene and mustard with fine discrimination. It had been first used by the Germans during an attack on Ypres in June 1917. In July of that year the casualties due to gas were almost as numerous as all the casualties during the previous years of the war. The phosgene element in the gas had an unpleasant odor and was a very severe respiratory irritant. The gas mask neutralized its severity. Mustard gas, however, was an oily liquid, a violent irritant, and had intense blistering properties. Even though the gas mask was in place, the mustard gas would burn into any exposed skin such as the ears, neck, and hands. It could also penetrate its irritation through light clothing. Although the men of the 77th Division were new at this war business, they were not careless; they quickly put on their gas masks with great speed and saved themselves from much suffering and many casualties. Somehow Eger, McGavis, Hatten, and Muth came through this ordeal unscathed, but Buchheit who was positioned directly under one of the exploding canisters and inundated with the gas, was not as lucky as they, but was somewhat fortunate on that day.

He was wearing a very long and heavy sweater that his mother had knitted for him. Fortunately it reached him just two days before the attack. The thickness of the sweater did not allow the gas to attack his torso but his hands and neck did blister. Because of these wounds he was removed from the trench and sent to the rear for medical attention. When released, he again joined his regiment. He was with it in August, just in time to leave the Baccarat; and, after two days on trains from Bayon and Charmes, it reached Coulommieres. Traveling on busses, it passed through the wreckage of the Marne River offensive, through Chateau Thierry and Fere-en-Tardenois, to Nesle Wood, near Seringes, a town about twelve miles northwest of Rheims. Buchheit's regiment was then attached to the 77th Division which gave relief to the tired and battle-worn 4th American and 52nd French Divisions.

The relief was effected on the night of August 11, in the *HellHole Valley of the Vesle River*, where the advance in the second battle of the Marne had been halted. By August 17, Buchheit, Eger, McGavis, Hatten, and Muth were in position with their respective groups in the 77th Division. With them, Bauer, Dearing, and Dietzel were among those in the 302nd Engineers who worked heroically night after night repairing bridges over the Vesle River under heavy shell and machine gun fire. It was on one of those bridges that Edward Bauer saw the first Buffalo man in the 302nd Engineers die; he was Private Wallace Parmenter. It was also on this day that Richard Eger of the 306th Infantry was severely wounded and brought to the rear. The division leaders, growing restless under severe strain of simply holding without the incentive of making an advance, decided to capture Bazoches. The 306th Infantry was selected for the job. Bazoches was a small town that rested in a deep pocket on the German side of the Vesle River. Hills stretched back from it on three sides. The attack started at 4:15 A.M. on August 27. It advanced into the town, but did not hold it. From concealed positions in the hills, the Germans bombed them on both flanks. By 10:00 A.M. the Americans withdrew; they had paid a big price for success and failure, but they had learned a great lesson that was their salvation in the greater struggles which followed. The Italians relieved the 77th Division on September 15. It moved over to Verrieres where it participated in the Argonne offensive.

With the organization of the American First Army on August 10, 1918 under the personal command of General John Joseph Pershing, nicknamed Black Jack Pershing, the history of the American Expeditionary Forces entered upon a new stage. The St. Mihiel and Meuse-Argonne offensives, which lasted from September 12, to November 11, were those planned by American generals and executed by American troops. St. Mihiel was a salient in the front line that had stood impregnable for four years. It lay slightly more than twenty miles south of Verdun and included towns and villages such as Xivray, Vigneulles, Thiacourt, and Fresnes-en-Woeuvre. Frank and Edward Bauer were engaged with the 78th Division, and Father Walter

Fornes, as chaplain, was a member of the 106th Field Artillery. The first attack of the offensive began on September 12, with a heavy barrage from the guns of the 106th. To the infantrymen it looked as though they were set in one vast circle of flashing skies and crashing thunder. So well lighted was the field from the blazing powder that they could now easily find their lines. After much fighting, the Germans sought healthier lines in the rear.

On the next day, at the beginning of a battle, which lasted continuously until October 9, Cyrus J. Marshall, a St. Louis Church parishioner, saw Captain Lawrence H. Platt and four other officers killed outright as a large German shell made a direct hit on headquarters. On September 21, Marshall saw fellow Buffalonians, Christ J. Klailer and Alexander Kuczkowski, fall victim to the artillery barrages of the Bosche, a name given to the Germans by the Allies. Klailer's family lived at 456 Jefferson Street; Kuczkowski's mother and father lived at 70 Woltz Avenue. Charles J. Fell, another member of St. Louis Church, witnessed the death of Edward W. Kindt, whose mother resided at 257 Howard Street, Buffalo. During these days of battle, more than five hundred and fifty thousand Americans were engaged, enduring seven thousand casualties while firing more than one million rounds of ammunition.

Following their successful engagement on the St. Mihiel Front the 78th Division moved northward to join the 77th Division in the offensive of the Meuse-Argonne Forest, which was carried out to draw the best German divisions to the front so as to consume them. It took forty-seven days of continuous fighting to do so. Here the men of St. Louis Church distinguished themselves; some were wounded and some died. By October 14, the 78th Division had made a forced march under orders to relieve the tired, weary, and shell-torn, but victorious, 77th Division. Though excessively fatigued by a long march through mud, the men of the 78th Division swung into the fighting line on the night

of October 14. Major General McRae commanded the division. For the 77th Division, it was a bad day; many men were left dead and wounded on the battlefield because of the horrendous enemy machine-gun fire.

The Bosche had made a last stand in the second phase of the offensive, but the 302nd Engineers went into action. Edward Bauer, Edward Dearing, and Frank Dietzel were among those who set out on October 15, to cut wires, clear mines, and construct two bridges across the Aire River in the direction of Grand Pre. Under heavy fire they did their work well. By October 16, the Americans had crossed the Grand Pre-St. Juvin Road, and were heading with great speed toward the town. On the next day the Buffalo Boys went over the top for the second time; they advanced across the open ground to the Aire River, a small, swiftly flowing stream. They waded through the chilly, waste deep water, and formed a skirmish line on the opposite side. Throughout the remainder of the day, however, the Americans lay huddled, cramped, and chilled while machine gun bullets whistled over them and high explosive and gas shells landed nearby. Back and forth the battle swayed for nine days with no one gaining an advantage; only death was the victor.

On October 25, the 311th Infantry tried to crash the Bosche's lines. At headquarters, just before dusk, Anthony Didley, one of two members of St. Louis' parish to die in World War I, was killed while lying behind an embankment south of Grand Pre. He was struck by fragments from a high explosive shell. He was one of three brothers serving in the armed forces, all of which had graduated from St. Louis' school. Anthony was the oldest of the Didleys having graduated in 1904. When he died at Grand Pre, he was twenty-seven years old. His brother, Joseph M., who was a year younger than he and chief petty officer in Naval Aviation, returned home after the war unscathed. Anthony's other brother, Eugene G., who, at the age of twenty-one, was at the Seaman's Institute of the United

States Navy at Newport, Rhode Island, when the news of his brother's death reached the family. He had graduated from St. Louis' school in 1909. Anthony's youngest brother Raymond E., being only fifteen, did not enter the service; he graduated in 1916.

Many of the Buffalonians were killed in fighting between October 16 and November 6, a day on which the 42nd Division relieved them. By this time General Pershing and his men were on their way to Sedan, reaching its outskirts on the eve of the armistice. In the cemeteries around Grand Pre many brave boys from Buffalo are sleeping. Every tree is stamped with an act of American valor; and, while the soldiers of the 77th and 78th Divisions were not aware of it at that time, they were engaged in smashing the western defenses of the famous Kriemhild Line as divisions on their right were going through it. The armistice was signed five days after they were relieved at 5:00 A.M. on November 11; and, at the eleventh hour of the eleventh day of the eleventh month of the year 1918, the bugles sang truce. Following this event, the American troops moved all the way to Coblenz, in German territory, and remained there until 1923. A formal peace treaty was signed on July 28, 1919 at Versailles, France. Many important anti-war conferences were held during the next fourteen years by the great European powers of England, France, Germany, and Italy. Most notable was the four-power peace pact signed by them on June 7, 1933; it renounced war as a national policy. It is ironic that three months before this pact was signed, Adolph Hitler had been appointed chancellor of Germany, the highest office next to President Paul von Hindenburg who at the age of more than eighty-three remained in office, but in name only. One year later, he died at Neudeck, and the German Republic became a dictatorship in the hands of Hitler and his Nazi Party. [1]

During the Great War, Kaiser Wilhelm, who had become the emperor of Germany in 1889, and who proclaimed himself to be equivalent to the Caesar of the Roman Empire, was considered in America as an ogre, the man-eating monster of children's fairy tales. Crowds of Buffalonians stood in long lines serpentinely bent around the block waiting to purchase tickets to see Douglas Fairbanks perform in the silent movie, *Swat the Kaiser*. Although the country had remained neutral from 1914 to 1917, the Kaiser was the butt of jokes and political cartoons; he was the spearhead of the destruction of Germanic pride in the United States. If the German-Americans, who represented a vast portion of the population of Buffalo, were not naturally inclined to support the foreign enemy, they surely were accused of doing so. In the summer of 1917, Charles Fuhrman, a man of German descent and the city's mayor, was not quite sure how his ancestry would damage his campaign for re-election in November. As a protection, he jumped on a political bandwagon and formed a Committee of Americanization. His message was clear, "Either a Buffalonian is an American and nothing else or he isn't an American at all!"

He pledged to make Buffalo *an English Speaking City*. He got his wish because the study of the German language was eliminated from the curriculum in the public schools even though, after the war, it was judged that this action was unconstitutional. His words struck fear and panic into the more than one hundred thousand German-American residents in the city. Although not required by law, students at St. Louis' school dropped their German classes; parental advice was to speak English only. By 1919, the German language was no longer a vehicle of learning whereas in 1916, by encouragement from the parents, the children were taught their lessons a half day in German and a half day in English. Pressure on the parents was intense. All through the nineteenth century German-Americans had been idealized as hard-working, thrifty, and successful immigrants. Following the declaration of war against Germany by the United States on April 6, 1917, they suddenly found themselves objects of suspicion, anger, resentment, prejudice, and discrimination. It was the sophisticated pressures such as the raising of eyebrows, at the Washington Street market, that hurt the most as a housewife using her English with a German accent bickered over a purchase price. It was the fixed gazes and the mumbled remarks passed by onlookers as clientele walked into the German Bank. It was the conversations in the privacy of homes where *Mayflower* Americans instilled the use of nicknames such as "Heine" and "Kraut" into their children to be later used by them as slings and arrows in slurring fellow playmates.

This attitude toward the Germanic population was in great contrast to events which took place in Buffalo in 1871 when all the small German kingdoms in Europe were united and Wilhelm I, King of Prussia, was crowned as emperor of them, and Bismarck, who had formed the North German Confederation, became chancellor of the new empire. In Buffalo on May 29, 1871, a gala jubilee day was celebrated honoring this great event which had taken place in Europe. It began with thundering cannon salutes. From roofs and windows the black, red, and white German flag fluttered gaily beside American banners, flowers in profusion adorned the houses, and the streets were alive with brightly garbed happy crowds of anxious people. From all parts of the city and suburbs they had come to surge and throng the avenues through which the jubilee procession was to pass. On Main Street, where the procession would be seen in its entirety, almost all the businesses were closed but very tastefully decorated. Even houses that were not along the parade route were decorated with flags, flowers, and greenery.

The starting point of the parade was at Niagara Square. At the appointed hour all the societies, unions, bands, flag bearers, and politicians were in place. Dr. Edward Storck, in the name of the Germans, opened the festival and welcomed the guests while flanked by the mayor, members of the Common Council, and other officials of the city and county. Through the crowded streets this entourage of dignitaries was then driven in carriages to Court House Park, which today is Lafayette Square, where from a large platform they could review the units which would proudly pass before them. Suddenly from that vantage point music could be heard in the distance and the grand parade came sweeping majestically by them. It was preceded by a detachment of mounted police followed by the first division including the 65th New York Regiment led by Colonel Richard Flach of the New York State National Guard. Next in order came the Lancaster Independent Guard, the garrison at Fort Porter, and the Buffalo Turnverein.

The second division wasted no time in following the first. It was composed of floats advertising the various singing societies of Buffalo. It was led by Marshal J. Adam Lautz, who was the founder of Lautz Brothers and Company, makers and dealers of acme soap, marble and onyx, and he was also chairman of the building committee of St. Louis' gothic church. The crowd gazed with delight and sounded forth its oohs and ahs as each float passed by. The members of the Liedertafel, the oldest singing society of the city, had a richly decorated wagon, upon which, encircled by the weapon trophies and coat of arms of the German States, rested an immense globe; and upon it, leaning on a gigantic sword, stood Arminius, the Cherusker, who had conquered the Roman legions in the Teutoburg Forest. It symbolized the warlike spirit of the Germans. The float of the Saengerbund featured a tableau representing the sleeping emperor Barbarossa dreaming of a united empire for the German people, a dream that had just come true. Next in line came the Buffalo Maennerchor, the Harugari Maennerchor, the Buffalo Orpheus, and other singing societies from Niagara Falls, Suspension Bridge, Dunkirk, and Erie, The officials of the German Young Men's Association brought up the rear.

The lodges of the Harugari's and Odd Fellows formed the third division, beneficiary societies the fourth, church societies the fifth, bakers, brewers, malsters, and coopers the sixth, and German business organizations made up the seventh and last division. It was a day in which German art, commerce, industry, and agriculture were praised and honored. In passing the reviewing platform, the parade occupied one hour and five minutes. The street sequence which the line of march followed was: Niagara, Main, Exchange, Michigan, Eagle, Main, Virginia, North Pearl, Allen, Main, Genesee, Hickory, and Batavia, and finally it reached the arsenal. As the procession passed St. Louis Church, Father Sorg, the trustees, and several parishioners standing on the front steps greeted it. Sorg raised his arm and hand so as to indicate his blessing. At the end of the march the orchestra under the leadership of Frederick Federlein introduced the strains of a *Peace Jubilee March* which he had composed for the occasion. The choral group bust forth with *Die Wacht am Rhein* followed by *Nun Danket Alle Gott*. Although the jubilee appeared to end with the orchestra playing *The Star Spangled Banner* at the arsenal, it in no way was concluded.

Afternoon picnics were held in all the parks and summer gardens, the most noteworthy being held in Koester's Park on Main Street near High Street. The Anglo-American press was unanimous in its praise of the festival. The *Buffalo Courier* published its satisfaction on the following day. It said, "The peace celebration by our German fellow-citizens was full of significance. No where else can there be found so numerous a body of expatriated Germans as in the United States; from no other country would so many impulses of sympathy and love go out to the Fatherland; and in no other country would such an open demonstration of foreign nationality have passed so peacefully, if indeed it had been permitted at all. The intelligent spectator could not fail to be impressed with two central ideas. One was the general thrift and prosperity of those who made up the great procession; and, the other was the strong assertion of nationality that was made. The whole demonstration seemed to

us to afford a justification of the American policy of welcoming all nations. It showed most conclusively that the instinct of nationality is not in conflict with true citizenship." Looking back on this occasion in 1918, it must have been quite disappointing to the Americans of German descent who were still living in Buffalo. Although their sons, brothers, and sweet-hearts went off to fight against the Fatherland, they had to remain at home and suffer the raised eyebrows, the snickers, and the slurs which tortured their belief that whatever their allegiance they could also be proud of their lineage and of their Fatherland. [2]

Four years before President Woodrow Wilson announced to the citizens of the United States that Congress had declared war on Germany, many young men at St. Louis Church, such as Cornelius F. Miller, Louis A. Buchheit, Cyrus J. Marshall, Albert T. Hardick, and Frank Bauer, never imagined that by 1918 they would be stationed in the trenches of France, dodging a hail of machine-gun bullets, cutting barbed-wire, building roads, repairing bridges, charging across no-man's land, and suffering the pain and injury of phosgene and mustard gas. In 1913, some of them were at the most twenty-four years of age; some others were just turning nineteen. Although they were military minded, it was not, however, to learn discipline and drill for the purpose of killing their fellowmen. They were romantic boys who had been fed upon the French, German, and English literature which featured the medieval knight in shining armor. Their idol was Sir Gawyne of King Arthur's Court who was found faultless in five virtues—purity, compassion, fellowship, courtesy, and frankness. They were inundated with the spirit of the German knight, Parsifal, who set out to find the Holy Grail. In May, 1913, a committee composed of Fred L. Hardick, George Koch, Fred L. Zwirlein, Cyrus J. Marshall, and Nelson Marshall called upon Monsignor Paul Hoelscher, D.D., pastor of St. Louis Church, requesting his endorsement of a plan which they had conceived to organize a commandery of the Knights of St. John in the parish.

They asked Hoelscher to be their chaplain. They informed him that although the Knights of St. John in the United States had no affiliation with the Military Hospitaler Order of St. John of Jerusalem, of Rhodes, and of Malta, that it did model itself on it in terms of spiritual and charitable works of mercy. Hoelscher looked upon these five eager and determined boys, turning into men, and said, "When St. Louis says yes, there must be no failure." With this seed, which fell upon fertile ground, St Louis Church's Knights of St. John Commandery 204 was given birth.

The concept of the Knights as a semi-military religious body active in Catholic Church circles was not new to Buffalo. Hoelscher had been aware of the existence of twelve other commanderies that had cropped up in the city since 1874 with the organization of Commandery 13 at St. Ann's Church at Broadway and Emslie Streets. This was a German Parish that began in 1858 and was under the spiritual direction of the Jesuits. At the time Hoelscher was about to give his encouragement and approval to the five young men who approached him in the summer of 1913, Reverend Peter W. Leonard S.J. was the pastor of St. Ann's Church and chaplain of its commandery. Hoelscher asked Fred L. Hardick, who appeared to be the leader of the request contingent if he thought that a discussion with the chaplains and representatives of the military staffs of the twelve commanderies already existing in Buffalo would be worthwhile. In the name of the members who had approached Hoelscher, Hardick gave his wholehearted approval.

In 1913, including active, retired, and honorary members, the twelve commanderies boasted of seven hundred and sixty-eight knights. The history of the Knights of St. John, as an organization on a national basis, paralleled the development of the Nord-Amerikanischen Turner-Bundes; a German gymnastic organization of decided political orientation that was established in the United States before the American Civil War. It was an outgrowth of the European organization founded by Friedrich Ludwig Jahn in 1811, near Berlin, Germany. In America, the first Turnverein was founded at Cincinnati, Ohio, in 1848, after which a numerous number of cities followed its lead, established local Turnvereins, and associated themselves with the National Turner-Bund. A unit was organized in Buffalo on March 3, 1853. Two years later, after being incorporated under the title of *Turners' Association of the City of Buffalo*, its group hosted the National Turner-Bund convention. Forty-seven societies represented by thirty delegates took part in this event.

Likewise, by 1870, the various spiritual and semi-spiritual societies of the German Catholic Churches in America had banded together in a national organization known as the *Deutschen Katholischen Zentralverein*, which held national conventions periodically. One such meeting was held in Rochester, New York, in June of 1874, at which the affiliated societies of the German Catholic Churches of Buffalo were in attendance. It was customary to open such conventions with a parade, and on this occasion the participants were overwhelmingly enthusiastic seeing for the first time a company of men uniformed with feathered hats, shoulder straps, sword and belt, who called themselves the *German Catholic Union of Knights of St. Maritius*. They were parishioners of St. Joseph's Church in Rochester, and had organized in 1873 with fifteen chartered members. The principal object of the Union was to promote musical and literary entertainment for the members and their families, and exercise in military movements. At the death of a member, the surviving ones paid one-dollar to the widow of the deceased. Furthermore they assumed the self-appointed mission of organizing uniformed societies such as theirs throughout various cities of the United States and Canada. Upon witnessing their military expertise in the Rochester parade, the Buffalo contingent participating in the convention returned home full of enthusiasm for *Knighthood* as the Knights of St. Maritius had explained it to them.

*I*n the first week of July 1874, St. Ann's Church held a picnic at Seckler Summer Garden on Jefferson Avenue. The first companies of knights for St. Ann's Church and St. Mary's Church were pledged that day during the festivities which included traditional German music, dancing, singing, and the hoisting of many steins. For St. Ann's Church, the promoters asked L.P. Kirchmeyer, who had served with distinction in the Civil War, to organize and serve as captain of a society which they called *Knights of St. George*. They also requested John Groh Jr., adjutant of the 65th New York Regiment, to do the same at St. Mary's Church. During the summer the wheels of enthusiasm were put into motion and on September 4. 1874 two companies were fully established at St. Ann's Church with L.P. Kirchmeyer as captain and Edward M. Hager as lieutenant. St. Mary's Church followed suit on September 19, 1874, with John Groh Jr., captain, and John W. Schlehr, lieutenant. St. Ann's Commandery 13 made its first public appearance on April 23, 1875, on St. George's feast day.

*T*hey paraded in Prince Albert coats, with slouch feathered hats, sashes, swords, and belts through Broadway and Emslie Streets, ending up at the church for Mass and the reception of Communion in honor of their patron saint, who in 303, during Diocletian's reign as emperor of Rome, held one of the highest military offices of the imperial ministry and suffered martyrdom for his christian faith. In 1875, St. Michael's Church and St. Stephen's Church put units on parade; they also were known as the *Knights of St. George*. In the summer of 1876, the three commanderies at Buffalo held a picnic in Taylor Park on the Erie Road near Alden, New York. The Rochester commandery of *St. Maritius* was invited to participate. Together they called themselves the first *Battalion of Knights*. Their drill led by Captain L.P. Kirchmeyer was reviewed by Colonel Michael Wiedrich, the respected leader of the 1st New York Artillery at the Battle of Gettysburg in 1863. Because of the excitement this event produced, three more units, known as *Knights of St. George*, were

assembled in Buffalo by 1883 at St. Boniface, Sacred Heart, and St. Francis Xavier Churches.

*W*ord had spread across the eastern part of the United States that Catholic churches in Buffalo and Rochester had formed units of knights. The call to semi-military arms of knighthood was heard and carried out in Washington D.C., Cincinnati, Ohio, and Baltimore, Maryland. As new commanderies were formed in these cities they did so without regard for any uniformity among separate units. Each one had its own individual by-laws, type of uniform, and ancillary equipment. Some had soft-feathered hats while others were donned with steel or brass helmets carrying plumes of various colors. Some wore shining breastplates while others were proud of their enormous boots. In June of 1879 several delegates from the various commanderies met in Baltimore to discuss uniformity and the formation of a national organization that could possibly be called *The Roman Catholic Union of the Knights of St. John*. The meeting ended without any positive action, however, a second convention was called for June 24, 1880 at Cincinnati, Ohio.

*W*hen this meeting was held, little attention was given to naming a national organization because a time and place to hold the sessions were unexpectedly entered into competition with the Democratic National Convention being held that year at the same time in Cincinnati for the nomination of General Winfield Scott Hancock as the party's candidate for president of the United States. Hancock had been raised to the rank of Major General of the United States Army in 1866 following the Civil War, in which he had distinguished himself in command of Union Forces at many battles from Chickahominy, through Gettysburg, to the siege at Petersburg. Although most of the business of the knights was tabled for a future date, the assembly did greet, with joy, delegates from the new commanderies which had been formed in Cleveland, Buffalo, Rochester, and Louisville, Kentucky, along with those which had been represented at the Baltimore convention. Also, new officers were elected to the national organization, but its name still was held in limbo. Buffalo, New York was given the nod for the next convention to be held in June of 1881. Many wondered if at that time a decision would be made to name the organization.

At that convention, held at Kehr's Hall on Genesee Street, a turning point in the history of Catholic Knights was reached. Although no move was made at that time to incorporate the national organization under the name *The Roman Catholic Union of the Knights of St. John*, it was agreed that when such an incorporation would take place all commanderies whose formation would have been made prior to that time would change their name to reflect the title of the national organization. Before the convention was held in Chicago, Illinois, in 1885, where the national organization was finally incorporated, the movement toward knighthood had accelerated. Besides the cities already mentioned new organizations cropped up in Syracuse, New York, New York City, Detroit, Michigan, and Vicksburg and Jackson, Mississippi. Prior to 1913, *The Knights of St. John* were well entrenched in twenty-eight cities in the United States and two in Canada. Each city had at least one commandery; and, in most of them, enough units had been formed so as to develop battalions and regiments. The membership grew to twenty thousand wearing standard uniforms when on drill or parade. *The Knights of St. John* were held in the highest esteem. They participated in church functions, civil functions, funerals, meetings, parades, picnics, outings, and drill competitions. At each affair they were honored with the presence of high dignitaries of church and state, and enjoyed their hearty approval.

In Buffalo, from 1894 to 1912, five more churches had commanderies incorporated under the name of *Knights of St. John*: St. Mary's of Sorrows, St. Mary Magdalene, St. Agnes, Blessed Trinity, and St. Gerard

Churches. After the representatives of all twelve commanderies in Buffalo had met with Hoelscher and the St. Louis Church committee, and they had reviewed all the aspects of forming a commandery at St. Louis Church, the decision was, "Go for it!" Once again Hoelscher repeated his former saying, "When St. Louis says yes, there must be no failure." The wheels to success were immediately on their way. By September 22, 1913, the day acclaimed as the organizational date, ten members of the parish had stepped forward and acclaimed their allegiance. They were: Frank Bauer, George W.J. Buchheit, Louis Buchheit, Albert Hardick, Joseph E. Koch, Cornelius F. Miller, Joseph E. Reade, Charles J. Schifferle, Lawrence Wagner, and Fred Zwerlein. By the spring of 1914, eighteen more names were added to the roster. They were: Eugene Bauer, George Bielman, Frank B. Bingeman, Joseph Eger, Fred L. Hardick, Edward Huber, George J. Koch, Alfred Kolb, Cyrus J. Marshall, Nelson W. Marshall, Clarence Meyer, Frank Pierott, Charles Ramsperger, George Sagen, Frank D. Schoenberger, W.E. Schwing, Charles G. Schwelle, and Anthony Selman. The *Knights of St. John* at St. Louis Church became known as Commandery 204; it was the "baby commandery" which brought the total number of commanderies in the city to thirteen. In 1883, when only six of them were in existence in the city, the Second Regiment of New York State had been formed. In 1913, Colonel John L. Schwartz was its ranking Senior Colonel, a position that he had held for twenty-four years. When St. Louis Church entered on to the stage, there were two battalions in that regiment and Commandery 204 was assigned to its Second Battalion.

The charter members of Commandery 204 first set out to determine their aims and objectives as knights, to determine what military training they needed, their duties in assisting at ceremonies in the church, the qualifications of the members, and the development of a set of by-laws which would include specifications for sick benefits and provisions for widows and orphans.

Using documentation from the other commanderies, they wrote a mission statement that pledged the practice of the noblest of Christian principles and the highest civic virtues. They wanted to infuse into human society a broad and lofty morality, foster and create fraternity among its members, inculcate sympathy and charity by alleviating conditions of sickness and misfortune of those unable to sustain themselves, to promote a generous and filial respect for the spiritual authority of the Roman Catholic Church, to infuse a broad and pure patriotism among its members and other citizens, and to exert a beneficial influence upon existing social conditions. To justify their claims of a charitable organization they pledged participation in the regiment's beneficiary plan of financial aid to those in need. They drew up a set of by-laws that were in conformity with the other commanderies in the regiment. They pledged to wear a uniform consisting of a chapeau, double-breasted coat, pantaloons, sword, belt, and necessary and complimentary trimmings in uniformity with all other units. They vowed to excel in military training, the precision of the drill, martial training, and self-reliance. Their qualifications for membership were simple but acute; a man had to be a practical Catholic, of sound body and mind, and between the ages of eighteen and fifty years. Every applicant was to have the signature of the pastor of his parish before admission was confirmed.

The by-laws outlined the duties of officers and sir knights, methods of election, annual dues, protection against incompetence and methods of removal from office, an outline of meeting dates and obligations of attendance, times and obligation of the reception of Holy Communion in a body, types of suspensions and fines for dereliction of duty, the obligations of the purchase and maintenance of uniforms, descriptions and mission statements of committees formed in the commandery, and the protocol to be observed at wakes and funerals, church functions on days of church feasts, days of the reception of the sacraments, and on days of official visitation of distinguished hierarchy. The determination of the charter members of Commandery 204 that "there must be no failure" intensely glowed during the first fifteen years of their existence. It grew from the first twenty-nine knights to fifty-one in 1928. In January 1914, it made its first official appearance. The parishioners were overjoyed when they first caught sight of a column of uniformed troops, moving with military precision down the long aisle of St. Louis Church and taking their positions before the altar rail. At the following Christmas Eve Midnight Mass, it was the first time the congregation witnessed the innovation of uniformed ushers directing people to their pews. The gracious comments voiced by the worshippers were sufficient to perpetuate this plan. The first great event in which the commandery participated was the dedication of the monument for the *Knights of St. John* in the United German and French Roman Catholic Cemetery.

In 1894, twenty years before this occasion, Colonel John L. Schwartz proposed a plan to the Second Regiment by which it would observe Memorial Day each year. It provided for the regiment to attend Holy Mass in a body on that day after which it would proceed to the United German and French Roman Catholic Cemetery, and there visit the graves of their departed comrades and attend a memorial service. Prior to the service a pre-chosen committee would decorate the graves of the departed with flowers, and place on each of them a flag of their order together with a flag of the United States. By 1907 it was confirmed that a large monument would be erected at the expense of the Knights in the confines of property owned by the United German and French Roman Catholic Cemetery Association, but the property upon which it would be built was to be donated by the Association to the *Knights of St. John*. Seven years later the task was completed. By the time of dedication, Commandery 204, the "baby commandery," was, for the first time, ready to participate fully with the entire regimental command.

First World War and the Roaring Twenties

On Pentecost Sunday, May 31, 1914, the Second Regiment, Knights of St. John, Buffalo, New York, together with the officers of the Supreme Command and a large representation of the Field and Staff Officers of the Rochester, Cleveland, and Detroit, assembled at Genesee Street and Pine Ridge Road, near the entrance to the United German and French Roman Catholic Cemetery; and, from there, proceeded to the entrance in escort of the Right Reverend Charles H. Colton, Bishop of Buffalo, together with the Right Reverend Thomas F. Hickey, Bishop of Rochester, and other invited dignitaries and priests. At an altar erected at the site of the monument, a Solemn Pontifical Field Mass was celebrated by Bishop Colton. He was assisted by a body of the clergy made up of Paul Hoelscher, pastor of St. Louis Church, Ferdinand Kolb, B.J. Cohausz S.J., George Weber, Thomas H. Barrett, J.C. Bubenheim, Charles V. Schaus, John F. Pfluger, and Thomas J. Walsh. The Right Reverend Thomas F. Hickey eloquently and impressively delivered the dedicatory address. The solemn and inspiring ceremonies were closed by Benediction of the Blessed Sacrament and Papal Blessings. In closing, over ten thousand Catholic men and women, and friends of the Buffalo Knights, who graced the dedication with their presence, raised their voices in unison singing, "Holy God, We Praise Thy Name!" The great choir in attendance that day, consisting of two hundred male voices and those of one hundred vested sanctuary boys, had been gathered and trained by Battalion Adjutant, Peter C. Meyers, who also arranged the music and organized the band which accompanied the choir.

Following the dedication ceremonies, Commandery 204 spent the summer practicing their techniques in drill. On October 27, 1914, it presented its first Review and Exhibition Drill under the direction of its own officers. Two years later at the biennial convention held at Detroit, Michigan, the drill team won second place prize in national competition. Over the fifteen years that followed its initiation, it enjoyed the unique distinction of being the only commandery to represent Buffalo at each national convention, and return home with a prize-winning pennant. Each year the Second Regiment held a drill in Buffalo for local commanderies. A gold badge was awarded to the commander of the best drill team. Only four years after it was organized, Commandery 204 was awarded this medal. Its captain, Fred L. Hardick, accepted the award on January 7, 1917. Later in that month sadness filled the hearts of the troop. Father Hoelscher, its pastor and chaplain died. It had the privilege to assist the clergy and the parishioners in bringing an aura of military honor and distinction to the spiritual rites of his Christian burial. It then turned its attention to greet, in a momentous display of enthusiasm, its new chaplain and pastor, Henry B. Laudenbach, who had been pastor at Sacred Heart Church, in Dunkirk, New York, and chaplain of its Knights' Commandery 90. He was well known by the congregation at St. Louis Church, having served as an assistant to Hoelscher in 1899. Immediately Commandery 204 raised him to the rank of captain.

World War I interrupted the activities of the Knights. Commandery 204 had its ranks depleted by eleven members who served in the army or navy of the United States during 1917 and 1918. They were: Frank Bauer, Louis Buchheit, Gregory J. Ducro, Christian Ecker, Richard Eger, Albert Hardick, Edward Huber, Charles Marshall, Cornelius F. Miller, and Frank Ross. The interruption of Knights' activities was national; no national convention was held in 1918. Two years later, however, Commandery 204 represented Buffalo at the convention held in Toledo, Ohio. In competitive drill, it returned home with first prize. On April 24, 1921, it gave an exhibition drill in Buffalo and received the first prize banner from Bishop William Turner. Upon receiving this award, Mister Norman Clement, president of the Citizens Trust Company, began a fund so as to provide the commandery with a special flag of its Order to be carried proudly in all ceremonial events. Soon after, Charles J. Schifferle, First Lieutenant, purchased the flag that was acknowledged as the most exquisite one among the Buffalo commanderies.

311

From 1922 to 1926 the commandery continued to participate at anniversary military concerts and balls at the Elmwood Music Hall, Cedar Point, St. Martin's parish, and in the various cities in which national conventions were held. One event that is most memorable took place on October 18, 1925. It was on this occasion that the Noble Degree, the highest degree that a Knight of St. John can receive and only awarded by the bishop, was initiated in a ceremony at St. Joseph's Cathedral, Buffalo. The four officers of Commandery 204 who received this honor on that day were: Captain Fred L. Hardick, Lieutenant Fred L. Zwerlein, Lieutenant Cornelius F. Miller, and Sergeant Joseph E. Reade. In 1928, the national convention was held in Buffalo and Commandery 204 took a lead role in hosting it. During the sessions, Colonel John L. Schwartz was elected Supreme Trustee, with the rank of Brigadier General. Frank Kreppel was raised to the rank of Lieutenant Colonel and Charles Hereth assumed the rank of Major. During its first fifteen years of history, Commandery 204 bowed four times in grief. On November 14, 1924, when Frank D. Schoenberger, the first treasurer, died; on November 17, 1921, when George H. Koch, the first financial secretary, was called; on May 26, 1926, and July 24, 1927, when Gregory Ducro and Anthony M. Selman ceased answering the roll. Their names were the first four of the commandery to be immortalized on the Knights' monument in the United German and French Roman Catholic Cemetery.

Ten more years passed by and on September 25, 1938 Commandery 204 celebrated its twenty-fifth anniversary with a special morning Mass at St. Louis Church and an evening banquet at the Trap and Field Club. Father Howard M. Adolf was the celebrant of the Mass and Father Laudenbach delivered the sermon. Laudenbach, who had been the spiritual director of the commandery for twenty-one years and chaplain for the Second Regiment for seventeen years, told the assemblage that the Knights were held in an uppermost place in fidelity and loyalty to the Catholic Church, the State, and to the Regiment. Following his remarks, the commandery received more accolades from a number of other speakers. Major John J. Schwab, vice president of the Supreme Command and son of Francis X. Schwab, former mayor of the City of Buffalo, praised the commandery for its participation in the annual Memorial Day ceremonies held at the United German and French Roman Catholic Cemetery. He was followed by Brigadier General Frank F. Kreppel, commander of the Second Regiment and aide-de-camp to the national president of the Knights of St. John. It was, however, the words of Fred L. Hardick, Lieutenant Colonel of the Second Regiment, who had led Commandery 204 until he was promoted to his higher post in 1929 that stirred the audience with high emotion. He said, "Perhaps at this time, someone else, a friend not a part of our ranks, might pen a description of the silver years of Commandery 204. No doubt it would have the value of an unprejudiced estimation and yet, could it tell the really fine part of the story? I believe not. Only those who have passed through the actual experiences, who have had the actual service to their credit, can tell of the *Golden Memories of Our Silver Years*." In response to these words the audience responded with a period of clapping which seemed interminable.

Hardick then continued recalling the prizes won for drill competitions at Detroit, Toledo, Cleveland, Rochester, and Sandusky. He gave special mention to Captain Clarence J. Meyer who had brought his winning team back from the Philadelphia convention that had been held that year. With a twinkle in his eye, he recalled how the commandery assumed a most terrifying expense by engaging the Goodrich Silvertown Cord Orchestra with the Silver Masked Tenor from New York City for an evening of dancing and entertainment at the armory of the 74th New York Regiment in 1927. After all, these were the Roaring Twenties and everyone had to try the rollicking pace of the Charleston. The affair, however, was extremely successful, both financially and socially. Hardick ended his talk saying, "Many are the sacrifices we have made since September 22, 1913, none of which are today regretted but rather we feel well repaid and satisfied." Captains Clarence J. Meyer and Cornelius F. Miller added their memories of the years gone by. They recalled the deaths in the summer of 1936 of Father Nelson Baker and Bishop William Turner, two important personages in the history of Buffalo. At their wakes and funerals Commandery 204 was prominent. They praised Charles B. Schreck and Louis Buchheit for being so devoted in their annual charge of decorating the graves of the deceased members on Memorial Day. They also described the attention the commandery received from the parishioners at St. Mary's, Swormville, when, in 1932, it brought a military aura to the blessing of the parish's new school at the invitation of Father Kraehn. On that day, the Knights escorted the clergy and Monsignor Duffy, who later became Bishop of Buffalo, in an elaborate program of flag raising, blessing the building, and Benediction of the Blessed Sacrament.

Following the Silver Jubilee year, the commandery once again experienced the outbreak of War. Germany invaded Poland in September 1939; England and France declared war on Germany. The United States, however, did not declare war on Germany until Japan, without warning, attacked Pearl Harbor on Sunday morning December 7, 1941. By June of 1943 the commandery had once again seen John J. Bauer serving his country in the armed forces. Allen Joseph Schneggenburger was on his way overseas while Richard L. Hecht was already fighting in North Africa. In the fall, the commandery had a farewell party for Harold Trapp, and Richard Ball who had been inducted subsequent to the stepped up draft allocations. At the party they each received a prayer book, rosary, and a check for $7.50. These were presented to them on behalf of the Second Regiment. By early 1945, Albert Leigl and John Widmer had left the city for their opportunity to join Uncle Sam in the war. Frank Ross was confined in Veteran's Hospital in Batavia. He was not a victim of World War II, but a wounded survivor of World War I who needed much medical attention, having bad lungs resulting from

his experience of phosgene exposure. By December 1945, the boys were coming home, the war in both Europe and Asia had come to an end. John Widmer and the rest of the members of the commandery were home by Christmas that year. Richard Ball had been in the Pacific campaign at Hawaii, Philippines, and Okinawa, and Allen Joseph Schneggenburger had spent thirty-three months in Africa, England, and Europe.

By a few years after the war, the number of Knights in the commandery had fallen to forty-nine and five more had moved on to their eternal rest. They were Raymond D. Schouten, Frank Bingeman, George Trapp, Clarence Bork, and Joseph Lambrix. The living officers, active and retired, were: George W. Buchheit, Louis Buchheit, Christian Ecker, Albert Eger, Albert T. Hardick, Fred L. Hardick, Paul Hardick, Ferdinand Koerner, Alfred Lang, Henry B. Laudenbach, Joseph Lux, Clarence J. Meyer, Cornelius F. Miller, Eugene W. Miller Sr., James Ogden, Charles W. Ramsperger, Joseph Reade, Frank J. Ross, Charles Schifferle Sr., Charles Schifferle Jr., Irving L. Sullivan, Joseph E. Koch, Lawrence Wagner, Fred J. Weigel, and Fred J. Zwerlein. Other active Knights were: Richard Ball, Frank Bauer, John Bauer, Charles Buchheit, Wilfred Cappell, Joseph Deck, Albert Gebhard, James Gillen, Dean Higgins, Robert Hecht, Richard Hecht, Casper Koch, Mathew Kruse, Albert Liegl, John Nolan, Martin Peltier, Francis Reuvain, Allen Joseph Schneggenburger Charles Schweizer, George Shields, George Schneller, Frank E. Summers, Edward Thomas, Harold Trapp, and John Widmer.

Through the next two decades the Knights of St. John at St. Louis Church continued to repeat year after year what they had done so well in the past by adding solemnity and dignity to solemn church services in the military uniform of their order. They did not, however, participate in drill competition because the group began to age and new members were becoming a premium. Eugene W. Miller Jr., however, with the encouragement of his father, Eugene W. Miller Sr., joined the commandery after his service in World War II. In 1951 and 1952, Miller Jr. was elected first vice president. From 1962 to 1964, he served as financial secretary. After his father died in 1964, Miller Jr. resigned. The Knights of Commandery 204 performed with distinction at the 125th anniversary of the founding of St. Louis Church in 1954. On this occasion Robert Hecht was the executive officer and president, Eugene W. Miller Sr. was the military captain and first vice president of the commandery, Paul Hardick was the second vice president, Edward Mescall was the secretary, Louis Buchheit was the financial secretary, and Albert Liegl was the treasurer.

The trustees of the commandery were Albert Eger, Eugene W. Miller Sr., Frank Ross, Joseph Lux, and Lawrence Wagner. Following the anniversary celebration it became more difficult to fill the ranks of knights, which were depleted by retirement, resignation, death, and movement away from Buffalo and Erie County. By 1964 a letter was sent to Battalion headquarters informing them that the membership in Commandry 204 was down by fifty percent, and that the retired members were requesting relief of delinquent dues and assessment payments. In 1965 no officers were elected and transfer to St. Barnabas Church, Depew, New York, was requested. Lieutenant Colonel, Clarence Neunder, who was a member of a commandery at St. John the Evangelist's Church on Seneca Street, Buffalo, began the necessary action to bring about a transfer of Commandery 204 to St. Barnabas Church. He did so at the encouragement of Father Howard Schwartz, who in 1964 had been transferred there by Bishop James McNulty from his pastorship at St. Louis Church as a replacement to Father Clarence Ott. Those members at St. Louis Church who were encouraged to transfer were: Joseph Abella, Richard Ball, Frank Bauer, Christian Ecker, Fred Hardick, Paul Hardick, Joseph Koch, John Juergens, Al Kratus, Joseph Lux, Edward Mescall, Robert Nebrick, Charles Schifferle, Allen Joseph Schneggenburger, Rudy Slevar, and Daniel Mescall.

On paper this transfer was completed by 1966, however, the personnel from St. Louis Church were never successfully absorbed into the new program. By the end of 1966 Joseph Abella had resigned and moved to Wisconsin. Richard Ball, Chris Ecker, Paul Hardick, and Charles Schifferle paid their dues, did not attend meetings, and retired by the end of 1968. Al Kratus, John Kratus, and Robert Nebrick resigned. Frank Bauer, Fred Hardick, and Joseph Koch died. Joseph Lux paid his dues each year but did not attend meetings. Allen Joseph Schneggenburger was the only original Knight at St. Louis Church who, having made his first degree on May 8, 1934, was still alive in 2001 and an active member at St. Barnabas Church. He received his noble degree from Bishop James McNulty on November 6, 1966. Captain Eugene W. Miller Sr. was the last military captain of Commandery 204 while it was still at St. Louis Church. His name was transferred to St. Barnabas but the process was never completed; he died December 15, 1964.

Of the other eighteen who were processed, Joseph F. Lux lived the longest; he died on September 16, 1980 at the age of 71. He was a man who achieved higher education because he had excellent abilities in sports. He graduated from St. Joseph's Collegiate Institute having been a star fullback on the football team. Accepting a scholarship to St. Bonaventure University, he achieved a bachelor's degree while excelling as the football team's star tackle. He married Paula Netter, was a funeral director at Mrs. Joseph J. Lux and Sons, and coached football, basketball, and baseball for St. Joseph's Collegiate from 1938 to 1942. The various other community activities in which he participated is a litany: president of the St. Bonaventure University's Alumni Association; Director of the Buffalo Council, Knights of Columbus; member of the First Friday Club and a fourth degree, Order of Alhambra; A Knight of St. John, Commandery 204; member of the Holy Name Society and the Usher's Guild, St. Louis Church; president of the Erie-Niagara County Funeral Directors Association; president of the Main Street

Lions' Club; president of the Greater Buffalo Advertising Club; member of the Brothers of the Christian Schools Founders' Club and its Circus Saints and Sinners; and a member of the Main-Amherst Businessmen's Association.

*I*t has been said in the past that to belong to St. Louis Church was to hobnob with the rich German families of Buffalo. Impressed in the minds of those who think this way are family names of parishioners such as Lang, Gittere, Wex, Lautz, Davis, Garono, Feist, Weyand, Hager, Kam, and Kraus. As one reads the roster of family names of the Knights of St. John such as Ball, Bauer, Buchheit, Hecht, Kruse, Hardick, Miller, Schifferle, Wagner, and Zwerlein, one does not see golden coins of great wealth hanging in their family trees. Commandery 204 was composed of many men who worked hard, made a good living, and provided well but not lavishly for their families. Joseph Deck, the brother of Gregory Deck, may have been considered to be quite well to do because the Deco Restaurants were so numerous and visible around the city. Joseph and his wife, Jean, had no children of their own, but they adopted two boys for whom they provided a good Catholic education. Barbara Steffan, who had married Charles Buchheit, a house painter, was proud as a peacock, displaying its iridescent golden and green feathers, when she would tell people that her three sons Charles, George, and Louis were Knights in Commandery 204. It was her family that traced its ancestry back to Michael Steffan one of its first parishioners.

*G*eorge Buchheit married Anna Schifferle who was the sister of Charles Schifferle, another distinguished member of Commandery 204. Anna was a regular member of the St. Louis Church choir; and, with George, she gave birth to two boys, Paul and Robert. Paul Buchheit sang with her in the choir. He was one of the Cadet Knights when the "corps of little knights" was attempted at the church. It was, however, short lived.

Paul continued, however, to be associated with the older knights and was a star player on their baseball team of inter-commandery competition. He graduated from Canisius College and served in the Chemical Corps during World War II. Robert Buchheit attended St. Louis' parochial school; he graduated in 1928 along with Edmond Dietzel, James Malone, and Eugene Wagner. This has been called the "holy class" because all four boys eventually were ordained priests in the Diocese of Buffalo. Father Robert Buchheit was the founder of St. Gregory the Great Church on Maple Road in Amherst. Eugene Wagner was the son of Lawrence Wagner, an active Till Eulenspiegel of the Knights of St. John. At various conventions, Lawrence carried a scissors in his pocket. At the most opportune time to himself and to the greatest embarrassment to his prey, he would approach a fellow knight and cut his tie in half. At work, however, he was very serious; for many years he was a salesman and a buyer for Adam, Meldrum, and Anderson's Department Store. A fellow knight, Frank Bauer was another self-confirmed trickster; he intermingled among the children at picnics bursting their balloons with a pin. George and Anna Buchheit also gave birth to Georgiana who later married Charles Besch; one of their daughters, Carolann, is presently a member of the Parish Council at St. Louis Church.

*C*harles J.M. Buchheit, son of Charles Buchheit and Barbara Steffan remained a Sir Knight during his entire life. Although he did not seek any office he was a most faithful attendee of meetings, military practice, and participation in all the ceremonial processions and escorts. He was consistently a winner of the annual prize for attendance when the candidate of excellence was presented a medal with an attached bar which symbolized the faithfulness of attendance. A gold bar was for first place with one hundred percent attendance and silver and bronze for second and third place provided the attendance was over ninety percent. In 1925, Clarence Meyer, Charles J.M. Buchheit, and Eugene W. Miller Sr. achieved third place; Fred L.

Hardick and Casper Koch were awarded second; and Charles J. Schifferle, Cornelius F. Miller, Joseph E. Koch, and Albert Gebhard took first place. Charles J.M. Buchheit was a self-employed interior decorator specializing in artistic wall paperhanging. He and his wife Mary Futterer lived at 42 Park Street where they had five children, Charles, Edward, Richard, William, and Marie. William died in infancy, but all the others attended St. Louis' school. Louis A. Buchheit, who had been wounded in World War I, was born on September 8, 1889. He, the youngest member of his family, lived with his mother and father at 20 Pearl Place. After the War he married Janet Hatten; they, however, had only one child, Louis John Anthony who married Carmene Didio at St. Louis Church on June 11, 1949.

𝓑esides having four boys, three of whom became Knights, Charles and Barbara Buchheit gave birth to two girls Frances and Rosina. Frances married George H. Koch, who was the second member of Commandery 204, following Frank D. Schoenberger, to experience eternal life beyond the grave. Sergeant Joseph Reade, a friend of the Buchheit family, was the maitre d'hôte, chief steward, at the Lafayette Hotel. Another family that gave multiple Knights to Commandery 204 was the Hardick's. Fred, Albert, and Paul all served. Fred Hardick moved up the military ladder and became Colonel in the Second Regiment. Paul and Albert, however, after more than thirty years of service resigned when the commandery was transferred to St. Barnabas Church. Also, prior to the transfer, Cornelius F. Miller, a charter member of the commandery and its president for eight years, resigned.

𝓘n fact twenty-nine members who had been at St. Louis Church will not have their names on the monument in the United German and French Roman Catholic Cemetery because they withdrew prior to their death. These are: Richard Ball, Wilfred Cappell, George Buchheit, Christian Ecker, Albert Eger, Albert Gebhard, James Gillen, Albert T. Hardick, Paul Hardick,

Robert Hecht, Richard Hecht, Dean Higgins, Ferdinand Koerner, Matthew Kruse, Alfred Lang, Albert Liegl, Cornelius F. Miller, Eugene W. Miller Jr., Robert Nebrick, John Nolan, Martin Peltier, Charles Schweizer, George Schneller, Frank Summer, Edward Thomas, Harold Trapp, Lawrence Wagner, and John Widmer. Of this group Richard Ball is noteworthy. He delivered ice for Gruber's Ice Company and built and repaired candy machines for Rittling Company. He married Dorris Dietzel who was the sister of Father Edmond Dietzel. One of his sisters is Dorothy Ball who married Allen Joseph Schneggenburger, the last of the original Knights of St. John Commandery 204. One day while young Schneggenburger was in attendance at St. Louis' school, Father Henry Laudenbach entered the room. Looking at this lad with a very long last name he said, "Son, what is your first name?" Schneggenburger replied, "Allen, Father." To this Laudenbach bellowed, "There is no saint named Allen. From now on you will be called Joseph."[3]

𝓓uring Hoelscher's tenure as pastor of St. Louis Church following the birth of Commandery 204, World War I erupted in Europe. He died in 1916 before the United States entered the war on the side of the Allies. Bishop Denis Dougherty appointed Henry B. Laudenbach, who had once been Hoelscher's assistant and later was made pastor at Sacred Heart Church, Dunkirk, New York, as Hoelscher's replacement. Laudenbach's reign spanned more than a quarter of the twentieth century from the armistice of World War I on November 11, 1918 to the year 1944, when the allied victory in World War II was still indecisive. Following the armistice of World War I, he had to emphasize and affirm that the Germanism of his parishioners' heritage was something beneficial, advantageous, and edifying. He raised their morale that had been sorely tested during the war; he made them feel buoyant, confident, aggressive, and resolute. He pointed out that it was young men of German descent from St. Louis Church who had been doughboys "over there." Several had been wounded and some died bringing an end to hostilities.

After Germany signed the peace treaty on June 29, 1919, like most Americans, the congregation at St. Louis Church turned its attention to conditions at home rather than abroad. Economic prosperity, experimentation with new products, especially the automobile, and indulgence in entertainment seemed to be high on the parishioners' priority list. Laudenbach was to flow with his flock through the roaring twenties that began with the acclamation of prohibition of the manufacture and consumption of alcoholic beverages, and ended with a mighty financial collapse of the stock market in 1929. He then spiritually guided them during the dark years of Depression, the repeal of Prohibition, and the ominous clouds predicting World War II.

On June 7, 1933, Italy, England, France, and Germany signed the four-power peace pact. It was to last for ten years and then automatically be renewed unless denounced on two years notice. On January 28, 1933, however, the Reichstag of Germany had voted to give Adolf Hitler the powers of dictator, Paul Ludwig von Hindenburg remained president of the Weimar Republic in name only, and an arsonist burned the Reichstag, for which act Hitler blamed the Communist Party. Besides attacking the Communists, Hitler silenced the Social Democrat, the Nationalist, and the Catholic People's Parties. On August 2, 1934, when von Hindenburg died, Hitler's Third Reich, with himself as Der Fuehrer, had been solidly established, and the Weimar Republic was only a memory. In September 1939, Hitler's armies invaded Poland and World War II was on. Laudenbach was in his pulpit on Sunday, December 7, 1941, when the Japanese, an Axis Power in league with Hitler, using an aerial attack and without warning, destroyed the United States' fleet anchored at Pearl Harbor. Once again America was jettisoned into another World War. Two years after it began, Laudenbach died, and St. Louis Church received a new pastor, Father Michael A. Anstett.

Henry B. Laudenbach was born at Schweinfurt, Lower Franconia, Bavaria, on January 8, 1883. His father Henry P. Laudenbach was a paving contractor who had been well educated in the methods of road building which had been handed down from the Romans, modified by John Loudon MacAdam and Thomas Telford of Scotland, and Joseph Aspden of Leeds, England. Henry P. Laudenbach was quite knowledgeable of digging out the earth down to a firm foundation between two trenches along a straight line from one point to another. In an excavation of approximately four feet, he would have his workers place slabs of stone at the base joined together by cement mortar. In layers on top of these slabs they placed rubble, fine concrete, and pavement stones to complete the roadway. The Romans named this method *munire viam*, to fortify the way. Following the methods of Aspden, Laudenbach created his own type of cement which was a mixture of calcium and aluminum silicates, hydrated, and placed in a kiln until the high temperature caused them to fuse and form a clinker. He then ground the clinker into a fine powder which he jocosely called *laude cement*. Many times he used asphalt limestone from Val de Travers, Switzerland, as an ingredient which when mixed with sand, gravel, stone fragments, and water formed concrete.

Although he had a well-established and successful business in Bavaria, Laudenbach had, since the birth of his son Henry B., toyed with the idea to immigrate to the United States. After the Franco-Prussian War that began in 1870, Bismarck had solidified the German states and pronounced his plan to have all groups subordinated to the state. In that same year Pope Pius IX, however, pronounced the dogma of papal infallibility. All Catholics were required to accept unreservedly papal pronouncements in matters of faith and morals. Misunderstanding what was meant by the pope speaking *ex cathedra*, Bismarck felt that he could not count on the undivided loyalty of the new Germany's citizens, especially the Bavarians who had organized a powerful political party called the Center

Party. In 1871 he launched his famed *Kulturkampf*, his battle for modern civilization. A series of anti-Catholic laws were enacted and inforced. Restrictions on Catholic worship and education were imposed, the Jesuits were expelled, and many Catholic bishops throughout Germany were arrested or went into exile. Although by 1879 Bismarck came to the conclusion that his anti-Catholic legislation was fruitless, the scars of being considered disloyal to the state still remained impressed in the minds of Bavarians. Henry P. Laudenbach had weathered the storm of *Kulturkampf*, but refused to live in a country where great trouble was festering between the theories of socialism and the anti-republican efforts. From 1878 to 1890 anti-socialist laws prohibited all socialist meetings and newspapers. Laudenbach considered this state of affairs as "bad for his business." In 1883, he brought his entire family to Buffalo, New York. Young Henry B. Laudenbach was seven years of age.

The Laudenbach family became parishioners of St. Mary's of Sorrows Church, which was founded in 1870 for those German parishioners of either St. Ann's Church or St. Louis Church who lived too far away from either so as to attend Mass and devotions with convenience. St. Mary's of Sorrows Church was located at the corner of Genesee and Rich Streets. A brand new church building was completed at the site a year after the Laudenbachs arrived. Young Henry attended the parish's parochial school, and was an altar boy in the procession accompanying Bishop Stephen Vincent Ryan at the blessing of the new church in 1884. He graduated at the age of thirteen in 1899. Following his graduation he was among those who had been selected to receive their First Holy Communion and Confirmation. On a beautiful Sunday in June, Bishop Ryan, at the invitation of Father Adolph Heiter, pastor, who had informed the bishop that his candidates were duly trained in their Catholic religion, came to St. Mary's of Sorrows Church to administer these sacraments. The children had assembled in the school, and preceded the bishop in a liturgical procession to the church. After entering, they marched up the main aisle took their places in the first pews closest to the altar rail. The bishop and his ecclesiastical entourage went through the open gate of the altar rail and took their assigned places on the altar. During the Mass, the children received Communion; for them it was their first. Following the Mass, Father Heiter introduced the bishop, who stood, holding his crosier and wearing his miter, to the candidates. The bishop said, "Confirmation is a Sacrament, instituted by Christ, in which, by the imposition of my hands, my anointing and my prayer, those of you who are already baptized are steadfastly strengthened by the Holy Ghost, so as to profess your faith in word and deed."

Ryan then raised his left hand and continued saying, "Children, I want you to know that your Confirmation which you will receive today at my hand will increase sanctifying grace within you, the Holy Ghost will enable you to resist evil and grow in virtue, and your souls will be imprinted with a mark that can never be effaced." The children were then asked by Father Heiter to approach the altar rail and kneel before the bishop. Ryan then came down the altar steps, gave his crosier to Heiter, and moved to the first kneeling applicant. He extended his hands over the applicant's head and said, "Holy Ghost, come down upon this child!" Using chrism, which signified inward strength and sanctification, he then made the sign of the cross on the child's forehead saying, "I sign thee with the sign of the cross and I confirm thee with the chrism of salvation, in the name of the Father, and of the Son, and of the Holy Ghost." Completing this prayer which reminded the confirmed Catholic that one is never to be ashamed of the Cross, but boldly profess faith in Christ crucified, he gave the child a slight blow on the cheek as a reminder that a good Catholic should be ready to suffer patiently any humiliation for the sake of Christ. After repeating this ritual with each and every applicant, he retired to the high step of the altar, turned to the recipients who were still kneeling, and gave them all in a body his blessing. On that day young Henry

318

Laudenbach returned home emotionally uplifted and repeating to himself the seven gifts of the Holy Ghost which he, on that day, had received: Wisdom, Understanding, Counsel, Fortitude, Knowledge, Piety, and Fear of the Lord.

The following September, Laudenbach entered classes of higher education with the Jesuits in their school on Washington Street, named for Peter Canisius, a saint of their Order who died in 1598. Laudenbach was a precocious lad, who accelerated his education and graduated in six years completing with honors all of his required college courses. It was in that same year that he informed his parents and Father Heiter of his intention to enter studies for the priesthood. Heiter decided to send Laudenbach to see Bishop Ryan who by that time was a venerable and benign figure. His long white hair graced a face of intelligence and serene character. He had moved from his home on Franklin Street to the new bishop's house on Delaware Avenue, built for him by the priests of the diocese and presented to him with the Chapel of the Blessed Sacrament as a mark of filial devotion. As Laudenbach entered the bishop's parlor, he was greeted by him with much fatherly concern. The bishop said, "Henry, your college days are over. Your seminary looms on the horizon! For you it will be the University of Innsbruck, Austria. Go home and tell your parents to pack your bags. As the mariner says, 'You will sail at high tide.' Have no worries my young protege, in four years, by the grace of God, you will be ordained and return to us as an adopted child into the Diocese of Buffalo."

So it came to be! Laudenbach was ordained at Brixen, South Tyrol, Austria, on March 19, 1899 by Prince Bishop Aichner. Post-haste, Laudenbach returned to Buffalo; but, sadly, he would not greet Bishop Ryan at his residence on Delaware Avenue; Ryan had died in 1896 and was replaced by Bishop James Quigley, who immediately assigned Laudenbach to be assistant to Father Paul Hoelscher at St. Louis Church. Three years

later the bishop sent him to St. Nicholas Church in North Java, New York. In 1905, he was given his first pastorship at a newly created church, St. Joachim's, located at 64 Titus Avenue on Buffalo's East Side. In 1909, he became pastor of St. Paul's Church, Delaware Avenue and Victoria Boulevard in Kenmore. Five years later he found himself as pastor of Sacred Heart Church, a very old establishment founded in 1858 at 21 Franklin Avenue in Dunkirk, New York. In 1917, upon the death of Father Paul Hoelscher, Bishop Denis Dougherty, the fifth bishop of Buffalo, asked him to return as pastor to St. Louis Church. Although Laudenbach, had a different personality than Hoelscher, he was immediately liked and respected by the parishioners. Laudenbach had an ever-ready smile, twinkling eyes, and a voice filled with kindliness and interest. In very little time he was seen as unmistakably their priest; he was their beloved Father and Confessor. Slowly but surely he made it his practice to know virtually all of his parishioners by their first names. Whenever he visited the children in the first grade of the school, they thought of him as the ideal Santa Claus!

One of Laudenbach's first priorities was to keep the lines of communication open with the young men from St. Louis Church who had joined or were drafted into service with the United States Army, Navy, or Marine Corps. Several of the lads had gone to Camp Wadsworth, South Carolina, where Father Walter Fornes was the chaplain. Laudenbach wrote several letters to Fornes and inquired about the boys. One of those young men who kept in contact with Laudenbach by mail was Frank Ross. Before going overseas, Frank had written to Laudenbach, who on February 19, 1918 wrote a reply. He said, "Dear Frank, It certainly was nice of you to remember me in sending your postal. You're far away from home indeed, and from all your old friends. As long as you're busy and keep close to your church, you're OK. Father Fornes was here from Camp Wadsworth; we've quite a roll of boys down there from our parish at this time. God be with you and keep you sturdy and brave in your country's service." When the war ended, Laudenbach was most enthusiastic about having a party for the returnees. He called upon the members of the Knights of St. John to welcome the boys home. He also was the energizer who got the congregation excited about placing a plaque on the wall of the church near the entrance from Main Street.

*F*ollowing World War I, all through the Roaring Twenties, and into the Painful Thirties, Laudenbach had a colorful and distinguished career while being pastor at St. Louis Church. He had great talents that he unostentatiously and generously dedicated in various fields for the welfare of his fellow citizens. In the literary field, he was founder, editor, and trustee of the *Echo*, the diocesan Catholic newspaper, in competition with the *Catholic Union and Times,* and head of the Catholic Library. He was also diocesan Censor Librorum, one who determines the dogmatic and moral acceptability of literary works, and moderator of clerical conferences in the diocese. In 1939, the Catholic Pamphlet Society published his short history of the first six bishops of the Buffalo Diocese. With unfailing optimism, forthrightness, broad sympathies, deep understanding, and scintillating humor he, by popular demand, served in many institutions. He was chaplain of the Buffalo Moose, regimental chaplain of the Knights of St. John, Director of the German Roman Catholic Orphan Asylum, Director of the Diocesan Priest's Eucharistic League, received an honorary law degree from Canisius College, obtained a friarship of the fourth degree assembly with the Knights of Columbus, and was an honored member of the Buffalo Club. In December 1942, Pope Pius XII raised him to the rank of monsignor; Bishop Duffy ceremoniously invested him several months later.

*A*s pastor of St. Louis Church, Laudenbach was a strong supporter of its various societies. He praised and encouraged the men of the Dramatic Circle who had established and continued a policy of presenting excellent entertainment. By 1934, it had produced thirty-four performances. He was delighted when he heard that the women of St. Louis Church had banded together in 1896 and developed a branch of the Ladies Catholic Benevolent Association. It was gratifying that they had continued for so many years providing insurance protection for so many ladies of the parish. This society was a complimentary one to the men's Catholic Mutual Benefit Association, which also had a branch at St. Louis Church. He was instrumental in assisting Bishop Turner in deciding to turn the activities of the St. Vincent de Paul Society, founded in 1833, over to the direction of laymen. Laudenbach brought a chapter of the society to St. Louis Church. In 1924, Father Albert J. Hoffmeyer was the chapter's spiritual director; Albert M. Wagner, president; Eugene Ebner, secretary; and Charles J. Schifferle, treasurer.

*L*audenbach always attended the meetings of the Christian Mothers who were in 1934, three hundred and fifty strong. They were originally established at St. Louis Church on March 21, 1897. Collectively, they were the powerhouse behind furnishing the funds that provided new vestments for the clergy, flowers and linens for the altar, and were the bulwark of many fine social affairs. High on Laudenbach's list of priorities were the spiritual societies: Young Ladies Sodality, St. Joseph's Sodality, Holy Name Society, and the Third Order of St. Francis. Besides his skill and talent as a writer, Laudenbach was also a life long student of church music. As pastor he appointed himself as moderator of the church choir. As such, he had a long, delightful, and fruitful relationship with Henry J. Zeinz, whom he always called Professor, and who was the able organist and director of the choir. Laudenbach was a large framed man, looking much bigger when he was in cassock and surplice. On Christmas Eve it was his custom to climb to the choir loft, drape his large frame tightly against the loft's railing, and, with his sonorous deep basso voice, sing, *O Jerusalem*, accompanied by Professor Zeinz.

On April 22, 1924, after having served as pastor at St. Louis Church for seven years, Laudenbach celebrated his silver sacerdotal jubilee. He sang a Solemn High Mass assisted by Fathers William J. Schreck and Albert F. Fritton. The Right Reverend William Turner, D.D., assisted in cope and miter. Monsignor Nelson H. Baker, Proto-Apostolic, was assistant to the bishop. The bishop's deacons of honor were Monsignors Charles E. Duffy, Francis Kasprzak, and Edmond J. Britt. Father Albert F. Hoffmeyer acted as the master of ceremonies. Monsignor John J. Nash delivered the sermon. Also in the sanctuary were: Monsignor Michael F. Gallagher, Bishop of Detroit; Monsignor Peter Petri, Atlantic City; Monsignor Thomas H. McLaughlin, President of the Immaculate Conception Theological Seminary, South Orange, New Jersey; J.M. Stadelman, Pittsburgh; Monsignor Ferdinand Kolb, and Father George J.Weber, Buffalo. Approximately one-hundred and fifty priests, from all parts of Western New York, filled the upper pews in the nave. Two days later, a dinner in honor of Laudenbach was given by the parishioners in the school auditorium. The following evening, the Knights of Columbus, the Fourth Degree Assembly and the Alhambra united in a testimonial dinner in Laudenbach's honor. Robert T. Bapst, Superintendent of Buffalo's public schools, delivered the principal address.

Following this almost weeklong celebration, Laudenbach prepared to travel to Europe, accepting the financial cost of it, which was $3,600, as a gift from the trustees and the parishioners. While in Europe he visited scenes of his early youth; it was refreshing to relive his boyhood days, but he was saddened when he saw its landscape torn and rent by World War I. After passing through several cities he saw his fellow classmates at Innsbruck. He also visited needy parishes, sisterhoods, and orphanages where he had unbounded generosity. As he traveled he wrote many articles which were published weekly in the *Echo*. By these, the congregation at St. Louis Church was able to keep in touch with him. Father Hoffmeyer, who was acting

pastor, wrote and told him of the Golden Jubilee Mass held at St. Louis Church honoring the parishioners who in 1874 had received their first Holy Communion. In that year, one hundred and sixteen boys and girls dressed in their black suits and white veiled dresses, had walked together down the long aisle of the church in anticipation of receiving that sacrament. Fifty years later only seventy-six remained alive, and forty-two were able to attend the ceremony. Two of the Knights of Commandery 204, Cornelius F. Miller and Eugene W. Miller Sr. were very proud to see that one of the participants was their mother, Catherine Grimm, who had married Charles Augustine Miller. On October 28, 1924, the Knights of St. John devoted their annual concert, dance, and military drill to welcoming Laudenbach home. They all stood as he entered the Elmwood Music Hall, and presented him with a tumultuous applause as they first caught sight of his jovial countenance. Following this greeting, Henry J. Zeinz, with Catherine Berger as piano accompanist, led the choir in a rousing song *Hail Bright Abode* from Tannhauser written by Richard Wagner.

During the celebration Father Laudenbach was asked by the Knights to tell them what the Europeans in the countries which he had visited thought of us back home. He, as he was well known to speak at the drop of a hat, said, "For some Germans that you meet the war has not ended yet. They look askance at you when you quote the fact that you are German-born. Thank God, they seem to be in a very decided minority." With this introduction, he then continued with a theme that was apocalyptic. He said, "For the rest of Europe, however, a future war-cloud has not been dissipated by the horrors of the Great War. In every country the active crowd are keeping up the idea of future war and huge armies are not damping the ardor of these dangerous jingoes. The fine and ancient art of fooling with the fates of peoples through diplomacy is as rife as ever. True, the overwhelming majority shudders at the prospect. It was not otherwise in years gone by, and yet wars came and came again. The League of Nations is the frailest imaginable reed for any true pacifist to lean on. It is on the contrary more an invitation and incentive to strife."

Speaking of how the Europeans thought of America, he said, "One other thing which must be considered is our national attitude toward the Ku Klux Klan. Despite the persecutions of the Church in Italy and in France the methods of these Klansmen are unintelligible to the people abroad. They would not be tolerated in what we please to call the backward and slow countries of Europe worn out with age and exhausted of energy. Men there cannot see how in America they are allowed to control such vast parts of our country with its wide and distinct promises of religious and civic freedom. They rightly fasten the blame on a weak and inefficient Federal Government, afraid, for the sake of votes, to call a spade a spade. The peoples of Europe ridicule our professions of liberty under such like foul and illiberal treatment. They place it on a level with universal disorder engendered by our Prohibition Law with its enormous ethical and financial losses, its hypocrisy and absolutely inefficient operation. Who would contradict and deny that we were a saner and happier people if the virtues of temperance and tolerance were not being pounded into us with a gun in the hands of a Prohibition sleuth or a hooded Klansman? Likewise, they ask, is government by and for the masses not just a phrase in America? To answer these questions for honest people in Europe is no easy task and puts one into a very embarrassing condition to say the least!" When he had finished, he was almost endlessly applauded; he had touched them to the core.

On September 23, 1928, the Knights of St. John celebrated their fifteen anniversary of the establishment of Commandery 204. Solemn High Mass was sung in the morning with Father Henry B. Laudenbach as the celebrant. In the evening a memorial banquet was arranged for only commandery members by a committee under the direction of Captain Fred L. Hardick. Their annual ball, however, did not take place until October 23, 1928. The executive chairman for that evening's activities was Sergeant Clarence J. Meyer, and Sir Knight Eugene W. Miller Sr. arranged the souvenir yearbook. The ball was held at the Elks Club at 297 Delaware Avenue, and all members of the parish were invited. This gathering of the Knights, who after fifteen years had become very visible and influential in the parish, provided Laudenbach with a vehicle for presenting his two major concerns. He spelled out the details of the ongoing debate between the trustees of St. Louis Church and the Buffalo City Council over the proposal to extend Pearl Street from Tupper, arching behind the Teck Theater, cutting the property of St. Louis Church so as to separate the rectory from the church, and destroying the school as it hooked up with North Pearl at Virginia Street. He was incensed by the plan that had been presented to the City Financial Committee by the Pearl Street and Main Street Businessmen's Associations.

Laudenbach was an accomplished lecturer and orator. When he spoke he did not ramble, but he came right to the point. On that evening he told the assembly what he had been saying since May 1, 1928 to the members of the City Council. He said, "The matter that most of our parishioners will want to know about naturally, the one that has exercised the City Council and the parish a great deal, to wit, the extension of a street through the middle of our property and the consequent destruction of our utility as a parish in the place which we have occupied just one century. The matter has been threshed out before the Finance Committee of the City, the counsel for the parish, and the pastor, and the result was a great silence on the part of the three delegations that were present at the hearing. Not one man had the courage to answer our arguments. Not one man stated that they were based on anything but solid truth. Not one man was heard to state that he would be willing to shoulder the responsibility for this action against the Catholics of the city as shown in this attempt on the Mother Church of the diocese."

He discussed the situation further, "As a consequence, the proposal made to the trustees of St. Louis Church to confer with the Main Street Association is a stop-gap, and may lead to something or nothing! The proposition as it stands today is to buy a large plot of land in the immediate vicinity of the church, and, possibly, to concede to us a sufficiently large sum of money to replace our buildings. Whether this can be legally done, whether the city will ever consent to do so, whether the Finance Committee of Buffalo will tolerate this purchase for a private corporation; all these are ticklish and, at the same time, interesting developments. We shall see what we shall see. In any case, we have won the first round and, it seems to us, decisively. We have relied upon the justice of our cause, not upon politics or upon the favor of anyone. We trust and believe that in the future this policy of ours will result in convincing our opponents, who are the Main Street Association, the Delaware Avenue Association, and the Automobile Club of Buffalo, that we are here in a permanent way and, with the help of God, intend to stay here for many years to come after these associations have passed into the limbo of forgotten and unnecessary things."

After Laudenbach finished his speech concerning the Pearl Street extension he discussed plans for the Jubilee Celebration which was to take place in 1929. He said, "You are undoubtedly anxiously waiting for further details regarding the Jubilee Celebration next year. Your Pastor has not been idle since the last announcement a year ago in this program. We have chosen the month of May, the date still being uncertain, but it is fairly sure to be around the middle of the month. We intend to have a dignified and, at the same time, simple celebration, confined to our parish and to the former members of the parish whose names are legion. There will be a Pontifical High Mass with the new and gorgeous gold brocade set of vestments now being finished in Germany. There will be a play by our Dramatic Circle. There will be a Children's Day and, finally, a dinner for the parish and for the clergy of

the whole diocese of Buffalo in the Elmwood Music Hall to sum up the celebration."

He encouraged their participation, saying, "We know that all the members of the parish will co-operate and be happy to make this a real family celebration. It is, of course, unique in this way that we are celebrating a centenary of the Catholic Church in this part of New York State and we feel the honor of doing so in our own parish which was established nearly twenty years before the beginning of the diocese of Buffalo itself. So, as the advertisements in the papers say, 'Watch this column for further news.' It will be interesting and, at the same time, will give you a clue to the nice things and the interesting things in store in May 1929, our golden year of jubilee and thanksgiving." Laudenbach finished his discourse that evening praising the Knights of St. John as the bearers of the Cross and Religion. He campaigned for more recruits to their ranks, and, in his humorous but sincere manner, said, "This 'ad' of our Knights of St. John is unsolicited on their part. It is the firm conviction of your pastor, who is also the chaplain of the local commandery, and assistant chaplain of the regiment, that they are worthy of full support, generous co-operation and praise for the leading part which they have played for fifteen years in the history of your old and venerable mother, St Louis Church."

All through the winter Laudenbach worked diligently with the trustees and other church organizations in bringing the plans for the centennial celebration to fruition. On Sunday, May 26, 1929, at 11:00 A.M., the church was filled to capacity. Approximately two thousand people were in attendance for a Pontifical High Mass celebrated by Bishop William Turner. The deacons at the Mass were Reverend Bernard C. Cohausz S.J., and Reverend Walter F. Fornes. Assisting the bishop were Right Reverend Monsignors George J. Weber, Alexander Pitass, and John J. Nash. The Right Reverend Edmund J. Britt, chancellor for the diocese and the Very Reverend James

H. Murphy were masters of ceremonies. Other clergy who were in the sanctuary were: Reverends William Martin, Eugene H. Selbert, Joseph Kennedy, Albert Winter, F. Cornelissen, Albert Rung, and John Szal. The sermon was preached by Reverend William Schreck, pastor of St. Gerard's Church, Buffalo. Being a graduate of St. Louis' parochial school, he began by recalling the joys and hardships, but the fine education that he had received at the hands of the Sisters of St. Joseph and the Brothers of the Christian Schools. Being a former member of the St. Louis' Dramatic Circle, he contributed his ability to emote in his sermons because of the early training he received under the direction of Otto Andrle.

He then said, "St. Louis Church is the nucleus from which all other parishes in this part of the country were formed. Erection of its first church was the giant step in the development of the Catholic religion in Western New York." He then sketched the history of the parish, recalling the difficulties under which the parish labored in testing out several administrative systems. He described the co-operative effort between the clergy, the trustees, and the congregation of St. Louis Church as being a Rare Tradition in American Catholicism. The program of sacred music was rendered by a choir of fifty voices under the direction of Henry J. Zeinz. They faultlessly executed the Mass in honor of the Sacred Heart of Jesus composed by Dr. Ignatius Mutterer, who was a former seminary professor at Innsbruck, Austria, while Laudenbach was there studying theology. The Introit, Gradual, and Communion prayers were sung in Gregorian Chant. Professor John Singenberger composed the Offertory motet, *Oremus Pro Pontifice*.

Following the Mass, the clergy dined together in the church hall at which Laudenbach opened the festivities by offering a toast to Bishop Turner. Zeinz, who had put together a double quartet, provided the musical entertainment. At 2:00 P.M., the children gathered at the Teck Theater for a matinee of the comedy, *The County Chairman*, written by George Ade and produced by the St. Louis' Dramatic Circle. At an evening performance of it, which began at 7:00 P.M., all adults were invited to attend. During the intermissions the Christian Mothers served soft drinks and snacks. On the following morning at 9:00 A.M. Laudenbach celebrated a Solemn Requiem Mass for the repose of the souls of all the deceased members of the parish. Reverends John Hippchen and Joseph A. Kennedy assisted him. Once again the church pews were filled to capacity with friends and relatives of families whose names had appeared on church rosters since 1829. At 2:00 P.M., a special form of entertainment was activated in the church hall for the children; classroom work was cancelled to the delight of all, snacks provided by the Christian Mothers were devoured with joy, and the games organized by the Sisters of St. Joseph were intently relished. In the evening at 7:00 P.M., the final event of the two-day celebration took place at the Elmwood Music Hall. One thousand people gathered at the tables set for a sumptuous banquet, whose menu, provided by Mr. B. Martin's catering service, included fruit cocktail, celery, olives, radishes, Long Island roast duck with dressing, sauerkraut, mashed potatoes, centenary ice cream, coffee, cake, and rolls. While this vast group ate and chatted, Fuller's Orchestra played wonderful dinner music.

At the dais were: the Mayor, Frank Xavier Schwab; the trustees, Edward J. Garono, Peter Schirra, Albert M. Wagner, John M. Fornes, Louis Ludaescher, William E. Swanz, and Peter M. Ginther; the wives of these distinguished guests; and Reverends William J. Schreck and Henry B. Laudenbach, who was the toastmaster. Laudenbach began the dinner by saying that regrettably Bishop Turner could not attend because he was unexpectedly called out of town. He then traced the history of the parish, paying tribute to the former pastors, and reiterated the sentiments expressed in Father Schreck's sermon concerning the greatness of the church because of the co-operative effort made in administrative details by the trustees and the pastor. He said, "In a stormy sea, the bark will not yield to the waves when all hands on deck, together, batten the hatches and secure the lines!" Mayor Schwab extended the felicitations of the City. He said that the parishioners of St. Louis Church had been a potent factor for good in the city, and he paid tribute to them for the sacrifices that they had made for God and country. He said, "This country was founded on the principle that its citizens owed allegiance to God and country, and if the nation forgets this principle it will not long endure." In the course of his address, he referred to the action of the council in overriding his veto in the matter of the Pearl Street extension, which he opposed for ethical and economic reasons. He stated that the plan, if carried out, would involve great injustice to St. Louis Church. He predicted, however, that eventually the Democratic majority of the Common Council would decide against the extension as unnecessary, refuse the appropriation of the funds needed to purchase land so as to make the project viable. He said that he would continue to impress the legislature with his opinion that their proposed fear of traffic congestion on the parallel streets of Pearl and Main was a myth.

Edward J. Garono, speaking on behalf of the parishioners, presented Father Laudenbach with a check for $1,000, as a mark of the esteem in which they held him and of the gratitude for his untiring labors in their behalf. He then added a word of tribute to the pioneer parishioners who built the church and contributed largely to the civic upbuilding of the city. The building of the first log church by these pioneers, he declared, was just as colossal an undertaking for them as the building of the great gothic edifice by a later generation. When Garono had finished, Laudenbach, who had gratefully accepted his gift from the parish stated that probably he would use it to take a trip to Alaska in July. He announced that since he had received so much gratitude for his travel letters to *The Echo* during his European trip that he would continue the practice when he would be on his Alaskan adventure. In a short address, Father Schreck paid tribute to Fathers Sorg, Hoelscher, and Laudenbach. These were the three pastors of St. Louis Church whom he had known during his lifetime. He also remarked of the generosity that had characterized the parishioners in their support of the church since its inception. He recalled incidents in the history of the parish for a half century, stressing the work of Professor Hemmerlein and others in the education of the youth of the parish. For the one thousand guests who had gathered for the banquet, and others who had attended the Masses and seen the production by the Dramatic Circle, the two-day celebration was one glorious reunion, one long to be remembered. [4]

Knights of St. John Insignia

REFERENCES AND NOTES ✣ CHAPTER THIRTEEN

1. The names of those members of St. Louis Church who participated in World War I were taken from the plaque which is on the wall of the Main Street vestibule of the church. Not all of the names on the plaque could be found and equated to a unit in which they served. The following are those names whose units were not located: Able, Aloysius; Argus, Aloysius; Bauer, Clarence; Berger, Norbert; Chandler, Herbert; Conboy, Arthur; Eger Albert; Freyburger, Joseph; Fisher, John C.; Dietsche, Karl J.; Deckof, James A.; Hecker, Fred; Helbringer, Alfred F.; Jehle, George A.; Koch, Leo Albert; Koch, August L.; Kohlbrenner, Edward; Missert, Alfred F.; Missert, Edwin J.; Noeltner, Edward J.; Noeltner, J.; Sasgen George N.; Schimpf, George L.; Schimpf, Henry F.; Schweitzer, Charles O.; Schwing, William E.; Shields, James; Sprage, William J.; Steffan, John; Stendts, Albert; Stoerr, William Edwin; Warner, Philip; Weigel, Norman; Welsch, John M.; Weppner, Raymond; Zuber, Harry. Names of those members of St. Louis Church who served in the armed forces of the United States during World War I, between the years 1914-1918 and whose units could be determined are as follows: Identification of rank and outfit served-with was taken from: Daniel J. Sweeney, *History of Buffalo and Erie County, 1914-1919*, committee of One Hundred, Finley H. Greene, Chairman, Under Authority of the City of Buffalo, July 4, 1919, pps.497-754; KA is Killed in Action; WA is wounded in Action, DW is died of wounds: Paul L. Abel, Ensign, *U.S.S. Castine;* Carl A. Albert, Corp., General Hospital 31; Charles J. Basset, 1st. Lieut., Engineering Staff, Ordinance Dept.; Edward Bauer, Pvt., Co.C., 302 Engineers; Frank Bauer, Pvt. Co.F., 303 Engineers; John Bauer, Pvt., Co.F., First Army Replacement Depot, Frank Bauer, Pvt. Co.E., 61st Infantry WA; Norbert M. Berberich, 310 U.S.G.F.; John P. Brach, 2nd Class Seaman, Naval Rifle Range, Annapolis; Louis A. Buchheit, Pvt., 307th Infantry, WA, June 28, 1918; Herbert Chandler, Edward G. Dearing, Corp., Co.D., 302 Engineers; James Deckop, Landsman for electrician, N.R.F.; Anthony Didley, Sgt., Headquarters 311th Infantry, KA, October 25, 1918 at Grand Pre; Eugene G. Didley, Seaman Inst., U.S. Navy, Newport, R.I.; Joseph M. Didley, Chief Petty Officer, Naval Aviation; Karl J. Dietsche, Frank Dietzel, Corp., Co.C., 302 Engineers; George Domedian, Cook Replacement, 2nd Provisional Regiment; Frank J. Drexelius, Landsman for Electrician, N.R.F.; Joseph E. Drexelius, Pvt., 68th Infantry; Gregory J. Ducro, Pvt., Headquarters Co., Air Service, 1st. Pursuit Group; Frank Eager, *U.S.S. Lake Wimico*; Albert H. Ecker, Pvt., Co.E., 362nd Infantry; Richard Eger, Pvt., Co.B., 306th Infantry, WA, August 17, 1918; Herbert C. Faust, Aviation Corps.; Charles J. Fell, Pvt., Headquarters, 311th Infantry; Rev. Walter F. Fornes, Catholic Chaplain, Camp Wadsworth S.C., and 106th Field Artillery A.E.F.; Edward C. Gangloff, Corp. Battery A., 7th Artillery; Paul A. Grupp, Radio Operator, *U.S.S. Canonicus*; Albert Hardick, Pvt., Co.E., R.U. 321st Motor Transport Corps; John Hatten, Pvt., 27th A.S.A.; George Howard Hess, Corp., Battery C., Tractor Artillery, 1st. Army; Edward F. Hoffman, Sgt., 287th Aero Squadron; Amil Huber, Corp., Co.G., 348th Infantry; Karl A. Kiefer,

Pvt., 3rd Provisional Regiment; Edwin H. Kolb, Engineers, Edgewood Arsenal; Charles J. Lazarus, Sgt., 5th Division, 9thBrigade, 14th Machine Gun Battalion; Raymond Lux, Corp., Co.M., 326th Infantry; Cyrus J. Marshall, Sgt., Co.J., 309th Infantry; Frank McGavis, Corp., Sanitary Squad No.44, 27th Division; Frank Hugo Merz, Cornelius F. Miller, Sgt., C., U.S. Guard; Albert Mockers, 1st. Class Pvt., 626th Aero Squadron; Paul J. Muth, Pvt., Co.E., 307th M.T.C.; Walter J. Rick, Regimental Sergeant Major, Headquarters; Frank J. Ross, Pvt., Co.C., 318th Engineers; George N. Sasgen, William J. Schifferle, Pvt., Co.A., 18th Infantry; Harold P. Schwartz, 2nd Class Seaman, N.R.F.; Clayton James Souter, Sgt. Intelligence Dept., 108th Infantry, DW, August 27, 1918, Mandalay Cross, Belgium; Alphonse J. Steinwachs, Pvt., S.A.T.C.; Matthew X. Wagner, Pvt., F.A.R.T.; Hadley Philip Warner, Radio Operator, *U.S.S. Lake Catherine*; Edgar W. Weigel, Corp., S.A.T.C.; Dr. Elmer P. Weigel, 1st. Lieut., Medical Corps; Edmond J. Welker, Pvt., Co.K., 347th Infantry Corps; Alexander Wendling, Oiler, N.R.F.; and Charles J. Zimmerman, Chemical Warfare Service. Details of the movements of the 77th and 78th Divisions, in which several of these above served, can be found Ibid, in the chapter "Buffalo Draft Men of the 78th Division in France," pps. 179-91; Details of the battle for St. Mihiel see: Ibid, pps. 223-35; Details of the 77th and 78th Divisions entering the Argonne Campaign see: Ibid, pps.238-51; For a review of the activities of the 106th Artillery at the Meuse River see: Ibid, pps. 253-4; For breaking the Hindenburg line see: Ibid, 255-65; for the occasion of the death of Anthony Didley and the battle of Grand-Pre see: Ibid, pps. 274-82; For details of the type of airborne operations which were conducted by Gregory J. Ducro, Edward F. Hoffman, and Albert Mockers, see: Ibid, pps. 309-13. Cornelius F. Miller was a Sergeant in the U. S. Guard. In Europe, the Guard became part of the 27th Division. The National Guard Regiments were hurried overseas following the declaration of war on April 6, 1917. The 27th division carried the old 74th, some of them in the 108th Infantry, some in the 55th Pioneers, some in the 102nd Engineers and Ammunition Train; the old 65th Regiment became the 106th Field Artillery, and Troop I became the 102nd Trench Mortar Battery. In Buffalo, the 74th Regiment had occupied the armory located opposite Prospect Park at Niagara and Connecticut Streets, the 65th Regiment had occupied the armory at Masten and Best Streets, while Troop I had occupied the armory on Delavan Avenue opposite Forest Lawn Cemetery. (It recently was torn down and replaced by dormitories for Canisius College). Troop I still has its meetings at the Hamlin House on Franklin Street near Virginia Street. The mustard gas used by the Germans was dichloraethyl sulphide, a most effective battle gas. It was first used by them during an attack on Ypres— today found on the maps as Leper—in June 1917. Although the British called it mustard gas, the French named it Yperite gas. The Allied gas casualties in July 1917 were almost as numerous as all casualties during the previous years of the war since 1914. This gas was first used by the American army in September 1918 in its attack on the Hindenburg line. The French employed it three months earlier. The gas had a very light smell with no immediate sensations or

The Knights of St. John Commandery 204 at St. Louis Church. *Top*: In the 35th year of their existence, the Knights of Commandery 204 are left to right: 1st row: A. Eger, L. Buchheit, F. Ross, C. Meyer, J. Lux, E.W. Miller Sr., C. Schifferle Sr. 2nd row: F. Ball, C. Buchheit, M. Peltier, F. Lambrix, Rev. E. Dietzel, Rev. M. Anstett, A.J. Schneggenburger, C. Schifferle Jr., C. Koch. 3rd row: L. Wagner, R. Nebrich, I. Sullivan, H. Trapp, R. Ball, F. Bauer, J. Widmer, C. Ecker. 4th row: A. Liegl, P. Hardick, E. Bauer, J. Ogden, G. Buchheit, E.W. Miller Jr., F. Summers. 5th row: J. Walsh. *Bottom*: September 1938; returning from Philadelphia after the drill team won 2nd place prize.

discomfort. Exposure, however, even in low concentrations put a man out of action by effecting his eyes and lungs. Severe blisters were eventually produced on the exposed skin and in areas of the torso underneath thin clothing. Phosgene is a colorless gas, unpleasant odor, and a severe respiratory irritant. Erich von Ludendorff was born at Kruszevnia, near Posen, Prussia, in 1865. In 1914 he achieved the rank of major general. He moved his troops into France as far as the Somme River at which time he was sent to East-Prussia as chief of staff under Hindenburg. The failure of the German leadership at the battle of Verdun in 1916 brought Ludendorff back to the Western Front. Thenceforth until the German collapse he was the outstanding military power in Germany. After the war he fled to Sweden but returned to oppose the newly-formed German Republic. Henri Petain was born in 1856. At the outbreak of the war he was a retired colonel. He distinguished himself at the first battle of the Marne and achieved the rank of general. His arrival at Verdun during the German attack of 1916, turned the tide at Douaumont; he was then promoted to the command of the central sector. From May 1917 to April 1918, he was commander-in-chief of the French armies on the Western Front. In December 1918 he was made Marshal of the French Army. He was replaced by General Ferdinand Foch, born at Tarbes in 1851, who assumed the roll of commander-in-chief of all Allied Forces at the close of the War. In 1914, Douglas Haig, born 1861, was the commanding officer at Aldershot, England, a permanent camp for training British troops, thirty-five miles southwest of London. He was commissioned to cross over to France and take command of the First Army. He was commander-in-chief of British Expeditionary Forces from 1915 to 1919. He died on January 30, 1928. Encyclopedic information for these paragraphs was taken from op. cit. *The Modern Encyclopedia*, from op. cit. *World's Popular Encyclopedia*, and from op. cit. *Illustrated World Encyclopedia*. Although the entire German defense system in France had been known as the *Hindenburg Line*, the portion between Cambrai and St. Quentin was considered the line proper. It was built by the Germans in the winter of 1916-1917 using French and Belgium civilians. It consisted of the most formidable system of trenches; the best of which military ingenuity could contrive. In front of it extending between six and eight miles, the land was a desert, void of buildings, trees, and water. This was *No Man's Land*! For the general defense system which extended down through Renthal, Grand-Pre, to the outskirts of Verdun there were systems of deep trenches protected by barb-wire entanglements, and detatched cement forts for machine guns. In the rear was heavy artillery. Some stretches of the line were more hazardous than others. One of the most difficult stretches was the *Kriemhilde Line* at Grand-Pre; it was so named after the heroine of Nibelungenlied and wife of Siegfried. It was at this line that Anthony Didley, parishioner of St. Louis Church, lost his life. The following is the list of those who served in the Army or the Navy and had graduated from St. Louis' school according to the existing school record in the St. Louis Church Archives. After each of their names, their year of graduation is given. Although all were taught by the Sisters of St. Joseph in their younger grades, these listed were also

taught by the Brothers of the Christian Schools F.S.C., for two extra years prior to graduation. Abel, Paul L., 1909; Albert, Carl, 1906; Bassett, Charles J., 1914; Bauer Edward, 1912; Bauer, John J., 1914; Berberich, Norbert, 1911; Buchheit, Louis, 1905; Didley, Anthony, 1904; Didley, Eugene, 1909; Didley, Joseph M., 1907; Drexelius, Frank J., 1908; Drexelius, Joseph E., 1910; Hardick, Albert J., 1912; Huber, Emil A., 1904; Kiefer, Carl A., 1909; Miller Cornelius F., 1909; Muth, Paul J., 1910; Rick, Walter, 1909; Wagner, Matthew X., 1913; Weigel, Edgar, 1914; Weigel, Elmer P., 1906; Although Carl A. Albert had achieved the rank of corporal and was in residence at General Hospital No. 31, he was never assigned to overseas duty. When it was found that he had knowledge and expertize in mathematics and medicine, he was transferred to the War College at Carlisle, Pennsylvania, where he taught soldiers who were going and coming from the front. He had a specialty in teaching those who had been shell-shocked in battle.

2. For the effect of World War I on the German population of Buffalo see: op. cit. *High Hopes*, pps.196-201; For the decrease in students at St. Louis' school taking German language classes see: *School Book Records of Graduates, 1893-1959*, in the St. Louis Church Archives. For a description of the celebration of the jubilee day following the Franco-Prussian War in 1871 see: op. cit. *History of Germans of Buffalo and Erie County*, pps. 180-84; Information concerning the formation of the German Empire 1870-1871 see: op. cit. *Wiorld's Popular Encyclopedia*. In 1701 the Prussian Kingdom was created. A member of the Hohenzollern family, as elector of Brandenburg, Frederick III reigned in that kingdom. He became Frederick I, King of Prussia, in 1701. His son, Frederick William I succeeded him in 1713 and ruled until 1786. He was followed by his son Frederick William II who succeeded to the throne in 1786 and ruled to 1797. He was succeeded by his son who became Frederick William III who reigned between 1797 and 1840. In 1793 Frederick William III married Louise Mecklenburg-Strelitz. They had two sons: Frederick William IV ruling from 1840 to 1861, and William I who ruled from 1861 to 1888. In 1871, however, following the Franco-Prussian War, William I became also the First Emperor of Germany, in which the thirty nine separate German States had been unified under the leadership of Otto Eduard Leopold Bismarck, who during the reign of William I became chancellor of the empire. Frederick William IV had married Elizabeth of Bavaria in 1823 and together they had Frederick III in 1831. In 1858, He married Princess Victoria, daughter of Queen Victoria of Britain and Albert, Duke of Saxe-Coburg. Frederick III and Princess Victoria had a son, William II. Frederick III succeeded to the throne in 1888 but only remained there three months. He died of a mortal disease which had bothered him for some time. He was succeeded, however, by his son William II who was 29 years of age. In 1890, William II demanded that Bismarck resign as chancellor, and he declared himself as the Caesar, the Kaiser, of the German Empire; ever afterwards he was known as Kaiser Wilhelm. He saw Germany through World War I, abdicated on November 28, 1918, went to Holland, and died there in 1941. In 1834 the Zollverein

had been created; it was a Custom Union headed by Prussia. In 1866, Austria the power competitor of Prussia was defeated by Prussian armies at Sandowa which ended the War of Spoliation. Prussia became the prominent and dominant power in Europe. In 1870, Bismarck, chancellor of Prussia, formed the North German Confederation; France was defeated in the Franco-Prussian War. Alsace and Lorraine became part of Germany. The other states of South Germany united with Prussia and the North German Confederation. In 1871 Wilhelm I who had been King of Prussia, now became Emperor of Germany. Bismarck remained as chancellor and ran a policy which was anti-democratic. He aimed at checking the power of France, pacifying Russia, and confirming an alliance between Germany, Austria, and Italy. His *Falk Laws* were directed mercilessly against Catholics; it was his *Kulturkampf*. Wilhelm II came to power in 1888 and pressured Bismarck to resign as chancellor. William II was a staunch believer in the Divine Right of Kings; war became the religion of Germany; over seven hundred books dealing with warfare were published in the Fatherland during the three years preceding World War I. On November 28, 1918, the Kaiser abdicated, and by December 6, 1918 the Allies had occupied Cologne, Coblenz, and Mainz along the Rhein River. A new armistice was signed on Jamuary 17, 1919. In that month Hindenburg resigned as the head of the army. In January 1923 France took complete possession of the Ruhr Valley because Germany did not pay its reparations. In 1925 President Ebert of the German Republic, which had been formed after the war, died. Paul von Hindenburg was elected president. In 1926 the Ruhr valley was evacuated.

3. From op. cit. *World's Popular Encyclopedia*, one finds that the Holy Grail is a miraculous vessel, which formed the subject of many medieval romances. In most versions of the legend, it was a cup sent by heaven, and used by Christ at the Last Supper, afterwards coming into the possession of Joseph of Arimathea, who collected the last drops of the Lord's blood in it. Upon the death of Joseph, the grail was taken to heaven and kept there until a hero worthy of it should appear on earth. The search for the Holy Grail enters into the legend of King Arthur and the Knights of the Round Table, many of whom, including Galahad, Perceval, and Gawain, set out in quest of it. In the text, the spellings of these names are as they appear in the German or the Old English literature. It is also the subject of Wagner's opera *Parsifal*. The source material for the discussion of the History of the Knights of St. John was provided by Donald Killian, 124 Wiltshire Road, Williamsville, New York, and Robert Ruszala, 44 Nadine Drive, Cheetowaga, New York. Both are members of Commandery 204 at St. Barnabas Church, 2049 George Urban Blvd., Depew, New York. In the archives of Commandery 204 is a copy of the brochure published at the time of the dedication of the Monument to the Knights of St. John in the United German and French Roman Catholic Cemetery in 1914. It is titled, *Monument Dedication, Knights of St. John*, Second Regiment, State of New York, Buffalo, New York, May 31, 1914, pps. 1-200. From this journal was taken extracts concerning commandery chaplains and military officers, commandery units

and the churches to which they were affiliated, early history of the Knights in New York State and other cities of the United States, and the aims and objectives of the Knights of St. John. Further, Monsignor Hoelscher was aware of the existence of Knights in Buffalo prior to 1913. He was founder and pastor of St. Agnes Church, Buffalo, in 1883; it formed a commandery of Knights in 1904. The meeting called by Hoelscher in 1913 included the following officers and chaplains. Frank X. Schwab and Father Peter W. Leonard S.J., St. Ann's Church, Commandery 13; Leo P. Frohe and Father Francis T. Parr, C.S.S.R., St. Mary's Church, Commandery 14; John L. Schwartz and Father B.J. Cohausz S.J., St. Michael's Church, Commandery 15; Richard W. Codd and Father Thomas H. Barrett, St. Stephen's Church, Commandery 16; Frank F. Kreppel and Father Ferdinand Kolb, St. Boniface Church, Commandery 22; Peter Pirrung and Father William M. Bernet, Sacred Heart Church, Commandery 23; Frank Barth and Father Charles Schaus, St. Francis Xavier Church, Commandery 47; Theodor Schilling and Father George Weber, St. Mary's of Sorrows Church, Commandery 292; George Schreckenberger and Father J.C. Bubenheim, St. Mary Magdelene's Church, Commandery 99; Peter Paulus and Father Joseph Fischer, St. Agnes Church, Commandery 135; Louis R. Cramer and Father John F. Pfluger, Blessed Trinity Church, Commandery 150; and Stephen Greil and Father William Schreck, St. Gerard's Church, Commandery 192. From 1913 to 1933, the number of commanderies in Buffalo increased from thirteen with two battalions to nineteen with three battalions. At present the Knights of St. John is an international organization. The Supreme Commandery is global. The Grand Commanderies are in the United States and Africa. A Grand Commandery was just begun in 2000 in England. The Buffalo Grand Commandery, the Second Regiment once had three battalions, but now it has only two. The Constitution of the Knights of St. John was first promulgated in New York State in 1886; it was revised in 1896; an international constitution was proposed on October 15, 1992, coded at Buffalo, New York in July 1996, and revised and adopted at Fort Mitchell, Kentucky, in 1998. Specific information concerning Commandery 204 at St. Louis Church was obtained from the following anniversary journals: *Twenty-eighth Anniversary, St. Louis Commandery 204, Knights of St. John*, Knights of Columbus Ballroom, Buffalo, New York, October 28, 1941; "Golden Memories of Silver Years," *Silver Jubilee Commemorating 25th Anniversary, St. Louis Commandery, Knights of St. John*, Buffalo Trap and Field Club, Buffalo, New York, September 25, 1938; *Drill and Ball*, St. Louis' Commandery No. 204, Second Regiment, Knights of St. John, Elmwood Music Hall, Buffalo, New York, October 26, 1937; *Twentieth Anniversary, Souvenir Program, St. Louis' Commandery, No. 204, Knights of St. John*, Elmwood Music Hall, Buffalo, New York, 1933; *St Louis' Commandery No. 204, Fifteenth Anniversary Souvenir*, Elmwood Music Hall, Buffalo, New York, 1928; *St. Louis' Commandery No 204*, Elmwood Music Hall, Buffalo, New York, October 27, 1925; *St. Louis Commandery No. 204*, Elmwood Music Hall, Buffalo, New York, October 28, 1924; The caption, "Golden Memories of Silver

Years" for the 25th anniversary was the design of Irving L. Sullivan, Sir Knight, of Commandery 204. When Sullivan was in his early twenties he told his mother that he was going to join the priesthood. She immediately went out and purchased him a cassock and surplice. The next day he was traveling on the streetcar going down Main Street. At one of the stops he saw a girl standing; her name was Ivy. He fell madly in love-at-first-sight. He forgot the seminary idea and vowed to marry his girl. His mother was so angry that she burned his cassock and surplice in front of his eyes. Another display of impulsiveness on his part occurred late in his life. In 1962, his wife, Ivy, died; Irving was alone. One night he went to Connie and Murph Battaglia's home on Norwood Avenue for dinner. He not only stayed that evening, but he never went home for three years; he died there on December 2, 1965 and was buried with all honors as a Knight of St. John at St. Louis Church. Monsignor Nelson H. Baker was born in Buffalo February 16, 1842, graduated from Old Central High School in 1859, joined the 74th New York Regiment during the Civil War, ordained at St. Joseph's Cathedral in 1876, was assistant pastor at St. Patrick's Church, Lackawanna, and became its pastor in 1882; he administered at St. John's Protectory and St. Joseph's Orphan Asylum; struck a reservoir of natural gas on August 22, 1891 in Lackawanna, was appointed vicar general in 1903, began construction of the Basilica of Our Lady of Victory in 1921, built a hospital and high school adjacent to it; he died July 29, 1836; he is now being considered for canonization by the Roman Catholic Church. On May 31, 1937, the Knights of St. John participated in Memorial Day Ceremonies at the United German and French Roman Catholic Cemetery at which Bishop John Aloysius Duffy delivered the sermon. The choir of St. Louis Church sang the responses at Mass. Regimental Quartermaster Captain Charles B. Schreck was in charge of decorating the graves assisted by Sergeant Louis Buchheit and Sergeant Lawrence Wagner of Commandery 204. The entire ceremony was broadcast by radio station WBNY; Monsignor Henry Laudenbach, pastor of St. Louis Church was the commentator. The 25th anniversary of Commandery 204 was held at the Trap and Field Club located on Cayuga Road in Cheektowaga, New York; when it was demolished it was replaced by the Sierra Aeronautical Company. Copies of these anniversary journals are in the St. Louis Church Archives. For a pictorial description of the dedication of St. Louis Church see: *Buffalo News*, September 14, 1913; a copy is in the archives of St. Louis Church. The Knights of St. John who appear in these pictures are not those of commandery 204; it was not formed until Sept. 22, 1913; It made its first appearance later that year and early Spring 1914 as described in the text. Further information concerning individual Knights was obtained from Marie Buchheit Miller, wife of C. Eugene Miller, author/editor; Louis Buchheit, son of Knight, Louis A. Buchheit; Allen Joseph Schneggenburger and his wife, formerly, Dorothy Ball; and from C. Eugene Miller, aka Carl Anthony Miller, author/editor, and son of Captain Eugene W. Miller Sr. The following information is given to indicate the type of business in which some of the Knights were engaged. Using the advertising which is found in the various anniversary

journals referred to above one finds the following information concerning some individual Knights in the text. Fred L. Zwirlein was a merchant tailor doing cleaning and repairing, located at 2213 Seneca Street; John Bauer and Sons were General Wall and Floor contractors, located at 286-88 High Street; The Trapp Family owned a restaurant at 1237 Michigan Street, served lunches, fish fry, steak dinners; G. Trapp and H. Gates later opened a restaurant at 1266 Jefferson Avenue, and had a room set aside for ladies to have card parties and teas; Jacob Gebhard ran a general Carting and Moving Company located at 128 Maple Street; Frank E. Summers ran a tourist home at 440 Franklin Street; Clarence Meyer was the son of Joseph Meyer who did furnace work and sold hardware at 567 Genesee Street; Joseph Lux was the son of Joseph Lux Sr., who ran a funeral home at 124 Goodell Street. When the father died his wife assumed responsibility for the home but put her two sons, Joseph and Raymond in charge. Fred Hardick became a major of the Second Regiment by 1937; In 1937, Eugene W. Miller Sr., Clarence Meyer, and Frank Ross were in charge of the Military committee for the Drill, Ball, and Concert held at the Elmwood Music Hall; The type of dancing in which the attendees participated was the Waltz, the Fox Trot, and the Charleston; In 1928 Cornelius F. Miller was the president of Commandery 204 and his brother Eugene W. Miller Sr. was first vice president; At that time Cornelius F. Miller was First Lieutenant and 3rd Battalion Adjutant. John L. Schwartz, Colonel of the Second Regiment, was a member of Commandery 204; J. F. Lambrix was in the Coal and Ice Carting Business located at 167 Mulberry Street; The Ross family ran a cafe and restaurant at 942 Michigan Street; In 1928, Eugene W. Miller Sr. became a partner with Anthony Zimmermann whose wagon and automobile body shop was at 136-38 Northampton Street. Miller was able to secure ads that year and subsequent years from Anthony Zimmermann and from George J. Herlan, Plumbing and Heating, at 128-32 Northampton Street; George Buchheit with John Kunz ran a wood turning business at Kunz's home at 670 Elm Street. They specialized in turning out wooden lamps of all sizes and railings for staircases. The following notes obtained from the archives of the Knights of St. John illustrate some of the aura of spiritual symbolism of the organization. The patron saint of the Knights of St. John is Saint John the Baptist. The prayer recited daily by the members and given the imprimatur of Walter A. Foery, D.D., Bishop of Syracuse is: "In thy strength , O Lord, the just man shall exalt, and in thy salvation he shall rejoice exceedingly. Thou hast given him his heart's desire. We beseech Thee, O Lord, that every thought, word, and action which we offer in memory of the sufferings of Thy Holy Martyr, St. John the Baptist, may by his intercession profit us unto salvation, through Our Lord Jesus Christ, Thy Son, who lives and reigns with thee in the unity of the Holy Spirit, God, world without end. Amen." In recognition of the Knights, Pope Pius XI, as a reward for services to the church by the Knights of St. John, has granted an indulgence to every Sir Knight and Officer, every time they donned their uniforms, every time they put on their caps or chapeaus for the purpose of discharging their duties with becoming religious spirit, or when taking part in any liturgical ceremony. Each Knight recites the following: When donning the uniform he says, "May the Lord clothe me a new man, who is created in justice and truth." Every time he enters into liturgical service he says, "Place, O Lord, on my head the helmet of salvation, that I may overcome the assaults of Satan." Each prayer carries a 300 days indulgence. The uniform of the Knight has the following symbolism: *Plume*, merciful judgment; *Chapeau*, ruling wisely, firmly, but fairly; *Belt*, self control in anger and the avoidance of sin; *Coat*, the armor worn by knights-of-old on the battlefield; *Epaulets*, weight of responsibility which rests on the knight's shoulders; *Buttons*, the fourteen stations of the cross; *Sword*, faith, hope, and charity. The ribbon, gold and white, represents the papal colors and the Knight's uniform patch, the emblem, is a modified Maltese Cross with a central circle containing the plumed helmet of a knight with the surrounding words, "Knights—St. John." Two swords crisscross through the circle. Each of the eight points of the Maltese Cross represents one of the Beatitudes: Poor in Spirit, Meekness, Sorrowfulness Over Sin, Justice, Mercifulness, Clean of Heart, Peaceable, and Suffering for Christ's sake. The following is a commemorative contribution from the author/editor of this book, "When my father, Eugene W. Miller Sr., died in December 1964, I was an engineering professor at Manhattan College. I was in class teaching when word came to me of his demise. Immediately I arranged to fly to Buffalo and be with my family at the wake and funeral. The Knights of St. John, Commandery 204, stood guard over my father's bier. In the evening before his burial, while the family was gathered, a large contingent of the commandery came into Joseph Lux's funeral home on Main Street, where my father's wake took place. Richard Ball was the president of the commandery, and he assumed the task of giving an address. I will never forget that occasion and how we all were emotionally touched by what Ball said, 'Brothers: Christ has promised us that everyone who believes in Him has Eternal Life. Christ says to us that it is His Father's will that whoever sees the Son and believes in Him shall have Eternal Life, and that the Father shall raise him up on the last day. We are here this evening to rejoice with one of our brothers among our fellowship who has believed and has life. Christ has called us into his Church, our Catholic Church. What we believe is the faith of that Church, that faith which goes back not only to the Apostles but even to the Risen Lord Himself. The life and death of each of us has its influence on others; if we live we live for the Lord; and if we die, we die for the Lord. In death, life is not taken away but merely changed. Our Brother, Eugene W. Miller Sr., testified through his life of service that he believed that God would not abandon his soul nor allow it to experience corruption. For while his body rests in the hope of its resurrection, his soul will be filled with the gladness of God's presence. Let us all be joyful in the fulfillment of the promises of Christ to our Brother, Eugene W. Miller Sr., and ask God to reveal that path of life to us all, which, in the end, will give us unbounded joy and everlasting pleasures.' In most awesome silent procession the Knights came, prayed, heard Richard Ball's address, and retired, leaving those in the room with an aura of most profound solemnity. For this my mother, my

brothers, and I were and always will be humbly grateful."

4. The St. Louis Church Archives has a letter sent from the church rectory at 35 Edward Street by Reverend Henry B. Laudenbach to Frank Ross dated January 18, 1918. Rev. Henry B. Laudenbach L.L.D., *Little Stories of Buffalo's Bishops*, Catholic Pamphlet Society, Buffalo, New York, 1939, pps.3-31; this booklet contains the history of Bishops John Timon, Stephen Vincent Ryan, James E. Quigley, Charles H. Colton, Dennis Dougherty, and William Turner spanning the years between 1847 and 1936. The book is prefaced by a letter of congratulation sent to Laudenbach on March 14, 1939, from John A. Duffy, the bishop of Buffalo at that time. In the text Laudenbach makes references to Fathers Sorg and Hoelscher in regards to St. Louis church. He also points out that the wall crosses in St. Louis Church were placed there as part of the rite of consecration of the church. Laudenbach explains that when Quigley was chosen as bishop in 1897 it was the first time in the history of the Catholic Church in America that a new bishop was chosen by a semi-democratic method of election by certain priests of the diocese. Before the Pope made his decision as to who would be bishop, they assembled in the diocese and made a list of three names, called the *Terna*, which they sent to Rome. According to the law of the Catholic Church initiated in 1866, the names were graded as Worthy, More Worthy, and Most Worthy. Paul Hoelscher's name was on the list three times. The ultimate choice, however, rested with the Apostolic Delegate and the Congregation of Cardinals intrusted with the choice of bishops. This system was later abandoned. Laudenbach makes it clear that the church is not by nature democratic, but autocratic. The new system had begun about 1915 when Pope Benedict XV gave the method a trial run. In every province of the Catholic Church the bishops have a biennial meeting under the supervision of the Archbishop. At the meeting candidates for a new bishop are presented, balloted upon, and sent to Rome. Again, the final decision rests in the Vatican. The method was first used in the Diocese of Buffalo in 1916 with the election of Dennis Dougherty. For the biographical material used in the text see: "St. Louis Church Mourns Death of Monsignor Laudenbach," *Buffalo Evening News*, December 29, 1943 and op. cit. *Little Stories of Buffalo's Bishops*. For the Rite used by Bishop Ryan in the administration of the Sacrament of Confirmation see: op. cit., *L'Arge Catechism*,pps. 92-4 and op. cit. *The Beauties of the Catholic Church*, pps. 303-09. For the story concerning Laudenbach's Sacerdotal Jubilee see: *The Echo*, Thursday, April 17, 1924. For Laudenbach's trip to Europe and his Welcoming Home Party see: *St. Louis Commandery No. 204*, Elmwood Music Hall, Tuesday October 28, 1924, and various "Travel Letters" by Laudenbach published in *The Echo* while he was in Europe. These were: May 29, 1924 (the Mediterranean), June 5, 1924 (Italy at First Glance), June 12, 1924 (Rome), June 19, 1924 (Churches of Rome), June 26, 1924 (Jungfrau in Bernice Oberland, Switzerland), July 3, 1924 (Geneva, Home of the League of Nations), July 10, 1924 (Southern Germany), July 17, 1924 (Germany Under Stress), July 24, 1924 (German Republic), July 31, 1924 (Germany Disarmed), August

7, 1924 (German politics), August 14, 1924 (Visits Rothenburg, Munich, Bamberg), August 28, 1924 (Palatinate), September 24, 1924 (Innsbruck, Austria), October 2, 1924 (Thuringia, Germany), October 9, 1924 (London), October 16, 1924 (Ireland), and October 23, 1924 (Coming Home, Travel Survey). The following is a summary of his impressions of the situation in Europe, especially Germany, six years after the World War I. "The German people are thoroughly discouraged; war had wiped out living conditions, but they have *Galgenhumor,* a grim humor of the condemned criminal; political situation is a hopeless muddle. There are monarchists, men who demand war, majority accepts the *status quo* of the Republic, Party arises upon Party until one does not know where one belongs; Catholic Party has lost importance, Socialists are split, and the old Tory Parties have been changed; everywhere is felt the threat of the *Entente*, the treaty of Versailles which was a crime; France wants Germany to be divided into small parts so there will be no threat to her, France controls the Ruhr and Saar Valleys, Germany is void of the possibility of getting her industry going, Germany must constantly keep paying France a high indemnity, Germany has no money in the banks and loans are set at annual interest rate of 40%, middle and working class German people are reduced to beggary, and all savings in banks, all mortgages, all insurance, all railroad securities are gone with no compensation and with no hope of validation; all this adds up to confusion in Germany. The people of Germany have the least animosity toward USA and praise Woodrow Wilson's fourteen points and his generosity toward the suffering people of Europe." The expression *Entente* used by Laudenbach means the *Triple Entente* or agreements of mutual protection established between France, England and Russia prior to the beginning of World War I. Laudenbach uses it as a term in speaking of the secret collusion which took place unilaterally, bilaterally, or trilaterally between these three nations after the World War I. Then Laudenbach gave voice to his apocalyptic observation, "The future war in Europe is not far off! Italy and France are not on good terms. England has disappointed Italy by refusing her the political command of the Mediterranean. France is too strong in every way and too arrogant for British tastes. Given this condition, plus the hopelessly divided and ambitious *Entente* in the East, the Balkan States and their everlasting quarrels: What has the *War to End all Wars* accomplished for genuine peace? Nothing at all! It is only financial exhaustion that keeps this pack from one another's throats." These thoughts were omens of the future: Adolph Hitler's armies invaded Poland on September 1, 1939 and World War II was on! (note by the author/editor.) For Laudenbach's speech concerning the Pearl Street Extension controversy and the preparations for the Centennial Celebration see: Sir Knight Eugene W. Miller Sr., " Some Parish News From the Pastor's Study," *St. Louis Commandery No. 204, Fifteenth Anniversary Souvenir 1913-1928*, Elks Club, Buffalo, New York, October 23, 1928. Map and articles concerning the Pearl Street Extension see: *Courier Express*, Buffalo, New York, May 1, 1928 and December, 18, 1928. These newspaper clippings are in the archives of St. Louis Church. For the sources used in developing the paragraphs on the Centennial Celebration see: op. cit. *St. Louis Church Centennial Celebration;* The Centenary Banquet Committee, *Centenary Banquet, St. Louis Church*, contains menu, and evening's events; "Partition of St. Louis Church Site Recalls Vivid History," *Buffalo Evening News*, Tuesday, April 9, 1929; "St. Louis Church Soon to Celebrate 100th Anniversary, *Buffalo Sunday Times*, Buffalo, New York, April 14, 1929; "Requiem Mass At St. Louis,"*Scripps-Howard Alliance*, Buffalo, New York, May 27, 1929; "Centennial Opens In St. Louis Church," *Buffalo Evening News*, Buffalo, New York, Monday, May 27, 1929, "St. Louis Church to Observe 100th Anniversary," *The Echo*, May 23, 1929; "St. Louis Observes Hundredth Anniversary," *The Echo*, Thursday, May 30, 1929. Those who participated in the Golden Jubilee of their first Holy Communion in 1924 were: Mrs. Joseph Sattler, Mrs. Mary Schoenle, Edward M. Roth, Mrs. Julia Ambs, Mrs. L. Huth, Conrad Denler, Mrs Emma Ochs, Mrs. A.G. Diebolt, Mrs. George Goethoffer, Mrs. Fred Potts, Mrs. Charles A. Miller, Frank J. Beck, Frank Bensler, John Zuber, Mrs. Emma Huber, John H. Strub, Fred Hoehn, Frank Brechtel, Nicholas Rothballer, Charles A. Weppner, Frank A. Weppner, Fred Jehle, John Mader, Louise Bitterman, Anna Hazenfratz, Martin Nicklas, Michael Paufler, Wendelin Gloen, Mrs. John Geiger, Mrs. C. Gollwitzer, Mrs. G. Cook, Mrs. M. Nebrich, Mrs. C. Bruicknern, Mrs. Valentine Specht, Mrs. C. Wittman, Mrs. Frank A. Kolb, Delia Dodds, Louis Deiter, Mrs. J.G. Lang, Mrs. Anna Bauml, Jacob Schoemann, and Mrs. J. Zimmerman. See newsclipping titled *First Communion Fifty Years Ago*, St. Louis Church Archives. op. cit. *The St. Louis Church Centennial Celebration* listed the names of all prelates, and priests who were either permanent, or temporary at St. Louis Church as assistant pastors, guests, or curates from 1843 to 1929. They are: (1843) P.B. Boyer, M. Arlig C. SS. R.: (1847) Bishop Timon; (1849) T. N. Arent, P.J. Kruze, Jos. Raffeiner; (1855) F.X. Wenninger, S.J., T. Kleinbucher, Dr. Arnold, Bernard Fritsch S.J.; (1858) Henry Feldman; (1861) J. Bletner S.J., P. Poutsch, Jos. Vetter; (1862) Dr. Gerber, Joseph Albinger; (1869) F.A. Keck, A.L. Neumayer, Peter J. Schmitt; (1871) Vincent Scheffels; (1872) Innocent Sager; (1873) Chas. J. Geppert, Anthony Adolph; (1875) James Schneider; (1876) Dr. A. Kister; (1877) Martin Philipps; (1880) Andrew Frey; (1881) Henry Plebs; (1884) Wm. Riszewski, G. Frederick S.J., Geo. J. Weber, Clemens Niemann; (1885) Theodore Hauser S.J., Albert M. Kork; (1888) F.J. Trautlein, N. Jasper; (1889) James C. Bubenheim; (1890) Chas. N. Schillo; (1891) Martin Philipps; (1892) John V. Schaus, James Franz; (1894) Henry Fuchs; (1897) Dr. August Mueller; (1899) Henry B. Laudenbach; (1901) August Ruffing, Cornelius C. Fischer; (1903) M. J. Weber; (1904) Henry Berg; (1906) E. M. Deck, Joseph L. Stephan; (1908) Walter Fornes; (1909) Michael Anstett; (1911) Albert G. Rung; (1916) A.J. Hoffmeyer; (1917) F. Trompeter; (1918) D. O'C. McAlister; (1919) J.D. Linehan; (1923) William Burchardt, Chas. Schreckenberber; (1924) Chas. Lukasik; (1926) Dr. L. Cornelissen, Ph. Hildebrand; (1927) J. A. Hippchen; (1928) J. A. Kennedy; (1929) T, J. Lynch.

CHAPTER FOURTEEN

Financial Disaster, Depression, World War II

Following the Jubilee Year banquet, members of the Steffan, Buchheit, and Fornes families discussed, with each other and their neighbors on Pearl Place, the optimism generated by Mayor Schwab's talk concerning the halting of litigation in regards to the Pearl Street extension project. If the project went through as planned, Pearl Place was to be widened to sixty-nine feet from curb to curb. Each of their properties would have been condemned and a price paid to them for their inconvenience as determined by the city. In 1929, the price which was on the table for reimbursement of condemned properties between Tupper and Virginia Streets was over a half million dollars. Some of the trustees of St. Louis Church, who were also leaving the banquet, joined in with these conversations. None, however, had any idea how long it would take before all the litigation proceedings would be finished, and the debates among the members of the City's Common Council and Finance Committee would result in finding a way to finance such a large sum of money. These families and the trustees had every reason to be concerned because the wrangling went on for three more years. On May 10, 1932 the project was finally doomed when the Common Council adopted a resolution to consider dropping the case. It was not, however, until December 14, 1932 that the last litigation took place and all parties, the City, as plaintiff, and a very long list of defendants, were satisfied. By this time the United States was deep into the Depression; the City was unable to finance any public works projects without Federal support.

Others who left the Elmwood Music Hall that evening talked about the prosperity which they and the City of Buffalo had enjoyed during the decade which had followed World War I. None of them, however, were aware of the financial disaster which they would witness late in October, 1929, five months in their future. Without perceivable warning the Stock Market crashed! Sixteen million shares of stock were sold in a single day. Investors who had played the market on a violin of margin struck a very sour note; a note heard around the world. Shares were sold abundantly, but people did not buy abundantly! Prices of stock fell further until panic struck, banks and businesses failed, and millions of people lost their jobs. Following the stock market crash, Herbert Clark Hoover, who had defeated Al Smith, a Catholic, in the presidential election of 1928, tried to tell the people that prosperity was just around the corner, but it seemed that the nation could not find the corner. His four years as president were the worst of the Depression, which followed that single day of financial disaster. During these years Hoover and the Congress of the United States were unable to re-instill people's confidence in government through remedial projects such as the Reconstruction Finance Corporation and the Home Owner's Loan Corporation. By 1933, the voters howled for change and Franklin Delano Roosevelt was inaugurated as President of the United States after being elected by a landslide. He had campaigned on a platform of a New Deal for the nation.

Others who had enjoyed the duck, potatoes, and sauerkraut served at the banquet decided to "wet their whistle." The eighteenth amendment, however, which prohibited the manufacture and sale of all beverages whose alcoholic content was above one-half of one percent in the United States, was still in vogue. The whistle wetters had to either retire to their homes where they had a stash of illicit liquor, most likely bootlegged into Buffalo using the alcoholic expressway of the Peace Bridge connecting it to Canada, or they could seek out one of the eight thousand speakeasies or drinkies where illegal liquor or beer could be obtained. They needed to know only the proper verbal code for admission. Several of these were in walking distance of the Elmwood Music Hall on Main Street, Elmwood Avenue, or Washington Street. One establishment well known to the parishioners, especially to Edward White, member of the Dramatic Circle, was Ulrich's Tavern located at 674 Ellicott Street at the corner of Virginia Street. Downstairs soft drinks and legal "near" beer were served, but upstairs one could be ushered into the Hasenpfeffer Club where beer was "needled" and real whiskey and ales were available. By 1929, it was well known by the citizens of Buffalo that Prohibition of alcoholic beverages was a legal experiment doomed to failure.

In fact it was this governmental attempt to legislate morality that most contributed to making the "Roaring Twenties" quite roaring for the youth of the nation as well as the adults. It is ironic that in the edition of *The Echo*, May 23, 1929, which advertised the forthcoming One Hundredth Jubilee Celebration at St. Louis Church at which Bishop William Turner was to preside, carried an article titled, "Bishop Turner seeks to promote Temperance." It was an item that related the events associated with the bishop's administration of the Sacrament of Confirmation at St. Joseph's Cathedral, Delaware Avenue, on the previous Sunday. Turner said, "I wish to re-introduce the custom of asking children who are to be confirmed to promise to abstain from the use of intoxicating liquors until they

have attained the age of twenty-one years. I think this would have a salutary effect in these days of moral laxity when drinking in excess is all too common even among girls. The pledge was the practice in the Church until ten years ago. When the Volstead Act took effect it was optimistically assumed that enforcement of the Act would make continuance of the pledge superfluous, so it was discontinued. With the growing evidence, however, that the child or youth still must face the temptation that formally evoked the promise of abstinence, I have decided it would do well again to re-introduce the custom." Turner administered the pledge in conjunction with the administration of the sacrament, although not an essential part of it, to seventy children. Parents and children had been previously indoctrinated by the bishop about total abstinence; but, although some of those being confirmed appeared to take the pledge, their lips were moving without positive intent.

Beer, wine, and whiskey were treasured alcoholic drinks of the human race throughout its history. From the banks of the Tigris and Euphrates Rivers, following the great flood, from which Noah, his family, and his animals survived, to the present time, juices and foods were fermented for consumption. Egyptians made beer and wine, Bohemians added hops to beer to preserve it longer and improve its taste, breweries and distilleries sprouted upon the land like weeds to make larger amounts of the elixir, and frontier America maintained drinking alcoholic beverages as a vital part of colonial social life. It seems that wine was always there. It was in existence when Jesus Christ walked on the dusty roads of Galilee, Samaria, and Judea. It was He who turned water into wine, performing the first miracle of His public life at the marriage feast of Cana. By 1700, brewing and distilling had become highly developed sciences in Europe and emigrants from England and the Continent brought the industry to America. In 1780, Elijah Pepper built a log cabin distillery near Lexington, Kentucky, and fermented his alcoholic beverage which he called "Old 1776; Born with the

Republic." In 1789, Reverend Elijah Craig, a Virginia Baptist minister, made the first bourbon whiskey at North Elkorn Creek near Georgetown, Kentucky.

Following a brewer's timeline in Buffalo, New York, one finds an entry for 1811 whereby Joseph Webb advertises his microbrewery at Black Rock. In 1828, a year before Louis Le Couteulx gave his property to Bishop Dubois so as to build the first Catholic Church in the city, a brewery opened at the corner of Niagara and Mohawk Streets under the direction of the brewmasters, Dennis Kane, Peter Peacock, and Charles Relay. In 1830, a year after Bishop Dubois blessed the land at Main and Edward Streets upon which the Lamb of God Church was built, Jacob Roos, one of its parishioners, built a tavern and brewery at the foot of Batavia Street. By the time the Civil War broke out in the United States there were nearly twenty breweries in Buffalo producing more than a million and a half gallons of beer each year. Most of it was consumed locally. The number of distilleries and breweries increased in proportion to the increase in the immigrant population of the city, mainly made up of thirsty Irish and Germans. The Irish favored their whiskey and the Germans loved their beer. These were the same Irish and Germans who were found in their pews reverently attentive at Mass on Sunday mornings.

Nowhere in the Catholic catechism can one find a condemnation of the use of alcoholic beverages, but the abuse of their use is condemned in the same manner as the abuse of food, tobacco, medicine, or sex. Instead of emphasizing negatives involved in the use of alcohol, the hierarchy and theologians of the Catholic Church stressed the positive by advocating the acquirement of temperance, one of the four cardinal virtues which also includes prudence, justice, and fortitude. Theologians agreed with scientists and sociologists that ten percent of all people were prone to the fate of alcoholism. For these, they advocated absolute abstinence. As an example, they used the experience of Matt Talbot, an Irish layman who was a scandalous alcoholic until at the age of twenty-eight he underwent a conversion and took "the pledge" against further drinking, and embarked on a life of penance and devotion as inspired by Saint Louis Grignion de Montfort.

Theologians looked upon abuse of alcohol as an addiction with genetic, biological, and social dimensions for which, as seen by St. Augustine, Bishop of Hippo, there was no amount of will power, promises, or resolutions that could liberate the addict. As such they promoted successful programs such as Alcoholics Anonymous, first introduced by Bill Wilson, or a method used by Father Edward Dowling, based on St. Ignatius Loyola's "rules for the discernment of spirits." Many Catholic parishes provided place, time, talent, and funds in the church complex for such programs. The type of temperance which theologians advocated for non-alcoholics who could become heavy drinkers, was the moral virtue that moderates the attraction of pleasures and provides balance in the use of created goods. It ensured the will's mastery over instincts and kept desires within the limits of the honorable; the temperate person maintained a healthy discretion. It was to this end, fostering temperance as a virtue into Buffalo's Irish society, that led Bishop Timon to encourage Father Matthew to administer the "pledge" to six thousand Irishmen during a temperance week program in 1851.

The temperance promoted and advocated by the Young Men's Temperance Society and newspapers such as *Temperance Standard* and *Western Temperance Standard* was not cause oriented, but source and symptom motivated. It was an indirect attack upon basic social evils, indecency, lawlessness, drunkenness, gambling, and prostitution. The great cry was, "Get rid of the alcohol, close the bars, taverns, and saloons; exile gambling joints and houses of prostitution." From the "grass roots" of America, citizens opposed to inebriation banded together to influence State and Federal legislators so as to destroy these sources of evil. Among the most influential organizations were the Women's Christian Temperance Union, the Prohibition Party, and the Anti-Saloon League. Their attacks were irrational. Statements such as "every man who takes a drink is an inebriate," "any homicide is a whiskey murder," and "children of drinkers will be mentally defective," were published or posted by them. The promotion of Prohibition, being a struggle between the rural voters and the rising power of the cities, was middle class American morality, as a fundamentalist religion, reacting to immigration and the flourishing Roman Catholic Communion in the cities.

Legislators developed ordinances and laws whereby high fees for licensing a saloon were enacted, sale of liquor was forbidden in certain residential areas; minors, habitual drunkards, and intoxicated persons were refused service; and counties, cities, and towns could decide if they wished to be "wet" or "dry." Finally, when it was found that these laws did little to curtail inebriation, State government's only recourse, under pressure of the non-drinking public, was to initiate Prohibition. By 1855, seven States had abolished booze, but they were required to repeal their laws under protest from the "drinkers." Social reform, however, got into high gear beginning in 1880 when Western States voted to be "dry." After 1900 almost the entire South followed in their footsteps. Even the Far West was in the temperance camp by 1916. By July 1917, when the Federal Congress forbade production of alcoholic beverages for the duration of World War I, twenty-three States had already outlawed the manufacture and sale of alcoholic beverages. The nationwide death knell to the consumption of alcohol was summoned by the enforcement of the Food Stimulation Act of June 30, 1919, which introduced prohibition of alcoholic beverages in all States and Territories until the demobilization of the army was effected. In October 1919, the Vostead Act was initiated; it limited the amount of alcohol in any

beverage to be less than one-half of one percent. By January 17, 1920, the eighteenth amendment initiated in Congress in 1917 had been ratified by two-thirds of the States and became law; from that date no intoxicating beverages were to be manufactured, sold, or purchased in the United States and its Territories.

For the dedication of the monument of the Knights of St. John at the United German and French Roman Catholic Cemetery in 1914, a dedication journal, which described the history of the Knights of St. John, also featured advertisements of establishments which were owned, managed, or operated by Catholic laymen in the City of Buffalo, many of whom were deeply involved in the activities of the various parishes which had a commandery of the Knights attached to it. Among these advertisements approximately forty pertained to breweries and other alcoholic enterprises. They showed the extent to which Catholic laymen had helped to make the beer, wine, and liquor trade grow in Buffalo prior to Prohibition. After January 29, 1920, however, these businesses were closed or highly curtailed, causing many church members to be unemployed.

Prior to 1920, many prominent members of St. Louis Church specifically influenced the brewing and malting industries in Buffalo. The litany of names are: Christian Weyand, Charles Weyand, J. Adam Lautz, Peter Seereiter, William Weigel, Andrew Kraus, George Roos, Jacob Roos, Gerhard Lang, Philip Born, Edwin Miller, Jacob Weppner, William Simon, Joseph Friedman, Magnus Beck, Jacob Scheu, Philip Scheu, Joseph L. Haberstro, John L. Schwartz, John Kam, John Kam Jr, and Joseph Kam. Among these names two of the most prominent are Gerhard Lang and Edwin Miller. Besides being in the brewing business, Lang was also an alderman for the Sixth ward, trustee of the Western Savings Bank, director of the German-American Bank, and an influential member of the building committee of the St. Louis Church between 1885 and 1889. He died July 14, 1892. His son-in-law Edwin Miller, who was born in Buffalo, March 9, 1854, succeeded him as director of Lang's Brewery.

Before becoming manager of Gerhard Lang's Brewery, Miller had been a partner in the George Urban and Son Milling Industry. In June 1884, when he became manager of the brewery, he married Annie E. Lang, Gerhard Lang's daughter. After her father had died, Edwin became president of the brewery. While serving in this capacity he also was director of the People's Bank, German-American Bank, Buffalo Savings Bank, the Buffalo Trust and Safe Deposit Company, and president of the streetcar facilities for the City of Buffalo. When Lang's beer was advertised, Miller had it carry the following statement, "This beer has been analyzed by the chief chemist of the Agricultural Department of the United States and pronounced pure and healthy and is equal to any in the country." No one would conclude from this advertisement that Lang was producing a product of mass destruction as one would be led to believe from circulars put out by the Temperance movement.

Although Albert Ziegele was not in communion with the members of St. Louis Church, his brewery employed many of its parishioners. He was born in Stuttgart, Wuerttemburg, in 1818. He came to Buffalo in 1849 and went to work for Jacob and Philip Scheu who ran a brewery on the corner of Spring and Genesee Streets. They were early arrivals to the city and members of St. Louis Church. After a year, Ziegele went into business for himself in a former brewery that had been owned by Gottlieb Boadamer with an attached saloon. Ziegele advertised that he had his saloon fixed with tables and chairs because his intention was to have an establishment for casual socializing and meetings. He wanted people to know that his saloon did not carry the temperance movement's concept of a place of quarrel, squabble, broil, brawl, or riot. Twice his breweries burned and he had to restart. In 1879 after he turned his business over to his sons, the second fire

burned the building to the ground. The Ziegele boys, Albert Jr. and William built a new brewery at the corner of Washington and Virginia Streets.

They dubbed it the Phoenix Brewery named for the legendary Greek bird that was born out of fire. In 1888, when St. Louis Church held its first bazaar to offset the cost of the new gothic church, the Phoenix Brewery employed eighty men and sold eighty thousand barrels of beer in one year. At that time J. Adam Lautz was president and Peter P. Seereiter was financial director. Both men were parishioners of St. Louis Church. Lautz was born at Dieburg, Germany in 1840. After coming to Buffalo he organized the Orpheus, the German Singing Society. He was also president of the German Young Men's Association, member of the Merchant Exchange, and chairman of the St. Louis Church building committee. He was also involved with his brothers in the Lautz Soap Industry and the production of monuments in marble and onyx. In order to offset the disparaging concepts about beer undermining family life as perpetrated by the Temperance movement, Lautz placed the following advertisement in the *St. Louis Bazar Chronicle*: "Drink Phoenix Beer: A pure and healthy beverage, bottled at the brewery for hotel and family use." Peter P. Seereiter was born in Buffalo on July 15, 1854. He attended St. Mary's School for early education and worked as a bookkeeper for Peter Paul and Brothers who were in the printing business. He was treasurer of the 1888 bazaar at St. Louis Church.

At the onset of Prohibition, Christian Weyand's brewery was located on the north corner of Main and Goodell Streets at the present site of the Catholic Center, formerly the Courier Express Building. In 1919, the brewery had a capacity of one hundred and twenty thousand barrels. Weyand was born in Lorraine, France, on May 11, 1826 and came to Buffalo in 1847. In 1888 Weyand was in business with another member of St. Louis Church, William J. Weigel, who was born in Buffalo on September 15, 1851, attended school at St.

Louis Church and was on the building committee for the new gothic church. After Prohibition, the Weigel family took ownership of the Iroquois Brewing Company which by 1950 was the largest brewery in Buffalo, bigger than Gerhard Lang's which had been the largest Pre-Prohibition brewery. Charles Weyand, Christian's son, was born on March 1, 1869 and at the beginning of the twentieth century was a member of his father's firm. He was also a member of the St. Louis Dramatic Circle and secretary and treasurer of the bazaar held at St. Louis Church in 1900. He developed the simple advertisement: "Weyand's; Lager and Dunkel Bier on Goodell Street."

Andrew Kraus who had been born in Buffalo on December 10, 1846, and in adult life became a member of St. Louis Church and vice president of its 1888 Bazaar, was also a member of the Catholic Mutual Benefit Association, the Orpheus, the German Young Men's Association, and incorporator of the Buffalo Co-operative Brewing Company which was in existence from 1880 to 1920. It brewed three brands: Extra 6, Stock Lager, and Muenchner. One would have to go a long way to describe Andrew as a man who wished to destroy the morals of humanity by operating his plant at Michigan and High Streets. Closely allied with the brewing industry were the several Malting Works operating within the city. Among these was one owned and operated by John Kam and his two sons, John Kam Jr. and Joseph Kam. All three were upstanding citizens and members of St. Louis Church. In 1888, John Kam Jr. married Miss Louise Simon, daughter of William Simon. John Kam Jr. was a member of the board of trustees of the St. Louis Church. It is most difficult to understand how these men could be such respected persons and be accused of developing a product that was destroying the very nature of man who partook of it. Repeal of Prohibition after thirteen years of experimentation proved that the product was not the cause of intoxication it was only the source, but it was equally a source of good, happy, and enthusiastic socializing, leading to positive expression of community life.

When one is asked to fast or abstain from something for devotional reasons, as a preliminary procedure of gastrointestinal examination, or blood testing which requires non-partaking of food for twelve hours, one usually has a psychological impetus to excite the body's pleasurable juices so as to desire what is forbidden. When God asked Adam and Eve to abstain from eating the fruit of the tree of knowledge of good and evil, the devil, lurking in the wings of the Garden of Eden, knew that they were ripe for temptation because of this sinister sinuous psychological twist of the brain. There are actions, which are coded by the rules of proper conduct as moral or immoral. The one who acts has the capability and must make a free choice to accept one or the other. If an outside agent should take away that free choice, the person will rebel even if the resulting choice would be to do the moral thing. If an action is moral in conscience but illegal by legislation, one begins to understand how choice can lose its freedom. One then proceeds to act persistently and defiantly in violating the legislation. Having only fear of being caught, charged, and convicted by authority, one's violation methods are inventive, imaginative, skillful, and daring. So it was in Buffalo after January 29, 1920 when the noble experiment of Prohibition became effective.

In 1922, Francis Xavier Schwab was elected Mayor of the City of Buffalo after he had vigorously campaigned on a platform that was decidedly Anti-Prohibition. His promise to work assiduously for repeal of the liquor legislation was very appealing to that portion of the population that annually consumed nearly eighty gallons of beer per person. At his State of the City Address during his time in office, he advocated licensing speakeasies that had the more polite names of "soda shops" and "drinkies." Knowing that Schwab allegedly used his influence as mayor to promote local law enforcement agencies to curtail the efficiency of federal agents as "booze busters," the Anti-Saloon League launched a vicious campaign to dry up Buffalo. The immigrants such as the Germans, Irish, and Polish fought back. Germans claimed that their businesses, which were extensive and traditional, were ruined. Poles and Irish demanded the reopening of their neighborhood taverns and saloons that were required to feed their social needs. All efforts of the "Feds" made only a dent in the liquor trade and consumption. After eight years of the law being ordained, there were still eight thousand speakeasies operating in Buffalo. Schwab, who had interest in brewing, was accused of being directly involved with production and distribution of illegal beverages; he pleaded "no contest" to one of these charges. He, however, was a good Catholic. He lived at 2 West Parade Street, and was a member of St. Ann's Church. There he had become an early member of the Knights of St. George; an organization that later was called the Knights of St. John. In 1914, he was a major of the Second Regiment. As mayor he would walk the streets and greet the little children. When he saw children with worn out shoes, he took them into the nearest shoe store and bought them new ones. Jesus Christ once said, "Whatsoever you have done to one of these the least of my brethren, you have done unto me." Jesus' peers, however, condemned Him because he ate with drinkers, publicans, and sinners. Mayor Schwab was happy to be in Jesus' camp!

*I*n 1884, John Feist, a member of St. Louis Church, was colonel of the Second Regiment of the Knights of St. John in Buffalo. He appointed John L. Schwartz, a Knight of St. George at St. Michael's Church, as his adjutant. On November 3, 1889, Schwartz was elected colonel of the Second Regiment, a position that he held for five successive terms. He became Regimental Brigadier General in 1928. From 1909 to 1920 he was the owner and president of John L. Schwartz Brewing Company, which was on Pratt Street in the vicinity of the Clinton Market. Before Prohibition it had a capacity which exceeded forty thousand barrels per year.

It closed in 1920 and did not reopen as Schwartz Brewing Company when the eighteenth amendment was repealed in 1933. He was broken hearted at the loss, but he never lost the esteem held for him by his fellow Knights and the parishioners and priests of his church.

*G*erhard Lang was by far the greatest star among the Pre-Prohibition brewers and a very esteemed affluent parishioner of St. Louis Church. People would wait on the steps of the church on Main Street on Sunday mornings to see his chauffeur driven Cadillac roll up to the front doors, and he and his family exit the car with a flourish and enter the church portals to partake of the Mass. Lang was also a member of the Knights of St. John, Commandery 14, attached to St. Mary's Church on Broadway and Pine Streets. He partially closed his brewery in 1920, but continued to make soda and the legal "near" beer. His brewmasters, however, were clever enough to have one of the vats on a rotating basis filled with "needle" beer which exceeded the limit of alcohol allowed by the Volstead Act. The "Feds" were highly suspicious of this comedy of musical chairs but were unable to get past the alleged stage. It appeared that some small leak from the local police kept the brewery one step ahead of the "Fed." Besides needling in "near" beer, Lang's business survived by producing dairy and soda products, baked goods, and creamery delights. Following the repeal of the eighteenth amendment Lang's brewery was the first in the city to start production under the able hands of Gerhard Lang's son Jacob. It did not close again until 1949; a year that marked the beginning of the end of a glorious era for the local brewing industry in Buffalo.

*T*wo organizations at St. Louis Church most affected by the Prohibition laws were the Knights of St. John and the Dramatic Circle. Both groups had made it a practice to socialize following each of their meetings; socializing which involved the partaking of alcoholic beverages. It was traditional that at a meeting one would stand and say, "Mit ein Trinkglas im Hand muess Ich der Trinkspruch machen und ein Trinklied singen." In the reign of Laudenbach as chaplain of the Knights and as moderator of the Dramatic Circle, he would respond, "Mit meinem Segen, spreche ich Amen dazu!" Prohibition outwardly changed this public expression of fraternalism. Many times the venue of brotherhood activity had to be changed. A short hop across the Peace Bridge was the small village of Fort Erie, Canada. There several of the Knights of St. John owned or rented cottages for the summer; some had year-round abodes. Albert J. Eger, a member of Commandery 204, owned a house at Erie Beach adjacent to Fort Erie. Almost as a religious devotion, weekly poker games were held; among the regulars in attendance were: Frank Bauer, Albert J. Gebhard, Joseph F. Lux, Eugene W. Miller Sr., Frank Ross, Charles J. Schifferle Jr., Lawrence Wagner, and Albert T. Hardick.

In those days no one advocated "Don't Drink and Drive" and accidents were not overly emphasized. Prior to 1923, it was legal to drink alcoholic beverages on a boat in foreign waters. One must assume that there was much more than soda pop available on the barge which the Knights of St. John and the Dramatic Circle used for their summer picnics, launching it from a port on Grand Island. Using the map that they had aboard they could determine where in the Niagara River they were outside the United States. In Canadian waters, it was a fine time to raise one's Stein! Likewise, families came in droves to the foot of Ferry Street to board the Niagara River Ferry that sailed every hour to Fort Erie. The Queen's Hotel greeted the tourists with open arms. Crystal Beach, eight miles west of Fort Erie became the summer recreational area of Buffalonians who could enjoy the rides at the amusement park, frolic on the beach in their swim suits, dance until late at night at the Ballroom to wonderful big band music, picnic in the shady park, and legally enjoy whatever beer, wine or whiskey they desired.

People had plenty of spending money because the economy of Buffalo was booming. Transportation was no problem. Each day, two steamships, the *Americana* and the *Canadiana* made round trips from the Port of Buffalo, near the lighthouse, to the long dock at Crystal Beach. On September 25, 1930, Senator Morris Sheppard told the editor of the Washington Post that there was no chance that the eighteenth amendment would be repealed; he insisted that the people of this country were for temperance and that they would continue to elect those in Congress who were for it. Three years later, where did all those people go? On April 7, 1933, at 12:05 A.M., Rupert Breweries of New York City delivered two cases of legal beer, repealed Prohibition beer, to the White House in Washington D.C. In Buffalo, William W. Weigel and J. Raymond Schwartz had a case of beer delivered to Buffalo's Mayor, Charles E. Roesch. In February 1934, all alleged liquor violations pending in Federal Courts were voided, but the country was deep in the Depression, struggling to recover. [1]

Following the Stock Market Crash of 1929, Laudenbach and the trustees of St. Louis Church knew that they had more to cope with than avoiding the appearance of consuming alcoholic beverages at societal functions of the church. When they held their monthly meeting in the school hall eight days before the "Crash," present, besides Laudenbach, were all seven enthusiastic trustees: John M. Fornes, Edward J. Garono, Peter M. Ginther, Louis Ludaescher, Peter Schirra, William Swanz, and Albert M. Wagner. That night they presented their annual report; little did they realize that it would form a baseline upon which they would judge the effect of the following Depression years on the church's financial solvency. The annual income of the church was derived from Sunday and Feast Day Mass collections, special Christmas and Easter collections, school tuition, coal collections, pew rent, rent from properties owned by the church on Delaware Avenue, Franklin Street, and Pearl Place, donations, foundations, special collections, refunds, and bank interest.

The special collections were funds donated for charitable and missionary activities extramural to the church; usually what funds were received were immediately forwarded to the group for which they were intended. Among these were Pope in Rome, St. Vincent de Paul Society, Catholic University in Washington D.C., and Missions in the United States and foreign lands. Funds which were collected specifically for the church's use were dispersed as follows: repairs on the church, school, rectory, rental properties, and the organ; salaries for the pastor and his assistants, the Sisters of St. Joseph, teachers at the school and custodians of the sacristy, the organist, janitor, and domestics; payments of utilities, operational bills, taxes, and cathedraticum; purchase of coal and altar supplies such as communion breads, wine, candles, and vestments. One can judge the effect of the Depression upon the church and the parishioners by observing the financial fluctuations in the average monthly receipts over the Depression years, in the decrease of rents received from the properties owned by the church, the trustees' struggle to balance the annual church budget, and the need for several generous parishioners to come forth and loan the church money at insignificant interest.

When the Great Depression hit the nation, Hoover was not blind to its impact. Working with his Congress he created the Reconstruction Finance Corporation on February 1, 1932. Its activities were to relieve financial institutions from frozen conditions, fund immediate relief to the unemployed, and use Federal funds targeted to the States so as to give help to the needy in urban areas and help farmers to obtain a fair profit on the sale of their crops. He likewise authorized the Federal government to make loans to banks, building and loan associations, insurance companies and the railroads. Among the public works which he advocated were: construction of toll bridges, power

plants, sewers, sanitary facilities in cities and towns, and improve the slums. When the Federal government saw that there was overproduction of wheat in 1930 followed by a nationwide drought in 1931, it stepped in and offered financial assistance. In all this remedial activity one flaw existed; Hoover and Congress could not agree as to what extent government should interfere in matters that had never confronted them before. It was this fact which brought the people to blame Hoover for the crisis; and, with a landslide vote, elected Franklin Delano Roosevelt president of the United States in 1932.

Along with Roosevelt's election, the people gave him a Democratic majority in Congress both in the Senate and the House of Representatives. He took the oath of office on March 4, 1933. To the panic stricken people who elected him, he said, "I will lead you out of the quicksand of Depression that is engulfing you, and bring you once more to the safe firm foothold of re-established credit, renewed industrial activity, and peaceful foreign relationships." The day after his inauguration he issued a bank holiday, which although it was to end on March 9, 1933 was extended until he was sure that the banking industry was stabilized. Without further ado, he had Congress pass laws that modified the Volstead Act so as to legalize the manufacture of beer and other alcoholic beverages. By April 7, 1933, the nation had beer and the government had a pocket-full of money gained in taxes on the production of it. Although the old-fashioned saloon was taboo, beer was readily available at restaurants, hotels, clubs, groceries, and drug stores.

Next in rapid succession came the enactment of legislation which put into operation such activities as the Blue Sky Laws, Economy Bill, Farm Bill, Farm Credit Administration, Farm Debt Relief Bill, National Industrial Recovery Act, National Employment System, Public Works, and the New Gold Policy. Putting it all together it carried the logo of Roosevelt's New Deal.

Hours that a laborer had to work in a week were reduced and wages were increased. Whereas in 1932 twenty-five percent of the work force in America was unemployed, by the fall of 1933, over one million workers had returned to employment status. Although this left nearly twelve million still unemployed, one could see that the effort was working. By August 31, 1934 only ten million were unemployed and financial relief was being given to another four million families. During the twelve-month period from December 1933 to December 1934, the Federal government had poured almost seven billion dollars into the activities of the National Recovery Act and the New Deal was making life palatable.

The New Deal, however, was slow in coming to Buffalo; and, when it came in 1935, it did not bring prosperity, an end to unemployment or hard times, but it kept the city from going bankrupt. Years later, people would realize what Buffalo gained: public housing, a modernized airport, downtown auditorium, concert hall and a symphonic orchestra, modernized zoo, a federal office building, civic stadium, police headquarters, improved schools and libraries, playgrounds, tennis courts, swimming pools, sewers, and widened and repaired streets. In the bailout by the Federal government, Buffalo employed seventy-five thousand men and women and spent over forty-five million dollars on salaries, materials, transportation, and supplies. One of the projects which affected St. Louis Church, attributed to Federal money appropriated for the Works Progress Administration, simply known as the WPA, was the repaving of Edward Street from Main Street to Delaware Avenue.

It had been first paved in 1899 at a cost of $5,714, but as years went by, more repairs were needed to prevent accidents. These cost $5,050, but the street was constantly impassable. The Common Council had been deliberating on a complete overhaul of it since 1926, but it was finally condemned. On July 17, 1935, the WPA began its work. Reverend Francis A. Kasprzak, assistant to Father Laudenbach and affectionately referred to by the school children as Father Kasper-Jack, was outside the rectory wearing his boater straw hat and inspecting the initial progress. A large steam shovel had just begun ripping up the thirty six-year-old pavement. Soon other by-standers joined him in offering sidewalk superintendent suggestions. The complete job took three weeks to complete; and, when finished, the street had an eight-inch concrete base over which was laid a three and one-half inch asphalt top. Commissioner George J. Summers of Public Works was on hand when the project was completed. He informed the community that the total cost was $14,380 of which the city was to pay two-thirds and the abutting owners were to pay one-third. Laudenbach and the trustees did not complain about the cost because they were so pleased that the Pearl Street extension project had been squelched. What Summers did not tell the community, however, was that WPA was paying the city's two-thirds.

Although many of the male parishioners at St. Louis Church boasted about their economic diversity in their business endeavors, they were quite curtailed because of the Depression. They were also helped when the bailout finally arrived at the hands of the Federal government. During the years between 1929 and 1936 the trustees did an excellent job of balancing the books, staying in the black, and balancing the budget. Many entries into their annual statements reflect how the church and the parishioners were hurting financially. Contributions that included cash on hand from the previous year, church, school, and fuel collections, and pew rent showed a decided variation. In October 1929 the sum of these contributions was $30,322.99. Over the next five years they progressively dropped until low tide was reached in 1934 when the sum amounted to $20,938.99. This was a thirty-one percent drop in the four years before Buffalo experienced Federal relief. At first the total drop in annual income did not seem to be too drastic because in 1930 the trustees had received six thousand dollars from the probate of Anna Marie

Born's will. She was the daughter of Philip Born, the owner of Born's Brewery from 1840 to 1862. He died in 1848, and his wife Barbara, Anna Marie's older sister, was remarried to Gerhard Lang.

Also near the end of 1931, Father Laudenbach felt that his assistant priests needed extra money to carry them through the crisis. Each year the trustees had allotted an annual salary of $3,400.08 for Laudenbach and his two assistants. Each assistant was receiving only $850.02 per annum. Laudenbach, who had continued the practice begun by Hoelscher of allowing the Christmas collection to go into the church fund rather than to the priests, decided to change the practice. That year the sum collected was $2,816.00. Under Laudenbach's pastorship the practice was an option which the trustees had approved, and in lieu of the clergy not receiving the Christmas collection the trustees purchased a large four door Cadillac for Laudenbach and paid for all its garage rental and maintenance. From 1917 to 1931, the sum of money donated in this way by the clergy to the church had amounted to approximately $72,000. On November 21, 1931, Laudenbach announced to the trustees that he would use his option to now accept the Christmas collection starting in December 1931, trade in his large Cadillac for a smaller Cadillac coupe; and, at his expense, be responsible for the maintenance of the vehicle. On May 1, 1932, the trustees paid the cost of the coupe to Buffalo Cadillac Company. From Christmas 1931, through the rest of the Depression and its recovery, the assistant priests each received an annual salary of $1,472.36.

In balancing the budget there was a category of donations given each year to outside charities and home and foreign missions. In this category, one found a sixty-six percent decrease in giving during the first five years of Depression. A third area most devastating to the church was in regards to the rentals received for the three pieces of property that it owned. In 1929 they

brought to the church an income of $10,694.00. By 1936 that income had decayed by eighty percent to $2,088.79. The situation was so bad in 1934 that the trustees turned to the parishioners and explained that if some money were not loaned to the church at very small interest it would experience a $19,000 deficit that year. Thirteen members were able to answer the clarion call. They were: William Mittling, Joseph Strigl, Laura Wollziefer, Ollie S. Hornung, Delia Schillo, Joseph E. Reade, Cecelia Koch, Laura Voltz, Joseph T. Kies, Louise M. Bauer, Susan Schifferle, Mary S. Conrad, and Bertha Breithecker. The average loan was $1,500 with the lowest being $500 and the largest $2,500. In 1935 and 1936 added help was needed. Father Laudenbach and his sister, Anna C. Laudenbach, came forth and presented the trustees with $2,500 each year. By the end of 1936, the financial situation began to ease as collections increased. During these trying times the trustees held salaries of the organist, janitor, teachers, and domestic help at the same level as in 1929. The number of domestic help was slightly decreased, Ed White, the janitor, was lowered $300 in salary after 1932; but, another man, John Kunz, was added to help him at an annual salary of $936. [2]

In the spring of 1931, the City of Buffalo was well on its way in preparation for the centennial celebration of its one-hundredth anniversary of its incorporation as a city. An entire centennial park was planned with a stadium, midway, airplane exhibits, and several large exposition halls. The organizers believed that, in those days of panic and despair, they had to have a mini remake with pomp and splendor of the Pan American Exposition of 1901. They were convinced that after the citizens recalled the glories of Buffalo's past history, they would have faith in the future of the city by participating in the events that the centennial park would offer. Radio, queen of the communication media, was in the process of preparing an eight-night serial, a musical drama of Buffalo's progress from pioneer days to the centennial; it was aimed to be aired in July 1932. As part of that preparation the staff members of the *Buffalo Times* traveled about the city documenting history wherever it could be found. On May 27, 1931 they knocked on the door of the rectory of St. Louis Church and interviewed Reverend Henry B. Laudenbach. The interviewers found him to be a large jovial man who had a citywide reputation as a master of ceremonies and after-dinner speaker. He was the founder of the *Echo*, a second Catholic newspaper in Buffalo in competition with *The Catholic Union and Times*. With Laudenbach the interviewers reviewed the days of Father Nicholas Mertz, the Lamb of God Church, the first brick church which burned in 1885, and the construction of the new gothic church. Laudenbach was very insistent to point out to them that his St. Louis Church was established before the incorporation of the City of Buffalo and before the Catholic Diocese of Buffalo. He said, "We are the first church, the first cemetery, and the first school of the Catholic persuasion. We are the Mother Church of the diocese."

He was then asked to describe any other positions that he had held while being pastor of St. Louis Church. He ran off a litany of activities: Director of the Catholic Library, Chaplain of the Knights of St. John, Director of the German Roman Catholic Orphanage, censor of books written by nuns and priests, judge at the Catholic marriage-relations court, and moderator of clerical conferences. When he was questioned as to how he could do all these things, including his after-dinner speeches, and still carry-on his pastorship, he replied, "All money matters pertaining to the church are handled by the trustees. I have nothing to do with the temporal affairs but to listen to the trustees, attend their meetings, and offer my suggestions. This is why I believe that I am able to keep my youthful appearance." When he was asked about his recent talk in which he expressed his ardent opposition to Prohibition he replied, "Long ago, I cultivated the dangerous art of speaking on any subject that came up. Prohibition came up, and I gave my honest and reasoned opinion." When asked what his thoughts were on the raging Depression

which was effecting Buffalo he said, "I think Bruce Shanks, cartoonist for the *Buffalo Times* has described the situation quite well. His cartoon of late, features two rather wealthy men dressed in tuxedoes, top hats, and black paten leathered shoes covered by gray spats, sitting inside a spherical gondola supported by a balloon floating placidly around the earth. Both are obviously very healthy because they sport large tummies underneath their expanded vests. Both are deeply asleep; Shanks is very expressive in detailing the extent of their snoring. On one man's vest is written, Mr. Prosperity, on the other the name Mr. Jobs. Below the gondola one sees a man standing on earth. He is a poor, forlorn man, wearing pants, coat, and hat that are extensively patched. As sweat pours forth from his brow, he cries-out to those gentleman in the gondola, 'When are you coming back?'"

During the panic years of the Depression and the slow recovery years that followed, millions of Americans turned to the new prophets who invaded the country. These were men such as Father Charles E. Coughlin, Huey Pierce Long, Francis E. Townsend, Louis C. Fraina, Earl Browder, and Eugene Debs. Although they preached competing gospels and seemed at times to vacillate within themselves, those who were in an unprecedented stage of frustration, fear, humiliation, dispossession, and poverty listened intently to them. Among this group were self-employed farmers, shopkeepers, and artisans. They were mostly men and women of native born old immigrant Anglo-Saxon, German, and Irish stock. When they searched for their enemies, they saw the bankers and large corporations above and the trade unions below. They were resentful of contemporary politics and economics, and they were weary of the disorder of a free society. They were swept down the river of despair until they reached a fork at which they believed they had to choose between Communism or Fascism, two ideologies spawned in Europe following World War I. For many Catholics, their ears were tuned to the radio where they heard the rolling and resonant brogue of

Father Charles E. Coughlin filling the airways with his colored rhetoric. In 1926, from his parish shrine in honor of St. Theresa of Lisieux, known as the Little Flower, he began hosting his *Golden Hour of the Little Flower,* which was aired by WJR, Detroit, Michigan. By 1930, after several stations in other cities carried his show, he announced the beginning of the *Radio League of the Little Flower* for which he received copious donations.

*I*n that year, using the Depression as a theme he shifted from religion to politics. He called himself a religious Walter Winchell. At first, this Radio Priest turned against the Communists. He said, "Choose today, it is either Christ or the Red Flag of Communism." Later he claimed he was teaching social justice when he opposed modern capitalism. Soon he joined with William Randolph Hearst in a crusade against the Communists after they had instigated a riot at Madison Square Garden in 1934, and organized the American Writers' Congress in 1935. At first Coughlin was in praise of Roosevelt and his New Deal, but by 1934, he felt that the Communists had infiltrated the Democratic Party in Congress, and that the international bankers controlled its legislative power. Thus he threw himself into the camp of the Fascists, men of the radical right influenced by Seward Collins, Huey Long, Francis Townsend, and Lawrence Dennis. In 1933, Collins had said, "Mussolini is the most constructive statesman of our age." Dennis, who hailed from Georgia and had been a boy evangelist, served the State Department in Honduras and Nicaragua where he became cynical about the United States' capitalist foreign policy. He led Coughlin to believe that usury and the Jews, who he claimed were the group that thrived on it, was the cause of capitalism's sins.

*C*oughlin agreed that the Jews alone had the power of hogging the harvest. By 1936 when Roosevelt ran for re-election, Coughlin's broadcasts had become saturated with Anti-Semitic, pro-Nazi, and Fascist rhetoric; his credibility was destroyed. One archbishop and two bishops rebuked him when he labeled Roosevelt as a liar. They said, "Coughlin is killing himself politically at a very rapid rate!" A priest from California said, "Everybody here, even the nuns, are for Roosevelt, and they resent Coughlin's attacks on him." The Irish Catholics from Connecticut responded saying that Coughlin had stepped from the high place of priest and holy man to the gutter of common unreasoned insult. Although besieged by these remarks, when asked what his opinions were concerning the presidential election, Coughlin said, "Democracy is doomed, this is our last election. We are at a crossroads, and I take the road of Fascism."

*A*fter the Japanese attacked Pearl Harbor on December 7, 1941, Coughlin, a member of the Basilian Order, gave up his public life and retired to one of its houses. In his heyday his influence on the general Catholic population was impressive. Because of his tendencies toward accepting the concepts of socialism, many German-Americans felt that he catered to their militaristic feeling and romantic idealism so well pronounced in Wagner's adaptation of the legends of Lohengrin, Parsifal, and Tannhauser. It seemed ingrained in the German psyche to be drawn toward parades, carrying of flags, and the playing of bands especially when these honored something German. In 1934 Paul von Hindenburg, German general of World War I and second president of the German Republic following the war, died. He was laid to rest at Neudeck, Germany, on August 2, 1934. Adolph Hitler, at the head of his Nazi Party, had been well entrenched as the leader of Germany before his death. One month later, German-Americans held a memorial for Hindenburg at the Elmwood Music Hall in Buffalo. He was lauded by speakers as a loyal friend of Germany, as a great commander, as a man who served Germany during its regime as a Republic, and as one who brought back proper significance to the German army. The program opened with an overture from the Wagnerian opera Tannhauser followed by musical selections from the works of Henrion, Hannemann, Meyerbeer, Kunoth, and

Radecki. It ended with the singing of the *Star Spangled Banner, Deutschland Ueber Alles*, and *Das Horst Wessel-Lied*, the Hitler song. Many arms were extended as it was played by the Steel Helmet Band and sung by members of the audience that filled the Hall.

During the musical program beer and sandwiches were served. Following the memorial ceremony, a grand parade marched from the Hall to Humboldt Park in a line of march over Virginia, Main, and Genesee Streets. It was led by members of the Steel Helmet Band composed of veterans who had served in the German Army in World War I and later became residents of New York City. Preceding the other groups in the parade were the flag bearers carrying dozens of German, American, and Nazi Swastika banners. Next in line after the band were boys and girls who were members of the German-American United Front carrying flaming torches. Later, the German-Austrian war veterans held their annual Veterans Day picnic at Genesee Park. The memorial, the parade, and the picnic were staged by German-American organizations whose main offices were based outside of Buffalo.

Represented were members of the German-American United Front, the German Legion, and the German-Austrian Veterans. Speakers at the Music Hall were: Herman Schmidt, president of the German-American Front; Ernest Wernet, commander of the German Legion; Ernst Schmidt, publisher of the *Daily Volksfreund*, and Reverend Doctor Joseph Asmuth S.J., professor at Fordham University. Although many German Catholics from churches such as St. Ann, St. Mary, St. Michael, St. Boniface and St. Louis may have been on the sidelines watching the parade, and may have been in the Music Hall witnessing the Hindenburg celebration, no organized church groups participated. The Knights of St. John might have been invited, but they were not. The St. Louis Church Dramatic Circle could have been asked to offer a recitation, but it was not. Besides, Laudenbach, after his visit to Germany in

1924 was well aware that the German Republic was under siege. He had known of Hitler's organized revolt called a "putsch" held at Munich, his incarceration, and his release from prison.

While in Germany, Laudenbach heard some of Hitler's oratorical fervor that was rallying millions to his cause. He saw that the *Nationalsozialistiche Partei*, led by Hitler, was well on its way to achieving votes necessary to have members elected to office and take control of the government. Although he looked upon the demonstration in Buffalo as an event to arouse the enthusiasm of the Germans, he was appalled at seeing the NAZI flags in the parade. As true to his nature, when asked his opinion, he did not hesitate, but responded frankly, "This is German Fascism, I do not like it!" In March 1938, his words were more than justified; they were reality. Hitler's Nazis swept into Austria; it was known as the *Anschluss*. One of their goals was to seize the University of Innsbruck where Laudenbach had studied theology. Immediately he went about Western New York seeking funds to carry on the University's work in Switzerland. At that time he was bitter in denouncing the Nazis, distinguishing the difference between them and other Germans. He said, "The Nazi regime is openly and strictly one of neopagans, and therefore unacceptable to the life of Christian or Catholic people and there still are many in Germany who are Christian and Catholic." [3]

Laudenbach was always ready to use his literary talent in whatever way it would be helpful to his parish and to the diocese in general. On Easter Sunday, 1938, a small card was presented to each parishioner; it contained an Easter message from Laudenbach and his two assistants, Fathers James Kirby and Howard Adolf. Laudenbach wrote, "This is the day the Lord has made, let us rejoice and be glad. Holy Mother Church sings joyously throughout Eastertime. May we, the priests, and trustees of your parish wish you the very best of spiritual and material success in the months to come.

May we remain united and generous to each other always. The cord of friendship between us shall never be frayed, if we try to keep it strong and fine." In these few words Laudenbach summed up the Rare Tradition in American Catholicism which had existed at St. Louis Church for an entire century, and showed that it was alive and well in the twentieth century after passing through some trying years. After Easter, Laudenbach began writing a booklet which contained the biographies of the first six bishops of the Diocese of Buffalo: Bishops John Timon, Stephen V. Ryan, James E. Quigley, Charles H. Colton, Denis Dougherty, and William Turner. He titled it *Little Stories of Buffalo's Bishops*. It was published on March 14, 1939 with an introductory letter from the reigning bishop of Buffalo, Right Reverend John A. Duffy. Laudenbach's artistic writing described the history surrounding his bishops with reverence, respect, feeling, understanding, and satire.

*I*n his biography of Bishop John Timon, Laudenbach makes some references to items which were of interest to the parishioners of St. Louis Church in 1939; some of these are still of interest to them in the year 2004. In regards to Timon's first coming to Buffalo in 1847, Laudenbach says, "On the record books here at St. Louis Church there are quite a few entries of baptisms and other parochial activities of our first bishop. His mahogany easy chair and the walnut throne made for him are still in the rectory and in use." Concerning Timon's interdict of St. Louis Church which ended in 1855, Laudenbach writes, "In regard to the trustees' problem, the matter was a *cause celebre* and stirred up lots of dust which does not concern the personal sketch of the pioneer and fearless man of the West. He held his own, and with the aid of a Jesuit missioner, Father Wenninger, peace was restored and the parish began to function again." In reference to St. Michael's Church which was established at Timon's request by the Jesuits at the time of interdict, Laudenbach says, "Until a few years ago, there were still good folks who belonged to the *Market-Church*

but also kept their pews at St. Louis Church on Main Street. This was the result of the interdict. There are no scars left and the two churches were neighborly and are so today." In regards to St. Joseph's Cathedral, Laudenbach writes, "The apple of the new bishop's eye was his cathedral, established in that sector of the city where everybody who was anybody lived. There was aristocratic Swan Street and the great section of Irish where now the sons of Italy hold undisputed sway. The stained glass in the rear of the sanctuary was a donation of Ludwig, King of Bavaria. Innsbruck windows were later imported for the nave. The style of English Gothic is today a very happy expression of the restrained building. Too bad that the north tower was never finished."

*T*urning his attention to the second bishop of Buffalo, Stephen Vincent Ryan, Laudenbach describes his coming and appearance. He says, "The news of his election to Buffalo came quite a long time after Bishop Timon's death in April 1867. It was in November 1868, that the colorful ceremony of consecration took place in St. Joseph's Cathedral on Franklin Street. The Metropolitan of the State, Archbishop McCloskey of New York performed it, assisted by Bishops Loughlin and Lynch. Ryan was a venerable and benign figure. His long, white hair graced a face of intelligence and serene character." While writing Ryan's biography, Laudenbach gave a description of the changing faces seen in old neighborhoods of Buffalo. He wrote, "During Bishop Ryan's tenure of more than a quarter of a century, the new diocese emerged from the cocoon of the old. Up to the time of his coming there were two races: German and Irish. They not only predominated, there just were no others. Then conditions in Europe brought the great Polish and Italian influx. The first settled on the East Side and like a tidal wave swept other nationals out of their path. Just stand at the spot where the New York Central station rears its tower: wherever you look, steeples of Polish churches, built through the piety of the poor immigrant and the energy of their clergy, headed by the grand old Roman Dean,

John Pitass. The Italian came later. The tide settled him in the old sectors of the Irish around the West Side. Soon there was no room for anyone else. A solid block of the city from the docks on Main to Black Rock is Italian today. Then almost unnoticed and in small numbers came the Catholic Syrians, Greeks, Hungarians, Bohemians, and Czechoslovaks." In this sketch, Laudenbach also did not want to forget Father Nelson Baker who was buried at Limestone Hill in Lackawanna. He said, "His simple and dignified tombstone justly bears the words: *In memory of Father Baker.* That's what he always wanted to be called, Father Baker. The titles given to him by his bishops meant nothing to him in his simplicity of soul and mind."

Next Laudenbach concentrated on Bishop James E. Quigley. He wrote, "The Diocese of Buffalo was celebrating its golden jubilee of its foundation when it received as a birthday present a new bishop from the Holy See. James Edward Quigley came from Canada, as did his predecessor. He grew up here from early childhood. At the time of his election he was pastor at St. Brigid's Church on Elk and Louisiana Streets." Prior to Quigley's election, Reverend Paul Hoelscher, later pastor of St. Louis Church was also being considered as a candidate for bishop. Laudenbach had the following to say, "Among the group considered was Dr. Hoelscher, the dogmatician and rubricist, which means in plain English, that he was thoroughly educated in religion and knew how to run the complicated affairs of sacristy and altar. It was no secret that Dr. Hoelscher was on the list of bishops-to-be three times. Later he good-naturedly acknowledged the fact that his high-strung temperament would have made the honor a terrible burden and would have shortened his life considerably." Quigley was Bishop of Buffalo for only six years. He then went on to reign in the Archdiocese of Chicago. Laudenbach speaks of the events in Buffalo that led Rome to make his new appointment. He says, "One of the outstanding accomplishments of Bishop Quigley was the decisive and rather sensational manifesto against Socialism.

Another big thing was his part in getting proper living conditions and wages for dock laborers. His struggle against Socialism drew the attention of Rome. We hated to see him go: he was fair and every inch a prelate and every bit a man."

Following Quigley was Charles Henry Colton. Laudenbach speaks about his election as bishop, he says, "Colton was made bishop here largely on account of his success in handling perilous parish-affairs in New York City. It's an open question, no doubt, as to which qualification of bishop is preferable: the professor, the official, or the pastor? I once heard Archbishop Messmer, late of Milwaukee, tell in my rectory, that a professor made a weaker overseer than a pastor. I don't think that to be true because Messmer was, as the professor, in the foreground of affairs besides being a prolific writer." Laudenbach then gave graphic snippets of Colton's character. He said, "It didn't take long for our gentle prelate to get into harness. Must I describe him? Then I would say that he had what the Germans call *eine Johannes-natur*, a St. John the Evangelist make-up. A fine, even aristocratic exterior, refined language, gentlemanly. He was not a magnetic preacher but he did love people, and loved to be near them. His sentences flowed from his lips in a tranquil stream, devoid of the Jovian diction of an Ireland or McQuaid. Although he allowed many churches to be open and bore the financial burdens involved, he was, however, never robust at any time. His vision and energy, which went into building the Cathedral on Delaware Avenue, took its toll and led to his death in May 1915. It was the eve of his departure for Confirmation at Salamanca. He was a soldier dying with his armor unstained, giving and giving to the end. So the stately marble pile on Delaware Avenue, for which he had made so many trips, had its first service: the funeral of its builder."

In 1916, Bishop Denis Dougherty came to Buffalo; he stayed only two years. Laudenbach wanted his readers to learn the background of the new bishop. He wrote, "The new occupant of the See in Buffalo was to be a distinct surprise. We got our bishop from the Philippine Islands, where American priests were sent to work in the new addition of our colonial expansion under difficult and embarrassing conditions. He was a native of Pennsylvania, born in the coal-regions at Girardville, and attended elementary school there. As a little boy he was one of the thousands employed in the *breakers* of the collieries, sorting coal; he knew hard work early. Before his ordination on May 31, 1890 he was a student at the American College in Rome. Crowned with a doctor of theology and famed for his dogmatic erudition, we cannot be astonished to find him immediately installed as professor at the College. Rome likes to pick bishops from academic men known to the authorities of the Eternal City."

Laudenbach then described the grand parade held in Buffalo, welcoming the new bishop. He wrote, "I saw our Bishop Dougherty for the first time in Boston at the Missionary Congress of 1912. Little did I think that I would be marching on Main Street a few years later and wondering, with the rest, 'How would he be?' It was a great parade in June 1916: about thirty thousand men in line and poor weather. And it was the last big turn out of its kind witnessed here for a new bishop. The parade was discontinued when Bishop Turner arrived, and a reception for Bishop Duffy, at the Central Terminal, plus radio, was a better substitute." Laudenbach then described Dougherty at work and his future status. He said, "For Bishop Dougherty, punctuality was one of his fondest and most enforced rules. He was always at our disposal for business. Preached at all Confirmations and rather long discourses at that, plus the children's questioning. A sociable man, full of stories, and merry quips. For him Buffalo proved to be a stepping stone to higher things. He became archbishop of Philadelphia, an ecclesiastical shepherd to eight hundred and forty thousand Catholic laity and one thousand two hundred and fifty-nine priests. Three years after his arrival he was 'created' Cardinal in that fair city of Brotherly Love. We don't see him very

often: cardinal-archbishops are tremendously occupied men. But we think of him a lot, are proud of him, and wish him long life in his toilsome and difficult task."

The last biography in Laudenbach's book was of Bishop William Turner who remained as bishop of the diocese for seventeen years. Laudenbach described the man coming into his maturity. He said, "God in His wisdom, sent us another professor in the person of William Turner. His few months as pastor of St. Luke's parish at St. Paul, Minnesota, was a help in understanding the difficulties which beset the clergy called secular, or as some have it: 'the Ordermen of St. Peter.' He flew through his early education. He was a Doctor of Philosophy at a time when most students were plowing through the preliminaries. He came from his studies with a highly polished knowledge of classic French, he spoke and wrote German better than most German-American students abroad, and Italian was as familiar to him as English. Ordained for and adopted by the Diocese of St. Augustine's, Florida, he never served a day. In Turner's case he was destined to be an honored 'guest' rather than a steady sojourner in the sunny Land of Flowers. He went on to great academic heights at Catholic University."

Laudenbach then wrote about Turner's work as bishop and his death. He said, "Pope Benedict XV appointed Dr. Turner as Bishop of Buffalo in 1919. As bishop, he began a vast building program of elaborate churches, especially in the northeastern sector of the city: St. Vincent's, Blessed Trinity, St. Gerard's, St. Bartholomew's, and St. Joseph's. Father Baker, Turner's vicar general finished the National shrine dedicated to Our Lady of Victory honored as a Minor Basilica. Turner took a keen interest in scholastic life and institutions. He assisted at all commencements. He established the St. Vincent de Paul Society in all parishes with the laity participating in the work of ministering to the poor. He was a worthy successor of the men who preceded him. When it became apparent that Father Baker was about

to die Bishop Turner prepared a eulogy for him. Unexpectedly, however, the bishop died first! The funerals of the two men were away the largest and most elaborate ever seen in the city. Bishop Turner came from a unique family. Three of his brothers were priests; three of his sisters were nuns. Seven members of one family given to the Church and her service!" [4]

Although Laudenbach's booklet was well received and widely read particularly by the new generation of Catholics in Buffalo, they were, however, more preoccupied with other matters. In 1939, war had once again broke out in Europe, and the United States, although not actually militarily involved, was called upon to produce steel, chemicals, trucks, airplanes, and munitions for the Allies who were opposing the Axis Powers. In Buffalo, business turned a handspring. Bethlehem Steel, Buffalo Copper and Brass, Curtiss Wright, Bell Aircraft, Buffalo's railroad systems, and harbor commerce were taxed to capacity. There was no more lethargy in industry and commerce. Buffalo had risen gloriously on the heels of war from the Great Depression and its slow recovery. On December 7, 1941, Japanese carrier based planes bombed Pearl Harbor, at Hawaii, in the Pacific Ocean, without warning. The

American battleship fleet anchored in the harbor was devastated. The United States was forced to declare war against the Axis Powers and join the other Allies in World War II. Once again young men, including parishioners of St. Louis Church, were off to war either by enlistment or by being drafted. One month and a half later, however, a joyous occasion took place at St. Louis Church. Father Laudenbach celebrated his twenty-fifth anniversary as pastor of the church.

For one fleeting moment on January 25, 1942, the war was forgotten so that the parish could honor this large man, their priest with the broad nose and large ears, which supported his wired-rimmed glasses. Observing his physique one might think that he might be a general in the old imperial army of Germany, or a beer baron, or a bass drummer in a German band. When asked if he had any faults, he said, "My sole fault is a gift of gab and I'll talk at the drop of a hat!" He carried a perpetual smile on his pronounced lips embedded in his dimpled cheeks. It was said of him that, as a particularly revealing sentence shaped itself in his mind, his lips pursed whimsically. As the thought reached his tongue, his lips spread until with its utterance his smile flowed outward so as to cover most of his broad kindly face. His white hair was sparse but neatly cut, his face cleanly shaven, and his eyes twinkled when he spoke. He had large powerful hands that gave each one who grasped them a quiver of strength in friendship. It was winter in Buffalo, and he wore a large, heavy black woolen overcoat with three large buttons and a very wide lapel. Underneath his coat he wore his black "dickey" front and his Roman collar. This was the priest and gentleman of distinction who had served St. Louis Church as pastor from 1917 to 1942.

On the morning of the daylong festivities a Solemn High Mass was sung at St. Louis Church. Father Laudenbach was the celebrant with Reverend Andrew H. Kunz, assistant pastor at Holy Angels' Church, as subdeacon, and Reverend Martin E. Norton, pastor of Holy Angels' Church, as deacon. Both men were members of the Order of Mary Immaculate. They wore the heavy golden vestments presented to St. Louis Church on its centennial jubilee in 1929, and used the gem-studded chalice obtained for the first time for that same occasion. The altar was lavishly bedecked with Madonna lilies with their trumpet shaped blossoms in imitation of the *fleur-de-lis,* a symbol of France in honor of the Church's patron, St. Louis, Saint, King, and Knight. Professor Henry Zeinz capably led his choir in all the responses as he played the organ.

Following the Mass a breakfast and reception were held in the church hall. In the evening a banquet was given in honor of Father Laudenbach at the Hotel Lafayette, located at 391 Washington Street at Lafayette Square. It was designed by Louise Blanchard Bethune, first woman member of the American Institute of Architects. Arrangements for the banquet were made by Joseph E. Reade, parishioner of St. Louis Church, Knight of St. John, Commandery 204, and maitre-d'hôte at the Lafayette. More than four hundred parishioners, friends, and public figures attended. Among the distinguished guests were Joseph J. Kelly, Mayor of Buffalo and Doctor Robert T. Bapst, superintendent of Buffalo's public schools. Bapst's ancestral home was on the corner of Franklin and Edward Streets; he had attended St. Louis' school as a boy. Both the mayor and the superintendent of schools were lavish in their tributes, citations, and panegyrics of Father Laudenbach filled with warmth, high praise, poetic elaboration, and compliments. In lauding Laudenbach, Bapst said, "He is not only my friend but he is a kindly priest, a humanitarian, and one of Buffalo's best known and respected clergymen. In a day when so many have fallen to the worship of materialism, pragmatism, and naturalism the need of the hour is for men of conviction. Father Laudenbach is such a man." Edward J. Garono, president of the Board of Trustees at St. Louis Church acted as the Master of Ceremonies. In Father Laudenbach's response to these encomiums he said, "I profoundly deny that I am anything but a *run-of-the-*

mine parish priest who likes to talk, work hard, be invited out, and flattered a little." At this point Reverend Francis Hall, assistant to Father Laudenbach delivered the invocation.

The war brought out an extraordinary surge of patriotism and charity among the Catholic population of Buffalo. Priests were enlisting in the service as chaplains, flag ceremonies were held in the churches, the pews were filled to capacity for Masses at which prayers were offered for the young boys who had enlisted or were drafted into the Armed Forces, and Catholic Charities continued with its annual Lenten Fund Drive, considered by some to be failure-proof. On Sunday September 27, 1942, American and Papal flags, purchased with funds collected by St. Louis Church's veterans of World War I, were blessed and dedicated at morning Mass. Soldiers from the 65th New York Regiment were on hand for the ceremony as were the Knights of St. John, Commandery 204. Members of the Coast Guard and Navy were also represented. The flags were brought forth to the altar rail leading to the sanctuary where the triumvirate of Fathers Henry B. Laudenbach, Francis J. Hall, and Walter Fornes raised their hands in simultaneous blessings. Francis Hall was Laudenbach's assistant pastor, and Walter Fornes, was a former member of the parish who had been chaplain of the 106th Artillery in World War I and, in 1942, chaplain of the veterans of the old 65th New York Regiment.

In October 1942, Laudenbach was toastmaster at a send-off banquet for Father Roman J. Nuwer, pastor of St. Joachim's Church at 54 Titus Avenue, Buffalo. On October 24, 1942, he left his parish and took up his duties as chaplain of the 106th artillery. The banquet also honored the twenty-fifth anniversary of the Holy Name Society at the parish. The chairman of the organizing committee was Clarence L. Neunder who in 1965 prepared the way for the Commandery 204 to be transferred from St. Louis Church to St. Barnabas

Church. In November 1942, immense numbers of parishioners and friends crowded into the Masses on Sundays to pray for the men in the Armed Forces. At the reading of the gospel and the preaching of the sermon, Laudenbach stood tall in the sculptured pulpit and emoted with a voice that needed no *Ersatz* acoustical equipment. At the conclusion of Mass the Leonine Prayers were recited for the conversion of Russia and the protection of the men serving in the military.

In the spring of 1943, Catholic Charities had its fourteenth anniversary Fund Drive in full swing. The drive first began during Lent 1929, following Laudenbach's appeal to Bishop William Turner explaining that his nuns from the German Roman Catholic Orphanage, who had been soliciting donations at the Washington Market, were bombarded with tomatoes by anti-begging activists. Turner said to Laudenbach, "This will never happen again." Turner then tried desperately to have charitable Catholic services included in the appropriations from the proceeds of the Secular Joint Charities of Buffalo. He was flatly refused. He then replied, "We'll go it alone!" At that time the Catholic needs for assistance included: four homes for the aged, fives homes for children, two proctectories, two nurseries, and three field agencies. He placed Monsignor John Carr as director of the drive. Carr's committee proposed a goal of $262,116. It successfully received $325,808.

In 1943, Father Laudenbach and Right Reverend Monsignor Kasprzak, pastor of Transfiguration Church on Mills Street were co-workers on the goals committee of the Catholic Charities Appeal. At one of the meetings of the committee, a *Buffalo Times* staff photographer snapped a close-up picture of the two prelates while speaking to each other. When their picture appeared in the newspaper the parishioners at St. Louis Church were confused. The two prelates looked so much alike that they thought Laudenbach had his twin brother hiding out in the diocese, unknown to them. From the pulpit Laudenbach told them, "If you wish to call me Monsignor, and call Kasprzak, Father, I will not mind in the least. If you ask him about affairs at St. Louis Church, he will tell you to talk to his holy likeness, Father Laudenbach, for although I did receive my title of monsignor in 1942, I still prefer to be addressed as Father Laudenbach."

Following the Catholic Charities Appeal Laudenbach began to experience periods of dizziness, fatigue, and shortness of breath. He asked his physician, Doctor H. E. Stadlinger, who resided at 1 North Pearl Street, to come to the rectory. The doctor examined Laudenbach and found that he had a heart arrhythmia that he explained to the priest as an atrial fibrillation and flutter. He also determined that Laudenbach's heart was a bit flabby, lacking contractual strength; he felt that the ventricles on each beat of the heart were pumping insufficient blood. He gave Laudenbach a prescription and told him to try to lose some weight and slow down a bit in his apostleship. Both men chuckled over the affair and the doctor left. The summer passed with little further physical incident and Laudenbach was feeling more confident that his brush with disaster was a thing of the past. It was, however, not so. In early December, he appeared to catch a cold. It was not just the flu bug that attacked him; it was an infiltration of a host of streptococci. Now he had a blush tinge in his skin, chest pains, and chills. These symptoms escalated with the addition of a cough containing bloody sputum accompanied with fever. His heart also began to act-up sending him into fits of dizziness and fainting spells. Stadlinger ordered him to complete bed rest. On December 14, 1943 the doctor announced that Laudenbach's condition was critical. He received the last rites, the Sacrament of Extreme Unction. He lingered in bed for fifteen days under severe stress. Early on Wednesday morning, December 29, 1943, he lapsed into a coma and died at 10:45 A.M. Stadlinger signed the death notice containing a cause that read, "terminal pneumonia, plus a heart complication."

When the end came he was surrounded in his sick room in the church rectory by his assistants, Raymond J. Talty and Bernard J. McLaughlin; his close friend, Reverend Cornelissen, Latin and Greek teacher at the Little Seminary; his nephew and only relative, Henry W. Keitzel, vice chairman of Buffalo's sewer authority, his wife and their daughters, Anita and Mrs. Marie Schneider; the rectory housekeepers, Mrs. Emma Kuntz and Miss Gertrude Volk; several nuns of the Sisters of St. Joseph who taught in the parish school; Brothers Servatius and Gabriel of the Brothers of Mercy, and his nurse, Miss Marian Burns. When the funeral arrangements were made, his body was moved from the rectory to the church at 4:00 P.M. on Sunday afternoon, and the diocesan priests sang the Office of the Dead, consisting of Vespers, Matins, and Lauds. From that time until 10:30 A.M., Monday, January 3, 1944, his body lay in state inside his beloved St. Louis Church. Members of the Knights of St. John, dressed in full military finery, stood as guards of honor, never leaving the casket until the Solemn High Requiem Mass was to begin. With tears in their eyes, more than two thousand parishioners, friends, civic servants, military personnel, and visitors to the city passed by his bier, pausing, praying, and touching. A solid stream of people processed down the long center aisle, from 6:00 P.M. on Sunday until Mass the next morning, each patiently waiting a turn to have one last glimpse of this most active and widely known of all Buffalo's diocesan priests.

By the time the Mass began the church was filled to overflowing capacity; more than two thousand were in attendance. Twenty-two pews of the left center aisle were filled with clergy of all ranks. Distinguished guests, nuns, and Knights of St. John filled the complimentary pews on the right center aisle. Every other pew and available places in the choir loft were filled with parishioners and friends. Across the entire sanctuary including the two side altars a drapery of black and white hung to denote the feeling of loss and the seriousness of the occasion. Approximately thirty altar boys dressed in black cassocks and white surplices surrounded the rear side of the altar. Both chancels and the main section of the sanctuary were filled with the distinguished clergy. At the high altar the celebrant, deacon, and subdeacon conducted the complete ritual of the Requiem Mass. The massive choir led by Henry Zeinz was enthusiastic in the responses; its rendition of its Gegrorian Chant was most moving. Hearts were touched and emotions flowered as the ritual went on and all gazed upon the single closed casket set in the center aisle of the nave immediately in front of the sanctuary. Among the dignitaries of the city present were: Mayor Joseph J. Kelly, Edwin G.S. Miller, City Judge Harry M. Zimmer, Rabbi Joseph L. Fink, Jacob Lang, Former Mayor Frank X. Schwab, George L. Kloepfer, Joseph W. Glenn, School Superintendent Robert T. Bapst, Surrogate George T. Vandermeulen, Health Commissioner Francis E. Fronczak, License Director Stanley Molik, Francis J. Downing, and City Treasurer Leo W. Kirshenstein.

The celebrant of the Solemn Requiem Mass was the Most Reverend Joseph A. Burke, auxiliary bishop of Buffalo's diocese. Participating also at the Mass were: Right Reverend John A. Weismantel, deacon; Right Reverend Edmund J. O'Conner, subdeacon; Reverend William M. Martin, assistant priest; Reverends Albert J. Hoffmeyer, and Lawrence Cornelissen, deacons of honor; Reverend Edward J. Walker, master of ceremonies; Reverends Earl J. Kleis and John L. McHugh, assistants; Reverend Francis J. Hall, cross bearer; Reverends John B. Schwert and Eugene L. Wagner, acolytes; Reverend Francis G. Ruby, thurifer. The priests who served as pall bearers were: Reverends Howard M. Adolph, Norman P. Batt, Robert L. Buchheit, Francis A. Kasprzak, Eugene H. Selbert, Alfred M. Mosack, Thaddeus J. Zablotny, and Timothy J. Lynch. The female religious who were present for the Mass were: the nuns from the German Roman

Catholic Orphanage, of which Monsignor Laudenbach was a past president and director; the Sisters of St. Joseph, St. Francis, and St. Mary Namur. The Supreme Officers of the Knights of St. John who attended were: General Frank H. Biel, Rochester; General Joseph Treppa, Detroit; General Clarence Schu, Evansville, Indiana; and General Frank K. Kreppel, Buffalo. Present also was a delegation of the Fourth Degree of the Knights of Columbus of which Laudenbach was a faithful friar.

Following all the rituals of the Mass the casket was taken down the center aisle and exited through the Main Street portals and down the church stairs to the awaiting hearse at the curb. Coming down the steps, the casket carried by the pallbearers was encased in a canopy of lifted swords of the Second Regiment of the Knights of St. John led by Colonel Philip Gerhard. It was these men who formed the escort and honor guard for the casket while entering the church, departing the church, and in its delivery to Laudenbach's family plot in the United German and French Roman Catholic Cemetery. Members of the police department traffic squad, directed by Captain George W. Rickard, escorted the hearse and the motorized funeral procession to the cemetery from St. Louis Church. Bishop Burke offered final prayers at the gravesite. His final comment to all that were present was, "His demise is a distinct loss to the Diocese of Buffalo and to the members of St. Louis Church whom he guided for more than a quarter of a century."

On January 10, 1944, at the regular monthly meeting of the Board of Trustees, the assembly eulogized Father Laudenbach. They said, "Throughout the twenty-seven years of his rectorship of our parish, he has been to us a true Ambassador of Christ, unctuously preaching the word of God, tirelessly caring for the sick, zealously administering the sacraments, lovingly providing for the poor, painstakingly educating our children, and paternally by word and deed directing us to be followers of Christ. He, by the spontaneity of his wit, the heartiness of his laughter, the geniality of his countenance, the keenness of his intellect, the wealth of his talents, and the diversity of his experiences—the benefit of which he denied to none but graciously expended upon all—has become universally beloved and respected far beyond the confines of St. Louis' parish and the Diocese of Buffalo, and this has redounded to the honor and credit of our church. We the trustees of St. Louis Church personally have in a special manner benefited by his counsel and encouragement. Because he can no longer be with us we, the trustees publicly testify to the greatness of the loss as well as the depth of the sorrow and regret that the parishioners of St. Louis Church and their trustees feel at the death of their pastor, Monsignor Laudenbach. We, the trustees, are therefore resolved that at the beginning of the monthly meetings of our board, for a period of one year, we recite three "Our Fathers" and three "Hail Marys" for the happy repose of his soul, and that this resolution be spread on the minutes of this meeting for all posterity to see and know how our hearts do grieve."

*I*n the beginning of February, 1944, Bishop John A. Duffy appointed Father Michael A. Anstett as pastor of St. Louis Church replacing Father Raymond J. Talty who had been temporary administrator of it for a month after Laudenbach's funeral. After being appointed, Anstett had, for a short time, the assistance of Monsignor William J. Schreck who helped him learn the ropes of being pastor and spiritual leader of the parish in cooperation with the trustees. As Anstett sat at his desk in the rectory, pouring over papers, one could see that he was a large framed man, right handed, receding forehead and beautiful white hair, wire rimmed glasses, and chubby face with pronounced ears. He was sixty-nine years of age. With Schreck's help, he caught on fast. He was no novice in the field of ecclesiastical administration having had a very successful pastorship at St. Agnes Church prior to coming to St. Louis Church.

*N*either the congregation nor the triune governmental system at St. Louis Church interlocking lay trustees, pastor, and bishop, considered as a Rare Tradition in American Catholicism, were enigmas to Michael A. Anstett. He had been previously assigned to the parish in 1909 as an assistant, a task which he graciously fulfilled for two years before being elevated to the first resident pastor at the Church of Our Lady of Good Counsel at Darien Center, New York, seventeen days after its dedication. In less than five years he freed the church of debt, opened a school, and built a rectory. In 1916, however, he returned to Buffalo as pastor of St. Bernard's Church on Clinton Street. It was here that Anstett's father, Michael Anstett, came from Lancaster, New York, to live at the rectory until he died on December 6, 1920. He had been a Union Soldier in the Civil War, captured by the Confederates at the Battle of the Wilderness, and incarcerated at Andersonville. He survived his ordeal there, returned home at the end of the war, married Mary Magdalena Stephan on November 9, 1865, purchased a farm in the Town of Lancaster, and gained the reputation of *Steeple Jack* after he repaired and painted the tower of its Town Hall in the center of the city. Six years after his father's death, Father Michael Anstett was given the nod by the bishop to assume the pastorship of St. Agnes Church.

*H*is first unhappy event as pastor at St. Louis Church was the death of Henry J. Zeinz, which occurred on June 21, 1944. He had been the church's organist for thirty-three years. At the time of his death he was living at 110 Dodge Street. Like Laudenbach he had been quite ill since Christmas of the previous year, but he managed to carry on his duties as organist until the first part of June. He was sixty-one years of age when God called him. He was born in 1883 at Cincinnati, Ohio, first trained in music at the Cincinnati School of Music, later studied in Chicago, and took his first professional position at St. Mary's Church, Covington, Kentucky. He left Kentucky to attend classes at Berlin, Germany, in the Conservatory of Music. Upon returning to America, he was hired by Father Hoelscher in 1911 at St. Louis Church. Immediately, with vigor, he took on both tasks of organist and choirmaster, while he gave private lessons in harmony, voice, piano, and organ. When he died he left behind his wife Martha Gottstein Zeinz, five daughters, Mary, Gertrude, Helen, Angela, and Mrs. Melvin Loatsch. His brother and two sisters lived in Brooklyn, New York. They were Joseph, Anna, and Josephine. Mary succeeded her father as organist at St. Louis Church after his death.

Two of Anstett's greatest joys were the celebration of the feast of Corpus Christi and the May Crowning of the statue of the Most Blessed Virgin. For both of these events he fondly looked forward to and elaborately prepared for. Both the clergy and the laity with great enthusiasm executed them. Corpus Christi was the solemnity of the Body and Blood of Christ. It originated in the diocese of Liege, France, in 1246, based on the revelations of a French nun, Juliana of Mont-Cornillon. It received universal promulgation by Pope Urban IV in 1264. He was convinced that since Holy Thursday, which also celebrated the Eucharist, was so close to Good Friday, with its sadness that the Church needed a special day to celebrate more joyously. The annual event took place on Thursday following Trinity Sunday. It was this feast which had been most honored by the early Alsatian-Lorrainers, Bavarians, and Rheinlanders who had immigrated to Buffalo in the early half of the nineteenth century.

The prominent feature of the ceremonial activities of the day was the grand procession. After Mass was completed in the morning, Anstett went to the tabernacle, dressed in his ankle-length cloak called a cope, took out the host contained in a pyx, and placed it into the monstrance. Schwartz, who was assisting, brought Anstett the large humeral veil, put it on his shoulders, and aided him in wrapping it around the monstrance. Anstett then proceeded to the altar rail where four of the trustees were waiting with the canopy,

which was a very large ornate cloth supported by two long rods with their ends attached to four poles. When opened, the canopy formed a portable tent over the priest carrying the monstrance. Led by a cross-bearer, several acolytes, and thurifers, and flanked by four officers of the Knights of St. John, they walked down the aisle so as to exit by the Main Street doors. As they did so the other three trustees and the remainder of Commandery 204 fell into position.

Behind the Knights, came the children, young boys and girls; the boys dressed in their black suits with a white silk scarf bowed in front; the girls wore white shoes, long white stockings, and white communion dresses with veils on their heads. Behind the children were the adults. The procession proceeded down Main Street to Edward Street and progressed upon the grassy area of the side of the church until it reached the walkway running parallel to the porch of the rectory. Following this lane the entire group entered into the lot in front of the school. At that point a huge tent had been constructed with an altar, covered with beautiful flowers. Anstett moved forward and placed the monstrance onto the altar. When all the accompanying personnel were in their proper positions the devotional rite of Benediction was carried out by Anstett with the entire compliment singing the *O Salutaris* and *Tantum Ergo*. The procession then reorganized and marched down the north side of the church to Main Street, and re-entered the church; members of the congregation took their places in the pews. Anstett, who had proceeded directly to the high altar in the sanctuary, conducted another Benediction. Following the recitation of the Divine Praises the ceremony was concluded.

The other festivity which the parish greatly enjoyed was called the May Crowning. St. John Chrysostom reinterpreted crowning as a sign of victory over concupiscence. The Blessed Virgin Mary was conceived without original sin, and conceived her Son, Jesus Christ, by the power of the Holy Ghost; she knew not

The Corpus Christi Procession at St. Louis Church.
Father Michael Anstett carries the monstrance followed by Father Howard Schwartz

man, she knew not concupiscence. As the Virgin Mary or as the Lady of Victory she symbolized all that was pure and holy. As such, each May, her statues as the Immaculate Conception and as the Lady of Victory were brought outside to be placed in a large tent constructed in front of the school. She, as the Lady of Victory, wearing a crown and holding her Son was placed center-stage upon the altar. Surrounding her on both sides were sprays of lilacs, bluish-red in hue with a medium saturation of high brilliance and fragrance. The altar was neatly decked out with white draperies and linen altar cloths with lace fringing. On the sides of the tent were blue draperies, in front of which stood large potted palm trees. To the left side of this altar was another one on which stood the statue of the Immaculate Conception. It too was surrounded by potted palm trees, gladioli and hydrangeas. It was upon this statue that a beautiful young girl of the parish in her white dress, after climbing a ladder behind it, ceremoniously placed a crown of flowers. Witnessing this event were the children from the school, the Knights of St. John who acted as escort to Anstett, the trustees, and the parishioners of the parish. Following the crowning, Anstett completed the ceremony with Benediction of the Blessed Sacrament as it was done for Corpus Christi.

Father Anstett was a deeply spiritual man, mild and unassuming. His stay at St. Louis Church, however, was short. He was born in Lancaster, New York, on August 20, 1875, attended grammar and high school at St. Mary's, Lancaster, did pre-seminary work at Canisius College, studied philosophy and theology at the Canisianum in Innsbruck, Austria. Returning to Buffalo, he was ordained by Bishop Charles Colton on March 31, 1906. Six days later he said his first Mass at St. Mary's, Lancaster. His first assignment in Western New York was as assistant pastor at St. Vincent de Paul Church on Main Street near Humboldt Parkway. While in this capacity, he also served as chaplain to the Sisters of St. Joseph, whose convent and academy were across Main Street opposite the church. Three years later

he was sent to be assistant to Paul Hoelscher, pastor of St. Louis Church. In 1911, he became pastor at Our Lady of Good Counsel, Darien Center. In 1916, Bishop Denis Doughtery, thinking of him as a successful fundraiser, sent Anstett to St. Bernard's Church, which was opened in 1908; he stayed as pastor until 1926. In that year, William Turner, who had become bishop made him pastor at St. Agnes' Church, which began in 1883. After serving there for eighteen years he returned as pastor to St. Louis Church.

On September 23, 1948, the feast of St. Linus, first Pope at Rome following St. Peter, Anstett rose early to say the 8:30 A.M. Mass at St. Louis Church. He did not, however, say the Mass in honor of the saintly Pope, instead he chose to don the black vestments and say a Requiem Mass for the repose of the soul of the late Helen Jerge. The Canon of the Mass had been completed and Communion distributed to the congregation. He returned to the altar, moved to the right side, and said the Post Communion Prayer. In Latin he said, "Grant we beseech You, O Lord, that the soul of your handmaid, Helen Jerge, of whose death we commemorate, may be cleansed by this sacrifice, and obtain forgiveness and eternal rest. Through our Lord, Jesus Christ, Your Son, Who lives and reigns with You in the unity of the Holy Spirit. Amen." He then closed the Missal and fell to the floor, struck by a massive heart attack. One of the two altar boys ran to the rectory and found Father Schwartz, the assistant, who, while going immediately to the church to anoint his pastor, told the cook to call General Hospital and the Fire Department for an ambulance. In church, surrounded by several women who had attended Mass and who were now praying the rosary, Schwartz administered the last rites as the physician arrived to pronounce Anstett dead. Schwartz commented to all present, he said, "Father Anstett's death was a perfect one; he died in harness. He once told me that when it was time for him to go, he hoped his end would come while in Mass vestments." For believers, one would be hard pressed not to say that on that day, at that hour, Anstett saw the Beatific Vision while being accompanied by the soul for whom he said the Mass, Helen Jerge. After Anstett's death Howard J. Schwartz assumed the temporary pastorship until he was appointed by the Bishop as the next pastor of St. Louis Church. [5]

Top: The Corpus Christi Procession winds around the neighborhood on its way to St. Louis Church. **Left:** The May Crowning Altar constructed in the school yard in honor of the Immaculate Conception and Our Lady of Victory. **Right:** A young girl crowns the statue of the Most Blessed Virgin during Father Michael Anstett's tenure as pastor.

REFERENCES AND NOTES ❖ CHAPTER FOURTEEN

1. As the people left the Jubilee party three items were considered: the Extension of Pearl Street, the prosperity that was preliminary to the Stock Market Crash, and Prohibition. For a map and explanation of the proposed extension of Pearl Street from Tupper Street to North Pearl Street see: *Buffalo Courier Express*, Tuesday, May 1, 1928. For an article, which indicated the enthusiasm of the City for its proposal of the extension of Pearl Street, see: *Buffalo Courier Express*, December 18, 1928. For the plan of the extension facing defeat, time frame, and defendants involved see: *Affidavit and Notice of Motion*, Charles Feldman, The City of Buffalo, Plaintiff against Charles R. Day, Defendants in Condemnation Proceedings No. 106, New York Supreme Court: Erie County, City Hall, Buffalo, New York, November 25, 1932. G. Peter Higgins, Real Estate Lawyer, residing on Tonawanda Creek Road, Pendleton, New York in February 2002, gave the following interpretative information of the document to the author/editor. The defendants who were served and involved in the property condemnation proceedings were: Western Savings Bank of Buffalo; Albany Savings Bank; James Venor Company through its attorneys Kileen and Sweeney; E. H. Close Realty Company; The Trustees of the Roman Catholic Church through their attorney Edward J. Garono; John M. Fornes and Michael J. Fornes; Julia B.S. Steffan, John J. Steffan, George E. Steffan, Albert J. Steffan, Julia L. Steffan, Charles J. Schruefer, Elizabeth Schruefer, Carl Schruefer, Bernice Schruefer, Marjorie Schruefer, George E. Steffan, and M. Salina Steffan through their attorney William S. Mann counsel for Colgan and Battaglia Law Firm; Charles R. Day counsel of the law firm of Shire and Jellinck; Teck Reality Company Incorporated through the law firm of Desbecker, Fisk, and Newcomb; Frank M. Buchheit, Charles J. M. Buchheit, and Rosina Buchheit as executors of the last will and testament of their mother Barbara M. Buchheit, deceased, through their attorney John V. Maloney; Frank M. Buchheit, Charles J. M. Buchheit, Rosina Buchheit, George W.J. Buchheit, and Louis A. Buchheit through their attorney John V. Maloney. Besides those above receiving the notice, the following were also included as defendants: Penn Mutual Life Insurance Co.; Trustees of the Grosvenor Library; The German Young Men's Association of Buffalo; Erie County Savings Bank; The Diocese of Buffalo; St. Louis Roman Catholic Church; Frances M. Koch; Block and Kurl Co.; Louis Le Couteulx de Chaumont; Henry Le Couteulx de Chaumont; Emanuel Baron de Bizi; and Massachusetts Mutual Life Insurance Co. The time table of events which took place in the Pearl Street extension project: December 10, 1929, Common Council adopts a resolution to make a study for the condemnation of lands on the right-away of the proposed extension; February 10, 1929, the study was completed and received by the Common Council; April 1, 1929, Common Council passed a resolution to take the lands, proposed appropriate fees to be rendered for them, and discussed the methods whereby the money would be raised by the City. On April 15, 1929, the resolution became effective; on May 13, 1929, the resolution was adopted by the Common Council; on November 8,

1929, names of those whose land was involved in condemnation was heard by the Supreme Court; on December 2, 1929, all defendants appeared in court and individual testimony was given from December 5, 1929 to December 10, 1929; on Jan 2, 1930, all of the December proceedings were filed at the office of the County Clerk, Erie County; on March 2, 1931, a formal trial at the Supreme Court, Erie County was held with Judge James E. Norton, presiding. Individual testimony was given between March 2, 1931 and October 6, 1931; on March 5, 1931, Rev. Henry B. Laudenbach, pastor of St. Louis Church testified; on March 8, 1932, the court made a decision to go ahead with the condemnation if the money would be available to pay the defendants for their property; on May 14, 1932, the decision was filed in county clerk's office; on May 10, 1932, the Common Council considered to adopt a resolution to discontinue all condemnation proceedings because the money did not appear to be available; on November 3, 1932, Common Council asked their Corporation Council to discontinue further legal negotiations; on November 25, 1932, all defendants were made aware to appear in court to reconsider the case; on December 14, 1932, the Supreme Court heard the case; the project was doomed. For a consideration of prosperity in America before October 1929 see: op. cit. *World's Popular Encyclopedia* and *Illustrated World Encyclopedia*, and Gabriel Costello F.S.C., *Arches of the Years*, Manhattan College, New York City, 1980, p.138. For the concepts of the Catholic Church regarding alcoholism and temperance see: op. cit. *Encyclopedia of Catholicism*, pps. 29, 410, 1240, 1244; and op. cit. *Catechism of the Catholic Church*, pps. 443(1805), 445(1809), 551-52(2290-91). Alcoholics Anonymous was co-founded by Bill Wilson in 1935 when he and his partner advocated the theory of the *Twelve Steps*, see: Milam, James R., and Ketcham, Katherine, *Under the Influence*, Bantam Books, New York, 1983, p. 139. Among the beer, wine, and liquor trade advertisements in the dedication journal for the Knights of St. John's installation of the monument in the United German and French Roman Catholic Cemetery were the following: The name of each establishment is given with some identifying characteristic: **George E. Meyer Malting Company**, Superior Qualities of Malt, offices at 1314-1316 Niagara Street, Malt Houses and Elevators at New York Central Railroad Terminal and Erie Canal, Foot of Lafayette Avenue; **John Kam Malting Company**, High Grade Malt, Capacity 2,500,000 Bushels of Malt, office at 377 Genesee Street corner of Pratt Street; **Lang's Bottled Beer**, Ale, or Porter, Edwin G.S. Miller, President; **Beck's**, Buffalo's Best Beer; **Iroquois** Brewing Company, Speaks for Itself; Drink Simon's Pure, brewed by **William Simon Brewery**; **Phoenix Brewery**, Albert Ziegele, Washington and Virginia Streets; Maltosia Beers, "Try a Case and be Convinced," **German-American Brewing Company**, Main and High Streets; **Manru**, "The King of Bottled Beers," **A. Schreiber Brewing Company**, 662-686 Fillmore Avenue; **Broadway Brewing and Malting Company**, 797-815 Broadway; **International Brewing Company**, "The Drink of the Temperate," Every normal human being desires stimulation, and is better for the right kind of stimulation. We live but once, and the only way we can enjoy it is by making it pleasant for others and for ourselves as we go along day by day. Drinking a glass or two of International Beer with your friends or family is a keen, healthful, and in every way beneficial pleasure; **Buffalo Co-Operative Brewing Company**, Beer and Ale; **John L. Schwartz** Brewing Company, Buffalo's Popular Leaders, Alma Beer, Sparkling Ale, Half and Half, 10-24 West Bennett Street; **Weyand's Brewery** Buffalo, Which is Best: To promise more than you fulfill, or to fulfill more than you promise? Sunnytop, the Quality Beer for the home has always been a little better than we declared it to be. **M. J. Bernard**, Manufacturer of Saloon Furniture, Largest Factory of its Kind in Western New York, Jefferson Street; **Frank X. Schwab Company**, Wholesale and Retail Liquor Dealers, Broadway and Jefferson Streets; **George J. Schwabl**, Broadway Hall, Wines, Liquors, and Cigars, 349-51 Broadway Street; **Lux-Hofbrau**, Buffalo's Famous German Cafe, H.J. Schwabl, proprietor, Imported Muenchener and Pilsener Beers, Business Men's Lunch, Ladies Dining Parlors, Fillmore Avenue near Broadway; **Shining Light Buffet**, Bowling Alleys, Pool Room, and Lodge Hall, Charles J. Schnellbach, proprietor, 270-72 Broadway; **August F. Meyer**, Beer Pumps, Bar Fixtures, Soda Fountains, and Accessories, 408 Broadway; **Buffalo's Brewer's Supply Company**, Dealers in Ammonia, Calcium, and Brewer's Supplies, 446 Genesee Street; **The Hofbrau**, Restaurant and Cafe, Buffalo's Famous German Restaurant, 199-201 Pearl Street and 21West Eagle Street. For information and source material about breweries in Buffalo before prohibition, speakeasies, bootlegging, and political ramifications of Prohibition see: Stephen R. Powell. *Rushing the Growler: A History of Brewing in Buffalo*, Apogee Productions, Buffalo, New York, 1999, pps. 15-20 (early history), 43-46 (pre-Prohibition breweries in Buffalo), 55-57 (temperance movement), 59-60 (Mayor Schwab), 60, 117 (Ulrich's Tavern and Hasenpfeffer Club). When St. Louis Church's parishioners left the Jubilee ceremony in 1929, they had an opportunity to visit Ray Flynn's speakeasy on Main Street opposite the church and adjacent to Weyand's brewery which was closed. For bishops such as Turner and Timon administering the "pledge" during the rite of the Sacrament of Confirmation see: *The Echo*, May 23, 1929, and David A. Gerber, *The Making of an American Pluralism, Buffalo, New York, 1825-60* (referred to in ibid, *Rushing the Growler*, p. 56), Illinois University Press, Illinois, 1989. For the history of Bourbon and other whiskies in the United States and the morality issue of prohibition see: Gerald Carson, *The Social History of Bourbon*, Dodd, Meade, and Company, New York, 1963, pps. 33-37, 204-205, 218-220. Biographies of brewers who were members of St. Louis Church see: op. cit., *St. Louis Church Bazar Chronicle* and *St. Louis Church Bazaar Herald*. For a biography of Edwin Miller see: op. cit. *History of the Catholic Church in Western New York*, p. 335; For Mayor Schwab's feelings about Prohibition and the Anti-Saloon Leagues' attempt to "dry up Buffalo" see: op. cit. *High Hopes*, p. 210. For information concerning Schwab, Schwartz, and Lang as Knights of St. John as well as advertising used by breweries in 1914 see: op. cit. *Monument Dedication: Knights of St. John*, May 31, 1914. Names of Knights of St. John who played poker together at Fort Erie and had picnics on Grand Island were

described by John E. Miller and C. Eugene Miller, sons of Eugene W. Miller Sr. The note concerning Mayor Schwab purchasing shoes for needy children was told by Rosina Buchheit (deceased) to Marie Buchheit Miller, her niece, who passed it on to the author/editor.

2. Financial information concerning St. Louis Church during the Depression was extracted from *Minutes of the Board of Trustees Meetings; 1929-1936*, a copy of these minutes is in the St. Louis Church Archives. Each year during the second week of September a meeting was held by the trustees with the congregation of the church. Father Laudenbach, a member of the trustees ex officio, was always present at this meeting which was held for the purpose of the congregation for nominating any trustees whose time of service had expired. Nomination was tantamount to being elected but a formal election always took place two weeks later in September. On the second week of October the regular meeting of the board of trustees took place. The annual audited report was read and approved. The new board, of which Father Laudenbach was always a member ex officio, which had been elected, made an election among themselves as to the officers for the year and appointed the heads of the Real Estate Committee and the Finance Committee. They then proceeded to review the financial transactions of September and consider any old and new business. The following made up the boards of trustees during the depression years: (1929-1930), Edward J. Garono, president; Fred L. Hardick, recording sec.; Louis Ludaescher, financial sec.; William E. Swanz, treas.; Peter M. Ginther, John M. Fornes, Albert E. Wagner. (1930-1931), same as year before except Edward A. Rick replaced Peter M. Ginther. (1931-1932), same as year before except Eugene B. Ebner replaced John M. Fornes. (1932-1933), same as year before. (1933-1934), same as year before. (1934-1935), same as year before. (1935-1936), same as year before. During the second week of every month a regular meeting was held at which time all finances were reviewed and the payment of all bills was approved. For information concerning unemployment in America during the Depression and the attempts of both Hoover and Roosevelt to solve the situation of panic see: op. cit. *The Modern Encyclopedia*, pps. 539, 1225-26, 1231-32; op, cit. *World's Popular Encyclopedia*, article on depression under United States history; op. cit. *Illustrated World Encyclopedia*, p. 1590; Arthur M. Schlesinger, Jr., *The Politics of Upheaval*, Houghton Mifflin Company, Boston, The Riverside Press, Cambridge, 1960, pps. 1-11. For Federal Financial Relief coming to Buffalo see: op. cit. *High Hopes, pps. 224-28*. For the paving of Edward Street see: *Newsclippings* in the St. Louis Church Archives. The details of the probate of Anna Marie Born's will appeared in the *Buffalo Courier Express*, Sunday, April 30, 1930. Anna Marie Born was a daughter of Philip Born and sister to Barbara Born who was the first wife of Philip. After Philip Born's death in 1848, Jacob Weppner and Barbara Born managed the brewery, which he ran at the corner of Genesee and Jefferson Streets. In 1862 Gerhard Lang married Barbara Born, bought out Weppner's interest in the brewery; Lang and Barbara then ran the company known as Mrs. Philip Born and Gerhard Lang until 1876 when Gerhard built a new plant

at Jefferson and Best Streets known as Gerhard Lang's Park Brewery. Anna Marie was unmarried. In her will she left $6,000 to St. Louis Church. Of this amount $4,000 was to be used for the general purposes of the church, and $2,000 was to be used for Foundation Masses said for the deceased. She also gave $1,000 to the German Roman Catholic Orphanage, Dodge Street, $1,000 to the St. Francis' Asylum, Pine Street, $500 to Sisters of Good Shepherd Home of Refuge, Best Street, and $400 to Rev. Albert Hoffmeyer, assistant to Father Laudenbach at St. Louis Church. The remaining estate was divided among five nieces and one nephew: to Annie E. Miller, daughter of Gerhard Lang and Barbara Born who had married Edwin G. S. Miller; to Gerhard and Barbara's other children, Katherine Lang, Bertha O'Neil, Marie M. Lang and Jacob G. Lang. After Prohibition Jacob G. Lang operated the Gerhard Lang Brewery.

3. For Centennial activities in Buffalo in 1932 see: op. cit. *High Hopes*, pps. 225-26, For interviews with Laudenbach concerning depression days see: *Buffalo Times*, May 29, 1931; *Buffalo Evening News*, Dec 21, 1939; and *Union and Echo*, February 10, 1961. For information about Father Coughlin, Communism, and Fascism during this period see: op. cit. *The Politics of Upheaval*, pp. 16-23, 556-61, 626-30; 92-5; 167, 177, 197, 185-87, 84-88; 70-78, 78-88. Also on Coughlin see: op. cit. *Encyclopedia of Catholicism*, p. 370. For the Hindenburg memorial and parade see: *Local Germans Hold Memorial for Hindenburg*, newsclipping, Sept. 4, 1934, a copy is in the St. Louis Church Archives. In the Music Hall the *Steel Helmet Band performed the Fackeltanz, the torch dance*. It was repeated in the parade. Another song, which aroused the audience, was the *Night Prayer of the German Army*. Genesee Park is the same place known as Schiller Park. Humboldt Park was named for Friedrich Heinrich Alexander, Baron von Humboldt (1769-1859), a German explorer and naturalist. During 1797-1804 he traveled in South America, Mexico, and the United States. He made many contributions to the philosophy of science. Today it is called Martin Luther King Park. A Swastika is an ornamental figure in the form of a Greek Cross with the ends of the arms turned at right angles, all to the right or all to the left. It is a very ancient device found in the remains of the Bronze Age in Europe, India, Asia Minor, and among the North American Indians. It was believed to be a religious symbol.

4. Source material for Laudenbach's quotes see: Rev. Henry B. Laudenbach, LL.D., *Little Stories of Buffalo's Bishops*, Catholic Pamphlet Society, Buffalo, New York, pp. 5-31. **Bishop John Timon**, born Conewago, Pennsylvania, 1797; resided in St. Louis, MO, 1823; ordained in Lazarist's Seminary of the Virgin at Barrens; on mission to Arkansas and Texas; parishes in Cape Girardeau, Jackson, and New Madrid, MO; appointed Visitor of the Lazarist Order, USA, 1835; refused position of assistant bishop of St. Louis, MO; made prefect apostolic to empire of Texas in 1840; appointed bishop of Buffalo in 1847; built St. Joseph's Cathedral on Franklin Street, died April 16, 1867. **Bishop Stephen Vincent Ryan**, born Almonte, Canada, January 1, 1825; entered

St. Charles Lazarist Seminary, Philadelphia, PA, 1840; ordained by Archbishop Kenrick at St. Louis, MO, 1849; made president of St. Vincent's College and Visitor of the Lazarist's Order in 1857; became bishop of Buffalo in 1868; a great educator, established parochial school system in Buffalo Diocese; died at Buffalo in 1896. **Bishop James Edward Quigley**, born in Canada but raised in Buffalo; became bishop of Buffalo in 1897, while being pastor at St. Brigid's Church; as bishop his vicar-general was Monsignor Gleason; as bishop he fought against socialism and advocated labor protection for workers; appointed archbishop of Chicago in 1903. **Bishop Charles Henry Colton**, descendant of an old and rich family of New York City; became bishop of Buffalo in 1903; laid corner stone of the new St. Joseph's Cathedral on Delaware Avenue in 1912; he died in May, 1915. **Bishop Denis Dougherty**, born in the coal region of Pennsylvania; went to St. Mary's College in Montreal; studied at St. Charles Borromeo Seminary in Overbrook; attended the American College in Rome; ordained May 31, 1890. The American College was an old nunnery transferred to the American Episcopacy by Pope Pius IX. After teaching 13 years at Overbrook he went to Nueva Segavia in Luzon, Philippine Islands; five years later transferred to the Island of Panay and the See of Jaro; made bishop of Buffalo 1916; made archbishop of Philadelphia in 1918; made cardinal three years later. **Bishop William Turner**, born in Ireland in 1871; studied at the Jesuit College in Nungret; went to the American College in Rome until 1893; attended the Catholic Institute in France for post graduate study; taught at Catholic University, Washington D.C.; made bishop of Buffalo in 1919; consecration took place in the Monastery of Mt. Sepulchre, Washington D.C., on March 30, 1919 by Cardinal James Gibbons; Laudenbach was deacon to Cardinal Gibbons at Turner's consecration; after 10 years in Buffalo the priests of the diocese presented Turner with a special crosier designed by Rev. Dr. Francis Wanenmacher, rector of St. Bernard's Church; he died in Buffalo 1936. One finds a discussion of Cathedraticum in op. cit. *Encyclopedia of Catholicism*. Historically it was a tax paid by each parish to the bishop ordained by a code of Canon Law initiated in 1917. Although at first it was a symbolic gesture of submission to the bishop, it later developed into a larger financial payment. In 1983, Canon Law Code 1263 imposed a moderate tax on all parishes.

5. For Laudenbach's 25th anniversary see: *Buffalo Courier Express*, January 26, 1942. For a description of Laudenbach see: Note of Gratitude from Father Laudenbach to the attendees of the banquet for his 25th anniversary. His picture is on the cover. A copy is in the St. Louis Church Archives. For information concerning Hotel Lafayette see: *Buffalo Architecture: A Guide*, Buffalo Architectural Guidebook Corporation, The MIT Press, Cambridge, Massachusetts, 1982, pp. 11, 45, 89. Louise Blanchard Bethune (1856-1913) was the first woman member of the American Institute of Architects, began her career after graduating from the University of Buffalo. From 1876 to 1881 she worked in the offices of Buffalo architects Richard A. Waite (1848-1911) and F.W. Caulkins, before becoming a partner with her husband

More than a century of spiritual and moral leadership in the City of Buffalo by five outstanding pastors at St Louis Church. *Left to right, top row*: Reverend Joseph M. Sorg (1867-1888), Right Reverend Paul Hoelscher, Doctor of Divinity (1888-1916). Bottom row: Right Reverend Henry B. Laudenbach (1917-1944), Rev. Michael A. Anstett (1944-1948) and Reverend Howard J. Schwartz (1948-1964).

Robert Bethune in the offices of Bethune, Bethune, and Fuchs. Hotel Lafayette was one of her last designs. Information concerning Joseph E. Reade was offered in 2002 by Marie Buchheit Miller who knew him through her aunt, Rosina Buchheit, who lived on Pearl Place. For the source material for the flag blessing, the chaplain send-off banquet, war-time church services, and Laudenbach and Kasprzak as members of the goals committee for Catholic Charities see: *newspaper clippings*, St. Louis Church Archives; *Courier Express*, September 28, 1942; *The Buffalo Times Rotogravure Section, Buffalo Evening News*, October 14, 1942; *Buffalo Times*. For the history of the Leonine Prayers see: op. cit. *Encyclopedia of Catholicism*, p. 766. These prayers were ordered to be said at the conclusion of Mass by Pope Leo XIII in 1886. They consist of three Hail Marys, a collect, and a prayer to St. Michael the Archangel. Pope Pius XI ordered their recitation for the conversion of Russia. The practice was discontinued after 1964. Monsignor George Yiengst, Pastor St. Pius X parish, continues to say these prayers after Mass for the men in the military during periods of armed conflict which involves the USA military. For background of the Catholic Charities see: op. cit. *Celebrating God's Life In Us*, pp. 97-99. The story concerning the beginning of the Catholic Charities Appeal was taken from Monsignor George Yiengst's sermon on Sunday, March 10, 2002 at St. Pius X Church. For the details of Father Laudenbach's sickness, death and funeral see: *Buffalo Evening News*, December 29, 1943; *Courier Express*, January 3, 1944; *Courier Express*, January 4, 1944; and newsclippings and pictures, "Body Lies in State," "St. Louis Church Mourns Death of Msgr. Laudenbach.""Throngs Attend Last Rites for Popular Priest," "Pontifical Mass Held at St. Louis Church for Msgr. Laudenbach," "Rites for Msgr Laudenbach Set This Morning." These clippings can be found in the St. Louis Church Archives. For the trustees statement of resolutions see: *Minutes of the Regular Monthly Meetings of the Board of Trustees of St. Louis*

Church, January 10, 1944, a copy is in the St. Louis Church Archives. For information concerning Father Anstett see: op. cit. *125th Anniversary, St. Louis Church, 1829-1954*; "Father Anstett Accepts His New Charge," *Courier Express*, February 16, 1944. For details about Father Anstett's father, Michael Anstett, and biological material about Father Anstett's education, ordination, and early church assignments see: *Genealogical Studies of the Stephan Family* preserved in the archives of William Kurzdorfer, curator of the 1903 Kimball Pipe Organ, St. Louis Church, Buffalo, New York. The Stephan family originated with Michael Stephan born circa 1771 in Reitzel, northeastern France, in the province of Alsace. He married Christina Beck and they had six children: Michael F., George, Franz, Peter, John and Jacob. These children eventually settled in Lancaster, New York. Father Anstett's father, Michael, was, after the Civil War, a member of the Chapin, New York, Post No. 12, Grand Army of the Republic. Father Anstett had a twin sister, Margaret. She died at the age of 15 in 1890. His other siblings were Bernard, Henry, Magdalena, Rose, Elizabeth, Joseph, Cecilia, and Frank. For obituary of Henry Zeinz see: newsclipping possibly *Courier Express*, copy in the St. Louis Church Archives. Information concerning the Corpus Christi celebration was obtained from Louis J. Buchheit who lives in Naples, Florida. He supplied the author/editor with many photographs,which will be found in the St. Louis Church Archives. Likewise, the St. Louis Church Archives contains photographs which describe the events of the May Day celebration during Anstett's pastorship. For details of Father Anstett's death see: *Buffalo Courier Express*, September 24, 1948; *Buffalo Evening News*, Thursday, September 23, 1948; *The Union and Echo*, Friday, September 24, 1948. For a description of Anstett's funeral service at St. Louis Church see: *The Union and Echo*, October 1, 1948. For the details of Anstett's last will and testament see: *Buffalo Evening News*, Friday, February 4, 1949.

CHAPTER FIFTEEN

Golden Age of Tridentine Catholicism in Buffalo

The history of Petrine Catholicism has been punctuated from its very beginning with terrible crises. It suffered through Roman persecutions, Arian heresies, barbarian invasions, lay investiture struggles, Eastern and Western Schisms, and Martin Luther's revolt, the most devastating of them all. Subsequently, Catholic altars were abandoned, priests and nuns deserted their cloisters, half of Europe was lost to obedience to the pontiff in Rome, and the unity of Christendom became only a memory. The Catholic Church, however, did not die! It turned inward upon itself and focused upon the remnants of its spirituality. It devised a plan to reconstruct its liturgy, parochial work, preaching, monastic communities, and social apostolate. It faced head-on the problems of doctrinal confusion, fiscal abuses, widespread ignorance, and organizational breakdown. Although it took twenty-eight years after Martin Luther raised his first cry, the Catholic Church of Rome, under the leadership of Pope Paul III, opened in the northern Italian city of Trent, on December 13, 1545, a Counter-Reformatory Council which took eighteen years to complete its work of spiritual reconstruction. Upon its completion the new Church, the Tridentine Church, was on its way to engender a tremendous movement of reform.

This remodeled Catholic Church had reaffirmed every jot and tittle of tradition that made it strong, self-confident, and spiritually revitalized. It had its Revised Roman Missal and its Tridentine Mass securing uniform religious expression for Catholics throughout the world. It had its Catechism of the Council of Trent that gave a clear, concise summary of Catholic beliefs and practices. It was, however, a highly conservative rule of order that it prescribed. A rigoristic and authoritarian institution was set up in which bishops had absolute control over their dioceses, and no room was left for the participation of the laity in the administration of the Church. The bishops could not afford to admit that the Protestants were right about anything, so the language of the liturgy remained clothed in Latin. Because of this, the Council of Trent failed to restore to the people a sense of participation; they became an audience who witnessed the mysticism of the liturgy, and were forced to run after a multitude of extra-liturgical devotions in order to satisfy their need of involvement in acts of worship. For Catholics, spiritual perfection involved a high degree of personal activity that combined a striving for self-control with the acquisition of virtue and a zeal for good works of mercy and charity. The new structure of the Church, even with its limitations, scored great spiritual, intellectual, cultural, and missionary victories that lasted unchanged until the second half of the twentieth century.

The Golden Age of Tridentine Catholicism in Buffalo was most gloriously expressed at the Eucharistic Congress held in Buffalo, September 22-25, 1947, which celebrated the one hundredth anniversary of the founding of the diocese. It was the Tridentine Church that had come to Buffalo in 1829 eighteen years before the Buffalo Diocese was formed. Then, only from St. Louis Church, known as the Lamb of God, did the acquisition of virtue and a zeal for good works of mercy and charity flow. Like a good mother, however, through pain and sorrow, she gave birth to other churches, she saw schools and seminaries formed, she became surrounded by health care institutions, and she greeted the influx of members of many religious orders. By 1850, with John Timon as Bishop, there were five churches and a convent chapel in the City of Buffalo, nine churches in rural Erie County, two churches in Genesee County, four churches in Niagara County, twelve parishes in Wyoming, Cattaraugus, and Chautauqua Counties. One church had been constructed in Portage, Allegany County, and parishes had arisen at Angelica, Scio, Cuba, and Friendship in that county. In that year the Very Reverend B. O'Reilly announced that he had begun a seminary in Buffalo in a rented house. In 1947, the Diocese of Buffalo counted within its boundaries two hundred and seventy churches, and seven hundred and seventy-seven priests. It boasted of five seminaries: Christ the King associated with St. Bonaventure's College, Seminary of St. Joseph, St. Columban's Seminary at Silver Creek, New York, Holy Cross Seminary at Dunkirk, New York, and Our Lady of the Angels associated with Niagara University.

By 1850, Timon had founded the College of St. Joseph under the direction of secular priests. By 1861 he relieved them of their teaching duties and employed the services of the Brothers of the Christian Schools. Between 1850 and 1868 the diocese saw the creation of St. Bonaventure's College; Niagara University; St. Elizabeth's Academy and St. Mary's Academy, under the direction of the Sisters of the Third Order of St. Francis; the Academy of St. Vincent, Buffalo; Academy of the Sisters of St. Francis, New Oregon; Academy of the Sisters of St. Francis, East Eden; St. Joseph's Academy of Our Lady of Mercy; Holy Angels Academy, under the direction of the Grey Sisters; and St. Joseph's Academy, Lockport, under the direction of the Sisters of St. Mary of Namur. Nearly one thousand students were being accommodated. In 1947 there were thirty-two business and academic high schools, private

or parochial in nature, under the direction of twenty Orders of Priests, Sisters, and Brothers. Parish grammar schools had increased from only one at St. Louis Church in 1848, to one hundred and sixty in 1947, in which forty-one thousand students were educated.

Besides the two colleges and academies founded before 1868, the diocese was serviced with higher education by Canisius College, Mt. St. Joseph's Teachers College, D'Youville College, Canisius High School, St. Joseph's Collegiate Institute, Buffalo Academy of the Sacred Heart, Holy Angels, Immaculata Academy, Immaculate Heart of Mary Academy, St. Mary's High School in Lancaster, Mount Mercy Academy, Seminary of Our Lady of the Sacred Heart at Stella Niagara, St. Mary's of the Cataract at Niagara Falls, St. Mary's Business School, St. Ann's Business School, St. Francis High School at Athol Springs, Mount St. Mary's in Kenmore, Annunciation High School, St. Nicholas Academy, St. William's High School at Winchester, De Sales Catholic High at Lockport, Bishop Duffy High School at Niagara Falls, and Our Lady of Victory Academy in Lackawanna. The Religious Orders involved with the administration of these schools were: Franciscan Fathers, Holy Cross Fathers, Jesuits, Sisters of St. Joseph, Sisters of the Third Order of St. Francis, Sisters of Charity, Sisters of Mercy, The Grey Sisters, The Order of Miss Nardin, Sisters of St. Mary of Namur, Brothers of the Christian Schools, Passionist Fathers, Oblates of Mary Immaculate, Franciscan Sisters, Felician Sisters, Sisters of Christian Charity, Sisters of St. Francis of Penance, Sisters of Notre Dame, Order of Friars Minor Conventional, and the Oblates of St. Francis de Sales.

In 1947, the mercy and charity advocated by Tridentine Catholicism was expressed in the operation of Catholic hospitals in the Buffalo Diocese. The Sisters of Charity, who began their first hospital in Buffalo on Pearl Place near Virginia Street, were administrating a large complex on Main Street near

Delavan Avenue. On the architect's drawing board, however, were plans for their new hospital to be placed at Main Street near Kensington on the site of the St. Louise de Marillac building that had taken the place of the former St. Mary's Hospital on Edward Street. Louise de Marillac hospital had been established in 1943. Previous to that time, its building was known as Providence Retreat, a Catholic hospital for the mentally ill, and an institution that had been in existence since 1860. The Sisters of Charity also operated Emergency Hospital in Buffalo. The Brothers of Mercy came to Buffalo in 1924 and opened an Infirmary that gained great renown. The Sisters of Mercy began St. Jerome's Hospital in Batavia in 1917 and Mercy Hospital in Buffalo in 1904. Besides teaching, the Sisters of St. Joseph took over the administration of Our Lady of Victory Hospital in Lackawanna in 1917, and staffed it with several nuns who had been trained as nurses in academia both in New York and in other states. Sisters of St. Francis and the Third Order of St. Francis were deeply involved in the operation of three hospitals: St. Francis Hospital in Williamsville, Mount St. Mary's Hospital in Niagara Falls, and St. Francis Hospital n Olean.

*B*esides hospitals, works of mercy were performed by the Religious Orders giving care to infants, orphans, homeless and wayward children, and the aged. The two infant homes were: St Mary's Infant Center staffed by the Sisters of Charity and Our Lady of Victory Infant home attended to by the Sisters of St. Joseph. The six homes for children were: German Roman Catholic Orphan Home, Immaculate Heart of Mary Home, St. Vincent's Manor, St. Mary's Home and St. Joseph's Farm and School at Dunkirk, and St. Joseph's Home for boys associated with Our Lady of Victory in Lackawanna. The four homes for the aged were: St. Francis Home in Buffalo, St. Francis Home in Gardenville, St. Anthony's Home in Hamburg, and St. Vincent's Home in Dunkirk. Our Lady of Refuge, conducted by the Sisters of Our Lady of Charity, was the only protective home for girls and women. The

diocese, however, did have organized programs for Catholic families and child welfare, a foster home program, and an adoptive service. The two large charitable volunteer societies were the St. Vincent de Paul Society for men and the Ladies of Charity for women.

*I*n order to support these institutions and organizations the diocese had organized The Catholic Charities of Buffalo and Our Lady of Victory Charities, Lackawanna. Catholic Charities was first initiated in 1923 by Bishop Turner. Its purpose was to aid financially, through an annual appeal, those institutions already founded and to develop more agencies of Catholic welfare throughout eight counties making up the diocese. The first year the campaign was held, the donations resulted in a financial success of $325,808.25. By 1947, the donations produced a gross sum of $1,084,469.31. Our Lady of Victory Charities was completely independent of Catholic Charities; and funds gathered in private donations from persons in every part of America were sufficient to grow a super complex of mercy in Lackawanna, which included an infant home, a hospital, an orphanage, and an academy. All these, as seen in 1947, could be attributed to the gigantic physical effort of a frail, saintly man, Monsignor Nelson Baker. He was called the Padre of the Poor; he was so filled with love for the unfortunate that he could turn no one away. Today his remains rest inside the great Basilica of Our Lady of Victory that he created.

*T*he preparation and execution of the Eucharistic Congress epitomized the rigoristic and authoritarian rule of the ecclesiastical clergy in which the laity had very little input or none at all, but were expected to be present in audience as witnesses rather than as active participators. At the liturgical receptions and pontifical Masses one observed with the presence of cardinals, archbishops, and bishops, the chain of command of the monarchial church from top to bottom of the ecclesiastical ladder. The formal use of titles, positions, and locations of residency indicated the sequential authority represented at the Eucharistic Congress. Although not present but featured first in the program of the Congress, which listed all the events of the four-day solemn commemoration of the Diocese of Buffalo's first centenary, was His Holiness Pope Pius XII. On the first day of celebration the liturgical reception in St. Joseph's New Cathedral on Delaware Avenue was presided over by His Eminence, Francis Cardinal Spellman, Archbishop of New York.

*T*he civic reception, held at Kleinhan's Music Hall was presided over by The Most Reverend John F. O'Hara, Bishop of Buffalo with The Most Reverend Joseph A. Burke, Auxiliary Bishop of Buffalo, acting as chairman. On this occasion Bernard J. Dowd, Mayor of the City of Buffalo, was given the podium so as to welcome the dignitaries to Buffalo. The following day the celebrant of the first Pontifical Mass was the Most Reverend Amleto Giovanni Cicognani, Titular Archbishop of Laodicea and Apostolic Delegate to the United States. He was, as the official representative of Pope Pius XII, a resident in Washington D.C. There were no laymen serving in any titular capacity of the liturgy. Diocesan priests acted as crossbearer, acolytes, thurifers, torchbearers, trainbearers, book-bearers, candle-bearers, crosier-bearer, and gremial-bearer. The choir was exclusively filled with priests and seminarians from St. Mary's of the Angels, Niagara University, and St. Bonaventure College. The choir director was Reverend Paul J. Eberz. Mrs. Celia Kenny, however, was listed as organist.

*I*n the ecclesiastical procession to the altar and at designed places in the sanctuary were the eminent visitors: Archbishops Samuel Cardinal Stritch from Chicago, Bernard Cardinal Griffin from Westminster, London, James Charles Cardinal McGuigan from Toronto, Canada, and Norman Cardinal Gilroy from Sidney, Australia. Accompanying these prelates were thirteen bishops, coadjutor bishops, or bishops of military ordinate from Rochester, Brooklyn, Albany, Ogdensburg, Syracuse, New York City, and Maryknoll on the Hudson River. Committee meetings, at which every facet of Catholic life was touched upon, were held at Hotel Statler, Lafayette Hotel, Civic Stadium, Memorial Auditorium, Kleinhans Music Hall, St. Stanislaus Church, and Our Lady of Victory. Grave consideration was given to the past, present, and future needs and duties of those involved in youth services, press and radio, clerical activity, teaching, nursing, office work, farming, law and order, public and social services, activities of nuns, mothers, and fathers, banking and business activities, and the professional life of college students, dentists, and physicians.

*P*residers at each of these meetings were pastors, associate pastors, and assistant pastors from the two hundred and seventy parishes in the Diocese of Buffalo. Clerics were also in charge of the committees devoted to the functional activities of the Congress such as arts, ceremonies, commercial exhibits, deaneries, decorations, health, history, housing, directorship of laymen and lay women, mission exhibits, music, oriental exhibits, processions, programs, publicity, public safety, radio, reception, records, registration, sacristy, school participation, seminary involvement, themes, traffic, transportation, and ushers. All seven hundred and seventy-seven priests of the diocese held either one or two positions of prime authority in conducting the operations of each of these committees. Secondary positions of leadership and directorship were allotted to laymen in fields and professions such as medical, dental, banking, law, nursing, office works, public service, home economics, and music. Ironically a layman, James F. Loftus, was chosen as the Grand Marshall of the procession held in Delaware Park. Also music conductors, organists, and a few choir directors were laypersons. Among them were: Mrs. Celia Kenny, Fred A. Ressel, Jerome Murphy, George Holovitch, Sister M. Agnes, and George Chambers. [1]

Because the bishops who had conducted the sessions of the Council of Trent, which ended in 1563, would not admit that the Protestants were right about anything, they kept Latin as the language of the Mass and as the musical expression of prayer in the liturgy. The Latin language, therefore, offered a mysticism and uniformity to the Mass that was unchangeable for four hundred years. The priest who did not face the people, but stood at his ornate altar, facing the tabernacle conducted it. Only on two occasions, once at the Offertory and again at the final blessing, did he turn toward the congregation. Otherwise, the Tridentine Mass was a personal interrelationship between God and priest, through whom Jesus Christ offered Himself and His Mystical Body, the Church, to His Father as Priest and Victim in a memorial of Calvary. The laity were present only to add to the priest's private and personal worship by witnessing this social public act of offering to God, the sacrifice of the most pleasing victim possible, His Divine Son, Jesus Christ. The consecration was the central point of the Mass, for then the priest, a man who offered sacrifice and mediated between man and God changed the bread and wine into the body and blood of Christ, by the power given to him by God. The appearances of bread and wine, such as size, color, taste, smell, called the matter of bread and wine, were not changed, but the form or soul of Jesus Christ entered into these substances by a process known as transubstantiation. Although the appearance of bread and wine remained after consecration, the substance was transmuted. From this point in the Mass, the real presence of the body and blood of Christ, the Victim remained on the altar until the priest completed the sacrifice by consuming the transmuted substances. There were various prayers and ceremonies prior to consecration, and, likewise, those also which followed it until the conclusion of the Mass.

Two types of Masses were distinguished; High Masses at which the prayers and invocations were sung and Low Masses at which they were read. For the simplest type of each category a single priest only was required as a celebrant. For special feasts or anniversaries where a deacon and a subdeacon assisted the celebrant, the Mass was referred to as a Solemn High Mass. If a bishop was the celebrant on such occasions, it was considered a Pontifical High Mass. For High Masses the organist filled the church with liturgical music and the choir sang the responses to the priest's invocations and prayers. For simplicity of explanatory purpose, one concentrates on the Low Mass. It began with the priest accompanied by an altar server entering the sanctuary from the sacristy. The server was dressed in black cassock and white surplice. The priest was clothed in six distinct garments. Around his shoulders, underneath his outer garments, he wore a square piece of white linen called the amice. It symbolized the helmet of salvation, the virtue of hope that helped the priest to overcome the attacks of Satan. Over the amice he wore a long white linen garment reaching to his feet. It was the alb. It symbolized the innocence and purity that adorned the soul of the man who ascended the altar. Around his waist, over the alb, the priest wore a tasseled cord called a cincture. It proclaimed the virtues of chastity and continence required of every priest. Over his left forearm he wore a maniple, an ornamental vestment of silk or damask. Originally used as a handkerchief, it symbolized the labor and hardships of the celibate's life. Around his neck the priest wore a stole, a long scarf originally worn by Roman magistrates as they conducted official duties connected with judicial practice. The stole was the official sign in any priestly function involved with the administration of the Sacraments. It was a garment representing the immortality forfeited by Adam and Eve in the Garden of Eden when they first sinned against God. Finally over these five garments, the priest wore a chasuble, a very full garment shaped like a bell. Originally it reached almost to his feet; but, following the Council of Trent, it suffered much from a process of shortening and stiffening.

By the middle of the twentieth century, the more historical chasuble, a draping garment that symbolized the virtue of charity and the yoke of unselfish service that the priest assumed at his ordination, replaced the shortened and stiffened one. The maniple, stole, and chasuble carried the liturgical colors required for the occasion on which the Mass was conducted. White was worn on joyful and glorious feasts of Jesus Christ, the Blessed Virgin Mary, and on feasts of angels and saints who were not martyred. Red, the color of blood, was used for feasts of Our Lord's Cross and Passion, Masses of the Holy Spirit, particularly Pentecost, and on feasts of the Apostles and Martyrs. Green, symbolized budding and living vegetation. It was worn representing hope during seasonal Masses following Epiphany and Pentecost. Special colors such as old rose, gold, and black were rarely worn. On the Third Sunday of Advent and the Fourth Sunday of Lent old rose made its appearance at the altar, tempering the sadness of these penitential seasons. Gold replaced white, red, and green on very special occasions. Black, the color of death and mourning, was worn at Masses of the Faithful Departed.

As the priest entered the sanctuary from the sacristy with his server, he carried the chalice, purificator, and paten, with an unconsecrated host upon it. Covering these were chalice veil and pall that were of the color of his outer vestments. Pausing at the center of the foot of the altar, they genuflected, and the priest went up the steps, kissed the relic, and placed the chalice upon the linen cover of the altar. He turned, came back to the foot of the altar, again turned, and made the sign of the cross as he said, "In Nomine Patris, et Filii, et Spiritus Sancti, Amen." With this the first part of the Mass began. It was known as the Mass of the Catechumens. The priest announced, "Introibo ad altare Dei." The server responded, "Ad Deum qui laetificat juventutem meam." The priest had proclaimed in Latin that he would go in to the altar of God, and the server responded that it was the God of his gladness and joy. The priest then said the Confiteor, his confession of sinfulness requesting God's forgiveness. Representing the entire congregation, the server repeated it.

After the priest offered prayers of petition for the remission of sins, he again rose up the steps, kissed the relic, and proceeded to the right hand side where an open missal had been previously placed. He announced the prayer, usually a psalm, known as the Introit, the entrance prayer, taken from what was known as the Proper of the Mass, a prayer pertinent to the feast or event being celebrated. Prayers like this one, said throughout the Mass, were variable and distinct from those of the Ordinary of the Mass that never varied. Upon completion of this prayer, he returned to the center; and, in a loud voice, proclaimed the triad of Greek words, a Christe Eleison sandwiched between two Kyrie Eleisons, the only Greek used in the Latin Mass. In a High Mass, the choir would take up the chant at this point; and, as representatives of the entire congregation, rendered an extensive musical performance sung in parts by altos, sopranos, tenors, and basses. Not only were the Kyrie Eleisons and Christe Eleison sung once but also several refrains of the same were often added. Remaining at the center of the altar, the priest then intoned the chant of joy, the Gloria in Excelsis Deo. The choir sonorously completed this prayer of praise. Only during Advent, Septuagesima, Lent, and Requiem Masses did the congregation not hear, say or sing this chant of joy.

The priest again returned to the right hand side of the altar and read the Prayer from the Proper of the Mass that asked God's favor to be spread upon His people. It invoked His favor in connection with the feast or season of the year being celebrated. At its conclusion, the priest immediately read from the Proper of the Mass an Epistle, Gradual, Alleluia, and possibly a Tract if it were required. The server who had been kneeling at the foot of the altar during these readings, rose, approached the right side, picked up the large missal, carried it to the center of the foot of the altar, genuflected, and brought it to the left side. While he was doing this the priest had returned to the center, said a prayer, from the Ordinary of the Mass, to cleanse his heart so as to proclaim the Holy Gospel, a reading from the New Testament. Following this recitation the priest went to the pulpit, read the same gospel and delivered a sermon to his congregation in the vernacular. After his sermon, he returned to the altar, genuflected in front of the tabernacle; and, on Sundays and important feast days, announced in Latin, *Credo in Unum Deum*, the beginning of the Nicene Creed. Once again, the choir burst into song, completing this extended rendition of an act of faith. The Mass of the Catechumens had ended.

After removing the corporal, a folded linen cloth, from the pall, the priest then leaned the pall against the shelf next to the tabernacle, unfolded the corporal on the altar linen before him underneath the chalice, removed the veil from the chalice, folded it neatly upon the altar, raised the host on the paten with outstretched arms, and in Latin said, "Accept, Holy Father, Almighty and Eternal God, this spotless host which I, Your unworthy servant, offer to You, my living and true God, to atone for my numberless sins, offenses, and negligences; on behalf of all here present and likewise for all faithful Christians living and dead, that it may profit me and them as a means of salvation to life everlasting. Amen." He then made the sign of the cross with the paten and host, and placed the host upon the corporal. At the right side of the altar, with the assistance of the server, he poured wine and water into the chalice, blessing the water prior to pouring it, and then, returning to the center, offered the chalice and its contents to God as he had done with the host. Then making the sign of the cross with the chalice, he placed it upon the corporal and covered it with the pall. He then prayed for union with God in Christ, asked mercy for the world, and begged God to accept the offering that was being made.

He then invoked the Holy Spirit to come upon these gifts and make them holy. Moving to the right hand side of the altar, where the server stood holding a dish, a cruet filled with water, and a linen cloth, the priest washed and wiped his fingers which were soon to hold the host which would be transubstantiated, and begged the Holy Trinity to accept his offering. Then for the first time, other than at his sermon, the priest turned and faced the server and the congregation. He said, "Orate Fratres, Pray brethren that my sacrifice and yours may be acceptable to God the Almighty Father." In Latin the server responded for all the faithful present; he said, "May the Lord accept this sacrifice from your hands to the praise and glory of His name, for our advantage and that of all His Holy Church." The priest ended with, "Amen." A final prayer called a Secret was offered, ending that part of the Mass of the Faithful known as the Offertory.

In the Tridentine catechism there were six commandments of the Catholic Church. The first of these was that all Catholics were required to rest from servile work and hear Mass on Sundays and Holy Days of Obligation; the required Mass was that of the Missal of Pope Pius V published in 1570. This was the same Mass that was in vogue nearly four hundred years later during the Golden Age of Tridentine Catholicism in Buffalo. Catholics were bound to keep this commandment under the pain of grievous sin, interpreted by most as mortal sin. To commit a mortal sin, however, one had to engage in an act of wrong-doing of a grave or grievous nature while the wrong-doer did so with sufficient reflection and full consent of one's will. The Catholic Church, therefore, had prescribed, with grave intent, the attendance at Mass on Sundays and Holy Days of Obligation. An individual was excused only for weighty reasons such as illness, nursing the sick, attention to the needs of infants, or residing in a location that was at a great distance from a church. Catholics were bound to fulfill that obligation under the pain of grievous sin because it was one given by the Church; for it was God Himself who gave this commandment to each Catholic through His Church.

All Catholics were bound to assist at the Holy Sacrifice of the Mass with attention and devotion. They sinned against the commandment when through their own fault they missed Mass altogether or missed part of it. Although present, they still sinned if they laughed, talked, or misbehaved during its conduct. The question arose, however, as to what part of the Mass could be missed because of one's tardiness, but not result in grave matter. Among the generality of Catholics, missing the Mass of the Catechumens would not constitute serious gravity. Missing any part of the Mass of the Faithful, however, would indeed be considered very grave. As the priest removed the corporal from the pall and spread it upon the altar, beginning the offertory, all Catholics knew that they had to be in their pews. This was their Mass; the Mass of the Faithful. Once the congregation had received Communion, however, many Catholics assumed that the Mass of the Faithful was completed and many immediately departed from the church. Sometimes very few remained following the final prayers and the rendition of the Last Gospel. In doing so they felt exonerated from any sense of serious sin. These were those Catholics who had come to Mass only to fulfill a duty by doing the minimum necessary for achieving it.

After the *Orate Fratres* had been completed the priest turned again toward the tabernacle and prayed the Preface to the Canon of the Mass of the Faithful. It was indeed a prayer of thanksgiving and praise to Almighty God, the Father. It ended, invoking the aid of the angels and archangels of heaven in a glorious chant of praise, "Sanctus, Sanctus, Sanctus, Holy, Holy, Holy, Lord God of hosts. Heaven and earth are filled with your glory. Hosanna in the highest. Blessed is He Who comes in the name of the Lord. Hosanna in the highest." At this point in Solemn High Masses, the organist would introduce a lavish display of chords and overtones while the choir enthusiastically sang in Latin the Sanctus with its Hosannas. At the conclusion of the singing, with hands folded and thumbs crossed, by ritual requirements, the priest prayed for the leaders of the Catholic Church, and the living members of the Communion of Saints, commemorated the Saints,

beginning with the Blessed Virgin Mary and ending with the early martyrs of Christianity. He then bent over the altar and consecrated the host on the paten saying, "Hoc est enim Corpus meum; for this is my Body." As he then elevated the host over his head so as to be viewed by the congregation, the server lifted, with his left hand, the tail of the chasuble; and three times he stroked the bell which was in his right hand. In like manner, the priest consecrated the wine in the chalice saying, "Hic est enim Calix Sanguinis mei, novi et aeterni testamenti: mysterium fidei: qui pro vobis et pro multis effundetur in remissionem peccatorum; for this is the chalice of my Blood of the new and eternal covenant: the mystery of faith: which shall be shed for you and for many unto the forgiveness of sins." Likewise, as with the host, the chalice was raised over the priest's head while the server lifted the chasuble and rang the bell three times.

Following the act of transubstantiation, the priest continued with his supplications to God the Father, imploring that Christ's sacrifice which had just been performed upon the altar be carried before the face of His Divine Majesty and have His grace showered upon all who had participated in the sacrifice. The souls of those members of the Communion of Saints who had died and gone to their eternal rest were then commemorated. The priest then, holding the chalice in his left hand with the host held in his right hand over the mouth of the chalice, elevated the Body and Blood of Christ once again toward heaven saying in Latin, "Through Him, and with Him, and in Him, is to You, God the Father Almighty, in the unity of the Holy Spirit, all honor and glory." With this act, the Canon of the Mass came to an end, and preparations were made to conduct the sacrificial banquet. It began with the recitation of the "Our Father." The priest then broke the host, mingled a small piece with the contents of the chalice, and pronounced the "Agnus Dei, qui tollis peccata mundi..." At this point at Solemn High Masses the choir accompanied by the organ gave a beautiful rendition of this solemn plea for forgiveness and peace through Jesus Christ, the Lamb of God.

After several more prayers, the priest consumed the Body of Christ and drank His Blood while the server rang the bell three times. Following his Communion the priest administered Communion to the faithful who approached the altar rail separating the nave from the sanctuary. They knelt and received the host upon their tongues. To each recipient, the priest said in Latin, "May the Body of Our Lord Jesus Christ preserve your soul to life everlasting. Amen" When all that had come forth received, the priest returned to the altar, wiped the chalice, and recovered it with the veil and pall. Meanwhile the server moved the missal from the left side to the right. The priest approached the missal and recited a Communion and Post Communion Prayer from the Proper of the Mass. Upon completion, he closed the book. He then came to the center of the altar, turned toward the server and the congregation and announced, "Ite, Missa est; Go you are dismissed." Immediately, raising his right arm, he blessed everyone saying, "Benedicat vos omnipotens Deus, Pater, et Filius, et Spiritus Santus." The server in the name of all responded, "Amen." Going to the left side of the altar, and reading from a card, the priest said the Last Gospel, a passage from the New Testament, John's Gospel, Chapter One, verses one through fourteen. At its completion the server said, "Deo gratias." The priest, carrying his chalice covered with the veil and pall, came to the foot of the altar, knelt with the server, and recited the Leonine prayers specified by Pope Pius XI to be said for the conversion of Russia. Upon completion, priest and server genuflected and walked into the sacristy. [2]

For the Tridentine Mass, there were standard sets of Propers of the Mass for Sunday, Holy Days, Feasts, and Requiems. Each Mass had its ironclad Introit, Collect or Prayer, Epistle, Gradual, Alleluia Invocation, Gospel, Offertory Prayer, Secret, Communion, and Post Communion. These never varied from year to year, and each liturgical year was coded and predictable. All could be placed neatly in a single Missal. It contained Sundays and Feasts whose dates on the calendar never changed, however, there were variable Sundays and Feasts that depended upon the cycle of the moon but could be solidly predictable over a span of hundreds or thousands of years if it were so desired. For movable feasts, the Tridentine Liturgical Calendar had its focal point with the date of Easter, the commemoration of the resurrection of Jesus Christ from the dead. It was always celebrated on the first Sunday following the first full moon after the vernal equinox. Hence it always fell on a Sunday between March 22 and April 25 each year.

Six weeks with six Sundays prior to Easter marked the Season of Lent. Ash Wednesday always occurred on the Wednesday before the First Sunday of Lent which, if one did not count Sundays of Lent, would be forty days. An introductory period to Lent, a semi-penitential period, ran for three Sundays before Ash Wednesday; they were called Quinquagesima, Sexagesima, and Septuagesima. For example, in 1957 Easter fell on April 21, Ash Wednesday on March 6, and Septuagesima on February 17. After Easter Sunday, there were always eight weeks and eight Sundays that made up the Easter Season. Low Sunday was the name given to the octave of Easter; after which, followed four Sundays simply titled Sundays after Easter. Ascension Thursday was held on the fortieth day after Easter followed by the Sunday after Ascension. Then came Pentecost Sunday, which was fifty days after Easter, and Trinity Sunday followed by the feast of Corpus Christi on the subsequent Thursday. With this feast, the annual predictable but variable part of the liturgical calendar came to an end.

On December 25, the Tridentine Church celebrated the birth of Jesus Christ. The time period, which included four Sundays prior to this date, constituted the liturgical period known as Advent. The fourth Sunday before Christmas, therefore, was the First Sunday of Advent and the beginning of the Tridentine Liturgical Year. For example, in 1945, Christmas fell on Tuesday; the previous Sunday was the Fourth Sunday of Advent.

The First Sunday of Advent was held on December 2. That year Advent had twenty-three days. In 1987, Christmas fell on Friday. Counting back four Sundays from this date one found that the First Sunday of Advent was November 29, and there were twenty-six days before Christmas. The Christmas Season ran from Christmas Day until the First Sunday after Epiphany that was celebrated on January 6. During the Christmas season, one observed the Sunday within the octave of Christmas, the feast of the Circumcision of Jesus on January 1, feast of the Holy Name of Jesus, celebrated on the Sunday between Circumcision and Epiphany, and the feast of the Holy Family celebrated on the First Sunday after Epiphany. At most, six Sundays constituted the liturgical period after Epiphany. Some years there would be a lesser number depending upon the date that was predicted for Septuagesima Sunday. On the Sunday after Pentecost the feast honoring the Trinity was celebrated. After the feast of Corpus Christi the Sundays were given numerical indicators of Sundays after Pentecost. On the Friday following the Second Sunday of Pentecost, the Tridentine Church always celebrated the feast of the Sacred Heart of Jesus. The number of Sundays after Pentecost varied from twenty-four to twenty-eight depending upon the length of time allowed to fill the entire time from Pentecost until the First Sunday of Advent that began the next liturgical cycle.

Even as late as 1962, prior to the Second Vatican Council, the mentality, which went into creating the liturgical calendar, was an agrarian one. It was for this reason that the Tridentine Church tenaciously held on to the celebration of Rogation Days and Ember Days. Each year, April 25, was the feast of St. Mark, the disciple of St. Peter, who is alleged to be the author of the second Gospel of the New Testament. He founded the Church of Alexandria and was later martyred there. Although not directly connected with his feast day, it was on that day that the Tridentine Church celebrated a Rogation Mass which followed a grand procession which included that which was called the *Greater Litanies*. It originated in Rome near the end of the fourth century by St. Gregory the Great. Only the celebration of Easter on that day would have caused the celebration to be delayed until the following Tuesday. On three other days, Monday, Tuesday, and Wednesday, preceding Ascension Thursday, Rogation Masses and processions were held. These, however, were titled, the *Lesser Litanies*. St. Mamertus, Bishop of Vienne, France, introduced them in 470. During the reign of Pope Leo III, who died June 12, 816, these litanies were celebrated in Rome and became part of the observance of the Universal Church.

The prayers offered on these days not only begged God to ward off natural calamities of both drought and flood which could destroy crops and bring about starvation, but also asked Him to bless the seeds which had been planted so as to bring forth an abundant harvest in late summer. The days of fast and abstinence known as Ember Days, held, each year, on Wednesdays, Fridays, and Saturdays of four weeks during each of the four seasons, winter, spring, summer, and fall, were held in the agrarian society so as to thank God for the blessings received during the previous season. They were progressively held during the week following the Third Sunday of Advent, the week following the First Sunday of Lent, the week of the Octave of Pentecost, and in the week following September 15, the feast of the Holy Cross. The prayers of the Proper of the Masses for these days begged God to be generous with vocations to the priesthood, grace for the priest to successfully fulfill his duties, and increase the spirituality of the laity.

The Tridentine laws of Fast and Abstinence, by today's standards, were rigorous. The rule of abstinence, which forbade the use of flesh-meat, and broth made from meat, was binding on all that had completed their seventh year. Fish, eggs and milk products were allowed, and lard was acceptable in preparing food. The rules of fasting, permitted only one full meal a day, but allowed food to be taken in the morning and the evening provided that the quantity of both occasions did not equal one full meal. Those who were bound to observe this rule were all that had reached their twenty-first birthday but had not reached their sixtieth year. Although in an agrarian society the full meal was taken at noon, the church allowed that Catholics could keep the observance even if the principal meal was taken in the evening. In the liturgical cycle, the days of abstinence were on all Fridays of the year. Days of fasting only, were all weekdays of Lent. Days of both fast and abstinence were on Wednesdays and Fridays of Lent, on Ember Days, and on the Vigil of Pentecost, of the Assumption of the Most Blessed Virgin, of All Saints Day, and of Christmas. If a Vigil fell on a Sunday the penitential observance was cancelled. At the time of the Golden Age of Tridentine Catholicism in Buffalo, by a special Apostolic Indult granted to the bishops of the United States, flesh-meat was allowed to be eaten by all working men and their families at the principal meal, except on all Fridays, Ash Wednesday, the forenoon of Holy Saturday, and the Vigil of Christmas. In the United States, each Catholic's Easter duty of making a good confession and receiving the Holy Eucharist at least once a year had to be fulfilled between Ash Wednesday and Trinity Sunday. [3]

The Golden Age of Tridentine Catholicism in Buffalo had begun to bud at St. Louis Church during the short pastorship of Michael A. Anstett, but it had had its roots in the innovations of the long reigning pastors, Joseph Sorg, Paul Hoelscher, and Henry B. Laudenbach. It was left to fully blossom under the guidance of Father Howard J. Schwartz, whom Bishop John O'Hara assigned there on Friday, December 4, 1949. Schwartz's tenure as pastor consumed sixteen years which one can truly mark in the history books as the "Last Hurrah" of four hundred years of Tridentine Catholicism. When Anstett was assigned to St. Louis Church in 1944, he had been pastor at St. Agnes Church, having been there since 1926. Howard Schwartz had been his assistant for a short time, arriving early in 1943.

Upon leaving St. Agnes, Anstett informed Schwartz that as soon as he was settled in his new assignment he would ask the bishop to assign him to St. Louis Church. Schwartz, however, did not come quickly. Anstett had to wait nearly two years before he would get him as an assistant. The United States had entered World War II, and Schwartz, who volunteered for service in the Army on December 1, 1943, attended classes at Harvard University in preparation to be a chaplain. He served from April 1944 until the end of the American occupation of Austria in March 1946. He was with the Allied invasion force at Normandy Beach in 1944. Returning from Europe that spring, he was assigned as assistant pastor at Our Lady Help of Christians.

When Anstett heard of his appointment there, he spoke to the trustees of St. Louis Church, and told them that he was bringing Schwartz to be his new assistant. He called him his "Left Bower." The trustees understood what he meant; they too were familiar with the game of cards called *Euchre*. In that game, using a reduced number of cards from the deck, the right bower, the highest card, was the knave of trump. The next highest card, the other knave of the same color, was the left bower. Schwartz arrived early in 1947. From then until his death, Anstett was a pastor and a leader who leaned heavily upon the companionship, loyalty, and advice of his new assistant. Although Schwartz had been the temporary administrator of St. Louis Church following Anstett's death, his appointment as pastor was not a "shoe-in." On June 25, 1949, Bishop John O'Hara named Father Martin H. Ebner, pastor of Fourteen Holy Helpers Church, Gardenville, New York, as the next pastor at St. Louis Church. Ebner accepted, and O'Hara transferred Schwartz, who was only forty-one years old, to the new St. Joseph's Cathedral on Delaware Avenue as an assistant. Schwartz, however, never got a chance to pack his bags. Within twenty-four hours, Ebner, who always kept inviolably his promise of obedience to his bishop, for once reneged, and prevailed upon him not to send him to Buffalo. Existing records claim that he wanted to stay at Gardenville. Rumor was circulated, however, that since Eugene Ebner, his brother, was one of the trustees at St. Louis Church, Martin, considered that accepting the bishop's new assignment would result in a real or imaginary conflict of interest. His decision not to accept it was an indication that The Rare Tradition in American Catholicism was alive and well at St. Louis Church in the Golden Age of Tridentine Catholicism in Buffalo.

The Bishop, too, realized the seriousness of Martin's concern because immediately his appointment was aborted and Schwartz was told to stay on at St. Louis as administrator. By December 4, 1949, O'Hara had made up his mind and had given the pastoral nod to Howard Schwartz. On that Sunday evening, a large contingent of the congregation gathered in their pews in church while a small conclave took place in the rectory. Sitting at a desk in the front office near the door to Edward Street, Monsignor William Schreck, pastor of St. Gerard's Church, dressed in black cassock and lace surplice, with pen in hand, proceeded to sign some chancery and parish documents. He had been appointed by the bishop to be director of Schwartz's installation. Standing next to him and looking over his shoulder was Howard Schwartz, waiting his turn to take up the pen. Besides Schreck, Edward J. Garono, president of the parish board of trustees, and Albert J. Eger, the board's secretary, were the other official witnesses.

Signing these documents was preliminary to the official installation service that was soon to take place in the church. Immediately following the signing, the four left the rectory, walked to the rear entrance of the church, and entered the sacristy. From there Howard Schwartz walked out onto the altar and was escorted down the main aisle by uniformed Knights of St. John, visiting priests, and torch bearing altar boys to the vestibule. Except for torchlight the church was in complete darkness. When the side door of the church to Main Street was reached, Edward J. Garono in the name of the trustees handed Schwartz a large key. He

went out the side door and came around to the center door that was locked, used his key, and unlocked the main entrance. When he entered through that portal, on that winter night, he fulfilled the ancient custom of a new pastor entering his assigned church. The lights went on inside, and he was again escorted up the aisle toward the altar as the choir sang *Laudate Dominum*, Praise the Lord, written by Caspar Ett, and accompanied by Miss Mary Zeinz on the organ. As the altar was approached, the Knights, with their white-plumed hats, stepped aside and raised swords as the procession ascended the altar steps to the sanctuary. The priests and altar boys knelt before the altar as Schwartz prayed silently.

Schreck then chanted several prayers in Latin, after which he was escorted to the beautiful hand-carved pulpit in the nave by Father James P. Cahill, assistant pastor. Facing the congregation, Schreck, who had been baptized, confirmed, received his first communion, and sang his first solemn Mass at St. Louis Church in August 1897, said, "I am very pleased to see such a goodly number of parishioners and friends of Father Schwartz here tonight." Schreck, sensing that he had the congregation's undivided attention, continued, "Whenever I install a pastor, I think of the words of James E. Quigley, the third bishop of our diocese, who spoke at the dedication of my church, St. Gerard's, in 1902. He told the people that the Catholic priest is not called—he is sent to serve. Father Schwartz has been sent to be with you, and he will remain with you for years to come. Bishop O'Hara has sent you a new pastor, a guide and a counselor. Father Schwartz's work in the past as an assistant and as a chaplain in the army gives us sufficient proof that he will work hard with you and for you."

Schreck then descended from the pulpit, returned to the altar, while Schwartz, simply dressed in his black cassock and white surplice, ascended the pulpit's steps. Once in place, he put his hands firmly on the ledge, bent slightly forward, and said, "I want to thank publicly Almighty God for this blessing and for all the blessings of the sixteen years that I have been in His vineyard. I thank, also, all of you for the wonderful help since I have been here and I certainly hope, as the years go on, friendships will lead to the one goal to which we all aim and aspire—the saving of souls. For me this is a tremendous responsibility that I accept with deep humility. I ask God to continue to bless me in my work so that I may have the strength to carry on and do the work for which Christ came into the world." Although the hearts of the members of the congregation were touched, there was no public emotional response on their part, such as clapping, because the spirit of Tridentine Catholicism was set in silent acceptance. The ceremony came to an end with the recitation of the Divine Praises that followed Benediction of the Blessed Sacrament officiated by Monsignor Schreck.

*F*ather Howard Schwartz, the youngest pastor had become the spiritual director of the oldest church in Buffalo. His appointment, in 1949, marked a unique milestone in pastorships at St. Louis Church. All three pastors, including him, who were born in the United States, hailed from Lancaster, New York. Joseph Sorg's parents had lived there and he was born there in 1838. Sorg's parents brought Joseph to Buffalo to be baptized at St. Louis Church. At that time, most residents, almost all of German or Alsatian descent, from Williamsville, Lancaster, and East Eden came into Buffalo to worship. East Eden was eighteen miles away, Lancaster was eleven miles, and Williamsville was ten miles. By 1850, however, St. Mary's of the Assumption was constructed in Lancaster, Sts. Peter and Paul Church was in Williamsville, and East Eden functioned with St. Mary's Church. Father Michael Anstett was born and baptized in Lancaster. So also was Father Howard Schwartz on June 2, 1908.

*S*chwartz obtained his elementary and high school education at St. Mary's of the Assumption Church. He attended St. Bonaventure College and prepared for the priesthood at the Canisianum in Innsbruck, Austria. He was ordained on March 18, 1934, and said his first Solemn High Mass at St. Mary's of the Assumption Church. Later, he was an assistant at St. Agnes, St. Rose of Lima, Sacred Heart, Dunkirk, and at Our Lady Help of Christians, Cheektowaga. He was an army chaplain from December 1, 1943 to March 31, 1946. He was with the army during the early days of the invasion of Normandy in June, 1944. He was, in 1945, with the rank of major, division chaplain during the American occupation of Linz, Austria. Because of this strong association with military service, it was not fortuitous that during his early tenure as pastor of St. Louis Church, he was chosen as the honorary chairman and cleric who performed the dedication and blessing of the memorial plaque for all military service personnel, men and women from St. Louis Church who participated in the activities of the Armed Forces of the United States in World War II, particularly those who fought, were wounded, or died. The ceremony took place on Sunday, October 1, 1950 at 7:30 P.M.

*T*he ceremony came about after four months of preparation by a committee made up of devoted laymen and veterans of World War I. Paul J. Muth was the chairman, Dr. Francis J. Stone represented the St. Louis Church Men's Club, and Edward Garono, president of the Board of Trustees, represented the temporal administration of the church. These men were competently assisted by Carl Albert, Edward A. Rick Sr., Edwin H. Kolb, Raymond Didley, Walter Rick, Frank Ross, Eugene W. Miller Sr., and Barney Quinn. Together they arranged and received commitment from the Knights of St. John; Troop I Post, American Legion; Veterans of Foreign Wars; Catholic War Veterans; Daly Post, American Legion; Disabled American Veterans; Boy Scouts and Girl Scouts; Amvets; Our Lady of Lourdes Band; and the St. Louis Church Choir; and as many veterans of World War II, as could be contacted. For the ritual of unveiling the memorial plaque, Edward A. Rick Jr., Catherine H.

Knecht, and Louis J. Buchheit represented the entire body of World War II veterans.

*I*n July 1943, Louis J. Buchheit volunteered for the United States Air Force and attended a specialized education program at Syracuse University. After classification, and cadet and gunnery training, he was commissioned a Second Lieutenant in November 1944. At age eighteen, he was one of the youngest officers in the Air Force. Assigned to the Eighth Air Force stationed at East Anglia, England, he flew missions over Germany. When the war in Europe ended in 1945, he was reassigned to the Pacific Theater where the war with Japan was still in progress. With the explosion of the atomic bombs on Hiroshima and Nagasaki, however, his services were aborted, and he was honorably discharged.

*E*dward A. Rick Jr. had joined the United States Army and fought in Sicily and *Up the Deadly Boot* in the Italian Peninsula campaign. In 1944, from somewhere mired in combat, he wrote the following poem that he sent to his parents.

I
I dream so often through the day
From dawn 'til setting sun
Of the loved ones that I left behind
At home, a cherished one.

II
I see my Mom and Dad so real
From the memories I hold
Of the guidance on my start of life
That can't be bought for gold.

III
I hear that voice that is so sweet
That told me right from wrong,
I hear that voice that is so clear
Which made my courage strong.

IV
I can feel the warmth of that boodbye
and the tear stained cheek I kissed

The pain so deep around our hearts,
Our eyes so filled with mist.

V
I know the hand that held mine fast,
In a grasp no one can word,
Our feelings were conveyed so true
Though no one heard a word.

VI
Those partings then I won't forget,
In the years that lie ahead
For those words and looks can't be erased
When "Goodbye, my son," they said.

VIII
But now I dream of brighter things,
Which the future holds I know
For the day is near when I shall come
To receive that warm "Hello."

IX
For time is all that's between us now
The partings they are o'er
My heart beats faster when I think
Who'll be standing at the door.

X
These days that seem so long will fade
To memories of a yester-year
And I shall be back home again
With those I love so dear.

*E*dward A. Rick Jr., Louis Buchheit, and Gerry Braun had been classmates at St. Joseph's Collegiate Institute and kept in touch with each other and their families during the war. When Charlotte Rick, Edward's mother received the poem that her son had sent from Italy, she was quick to send a copy to Gerry Braun's mother, Philomena. Gerry's father was Adolph. In a letter dated April 26, 1944 Charlotte said, " Enclosed are two copies of the poem we spoke of and I thank you for being so interested. St. Joes mailed the *Student Prints* to Ed since he has been 'over there' and he surely enjoys it. Let's keep in touch with each other. I'm always interested to know about my friends' sons, and Ed will also like to hear."

*D*uring the war Edward A. Rick Jr. served in the Army's 194th Field Artillery Unit. After the war he was a member of Kensington Post 708, American Legion. He was a sales representative for International Harvester, Cottrell Bus Company, and Dobmeier Janitor Supply. He retired in 1986. He also had been president of the Kenilworth Fire Department and Kenilworth Exempt Firefighters. He died at his home on July 29, 1991 in the Town of Tonawanda at the age of sixty-seven. Catherine H. Knecht who was present at the unveiling represented the nurses in the United States Navy. The plaque which today can be seen in the church on the Main Street wall of the vestibule carries the following inscription, "This tablet is dedicated in honor of the men and women of St. Louis Church who served in the Armed Forces of their Country during World War II from December 7, 1941 until September 2, 1945. May those who gave their lives for God and Country Rest in Peace. Erected by the Congregation."

*P*rior to the actual unveiling, Father Howard Schwartz delivered an address. He said, "There will be world peace only when man observes the Ten Commandments, practices the Golden Rule, and accepts the Beatitudes of Christ. Blessed are the peacemakers for they shall be called the children of God. Unfortunately, God is still kept from the meeting rooms and peace plans. There is no prayer for enlightenment, strength, or guidance. Man is still trying to do the mighty job alone, forgetting that peace is the work of the Almighty." In reference to the Korean War which had broken out in June 1950, when the Communist Army of North Korea crossed the 38th Parallel and invaded South Korea, he said, "Once more our boys and girls are being sent into battle to settle world problems. And what will be the result? Land may be won, armies destroyed, governments overthrown, cities leveled, but will there be peace? No, not until men change. There is

hope; however, sooner or later we must realize that there is a God above us. There will be peace as soon as we realize that God is our living Father, and that makes all of us brothers." Following his address, Schwartz blessed the unveiled plaque.

*T*here was a parade around the exterior of the church before and after the unveiling. There were units in the parade from all the participating organizations that were contacted by the committee. One proud moment was displayed when Dr. Francis J. Stone and Paul J. Muth made a roll call of all veterans present; one after another more than sixty of them, when their name was called, responded, "Here!" Our Lady of Lourdes' school band played several marches during each parade and tears were brought to many when, as in echo, Charles J. Knowles and John W. Johnson played Taps. Father Schwartz assisted by Fathers Raymond F. Herzing and Albert Bosack offered Benediction of the Blessed Sacrament that concluded with the St. Louis Church choir singing *Holy God We Praise Thy Name*. Upon its completion the band played the national anthem and everyone present joined in singing the *Star Spangled Banner*. Each of the units then broke ranks, but the Knights of St. John escorted the priests who returned the Blessed Sacrament to the tabernacle. Many observers, non-Catholics as well as Catholics, had lined the edge of Main Street and Edward Street to observe the event. It was an example, in the Golden Age of Tridentine Catholicism in Buffalo, how a mix of the patriotic and the ecclesiastical could be enthusiastically displayed inside the church walls and overflow into the streets.

*T*he Tridentine Church may have been considered rigid and set in stone in reference to laws and policies, however, there was always room for dispensations. One such involved a life long member of St. Louis Church, Robert T. Bapst, who lived but a stone's throw away at 388 Franklin Street at the corner of Edward Street. Today his house still stands and is occupied by nuns who use it as a kindergarten. On Sunday, December 18, 1951, Gaudete Sunday, the Third Sunday of Advent, Bapst sang his first Solemn High Mass at St. Louis Church. In October 1949, his dispensation had come from Rome, signed by Pope Pius XII, giving him permission, at the age of seventy, to attend St. Bernard's Seminary, Rochester, which upon successful completion of his studies, he was ordained to the priesthood on December 8, 1951, the feast of the Immaculate Conception. As a layman, he had been a teacher at Canisius High School, principal of South Park High School, and superintendent of the Buffalo Public Schools for thirteen years. Howard Schwartz was chosen to give the sermon at Bapst's first Mass. He said, "Father Bapst is now one of us, and I want to welcome him to our ranks." It was ironic that a man of forty-three years of age welcomed a man who was almost thirty years his senior and full of grand academic achievements. Undaunted, Schwartz went on, "We honor him today not so much for his past achievements, but because of his present dignity in the priesthood. Almost at the sunset of his life this great honor is bestowed upon him. We will always respect him as a priest of God, and we extend to him our best wishes for a fruitful ministry. He will prosper spiritually and when the end comes he can look back not only on a long life of positions of honor in public life, but also as a laborer in God's church. Then the Lord will take him home as a good and faithful servant who did all things well."

From the sanctuary, the Most Reverend Joseph A. Burke, Vicar General and Auxiliary Bishop of Buffalo, addressed the congregation, he said, "As a priest of God and a citizen of Buffalo, I welcome the opportunity of expressing the joy of countless citizens of Western New York on Father Bapst's reaching the goal of a life-long ambition. His influence spread beyond the confines of this region; many of his former students have become priests and honored members of several professions." Present for Bapst's Mass were former students who had achieved prominence in the priestly vocation; the list was a litany of monsignori: Joseph C. Kelly S.J.,

Edward J. Walker, Edmund J. Britt, Joseph Glapinski, Joseph H. Hoernschemeyer, Albert Rung, David A. Coughlin, Charles H. Schreckenberger, William E. Crotty, and Frank J. Walker. Besides his former students, sixteen other priests whom had had association with him in the past were present in the sanctuary. Besides these prelates, there were one thousand eight hundred persons occupying the pews, including many schoolteachers and principals. The Mass, addresses, and ceremonial activity took ninety minutes to complete. Newspapers around the country as far south as Washington D.C. and as far west as Los Angeles, California, enthusiastically gave an account of the event. [4]

By 1953, Fathers Bapst, Bosack, and Coveney were assistants to Father Howard J. Schwartz at St. Louis Church. Following the tenets of Tridentine Catholicism the parishioners, without fanfare or showy piety, worked to gain a high degree of perfection by acquisition of virtue and zeal for good works of mercy and charity. The pastor and his assistants encouraged the members of the congregation; not only to attend liturgical services, but also to wholeheartedly participate in all extra-liturgical devotions afforded by the various parish societies that were in existence. In preparation for the celebration of the one hundredth and twenty-fifth anniversary of the founding of St. Louis Church, the preparatory committee, encouraged by the trustees, asked Father Albert Bosack to present a critique on the various parish societies which were actively engaged in fulfilling their respective missions. He listed each of them and then proceeded to explain their history, mission, and fruitfulness. In existence were: The St. Louis Men's Club and Holy Name Society, The Knights of St. John, Commandery 204, The Saint Vincent de Paul Society, The Third Order of St. Francis, Apostleship of Prayer, Catholic Youth Council, The Dramatic Circle, The Confraternity of Christian Mothers, St. Louis Home School Association, St. Veronica's Altar and Rosary Society, The Altar Boys, and The St. Louis Church Choir. After listing the group

Bosack said, "Each parish society exists chiefly for the personal sanctification of its members. It is evident that collectively these societies are the pulse of the congregation. Each is open to all that might be interested and has the talent required for membership. Every person in the parish should be, or become, an active member in good standing of one or more of these organizations. By doing so, one enters actively into the life of the parish, is afforded an opportunity of widening one's circle of friends and acquaintances, develops new interests, and shares in the spiritual benefits of such membership."

The history of devotion to the Holy Name of Jesus, the basis for the Holy Name Society and Men's Catholic Clubs, found a beginning in the fifteenth century through a three pronged approach. A Franciscan, Bernardino of Siena, vigorously preached this devotion as a means to combat blasphemy. Jesuits later took up the promotion of the devotion and fostered a pious group that called themselves the Holy Name Society. The greatest impetus to the devotion, however, came from the fifteenth century preaching of a Spanish Dominican Friar, Diego of Victoria. He established the *Confraternity of the Name of God*. Its growth in the United States was attributed to the enthusiasm of another Dominican, Father Charles H. McKenna. In 1896, the United States' bishops obtained permission from the Vatican to establish the devotion in every parish under the title, *Holy Name Association*. By 1910 the nation's membership had grown to five hundred thousand. By 1963 there were five million men registered worldwide. At St. Louis Church the Holy Name Society and Men's Club was the successor of the St. Joseph's Men's Sodality, founded in 1890, and open to young men between the ages of seventeen and twenty-five, and the St. Aloysius Sodality, open to young boys between the ages of twelve and sixteen. It was founded in 1891, so as to parallel the spiritual activities of the St. Joseph Sodality. It began in the year of the tercentenary of the death of St. Aloysius Gonzaga in 1591. Since 1926, he has been acclaimed as patron saint

of youth in the universal church. In St. Louis Church, his statue is in a niche to the right of the Sacred Heart of Jesus. The aim of the Holy Name Society and Men's Club was a spiritual one. The members participated in parades and rallies that demonstrated Catholic strength. They had a corporate communion on the second Sunday of each month, their monthly meetings were divided between business and social activities, and their social get-togethers during the course of the year were always pleasant. In 1954, John Rembold was the president.

Prior to 1890, the only sodality functioning at St. Louis Church was that of St. Ann's. It was designed for older women of the parish, mostly mothers, who wished to develop their own spirituality and have a social outlet. The motivation to establish spiritual societies for the young adults in the parish was one result of a weeklong mission conducted at St. Louis Church in the winter of that year by Father Carlstaeter S.J. He invited all parishioners to join him. Hoelscher, the pastor, added his enthusiasm to the invitation. As a result, a very large number of the congregation prayed together, attended daily Mass, listened to inspiring sermons, confessed their sins, and received Holy Communion. At the end of the mission many men and women approached Carlstaeter and asked about the requirements needed of them to form the Society of St. Joseph for the young men and the Society of the Children of Mary for the young women.

Both societies had the same purpose: the steady and unobtrusive strengthening of piety among the men and women of the parish. Both groups were open to individuals between the ages of sixteen and twenty-five. The social activities, which each group conducted, allowed for an intermingling of the two sexes so that acquaintances could be made, pre-marital discussions could be privately held, and engagements leading to marriage could be developed. Many a St. Joseph man married a Child of Mary! Once marriage was contracted, however, each would drop out of their respective societies. Within a year, younger boys and girls saw the advantages of their elder brothers and sisters and formed the St. Aloysius Society for boys and the Guardian Angels for girls. Both groups were limited to those between the ages of twelve and sixteen. By 1929 both women's groups ceased to exist along with the demise of the St. Aloysius Society. Members of the Children of Mary joined either the St. Cecilia Society or the St. Agnes Sodality. Both groups met their demise following World War II. The St. Joseph's Society continued, with a membership of about one hundred; but, by 1954, it too met its demise. Most of the members joined the Holy Name Society and Men's Club.

The Knights of St. John, Commandery 204, was organized in 1913. Its aims were both spiritual and social. One of its chief purposes was to add solemnity and dignity to solemn church services by assisting in the military uniform of their order. The Knights took a regular part in church activities such as installations, Forty Hours, Corpus Christi, Christmas' Midnight Mass, Easter Sunday, and guard duty during wakes and funerals. In 1954, Robert Hecht was the president and chief executive officer. Eugene W. Miller Sr. was captain and chief military officer. Other executive officers were Paul Hardick, Edward Mescall, Louis Buchheit Sr., Eugene W. Miller Sr., and Albert Liegl. In 1954, the Dramatic Circle, was the oldest of its kind in the United States, having had a continuous existence for almost sixty years. Founded after the great fire of 1885 that destroyed the church, it assisted, by means of dramatic productions, to provide funds for the building of a new church. In its heyday it enjoyed a well-merited reputation as a unique amateur group of thespians. The legitimate theater, so popular at the turn of the century, yielded to the "movie" on the silver screen, and the Dramatic Circle ceased to produce plays because the cost was prohibitive and the net return scant. The members, however, retained their affiliation as a social organization. In 1954, Edward A. Rick Jr. was the president.

At St. Louis Church the Third Order of St. Francis, through its monthly conferences, its yearly triduum, and corporate communions and breakfasts strove to inculcate in its members the practice of prayer and self-denial in the spirit of the Poor Man of Assisi. Third Orders in Catholicism, such as the one at St. Louis Church, were associations of laity who were not religious, did not take public vows of poverty, chastity, and obedience, did not live in community, and did not follow the rule of the Third Order Regular of St. Francis, which was founded by the Poor Man of Assisi in 1221. In 1929, the chapter of the Third Order at St. Louis Church, which was open to both men and women, counted three hundred members. They hailed from all parts of the city and suburbs. The Apostleship of Prayer was an association of Catholics designed to foster special devotion to the Sacred Heart of Jesus, especially through the daily recitation of a prayer for a specified intention determined by the Holy Father the Pope each month. It was founded in Vals, France, in 1844 by Francis Gautrelet S.J. Devotion to the Sacred Heart inspired by the popular sense of the heart as the seat of a person's inner life, both natural and supernatural, centered around Christ's threefold love which was emphasized by Gautrelet as human, infused, and divine. Prior to him others helped to promote and shape this devotion: Ignatius of Loyola, Francis de Sales, John Eudes, and Margaret Mary Alacoque. The feast of the Sacred Heart was extended to the Universal Church in 1856 and celebrated on the Friday after Corpus Christi. The practice of enthroning an image of the Sacred Heart in homes began in Paray-le-Monial, France, in 1907. Pope Pius XII described the theological foundation of this devotion in his encyclical *Haurietis Aquas* in 1956. The Apostleship of Prayer in the United States published the magazine titled *Messenger of the Sacred Heart*.

Frederic Ozanam founded the Society of St. Vincent de Paul in Paris in 1833. He, a layman, was so discouraged and outraged by the poverty and disorder that gripped Paris in the early days of industrialization that he felt obliged to do something about reversing the situation. His followers devoted themselves to personal holiness, made contact with the poor, and organized a system of distributing alms to them. They established Vincent de Paul as their patron saint. From a humble local beginning, it developed diocesan, national, and international councils. It first appeared in the United States at St. Louis, Missouri, in 1845. At St. Louis Church, the men of its branch supported Buffalo's diocesan center of the Society of St. Vincent de Paul, collected money, clothing, and furniture for the poor, and did other prescribed corporal works of mercy. In 1954, Eugene Ebner, who was also a trustee of the church, was president, and John Broderick was treasurer. This lay activity was not to be confused with the Congregation of the Missions (C.M.), founded in France in 1625 by St. Vincent de Paul. This group of religious priests was commonly known either as Vincentians and or as Lazarists. In its early history, it had a priory at St. Lazare, France. After 1803, the Order came to the United States where it established parishes, schools, and seminaries. In New York State it was in service at St. John's University on Long Island and Niagara University near Niagara Falls. DePaul University in Chicago was also established by the Vincentian Order.

*I*n 1914, Father Paul Hoelscher advocated an increase in enrollment in the Chapter of the Confraternity of Christian Mothers at St. Louis Church. It had been organized at the church on March 21, 1897. The origin of the international Archconfraternity dated to 1846 when at Lille, in northern France, Louise Josson de Bilhem, a model wife and mother in an aristocratic family invited her friends, also wives and mothers, to her house to express concern about the infiltration of secularization into their Christian homes. On May 1, 1850, these women founded a scapular confraternity under the guidance of the Capuchin Fathers and

Brothers. Its mission was to bring mothers together to pray for their families, to learn the ways to instruct their children about Christian faith, and to carry out locally social and charitable events. The Blessed Virgin Mary as the Mother of Sorrows was the patroness of the sodality. At the time of its acceptance by the Vatican, Pope Pius IX had anathematized the ideology of modern secular liberalism. By the time Hoelscher had encouraged the women to increase their enrollment in their chapter, Pope Pius X had already denounced the culture of modernism to be irreconcilable with Catholicism. The Christian Mothers became the vanguard to protect their children by vigilance against these two ideologies. They also carried out ancillary activities in the parish. They aided the Altar and Rosary Society, organized card parties, and donated many financial contributions to purchase new vestments, repair the organ, and redecorate the church. They had monthly meetings and met on the third Sunday of each month for a corporate communion and breakfast. In 1954, Karolyne Mathers was the president.

*A*fter Father Schwartz became pastor he organized the St. Louis Home School Guild. It was an organization of parents whose children were in the parochial school, and wanted to become better acquainted with the school life of their children in cooperation with the Sisters of St. Joseph who were their teachers. It was loosely connected to the National Federation of Home-School Associations, which was a subset of the National Catholic Educational Association founded in 1904 but reorganized in 1927. Both associations had the purpose to improve Catholic Education at all levels. The Home-School Association particularly endeavored to build on one of the strengths of Catholic Education—the parental involvement in the child's educational progress and spiritual development. Regular meetings were held on the third Thursday of each month and a corporate communion and breakfast were held on the third Sunday of the month.

It was not difficult for one to understand why conflicts of interest did arise between the Home-School Guild, which in 1954 was directed by Margaret Broderick, and the Christian Mothers. Both organizations held their corporate communions on the same Sunday. Both had a similar mission, although the Christian Mothers had, in the middle of the twentieth century, shifted more toward their ancillary activities rather than those involved in their pristine educational mission. Some members of the Christian Mothers openly denounced Schwartz for having created the conflict; they felt that he favored the Home-School more than he did the Christian Mothers. This was not, however, the attitude of all members of the Christian Mothers. Hence, dissention arose within their own ranks and rancor prevailed in their meetings. Peace was finally restored when the two organizations learned how to work with each other; the Christian Mothers becoming the fuel whereby fund raising activities successfully obtained the funds needed to improve educational activities in the school. Parents, teachers, and Christian Mothers eventually worked hand-in-hand in harmony with an occasional mild scurrilous remark spoken softly under one's breath.

Closely associated with the spiritual education of the children was the Confraternity of Christian Doctrine (CCD). It was the official organ of the catechetical instruction of the Catholic laity, both adults and children, who did not attend parochial school. In 1954 at St. Louis Church, the mission of its activities was directed by Father Schwartz and his assistants, in conjunction with the Sisters of St. Joseph. The Confraternity was a Tridentine creation, first proposed in the period of church reform in the sixteenth century. Pope Pius X gave it a rebirth in 1905. His encyclical titled *Acerbo Nimis* commanded the establishment of CCD in every Catholic parish. In 1935 its inauguration as an independent apostolate with a national director and a publishing arm became closely tied to the administrative structure of the Office of the United States' Bishops. Besides CCD, the bishop of Buffalo

also asked all parishes of his diocese to participate in the mission of the Legion of Decency. It reviewed weekly the major movies that were shown in the theaters. In the Buffalo Catholic newspaper, *The Union and Echo*, published weekly, the movies were classified as that worthy of family viewing, those that were for adults only, those that were partly objectionable, and those that were condemned. These movies were also given lengthy reviews. Besides this form of screening, the Legion also became a watchdog of lewd, salacious, and suggestive magazines and comics. *The Union and Echo* listed Catholic Radio Programs along with the stations and times when they could be heard. Two priests who had been associated with St. Louis Church, Fathers Eugene Kolb and James Cahill were regular newscasters on stations WUSJ, Lockport, and WJJL, Niagara Falls. The newspaper also listed weekly the feast-days that would be observed by the diocesan churches during the week. Parents had an excellent opportunity of reading, each week, scholarly and devotional articles, which included editorials by Fathers James M. Gillis C.S.P., William J. Smith S.J., Daniel A. Lord S.J., and Fulton J. Sheen.

St. Veronica's Altar and Rosary Society was the most loosely organized of all those at St. Louis Church. It was founded to give assistance to the Sisters of St. Joseph who were engaged by the trustees to care for the sacristy, vestry, and sanctuary. In the Depression years the Sisters were paid collectively an annual salary of $1,700.00 for teaching and care of the sacristy. The Order provided one nun each year to care for the linens, vestments, and other liturgical supplies. Her part of the total salary was $300 for twelve months of the year whereas the teaching nuns were paid for ten months. The ladies of the St. Veronica's Society did the sewing on the linens and vestments when they would become torn or frayed. They worked closely with the Christian Mothers because several members belonged to both groups simultaneously. Because they were loosely organized, members of the St. Veronica's Society only held one meeting per year in January. The

St. Louis Business Women's Club was not founded until 1953 and contended that it was in principle a successor of the former St. Cecilia Society. Its purpose was manifold: spiritual, material, cultural, clerical, and social. In 1954, under the leadership of Miss Louise Haas, it made generous contributions for church maintenance and met at the communion rail on the first Sunday of each month. Many of its members were also involved with the Ladies Catholic Benevolent Association of which in 1954 Miss Ann Strigl was the president. Other Business Ladies were associated with the diocesan organization known as the Ladies of Charity. In 1954, Edith Ebner directed the chapter at St. Louis Church.

Under the guidance of their moderator, Father Albert Bosack, the youth of the parish, both boys and girls, were organized into groups according to the interests manifested by the young people joining the various divisions. Athletics, theatricals, and forensics were but a few popular objectives that filled their leisure time in a wholesome and profitable manner. The common object of any youth activity, as understood by the priests and the trustees, was to keep the young close to God and their church, and far from the distractions and allurements, which even if they were non-productive of harm, were also deemed non-productive of good. On a national level the bishops had created an office of Catholic Youth in Washington D.C. under the direction of Monsignor Joseph E. Schieder. He had been the former chaplain of students at St. Joseph's Collegiate Institute, Buffalo. In 1954 he claimed that six million Catholic Youth were under his office's influence. In Buffalo, the Catholic Youth Council (CYC) was in vogue, conducting intramural parish sports, summer camping, and youth work.

Auxiliary Bishop Bernard J. Sheil, however, founded the Catholic Youth Organization (CYO), in 1930 at Chicago, Illinois. It sought to solve the teen-age problems of that city by offering its young people worthwhile activities such as scouting, day camps, vocational training, and emphasis on athletics including track meets, swim meets, golf tournaments, and parish-based sports' leagues in basketball and baseball. In 1932, a CYO center was built in downtown Chicago. By 1934 an attempt was made to make the CYO a national organization, however, only Los Angeles and San Francisco cooperated with Chicago in this endeavor. Overcoming this apparent disappointment, the idea caught fire during the next four years and a national conference of CYO was held at Chicago in 1938 because it had expanded to most dioceses in the United States. In 1954, the Buffalo diocese, according to articles in the *Union and Echo,* was still crediting all youth activity as coming under the umbrella of the CYC. It organized and scheduled bowling, baseball, and basketball leagues. It promoted the annual Cub Scout pilgrimage to Our Lady of Victory Basilica in Lackawanna. It provided opportunity for religious exercises, such as recollections and conferences during camping situations. It provided awards for Camp Fire Girls, Girl Scouts of America, and Junior Catholic Daughters of America who would compete in religious study and practice. A chapter of the Boy Scouts and the Girl Scouts had been first organized at St. Louis Church in 1946 and continued uninterrupted for the next eight years.

In 1954, in preparation for the one hundred and twenty-fifth anniversary of the beginning of St. Louis Church, Father Bosack made special mention of the altar boys that served the priests at Mass. He said, "How few there are who appreciate the altar boy! In all kinds of weather, even before the sun has risen, he leaves his bed; and, while the rest of the world sleeps, wends his way to *Ad Altari Dei.* Never known to complain or to murmur, he takes his assignment like a man. A word of thanks, provided it be forthcoming, is his only reward. And yet, the importance of his service must be measured by the fact that without it, there may be no Mass, excepting where urgent necessity warrants making an exception to the law of the Church." In

Tridentine Catholicism, the altar boy represented all the faithful at Mass. Because he did so, his presence was indispensable. Bosack then proceeded to mention the names of those faithful, indispensable, representatives of the congregation. He said, "Those in the senior division, boys who are attending high school and serving Mass on Sundays and festive occasions throughout the year, are: Carl Albert, Michael Broderick, Carlos Carballada, Walter Mohler, Charles Schifferle, Ralph Rentz, and Joseph Valvo. Boys who are attending the parochial school and serve Mass during weekdays are: Frank Bova, Donald Buchanovich, Ronald Foegen, Richard Hardick, Anthony Jubilis, Robert Straveski, Michael Bova, Pat Broderick, John Jubilis, Paul McCarville, Enzo Paoletti, George Schifferstein, and Robert Zeiss."

During the Golden Age of Tridentine Catholicism, entire congregations in parish churches were not called upon to sing the Latin responses at High, Solemn High, or Pontifical High Masses. This task was left to a select few, called the church choir, which would be accompanied by a musician on an organ, preferably a pipe organ. Each church, therefore, needed to employ a professional who would be both organist and a choir director. From 1889 until the end of the Golden Age of Tridentine Catholicism, St. Louis Church was fortunate to have had extremely professional directors. The long chain began with Ignatz Czerwinski who performed for twenty-one years, went through a thirty-three year period with Henry Zeinz, followed by eight years with his daughter, Mary M. Zeinz, a short interlude with the notable Louis H. Huybrechts, and ending with a nine year stretch with Joseph Kurzdorfer. Zeinz's choir consisted of thirteen male tenors and basses joined by thirty-two female voices spread through the categories of sopranos and altos. Kurzdorfer had inherited Huybrechts' choir of nine male voices and those of twenty-two females. The playing of the organ and the singing of the choir followed the musical tradition of the Universal Tridentine Church. It was a treasure of inestimable value, greater even than that of any

other art. Its pre-eminence existed because it was a combination of sacred music and words, and formed a necessary and integral part of solemn liturgy. The long chain of musical directors at St. Louis Church insisted that the harmony of song, music, words and actions from the choir loft were to be most fruitful when expressed in the cultural richness of the people of God who celebrated the liturgy. Kurzdorfer often remarked, "Texts which are intended to be sung by us must always be in conformity with Catholic doctrine, drawn from Sacred Scripture or liturgical sources. Our main task is to produce song and music for the Glory of God and the sanctification of the people."

In an interview with Elizabeth Kurzdorfer, wife of Joseph Kurzdorfer, she said, "We musicians owe a great debt to Pope Pius X for his insistence on keeping the original purity of Gregorian Chant as part of the liturgical celebrations. In 1903, he issued his *motu proprio* in the document titled, *Tra le Sollicitudini*, which instructed the faithful on which music should be used as proper and fitting in liturgical services. He wrote this encyclical because he knew that there were organists and choir directors, who, out of sheer boredom, bent the rules and inserted music that he contended was too emotional and stimulating for sacred music. When I joined my husband in the choir that he directed at St. Louis Church, he was strictly following all the rules set down in *motu proprio*. He made us use the *Liber*, the official book containing the music for the chant Masses and the Propers which we sang on Sundays and feast days. He also made us aware of the *Diocesan Black-List* that forbade certain emotional and cheap renditions of hymns such as Rossiwig's and Bonvin's tawdry *Ave Marias*. This *Black-List* weeded out a lot of the sentimental and trashy Masses which were being published by nuns who had no thought of what was appropriate to church services. After listening to my husband, Joe, expound on the sacred rules, I was very upset with some organists who played what they felt like playing. As a teen-ager and lover of opera, however, long before Joe entered my

St. Louis Church Choir during the Golden Age of Tridentine Catholicism in Buffalo. Mary Zeinz, the organist and director, is seated at the table between the pastor, Father Howard Schwartz, on her left and his assistant, Father Albert J. Bosack, on her right.

life, I attended noon Mass on Sundays at St. Mary's Church at Broadway and Pine Streets because the organist, Mr. Louis Zimmerman, would play the *Triumphal March* from Aida, the *Ride of the Valkyries* by Wagner, or some other expressive theatrical music. Although this was music with melody, harmony, and rhythm which pleased my ear and moved my emotions very much, I came to realize that it belonged in the Music Hall and not in the church."

*B*esides Gregorian Chant, organists and choirs in preparation for Solemn High and Pontifical High Masses, practiced so as to perfect the singing of Palestrina styled polyphony. Pope Julius III brought Giovanni Palestrina, a foremost composer of the sixteenth century, to Rome in 1551. He created rich and complex polyphonic settings of the Mass, one such composition being *Missa di Papa Marcello*. The Pope approved of his work saying that it was an artistic

expression of the Counter-Reformation and Tridentine Catholicism. His polyphonic music consisted of many sounds or voices consisting of two or more melodies combined, contrapuntal, and capable of giving more than one tone at a time. These multiplicities of sounds were like reverberations of an echo; they were simultaneous and harmonizing but melodically independent. Choirs that sang these Masses had to be well disciplined, eager to practice, and determined to obtain perfection. At St. Louis Church, Kurzdorfer was a director who inspired his men and women to such heights of achievement. They were very successful in developing a combination of tones that blended harmoniously when sounded together. They well mastered the science of structure, relation, and progression of chords. Kurzdorfer taught them to sing with rhythm, whereby their symmetrical and regularly grouping of tones was carried out according to accent and time value. By Sunday, October 3, 1954, Kurzdorfer and his magnificent choir were ready with their

Gregorian Chant and Palestrina to embellish the walls of the great gothic structure as the Most Reverend Joseph A. Burke, D.D., Bishop of the Buffalo Diocese, celebrated the Solemn Pontifical High Mass of Thanksgiving which opened the week long festivities celebrating the one hundred and twenty-fifth anniversary of St. Louis Church. (5)

On Sunday, October 3, 1954, the series of celebrations began at 10:45 A.M. The soaring gothic church was resplendent in papal gold-and-white bunting. It had been completely redecorated, repainted, and rewired. The organ had been electrified and all the church kneelers had been recovered with sponge and foam rubber under mohair. When Bishop Burke had completed his celebration of the Pontifical Solemn High Mass of Thanksgiving, the congregation had much to be proud of and nostalgic about. On that day they could stick out their chests and proclaim that they were the descendants of the first Catholic congregation in Buffalo, the first resident priest in Buffalo, the first Catholic cemetery in Buffalo, the first Catholic school in Buffalo, and the first Catholic choir in Buffalo. Over three days the celebration continued. In the evening of the first day solemn vespers was sung and Benediction of the Blessed Sacrament was observed. On Monday, the following day, Monsignor Albert Rung, former assistant at St. Louis Church and then pastor of St. Joseph's Church, offered a Solemn High Mass for all living members of the parish. The bishop administered the sacrament of Confirmation in the evening.

On Tuesday morning, Father Robert T. Bapst celebrated the Solemn Mass of Requiem for all deceased parishioners with special mention of those among them who had accepted and persevered in their vocations as priests, sisters, and brothers. Following Mass the diocesan clergy attended a breakfast in the church hall. In the evening at 7:00 P.M. a banquet for the entire congregation was held at the Knights of Columbus Hall on Delaware Avenue. The grand observance closed on Wednesday with Father Howard Schwartz offering a special Solemn High Mass for the children at which they received Holy Communion in a body. At Mass Schwartz reminded them that the preceding one hundred and twenty-five years was like a giant tapestry held together by very strong threads. Some of these were the pastors: John Nicholas Mertz, Alexander Pax, Joseph Sorg, Paul Hoelscher, Henry B. Laudenbach, and Michael J. Anstett. The other threads were the long lines of trustees, the laymen who had provided the intellectual and moral fiber that kept the temporal affairs of the church moving along smoothly.

Speaking at the banquet, Father Schwartz emphasized what he considered was the real meaning of the anniversary celebration. He said, "We of the present look back over the past and study the achievements, failures, nobility, and courage of those who have gone before us. Our happiness and our joy, on this night, are not just measured merely in the number of years but rather in the constant flow of God's grace throughout the years. Four volumes of baptismal records tell the story of the first entrance of Sanctifying Grace into the souls of thousands. God alone knows how many believing souls, over the course of years, have approached the altar rail to receive in Holy Communion the Giver of every good and perfect gift. Troubled and despairing souls sought out the tribunal of the Sacrament of Penance only to come away consoled in spirit, with the courage to build anew a better life. True love brought many a couple to the altar of God to pledge a mutual life-long fidelity and to receive the nuptial blessing. Finally, at life's end, how many a faithful parishioner, started out on that long journey, fortified by the Holy Sacraments? Let us then not speak of one hundred and twenty-five years of mere existence of a parish, rather let us thank God for the multitude of blessings that He has showered upon us during the long span of time and so commit ourselves wholeheartedly to His guiding Providence until the day when our summons comes."

During the ten years which followed the one hundred and twenty-fifth anniversary celebration, the trustees, parishioners, and the clergy of St. Louis Church enjoyed a spiritual and temporal coexistence which was filled with certainty, attention to principle and dogma, strong faith, devotion, and mutual cooperation. To the uncritical eye and the non-prognostic mind, this complacency, especially self-satisfaction, was a crowning achievement of the Golden Age of Catholicism and the Rare Tradition in American Catholicism, which had survived at St. Louis Church for more than a century. One witness, Father Albert Bosack, former assistant to Father Howard Schwartz during these years, has given testimony of affirmation and has demonstrated, by his experiences, the evidence sufficient to verify this achievement. He has given a clear description of the clergy, the trustees, and the interaction between them. His review of the parishioners' participation in liturgical, devotional, and social activities was filled with fond memories of their enthusiasm. Bosack had served as an assistant at St. Louis Church from 1950 to 1962. Following this tenure, he was assigned as pastor at St. Joseph's Church in Lyndonville, New York.

Bosack described Schwartz as a slightly heavy man of about five feet nine inches tall, who was easy going, congenial, and likeable. Although Schwartz couldn't remember their names very well, the parishioners showed no distaste of this flaw because he was such a likeable character. Bosack remarked, "He had two dogs, one a German Shepherd named Julie and a Boxer named Foot-Prints. Sometimes he also got their names mixed up!" Outside the church, Schwartz was rarely seen without his black sherlock, a tobacco pipe named after Sir Arthur Conon Doyle's famous detective, Sherlock Holmes. He always clenched its crooked stem by his teeth on the right side of his face; and, while speaking, his right hand clutched the bowl. Besides Bosack, Fathers Edwin J. Coveney and Robert T. Bapst assisted Schwartz. Coveney lived in the rectory, but Bapst lived in his family home that was

located on the corner of Franklin and Edward Streets. Speaking of Bapst, Bosack said, "He had always wanted to be a priest from early childhood, but he did not enter the seminary until very late in life because he wanted to take care of his mother with whom he lived. When he was a very small boy, she made vestments for him, dressed him in them, and watched him play as if saying Mass at a simply constructed altar." Also, for about two years, Monsignor Raymond Herzing lived in the rectory; he was the Diocesan Director of the Confraternity of Christian Doctrine (CCD). When he left, Monsignor Maurice Woulfe, Diocesan Director of Youth, replaced him, for two more years.

Bosack named the trustees: Edwin Garono, president, Edwin Kolb, Edward A. Rick, Frank Ross, Paul Hardick, and Louis Ludaescher. He could not remember who the seventh trustee was, but later it was verified to be Albert Eger. When Garono died Francis Cole joined the trustees and Edward Rick became president. In regards to the relationship between the trustees and Schwartz, Bosack said, "On some occasions, Schwartz liked the actions of the trustees but on others he didn't. He went to all their meetings that were held in the school once each month. He was most appreciative that they took care of all the finances, including budgeting, paying bills, and keeping up the heat, plumbing, and repairs. When the trustees knew that he liked carpentry as a hobby, they bought him a cellar-full of power and hand tools so that he could putter-around during his leisure time. No trustee voiced any opposition to the cost of the equipment. On one occasion, though, Schwartz did have a bit of a "to-do" with them. He wanted a three-car garage so that each of us permanent priests could have a private parking space. Father Bapst did not need one; he had his own on Franklin Street. The trustees initially gave the pastor a hard time, claiming that he could keep the cars at the Edward Street Garage as did Laudenbach and Anstett. Schwartz simply said that he didn't want to do that. Because they liked him very much, they decided not only to give him a three-car garage but also to build

The "Four Musketeers of the Altar" at St. Louis Church during the Golden Age of Catholicism in Buffalo. Left to right, top: Howard J. Schwartz, pastor; Albert J. Bosack, assistant pastor; bottom: Robert T. Bapst and Edward J. Coveney, assistant pastors.

The Board of Trustees

EDWARD A. RICK   EDWIN H. KOLB   LOUIS LUDAESCHER

EDWARD J. GARONO, *President*

FRANK J. ROSS   ALBERT J. EGER   PAUL G. HARDICK

Above are the trustees who were the corporation at St. Louis Church at its 125th anniversary celebration. Left to right, top row: Edward A. Rick, Edwin H. Kolb, Louis Ludaescher, middle: Edward J. Garono, *president*; bottom: Frank J. Ross, Albert J. Eger and Paul G. Hardick. During the latter half of the Golden Age of Catholicism in Buffalo, Francis Cole, Arthur Grupp and John Rembold replaced Garono, Eger and Ludaescher. Edward A. Rick assumed the presidency. During the last decade of Trusteeism preceding 1979, the trustees were: George Reinagel, *president*, Arthur Ball, Francis Cole, Thomas Driscoll, Arthur Grupp and John Rembold. When Paul Hardick died, his position was not filled.

it strong enough so that later an apartment could be constructed as a second floor. It was usually difficult for the trustees to refuse Schwartz; he was a devoted priest who immediately dropped everything to go visit the sick or administer the last rites. He gave inspiring sermons, conducted the liturgy with the utmost care, and gave special consideration to the elderly."

During Bosack's service at St. Louis Church, Mary Zeinz was the organist, followed by Huybrechts for two years. Although she directed the choir Huybrechts did not. He had Edward Mischka do that service. When Huybrechts left in 1954, Joseph Kurzdorfer came from St. Bonifice Church to be the organist and direct the choir. The custodian who lived in the north wing of the school building was Paul McCarville; his wife was Rosemary. The Sacristan was Caroline Starck who took over the job from the Sisters of St. Joseph. The housekeeper was Ann Smith and the secretary was Mrs. Gibson. While Schwartz was pastor, Catholic Charities sponsored several families of Latvian immigrants who had come to America fleeing the atrocities of the Russian Communists who had occupied their native land. Although some families settled in Niagara Falls, Schwartz opened the doors of St. Louis Church to about sixty adults and their families. Bosack said, "They, like all first immigrants, were clannish people. They didn't mingle much with the Germans, Italians, or Irish, but no animosity was openly displayed by any parishioners to these newcomers."

He continued, "The Latvians would meet regularly for a Mass and a corporate communion followed by a breakfast in the church hall. On one occasion the Vicar General and Chancellor of Riga, Latvia, who was living in New York City in exile, came to sing Mass and be a guest speaker at their gathering. It was the occasion when they donated the painting of the Madonna that is located next to the Most Blessed Virgin's altar. On this occasion, Schwartz gave him the purple robes that had been given to St. Louis Church during Laudenbach's tenure as pastor. Several years later when Ed Kolb started the museum, Schwartz sent me to New York to get the robes back. I also remember the wedding when a daughter in the Jubulis family got married. The entire clan of Latvians came together dressed in their native costumes. After the ceremony in church, which was on Saturday, the celebration went on for three days. On Sunday Father Bapst, who had been away, called me, and I asked him if he were going to attend the Jubulis' reception. He said that he missed it because the wedding was on Saturday; he was really surprised to know that getting to it even on Monday would mean that he really wouldn't miss it."

In continuing his testimony, Bosack touched on several disconnected items. He told how impressed he was with the Corpus Christi and Forty Hours processions and devotions. In a Forty Hours procession there would be ten to twelve priests, twenty-five altar boys, the Commandery of the Knights of St. John, about twenty members of the choir, and a representation from all the men's and ladies' societies. Dinner usually followed for all in the church hall. He had special praise for Rose Kolb, Edwin Kolb, Ed Simon, Annie Buchheit, Rose Buchheit, and Paul Buchheit who were long time members of the choir. One thing that most impressed him as an assistant was an event that took place on June 6, 1960. The parishioners had arranged for a banquet to be held in his honor as an appreciation for the ten years of service that he was completing. To him it seemed unprecedented that a parish should honor an assistant in this manner. It was at the banquet, however, that emotion really swelled up in his heart. The parishioners presented him with a beautiful gold plated chalice. He has never forgotten this act of generosity. Bosack said, "This act was the culmination of a parish spirit which I had lived with for ten years. I truly believe that this spirit was generated because the parishioners could look at the four priests at St. Louis Church and see how well they got along together. Each priest always had a good word for his fellow priest, and each priest was generous with his time to support the efforts of his fellow priests. Neither assistant ever had a harsh word in describing the acts and decisions of the pastor. The 'four musketeers of the altar' could even laugh at their own foibles and look upon life's troubles with humor. This joviality spread like a brush fire through the parish and the congregation followed suit. Even though large numbers of parishioners were moving away from downtown to the suburbs in the latter years of the fifties and early sixties, and their children were attending parochial schools in their new neighborhoods, they still came to Mass at St. Louis Church on Sunday."

The interview with Bosack finished with his recitation of a humorous story about Howard Schwartz. Bosack said, "Howard always loved to hunt; with him it was a passion. Whenever he returned home with the spoils of his safari, he would call a great number of his priestly friends either to the church or to his cottage in southern Erie County for a feast. One year he joined up with Monsignor Kelleher, and both of them went far up into Canada, above Toronto, to hunt. They bagged a big one! It was a huge Moose! It was late on a Friday night that I, while preparing for bed at the rectory, received a phone call from Schwartz. He told me that by noon on Saturday I would receive more than a hundred pounds of moose-meat and a very large moose-head. His only instruction was that I should refrigerate them immediately. He did not, however, tell me how I was to go about getting these items refrigerated. Needless to say I had a very restless sleep that night. Next day, I put on my thinking cap, went over to the Washington Street Market, found a man who had refrigeration equipment, made a deal, returned home, and waited for the shipment to arrive. It came in all of its glory! When Schwartz and Kelleher returned they prepared for a great party. Seventy-five to one hundred priests came to the church hall where Ann Smith, ably assisted by the Christian Mothers put on a glorious dinner of salad, moose-meat, sauerkraut, and sweet potatoes. While eating, all were in awe seeing the end result of the taxidermist who had expertly

mounted the moose's head. It was an event I shall never forget."

Among the Latvian families that Father Bosack spoke about were the Ozolins, Jubulis, and Kudins. Some had homes on Franklin Street, others lived on Park Street. They immigrated to America because of the upheaval created in their native country by the occupations of the Russian Bolsheviks and the German Nazis. The Bolsheviks first occupied the country but they failed to win popular support of their established Soviet Latvian regime. On June 13, 1941, Andrei Vyshinsky, the angered Russian leader, deported fourteen thousand Latvian citizens to Siberia, Russia. Within the next few weeks thirty-five thousand more met with the same fate. In 1945, following the Nazi occupation, the Russians, who had been defeated for a time by the Germans, returned. Again the Latvians were brutalized; the number of mass graves scattered throughout the country was legion. Those who escaped with only their lives were able to seek refuge in areas of Europe controlled by the Western Powers. Eventually many came to America, and a small representation found a peaceful home in Buffalo. Father Schwartz took them under his wing.

Although by February 1955, the parish had paid $37,456.94 of the cost of redecorating the church for the anniversary celebration, another $12,000 was still needed to replace the entire floor in the church basement, rehabilitate the rectory, build a three car garage, install a fire alarm system in the school, and make alterations of the classrooms. By having a second collection on one Sunday each month for six months the trustees predicted that the financial goal would be met. The parish responded generously and within four months Edward A. Rick Sr., president of the Board of Trustees, and Father Schwartz were able to announce that the congregation was free of debt. Fear, however, struck in the hearts of the parishioners at the beginning of summer that year. Although construction on the first sections of the Kensington Expressway had not yet been started, the plan to build the entire arterial highway, connecting the Thruway looping around the eastern side of Buffalo with downtown and the Niagara section of the Thruway at La Salle Park, had already been approved. On June 27, 1957, a plan for diffusing the traffic expected to roll off the Kensington Expressway, between Main Street and Tupper Street, was submitted to the City Planning Commission by Eugene W. Fitzgerald, the Planning Director. The confusion of the proposed exits and entrances to the expressway at Franklin and Edward Streets as well as at Franklin and East Tupper Streets brought back to the minds of the parishioners, visions of the Pearl Street Extension fiasco of 1928.

The arterial diffuser route was scheduled to go down the middle of the block between Goodell and Tupper Streets from Michigan Avenue to Franklin Street. It would then veer northward to intersect the area at Elmwood Avenue between Virginia and Edward Streets. It would then go westward down the middle of the blocks between Maryland and Virginia Streets to connect with the Niagara section of the Thruway. Approximately four hundred and forty-two buildings were scheduled to be demolished, including the Grosvenor Library, the Montefiore Club, the Midtown Hotel, and School 46. It was not the cost of $6,000,000 that frightened the parishioners; it was the mess, confusion, and upheaval of parish life. When the expressway would be finished, however, they knew that it would be a quick, convenient transportation route to bring those of the congregation who lived in the suburbs to Mass on Sundays. The Kensington Expressway was built, but the diffuser plan never got off the drawing board. The arterial ended at Locust Street and channeled traffic over to Main Street via Goodell Street. The congregation was relieved for a time but several years later the City Council again devised another plan of diffusion and confusion that brought concern to the trustees, the congregation, and the diocesan clergy.

Once again on August 11, 1957, the City of Buffalo hosted a display of public Catholicism. The oldest Catholic Church in Western New York, St. Louis Church, was honored by the Order of Alhambra. With an unveiling of an historic six-foot granite monument set before the church on the corner of Main and Edward Streets, the Order opened its twenty-seventh biennial, four-day convention held at the Statler Hotel. It was the only time the convention had been held in Buffalo. The dedication ceremony, which was performed by the Most Reverend Joseph A. Burke, D.D., Bishop of Buffalo, began with a parade which formed in Niagara Square opposite the hotel, led across Genesee Street and up Main Street to Allen Street. The reviewing stand was set up in front of St. Louis Church, and traffic was curtailed so as the large number of attendees could be conveniently accommodated. Among those on the reviewing stand were: Philip L. Le Comte from Baltimore, Maryland, the supreme commander of Alhambra, with his wife; Right Reverend Monsignor A. D. Canon, past supreme chaplain who resided in Corpus Christi, Texas; Reverend James Ennis from North Evans, supreme active chaplain; Reverend Howard J. Schwartz, pastor of St. Louis Church; and the Right Reverend Monsignor John P. Boland, pastor of St. Thomas Aquinas Church. Following the unveiling all entered the church for Mass. Father Ennis was the celebrant with assistants: Monsignor Boland as archpriest; Father W. Vincent Egan from Toronto, Canada, as deacon; and Father Basil A. Ormsby, pastor of St. Mary's Church, Niagara Falls, New York, as subdeacon. The left hand side of the monument carried the Greek symbol for Christ, The right hand side carried the castle surrounded by a crescent, the symbol of the Alhambra, the center bore the bust of St. Louis, King of France, holding a silk pillow upon which rested Jesus Christ's crown of thorns. Below the king's image was a picture of the Lamb of God Church, the first Catholic Church in Western New York.

The Order of Alhambra had its beginning in Brooklyn, New York, in 1904. The first Caravan, as each local chapter is called, was ABD ER RAHMAN organized by William Harper Bennett. From that date, it grew into an international fraternal organization having chapters in the United States, Canada, and Mexico. The name 'Alhambra' and its symbols, the red tower of Castille and the crescent of the Saracen are vestiges of the Moorish occupation of Spain between 711 and 1492. In the latter year King Ferdinand and Queen Isabella led victoriously their armies against the Moors. Local chapters of Alhambra took names of Spanish cities that existed during the Moorish occupation. Such names as Salamanca, Algeciras, Guzera, Zamora, and Alcala, are representative. The Buffalo contingent was called, and still is known as, the Cordova Caravan No. 26. Today it is alive and well with one hundred and forty six members. In 1957, when the dedication took place there were over nine hundred members. The duties of the officers have a Moorish tone: the president and vice president are Grand and Vice Grand Commanders. The secretary is a Scribe and the treasurer is an Exchequer. The mission of the Order is to promote social and fraternal association among its members, to commemorate Catholic historic places, persons, or events of international significance, and to assist and provide means to further the cause of the developmentally disabled. It is open to all men of Catholic faith who are interested in carrying out the mission of the Order. Each member wears a white Fez, a cloth hat with a tassel, formerly worn as a national headdress of the Turks. The Roman Catholic Church approves wholeheartedly of the fraternity, its mission, and its ancillary activities. Many archbishops, bishops, monsignori, and priests have been members. Even Pope John Paul II has been "fezzed."

One might often wonder how well after more than one hundred years, the Rare Tradition in American Catholicism, the interrelation of trustees and clergy in the government of St. Louis Church, was functioning. By late in the fall of 1957, one had the opportunity to see the system in action in what one could have concluded was a trivial matter, but in reality expressed the power of the trustee system, the interrelation of its power between parishioners and clergy, and its concern to bring about good service to the congregation's participation in liturgy and devotional activities. At their monthly meeting in October, the trustees set out to form an Ushers Club at the church. Up until this date the responsibility of providing ushers on Sundays, Holy Days of Obligation, Corpus Christi, Forty Hour Devotions, Benedictions of the Blessed Sacrament, and other devotional activities, fell directly upon the shoulders of the seven trustees. Any action taken on their part to recruit ushers and to divide their assignments equitably and conveniently had been informally done at the trustees' monthly meetings in the presence of the pastor, Father Schwartz. He suggested to them that it was time to put the service of ushers on a more formal basis. Once he made his suggestion, he left the details up to them. They, seeing the rational behind his observation, scheduled a special meeting for November 14, 1957. At it both Frank J. Ross, one of the trustees, and Father Schwartz explained the need for better arrangements for providing adequate coverage of ushers at church services. Both recommended the formation of an organization of ushers in the parish separate from the trustees but responsible to them. In response to their proposal, a committee was immediately formed of John W. Rembold, Arthur L. Grupp, and Francis V. Cole. It was their task to consider the ways and means of establishing such an organization.

The wheels were put into motion! Within a month, the problem was analyzed, recommended interim steps were taken to maintain and improve usher service, an outline of the proposed permanent organization was written, and a procedure to carry out the desired objectives was issued. On December 15, 1957, Frank Ross sent a letter to all perspective male members of the congregation asking them to attend an organizational meeting of the ushers club. The letter stressed how important the recipient of the letter was to the creation of the club, how a permanent club would lessen rather than increase the demands on the volunteers, and that participants' suggestions would be considered and discussed. The meeting was held on December 20, 1957; a most gratifying number of men enthusiastically attended the meeting. An outline of the organization was established. The title chosen was *The St. Louis Ushers' Organization*, a charter was issued by the Board of Trustees, membership was limited to those specifically selected and invited by the Board, and a concise constitution and set of by-laws were drafted. After the holiday season a first meeting of the newly formed club was held in January 1958. Officers were elected, the constitution, by-laws, schedules, and regulations were adopted, and approval was requested of the Board of Trustees. Once it was given, the members of the club were ready to set sail in the early morning twilight on a voyage which would supposedly maintain constant and effective communication between them and the Board of Trustees, the clergy, and the parishioners while giving their service during the liturgy and other devotional activities.

One outstanding devotion of Tridentine Catholicism centered around Mariology, a branch of theology that focused on the person and the role of the Blessed Virgin Mary within the Catholic Church and the work of redemption. In 1854, Pope Pius IX defined the dogma of the Immaculate Conception, proclaiming Mary conceived without original sin. Between February 11, and July 16, 1858, the Blessed Virgin Mary allegedly appeared to a fourteen year old peasant girl, Bernadette Soubirous, eighteen times at the Grotto of Manabielle, Lourdes, France. On March 25, 1858, in one of the apparitions, Mary identified herself as *The Immaculate Conception*, confirming Pius IX's dogmatic declaration. In 1862, the Bishop of Tarbes, France, proclaimed the legitimacy of the apparitions and authorized the cult of Our Lady of Lourdes. The Grotto became one of the most important pilgrimage sites in the world. The apparitions at Lourdes followed two important others. One occurred at Guadalupe, Mexico, on December 9, 1531 to an Aztec Indian whose christian name was Juan Diego and another at La Salette, France, on September 19, 1846, to young cattle herders, Melanie Mathieu and Maximin Giraud. Following the experience at Lourdes, apparitions of world renown, featuring the Blessed Virgin Mary, took place at Fatima, Portugal, in 1917, to three young shepherds, Lucia dos Santos and her cousins Francisco and Jacinta Marto and again starting in 1981 to young children in the town of Medjugorie, Yugoslavia.

On April 13, 1958, the pilgrim statue of Our Lady of Lourdes, which had been circulating throughout the cities of the United States, came to Buffalo under the charge of Bishop Arthur P. Connors, O.M.I. With its arrival, Catholics in the city were able to participate in the one-hundredth anniversary of the original apparitions. Three thousand people went to St. Joseph's Cathedral, on Delaware Avenue, to see Bishop Joseph Burke inaugurate the statue's tour through the City's Catholic Churches. The ceremony was elaborate and terminated in the crowning of the Madonna. A five-year-old girl, Diane Steffan was chosen to place the wreath upon the head of the Virgin Mary. Earlier that year she, accompanied by her parents, Walter John Steffan and Norma Mary Lankes Steffan, had made a pilgrimage to Lourdes under the direction of Buffalo's Auxiliary Bishop, Leo R. Smith D.D. Diane who, had been an invalid from birth, asked for a miraculous recovery from her inability to walk, however, no miracle happened. Her faith, as well as that of her parents, however, was not weakened but only made stronger because she believed that if it had been the will of God, she was convinced that a miracle would have been granted through the intercession of the Most Blessed Virgin Mary as the Immaculate Conception. Walter Steffan had been a graduate of St. Louis' school in the year 1929. Between 1901 and 1936, eighteen Steffans graduated as did Walter. All were direct descendants of Michael Steffan who had immigrated to Buffalo in 1829, developed his leather business directly across Main Street facing the Lamb of God Church, and became a faithful aid to Father John Nicholas Mertz.

Although Walter was a successful businessman associated with the Walnor Realty Corporation, the Kenmore Motor Company Incorporated, Walter Steffan Chevrolet Incorporated, and once a candidate for mayor of Hamburg, New York, he was closely associated and involved in the affairs of the Catholic Church in Western New York. From 1964, he had been a member of the Bishop's Council, and in 1969, Bishop McNulty appointed him its chairman. Besides this prestigious position he was Chairman of the Board of Trustees at Hilbert College, Chairman of the Board of Advisors to School 84 for the Handicapped, Chairman of the Advisory Board of the Rehabilitation Medical Engineering Laboratory, Trustee of Catholic Charities, and associated with Baker Hall, Our Lady of Victory Homes of Charity, Brothers of Mercy, Cantalician Center, St. Francis High School, and the Diocesan Pastoral Council. Many of his generous financial donations were aimed at Canisius College and the Blessed Sacrament Church on Delaware Avenue. For the latter, he gave two-thirds of the cost of its construction. It was designed by Edward A. Pauly, architect, and dedicated by Bishop James McNulty on May 16, 1965. Pope Paul VI knighted him in the Equestrian Order of the Holy Sepulcher and in the Order of St. Gregory. Besides Diane, Walter and his wife Norma had three other children: Anne Mary, Walter J. Jr., and Mark. Anne was the oldest and born in 1941 while her mother and father lived in Hamburg and attended Saints Peter and Paul Church in that city.

Anne Steffan graduated from Rosary Hill College with a Bachelor's of Fine Arts Degree in 1963 following her marriage to Robert Dale Gunderman, a lawyer, on November 17, 1962 at Canisius College where the couple pronounced their vows before Father Charles J. Lehmkuhl S.J. In college she was strongly influenced by her teacher Jame Kuo, who told her that some day she would be a successful, prolific, and renowned artist. In 1973, the mother of four children under ten years of age, she was chosen as the New York State Young Mother of the Year in Visual Arts. Her painting that won her the award was a self-portrait holding her young daughter, Suzie, who at the time was four months old. In receiving the award Anne was accompanied by her husband and Bobby, age nine, Karen, eight, John, seven, and Suzie, two. By this time Anne had had her art exhibited at the Wanakah Country Club, Nationwide Art Center, Oliver's Restaurant, Boulevard Mall, Rosary Hill College, Main Place Mall, Canisius College, Sisti Galleries, and the Post Arts Galleries. The Archdiocese of New York had one of her paintings, *Madonna of the Broken Rosary*. Anne often said that she was ready to paint anywhere, anybody, and anytime. "Once, I painted sitting in a boat on Lake Chautauqua; thank God it was not too windy even though it was a bit hazy," she said. She loved to do atmospheric landscapes, portraits, flower studies, and abstracts. Painting in oils or acrylics, she concentrated on her children as subjects. They were also her best critics. Once Bobby said, "Gee, Mommy, I'm proud of you. I can't believe my mommy's a famous artist." Anne replied, "Of course I wasn't, but it's a great feeling that he thinks so. He's my scholar, and painting is a growing and learning process." It's also a great feeling for the congregation at St. Louis Church to have Anne Mary Steffan Gunderman as the designer of the Book Cover for *Gothic Grandeur: A Rare Tradition in American Catholicism*.

On June 20, 1958, a Pan-American World Airways tourist flight took off from New York with its destination at Lisbon, Portugal. On the flight were Reverend Howard J. Schwartz and a sold out occupancy of passengers making a historic centennial pilgrimage to Lourdes, France. Schwartz was their spiritual director. After the crowning ceremony of the Lourdes statue of the Blessed Virgin Mary in Buffalo, he was encouraged by the parishioners at St. Louis Church to organize it. The American Express World Travel Service had a Catholic travel division which was eager to provide the tour for seventeen days for $863, including roundtrip air tourist transatlantic transportation. Although the tour stressed the pilgrimage at Lourdes it also included visits to Lisbon, Barcelona, Rome, and Paris. On June 6, 1958, all were safely back in New York, full of stories about their wonderful time abroad. They recalled the Masses that were celebrated throughout the morning at the Miraculous Grotto and Basilica of Our Lady. During the day, they had joined the Procession of the Blessed Sacrament, followed by the Blessing of the Sick. None of them could forget the torchlight procession in the evening, during which they chanted the *Ave Maria* in concert with thousands of pilgrims carrying lighted tapers; it was climaxed by the recitation of the Rosary and Benediction of the Blessed Sacrament in the Grotto. The participants were so pleased with the arrangements made by Schwartz and with his enthusiasm that they encouraged him to organize a second pilgrimage. He did so, a year later, which took the group to the Shrine of Our Lady of Guadalupe in Mexico. It included sightseeing in Mexico City, the Pyramids of Cholula, Puebla, Rancho Telva, Taxco, Cuernavaca, and Acapulco.

*I*n between these two pilgrimages, in cooperation with the trustees and the assistant pastors, a celebration of Father Howard Schwartz's twenty-fifth anniversary of his ordination was planned and executed. On April 28, 1959, Edward A. Rick Sr., president of the Board of Trustees and Father Albert J. Bosack, representing himself and Fathers Edwin J. Coveney and Robert T. Bapst, sent a letter to all the parishioners detailing the plan. It included the dates and times of the activities to be included in the observance. Although Father Schwartz had been ordained on March 18, 1934, the members of the various committees thought that it would be appropriate to have a banquet in his honor on his birthday that was Tuesday, June 2, 1959. On the previous Sunday, at 10:45 A.M., Schwartz offered a Solemn High Mass of Thanksgiving at St. Louis Church. Fathers Bosack, Coveney, and Bapst assisted him. On

Tuesday at 6:30 P.M. all parishioners and friends of Schwartz, who had purchased tickets from the trustees for $2.50, joined each other at a banquet in his honor at Troop I, American Legion Post, on Franklin Street near Virginia Street. All the members of the various societies of the parish participated enthusiastically. Their long list illustrated the strength of the parish's faith in the Tridentine Church. In the reception line to greet Schwartz and his distinguished guests was a representative from each group: The Knights of St. John, Ushers Club, Board of Trustees, Boy Scout Troop 153, St. Louis Church Choir, St. Vincent de Paul Conference, Ladies of Charity, Christian Mothers Sodality, Bishop's Committee for Christian Home and Family, Dramatic Circle, Girl Scouts, Business Women's Club, Home School Guild, Holy Name Society and Men's Club, Catholic Youth Council, Altar and Rosary Society, Ladies Catholic Benevolent Association, and Third Order of St. Francis.

*W*hen all were seated the Kurzdorfer family, who supplied the instrumentation and singing burst forth with the National Anthem, *The Star Spangled Banner*. All stood in their places at attention. Father Albert J. Bosack then gave an invocation, followed by dinner, and an introduction of honored guests. The banquet speaker was the right Reverend Monsignor Roman J. Newer, pastor of St. Mary of Sorrows Church. He reviewed the salient features of Schwartz's clerical career, but giving special attention to his compassion for the sufferings of others. He described the attention given to the poor, ravished, and demoralized victims of war in Linz, Austria, in 1946, by Major Schwartz, Division chaplain of the American occupation forces. He also illustrated Schwartz's compassion, as pastor of St. Louis Church, in giving succor to the immigrant Latvian families who sought refuge in Buffalo after experiencing the Soviet occupation of their native land. Newer said, "Schwartz's heart is as big as his smile, and the continuous column of smoke which rises from his pipe is a symbol of his perseverance in compassion." Following Newer's talk, Edward A. Rick

Sr. presented Schwartz with a most generous purse that the parishioners had prepared, and Schwartz responded with a short and grateful acknowledgement of the gift. The banquet ended with added comments and a prayer of Thanksgiving by Father Coveney, and the Kurzdorfer family sang the closing hymn, *Te Deum Laudamus*.

*F*our months after the banquet, Father Robert T. Bapst died. He was 79 years old and had been an ordained priest for almost nine years. Prior to his ordination he had been superintendent of the entire public school system in Buffalo. When he died he had an estate of $50,000. For all the years that he was assistant pastor at St. Louis Church, he lived in his family's home on Franklin Street. There he had employed Helen C. Buehl as his housekeeper. He bequeathed to her $7,000 in grateful recognition of her devoted service. He established a foundation of $950 for Masses to be said at St. Louis Church for the repose of his soul, made an outright legacy to the church for $5,000, and provided $1,000 for his pastor, Father Schwartz. Among the other charitable beneficiaries were: St. Michael's Church, Mercy Hospital, Society for the Propagation of the Faith, Chicago's Catholic Church Extension Society, Franciscan Sisters at Stella Niagara Convent, Saint Francis' Home for the Aged, Brothers of Mercy, Our Lady of Refuge Charity, and the Immaculate Heart of Mary Home for Children. He was also generous to Mildred M. Cochrane, his former secretary, Doctor Joseph P. O'Brien, Mrs. Josephine Bapst, his sister-in-law and William J. Bapst, his nephew. The executors of his will were Howard Schwartz, Kevin Kennedy, and Helen Buehl.

*F*or five more years St. Louis Church enjoyed the waning years of Schwartz's pastorship. An administrative problem associated with a personality problem was smoldering within the diocese. One might consider it the tale of two priests, Fathers Howard Schwartz and Clarence Ott. Both were approximately the same age, and both had attended St. Bonaventure University, Christ the King Seminary, the Canisianum in Innsbruck, Austria, and ordained on the same day, March 18, 1934. Schwartz, however, was a popular, well liked priest, whom, after only a few assignments as an assistant, became the youngest pastor of the oldest church in Buffalo. Ott was a liturgical zealot, who, once he put on the vestments, was dogmatic, intolerant, and inflexible with anyone who did not precisely conform to ritual. In clerical street-dress, he was talkative and civil, almost friendly. From the time he returned to America after ordination he averaged less than two years in each church to which he was assigned. The list of parishes which experienced his antics as assistant pastor were: in Buffalo, St. Joachim's, St. Nicholas, St. Agnes, St. James, and All Saints; in Jamestown, Sts. Peter and Paul and St. John's. Before 1946 he was appointed pastor of St. Joseph's Church, Varysburg, New York, and administrator at St. Mary's Church, East Arcade, New York.

*F*inally the bishop made him pastor at St. Barnabas Church in Depew, New York, where, in 1964, the parishioners strongly petitioned Bishop James McNulty to have him removed. The time was ripe for Schwartz's and Ott's paths to again cross; the great swap was on. It satisfied the parishioners at St. Barnabas but sacrificed the lambs at St. Louis Church. Schwartz was assigned as pastor in Depew, and Ott came to Main and Edward Streets in Buffalo. On Monday evening, March 16, 1964, Ott was installed as pastor by Right Reverend Monsignor Francis Garvey, administrator of St. Joseph's New Cathedral. Garvey knew that he was not presenting the congregation with a prize. He said, "I want you all to know that priests are human. Because they are human, they need the prayers of the people to help them carry on the responsibilities of the parish. Today, I give the keys of St. Louis Church to Father Ott. They represent his responsibility to keep the physical part of the church in first class condition. They also symbolize his responsibility to keep the spiritual life of the parish in first class condition." One year later, under heavy protest to the bishop from the trustees, who were attempting to keep the church first class, and from the parishioners, who were trying to keep the societies first class, Ott was reassigned to Sacred Heart Church which ironically was in Friendship, New York.

*W*hile Ott was on his way to the Southern Tier of Western New York, and the trustees and congregation awaited a new pastor at St. Louis Church, the Second Vatican Council in Rome, Italy was ending its three-year mission. In 1962, Angelo Roncalli, the seventy-six year old cardinal from Venice, who took the name of the former anti-pope John XXIII, set the wheels in motion for a revolution in the Catholic Church which brought an end to the Tridentine era. The walls of "fortress mentality" created at Trent, which lasted unchanged for four hundred years, crumbled. Like the clock in the tower of the great gothic structure at Main and Edward Streets in Buffalo, time was running out on traditional institutions of established practices, laws, and customs. A subtle aura of change charged the atmosphere of the world. All things, including the Catholic Church, needed repair, and the clock in the tower was symbolic. When St. Louis Church was

gutted by fire in 1885, a new church, an architectural pillar of strength and beauty rose from its ashes. It was completed in 1889. While the old church was burning, Joseph Grimm had jumped from the tower to his death below. For the new church, Elbridge G. Spaulding, "father of the greenback" and a non-Catholic, who lived diagonally across the street from the church donated a large clock which he requested placed at the approximate spot from which Grimm leaped in desperation. Spaulding wanted to be part of the rebuilding, and to have time readily available on his corner. On August 10, 1959, that clock stopped for the first time in nearly seventy years. Ironically it stopped just when news arrived that Dr. Harold Lyons was being honored for inventing the atomic clock. Many in the street asked, "Has the clock given up at three score and ten or is it just protesting atomic time?" By December 15, 1959, Buffalonians had the answer. The clock tolled again after the Shields Brothers, whose shop was at 1410 Main Street, forged and installed two stainless steel counter weights for the hour and minute hands. Once again a passerby could mark the correct time on his own personal watch. [6]

Commemorative plate issued in 1979 for the 150th Anniversary of St. Louis Church

REFERENCES AND NOTES ✠ CHAPTER FIFTEEN

1. For the effect of the Council of Trent (1545-63) on the conduct of the Catholic Church for the following four hundred years see: op. cit. *A Concise History of the Catholic Church*, pp. 216-19, 226, 228; It is contended that the Diocese of Buffalo witnessed its Golden Age of Tridentine Catholicism during the years between the end of World War II and the Second Vatican Council I (1962-65). For understanding the Tridentine Church in Buffalo at that time as a rigorous authoritarian institution, dominated by a decided gradation of clergy, with no room for the laity, but seen as an institution deeply involved in reducing ignorance and enhancing charity, mercy, and care for the needy, see: Province of New York, *Buffalo Centennial Eucharistic Congress: 1847-1947*, Holling Press, Buffalo, New York, 1947, pp. 5-11, 35-40, 43-51, 56-60. A copy is in the St. Louis Church archives. A Eucharistic Congress is a name given to one of over forty-five major meetings or assemblies held since 1881 for the purpose of deepening understanding of, and devotion to the Eucharist. The term may refer to local, regional, or international meetings. They are sometimes held in conjunction with a celebration of an anniversary of a milestone in a diocese's history. Marie Martha Emilia Tamisier (1834-1910) was the first to conceive the idea of holding one. In 1881 she obtained the approval of Pope Leo XIII to hold one at the University of Lille, France. see: op. cit. *Encyclopedia of Catholicism*, p.480.

2. For the reason why the Council of Trent insisted on the retention of Latin to be used in the Catholic Church's liturgy see: op. cit. *A Concise History of the Catholic Church*, p. 218. For a description of the vestments, sacred vessels, and cloths, used at the Tridentine Mass see: op. cit. *St. Joseph's Daily Missal*, Catholic Book Publishing Company, New York, 1957, pp. 9-13. For a pictorial description of the priest saying a Tridentine Mass see: Bradley, Paul J., editor, *The Holy Bible*, Catholic Action Edition, Good Will Publishers, Inc., Gastonia, North Carolina, 1953, thirty-one inserted pages between 30-31. For a short discussion of the Tridentine Mass see: op. cit. *Encyclopedia of Catholicism*, p. 1268-69. For the plan of the Tridentine Mass see: op. cit., *St. Joseph's Daily Missal*, pp. 643-703. This missal also contains the Propers of the Mass for the entire liturgical year and the feasts of Jesus Christ, Most Blessed Virgin Mary, Saints, and Martyrs. A High Mass at which there was only one priest was called a Missa Cantata. For the Tridentine version of the Commandments of the Church, of which the obligation to hear Mass on Sundays and Holy Days is included in Commandment One, see: op. cit., *Deharbe's L'Arge Catechism*, pp. 70-75. According to this catechism, grievous sins are called mortal because they deprive the soul of sanctifying grace, which is the supernatural life of the soul, and make it guilty of eternal death and damnation. We commit mortal sin, when we knowingly and willingly transgress the law of God in a serious matter. We are bound to keep the commandments of the church, under pain of grievous sin; for it is God Himself who has given us these commandments through his Church. "Whatsoever

you shall bind on earth shall be bound in heaven," Matthew, XVIII, 18 and "He that heareth you heareth me, and he that despiseth you despiseth me," Luke X, 16. During the Golden Age of Tridentine Catholicism in Buffalo, the six Holy Days of Obligation in the United States were: Feast of the Immaculate Conception (Dec. 8.), Christmas (Dec. 25.), The Circumcision of Our Lord (Jan. 1.), The Ascension of Our Lord (40 days after Easter Sunday), The Assumption of the Most Blessed Virgin Mary (Aug. 15.), and the Feast of All Saints (Nov. 1.). For reference to the commandment of the Church regarding the Sunday and Holy-Day obligation since the end of Vatican II, see: op. cit., *Catechism of the Catholic Church*, pp. 350, 493, 526-27. The prayers said at the foot of the altar at the end of Mass called the Leonine Prayers were ordered by Pope Leo XIII in 1886 as an aid to the missionary expansion of the church throughout the world. They consisted of three Hail Marys, followed by the *Salve Regina*, a collect, and a prayer to St. Michael the Archangel. Pope Pius XI ordered their continued recitation for the conversion of Russia. The practice of reciting the prayers after Mass was discontinued in 1964.

3. For the Tridentine liturgical calendar see: op. cit. *St. Joseph's Daily Missal*, 16-33; Also consult: *Crusader's Almanac*, Franciscan Monastery, Washington D.C., October 1, 1944, vol. LIII, No.1, pp. 4-15. The day of the celebration of Easter depended upon the phases of the moon, which is the earth's satellite and rotates about it once in 27 days, 7 hrs., and 43 min. It rotates about its own axis, as its axis rotates about the earth, in such a way that it always turns the same face to the terrestrial observer. The earth rotates about the sun once every twenty-four hours. The moon, therefore, has, to the earthly observer, four phases. A new moon appears when the moon is almost between the sun and the earth, and is hardly visible. The new moon is called a black moon. A full moon appears when the moon is opposite the sun; its full face is brightly lit. First and last quarter moons appear when the moon is at right angles to the sun. The vernal equinox is about March 21. If the full moon appears on this day and the next day is a Sunday then this is Easter, the earliest it can be scheduled. If the full moon appears on March 22, one must wait another almost 28 days and Easter would fall on April 25; the latest it would be scheduled. Between 1957 and 1997 Easter occurred, the earliest for this span of years, on March 26, in the years 1967, 1978, and 1989. During the same period, Easter occurred on April 22, in the years 1962, 1973, and 1984. In the period between 1957 and 1997 whenever Easter fell on a Sunday between April 17, and April 22, there were 24 Sundays after Pentecost. In the three years it fell on April 22, Septuagesima Sunday was February 18 that allowed for six Sundays after Epiphany to be observed. In the three years Easter fell on March 26, there were 28 Sundays after Pentecost, Septuagesima Sunday was January 22, and there were only three Sundays after Epiphany, which were observed. The Prayers and readings of the Proper of the Mass for the 24th Sunday after Pentecost were always used on the last Sunday after Pentecost whether this was the 24th or the 28th Sunday. The laws of fast and abstinence were taken from op. cit. *The Crusader's Almanac*, p.3.

4. For Martin Ebner's aborted appointment to St. Louis Church see: *Buffalo Evening News*, December 2, 1949. Monsignor Martin Ebner was Eugene Ebner's brother. Eugene married Edith Rick, the aunt of Dorothy Zobel. Edith Rick was a sister to Edward A. Rick and Walter Rick. Edward Rick was Dorothy Zobel's father. Monsignor Paul Juenker, retired, living at the O'Hara apartments in Tonawanda to the author/editor on May 9, 2002 expounded the faithfulness of Martin Ebner in keeping his promise of obedience inviolably to his bishop. For Father Howard Schwartz's appointment as pastor to St. Louis Church and his installation see: *Buffalo Courier Express*, Monday, December 5, 1949. Information concerning Schwartz's biographical sketch and events surrounding his 25th anniversary as a priest see: *Courier Express*, May 28, 1959. For Father Schwartz's speech at the unveiling of the Veterans' memorial plaque see: *Courier Express*, October 2, 1950. Some copies of the activities are held in the St. Louis Church Archives: Dedication Program, picture of Schwartz, Knecht, Buchheit, and Rick standing in the church before the plaque. Information concerning Louis Buchheit's war status was obtained from an interview with him in the summer of 2001 by Marie Buchheit Miller, his cousin. After the war Louis met Carmene Didio on a blind date in 1946; they were married at St. Louis Church on June 11, 1949. In 1999 they celebrated their 50th wedding anniversary at St. Louis Church with Father Robert Mack, as the celebrant of Mass. Carmene was a sibling of the Didio Brothers who operated Didio Brothers Cut Glass Company, Buffalo, New York. At present Louis Buchheit and his wife live in Naples, Florida. Edward A. Rick Jr. was the son of Edward A. Rick Sr. and Charlotte; Ed Rick Sr. has been given biographical space in the chapter on the Dramatic Circle. Ed Rick Jr. died on July 29, 1991 and was buried from St. Louis Church. In the genealogical notes of William Kurzdorfer concerning Schwartz and Anstett being natives of Lancaster, it was also mentioned that Reverend Joseph Stephan, born 1875, son of John and Catherine Stephan, and ordained in Austria on August 13, 1906, was appointed as an assistant to the pastor, Rev. Dr. Paul Hoelscher following his ordination and return to the United States. The other assistant there at the same time was Rev. E. M. Deck. Joseph Stephan is buried at St. Mary's Church cemetery in Lancaster. For the educational achievements, preparation for the priesthood, ordination, and celebration of a first solemn high Mass of Reverend Robert T. Bapst see: *Buffalo Courier Express*, editorial, Tuesday, December 18, 1951; *Buffalo Evening News*, Monday, December 17, 1951; *Buffalo Courier Express*, Monday, December17, 1951; *The Evening Star*, January 2, 1952; *The Washington Post*, January 2, 1952; *Los Angeles Examiner*, Sunday, April 6, 1952.

5. For a review of the various parish societies that existed at St. Louis Church in 1929 and 1954 see: op. cit. *The St. Louis Church Centennial Celebration: 1829-1929* and op. cit. *Souvenir Book: 125th Anniversary of the Founding of St. Louis Church: 1829-1954*, p.42-50. For the history of the Holy Name Society see: op. cit. *Encyclopedia of Catholicism*, p. 619, 626; and op. cit. *Souvenir Book: 125th Anniversary*, p.42. For background on St. Ann's

Society, St. Joseph's Society, St. Aloysius Society, Children of Mary, and Guardian Angels see: op. cit. *Good Shepherd: The Church on the Canal*, p.39; St. Aloysius Gonzaga was a member of the Society of Jesus S.J., a scholar and a nurse. He is known and honored for his devotion to the Eucharist, interior prayer, and charitable service to others. He was canonized in 1726 and his feast is celebrated each year on June 21. In 1930, the St. Joseph's Society at St. Louis Church sent out post cards (postage was one-cent), to encourage participation of the membership at corporate communion. It carried the message that Father Laudenbach expected a 100% attendance. Charles J. M. Buchheit, president and Fred L. Hardick, secretary signed it. For extended notes on the St. Joseph's Society see: *St. Joseph's Society, Pendleton, New York, Organized October 26, 1890, Church of Good Shepherd, Secretary's Book*, the original is held in the archives of Good Shepherd Church, Pendleton, New York. For St. Ann Society and the Confraternity of the Christian Mothers see: op. cit. *Good Shepherd: The Church on the Canal*, p.39-40. At the head of each Confraternity was a priest as director; he approved of a president and a vice-president who served for three years. Among other activities, sick members were to be visited, consoled, and assisted in enjoying a happy death. Departed members were remembered with Requiem Masses said for their intentions. All members were required to be present at a departed member's funeral and again on the seventh day following the funeral; plus, prayers were to be said for the repose of the soul of the deceased. Pope Leo XIII granted both plenary and partial indulgences as follows: May 7, 1878; July 20, 1884; March 26, 1886; and February 17, 1889; all indulgences were applicable to the poor souls in purgatory. Also Pope Pius IX reigned from 1846 until 1878. He is noted for establishing the *Syllabus of Errors* that anathematized the ideology of modern secular liberalism, op. cit. *A Concise History of the Catholic Church*. Confraternities of Christian Mothers, canonically affiliated with the Archconfraternity, form a spiritual school of wives and mothers to aid them in the character formation of their children. See: *A Letter from Father Bertin Roll OFM, Cap., to Reverend Father Belzer, Pastor of Good Shepherd Church*, January 8, 1986. Letter is in the archives of Good Shepherd Church, Pendleton, New York. The Archconfraternity of Christian Mothers is a national affiliate of the N.C.C.W. operated under the direction of the Capuchin Fathers located at 220-37th Street, Pittsburgh, Pennsylvania, 15201-9990. In 1996 Bertin Roll OFM, Cap., was the director general of the confraternity and Mrs. Catherine Bulger was the national secretary. In 1970 there were 3,100 units in the United States affiliated with the Pittsburgh Archconfraternity. Any woman married or widowed was eligible for membership. In 1990 the title of the organization was changed to Confraternity of Christian Women. This was done so that women not married could join the organization. Also see: *Society of Christian Mothers, Pendleton, New York, Scapular Confraternity, 1886*, p. 4. An original is in the archives of Good Shepherd Church, Pendleton, New York. For more information on the Knights of St. John see notes for Chapter 13 of this text. For more information on the Dramatic Circle see notes for Chapter 11 of this text. For details of the Third Order of St. Francis, the Apostleship of Prayer, and Devotion to the Sacred Heart see: op. cit. *Encyclopedia of Catholicism*, 76, 1150, 1252-53. Also see: Father Aloysius G. Siracuse O.F.M., The *Tertiary's Notebook; A Complete Summary of the Franciscan Third Order Rule*, St. Elizabeth Mission Society, Allegany, New York, 1955, it carries the nihil obstat by Robert T. Bapst, Ph.D., censor librorum, 1955. For those participating in the Apostleship of Prayer, the morning prayer was: "O Jesus through the Immaculate Heart of Mary, I offer thee the prayers, works, and sufferings of this day for all the intentions of Thy Divine Heart, in union with the Holy Sacrifice of the Mass, and in particular for (inserted here was the intention given by the Holy Father, the Pope, for the month in question.) During July 1895 the intention given by Leo XIII was for "Christian Education." In the United States an Apostleship of Prayer leaflet was published and distributed each month from 801 West 181st Street, New York City, NY. For St. Vincent de Paul Society see: Ibid., 1205. For details of the Home School Association see: *Good Shepherd School, Book of Announcements, 1970-1*, Individual local schools which had a Home School Association HSA were associated with the National Federation of Home School Associations. For information concerning the Confraternity of Christian Doctrine CCD see: op. cit. *Encyclopedia of Catholicism*, 351-2. For salary given to the sisters of St. Joseph for attending to the needs of the sacristy and altar see: op. cit. *Minutes of the Board of Trustees, St. Louis Church, 1929-1936*. On Catholic Youth activities in Buffalo during the Golden Age of Tridentine Catholicism, Legion of Decency Ratings, Catholic School population; see: *Union and Echo*, Sunday, December 20, 1953; Sunday September 26, 1954; Sunday, October 3, 1954; For a description of history of CYO see: op. cit. *Encyclopedia of Catholicism*, p. 288. For Altar Boys at St. Louis Church in 1954 see: op. cit. *A Souvenir Book, 125th Anniversary*, p.48. For a description of the choir at St. Louis Church see: Chapter 12 of this text and Ibid., p.50. For a description of Palestrina see: op. cit. *Encyclopedia of Catholicism*, p. 274, 951. Also William Kurzdorfer carried out the interview with Elizabeth Kurzdorfer, wife of the late Joseph Kurzdorfer, in May 2002. He is presently curator of the 1903 Kimball Organ at St. Louis Church, and nephew of Elizabeth Kurzdorfer.

6. For information concerning the 125th anniversary celebration see: *Buffalo Evening News*, September 29, 1954 and *Catholic Union and Echo*, October 3, 1954. The kneelers in the church were covered by Eugene W. Miller Sr. over a period of several months before the celebration. Miller had his business, Niagara Trailer Corporation, on Genesee Street near Jefferson. The kneelers were collected, in shifts of approximately ten at a time, by Paul McCarville, the maintenance person at St. Louis Church, brought to Miller's shop, and when completed returned to church and installed. The work of rebuilding and electrification of the W.W. Kimball Organ of 1903 was done by Tellers Organ Company, Erie, Pennsylvania of which locally Stephen Po-Chedley was the representative. Louis H. Huybrechts, organist and choirmaster

at St. Louis Church, from 1952 to 1954, had a dedicatory organ recital on the completed product on October 29, 1952. That night he played several classical pieces: *Magnificat Pimi Toni*, by D. Buxtehude; *Aria Con Variazione*, by P. Martini; *Passacaglia and Thema Fugatum in C Minor*, by J. S. Bach; *The Cathedral at Night*, by Fr. Marriott; *Toccata*, by Leo Sowerby; *Three Pieces De Fantaisie*, by Louis Vierne; *Adagio From the First Symphony, Prelude and Fuge*, by Louis Huybrechts; and *Variations and Finale Over an Old Flemish Song*, by Flor Peeters. The full text of Father Schwartz's speech at the banquet can be found in op. cit. *125th Anniversary: St. Louis Church: 1829-1954*, p.7. Information concerning the parish activities at St. Louis Church during the tenure of Father Schwartz was obtained in an interview with Father Albert Bosack, who was an assistant pastor with Father Schwartz. The interview was led by the author/editor and his wife Marie Buchheit Miller, with Bosack (retired) at St. Joseph's Church, Lyndonville, New York, on October 9, 2000. The interview was taped and a copy is in the St. Louis Church Archives. For historical background on the Latvians at St. Louis see: *Latvia 1918-1958*, Latvian Legation, Washington, D.C., 1958, Action Printing Company, U.S.A.; *Communist Takeover and Occupation of Latvia*, House of Representatives, 83 Congress, 2nd Session, H. Res. 346, 438, Dec. 30, 1954, United States Govt. Printing Office, House Report No. 2684, Part 1; " The Soviet Occupation and Incorporation of Latvia: June 17 to Aug, 5, 1940," *The Baltic Review*, New York, 1957; Rt. H. Voldemars and K.M. Vicis, *We Accuse the East; We Warn the West*, Dzintarzeme and Scholar, Germany, 1948; Dr. A. Trimakas, chief ed., *The Baltic Review*, New York, October, 1962., No. 25. Concerning the St. Louis Church's clock, steeple, repairs, and satellite balloons see: *Catholic Union and Echo*, Aug. 19, 1960; *Courier Express*, Dec. 16, 1959; *Courier Express*, Dec. 6, 1960; *Courier Express*, Sept. 17, 1966; *Courier Express*, June 24, 1938; *Courier Express*, Aug. 13, 1958. For St. Louis Church as one of the most architectural beauties of Buffalo see: *Catholic Union and Echo*, Feb. 10, 1961. For detailing the relation between the Kensington Expressway and St. Louis Church see: *Buffalo Evening News*, June 27, 1957. For the second annual diocesan Corpus Christi procession, which involved St. Louis Church, see: *Courier Express*, June 4, 1956; also see a set of photographs in the St. Louis Church Archives. For information concerning the Alhambra and its placing a memorial at Main and Edward Streets, honoring St. Louis Church as the first church in Buffalo see: Letter to Edwin H. Kolb, chair of trustees of St. Louis Church, by John H. Stone Jr., Grand Commander of the Cardova Caravan No. 26, Aug. 5, 1957 and the *Courier Express*, Aug. 12, 1957. The other officers of the Cardova Caravan No. 26. were: Lawrence V. Dirnberger, Charles E. Hetterich, Karl J. Dietsche, Norman G. Schueckler, Anthony L. Amatuzio, J. Clarence Haberman, William E. Clark, Edwin E. Berst, Arthur P. Diebold, Charles Eich Jr., and Rev. James V. Ennis. For further information on Alhambra contact: Donald Webster, 9160 Wolcott Rd., Clarence Center, NY 14032; Sister Patricia, Cantalician Center, 3233 Main Street, Buffalo, NY 14214, near St. Joseph's University Church. For formation of the Usher's Club at St. Louis Church see: Letter sent by Frank Ross, trustee, to all possible members, a copy is in the archives of St. Louis Church. Attached to the letter is a memo by Francis V. Cole to Edwin Kolb, directing his attention to the enclosed draft of the Committee Report on the Usher's Club. He says that Art Grupp and John Rembold have copies. He asks for Kolb's comments. For the 25th anniversary of Father Schwartz's ordination held by St. Louis Church at Troop I, on Franklin Street, see: Letter to the parishioners and friends of St. Louis Church from Father Albert Bosack and Edward Rick, trustee, on April 29, 1959 concerning plans in preparation for Schwartz's celebration; *Buffalo Evening News*, Jan 29, 1959; *Courier Express*, May 28, 1959; *Buffalo Evening News*, May 28, 1959; the banquet menu and party book, June 2, 1959. The names of those prominent in making preparations for the banquet were: Edward A. Rick Sr., Miss Kathyrn M. McGuire, Richard Ball, Frank Breitweiser, Francis V. Cole, Steven Cotter, Miss Jane Demme, Eugene B. Ebner, Mrs. Anthony Guadagno, Mrs. William L. Hock, Edwin H. Kolb, Mrs. Kenneth McNulty, Miss Marie Meisreimer, Mrs. John Mortimer, George Reinagel, Ralph Rentz, Miss Caroline Stark, Miss Anne Strigl, Miss Rosemary Vallone, Paul Hardick, Eugene W. Miller Sr., John W. Rembold, Lawrence Wagner, Joseph Kurzdorfer, Mrs. John O'Brien, Mrs. George Reinagel, Mrs. John W. Rembold, Carl A. Albert, and Miss Ruth A. Kolb. A brief biography of Howard Schwartz was presented in the banquet program: Ordained—March 18, 1934; St. Agnes Church—1934-1937; Sacred Heart Church, Dunkirk—1937-1940; St. Rose of Lima Church, Buffalo—1940-1941; Armed Services, European Theater—1943-1946; Division Chaplain with rank of Major, Linz, Austria—1946; Our Lady Help of Christians—1946 (four months); Assistant pastor St. Louis Church—1946-1947; Administrator of St. Louis Church—1948-1949; Pastor St. Louis Church—1949-1964. For the biographical material about Walter J. Steffan, Diane Steffan, Anne Mary Gunderman, and Buffalo's celebration of the 100th anniversary of the Lourdes' apparitions of the Most Blessed Virgin Mary in 1958, see: Archives of the Steffan Family, Cathy Steffan, curator, 464 Thorncliff Rd., Kenmore, NY 14223. For Rev. Schwartz leading pilgrimages to Lourdes, Fatima, Rome, and Guadelupe, Mexico, see: *Travel Notices* in the St. Louis Church Archives. Also note the association of his pilgrimage with the diocesan devotional processions and crowning of Our Lady of Lourdes, Buffalo, New York, see: *Catholic Union and Echo*, April 13, 1958. For Father Bapst's death see: *Buffalo Evening News*, Oct. 29, 1959. For Father Ott accepting the post as pastor at St. Louis Church and Schwartz's change to St. Barnabas see: *Catholic Union and Echo*, March 3, 1964. For the discussion of Time Running Out on the Tridentine Church with a comparison with the clock in the steeple of St. Louis Church see: *Buffalo Courier Express*, June 24, 1936; *Buffalo Courier Express*, August 13, 1959; *Buffalo Courier Express*, December 16, 1959; *Catholic Union and Echo*, August 19, 1960; *Buffalo Courier Express*, December 6, 1960; *Buffalo Courier Express*, September 17, 1966; op. cit. *A Concise History of the Catholic Church*, pp. 354-55, 357. The following is the list of those who contributed toward the church improvements preceding the 125th anniversary celebration. They are parishioners, faithful friends, or relatives of former parishioners. The names are listed in strict accordance with each patron's request and as printed in the 125th Anniversary Journal. Mr. and Mrs.Willam Able, Joseph and Josephine Abrickis, Mr. and Mrs. Louis Aquisto, Miss Louise C. Adams, Mr. Carl A. Albert, Mr. and Mrs. Carl J. Albert, Mr. and Mrs. Robert P. Albert. Mr. and Mrs. S. Peter Altman, Miss Marie Amedick, Frank Andrzejewski and Family, Martin Armbruster Heating and Plumbing, Mr. and Mrs. Janis Audze, Mr. and Mrs. Morgan Baker and Family, Mrs. D.F. Baldwin, Mr. and Mrs. Arthur Ball, Mr. and Mrs. Emil Ball, Mr. and Mrs. Henry J. Ball, Mr. and Mrs. Richard E. Ball, Catherine and James Bartlett, Mrs.Teresa A. Bastedo, Miss Louise M. Bauer, Mr. and Mrs. Robert G. Bavisotto, Ella Beach, Mrs. Albert N. Beaser, Anna and Veronica Beck, In Memory of Frank J. and Lillian Beck, Mr. and Mrs. Robert Emmett Beck, Donald Beechler, Mrs. Walter B. Beechler, Mr. and Mrs. Edward K. Bennett, Joan Bennett, Antoinette M. Bensler, Norbert Berger Family, Francisco Bidegain, The Bielmann Family, In Memory of the Biesinger Family, Mr. and Mrs. Edward Q. Billiar, Henry M. Bitterman, Dr. and Mrs. Charles D. Blaser, Mrs. Samuel Blaser and William, Joseph M. Bogold, Mr. and Mrs. Charles F. Bohn, Mrs Carrie F. Boldt, Boncaldo Family, The Misses Bork, Ed Boyd, Mrs. Diane Bradford, Mrs. John (Cecelia) Bralla, Dr. and Mrs. James Brennan, Miss Berth Breithecker, Breitweiser Printing Co., Mr. and Mrs. Frank J. Breitweiser, Mr. and Mrs. Joseph J. Breitweiser, William Breitweiser, Brother Peter Albert O.F.M., Brother C. Eugene F.S.C. (Carl Anthony Miller), Brother C. Robert F.S.C. (Robert Beechler) In Memory of Charles and Barbara Buchheit, Mr. and Mrs. Charles J. Buchheit, Mr. and Mrs. George Buchheit, Mr. and Mrs. Louis A.J. Buchheit, Mr. and Mrs. Louis J. Buchheit, Miss Marie Buchheit, Mr. and Mrs. Paul Buchheit, Rose M. Buchheit, Helen C. Buehl, August F. Buchler, Mr. and Mrs. Emmet J. Buckley, Mrs. Josephine Buggby, Miss Emma L. Buhr, Mr. Bernard John Burchalewski, Burget Family, Mrs. Joseph Burkard, Verena Burkhart, Mrs. Frederick J. Burke, John M. Burns, Mr. and Mrs. James L. Butts, Rev. James Cahill, Mrs. Rose Caito, Susan E. Carey, Marie Chase, Ann Cherry, Mr. and Mrs. Philip Cipolla, Mary B. Coffey, Francis V. Cole, Mrs. Helen G. Cole, Mr. and Mrs. Howard Compton, Daniel Connor, Mary Conrad, Miss Esther Conroy, Margaret M. Conway, Dr. and Mrs. William J. Cook, Frank A. Coon, Simon Cordner, Robert P. Corrigan, Mrs. James Crage, Mrs. Lucille C. Caugh, Beatrice M. Cullen, Mr. and Mrs. Alfred J. Curtis, Mr. and Mrs. Charles Cutrona, Carlo and Oliva D'Alessandro, Mrs. James F. Danahy, Mr. and Mrs. Fred Cormier & Darlene, Mrs. Rose F. Danser, Mr. and Mrs. Edward Dearing, George and Mary Deliganes, Mrs. Marth Dembek, Elizabeth DeRusia, Mr. and Mrs. Paul Dewes, Mr. and Mrs, Charles Dewsberry, George A. Diamond, Mr. and Mrs. John Didio, Anthony Didley Family, Raymond M. Didley, In Memory of Mr. and Mrs. Frank L. Diebold, Mr. and Mrs. Thomas Diebow, Mrs. Edward Dietsche, Mr. and Mrs. William J. Dietzel, Loretta Zahm Dikeman, Mr. and Mrs, James Dispenza, Dobmeier Janitor Supply Company, The Doerr Family, James P. Dolan, Misses Doll, Mathew V. Doyle, Mrs. Charles A. Drescher, Dr. Robert Fraser Drew, Mrs. Henry J. Druar, Kenneth J.

Duffy, Evelyn M. Duffy, Mrs. Agnes Dunlap, Mr. and Mrs. C. Allen Dunham, Mr. and Mrs. John L. Dwyer, Mr. and Mrs. Walter Dziwulski, Christian Ecker, Mr. and Mrs. Arthur Eddy, Rose H. Eddy, Mr. and Mrs. Albert J. Eger, Cyril P. Ehrenreich, Mr. and Mrs. Jerome J. Endres, Mr. and Mrs. Frank English & Family, Mrs. Ida Ess, Mrs. George J. Faber, Mary Fagen, Mrs. Rose Fagen, Mr. and Mrs. Frank Farley, Norman Fath, The Fath Family, Veronica Federle, Mr. W.L. Fehrs, Mr. and Mrs. John Feist, Helen M. Feldman, Mrs. Harry Feltes, Florence L. Fischer, Marie F. Fischer, L. Norman Fischer, Mr. and Mrs. Franklin L. Fitch, Miss Grace L. Fix, Grace M. Fleiner, Anthony L. Foegen, Mr. and Mrs. Bernard Foegen, Mr. and Mrs. J.E. Foegen & Family, Francis J.D. Frank, Mrs. Margaret D. Frank, Beatrice M. Frappier, Sebastian Joseph Fraschella, Miss Teresa J. Freiburger, Mr. and Mrs. Martin Friegl, Mr. and Mrs. Melvin C. Froelich, Sharon Froelich, George Gagear, Joan Garin, Edward J. Garono, Miss Dorothy J. Gentesh, Mrs. L.H. Gentesh, Grace L. Georger, Dr. and Mrs. R.M. Gibbons, In Memory of Fred E. Gibson, Mr. and Mrs. John B. Giese, Mrs. Cyril F. Ginther, Giorgiano Family, Mrs. James J. Glavon, Mr. and Mrs. Thomas F. Goggin, Miss Mary Goldschagg, Emanuel L. Gollwitzer, Miss Mary Gottstein, Mary L. Graney, Frederick H. Grass, Mr. Joseph Grimm, Mrs. F. Grimm, Mrs. Arthur Griswold, Mr. and Mrs. Arthur L. Grupp, Mr. and Mrs. Emil J. Grupp, Guadagno Family, Theodore Guenther, Harry Gueth, Marian Gueth, Mr. and Mrs. John Guggisburg, Mr. and Mrs. Anthony Haas, Marguerite and Louise Haas, Miss Margaret C. Hacker, Mr. and Mrs. Fred L. Hardick, George and Elizabeth Hardick, Mr. and Mrs. Paul Hardick, Miss Helen Hammer, Mr. and Mrs. W.H. Hauser, Mr. and Mrs. Paul F. Hausle, Richard L. Hecht, Mrs. Elizabeth G. Heineman, Mr. and Mrs. Francis J. Henkel, Francis P. Hickey, Mrs. Arthur Hicks, Ann Henesy, Duronda Hobdy, Mrs. Velma Allen Hobdy, Mr. and Mrs. William L. Hock, Mr. and Mrs. Leo Hoerbelt, Miss Alice C. Hoffman, Edward F. Hoffman, Miss Sophia Hoffman, Mr. and Mrs. Thomas L. Holling, Ira J. Hoover, Mrs. Michael Hughes, Dr. and Mrs. A.S. Huebschwerlen, Louise M. Jehle, Margaret Jodd, Miss Mary V. Johnston, Mr. and Mrs. Charles J. Jones, Miss Josephine Jones, Mr. and Mrs. August Jubulis, John H. Juergens, Mrs. Joseph Kam, Marie English Kates, Mr. and Mrs. Anthony Kaiser, August A. Kaiser, Mr. and Mrs. Paul E. Kemp, Miss Helen G. Kennedy, Lillian F. Kennedy, Mr. and Mrs. Henry F. Kerker, Mrs. James R. Kerr Sr., In Memory of Fred J. Kessel, Mr. and Mrs. Raymond G. Kessel, Edward K. Killian, Miss Hilda M. Kirchgessner, Mrs. Frank J. Kirchgessner, Mr. and Mrs. Lawrence Klas, Arthur C. Klein, Mr. and Mrs. Charles M. Knopf, Mr. and Mrs. Arthur A. Koch, Mr. Arthur F. Koch, August P. Koch Family, Mrs. Caroline Koch, Joseph E. Koch, Miss Lucy M. Koch, Miss Mary Koch, Miss Rose Koch, Dorothy Koehler, The Komrek Family, The Misses Kolb, Mr. and Mrs. Edwin H. Kolb, Mr. and Mrs. Edwin R. Kolb, Rev. Eugene F. Kolb, In Memory of Frank and Mary Kolb, Mr. and Mrs. Paul E. Kolb, Harold W. and Ruth A. Kolb, Mrs. Frank A. Kraft, Mrs. Frank Schwartz Kraft, Kramer's Studio, Mr. and Mrs. Gerard Kraus, Katherine E. Krauss, Julians Kudins, Christian Kurtzman, Mr. and Mrs, Christian Kurtzmann, Joseph A. Kusch, Mr. and Mrs. Joseph Kurzdorfer, Mr. and Mrs.

Leo La Belle, Mrs. Christine Lambrix, Mr. and Mrs. Francis J. Lambrix, In Memory of Hildegarde Lamm, Howard J. Lamm, Mr. and Mrs. J.M. Lamm, Fred Lang, Mrs. Grace M. Lang, Jacob Gerhard Lang, Mr. and Mrs. Raymond Lang, Mrs. William J. Lang, Miss Florence La Rock, Mrs. Theodore Larsen, Joan S. Laughlin, Mrs. Julia Laughlin, Mr. Nicholas Laughlin, Mr. and Mrs. George LeBar, Anna Leeb, Edwin J. Leonard, Mary T. Lesch, Noreen M. Leslie, Arthur G. Lewis, Mrs. Louise G. Lewis, Miss Janet M. Lindner, Theodore C. Lipp, Miss Elizabeth Lochner, Mr. and Mrs. George Lockhart, Mrs. Emma Loesch, Mr. and Mrs. Bartholomew Long, Mrs. Mary Luber, Mr. and Mrs. Joseph Luckney, Mr. and Mrs, Louis Ludaescher, Majorie Ludaescher, Ludaescher & Reinecke, Inc., Mrs. Charles Ludwig, Lux & Sons, Mr. and Mrs. Joseph F. Lux, Raymond P. Lux, Mr. and Mrs. Joseph Machnica, Miss Anna M. Mandel, Rose Manner, Miss Rita Mars, Memory of Bertha M. Marten, Mrs. Bernard Martin and Family, Mr. and Mrs. Daniel J. Martin, Mr. and Mrs. W.E.J. Martin, John E. Martz, Mr. and Mrs. Harry J. Mathers, Mary Ann Mathers, John McArtney, Mr. and Mrs. A.J. McBride, Mr. and Mrs. Thomas J. McCarthy, Mr. and Mrs. Paul McCarville, Mrs. Mary McGarel, Joseph McGuire, Miss Kathryn M. McGuire, McKay & Gill, Inc., Mr. and Mrs. Thomas J. McKeon, Mr. and Mrs. Kenneth McNulty, Thomas P. Meehan, Loretta, Marie, and Irene Meisreimer, Mr. and Mrs. Myron Mercurio & Family, Mr. and Mrs. Frank Mergenhagen, Mr. Jacob P. Metz and Family, Mrs. Caroline M. Meyer, Mr. and Mrs. Clarence J. Meyer, Miss Florence C. Meyer, Mr. and Mrs. Michael Meyer, Mr. and Mrs. Michael X. Meyer, Miss Otilda Meyer, Rebecca D. Meyer, Tillie and George Meyer, Bertha Michel, Mr. and Mrs. Eugene W. Miller Sr., Frank L. Miller, In Memory of Frank and Caroline Miller, Harry G. Miller, Mr. and Mrs. Carl B. Mischka, Dr. Carl B. Mischka, Mrs. Carmelo Healey Modica, Mrs. Mildred Mooney, Peter J. Morgan, The John Mortimer Family, In Memory of Anatole Mpelezos, Mr. and Mrs. Harold F. Mueller, In Memory of Jacob E. Mueller, Margaret Mueller, Mr. and Mrs. Otto W. Mueller, Mr. and Mrs. Walter J. Mueller, Frank A. Mumm, Mr. and Mrs. Frederick E. Munschauer, Mr. and Mrs. Edward J. Murphy, Mr. and Mrs. Paul J. Muth, Mr. and Mrs. John Mysker, Miss Margaret M. Nagel, Henry J. Nebrich, Mr. and Mrs. Joseph J. Niederpruem, Nino's Restaurant, Julia Nolan, Thomas M. Nolan, Caroline Wollziefer Noonan, Edward Francis Norton, Mr. and Mrs. James Norton, Mr. and Mrs. Edward L. Nowak, Anne O'Brien, Mrs. Charlotte O'Hagen, Mr. and Mrs. John T. O'Neill, Mr. and Mrs. Mark Orth, Mrs. Virgina Orzechowski, Mrs. Joseph Panzica, John Paulin, Mrs. Frances Parisi, Henry Stephen Pentney, The Perner Family, Mr. William Peskley, Miss Mary R. Petrino, Mr. and Mrs. Louis Pfeffer, Mrs. Dora Philpot, George Picoly, Morgan Pierce, Frank J. Pierrot, Ernestina Planas, Mrs. Julia Ponicsan, Mrs. Gertrude Prizel, Mr. and Mrs. Bernard M. Quinn, Dorothy Ramsden, Harry W. Randall, Mr. and Mrs. George Reinagel, Joseph E. Reade, Charles R. Rembold, Miss Florence Rembold, Mr. and Mrs. John W. Rembold, Mr. and Mrs. William M. Repp, Mr. and Mrs. Francis L. Reuvain, Frank J. Reynold, John Taylor Reynolds, Mr. and Mrs. John S. Richthammer, Mr. and Mrs. Edward A. Rick, Mr. and Mrs. Edward A. Rick Jr., In Memory of Mr. and Mrs. Edward J. Rick,

Mr. and Mrs. Walter J. Rick, Edward J. Riedy, In memory of the Rieffel Family, Mrs. Carl A. Rieman, Charlotte Ritter, Nora Rochford, Mr. and Mrs. Gerald F. Rogan, Mrs. Henry Rohm, Mr. and Mrs. Bernard J. Rooney, Mr. and Mrs. Frank J. Ross, Martha Stockhausen Ross, Miss Carol L. Rothballer, Daniel M. Rubach, Mr. and Mrs. James F. Ryan, James Owen Ryan, Mrs. Catherine C. Ryan, Joseph and Martha Sahlen, Mr. and Mrs. Philip J. Salamone, William S. Schaff, Barbara and Lee Scheg, Mr. and Mrs. George Scheg, Mr. and Mrs. Harold Scheg, Harold Jr. and Paul Scheg, Mr. and Mrs. Robert Scheg, Miss Mildred M. Schemm, Miss Margaret A. Scheuer, Miss Margaret Scherf, Marie and Larry Schieber, Mr. and Mrs. Charles J. Schifferle Jr., David, Nadine, and Paul Schirra, Mr. and Mrs. K. Irlbacker Schirra, Mrs. Lillian Schleeweis, Mrs. John Schmauss, Mr. S.A. Schmitt, In Memory of Simon A. Schmitt, Mr. and Mrs. Allen Joseph Schneggenburger, Walter W. Schnell, Mrs. Walter W. Schnell, Mr. and Mrs. B. Schuldaski, Mrs. Elizabeth A. Schwartz, Karl A. Schwartz, Mr. and Mrs. Rudolph L. Schwartz, Mr. and Mrs. John P. Sedlak, Rev. Eugene H. Selbert, Miss Margaret A. Selbert, In Memory of Selbert and Scherf Families, Mr. and Mrs. Albert J. Sendker, Mr. and Mrs. Hugh Shannon, John J. Sharkey, Mr. and Mrs. Paul Vinton Sheehan, Miss Elizbeth Sidon, Professor William V. Sieller, Mr. and Mrs. Edward M. Simon, Martin Sinnott, Sister Mary Edwin, George Skelton, Mr. and Mrs. Leon Skier, Miss Mary Smerski, Mrs. Anne Marie Smith, Mrs. Edward T. Smith, Francis A. Smith M.D., Martin J. Smith, Mr. and Mrs. Peter F. Smith, Mr. Stephen J. Smith, Mrs. Henry E. Stadlinger, Miss Caroline A. Starck, Mrs. Katherine Stapf, Mr. and Mrs. Vincent C. Stark, The Steck Family, In Memory of Anna W. Stedler, Miss Martha Steffan, Mr. and Mrs. Alphonse R. Steinmann, Miss Althea Stevenson, Mr. and Mrs. Louis Stoll, Dr. and Mrs. Francis J. Stone, Edward H. Stratemeyer, Dr. and Mrs. Clarence A. Staubinger, John B. Strigl and Family, Mr. and Mrs. Joseph Striker, Anna Laura Strong, Victoria Sturiska, Mr. and Mrs. Irving L. Sullivan, Miss Mary Sullivan, Mr. and Mrs. Robert J. Sullivan, Professor J. Robert Sullivan, Mrs. William E. Swanz, Mr. and Mrs. Edward Sweeney Sr., Miss Lulu S. Tighe, Miss Agnes H. Trachenberg, Mr. and Mrs. Michael C. Treiber, Mr. and Mrs. Frank Tronolone, Mrs. Fred Vanderlinden, Francis A. Vetter, Mr. and Mrs. Frank Vetter, Mr. and Mrs. Charles Vincent, Mr. and Mrs. Lee J. Vold, Rev. Eugene L. Wagner, Mr. and Mrs. Lawrence H. Wagner, Mr. and Mrs. Lawrence J. Wagner, Redmond J. Walsh, Mr. and Mrs. William P. Walters, Mr. and Mrs. Robert B. Watkins, Mr. and Mrs. A.L. Weber, Mr. and Mrs. Carl C. Weber, Mr. and Mrs. Leo A. Weigand, Mr. and Mrs. Fred J. Weigel, Mr. and Mrs. William W. Weigel, Mr. and Mrs. F.L. Weitz, Mrs. Mary and Marion A. Wendling, Mr. and Mrs. Arnold H. Weppner, Miss Josephine B. Weppner, Mr. and Mrs. William J. Weppner, Mrs. Dorothea K. Werder, Mrs. Rozalia Wilczak, Clara K. Williams, Miss Leah Wilson, Grace M. Winter, Laura E. Wollziefer, Mr. and Mrs. Joseph W. Zahm, In Memory of Mr. and Mrs. Peter Zahm, George A. Zammit, Joseph D. Zammit, Mr. and Mrs. Maurice J. Zeder, Gertrude R. Zeinz, Mrs. Henry J. Zeinz, Mary M. Zeinz, Edward Zeis, In Memory of George Zeis, Mr. and Mrs. Robert J. Zeis, Mr. and Mrs. Joseph Zeuger, Henrietta M. Zillig, Mr. and Mrs. Michael J. Zobel, Bertha Zones, Dr. and Mrs. John G. Zoll, Mrs. Fred Zorn, John C. Zwilling.

CHAPTER SIXTEEN

Challenge, Confusion, Convulsion and Cataclysm

Someone standing at Battery Park, Manhattan Island, New York City, looking across the four thousand foot width of the Hudson River as it flows into New York harbor, might not imagine that it is possible to gingerly walk in ankle deep water across that same river as it trickles forth out of its source at Lake Tear in the Cloud in the Adirondack Mountains. Likewise the one who traverses the rivulet might not believe that it would become a mighty effluence downstream. Similarly, great sadness can underlie a single teardrop in the corner of a person's eye. A human character flaw can be the beginning of the tragic end of the life of a strong, noble human who experiences the effects of psychological, moral, and physical decay. Shakespeare capitalized on this theory in his productions of Hamlet, Macbeth, Romeo and Juliet, Julius Caesar, Othello, and King Lear. Similarly societal rumblings and discontents unnoticed and unheeded, can bring about challenge, confusion, convulsion, and cataclysm within cultural, social, and religious institutions of cities and nations throughout the world. Long before 1960, such flaws existed in black and white race relationships, red and white relationships, ethnic relationships, man and women relationships, management and labor relationships, prison officials and prisoner relationships, big and small nation relationships, law makers and law abiders relationships, and greed and justice relationships. Recognizing the flaws as good or evil was in the eye of the beholder; and, in many cases, their existence was unheeded. Complacency and procrastination spawned cliches such as: the grass is greener on the other side of the fence; butter and guns can have a generous coexistence; eat, drink, and be merry, for tomorrow we die; prosperity is around the corner; let's not get involved, its not our problem; what's good for the goose is good for the gander; and what is one person's trash is another's treasure.

In 1959 President Eisenhower and Queen Elizabeth ceremoniously opened the St. Lawrence Seaway. Buffalo feared while the nation cheered. The Midwest was open to world trade. Chicago became a world port in inland America. The Thruway had already come to Buffalo and was prepared to loop the city, opening it to the second age of the automobile. The suburbs were becoming self-sustaining and independent. City planners concentrated more on the smooth flow of traffic into the city rather than on the hemorrhage of people into the suburbs. Yet in 1960, the mood of Buffalonians was upbeat. Traders in tourism and advertisers of good will claimed Buffalo to be the hub of the greatest industrial and commercial activity of North America. Why not make such a claim? It had a population of over six hundred thousand, it was the second largest city in New York State, it had a metropolitan population of nearly one and a half million, was first in the world in flour and feed milling with sixty million barrels of wheat annually, had diversified industry and research in plastics, steel, automobiles, airplanes, helicopters, and electrochemical and metallurgical products.

It was the second largest railroad center in the

407

United States with twelve freight and five passenger terminals servicing ninety-five thousand trains annually. The terminals covered six hundred miles of track with a car capacity of fifty-seven thousand. The inner city was "a metropolis in a forest of trees." In forty-two square miles within the city limits, it hosted four hundred thousand trees arching over boulevards and parkways that linked ten public parks. The most beautiful of which was the three hundred and sixty-five acre Delaware Park with a zoo, picnic grounds, baseball infields and outfields, and a lake for boating in the summer and ice skating in the winter. Culture was preserved in the Buffalo and Erie County Historical Society Museum, the Albright Art Gallery, and the Museum of Natural Science. As a convention center, the city had Municipal Auditorium and Convention Hall with one hundred and twenty-five thousand square feet of exhibit space. For education, the city boasted of the University of Buffalo, Erie County Technical Institute, Canisius College, State Teachers College, and D'Youville College.

*I*n Buffalo and its suburbs, descendants of Polish, German, Italian, and Irish immigrants hung tenaciously to their ancestors' Catholicism. In the 1958 census, they outnumbered the rest of the population with sixty-three percent in the city and fifty-three percent in the suburbs. Among the six hundred thousand registered Catholics one-third were Polish. By 1900, downtown Buffalo had given birth to sixteen Catholic churches. The generality of them survived through the first half of the twentieth century; only six closed: Our Lady of Mercy Chapel, Our Lady of Mount Carmel, Sacred Heart, St. Augustine Mission, St. Lucy, and Old St. Patrick. In 1900 St. Peter's French Church moved and became known as Our Lady of Lourdes; it did not close until 1993. The faith of the Polish Catholics was deeply imbedded and preserved at Corpus Christi, Queen of the Most Holy Rosary, St. Casimir, and St. John Kanty that were in the heart of the Polish Ghetto. In 1958, Bishop Joseph A. Burke asked the Catholics of his diocese for two and a half million dollars for the

construction of a seminary. Since that was a lot of groceries, children's shoes, and gas bills that had to come out of workingmen's pockets, he allowed an entire week for the campaign. Within seven hours, however, his goal was not only met but also topped. By the end of the week, he had obtained nearly four and one-half million dollars. The Protestant population was as bewildered with this response as they were on Holy Saturday seeing Polish families walking through the streets carrying their baskets filled with food prepared for Easter. They were to be blessed by the priest at church in a ceremony called *Swieconka*. Italian neighborhoods held great displays and marches on St. Joseph's feast day. On March 17, however, the entire city's population put on green ties and claimed that it hailed from County Cork as it participated in the St. Patrick's Day parade.

*I*n 1960, the majority of factory workers, salesmen, self-employed laborers, artists, musicians, the retired, housewives, working ladies, ministers, priests, and students were still following traditional ways of life while the embers of a spirit of astronomical change were smoldering under a thin layer of complacency. Although World War I, which began in 1914 and had an armistice, signed in 1918, it really never ended. Its embers flared up again as World War II, the Korean War, and the Vietnam War. Cities and their populations became victims in the name of political and economical progress. Love of freedom from restraint, so desperately desired but falsely promised by the executors of twentieth century wars, spawned activists who waited to revolt against the establishment and tear down long honored institutions. War, fought and won, did not build a better world, only a different world with different problems. Could dialogue be opened up with the world? Angelo Roncalli, who had taken the despised name of Pope John XXIII, believed that it could and convoked the Second Vatican Council in 1962. Throughout the world, the atmosphere was full of the winds of change, change, and more change. For two subsequent decades the world saw the revolution of change. The promoters of which surged as waves, billowed as smoke, and gushed forth as flame. As with all revolutions some people won, others lost. Birth of the new was not obtained without death of the old. In the end the old proverb stood, "The spoils of the revolution are not for those who participate but for those who follow after." Allegorically using the Niagara River, the revolution of change was like a ride from Lake Erie on the white waters of the rapids, the descent over the falls, the twisting in the whirlpool and the smooth entrance into Lake Ontario.

Franklin Delano Roosevelt died in April 1945, the war in Europe ended in May, and hostilities ceased in the Pacific in August. Harry S. Truman, who succeeded Roosevelt as president of the United States, created an atmosphere of crisis and cold war. Although Russia's economy had been wrecked by World War II, and twenty million of her people were dead because of it, she rebuilt her industries and regained her military strength. She also developed a strong nuclear capability. In the United States, fear and hysteria promoted Russians as terrorists spewing oppression and suppressing personal freedoms. In China, the Communist Red Army ousted Chiang Kai-Shek's forces that were allied to American interests. By January 1949, the Communists were rulers in Peking and Chiang's people were huddled on the island of Taiwan. Korea, which had been occupied by Japan for thirty-five years was liberated, and divided into Northern and Southern provinces. The North was under a dictatorship joined to the Soviet Sphere of Influence. The South, allied to the United States, expressed protection from the Western Powers. The world awoke to find that World War II had only abated; local hot and cold wars flared up. In the winter of 1948, the Soviet Union blockaded Berlin; the United States airlifted supplies into the city and saved the West Germans from starvation.

On June 25, 1950, North Korean soldiers crossed the 38th Parallel, invaded South Korea. As a result, a United Nations war led by the United States saved the South, brought China into the War, and produced a stalemate which still exists. Vietnam, a French Colony in Southeast Asia, obtained its independence after its victory at Dien Bien Phu by the Vietminh on May 7, 1954. With the defeat of the French, the United States felt that it also had suffered defeat because it had financed more than eighty percent of the French effort in the war with the Vietminh. The United States moved quickly to prevent the unification of the country and to bring South Vietnam into its sphere of control. This was the beginning of a war that for America had an impossible victory, but lasted for two decades. Although by 1965 Communism was on the wane in the United States, the country was still left with the scars of the Communist witch hunting antics of Senator Joseph McCarthy, the Bay of Pigs scandal in Cuba with Fidel Castro thumbing his nose at the United States government, the missile crisis in Cuba, the Rosenbergs espionage trial and execution, and the billions of dollars spent on the Cold War with the Soviet Union in defense of Western Europe. The man in the street could only ask, "When will all this be resolved; when will all this stop?"

The world politics in which the United States found itself did not begin to directly effect demographic change in Buffalo until anger against the Vietnam War reached its peak. Politico-economic decisions of the Federal government and that of New York State did however effect that change. Before World War II there were many hints and articles in the press that leaders in Washington D.C. and in Quebec, Canada, were seeking ways to build a "seaway" to connect Lake Ontario with the Atlantic Ocean. After the war lobbyists against the "seaway" lost, and by 1950 passage of the St. Lawrence Seaway legislation seemed inevitable. Although virtually every interest group in Buffalo opposed the legislation it was enacted in 1954. By 1960, while the mood of Buffalo was upbeat, ocean-going vessels carried goods both to and from the Midwest bypassing Buffalo. Coming from Europe, all goods went directly to the Midwest with a short stop at Cleveland. On the return leg of their journey, the big ships stopped at Duluth, Chicago, Detroit, and Cleveland, but headed directly to the Welland Canal, which had been widened and deepened, and entered Lake Ontario. Both ways, Buffalo was not on the laden vessels' lists of embarkation or debarkation. It horribly sat at the end of a long dead-end street. By 1966, five flourmills had shut down; and, by 1981, Standard Milling, the largest, closed. Employment fell from nearly five thousand workers to one thousand. The entire range of waterfront industries, such as boat companies; ship chandlers, ship repairers, and ship builders went bankrupt or left for better ports of entry. With this exodus much change in the demography of downtown residential Buffalo took place.

Except for the marine industries, however, the economy in Buffalo seemed indomitable until 1969. With over twenty thousand employees at work at General Motors and Ford, Harrison Radiator, and ancillary industries, both management and labor had high hopes. Lewis Foy, president of Bethlehem Steel in Lackawanna, said, "You can't help but believe that a great decade lies ahead." Oh! How wrong he was! In 1971 half of the eighteen thousand employees at Bethlehem were permanently laid off. Foy blamed the sickness of the industry on oppressive taxes, unrealistic environmental control laws, and an uncooperative work force. Behind the scenes it was, however, more of a management fault than that of the employees. Even so, many senior members of the workforce were continually laid off. Why was it impossible for management to understand that the whole-industrialized world had found itself in the midst of a major, worldwide economic transformation? It did not automate, did not adopt other new technological means to cut costs, nor did it offer education so that its workforce could become more skilled. It tried to compete with rivals in Europe and Japan with physical plants that were antiquated. Above all it was shortsighted and greedy. So the Niagara Frontier was flushed of many

good companies such as National Gypsum and Houdaille, who were bound for the Sunbelt, and Carborundum and Western Electric, who journeyed to the Midwest. With the demise of industrial powerhouses such as these, came the death of many department stores, restaurants, shops, and service organizations. Buffalo even feared that its cherished institutions such as the Philharmonic Orchestra, the Science Museum, the Albright-Knox Art Gallery, and the Historical Society would face bankruptcy. Such a mess cried out for change.

City planners were victims of their own history. What they started through the slow process of democracy could not readily be changed quickly. Before 1969 they saw the city growing with a viable downtown. Knowing that many residents had moved to the suburbs, their vision of the city focused on a large downtown business district which would be surrounded by those multitudes of people living in suburbia; who, they believed, were ever ready and willing to flood the inner city for all their major shopping desires, banking needs, legal transactions, entertainment, and social life. To them, all that was required to bring this about was to methodically, dramatically, and immediately accommodate the vast increase in private motor vehicles expected to flow into the downtown. Although some of the vehicular invasion began around 1920, the new golden age of the automobile came after World War II. Gone were the gasoline rations, and gone were the waiting at stops for public transportation. Now the city planners cried out for a sweeping plan for the construction of a whole new system of citywide highways and arteries. The planners' motto was, "If you build it they will come."

One needs only to view the map of greater Buffalo to see the result: Niagara Section of the Thruway, Youngman Expressway, and Thruway Connection passing the Galleria, Kensington Expressway, and Scajaquada Expressway. Did suburbia come to downtown as planned? No! Suburbia became self-sufficient. Malls with expansive free parking lots became independent "downtowns" under a closed roof that afforded shopping, banking, legal advice, entertainment, and social life at moderate temperature and humidity mechanically controlled in all seasons of the year. Beginning with 1953 the City Council continually backed the highway plan, paid an enormous price to execute it, and did irreparable damage to the inner city. Amidst this damage, however, one can relate a benefit. Although St. Louis Church had many of its members living in suburbia, it did not lose all of them as parishioners. The highway system made it easy for suburbanites to have unobstructed travel on a Sunday morning for attendance and participation at Mass.

*W*hat was the motivation that caused residents of the inner city to flee to suburbia? It was a tangled web of intersecting political procrastination, an influx of desperately poor blacks, hispanics, and whites, racist intent of the local housing policy, and general federal subsidies for the selling of inner city homes. Before 1960, more than eighty thousand white Buffalonians had moved to the suburbs. By 1980, Buffalo's population had fallen to three hundred and fifty-seven thousand people. The whole vast East Side, the Fruit Belt, Hamlin Park, and St. Lucy's parish which were so predominately German in bygone days, had become a poor ghetto. Buffalo's Municipal Housing Authority and the policies of the federal government literally drew a circle around low-income communities, and attempted to preserve racial purity. The private real estate market followed suit. Blacks were not shown property in white neighborhoods and brokers refused to sell homes to whites in neighborhoods that were still integrated. Blacks also were constantly discriminated against when they desired to rent apartments in white neighborhoods.

*I*t was these kinds of racial discriminatory attitudes that infiltrated the policies of redevelopment of decayed and unrepairable communities. When a redevelopment plan was put into action, the area was cleared and all residents indiscriminately removed. Because of such a plan, by 1960, sixteen hundred Black families and one thousand Italian-American families had been removed from the confines of the parish of St. Lucy's Church at the corner of Swan and Chicago Streets. In 1970, Monsignor Carl J. Fenice, the former pastor of St. Lucy's that had been razed said, "My entire congregation was bewildered by this onslaught called a development. What galls me the most is that the plot of land upon which my church stood still remains vacant." Those Blacks who were ousted from their homes around his church and in other parts of the city needed new residences, but neither banks nor federal agencies were willing to oblige them. Excessive collateral was required. Some more influential activists among the Blacks had recourse to blockbusting, especially in the northern part of the old East Side. Fear and panic spread, more whites fled to the suburbs, the Black ghetto grew, and race relations were poisoned beyond repair. For the more than seventy thousand Blacks who were living in Buffalo, the whites had a phrase, "Let them be! Let them keep their ethnic purity equal to ours but separate!"

*B*uffalo's black and white relationships simply mirrored the entire Black revolution that took place for almost two decades in the latter twentieth century in the United States. All through the sixties, especially in the South, there were civil rights actions. Mrs. Rosa Parks refused to move to the back of the bus where Negroes were supposed to sit. The Student Nonviolent Coordinating Committee (SNCC) was formed, Freedom Riders put on mass demonstrations, and Martin Luther King Jr., a minister born in Atlanta, Georgia, thrilled two hundred thousand Black and White Americans with his speech, "I have a dream." After President John F. Kennedy was shot during a motorcade in Texas, his vice president, Lyndon Johnson immediately replaced him. He sponsored, and Congress passed, stronger voting rights for Blacks. Malcom X, a Black activist, spoke to students from Mississippi who were visiting Harlem, New York City, he said, "You'll get freedom by letting your enemy know that you'll do anything to get it. When you get that attitude, however, they'll still call you crazy nigger. They won't say Negro. You'll be an extremist, a subversive, seditious, a red, and a radical. But when you stay radical long enough and get enough people to be like you, you'll get your freedom."

By 1965, eighty percent of all Blacks lived in the cities of America. Fifty percent of these lived in the North. The words of the activists propelled them to violence that erupted with a fury in 1967. Every day, the newspapers were reporting racial riots in cities throughout the North and South. Finally Congress passed the Civil Rights Act of 1968. Although the legislation was in place, which appeared to bring about not just equality but integration as well, poor blacks were still economically pitted against poor whites. Blacks, who were freed from domination, were forced to take their place under capitalism and forced into conflict with whites for scarce jobs. In 1977, the Department of Labor reported that nearly thirty-five percent of young Blacks were unemployed. Despite new opportunities for a small number of Blacks, the generality still suffered in poverty, subject to unattended sickness, homicidal violence, drug addiction, and despair. What was to happen if Martin Luther King's dream was deferred? Obviously change was inevitable!

Like the Black revolution, another societal upheaval, which ruptured after 1965, was women's escape from the prison of wifeliness, motherhood, femininity, housework, beautification, and isolation. The control of women, however, had not been effected by the state but ingeniously by the traditional concept of family. Men controlled women, women controlled children, all were preoccupied with one another, turned to one another for help, blamed one another for trouble, and did violence to one another when things did not go right. When the nation went off to World War II,

however, industrial needs to produce massive amounts of war materials called a halt to the age-old doctrine of family control. Men had donned their uniforms, picked up their rifles, and joined the Army, Navy, Air Force, Coast Guard, or Marine Corps. Women came out of their prisons on a work parole program—they entered the factories that supplied their husbands, brothers, and boyfriends with tanks, planes, ships, and ammunition needed to defeat an ugly enemy. When the conflict was over it was not an easy task to get "Rosie the Riveter" to give up her spot on the assembly line. By 1960, twenty-three million American women worked for wages. Unlike men, however, women in the workplace had a problem; it was their bodies. They were the farmlands from which the vast number of children sprang forth. They had to be attractive enough to entice the farmer, the seed bearer, to carry out the planting. Women began to view their attraction as exploitation by men and society. As sex play things, they felt themselves weak and incompetent. As pregnant women they saw themselves as helpless. They feared the decline in beauty of middle age. Would the seed bearer ignore them completely in old age?

Unlike men, women were childbearers who wished to have complete control over the process of nurturing their unborn until it was time for delivery. Many, however, wanted to stay in the workforce where a newborn was an industrial burden. For some, abortion was a solution; but, before 1970, it was generally illegal. Each year approximately one million abortions were performed in the United States with only one percent being legal. Approximately one-third of those who had illegal abortions, mostly those considered poor, suffered hospitalization from complications. By 1969, the female clamor for change was recorded in a Harris poll which showed that sixty-four percent of those questioned claimed that a decision on abortion was a private matter and that no one should be able to compel a woman to bear a child against her will. In 1973, the Supreme Court ruled in the cases *Roe v. Wade* and *Doe v. Bolton* that the state could prohibit abortions only in the last three months of pregnancy, that it could regulate abortion for health purposes during the second three months of pregnancy, and during the first three months, a women and her doctor had the right to decide.

In the next ten years the number of abortions skyrocketed, abortionist and anti-abortionist groups pitted themselves against each other, the Catholic Church forcefully denounced the decision of the Supreme Court as immoral, but medical abortion mills blossomed throughout the nation. The change in America was startling. For the first time the biological uniqueness of women was openly discussed. The media jumped on the bandwagon. What for so long had been a deep, dark secret, and a hidden embarrassment now became common place on afternoon and evening TV talk shows. Menstruation, masturbation, menopause, abortion, lesbianism, sexual relationships, rape and self-defense, venereal disease, birth control, pregnancy, and childbirth became their common menu. The traditionalists were dumbstruck when the results of change became so blatant. They could only ask, "Will women liberating themselves, children freeing themselves, and men and women exposing their secrets in public, make society a better place to live than it was before?" One cannot deny, however, that change was affecting human sensitivities and conscience.

*W*omen were not alone in seeking their freedom. Native Americans and prisoners hopped on the bandwagon so as to play their tune of liberation. George Jackson, a Black inmate at Soledad prison, California, became a revolutionary who published his book *Soledad Brother*. Although it was well read by prisoners, black people, and white people, it was his death warrant. In August 1971, he was shot in the back by guards at San Quentin prison while he allegedly tried to escape. Disclosures suggested a government plot to kill Jackson. A chain of rebellions erupted at prisons in Texas, Massachusetts, New Jersey, and New York. Most

noteworthy was that at Attica prison, New York, where fifty-four percent of the inmates were black and one hundred percent of the guards were white. The prisoners were disgusted with their way of life. They spent almost sixteen hours a day in their cells, their mail was read, their reading material was restricted, their visits from their families were conducted through a mesh screen, their medical care was inadequate, and their parole system was biased. On September 9, 1971, protesting in honor of George Jackson, prisoners fought the guards within four prison yards. The prisoners got the upper hand and held forty guards as hostages. The news media was brought in to observe, the state officials lost patience, and Governor Nelson Rockefeller ordered a military attack on the prison. Thirty-one prisoners and nine guards died before peace was secured. The authorities made some moderate concessions, but the prisoners learned that law would not change their condition.

*A*nother group that found limited success in obtaining relief of sad conditions was the Native Americans. After the Sioux massacre at Pine Ridge, South Dakota, near Wounded Knee Creek in 1890, the white man thought that the red man's voice would never be again heard above a whimper. In 1969, however, the trickle of discontent, which the tribes showed toward the government in Washington D.C. for nearly four score years, came to a head. Indian literature, well publicized in the white media, showed that the United States government had signed more than four hundred treaties with the Indians and violated every single one. It now was bombarded with complaints from the Mohawk, Navajo, Sioux, Seneca, Cherokee, and Hopi tribes. On February 27, 1973, about three hundred Sioux entered the village of Wounded Knee and declared it liberated territory. Within hours the FBI agents, federal marshals, and police from the Bureau of Indian Affairs encircled the area and blockaded the town. A gun battle ensued, the Indians were forced to give in; and, although they gained little in fact, they were winners in the world of public opinion. Many sympathetic people began to appreciate the words of Frank James, a Wampanoag Indian who said, "Our spirit refuses to die. Yesterday we walked the woodland paths and sandy trails. Today we must walk the macadam highways and roads. We are uniting. We're standing not in our wigwams but in your concrete tent. We stand tall and proud and before too many moons pass we'll right the wrongs we have allowed to happen to us."

From 1965 until 1979, America did not just experience black revolt, women's movement, prisoner discontent, and Indian uprisings. The quest for change was in the air. Oppressive, artificial, and previously unquestioned ways of living were placed under the microscope. Every aspect of personal life: childbirth, childhood, love, sex, marriage, dress, music, art, sports, language, food, housing, religion, literature, death, and schools, were scrutinized. Sexual behavior went through startling changes. Premarital sex was on the lips of young and old. Men and women lived together outside of marriage without embarrassment. Married couples spoke about their sex life as they did about child rearing. Young men and women admitted openly their satisfaction with masturbation. The dark closets were opened, and out stepped the homosexuals and lesbians into the light of day. On many occasions the courts overruled the local banning of erotic and pornographic books.

It appeared that both men and women refused to be restrained in any way. Men stopped wearing neckties and stripped off their suit coats. Women disposed of their bras, discarded their girdles, and wore slacks in place of dresses. Casual was in vogue. Popular music of protest made singers such as Bob Dylan and Joan Baez gold label record winners. Within the Catholic Church, a bulwark of conservatism, there were signs of strong dissatisfaction. Priests and nuns resigned their way of life, sought dispensations from Rome, and set up new secular lives in a world outside their chapels, convents, and monasteries. With a loss of

traditional faith in business, government, and religion, a strong belief in self arose. Experts in all fields could not be trusted; individuals believed that they had the power and intelligence to know what was good to eat, how to live their lives, and be healthy. The scientific evils of smoking cigars and cigarettes, chewing tobacco, or puffing away on a pipe were so powerful that individuals equated this addiction to slow suicide. The values of traditional education were questioned. The new breed asked, "Has not our schools taught entire generations the values of patriotism and obedience to authority, but has perpetuated ignorance of and contempt for people of other nations and races?" Modern students even challenged the style of their education; they hated formality, bureaucracy, and insistence upon subordination to authority.

Although seeing change, change, and more change spreading like a low hung cloud, slowly creeping across the sky as a prelude to a great rain storm on a hot, humid, summer day, the Roman Curia of the Catholic Church tenaciously held to its Tridentine conservatism, with belief that the storm would quickly pass without destructive power. The Curia is the collective papal bureaucracy, composed mainly of cardinals and archbishops who assist the pope in matters of service and governance beyond the diocese of Rome. Chief among them is the Secretariat of State who not only deals with diplomatic relations but also is in charge of the overall supervision of councils, tribunals, and prefectures, which set the guidelines for all aspects of life in the Church, pastoral matters, and liturgy. Pope John XXIII, however, was not as conservative as the members of the Curia were. He wanted to open a dialogue with the whole world so as to make it better. He convened the Second Vatican Council in Rome that began ceremoniously on October 11, 1962. All bishops of the Catholic world, who were physically able, were in attendance. The Curia, after reviewing thousands of suggestions offered by them, drew up seventy proposals, called schemata, which they presented to the first session of the council. The Curia expected the bishops to accept their scholarly work, rubber-stamp it, and go home. John XXIII was outraged. This was not what he wanted. Unlike the prophets of doom and gloom among his counselors, he preferred an optimistic view of the course of modern history. He told the bishops that they were invited to Rome, not to engage in sterile, academic controversies, but to find meaningful, positive, and fresh ways of stating the Church's age-old doctrine. With vigor, he dismissed the seventy ludicrously medieval and outdated proposals prepared by the Curia and demanded a fresh agenda.

*I*n the first session convened in the Council, the bishops gained the upper hand over the Curia, got their own nominees elected to the various commissions, and banished sixty-nine of the seventy proposals on the Curia's draft document as outdated, textbookish, and useless. For these, a new schemata was drawn up. Only the Curia's proposal concerning the liturgy was retained for immediate discussion. John XXIII was pleased with the bishops' actions; they confirmed his genial intuition that powerful, if latent, force for change was running strong within the Church. The first session took its first recess on December 8, 1962. By then the world saw that the Catholic Church had seriously entered into a triple dialogue with the faithful themselves, with the separated brethren, and with the world outside. During recess, John XXIII died and John Baptist Montini, who chose the name of Pope Paul VI, succeeded him and opened the second session on September 29, 1963. Debates in this session centered on ecumenism, religious liberty, modern communications, and anti-semitism. Before it ended the bishops prevailed over the conservatives of the Curia and voted in favor of collegiality, a doctrine deeply rooted in tradition that expressed the right of the bishops to participate as a body in the full and supreme authority of the Pope over the Church.

*T*he second session ended on December 4, 1963. The Council was reconvened on September 14, 1964.

Delicate topics were debated in this third session: the official teaching on marital morality, the problem of artificial birth control, and religious liberty. It ended in compromise between the liberals and the conservatives. Paul VI, in order to pacify the minority, who was the conservatives, made last minute changes in key documents. He emphasized papal primacy and the independence of the pope at the expense of collegiality and rendered a decree on ecumenism less conciliatory toward Protestants than authorized by most bishops. The session ended on November 21, 1964. Paul VI opened the fourth session on September 14, 1965. Again the topic of religious liberty was on the agenda as well as documents concerning the missions, religious life, priestly formation, priestly ministry, and non-Christian religions. When it ended on December 8, 1965 the final vote on all documents proposed in the agenda was recorded. Two thousand three hundred and ninety-nine bishops cast their ballots.

*D*uring the four years in which the Council was held, sixteen documents were debated, edited, and voted upon. They covered a wide range of topics; and, when written up in final form, they became the dogmatic constitutions, decrees, and declarations that defined the Modern Catholic Church. The clergy and the laity had a new way of thinking about the definition and meaning of Church, divine revelation, sacred liturgy, pastoral function in the modern world, instruments of social communication, ecumenism, relationship to the Eastern Catholic Churches, a bishop's pastoral office in the Church, priestly formation, renewal of religious life, apostolate of the laity, ministry and life of the priests, the Church's missionary activity, Christian education, the Catholic Church as related to non-Christian religions, and religious freedom. Under the edicts of the Tridentine Church that served for four hundred years, ten items can be formulated and then contrasted with their redefinition by the Second Vatican Council. The first six deal with the concept of the Catholic Church. It had been previously considered primarily as an organization or institution. Its new definition made the Church a mystery or sacrament. Of old, it was the hierarchy, clergy, and religious. Now it was defined as the whole people of God. The laity had been included as partakers not viewers.

*I*n the Tridentine Church, its mission was preaching of the Word of God and celebrating the sacraments. In the Modern Church, the mission also included action on behalf of justice and peace. For four centuries the definition of the Church of Salvation meant exclusively members of the Catholic Church. Following Vatican II, all Christians were members of the Church of Salvation. Before the Council met, the local Church, the individual's parish was considered as an administrative subdivision of the universal Church. When the Council finished its work, the universal Church was defined as a communion, or college, of local churches. Finally, through the years of Tridentine theology, Catholics were asked to consider themselves as having become members of the Kingdom of God. The Modern Church was defined as an eschatological community that is a grouping of individuals who are moving toward the final state of the universe, the goal toward which God is moving all creation. The power to achieve this is found in the Risen Christ who will supervise each one in the community at their individual death, resurrection, immortality, and judgment. Those whom He selects will then enter into the Kingdom of God.

*T*he final four items concerned the individual Catholic as a person who was anxious about one's own evaluation of mission, truth, salvation, and dignity. In the Tridentine Church, the Catholic merely shared in the mission of the hierarchy. Now the Catholic had to be committed to a direct participation in the mission of the Church; it was a condition called lay apostolate. Before the Council met, all the teachings of the Church were equally binding or essential to the integrity of the Catholic faith. Now, by definition, there was a hierarchy of truths. Some truths were essential, others

were peripheral. If one distinguished between these two types, ecumenical dialogue would be enhanced and legitimate diversity would be promoted while essential unity would be ensured. Hence all truths were not equally important even though they were believed with the same faith and kept with equal fidelity. Under the influence of Tridentine theology, many clerics promoted the concept that the Catholic Church was the only means of salvation. The Second Vatican Council made it clear that God uses all other Christian churches and non-Christian religions in offering salvation to all humankind. The Tridentine Church promoted the concept that "error has no rights." It took away an individual's religious freedom because it argued that the rights of an erroneous conscience, even if sincere, cannot be considered equal to the rights of a conscience that is both sincere and correct. In the Modern Church the dignity of the human person and the freedom of the act of faith are the foundations of religious liberty for all. Through an understanding of these ten comparisons, one can see that the Catholic Church intended to shift its emphasis from being a pyramidal structure to one that includes the whole people of God, and it lays stress on the fundamental equality of all as regards basic vocation, dignity, and commitment by dwelling on the common priesthood of the faithful.

*C*onstitutional documents emanating from Vatican II touched upon doctrinal and universal pastoral matters that pertained to the very essence of the Church. Of the several, whose titles have been listed above, *Sacrosanctum Concilium*, the Constitution on the Sacred Liturgy, was the first major document completed and published. It was issued on December 4, 1963. Since Liturgy is so important to the communal activity of the laity in conjunction with the clergy, who together make up the Body of the Church which with Christ as its Head is the Mystical Body of Christ, one needs to understand in detail the ramifications of this document, and make comparisons with the Liturgy as practiced in The Tridentine Church. Before Vatican II, three major liturgical reforms took place consecutively in the

Catholic Church, during the reigns of Popes Gregory VII, Innocent III, and Pius IV. The last was made at the Council of Trent which ended in 1563 and sought to accomplish renewal by eliminating cultural and ethnic diversity and bring worship in European churches under the control of Rome. By contrast, Vatican II recognized that worship must be adapted to the varying temperaments and traditions of people. It expressed a clear desire for the liturgy to be carried out in the vernacular with clarified and simplified rites. The Tridentine Church was most concerned about validity in the execution of the liturgy. It questioned, "Are these services licit? What are the minimum requirements which make them effective even if they are not licit?" The Modern Church stated that individuals must celebrate sacramental events so as not to hinder their reception. God desires to save all people and so must the Church. God meets the people in and through the sacraments, and the Church must not hinder, even as it must regulate, the circumstances of that meeting.

Although it was a slow and frustrating learning process, Catholics became comfortable with the inclusion of more Scripture in the liturgy, the exercise of different ministerial roles by the laity, the active participation of the congregation in word and song in the vernacular, the restoration of the biblically and liturgically based homily at most Masses, the prayers of the faithful, the reception of Communion under both species for all the faithful, restoration of the catechumenate, the rite of Christian initiation of adults, and the revision of the rites of all sacraments and sacramentals. When the church first restored Sundays and feasts of the Lord to their central importance, while leaving the feasts of saints to local churches except in those cases where the individual saints have a universal significance, there was much uproar among the laity who regularly attended daily Mass. They missed devotion to several of their saints that had been relegated to oblivion. Many, however, enjoyed the recommendation that singing should no longer be limited to the choir and clergy, but they were confused

by the disappearance of statues from their churches while they heard that sacred art and furnishings should serve the dignity of worship.

Almost immediately following the publication of the Vatican II document on the liturgy, some Catholics around the world abandoned their elaborate altars at which the priest celebrated Mass with his back to the congregation. Instead they built slightly rectangular, attractive, impressive, and dignified tables with solid and beautiful materials in pure and simple proportions. They placed them in the sanctuary near or in the midst of the congregation with the priest facing the people as he said Mass. They set two lecterns made of the same materials as the altar, one to the right and one to the left of it, to be used for scriptural readings, responsive psalms, sermons, and instructions. The agenda of the Eucharistic celebration, the Mass, was simplified. It included an introductory and penitential rite, readings and prayers, homily, intercessory prayers, creed on Sundays and major feast days, presentation of gifts, Eucharistic prayer, Communion rite, and dismissal. Concelebrating by several priests replaced the combination of celebrant, deacon, and subdeacon at Solemn High Masses of the Tridentine era.

The seven sacraments in vogue during the Scholastic period of Church History from the eleventh to the thirteenth century, and held in honor by the Tridentine Church, still remained intact in the post Vatican II Church with revision and redefinition. Baptism for adults was revised in 1972 according to the Rite of Christian Initiation of Adults. A revision in the ceremony for the baptism of children was introduced in 1969. The former Sacrament of Penance was titled the Sacrament of Reconciliation. Four forms of reconciliation were advocated: an individual ritual of confession to a priest and the reception of his absolution; a communal ritual followed by individual confession and absolution; a communal ritual followed by general absolution; and an abbreviated, emergency ritual at the time of imminent death. Liturgically, a communal rite was advocated; however, individual confession was still required, if not immediately, at least at some convenient time following general absolution. The revised edition for the Sacrament of Confirmation came in 1971.

The revisions for the Sacrament of Matrimony were mainly in terminology. Although the Church still considered marriage and marital love of the spouses as ordained for the procreation and education of children, it did not make the other ends of marriage of less account. It proclaimed that it was not solely instituted for procreation. It is a loving partnership of the whole of life; it is both a covenant and a sacrament. In teaching the doctrine concerning Holy Orders, the Second Vatican Council stressed that all the faithful share in the mission of the Church; and, that by baptism, all are called to be a priestly people. There remained, however, an essential difference between the priesthood of the ordained and the priesthood of the people. Besides it was stated that the fullness of the ordained priesthood resides in the episcopacy. Each bishop received the threefold ministry of preaching and teaching, of sanctifying, and of governing. Although the priest received the ministry of sanctifying by his ordination, he only shared in the other two ministries in accordance to the authority of the bishop who gave him jurisdiction. Between 1972 and 1983, the Sacrament of Extreme Unction went through a rigorous metamorphosis. Its title was changed to Sacrament of the Sick. As a reformed rite, it restored the more traditional, antemedieval perspective as the ordinary rite for the strengthening of those whose health had been debilitated by physical illness or old age, and it called for the participation of members of the family and friends in its celebration.

As the various changes in liturgy trickled into existence with the disappearance of an altar rail here and altar rail there, Communion under two forms being given, statues being placed behind old ornate, unusable altars, never to be seen again, and several other unexplained changes being initiated, the average Catholic was bewildered. Among the more educated and scholarly, a tidal wave of unrest was set in motion during the decade following the Second Vatican Council. Old roots, families, nations, communities, and professions shook under the hurricane impact of the implantation of the substance contained in the various documents emanating from the Council. Few of those who had had the benefits of a Catholic college or university education were intellectually, spiritually, or emotionally prepared for what happened. Some were angered, felt betrayed, and stopped going to church. Others hooked-up with sympathetic, vagabond priests who clung tenaciously to the Tridentine liturgy. Those laity, who had advanced academically only as far as completing high school, accepted the changes with more or less grace but with little enthusiasm. The media had a heyday reporting whenever a priest or nun openly opposed a bishop, when a bishop squared off against a cardinal, or when a cardinal blatantly disagreed with the Pope. Although the seeds of a democratic revolution were sown at Vatican II, they were incased in a shell of words that remained only words. In practice following the close of the Council, little change was made in the pyramidal structure of the Catholic Church. Emphasis on it as being the whole people of God, the call for dialogue between all of its members, the assertion of the collegiality of Pope and bishops, and the erection of priests' senates and pastoral councils that included the laity, lay in limbo for more than a decade.

The Vatican continued to react unfavorably with the bishops' exercising decision making, with absolute power in their own dioceses, on moral issues which were in conflict with Rome. It was determined to keep the bishops in line on matters of the use of individual conscience as a guideline. In the Tridentine Church the independence of the individual conscience was kept at a minimum. After Vatican II, however, many Catholics suddenly found themselves no longer willing to give blind obedience to church authority. They looked more to the reasoning intellects of academic theologians for an influence of their consciences. Some theories, such as the principle of human dignity, affected their mentalities in giving guidance to personal morality. They were convinced that new data from the human sciences could lead to a change in deciding what was and what was not a correct moral code. Father Charles E. Curran, a theological professor at Catholic University, Washington D.C., opposed the declarations on sexual ethics issued by the Vatican on January 15, 1976. He claimed that the document, which it issued, was inaccurate, psychologically harmful, and pedagogically counter-productive. Argumentation ensued and the media popularly publicized the details. Many priests and religious were left in confusion.

From 1962 to 1974 the total number of seminarians decreased by thirty-one percent, religious brothers by twenty percent, and religious sisters by eighteen percent. Within seven years following the end of the Council eight thousand priests left the ministry. Ironically, the worldwide Catholic population increased from five hundred million to six hundred and fifty million. Such a process as Vatican II and the implantation of its radical changes in the Church was bound to be disruptive, but the shear magnitude of the crisis it provoked astounded everyone. Many theologians who had acted as advisors at Vatican II returned to their respective academic institutions sharing their interpretations of the document which emanated from the Council. Upon arriving on the campus of their colleges or universities they found that the aura of change and turmoil had preceded them. Old foundations of confidence, patriotic idealism, moral traditionalism, and Judeo-Christian theism had already gone awash. These centers of academia had become microcosms of the world at large where paradoxically the problems of the general society were reflected in an intensified manner. It was the year 1965, which saw the turning point from complacency to unrest. The first

symptom was the rebellion against dress regulations.

At Manhattan College, Bronx, New York, an institution of higher learning operated by the Brothers of the Christian Schools, a dress code which required suit coats and ties as the proper attire for all four thousand three hundred and fifty-four students while they attended class sessions was in vogue. When the students rebelled against this code, Brother Edward O'Neill, Vice President of Student Services, gave his approval to attend class without a jacket and tie. He stipulated, however, that dungarees, sweat shirts, T-shirts, sneakers, and shoes without socks were prohibited. Neatness in grooming was required at all times. The wedge of change, however, kept widening and some students defied all regulations. Although most of the faculty considered dress as trivial, it signaled that a deeper cultural change was taking place. When the graduating class of 1969 were freshman, a strong move on the part of the activists in the class was initiated to sell T-shirts with a huge number "69" implanted upon them. Brother Calixtus Eugene Miller, who was the freshman moderator, was asked by Brother Edward O'Neill to look into the situation. Obediently Miller did so, exposed the basis for the choice of the lettering; and, in thwarting the attempt of the editors of the *Quadrangle*, the college newspaper, to minimize the seriousness of his findings, blew up quite a wind which bewildered innocents from sixteen to sixty who learned that "69" was an erotic, obscene symbol.

The *Quadrangle* continued its erratic and erotic course of reporting and was suspended for an article which attacked Cardinal Spellman, in a disrespectful way, for forbidding fraternity houses on Catholic campuses and forbidding "folk" Masses. The editor said, "What was there about fraternity houses that worried you Sir? Did you fear that they were dens of iniquity, stocked with stewed-to-the-gills fraternity brothers and baited by madras-clad Whores of Babylon, all conspiring to work poor, naive Freddy Frosh into a life of sin, debauchery and all that *vanitas vanitatum?*" As time passed the editors of the newspaper were obsessed with explaining all kinds of dissent in terms of sexual hyperbole. They denounced residence rules, requirements on attendance at class, retreats, and mocked most religious practices on campus. In 1967, at the other end of the State of New York, at the University of Buffalo, the *Spectrum*, the school newspaper, dabbled in the same kind of newscasting which tested the limits of the trivial and the tasteless so as to attract readers who wanted to be shocked and titillated. It was outspoken and critical of selective service tests and policies of dress regulations, but supported campus groups that advocated the legalization of marijuana. Like the *Quadrangle*, it was eager to print scatological material. It received the condemnation of university authorities when, in dislike of governmental action of local legislators, it attempted to publish an undergraduate's poem that compared "Buffalo's City Hall" to a "limp penis." The ensuing uproar on campus led three hundred students to occupy President Martin Meyerson's office and demand "Freedom of the Press." In the aftermath, however, the editor was forced to resign.

*I*t would be unfair to conclude that during the sixties and seventies all college students were negative in their attitudes. Obviously the group of vocal minorities received the greatest attention, but the majority of students did what they were in college for—to get an education. Although at Manhattan College the regular religion classes taught by brothers and priests were removed from the curriculum, and the old formulation that colleges stood in *loco parentis* was abolished, the college did introduce the Christian Life Council and College Ministry in order to stimulate meaningful religious life on campus. In 1967, the Council launched a student opinion survey that was answered by nearly two thousand five hundred students. The answers were discouraging to the traditionalists. In regards to sexual morality: seventy-five percent of the students could not see abortion as a serious wrong;

nearly eighty percent found no fault with premarital sex; ninety-two percent favored contraception; and one-half of the seniors and one-fifth of the freshman admitted to have had sexual intercourse. In their relationships to the clergy and church: seventy-three percent claimed that their bishops and priests had no influence on their daily lives; sixty-two percent were indifferent to attending Sunday Mass; and forty-eight percent prided themselves more as a Christian than as a Roman Catholic.

*S*ome other answers, however, were encouraging. Seventy-two percent said that they would not go to Communion without first confessing serious sin in the confessional. Seventy-three percent favored the continuation of Catholic parochial school education, and claimed that their children would be enrolled there. Although no poll, particularly one like this that was not scientific, could probe the recesses of the human soul, it did reflect human impatience with moral restraints in a period when hedonism, the idolism of pleasure, was the sole good in life and the general cultural climate of the time. In Catholic colleges around the country, as at Manhattan College, few of the values and assumptions of society were unchallenged and unaltered; lifestyles and relationships were radically changed. [1]

*F*or St. Louis Church, the philosophy and psychology of the trustees, clergy, and parishioners, generated by the aura of change in society in general, and in the Catholic Church in particular, brought about the demise of a Rare Tradition in American Catholicism and initiated a new growth of lay involvement in church administration. This end result did not come about quickly nor without great pain. The journey was down a labyrinth of overlapping and interconnecting decisions, procrastination, and procedures on the part of the trustees, bishop and pastor, and the congregation. In 1965, Father Ott, under a cloud of dissatisfaction had left St. Louis Church for an assignment deep into the Southern Tier of Western New York. Bishop James McNulty chose Father Alfred M. Mosack as his successor. Mosack, who traced his ancestry to Alsace, France, joined Joseph Sorg, Michael Anstett, and Howard Schwartz in the chain of pastors at St. Louis Church who were both German language speaking and natives of Lancaster, New York. He attended St. Mary's elementary school and high school in that city, matriculated in his college studies at St. Bonaventure University, Olean, New York, and continued there in the Seminary of Christ the King, studying philosophy and theology on his road to the priesthood. He was ordained there by Bishop Tief of Kansas on May 19, 1934.

*F*ollowing his ordination he served as an assistant to the pastor at four Buffalo churches: St. Bernard's, St. Louis, St. Mary Magdalene's, and St. James. During World War II, he was an army chaplain assigned to the hospital ship *Louis A. Milne*. After the war he continued as an assistant at St. Francis de Sales, 407 Northland Avenue, and at St. Agnes, 194 Ludington Street. He received his first pastorship at St. Joan of Arc Church in Perrysburg, Cattaraugus County, New York. Simultaneously he served there as chaplain of J.N. Adam Hospital, and was administrator at St. Paul of the Cross Church at South Dayton, eight miles south. In 1960, he was transferred to St. Martin's Church, Langford, Erie County, where he was pastor for five years. While there he supervised the planning and construction of a school and a social hall. His appointment to St. Louis Church, in 1965, followed. He served there as pastor for fourteen years, not leaving until the church had celebrated its anniversary of one hundred and fifty years. On September 20, 1979, Bishop Edward Head assigned him as pastor at St. Mary's of the Immaculate Conception at New Oregon, New York, a parish of ninety-five parishioners which was only a "stones-throw" from his former parish at Langford. Mosack often commented, "In a small community, acting like a family is the way to get things done. In the city, I was always greeted as Father Mosack. Here in the country, I am simply Father Moe." The

parish conducted itself as he had said. There were blessings of snowmobiles and outdoor Masses followed by coffee and doughnuts. Mosack was always gregarious especially at the Local Volunteer Fire Company where he was chaplain. His parishioners gave him a lavish party in honor of his fiftieth anniversary of his ordination on May 20, 1984. Because of illness, which retired him to St. Francis' Home in Williamsville, he had to be replaced in 1985. He died on February 14, 1986 at the age of seventy-seven. His body was buried in St. Mary's of the Immaculate Conception's cemetery.

*M*osack, as pastor at St. Louis Church was responsible for leading his congregation down the road of confusion by which the constitutions, instructions, and guidelines of Vatican II, as interpreted by the Holy See in Rome and the Diocese of Buffalo were to be implemented. The wheels of progress from initiation to practice moved slowly. In 1964, the Catholic world was introduced to the articles of the Constitution of the Liturgy as approved by Vatican II. Instruction on the proper implementation of the new liturgy came a little later that year. In 1969 the general instructions of the new order of the Mass made their way into the local churches. This was followed by a third instruction on proper implementation in 1970. It was not until May 31, 1971, however, that Bishop McNulty of the Buffalo Diocese presented the pastors with the revised guidelines for building and renovation of the churches in Buffalo so that they would conform to the new liturgy. Meanwhile the pastors were befuddled as to how to introduce all of the changes to their congregations in a reasonable manner. Their previous pastoral experience had never prepared them for such a momentous educational program.

*I*n 1965, Mosack had learned that a new book, *Our Parish Prays and Sings*, published by Liturgical Press, Collegeville, Minnesota, was ready for purchase in every parish in the United States. It contained eight hundred pages, cost $1.25, and contained the Mass

On Ash Wednesday, 1969, Father **Alfred M. Mosack**, pastor of St. Louis Church, administered ashes, beginning a new Lenten season. Receiving the ashes is Patricia Nowak. Photo by Bill Dyviniak, *Buffalo Evening News*.

Propers, Liturgy of the Sacraments, Directions for Forty Hours, and Stations of the Cross. He obtained sufficient copies so that they would be on hand to be distributed at Sunday Masses, used by the congregation, and returned to the rack at the ends of the aisles at the end of Mass. Many were reluctant to use the books; they were entrenched and satisfied with the prayers in their personal missals and prayer books that they had used all their lives while assisting at Mass. When the new books were distributed on January 16, 1966, the parishioners had had no previous education that in the Tridentine Mass they were observers; the server was the participant at Mass for them. Now in the new concept of Mass, they were the participants and without their involvement, the Mass was not complete. Although the books were issued, however, Mosack still said and sang the Mass as if it were in the Tridentine form, at the high altar, not facing the people. Within a short time, however, a simple table was installed in the sanctuary and the Tridentine form was continued facing the people. On March 23, 1966, Mosack came forth from the sacristy before morning Mass and said, "Today at Mass we have a new change. The Collect, Secret, Libera, and Post Communion prayers of the Proper of the Mass will be said in English rather than Latin." A few weeks later he told them that the prayers at the foot of the altar and the Orate Fratres would be said in English. For the next two years the Mass was said and sung in this manner. Many parishioners asked, "Where are we going with this? Are we supposed to learn the meaning of the liturgical changes by osmosis?"

During 1967, four years before McNulty gave the diocese his revised guidelines for church furniture, Edward A. Rick Sr., representing the trustees, contracted with E. M. Hager and Sons, to construct a new altar, lecterns, credence table, three chairs for celebrant and servers, kneelers and chairs for the commentators, and kneelers on the sides of the altar for the servers. Two lecterns were built on raised platforms so as to be easily seen by the congregation. Also added to one side

of the sanctuary were three prie-dieux for the lay ministers of the Eucharist. Upholstery on these kneelers was in mohair and color in keeping with the kneeler padding in the pews in the nave of the church, which had been designed and installed by Eugene W. Miller Sr. in 1954. All of the furniture was made of comb-grained oak with a rubbed varnish finish. Each piece was patterned after the gothic cathedral in Cologne, Germany, and in keeping with the gothic concept which Hager's company had worked into the pulpit, confessionals, and pews several decades before. Mosack had remarked, "Although the furnishings are gothic, they are clearly molded and exquisitely carved, avoiding over-ornamentation." He said this to indicate that they were in conformity with the Constitution on the Liturgy approved by Vatican II. The work was completed and installed by the dedication date of January 28, 1968.

Placed also around the altar were six bronze and onyx candelabra, fitted with specially designed oak bases carved similar to the altar. They were floor-mounted, and arranged on both sides of the altar consistent with the new liturgical dictums. To enhance the new altar, overhead lighting was installed, and a new public address system was added with internal wiring in both the altar and the lecterns. At the time of installation Mosack said, "This altar and these furnishings have been made possible by the generous donation of George Howard Hess a former parishioner of St. Louis Church who now lives in Ohio. It will always be a memorial to his father Michael Hess and the Hess family." The Hager Company followed the design of the entire set of furnishings, which was provided by John G. Schwartz whose office was in the Ellicott Square Building. Edwin H. Kolb chaired the building committee for this undertaking. At the time that these items were dedicated the method of celebrating Mass had not been completely converted to the new liturgy. Indicative of this is the fact that at the ceremony, the Tridentine form of a Solemn High Mass was sung with Mosack as the celebrant assisted by a deacon and subdeacon. In 1970 the Tridentine Mass, which had remained in force with modifications, was discarded and a new form, codified in the Missal of Pope Paul VI, was added. In 1972, he abrogated the order of subdeacon in the Roman Catholic Church.

While these changes were being put into place, many parishioners whispered to each other their fears as to what might be next to go? What a tragedy it would have been had the rules been strictly followed and the old altar was removed and replaced by the celebrant's chair. Members of the Gerhard Lang family would have rolled over in their graves! In 1970, the *Notitiae*, the Official Publication of the Concilium of the Congregation for Divine Worship, allowed only two places for proclaiming the "Word of God" through passages from scripture. These were the ambo and the lectern. This meant that the pulpit might have to go. If the beautiful gothic pulpit in the nave of the church, featuring Matthew, Mark, Luke, and John, had to be dismantled, many parishioners would have permanently withdrew their financial support to the church. Hints that the altar rail was to be removed so that the congregation would foster active participation in the Mass brought many a raised eyebrow. Most of the congregation was happy when Mosack said, "The trustees and I will retain the altar rail because the bishop has not given us any specific directive to retain or remove it. One specification seems to be fulfilled by us. The lecterns, being raised, stand out as they should according to the directives."

The dictates of the *Notitiae* ordered that, if possible, the tabernacle be moved to a Blessed Sacrament Chapel, or be kept in a place in the church that was prominent. The congregation was satisfied with it being where it had always been. Both the trustees and Mosack opted for this position. This became a slight bone of contention after Reverend Leo A. Ramsperger, a former rector of the Mother Church of Toronto, Canada, had visited St. Louis Church and announced that he could not find where the tabernacle was located. On July 1, 1976, he wrote to Mosack saying, "On a visit to your splendid cathedral-like church a few weeks ago, Father Roy F. McGinn and myself, of the Toronto Archdiocese, could not discover where the Blessed Sacrament was reserved for the faithful. There were red lights burning on both sides of the church, but being strangers we were unable to know the location of the Most Holy Sacrament. Forgive my temerity, Dear Father, but perhaps you could indicate more clearly where the Blessed Sacrament is in your beautiful church?" Mosack had only one answer to give. His reply was, "None of the members of our congregation have any problem finding Him!" As time passed the trustees and Mosack were able to keep the church's devotional statues, stations of the cross, the side chapels, and recognized works of art as they had been since the restoration in 1929. [2]

On July 4, 1976, the United States of America celebrated the bicentennial of its independence from British rule. Although the country had gone casual, shedding its suit coats and ties, it did not lose sight of its roots. Celebration of this great historical event made believers out of the most die-hard beatniks. New York City's harbor was filled with a flotilla of old time sailing ships, schooners, packets, clippers, cutters and sloops, passing in review. In the evening a marvelous display of fireworks filled the sky over the Statue of Liberty in the harbor, a gift from France which had been unveiled for the first time in 1886. Similar celebrations were conducted in every city in the country. The French connection with American independence had always been prominent, and J. Edmund de Castro, a Buffalo lawyer, had arranged to have the French antisubmarine destroyer, *Duperre*, a four hundred and thirty-five-foot vessel which was on its American tour, visit Buffalo. Although it could not be present for the Fourth of July celebration, it did manage to overcome several obstacles on its journey down the St. Lawrence Seaway and through the Welland Canal so as to reach Buffalo on Monday, July 19, 1976. It was fortuitous that the occasion of its arrival would combine the two celebrations of American and French independence. The French wholeheartedly celebrated Bastille Day on July 14, each year. It arrived early in the morning, escorted by one hundred pleasure craft, a Coast Guard patrol boat, and the Edward M. Cotter, Buffalo harbor's fireboat. It moored at the docks of the Niagara Frontier Transit Authority off Fuhrmann Boulevard. The Junior Band from the George E. Lamm, American Legion Post, Williamsville, welcomed it. As the lines were being secured, it played the French National Anthem, *Les Marseillaise*, and the American National Anthem, *The Star Spangled Banner*. The Commander of the ship, Christian Bonbon, was heartily greeted by Mayor Makowski.

On Monday evening a dinner was served on board followed by a dance held on the pier adjacent to the ship. Attendance, however, was by invitation only. On Tuesday, at 10:00 A.M., a special Mass sung in the French language was conducted at St. Louis Church in honor of the officers and crew of the *Duperre*. The entire compliment of the ship attended the Mass accompanied by city officials, visiting clergy, parishioners, and other interested citizens of Buffalo. One of the officers of the ship was particularly honored; he was Lieutenant Yann Baggio, the great-great-grandson of Louis Stephen Le Couteulx, who donated the property, in 1829, upon which St. Louis Church was built. At Mass Father Mosack presented Baggio with a reproduction of an artistic portrait of Le Couteulx. The original had hung side by side with mayors of the City in Buffalo's Common Council Chambers for many years. It was later transferred to the Buffalo and Erie County Historical Society. Upon receiving the gift Baggio, who was twenty-seven years of age, replied, "Since I was a tiny boy I have known of the special meaning that Buffalo had for my great-great-grandfather. Coming here is like a rediscovery." When Mass was over Mosack took him on a tour showing him the place of the original Le Couteulx residence on Main and Exchange Streets and the gravesite of him

and his family at the United German and French Roman Catholic Cemetery on Pine Ridge Road.

In the afternoon a soccer match was held between a team of crewmembers of the *Duperre* and some Buffalonians. Other members of the crew took a tour of Niagara Falls and Fort Niagara. Some of them said, "We were not aware that the Fort was first a residence for the French. We are excited to see the three flags of the great allies of World War II, French, British, and American, flying over this bastion." Some officers were entertained at a luncheon at the Saturn Club located on Delaware Avenue. Other officers who had accompanied the crew going to Fort Niagara were guests of the Youngstown Yacht Club for cocktails and a luncheon. In the evening, the tired crewmembers, who had been enthusiastic tourists, were taken in as guests into the homes of gracious Buffalonians. Late in the day, the *Duperre* was opened to the public for their inspection. A skeleton crew on board acted as hosts. They were swamped with sightseers; twenty-five thousand came in their cars causing one of the greatest traffic jams the city had ever seen. Only fifteen thousand managed to visit the vessel even though the scheduled time was increased by one hour. On the deck, where the helicopter landed, some children were not investigating equipment; they were looking for something elusive. When asked by an officer what it was they replied, "Where's the blood?" On the same deck several sailors sold T-shirts with the ships name on them for five dollars. Long before the tourists were requested to leave the ship they had completely sold out their supply. The ship sailed the next day, about noon; its next port of call was Detroit. [3]

Although the second age of the automobile, the influx of blacks, and the development of independent suburbs took parishioners away from residential areas surrounding St. Louis Church many remained as weekly communicants. When asked the condition of the church, Mosack replied, "Standing as it does between downtown business places and neighbor to a few homes, the church still has a loyal following of four hundred in the parish that includes suburban commuters." In a way Mosack was an enigma in his treatment of the value of the church and his expression of hope for its successful future. When approached by young people interested in joining the congregation he would say, "Why do you want to come here? You live closer to Our Lady of Lourdes. I think you should go there." In 1978, however, he was advertising a rebirth of downtown. He said, "We hope that the new convention center will bring business for us too!" At a party one evening while speaking to some influential friends about the administration of the church, he said, "Although I and the church staff are diocesan employees, the church is independently run by a board of trustees, and financed mostly through funds which came some years ago when the parish was blessed with stocks and bonds from affluent parishioners."

The enigma lies in the fact that one cannot understand if he is being facetious in this remark. Does he really consider himself, a priest, as an employee of the diocese? If he is only an employee, what does he do in the church? Does he dislike the trustees whom he believes are sitting on a gold mine of stocks and bonds? If his intention was to try to build a more successful parish one would not find it in his words describing the services conducted at the church. At one luncheon he attended he said, "Today's services at St. Louis Church are apt to be attended only by senior citizens, downtown workers, and tourists." When he said this he was sixty-nine years old, his church was one hundred and forty-nine years old, his school was closed, and he had seen the demise of almost all of the church's devotional societies. Although one understood his disappointment and frustration one could not fathom why his mood changed on other occasions. At the one hundred and fiftieth-anniversary banquet, for example, he pleaded to the congregation; "This is an aging church that's thinking young. Let's keep our church going another decade and after that another decade."

At that banquet, Monsignor Dino J. Lorenzetti, pastor of Our Lady of the Sacred Heart Church in Orchard Park, was the main speaker. On the dais that evening, flanking Lorenzetti were Chuck Healy, master of ceremonies, County Executive Edward J. Rutkowski, Mayor James D. Griffin, Honorable Thaddeus J. Dulski, representing Governor Hugh Carey, Bishop Edward Head of Buffalo, and Bishop Harold Robinson of Western New York's Episcopal Diocese. Lorenzetti's words, which could have been full of positive ideas for the success of St. Louis Church, seemed to be naive. He began, "The future of St. Louis Church, which like most city churches has suffered from the population shift to the suburbs, is closely tied to the theater district redevelopment. On the periphery of the parish, great things are happening. Just look at the influx of out-of-town investment, rapid transit, and the commitment of Mayor Griffin's administration to the area. Gee, they all can't be wrong." Without explaining any details, his remarks continued in a similar manner, he said, "Since the church is near Roswell Park Memorial Institute, it could become a center offering special training to doctors, nurses, and educators. It could be a center of education as well as compassion. St. Louis has a part in a new vision for the Buffalo of the future, one that is filled with joy and expectation." This meandering of ideas surely ran counter to the more mature view of Buffalo given by Mark Goldman in his discussion of the Rise and Decline of Buffalo. Goldman said, "Buffalo has not been a growing city for almost half a century and will never be again. Once we have discarded this image of growth we must begin to think in terms of trying to create a vital community within the contexts of a shrinking population. This is perhaps the greatest challenge for local leaders in years to come. It is not easy. It may even be impossible. We do not have any models of graceful decline."

When all the other speakers had finished Bishop Edward Head approached the podium and said, "While the emphasis for St. Louis Church is on the future, parishioners should not forget the thirteen pastors and hundreds of associates, sisters, brothers, trustees, and the laity who wrote the church's history. It was this very idea which had impressed Edwin H. Kolb, a member of the board of trustees, who, in 1957, conceived the idea that a permanent exhibit be set up to house the many irreplaceable souvenirs of the past already made sacred by the passing of time. With the approval of the pastor, Father Howard Schwartz, and the Board of Trustees, he threw himself wholeheartedly into the project. He formed a committee consisting of Carl Albert, Lawrence Wagner, and Lawrence Vincent. They immediately went about their task with compelling enthusiasm, zeal, and labor. They gathered artifacts and literature from past and present parishioners and called upon various organizations and companies to help them in making display cases and cabinets, providing lighting, and framing of pictures. Among those who gave assistance the following were prominent: Armento Metal Arts Company, Breitweiser Printing Company, Business Women's Club, Christian Mothers Society, Dramatic Circle, Holy Name Society, Knights of St. John, Eugene W. Miller and Son, and Reinagle Lighting Company. Upon completion the exhibit had a very fine, well lighted home at the south end of the Church Hall in the basement. The formal opening was September 29, 1957 at 12:15 PM. It was viewed that day by an extremely large group who had attended the morning Masses at St. Louis Church. The Christian Mothers provided refreshments.

Over the next twenty-two years the exhibit received only minor attention. Poor atmospheric conditions in the basement of the church brought quite a bit of deterioration to some of the artifacts. After its initial installation, the trustees never again placed historical preservation high on their priority list. The artifacts, however, received a rebirth of enthusiasm during the sesquicentennial of St. Louis Church in 1979. Many items were cleaned and placed around the interior of the church for viewing. Several parishioners, other than the trustees had approached Mosack, and

asked his approval to make this presentation. He was highly in favor of the idea, but the trustees disapproved. Now for the first time in one hundred and twenty-four years the trustees were not only at loggerheads with the clergy but also with an enthusiastic and determined group of parishioners. These were led by Larry Schieber and Frank L. Wodzicki. The trustees, especially George F. Reinagel, were further angered because the exhibit received much attention by the congregation and friends of St. Louis Church who had come from far and wide to participate in the sesquicentennial celebration which began with Mass on the First Sunday of Advent in 1978. Edward Head was the celebrant; his concelebrants were: Francis J. Hall, former associate pastor for six years, and Monsignor Eugene Selbert, born and reared in St. Louis' parish, and former pastor of St. Gerard's Church who retired in 1978.

Following Mass, Mosack, assisted by Joseph Lux, was very happy to take visitors on a tour and show them the artifacts. Mosack pointed out the oil painting of Louis Le Couteulx that had been done by Bernard J. Rooney, former assistant superintendent of school planning in Buffalo. Joseph Lux commented on the case containing the news clippings from the early 1900's pertaining to the great-grandchildren of Le Couteulx coming from France to break the old will and retrieve for themselves the property upon which St. Louis Church was built. He then turned and showed them the entire case that was devoted to Bishop John Timon. Many of the visitors were interested in trivial things such as the badly singed key which was pulled from the door of the flaming church in 1885, the stole of beige silk worn by the first pastor, John Nicholas Mertz, an ash tray made from the horn of an animal, and two gold gilded German Missals each titled *Die Heilige Schrift*. At the end of the tour Mosack announced that cover envelopes had been designed and were ready for distribution so that they could receive a cancelled stamp at the Post Office on January 5, 1979. It featured St. Louis Church with the inscription *"150th Birthday."* [4]

On December 3, 1978, the First Sunday of Advent, **Bishop Edward D. Head** celebrated Mass at St. Louis Church, initiating the Sesquicentennial Anniversary of Western New York's Mother Church. From left to right, the participants are: Rev. Francis J. Hall, Monsignor Eugene Selbert, Bishop Head, and Monsignor Peter Popadick

Challenge, Confusion, Convulsion and Cataclysm

The trustees, who had had a good working relationship with Father Schwartz, were very much disturbed when Bishop James McNulty switched him with Father Ott who had been pastor at St. Barnabas Church. They did not get along very well with Ott when he came to St. Louis Church because the parishioners were constantly pushing them to have Ott removed. After one year of residency, he was transferred to Friendship, New York. Mosack replaced him. The trustees were also disenchanted with him right from the start. Although he liked to party and carry on conversation while enjoying a bit of social libation, as did also the trustees, he was no charmer as Schwartz had been. By 1974, the relationship between George F. Reinagel, president of the trustees, and Mosack was so bad that they hardly spoke to each other even at the monthly trustee meetings. Reinagel also influenced the other members of the board: Arthur H. Ball, Francis V. Cole, Thomas P. Driscoll, Arthur L. Grupp, John W. Rembold, and Paul Hardick. Each of these men had held their positions, as trustees for a very long time; and, as a group, became extremely introverted.

If someone in the parish was interested in knowing what decisions were being made behind the closed doors of the trustees' office, they could not find out from Mosack, he was not in their inner circle. Parishioners could, however, keep their ears attuned to the whisperings of the wives of the board members; what they heard, spread as rumor throughout the parish and sometimes it was so embellished that it came out untrue. One truth, however, concerned the cathedral. Shortly after Edward Head had been appointed bishop in 1973, St. Joseph's Cathedral on Delaware Avenue was crumbling and sinking after only sixty-one years of existence. Architects examined the building, and offered no guarantee that it could be saved. Head decided to raze it and find himself another cathedral. When the trustees at St. Louis Church heard that Father Welker, pastor of St. Mary's of Sorrows Church, Genesee and Rich Streets, had offered his church as the cathedral, they approached Head and offered St. Louis

Church for this privilege. Mosack heard of the offer from the Chancery, and the parishioners learned of it through a host of rumors.

William Kurzdorfer, who had taken it upon himself to save the organ from decay, pointed out to Mosack that it was in dire need of repair. On one rare occasion when Mosack had an opportunity to verbally communicate with one of the trustees, John W. Rembold, he told him that some money would have to be spent to make needed repairs on the organ. Rembold, was the one trustee who had compassion. In 1972 he had received the diocese's St. Joseph the Worker award and the Holy Name Society's Man of the Year award for excellent service offered by a lay Catholic. He was born in Buffalo in 1900, attended School 37 and Our Lady of Lourdes' parochial school, went to Chownes Business School, and became a member of St. Louis Church in 1929. He and his wife Florence had two children: Charles R. and Florence H. At St. Louis Church, he founded the Ushers Club, chaired the Catholic Charities Drive for twenty-five years, and established the local chapter of the St. Columban Retreat League.

Rembold listened intently to Mosack's plea and said that he would present the condition of the organ at the next trustee meeting. Reinagel would not allow any discussion; he simply tabled the request and said that no money was available. It didn't make any difference to him that four sequential organists and choirmasters had made the same complaint that Kurzdorfer did. They were Leonard Weigand, Jim Kosnick, Susie Swinnich, and Dona Vasey. During the sesquicentennial year, choirs of twenty-five or more members were coming once each month to sing at St. Louis Church. In some cases, the music could have been tragic, however, organists such as Bob Chambers, from Holy Angels Church, had a way of dubbing out sounds that were unworthy on the organ, but he kept insisting that it needed repair. Leaving the organ's problems in limbo,

Reinagel talked the trustees into changing the lighting in the church. He became the beneficiary of this idea; the Reinagel Lighting Company was called upon to do the job. All the cluster lights in the church were removed and replaced by hideous canister fixtures more comfortable in a modern art studio than in a gothic church. They hung down into the nave of the church in such a way that even the most liberal liturgists could not say that they conformed to the new architectural movement of Vatican II. Again in secret this program of beautification was initiated behind the closed doors of the trustees' office and the parishioners were the last to know about it.

In late spring of 1978, St. Louis Church and its surrounding property were a disgrace. Among a legion of problems, the roof of the building leaked in many places, downspouts needed repair, the paint was peeling off the walls, and kneelers in the pews needed fixing. On the property, the old school building was fast deteriorating, grass and weeds were as high as an elephant's eye behind the school facing Franklin Street, and bundles of leaves were piled grotesquely in all the nooks and crevices of the buildings surrounding the parking lot. The trustees did not seem to care that flowers were not growing, trees were not pruned, and grass was not groomed. They ignored the condition of the church hall, the kitchen, the utensils, the bathrooms, and the museum. How was St. Louis Church supposed to celebrate the sesquicentennial amidst such squalor? The trustees said that only enough money was on hand to paint the lower portion of the church. They probably thought that the aging congregation would be so impregnated with visual cataracts that they would not see the upper portion. They also did not think that anything elaborate for a celebration was needed for a church undergoing erosion and decay. Their idea of celebrating was one single Mass on the feast of St. Louis, King of France. They had given up hope in the future of the church, and their voices were those of gloom and doom. [5]

This, however, was not the sentiment of a group of energetic parishioners led by Frank Wodzicki, Larry Schieber, Rose Kennedy, Josephine Weppner, and Michael Riester. On June 10, 1978, Larry Schieber sent a passionate letter to the members of the Board of Trustees. He pleaded with them to reconsider their reticence to enthusiastically celebrate. He told them that many of the parishioners understood the financial inability of their small number to contribute an adequate sum of money to redecorate the church and clean up the property. He realized that it might cost more than one-half million dollars to do the job. He was convinced, however, that through the use of television, radio, and newspaper articles concerning the magnificent history of St. Louis Church that the community would be moved to give financial assistance. He even insisted that large area foundations and corporations would graciously donate if approached properly. He then offered the trustees the names of a number of volunteers who would form committees and work hard to put out a souvenir program, develop an historical booklet, purchase a one hundred and fiftieth anniversary banner, and strike a commemorative medal. He told them that the group of volunteers had the backing of Father Mosack who would make arrangements with the diocese for representation by the clergy, singing groups from other Catholic churches, participation of Commandaries of the Knights of St. John from local churches, and obtain the use of facilities from the Knights of Columbus. In desperation Schieber begged the trustees to give their approval to his suggestions and draft letters to be sent to local painters' unions asking for a donation of services, to paint manufacturers so as to obtain gratis supplies of paint or at least sell them to the church at factory cost, and to solicit volunteers from among the areas most reputable artists' organizations so as to painstakingly paint and refinish statues and other artifacts. He insisted that the trustees would not be inconvenienced in anyway except to publicly give their approval. Once again, however, the trustees procrastinated, but the parish activists and their volunteers moved ahead without them.

Challenge, Confusion, Convulsion and Cataclysm

Seeing the congregation's approval of the motivation of the activists and their volunteers, the trustees felt embarrassed. Although once again the wives of the trustees knew what was going to happen, the parishioners were never informed. Through the efforts of Rembold, the trustees sold some Trico stock, raised $160,000, and had the church totally repainted. At the time, only two active organizations operated within the church, the Holy Name Society and the Ushers Club. Besides being trustees, John W. Rembold and Arthur Ball were officers in the Holy Name Society. No trustees were officers of the Ushers Club. The sesquicentennial committee was composed as follows: Frank L. Wodzicki, chairman; Larry Schieber, co-chairman; Rose Kennedy, coordinator; Josephine Weppner, treasurer; Sister Therese Marie, spiritual coordinator; Michael A. Riester, historical activities; Irene T. and Marie A. Meisriemer, souvenirs; Ruth A. Kolb, choral activities; Anna Marie Barone, correspondence; James J. Bartlett, coordinator of decorations and services in the church hall; Patricia M. Walters, social activities; Albert W. Riester, federal postage stamp preparation; and Frank J. Breitweiser, printing of the programs. The committee was given further assistance by Walter Swanigan, Joseph Lux, and Arthur Bond. Reverend Alfred M. Mosack and his assistant Reverend Frank F. Barone were, respectively, honorary chairman and co-chairman of the committee.

Although the museum had been cleaned and the artifacts put on display by November 3, 1978, the year of celebration did not begin until December 3, 1978, the First Sunday of Advent. The postage stamp was issued on January 5, 1979. On Tuesday, August 14, Mayor Griffin signed a proclamation designating the week of August 20-25, as *St. Louis Week*. The big day, the feast of St. Louis, King of France, August 25, 1979, began with a musical recital at 4:00 P.M. featuring the St. Louis Choir assisted by many members of other church choirs directed by David Wagner. It was followed by a procession formed outside the church and proceeded inside where Mass was concelebrated by

Bishop Head and several priests. After Mass everyone retired to the Hotel Statler for a banquet, entertainment, speeches, and good cheer. Bob Curran, a well-known writer for the *Buffalo News*, who was in attendance, asked Larry Schieber, "I understand that there are only two hundred parishioners on the St. Louis official membership list. And I know that you live in Snyder. So I have to figure that when my friend Clyde, a fellow alumnus of Notre Dame, spoke about the uniqueness of this big event, he was talking about help from outsiders." Larry replied to Curran, "Your two hundred figure is correct, but there are between four and five hundred people who live outside the parish, but attend Mass at St. Louis Church each week. I am sure that each of those who keep returning has a special reason. In my case I became involved with the church through my mother-in-law, Anna Hacker. When I first came around, I saw that volunteer workers were needed, and so I joined the Holy Name Society, and I am very happy with the association."

At the banquet the names of only six trustees were listed in the program; there had always been seven on the board. For several years, however, Paul Hardick, had been ill and diagnosed with a brain tumor. When his position as a trustee had been vacated it was never filled. He died before the one hundred and fiftieth-anniversary celebration. Frank L. Wodzicki, chairman of the celebration committee, had several times volunteered to join the trustees. He was refused. Did the trustees consider him a revolutionist within the parish? Time had to pass, however, before the real reason of their refusal would be understood. Even before the celebration, as early as January 1979, behind the closed doors of the chancery, Arthur Grupp and Francis Cole had been carrying on serious conversations with Monsignor Donald W. Trautman, diocesan chancellor, concerning a change in administrative policy at St. Louis Church. Trautman encouraged Grupp and Cole to speak with the other trustees to see if this would be an opportune time to have such a change. They were impressed with

Trautman's ideas and agreed that the time was opportune, especially since Cole, a lawyer, was having problems filling out Tax Exemption papers for the City Assessors. He knew that if the church were under the umbrella of the diocese that this difficulty would be removed.

Grupp was particularly enthusiastic about placing the church into the hands of the diocese. He had been a successful businessman. He was the owner of the E. J. Grupp Company, a paper-distributing firm located in Orchard Park. He was born in Buffalo on November 28, 1907, graduated from Canisius College in 1930, and married Marie Angeline Faber at St. Louis Church in 1938. Later he received an honorary doctorate from Canisius and held an annual class reunion for fifty years until his illness brought about his death on July 27, 1984. He was seventy-six years old. In life he had been a member of the Buffalo Rotary Club, a Knight of the Holy Sepulchre, Trustee of St. Louis Church, and a member of its Holy Name Society. It was Bishop Head who was instrumental in having Arthur inducted into the Knights and Ladies of the Equestrian Order of the Holy Sepulchre in 1982. At the same time Jerome B. Magee, Frank J. Maher Jr., William F. Brown, James G. Hurley, Stanley F. Phillips, James V. Glynn, Pasquale A. Greco, Charles S. Desmond, and Charles A Bauda were inducted by Cardinal Terrance J. Cooke at St. Patrick's Cathedral, New York City.

Grupp and Cole told George Reinagel, President of the Board of Trustees, what had transpired between themselves and Trautman, and Reinagel reluctantly decided that it would be acceptable for all the trustees to meet with Trautman and Bishop Head. Angered with the initiatives of Wodzicki and Schieber, the beginning of a sesquicentennial celebration on the First Sunday of Advent in 1978 against their wishes, the issuance of an anniversary postage stamp, and the embarrassment which forced them to spend $174,662 redecorating, repairing, and cleaning the church, the trustees decided

to conclude discussions concerning a change in the administrative policy of the church. Lawyers were hired so as to carry out the writing of the necessary legal papers that would essentially turn St. Louis Church over to the diocese and end the Rare Tradition in American Catholicism that had existed since 1838. Trautman told the trustees that the lawyers would have the papers ready for signatures by late September. Once again, the parishioners were the last to know what was taking place.

As another show of their displeasure with the way the sesquicentennial committee launched its administrative revolution, the trustees, on the eve of the Feast of St. Louis, August 24, 1979, formulated a letter which was to be sent to the congregation informing them of the transfer. It read, "Conscious of the many forces, economic and evolutionary, which endanger our beloved church, the trustees find it most reasonable and compelling that St. Louis Parish be entrusted to the Diocese of Buffalo to ensure its stability and longevity. The old adage, 'In union there is strength,' prompts us to recommend that our parish join with the other parishes in the diocese and make unanimous the management of the Catholic Church in this area. The decision is a fitting climax to our one hundred and fiftieth anniversary year. It will be announced publicly on Sunday, September 2nd, and will take effect immediately." The letter, however, was dated August 27, 1979, but was not postmarked until September 25, 1979.

On Saturday, September 22, 1979, Father William A. Schwinger entered the rectory on Edward Street; he had been appointed the new pastor of St. Louis Church. He was the former principal of Bishop Fallon High School at Main and Northampton Streets. It had been closed for some time having been the successor of the old St. Joseph's Collegiate Institute, which had moved to Kenmore. He had also served with the United States Marines during World War II. Before coming to St.

Louis Church as pastor, he was the chaplain of the Erie County Holding Center, a residence for convicts awaiting transfer or alleged convicts waiting trial. On the surface of things it looked as if one could consider him dynamic but not young. He, also, had never even been inside St. Louis Church or ever visited the rectory. Mosack, who had been pastor for fourteen years, and had prepared the congregation for the sesquicentennial celebration twenty nine days before, was in the process of packing so as to assume the pastorship of a rural church, St. Mary's of the Immaculate Conception.

*O*n October 1, 1979, Bishop Head accepted the transfer from the trustees and signed the papers that formed a new corporation for the church. On that day the church legally became known as St. Louis Roman Catholic Church of Buffalo. The by-laws, which had been drawn up by the lawyers, were filed with the County Clerk's Office on October 4, 1979. The New York Supreme Court had approved the certificate of incorporation and the by-laws on September 23, 1979. Bishop Head informed the Apostolic Delegate, Right Reverend Jean Jadot, of the transfer on October 15, 1979. He was a resident of Washington D.C. The Bishop made it clear to the congregation that the action had been taken in order to assure the stability and longevity of the church. He said, "St. Louis Church's historical background, good physical condition, and financial stability are the basis upon which your church will survive; it shall remain open. The first one hundred and fifty year chapter of its history, however, has come to an end." [6]

Above: **Reverend Monsignor William A. Schwinger**, who was the first pastor at St. Louis Church following the creation of the New Trustee System based on the New York State Corporation Law, first initiated in 1863. He was an ecclesiastical member of the Church's Trustees along with Edward Head, Bishop; and Donald Trautman, Vicar General. The two appointed laymen were Arthur Grupp and Thomas Driscoll.

REFERENCES AND NOTES ✤ CHAPTER SIXTEEN

1. For the statistics of Buffalo in 1960, and the condition of its streets, parks, universities and colleges, hospitals, hotels, post offices, theaters, and museums; a metropolis in a forest of trees, see: Empire State News Corporation, *Street Guide of Greater Buffalo and Niagara Falls*, Interstate Publishing Company, Boston, Mass., 1960, pp. 177-79; and Walter G. Young, "Buffalo City of Good Neighbors, *Catholic Digest*, March 1960, pp. 73-8. For Information concerning the St. Lawrence Seaway and its effect on Buffalo, the decline of business in Buffalo following its opening in 1959, the second automobile age, highway construction in Buffalo, the Black ghetto, and white flight to suburbia see: op. cit. *High Hopes*, pp. 267-291, 276-77, 270-71, 284-88, 296. For surviving churches in Buffalo during the decades of unrest see: op. cit. *Celebrating God's Life In Us*, pp. 151-52. For background during 1960-1979, on Black revolt in America, Vietnam, the impossible victory, Women's rights movement, Indian's unrest, prisoners' movement, see: Howard Zinn, *Peoples History of the United States*, Harper Perennial, A division of Harper Collins Publishers, New York, 1990, pp. 416-17, 422-29, 432-36, 442-48, 451-52, 457-59, 460-64, 492, 493-504, 509-13, 524-28. For discussion of the Second Vatican Council see: op. cit. *Encyclopedia of Catholicism*, pp. 787-88, 1299-1306; Also see: op. cit. *A Concise History of the Catholic Church*, pp. 355-68. Also see: Alvin Toffler, *Future Shock*, New York Random House, Inc., 1971, p. 35. Charles E. Curran, a priest and theologian at Catholic University in 1968, who led the public dissent against *Humanae Vitae*, the encyclical prohibiting birth control by artificial means, resulted in his being considered no longer suitable or eligible to exercise his role as professor of theology at the university. For college unrest, particularly at Manhattan College see: Gabriel Costello F.S.C., *Arches of the Years, Manhattan College, 1853-1979*, Manhattan College, Riverdale, New York, 1980, pp. 293-296, 298-300, 303, 316-17; Also for campus newspapers' responses see: *Quadrangle*, March 11, 1966, *Quadrangle*, November 5, 1965, and reference to the University of Buffalo's *Spectrum*, op. cit. *High Hopes*, pp. 253-54.

2. The biographical sketch of Father Alfred Mosack was gleaned from information provided by *Western New York Catholic*, May, 1984; *Buffalo Courier Express*, Saturday, February 15, 1986; *Buffalo News*, February 15, 1986. For the implementation of the New Catholic liturgy in the local churches following Vatican II see: op. cit. *Encyclopedia of Catholicism*, 362-63, 786, 787-88, 791; op. cit. *Good Shepherd; The Church on the Canal*, pp. 107-8; The Libera was the prayer said right after the Our Father; "Deliver us O Lord, from all evils, past present, and future etc." The complete outline of the implementation is as follows: 1964, Vatican II, Constitution of the Liturgy published; 1965, instructions for the implementation drawn up, books for distribution in the local churches are ordered; 1965, Although Latin could still be used by the people in their responses at Mass, an *Introduction to English*

Translations of the Ordinary of the Mass for Liturgical Use in the United States was issued by the Bishops' Commission on the Liturgical Apostolate; 1966, Copies of the *Peoples Mass Book* were used for the first time in the local churches, some Mass prayers were said in English, the canon of the Mass was still in Latin; 1967, St. Louis Church ordered new sanctuary furniture according to the dictums of Vatican II; 1968, the new furniture was installed and dedicated at St. Louis Church, but Mass was still celebrated in the Tridentine form; 1969, the general order was given to the pastors to have instruction for the faithful on the conduct of the new Mass form; 1970, the Tridentine form of Mass was discarded and the new form was put in place; 1972, Pope Paul VI abolished the subdeaconship. For the Liturgical Regulations to be followed in Renovating Churches see: *Western New York Catholic*, July 29, 1976. For understanding the liturgy during the five year interim of implementing it into the local churches see: *Peoples Mass Book*, World Library of Sacred Music, Inc., Cincinnati, Ohio, 1966. For the type of hymns sung at St. Louis Church during the interim see: *New Community Mass*, Cantate Omnes Publications, Buffalo, New York, 1964. For the distinction between pulpit, lectern, and ambo, Permanent Deacon, Don Seyfried, St. Pius X Church, Getzville, New York, has contributed the concepts contained in a book by Rev. Jovian P. Lang, O.F.M., *Dictionary of the Liturgy*, Catholic Book Publishing Company, New York, 1989, pp. 26, 311, 533. Ambo comes from the Greek word *ambon* meaning pulpit. In the Byzantine rite it was the pulpit, usually in the center of the nave, from which were rendered litanies, diptychs, scriptures, programs of imperial coronations, exaltations of the cross, promulgation of councils, and pronouncements of anathema. Preaching was usually carried out from the throne that was in the apse of the church. In the Roman rite the pulpit was an elevated stand for the preacher or reader. In the early church these things were done from the cathedra and episcopal chair, and later from an ambo which was an elevated platform. Since Vatican II ambo has been replaced by the lectern which is a place from which the Word of God is proclaimed; it is the focal point of the Liturgy of the Word in the post Vatican II Mass. It is a stationary reading stand reserved for scriptural readings, responsorial psalms, and the Easter Proclamation that in Latin is Exultet. It may be used for the homily and general intercessions that are like the old diptychs now called prayers of the faithful. In general practice, however, the modern Catholic will see the old pulpit not being used or it has been taken out of the church, and one will find one or possibly two lecterns in the sanctuary on opposite sides and forward from the altar from which the priest says Mass facing the people.

3. For the account of the French destroyer, *Duperre*, visiting Buffalo in July 1976 see: *Courier Express*, Wednesday, July 14, 1976; *Courier Express*, Wednesday, July 21, 1976. For a pictorial of St. Louis Church see: *Buffalo Courier Express*, December 21, 1941; picture of the church burned-out in the fire of 1885 see: *Buffalo Courier Express Pictorial*, October 24, 1954; picture of Buffalo looking up Main Street from downtown and seeing St. Louis Church's steeple in the background see: *Buffalo Courier Express*

Pictorial, October 24, 1954; For a full page of St. Louis Church, featuring it as the church of Laudenbach see: *The Buffalo Times*, Sunday, March 31, 1935.

4. For remarks by Alfred Mosack concerning the future of St. Louis Church and its conditions involved in being within the success or failure of downtown see: *Buffalo Courier Express*, November 3, 1978; *The Buffalo News*, Sunday, August 12, 1979; *The Buffalo News*, Sunday, August 26, 1979. Mosack puts ashes on head of Patricia Nowak see: *Buffalo News*, February 20, 1969. Photo of Bishop Head celebrating Mass at St. Louis Church. Altar is turned so he faces the congregation see: *Buffalo Evening News*, December 3, 1978. For information concerning the exhibits in the St. Louis Church museum see: *Formal Opening of the St. Louis Church Historical Museum; 1829-1957*, four-page pamphlet, St. Louis Church, September 29, 1957. Also see artifacts discussed in: *Buffalo Courier Express*, Friday, November 3, 1978; *Buffalo Courier Express*, August 25, 1979. For historical reasons for issuing the stamp see: Mary Borrelli, *Western New York Catholic Visitor*, December 31, 1978. For biographical information concerning Arthur L. Grupp see: *The Buffalo News*, July 29, 1984 and *The Buffalo News*, Monday, September 27, 1982.

5. Information concerning the conditions of the church prior to the sesquicentennial was gained through conversations of the author/editor with Rose Kennedy, Michael Riester, Florence Rembold, William Kurzdorfer, and Mary Hardick. The degrading conditions of the organ and the church property were attributed to the procrastination and conservatism of the aging trustees. So also were the degrading conditions between the trustees and members of the youth of the parish involved in CYO/CYC. See *interview Between Francis V. Tonello and Michael Riester*, May 11, 2002, an oral history, a copy of which is in the St. Louis Church Archives. The following are three observations rendered to Michael Riester by Francis V. Tonello who graduated from St. Louis School in 1943. (1) Lack of enthusiasm on the part of the trustees as expressed in preparation for the sesquicentennial was not something that developed overnight. The mood of aloofness and conservatism may have always been the basis of their actions, but it became pronounced to some of the youth of the parish even during Anstett's and Schwartz's pastorships. The trustees had a particularly ambivalent attitude toward the activities of the CYO/CYC chapter at St. Louis Church. Father James Cahill, assistant to the pastor, was its director. Francis V. Tonello an elected officer, described Cahill, who first came to St. Louis Church in 1947, as a Bing Crosby playing the role of a parish priest in the movie *Going My Way*. Tonello said, "Father Cahill was twenty-seven years of age when he came here. He came in like a dynamo; he was all over the place, bumping into everyone, young and naive, and working out his teenage years which we assumed he never really had because he went to the seminary at a very early age. The trustees didn't relate to us, they were the institution that was against us. Father Cahill was our hero; he showed us a type of church authority different than that expressed by the trustees. Even Father Anstett was not a

social guy, but he gave Father Cahill "carte blanche" in his relations to us." (2) Cahill was born in Lockport in 1920, did his high school and college studies at the Little Seminary of St. Joseph and the Little Flower in Buffalo, attended St. Bernard's Major Seminary in Rochester, ordained on September 21, 1944, and immediately assigned to St. Mary's Church in Niagara Falls as an assistant. His other assistantship assignments were St. Louis Church, and St. Thomas Aquinas, Buffalo, Saints Peter and Paul, Williamsville, and St. John de La Salle, Niagara Falls. He also was the military chaplain of the 339th National Guard Anti-Aircraft Unit before being appointed pastor, in 1964, at Our Lady of Lourdes at Bemus Point. Following this assignment he served as chaplain at St. Mary's Manor, Niagara Falls, until he was named pastor at Nativity of the Blessed Virgin Mary, Herkimer Street, on June 6, 1970. He died on Wednesday, July 13, 1983 at the Buffalo General Hospital and was interred in the priest's plot at Mount Olivet Cemetery in Tonawanda. (3) Cahill had a talent for writing plays, putting shows together, recruiting talent, and using it successfully. Tonello said, "He wrote little teeny be-bop skits, silly boy and girl routines which lasted about five minutes during the intermissions of our dances. In a way he was more of a kid than any of us." Cahill wanted the members of the CYO/CYC to become a junior drama club and extend the work of the Dramatic Circle. He approached the members of the Dramatic Circle hoping that they would think that he had a good idea. "They wouldn't even give him the time of day," Tonello said. "That outfit was a walled-in group that had absolutely no connection with us. They came to their meetings for drinking, smoking, and sharing their fellowship. They could care less about Father Cahill's ideas. They and the trustees hated us kids; they would never think of coming to see one of our plays, or one of our basketball or football games. Maybe they didn't like us because we lost all our games; we really stunk in sports, but we were terrific in drama. They only tolerated us, but we showed them a thing or two. With Father Cahill's approval, we ran dances in the school yard and the church hall, put up our own advertising, hired a band, and lighted the area with a crystal ball supported by a rope across the yard. We paid for everything; they didn't offer us a dime. After the school closed in 1959, the trustees seemed very satisfied to pay the tuition for the children to go to other parochial schools such as St. Boniface, Our Lady of Lourdes, or Immaculate Conception. They lost all interest in giving financial assistance to anything that smacked of youthful endeavors. Fathers Schwartz, Cahill, Bosack, and Coveney kept them alive." Robert Albert was able to verify several observations made by Tonello concerning CYO/CYC at St. Louis Church. Albert said, "We had a large group of enthusiastic young people. I can remember the following names: Francis V. Tonello, Victor Mistretta, Sal Mistretta, Tony Mistretta, Mary Jane Tulapane, Pat Riley, Bob Albert, Rick Carballada, Donald Gibson, Betty Grady, Joan Kennedy, Rose Varco, Alma Jean Didio, Rosalyn Jean Le Bar Gibson, Pete Keeley, Dan Healy, Jim Hines, Joan Howard, Tom Powers, Nola Richardson, and Pat Nolan. Father Cahill was surely a whiz at putting on plays. They always had a strong religious lesson, and many were written by himself and Nick Santaserio.

Nick was the assistant manager of the Erlanger Theater at Delaware Avenue and Mohawk Street. Stage construction and make-up were provided by Lew and Josephine Fisher who originated and operated Melody Fair, North Tonawanda, for many years after having run the Lake Shore Playhouse in Derby. The St. Louis CYO group won first place prize in one act plays many times; the award was given by Father Joseph McPherson, director of the diocesan CYO. Most of these prize-winning plays were presented in the school hall on the third floor. During days of fine weather, Father Cahill enjoyed having picnics for his group at his cousin's cottage at Olcott Beach."

6. For newspaper articles concerning the sesquicentennial see: *The Buffalo News*, Sunday, August 12, 1979; *The Buffalo News*, August 26, 1979; and the letter to the Trustees by Larry Schieber, June 10, 1978, copy in the St. Louis Church Archives. Biographical material on Arthur L Grupp see: *Canisius College Chronicle*, October 1984; *The Buffalo News*, July 29, 1984; *The Buffalo News*, September 27, 1982. Letter concerning the location of the Blessed Sacrament in St. Louis Church see: Letter, July 1, 1976, sent by Rev. Leo A. Ramsperger, P.P., St. John's Church, Albion , Caldeon, East Ontario, Canada, to Reverend Alfred Mosack, copy in the St. Louis Church Archives. Photographs of the Mass celebration on Dec. 3, 1979 for the beginning of the sesquicentennial, by Bill Dyviniak, *Buffalo Evening News*. In preparation for the celebration see: Letter sent to Bishop Edward Head, from Larry Schieber requesting him to celebrate the Mass on August 25, 1979 and be present at the Statler Hotel for the banquet which was to follow Mass. He mentions that the banquet would also celebrate the 45th anniversary of Father Mosack's ordination. Copy in St. Louis Church Archives. The letterhead was another reason for anger on the part of the trustees. It identifies St. Louis Church, the new banner that was designed for the anniversary, and contains the officers as Mosack, Schieber,

and Wodzicki; no mention is made of the trustees. Another point of rift between trustees and Mosack, seven years before the celebration, can be seen from the *St. Louis Church Report of Operations*, fiscal year ending September 30, 1972. The total income was $81,467.49. The note to the parishioners only carries the name of The Board of Trustees with Mosack's name omitted. This was contrary to the practice of having the names of both pastor and trustees appear on documents such as letterheads, Christmas cards, Summaries of Financial Activities, and Annual Financial Reports during the tenure of previous pastors. For the arrival of Father Schwinger as pastor of St. Louis Church see: *Buffalo Courier Express*, Sunday, September 23, 1979. For Schwinger being raised to the rank of Monsignor see: *The Buffalo News*, Thursday, October 18, 1984; this was also the time that the present pastor Robert J. Cunningham was made a Monsignor by Pope Paul II. At the time he was Vice Chancellor. On that day the pope had raised twenty-five priests of the Buffalo diocese to this rank. For the banquet celebration see: *Program for the Sesquicentennial Dinner at the Statler Hotel*, a copy is in the St. Louis Church Archives. Rev. Donald Trautman was at the time of the sesquicentennial banquet the Chancellor and Vicar General of the Diocese of Buffalo. As chancellor he was the principal archivist of the diocesan curia which was the collective diocesan governing agency. He was a notary by law. He systematized and authenticated curial acts. His governance powers belonged to the vicar general by office. So he held both positions. A chancellor did not, however, have to be a priest, but in practice he was. Acts of the curia were those which set forth the laws, pronouncements, and addresses and principal documents issued by the bishop. The vicar general was a priest who functioned as the bishop's deputy. He had a wide range of responsibility; there could have been more than one vicar general at a time but with a defining role, an example of which would be Vicar General for the Germans. Vicar simply meant someone who acted for another.

CHAPTER SEVENTEEN

Anticipation Hailed a New Clarion Call

The clarion call at St. Louis Church in 1979, transferring the nineteenth century trusteeship of the church to a Diocesan form of administration, which brought civic legalism into conformity with ecclesiastical legalism, was the clear and shrill tone of heavenly angels' trumpets which announced the voice of the Holy Spirit, who proclaimed a new spiritual and corporate organization for the congregation of the church. His announcement, however, energized conflicting human responses. A thrill of satisfaction in victory ran through the ranks of the diocesan leadership, a ferment of revenge toward the pastor, Father Mosack, and the sesquicentennial activists consumed the trustees who dissolved the old structure of temporal administration, and a deep sense of betrayal toward both the trustees and the diocesan leadership permeated the minds and hearts of the congregation. In his letter to the Most Reverend Jean Jadot, Apostolic Delegate of Rome to the United States, Edward D. Head, Bishop of the Diocese of Buffalo, delighted in expressing his happiness that St. Louis Parish had been returned to the diocese. He said, "The hundred and fifty year chapter in the history of the diocese has come to an end! For the past one hundred and fifty years, a corporation under lay trustees has owned this parish. The parish history is steeped in lay trusteeism, which had national ramifications for the early American Church. In 1843, the parish was placed under an interdict. In 1847, Bishop Timon again placed the Church under interdict, which lasted until 1855. Time has proven a great healer." Bishop Head in his haste and enthusiasm to spread the news to the Apostolic Delegate, however, riddled his letter with several inaccurate historical facts.

His reference to St. Louis Parish being, according to civic legalism, returned to the diocese was erroneous. The church never legally belonged to the diocese; it was incorporated on December 2, 1838, nine years before the diocese came into existence. The church, founded in 1829, pre-dated the diocese by eighteen years. Bishop Hughes placed the church under interdict on April 4, 1843, because the church would not conform to the regulations set down by his synod of priests that had been called in 1842. The whole intent of the legislature in the *Act of Incorporation of Religious Societies, 1813*, under which the Trustees of St. Louis Church had incorporated, was to place the control of the temporal affairs of religious societies in the hands of the majority of corporators, independent of priests and bishops, presbyters, synods, or ecclesiastical judicatory. According to this civic legalism, the trustees of St. Louis Church, in the eyes of the laws of the State of New York, did not have to honor the ecclesiastical legalisms of Hughes' synod. On August 10, 1844, sixteen months after Hughes brought down his iron authoritative fist, he lifted the interdict. Bishop Timon did not place St. Louis Church under interdict in 1847 as maintained by Bishop Head in his letter to Jadot. Timon applied it on June 14, 1851 and officially lifted it on May 27, 1855. One observes, in a review of this history, the extent of the cleavage between civic legalism and ecclesiastical legalism, a cleavage which, by an evolutionary process, was mended in time. Bishop Head did not seem to be aware of this evolution. If he had been, one would assume that his remark, "time has proven a great healer," would have been applied to the evolution rather than to the erroneous indication that St. Louis Church was returned to the diocese. [1]

Since 1974, the trustees had been extremely antagonistic toward Father Alfred Mosack. They accused him of poor stewardship, lack of leadership, and rough handling of parishioners. They criticized his extensive visits to Troop I so as to fraternize with veterans in late hours of the evening, and of spending long hours at the racetrack at Hamburg, New York, or in Fort Erie, Canada. They confronted him with the fact that he was primarily pastor of St. Louis Church and secondarily chaplain of Troop I. They hardly ever spoke to him, disliked it when he showed up for trustee meetings, and abhorred his tone of temper and anger toward them. They refused to place his name on the annual financial operating statement, as had been the custom with former pastors. Above all, they were disgusted with the sesquicentennial committee's choice of Fathers Alfred Mosack and Frank Barone as honorary chairman and co-chairman with their pictures in the program while the trustees' names were only listed with no particular part to play in the ceremonies. In the confidential meetings that they had with Monsignor Trautman, Chancellor for the Diocese of Buffalo, preliminary to the dissolution of the Trusteeship, they savored a sense of victory when they were told that Mosack would be replaced as pastor at St. Louis Church by Father William Schwinger. They did not know him, but Trautman told them that he bore a German name and was a younger and more dynamic person than Mosack. Their faces were aglow with satisfaction.

The trustees told Monsignor Trautman that the reason they would be willing to dissolve the nineteen-century trusteeship was because they did not believe that St. Louis Church could be perpetuated beyond the next generation. They implied to him that the parish

could not provide the leadership necessary to carry on the tradition of trusteeship, as they understood it, and as it had been handed down from past generations in its pristine state to its present time. George Reinagel, president of the trustees said, "This concern of leadership has been on our minds for some time. The position held by Paul G. Hardick had been held in limbo since he was diagnosed with cancer. We are but six trustees rather than seven as prescribed by our original by-laws: Arthur H. Ball, Francis V. Cole, Thomas P. Driscoll, Arthur L. Grupp, John Rembold, and myself. When Paul Hardick finally died, after suffering many years, we were unable to find a proper replacement. We are also concerned about ourselves being able to continue in leadership. We too are aging, and some of us also have poor health." They withheld from Trautman, however, their deep feeling of resentment toward certain activist individuals in the parish such as Frank L. Wodzicki, Larry Schieber, Rose S. Kennedy, Josephine Weppner, James J. Bartlett, Michael Riester, and several others who were prominent on the sesquicentennial committee. They saw several women gaining prominence in the parish, and it was beyond their capacity to think that women could sit on their Board of Trustees.

They were most disgusted with the gall of Larry Schieber who wrote to them on June 10, 1978 proposing directives as to how the church should prepare for the sesquicentennial celebration. He had pointed out that the church needed to be painted, windows repaired, and all furniture cleaned. He said that public awareness needed to be stirred up with news flashes on TV, radio, and in the press. He said, "Money will be needed to support these activities, get out a souvenir program, write an historical booklet, design a church flag featuring a shield enclosing the form of St. Louis King of France surrounded by fleur-de-lis, forge commemorative medals, and apply for a Federal Postage Stamp wishing happy birthday to St. Louis Church." Reinagel did not reply to Schieber's letter, but let information slip through the rumor mill that the trustees' idea of a celebration was simply a special Mass to be said on the twenty-fifth of August, the feast of St. Louis, King of France; and, if the church needed painting, it would only be the lower half which would receive the brush. The parishioners, however, were appalled with the trustees' attitude and voiced their discontent. The trustees were so embarrassed that they commissioned Francis V. Cole to sell some Trico stock for $160,000. They added money to it from the general fund and had the church painted, the windows repaired, and the church cleaned. They were irritated that they had to spend a total of $174, 662 to appease the crowd.

*O*utside of this action the trustees did nothing, but the sesquicentennial committee plodded on. The celebration started with a Mass concelebrated by Bishop Head and several other priests of the diocese on December 3, 1978, the First Sunday of Advent. Through the initiative of Albert W. Riester, a Federal Postage Stamp was issued on January 5, 1979 in commemoration of the day Louis Le Couteulx sent the deed of the property to Bishop Dubois in New York City in 1829. During the summer, Mayor James D. Griffin issued an order naming the week beginning with August 20, St. Louis Week in Buffalo, New York. On the feast of St. Louis, August 25, Bishop Head again concelebrated Mass in the afternoon. Preceding it, the congregation enjoyed a special musical recital conducted by the former church organist, David Wagner. The choir was made up of a large number of voices from St. Louis Church and other downtown churches. Following the Mass all retired to the Statler Hotel for a banquet and speeches by dignitaries. The trustees considered all of this to be in extreme disobedience to their will; and because of it, they were willing to dissolve the trusteeship rather than allow the administration of the church to flow into the hands of activists such as those on the sesquicentennial committee.

*N*either Frank Wodzicki nor Larry Schieber

deserved these epithets. Wodzicki and his wife were Polish born. They had twin boys, lived in Allentown, and joined the church in 1978. Wodzicki had a very good job with *Lufthansa Airlines*; and, immediately after joining the church, he volunteered his services as a lector. Father Mosack liked him and allowed him to organize a crew so as to clean up the pitifully unkempt lot behind the school building. Larry Schieber was an administrator with the Niagara Frontier Transit Authority; he played a significant role in the construction of the underground rapid transit system on Main Street. Although he was a very mild mannered person, he displayed a tenacious determination to correct any neglects and wrongs that he saw in the church. He had married Marie Hoover, nee Hacker. For an entire decade from 1903 to 1913, five children from the Hacker family graduated from St. Louis' School: Joseph F., Frank, Carl, Catherine, and Helen.

*T*he trustees were not totally honest in their conversations with Trautman. They withheld the fact that several times Frank Wodzicki, chairman of the sesquicentennial committee, had volunteered to take the place of Paul Hardick as a trustee. Each time his request was made they disdainfully spurned it. The trustees were so totally wrong in claiming that the members of the sesquicentennial committee were incapable of providing leadership. After the dissolution of the trustee system, these members surfaced into the sunlight and became leaders in the new corporation that was formed following the demise of the old. Again if the trustees in power in 1979 had reviewed the history of the evolution of Corporation Law for Religious Societies in New York State, they would have found that they were skating on very thin ice by opposing and rejecting these emerging leaders of the congregation. Even Kevin Kennedy and Joseph A. Stoeckl, attorneys for the diocese, and Francis V. Cole, attorney for the trustees, who were putting together the necessary papers for dissolution of the trustee system, were apparently unaware of the history which had brought civic legalism more in conformity with ecclesiastical legalism.

Nowhere in the Confidential Chancery Memos between Monsignor Trautman and Bishop Head does one find that Kennedy, Stoeckl, or Cole advised Trautman of the existence of any historical information. Prior to 1854, all religious societies, both Protestant and Catholic were incorporated under the provisions of the Corporation Law of 1813. The law considered a church under three aspects: the spiritual organization, the society, and the trustee corporation. The law had nothing to say concerning the spiritual organization. This was that part of the system in which ecclesiastical legalism reigned supreme. Any interference with the spiritual organization by the civil courts would have been a breach of the First Amendment to the Constitution which provided that Congress shall make no law respecting an establishment of religion, or prohibit the free exercise thereof. Concerning the society, the law took cognizance. This meant that the law could judicially hear controversies. The society, however, was in limbo. In controversy against ecclesiastical power that was absolute, it could not dialogue or win. In controversy against the trustees it too was not heard because it did not belong to the corporation; only the trustees were the corporation and the legal representation of the society.

In June of 1854, however, the case of *Robertson v. Bullions* came before the New York Court of Appeals. The case involved a Presbyterian minister who had been excommunicated by the presbytery and synod, but whom the trustees of the Associate Church of Cambridge, New York, wished to retain. The decision of the Court of Appeals was in favor of the presbytery stating that there was to be considered no legal distinction between societal corporation and trustee corporation. The society, as far as civil legalism was concerned, was taken out of limbo. Thenceforth in the State of New York, a trustee corporation gave way to a

corporation aggregate in which the congregation as such was held to be incorporated. Corporate franchise was extended to all members of the society; and, from being exclusive corporators, the trustees were reduced to mere officers of the corporation. The society became the corporation, the owner of the property, and responsible for the temporal affairs with the trustees as officers of the board of directors. In a controversy, however, the society could bring legal action against the trustees. If in 1979, the congregation had been aware that the trustees were going to dissolve the corporation without their knowledge, it could have opposed them in a court of law. It seems reasonable that the trustees and the diocese should have been so advised by Kennedy, Stoeckl, and Cole of this possibility. Because of laws passed in 1863, civil legalism had grown positively in agreement with ecclesiastical law. If, in 1979, the congregation had carried on a civil dispute, the concept of a Trustee Corporation by the Laws of 1813 would have been shown to be an illusion. The trustees really dissolved something that had already become a ghost of the past. The historical importance of this Rare Tradition in American Catholicism existing at St. Louis Church is that it had not been firmly challenged in the courts for a hundred and sixteen years.

When the news of the transfer of the trustee corporation was announced by Father Schwinger on Sunday, September 30, 1979, and distributed by the press following the actual take-over by a newly formed corporation on October 1, the parishioners were appalled. Fear, horror, dismay, and shock ran rampantly through the pews and households of the congregation. Larry Schieber said that the transfer was callous and unchristian like. Rose Kennedy said that it was insulting. The entire sesquicentennial committee met in special session on Thursday evening following the announcement in the press on October 2. Its members called for legal action to be taken against the trustees, forcing them to make a full accounting of the church's assets. Up to that time they had refused to do so. Schieber said, "The trustees didn't notify us until the decision was made. They are supposed to represent the parishioners." Rose Kennedy said, "The trustees formulated a letter which they dated August 27, to inform us of the transfer. It was postmarked September 25, and we did not hear of its contents until Schwinger read it to us. Why did they delay for a whole month?"

The committee did not, however, challenge the trustees' decision to transfer the church to the Catholic Diocese of Buffalo, nor did they follow through with any lawsuits. If their knowledge of past history had been honed to the nature of the evolution of incorporation of religious societies, they may have attacked the situation with more vigor. Since 1854, they, the society of the church, were the corporation and the trustees were merely officers of it. The action of transfer of property and assets to a new corporation and dissolution of the trustees' corporation without a consensus of the parish might have been proven to be illegal and possibly null and void. Without realizing it, however, the parishioners were victorious because the new corporation which was formed allowed ecclesiastical legalism and civil legalism to coexist without conflict. From an historical standpoint the parishioners could say to the old system, "Good Riddance!"

In order to better understand the ramifications of what has been said about the transfer, one should consider the significant historical facts regarding the development of the New York Law on religious corporations and review the time table of events in the transfer process. The first general law permitting the creation of corporations for churches was the *Religious Incorporation Act of April 6, 1784*. No longer did churches have to be incorporated by a special legislative act. Under this statute, the trustees of the first Catholic Church in New York, St. Peter's Church, were incorporated. It was in this board of trustees that ownership of the church property was vested. In 1813, the New York State Legislature passed into law, *An Act for the Incorporation of Religious Societies*. In that Act

any church belonging to the Catholic denomination was included in the general regulations applied to all religious societies. As in the Act of 1784, the ownership of property was vested in the trustees, however, by the Act of 1813, the control of the temporal affairs was also placed in the hands of the majority of corporators rather than in the hands of any priest, bishop, or synod. It was under the statutes of these two acts that the Trustees of St. Louis Church were incorporated in 1838. From 1852 to 1863 the bishops of the dioceses in New York State tried unsuccessfully to have the legislature enact laws which would give them control over the temporal affairs in their churches. They suffered the most serious blow in 1855 when New York State passed the Putnam Bill into law. By it, all Catholic churches in the State had to incorporate in accordance with the Act of 1813 under penalty of escheatment to the State of church property thenceforth handed down in any other way. In effect, it gave the lay corporations the power to overrule the bishop if they were so inclined.

It was because of the enactment of the Putnam Bill, which remained in effect until it was repealed by the New York State Senate in 1863, that Bishop Timon had all of the churches of his diocese incorporated according to the Act of 1813. He placed as many of them as possible into the hands of Religious Orders. Although the Orders of Priests were not directly subservient to him because their affiliation was directly regulated by Rome, it was a way for him to keep the churches out of control of laymen. The Jesuits took over St. Ann's Church, St. Francis Xavier Church, and St. Michael's Church. Oblates of Mary Immaculate served at Holy Angels Church and Immaculate Conception Church. The Redemptorists continued to control St. Mary's Church on Broadway. A battery of Religious Orders serviced St. Joseph's Parish on Main Street at Ellysville: Jesuits, Redemptorists, and Franciscans. St. Vincent de Paul Church was host to Jesuits and Redemptorists. Passionists Fathers serviced Sacred Heart Church in Dunkirk, New York.

Four parishes that Timon had to operate with secular priests were St. Boniface, Buffalo, Sts. Peter and Paul, Hamburg, St. Mary's, Lockport, and Good Shepherd, Pendleton. At various times before 1891 trouble brewed in each of these churches between the lay trustees and the resident pastor. Another tactic used by Timon to keep the trustees of these incorporated churches off guard was to change pastors frequently. The bishop's one defense against lay abuses, as he called them, was to get the congregations to elect trustees favorable to the clergy. He had to continually work hard to get priests' and trustees' personalities in tune. Observe the pastoral turnover at St. Mary's, Lockport, from 1859 to 1896: Francis Stephen Uhrich from 1859 to 1863; Zoegel, one year to 1864; Hechinger, two years to 1866; Zoegel returns for two years to 1868; Wensierski, one year to 1869; Kofler, two years to 1871; Wensierski returns for a year to 1872; Uhrich returns and stays from 1872 to 1877; Scheffels follows until 1881; Soemer enters and stays until 1883. Finally stability was reached and Father Grill assumed the pastorship for the next thirteen years, as it had been reached in most other parishes by 1891.

On March 25, 1863, through the legal maneuvers of Archbishop Hughes and his diocesan council, Charles O'Connor, a new provision favorable to the clerical leadership of the Catholic Church was enacted. It was called *An Act Supplementary to the Act entitled An Act to provide for the Incorporation of Religious Societies, passed April 5, 1813.* It read, "It shall be lawful for any Roman Catholic Church or congregation now or hereafter existing in this State to be incorporated according to the provisions of this Act. The Roman Catholic archbishop or bishop of the diocese in which such church may be erected or intended to be, the vicar-general of such diocese, and the pastor of such church for the time being, acting as trustees ex-officio, respectively or the majority of them, may select and appoint two laymen, sign a certificate, showing the name or title by which they and their successors shall be known and distinguished as a body corporate by virtue

of this act." By this Act, New York State law removed the danger of lay interference with ecclesiastical jurisdiction by giving ecclesiastics a predominant place on the trustee board, and by granting to them the nomination of the lay trustees. In 1895, an amendment was added to the Act. It required the sanction of the Catholic bishop or administrator for the validity of any corporate acts of the board of trustees. A second amendment was added in 1902. It permitted the bishop to transfer the property of a divided parish newly established by division, and to divide assets proportionately. On July 29, 1911, the Sacred Congregation of the Council at Rome asked all bishops of the United States to adopt the model of Religious Corporation Law as developed in New York State and introduce it into their dioceses for the control of all temporal possessions.

After the Supplementary Act of 1863 was passed, procrastination in applying the law by the reigning bishops prevailed in the diocese of Buffalo. Both Timon and Ryan realized that forced application of the law would not be well received by trustees already entrenched. Each parish, therefore, was given ten years to initiate the law. In a study of the history of Good Shepherd Parish, Pendleton, one finds an example of the results of this procrastination and sensitivity. Good Shepherd Parish was founded in 1847. By 1849, the land upon which the first permanent church structure was built had been purchased by Bishop Timon. In 1854 the parishioners began construction of a brick church on the property. It was finished by 1858, became debt free, and dedicated by Timon on August 28, 1859. On August 9, 1858, however, the church had been incorporated according to the New York State law of 1813. The corporation was called The Trustees of the Roman Catholic Church of Good Shepherd, at Pendleton. One can see that this title reads the same as that of St. Louis Church in its incorporation of 1838. One also observes that the action was done following the passing of the Putnam Bill by the State Legislature. Although the Supplementary Act was passed in 1863, the Trustees at Good Shepherd Church did not respond immediately, and no pressure by Timon to do so was made upon them.

*I*t was not until November 2, 1873, that the then reigning pastor, Father Charles Geppert, informed the congregation that the incorporation, which they had made in 1858, was to be revised according to the Act of 1863. This was the first that the congregation heard of this revision. Geppert informed the trustees that the old system would be dissolved and a new one started. He said, "We must complete the transfer by the beginning of the New Year." The old trustees went into revolt. New trustees favorable to the clergy were elected, but were not well received by many. The congregation became divided some favoring the old system and some willing to accept the new. Two of the former trustees, Henry Hebler and John Dehn resigned. A third member's time had already lapsed and was not filled. The January 1, deadline was not met because a fist and snowball fight erupted outside the church after a Sunday Mass. On January 26, 1874, Bishop Ryan came to Pendleton and threatened the congregation. He made all the members aware that he had the power of interdiction. He spewed forth to them the consequences of that interdiction if he applied it. The congregation relented and the bishop said, "Ah! My children, I thank you for your cooperation, and I am happy that you have made the right decision. Other German congregations such as those at Sts. Peter and Paul, Hamburg; St. Boniface, Buffalo; and St. Mary's, Lockport experienced similar upheavals.

*O*ver a century later the transfer at St. Louis Church took place, but not because the trustees were pressured by the bishop. After the postage stamp wishing a happy birthday to the church was issued by the federal government, Arthur Grupp and Francis Cole, two trustees at St. Louis Church, had several luncheon meetings with Monsignor Trautman, chancellor of the Diocese of Buffalo. At first, conversations centered on topics such as the exodus of parishioners from downtown Buffalo heading for the suburbs, the deterioration of the city, and the closing of several businesses in the downtown area. Later Cole quizzed Trautman about the method by which the diocese handled tax exemptions on properties owned by other churches in the diocese. He had been having problems in filling out his tax exemption papers for the City Assessors. While Trautman was having dinner at Grupp's home one evening, Trautman made a hint that the St. Louis Parish Corporation, by owning income producing property on Delaware Avenue, but not the building on it, was in a vulnerable position for obtaining a tax exemption. He mentioned that the other churches of the diocese, all of which were under a system of diocesan corporate protection, enjoyed the tax protection under an ecclesiastical umbrella.

*B*y May 31, 1979, Trautman was in a position to write a memo to Bishop Head informing him that there was a positive movement on the part of the trustees at St. Louis Church to return the parish to the Diocesan Corporation. This meant that the corporation known as *The Trustees of the Roman Catholic Church of St. Louis, Buffalo, New York* would be dissolved, and all properties and assets turned over to the diocese. On June 15, 1979, all six trustees met with Trautman at a luncheon at the Chancery so as to finalize their position. Only George Reinagel was reluctant to make a change; but, when he realized that such a move was in the best interest to the parish, he nodded approval. He had only one request, he said, "I don't believe that Father Mosack should be involved in any of the proceedings. He is not a member of the Board of Trustees." Trautman agreed. When satisfaction of all parties was achieved they settled down to develop the verbal expression which, when made public, would dissipate the fears of the congregation which, to that time, had no knowledge that negotiations were being conducted.

It was decided that if the return of the parish to the diocese were done in conjunction with the sesquicentennial anniversary it would be a crowning achievement for the trustees. They would look very good by making this the final event of the Jubilee Year. Trautman injected his thought, he said, "If it comes at any other time, it will appear as a default." All agreed that they did not wish to look as failures, men who could not carry on the burdens of administration. They reflected that it would look good that the Mother Church of the diocese, a prominent Catholic church, would join all two hundred and ninety-eight other Catholic parishes that were really her children. Trautman said, "The historical tradition and proud heritage of St. Louis Church remain, but now is the historic moment for the parish to give up *Trustee-ism* and be returned to the diocese." Reinagel then proposed that something be said concerning finances so that the congregation would be appeased. Trautman said, "We can tell them that more and more there will be the question of tax exemption. We can stress that it will be difficult for a solitary non-profit corporation, not related to the diocese, to cope with the intricacies of this situation. We must be realistic and provide for the future of St. Louis Parish. This can only be adequately done if the parish is returned to the diocese." The luncheon ended in an atmosphere of jovial fellowship. The trustees told Trautman that they would conduct a meeting in the near future and formally vote to dissolve the trusteeship and transfer all property and assets of the parish to the diocese. They assured him that the return would be made in August. Trautman told them that until then there would be no need to involve the bishop or Kevin Kennedy, the diocesan lawyer.

Although twenty five years had passed since the transfer took place, Monsignor Donald Trautman, presently Bishop of Erie, Pennsylvania, recalled that George Reinagel was a tall, slender man who was very intelligent, but a man living in the past. Trautman said, "He was a real German to the core!" Trautman then continued saying, "I believe that all the trustees bonded with me because I had a German name, was a native of Buffalo, had my schooling at St. Mark's on Woodward Avenue near the Zoological Gardens, and had my seminary education and ordination at Innsbruck, Austria. They could sense that I truly loved St. Louis Church and they knew that I was seeking the best for it. They also sensed how sympathetic I was to their situation; they truly believed that they had to be faithful to their tradition of authority, responsibility, and heritage. They wanted to continue in the tradition, but felt that they were unable to do so as the many trustees before them had done. Because I had been a student at Innsbruck, I reminded them of the pastors that they worked so well with such as Laudenbach and Schwartz who also were products of Innsbruck. I knew Arthur Grupp very well. He was the first to approach me. I believe that his desire to make a change grew out of a spirit of pragmatism whereby the truth of his situation was pre-eminently to be tested by the practical consequences of his belief. He believed as I did that the trustees had a burden. The truth was that a solitary non-profit organization could not handle the tax problem alone. This began our series of discussions and the rest is history. The voice of the Holy Spirit was heard."

The trustees met in their room in St. Louis' schoolhouse just before July 12, 1979. They voted unanimously that the ownership of St. Louis Church and all its assets be transferred to the Diocese of Buffalo, which was also a corporation having its board of trustees. Unlike the Religious Society Corporations, it was brought into existence by a special act of the Legislature. The most influential person on its board was Bishop Edward D. Head, president and treasurer. His chancellor Monsignor Donald W. Trautman was the secretary, and Auxiliary Bishop Bernard J. McLaughlin was vice-president. Following their meeting, the trustees approached Trautman and verified the fact that Father Mosack would be transferred and Father William Schwinger would be appointed as the new pastor. They then said that they would formulate a letter on August 24, 1979,

444

to be sent to the congregation announcing the transfer. Their plan was to have it read from the pulpit by Mosack on Sunday, September 2.

*T*rautman, receiving their messages, immediately engaged Joseph Stoeckl to research the finances of the parish. He met with Cole and they went over all the records, which showed that St. Louis Church had a total amount of assets slightly in excess of $400,000. These brought an annual interest earning to the parish of nearly $29,000. The assets were spread out in Common Stocks, Preferred Stocks, U.S. Treasury Bonds and Notes, Time Deposits, Rental Real Estate, and the jeweled monstrance with a precious diamond studded luna in its face. It had been last appraised in 1949 with a value of $50,000. Two rental real estate properties were: one on Delaware Avenue on which had been built the Interlude Restaurant; and, the other, a parking lot on Franklin Street rented to an Oil Company. By the middle of August, Trautman had asked Arthur Grupp and George Reinagel if they would like to serve as the two lay trustees in a new corporation that was to be formed since the old had been dissolved. Reinagel declined but Grupp accepted. Thomas Driscoll accepted in place of Reinagel.

*T*he trustees formulated their letter to the parishioners on August 24, but reneged on the date of sending it. They didn't think that it was a good idea to have Mosack read it to the congregation. They were informed that Schwinger would be assigned by September 22, and they planned that he receive the letter on September 27, so as to read it from the pulpit at his first Sunday Mass, September 30, 1979. Schwinger recalled some of the events of that time, he said, "Before September 22, the bishop had appointed me to be pastor at St. Louis Church. I said to him, 'Why me?' I've heard of it, but I've never been in it. The bishop said, 'You'll like it.' When I got to the rectory Father Mosack was still there, and I tried to get him to tell me something about it. I wanted to learn, but he

was too busy. He said, 'around here I only have two positions, slow and stop.' Scattered all over the dining room table were racing forms. He said, 'Don't talk to me until I get through my racing forms, and don't disturb them. If you want to go somewhere there's an old vintage car in the garage. I don't use it because I don't drive.' I soon found out from the chancery that Kevin Kennedy was in the act of dissolving the corporation. I didn't know what a corporation was. He was doing all the legal work and he handed me the deed. When I first held that deed, my hand trembled because I knew that I was holding something monumental. I quickly learned that it was a beautiful church but it had no money" On Monday following Schwinger's reading of the trustees' announcement, the Diocese of Buffalo went into action. It was October 1, 1979.

*O*n Monday at 3:00 P.M. at 35 Lincoln Parkway, Bishop Edward Head and Monsignor Donald Trautman, representing the Trustees of the Diocese of Buffalo, New York met in conclave. All the proper formalities of conducting a bona fide Board of Directors meeting were followed. Bishop Head called the meeting to order and stated that the purpose thereof was to arrange for the transfer of real property and all other assets received from the corporation *The Trustees of the Roman Catholic Church of St. Louis* to the new parish corporation being formed under the name and style of *St. Louis Roman Catholic Church of Buffalo, N.Y.* After a brief discussion the following resolution was duly made, seconded, and carried by unanimous vote: "Resolved that this corporation convey and transfer all the real property and the assets received from the Trustees of the Roman Catholic Church of St. Louis to a new corporation to be formed under the name and style St. Louis Roman Catholic Church of Buffalo, N.Y." There being no further business the meeting was adjourned.

*A*lthough the resolution had been unanimously approved, the new corporation had not yet been formally established. The news of its establishment, however, was released to the press later that same day. The following day the *Buffalo News* said, "Under the new arrangement, Bishop Head will lead a new parish corporation with four other trustee members: Monsignor Donald W. Trautman, diocesan chancellor; St. Louis' pastor, the Rev. William A. Schwinger; and two parishioners, Arthur Grupp and Thomas Driscoll." Some people concluded that this was more of a *coup d'etat* rather than a smooth legal transfer because on October 9, 1979 at 11:30 A.M., in the rectory of St. Louis Church, a meeting of *The Trustees of the St. Louis Roman Catholic Church of Buffalo, N.Y.* was conducted to report that their corporation was formed on October 4, 1979, the date the certificate of incorporation was filed in the Erie County Clerk's Office and that Bishop Head, the vicar general, and the pastor had appointed Arthur Grupp and Thomas P. Driscoll, lay members of the parish, as lay trustees.

Although at the time, no parishioner asked, but every one of them had the right to know when the formation actually took place, who made the formation, and did they who made it have the legal right to do so? According to the certificate of incorporation the five original members of the new corporation, Bishop Head, Donald Trautman, William Schwinger, Arthur Grupp and Thomas Driscoll did have that right. It was a right pursuant to Article Five of the Religious Corporation Law of the State of New York enacted on February 17, 1909. The group had filled out all the application forms and had had them approved by the State Supreme Court of New York before the Diocesan Corporation meeting on October 1. Because the certificate of incorporation which carried the signatures of the five trustees stated, "In witness whereof, we have signed these presents and have acknowledged the same according to law this first day of October 1979," one speculated that immediately after the meeting, Bishop Head and Donald Trautman ushered William Schwinger, Arthur Grupp, and Thomas Driscoll into the room, the document for the incorporation was signed by the five;

and, at that point, the corporation was duly formed. At that same gathering, the by-laws of the new corporation were approved and signed by Bishop Head and Donald Trautman. Further, Head, Trautman, and Schwinger signed the document appointing Grupp and Driscoll as the two lay trustees. *The Buffalo News*, however, reported on October 2, 1979, that the transfer had been approved by the Supreme Court, and appropriate papers signed and recorded on Friday, September 28, 1979, two days before Schwinger made his announcement from the pulpit. Because of this incongruity it is understandable why several people cried out *coup d'etat!*

With this action on the part of the Diocesan leadership one could consider the legal transfer complete. According to civil law, St. Louis Church was under new management. For some that heard the news it was a tragedy. For them, it was like looking at the burned out gutted shell of St. Louis Church on the morning of March 26, 1885. For others, it was a challenge; and, like the great gothic structure which stands in its place today, so also, a new management grew in the shadow of the Constitutions, Decrees, and Declarations of the Second Vatican Council. Michael Riester, Parish Council Member and author of *Lay-Trusteeism at St. Louis Roman Catholic Church, Buffalo, New York*, has said, "One of the greatest attributes of St. Louis Church has been its ability, throughout its history, to recreate itself." Riester had grown up in the Parkside region of Buffalo. His parents were married at St. Vincent de Paul's Church, but gave great allegiance to St. Louis Church. Riester said, "When I first saw St. Louis Church, I was a very small boy. My mother had an errand to run downtown and my father had time to kill. He took me into it. Walking down the long aisle and standing before the altar I was in awe with the size and beauty which I saw before my eyes. As I aged, I took the bus downtown, met some friends, went into the church, sat in the choir loft, listened to Leonard Weigand practice on the organ, and sneaked up into the tower."

Riester continued, "During the decade of the seventies, I became an altar server and a lector. To me, the sesquicentennial was a turning point for the parish. The trustees planned nothing for the anniversary. A group of parishioners, however, emerged, met on their own, and planned a suitable celebration while the trustees remained silent. I remember that each month of the celebration year we had several musical activities conducted by guest choirs and soloists. The Bayerische Maennerchor and the Chopin Singing Society sang at some Masses. The sesquicentennial banquet was held in the Golden Ballroom of the Statler Hotel. I was given special mention that evening because on the following morning I was leaving Buffalo to enter the Franciscans. I was the first vocation in the parish for many years. I believe that the trustee system eventually became much like a cancer cell that would be a perpetrator of death to the church. The emerging leaders such as Frank Wodzicki; Larry Schieber and his wife, Marie, nee Hoover, who was a direct descendant of the Hacker family; Rose Kennedy; Trudy Demo; Pat Walters; my father, Albert Riester; Frank Breitweiser, Josephine Weppner; Ruth A. Kolb; Anna Marie Barone; and James Bartlett were like living cells. Here in incubation was the parish management of the future, and all that was needed was hope in that future." One can truly say that Riester's words echoed the congregation's anticipation as it hailed a new clarion call. [2]

Was Father William A. Schwinger the poor scapegoat of the transfer? Did the leaders of the Diocese send him to St. Louis Church to bear the burden of closing it? Was he to receive the congregation's blame while it was taken away from the trustees? As Schwinger stepped down from the pulpit on Sunday, September 30, 1979, after reading the trustees' letter with the delayed postmark, he could feel all the ingredients of suspicion: fear, incredulity, and doubt. The parishioners did not believe that he had come to revitalize the parish, yet he was the principal ex-officio leader of the three local trustees in the new corporation. They doubted his abilities; he had never been a pastor before, he had spent the majority of his priestly life since his ordination on March 1, 1958, as a schoolmaster, and he was no natural or self made political savant in dealing with parishioners. He, likewise, had similar feelings of suspicion toward them. He thought that he was sitting upon a crown of thorns. He distrusted the parishioners, and acted with hesitation. His academic abilities of supposition, assumption, and postulation seemed useless, as he doubted what to do about his sad situation. Could he ever understand that learning, lore, and scholarship had little to do with dealing with a diverse group of people?

On one occasion he described his fear of the congregation in terms of another fear which he experienced in an event that had taken place almost immediately after his ordination. He had been assigned to live in a large house in Albion, New York, from which each day he would travel south to St. Mary's Church in Pavilion so as to say Mass. This was an historic church that had been established in 1865 in the hilly country north of Letchworth State Park on the road to Hornell, New York. Jimmy Bay, who acted as his altar boy, accompanied him on these excursions of about thirty miles, one way. Schwinger said, "On one winter morning after a heavy snowfall, Jimmy and I traveled south. We were almost at the intersection of the road that went down to Hornell. As I proceeded slowly down the long hill, my tires lost traction, and I began to slide. I put on my breaks, but they would not hold. As we reached the bottom, we went right across the intersection. The nose of the car, like a projectile, was aimed directly at Mr. Costello's tavern ironically named, *Can't U Come In?* Well Jimmy and I went in! Great fear engulfed us as we smashed right through the front door! The front wheels ended up facing the bar! Costello was a Catholic, and his wife was a daily communicant at St. Mary's. Witnessing that catastrophe was the postmaster, a Protestant. He got a lot of mileage out of that event. He would tell the story over and over, especially each time that a new priest came to say Mass.

447

He would say, 'Wow! That other priest just had to have a drink before Mass!' Needless to say, I was the priest who answered, in style, the call, *Can't U Come In!*" Following his stay at Albion, Schwinger received his Master's degree and was appointed as a teacher at Turner High School. Subsequently, he was assigned to Fallon High School in Buffalo.

Schwinger spent his first year at St. Louis Church in confusion. His first embarrassing task was to get out the financial statement that covered a period from October 1, 1978 to September 30, 1979, the very day he read the trustees' letter from the pulpit. He had only eight days to look over the report that the trustees of the defunct corporation had handed to him. His eyes settled immediately on an entry that read,"$12,833.17 deficit." He said, "I'm here only one day and the red ink is making my heart bleed. Look at those expenses for repairs on the church tower, roof, and furnace installation; it's close to $17,000!" For the first few months, Arthur Grupp and Thomas Driscoll, the new lay trustees, had the former ones stay on and help with the collections and purchases for the coming year. Schwinger later remarked, "I don't think that they were much help. They would meet once a month in their old office in the schoolhouse, count money, sell tickets to each other, and complain a lot about everything. Then they would play cards, eat Limburger sandwiches, drink beer, and go home."

Schwinger continued, "Most weeks the collection only amounted to $500. For almost an entire year I couldn't even take a salary. By the time my first full year was completed as pastor on September 30, 1980, I again ran an operating deficit of $14,964.85 with total disbursements of almost $100,000. All during that time, I knew nothing about the Diocesan Bank where bequests to the church in the form of government bonds and investments were supposedly saved. Monsignor Trautman called me one day and said that he knew how much money St. Louis Church had in several bank accounts. He wanted me to deposit all of it in the Diocesan Bank. An accountant, a layman who worked for the diocese, and I went to a bank on Delaware Avenue near North Street where we found my checking and savings account. My money totaled about $400,000. When I first deposited it with the diocese, I was given an annual rate of eight percent. Since so many things, however, were falling apart in the church, and the organ badly needed repair, I decided on starting a Fund Drive in 1981."

One of the members of the old trusteeship, who was most helpful to Schwinger, was John Rembold. He was a man of medium height and gray hair. After he graduated from Chownes Business School, he took night classes at the University of Buffalo. He then became a successful accountant, worked for a leather manufacturer, G.F. Zeller, on Smith and William Streets, and Continental Grain whose office was located in the Marine Trust Building. He married Florence Blaser, who was the daughter of Charles Blaser, a graduate of St. Louis parochial school in the late nineteenth century. John and Florence were married in 1928 at St. Mary's of Sorrows Church on Genesee and Rich Streets. Their first home was located at the corner of Best and Fox Streets where their daughter, Florence, was born in 1929. John Rembold had worked with Edwin Kolb and Edward Rick in establishing the St. Louis Church Museum. Rembold and Rick obtained the cabinets in which the artifacts were displayed from Adam Meldrum and Anderson Department Store. During Schwinger's first hectic years, Rembold, was a great help to him, doing necessary financial work such as filling out tax forms and making an audit of the annual financial statement. He often told his daughter that while he had been a member of the old trusteeship, he thought of himself as merely a rubber stamp! He died in 1994.

The new post Vatican II Corporation which had been established at St. Louis Church presented the congregation with a form of management which was entirely different from what it had experienced for one hundred and fifty years. The trustees were only officers of the Board; their job was to protect the congregation as a society against the invasion of civil activities impacting upon its ecclesiastical rights to property, the maintenance of it, and protection of the structures placed upon it. The prime power in the corporation and the essential leader in external conflicts against the church was the bishop of the diocese. The two lay members of the board were spokesmen for the society. The pastor was the spokesman for the bishop. Within the community of the church, interrelations and conflicts between ecclesiastical authority and laity effecting temporal needs, duties, and rights were governed by codes of canon law, interpretations of these codes, and due process.

*V*atican II provided the modern Catholic Church with the vehicles to achieve proper administrative procedure and successful cooperation between laity and clergy. The Decree on the Apostolate of the Laity, published in 1965, which called for lay involvement in diocesan councils also encouraged a parallel development on the parish level by suggesting the establishment in each church of a parish council. It was a body of representatives elected, chosen, or appointed for the purpose of sharing administrative and ministerial responsibilities with the pastor. Although activation of a parish council was not mandated by canon law, diocesan leadership could require it. Canon law stipulated, however, that the council would be governed by the norms of the bishop, the pastor would be the president, and the authority and vote of the council members would be consultative. The decision-making process between pastor and council members was to be guided, however, by a form of checks and balances provided by canonical equity, a virtue that sought reasonable justice.

*T*he first civic crisis which required the attention of the Board of Trustees of the new corporation since St.

Louis Church had responded to the clarion call in 1979 was the conflict between them and the Mayor of Buffalo and the City Council. These civic leaders had proposed to formulate a Pearl Street Connector that would impact upon property owned by the corporation. The Niagara Frontier Transportation Authority, which had been building the underground light rail rapid transit system from the University of Buffalo's South Campus under Main Street, was to have its tracks rise to grade level just south of Edward Street by 1982. From that point to the south, Main Street was to be closed to all automobile traffic so that it could become a pedestrian mall. Automobiles going south on Main Street would have to exit on to Edward Street and find an alternative route downtown. Likewise the traffic coming from the Kensington Expressway via Goodell Street would need to cross Main into Edward Street and follow that alternative route. David Jaros, the Buffalo Commissioner of Transportation, and Donald H. Ketcham, the New York State Regional Director of Transportation, agreed that the alternative route should be via Pearl Street. Before May 6, 1980, James Giardinas, the New York State Regional Design Engineer, had proposed six possible routes to take traffic around Main Street and down Pearl, which ran one-way southbound into Downtown. He said, "New York State needs the approval of the local governing body before it constructs new roadways. If the State approves your recommended route, bids will go out on the connector in May 1982 with completion scheduled before 1984. We estimate the project at seven million dollars of which the Federal Government will pay eighty percent and the remainder will be paid by the State. If the design is not completed and approved by 1982, the Federal Highway Administration grant will be withdrawn and the project aborted."

*A*fter a short period of time all plans were eliminated except two. Each of these included a provision to take property away from St. Louis Church. The plan backed by Mayor James Griffin, the Theater District Businessmen's Association, and David Jaros would cut into the church property thirty-six feet at its deepest point, require the purchase of two thousand square feet along Edward Street, eliminate trees and grass, and allow the widened Edward Street to be extremely close to the walls of the church. This plan was absolutely unacceptable to the Trustees of St. Louis Church. On May 12, 1980, William A. Schwinger, pastor and spokesman for the trustees of which Bishop Edward D. Head was the president, wrote a letter to Mayor Griffin. He said, "The position of St. Louis Church is that your present plan is totally unacceptable. Our desire is that no property of ours should be given up at any time. If, however, you modify the plan so that you will cut into St. Louis Church property by only six feet at deepest penetration and require purchase of no more than one hundred and forty square feet, we might consider it as less objectionable than your present plan. This modified plan would also have the approval of Bruce Fullem, Compliance Officer of the State Office of Historic Preservation, the majority of the Allentown and West side residents, and Delaware Council Member, William J. Marcy Jr." Griffin never answered Schwinger's letter.

The debate was well publicized in the newspapers and on television news briefs. The wrangling continued for the remainder of the summer and into the fall. Schwinger was relentless in his opposition. To the comments of the Theater Businessmen he said, "The Teck Theater is only used occasionally for late night movies. It is not a landmark as St. Louis Church is! It's just a big ugly building; let it go!" John C. Berlin, president of the Building Owners and Managers Association of Buffalo said, "The City is on the threshold of a gigantic new experience. We need this connector to help that, and we need it not only now but for generations to come." Schwinger was quick to reply, he said, "If you wanted our land for housing for the poor that would be one thing, I'd say fine, take it, but it is just for automobiles! This is the only beautiful parkland, restful to the eye, in the immediate area. Why should we surrender that to cars?" David Jaros disagreed

with Schwinger, he said, "What we have to do is weigh the disadvantages of taking land from the church against the disadvantages of disrupting a very important business district." Schwinger sarcastically replied, "You are right, and I insist that the church's disadvantages outweigh those of the business district!"

Back and forth, tooth and nail, the contenders verbally fought the battle until members of the City Council realized that the entire affair was to be caught up in an environmental hassle with deed restrictions concerning the use of the property upon which existed a former cemetery. They were concerned that bodies might still have been buried there. Further they debated the length of time it would take to have hearings on the feasibility of using historical church property in the project. Although the preservationists would not have had an open and shut case because the route only took the lawn and not the building, nevertheless, Griffin agreed that there could have been a real difficulty when the historic preservation debate hit the table. Before this happened, Griffin agreed to accept the offer of the Trustees of St. Louis Church and take only one hundred and forty square feet of the church's property. The City purchased the land from the trustees for $1,334.67. This amount of money was the equivalent of purchasing land for the sum of $444,890 per acre. One could say that the trustees' first encounter with a civil dispute was a successful one. It showed that the new fledgling corporation had power because of its prime position under the umbrella of the Diocese of Buffalo, as had been predicted by Monsignor Donald Trautman.

The internal affairs at St. Louis Church were a greater challenge than the external ones. For almost two years Schwinger had been sailing on stormy waters with an uncertain steering mechanism. In an interview, he said, "We didn't have enough people to put into effect any of the changes of Vatican II. I started using lay Eucharistic ministers only after I had been here a couple of years. Although I was agreeable to having a woman as a Eucharistic Minister, several parishioners squawked and said, 'No women!' I ignored them and did it anyway. I liked Al and Dorothy Schneggenburger; they did a lot for the church. One Sunday I trotted her out wearing a white alb. Eventually the congregation got used to her; she was not ignored, and her line for the reception of communion was as full as mine. Later we added more women; even included them as lectors."

*I*n an interview on August 14, 1981, with John Sinclair, a writer for the Religion Section of Saturday's *Buffalo News*, Schwinger told him that the Spirit of St. Louis Church was high. He said, "Despite its age and the changes which have altered the neighborhood in the last thirty years I can tell you that the parish retains its vitality. We have an active Ladies Guild and Men's Holy Name Society. We have a choir that sings at 10:30 A.M. Mass every Sunday. I also have established an effective parish council." This was his first attempt at a parish council but his enthusiasm about it was short lived. Once he said, "I remember that I had a parish council at the end of 1981, and I thought that I had appointed people who were friendly to me. They were, however, vicious and turned on me! I would propose something, but they would ignore me. They mumbled things under their breath, but loud enough so I could hear. After awhile, I ignored them and they went out of business. I was then advised by the members of the Holy Name Society and the Ushers Club. I attended their meetings. I also had some other limited advisors such as Arthur and Marie Grupp, Thomas and Mary Driscoll, and Bob and Pat Albert."

*I*n 1980, Father Richard J. Bohm came to live in the rectory with Schwinger. He had the title of Weekend Associate to the Pastor. Schwinger had first made his acquaintance at Fallon High School where Schwinger had been made principal. Bohm was in residence at St. Louis Church for four years. While there,

he was also chaplain at the Erie County Holding Center. On the evening of October 21, 1984, Bohm came into Schwinger's room and said, "Bill, I can't breathe!" Schwinger called 911 and waited for the ambulance to arrive at the rectory. Schwinger said, "I heard the ambulance go past the house so I thought they didn't know the address. When I got downstairs, however, I saw it coming in the gate from St. Louis Place. They quickly checked Bohm's pulse; it was extremely weak. They got him into the vehicle and rushed him over to Buffalo General Hospital on High Street. I called his folks in Batavia and they came right to the hospital. Dick, however, had gone into a coma and died the next day. To me the event was extremely tragic!" For the next two years Schwinger lived alone in the rectory. In 1986, Bishop Head assigned Father William F. White to be a Weekend Associate. He stayed for six years. Arthur Grupp died before the Financial Statement in 1985 was completed. His wife Marie Grupp, nee Faber, stepped in immediately to fill his position as a trustee. Thomas Driscoll died in May of 1987; his position as a trustee remained vacant for a year until Dr. John G. Zoll filled it. When Marie Grupp died in 1995, Rose Kennedy filled her position. Zoll and Kennedy continued as trustees into the new millennium..

*I*n the first decade after Vatican II, more than ten thousand parish councils were founded. By 1989 approximately seventy-five percent of all parishes in the United States had had them in place. Each of these had committees responsible for guiding administrative and pastoral ministries such as finance, liturgy, education, social justice, spiritual development, ecumenism, and parish activities. Many pastors who had been brought up in the spirit of the Tridentine Church appeared incapable of administering their churches according to this new concept of lay involvement. Father William Schwinger was one of those. Because he had chosen to cancel his first attempt to try it out, he found himself running amuck in a quagmire of financial difficulties that he had inherited. During his sixteen years as pastor he experienced an average annual deficit of $17,740. A second attempt at beginning a parish council came in 1989, at the suggestion of Benedict J. Pancamo, affectionately known as "Dick." On the steering committee for that council with him were Leonard Giarrano, Vinney Giarrano, Joe Bullion, Beverley Bullion, and Genevieve Moss. Because it did not have the backing of Schwinger, it too ran out of gas in a very short time. St. Louis Church had to wait until 1993 before a third and lasting attempt was made. By that time, however, Schwinger had withdrawn $284,000 from his reserve fund in order to keep the parish afloat and balance his financial statement each year.

*D*uring Schwinger's first year as pastor, the weekly collection amounted to a paltry $753. Although this sum tripled in sixteen years it was not until 1990 that it passed the $2,000 mark per week. His annual expenses for maintenance, repair, and purchase of equipment for the church were overwhelming. In his total tenure he had spent over $300,000 just to keep the church out of danger from rain, snow, cold, heat, humidity and general deterioration. He often said, "Every time we had a heavy rain the floor of the church hall was flooded because there was only one drain in the middle of the floor, and it malfunctioned. I would spend hours mopping up the mess. Time after time I'd call Mike Caligiuri to come over and put in a new drain." The salaries, which Schwinger paid for regular help both in the church and the rectory, ballooned from $13,000 in 1980 to over $93,000 in 1994. He kept the grim reaper of bankruptcy away from his front door by initiating an annual fund drive, and rewarding the parishioners with an annual picnic on the north lawn of the church.

*W*hen the organ's bellows "blew-out" at the twelve o'clock Mass on Sunday, June 28, 1981, Schwinger called William Kurzdorfer, a member of the parish since 1977 and a licensed electrician. Kurzdorfer looked over the situation and knew immediately that some serious repair work was needed. He explained to Schwinger,

"A rotted leather covering on the organ's bellows is the culprit. When the electric pump releases air into it, sound is produced, and the air is kept in there by the leather covering. When that covering wore away, the air in the bellows escaped, making it impossible for the organ to make any sound. Meanwhile the pump continued to push air into the bellows until the pump overloaded and shut itself off." Schwinger replied, "Gee, Bill, the automatic shut-off was a godsend. Without it we could have had a fire!" Kurzdorfer said, "Father, replacing the leather cover for bellows will be delicate business. The leather used in 1903, when the organ was installed, was treated by special chemicals. Today's leather may not be suitable; it may even harm the bellows. I think that you better make a careful investigation and locate the right individual to make the installation." Later, Schwinger read an article in the newspaper which described organ-work performed by Ron Kinard. He told Kurzdorfer, "I'll call that fellow and get him over here." Kurzdorfer disagreed, he said, "Father, You don't know this man's abilities, nor do you have any idea of his credentials."

*S*chwinger ignored these warnings and hired Kinard to do the job; one which was done poorly, but cost about $10,000. In order for Schwinger to pay for the work, he decided to run a special fund drive that he called an organ drive. It netted $8,000. It was so successful that he had a plaque struck with all the names of the donors listed. He also decided to continue it every year so as to pay not only for the organ but also for other needed repairs around the church. The organ, however, never worked right and in 1985, Schwinger called upon Kurzdorfer once again. Kurzdorfer responded, "Father, Kinard never did his work right. Get him back here and tell him to complete the job at no extra cost or hire me." Schwinger replied, "Look, Bill, I don't care what you do with the organ as long as it doesn't cost me anything." This was the beginning of a new loving relationship between Kurzdorfer and the Kimball Organ of 1903, which brought him no remuneration, and put a strain on his wallet which has lasted to the present time. It was also the beginning of the Annual Summer Fund Drive which ran each year for several weeks ending on August twenty-fifth, the feast of St. Louis, King of France. In 1984, it brought into the parish coffers the sum of $15,760.03. This amount steadily increased each year until 1995 at which time Schwinger announced a collection of $38,717.00. Over his sixteen years, the drive succeeded in obtaining a total of $302,275. Although this amount fell shy of the $311,268 that was paid for maintenance, repairs, equipment, furnishings, and the demolition of the school building, it did help to plug the financial holes in a leaky boat on a stormy sea.

The occasion of replacing the leather covering on the organ gave Schwinger the opportunity to show that he was an unsophisticated, unadulterated, and unvarnished person. To Audrey Lipford, a *Courier Express* staff reporter, he said, "The organ's music has become a way of life for St. Louis parishioners, and will be sorely missed. It has a magnificent sound; it fills the church. The acoustics here are probably among the best of any church in Western New York. My own voice seems fuller, richer when I intone the prayers at Mass. Although I'm one who likes to sing in the shower because no one can hear me, I'm also not afraid to sing in my church. We also need that beautiful organ because of weddings. Every bride wants organ music when she walks down our long center aisle. I'm appealing to the parishioners for donations. They've been coming to St. Louis every Sunday; they know the organ, and have come to expect music. They have always been generous."

Before he put his plug in for donations in his Sunday bulletin of July 4/5, 1981, he considered people first. He wrote, "Many of us remember Jim Ryan. A few weeks ago he appeared well and jovial as usual. His sudden death, however, really shocked everyone. Jim was an 'all right' guy, 'big' in mind, 'big' in concern for a great many people. He will be truly missed, and we shall remember him with the greatest affection. Every Sunday, he came to the twelve-noon Mass. All the worshippers and I extend our sympathy to Jim's wife, Pat, and to the Ryan, McNaughton, and Nolan families. Till we meet again, Jim, fond farewell!" Neither did Schwinger neglect a good quality of life for the old, who were frail and feeble; he wrote, "Happy ninety-fifth birthday, Sue Hardick. Glad to see you at Mass last Sunday. You are as sharp as a tack! St. Louis Parish congratulates you and we hope you can be with us each Sunday. Thanks to your relatives who bring you to church, and are so good to you." Only when he had finished these recollections, did he come forth with his advertisement. Again he wrote, "We thank Bill Kurzdorfer, our licensed electrician and one of the finest organists in the country, for his free time and free materials for the emergency repair of our organ, but the time has come to make those repairs more extensive. Your pastor wants to know what you think about starting an organ fund to keep the organ playing. We do need it so please let the pastor know your mind on this, and how to go about getting this fund drive started." This was brave talk considering that he also had to list at the bottom of the bulletin that the regular collection on the day the organ stopped playing was only $563.87. [3]

Although Schwinger's financial woes were a heavy burden to bear, his good will and enthusiasm for the success of his new parish brought him a distinguished reward. It was announced on October 18, 1984 that Pope John Paul II had raised him to the dignity of Monsignor. In that year Edward D. Head had completed eleven years as bishop of the Diocese of Buffalo. Since he had been installed, six churches in the City of Buffalo had been closed, suppressed, or merged. Since the end of Vatican II, the diocese had suffered a decided thinning in the ranks of the clergy along with a decline in Religious Brothers and Nuns who served in Catholic schools, hospitals, and homes for the aged. More rather than less was expected from the laity. Devotional organizations in the parishes such as the Knights of St. John, Christian Mothers, and Altar Societies, which had been prospering in the Tridentine Church, ceased to exist or were gravely diminished. It was obvious that the Catholic Church in the United States needed a social program that would give it a spiritual shot in the arm.

Although at first it seemed that Peter Gerety, Archbishop of Newark, New Jersey, had attempted to reinvent the wheel in 1978 with his plan for developing parish spirituality called *Renew,* it had, by 1984, received the enthusiastic support of bishops in sixty dioceses in the United States. Even the National Conference of Catholic Bishops gave it a general commendation. The plan was described as a spiritual renewal process for the parish to help parishioners develop a closer relationship with Christ, to make adult commitment to Jesus as central in their lives, and to open them to the power of the Holy Spirit so as to become more authentic witnesses. It was, furthermore, seen as a process that developed community, strengthened faith, and inspired the believer to witness more fully Jesus and His message. Gerety truly intended that it would be implemented nationally on the diocesan level or at least in a significant cluster of parishes within a diocese. The *Renew Process* was intended to extend over a three and one-half year period including a preparation and training year. The parish experience was divided into six-week sessions; one offered in the fall of one year and the other during Lent of the following year. The process had six goals: unification of the parish, increases in prayer, develop parish leaders, involvement of people in church and community, bring back wayward Catholics, and foster evangelization.

In the summer of 1984, the Buffalo Diocese became the sixty-seventh diocese in the United States to consider being involved in *Renew*. The Diocese of St. Catharine's, Ontario, Canada, had already finished their training sessions, and started the parish programs in the fall of 1983. Father Richard Greco directed its endeavor from his office adjacent to the Carmelite Monastery overlooking the Horseshoe Falls on the Niagara River. Under the direction of Monsignor Joseph Chaplin, one hundred and thirty-eight parishes in Syracuse, New York, began their parish programs in the fall of 1984. In Albany, New York, Bishop Howard Hubbard, had *Renew* well under way by the Fall of 1983. In Buffalo, Bishop Edward D. Head appointed Father Thomas Maloney as the director of the program in Western New York. Maloney chose Sister Louise Alff and Ellen Rose as his associate directors. By April 5, 1985, they had eighty percent of the parishes in the diocese committed to participate. On that day training sessions were initiated in various centers throughout the city and rural areas.

When Sister Louise Alff met her first group of volunteers she said, "A person's life can be touched either through the Sunday Liturgy, take home material, large group activities, or small groups of people sharing themselves with each other. *Renew* is a challenge to new spiritual growth for the whole parish." Father Henry Boyle S.J., who had come to St. Michael's Church on Washington Street, was most eager to begin *Renew* as he had done so when he was at St. Aiden's Parish, Welliston Park, Long Island, in the Diocese of Rockville Center. After all the trainees had been indoctrinated during the fall of 1984 and the spring of 1985, Bishop Head had his "kick-off" day at St. Joseph's Cathedral on September 15, 1985. Representatives from two hundred and forty parishes were present. Thirty thousand Catholics were expected to be involved. Speaking to the gathering of enthusiastic facilitators, Father Maloney said, "We do not expect or ask people to question defined doctrines of the Church, but we encourage them to probe how the tenets of faith can be lived. *Renew* encourages people to take their faith seriously, believing and trusting in God."

The first six-week session began in Buffalo on October 13, 1985. It finished one week before the First Sunday of Advent. During that period the participants gave profound consideration through serious reflection about the nature of themselves as members of a parish and as a member of a community. Much success in this regard came in the small groups that were formed with about ten members with a leader. Each meeting opened with a prayer followed by a Scripture reading. The leader would then suggest some questions to stimulate faith sharing on the part of the participants. Discussions then centered on the reflections of each person in the group, based on their personal experience. Above all, the speakers could take pride in their sincerity, honesty, and openness. The spring session began on Ash Wednesday, February 16, 1986. Ellen Rose summed up the theme of the session saying, "What are we doing to respond to God's call in our lives? We must make a personal decision to follow Christ wherever he leads us! We must think about social justice and share our abundance with the less fortunate." On October 12, 1986, the fall session began. For six weeks the participants experienced the empowerment of the Holy Spirit. They discerned their own gifts and talents and discussed how they could use them to do right and overcome evil in the world. They looked within themselves to find how they could make the world a better place to live. On Ash Wednesday, March 4, 1987, the fourth session began with the discussion of discipleship that centered on the day-to-day struggle to take on the mind of Christ and live the Gospel values. The last session began on October 11, 1987. The theme was evangelization. Father Maloney said, "Now my people, go forth and share your faith with others in the workplace, at recreation, and among all your friends no matter what may be their religious beliefs. Be ecumenical."

At St. Louis Church, Joseph and Beverly Bullion, Leonard and Vinnie Giarrano, Benedict Pancamo, Gary Romyak, Pete Murray, Sister Therese Marie Santos, Lois Riester, Larry and Marie Schieber and a few others met with Monsignor Schwinger at the rectory once each week so as to share their experiences in a small group as it was suggested by the designers of *Renew*. Joe Bullion said, "I remember that we discussed spiritual issues such as how to develop a community in the church and how we as people blessed with abundance were to share it with the poor. During these discussions Schwinger came up with the idea of feeding the various downtrodden that came to the rectory requesting handouts. Although he named it *The Sandwich Program*, there was more to it than just a sandwich. Each day after its initiation, he answered the doorbell to greet an entire spectrum of needy folk: prostitutes, addicts, alcoholics, urban nomads, unemployed, unemployable, and the working poor. Each day they were given something to eat and many times some cash so as to sustain life or squander it. In 1986, he distributed $868.28 in this fashion, but did not ask the parishioners to donate anything.

For ten subsequent years, he continued what had begun with *Renew*. In 1989 he set aside one Sunday on which he asked the congregation to participate in this charitable activity. That year he received $895.00 for food for the poor. For the next six years, until his retirement as pastor, the donations increased steadily. In 1992 they exceeded $4,000. Until 1991, the amount donated each year was less than he gave away. After that year the amount given away was only seven percent of what was donated. This was probably due to the fact that only sandwiches and packaged foods were distributed, and actual food products were brought to St. Louis Church from other local churches and supermarkets. Also his generosity in cash flow had ceased because his overt gentleness and generosity sometimes caused him problems. He had employed two men released from the Holding Center as janitors. They told Schwinger that they were going to grow flowers for the church in its basement. The flowers turned out to be marijuana. Three other questionable characters employed as janitors spent many work hours clandestinely quaffing alcoholic elixirs in the clock room of the church tower or at Clancy's bar on Main Street while their mops and brooms remained idle in a closet.

Rose Kennedy, presently a lay trustee, said that there were at least four small groups organized at St. Louis Church during the period of *Renew*. Kennedy said, "I was a leader of one of them. I held my meetings at the Roosevelt Apartments. In attendance were about fifteen senior citizens. They were a mixture of Catholics and non-Catholics, and many were African-Americans. We had discussions interpreting passages of Scripture, both in the Old and New Testaments. The Protestants knew the Bible better than the Catholics." Margaret Foegen ran a *Renew* group in her home. Several of those who attended the sessions that she facilitated were well pleased. One lady said, "My religion is beginning to make more sense. Slowly it's starting to piece together. Really this is the first time we have been able to talk about our faith." Many others admitted that they were better persons because of the group experience. Joe Bullion spoke about some of the offshoots and aftermath of *Renew* as conducted at St. Louis Church. He said, "Before our discussions few people ever shook hands with each other at church. A sort of coldness prevailed. I think our quest for establishing a community helped us all to be friendlier. We started having coffee and doughnuts at the end of some Masses on Sundays. The bake sale was initiated, and Gary Romyak began the St. Louis Gardening Society affectionately called *The Slugs*. He and his cohorts wanted to beautify the grounds around the church. We also had to organize a group to clean the church; it, like the property, was dirty. The janitors wouldn't do that work; they were hiding out somewhere. They were nowhere to be seen on the day Dick Pancamo caught some men carrying away the lawn mowers which the janitors had left in the yard." [4]

At St. Louis Church, Pancamo was a dedicated person. He was always nice to people and very helpful,

especially to older folks. As a security guard he kept a good eye on the church. He was, however, more than a security guard; he was a business manager, helped Frances Frankenberger, who was secretary in the office, and later helped get Dolores Vasi oriented when Frances retired. Bill Kurzdorfer said, "Dick would come to church at 6:00 P.M. and stay on as guard all night. Father Schwinger could rest peacefully in the night knowing that Dick was there. Pancamo went home during the day and slept so as to be back on his security rounds each night. He also ran one of the picnics and started the second attempt at forming a parish council." The first picnic was held on the church's north lawn in 1989. At first Schwinger would not agree to have it. Joe Bullion, however, belonged to the Knights of Columbus whose hall and athletic club were on Delaware Avenue. Joe talked Schwinger into coming with him and some other members of the church with whom Schwinger was friendly, as a guest of the club. Schwinger liked to swim, and they could frolic together at water games in the pool. Bullion said, "One night while swimming, we brought up the topic of a parish picnic. Schwinger still didn't want it. The guys began to ride him about his decision saying, 'If you had it, what could you lose if it didn't cost you anything?' Schwinger then said, 'Well OK! If it doesn't cost me anything go ahead and have it!' We did. There were no chairs or tables the first year. People brought blankets to sit on and food to pass. In the second year they began to donate toward it. Then Schwinger started to like the idea; he even told everyone that he started it. That first picnic was run by Leonard and Vinnie Giarrano."

Every year after 1989, the picnic was held uninterruptedly on a Sunday closest to the feast of St. Louis on the small plot of land next to the church facing Main Street affectionately referred to as the North Lawn. A most memorable one was that held in 1995 when Henry J. Mansell, who had been appointed by Pope John Paul II as the twelfth bishop of Buffalo on January 18, 1995, came to St. Louis Church, celebrated

Mass, and stayed for the picnic. At his inauguration as bishop, Mansell said, "I want to know well all the people of my diocese." By being at the picnic, he had an opportunity to meet those devoted to St. Louis Church. Fortunately the committee had invited all former graduates of St. Louis' parochial school to attend. The word had been sent out far and wide, and they responded with enthusiasm and came in great numbers. Monsignor Schwinger said, "Bishop Mansell was as amazed at seeing the vast number present as was Bishop Dubois who, when he visited Buffalo in 1829, and thought he would find only a few Catholics, found instead eight hundred souls straining to get a glimpse of him."

One recalls the last two picnics of the twentieth century and the one, which ushered in the twenty-first century which the Catholic Church, denoted as a Jubilee Year. For the picnic held on August 23, 1998, Benedict "Dick" Pancamo was the chairman. The weather was not only beautiful, it was terrific. The food was abundant, the quality was great, and the help from the workers was superb. From the planning sessions on July 29, to the end of the festival day many hands, hearts, and minds went into set-up, food preparation and transportation, grilling, clean-up, and take-down. What is a St. Louis family picnic? It is the gathering of parishioners of the past and present, old and young, who come to see the gothic grandeur, participate at Mass, gather on the lawn, eat, drink, and enjoy merriment while mingling and reminiscing. It's an annual event that keeps the Communion of Saints on earth in contact with each other even though their residences are spread far and wide over Western New York and in some cases out of state and country.

No picnic is complete without the aroma of hot dogs, hamburgers, and sausages being grilled in the open air. The directors of the St. Louis Church picnic have been so fortunate to have the meats donated by one of the old-time families, the Sahlens. As a gracious donation Joseph and Anita Sahlen have annually supplied the committee with as much as thirty pounds of dogs, burgers, and sausages. Henry "Bernie" Gerling and Lee Volo were the chefs for the day, grilling outdoors. They kept their food warm in a heat cabinet and served with utensils loaned to the committee by Al Caldiero, Director of Support Services at Our Lady of Victory Hospital. One could not have these grilled delights without the rolls and condiments. Mary Prenevau arranged with Joe Barruca, general manager, and Tim Gorecki, bakery manager, at Tops D&L Plaza, Depew, to supply the breads at double discount. Bart Siener also arranged for rolls to be brought in from Kaufmann's Bakery.

Weather and other seasonable disturbances can play havoc in the open air. One year the North Lawn and most of Western New York were inundated with yellow jacket bees. They were buzzing everywhere, on the plates and in the cups, denying everyone a peaceful bite to eat. Since the picnic was scheduled, rain or shine, tents were needed as well as chairs and tables. These ironically had been traditionally supplied by Rain and Shine Rental Incorporated from Lancaster, New York. When Jo Ann Decker chaired the picnic in 1999, these items cost $354.00. They were installed before 9:00 A.M. and taken down immediately after 4:00 P.M. In that year, the church was still in the process of completing the ramp for the disabled, and installing the bathroom in the vestibule of the church. Outdoor toilet and septic services were needed. These were supplied by Donna Ball whose company has its main offices in Blasdell, New York. Each year Bill Kurzdorfer was on hand to install the electrical hook-ups while the set-ups were being made.

As the party rolled into high gear, John and Nancy Pax took over the distribution of drinks with help in the kitchen from Francis and Stasia Lukomski, Jack and Arline Hoyt, John and Debra Beller, John Regan, Herbert Bucki, and Mike Mikos. Delicious popcorn came as an artistic creation from Kathleen Tyler while her husband Wilbur was on hand to help. While the folks were enjoying their food and drink, balloons, donated by Gary Romyak, were inflated and passed to the clown who entertained the children. Moving in and out of the crowd, always busy arranging and helping, were Margaret Considine, Dolores Monahan, Marilyn McNamara, Jane Cudmore, Devon Klein, Cynthia Doerr, Lucille Decker, Margaret Foegen, Marilyn Young, Natalie Gerling, Christa Behr, Elizabeth Pirrung, Kathryn Missert, Bob and Pat Albert, Bridget Griffin, Mary Kintos, Ginger Gibbons, Sarah Muscarella, and Sister Therese Marie Santos. Off in the distance were Daniel McCarthy and Jonathan Vasey doing their yo-yo antics.

*O*ne of the highlights of the picnic, one which allowed many to actively participate even though they were not planners and workers, were those who prepared some food delights which graced the long line of delicacies on the tables under the serving tent. Tortellini, Greek pasta, macaroni and tuna, three bean, German potato, shrimp pasta, veggie pasta, American potato, Brazilian, tossed, and coleslaw were all salads brought by Terry Wegler, Nancy Pax, Augie Gutowski, Betty Moineau, Rita Foegen, Michael Riester, Rose Kennedy, Patricia Siener, and Marilyn Young. To arrive on the table these salads made quite a trip coming from Tonawanda, Grand Island, Northeast Buffalo, West Seneca, and Kenmore. Rose Kennedy, Betty Monieu, and Augie Gutowski were Westsiders living nearby. Rose resided on Delaware Avenue near Bryant, Betty lived on Elmwood Avenue near Summer, and Augie had her home on Richmond Avenue near Highland. Sister Therese Marie Santos had the shortest distance to bring her specialty, not from Brazil, but just around the corner from her Kindergarten-K on Franklin Street.

*B*aked beans, meatballs and sauce, scalloped potatoes, and relish tray were contributions from Mary Driscoll, Sue Danieu, Terry Pirrung, Bart Siener, Lucille Decker, and Marilyn Young. What is a picnic without dessert? There were many delicious ones provided by Marie Buchheit Miller, Rose Marie Bloch, Debra Beller, Margaret Scaduto, Carolann Besch, and Arline Hoyt. Those who had eager hearts but could not provide food or active service were gracious in making financial contributions to pay for needed items that were not donated. Among these were Doctor John Zoll, Esther Fest, Josephine Pelicano, Mary Lou Geoghan, and Pat Walters. Always on hand and perspective leaders of activities at the church were: Grant and Lynda Violino, Fred and Melanie Luongo, Bill and Susan Lynn Fiden, Judy Perkowski, Bob and Ann McCarthy, Geoffrey and Cheryl Klass, and Linda Holben. [5]

*T*he picnic was one of the internal affairs at St. Louis Church that required only the suggestion and energy of some members of the congregation, the backing of the parish's lay leadership, and the approval of the pastor. Because St. Louis Church had become a member of the diocesan family, as expressed by Monsignor Trautman, it also became, however, intensely involved in the struggles and decisions of the diocese. On March 19, 1973 when Edward D. Head became the eleventh bishop of the Buffalo Diocese, he inherited many problems mostly unforeseen. His watch was only into its second year when he was required to raze St. Joseph's Cathedral, the New Cathedral, on Delaware Avenue. It was a young sixty-one years old but found to be crumbling and sinking before the very eyes of the faithful. He then had to have St. Joseph's Old Cathedral on Franklin Street renovated according to the codes of the new liturgy expounded by decrees of Vatican II, and use it as the diocesan cathedral. He had to appoint a lay advisory board, develop the three year *Renew* program, consolidate all religious education into one department and form a Board of Catholic Education, and purchase the *Courier Express* building on Main and Goodell Streets opposite St. Louis Church as a Catholic Center.

Above all he had to cope with the reorganization of churches and schools because of the decline in the number of active priests and male and female religious teachers. The seriousness of this situation required that many schools and churches had to be closed, merged, absorbed, linked, or suppressed. By 1993, Head therefore organized the diocese of Western New York into twenty-seven regions containing two hundred and seventy-one parishes, three hundred and twenty-two priests, and a total Catholic membership of five hundred and ninety-eight thousand, which had at its disposal one thousand weekend Masses. Although the churches of the diocese offered a seating capacity of nearly one hundred and twenty-eight thousand seats only forty-seven percent of them were ever filled each weekend. The majority of Catholics were no longer faithfully observing the First Precept of the Church's Commandments, "You shall attend Mass on Sundays and Holy Days of Obligation," which since Vatican II required the faithful, not to just attend, but to actively participate in the Eucharistic celebration on those specified days or on the vigils of them.

In the spring of 1993 Bishop Head said, "In recent years many factors have impacted on our local church, particularly the movement of industry from Western New York, economic decline, rising costs, social mobility, and fewer vocations to the priesthood and religious life. We must address these changes and adapt to them if we are to effectively continue the mission of Jesus Christ. Over the past ten years, the number of active diocesan priests has declined twenty-one percent, and resident priests are not available for each parish community. In some areas the Catholic population has declined sharply, while in others there is significant growth. Some parishes have adequate fiscal resources while others do not. Some parishes own buildings which are old and unutilized, while others need to construct new ones. So we need to undertake a diocesan-wide planning process of parish life and ministry. How can we achieve viability in our parishes? How can we minister effectively to all? Our future will involve many

changes, which are difficult to accept, no matter how necessary. What is essential to all of us, the Mission of God, will not change, but will endure." The first phase of the bishop's bold plan began with an educational program in April 1993 and finished with all parishes making a self-study of them by December of that year. During the following year studies were made on the regional and diocesan level and ended with the bishop's review by November 1994. Implementation of the plan that was named *New Visions* was scheduled for the First Sunday of Advent.

Two years prior to the general thrust of the *New Visions Program,* studies had been made of conditions of population shifts effecting the vitality of churches in the Central City and on the East Side. Auxiliary Bishop Edward M. Grosz acted as a liaison between Bishop Head and the Study Commission. On the East Side, in what was the Polish fortress of faith, eight churches had a parishioner decline over a fifty-year period that reduced attendance at Mass on weekends from forty-three thousand to three thousand one hundred. Because of this finding, St. Luke's Church on Sycamore Street and Miller Avenue, Queen of the Most Holy Rosary on Sycamore and Sobieski Streets, Transfiguration on Sycamore and Mill Streets, and St. Joachim's Church at 64 Titus Street were closed outright in 1993. Father Jerome E. Kopec had headed the commission that advised Grosz to have these parishes locked out. The commission, however, advised that within the two and one-quarter square mile area four other churches would remain open because they could show their vitality. They were: St. Adalbert's Church on Stanislaus and Kosciuszko Streets, St. John Kanty on Broadway and Swinburne Streets, Corpus Christi at 189 Clark Street, and St. Stanislaus at 123 Townsend Street. Diocesan priests spiritually serviced three of the churches, but Corpus Christi was owned and administered by the Conventual Franciscan Friars.

The Commission likewise pursued its study into

the Central City and found the need to close four parishes and merge their congregations into one parish, St. Martin de Porres Church at 80 Durham Avenue, east of the present Erie County Medical Center. The areas in which these churches existed had become fully inundated with African-Americans of which very few were Catholics. The four churches which merged were St. Mathew's, St. Boniface, Our Lady of Lourdes, and St. Benedict the Moor. Recently a new St. Martin de Porres Church opened at 555 Northampton Street. It is adorned with many of the artifacts which had been taken from the previously merged churches. In 1993, three other parishes were clustered into one single parish. They were: St. Mary of Sorrows at 333 Guilford Street, St. Columba at Eagle and Hickory Streets, and St. Ann's Church on Broadway and Emslie Streets. Two other churches were also closed and their parishioners merged into Blessed Trinity at 323 Leroy Street. These were St. Vincent de Paul and St. Bartholomew Churches.

After the coordinators of the twenty-seven regions had met on April 27, 1993, the congregation at St. Louis Church found itself involved automatically into the Planning Process for Parish Life and Ministry in the Diocese of Buffalo. By May 3, Monsignor Schwinger provided the Diocesan New Visions Committee with the names of two facilitators from St. Louis Church. They were John Pax and Mike Mikos. Both men were soon indoctrinated with a new outlook for parish life as described by Sister Regina Murphy, director of the diocesan Department of Research and Planning. Murphy said, "Bishop Head has established the New Visions Commission because there are many factors that are affecting the lives of parishes, factors quite different from those which existed years ago when many of them were established. Today they are being challenged and there are new possibilities already in place that can help them. See the new forms of ministry: permanent deacons, pastoral associates, parish life coordinators, and other lay ministers who can do the work which priests do. See the new structural forms for a parish: merging, linking, clustering, and interconnecting them.

Don't get hung up on having your own building. It's more important that you have a living, vibrant community."

She then continued, "Parochialism can get in your way. People must realize that a parish is not just a place where they come to Mass every Sunday; it is a place where the community comes together to cultivate their spiritual life and spread it. How alive and how much activity is going on in your parish? Once each parish has cultivated the correct frame of mind it can begin the process of self-study." Pax and Mikos were in dire fear that her words echoed a possible demise of St. Louis Church. They felt that the New Visions Commission was bias in favor of geographical suburban parishes and failed to recognize the unique ministry of the likes of St. Louis' parish. They feared that the shortage of clergy might work against their strategy for insuring the viability of St. Louis Church. Monsignor Schwinger, however, was optimistic. He said, "I don't think our church is in danger of being closed. Mikos replied, "Father, it will be difficult for you, alone, to handle all the Masses at Christmas and Easter." Pax said, "What do we do about finances?" Schwinger replied, "Bequests have helped in the past, and they can continue in the future. Also, I don't think that the bishop would merge us in with Immaculate Conception. Because of its catering to the Hispanic population, it is not compatible with us."

Pax and Mikos attended facilitator-training sessions during the month of August and were ready to hold a meeting of task force leaders at St. Louis Church on September 23, 1993. Present were Monsignor Schwinger, John Pax, Mike Mikos, Rosemary Block, and Rose Kennedy. They discussed the methods to attract a large number of parishioners and broaden the size of the task force, set dates for a series of parish training sessions, and set up a program to gather self-assessment data and evaluate it before submitting it to the diocesan commission. By November 24, 1993, it had been completed and the results prepared to be seen by the entire congregation. The strengths and weaknesses of St. Louis Church were self-evaluated under three general categories. To describe how well they considered themselves as a people of God, twenty-two members of the task force considered the parish's prayer and worship experience, the spirit generated in the congregation, and the extent of lay involvement in its ministry. In all three aspects, they considered themselves to be above a satisfactory level, but did admit that some improvement was needed.

Nineteen members of the task force made judgment upon the parish sharing in the mission of Christ. They considered the extent of efforts made in catechesis, the quality of pastoral ministry, and the extent of the parish's involvement in outreach endeavors. They rated themselves as poor in regards to catechesis. Although they rated themselves as good in sacramental preparation programs and in the Rite of Christian Initiation of Adults, they considered themselves as poor in youth ministries, continuing religious education, and participation in renewal programs such as Mission and Cursillo. They considered themselves to have strengths in both pastoral ministry and outreach programs. They also considered themselves to be very satisfied with a collaborative administration that involved lay leadership in cooperation with the clergy. The nineteen members of the task force, who considered themselves to be financially stable, realized later that the stability was only a myth.

The process of self-evaluation sparked enthusiasm for the implementation of a workable parish council at St. Louis Church. The first attempt at having a council in 1981 was dealt the death knoll by Schwinger only a few weeks after he had informed the news media that he had a prospering council in operation. The second attempt began on May 20, 1989, when a Steering Committee composed of Dick Pancamo, Leonard and

Vinnie Giarrano, John and Nancy Pax, Joseph and Beverly Bullion, Sister Therese Marie Santos, and John Rembold met at the home of Leonard Giarrano. The meeting had a two-fold purpose, one of which was the development of a constitution for a proposed parish council. They hoped to complete their work by the middle of August. Once again, however, their endeavor did not receive an enthusiastic endorsement from Schwinger, and it had to be squelched.

On December 4, 1993, however, a third attempt was conceived, riding on the coattails of New Visions. Following a meeting of the task force for the parish self-assessment, twenty-five members stayed on so as to form a parish council steering committee, and discuss creative action. They were: Rosemary Bloch, Joseph and Beverly Bullion, Mary Di Lapo, Margaret Foegen, Bernard Gerling, Lennie and Vinnie Giarrano, Marie Hermann, Jack and Arline Hoyt, Trudy Demo, Robert Lannigan, Rose Kennedy, Mike Mikos, Bill Kurzdorfer, Peter Murray, Dick Pancamo, Genevieve Moss, John Pax, Dr. John Zoll, Susan Peters, Jim Mrozek, Sam Fiorella, and Monsignor Schwinger. By February 12, 1994, the concept of a council had achieved the endorsement of Monsignor Schwinger, who saw the handwriting on the wall when more than thirty candidates were nominated for a position on the council of which fifteen were elected. The elected members were announced at the last meeting of the steering committee on April 27, 1994. They were: Robert Albert, Joseph and Beverly Bullion, Sam Fiorella, Margaret M. Foegen, William Kurzdorfer, Margaret L. Maloney, Sister Therese Marie Santos, Dr. Thomas Aquinas O'Connor, Dick Pancamo, John Y. Pax, Susan Peters, Rae Reines, and Dr. John Zoll. Installation took place on May 22, and the first meeting at which the officers were elected was held on June 1, 1994. A Constitution and By-laws were drawn up and approved.

The Council was intact six months before Bishop

Head inaugurated New Visions. Its mission was to provide assistance to the pastor and leadership in the parish. It provided a forum in which the consensus of the congregation could be voiced. It vowed to preserve the unique history and tradition of St. Louis Church as it cared for the future needs of the parish. It determined to foster parish growth spiritually, numerically, and financially within the context of the unique nature of the congregation while providing liaison for and promotion of parish activities. Above all it demanded that, with all its energy, it would provide insurance of the perpetuity of the parish. With the words of Article Two of its Constitution the founding members once again allowed St. Louis Church to recreate itself fifteen years after the one hundred and forty-one year trustee system had met its demise. It read, "We the Catholic Community of St. Louis Parish, led by the Holy Spirit, united by faith in Christ Jesus, create a Parish Council for the spiritual good and welfare of the parish; in a sincere spirit of collegiality of the laity working in cooperation and support of the clergy to recreate and revitalize our Christian Community so as to live a life that is fundamentally Christian, to celebrate our Eucharistic charisma, and to radiate the love of Christ to all." This bold intention was carried out through the initiation and development of five standing committees: Building and Grounds, Spiritual Life, Finance, Social Action, and Membership.

With its Parish Council intact, approved and backed by the pastor, St. Louis Church, through the action of its facilitators, John Pax and Mike Mikos, were ready to participate in a preparation of a final report on their status in Region II. Their primary objective was to keep the doors of St. Louis Church open as a single parish, serviced by one priest not involved in combination with any other parish. The twelve parishes in Region II were: Annunciation, Blessed Sacrament, Coronation of the Most Blessed Virgin, Holy Angels, Holy Cross, Immaculate Conception, Nativity of the Blessed Virgin Mary, Our Lady of Loretto, St. Anthony of Padua, St. Joseph's Cathedral, St. Louis, and St.

Michael. By the year 2000 it was estimated that these twelve churches would be serviced by only nine priests. Discussions aimed at this dilemma wrangled on until March 20, 1995; three months after Bishop Head had planned to implement his New Visions program in the twenty-seven regions of Western New York. In the end the diocese wanted a merger of St. Louis Church with Blessed Sacrament. Schwinger, without neither the consensus of the congregation nor advice of the Parish Council, publicly voiced his approval of this recommendation. Rae Reines, president of the Parish Council, wrote to the New Visions Regional Committee stating that Schwinger's views were not those of the Council's. Schwinger moved by the reaction of the congregation apologized for having made his statement, he said, "I do not wish you to think that I had sold you down the drain." John Pax rose in the pulpit one Sunday and reported that St. Louis Church had financial problems. He opined that if Schwinger continued to use large amounts of money from the reserve fund that the church would be broke in twenty years.

The decisions of the Diocesan New Visions Committee, however, soon became academic. In January 1995, Bishop Head celebrated his fiftieth anniversary as a priest and his twenty-fifth anniversary as a bishop. Following the celebration he proposed the date of his retirement. On April 18, 1995, one month after the New Visions Committee produced its final report, Pope John Paul II appointed Henry J. Mansell as the new bishop of the Diocese of Buffalo. Mansell did not initiate any of the decisions made by the various regions and proceeded to initiate his own ideas that included a strong determination not to close any schools or churches in the near future. Using a cliche, one might say that St. Louis Church was saved by the bell! [6]

At the weekend Masses of September 16/17, 1995, Monsignor Schwinger announced his retirement, he said, "I would like to tell you something about my plans. On November 3, of this year, I will be seventy-five. Having been your pastor for the last fifteen years, I now look forward to my retirement. I will not be far away. Monsignor William Gallagher, rector of St. Joseph's Cathedral, has invited me to reside there. You can all attend the weekly noon-day Mass which I will celebrate starting with the commencement of the Season of Advent." The Parish Council had established a *Newsletter* committee of which Bob McCarthy and Sam Fiorella were editors. In its October 1995 issue, they announced that Schwinger would be honored at a retirement brunch on Sunday, November 5, at the American Legion Troop I Post at 341 Franklin Street following a noonday Mass. The *Newsletter* said, "Tickets, the price of which include a gift for Monsignor Schwinger, are available for purchase after each weekend Mass at the rear of the church or by calling Joe Bullion at 822-4138. John Pax is the chairman of the Retirement Planning Committee."

On November 5, at the Mass of Thanksgiving for the Priesthood in honor of Monsignor Schwinger, Bishops Henry J. Mansell and Edward D. Head concelebrated. In attendance were: Monsignor Robert J. Cunningham, Chancellor of the Buffalo Diocese; Monsignor Peter J. Popadick, Secretary to Bishop Mansell; Father Paul L. Golden C.M., President of Niagara University; Father Francis X. Prior C.M., Vice President at Niagara University; Monsignor William G. Stanton, Pastor of St. Ambrose Church; Monsignor Ronald P. Sciera, Pastor of Precious Blood Church; Monsignor Richard M. Cahill, Pastor of St. Stephen's Church on Grand Island; Monsignor Daniel J. Myska, Pastor of Assumption Church; Monsignor Edward J. Ulaszeski, St. Jude Center; Father Angelo M. Chimera, Pastor of Nativity of the Blessed Virgin Mary Church; Father Patrick T. Sullivan S.J., Pastor of St. Michael's Church; Father Paul R. Bossi, Pastor of Blessed Sacrament Church; and Father Michael J. Parker, Parochial Vicar at St. Amelia's Church.

Members of the retirement committee were: John Y. Pax, Chairman; Joe and Beverly Bullion; Rosemary Bloch, Herb Bucki; Bernie Gerling; Jack and Arline Hoyt; Lewis Mancini; Michael Mikos; Robert and Ann McCarthy; Dick Pancamo; Susan Peters; Mary Prenevau; John Regan; Gary Romyak, and Bart Siener. The lectors were Matthew and Julie Wojick; the prayers of the faithful were conducted by Jodie Laughlin and Monsignor Cahill; the gifts were presented by John and Debbie Beller, Kathy Missert, and Jodie Laughlin; the altar boys were Michael and Jason Hall; and the organist and choir director was Dona Vasey. Susan Peters requested that all sing a song much liked by Father Schwinger. It was titled *A Parting Blessing*, a song which an Irishman rather than a German was expected to hold dear. It read, "May the road rise to meet you: May the wind be always at your back: May the sun shine warm upon your face. May the rain fall soft upon your fields: and until we meet again, May God hold you in the palm of his hand." When it was finished Schwinger said in truly German fashion, "Auf Wiedersehen, and thank you Lord for the blessings I have received as pastor of St. Louis Church. May the benediction of God, the Father, Son, and Holy Spirit be with us always." Knowing how hard it was to break away, Schwinger had to make one more note of thankfulness. On Thursday, November 23, 1995, he said, "Dear Parishioners and good friends of St. Louis Parish—A Blessed and Joyful Thanksgiving. It's my last with you." On Saturday December 2, 1995, he moved to the rectory at St. Joseph's Cathedral. His tenure at St. Louis had been blessed with spiritual benefits: He had conducted three hundred and sixty-five baptisms, three hundred and eleven marriages, and two hundred and seventy-nine funerals. Through all the trials and vicissitudes of administrative life this man, who had never been a pastor before coming to St. Louis Church, was pre-eminent in bringing the sanctifying grace of God, into nearly two thousand souls in the space of fifteen years.

Anticipation Hailed a New Clarion Call

Through the period of preparation for Schwinger's retirement celebration, the members of the Parish Council were active in consideration of the type of pastor whom they would like to see appointed by the bishop. In October 1995, Monsignor David Lee, communications officer for the diocese, told the council, "Although various scenarios over the past year or so have pointed to a shared pastor for St. Louis Church, no final decision has been made by Bishop Mansell as yet. I have every indication, however, that you will receive your own pastor. Although Rae Reines, president of the council was aware that the final decision rested with Bishop Mansell, she initiated plans to suggest an appropriate type of pastor for the church. She said, "A pastor at St. Louis Church should be vigorous and enthusiastic in his approach to the continued re-building of it. Optimism and confidence in the process of moving it forward in the twenty-first century is of paramount importance for our inner city parish with its multi-cultural and diverse backgrounds. The new pastor, however, must maintain, preserve, and appreciate the historic and architectural significance and deeply rooted traditions inherent in it. Spirituality, guidance, buoyancy, idealism, and enthusiasm should be the bench mark of our new pastor."

Priests from the diocesan office of personnel came to visit the Parish Council and all other interested parishioners seeking their advice on the selection of a new pastor. According to Michael Riester it seemed as if the Holy Spirit was working overtime. Riester said, "As Monsignor Robert Mack was crossing the parking lot one day, he was met by Bishop Mansell. The bishop said, 'Bob, I think that you would make a good pastor for St. Louis Church.' So it came to pass. On the weekend of December 16/17, 1995, the church bulletin carried the message of welcome to Mack with anticipation that his spiritual warmth and shepherding of his flock would continue to keep the spirit of St. Louis alive and well for many years." For the following six years Mack profoundly fulfilled the *Parish Dream* which Reines had expounded when defining the nature of a proposed incoming pastor the previous October.

Monsignor Mack inherited a non-residential parish where two hundred and fifty individuals were registered. Each weekend the church was graced at its Masses with an extra three hundred and fifty "drive-ins," who, although not registered, still financially supported the church. There were four Masses on weekends and two Masses each weekday. For lay help there were on hand six lectors, nine special ministers of Holy Communion, two altar servers, and eight ushers. Pre-Baptismal instructions had been scheduled to be given in the rectory. Instructions in Penance, Holy Communion, and Rite of Christian Initiation for Adults were to be conducted in other parishes of Region II. Intact at St. Louis was a Parish Council of fifteen members with five standing committees. Staff on deck was a cook, secretary/computer operator, housekeeper, and food-preparer for the outreach program, all part-time, and one security guard. The only organization from the Tridentine Church era was the Holy Name Society. Besides his parish work the pastor was expected to visit the shut-ins, and the sick in Hospitals: Buffalo General, Millard Fillmore, Children's, Mercy-Buffalo, and Mercy-Kenmore. The pastor was also required to celebrate Mass at Roosevelt Apartments. As an ecumenical participation, the Choir of Central Presbyterian Church came to St. Louis twice a year to perform acappella concerts. By 1995, the church again needed repair and redecoration. Much old paint had fallen from the ceiling and side aisles. The church hall in the basement was in need of remodeling. The constant cry was, "Stop the flooding on rainy days!" The rectory, dating from the Civil War was in need of an overhaul. There was, however, no debt; all assessments to the diocese and to the Catholic Academy of West Buffalo had been paid. Food, pastries, and sandwich meat came daily to the rectory for distribution. The housekeeper started preparing food at 6:00 A.M.; the distribution was scheduled for hours between 7:30 A.M. and 1:00 P.M.

Anticipation Hailed a New Clarion Call

The charisma generated by Monsignor Mack and the Parish Council during the last years of the old millennium brought maturity to the hopes of those who had first heard the angels' clarion call in 1979, announcing the new society proclaimed by the Holy Spirit at St. Louis Church. From the time that Monsignor Schwinger retired to Monsignor Mack's farewell, the registered enrollment at the church had increased by ninety-three percent. Regular offertory, monthly, and pew rent collections increased one hundred and twenty-nine percent. The annual parish fund drive, started by Schwinger, increased one hundred and fifty-six percent. Mack also fulfilled the desires of Rae Reines for an increase of spirituality, guidance, buoyancy, idealism, and enthusiasm. The percent of the number of souls especially served through the sacraments of baptism, and matrimony doubled. During his tenure, he witnessed more than two hundred brides who walked down the long aisle to meet their grooms at the entrance to the sanctuary. Every Sunday, his sermons had such content and distinct expression that people far and wide came to hear him preach. Many often said, "If only the pastor in our local church could preach as this man does!" His introductions to every Mass and his prayers for the faithful included references to the entire Communion of Saints of St. Louis Church and all those who suffered from the most heinous crimes, unacceptable social injustices, and crushing diseases. Although a man's life has been defined as something to be, to do, to do without, and to depart, Monsignor Mack did not want people to dwell on the final goal as much as enjoying the journey to that goal. People could empathize with his description of humanity in which he said, "We can find bad in the best of us, and find good in the worst of us!"

While Mack professionally handled the spiritual aspects of the church, the members of the Parish Council were active in the temporal. Their cooperative efforts and sound advice brought about profound changes with a capital expenditure of a half million dollars over a six year period. The greater expenditures were made in the last two years of the old millennium. Before anyone had vision of cleaning the stone surface of the church, pointing up all the exterior sandstone, and remodeling and redecorating for the one hundred and seventy-fifth anniversary in 2004, the handicap ramp, the two side entrances and sacristy vestibules, a modern bathroom, and repair of several stained glass windows became fulfilled projects. In the realm of social and community activities, the members of the council promoted the beginning or continuation of spaghetti dinners, golf tournaments, wreath sales at Christmas, baked goods sales, picnics, coffee hours, church lectures followed by German dinners at Ulrich's Restaurant, cook books, and holiday festivals. These activities not only brought a financial profit to the church of nine thousand dollars annually, but allowed friends, present and former parishioners, and tourists to come together and share their circles of life, which otherwise would not have been entwined.

A short review of some of the active members in the church along with their wide variety of secular occupations is like a flash back in the history of its membership of beer barons, butchers, bankers, and businessmen of many sorts in the nineteenth century. They are: Robert Albert, Fire Inspector; Debbie Beller, Manager, Finance Company; John Beller, Traffic Manager, Del-Rain Corporation; Beverly Bullion, Family Court Clerk; Joseph Bullion, President, Winter Brothers Bank Supplies; James Burns, American Light Company; Sam Fiorella, Retired from Conrail Railroad; Margaret Foegen, Buffalo Public School Teacher; Bernie Gerling, Human Resources Professional; Jack Haber, Loan Officer; Marlon Holt, Contractor and Builder; John Hoyt, President, Photographic Business; Christopher Jadoch, Attorney and Pharmacist; Joe Palladino, Real Estate; Rita Palladino, Homemaker; Dick Pancamo, Security Officer; John Pax, Attorney and Executive Director, Consumer Credit Counseling Service of Buffalo; Susan Peters, Writer and Educator; James Pieczynski, Teacher and Allentown Businessman;

Rae Reines, Educational Administrator, Buffalo Board of Education; Lee Volo, Businessman; Eunice Wozniak, Retirement Administrator, Erie County Community College; John Zoll, Physician; Rose Kennedy, Military Nurse with the Veterans Administration; Bill Kurzdorfer, Organist and Electrician at University of Buffalo; William Keenan, Attorney, Law Firm of Heimerl, Keenan, and Longo; Judy Laughlin, Marketing; Melanie Luongo, Homemaker; Margaret Maloney, Vice President, Marine Midland Bank; Sister Therese Marie, Teacher; Mike Mikos, Production Coordinator; Robert McCarthy, Political Reporter for *The Buffalo News*, Fenton Moore, Art Dealer; Peter Murray, Comptroller; Thomas Aquinas O'Connor, Physician; and Michael Oaika, Comptroller.

Two of those mentioned above are worthy of further scrutiny. They are Rose Kennedy and Sister Therese Marie Santos. The former trustees, in their wildest dreams, would never have believed that these would be listed as leaders in St. Louis Church. Besides not being solidly rooted in the long history of the church, they were also women. Rose Kennedy joined the parish with her husband, Doctor Francis J. Kennedy, in 1966. He died three years later, but she carried on to the present. Sister Therese Marie Santos born of Portuguese and Italian parents, and a nun in the Order of the Missionary Sisters of Our Lady of Mercy, became active in the church in 1969. Rose Kennedy was born in Rochester, New York, in 1918, graduated from a one-room schoolhouse in District eight, Barre School, near Albion, New York, and attended the Edward J. Meyer Memorial Hospital School of Nursing in Buffalo. When she graduated in 1941 her class was referred to as the *Pearl Harbor Class*. Following her Army nursing career in the Pacific Theater of War, she earned Bachelor's and Master's degrees in Nursing Administration at the University of Buffalo from whence she labored in Veterans' Hospitals in California, Washington D.C., and New York. When women were allowed to join the Holy Name Society, she became a member at St. Louis

Church. It dissolved in 1998. She was a member of the sesquicentennial celebration in 1979, was actively engaged in the Renew program for three years, worked diligently on the New Visions committees, was appointed a trustee in 1995 when Marie Faber Grupp died, received the St. Joseph the Worker Award in 1998, and is presently active on the Finance and Spiritual Life Committees of the Parish Council.

Father Bapst's house on the corner of Franklin and Edward Streets is now owned and occupied by the Missionary Sisters of Our Lady of Mercy, a Religious Order which originated in Brazil in 1938, but had its roots in an Order founded by Peter Nolasco in 1218. Sisters Stella, Neves, Victoria, Therese, and Catherine have occupied its rooms, since June 6, 1969. Their original aim was to gather children together from slum areas into day care so as to prevent them from falling into delinquency. They began the *Father Bapst Day Care Center*. Catholic Charities had owned the building before the Sisters came; it was a home for unwed mothers, but was closed in 1965. Under the direction of Sister Stella, the nuns also took care of the sacristy at St. Louis Church. Father Mosack, pastor, paid them $100 per month for this service. They discontinued their service in 1983 during the tenure of Monsignor Schwinger. Sister Therese loved to sing, and joined the church choir under the direction of David Wagner soon after she arrived in 1969 with the encouragement of Ruth Kolb and Marie Meisriemer. Her voice has been heard at the 10:30 A.M. Mass on Sunday for the past thirty-three years.

The enrollment at the day care center dropped drastically in 1983; it was closed. The Sisters' Order, however, purchased the building, and reopened it as a school called *Rainbow K. Kindergarten*. Today the school caters to children whose parents are the working poor and cannot afford to pay the price of $150 or more each week for the education of their children from ages three to seven. For a far less cost, the Sisters carry these children through Kindergarten, and first and second grades. They truly form a Rainbow whose nationalities are Laotian, Vietnamese, Puerto Rican, African-American, Chinese, and Korean. Like Rose Kennedy, Sister Therese was a member of the sesquicentennial anniversary celebration at St. Louis Church. She was also a member with John Rembold of the defaulted Parish Council begun by Dick Pancamo and Leonard Giarrano in 1989. In 1994, she was elected to a three-year term on the Parish Council that grew out of the need to complete the process of New Visions. Her name does not appear as a member in 1995 because she had to return to Brazil at the request of her Superiors. Upon returning to Buffalo, she again appeared as a member of the council in the year 2000 along with Bart Siener, president, John Zoll, secretary, Grant Violino, Mike Mikos, Melanie Luongo, Bill Fiden, Judy Perkowski, John Pax, Rose Kennedy, Kathryn Missert, Mike Riester, Jo Ann Decker, Bob McCarthy, Bridget Griffin, Linda Holben, and Cheryl Klass. Besides her many contributions, Sister Therese has always been a big help at the annual picnics.

Like Sister Therese, there are nine others who love to sing and have joined the St. Louis Church Choir as an outlet for their talent. At present the organist and choirmaster is Dona Vasey, a position she has held for thirty-one years. She has been a church organist ever since her high school days playing at Queen of Heaven Church in West Seneca. After earning her Master's degree in 1973, working part time at Depew Public Schools, and substituting for Susan Swinnich, who was the organist at St. Louis Church, Vasey was offered a full time job in replacing her. She has played at Masses for a legion of priests: Monsignor Vogel, Father Barone, Father White, Father Bohm, Father Mosack, Monsignor Schwinger, Monsignor Mack, and Monsignor Cunningham. Her children follow in her footsteps; her one daughter, Teri, plays flute, her son, Jon, enjoys his drums, and her other daughter, Monika, brings her harp to church and sings whenever she returns from college.

The choir is filled with well-educated people. Marylin Smith had her school years at St. Thomas Aquinas, Mount Mercy Academy, and Canisius College. She has had an eclectic career as an English and Religion teacher, an administrative assistant, and as a legal and medical secretary. She joined the choir in 2001. Colleen M. Burke joined the choir in 1980 because her mother and friends while seeking out a traditional church hitched on to St. Louis. Each Sunday at the 10:30 A.M. Mass the congregation then heard the new voices of Janet Burke, Coleen Burke, Sue Huston, Donna Huston, Judy Caratta, Tiena Laughlin, and Pat Huston. Today, only Sue and Coleen are still on hand each Sunday. Chuck Thomas is the most recent member having joined in May 2002. Although he studied voice and saxophone since he was in the third grade, majored in voice with a Philharmonic Choir, and received his Bachelor of Arts degree from the University of Buffalo in 1977, he had a thirty-four year hiatus in his singing career until he returned to it by singing with the Lutheran Chorale in 2001. Roy Butz is a true German, who speaks the language fluently. He's been in the St. Louis Choir since 1990. In his early days he passionately wanted to be in a barbershop quartet, but the director found out that he was a boy soprano. Finally, Patricia Albert, nee Riley, was a graduate of St. Louis' school in 1943, sang in the choir from fifth to eighth grade, and joined the present choir in 1984. Graduating with a degree from Bryant and Stratton Business School, she enjoyed her work as a civil servant with the Buffalo Board of Education. She is very proud to be the wife of Robert Albert, with whom she had two sons and a daughter. Her five grandchildren love to hear her voice when they attend Mass.

In 1995, the five council members who were elected for three years voiced their opinions of the goals for St. Louis Church. In retrospect these were omens of the future and in synch with the ideas of the new pastor, Monsignor Mack. Carolann Besch, who had chaired the Constitution and By-Laws Committee the year before, said, "We should increase the parish membership by twenty-five percent, increase weekly collections by five hundred dollars, institute a fundraiser to rehabilitate the church's interior and exterior, and make the church handicapped accessible in a practical manner that would be in keeping with the church's architecture." By the year 2001 these projects had been exceeded, accomplished, or seriously underway. Sam Fiorella said, "We should continue the high level of discussion and spirituality that has been developed during the Parish Council's first year." The joy of seeing the expression of that spirituality was witnessed in the year 2000 on the eve of the feast of St. Louis when twenty-two parishes in the Vicariate of which St. Louis Church was a member, came together within its walls to celebrate Mass with Bishop Mansell in honor of the Jubilee Year. Jack Haber said, "We should encourage parish growth by encouraging younger people and new families to attend while we preserve the beauty and history of St. Louis Church for the future." During his six years as pastor, Monsignor Mack made a strong financial commitment of $200,000 to the Catholic Academy of West Buffalo that has become the parochial school for children of parishioners of St. Louis Church if they should so choose. In the long lines of the Communion processional at Sunday Masses one sees a large number of small children which shows the growth of younger families in the parish. Monsignor Mack was always ready to greet young ones with a handshake or a high-five. For the babies he had a light tap on the forehead.

Craig Coyne said, "We should ensure the financial stability of the parish with revenues exceeding expenses." In 1997, the year end financial statement showed an ending balance of $53,087.69. This was two years after Mack had assumed the pastorship. Because of improvements made in the church and rectory, this balance declined to $22,176.25 in 1999. By the year 2001, however, it had increased to $33,295.88 even though many more capital expenditures had been made. Finally Doctor John Zoll, who has been a member of the church for a long time, a

parish trustee, and a communicant at the 8:30 A.M. Mass, said, "We want the parish council to serve the parishioners so that individuals who want to be active have the opportunity to do so, and those who only wish to attend services will feel comfortable and accepted as true St. Louis Parishioners." St. Louis Church has always been the historic Mother Church of the Diocese. Both the Parish Council and Monsignor Mack have insisted that the church is open to all: the downtown workers, the old parishioners and friends in the suburbs, the refugees, the tourists, the wanderers, and casual ecumenical observers.

Monsignor Robert Mack, who came to St. Louis Church to fulfill the dreams of the Parish Council, was ordained in 1957 at the age of twenty-six. In the immediate years that followed, he served as parochial vicar at St. Stephen's Church, Buffalo, and at St. Joseph's Old Cathedral. From 1962 to 1971, he was chaplain of the Buffalo Fire Department. His first pastorate was at the former St. Mathew's parish, Buffalo, followed by St. Brigid's Church, Newfane. During the years of *Renew* and its aftermath, he was pastor at St. Francis Xavier and All Saints Church, Buffalo. He was administrator of Our Lady of the Rosary Church in Niagara Falls before becoming pastor at St. Louis Church in December 1995. On June 17, 2001, in an interview with Louise Continelli, staff reporter for the *Buffalo News*, he said, "Nationally recognized as one of Buffalo's most architecturally significant buildings, St. Louis Church is the jewel of its downtown neighbors. It needs, however, restoration which when done will benefit the whole downtown community." His remarks came on the heels of Representative John L. LaFalce's presentation to the church of a Federal check for a quarter-million dollars as seed money toward this million dollar project planned for completion by 2004, for the one hundred and seventy-fifth anniversary of the church. LaFalce said, "St. Louis Church is one of the first buildings you see when entering downtown Buffalo off the Kensington Expressway. Through the nineteenth and twentieth centuries this landmark has provided a steady spiritual presence in a changing city."

One of the parishioners who strongly believed in the historic preservation of St. Louis Church was William Fiden, the fourth president of the Parish Council. He had deep roots in the church. His mother, nee Fath, attended St. Louis School to which she walked each day from the old family home on Mulberry Street. Bill and his wife Sue were married at St. Louis Church in 1969. There first child of four, Adam was baptized there. Soon after, however, Bill's military and medical career demanded that he serve in various parts of the country other than Buffalo. Upon returning to keep a permanent residence in Western New York, Bill and Sue rejoined the church in 1996. Two years later, after a tour of all its nooks and crannies given to him by Bill Kurzdorfer, a former classmate at Fallon High School, he decided that the tomb of Father Joseph Sorg, tucked away in a room which was being used as a closet, needed attention. As a clinical director of family medicine at Erie County Medical Center, he knew that he had to prescribe the right dose of elbow grease and architectural appreciation to lead a team of workers who would make the area around Father Sorg's tomb a beautiful and restful place for prayer and meditation. After the clean up was finished, Fiden quipped, "We all got to know Father Sorg pretty well down there!" As president of the Council, Fiden was most eager to have a large number of people participating in the activities of the church as lectors, ushers, and Eucharistic ministers. His remodeling of the tomb, however, was his crowning achievement and brought much publicity to the church.

St. Louis Church received further publicity on July, 18, 2001 when Guillame, Christian, Sophia, and Isabelle Le Couteulx, descendants of Louis Etienne Le Couteulx, who had donated the property upon which St. Louis Church was built, came to Buffalo. After the family had an opportunity to visit Louis' gravesite in the United German and French Roman Catholic Cemetery, Isabelle said, "We didn't know that his grave still existed; the experience was emotional." Besides visiting the cemetery they also saw the section of Buffalo where Louis Le Couteulx had lived, they saw the sites of several properties which he had donated to the Buffalo Diocese and to Religious Orders, and they were hosted by the congregation at St. Louis Church at a reception in the rectory. Two months before they came to America, they had received a letter from Molly Hauck, an historical researcher, writer, speaker, and consultant who had had her office at Mount Calvary Cemetery. In that letter she informed the members of the Le Couteulx family of her findings, and how rewarding she thought a visit to Buffalo would be for them. At the reception, Isabelle said, "It was a good mission for us. We are very grateful to Molly, Monsignor Mack, and to all the parishioners of St. Louis Church."

On the weekend of September 8/9, 2001, Monsignor Mack made a stunning remark to the congregation; he said, "Priests of the diocese of Buffalo have the option to retire at age seventy or accept mandatory retirement at age seventy-five. In October, I will reach the age of seventy and because of some health concerns, I have decided to exercise my option to retire from the pastorate of our parish." This was a blow which many thought was unbelievable; only a year earlier he had sent a holiday card to them picturing himself dressed like an Arabian nomad riding on a burley camel through the Holy Land. The caption under the picture read, "Merry Christmas and Happy New Year from the Fourth Wiseman trekking toward Bethlehem." He was, however, extremely serious; he said, "Bishop Mansell expressed great fraternal support and granted me permission to retire. The date of January 7, 2002 was agreed upon as an appropriate time." Although he wished not to be honored with any farewell party, one was arranged in the church hall on Sunday, January 6, 2002. The highlight of the gathering was a presentation to Monsignor Mack of a Proclamation issued by Joel A. Giambra, Erie County

Executive, defining that Sunday as *Monsignor Robert Mack Day*. Giambra gave his reasons for the proclamation; he wrote, "Monsignor Mack has worked diligently to foster an appreciation and knowledge of the long and glorious history of St. Louis parish as the Mother Church of the Diocese of Buffalo. With his support, the writing of an official parish history has begun in anticipation of St. Louis parish's one hundredth and seventy-fifth anniversary in 2004. During his six-year pastorate, the exterior restoration of the historic 1868 parish house has been completed and the restoration of the church exterior has now begun, as well as completion of several major improvements such as a new restroom and handicap ramp into the church. Under Monsignor Mack's spiritual leadership, St. Louis Parish has witnessed tremendous growth and prosperity; parish membership has doubled, and the church has succeeded in raising more money than ever in its long history."

Giambra continued, "Today, St. Louis Church, its directors, parishioners, and all of its many friends honor a great man and a long-time supporter of St. Louis Church, Monsignor Robert Mack, on the occasion of his retirement from active service to the parish, and we all are most grateful for his role in strengthening this beautiful downtown Buffalo institution, and helping to secure St. Louis parish as an historic landmark in the community." Monsignor Mack then replied, "You have been kind, thoughtful, concerned, and considerate, Thank You. Your loyalty, faithfulness, and dedication to St. Louis will guarantee it a great future. The past is prologue—the best is yet to be!" On the weekend following Mack's reception, Monsignor Robert Cunningham, chancellor and vicar general of the Diocese of Buffalo, celebrated Mass in St. Louis Church for the first time as its pastor. During his sermon, he announced his presence, and indicated that his acceptance of Bishop Mansell's request to replace Monsignor Mack had similarities to Reverend Paul Hoelscher; who, as the first chancellor of the diocese of Buffalo, was appointed pastor at St. Louis Church

on September 18, 1888. Hoelscher arrived three days after Father Joseph Sorg, the former pastor, had died. Sorg had begun the construction of the present grand gothic church, but Hoelscher had to see to its completion and make it debt free. A similar task of remodeling and fund-raising was laid in the lap of Monsignor Cunningham in preparation for the one hundredth and seventy-fifth anniversary to be celebrated in 2004. Historians writing in 2029, at the bicentennial celebration of the church, will tell the "rest of the story."

Although at this point one might wish to end this long and glorious history, one is urged to pause and reflect. As one enters the side door to the church from Edward Street, turns right to the first aisle, and again turns toward the first set of pews, one feels the presence of a former parishioner who always sat there and embodied the full spirit of St. Louis Church. She was Anna Beck who died January 4, 1998 at the age of ninety-seven. She was neither a famous politician, scientist, nor tycoon, but she was an ordinary feisty citizen who was hard working, law abiding, and frugal. Never married, she had only two loves: her family and St. Louis Church. When she died, she willed the bulk of her estate, $150,000, to the church, gave the city of Buffalo the option to buy her property at 923 Washington Street for $100, but demanded that her small cottage there be razed. Before she died, she said, "After I die, the house will be torn down. I am the last of my family and no one else shall live there when I'm gone!" Her life revolved around St. Louis Church, and her great disappointment came when she could not walk to church anymore. Right to the end, however, Anna Beck could look out her front door and over the neighborhood rooftops, and see the spire of her church reaching skyward.

Anna Beck's father was Frank Beck who had come to America from Germany with his widowed mother Marie Anna Beck in 1865 following the American Civil War. In 1868, Marie married Andrew

Kraus who built her a one and one-half story wooden frame house with clapboard siding at 42 Ralph Place. It was telescopic with some Italianate influence. Reaching maturity, Frank Beck married Lillian Schlenker. They had two daughters, Anna, born in 1900 and Veronica, born in 1903. Both children were born in the house on Ralph Place, never married, and lived in it their entire lives. What is unique is that the abandonment of family homes and parish churches, which often occurred in subsequent generations, did not happen with the Beck sisters. In 1973, their house was in the midst of controversy when the Buffalo Urban Renewal Agency (BURA) took action against them in an attempt to have it demolished in order to make way for the Oak Street Redevelopment Project. Anna said, "I will fight the city tooth and nail. I don't care if they do call me Annie the Menace!" On March 17, 1982, the sisters entered into an agreement with BURA that gave them ownership of a lot located at 923 Washington Street with the provision that their home on Ralph Place would be moved there "lock, stock, and barrel, and the iron fence too!" Anna had insisted that she and Veronica be in a place where they could see the steeple of St. Louis Church. In the move, her wish was fulfilled. After Veronica died, Anna stayed on alone in the house. Still a fiercely independent, five-foot dynamo, she carried on keeping it as neat as a pin. One night she awoke to find a robber standing by her bedside. She grabbed a broom and beat him so mercilessly that he begged her to stop and let him go. Monsignor Mack also learned quickly of her spunkiness. He said, "I soon learned that nothing happened at St. Louis Church without Miss Beck's approval. She counted the bulbs that had blown out in the ceiling clusters and demanded their replacement. When I first became pastor, I decided to change the cover of the church bulletin from a picture of St. Louis to one of the church tower. Anna was so shocked and unhappy that I put St. Louis back on the cover." Jack and Arline Hoyt, who had been life long friends with her because of family ties, said, "Inside her house, time stopped around 1930. One could see an eighty-year-old cast iron stove, a treadle sewing machine, an early Hoover vacuum cleaner, a refrigerator one step above an icebox, a washing machine with a hand wringer, an ancient rug beater, and vintage furniture."

*I*n her later years, a support network of neighbors, priests, fellow parishioners, and friends looked after her. Anna, however, would not give anyone a key. She was afraid that whoever had a key might someday find her very ill, and send her to the hospital, a place in which she did not wish to die. She often said, "Here I was born, here I will die." Doctor Phillips who cared for her said, "Annie, some day they will find you dead on the floor." It almost happened that way. Joe Marasi, an Eucharistic Minister at St. Louis Church, looked through the window on her near fatal day and saw her on the floor, but her legs moved. He called the police who broke the window, and phoned for an ambulance. Very reluctantly she allowed herself to be taken to General Hospital where, after going into a coma, she died three days later. Arline Hoyt was at her side at that last hour when she succumbed to a fatal heart attack and Monsignor Mack had given her the last rites.

*F*or nearly thirteen months following her death the Common Council, the Preservation Board, the Buffalo Urban Renewal Agency, and the Erie County Surrogate Court debated the feisty lady's will, which demanded her home demolished upon her death. Finally, under a ruling by Judge Joseph S. Mattina, at the urging of Anna Beck's attorney, Ms. Kennedy Martin, the clam-like derrick-shovel was given the green light to take down Anna's tiny yellow cottage. The judge said, "Ironically, the agency which now claims to champion its preservation was the same agency that went to court seeking its demolition in 1973. That twist of fate is not lost on this court." Michael McCarthy, attorney for the Buffalo Urban Renewal Agency replied, "We accept Judge Mattina's ruling and there will be no appeal. We will further exercise our option to acquire the property and use it to provide parking for nearby apartments." The Buffalo Common Council, however, made an appeal, but withdrew it on January 12, 1999. Eight days later, Jack and Arline Hoyt were on hand with tears in their eyes to see Annie get her wish. The clam-mouthed shovel opened wide, grabbed the little yellow cottage, and squeezed it into obliteration. As the walls crumbled, reams of newspapers, which Annie had plastered over the interior shell of the attic to keep out the weather, burst into the air, were carried upward by the wind, flew gracefully above Washington Street, and floated toward the steeple of St. Louis Church. [7]

REFERENCES AND NOTES ⚜ CHAPTER SEVENTEEN

1. Letter of Most Reverend Edward D. Head D.D. to The Most Reverend Jean Jadot D.D., Apostolic Delegate, 3339 Massachusetts Avenue, N.W., Washington, D.C., 20008, October 15, 1979. See the Archives of St. Louis Church. Also, Letter of the Apostolic Delegate, Jean Jadot, to The Most Reverend Edward D. Head, Bishop of Buffalo, 35 Lincoln Parkway, Buffalo, New York, 14222, October 19, 1979. See the archives of St. Louis Church. For a historical review of facts see: op. cit. *Lay-Trusteeism at St. Louis Roman Catholic Church, Buffalo, New York*, pp. 30, 37, 49, 63, 81. For the intent of the New York State Law, *An Act of Incorporation of Religious Societies, 1813*, see op. cit. *Laws of the State of New York Affecting Church Property*, pp. 45-6. For fifty years of problems in Catholic dioceses in New York State because of the Incorporation Act of 1813, see: McNamara, "Trusteeism in the Atlantic States, 1785-1863," *Catholic Historical Review*, XXX, 1944, 135-154.

2. Chancery Memos to Bishop Head from Monsignor Trautman, May 31, 1979, and July 12, 1979. These are in the Archives of the Diocese of Buffalo and the Archives of St. Louis Church, see: Michael Riester, and Sister Martin Joseph. Facts and intent of information contained in these memos were verified by the author/editor in an interview with Most Reverend Donald W. Trautman, Bishop of Erie, Pennsylvania, formerly Auxiliary Bishop of Buffalo, on August 7, 2002. The attitudes of the Trustees toward Father Alfred Mosack were gleaned from conversations by the author/editor with many present day parishioners, who wish to remain anonymous. The content of these conversations has so many collaborating points, however, that it is impossible to deny their veracity. One can conclude that the trustees had not just stormy relations with Mosack, they were in fact very hostile toward him. In reference to the charge of rough handling of people one informant said that the family of William Kastings, owner of a wholesale florist business in Buffalo and parishioner of St. Louis Church, was outraged with the attitude of Mosack at Bill Kastings

funeral. The family had arrived early at church for the funeral that was scheduled for 11:00 A.M. Ten minutes before the hour, Mosack was not in the church and someone went to the rectory to fetch him. In a rough voice, Mosack rebuffed him saying, "I will not be over to the church until I have finished my breakfast." In his short memo titled *My Own Thoughts*, Michael Riester has said, "Father Mosack was a very likable but ineffective pastor. His main interests were Troop I on Franklin Street and the horse races. He freely spoke of his dislike for the trustees in his homilies. In one homily, he said that he needed a new typewriter, but the trustees refused to buy it for him. Also in his sermons he used the term "winners circle" as a place where those who died received their eternal reward. Father Mosack organized the "St. Louis Nite at the Races," an annual outing at the Hamburg Trotters Race Track. It was the only social outing sponsored by the parish." Members of the sesquicentennial committee worked very smoothly with Mosack. The author/editor and his wife Marie Buchheit Miller were married in 1969 at St. Louis Church with Mosack presiding. They had no dislike for him; and, on the contrary, often visited him when he was pastor of St. Mary's in New Oregon. James Bartlett spoke of Mosack in very good terms. Donald W. Trautman, now Bishop of Erie, Pennsylvania, said, "Father Mosack was from the old school, a man who sincerely and positively fulfilled his priestly duties, but with the trustees he could be a man of little political tact." Information concerning the members of the sesquicentennial committee was obtained from Michael Riester, Rose Kennedy, James Bartlett, and the recollections of Father William Schwinger. For information concerning preparations for the sesquicentennial celebration see: Letter to Board of Trustees from Larry Schieber, June 10, 1979; a copy exists in the archives of St. Louis Church. For the laws and legal cases effecting Trustee Corporations of Religious Societies see the following: Zollman, *American Church Law*, West Publishing Company, St. Paul, Minnesota, 1933, p.117; Case of *Lawyer v. Cipperly*, 7 Paige 231, New York, 1838; Case of *Robertson v. Bullions*, 11, New York, 243, 1854; Case of *Petty v. Tooker*, 21, New York, 267, 1860; Dignan, *A History of the Legal Incorporation of the Catholic Church in the United States*, Kennedy Pub. New York, 1935, pp. 27, 96, 196, 207; Jones and Warwick, *Laws of the State of New York*, vol 1., New York, 1789, pp. 104-109; Jones and Warwick, *Laws of the State of New York, 1812-1813*, vol. 2., Albany, NY, 1813, pp. 214-216. In September, 1854, the trustees at St. Louis Church brought suit against Stephen Bettinger for not paying his pew rent. He had challenged the trustees' right to collect saying, "Only the bishop has the power to say who does or does not have the right to sit in the church." The case was tried before Judge Sheldon who ruled in favor of the trustees in so far as collection was concerned, but did not pass on right of title between bishop and trustees. The ruling forced Bettinger to pay six shillings and six pence per seat per quarter for four seats; it was granted on January 9, 1855. It was understandable that Sheldon so made his decision. It was made three months before the Putnam Bill was passed into law, and six months after the case of *Robertson v. Bullions* which decided against the trustees of a Presbyterian church by the New York Court of

Trustees of the Post Vatican II Corporation known as "St. Louis Roman Catholic Church of Buffalo, New York," during the Jubilee Year 2000. This corporation had replaced that known as "The Trustees of the Roman Catholic Church of St. Louis, Buffalo, New York" on October 4, 1979. Moving clockwise from top left, the featured trustees are: Reverend Monsignor Robert J. Cunningham, P.A., J.C.L., Vicar General of the Buffalo Diocese; The Most Reverend Henry J. Mansell, D.D., Bishop of the Buffalo Diocese; Reverend Monsignor Robert A. Mack, Pastor of St. Louis Church; Doctor John G. Zoll, M.D.; and Mrs. Rose S. Kennedy.

Appeals. If Bettinger had taken his case to the Court of Appeals, he too, based on *Robertson v. Bullions*, may have reversed the decision of Judge Sheldon. Another possible challenge came in 1978 when Reinagel told Rose Kennedy that only the trustees had the right to decide who would be allowed to be buried from St. Louis Church; these would be only pew holders. She complained to Father Mosack but he failed to follow through and challenge the trustees on the basis of *Robertson v. Bullions*. In fact he was unaware, as was Rose Kennedy, that the case was ever heard. Her challenge was aborted. For dissatisfaction on the part of the parishioners at St. Louis Church over the transfer see: Paul Batt, "Historic St. Louis Church is Taken Over by Diocese," *Buffalo News, October 2, 1979*; "City Church Laymen Upset By transfer," *Buffalo News*, October 2, 1979; Paul Batt, "Parishioners To Mull Suit in Transfer," *Buffalo News*, October 3, 1979. Also see: *Courier Express*, Tuesday, October 2, 1979. For laws recognized in the historical review see: op. cit. *Laws of the State of New York*, vol. 1., pp. 104-109; op. cit., *Laws of the State of New York, 1812-1813*, vol. 2., pp. 214-216; op. cit. *A History of the Legal Incorporation of Catholic Church in the United States*, pp. 96, 185; McNamara, *Catholic Historical Review*, XX, 1944, p.150; Farley, *The Life of Cardinal McCloskey*, New York, 1918, p.193; op. cit. *American Church Law*, pp. 120-122; For the New York State law of 1863 see: op. cit. *A History of Legal Incorporation of the Catholic Church in the United States*, p.27; *Laws of the State of New York passed at the Eighty-sixth Session of the Legislature*, Albany, 1863, pp.65-67. For the amendment of 1895 see: *General Laws of New York*, vol. 1., Albany, 1895, 449. For the second amendment see: *Consolidated Laws of the State of New York*, Vol. 2., Albany, 1909, art. 5, p. 92. For the recommendation of the Sacred Congregation see: *The Ecclesiastical Review*, XLV, 1911, p. 585; Bouscaren, *Canon Law Digest*, Bruce Publishing, Milwaukee, Wisconsin, vol. 2., 1943, pp. 444-445. In 1917 the New York State Law was extended to all dioceses in the United States not only of the Latin rite but also to church corporations of the Ruthenian-Greek Rite. For the incorporation problems experienced at Good Shepherd, Pendleton see: op. cit. *Good Shepherd, the Church on the Canal*, pp. 12, 15. For Trusteeism according to the law of 1813 as it existed in other churches, St. Boniface; Sts. Peter and Paul, Hamburg, St. Mary's, Lockport; St. James Church, Angelica; St. John Baptist Church, Boston, NY, see: op. cit. *History of the Catholic Church in Western New York*, pp. 245, 272, 274, 283, 284, 293, 299. In 1857, A brick church was built at St. Boniface during the pastorship of Father Follenius. It was then incorporated according to the New York State's Law of 1813. On May 30, 1884, Bishop Ryan appointed Father Ferdinand Kolb as pastor and re-incorporated the church according to the revised laws of 1863; taken from *Brief History of St. Boniface Parish*, published by St. Boniface Church of which a copy supplied to the author/editor by William Kurzdorfer is in their archives. For the formation of the new corporation at St. Louis Church see: op. cit. *Minutes of the Meeting of the Trustees of the Diocese of Buffalo, New York*, 35 Lincoln Parkway, October 1, 1979 in archives of St. Louis Church. The trustees of the Diocesan Corporation, which had been incorporated in 1898 and re-incorporated in 1954 by a special act of the Legislature of New York State, were in 1979, Bishop Edward Head, president and treasurer; Auxiliary Bishop Bernard J. McLaughlin, vice-president; and Donald W. Trautman, secretary. Only Head and Trautman were present for the meeting. McLaughlin retired in 1988 and Trautman was consecrated Auxiliary Bishop in 1985. When Trautman became Bishop of Erie, Pennsylvania, Auxiliary Bishop Edward M. Grosz replaced him in Buffalo. A note was attached to the bottom of the minutes. It reads: "I, the undersigned Secretary of the Board of Trustees of the Diocese of Buffalo, New York, do hereby certify that the above is a true copy of the original minutes of the meeting held October 1, 1979, and that the resolution therein is still in full force and effect." It is signed Monsignor Robert W. Trautman and dated November 27, 1979. Also see: *Minutes of the Board of Trustees of St. Louis Roman Catholic Church of Buffalo, New York*, 35 Edward Street, October 9, 1979. It was also resolved, duly made, seconded, and passed unanimously that the proposed by-laws be accepted. Copies of the certificate of Incorporation and by-laws are in the Archives of St. Louis Church. It was also resolved that the safe deposit boxes be opened and all legal documents signed so that checks could be used and withdrawals on bank accounts could be made. For the news release see: *Buffalo News*, October 2, 1979. For Michael Riester's comments see: *My Own Thoughts*, submitted to the author/editor on August 4, 2002, a copy is in the archives of St. Louis Church.

3. Chronology in the life of Father William A. Schwinger: 1942, joins the Marine Corp.; 1946, his first enlistment period is up; 1948, after a second enlistment he is discharged with the benefits of the GI Bill of Rights; 1948, he attends classes at Niagara University; 1953, graduates from Niagara U.; 1953-54, teaches at Gaskill Junior High School; 1955, enters the seminary; 1958, finishes his studies and is ordained on March 1, 1958, and is sent to Albion; 1961, appointment at Bishop Turner High School; 1967, appointed as teacher at Bishop Fallon High School; 1974, appointed principal of Bishop Fallon High School and chaplain at the Erie County Holding Center; 1979, appointed pastor at St. Louis Church; 1984, raised to the dignity of Monsignor by Pope John Paul II. See: *Buffalo News*, Thursday, October 18, 1984, and *Buffalo Courier Express*, Sunday, September 23, 1979. Schwinger said that he lived in a big house in Albion. It was the rectory associated with St. Joseph's Church established in 1852 at 106 South Main Street. Another church, St. Mary's of the Assumption Church was established at 47 Brown Street in 1891. St. Joseph's was linked with St. Mary's in 1990. In his interview with Michael Riester, Schwinger said, "In 1981, I had problems with the organ. It blew, but its bellows were very bad. One was large the other small; they were covered over with deerskin. One day the organist, Dona Vasey, was playing and she stopped because the organ stopped. So I had to have an organ fund drive. Today you can see the names of all the generous donors on a plaque near the large crucifix on the right hand side of the front wall of the church. Then came early spring with strong winds blowing at 72 miles per hour. The huge stone

cross on the main spire fell off onto Edward Street. We had to get it removed immediately. I had no money to pay for this tragedy's clean-up so I decided to have another fund drive." Both drives were successful; by the end of the fiscal year, 1983, the reserve fund from the organ drive and the first fund drive was $41,220. For the story of the organ being silenced see: Audrey Lipford, *Courier Express*, Monday, July 6, 1981. Also see: *St. Louis Church Bulletin*, Courtesy of William J. Dengler, successor to Lux and Sons Funeral Home, 2540 Main Street, Buffalo, New York, July 4/5, 1981. Sources used to discuss the Pearl Street Connector dispute between the Trustees of St. Louis Church and the City of Buffalo see: Dan Herbeck, *The Buffalo News*, Sunday, June, 8, 1980; Charles Haddad, *Buffalo Courier Express*, Thursday, July 3, 1980; Charles Haddad, *Buffalo Courier Express*, Sunday, July 13, 1980; *Courier Express*, Tuesday, July 15, 1980; St. *Louis Roman Catholic Church Financial Statement*, September 1, 1982 to August 31, 1983, a copy is in the St. Louis Church Archives; and a Letter from Rev. William A. Schwinger to Mayor James D. Griffin, May 12, 1980, with cc. to Bishop Edward D. Head, Trustees' lawyers, Kennedy and Stoeckl, and City Director of the Planning Board, Michelle Penca; see the St. Louis Church Archives.

4. For source material upon which the topic of *Renew* was discussed see: Father Tom Maloney, "American Bishops Endorse Renew," *Western New York Catholic*, July, 1984; "Local Parishes to Participate in National Renew Process," *Amherst Bee*, April 11, 1985; Joan Bombarger, "Renew is Moving Forward in Lockport," *Union-Sun Journal*, April 29, 1985, sec. 2, p.11; David Briggs, "Renew Will Prompt Catholics to Live Their Faith," with pictures of Rev. Thomas Maloney, Sister Louise Alff, and Ellen Rose, The *Buffalo News*, Saturday, August 31, 1985; The National Renew Service Team, *Renew Guidelines, Thoughts and Renew, A Proven and Effective Way to Vitalize Spirituality in Your Diocese/Parish*, Paulist Press, Ramsey, New Jersey, 1982; Philip J. Murnion, "Parish Renewal," *America*, April 24, 1982, pp. 314-17; Bishop Edward D. Head, "My Personal Experience," *Western New York Catholic*, January 1985; "Young People Find Something Special in Renew Sharing Groups," *Western New York Catholic*, December 1986; David Briggs, "Panel of Catholic Bishops Commends Renew Program," *The Buffalo News*, Wednesday, December 31, 1986; Advertisement on Renew, *Buffalo News*, December 22, 1986; Father Thomas Maloney, "Renew Action Groups Respond to Hungry People," In the article one finds that Monsignor Robert A. Mack, then pastor of St. Francis Xavier Parish, East Street near Amherst Street, and later pastor at St. Louis Church, 1995 to 2002, ran a soup kitchen on Saturday afternoons at St. Francis in 1987, *Western New York Catholic*, January 1987; Concerning Schwinger's sandwich program see: Don Esmonde, "A Kind Word, and a Sandwich, for the Outcasts," *The Buffalo News*, Sunday, December 10, 1995; David Briggs, "Bishops' Changes in Renew Aren't Due until Fall," *The Buffalo News*, Saturday, February, 21, 1987; Louis H. Pumphrey, "Renew," *Catholic Universe Bulletin*, June 5, 1987; James R. Kelly, "Does the Renew Program Renew?" *America*, March 7, 1987, pp. 197-

99; David Briggs, "Renew Ends Amid Calls to Extend It," *The Buffalo News*, Saturday, January 16, 1988; For attacks against the Renew Program see: David Briggs, "Group Aims to Lure Catholics from Church," *The Buffalo News*, Sunday, March 29, 1987; Richard A. Maussner, "Renew Facts vs. 'Renew,' *Metro Community News*, Tuesday, October 1, 1985, vol. 8, no. 6, it contains an open and challenging letter to Bishop Edward D. Head, Bishop Of Buffalo; Sharon Johnson, "Renew Program Debated by WNY Catholics, *Niagara Gazette*, November 1985; *Renew What's Wrong With It? A Wanderer Supplement*, Wanderer Press, St. Paul, Minnesota, 1985; "Letters to the Editor," *Metro Community News*, September 17, 1985. In 1995, Mary Prenevau donated $2,400.00 to the St. Louis' sandwich program, thanks to the charity of the employees of Top's International Supermarket of Amherst, New York. The donations had been received on a regular basis since 1991, see: *St. Louis Church Parish Bulletin*, October 7/8, 1995.

5. Dick Pancamo's care for Monsignor Schwinger was described to the author/editor by Bill Kurzdorfer, Curator of the 1903 Kimball organ. The story of enticing Monsignor Schwinger to allow a first picnic at the church and details of it were related to the author/editor by Joseph Bullion, former member of the Parish Council Steering Committee and active in New Visions. Melanie Luongo, chairperson of the picnics, supplied details of the picnics of 1998, 1999, 2000, 2001, and 2002. Jo Ann Decker was the chairperson of the 1999 picnic. Luongo supplied the author/editor with order sheets for meats, rolls, drinks, and donated material on loan. She also included lists of workers, jobs to be performed, and the kinds of foodstuffs made by the various parishioners. Dates and minutes of planning sessions' meetings were also provided. Financial statements for the costs of the various purchased items were given. The financial success of the various picnics can be found in the *Annual Financial Statements of St. Louis Church*, for the years 1989 through 2002.

6. For Bishop Head's appointment and work in the Diocese of Buffalo see: op. cit. *Celebrating God's Life In Us*, pp. 73-77; For the closing of churches by Bishop Head see data in Ibid., pp. 151-55. For the obligation to participate at Mass on Sundays and Holy Days of Obligation or on their vigils see: op. cit. *Catechism of the Catholic Church*, p. 493, article 2042 and note 82. For Bishop Edward D. Head's plan known as *New Visions* see: Pastoral Ministry Commission, A *Planning Process for Parish Life and Ministry in the Diocese of Buffalo*, Diocese of Buffalo, Spring 1993, pp. 1-52. Sister Regina Murphy whose office is at the Catholic Center, 795 Main Street, directed the statistical team that mathematically analyzed the data, set a baseline of activity for 1993, and predicted the diocesan situation in 2000. Prior to the main thrust of New Visions churches had been closed, merged, or clustered in the Central City and on the East Side; see: Dave Condren, "Buffalo Diocese Faced With Aging Clergy, Dwindling Ordinations," *The Buffalo News*, Sunday, May 2, 1993 and Dave Condren, "Four East Side Catholic Parishes to Close," *The Buffalo News*, Sunday, May 23, 1993. Also see: Ellen Jean Klein,

"Collaborate or Close," *Today's Parish*, March 8, 1994, and Harry W. Paige, "Abandoned Churches," *Liguorian*, June 1994. For a discussion of the beginnings of parish self-evaluations see: Msgr. David M. Lee, "Diocesan New Visions Committee Begins Parish Self-evaluation Steps," *Western New York Catholic*, June 1993 and Keith Kidder, "Parishes Begin Self Study," *Western New York Catholic*, June 1993. For evidence at a second attempt of developing parish council see: Letter from Leonard Giarrano to Father Schwinger on May 22, 1989. Letter was provided from the archives of John Pax, Grand Island, New York. The following attended the Parish self-assessment meeting on December 4, 1993: Robert J. Lannigan, Trudy Demo, Sophie C. Stasz, Marie Hermann, Josephine Weppner, Mary Hardick, Jack and Arline Hoyt, Joan Cummings, Barry Kraus, Larry and Marie Schieber, Joe Hoover, Mary Prenevau, John and Nancy Pax, Mary Di Lapo, Joseph and Beverly Bullion, Rosemary Bloch, Benedict Pancamo, James and Susan Mrozek, Genevieve Moss, Bill Kurzdorfer, Margaret R. Foegen, Susan Peters, Sam Fiorella, Mike Mikos, Rose Kennedy, Allen and Dorothy Schneggenburger, and Bernie Gerling. For appointment of delegates, John Y. Pax and Michael T. Mikos, from St. Louis Church to the Regional Task Force see: Letter of Msgr. William Schwinger to Sister Regina Murphy, December 9, 1993 and Letter of Msgr. William Schwinger to Rev. Anthony Rigoli, OMI, Regional Coordinator of Region II, December 9, 1993. For a prelim draft report to New Visions Commission naming the churches and subcommittee members of Region II see: Letter of John Y. Pax to Region II-West side-Document Subcommittee in reference to Subcommittee meeting to be held on April 11, 1994, March 31, 1994. Subcommittee members of Region II were: John Pax, Ileana Cappuzzello, Charles Birdie, Gamaliel, F. Colon, Lucy Cullens, Nancy Starzynski, Kate Wolf, and Mike Mikos. Also see: *Minutes of Region II at Holy Angels Parish*, April 18, 1994; *Prelim Draft Report to New Visions Commission*, April 18, 1994; it included discussion of non-homogeneous grouping of parishes in Region II; How four parishes: Holy Angels, Holy Cross, Immaculate Conception, and Our Lady of Loretto embraced a Hispanic population; How St. Michael's, St. Anthony's and Holy Angels were serviced by priests of Religious Orders; How St. Louis Church was the Mother Church of the Diocese; How St. Joseph's Cathedral was the bishop's church, the seat of the diocese. It also included a discussion of how a West Side School could provide Catholic Educational possibilities. For acknowledgement of the reception of the final report from Region II see: Letter from Sister Regina Murphy to Mr. John Pax and Ms. Ileana Cappuzzello, May 31, 1994. Also see: *Minutes of Region II, General Meetings at Holy Angels Hall*, October 17, 1994, November 14, 1994, and December 12, 1994. Three models were proposed so as to keep all twelve churches open but spiritually serviced by nine priests, which was Sister Regina Murphy's statistical estimation for the year 2000. For the final outcome of the diocesan decisions regarding Region II see: John Pax, Chairman of New Visions Committee, *Report to St. Louis Parish Council*, January 1, 1995; *Minutes of New Visions Committee Meeting, Region II*, January 30, 1995; Letter and enclosures from John Y. Pax and Ileana Cappuzzello, co-

chairpersons of Region II, to Sister Regina Murphy, February 20, 1995; Letter to New Visions Committee from Rae Reines, president of the St. Louis Parish Council, January 25, 1995. The Parish Council did not endorse the recommendations of the New Visions Committee that St. Louis Church and Blessed Sacrament be serviced by one priest, and recommended that both would keep their identity. The finalized version repeating the February 20, 1995 recommendations, however, were sent to Sister Regina Murphy by John Pax and Ileana Cappuzzello on March 20, 1995; this was three months after the proposed implementation date originally set by the diocese. From the library of John Pax the following schedule of the beginnings of the St. Louis Parish Council was: October 21, 1993 and November 4, 1993, preliminary meetings on need of Parish Council to be held to get task of New Visions under way at St. Louis Church; December 4, 1993, self-assessment of New Visions and the Council Steering Committee of 18 members; January 11, 1994, February 12, 1994, and February 27, 1994, Draft the Council's Constitution and by-laws; March 5/6, 1994, speakers explain the Council to all the congregation at weekend Masses; March 12, 1994, attendance of interested persons was 35; March 17, 1994, nominees are taken for election to the first Council and biographies of candidates are distributed; March 23/24, 1994, Constitution and by-laws are ratified and 15 parishioners are elected for the first sustaining Parish Council; May 22, 1994, the first Council members are installed on the Vigil of Pentecost, Monsignor Schwinger approves reluctantly; March 29/30, 1995, the second set of elections takes place for seven open positions, there are 10 nominees. The second year of the Council is brought to full strength on May 21, 1995 with formal installation of all members, both new ones and repeaters. The Council is now well on its way to success. Members of the Parish Council as of May 21, 1995 were: Carolann Besch, Craig Coyne, Sam Fiorella, Jack Haber, Dr. John Zoll, Dung Ahn Tran, Michael Mikos, Joe Bullion, Beverly Bullion, Maggie Maloney-Scaduto, Robert McCarthy, Dick Pancamo, John Pax, Susan Peters, Rae Reines, and Msgr. Schwinger. Because of an unfortunate, off-handed, and uncomplimentary remark by Schwinger concerning Dung Ahn Tran's sister proposing a Vietnamese hymn for the choir, Dung Ahn Tran took his family out of the church. Sister Therese Marie replaced him when she returned from Brazil. During the Jubilee Year 2000, the members of the council were: Dr. John Zoll, Grant Violino, Mike Mikos, Melanie Luongo, Bill Fiden, Judy Perkowski, John Pax, Bart Siener, Sister Therese Marie, Rose Kennedy, Kathryn Missert, Mike Riester, Jo Ann Decker, Bob McCarthy, Bridget Griffin, Linda Holben, and Cheryl Klass. Rae Reines was the president during the regional debate concerning New Visions and Judy Perkowski was the president when the pastorship exchanged hands between Msgr. Robert Mack and Msgr. Robert Cunningham. By the year 2000, besides the standing committees of Membership, Building and Grounds, Spiritual Life, Social Action, and Finance, the parish council directed the activities of the Garden Society, Historical Committee, Parish Life Committee, and Public Relations Committee. For Rae Reines's suggestions see: Rae Reines, President St. Louis Parish Council, *A*

Parish Dream, St. Louis Parish Council, Buffalo, NY, October 1995. Also see: Bernie Gerling, chairman of social action committee, *Memorandum: Some Thoughts, Ideas, and Reflections on a New Pastor*, October 24, 1995. *Letter to Rae Reines, President of the Parish Council* from Sam Fiorella, council member, October 22, 1995. For Msgr. David Lee's remarks see: Bob McCarthy and Sam Fiorella, eds., *St. Louis Parish Council Newsletter*, vol. 2, no.1, October 1995.

7. For Bishop Mansell celebrating Mass on August 27, 1995 and attending the annual picnic on the North Lawn of the church see: "Double Welcome," *St. Louis Church Bulletin*, August 26/27, 1995. For announcements and details of a retirement party for Monsignor Schwinger see: "And A Time To Retire," *St. Louis Church Bulletin*, September 16/17, 1995; "Retirement Dinner — November 5th" *St. Louis Church Bulletin*, October 7/8, 1995; Bob McCarthy and Sam Fiorella, editors, *St. Louis Parish Council Newsletter*, October 1995, vol. 2, no. 1; "Retirement Committee Update," *St. Louis Church Bulletin*, October 14/15, 1995; "Retirement Party Update," *St. Louis Church Bulletin*, October 21/22, 1995; "Retirement Party," *St. Louis Church Bulletin*, October 28/29, 1995; *Program of Mass On the Occasion of Monsignor William A, Schwinger's Retirement as Pastor of St. Louis Church*, Published by the Parish Council, Rae Reines, Chairperson, November 5, 1995; "The Noonday Mass of Thanksgiving," *St. Louis Church Bulletin*, November 11/12, 1995; "Final Words of Gratitude From Monsignor Schwinger," *St. Louis Church Bulletin*, November 18/19, 1995. Conditions found at St. Louis Church when Monsignor Mack arrived as pastor see: Diocese of Buffalo Priests' Personnel Board, *Conditions at St. Louis Church*, October 1995. It gave statistics and comments on the following topics: Composition, Liturgy, Sacramental Preparation, Parish Council, Parish Staff, Organizations, Apostolate to the Sick, Ecumenical Activity, Buildings, Financial, Statistics on Baptisms, First Communions, Marriages, and Funerals, and New Visions Status. For type of pastor desired by the Parish Council see: Letter of Sam Fiorella to Rae Reines, Chairperson, October 22, 1995; Memorandum to the St. Louis Church Council from Bernie Gerling, Chair, Social Action Committee, Re: Some Thoughts, Ideas, Reflections on a New Pastor, October 24, 1995; Rae Reines, President, St. Louis Parish Council, *A Parish Dream*, October 1995. Michael Riester, co-editor, made the following entry: "In 1997, while Monsignor Mack was pastor, a committee of parishioners was formed to identify the religious education needs of St. Louis' parish. The committee comprised Michael Riester, Rae Reines, Carolann Besch, Linda Holben, and Andrew Mattle (a recruit from St. Joseph's University Church). Five young men and women as well as seven adults were identified as needing the Sacrament of Confirmation. After consultation with the Catholic Center, an 18-month instructional program was planned. The sacrament was celebrated at noon on Sunday April 26, 1998 by Bishop Bernard McLaughlin, who in his homily made a commentary on the words in the program which were, " St Louis Parish, 1829-1998; into the new millennium, serving God's people." A reception followed the ceremonies. Those who received the sacrament were: Linda Carbone, Claire A. Coyne, Michael Hall, Carolyn Hunter, Carolyn Huonker, Kyle Krawczyk, Thomas Krug, Alexander Sahlen, Joseph Sahlen, Jennifer Scholl, Martin Scholl, and Lindsay Violino. This is the first time that this sacrament had been celebrated at St. Louis Church since the 1950's. In many ways it demonstrated that the parish not only had religious education needs but that it could recruit and sustain volunteers to plan and execute a program designed to meet the diverse needs of the parish." For background on Monsignor Mack see: "Paradise Means Basking in the Love of God," Sermon by Monsignor Mack, *Buffalo News*, January 6, 2002. For other sermon topics discussed see: "Max Facts," *St. Louis Church Bulletin*, during the years that he was pastor. During Mack's time as pastor the activities of the Parish Council such as Bake Goods Sales, Christmas Parties, Wreath Sales, Coffee and Doughnut Gatherings were told to the author/editor by Joseph and Beverly Bullion, Jack and Arline Hoyt, and Michael Riester. For celebration of the Jubilee Year at St. Louis Church see: "Jubilee Celebration for Our Vicariate," *St. Louis Church Bulletin*, August 19/20, 2000; *Northwest Buffalo Vicariate Celebration*, St. Louis Church, Buffalo, New York, August 24, 2000; the Vicariate of Northwest Buffalo was composed of 22 parishes and 14 institutions with Rev. Paul R. Bossi as the Episcopal Vicar. Most Rev. Henry J. Mansell, Bishop of Buffalo, *Decree Designating St. Louis Church, Buffalo, As a Pilgrimage Site for the Jubilee Year*, December 8, 1999. For remodeling of the Church during Mack's pastorate see: *St. Louis Parish Council Newsletter*, Fall 1999; the ramp project alone cost $85,000. For the presentation of St. Louis Church with $250,000 from the Federal Government see: "The Jewel of Main Street," *The Buffalo News*, Sunday, June 17, 2001. For the visitation of the Le Couteulx family to Buffalo see: "Unbroken Family Ties," *Buffalo News*, Friday, July 20, 2001. Short biographies of the candidates for the Parish Council were supplied to the author/editor by Mike Mikos and dated March 15, 1994. These listings also include the contribution that each candidate would bring to the administration if elected. Mike Mikos also supplied another list of Parish Council Nominees including the goals they expected for St. Louis Church once the Council was organized in 1994 and 1995. Biographical Material of Rose Kennedy was taken from Letter of Rose S. Kennedy to Professor C. Eugene Miller, August 24, 2002. Biographical Material of Sister Therese Marie was obtained from an interview with her by the author/editor at the Rainbow K. Kindergarten, August 29, 2002 and from Sister Mary Neves, *The Missionary Sisters of Our Lady of Mercy*, pamphlet distributed from 388 Franklin Street, Buffalo, New York, 14202. Biographies of St. Louis Church Choir Members were obtained by Dona M. Vasey, collated, and given to the author/editor on Sunday, September 1, 2002. Michael Riester obtained information on the Catholic Academy of West Buffalo from Louise M. Myszka, Supervising Principal. There are two campuses. One, the former Cathedral School, at 1069 Delaware Avenue, 14209 (Grades 3-8) and the other, the former Annunciation School, at 279 Lafayette Avenue, 14213 (Grades Pre-K to Grade 2). Present enrollment is 312, however, Myszka says

that there are 400 students from outside the region as well as from the original 11 parishes. Sponsoring Parishes are: St. Joseph's Cathedral, Annunciation, St. Anthony of Padua, Blessed Sacrament, Holy Angels, Holy Cross, Immaculate Conception, St. Louis, St. Michael, Nativity of the Blessed Virgin Mary, and Our Lady of Loretto. School was founded in 1988. Cost per student/year is $2,200 as compared to Public School that is cost per student/year of $7,600. The amount is paid by tuition of $975/year, financial support of the 11 parishes, Home-School Association fundraisers, and private donations. Students from St. Louis Church who have gone through the programs since 1990 are: (From Buffalo) Shaterrria Aultman, Annabel Almazan, Eugene Almazan, Milessa Bonner, Joseph Bonner, Derek Brennen, Anai Clark, Sarah Draper, William Dorsey, Jessica Dorsey, Paul Dorsey, Jacob Foss, Gabriella Gambino, Jason Hall, Michael Hall, Kevin Henry, George Kirkendoll, Sterling Lee, Lyle Nowak, Casey Nowak, Long Nguyen, Quynh Nguyen, James Peruzzini, Carmen Sample, Nicole Smith. (From Kenmore) Nicholas Orrange, Samantha Orrange. (From Lackawanna) Catherine Wyatt, Rhianna Wyatt. For Monsignor Mack's retirement see: "Mack's Facts—Max Fax," *St. Louis Church Bulletin*, September 8/9, 2001; "Mack's Facts—Max Fax," *St. Louis Church Bulletin*, September 15/16, 2001; Joel A. Giambra, Erie County Executive, *Proclamation, County of Erie, Executive Chamber*, January 4, 2002. This document gave the reasons for the County Executive to proclaim Sunday January 6, 2002 as *Monsignor Robert Mack Day*. A copy of this proclamation was obtained by Marie Buchheit Miller from Joel Giambra and given to the author/editor. For a review of Monsignor Mack's financial kudos see: *St. Louis Church Financial Statements*, for years 1995-2002. Since the year 2000, the following have been faithful in the weekend liturgy. *Lectors*: Jim Pieczynski, Dr. John Zoll, Roger Beamer, Dave Paschall, Wendy Mistretta, Joe Sahlen, John Pax, Mike Mikos, Michelle Cefaratti, Nicole Tzetzo, Richard Morrison, and Gary Romyak. *Eucharistic Ministers*: Dorothy Schneggenburger, John Farrell, Ted Guzowski, Mary Guzowski, Doctor Raymond Gibbons, Dr. John Zoll, Paul Schrems, Linda Holben, Jo Ann Decker, Carolann Besch, Judy Perkowski, Nancy Pax, John Pax, Maryann Petrella, Bridget Griffin Russo, Angela Esquilin, Joseph Marasi, Suellen Brewster, Susan Borodzik, Bart Siener, and Rae Reines. These names were taken from the *St. Louis Church Bulletin*, for the years 2000, 2001, and 2002. Dolores Vasi provided the names of the altar servers upon request of Marie Buchheit Miller. They are Joelle Luongo, Daniel McCarthy, Thomas O'Connor, Matthew O'Shea, and Jonathan Vasey. The discussion of the story-line for Anna Beck was gleaned from all material such as letters, newsclippings, and court papers supplied to the author/editor by Jack and Arline Hoyt, parishioners of St. Louis Church, close friends of Anna and Veronica Beck, and

defenders of Anna's right to have her will probated properly. The full story can be found in the following sources of which the author/editor had access; see: Agnes Palazetti, "The City vs. Anna Beck, *Buffalo News*, Sunday, May 3, 1998; Herbert Hoegel, "Why Have A Will If Wishes Can Be Ignored?" Letter to the Editor, *Buffalo News*, Monday, May 11, 1998; Floyd Baker, "Why Bother With a Will?" Letter to the Editor, *Buffalo News*, May 15, 1998; Mike Vogel, "Deceased Women's Estate Wins Fight to Demolish Home," *Buffalo News*, July 3, 1998; Agnes Palazzetti, "Council Votes to Delay House Razing," *Buffalo News*, Wednesday, July 22, 1998; Agnes Palazzetti, "Beck House Demolition Order Challenged," *Buffalo News*, August, 27, 1998; Letter of Arline M. Hoyt to John M. Laping, Chairman of the Buffalo Preservation Board, November 2, 1998, The letter states that the house should be destroyed; it has no historic significance, Anna's will was valid and she was mentally clear when she made it, the description of the house making it valuable was in error, and the house was formerly scheduled for demolition in 1973; Agnes Palazzetti, "Denial of Landmark Status Aids Cause of Estate," *Buffalo News*, Friday, November 6, 1998; Carolyn Thompson, "Dying Wish Denied," *Tribune Chronicle*, Ohio, Sunday, December 6, 1998; Carolyn Thompson, "Sides Shift in Tug of War Over Old House," *The Honolulu Advertiser*, Sunday, December 20, 1998; Carolyn Thompson, "Even In Death Woman Fights Buffalo, " *The Detroit News*, Tuesday, December 29, 1998; Letter of Richard J. Shanley, Cheektowaga, New York, Banker and Friend of Anna Beck, sent to Honorable Mayor Masiello, December 30, 1998, it favors demolition of Anna's cottage and states formidable reasons; Harold McNeil, "Council Fails to Act on Saving Cottage," *Buffalo News*, December 30, 1998, it is in an article titled "Allendale;" Phil Fairbanks, "Council Vote Clears Way for Demolition of Beck House," *Buffalo News*, January 13, 1999. In this article one sees that to the very end David A. Franczyk wanted the house declared a landmark. His aide James Brem said he wanted to buy the house. On Tuesday, January 12, 1999, the Buffalo Preservation Board disagreed with Franczyk and the Common Council dropped all appeals that the building should remain intact; Fax Letter from firm of Kennedy, Stoeckl, and Martin to Rev. Msgr. Robert Mack, January 14, 1999, notifying him that the demolition permit would be applied for because the City had withdrawn its appeal; Letter from David R. Hayes, Assistant Corporate Counsel, City of Buffalo, Dept. of Law, to Arline M. Hoyt, January 21, 1999, stated that since the Common Council had approved of demolition and that since it had taken place on January 20, 1999, there was no need to involve Mayor Masiello any further. His intercession was unnecessary; *The St. Louis Church Bulletin*, February 7, 1999, states that the Beck House is gone, Thanks are due to Jack and Arline Hoyt for their hard work in bringing about a settlement.

Bibliography

The literature sources cited in each category below are not in alphabetical order but are listed in the order that they first appear in the narrative. Specific elaboration of the information as taken from each source and used in the narrative is given in the references and notes that follow each chapter.

BOOKS

1. Thomas Bokenkotter, *A Concise History of the Catholic Church*, Revised and Expanded Edition, Image Books, Doubleday, New York, NY, 1990.
2. Richard P. McBrien, *Encyclopedia of Catholicism*, Harper Collins, New York, NY, 1995,
3. Michael P. Fogarty, *Christian Democracy in Western Europe, 1820-1953,* London, England,1957.
4. A. H. McDannald, Editor-in-Chief, *The Modern Encyclopedia*, W.H. Wise and Co., New York, NY, 1935.
5. Francis J. Reynolds, Editor-in-Chief, *World's Popular Encyclopedia*, The World Syndicate Publishing Co., New York, NY, 1937, 10 vols.
6. Harold J. Blum, Exec. Editor, *Illustrated World Encyclopedia*, The National Lexicographic Board, Woodbury, NY, 1970, 21 vols.
7. R.R. Palmer and Joel Colton, *A History of the Modern World Since 1815,* Alfred Knopf, New York, NY, 5th edition, 1978.
8. Richard Shaw, *John Dubois, Founding Father*, United States Catholic Historical Society, Yonkers, NY, and Mount St. Mary's College, Emmitsburg, MD, 1983.
9. Richard Shaw, *Dagger John, The Unquiet Life and Times of Archbishop John Hughes of New York*, Paulist Press, New York, NY, 1977.
10. C. Eugene Miller and Forrest Steinlage, *Der Turner Soldat; A Turner Soldier in the Civil War; Germany to Antietam*, Calmar Publications, Louisville, KY, 1988.
11. James R. Bayley, *A Brief Sketch of the Early History of the Catholic Church on the Island of Manhattan*, New York, NY, 1870.
12. Peter Guilday, *The Life and Times of John Carroll*, New York, NY, 1922, vol. 2.
13. Sister Mary Agnes McCann, *The History of Mother Seton's Daughters*, New York, NY, 1917, vol. 1.
14. Ronen John Murtha, *The Life of the Most Reverend Ambrose Marechal*, Ann Arbor, MI, 1975.
15. C. Eugene Miller, Gen. Editor, *Good Shepherd, The Church on the Canal, 1847-1997*, Good Shepherd Roman Catholic Church Society, Pendleton, NY, 1997.
16. Richard C. Brown and Bob Watson, *Buffalo: Lake City in Niagara Land*, Windsor Publication, Buffalo, NY, 1981.
17. Mark Goldman, *High Hopes, The Rise and Decline of Buffalo, New York*, State University of New York Press, Albany, NY, 1983.
18. *Andenken Hockw. Herrn Joh. Nik. Mertz einem der ersten deutschen Priester der Ver. Staaten und ersten Mission-Priester von Buffalo, N.Y., Kath. Volks-Ztg,* Baltimore, MD, 1868.
19. Glen Atwell and Ronald Elmer Batt, *The Chapel: A Comprehensive History of the Chapel and Pilgrimage of Our Lady Help of Christians, Cheektowaga, New York and the Alsatian Immigrant Community at Williamsville, New York*, The Holling Press Inc., Buffalo, NY, 1981.
20. J. Berger, *Leben und Wirken des hochseligen Johannes Nep. Neumann, C.S.S.R., Bischofs von Philadelphia*, New York, NY, 1883.
21. Ratzinger, Joseph, Imprimi Potest for Interdicasterial Commission, *Catechism of the Catholic Church*, Liguori Publications, Liguori, MI, 1992.
22. Philip Becker, *History of Germans of Buffalo and Erie County*, Verlag und Druck von Reinecke and Zesch, Buffalo, NY, 1898.
23. Thomas Donohue, *History of the Catholic Church in Western New York*, Buffalo: Catholic Historical Publishing Inc., 1904.
24. *Andenken an den hochwuerdigen herrn Alexander Pax*, Buffalo Deutschen Press, Translation by Victor Pax; *Un Centenaire: Un pretre lorrain en Amerique:*

Bibliography

Alexander Pax, 1799-1874.

25. Charles G. Deuther, *The Life and Times of Rt. Rev. John Timon, D.D.*, Deuther Press, Buffalo, NY, 1870.

26. Martha J. F. Murray, *Memoire of Stephen Louis Le Couteulx de Chaumont*, Publication of the Buffalo Historical Society, Buffalo, NY, 1906.

27. J. David Valaik et. al., *Celebrating God's Life in Us, The Catholic Diocese of Buffalo, 1847-1997*, The Heritage Press, Western New York Heritage Institute, Buffalo, NY, 1997.

28. Sister Mary Ramona Mattingly, *The Catholic Church on the Kentucky Frontier 1785-1812*, Catholic University of America, Studies in American Church History, vol.25, Washington, D.C., 1936.

29. Goldman, Mark, *The Rise and Decline of Buffalo, New York*, State University of New York Press, Albany, NY, 1933.

30. Shadler, F.J., *The Beauties of the Catholic Church*, Frederick Pustet & Co., Cincinnati, OH, 1881.

31. Deharbe, Joseph S.J., *L'Arge Catechism*, Benziger Brothers, Cincinnati, OH, 1921.

32. Martos, Joseph, *Doors to the Sacred*, Triumph Books, Liguori, MI, 1991.

33. Maps and articles on towns, cities, villages, and environment in Baden-Wuerttemberg, Germany, Gerd Doerr, *Baden-Wuerttemberg*, Baden-Wuerttembergische Bank, Hamburg, Germany, 1995.

34. Mark M. Boatner III, *The Civil War Dictionary*, Vantage Books, New York, NY, 1988.

35. *Buffalo of Today, Queen City of the Lakes*, Interstate Publishing Co., Buffalo, NY, 1898.

36. H. Perry Smith, *History of the City of Buffalo and Erie County, 1620-1884*, D. Mason and Co., Syracuse, NY, 1882, vol. 2.

37. Rev. Thomas Donohue D.D., *History of the Diocese of Buffalo*, The Buffalo Catholic Publication Co., Buffalo, NY, 1929.

38. Rev. Hugo H. Hoever, *St. Joseph's Daily Missal*, Catholic Book Co., New York City, N.Y., 1957.

39. Metcalf, Robert, and Metcalf, Gertrude, *Making Stained Glass*, McGraw-Hill Book Company, New York, NY, 1972.

40. Isenberg , Anita and Seymour, *How to Work in Stained Glass*, Chilton Book Company, Philadelphia, PA, 1972.

41. Irwin, Stevens, *Dictionary of Pipe Organ Stops*, G. Schirmer, Inc., New York, NY, 1962.

42. Barnes, William Harrison, *The Contemporary American Organ*, J. Fisher and Bros., Harrison Road, Glen Rock, NJ, 1959.

43. Leon Aroz F.S.C., etal, with an English translation by Luke Salm F.S.C., *Beginnings: De La Salle and His Brothers*, Christian Brothers National Office, Romeoville, IL, 1980.

44. Battersby, W.J., *De La Salle: A Pioneer of Modern Education*, Longmans, Green and Co., London, England, 1949.

45. Immaculata S.S.J., *Like a Swarm of Bees*, Society of St. Paul, Derby, NY, 1957.

46. Dunne, M.A. S.S.J., (Sister Mary of the Sacred Heart), *A Brief Account of Its Origin and Work: The Congregation of St. Joseph of the Diocese of Buffalo*, Holling Press, Buffalo, NY, 1934.

47. Germain Bazin, *A History of Art: From Prehistoric Times to the Present*, Bonanza Books, New York, NY, 1950.

48. Daniel J. Sweeney, *History of Buffalo and Erie County, 1914-1919*, Committee of One Hundred, Finley H. Greene, Chairman, Under Authority of the City of Buffalo,NY, July 4, 1919.

49. Henry B. Laudenbach, *Little Stories of Buffalo's Bishops*, Catholic Pamphlet Society, Buffalo, NY, 1939.

50. Ketchum, Katherine, *Under the Influence*, Bantam Books, New York, NY, 1983.

51. Powell, Stephen, R., *Rushing the Growler, A History of Brewing in Buffalo*, Apogee Publications, Buffalo, NY, 1999.

52. Schlesinger Jr., Arthur, M., *The Politics of Upheaval*, Houghton Mifflin Co., Boston, Riverside Press, Cambridge, MA, 1960.

53. *Architecture: A Guide*, Buffalo Architectural Guide Book Corporation, The MIT Press, Cambridge, MA, 1982.

54. Gerald Carson, *The Social History of Bourbon*, Dodd, Meade, and Co., New York, NY. 1963.

55. Costello, Gabriel F.S.C., *Arches of the Years*, Manhattan College, Riverdale, NY , 1980.

56. Province of New York, *Buffalo Centennial Eucharistic Congress: 1847-1947*, Holling Press, Buffalo, NY, 1947.

57. *Latvia 1918-1958*, Latvian Legation, Washington, D.C., 1958, Action Printing Company, U.S.A.

58. *Communist Takeover and Occupation of Latvia*, House of Representatives, 83rd Congress, 2nd Session, H. Res. 346, 438, Dec. 30, 1954, United States Govt. Printing Office, House Report No. 2684, Part 1.

59. Empire State News Corporation, *Street Guide of Greater Buffalo and Niagara Falls*, Interstate Publishing Company, Boston, MA., 1960.

60. Howard Zinn, *Peoples History of the United States*, Harper Perennial, A division of Harper Collins Publishers, New York, NY, 1990.

61. Zollman, *American Church Law*, West Publishing Company, St. Paul, MI, 1933. Case of *Lawyer v. Cipperly*, 7 Page 231, New York, 1838; Case of *Robertson v. Bullions*, 11, New York, 243, 1854; Case of *Petty v. Tooker*, 21, New York, 267, 1860.

62. Dignan, *A History of the Legal Incorporation of the Catholic Church in the United States*, Kennedy Pub. New York, NY, 1935.
63. Jones and Warwick, *Laws of the State of New York*, vol 1., New York, NY, 1789.
64. Jones and Warwick, *Laws of the State of New York, 1812-1813*, vol. 2., Albany, NY, 1813.
65. *Consolidated Laws of the State of New York*, Vol. 2., Albany, NY, 1909.
66. *Laws of the State of New York passed at the Eighty-sixth Session of the Legislature*, Albany, NY, 1863.
67. Farley, *The Life of Cardinal McCloskey*, New York, NY, 1918.
68. *A History of Legal Incorporation of the Catholic Church in the United States*.
69. *General Laws of New York*, vol. 1., Albany, NY, 1895.
70. *Laws of the State of New York*, vol. 1.
71. *Laws of the State of New York, 1812-1813*, vol. 2.
72. The National Renew Service Team, *Renew Guidelines, Thoughts and Renew, A Proven and Effective Way to Vitalize Spirituality in Your Diocese/Parish*, Paulist Press, Ramsey, NJ, 1982.

JOURNALS

1. John Bossy, "the Counter-Reformation and The Catholic People of Europe," *Past and Present, 1970.*
2. Rev. H.J. Schroeder, *Canons and Decrees of the Council of Trent,* St. Louis, MO, 1941.
3. L. Pfleger, "Untersuchungen zur Geschicte des Pfarrei-Institute in Elsass," 3 parts, "Die Einkommensquellen, i. Das Kirchenvermoegen," part 3, *Archiv fuer Elsassiche Kirchengeschicte* VIII (1932): 14.
3. Andre Schaer, "Le Chapitre Rural Ultra Colles Ottinis en Haute-Alsac, Aprcs La Guerre de Trente Ans Jusque a La Revolution. La Vie Paroissale dans Un Doyen Alsacien D'Ancien Regime (1648-1789)," *Archv. de L'Eglise D'Alsace,* XVI (new series), 1967-68.
4. Robert R. Palmer, *The School of the French Revolution,* Princeton, NJ, 1975.
5. Sarah Trainer Smith, "Philadelphia's First Nun," *Records of the American Catholic Historical Society of Philadelphia,* 1894, vol. 5.
6. *Historical Records and Studies*, New York, NY, 1909, vol. 5.
7. Letter of John Dubois Bishop of New York, *Annals of the Association for the Propagation of the Faith,* Lyon, Rusand, 1830, vol. 4.
8. Andrew P. Yox, "The Parochial Context of Trusteeism: Buffalo's St. Louis Church, 1828-1855," *Catholic Historical Review*, 1976.
9. Robert F. McNamara, "Trusteeism in the Atlantic States 1785-1863," *The Catholic Historical Review,* Vol. XXX, July 1944, no. 2.
10. George Krim S.J., "Diary of Fathers Fritsch, Frizzini, Kettner, and Ebner, 1848-51," *Canisius Monthly,* Canisius College Publication, Buffalo, NY, 1915-16.
11. Rev. Laurence Kenny, "The Gallipolis Colony," *Catholic Historical Review*, vol. 4, 1918-19.
12. "Dedication of St. Michael's Church," Leaves of An Old Diary, *Canisius Monthly*, 1916.
13. "On Arthur Grupp, Trustee at St. Louis Church," *Canisius College Chronicle*, October, 1984.
14. "On Marie Faber Grupp, Trustee at St. Louis Church," *Nardin Today,* Winter, 1995.
15. *Fest Zeitung fuer das 23ste Nord Amerikanische Saengerfest*, Buffalo, NY, August 23, 1883, no. 20.
16. Biography of Otto Rick, and etal: *History of Niagara Frontier.*
17. *Crusader's Almanac*, Franciscan Monastery, Washington D.C., October 1, 1944, vol. LIII, No.1.
18. " The Soviet Occupation and Incorporation of Latvia: June 17 to Aug, 5, 1940," *The Baltic Review*, New York, NY, 1957.
19. Voldemars, R.H. and Vicis, K.M., *We Accuse the East; We Warn the West*, Dzintarzeme and Scholar, Germany, 1948; Dr. A. Trimakas, chief ed., *The Baltic Review*, New York, October, 1962., No. 25.
20. Walter G. Young, "Buffalo City of Good Neighbors," *Catholic Digest*, March 1960.
21. McNamara, "Trusteeism in the Atlantic States, 1785-1863," *Catholic Historical Review*, XXX, 1944.
22. *The Ecclesiastical Review*, XLV, 1911.
23. Bouscaren, *Canon Law Digest*, Bruce Publishing, Milwaukee, WI, vol. 2., 1943.
24. McNamara, Robert F., *Catholic Historical Review*, XX, 1944.
25. Philip J. Murnion, "Parish Renewal," *America*, April 24, 1982.
26. James R. Kelly, "Does the Renew Program Renew?" *America*, March 7, 1987.
27. *Renew What's Wrong With It? A Wanderer Supplement*, Wanderer Press, St. Paul, MI, 1985.
28. Ellen Jean Klein, "Collaborate or Close," *Today's Parish*, March 8, 1994.
29. Harry W. Paige, "Abandoned Churches," *Liguorian*, June 1994.

MANUSCRIPT COLLECTIONS

1. J. Berger C.SS.R., *Theodore Noethen Report*, Berger Papers, Redemptorist Archives of Baltimore

Bibliography

Province—Neumann section, Brooklyn, NY, 1833.

2. George Zimpfer *History of the Roman Catholic Parish of Sts. Peter and Paul, From the Origins to 1928*, Archives of the Sts. Peter and Paul Church, Williamsville, NY, 1928.

3. St. Louis Dramatic Circle, *Anniversary Souvenir and Programme of St. Louis Dramatic Circle*, St. Louis Church Archives, 1896.

4. Robert T. Bapst, *One Hundred and Twenty Fifth Anniversary, St. Louis Church, 1829-1954*, St. Louis Church Archives, 1954.

5. *Records of the Trustees' Meetings at St. Louis Church*, Archives of the St. Louis Church, Buffalo, NY, Feb., 12, 1843.

6. *Records of the American Catholic Historical Society of Philadelphia*, vol.19, 1908.

7. Archival sources concerning Badin's life and his activities in Kentucky and the Old Northwest are:
   a) Loretto Motherhouse, Nerinckx, Kentucky; an original of op. cit. *Origine et Progress* are kept there.
   b) Nazareth Motherhouse, Nazareth, Kentucky. The Sisters at this establishment have a large collection of Badin's letters, newspaper clippings, and Catholic Church history of the early days of Kentucky. c) The University of Notre Dame, South Bend, Indiana, a complete set of the *Badin Papers*.

8. Severance, Frank, ed., *Publications of the Buffalo and Erie County Historical Society*.

9. Riester, Michael, *The 167th Anniversary History of St. Louis Church*, St. Louis Church Archives.

10. *Abstract of Title to Property in Pendale, Pendleton, New York, No. 93-04643*, Ticor Guarantee Company, Buffalo, NY, 1993.

11. "A List of Early Members of St. Louis Church," *Program for St. Louis Commandery 204*, Elmwood Music Hall, October 27, 1925.

12. Genealogical Studies of the Miller Family by Urban Lehner, Grand Rapids, Michigan, 1985.

13. Genealogical Studies of the Miller Family by Alice Grupp Miller, Buffalo, NY, 1990-2000.

14. Genealogical Studies of the Miller Family by Joseph Kellas, West Seneca, NY, 1985.

15. Early marriage records of both Germans and Irish, *Marriage Book I, 1829-1839*, St. Louis Church Archives.

16. St. Louis Church File in the Buffalo and Erie County Historical Society, Buffalo, NY.

17. *Minutes of the Board of Trustees of St. Louis Church, 1838-1874, Book 1,* Archives of St. Louis Church.

18. Chrisfield Johnson, *Centennial, History of Erie County, New York*, Printing House of Matthews and Warren, Office of the *Buffalo Commercial Advertiser*, 1876.

19. *Mass Foundations, Mass Bequests* Books II, III, IV, and V in St. Louis Church Archives.

20. *Minutes, United German and French Roman Catholic Cemetery, organizational meeting at St. Mary's School House, February 21, 1859*, copies of the minutes are in the Mount Calvary Cemetery Archives, Buffalo, NY.

21. *One Hundred and Twenty-Fifth Anniversary: 1829-1954*, St. Louis Souvenir Book, October 3-6, 1954. Copy in the St. Louis Church Archives.

22. *Cash, St. Louis Church Building Fund, 1885-1886*, Copy in the St. Louis Church Archives.

23. *Men of the Time*, A Collection of Biographies and Portraits of citizens of the Empire State, Buffalo and Erie County Scrapbook Collection, Buffalo, N.Y.

24. *Solemn Commemoration of the Centenary of the Founding of St. Louis Church, Buffalo, New York, 1929*, copy in the St. Louis Church Archives.

25. *Financial Reports of the Trustees of Good Shepherd Church, 1889-1972*, Archives of Good Shepherd Church, Pendleton, NY.

26. *History of the Pendleton Mission*, Archives of Good Shepherd Church, Pendleton, NY.

27. *Minutes of the St. Louis Board of Trustees, 1909*, St. Louis Church Archives.

28. *Anniversary Souvenir and Program of the St. Louis Dramatic Circle*, Music Hall, Buffalo, NY, January 7, 1896.

29. *A Century of Service in the Woodworking Business*, E.M. Hager and Sons, 141 Elm Street, Buffalo, NY, 1968.

30. *Minutes of the St. Louis Church Trustees, January 1901 to October 1904*, St. Louis Church Archives.

31. *Minutes of the Board of Trustees of St. Louis* Church, *February 2, 1863*.

32. *Specifications, Details of Construction, Contract*, W.W. Kimball Co., Chicago, IL., Nov. 5, 1902.

33. *Tellers Organ Company Contract for Teller's opus 781*, copy in the St. Louis Church Archives.

34. On the Dramatic Circle: Buffalo and Erie County Public Library, *Special Collections File*, and at the Buffalo and Erie County Historical Research Library.

35. Genealogical Studies of Edmond Sendker, Pendleton, New York, June 2001, on the Sendker family who were participators in the Dramatic Circle's plays.

36. Collection of memorabilia from the Dramatic Circle preserved by Michael Zobel Jr. intended for the Archives of St. Louis Church. It contains news articles, play programs, membership, actors and actress lists, and dates, names and places of productions.

37. For reference to Henry Hemmerlein, the Schulmeister, see op. cit. *Anniversary Souvenir and Programme of St. Louis Dramatic Circle: January 7, 1896*, p. 52.

38. Brother Eugene O'Gara, F.S.C., *The Community*

Register of St. Joseph's Collegiate Institute, Buffalo, NY; *Etat nominatif & statistique forms*. They are preserved in the archives of the Brothers in the Motherhouse in Rome, Italy; Personnel cards of individual Brothers. These cards are in the provincial headquarters of the New York District in Lincroft, NJ.

39. *Our Graduates, 1893 to 1959*, a book containing grades of the graduates. Original book is in the St. Louis Church Archives.

40. *Monument Dedication, Knights of St. John*, Second Regiment, State of New York, Buffalo, NY, May 31, 1914

41. Specific information concerning Commandery 204 at St. Louis Church: *Twenty-eighth Anniversary, St. Louis Commandery 204, Knights of St. John*, Knights of Columbus Ballroom, Buffalo, NY, October 28, 1941; "Golden Memories of Silver Years," *Silver Jubilee Commemorating 25th Anniversary, St. Louis Commandery, Knights of St. John*, Buffalo Trap and Field Club, Buffalo, NY, September 25, 1938; *Drill and Ball*, St. Louis' Commandery No. 204, Second Regiment, Knights of St. John, Elmwood Music Hall, Buffalo, NY, October 26, 1937; *Twentieth Anniversary, Souvenir Program, St. Louis' Commandery, No. 204, Knights of St. John*, Elmwood Music Hall, Buffalo, NY, 1933; *St Louis' Commandery No. 204, Fifteenth Anniversary Souvenir*, Elmwood Music Hall, Buffalo, NY, 1928; *St. Louis' Commandery No 204*, Elmwood Music Hall, Buffalo, NY, October 27, 1925; *St. Louis Commandery No. 204*, Elmwood Music Hall, Buffalo, NY, October 28, 1924. St.Louis Church archives.

42. *St. Louis Church Centennial Celebration*, Buffalo, NY, 1829-1929. St. Louis Church Archives.

43. The Hindenburg Celebration and Parade in Buffalo, Newspaper clippings contained in the St. Louis Church Archives.

44. In honor of Father Henry Laudenbach: *Minutes of the Regular Monthly Meeting of the Board of Trustees of St. Louis Church*, January 10, 1944.

45. During the Depression: *Minutes of the Board of Trustees of St. Louis Church, 1929-1936.*

46. *Affidavit and Notice of Motion*, Charles Feldman, The City of Buffalo, Plaintiff against Charles R. Day, Defendants in Condemnation Proceedings No. 106, New York Supreme Court: Erie County, City Hall, Buffalo, NY, November 25, 1932.

47. *Society of Christian Mothers, Pendleton, New York, Scapular Confraternity, 1886*. An original is in the archives of Good Shepherd Church, Pendleton, NY.

48. *A Souvenir Book: The 125th Anniversary of the Founding of St. Louis Church, Buffalo, New York, 1829-1954*, October 3, 1954. A copy is in the St. Louis Church Archives.

49. "Why Should I Become a Member…" *International Order of Alhambra*, 4200 Leeds Avenue, Baltimore, MD. Copy in the Archives of St. Louis Church.

50. A List of Alhambra Caravans with their Home Addresses supplied by the International Order of Alhambra on May 20, 2002. St. Louis Church Archives.

51. *New Community Mass*, Cantate Omnes Publications, Buffalo, NY, 1964.

52. *Program for the Sesquicentennial Dinner at the Statler Hotel*, August 25, 1979. Archives of St. Louis Church.

53. *Formal Opening of the St. Louis Church Historical Museum, 1829-1957*, September 29, 1957. Archives of St. Louis Church.

54. *Minutes of the Board of Trustees of St. Louis Roman Catholic Church of Buffalo, New York*, 35 Edward Street, October 9, 1979. Copies of the certificate of incorporation and by-laws are in the Archives of St. Louis Church.

55. On New Visions: Sister Regina Murphy, Pastoral Ministry Commission, A *Planning Process for Parish Life and Ministry in the Diocese of Buffalo*, Diocese of Buffalo, NY, Spring 1993.

56. *St. Louis Roman Catholic Church Financial Statements, 1979-2002*. Copies in the St. Louis Church Archives.

57. *Minutes of Region II at Holy Angels Parish*, April 18, 1994. St. Louis Church Archives.

58. *Prelim Draft Reports to New Visions Commission*: April 18, 1994; October 17, 1994; October 18, 1994; November 14, 1994; December 12, 1994. These documents are in the archives of Mike Mikos, St. Louis Church Archives.

59. Rae Reines, President St. Louis Parish Council, *A Parish Dream*, St. Louis Parish Council, Buffalo, NY, October 1995.

60. Bernie Gerling, chairman of social action committee, *Memorandum: Some Thoughts, Ideas, and Reflections on a New Pastor*, October 24, 1995.

61. *Program of Mass On the Occasion of Monsignor William A, Schwinger's Retirement as Pastor of St. Louis Church*, Published by the Parish Council, Rae Reines, Chairperson, November 5, 1995.

62. Diocese of Buffalo Priests' Personnel Board, *Conditions at St. Louis Church*, October 1995.

63. Joel A. Giambra, Erie County Executive, *Proclamation, County of Erie, Executive Chamber*, January 4, 2002.

64. *The Missionary Sisters of Our Lady of Mercy*, pamphlet distributed from 388 Franklin Street, Buffalo, NY, 14202.

65. Article on the Catholic Academy of West Buffalo by Louise M. Myszka, Supervising Principal.

Bibliography

NEWSPAPERS AND BULLETINS

1. *The St. Louis Bazar Chronicle*, October 22, 1888 to December 29, 1888; thirteen issues.
2. *The St. Louis Bazaar Herald*, September 17, 1900 to December 8, 1900; thirteen issues
3. "The Holland Land Company," *Buffalo Evening News*, October 3, 1953
4. "St. Louis Deed Valid," *Buffalo Express*, Aug., 12, 1914.
5. *Buffalo Daily Gazette*, October 19, 1843.
6. *Buffalo Commercial Advertiser*, August 10, 1844.
7. *The Buffalo News*, Thursday, August 15, 1996.
8. "The Holland Land Company," *Buffalo Evening News*, October 3, 1953.
9. Powell, Roland, "Were the Indians Given Fair Price for WNY? U.S. Reopens the Case," *Buffalo Evening News*, July 18, 1970.
10. "St. Cecilia's Celebrates Anniversary,"*Western New York Catholic*, July 1998.
11. Paul V. Hale Ph.D., "The Jesuits Downtown Church of Buffalo," *St. Michael's Church Bulletin*, June 3, 2001 and June 10, 2001.
12. "On Marie Faber Grupp," *The Buffalo News*, February 25, 1996.
13. "On Interdict, 1851-1855," *The Buffalo Morning Express*, June 21, 1851; June 24, 1851; June 28, 1851.
14. List of Trustees, 1851-1855, *The Buffalo Democrat*, July 26, 1851.
15. Alphonse Le Couteulx and his deed during Timon's tenure, *Catholic Union and Times*, January 23, 1913.
16. Interdiction at St. Louis Church, *The Buffalo Sentinel*, June 2, 1854.
17. Interdiction at St. Louis Church, *Taeglicher Buffalo Demokrat und Weltbueger*, June 7, 1854.
18. *Buffalo Commercial Advertiser*, June 29, 1855; August 8, 1889.
19. *Buffalo Express*, June 30, 1909; August 12, 1914; June 16, 1916.
20. *Buffalo Times*, January 13, 1915.
21. *Buffalo Evening News*, October 2, 1979.
22. Cemetery Activity in Buffalo: *Buffalo Express*, May 12, 1901, May 14, 1902, Nov. 20, 1902, Jan. 5, 1903, Feb. 26, 1903, Mar. 3, 1903; *Commercial Advertiser*, July 22, 1899; *Buffalo Evening News*, 1906, Mar. 14, 1906, Mar. 16, 1906, Mar. 17, 1906, Mar 21, 1906, Mar. 28, 1906, July 25, 1906, Aug. 12, 1906, Nov. 12, 1906, Nov 13, 1906, Nov. 12, 1907.
23. Newspaper articles on fire at the German Music Hall and St. Louis Church: *Buffalo Volksfreund*, March 27, 1885; *Buffalo Express*, March 27, 1885 and March 29, 1885.
28. Articles on Rev. Paul Hoelscher: *The Buffalo Echo*, Dec. 28, 1916 and Jan. 4, 1917.
29. Article on Rev. Joseph Sorg: *Catholic Union and Times*, October 4, 1888.
30. Article on Gerhard Lang: *The Buffalo Courier*, July 15, 1892.
31. Articles on Jonathan Scoville: *Buffalo Courier*, March 5, 1891, and *Buffalo Express*, January 1,1892.
32. Articles on Rev. Walter Fornes: *Union and Echo*, Feb. 25, 1945; *Buffalo News*, Feb. 23, 1945; *Amherst Bee*, Feb. 22, 1945.
33. "The St. Louis Church Pulpit," *Buffalo Courier Express*, May 26, 1968.
34. Articles on the organ at St. Louis Church, *Buffalo Commercial*, June 6, 1900; *The Courier*, September 9, 1900; *Buffalo Evening News*, May 2, 1901.
35. Concerning Louis H. Huybrechts, *Buffalo Evening News*, Oct. 30, 1952; *Buffalo Courier Express*, April 13, 1952.
36. On the Dramatic Circle: *The Buffalo Times, The Buffalo Courier Express, The Buffalo Commercial Advertiser*, and the *Buffalo Courier Express*, Buffalo, New York, January 15, 1950.
37. *Buffalo Times*, May 26, 1929.
38. Obituary of Father Edmund Dietzel, *Islan Dispatch*, April 28, 1989; *Western New York Catholic*, June 1989.
39. On closing the school: *Courier Express*, August 3, 1959.
40. Newspaper articles referring to the Brothers of the Christian Schools in Buffalo are: *Courier Express*, August 3, 1959; *The Express*, February 27, 1897; *Buffalo News*, January 20, 1950; *Buffalo News*, November 12, 1947; *Buffalo News*, October 12, 1946.
41. One Hundredth Anniversary of St. Louis Church: *Buffalo Evening News*, April 9, 1929; *Buffalo Evening News*, May 29, 1929; *Buffalo Times*, April 14, 1929; *The Echo*, May 30, 1929.
42. Concerning Father Henry B Laudenbach: *The Echo*, April 17, 1924; *The Buffalo Times*, March 31, 1935; *Buffalo Courier Express*, January 26, 1942; *Buffalo Evening News*, December 29, 1943; *Buffalo Courier Express*, January 3, 1944.
43. "Travel Letters" by Laudenbach: *The Echo,* May 29, 1924 (the Mediterranean), June 5, 1924 (Italy at First Glance), June 12, 1924 (Rome), June 19, 1924 (Churches of Rome), June 26, 1924 (Jungfrau in Bernice Oberland, Switzerland), July 3, 1924 (Geneva, Home of the League of Nations), July 10, 1924 (Southern Germany), July 17, 1924 (Germany Under Stress), July 24, 1924 (German Republic), July 31, 1924 (Germany Disarmed), August 7, 1924 (German politics), August 14, 1924 (Visits Rothenburg, Munich, Bamberg), August 28, 1924 (Palatinate), September 24, 1924 (Innsbruck,

Austria), October 2, 1924 (Thuringia, Germany), October 9, 1924 (London), October 16, 1924 (Ireland), and October 23, 1924 (Coming Home, Travel Survey).

44. Beginning of the Catholic Charities Appeal: *Courier Express*, September 28, 1942; *Buffalo Times*, October 14, 1942; *Buffalo Evening News*, October 14, 1942.

43. Anna Maria Born's Will: *Buffalo Courier Express*, April 30, 1930.

44. Concerning Father Michael A. Anstett: *Buffalo Courier Express*, September 24, 1948; *Buffalo Evening News*, September 23, 1948; *The Union an Echo*, September 24, 1948; *The Union and Echo*, October 1, 1948; *Buffalo Evening News*, February 4, 1949.

45. The Pearl Street Extension: *Buffalo Courier Express*, May 1, 1928; *Buffalo Courier Express*, May 18, 1928.

46. Concerning Father Howard J. Schwartz: *Buffalo Courier Express*, December 21, 1941; *Buffalo Evening News*, December 2, 1949; *Buffalo Courier Express*, December 5, 1949; *Buffalo Courier Express*, October 24, 1954; *Buffalo Courier Express*, May 28, 1959; *Buffalo Courier Express*, October 2, 1950; *Buffalo Evening News*, January 29, 1959; *Catholic Union and Echo*, March 3, 1964.

47. Concerning Father Robert T. Bapst: *Buffalo Courier Express*, December 18, 1951; *Buffalo Evening News*, December 17, 1951; *Buffalo Courier Express*, December 17, 1951; *The Evening Star*, January 2, 1952; *Washington Post*, January 2, 1952; *Los Angeles Examiner*, April 6, 1952; *Buffalo Evening News*, October 29, 1959.

48. For the 125th Anniversary Celebration of St. Louis Church: *Buffalo Evening News*, September 29, 1954; *Catholic Union and Echo*, October 3, 1954.

49. Dedication of the Landmark Stone at St. Louis Church by the Order of Alhambra: *Courier Express*, August 12, 1957.

50. *The Quadrangle*, Manhattan College, Bronx, NY, November 5, 1965 and March 11, 1966.

51. *The Spectrum*, University of Buffalo Student Publication, Spring 1967.

52. Concerning Father Alfred Mosack: *Western New York Catholic*, May 1984; *Buffalo Courier Express*, February 15, 1986; *Buffalo Evening News*, February 15, 1986, *Buffalo News*, February 20, 1969; *Buffalo Courier Express*, November 2, 1978; *Buffalo Courier Express*, November 3, 1978; *Buffalo Evening News*, December 3, 1978; *Buffalo News*, August 12, 1979; *Buffalo News*, August 26, 1979.

53. French Destroyer, *Duperre*, visits Buffalo: *Buffalo Courier Express*, July 14, 1976; *Buffalo Courier*

Express, July 21, 1976.

54. On St. Louis Church Sesquicentennial Celebration: *Western New York Catholic Visitor*, December 31, 1978; *Buffalo Courier* Express, September 23, 1979; Buffalo *News*, September 27, 1982; *Buffalo News*, July 29, 1984; *Buffalo News*, October 18, 1984 .

55. On transfer of the St. Louis Church Corporation to the Diocese of Buffalo: Paul Batt, "Historic St. Louis Church is Taken Over by Diocese," *Buffalo News, October 2, 1979*; "City Church Laymen Upset By Transfer," *Buffalo News*, October 2, 1979; Paul Batt, "Parishioners To Mull Suit in Transfer," *Buffalo News*, October 3, 1979. Also see: *Courier Express*, Tuesday, October 2, 1979.

56. Father Tom Maloney, "American Bishops Endorse Renew," *Western New York Catholic*, July, 1984.

57. "Local Parishes to Participate in National Renew Process," *Amherst Bee*, April 11, 1985.

58. Joan Bombarger, "Renew is Moving Forward in Lockport," *Union-Sun Journal*, April 29, 1985.

59. David Briggs, "Renew Will Prompt Catholics to Live Their Faith," with pictures of Rev. Thomas Maloney, Sister Louise Alff, and Ellen Rose, The *Buffalo News*, Saturday, August 31, 1985.

60. Bishop Edward D. Head, "My Personal Experience," *Western New York Catholic*, January 1985.

61. "Young People Find Something Special in Renew Sharing Groups," *Western New York Catholic*, December 1986.

62. David Briggs, "Panel of Catholic Bishops Commends Renew Program," *The Buffalo News*, Wednesday, December 31, 1986.

63. Advertisement on Renew, *Buffalo News*, December 22, 1986.

64. Father Thomas Maloney, "Renew Action Groups Respond to Hungry People," *Western New York Catholic*, January 1987.

65. Don Esmonde, "A Kind Word, and a Sandwich, for the Outcasts," *The Buffalo News*, Sunday, December 10, 1995.

66. David Briggs, "Bishops' Changes in Renew Aren't Due until Fall," *The Buffalo News*, Saturday, February, 21, 1987.

67. Louis H. Pumphrey, "Renew," *Catholic Universe Bulletin*, June 5, 1987.

68. David Briggs, "Renew Ends Amid Calls to Extend It," *The Buffalo News*, Saturday, January 16, 1988.

69. David Briggs, "Group Aims to Lure Catholics from Church," *The Buffalo News*, Sunday, March 29, 1987.

70. Richard A. Maussner, "Renew Facts vs. 'Renew,' *Metro Community News*, Tuesday, October 1, 1985, vol. 8, no. 6.

71. Sharon Johnson, "Renew Program Debated by WNY

Catholics, *Niagara Gazette*, November 1985.

72. "Letters to the Editor," *Metro Community News*, September 17, 1985. *St. Louis Church Parish Bulletin*, October 7/8, 1995.

73. On Father William A. Schwinger: *Buffalo Courier Express*, September 23, 1979; *Buffalo Courier Express*, July 6, 1981; *The Buffalo News*, June 8, 1980; *Courier Express*, July 15, 1980; *St. Louis Church Bulletin*, July 4/5, 1980.

74. On New Visions: Dave Condren, "Buffalo Diocese Faced With Aging Clergy, Dwindling Ordinations," *The Buffalo News*, Sunday, May 2, 1993.

75. Dave Condren, "Four East Side Catholic Parishes to Close," *The Buffalo News*, Sunday, May 23, 1993.

76. Bob McCarthy and Sam Fiorella, eds., *St. Louis Parish Council Newsletter*, vol. 2, no.1, October 1995.

77. "Double Welcome," *St. Louis Church Bulletin*, August 26/27, 1995.

78. "And A Time To Retire," *St. Louis Church Bulletin*, September 16/17, 1995.

79. "Retirement Dinner —November 5th" *St. Louis Church Bulletin*, October 7/8, 1995.

80. "Retirement Committee Update," *St. Louis Church Bulletin*, October 14/15, 1995.

81. "Retirement Party Update," *St. Louis Church Bulletin*, October 21/22, 1995.

82. "Retirement Party," *St. Louis Church Bulletin*, October 28/29, 1995.

83. "The Noonday Mass of Thanksgiving," *St. Louis Church Bulletin*, November 11/12, 1995.

84. "Final Words of Gratitude From Monsignor Schwinger," *St. Louis Church Bulletin*, November 18/19, 1995.

85. *St. Louis Church Bulletin*, for the years 2000, 2001, and 2002.

86. On Monsignor Robert Mack: "Paradise Means Basking in the Love of God," Sermon by Monsignor Mack, *Buffalo News*, January 6, 2002; "Max Facts," *St. Louis Church Bulletin;* "Jubilee Celebration for Our Vicariate," *St. Louis Church Bulletin*, August 19/20, 2000; *Northwest Buffalo Vicariate Celebration*, St. Louis Church, Buffalo, New York, August 24, 2000; *St. Louis Parish Council Newsletter*, Fall 1999; "The Jewel of Main Street," *The Buffalo News*, Sunday, June 17, 2001. "Unbroken Family Ties," *Buffalo News*, Friday, July 20, 2001.

87. "Mack's Facts—Max Fax," *St. Louis Church Bulletin*, September 8/9, 2001; "Mack's Facts—Max Fax," *St. Louis Church Bulletin*, September 15/16, 2001.

88. On Anna Beck: Agnes Palazzetti, "The City vs. Anna Beck, *Buffalo News*, Sunday, May 3, 1998; Herbert Hoegel, "Why Have A Will If Wishes Can Be Ignored?" Letter to the Editor, *Buffalo News*, Monday, May 11, 1998; Floyd Baker, "Why Bother With a Will?" Letter to the Editor, *Buffalo News*, May 15, 1998; Mike Vogel, "Deceased Women's Estate Wins Fight to Demolish Home," *Buffalo News*, July 3, 1998; Agnes Palazzetti, "Council Votes to Delay House Razing," *Buffalo News*, Wednesday, July 22, 1998; Agnes Palazzetti, "Beck House Demolition Order Challenged," *Buffalo News*, August, 27, 1998; Agnes Palazzetti, "Denial of Landmark Status Aids Cause of Estate," *Buffalo News*, Friday, November 6, 1998; Carolyn Thompson, "Dying Wish Denied," *Tribune Chronicle*, Ohio, Sunday, December 6, 1998; Carolyn Thompson, "Sides Shift in Tug of War Over Old House," *The Honolulu Advertiser*, Sunday, December 20, 1998; Carolyn Thompson, "Even In Death Woman Fights Buffalo, " *The Detroit News*, Tuesday, December 29, 1998; Harold McNeil, "Council Fails to Act on Saving Cottage," *Buffalo News*, December 30, 1998, it is in an article titled "Allendale;" Phil Fairbanks, "Council Vote Clears Way for Demolition of Beck House," *Buffalo News*, January 13, 1999; *The St. Louis Church Bulletin*, February 7, 1999.

UNPUBLISHED PAPERS AND THESES

1. Anita Louise Beaudette, *A Man And a Church Named Louis*, Unpublished Paper, D'Youville College, Buffalo, NY, 1954.

2. Molly B. Hauck, Historian, *Louis Le Couteulx, Buffalo Pioneer and Philanthropist*, Mount Calvary Archives, Buffalo, NY, 1999.

3. Michael A. Riester, *Lay Trusteeism at St. Louis Roman Catholic Church, Buffalo, New York*, M.A. Dissertation, Washington Theological Union, Silver Spring, MD, 1987.

4. Joseph P. Murphy, *The Laws of the State of New York Affecting Church Property*, Dissertation Ph.D., Catholic University of America Press, Washington D.C., 1957.

5. David Read Driscoll Jr., *Stephen Theodore Badin*, Thesis, Master of Arts Degree, Department of History, Graduate School of the University of Louisville, Louisville, KY, 1953.

6. Badin, S. T., *Origine et Progres de la Mission du Kentucky*, Paris, France, 1821.

7. Hauck, Molly B., *Louis Etienne Le Couteulx de Chaumont: 1756-1840*, Mount Calvary Cemetery Inc., Buffalo, NY, 2001.

8. Edward Zimmermann, *The Gitteres of Lorraine*, Buffalo, NY, 1997.

9. Literature cited by Zimmermann follows: Blaul, F., *Trauemen und Schauemen vom Rhein*, Germany, 1938; Coleman, Barry, *The Catholic Church and*

German Americans, Milwaukee, WI, 1952;
Salzbacher, J., *Meine Reise nach Nord-Amerika im Jahre 1842*,Wien, 1845; Dolan J., *The Immigrant Church*, Baltimore, MD, 1875; Albion R., *The Rise of New York Port*, New York, NY, 1970; Shaw, R., *Erie Water West*, Lexington, KY, 1966; Harlow, A., *The Road of the Century*, New York, NY, 1947; Hill, H.W., *Municipality of Buffalo, New York*, NY, 1923.

10. The entire story of the Hausle family is contained in Leo H. Hausle, *Family Record Book of the Hausle Family: Biographical Sketches*, unpublished, Buffalo, NY, 1905. A copy of this document is in the St. Louis Church Archives.

11. Riester, William, *Voyage to America*, A Diary, July 29, 1849 to October 1, 1849.

12. Riester, Michael, *A Short History of the Riester Family*, Buffalo, NY, 1995. A copy in the St. Louis Church Archives.

13. Lehner, Urban, *John Miller and Anna Maria Yax*, Grand Rapids, MI, 1985.

14. Hauck, Molly B., Louis Etienne Le Couteulx de Chaumont, 1756-1840, Pioneer Philanthropist, Financier, Druggist, First Clerk of Niagara County, Mount Calvary Cemetery Inc., Heritage Blvd, 800 Pine Ridge Road, Cheektowaga, NY, June 2001

15. Notes by Patrick Kavanaugh, Buffalo, NY, 2001, presented to the editors, copy in the St. Louis Church Archives

16. Written notes and contributions concerning the Dramatic Circle from Christopher Andrle, 5554 Juno Drive, Lake View, NY 14085-9724. Copies in the Archives of St. Louis Church.

17. *St. Louis Dramatic Circle Constitution Book*, *St. Louis Dramatic Circle Minutes*, and *St. Louis Dramatic Circle Correspondence*, which are preserved in the St. Louis Church Archives.

18. Michael Riester, *My Own Thoughts*, August 4, 2002. Archives of St. Louis Church.

19. Msgr. David M. Lee, "Diocesan New Visions Committee Begins Parish Self-evaluation Steps," *Western New York Catholic*, June 1993.

20. Keith Kidder, "Parishes Begin Self Study," *Western New York Catholic*, June 1993.

ORAL HISTORY REPORTS

1. Direct conversations of Patrick Wiessend, Director of the Holland Land Company Museum, Batavia, NY with Michael Riester, Archivist and Historian at St. Louis Church, 1999.

2. Ronald Pazek, superintendent of Holy Cross Cemetery, in an interview with the author/editor, Nov. 1, 1996,

3. Editor's interview with John E. Miller, Tonawanda,

New York, January 1, 2002.

4. Marie Buchheit Miller's interviews with the following: Blanche Buchheit, sister-in-law to Father Robert Buchheit; Donna Ball, niece to Father Edmund Dietzel; Father Eugene Wagner; Cathy Steffan; Father Philip Judge S.J., McQuaid High School, Rochester, NY; Sister Mary Anne Butler, Mother House, Sisters of St. Joseph, Strickler Road, Clarence, NY; Dorothy Ball, wife of Allen Joseph Schneggenburger; John Marciano; Helen Miller Roche concerning Cornelius Miller, her father; Rita Ball Foegen; Dorothy B. Reuvain, wife of Francis Reuvain; Saltvatore Mistretta; Monsignor Anthony Caliguri. Interviews were conducted January 1, 2001 to September 10, 2002.

5. A taped oral history interview between Michael Riester and Francis V. Tonello, May 11, 2002.

6. A taped oral history interview between Marie Buchheit Miller, C. Eugene Miller, Louis Buchheit, and Carmene Didio Buchheit on July 13, 2001.

7. A taped oral history interview between Marie Buchheit Miller, C. Eugene Miller, and Father Albert J. Bosack, October 9, 2000.

8. A taped oral history interview between Michael Riester, C. Eugene Miller, and Monsignor William Schwinger, Winter 2001.

9. A taped oral history interview between Michael Riester and Catherine Berger Almeter.

10. Robert McCarthy's interviews with the following: Catherine Berger Almeter; Robert and Patricia Albert; Sister Rita Kane SSJ; Sister Cecile Ferland SSJ; Sister Mary Ann Kolb SSJ; Marie Buchheit Miller; Carlos Carballada.

11. A taped oral history interview between Michael Riester and Norman White, son of Ed White, superintendent of the vast physical plant of St. Louis' parish.

12. Interview by C. Eugene Miller and Marie Buchheit Miller with Bishop Donald W. Trautman, Erie, PA, Summer 2002.

LETTERS AND SPEECHES

1. Rev. William Taylor, *An Address to the Roman Catholics of New York*, New York, NY, 1815.

2. Letter of Anthony Kohlmann to Propaganda Fide," New York Archdiocesan Archives, 1815.

3. "Letter from Rev. Alig, " St. Louis Church Archives, Buffalo, NY, dated 1844.

4. Speech of William Le Couteulx delivered to the parishioners at St. Louis Church on August 21, 1836 is a manuscript in the St. Louis Church File of the Buffalo and Erie County Historical Society's Library, Buffalo, NY.

5. Letter of the Congregation of St. Louis Church to Rt. Rev. John Hughes dated Feb., 12, 1843, St. Louis Church Archives, Buffalo, NY.

6. The text of the letter sent by the Congregation of St. Louis Church to Pope Gregory XVI can be found in op. cit. *Records of the Trustees' Meetings at St. Louis Church*, 1843.

7. William Hodge, *Buffalo Cemeteries*, a paper read before the Cemetery Society, Buffalo, NY, February 4, 1879.

8. Christmas Message of Rev. Paul Hoelscher, December 12, 1898. St. Louis Church Archives.

9. Letter from James O. Putnam to Peter Paul Esq. and Others, Trustees of the St. Louis Church in Buffalo, August 13, 1898. Also see *Commercial Advertiser*, August 8, 1889.

10. Concerning the Archconfraternity of the Christian Mothers: *A Letter from Father Bertin Roll OFM, Cap., to Reverend Father Belzer, Pastor of Good Shepherd Church*, January 8, 1986. Letter is in the archives of Good Shepherd Church, Pendleton, NY.

11. Letter to Edwin H. Kolb, chair of trustees of St. Louis Church, by John H. Stone Jr., Grand Commander of the Cardova Caravan No. 26, Aug. 5, 1957 and the *Courier Express*, Aug. 12, 1957.

12. *Chancery Memos to Bishop Head from Monsignor Trautman*, May 31, 1979; July 12, 1979. Copies in the St. Louis Church Archives.

13. Letter from Rev. William A. Schwinger to Mayor James D. Griffin, May 12, 1980.

14. Letter from Leonard Giarrano to Father Schwinger on May 22, 1989. Letter was provided from the archives of John Pax, Grand Island, NY.

15. Letter to Rae Reines, President of the Parish Council from Sam Fiorella, council member, October 22, 1995.

16. Bishop Henry Mansell, Decree Designating St. Louis Church, Buffalo, As a Pilgrimage Site for the Jubilee Year, December 8, 1999.

17. Letter of Arline M. Hoyt to John M. Laping, Chairman of the Buffalo Preservation Board, November 2, 1998.

18. Letter of Richard J. Shanley, Cheektowaga, NY, Banker and Friend of Anna Beck, sent to Honorable Mayor Masiello, December 30, 1998.

19. Fax Letter from firm of Kennedy, Stoeckl, and Martin to Rev. Msgr. Robert Mack, January 14, 1999.

20. Letter from David R. Hayes, Assistant Corporate Counsel, City of Buffalo, Dept. of Law, to Arline M. Hoyt, January 21, 1999.

Index

Index

Turner, William, 311, 313, 321, 323, 334, 347, 349, 352, 358
Turnerzeitung, 115
Turnverein, 78, 115, 185, 235, 305, 307
Tympanum, 200, 201

Uhrich, Francis Stephen, 118, 154
Underground Railroad, 117
Union and Echo, 384, 385
United German and French Roman Catholic Cemetery, 45, 129, 145, 290, 469
University of Notre Dame, 35, 38, 431
Ushers Club, 395, 398, 429, 431, 451

Vasey, Dona, 429, 463, 467
Vasi, Dolores, 456
Vatican II, 416, 417, 418, 419, 421, 423, 430, 448, 449, 450, 451, 453, 458, 459
Versailles, 153, 304
Verwaltung, 26, 27, 28, 67, 97
Vespers, 13, 23, 27, 76, 86, 97, 157, 268, 270, 353, 388
Vestibule, 198, 300, 376, 379, 457
Vestments, 50, 138, 139, 149, 202, 203, 216, 320, 323, 341, 351, 358, 370, 383, 384, 389, 399
Vietnam War, 408, 409
Vincentians, 62, 96, 383
Volstead Act, 334, 339, 341

Wagner, Eugene, 268, 269, 270, 271, 273
Wagner, Lawrence Sr., 269
Wagner, Matthew X., 284
Wallenhorst, Henry, 147
Walsh, Thomas J., 169
Wanderjahr, 83, 116, 142
Wanderschaft, 82
Wandling, Joseph, 13
Weber, Lawrence, 29, 83
Wehrle, Anna, 173
Wehrle, Clara, 173
Wehrle, Michael, 151
Weigand, Leonard, 429, 446
Weigel, William, 174
Welland Canal, 120
Wenninger, Francis X., 118
Weppner, Al, 242
Weppner, Arnold, 203
Weppner, Augustus F., 173, 174
Weppner, Delia E., 130
Weppner, Emma, 128, 181

Weppner, Jacob, 128, 200, 336
Weppner, May, 143, 172
West Indian Company, 1
West Indies, 1, 3, 41, 249
Western New York Catholic, 154
Wex, John L., 236, 237, 239, 240, 242, 243, 253
Weyand, Charles M., 145, 235, 237, 238, 239, 240, 241, 243, 246, 254
Weyand, Norman P., 240
Whig Party, 106
Whiskey, 43, 77, 334, 335, 336, 340
White, Edward J., 236, 237, 239, 240, 243, 246, 247, 254
White, Norman, 251, 280
Whitefield, James, 6, 9, 52, 95
Wilcox, Birdseye, 122
Wilhelm, Edward, 173
Wilhelm, Jacob, 83, 100
Wilhelm, William, 174
Williams, Charles, 143, 147, 166
Wine, 36, 40, 50, 79, 82, 84, 86, 150, 215, 217, 218, 244, 334, 336, 340, 341, 369, 371, 372
Winter, Alice, 240
Wodzicki, Frank L., 427, 431, 438
Wolmuenster, Alsace, 72, 75
Women's Christian Temperance Union, 336
Works Progress Administration, WPA, 342
Wounded Knee, 413
Wuerttemberg, Germany, 72, 78, 81, 82, 83, 142, 220
Yager, Margaretha, 72
Youngmann Expressway, 410

Zahm, George, 22, 24, 83, 151
Zahm, Loretta, 240
Zehnle, Christine, 238, 240
Zeinz, Gertrude, 226
Zeinz, Henry J., 223, 320, 321, 324, 355
Zeinz, Mary M., 223, 386
Zeller, Adolph, 235, 240, 253
Ziegele, Albert, 136, 337
Ziegele Brewing Company, 174
Zillig, Andrew, 240
Zimmermann, Anthony, 221, 288
Zimmermann, Brumpter, 55
Zimmermann, George, 27, 29, 83, 100
Zimpfer, Edward L., 240
Zinns, Peter, 22, 27, 83, 151
Zobel, Michael John Jr., 253
Zoll, John, M.D., 458, 461, 467, 468
Zollverein, 82, 83
Zorn, Fred A., 236, 237, 239, 240, 243, 246, 254
Zwirlein, Fred L., 306